MISES

The Last Knight of Liberalism

MISES

The Last Knight of Liberalism

JÖRG GUIDO HÜLSMANN

Ludwig
von Mises
Institute
AUBURN, ALABAMA

Photos:
Bettina Bien Greaves, cover, 1, 8, 9, 18, 20, 32, 40, 76, 77, 98, 99, 210, 255, 324, 404, 446, 447, 473, 519, 521, 522, 562, 563, 567, 610, 681, 758, 787, 809, 817, 825, 829, 835, 836, 847, 851, 882, 889, 890, 923, 934, 945, 986, 988, 1011, 1012, 1014, 1034, 1042, 1050
Archival Repository of the Center for Advanced Research in Phenomenology, University of Memphis, 365
David Jarrett photographs, 946
George Koether photographs, 888, 988
Harvard University Archives, 163
Hazlitt Photo Archive, Mises Institute, 795, 840, 852
Herbert Hoover Presidential Library, RWL #22, 840
Institut für Sozialforschung, 68
John Chamberlain Papers, Syracuse University, 840
Macmillan Publishers, 571,
Mises Archive at Grove City College, 833, 989
Mises Institute Photo Archive, 13, 94, 99, 111, 143, 145, 182, 253, 268, 365, 564, 840, 943, 928, 1036
Mont Pèlerin Society, 587, 679, 869, 870, 872
Moscow Archives, Mises, 262, 463
Österreich Lexikon, 83, 328, 366
Rothbard Photo Archive, Mises Institute, 840, 893, 929, 936, 939
Rubbettino Publishers, 476, 631
Ruprecht-Karls-Universität Heidelberg online, 336
University of Vienna, 99, 453
Warren J. Samuels Portrait Collection, Duke University, 99, 102, 109, 139, 118, 155, 424
Wikipedia, 23, 113, 128, 137, 335, 396, 840

ISBN: 978-1-933550-18-3

Contents

Preface

In the summer of 1940, with Hitler's troops moving through France to encircle Switzerland, Ludwig von Mises sat beside his wife Margit on a bus filled with Jews fleeing Europe. To avoid capture, the bus driver took back roads through the French countryside, stopping to ask locals if the Germans had been spotted ahead—reversing and finding alternative routes if they had been.

Mises was two months shy of his fifty-ninth birthday. He was on the invaders' list of wanted men. Two years earlier, they had ransacked his Vienna apartment, confiscating his records, and freezing his assets. Mises then hoped to be safe in Geneva. Now nowhere in Europe seemed safe. Not only was he a prominent intellectual of Jewish descent; he was widely known to be an arch-enemy of National Socialism and of every other form of socialism. Some called him "the last knight of liberalism."

He had personally steered Austria away from Bolshevism, saved his country from the level of hyperinflation that destroyed inter-war Germany, and convinced a generation of young socialist intellectuals to embrace the market. Now he was a political refugee headed for a foreign continent.

The couple arrived in the United States with barely any money and no prospects for income. Mises's former students and disciples had found prestigious positions in British and American universities (often with his help), but Mises himself was considered an anachronism. In an age of growing government and central planning, he was a defender of private property and an opponent of all government intervention in the economy. Perhaps worst of all, he was a proponent of verbal logic and realism in the beginning heyday of positivism and mathematical modeling. No university would have him. Margit began to train as a secretary.

Over the next decade, they would slowly rebuild and Mises would find new allies. He would also publish his most important book, *Human Action*. It would earn him a following whose admiration and devotion were beyond anything he had known in Europe.

When he died in October 1973, he had only a small circle of admirers and disciples, but this group became the nucleus of a movement that has grown exponentially. Today his writings inspire economists and libertarians throughout the world, and are avidly read by an increasing number of students in all the social sciences. There is an entire school of "Misesian" economists flourishing most notably in the United States, but also in Spain, France, the Czech Republic, Argentina, Romania, and Italy. This movement is testimony to the lasting power and impact of his ideas.

The purpose of the present book is to tell the story of how these ideas emerged in their time. It is the story of an amazing economist, of his life and deeds. It is the story of his personal impact on the Austrian School and the libertarian movement. It is above all the story of a man who transformed himself in an uncompromising pursuit of the truth, of a man who adopted his ideas step-by-step, often against his initial inclinations.

Once a student of the historical method in the social sciences, he would become the dean of the opposition Austrian School and humanistic social theory. He went from left-leaning young idealist in Vienna to grand old man of the American Right. Dismissive of "the metallists" early in his career, he became an unwavering spokesman for a 100 percent gold standard. His example inspired students and followers, many of whom would take his message and method farther than he himself would go.

The portrait of Ludwig von Mises offered here is primarily concerned with his intellectual development in the context of his time. Not much is known about the emotional layer of his personality. Early on he conceived of himself as a public persona: Professor

Mises. He took great care to destroy any evidence—from receipts to love letters—anything that could have been useful to potential opponents. We can report on some of the more intimate episodes of his life only because of the private records stolen from his Vienna apartment by Hitler's agents in March of 1938. These documents eventually fell into the hands of the Red Army, were rediscovered in a secret Moscow archive in 1991, and have been for us a precious source of information.

The present book is squarely based on Mises's personal documents in the Moscow archive and in the archive at Grove City College. I have also used relevant documents available from the Vienna Chamber of Commerce, the *Akademisches Gymnasium* in Vienna, the Graduate Institute of International Studies in Geneva, the Hoover Institution at Stanford University, as well as the materials that Mrs. Bettina Bien Greaves has inherited from the Mises estate. It goes without saying that I have studied Mises's writings in great detail, as well as those of the most significant other economists of his time. Furthermore, I have tried to familiarize myself with the historical context of his work, although remaining an amateur on these general questions. All this material is brought together here for the first time. I hope it will be a useful starting point for future research on Mises.

This brings me to a final remark on the scope and purpose of this book. Though I never met Mises in person, I have been a student and admirer of his works for many years. The following pages are last but not least a token of my gratitude toward this great thinker. In my economic research, I have tried to go on where he had left off, though not necessarily in the direction he seemed to be taking. This raised a few basic questions for my work on this biography: Should I talk about the research that Mises has inspired in our day? Should I discuss the sometimes different interpretations of Mises that are now current? It might have enhanced the present work and been more interesting to the present-day experts in the field to have included critical annotations on the literature, and there are many, but I decided to refrain from this. It would have drawn me away from speaking about *Mises himself* and into speaking about the *literature on* Mises. To keep a book that is already rather voluminous focused on its main subject, it was necessary to minimize the discussion of the secondary literature, including not only my own works, but also the works of eminent Mises scholars such as Murray Rothbard, Richard Ebeling, Israel Kirzner, Joseph Salerno, Hans-Hermann Hoppe, Bettina Bien Greaves, Julian DelGaudio, Eamonn Butler, Patrick Gunning, Jeffrey Herbener, Percy Greaves, Hans Sennholz, Ralph Raico, James Rolph Edwards, Laurence Moss, Gary North, Carsten Pallas, and David Gordon. This is an inconvenience, but an acceptable one in the age of the Internet.

The main point of a Mises biography in our present day, when so little is known about the man and biographical research is still in its infancy, is to come to grips with a figure who, without any significant institutional backing, by the sheer power of his ideas, inspires, more than thirty years after his death, a growing international intellectual movement. What are these ideas that have such magnetic power? Who was this man? What were his aims, his struggles, his triumphs, his defeats? How did his ideas originate in the context of his time and against the odds he faced? These, I think, are the main questions at the present stage. Those who love ideas—especially those who believe that ideas shape our world— may find the following pages worthwhile reading. If it does no more than raise further interest in Ludwig von Mises and his work, this book will have attained its goal.

Jörg Guido Hülsmann
Angers, France
May 2007

Acknowledgments

THIS WORK WOULD NOT have been possible without the initiative of Lew Rockwell, who encouraged me to write a Mises biography and then provided relentless support when the project grew bigger and bigger, far beyond our initial plans. It would not have been possible without the financial support of numerous dedicated men and women, and in particular of those patrons who are mentioned on the front pages of this book. Many other persons have helped and encouraged me in the course of my work. I have been especially blessed with generous aid from Mrs. Bettina Bien Greaves, who at the beginning of my research put me on the right tracks and made available to me the materials she had inherited from the Mises estate, as well as her own biographical research on Ludwig von Mises. She has also readily made available the wonderful collection of photographs of Ludwig and Margit von Mises that have been in her care. I gratefully acknowledge friendly help from the staff of the Special Archive for Historico-Documentary Collections in Moscow: Vladimir Kuselenkov (director), Vladimir Kurutajev (vice-director), Rostislav Sokolov (translator), and Natacha Samsonova (archivist). Similarly, I received liberal on-site support from Herr Magister Siegel, director of the Akademische Gymnasium in Vienna, and from Professor Jeffrey Herbener, custodian of the Mises Archive at Grove City College. I have benefited from the kind assistance of Professor Hans-Hermann Hoppe, who shared with me the archival material he had obtained from the Vienna Chamber of Commerce; of Professor Jesús Huerta de Soto, who shared with me his archival material from the Vienna Staatsarchiv; and of Mr. Ivo Sarjanovich, who researched for me the archives of the Graduate Institute of International Studies in Geneva. Many other individuals have graciously pointed out references or provided hard to find material. I should like to thank in particular Mr. Philipp Bagus, Professor Gabriel Calzada Alvarez, Professor Paul Cwik, Dr. Nikolay Gertchev, Dr. Floy Lilly, Dr. Anthony de Jasay, Professor Ralph Raico, Mr. Reinhard Stiebler, Mr. Joseph Stromberg, Dr. Mark Thornton, Professor Shigeki Tomo, Mr. Jeffrey Tucker, and Professor Ki'ichiro Yagi. To the great benefit of my readers, I have enjoyed the services of a competent and efficient editorial team under the leadership of Mr. Jeffrey Tucker, including Mr. B.K. Marcus, Mrs. Arlene Oost-Zinner, Mrs. Judy Thommesen, Dr. David Gordon, Mr. Jule Herbert, Jr., Mrs. Kathy White, and Mr. Harry David. Moreover, I have the honor to acknowledge my debt and immense gratitude to the readers and referees who helped improve the quality of this book, in particular Professor Walter Block, Dr. David Gordon, Mr. B.K. Marcus, Mr. Joseph Potts, Professor Ralph Raico, and Herr Dr. Herbert Unterköfler. Last but not least, I thank my dear wife Nathalie for bearing with me during all the years invested in this project, and for sharing a beautiful life beyond economics and great economists.

Part I
Young Ludwig

1

Roots

ON SEPTEMBER 29, 1881, Ludwig Heinrich Edler von Mises was the first in his family to be born a nobleman. A few months earlier, the Austrian emperor had ennobled Ludwig's great-grandfather, Meyer Rachmiel Mises. The family would henceforth bear the new name "von Mises." The emperor also conferred on them the honorific "Edler" which literally translates into "the noble" and was frequently accorded to Jews.[1]

Ludwig's birthplace was the city of Lemberg, the capital of the bygone "Kingdom of Galicia and Lodomeria." For centuries Galicia had belonged to Poland before it fell to the house of Habsburg in 1772 when large chunks of Poland were divided among its three mighty neighbors: Russia, Prussia, and Austria.[2] Even though the Habsburgs were the emperors of the German Reich, they never incorporated Galicia into Germany, but kept

---

[1]On the Mises family, see in particular the 1881 Adelsakt (Ennoblement Act) for Meyer (or Mayer) Rachmiel Mises, *Österreichisches Staatsarchiv*. See also *Österreichisches Biographisches Lexikon 1815–1950* (Vienna: Verlag der Österreichischen Akademie der Wissenschaften, 1975), vol. 6.

[2]The "Kingdom of Galicia and Lodomeria" had not existed before the division of Poland. The Habsburgs chose this name as a quasi-historical justification of the annexation. In the late Middle Ages, the Hungarian King Andrew had been a *Rex Galiciae et Lodomeriae*, that is, a king of the old Ruthenian principalities of Halitsch and Wladimir. See Isabel Röskau-Rydel, "Galizien, Bukowina, Moldau," in idem, *Deutsche Geschichte im Osten Europas: Galizien, Bukowina, Moldau* (Berlin: Siedler, 1999), pp. 11, 16.

it the northeasternmost province of Austria, the Habsburgs' personal dominion.

At the time of Ludwig's birth, the Habsburg Empire was the second-largest political entity in Europe, second only to Russia. Until the end of the seventeenth century, the Habsburg dynasty had also ruled Spain and its overseas colonies all around the world. Not long before Mises was born, the Habsburgs had ruled northern Italy, as well as Belgium and the Black Forest region in Germany. By 1881 the empire had lost these latter dominions but was still composed of twelve major ethnic groups and hosted six large religious bodies. Young Ludwig grew up in a powerful nation with a rich mix of cultures and a diverse ethnic heritage.[3]

Even by Austrian standards, Galicia was an extreme case of ethnic richness. Most of its citizens were Poles, Ruthenians, Jews, and Germans, but there were also substantial numbers of Armenians, Greeks, and Italians. While Jews were an often-tiny minority in virtually all other Habsburg lands, eastern Galicia's Jews represented an actual majority. At the time of Ludwig's birth, they were nearly the largest group in the city of Lemberg, second only to the Polish majority.[4] They had come to the country because the Catholic rulers of Poland, for more than 500 years, had been more tolerant toward Jews than had any other government. Legal protection for Jews started with the Statute of Kalisz (1264), and the fourteenth century King Casimir the Great and his successors upheld and extended these

---

[3]In 1918, Galicia fell back to Poland, and today Lemberg and the adjacent lands belong to Ukraine. Other historical names of Lemberg were Lviv, Lwow, Lvov, Leopoli, L'wiw, L'vov, Lwiw, Leopolis, L'viv.

[4]In 1848, the Galician population totalled 5.2 million. Among them were 2.2 million Roman Catholics (essentially Poles, but also Germans), 2.2 million Greek Catholics (Ruthenians), 333,000 Greek Orthodox, and 333,000 Jews. The city of Lemberg had some 63,000 residents in 1840, of which 30,000 were Roman Catholics, 4,500 Greek Catholics, and 25,000 Jews. See Röskau-Rydel, "Galizien, Bukowina, Moldau," p. 48.

rights during the next 200 years, at a time when Jews were expelled from virtually all other countries of Europe. Over the centuries, the Jewish community in Poland gained ever-greater legal autonomy, and by the end of the eighteenth century there was virtually a Jewish state within Poland. This country had become a homeland for the Jews of the entire world, a new Holy Land, many of them believed. By 1750, some 70 percent of all Jews lived in Poland, a number that grew even during the Polish partitions: by 1780, Poland was home to more than 80 percent of all Jews worldwide.[5]

Because the early influx of Jews was from Germany, the German Jewish dialect of Yiddish became the common language, even among later waves of Jewish immigrants from other parts of the world. Assimilation to the Polish language and culture was slow, if it happened at all. The strongest assimilation occurred among the Jewish intellectual and economic leaders, who shared business ties and other common interests with the Polish ruling class. The eminent Austrian historian and political philosopher Erik Ritter von Kuehnelt-Leddihn claims that this Polish background had an important impact on Ludwig von Mises's early development. Kuehnelt-Leddihn argues that young Ludwig was influenced by Polish political thought and political institutions, which cherished an aristocratic ideal of republican liberty.

> Movements for liberty, as a matter of fact, have typically been carried on by the nobility, which always opposed centralizing pressure and control. We saw this in England with the Magna Carta, in Hungary with the Golden Bull, in Aragon by the stubborn *Grandes*, and in France by the *Fronde*. In this respect,

---

[5] See Cyprian Pogonowski, *Jews in Poland* (New York: Hippocrene Books, 1993). Jews were evicted from England (1290), France (1306), Croatia (1349), Crimea (1350), Hungary (1360), Germany, Bohemia, Italy and Provence (1394), Austria (1421), Spain (1497), Estonia and Latvia (1495), and Portugal (1497); see ibid., p. 275.

Poland went further; it became an elective monarchy in 1572 and called itself a republic. One of the slogans of this very independent nobility was: "Menace the foreign kings and resist your own!" Political power rested with the nobility, which (before the partitions) had no titles, and its claimants comprised a fifth of the population. . . . It was a nobility without legal distinctions and a proverb said: "The nobleman in his farmhouse is equal to the magnate in his castle." And since all noblemen were equals, they could not be ruled by majorities. In the parliament, the *Sejm*, the opposition of a single man—the *Liberum Veto*—annulled any legal proposition.[6]

This Polish political tradition permeated the culture of the Polish upper class in Galicia and must have had a considerable impact on families such as the Miseses, who strove to be received into the higher social strata at the turn of the eighteenth and nineteenth centuries.

While his Polish heritage had its impact on the political thought of Ludwig von Mises, the cultural aspirations of his ancestors pointed in a completely different direction. Throughout the nineteenth century, in fact, the Mises family helped spearhead the Germanization of their native Galicia. In their eyes, German culture was the embodiment of social progress. The liberal policies pursued under Joseph II at the end of the eighteenth century promised to bring greater liberty for the Galician masses and emancipation for the Jews. This was exactly what "left-wing" secular Jews had been striving for. At the turn of the eighteenth and nineteenth centuries, these groups became pro-German under the determined leadership of wealthy merchants such as the Mises family.[7] They supported

---

[6]Erik von Kuehnelt-Leddihn, *The Cultural Background of Ludwig von Mises* (Auburn, Ala.: Ludwig von Mises Institute, 1999), p. 2.

[7]The Jewish community in Krakow had remained pro-Polish under orthodox religious leadership. In Lemberg, by contrast, the pro-German secular

the new political administration; they welcomed immigration of non-Jewish ethnic Germans; and they promoted the infusion of secular German culture into Jewish circles. Members of the Mises family played a leading role in advancing the study of philosophy and secular science among local Jews. Heinrich Graetz reports:

> Since the wars with Napoleon, there had arisen small circles in the three largest Galician communities of Brody, Lemberg, and Tarnopol, banded together for self-culture, the promotion of education, and a war of annihilation against Chassidism. . . . In Lemberg . . . a kind of literary circle was founded, at whose head was a wealthy, highly-cultured man, Jehuda Löb Mises (died 1831). He provided ambitious young men in Lemberg with money, counsel, and, what was of special value to them, with an excellent library of Hebrew and European books.[8]

After 1772, the Habsburgs imposed a caste of German-speaking bureaucrats on the country and also encouraged German settlements on land confiscated from the Polish kings, the Jesuit order, and various monasteries.[9] The Germanization of Poland went on for almost a century, during which the Polish aristocracy repeatedly tried to shake off Austrian rule. After a failed attempt in 1863, the old political establishment of Poland finally came to terms with the Habsburgs, promising loyalty of its *Kolo Polske* ("Polish Club") to the Austrian crown in exchange for a free hand in ruling Galicia. In 1867, the Polish aristocracy obtained a "Galician Resolution" in the Austrian parliament, which granted them a large degree of autonomy in this eastern-most part of the empire. The *Polenklub* in Vienna became one

---

faction had its way. See Röskau-Rydel, "Galizien, Bukowina, Moldau," pp. 88f., 145.

[8]Heinrich Graetz, *History of the Jews* (Philadelphia: Jewish Publishers, 1895), vol. 5, p. 612.

[9]Röskau-Rydel, "Galizien, Bukowina, Moldau," pp. 27–29.

of the main factions supporting the Austrian governments until
the eventual disintegration of the empire in 1918.[10] At the same
time, the Germanization of Galicia was rolled back and eventually died out. Only the traditional pillars of German language
and culture remained: civil servants and secular Jews.[11]

Until 1867, pro-German orientation was the basis of the
Mises family's influence in local political affairs. It made their

Mises at two years old

influence felt even in national circles once
the appearance of railroads brought Galicia into ever-closer economic ties with the
rest of the Habsburg Empire.[12]

In the second half of the nineteenth
century, railroads were an advanced technology that profoundly transformed economic, political, and social relationships.
Railroad companies paid the highest
salaries, provided opportunities for rapid
career advancement, and attracted the
most energetic and best-trained young men of the time. Virtually all these men belonged to a new intellectual class that had
emerged during the nineteenth century: the engineers. Typically
the children of bourgeois families, engineers epitomized intelligence, hands-on pragmatism, goal-orientation, and success.

---

[10]See Rudolf Sieghart, *Die letzten Jahrzehnte einer Grossmacht* (Berlin: Ullstein, 1932), pp. 334f.

[11]In 1880, there were some 324,000 Galicians whose first language was
German; in 1910, only some 90,000 were left. Thus even at its high point, the
Germanization movement had a weak numerical impact in the part of Poland
annexed by the house of Habsburg. The main reason was that most of the
new settlers were Catholics and were therefore integrated into the existing
Polish parishes and schools. See Röskau-Rydel, "Galizien, Bukowina,
Moldau," pp. 88f., 130, 152.

[12]It seems that railroad construction was a spin-off of Jewish initiatives to
promote the industrialization of Austria. Thus William Johnston states that a
few years after 1831, "Salomon Rothschild persuaded Metternich to promote
industrialization in the Habsburg domains." William M. Johnston, *Vienna,
Vienna—The Golden Age, 1815–1914* (Milan: Arnoldo Mondadori, 1981), p. 29.

Railroads came to Austria in the 1820s and by the early 1840s, the government was trying to take them over. During the next ten years, many Austrian lines were socialized until the cataclysmic events of 1848–1849 brought the state finances into such disarray that, starting in 1854, a re-privatization became necessary.[13] Once again under private ownership, the railroads reached Galicia. The Mises family was strongly involved in both of the two major Galician railroad ventures, serving as board members and bankers. A generation later, in the 1870s and 1880s, Ludwig's father, Arthur Edler von Mises (born on September 6, 1854) worked for the Czernowitz railroad company while his uncle Emil was an engineer for the Carl-Ludwig company.

Arthur von Mises had married Adele Landau (born on June 4, 1858) from Vienna.[14] Her family came from Brody, an almost exclusively Jewish town on the border of the Habsburg empire.

Mises's parents, Adele and Arthur, circa 1880

Her father was Fischel Landau and her mother Klara Kallir. Adele had followed Arthur to Lemberg, where she gave birth to Ludwig and his younger brother Richard Martin (born 1883). A few years later they had a third boy, Karl, but he died of scarlet fever when Ludwig was twelve years old. Adele's native Brody

---

[13]See Alois Gratz, "Die österreichische Finanzpolitik," Hans Mayer, ed., *Hundert Jahre österreichische Wirtschaftsentwicklung, 1848–1948* (Vienna: Springer, 1949), pp. 254f.

[14]They married on October 17, 1880. See the marriage certificate in the Grove City Archive: file #6/9/1/1. Witnesses were Fischel Landau (Adele's father) and Isidor Nirenstein.

was in those days a free trade zone for commerce with Poland and Russia. Her family had made good use of the profit opportunities and become affluent and influential. Her marriage with Arthur was not only a matter of love. It was also meant to cement a more encompassing alliance between two of the leading families of Eastern Galicia. Significantly, at the 1873 elections to the Austrian parliament, all three Jewish MPs from Galicia had family ties: Joachim Landau was elected for the city of Brody, Nathan Kallir joined the parliament as a representative of the Brody chamber of commerce, and Ludwig's uncle Hermann was elected for the county of Drohobycz.[15]

More than any other male family member of this generation, Hermann Mises featured the virtues that had made the Mises family so successful, and which, a generation later, would also characterize his nephew Ludwig: enthusiasm, determination, intelligence, love of his fatherland, leadership, and unpretentious and clear writing.[16] After directing a branch office for a large insurance company and exploring for petroleum in Galicia, Hermann moved to Vienna in the early 1870s to work for a major newspaper, the *Morgenpost*. In 1873 he became a one-term member of the *Reichsrat* (the Austrian parliament) for the Galician district of Sambor-Stryj-Drohobycz, then returned to journalism, writing for another major paper, the *Wiener Allgemeine Zeitung*, where he was a tireless advocate for the industrialization of Galicia.[17]

---

[15]Röskau-Rydel, "Galizien, Bukowina, Moldau," pp. 70, 147. Joachim Landau was the brother of Ludwig von Mises's grandfather on the maternal side. See Mises, *Erinnerungen* (Stuttgart: Gustav Fischer Verlag, 1978), p. 20. Ludwig's grandmother on the maternal side was a Kallir, his grandfather a Landau.

[16]On Hermann von Mises, see the entry in *Österreichisches Biographisches Lexikon, 1815–1950* (Vienna: Verlag der österreichischen Akademie der Wissenschaften), vol. 6, p. 317.

[17]There seems to have been an oil boom in what came to be called the "Galician Pennsylvania"—Hermann's election district around Drohobycz, an

Hermann and his brothers and cousins continued a tradition of achievement that can be traced back at least to their great-grandfather—Ludwig's great-great grandfather—Efraim Fischel Mises. Fischel was a large-scale fabric merchant and real estate owner in Lemberg. After the Polish partition of 1772, the inhabitants of this poor rural area greatly profited from the new Austrian rule, which brought unprecedented liberties for the rural population and also for the cities, even though Maria Theresa, empress at the time of the partition, was not a champion of Jewish liberties. Some of her most important consultants—the famous Sonnenfels, for example—were of Jewish origin, but she would not tolerate Jewish residents in Vienna.[18] In the cities that did tolerate Jewish residents, such as Lemberg, Jews were forced to live within special areas, the *Judenviertel*. They were generally prohibited from trading in the "forbidden districts" of the empire, and even those who had permission to trade there on business days could not stay overnight. So it remained, from her reign well into the nineteenth century.

---

area southwest of Lemberg. At the turn of the nineteenth and twentieth century, Galicia was the number four producer of petroleum worldwide, after Russia, the United States, and the Dutch East Indies. See Balduin Winter, "Die Rückkehr zum Kind. Wirklichkeit ist mehr als Realität. Drohobycz, die Heimat des Dichters und Traumtänzers Bruno Schulz im vergessenen Europa," *Die Ost-West-Wochenzeitung* (literature section; March 30, 2001).

[18]Jews were expelled from Vienna under Leopold I in 1669–1670. A few years later these measures were rescinded rather half-heartedly, and so things remained as in 1670. As far as Maria Theresa is concerned, cultural historian Robert Kann states:

> Within the first five years of Maria Theresa's reign the Jews were driven out of Bohemia (1745), and less than three years before her death, less than five years before Joseph II issued the famous *Toleranzpatent*, in 1777 she wrote these words: "'In the future no Jew shall be allowed to remain in Vienna without my special permission." (Robert A. Kann, *A Study in Austrian Intellectual History: From Later Baroque to Romanticism* [New York: Praeger, 1960], p. 158)

Despicable as the system of regulations was, it allowed for exceptions. Thus the city of Lemberg would authorize Jewish residence outside of the *Judenviertel* if the person in question fulfilled three conditions: he had to be wealthy; he had to be educated; and he could not wear traditional Jewish clothes.[19] A case in point was Fischel Mises, who enjoyed the privilege of living and trading in the forbidden district of Lemberg, where he also acted as the president of the secular organization of local Jews, the Jewish Cultural Community (*israelitische Kultusgemeinde*).

On June 23, 1800, Fischel's wife gave birth to the true founder of the Mises dynasty, the inexhaustible polymath Meyer Rachmiel Mises.[20] The boy quickly proved to be successful in many fields and his father made him a partner in his firm early on. He also arranged a suitable marriage with Rosa Halberstamm, whose father ran an important German-Russian export business. Barely thirty years old, Meyer became president of the Lemberg Jewish Cultural Community, and a year later he took on the role of auditor for the provincial court in charge of trade issues, the *Lemberger Wechselgericht*. When his father died in 1842, he set up his own trade firm. Still in his forties, he was not only a successful businessman, but also an influential social leader, elected several times into the Lemberg city council; founder of an orphanage, of a Jewish school, and a Jewish kitchen for the poor. He also created several institutions providing funds for scholarships and other public-welfare oriented purposes.[21]

Meyer was the leader of the secular, pro-German wing within the Lemberg Jewish religious community, in which he

---

[19]Röskau-Rydel, "Galizien, Bukowina, Moldau," p. 68.

[20]On Meyer Rachmiel Mises, see the entry (Mises, Majer Jerachmiel von) in *Österreichisches Biographisches Lexikon, 1815–1950*, vol. 6, pp. 317f.

[21]These activities must have played a decisive role in his eventual ennoblement. Throughout Franz Joseph's reign, contributions to public objectives or the creation of public-welfare oriented funds were instrumental in the ennoblement of wealthy industrialists, merchants, or bankers. See Sieghart, *Die letzten Jahrzehnte einer Grossmacht*, p. 256.

held various positions beginning in 1840. The top three items on the agenda of the "enlightened" Jewish faction under Meyer were (1) spreading the German language, (2) creation of a *deutsch-israelisches Bethaus*—a progressive synagogue in which services were held in German, and (3) the creation of a German-language Jewish school. The main stumbling block for these projects was the local rabbi, a leader of the orthodox Ashkenazi. After the death of this man in the early 1840s, the Mises faction brought in Rabbi Abraham Kohn, who was well known for his progressive views. Once in Lemberg, Kohn was adamant in pursuing his agenda and must have driven his opponents to despair. In September 1848 he was murdered.[22]

Meyer Rachmiel Mises was probably among those who, after 1846, successfully led the country's bloody insurrection against the Polish nobility. These aristocrats had tried to reestablish the

This coin, commissioned by the Mises family, was struck in 1880 to commemorate the 80th birthday of Meyer Rachmiel Mises. The obverse side carries Meyer's likeness and birth date. The words surrounding the Mises family crest, on the inverse, say "80th birthday anniversary," and below the line, "with gratitude from the family, 1880."

---

[22]Röskau-Rydel, "Galizien, Bukowina, Moldau," pp. 73f. Graetz remarks,

> [I]n almost every large community, there arose a party of the "Enlightenment" or "the Left," which had not yet broken with the old school, but whose action bordered upon secession. By the ultra-orthodox they were denounced as heretics, on account of their preference for pure language and form, both in Hebrew and European literature. (Graetz, *History of the Jews*, vol. 5, p. 403)

ancient custom of *Robot*—part-time serf labor for the nobility—
that had slowly declined after the Austrian takeover of Galicia
at the end of the eighteenth century. Two years later, when revolutionary insurrections broke out in Paris, Berlin, and Vienna,
Meyer helped bring the fight to Galicia. He was one of four
Jewish signers of a March 1848 Galician petition to the
emperor, demanding among other things legal equality for all
social classes, emancipation of the Jews, the creation of a Galician militia and of a Galician parliament.[23] As an initial result,
all forms of serfdom in Galicia were affirmatively abolished on
April 17, 1848—though the Polish aristocrats received some
compensation from the public treasury. In the same year, Meyer
Rachmiel Mises was elected to the Galician parliament. He had
now become a visible member of the unofficial "Jewish nobility" and was actively involved in major political reforms in this
easternmost province of the Habsburg Empire. He may even
have been one of the "democratic agitators" who caused such
headaches for the defenders of the monarchy.

This was more than enough for a lifetime, one would think,
but the most active and challenging part of his life still lay
ahead. It came when the railways, which had begun crossing the
European continent in the 1840s, reached Galicia in the mid-
1850s. Meyer and his son Abraham positioned themselves in
this business and were contracted by the Austrian army to transport wheat from Galicia in 1859. The army was preparing for
its Italian campaign. The wheat deal brought them in touch
with the financial empire of the Rothschild family. In 1855,
Anselm von Rothschild had established the Credit-Anstalt
bank, which specialized in financing industrial ventures and
would soon become the largest bank on the Vienna stock
exchange. One of its first major operations was to finance the

---

[23]Röskau-Rydel, "Galizien, Bukowina, Moldau," p. 91. The petition had
been initiated by the Polish politicians Smolka, Ziemalkowski, and Kulczycki.
It also demanded the introduction of the Polish language in public schools
and civil service.

The coat of arms was awarded in 1881 when Ludwig von Mises's great-grandfather Meyer Rachmiel Mises was ennobled by the Emperor Franz Joseph. In the upper right-hand quadrant is the staff of Mercury, god of commerce and communication. In the lower left-hand quadrant is a representation of the Ten Commandments.

Meyer Rachmiel, as well as his father, presided over various Jewish cultural organizations in Lemberg. The banner, in red, displays the Rose of Sharon, which in the litany is one of the names given to the Blessed Mother, as well as the Stars of the Royal House of David, a symbol of the Jewish people.

Italian campaign. The deal must have gone well, for in 1860, Abraham accepted a position as director of Credit-Anstalt's new Lemberg branch office. Meyer had moved to banking three years earlier, becoming a director of the Lemberg branch office of the Austrian National bank—the central bank of the empire until the creation of the Austro-Hungarian bank in 1879.[24] The thorough repositioning of the Mises family was complete when Meyer's younger son, Hirsche (Ludwig von Mises's grandfather), became a partner and managing director of the Hallerstein and Nirenstein bank, and his first-born grandson, Hermann, rose to the directorship of the Lemberg office of the Phoenix insurance company.[25] The Mises's economic interests, starting in a provincial trade company, had now shifted to the most profitable national industries: railroads and banking.

In April 1881, Emperor Franz Joseph granted Meyer a patent of nobility, and in September of the same year, granted him and his lawful offspring the right to bear the honorific title

---

[24]Anselm von Rothschild's son Albert became a general counselor to the Austro-Hungarian bank and was commonly regarded as the key figure in the Austrian financial market. It is likely that his father played a similar though less publicized role in the National bank.

[25]Hirsche Mises was married to a member of the Nirenstein family, Marie Nirenstein. See Grove City Archive: file #6/9/1/1.

"Edler." A lonely patriarch, Meyer Rachmiel Edler von Mises survived both of his sons and his youngest daughter, Clara.[26] When he died on February 28, 1891 in Lemberg, all of his grandsons had left for Vienna.

This exodus was by no means exceptional. Tens of thousands of Jewish families from the eastern provinces had seized the opportunities provided by the liberal post-1867 regime, which had abolished all legal impediments to Jewish migration, and established themselves in Vienna. Most of them held more secular views than those who remained in Galicia. Liberal Vienna held the promise of escape from the restrictions of small religious communities, and of secular integration into the larger world. Before 1867, city life in Lemberg and other major towns could offer similar prospects in Galicia. But by giving cultural supremacy in Galicia to the Polish Club, the Galician Resolution had quickly destroyed these prospects. The Polish aristocracy was adamant in suppressing any threat of social change. Liberalism and capitalism were not welcome. Neither were German-language schools, the great harbingers of social change in the preceding decades. In the Lemberg Jewish community, the rollback of German cultural supremacy was completed in 1882, when a pro-Polish president was elected to the Jewish Cultural Community.[27]

In the case of Ludwig's father Arthur, however, the crucial circumstance prompting his departure for Vienna may have been more prosaic. Austrian state finances had recovered in the 1870s and in the 1880s the government again took control of the railroad industry.[28] The lines that had the greatest military importance were nationalized first, including those connecting Vienna with the borders of Russia, in Galicia.[29] In the wake of

---

[26]Two of his daughters were still living in 1881: Stella Klarmann and Elise Bernstein.

[27]Röskau-Rydel, "Galizien, Bukowina, Moldau," p. 147.

[28]See Gratz, "Die österreichische Finanzpolitik," p. 255.

[29]Ibid., pp. 270f.

this takeover, Arthur von Mises was accepted into the civil service as a construction counselor to the railroad ministry in Vienna.[30]

In those days, joining the civil service in Vienna was a big improvement in any man's career: employment in public administration was comparatively rare and far more prestigious than any other field of activity. The family moved into an apartment at Friedrichstrasse 4, its home for the next fifteen years. Adele had a maid and a cook to assist her in running the household—standard in bourgeois families—while her main duty and passion was the education of her sons. This involved, most notably, placing them in good schools to prepare them for their future careers.

The Miseses had become a typical Jewish family for the Vienna of that time, as described by cultural historian William Johnston:

> It was characteristic of them that a businessman father would marry a wife who was more cultivated than he was. Together the couple would settle in Vienna, often in the Leopoldstadt district, where he established a career while she supervised the education of the children. The cultural ambition of the wife was then passed on to the sons, who aspired to excel their fathers by entering one of the liberal professions.[31]

By all human standards, Adele von Mises did an outstanding job educating her two sons. Each did far more than just surpass his father. They both turned out to be scientific geniuses: Ludwig in the social sciences and Richard in the natural sciences. Ample administrations of motherly love provided the foundation for

---

[30]Other family members had followed in the same path. By the 1890s at least three of Arthur's brothers and cousins—Emil, Felix, and Hermann—had left for Vienna, too. Felix was a chief physician at the Vienna general hospital, and Hermann was a reputable journalist and politician.

[31]Johnston, *Vienna, Vienna*, p. 200.

Richard, Ludwig, mother Adele, and Karl

their astounding achievements. But there was more. Adele taught her sons to care for others.[32] She taught them to be modest and frugal.[33] She taught them to honor truth and virtue more than the encomiums of the world. She taught them the art of writing. And she taught them always to strive for excellence.

In all of their later endeavors, Ludwig and Richard would be thorough and systematic. In their professional lives this was a matter of course. But it also permeated all their other activities. Ludwig for instance sought instruction even in popular sports such as mountain hiking, and when he played tennis it was always with a trainer.[34] Like their mother, Ludwig and Richard wrote with a clear and unpretentious style. From childhood they set for themselves the highest standards. And as they developed taste and

---

[32]Charitable works were a quintessential part of her upbringing. See her autobiographical recollections in Adele von Mises, "A Day in the House of My Parents," *Tante Adele erzählt* (unpublished manuscript, 1929). The chapter has been translated and put online by John Kallir.

[33]Ludwig was a rigorous bookkeeper throughout his life. He kept track of his income and daily expenditure in a personal ledger.

[34]On his training in these sports see Margit von Mises, *My Years with Ludwig von Mises* (Cedar Falls, Iowa: Center for Futures Education, 1978), p. 20.

expertise, they would judge their own achievements and those of others in the light of these standards.

Ludwig was especially adamant in his refusal to allow social or political considerations into his judgment of persons and deeds. He had a lifelong disdain for people who had attained positions of leadership without true competence. As a mature man, he would openly despise the great majority of his professorial colleagues, not for their errors, but for their dilettantism.[35] His complete inability to suffer fools would make him many enemies and almost ruin his career; it gained him the reputation of a stubborn doctrinaire.

Mises nevertheless got along on his rocky road, thanks to his outstanding gifts; among them the natural gifts from his native Galicia. In this respect too he was a typical case:

> Jewish lawyers, doctors, professors, and journalists abounded after 1880, and there were not a few rentiers like Stefan Zweig or Otto Weininger. These men, who had attended gymnasium and university in Vienna, often had grandparents who had lived in villages in Galicia or Moravia, close to the soil and to traditional Jewish culture. However ardently these young sophisticates might try to secularize themselves, they could not cut off all roots in the Jewish

---

[35]About the typical German economist he wrote:

> Such study of "economic state science" necessarily repelled young people with intelligence and thirst for knowledge. Instead, it strongly attracted simpletons. . . . They were dilettantes in everything they undertook. They pretended to be historians, but they scarcely looked at the collaborative sciences, which are the most important tools of the historian. The spirit of historical research was alien to them. They were unaware of the basic mathematical problems in the use of statistics. They were laymen in jurisprudence, technology, banking, and trade techniques. With amazing unconcern they published books and essays on things of which they understood nothing. (Mises, *Erinnerungen*, pp. 7, 67f.; *Notes and Recollections* [Spring Mills, Penn.: Libertarian Press, 1978], pp. 7, 102)

villages. They retained an earthy energy, a love of
nature, a breadth of horizon that served them well
and accorded with Vienna's traditions. After 1860,
Vienna's Jews were not products of generations in an
urban ghetto like that of Berlin or Frankfurt. They
were newcomers to the city, who brought an energy,
an ambition, an appetite for culture that made them
capable of astonishing innovations.[36]

Earthy energy, breadth of horizon, ambition, and appetite
for culture also characterized young Ludwig, and these qualities
would lead him to astonishing innovations. The next chapters
show how this newcomer conquered first Vienna, and eventually the world of ideas. ✍

The three Mises brothers, left to right, *Karl,*
Ludwig, and Richard

---

[36]Johnston, *Vienna, Vienna,* p. 200.

2
School Years

THE MISES FAMILY MOVED to Vienna some time between 1883 (when Ludwig's brother Richard was born) and 1891. The move probably occurred before the fall of 1887, when six-year-old Ludwig began the mandatory four years of elementary schooling. The family settled in a suburban apartment in close proximity to what was then the city of Vienna and today is its first district. From his home at Friedrichstrasse 4, young Mises set out for many excursions and became acquainted with the city, its history, and its people.

Vienna

For many centuries, Vienna had been the administrative center of the Habsburg Empire. After the revolution of 1848–1849 and Franz Joseph's abortive attempt to reintroduce royal absolutism, the Austrian liberals had risen to power at the end of the 1850s. Their reign lasted about thirty years, enough time to reshape the city to reflect their ideals. They demolished the ramparts that separated the old city of Vienna from the surrounding suburbs, replacing them with the *Ringstrasse*, a magnificent U-shaped boulevard that now enclosed the old center from three sides; the fourth border was an arm of the Danube River. The Ringstrasse became an architectural and aesthetic triumph which "by virtue of its geographical concentration, surpassed in visual impact any urban reconstruction of the nineteenth century—

even that of Paris."[1] The nobility too had its palaces on the new boulevard, but the dominant edifices embodied the liberal bourgeoisie's political and cultural values. On the very spot where the large city ramparts had once symbolized the military presence of monarchical rule, now an opera and a Hofburgtheater celebrated the performing arts, splendid museums for natural history and art displayed human achievements and discoveries, parliament buildings[2] hosted the new political forces present in the Reichsrat, new buildings for the university and the stock exchange represented the forces of economic progress, and a magnificent neo-Gothic city hall symbolized the rebirth of municipal autonomy after ages of imperial supremacy.

Young Mises could reach all of these places within a twenty-minute walk. Unlike most other major European capitals, the city of Vienna was surprisingly small.[3] It hosted all central political institutions and administrations, the most important cultural centers, and the headquarters of the largest corporations of the entire empire, but one could walk across the entire concentration in a half-hour's stroll.[4]

It was easy to encounter the empire's most famous and powerful people on the streets of Vienna. It was almost impossible not to see someone in some eminent position. Among the most

---

[1] Carl E. Schorkse, *Fin-de-siècle Vienna* (New York: Knopf, 1980), p. 6.

[2] Roman classicism for the lower chamber, the *Abgeordnetenhaus*, Greek classicism for the upper chamber, the *Herrenhaus*.

[3] Until the 1890s, Vienna counted barely more than 60,000 inhabitants. Felix Somary recalls: "Everything outside the centre was known as '*Vorstadt*'—the suburbs—which almost meant the same as 'provinces'." Felix Somary, *The Raven of Zurich: The Memoirs of Felix Somary* (London: Hurst & Co., 1960), p. 1. After 1900 a municipal reform merged Vienna with its proximate suburbs. The old Vienna thereafter became the first district of the new city.

[4] By comparison, it takes more than two hours of walking to cross Paris within the *Boulevard Périphérique*, and it takes roughly the same time to walk through the city of London.

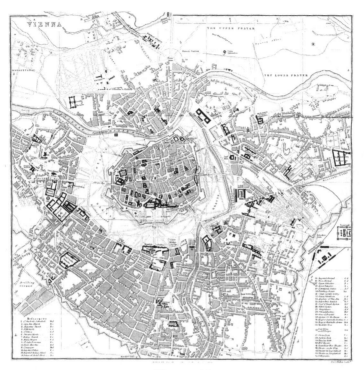

Vienna 1858

popular individuals were opera singers, stage actors, and members of the royal family. When a famous singer walked by, or one of the more than sixty archdukes or archduchesses drove by in their carriage, people would greet them with spontaneous applause. And when a star from the opera or Hofburgtheater died, flags flew at half-mast.[5] Yet the best example—and almost unbelievable for us today—was Franz Joseph himself, who frequently departed in just his carriage from the Hofburgtheater in the city to Schönbrunn Palace on the outskirts of Vienna. Anyone could walk within reach of the carriage and lift his hat to the white-haired emperor.

---

[5]William M. Johnston, *Vienna, Vienna—The Golden Age, 1815–1914* (Milan: Arnoldo Mondadori, 1981), p. 104. Johnston observes that even simple members of the opera or Philharmonic orchestras were greeted in public and that "many of them performed chamber music in the salons of the wealthy."

It was similarly impossible not to meet one's friends, relatives, and colleagues on the way to or from the office, shop, or school. It was in the cafés that the Viennese exchanged ideas, discussed events, debated issues, but they were already acquainted with one another just by walking from home to the office, by going to the opera, or to the museums.

The Viennese cultural elites did not live in secluded social circles. They perceived themselves as taking part in an all-encompassing social life that brought together ministers and students, opera singers and scientists, stock brokers and historians of art, philosophers and painters, psychologists and novelists, office clerks and architects, and so on in countless variations. Having so many people in so small a city contributed to making Vienna—from the 1870s to the 1930s—a cultural hothouse that would shape much of what was most valuable in twentieth-century civilization. In those years Vienna became the birthplace of phenomenology, medicine, psychoanalysis, Zionism, and *Jugendstil* (art nouveau). It was one of the cradles of modern analytical philosophy and, most importantly, it was the birthplace and home of Austrian economics—that school of thought that Ludwig von Mises was to lead and transform. In the words of cultural historian Carl Schorske:

> In London, Paris, or Berlin . . . the intellectuals in the various branches of high culture, whether academic or aesthetic, journalistic or literary, political or intellectual, scarcely knew each other. They lived in relatively segregated professional communities. In Vienna, by contrast, until about 1900, the cohesiveness of the whole élite was strong. The salon and the café retained their vitality as institutions where intellectuals of different kinds shared ideas and values with each other and still mingled with a business and professional élite proud of its general education and artistic culture.[6]

---

[6]Schorkse, *Fin-de-siècle Vienna*, p. xxvii.

The cafés had a decisive impact on the education of Vienna's young intellectuals.[7] The café was of course a place to have coffee or a small meal, but it was also where professional people met to talk business, and everyone else met to discuss current interests. For students, the café was also an institution of learning. The better cafés subscribed to the major international journals of science, art, and literature. Designed for the entertainment of customers, these subscriptions made the cafés function as a kind of private library. As a teenager, Mises must have spent many afternoon hours here, reading the latest articles in all fields of knowledge and achievement, and discussing them with his peers. It was probably here that he first encountered the writings of the German Historical School under Gustav Schmoller and found them less then fully convincing. He later recalled:

> I was still in high school when I noticed a contradiction in the position of the Schmoller circle. On the one hand, they rejected the positivistic demand for a science of law that was to be built from the historical experiences of society; on the other hand, they believed that economic theory was to be abstracted from economic experiences. It was astonishing to me that this contradiction was barely noticed and rarely mentioned.[8]

He was equally bewildered by the way the Historical School presented its case against *laissez-faire* liberalism. Schmoller and his friends seemed to argue that the modern

---

[7]On Vienna café culture, see Gustav Gugitz, *Das Wiener Kaffeehaus. Ein Stück Kultur- und Lokalgeschichte* (Vienna: Deutscher Verlag für Jugend und Volk, 1940). On the role of cafés in the education of young intellectuals see Stefan Zweig, *Die Welt von Gestern—Erinnerungen eines Europäers* (Frankfurt a.M.: Gustav Fischer, 1988), pp. 56f.

[8]Mises, *Erinnerungen* (Stuttgart: Gustav Fischer Verlag, 1978), p. 4; *Notes and Recollections* (Spring Mills, Penn.: Libertarian Press, 1978), p. 2.

liberal era contrasted unfavorably with older collectivist times. But this made no sense:

> At that time I did not yet understand the significance of Liberalism. But to me, the fact alone that Liberalism was an achievement of the eighteenth century, and that it was not known in former times, was no cogent argument against it. . . . It was not quite clear to me how an argument could be derived from the fact that in the distant past there had been community property in land. Nor could I understand why monogamy and family should be abolished because there had been promiscuity in the past. To me such arguments were nothing but nonsense.[9]

The sheer cultural density of the city almost forced the Viennese to take an interest in science, beauty, and art. Thinking and talking about such things were not reserved for the elite or particular occasions. They were a part of Vienna's daily common life. Virtually everybody, from the emperor to the housewife, knew something about the latest achievements of science and held some opinion about this actor or that novel. In fact, any kind of culinary, artistic, scientific, or technological achievement met with well-informed appreciation and critique. This permanent criticism—the famous Viennese *granteln*—sharpened everyone's minds and attained standards virtually without equal.

While the Viennese were interested in all fields of endeavor and refinement, what they were truly enthusiastic about was music. From about 1770 to 1810, they had witnessed the most extraordinary explosion of musical creation the world has ever experienced, when the geniuses of Haydn, Mozart, Beethoven, and Schubert burst onto Vienna's stages in rapid succession.[10]

---

[9]Mises, *Erinnerungen*, p. 4; *Notes and Recollections*, p. 2.

[10]Johnston, *Vienna, Vienna*, p. 20:

> The concentration of the supreme genius of Haydn, Mozart, Beethoven, and Schubert in one city over two generations

The city on the Danube became the world capital of music and remained so into the twentieth century. Passion for music united all ethnic, social, and political strata of the population. Differences that made them opponents in politics could not separate them when it came to enjoying old and new masters in music. And in distinct contrast to politics, where irreconcilable worldviews seemed to rule out any objective standards and true expertise, a widespread consensus determined what was good and bad in music, and these musical standards were applied to the performances of the Vienna Philharmonic and of the opera without mercy. In the words of William Johnston: "Slovenliness (*Schlamperei*) might be tolerated in politics, but not in musical or theatrical performance."[11]

Mises did not share the Viennese acceptance of *Schlamperei* when it came to politics, but he did share their passion for music. It would endure throughout his life. His stepdaughter, Gitta Serény recalled her ninety-year-old stepfather sitting next to her at a performance of Strauss's "Blue Danube" in New York City. The old man's eyes were shining as he hummed along with the music.

Viennese Jews

Ludwig's parents could rely on a closely-knit network of relatives that greatly helped their integration in Vienna. In particular, Arthur and Adele could build on blood ties with the local members of the Mises and Landau clans, as well as with the Nirensteins and Kallirs. Ludwig and Richard would have life-long friendships with the young Nirensteins and Kallirs. On

---

has no parallel in the entire history of culture. The closest parallel would be the Rome of Raphael and Michelangelo, or the Athens of Sophocles and Euripides. Yet in no other art do the greatest geniuses so outstrip lesser creators as in musical composition.

[11]Ibid., p. 104.

weekends Ludwig often saw his maternal grandfather, Fischer Landau, whom he admired very much (his paternal grandfather had died before he entered the gymnasium). Summer vacations were spent in the countryside with the Nirensteins and other cousins.

Social contacts outside the network of Jewish families must have been rare. The old Viennese establishment remained closed to newcomers, and even the noble pedigree of the Mises family was too recent to be taken seriously by them. Ludwig would see the day when titles no longer counted (officially at least). After the destruction of the monarchy in November 1918, the new republican government abolished all titles and banned their use in print. Ludwig Heinrich Edler von Mises became Ludwig Mises according to Austrian law. Outside the country, however, he would continue to use the title that his great-grandfather had earned for his family.

The liberal era in Austria had reached its peak in the 1870s. While the following decades would see its decline, it remained strong enough to accommodate the Galician and Moravian Jewish migration to Vienna. All great metropolitan cities of the world derive their dynamics through the influx of new blood from rural provinces. Ambitious young people bring with them innovations in art, science, and business.[12] In the case of Austria-Hungary, the eagerness of the provincial newcomer was compounded by the motivation of the Jewish upstart who for the first time ever had the opportunity to integrate himself into a cosmopolitan society. Art and science offered opportunities for social mobility that Jews enjoyed in no other area. Business, the press, literature and theater, music and opera, and the sciences became the great vehicles for the integration of secular Jews.[13]

---

[12]William Johnston observes that the majority of great "Viennese" pioneers had been born outside of Vienna. See ibid., p. 198.

[13]Heinrich Graetz reports that the first cautious steps toward Jewish integration into Viennese social life were undertaken when Fanny Itzig, a Jewish

By the 1890s, the Jewish impact on Viennese culture could not be overlooked. William Johnston remarks that at the turn of the century, when the Jewish population represented less than 9 percent of Vienna, it was responsible for almost half of the overall artistic and scientific achievement. This overwhelming success was due in part to the absence of a ghetto mentality among the new immigrants. The Jews from Moravia, Bohemia, and Galicia had been living for centuries under an oppressive rabbinical order, but they had not yet experienced any similar constraints in their dealings with gentiles.[14]

> In contrast to German cities like Frankfurt and Berlin, which had long had a Jewish settlement, Vienna first attracted Jews in large numbers after 1848. They came from small villages in Bohemia, Moravia, and Galicia, where Jewish culture had been preserved in relative isolation for hundreds of years. These were Jews who had lived in the countryside. In Bohemia, some of them had been farmers, and few had been touched by city life. They had been small merchants, often trading between towns or providing financial services to gentile landowners. Anti-Semitism had been rare in these regions because the Jews provided services that the gentile lords and peasants wanted but would not perform themselves. The economic complementarity of the countryside had guaranteed the Jews security and modest prosperity.[15]

The Jewish families who moved to Vienna from the eastern provinces formed the nucleus of a new, progressive and liberal

---

woman from Berlin (that is, from the Mendelssohn circle) moved to Vienna in the 1780s and opened a brilliant salon. See Heinrich Graetz, *History of the Jews* (Philadelphia, 1895), vol. 5, pp. 413f.

[14]See Israel Shahak, *Jewish History, Jewish Religion* (London: Pluto Press, 1994).

[15]Johnston, *Vienna, Vienna,* p. 200.

society. Vienna offered them the best schools in the world and
equally unique cultural facilities. And the cosmopolitan atmosphere of the country's largest city offered progressive Jews the
prospect of escaping the narrow confines of a life directed by
the traditional precepts of their religion. The leading organ of
this liberal Jewish immigrant community was the *Neue Freie
Presse*, which relied on the financial backing of the Credit-
Anstalt bank, the Austrian flagship of the house of Rothschild.[16]

Although the Miseses were more conservative than most
other Jewish families in Vienna (Arthur was a board member of
the Vienna Jewish Cultural Community, and Adele was very
religious[17]) Ludwig grew up in an atmosphere that tended to
equate progress and secularization, where prophets and saints
were increasingly replaced by the inventors of engines and the
heroes of philosophy, art, and science.[18]

---

[16]Ibid., p. 98:

> [T]he paper took an increasingly pro-German and anti-Slav
> stand. Under its mentor and editor Moritz Benedikt
> (1849–1920), it fanned anti-Slav feelings among Austro-Ger-
> mans. It lauded the post-1880 alliance with Germany, and in
> 1914 positively welcomed war as an ally of Wilhelm II. . . .
> The *Neue Freie Presse* resembled the liberal bourgeoisie who
> read it: exquisite taste in culture accompanied by naivete in
> politics.

[17]See her recollections, Adele von Mises, "A Day in the House of My Parents," *Tante Adele erzählt* (unpublished manuscript, 1929). Graetz mentions
one "great rabbi Landau" as condemning the study of philosophy and science. See Graetz, *History of the Jews*, vol. 5, p. 402.

[18]What Schorske says about Theodor Herzl, the founder of the Zionist
movement, also applies to Ludwig von Mises:

> When Theodor was born in 1860, his family was well out of
> the ghetto: economically established, religiously "enlight-
> ened," politically liberal, and culturally German. Their
> Judaism amounted to little more than what Theodor Gom-
> perz, the assimilated Jewish classicist, liked to call "un pieux
> souvenir de famille." (Schorkse, *Fin-de-siècle Vienna*, p. 147)

Schorske's parents even liked to call his bar mitzvah his "Konfirmation."

For young Mises, the transformation of Vienna through the exploits of science and technology was a continual process of never-ending improvements. When he arrived in the city as a young boy, the liberal governments had already put their stamp on the streets and architecture. Everything was new; everything breathed the spirit of the time. As a young man, Ludwig saw gas lamps replaced by electric lighting, horse and carriage by motorized vehicles, the daily excursion to the public water fountain by new plumbing systems. He saw telephone lines installed throughout the city, and eventually saw airplanes taking off and landing in Vienna. The famous writer Stefan Zweig, one of Mises's contemporaries, claimed that the same progress seemed to manifest itself in social and political matters, for example, in the extension of suffrage and in pro-labor legislation. The new urban middle class came to believe that all social and political problems would disappear in due course. Conflicts between ethnic and religious groups would vanish and mankind would eventually reach the state of universal brotherhood.[19]

It was no accident that the overwhelming majority of the Jewish immigrants to Vienna were liberals. Happy to have escaped the religious and moral constraints of their rural hometowns, they tended to oppose the limitations of their new environment as well. This concerned not only the political order, which officially privileged Catholics of German ethnicity, but also the social role of the Catholic Church, whose prominence painfully reminded them of the rabbinical order at home.

Two issues united Jewish and gentile liberals: opposition to the Church, and the fight against censorship. The latter had survived from the times of Franz I, who after the Napoleonic wars had turned Austria, and Vienna in particular, into a police

---

[19]Zweig, *Die Welt von Gestern*, p. 17. Zweig was born in the same year as Mises, 1881, and also was a Jewish intellectual whose family had settled in Vienna only recently. Zweig's testimony is therefore representative of experiences and sentiments of the milieu in which Mises spent his childhood.

state that sought to monitor all the intellectual activities of its citizens. Police spies infiltrated the cafés and theaters, and concierges acted as informers. Foreign books had to be

approved before they could be released on the Austrian market, and many foreign authors were prohibited. Newspapers were monitored as a matter of course and even theatrical productions needed the authorities' prior approval.[20] When the Mises family moved to Vienna in the 1880s, the stringency of the censorship laws had already faded under the impact of the liberal 1848 revolution, but the

Mises at about age 15

effects of the old laws on the Viennese mentality remained. Traditional city dwellers were reluctant to pursue what were possibly unbecoming innovations in business, science, or art. They were educated men and women of good taste and manners, but they lacked the initiative and drive necessary to realize projects against the resistance of a conformist environment. The entrepreneurial spirit came with the "impatient eastern Jew"[21] from Galicia.[22] These men cared far less about social disapproval than the old Viennese. Their rugged individualism transformed Vienna and western culture in the course of a few glorious decades.

---

[20]Johnston, *Vienna, Vienna*, p. 17. Newspaper censorship continued in force until after 1900 (see ibid., p. 97).

[21]The expression is Stefan Zweig's.

[22]Why had Franz's police state tamed the Viennese more than the provincials? Johnston gives this explanation:

> Vienna suffered far more harshly from censorship and police surveillance than any other region of the Habsburg Empire. In the days before the electric telegraph and the railroad, it was nearly impossible to harass a hinterland as effectively as a capital city. . . . At no other time since Maria Theresa centralised Austrian administration did the provinces compete so successfully with the capital in cultural prominence as during the Biedermeier period. (Johnston, *Vienna, Vienna*, pp. 17f.)

Akademisches Gymnasium

In September 1892, shortly before his eleventh birthday, Mises entered the *Akademische Gymnasium* where he would be schooled for the next eight years. The gymnasium schools were very particular institutions, more demanding and quite dissimilar from their present-day successors. A product of the nineteenth-century Continental system of education, they can best be described as "a combination of high school and college."[23] The children of ambitious and well-to-do parents began attending around the age of ten, after four years of elementary training. Three gymnasium models were available: a classical model featuring eight years of Latin and six of Greek; a semi-classical with Latin and one or two modern languages; and a thoroughly modern option with only modern languages. Erik von Kuehnelt-Leddihn states that the classical model had more prestige than the others, but they were all demanding.

> Often these very hard school years hung like a black cloud over families. Failure in just one subject required repetition of a whole year. This was the fate of Nietzsche, of Albert Einstein, and also of Friedrich August von Hayek! Young Mises, of course, got a classical education: the modern languages he learned privately.[24]

While at the Akademischen Gymnasium, Mises read Caesar, Livy, Ovid, Sallust Jugurtha, Cicero, Virgil, and Tacitus in Latin. In Greek, he studied Xenophon, Homer, Herodotus, Demosthenes, Plato, and Sophocles.[25] One verse from Virgil so deeply impressed him that it became his maxim for a lifetime:

---

[23]Erik von Kuehnelt-Leddihn, *The Cultural Background of Ludwig von Mises* (Auburn, Ala.: Ludwig von Mises Institute, 1999), p. 3.

[24]Ibid.

[25]Detailed information on the classes taught at Mises's school is contained in *Jahres-Bericht über das k.k. Akademkische Gymnasium in Wien für das*

Tu ne cede malis sed contra audentior ito.[26]

(Do not give in to evil, but proceed ever more
boldly against it.)

Many years later, he pointed out the crucial role that the immersion in classical literature—and the writings of the ancient
Greeks in particular—played for the emergence of liberal social
philosophy and thus in his own intellectual development:

> It was the political literature of the ancient Greeks
> that begot the ideas of the Monarchomachs, the phi-
> losophy of the Whigs, the doctrines of Althusius,
> Grotius and John Locke and the ideology of the
> fathers of modern constitutions and bills of rights. It
> was the classical studies, the essential feature of a lib-
> eral education, that kept awake the spirit of freedom
> in the England of the Stuarts, in the France of the
> Bourbons, and in Italy subject to the despotism of a
> galaxy of princes. No less a man than Bismarck,
> among the nineteenth-century statesmen next to
> Metternich the foremost foe of liberty, bears witness
> to the fact that, even in the Prussia of Frederick
> William III, the *Gymnasium*, the education based on
> Greek and Roman literature, was a stronghold of
> republicanism.[27]

Schuljahr 1899/1900 (Vienna: Verlag des k.k. Akademkischen Gymnasiums,
1900) and the annual reports for the previous years.

[26]Virgil, *The Aeneid*, VI, 95.

[27]Mises, *The Anti-Capitalistic Mentality* (Princeton, N.J.: Van Nostrand,
1956), pp. 93–94. Mises argued:

> The liberty which the Greek statesmen, philosophers and
> historians glorified as the most precious good of man was a
> privilege reserved to a minority. In denying it to metics and
> slaves they virtually advocated the despotic rule of a heredi-
> tary caste of oligarchs. Yet it would be a grave error to dis-
> miss their hymns to liberty as mendacious. They were no less
> sincere in their praise and quest of freedom than were, two
> thousand years later, the slave-holders among the signers of
> the American Declaration of Independence. (p. 93)

The Austrian schools had been reformed in 1851, at the beginning of the absolutist phase of Franz Joseph's reign. Under the leadership of Count Leo Thun von Hohenstein, the government seized control of secondary education, which had been the exclusive domain of the Catholic Church, and imposed a new curriculum that was meant to prepare the graduates for scientific studies and executive positions within the Austrian bureaucracy. The teaching of religion remained mandatory and was assured by representatives of the relevant religious organizations—Catholic priests and Jewish rabbis. But even the teaching of religion was supposed to be respectful of facts and laws established by scientific research.[28]

Public schooling had become compulsory in 1869. Children had to have four years of elementary school (which prepared them to be good subjects of the state) before they could enter a secondary school. The Gymnasien taught the humanities to the future elite of the country. Only about 5 percent of an age group was admitted. This number tells more about the nature of the gymnasium than any description of its curricula. To be admitted to a gymnasium was to be part of a tiny intellectual elite. It meant learning from teachers who were respectfully called "Herr Professor" and who were in fact the peers of today's

---

And he went on:

> The passionate endeavors to eliminate the classical studies from the curriculum of the liberal education and thus virtually to destroy its very character were one of the major manifestations of the revival of the servile ideology. (p. 94)

For a diametrically opposed assessment of the relationship between classical literature and liberty see Frédéric Bastiat, "Baccalauréat et socialisme," *Oeuvres complètes* (2nd ed., Paris: Guillaumin, 1863), vol. 4, pp. 442–503. Bastiat argues in particular that the classics have bequeathed to us the notion that society is a purely conventional construct, as well as the idea that legislation could fabricate society according to just any design.

[28]Johnston, *Vienna, Vienna*, p. 97. The other reformers were the professors Franz Bexner and Hermann Bonitz.

college and university professors rather than of today's high-school teachers. (Positions at the universities were extremely rare.) And it meant being measured by standards that were incomparably higher than those of modern high schools.

Being among the best students did not guarantee a place in a gymnasium: tuition was high and outside assistance was rare. (Only one of Mises's classmates had such assistance.) But because the schools competed for the best pupils, they often waived the fees for exceptional young men who could not afford them—about 20 percent of the pupils in Mises's class. The typical gymnasium pupil was the intelligent son of middle-class or wealthy parents. Pupils with a working-class background were an exception.

While the gymnasium was the best type of school, the various Gymnasien were not equal in quality or reputation. The best schools were in Vienna, both in terms of the family background of the pupils and of the quality of the professors. The latter were often published scholars who actively engaged in research and made important contributions in their fields. For example, Ludwig's Latin teacher, Dr. Valentin Hintner, was a member of the Royal Prussian Academy of the Socially Beneficial Sciences in Erfurt.[29]

In Vienna, three schools stood above the rest: the Theresianum, the Schottengymnasium, and the Akademische Gymnasium. These were all-male schools. (Vienna girls were taught in separate gymnasien, yet they could take the graduation exam in one of the top schools.) Empress Maria Theresa had created the Theresianum in the mid-1700s as a "knight's academy"—a school to prepare young aristocrats for future responsibilities as administrative and political leaders of the empire. In Mises's day, it remained a school for the sons of the high aristocracy and admitted bourgeois pupils only as day students. Among the latter were Karl Lueger (who eventually became the first non-liberal mayor

---

[29]Königlich preussische Akademie der gemeinnützigen Wissenschaften.

of Vienna), Rudolf Hilferding, and Joseph Schumpeter. There were, however, many families who abhorred the snobbish atmosphere of the Theresianum and preferred other schools such as the Benedictine Schottengymnasium, and the Akademische Gymnasium.[30]

The Akademische Gymnasium was the most thoroughly secularized secondary school in Vienna. It was therefore the favorite place of education for the sons of the liberal bourgeoisie, and in particular of Vienna's better Jewish families.[31] In Ludwig's terminal class, nineteen out of thirty-five pupils were Jewish, thirteen Catholic, and two Protestant. The school had been established in 1453. Today it is located on Beethovenplatz, near the eastern Ringstrasse. The tall neo-gothic building was constructed in the 1860s with romantic towers and high windows on ivied brick walls. This is where Ludwig spent the next eight years. His weekly schedule in the first year: religion (2 hours), Latin (8 hours), German (4 hours), geography (3 hours), mathematics (3 hours), natural history (2 hours), calligraphy (1 hour). By and large, the same subjects were taught throughout the entire eight-year program; the only major exception was Greek, which was taught starting in the third year. Mises was one of the best students, although not at the very top (the only class where he truly excelled was history) and he eventually graduated sixth out of thirty-three pupils.

The pupils were however somewhat disenchanted with their school because of the dour indifference of their teachers. Before the 1851 liberal education reform under Thun-Hohenstein, the Austrian schools had been run by Catholic clerics. Accordingly, classroom instruction featured mainly Church history and *philosophia perennis*. After the reform, civil servants replaced the

---

[30]Eugen Guglia, *Das Theresianum in Wien* (Vienna: Schroll, 1912). Somary, *The Raven of Zürich*.

[31]Schorske, *Fin-de-siècle Vienna*, p. 135; Karl Kautsky, *Erinnerungen und Erörterungen* (The Hague: Mouton, 1960), p. 211.

clerics. These new secular professors were entirely steeped in the traditions and mentality of the Austrian bureaucracy, and performed in the classroom with the same detached attitude of other state bureaucrats. Their main interest was not to educate students, but to present their material efficiently.[32]

Apart from the insufficient motivation of the teachers, there was another reason for student dissatisfaction, a reason that also explains the explosion of creative energies in Vienna that began in the liberal era. The schools did not offer enough intellectual stimulation for the Jewish boys, who came from families nurturing a long tradition of literacy and of careful and sustained intellectual work.

Then as now, young students endured school as a routine. It was not where they found their interests or passions. But while students today might look forward to sports or movies after school, their Viennese counterparts at the end of the nineteenth century looked forward to reading and writing what was not taught in school—in other words, to their real educations. In school, a fourteen-year-old would read the Latin and Greek classics; he stuffed his brain with the minutiae of German and European history, and he did so without enthusiasm. But after school he would devour modern writings on science and the arts. Why did these Viennese boys have such a different notion of having a good time from virtually all other generations at virtually all other places? The answer is, in brief: traditionalist Jewish culture let loose in a secular environment.

William Johnston observes:

> Jews had enjoyed many centuries of literacy before the rest of Europe started to become literate in the eighteenth century. Thereafter Jews entered as if by predestination into professions that required facility with words.[33]

---

[32]Rudolf Sieghart, *Die letzten Jahrzehnte einer Grossmacht* (Berlin: Ullstein, 1932), pp. 15f.

[33]Johnston, *Vienna, Vienna*, p. 217.

The true passion of these young men, who came from families that just a generation before had left the rural rabbinical order, was intellectual adventure in the secular realm—a pursuit unavailable to their ancestors. They threw themselves into literature, theater, opera, whatever aroused their curiosity. Raised to value religious scholarship, they found in Vienna the intellectual delights of the secular world.

Ludwig von Mises seems to have been a typical specimen of this generation. He recalled that his interest in history was piqued in 1888 when he read articles in a family journal on the lives of the German Kaisers, Wilhelm I and Friedrich III, who had died that year. He was then barely seven years old. According to his wife, he set out to write a history of the Crimean War when he was ten. After writing his first page, however, he abandoned the project when he discovered that an English historian had published ten volumes on the topic.[34] During his gymnasium years, he devoured the writings of the German historians justifying the new Prussian supremacy in German lands. These readings provided a lifelong lesson. He realized that the acclaimed authors were in fact writing with a distinct bias.[35] Thus, early on he trained the critical mind that would serve him so well throughout his life and eventually turn him into the twentieth century's greatest intellectual champion of liberty.

One of the few surviving photographs from his youth seems to forebode these events. Lew Rockwell comments:

> I often think back to a photograph of Mises when he
> was a young boy of perhaps 12, standing with his

---

[34]See Margit von Mises, *My Years with Ludwig von Mises* (Cedar Falls, Iowa: Center for Futures Education), p. 15.

[35]See Mises, *Erinnerungen*, p. 3. There he states: "As an Austrian it was not difficult for me to realize the overtones of these writers. And I soon discerned the method of their analysis, which had rudely been called the falsification of history." Mises, *Notes and Recollections*, p. 3. *See also* Margit von Mises, *My Years with Ludwig von Mises*, p. 15.

*Ludwig von Mises with his
father, Arthur, circa 1893*

father. He was wearing the traditional Austrian garb
popular in the 1890s, and holding a racket for sports.
The picture was grainy and distant. And yet you sense
that there was something in Mises's eyes, a certain
determination and intellectual fire, even at such a
young age. His eyes seem knowing, as if he were
already preparing himself for what he might face. . . .
We look and try to discern what it was about him that
caused him to be such a fighter, that caused him to
stand while others fell, that gave him that sense of
moral certitude to fight for enduring truths regardless

of the political winds. Even in that grainy photo-
graph, we have some sense that we see it in his eyes,
that glimmer that reflects a heart that would never
compromise with despotism but rather advance the
truth of human freedom until his last breath.[36]

These things appear clearer today than they were at the time.
Ludwig's passionate interest in the sciences was typical for boys
of his background and generation. So was his enthusiasm for the
arts. We must imagine him as a teenager standing in line before
premieres at the Hofburgtheater or Volkstheater. After school
he would meet friends such as Hans Kelsen at a café to read
journals and discuss their discoveries.

The lives of Mises and Kelsen bear many surprising parallels
that make this friendship particularly interesting. They were born
in the same year and attended the same school. Later they would
enter the same department at the University of Vienna, prepare
for a scholarly career, and publish their first major treatises
shortly before Word War I. Both became ardent defenders of
the notion that there is no such thing as a science of ethics, but
that all judgments of value are merely subjective. While Mises
would become famous for his studies of *a priori* laws in economics, Kelsen became a pioneer of the "pure theory of law." Also,
both would marry women named Grete, move to the United
States at the advent of World War II, and eventually die in the
same year, far from Vienna—Mises in New York, and Kelsen in
California.

Kelsen's family background was lower than average
Akademische Gymnasium standards, while Mises's was higher.
(Mises was the only aristocrat in his class.) This did not prevent
the ambitious nobleman from befriending the ambitious son of
a clerk and remaining his friend for a lifetime. It is likely that
they became acquainted with the philosophy of Immanuel

---

[36]Lew Rockwell, "Heart of a Fighter," *The Free Market* 23, no. 7 (2005):
4f.

Kant, and especially with Kant's epistemology, at the same time, when they were about sixteen years old. German "idealistic" philosophy—the philosophy of Kant, Fichte, Hegel, and their followers—exercised an enormous influence on many young minds in Vienna, not least of all because these books had been on the Catholic index of forbidden works.

Kelsen was profoundly shaken by his confrontation with idealist philosophy. Through his reading of Kant, Kelsen had come to the conclusion that the reality of the exterior world was problematic. During the rest of his life he seems to have applied his early subjectivist interpretation of Kant to the field of law. As an old man, Kelsen still recalled his reading of Kant as a crucial juncture in his intellectual development.[37]

The philosopher from Königsberg did not have the same impact on Mises. In distinct contrast to Kelsen, Mises did not have a Kantian epiphany and then set out to reconstruct economic science in the light of this idealist philosophy. Rather, Mises started from case studies and moved up to ever wider generalizations and greater abstractions. Eventually, he would realize that he could not avoid dealing with epistemological questions and then stressed the *a priori* nature of economic laws. But even at this point, Kantian epistemology did not have a noticeable impact on his thought.[38]

Mises's true primary interest was in political history and political action. All the other disciplines he eventually came to master—law, economics, epistemology, political philosophy—were subservient to these primary goals. In his final exam in German at the Akademischen Gymnasium, he had to write an essay on

---

[37]See Rudolf A. Métall, *Hans Kelsen* (Vienna: Verlag Franz Deuticke, 1968), p. 4.

[38]Many years later, he had nothing favorable to say about the neo-Kantian movement (in particular Cohen and Natorp), which blossomed at the turn of the century. He said it was an era of decline and neo-Kantianism was its philosophical reflection. See Mises to Lachmann, letter dated October 11, 1956; Grove City Archive: Lachmann file.

the following question: "What are the moral inspirations that we derive from the study of the history of Austria?"[39] Though his answer is lost, a statement that he made many years later gives us a hint as to what he might have written in May 1900. Speaking of the benefits of studying history, Mises wrote:

> It opens the mind toward an understanding of human nature and destiny. It increases wisdom. It is the very essence of that much misinterpreted concept, a liberal education. It is the foremost approach to humanism, the lore of the specifically human concerns that distinguish man from other living beings. . . . Personal culture is more than mere familiarity with the present state of science, technology, and civic affairs. It is more than acquaintance with books and paintings and the experience of travel and of visits to museums. It is the assimilation of the ideas that roused mankind from the inert routine of a merely animal existence to a life of reasoning and speculating. It is the individual's effort to humanize himself by partaking in the tradition of all the best that earlier generations have bequeathed.[40]

The complicated political history of Austria was certainly interesting enough to attract the attention of a bright teenager. In fact, much of Mises's later work can be seen as an attempt to understand the problems of his age from the point of view of economic theory and social philosophy. But even more fundamentally, he was interested in practical questions: What could

---

[39]*Jahres-Bericht über das k.k. Akademische Gymnasium in Wien für das Schuljahr 1899/1900*, p. 13. The written part of the exam also included mathematics and geometry (requiring among other things that he deliver a mathematical proof for a geometric theorem), as well as translations. Mises had to translate from Latin into German, from German into Latin, and from Greek into German.

[40]Mises, *Theory and History* (New Haven, Conn.: Yale University Press, 1957), pp. 293–94.

governments do to make their country a better place? Mises was never interested in merely collecting historical data. He wanted to explain history—to trace observed events back to their causes—and he wanted to apply these insights in practice. How did the political and social institutions of his fatherland come into being? What were the causes of ethnic and social strife and how could one combat them? What were the roots of imperialism? What were the causes of the great social progress of the nineteenth century, in rising literacy, declining infant mortality, and higher mass consumption?

All these questions and their answers were preliminaries to action. Given our knowledge about causes and effects in social life, what is to be done now? For example, how could one promote the welfare of the working classes now more than in past decades? A family tradition of commerce and social leadership had made young Mises used to seeing and seeking the bottom line. He brought this emphasis on results to the study of social life and social strife, which prepared him, as he would say, "to take an active part in the great issues of his age." Thus he turned to the study of intellectual disciplines that promised to give guidance in political matters. And because the conflicts of his era—and ours—were largely economic ones, Mises ultimately became an economist. Many years later he wrote these lines:

> All the political antagonisms and conflicts of our age turn on economic issues.
>
> It has not always been so. In the sixteenth and seventeenth century the controversies that split the peoples of Western civilization into feuding parties were religious. Protestantism stood against Catholicism, and within the Protestant camp various interpretations of the Gospels begot discord. In the eighteenth century and in a great part of the nineteenth century constitutional conflicts prevailed in politics. The principles of royal absolutism and oligarchic government were resisted by liberalism (in the classical European meaning of the term) that advocated

representative government. In those days a man who wanted to take an active part in the great issues of his age had to study seriously the matter of these controversies. . . . Only boors neglected to inform themselves about the great problems that agitated the minds of their contemporaries.

In our age the conflict between economic freedom as represented in the market economy and totalitarian government omnipotence as realized by socialism is the paramount matter. All political controversies refer to these economic problems. Only the study of economics can tell a man what all these conflicts mean. Nothing can be known about such matters as inflation, economic crises, unemployment, unionism, protectionism, taxation, economic controls, and all similar issues, that does not involve and presuppose economic analysis. . . . A man who talks about these problems without having acquainted himself with the fundamental ideas of economic theory is simply a babbler who parrot-like repeats what he has picked up incidentally from other fellows who are not better informed than he himself. A citizen who casts his ballot without having to the best of his abilities studied as much economics as he can fails in his civic duties.[41]

Economic conflicts were at the forefront of social dissension in Austria-Hungary during Mises's early years and were debated each day in the press, in new books, in cafés and in the streets. Let us look more closely then at the fundamental political problems of *fin de siècle* Austria.

---

[41]Mises, "Eugen von Böhm-Bawerk and the Discriminating Reader," *The Freeman* (August 1959).

Austria-Hungary

Austria-Hungary as a political entity came into being after the defeat of the older Austrian Empire in 1866 by the Prussian armies at the Bohemian town of Königgrätz. The conflict with Prussia was over supremacy within the Germanies. The military defeat settled the question in favor of Prussia, but the Habsburg family did not abandon its plans to regain its traditional position of leadership.

The greatest problem for the Habsburgs' ambitions in the age of the nation-state was that their empire was not predominantly German. The Hungarian population was approximately the same size as the Austro-German population, and the empire contained several million each of Czechs, Poles, Romanians, and Ruthenians, as well as a handful of smaller nationalities. In the eyes of the liberals—in those days the strongest political force in the Germanies—this hodgepodge of nationalities disqualified the Habsburg family from leadership of the German Reich. After the defeat in the 1859 Italian campaign, various Austrian governments sought ways to make the empire more German and more liberal to emulate the ideal of a liberal nation-state.[42]

A constitutional reform in February 1861 under Prime Minister Schmerling addressed the nationalities problem through the introduction of estate parliaments (*Kurienparlamente*). The idea was to use parliamentary representation as a means to settle political conflicts between different ethnicities and different social classes without resorting to the nefarious one-man-one-vote principle. The constitution guaranteed a majority of seats to the political and economic establishment. Primarily, it guaranteed the ethnic Germans and their allies a majority of seats, even where they were in the numerical minority.

---

[42]Sieghart, *Die letzten Jahrzehnte einer Grossmacht*, pp. 377ff.

The Schmerling constitution tried to make up for Austria's lack of German character. But with the military defeat at the hands of Prussia, a more pressing problem suddenly appeared: separatism. The Habsburgs felt they had to secure their power base by finding a way to guarantee the continued loyalty of the Hungarians. This was done in the so-called *Ausgleich* ("settlement") that was hurriedly crafted and ratified within weeks after Königgrätz.[43] The *Ausgleich* established the principle of political dualism in Habsburg lands—the subdivision of the empire into two spheres of influence, one under German rule, the other Hungarian. The *Ausgleich* granted far-reaching autonomy to the Hungarian gentry and made them *de facto* rulers over other peoples within the confines of "Hungary."[44] In exchange, the Hungarian establishment did not contest German hegemony in the other lands of the empire, and they consented to the continued existence of a common dynasty, a common foreign policy, and a common army. The *Ausgleich* also guaranteed the economic unity of the empire.

From its very inception, however, the *Ausgleich* was prevented from securing internal peace because its stipulations were interpreted in fundamentally different ways. In the eyes of the German side, the *Ausgleich* was an agreement reached between the different nations of the empire, which implied that the signatories from the very outset conceived of themselves as parts of a larger political entity. The emperor was not one of the contracting parties; rather, he presided over the whole political entity and the contract was between different parts of that whole. In contrast, the Hungarians saw the *Ausgleich* as a bilateral affair between themselves and the king of Hungary

---

[43]The Austrian Reichsrat voted a new constitution on December 21, 1867. On the *Ausgleich* see, in particular, ibid., pp. 111ff.

[44]This concerned in particular Slovaks and Romanians. The "Kingdom of Croatia and Slavonia" was also part of Hungary, but it was relatively autonomous.

(who also happened to be the ruler of Austria and various other foreign countries). It was only incidental that the agreement with their monarch was mirrored by a parallel agreement between the Austrians and their emperor. In short, the Hungarians considered themselves a sovereign nation on its way to full autonomy, and the *Ausgleich* merely one step on this path.[45]

For this reason alone, the *Ausgleich* failed miserably in providing a basis for the continued peaceful coexistence of the various Austrian nations, and thus for Habsburg power. Year after year, the Hungarians presented new claims and reached new compromises at the cost of the rest of the empire. German Austrians interpreted these ever-increasing demands as political extortion. They despaired of the disputatious behavior of the Hungarians, which undermined the very existence of the empire. But the Hungarian campaign did not suffer the slightest trace of remorse, and it steadily gained ground.

How successful it was can be inferred from its impact on political language. The words "Austria" and "Reich" were increasingly abandoned to suit Hungarian-style political correctness. Common institutions of the empire were no longer called by the prefix *Reich-* (as in *Reichskriegsminister*), but by the prefix "k.u.k." (*kaiserlich und königlich*—Imperial and Royal), thus "k.u.k. Kriegsminister." By contrast, Hungarian state institutions were prefixed with "k." as in "kingly" (referring to the Hungarian crown), and the state institutions of the other, non-Hungarian territories, which shared a common parliament under German supremacy (the *Reichsrat*), were prefixed with "k.k." (Imperial-Royal). Curiously, these other territories did not even have a common name. They were only the "kingdoms and lands represented in the Reichsrat."[46] In a great satire on this abbreviation orgy, Robert Musil, in his famous *fin de siècle*

---

[45]They were pressing these demands on their legal representative, the King of Hungary. This king was of course Franz Joseph himself.

[46]Sieghart, *Die letzten Jahrzehnte einer Grossmacht*, p. 113.

novel *The Man without Qualities* called the country of his hero Kakanien ("k-k-land") and said it was the only country that declined for lack of a name.

The *Ausgleich* also provoked resistance from others, most notably from the Croats and the Czechs.[47] Both saw the *Ausgleich*—correctly—as a scheme to perpetuate the current political privileges of Germans and Hungarians. The Czech radicals, calling themselves the Young Czechs, became famous for their ruthlessness in adopting the Hungarian strategy. Their representatives boycotted the sessions of the Reichsrat (the parliament of the "Austrian half" of the empire) and claimed to be one sovereign nation, which would deal only with its own King of Bohemia (who happened also to be the emperor), and they would do so only to secure more liberties for the Czechs.

The ultimate effect of the *Ausgleich* was to alienate step by step all nations from the empire. The radical elements in each nation increasingly refused to perceive themselves as parts of a larger whole. They considered disputes with other nations of the Habsburg crown to be matters of their own foreign policy that did not involve the empire or the monarchy. This tendency was reinforced in a fateful way when, in 1878, the southern Slav lands of Bosnia and Herzegovina fell under the dominion of Austria-Hungary.[48] Rather than granting autonomous status to the new territories, the Hungarians immediately claimed the right to rule them, arguing that at some point in the

---

[47]Support for the *Ausgleich* came from the Poles and the Italians. Both nations were settled predominantly in areas where they had the economic and political power, but were numerically inferior to other local nations (Ruthenians, southern Slavs).

[48]This was one of the stipulations of an agreement of seven governments at a congress in Berlin in August 1878. The Berlin Congress dealt with territorial questions in southeastern Europe and the Middle East. It was prompted by a crushing Russian victory over Turkey and signed by these two states, as well as by the governments of Austria-Hungary, Germany, France, England, and Italy.

distant past they had been conquered by a Hungarian king. Bosnia-Herzegovina therefore came under the co-dominion of Hungary and "the kingdoms and lands represented in the Reichsrat." Over the next thirty years, this divided rule from Vienna and Budapest created fertile ground for southern Slav nationalism and Serb agitation. It was a major factor in the events that eventually precipitated the world into the Great War, and destroyed the Austrian monarchy.

Following the Hungarian strategy, the radicals of all nations eventually refused to deal with any other nation at all. The central government in Vienna made concessions concerning the use of language in the local branch offices of its bureaucracy and so, around the year 1900, German, Hungarian, Italian, Czech, Polish, and Serbo-Croatian were all in official use. But such concessions could not satisfy the aspirations of the radicals. At the turn of the century, many Italians, Czechs, Slovaks, Poles, Ukrainians, Magyars, Romanians, Serbs, Croats, and Slovenes strove for national independence.[49] They insisted on the sovereign status of their ethnic group and argued that matters of "domestic" policy existed only insofar as they pertained to their relationship with the local monarch.[50] Franz Joseph slipped more and more into the impossible situation of being the sole embodiment of a political entity scorned by millions of his subjects: the empire.[51] He was still acceptable as a political partner, but only in his capacity as a king, that is, as King of Bohemia, King of Hungary, King of Croatia, etc. In the minds of his subjects, the monarch was the only element that tied together the various lands and nations, who felt no desire or need to come to terms with one another. One of Mises's fellow students recalled:

---

[49]Johnston, *Vienna, Vienna*, p. 8.

[50]The greatest problem of this stance was that the traditional political territories (the "kingdoms and lands") did not have nationally homogeneous populations. Except for some of the Alpine regions, all these traditional territories hosted at least two nationalities, often more.

[51]Sieghart, *Die letzten Jahrzehnte einer Grossmacht*, p. 391.

No more than 300 metres separated the University
from the parliament building in the Vienna
Ringstrasse; if the young people fought almost daily at
the University, the conflicts of the deputies were of
equal violence, and were battled with a fanatical passion unknown in other countries. If you went only a
hundred steps further on from parliament, you could
see every day—and usually more often—a carriage
drawn by two horses drive out of the Hofburg. In it
sat the old Emperor and his equally elderly adjutant,
and they would set out for Schönbrunn at an easy
trot, always at the same hour, and always down the
same street. There was no security escort ahead of or
behind the carriage, no policeman sat in the vehicle
itself; any assassin would have had an easy job. But
nobody took the opportunity.[52]

Franz Joseph, who had begun his reign as an arch-reac-
tionary and gave his consent to constitutional government only
after two lost wars, eventually became the glorified, almost mys-
tic embodiment of a state that few of his subjects really desired.
He presided over the radical transformation of Austria that
started after the revolution of 1848, and stretched until the very
end of his reign in 1916, a transformation that left no sphere of
social life untouched. A contemporary witness, himself a democrat born around the time Franz Joseph ascended the throne,
recalls the awe that the emperor inspired in all his subjects:

And the Kaiser had lived through—in fact co-spon-
sored—truly monumental changes. The almost feu-
dal landed lordship with its peasants subject to the

---

[52]Somary, *The Raven of Zurich*, p. 11. He goes on to observe:

The leaders of our modern great empires are driven rapidly
in bullet-proof cars, protected by countless bodyguards.
Aristotle thus defined the difference between a monarch and
a tyrant: the monarch protects his people, the tyrant has to
protect himself from them.

estate, sleepy little towns with their handicrafts
organized in guilds, a capital city with concentric
walls and bastions, with large ramparts and glacis, a
society the ruling intellectual power of which was the
Church and the materially moving power of which
was still the stagecoach and the horse—all this
formed the environment of the beginning reign of
Francis Joseph, which was to encounter so many
material and intellectual innovations. Almost all laws
that created or made possible landed property for citizens, free peasants and country workers, handicrafts
and industry, large-scale trade, railroads and
steamship transport, and insurance and banking services were signed with his name. The tremendous
development of modern capitalism fell into the
period of his reign; and thereby the transformation of
the absolutistic patrimonial state into a constitutional
monarchy, the rise of the free citizenry, the flowering
of the citizens' parliament, the cultural unfolding of
all nations of the Reich, along with the inevitable frictions of the maturing process and, finally, the rise of
the working class, the spreading of the social idea,
and the beginnings of social legislation. Whoever
met Francis Joseph at my time felt the breath of a
long and grand period of history that he has carried
on. Seldom a single human life has encompassed such
immensity.[53]

But even those who had not inherited sentimental feelings
for the emperor could hardly fail to perceive his pivotal role
within Austria-Hungary's political system. Ludwig von Mises's
contemporary and fellow student Felix Somary recalled his
father telling him,

> This Empire is quite different from the rest of the
> world. Imagine the Emperor and his Government
> gone for even one year, and the nationalists would

---

[53]Sieghart, *Die letzten Jahrzehnte einer Grossmacht*, p. 210.

> tear each other to pieces. The Government is the
> fence that separates the zoo of wild animals from the
> outside world, and nowhere else are there so many
> and such dangerous political beasts as we have.

Young lads such as Felix learned early on to appreciate the benefits of the monarchical order in Austria, understanding that

> the Monarchy was not some historical relic, but the
> sole possible institutional framework for holding
> eight nationalities together on Europe's most dangerous frontier.[54]

It was to no avail. Imitation of the Hungarian strategy mushroomed after 1867 and culminated in the late 1890s, when Prime Minister Count Badeni sought to solve national conflicts between Germans and Czechs through legislation that put the two languages on an equal footing within the Bohemian government. Ethnic Germans saw the ordinance as the "last straw" in an ongoing series of concessions to the Czechs. Badeni was not prepared for the level of animosity the Germans of Bohemia and the rest of the empire directed at him as a result of his legislation. They began disrupting parliamentary proceedings and instigated violent protests. The emperor, frightened by the mass agitation of some of the most important segments of society, dismissed Badeni in November 1897.

Socialisms, Austrian Style

The national conflicts within the empire were compounded by social conflicts resulting directly or indirectly from the liberal reforms of the 1850s and 1860s. The liberalization of trade, transport, banking, and industry had completely transformed the Austrian economy, undermining the social and political position of the old elites. The aristocracy and clergy despised

---

[54]Somary, *The Raven of Zurich*, p. 10.

the emerging coterie of capitalist upstarts, and in their political rearguard action against liberalism and capitalism they allied themselves with the economic losers of the transformation process: the great number of people employed in traditional forms of production, including small-scale farming and those handicrafts that had become obsolete in an era of more efficient factory production. They were not necessarily "losers" in the sense that their income had been reduced in absolute terms. It was rather that their relative economic and social positions had deteriorated in comparison to those of their relatives, friends, and neighbors who had found employment in the new capitalist corporations.

Petit-bourgeois residents of *fin de siècle* Vienna especially resented the success of the new Jewish middle and upper classes, which most visibly represented the changes in Austrian society induced by the liberal reforms. There had been virtually no Jewish residents in Vienna before 1848 because Jews were not allowed to own land in the city or to stay longer than three days within its walls. Only about 200 distinguished Jewish families such as the Rothschilds had obtained an exemption from this policy. All others had to leave the city after three days and re-enter it at another gate to obtain a new visa. As a consequence, Jews were virtually unknown to the general population, and those who had actually met Jews in person remembered them as impoverished Talmud students in Galicia and other rural regions of the empire. Things changed radically in the wake of the revolution of 1848, when the restrictions on Jewish real estate ownership were abolished. By 1857, about 7,000 Jews had settled in Vienna. This was the beginning of a great wave of Jewish middle- and upper-class immigration. Starting in the 1860s, well-to-do Jewish families flocked into the capital. By the turn of the century, there were 145,000 Jews in Vienna. By 1910, it was 175,000. Only Warsaw hosted a larger Jewish population.[55]

---

[55]These figures are taken from Johnston, *Vienna, Vienna*, pp. 199f.

In a city as small as Vienna it was now impossible to overlook the Jewish presence. The new wealthy Jewish residents clearly outnumbered the Catholic *nouveaux riches*. For traditional city dwellers, liberalism, capitalism, and Jews were all alien intruders. These urban masses in Vienna were easy prey to the old elites when they began to organize a political backlash against the capitalist movement. Two parties were particularly effective: the German Nationalists and the Christian Socialists.

As a schoolboy, Ludwig von Mises witnessed firsthand the rise of the Christian Social Party in Vienna. In 1882, the Vienna election law had been modified to extend suffrage to lower-income groups.[56] These voters eventually secured the sweeping victory of the Christian Socialists under Karl Lueger in the communal elections of 1895. Lueger—commonly called "Handsome Karl" (*der schöne Karl*)—was the incarnation of the modern politician. He knew how to flatter the "man on the street." He did not count on winning by argument, but relied entirely on appeals to voters' feelings, fears, and resentments. Although he had risen from lower-class origins in a liberal age and harbored no personal ill will toward Jews, he built his election campaign squarely on anti-capitalism and anti-Semitism.

The emperor despised Lueger's anti-Semitic tactics and refused to appoint him mayor of Vienna. But after three consecutive election victories, Franz Joseph eventually gave in and Handsome Karl became mayor on April 20, 1897. Lueger immediately proceeded to enlarge his power base by incorporating many suburbs into the city of Vienna. After the incorporation had been completed in 1902, Vienna became a secure dominion of the Christian Social Party. It would remain so until the end of World War I, when the red socialists won the majority in the city and started one of the greatest experiments in communal socialism ever, turning the capital of Austria into Red Vienna.

---

[56]Sieghart, *Die letzten Jahrzehnte einer Grossmacht*, p. 311.

Like the Christian Socialists and the German Nationalists, the socialist movement was ultimately an offshoot of the liberal transformation of Austria-Hungary. But whereas the former groups resisted this transformation, the socialists were carried along with it, and its leaders were quite conscious of the irony—or, as they would say, "dialectics"—that they were "children of the capitalist revolution." They were spoiled brats bound for patricide, praising the economic achievements of liberalism while silently preparing the violent overthrow of this very system.

Socialism and capitalism were but two faces of the same radical and rapid transformation of the economy, society, and politics. For this very reason, both of them lent themselves to the integration of Jewish elites into leadership positions. Just as capitalism enabled a great number of Jewish entrepreneurs, statesmen, and intellectuals such as David Ricardo, Disraeli, and Ludwig Bamberger to rise to wealth and influence, so the socialist movement was a predominantly Jewish movement at the leadership level. Lassalle and Luxemburg in Germany, as well as Kautsky, Bauer, and the Adlers in Austria were all of Jewish origin. In short, liberalism had paved the way for freely experimenting with new modes of production and thus led to the emergence of the factory system. With the large factories came many Jewish capitalists and a proletariat with a Jewish leadership.[57]

In contrast, the new urban proletariat was a largely non-Jewish group without traditions. It therefore lacked social and political institutions and quite naturally became fair game for politicians and political movements. All parties tried to mobilize the new urban masses for their causes, and until the 1880s the German Nationalists and the Christian Socialists had the upper

---

[57]Georg Franz has argued that the rising Austro-Jewish establishment was instrumental in promoting a homegrown brand of classical-liberal doctrine. See Franz, *Liberalismus—Die deutschliberale Bewegung in der habsburgischen Monarchie* (Munich: Callwey, 1955), pp. 145–220, 439.

hand in this endeavor. Things changed only when the socialists triumphed in German elections. Their popularity extended to the Austrian proletariat, winning many over to the socialist cause—but not all of them.[58] When Handsome Karl made anti-Semitic slurs at election rallies, he knew what he was doing. It was the one sure way to lure voters away from both the liberals and the socialists.

Like all social democratic parties in central Europe, the Austrian organization was entirely under the sway of Karl Marx's doctrines. Marx had reconstructed the theory of socialism in a way that made it especially appealing to the urban proletarian masses. In his account, the proletariat was the social class that embodied the future of socialism. Liberalism and capitalism, Marx argued, were merely an intermediate phase of social evolution. Their main function was to give birth to the proletariat and then to impoverish it, thus inciting the working masses to the final revolution, which would create a classless society and bring about the end of history.

By the time twelve-year old Mises had completed his first year of school in Vienna in 1893, Marxism had already lost much respect and attraction. Twenty-five years had passed since the first publication of *Das Kapital,* and events had clearly refuted Marx's predictions about capitalism's propensity to create misery among the working classes. The uncomfortable evidence induced a split among socialist intellectual leaders. Eduard Bernstein criticized Marxism and proposed a "revised" theory of socialism. He recognized the ability of capitalism to improve the material lot of the proletariat. Rather than seeking to overhaul capitalism, he argued, socialists should strive to correct its flaws through democratically elected governments.

Bernsteinian revisionism was part of a more general effort to turn the socialist movement away from its Marxist fixation on a violent overthrow of present social conditions. Under the

---

[58]Sieghart, *Die letzten Jahrzehnte einer Grossmacht,* p. 348.

leadership of the Vienna doctor Viktor Adler and of the Marxist theoretician Karl Kautsky, the Austrian social democrats gave a clear endorsement of the principles of non-violence and legality in political struggle.[59] At the Hainfeld party congress in 1888–1889, which united the violence-prone ideological radicals and the union-dominated moderates, Adler and Kautsky championed piecemeal social reform through universal suffrage and parliamentary legislation. Marxist radicals in other countries heaped ridicule on this affirmation of the legitimacy of the state and its organs, calling the approach of their moderate Austrian comrades "k.k. social democracy."[60] But the new strategy was undeniably successful.

During his school years, Mises followed the progress of the social democratic agitation in favor of universal suffrage. He lived first-hand the conflicts he would later spend so much time analyzing. His contemporary, Felix Somary, recalls:

> It had been eighty-four years since the Congress of Vienna, and both Europe and America basked in the long peace and looked down on the Austrians as incompetents, immature, patiently enduring a tyrant's yoke. The reality was quite different, for the big issues that we were struggling over in Austria had not been dealt with in other countries; on the contrary, they

---

[59]On Adler see Karl R. Stadler, "Victor Adler," *Tausend Jahre Österreich*, Walter Pollack, ed. (Vienna: Verlag Jugend und Volk, 1974), vol. 3, pp. 50ff. Kautsky distinguished himself by advocating a determinist brand of Marxism, that is, he believed that Marx had discovered strict laws of social evolution. Capitalism necessarily led to socialism and communism, and it was therefore devoid of sense to try to "push" things through violent overhaul. Norbert Leser argued that Kautsky thereby exercised a nefarious influence on Austrian socialism. Kautsky's determinist views spread fatalism and paralyzed the activities of socialist "practitioners." See Norbert Leser, "Otto Bauer— Friedrich Adler—Max Adler," in ibid., p. 256.

[60]Sieghart, *Die letzten Jahrzehnte einer Grossmacht*, p. 351. (German pronunciation of the letter "k" renders the epithet identical to international slang for excrement.)

had not even surfaced in those countries, and were to do so only decades later. Nationalism, political anti-Semitism, even Communism, were already fighting issues with us, while in the rest of the world the curious duality of liberalism and imperialism still held sway.

While all the rest in their smug peace and quiet looked down at the Austrian turmoil as if at some curiosity, we young people felt ourselves at the very centre of political events. For our world was far more real than the other: we didn't discuss, we fought; and not, as outsiders imagined, over the questions of the day before yesterday, but about those of the day after tomorrow. When in later decades the new barbarianism came flooding in, it surprised the West; for us it was a familiar phenomenon, we had seen it churning with wild and uninterrupted turbulence at the heart of a highly developed and refined civilization. I say "we," meaning the entire intellectual youth of Vienna at that time: we stood at a decisive turning-point in history and felt it in our innermost being.[61]

Which Career?

As the nineteenth century drew to a close, and Ludwig reached the age of legal maturity, he took some time to consider the path that lay ahead. Austria-Hungary offered four career options for well-educated young men. These were, in order of their prestige: the military, public service, the liberal arts, and commerce.

In liberal post-1848 Austria, industry and commerce were—with some exceptions—open to anyone, even though they were often subject to countless regulations, remnants of the pre-1848 police state. Activity in these fields attracted the educated young men of the bourgeoisie, and entrepreneurial leadership was

---

[61]Somary, *The Raven of Zurich*, p. 7.

exercised by the most daring strata of the population, including Jews who excelled as merchants, bankers, and insurers. The liberal economy had given these entrepreneurs great opportunities to serve their fellow-citizens and thereby earn great fortunes for themselves. They usually started in a province of the empire and then expanded to all of Austria-Hungary, and sometimes to an international scale. Once they reached this size they transferred company headquarters and moved their families to Vienna.

However, the great majority of the sons of provincial engineers and entrepreneurs did not aspire to follow in the footsteps of their fathers. Encouraged by their parents, and with the constant personal support of their mothers, they sought to become lawyers, physicians, scientists, artists, public servants, or politicians. Young Ludwig was no exception. His father's example had inspired him with respect for the civil service and with a desire to use his energies to the benefit of the commonwealth. Philosophy, politics, and history were more attractive to him than the old trades of his family. He decided to study at the University of Vienna, get a degree, and seek employment in the civil service. He passed the final written exam at the Akademischen Gymnasium in May 1900, and the orals in mid-July of that year. In the fall, together with his classmates Hans Kelsen and Eugen Engel, Mises enrolled in the Department of Law and Government Science.[62] He was a handsome young man with blue eyes, 5 feet 8 1/2 inches tall (171 cm).[63] He came with a great education, a razor-sharp mind, and passion for ideas that could be applied for social progress. He was made for the university. ✺

---

[62]Rechts- und staatswissenschaftliche Fakultät der k.k. University of Vienna.

[63]According to his 1941 U.S. "Affidavit of Identity and Nationality," see Grove City Archive: Mexico 1942 files.

3

Alma Mater Rudolphina

WHEN MISES STUDIED LAW and government science, the University of Vienna was one of the best institutions of higher learning in the world. It had been founded in 1365 by Emperor Rudolf IV, thus the school's Latin name, *Alma Mater Rudolphina*. For centuries it preserved the three typical features of medieval universities: political and legal autonomy; only four departments (law, medicine, the arts, and theology); and management by the Catholic Church.

> The medieval autonomy of the Continental universities was legendary. It went beyond intellectual affairs, extending to jurisdiction over virtually all the legal relationships between university members.[1] When Ludwig von Mises was a student at the University of Vienna, the police still had no authority to enter its premises.

By the early twentieth century, however, its legal independence was not quite what it had been in ancient times. One of the causes of this reduced autonomy was the imposed change of patrons that, in the Age of Enlightened Despotism, shifted control over the Catholic Church in Austria—and thus over

---

[1]The very expression "academic freedom" is in fact a term translated from the German. See Erik von Kuehnelt-Leddihn, *The Cultural Background of Ludwig von Mises* (Auburn, Ala.: Ludwig von Mises Institute, 1999), p. 3.

the University of Vienna—to the House of Habsburg. Starting in the mid-eighteenth century, the Austrian monarchs success-fully initiated a grand campaign to break the influence of inter-national Catholicism, a process that was completed by 1790. The bureaucratization of the clergy—known as *Staatskirchen-tum*—also brought the University of Vienna under the control of the Habsburg state.[2]

As a consequence of this takeover, Protestants could acquire academic degrees after 1778, and in 1782 Jews were admitted to the departments of law and medicine. A century later, women too were admitted, first to the department of philosophy (1897), then to medicine (1900), and law (1919).[3] Another consequence of the government takeover of the University of Vienna was the proliferation of departments and institutes. Among the new departments were philosophy, which at first had only the sub-servient function of preparing the students for study in other fields, and the department of law and government science.

The first full professor's chair in the field of government sci-ence had been created in 1763 for Maria Theresa's counselor Joseph von Sonnenfels (1732–1817), one of the few Jews the empress tolerated in her residential city.[4] A towering personality, Sonnenfels initiated several important traditions. Not only was he the first professor of applied political science, but also the

---

[2]Appointments of professors had to be approved by the emperor, as with other high civil servants. See William M. Johnston, *Vienna, Vienna—The Golden Age, 1815–1914* (Milan: Arnoldo Mondadori, 1981), p. 97.

[3]On the University of Vienna see Rudolf Kink, *Geschichte der kaiserlichen Universität zu Wien*, 2 vols. (Vienna: Gerold, 1854); Franz Gall, *Alma Mater Rudolphina 1365–1965—die Wiener Universität und ihre Studenten* (Vienna: Austria Press, 1965).

[4]The exact name of his chair was *Lehrstuhl für Polizei und Kameralwis-senschaften*. On Sonnenfels see Robert A. Kann, *A Study in Austrian Intellec-tual History: From Later Baroque to Romanticism* (New York: Praeger, 1960), pp. 153ff.; see also Hans Tietze, *Die Juden Wiens* (Vienna & Leipzig: Tal, 1933), pp. 107ff.

first Jew to influence intellectual life in Vienna, and the first great proponent of the "economic point of view," that is, of a strict utilitarian perspective in judging political problems. An engaging teacher and gifted writer, Sonnenfels also started the characteristically Viennese tradition of economist-journalists that in later generations included Carl Menger, Eugen von Böhm-Bawerk, Eugen von Philippovich, and Ludwig von Mises. Because of their academic pedigree and their clear, concise, and unpretentious writing style, these thinkers would exercise considerable influence on political reform processes in Austria.

In Mises's day, studies at the department of law and government science were organized in two phases. The first two years featured lectures and seminars on the history of law and legal institutions, and they ended with the first of three exams, called the *Staatsexamen* because the examiners were specially appointed to act as agents of the Austro-Hungarian state. Then the students spent another two years in lectures and seminars to acquaint themselves with the current civil, penal, and legal-process laws of the Austro-Hungarian Empire, and with government science, which included economics, economic history, and courses on technical and legal aspects of public administration. The *Staatsexamen* for current law and for government science completed this second phase.[5]

Passing these exams completed the university requirement for a career in law, but a mandatory two-year apprenticeship still stood between the graduate and his career. Some students, in particular those interested in becoming professional scholars, also acquired the degree of *doctor juris* (doctor of law), which

---

[5]The two phases had nothing to do with our present-day distinction between undergraduate studies and graduate studies. As Kuehnelt-Leddihn points out, in Mises's day, Continental universities had no undergraduates— "they were graduate schools pure and simple." Kuehnelt-Leddihn, *The Cultural Background of Ludwig von Mises*, p. 3.

required them to pass three additional exams—the *Examina Rigorosa*—after the three *Staatsexamen*.

Mises went through all these stages. In October 1900 he began his two-year study of the history of law, Roman and Canon Law in particular, and of medieval legal institutions and economic conditions. Today, the study of Church and medieval law is reserved for a handful of scholars. But in the Austria-Hungary of Mises's time, a career in law or government required both a familiarity with these traditions and a solid command of Latin. Hungarian politics was built on medieval thought and institutions, and Latin had been the language of instruction in Hungarian middle schools until 1867. Up to the very end of the monarchy in 1918, Hungarian intellectuals and politicians did not yield an inch when it came to the mystical foundations of their nation.[6]

While students needed to know Austria-Hungary's legal and institutional traditions, these subjects were not particularly popular among non-Hungarian students. Mises did not deem this period of his studies worth mentioning in his autobiographical recollections.

The lectures were infamously bad, resulting in part from a distinctive lack of consumer orientation on the part of the professors. After the government takeover of the Austrian universities, the professors had become financially independent of their audience and had little incentive to accommodate the needs of their students. This affected both their behavior and their public status. The government had turned them into civil-servant scholars—or to put it less flatteringly, into court intellectuals. "Academic freedom" no longer meant political autonomy. When the public spoke of "limitless academic liberty," they referred to freedom from responsibility or consequences. In the words of Kuehnelt-Leddihn:

---

[6]Rudolf Sieghart, *Die letzten Jahrzehnte einer Grossmacht* (Berlin: Ullstein, 1932), pp. 115ff.

> The freedom to teach was limitless. . . . Even a pro-
> fessor, who, instead of lecturing, read newspapers,
> could not be dismissed. Every professor had tenure
> up to the age of sixty-five or sixty-seven, when he had
> to retire at eighty-two percent of his final salary. The
> quality of the professor as a teacher bore no weight:
> the professor was expected not to be an educator, but
> a scholar who gave the students a chance to listen to
> him.[7]

Mises's early university years were a mixed experience. In addition to the poor lectures, there was rampant hostility between students of different nationalities and widespread anti-Semitism. Student life was generally organized through fraternities, which tended to segregate based on place of origin. This provided newcomers to the capital city with a network of their countrymen for mutual support; it also introduced them to established former members who could later be helpful in finding suitable employment. But the fraternities often degenerated into associations dedicated to excessive collective alcohol consumption, and tended to glorify violence and a militaristic lifestyle, with variants of a half-baked nationalistic ideology. There were frequent violent confrontations between members of different fraternities, especially between students of different nationalities. The largest non-German student group in Vienna, the Czechs, clashed with German students on an almost daily basis.[8]

Because the University of Vienna still enjoyed its status of legal autonomy, the police were helpless to prevent these confrontations, and the aggressive students took full advantage of the situation. Students from Vienna were less dependent on the support of compatriots and therefore had less incentive to join

---

[7]Kuehnelt-Leddihn, *The Cultural Background of Ludwig von Mises*, p. 3.

[8]At the turn of the century, several hundred thousand Czechs lived in Vienna. See Johnston, *Vienna, Vienna*, p. 200.

one of the fraternities. More importantly, however, many Viennese students were Jews, and while few of them identified themselves along religious lines, the fraternities despised these identifiable and highly efficient competitors.

Mises managed to steer clear of both the ethnic unrest and collegiate debauchery. He threw himself into his work and pursued the opportunities that now opened up. Aside from lectures and seminars, in the first two years he took part in the meetings of the *Sozialwissenschaftlicher Bildungsverein* (Association for Social Science Education). This association was non-partisan and brought the students in touch with some of the leading intellectuals. It was here that Mises first met the historians Ludo Hartmann and Kurt Kaser, the socialist leader Karl Renner, and Michael Hainisch, who would later become president of the Republic of Austria. Among the student members were Friedrich Otto Herz, Otto Bauer, and Hans Kelsen.[9]

The most fascinating and at the same time bewildering personality among the students was Otto Weininger (1880–1903), who would become famous throughout Austria and Germany almost overnight when he published his 1903 doctoral dissertation, *Geschlecht und Charakter* (*Sex and Character*). The book would be republished in more than thirty editions until the 1930s. It had a great impact on how German-speaking intellectuals thought about gender differences and gender relations. Weininger undoubtedly presented his ideas first to the smaller circles of friends and admirers with Hans Kelsen first in line. Mises probably took part in some of the meetings of the Weininger circle, and his 1922 treatise on socialism would reflect this influence.

The Grünberg Seminar

The university seminars gathered smaller groups of students around a professor who directed their reading and research in his

---

[9]Luwig von Mises, *Erinnerungen* (Stuttgart: Gustav Fischer, 1978), p. 13.

field of expertise. Mises profited in particular from his participation in the seminar of Carl Grünberg, a young and energetic professor who had just received a full professorship at the department.[10]

Grünberg knew what he could expect of the brilliant members of his seminar and encouraged even first-year students to do publishable research under his guidance. After only one semester, he assigned Mises a research project on the Galician peasants' liberation movement from 1772 to 1848. Mises started the work shortly after Easter 1901 and within a year produced a comprehensive study on the subject. He had spent several months in the *Vienna Staatsarchiv* researching all available literature on the evolution of the legal status of Galician peasants, on the reforms enacted by Emperor Joseph II, and on the events leading to the revolution of 1848. His meticulous notes filled several hundred handwritten pages from which he eventually distilled a manuscript. His work was published immediately, under the innocent title "The Development of the Relationship Between Lords and Peasants in Galicia, 1772–1848," in the department's prestigious series, *Vienna Studies in Government Science.*[11]

---

[10]It is likely that in this first phase of his studies he attended a class of Karl Theodor von Inama-Sternegg on medieval economic history. Inama-Sternegg was an old rival of Carl Menger's. Already in 1879, then still under the leadership of Lorenz, the department of law and government science had supported his attempt to gain the chair of political economy that eventually went to Menger. Inama-Sternegg was an economic historian through and through. His main field of research was German economic history from the late ninth to the sixteenth century. See K.T. von Inama-Sternegg, *Deutsche Wirtschaftsgeschichte*, 4 vols. (Leipzig: Duncker & Humblot, 1879–1901).

[11]Mises, *Entwicklung des gutsherrlich-bäuerlichen Verhältnisses in Galizien (1772–1848)*, Eduard Bernatzik and Eugen von Philippovich, eds., *Wiener staatswissenschaftliche Studie* 4, no. 2 (Vienna & Leipzig: Deuticke, 1902): vi + 144. After him, some of his fellow students and friends published research in the same series. See for example, Karl Pribram, *Der Lohnschutz des gewerblichen Arbeiters nach österreichischem Recht* (1904); Hans Kelsen, *Die Staatslehre des Dante Alighieri* (Vienna: Deuticke, 1906); Alfred Amonn, *Objekt und Grundbegriffe der theoretischen Nationalökonomie* (Vienna: Deuticke, 1911).

The subject of peasant liberation drew much attention due to the widely acclaimed research of Georg F. Knapp into the causes and consequences of the liberation of Prussian peasants, which had resulted from various agrarian reforms starting in the eighteenth century.[12] Knapp's research essentially relied on archival evidence. His approach soon found disciples in the German scholars Ludwig and Wittich, who further extended and reinforced his analysis of German conditions. Knapp's approach was later applied to Austria, most notably in the work of Carl Grünberg, *Die Bauernbefreiung in Böhmen, Mähren und Schlesien* (Peasant Liberation in Bohemia, Moravia, and Silesia).[13] It was this work that brought Grünberg to the University of Vienna, where he set out to train his

Carl Grünberg

students in questions of Austrian peasants' liberation and especially encouraged them to research with him the conditions of those parts of the empire which he had not himself covered. Grünberg then produced another volume on agrarian reforms in the Bukovina, which was complemented by Mises's work on peasants' liberation in Galicia.[14]

---

[12]See in particular Georg Knapp, *Die Bauernbefreiung und der Ursprung der Landarbeiter in den älteren Teilen Preussens*, 2 vols. (Leipzig: Duncker & Humblot, 1887); see also Knapp, *Die Landarbeiter in Knechtschaft und Freiheit* (Leipzig: Duncker & Humblot, 1891). This is the same Knapp who today is better known among economists for his *Staatliche Theorie des Geldes* (Government approach to the theory of money) (Leipzig: Duncker & Humblot, 1905). We will discuss Knapp's work in our presentation of Mises's theory of money.

[13]See C. Grünberg, *Die Bauernbefreiung und die Auflösung des gutsherrlich-bäuerlichen Verhältnisses in Böhmen, Mähren und Schlesien*, 2 vols. (Leipzig: Duncker & Humblot, 1893–1894).

[14]Some years later, a young man by the name of Leo Fishman (Fischmann) wrote on peasant liberation in central Austria (*Inneroesterreich*). See Fishman to Mises, letter dated November 11, 1950; Grove City Archive: "F" file.

In his general exposition Mises closely followed his teacher. He made exhaustive use of the literature in Polish and German that was available in the largest Austrian archive, where he had unearthed hitherto unknown material. He could be proud of the result and congratulate himself on having landed, at the age of twenty, a first scholarly publication in a highly respected series. But he later recalled:

> [C]arl Grünberg had worked for a while with professor Knapp in Strasbourg. . . . His work slavishly followed in form, presentation, and method, Knapp's book on the old provinces of Prussia. It was neither economic history nor administrative history. It was merely an extract from government documents, a description of policy as found in government reports. Any able government official could easily have written it.
>
> It was Professor Grünberg's ambition to found in Vienna a center for economic history like that created by Knapp in Strasbourg. . . . As far as possible, I endeavored to free myself from too close an association with Knapp's system. But I succeeded only in part, which made my study, published in 1902, more a history of government measures than economic history.[15]

In the introduction of the book, Mises describes the evolution of the condition of Galician peasants from the fifteenth through the eighteenth century. In the late Middle Ages, he points out, the Galician peasants had a comparatively favorable lot. They paid low taxes to their lords, could not be coercively removed from their land, often enjoyed autonomous jurisdiction, and even had a limited right to leave the country. The lords were not interested in agriculture and left the management of all farming affairs to the discretion of the peasants and their representatives.

---

[15]Mises, *Notes and Recollections* (Spring Mills, Penn.: Libertarian Press, 1978), p. 6.

Things began to change drastically after two consecutive Polish victories against the German Order, which had ruled large parts of the East Baltic in the fifteenth century. After 1466, the Poles controlled the ports of Danzig, Memel, and Elbing, and as a consequence export of agricultural products of the Polish hinterland became more profitable. The local aristocracy tried to gain ever more control over agricultural production and in particular over the work force of their peasants. These attempts proved to be very successful: at the beginning of the eighteenth century, the Polish aristocracy in Galicia controlled all lands, and the Galician peasant was the slave of his lord, destitute of any rights, liable to be sold or traded away.

Mises analyzed the state of affairs prevailing in the early eighteenth century in his first chapter. He explained that the Polish aristocracy was essentially a club of slaveholders with no backing in the wider population. This was a major reason why they were unable to avoid partitioning of the country (1772 to 1795) and could not re-establish its independence thereafter. Ruthenian slave-peasants liable to come under Prussian or Austrian dominion had nothing to lose; they could only expect an improvement in their situation.[16]

The new rulers in Vienna were keen enough to realize the political opportunity in this state of affairs. "The policies of the Austrian government in Galicia," Mises wrote, "had the objective of benefiting the peasant class at the expense of the nobility."[17] This tendency was further reinforced by the adherence of

---

[16]In Eastern Galicia (the area around Lemberg), the Ruthenians represented two thirds of the population, whereas the nobility was almost exclusively Polish. See Isabel Röskau-Rydel, "Galizien, Bukowina, Moldau," in idem, *Deutsche Geschichte im Osten Europas: Galizien, Bukowina, Moldau* (Berlin: Siedler, 1999), p. 49.

[17]Mises, *Entwicklung des gutsherrlich-bäuerlichen Verhältnisses in Galizien (1772–1848)*, p. 79.

Emperor Joseph II to the ideals of Enlightenment liberalism. After Galicia's annexation to Austria, taxes were reduced, legal protection for peasants established, and the property rights of lords and peasants were now more clearly distinguished. Most importantly, slavery received a fatal blow. The peasants were no longer considered the property of their lords, but they were still forced to work a certain number of hours—a duty called *Robot*, originally established by Empress Maria Theresa.

But Joseph II died in February 1790, before his vast program of social reform could be brought to completion. The reforms had failed to specify the rights and duties of all parties; in particular, that the peasants were no longer forced to complete certain types of tasks, but merely to work a certain number of hours. The result was sloppy work and a sharp decline in productivity. The aristocracy then resorted to stronger punishments, which further poisoned social relations. In the first four decades of the nineteenth century, democratic agitators believed Galicia to be fertile ground for their activities, because the rural population seemed to be ripe for revolution. Mises argued that the great majority of the peasants did not trust these agitators any more than they trusted the local aristocracy. They did trust the emperor and believed him to have abolished the *Robot*, despite what the Polish aristocrats said. When in February 1846 the aristocrats rebelled against Austria in an attempt to restore their ancient privileges, they confronted a united rural peasantry, which smashed this rebellion without any assistance from the Austrian army.[18]

Mises gave a detailed account of this failed aristocratic rebellion and of its consequences in his fourth chapter. He had many things to say on the issue. After all, his great-grandfather had been an eyewitness to the event and had welcomed the peasants' success.

---

[18]Ibid., p. 114.

The victorious peasants believed they had now earned both liberty and imperial recognition. But the government in Vienna was not ready for Galician peasant liberty and feared its repercussions in other parts of the empire, where forced labor still existed. When a law was passed in December 1846 that essentially preserved the *status quo*, the Galician peasants felt betrayed. They were now ready for the revolution of 1848, which eventually succeeded in abolishing the *Robot*, root and branch.

Although presented as a work of purely historic interest, Mises's research touched important political sensibilities of the day. For the gist of the Knapp-Grünberg-Mises argument was that slavery was the typical condition of peasants under a Slavic regime, and that serious attempts at their liberation were begun only under Germanic rulers. Mises argued that the various Polish rebellions following the 1772 partition failed because they were not genuine national upheavals, but purely aristocratic ventures that antagonized both the imperial central government in Vienna and the local population. Because the democratic movement did not find support within the rural working classes, its leadership allied itself to the higher aristocracy, thus supporting the political *status quo*. In Mises's words:

> How [the peasants'] eyes shone when they heard talk
> of a better, more beautiful future; one in which there
> would be no more lords and servants, and all would
> be brothers. But what they took away from the words
> of the [democratic] insurgents fueled yet further their
> hatred of the aristocracy. They did not wish to hear
> about the reestablishment of the Polish state. What
> was Poland to them? Whether it was Polish or Ger-
> man met with their indifference. But they did know
> that the Austrian civil servants provided their only
> help against the oppressive landlords. The injustice
> once suffered by the peasants was still alive in the
> memory of the older people, and thanks to the inter-
> vention of the Kaiser, it no longer had to be endured.
> But because their oppressors were Polish, they felt

only disdain for all "Polish" things. They now called themselves "kaiserlich" [Imperial] and "Austrian."[19]

Mises's conclusions were unwelcome among Poles and other Slavic nationals, especially in early twentieth century Vienna's heated climate of ethnic sensibilities. How much these questions of apparently mere academic interest were fought over can be gathered from the fact that in the very same year in which Mises's study appeared, a young Polish historian had published a dissertation in which he claimed the exact opposite—that the condition of the eighteenth-century Polish peasants was significantly better than that of peasants living under German rule.[20]

Mises's research also had personal resonance for him. It presented his compatriots, who had shrugged off the aristocratic rebellion, as freedom fighters and, hence, as motors of the "historic" trend toward liberty in Galicia.

Mises's work was positively reviewed by one of the main authorities in the field, Knapp's disciple Ludwig from the University of Strasbourg, who called it a model study and praised the clarity of Mises's style, which he seemed to have inherited from his teacher Grünberg.[21] A review in the principal organ of the German socialists of the chair, Schmoller's *Jahrbuch*, said that the study contained much new material, and that it was an extremely sound and informative work.[22] Another expert, Professor R.F. Kaindl from the University of Czernowitz praised Grünberg for his brilliant student, mentioning especially

---

[19]Ibid., pp. 104f.

[20]August Rodakiewicz, *Die galizischen Bauern unter der polnischen Republik: eine agrarpolitische Untersuchung* (Brünn: Rohrer, 1902). In the same year, he published some results of this work in an article for Eugen von Böhm-Bawerk's *Zeitschrift für Volkswirtschaft, Sozialpolitik und Verwaltung* 11 (1902): 153ff.

[21]Mises Archive 107: 26f.

[22]*Schmoller's Jahrbuch* 28 (1): 374–79; see Mises Archive 107: 28ff.

Mises's thorough analysis—"from the generally higher stand-point"—of the material available in the Vienna *Staatsarchiv* on the Galician reforms that were implemented during the reign of Joseph II.[23]

On July 15, 1902, Mises completed the initial phase of his studies by passing the first *Staatsexamen* on the history of law. His examiners focused particularly on the history of the Austrian Empire; Mises passed with distinction and the twenty-year-old seemed headed for a brilliant career in academia. Before entering the second phase of studies, however, he had to fulfill his military obligations.

Military Service and Death of His Father

On October 1, 1902 Mises presented himself as a one-year volunteer at the Imperial and Royal Division Artillery Regiment number 6 (later renamed the Imperial and Royal Field Cannon Regiment number 30).[24] Jews had been subject to military obligations after 1788. They were usually employed in transport and the artillery, thus Mises was a typical case.[25] He spent exactly one year in his regiment, which was stationed near Vienna, and returned on September 30, 1903 to his studies. In the following years, he was mobilized twice as a reserve officer within the same regiment, in 1908 and 1912, during political crises between Austria-Hungary and Russia. He would have to resume his duties in 1914, under even less pleasant circumstances.

The Austrian army had not won a war since the defeat of Napoleon in 1815. It had lost the Italian campaign in 1859 with the battle at Solferino and had also lost the important battle against the Prussian forces at Königgrätz in 1866. But this lack of success did not prevent it from enjoying an overwhelmingly

---

[23]Mises Archive 50.

[24]K.u.k. Divisions Artillerie Regiment Nr. 6; k.u.k. Feld Kanonen Regiment Nr. 30; Einjährig-Freiwilliger.

[25]Röskau-Rydel, "Galizien, Bukowina, Moldau," p. 70.

positive reputation in all parts of the Habsburg empire. It was the most visible sign of the empire's unity and security. In those days, army troops and their activities were a highly visible element of everyday life. Where present-day troops are typically stationed away from cities, their activities hidden from the eyes of the average citizen, the Austro-Hungarian troops were stationed inside the towns and cities of the empire. They exercised within view of the civilian population and their appearance set a standard for discipline and elegance.

Of the old institutions of the empire, the army seems to have been the most democratic in character. The career of an officer was open to virtually all strata of the population, and officers paid each other tribute and solidarity regardless of social background. Most of them addressed one another in private conversation with the familiar "*Du*"—insinuating that each bearer of His Majesty's *port epée* was a nobleman and an equal among equals. Yet while recognition and prestige within the officer corps depended mainly on individual performance, admission to the higher ranks required admission to the *Kriegsschule* (war school), which necessitated personal connections. Here the old nobility had a net advantage whereas Jewish origin was a handicap.[26]

The bottom line was that the majority of ambitious and talented young men from low nobility or bourgeois circles were effectively deterred from considering a military career. Alumni from a gymnasium could obtain the commission of a reserve officer by volunteering for one year, and virtually all of them did

---

[26]Things began to change slowly after the Austrian republic was created in 1918. Quick and thorough changes occurred only under the (national) socialist regime: under Hitler, the Wehrmacht employed tens of thousands of "partial Jews" (*Mischlinge*) as regular soldiers, and some of them even as generals, admirals, and field marshals—unthinkable in the old regime. See Erik von Kuehnelt-Leddihn, *Von Sarajevo nach Sarajevo* (Vienna: Karolinger, 1996); Bryan Mark Rigg, *Hitler's Jewish Soldiers* (Lawrence: Kansas University Press, 2004).

this because of the military prestige it conveyed, which in turn was very helpful for obtaining employment in all other fields. Many of them volunteered directly after leaving the gymnasium and then enrolled in university afterward. Others, like Mises, chose to volunteer after the first two years of university because the service gave them a break from their intense studies. They received the officer's commission after a year of service and an easy-to-pass exam that certified their ability to be an officer.

Mises was patriotic and proud to wear the uniform of the Imperial and Royal army, but he had no militaristic inclinations. He never related details or boasted about his one-year service. All in all, this period seems to have been unexciting for him.

It was also a sad period of his life, marked by three tragic deaths. One of the last times Ludwig saw his father alive was at the burial of his uncle Felix. As saddened as he was by his uncle's passing, it could not compare with the death of his father later the same year. Arthur von Mises had suffered from a gall bladder condition for years and regularly sought relief in health resorts. Following his brother's death in the summer of 1903, Arthur and his wife went to Karls-

Lieutenant Mises of the Imperial and Royal Field Cannon Regiment 30

bad. By September his condition had noticeably deteriorated so they left for Halberstadt where he underwent surgery on October 1. He died the same day. He was forty-nine. Ludwig attended his burial four days later.

On the day before, October 4, twenty-three your old Otto Weininger had killed himself, to the great consternation of his friends Kelsen and Mises. Suicide was in vogue in those days, especially among young people. Even Prince Rudoph, the Habsburg dauphin, had killed himself in 1889. Weininger sought a theatrical exit. Only six months after he had made a splash with the first edition of his *Sex and Character*, he rented an apartment in the house where Beethoven had died and shot himself on the master's piano.

Mises's father, Arthur Edler von Mises, at 42

In the Philippovich Seminar

At the onset of the twentieth century, most German economists held the teaching of economic theory in disdain. They thought that political economy, insofar as it was a science at all, was a historical discipline ("historicism"). Mises recalled, certainly with his teacher Grünberg in mind:

> At that time, around 1900, historicism was at the zenith of its career. The historical method was believed to be the only scientific method for the sciences of human action. From the height of his historical clarity, the "historical political economist" was looking with unspeakable disgust on the "orthodox dogmatist."[27]

Many members of this school of thought had strong socialist leanings and openly called for more government intervention. Some even advocated the complete abolition of private

---

[27]Mises, *Erinnerungen*, p. 3; *Notes and Recollections*, p. 2.

property. This attitude had earned them the epithet *Katheder-sozialisten* (Socialists of the Chair).[28] The *Kathedersozialisten* had risen to dominance at the universities of the German Reich in the wake of the creation of a German central state under Pruss-ian leadership. Their political ascension seemed unstoppable and contributed to their reputation as the avant-garde of their discipline.[29] By the turn of the century, they had virtually monopolized the chairs in political economy in the German Reich and were on the verge of becoming dominant in Austria too. Carl Grünberg, Mises's main teacher during the first two years, was one of them; in fact, he had been brought to the Uni-versity of Vienna precisely in order to bring research and teach-ing of government science up to date—that is, up to the his-toricist standards of the other German-language universities.

Grünberg's call to the University of Vienna had been a terri-ble mistake. In the case of new appointments, the other faculty members—all lawyers except for two economists—had to select the new incumbent. These men were unlikely to give the posi-tion to an "Austrian economist." Mises explained:

> They had to choose between two opposed schools of thought, the "Austrian School" on the one hand, and the allegedly "modern" historical school as taught at the universities of the German Reich on the other hand. Even if no political and nationalistic preposses-sions had disturbed their judgment, they could not help becoming somewhat suspicious of a line of thought which the professors of the universities of the German Reich dubbed specifically Austrian. Never before had any new mode of thinking originated in

---

[28]This may sound similar to the English-language epithet, "armchair socialists," but *chair* in this case refers to a full professorship in the European university system. Perhaps "ivory-tower socialists" would be more on the mark.

[29]Ralph Raico, *Die Partei der Freiheit* (Stuttgart: Lucius & Lucius, 1999), p. 185.

Austria. The Austrian universities had been sterile until—after the revolution of 1848—they had been reorganized according to the model of the German universities. For people who were not familiar with economics, the predicate "Austrian" as applied to a doctrine carried strong overtones of the dark days of the Counter-Reformation and of Metternich. To an Austrian intellectual, nothing could appear more disastrous than a relapse of his country into the spiritual inanity of the good old days.[30]

The Grünberg seminar had reinforced for Mises the worldview of his adolescence, a vision of a glorified government as the prime mover in the enlightened management of the economy and of society. Mises grew up in an atmosphere of almost unlimited confidence in the state's ability to make human society safe for its constant improvement. This faith in the state went along with a distrust of private individuals and associations to match the good deeds of government. He later recalled:

By 1900 practically everyone in the German-speaking countries was either a statist (interventionist) or a state socialist. Capitalism was seen as a bad episode which fortunately had ended forever. The future belonged to the "State." All enterprises suitable for expropriation were to be taken over by the state. All others were to be regulated in a way that would prevent businessmen from exploiting workers and consumers. . . . When I entered the university, I, too, was a thorough statist.[31]

---

[30]Mises, *The Historical Setting of the Austrian School of Economics* (Auburn, Ala.: Ludwig von Mises Institute, [1969] 1984), p. 14.

[31]Mises, *Erinnerungen*, pp. 10f.; *Notes and Recollections*, pp. 13, 16. Mises adds that only in one respect were his views not quite as wrong as those of his fellow students: he was "consciously anti-Marxian."

Most objections to this statist view were moral objections, defending the individual's rights against bureaucratic encroachments. These arguments fell on deaf ears. They could not withstand the appeal of the utilitarian case for government intervention—especially since so many nineteenth-century liberals had themselves promoted utilitarianism as the basis for social policy. Surely, the improvement of the vast majority could not be sacrificed to selfish interests. Thus, when he started his legal studies, Mises was a champion of interventionist statism. He believed that government was able to fix a wide variety of social problems, and he was eager to engage in the scientific discovery of the dangerous consequences of unhampered capitalism.

It so happened, however, that the department of law and government science at the University of Vienna was home to some of the most outspoken opponents of historicism and thus by implication of the *Kathedersozialist* program. These scholars denied that economic affairs could only be studied by historical methods and they made the case for a rational economic theory which, they held, was indispensable for the understanding of certain economic phenomena such as value, interest, money, income, and so on. The most important theorist of this group was a man by the name of Carl Menger.

In 1871, Menger had published a book with the title *Grundsätze der Volkswirtschaftslehre* (Principles of Economics), in which he co-pioneered the marginalist approach to the theory of value—the standard analysis still in use today. This book had earned him a chair in political economy at the University of Vienna, where he taught until the spring of 1903. In the 1880s, Menger had become famous throughout the academic world because of a highly polemical dispute with Gustav Schmoller on the respective merits of the historical and theoretical methods. The *Methodenstreit* (dispute on method), as their debate came to be known, polarized German economists between the *historicists* and what would come to be known as the Austrian School.

At the turn of the century, Menger had about twenty followers among the Austrian professors of political economy, which
was a considerable number in those days.[32] The most significant
theorists were two brothers-in-law: Eugen von Böhm-Bawerk,
Austria's four-time Minister of Finance and holder of a chair of
political economy at the University of Innsbruck, and Friedrich
von Wieser, who held a chair of political economy at the German University of Prague and would succeed Menger at the
University of Vienna in 1903. Another follower, Eugen von
Philippovich, was a full professor at the University of Vienna,
and although he was not an important theoretician of the Aus
trian School, he excelled as a pedagogue. His textbook, which
was at that time the most successful German-language textbook
on economics, almost single-handedly ensured that the avalanche of historicism would not wipe out the teaching of economic theory in the German-speaking world.[33]

Mises's first years at the university overlapped with Menger's
last, but during the first phase of his studies, Mises did not attend
Menger's last lectures. When he began the second phase, after
returning from military service, Menger had retired to live the
life of a private scholar. It is likely, however, that Mises attended
Friedrich von Wieser's inaugural lecture as Menger's successor
on October 26, 1903. In this lecture, Wieser attempted to
expand on Menger's monetary writings with an original analysis

---

[32]See Menger's letter to the (Austrian) Ministry of Culture, dated March 19,
1902, quoted in Yukihiro Ikeda, *Die Entstehungsgeschichte der "Grundsätze" Carl
Mengers* (St. Katharinen: Scripta Mercaturae Verlag, 1997), pp. 1f.

[33]Eugen von Philippovich, *Grundriss der politischen Oekonomie*, 9th ed., 3
vols. (Tübingen: Mohr, 1911). On Philippovich see Mises, "Eugen von Philippovich," *Neue Österreichische Biographie*, 1st section, vol. 3 (1926), pp. 53–62;
Ludwig Elster, "Philippovich von Philippsberg, Eugen," *Handwörterbuch der
Staatswissenschaften* 6 (1925). See also the obituaries by Amonn in *Jahrbücher
für Nationalökonomie und Statistik*, 3rd series, vol. 58, pp. 158–63, and by
Hainisch in *Schriften des Vereins für Sozialpolitik* 159: 25–29.

of the value of money and its changes through time.[34] The lecture was different in style and content from what the students of government science were used to in Grünberg's seminars. Wieser was a pure theorist, in the sense that his ideas were removed from the hard data studied under Grünberg. But Wieser was an impressive speaker, and his lecture might have been the event that prompted Mises to become acquainted with Menger's *Principles*, which he started reading about two months later. In any case, the lecture was in many ways the basis and starting point for Mises's later work on the theory of money, as we will see in more detail in a later chapter.

Mises joined the government science seminar of Philippovich, where he met and befriended Emil Lederer, who later became Germany's top Marxist economist. The seminar was a rallying ground for the most fervent social reformers, with the possible exception of Philippovich's assistant, Felix Somary, who already held radical free-market views.[35] Professor Philippovich was a very influential public figure, known equally for his Mengerian inclinations in economic science and his interventionist position on politics. Of all academics with *Kathedersozialist* inclinations, his writings had the most thorough grounding in economic theory, and Mises later praised him as the most thorough theorist ever of third-way policies. "History," Mises wrote without irony, "will see in Philippovich the most outstanding advocate

---

[34]Friedrich von Wieser, "Der Geldwert und seine geschichtlichen Veränderungen," *Zeitschrift für Volkswirtschaft, Sozialpolitik und Verwaltung* 13 (1904); reprinted in Wieser, *Gesammelte Abhandlungen*, F.A. Hayek, ed. (Tübingen: Mohr, 1929), pp. 164–92.

[35]Felix Somary, *The Raven of Zurich: The Memoirs of Felix Somary* (London: Hurst & Co., 1960), pp. 12f. Somary had first been hired by Carl Menger to assist him in extended sociological studies. But Menger did not anticipate publication any time soon and felt he might be wasting his brilliant young assistant's time. He put Somary in touch with Philippovich, who was looking for help with a new edition of his textbook.

of the ideology of statism, the characteristic representative of the spirit of social reform."[36]

Eugen Philippovich von Philippsberg (1858–1917) was the product of an old Austrian family of military officers. After studies in Graz, Vienna, Berlin, and London, he received his *Habilitation* diploma under Menger, then quickly became a tenured professor at the University of Freiburg im Breisgau. In 1893, he returned to Vienna as a full professor of political economy and public finance. Philip-povich was active in various political associations and over the years gained great influence at the University and in Austrian politics. As a young man, he had been an enthusiastic champion of the Schmollerite program, advocating histori-cism in economics and heavy government inter-ventionism in politics. Under the influence of Menger and Böhm-Bawerk, however, he began

Eugen von Philippovich

to reconsider the case for economic theory and economic liber-alism during his years in Freiburg. The result of this research on economic theory became visible in the first of the three vol-umes of his *Grundriss der politischen Oekonomie*, which dealt with general economic theory. Here Philippovich showed great apti-tude in putting economic theory in the service of political views that, while less statist than the official line of the *Kathedersozial-isten*, still called for far-reaching government control.

When he returned to Vienna, he immediately joined the Vienna Fabians.[37] The group organized public conferences and discussions to promote the idea of government intervention in the service of a "social" agenda, which primarily concerned the support of the working-class poor. Philippovich's personal and

---

[36]Mises, "Eugen von Philippovich," p. 60.

[37]Wiener Fabier-Gesellschaft, established 1891. The main protagonists were Hainisch, Pernerstorfer, and Philippovich.

intellectual qualities made him the center of the Vienna Fabians and helped spread their influence among academics and businessmen. These activities were so successful that Fabian ideas eventually were incorporated into the programs of all Austrian political parties.

Philippovich also left a deep impression on his seminar students. In the classroom, matters of social policy took center stage. While the students usually jumped head-on into championing various practical welfare schemes, Philippovich again and again drew them into discussions of the theoretical foundations of government intervention. He clearly perceived that emotional appeals or references to we-all-know convictions were not enough to justify the use of the public organization of coercion and compulsion. He urged his students to make a scientific case for interventionism and constantly raised problems that they had not considered—problems for which he himself had not found adequate solutions.[38] It was in these exchanges that he was most impressive, especially in the eyes of his most critical students. Mises recalled the atmosphere in the Philippovich seminar:

> Here he could utter his doubts without being misunderstood. Here he was not the famous writer who presented his reader with something that was finished, complete, and apparently unshakable. Here he showed himself in his true nature, as the critical

---

[38]This seems to have been rather exceptional among economics professors. Mises, who knew well the economics profession of the turn of the century, later said:

> In the decades between the Prussian constitutional conflict (1862) and the Weimar constitution (1919), only three men sensed the problems of social reform: Philippovich, Stolzmann, and Max Weber. Among these three, only Philippovich had any knowledge of the nature and content of theoretical economics. (Mises, *A Critique of Interventionism* [New Rochelle, N.Y.: Arlington House, 1977], p. 38)

thinker and explorer who wrestled laboriously (*müh-sam*) in his quest for knowledge.[39]

Philippovich was in fact only too conscious of the existence of unintended consequences that result from government intervention. In a speech delivered in his capacity as a university president, he warned:

> May none of you have the painful experience, at times not even spared the man of the best intentions, of having to say of one's activities: I drew pure fire from the altar, but what I ignited is not a pure flame.[40]

But such experiences did not shake his conviction that government interventions were necessary. They were needed despite all the economic achievements of liberalism that Philippovich praised in his seminar and in other public appearances. He stressed that liberalism made it possible for Europe's population to grow during the nineteenth century from 187 to 393 million, while simultaneously increasing the living standards of the masses—a development unprecedented in history. He even claimed that no previous era had done as much for humanity as liberalism, with the possible exception of Christianity's acknowledgment of human dignity. Celebrating the liberating and creative powers of liberalism in political and economic affairs, he argued that the only relevant question was whether one could avoid full-blown individual liberty:

> The economic forces that the liberal system called forth—capitalistic large-scale organization of production and exchange—as well as the personal values and energies that it brought into being, form a component of social life that we can no longer do without.

---

[39]Mises, "Eugen von Philippovich," p. 61.
[40]Ibid., p. 62.

> The present and future cannot be based on for-
> going the products of economic liberty: the power
> of fruitful initiative and economic organization.
> The question that must be asked is whether the
> acknowledgment of the basic ideas of the liberal
> system necessarily implies the acceptance of the
> ultimate consequences of its unrestricted application,
> that is, whether clinging to the principle of economic
> liberty is identical with accepting the social system of
> individualism.[41]

Philippovich argued that one could enjoy all the blessings of individual liberty and remedy its shortcomings on an ad-hoc basis. Pointing to specific fields where such remedial action was required, he argued that unrestricted individualism leads to the dissolution of communities, that the interests of the individual are not always identical with the interests of the social whole, and that unrestricted economic liberty might destroy its own foundations through the formation of monopolies. Government interventions were necessary to counteract these short-comings.[42]

The Philippovich seminar was an important training ground for Vienna's fervent young social reformers—of whom Mises was one. Philippovich did not deny the validity of the traditional case for economic freedom and he made sure his students were familiar with the theory and history of classical liberalism. This was probably as much liberalism as most of them could take. But for Mises, the seminar proved to be his first step in an unexpected direction—one that would ultimately change his path radically and for his entire life.

---

[41]Eugen von Philippovich, *Die Entwicklung der wirtschaftspolitischen Ideen im 19. Jahrhundert* (Tübingen: Mohr, 1910), p. 131.

[42]Ibid., pp. 132–38.

Birth of an Economist

Around Christmas of 1903, Mises had just received his officer's commission and had recently returned to his studies when he first read Menger's *Principles*. It was an intellectual encounter that would forever change his outlook on science and the world.

Mises later emphasized that the book "made an 'economist' of me"[43]—that is, practically speaking, it made him skeptical of the benefits of government action. To be an economist is in fact to understand the limitations of government. It is to have grasped that the state is not omnipotent, and that it cannot do all it claims it can do. Today most professional economists would probably reject this definition, but that is because the economics profession underwent such dramatic changes after World War II that present-day economists share only the title with their pre-war predecessors. At any rate, Mises understood the practical essence of economic science to be the insight that free enterprise and the voluntary association of individuals is superior to the coercive schemes of the state. In this understanding he continued the tradition of the British classical economists and of the great eighteenth- and nineteenth-century French *économistes*.

In 1904 Vienna, Mises was quite alone in his new orientation. Reading Menger's *Principles* alienated him from his fellow students, from his professors, and then later from his colleagues. His discovery made him richer intellectually and spiritually, but it also made him a very lonely man. Twenty-five years later, Franz Weiss remembered vividly how Mises had suddenly turned away from the ideals he had shared with Weiss and other peers. Weiss warned young Friedrich August von Hayek not to follow Mises in his betrayal of "social values" for the old doctrine of liberalism. Hayek surmised:

---

[43]Mises, *Erinnerungen*, p. 19; *Notes and Recollections*, p. 33.

> If Carl Menger had not aged at such a relatively early
> date, and if Böhm-Bawerk had not died so early,
> Mises probably would have found support in them.
> But the only survivor of the earlier Austrian School,
> my very dear teacher Friedrich von Wieser, was him-
> self rather a Fabian, proud, as he thought, to have
> delivered with his development of marginal-utility
> theory a scientific justification of the progressive
> income tax.[44]

Reading Carl Menger did not immediately produce the
author of *Human Action*. Mises's own statism was too deep-
rooted: he had absorbed it from the earliest days of his childhood, and he unconsciously applied it in his research for the
Grünberg and Philippovich seminars. Everyone he knew shared
the fundamental conviction that government intervention is
inherently beneficial while the free market is only accidentally
so at best.

What Menger's *Principles* did was to change fundamentally
Mises's outlook on the analysis of social problems. Menger's
book showed that individual consumer values are paramount on
the market because they not only determine the values of all
consumers' goods, but also the values of all factors of production. It is consumers who steer the entire market system
through their spending decisions; capitalist-entrepreneurs
merely carry out (or anticipate) their wishes. The market is not
beneficial by accident but is inherently so. It is eminently just
and it is elegant. All government intervention must therefore be
considered carefully before it is allowed to disrupt the order of
the market.

It took Mises a while to digest the Mengerian message, to
analyze its weaknesses and strengths, and to think through its
political implications. He could not jump directly from his

---

[44]See F.A. Hayek, "Einleitung," introduction to Mises, *Erinnerungen*
(Stuttgart: Gustav Fischer Verlag, 1978), p. xiv.

former statist convictions to embrace complete *laissez-faire* liberalism. This was the main challenge of Menger's book. Mises did not have to be convinced of the merits of Menger's theory. From his childhood days, he had had doubts about the purely historical approach. He had a passionate interest in deriving practical lessons from the study of history, but did not know how to do it. The writings of the Historical School that he digested while at the gymnasium did not seem to solve the problem either.[45] His years in the Grünberg seminar finally convinced him that the champions of the Historical School had indeed failed to solve this problem. He later summarized their failure:

> Historicism was right in stressing the fact that in order to know something in the field of human affairs one has to familiarize oneself with the way in which it developed. The historicists' fateful error consisted in the belief that this analysis of the past in itself conveys information about the course future action *has to* take. What the historical account provides is the description of the situation; the reaction depends on the meaning the actor gives it, on the ends he wants to attain, and on the means he chooses for their attainment. In 1860 there was slavery in many states of the Union. The most careful and faithful record of the history of this institution in general and in the United States in particular did not map out the future policies of the nation with regard to slavery. The situation in the manufacturing and marketing of motorcars that Ford found on the eve of his embarking upon mass

---

[45]Mises, *Erinnerungen*, p. 7; *Notes and Recollections*, p. 7.

> It was my intense interest in historical knowledge that enabled me to perceive readily the inadequacy of German historicism. It did not deal with scientific problems, but with the glorification and justification of Prussian policies and Prussian authoritarian government.

production did not indicate what had to be done in
this field of business.[46]

Practical guidance could not be obtained at all through historical inquiry. Only theory of the Mengerian sort could do this.
But to go from theory to endorsing the political program that
seemed to follow from the Mengerian premises was quite a step.
It took Mises years to gradually overcome his prejudices. His
ongoing political radicalization shows that the process continued late into his life. He recalled its very beginning:

> My first doubts about the excellence of intervention-
> ism came to me when, in my fifth semester, Professor
> Philippovich induced me to research housing condi-
> tions and when, in the following semester in the Sem-
> inar on Criminal Law, Professor Löffler asked me to
> research the changes in law regarding domestic ser-
> vants, who at that time were still subject to corporal
> punishment by their employers. It then dawned on
> me that all real improvements in the conditions of the
> working classes were the result of capitalism; and that
> social laws frequently brought about the very oppo-
> site of what the legislation was intended to achieve.
>
> It was only after further study of economics that
> the true nature of interventionism was revealed to
> me.[47]

Two years later, he was already fairly critical of the benefits of
organized labor. On November 28, 1905 he watched 250,000
labor union members defy the law that prohibited demonstrations before the parliament while the MPs were in session. That
night, his friend Otto Bauer rejoiced over the triumph of the proletarian masses. Mises saw it as anarchy. What if another mass
organization arose and similarly defied the law? Would that not

---

[46]Mises, *Theory and History* (New Haven, Conn.: Yale University Press,
1957), p. 288; emphasis added.

[47]Mises, *Erinnerungen*, pp. 13f.; *Notes and Recollections*, pp. 19f.

lead to civil war? Bauer scorned Mises for this question, which he thought betrayed a petty bourgeois mindset. The future belonged to social democracy.[48]

Mises's early transition period from statism to liberalism is well documented in a lengthy study he wrote for the Philippovich seminar on "The History of Austrian Factory Legislation." Mises presented the paper in 1904 or early 1905 and subsequently published it in Böhm-Bawerk's *Zeitschrift*.[49] In it Mises pointed out that in Austria organized child labor was a creation of the state. Under Empress Maria Theresa, coercive child labor had been instituted in an effort to combat "laziness, misery, and sin [sexual activities]." Thus the state could pursue several goals through a single measure: it got the children off the streets—ostensibly in their own interest—and as a beneficial side effect it promoted large-scale industry and reduced public welfare expenditures.

Not surprisingly, many factory owners abused the situation. In 1785, Emperor Joseph II visited a factory in the town of Traiskirchen and, shocked by what he saw, ordered legislation to remedy the children's misery. Mises proudly noted that the emperor's order preceded the British Morals and Health Act by sixteen years, but he also emphasized that the market was not the cause of the problem. The root of the children's misery lay not in the factory owners' entrepreneurial function but in the lack of a contractual relationship. Commenting on the eventual suppression of the *Kinderhäuser* where the children were kept after work, he said:

> The children's houses might have offered better room and board to the adolescent worker than his parents' home, but they delivered him entirely into

---

[48]Mises, *Erinnerungen*, p. 58.

[49]Ludwg von Mises, "Zur Geschichte der österreichischen Fabriksgesetzgebung," *Zeitschrift für Volkswirtschaft, Socialpolitik und Verwaltung* 14 (1905): 209–71.

the power of the factory owner. This legal relationship could be interpreted as a wage contract only
from a formal point of view; in its essence, it was
more similar to slavery.[50]

While these facts did not fit the mainstream view of government's role in child labor, Mises was not yet ready to deny the
Austrian government a role in improving the children's situation. He ferociously criticized a favorable report on free-market
child labor as "tendentious" and "exaggerated" though he did
not provide a single counter-argument.[51] In his conclusion he
hailed the "progressive" Emperor Joseph II for instigating the
epoch of social-policy:

> The double insight that we first encounter in this law
> [Joseph II's bill dated November 20, 1785]—that fac-
> tory work involves grave disadvantages for children
> from a hygienic and moral point of view, and that
> these ills can only be eliminated through the inter-
> vention of the state and through continuous control
> by the state—has become the point of departure of
> modern social policy.[52]

We can see the remnants of unquestioned suppositions in
young Mises's thought. But he had learned the first step: how to
think as an economist. This shift was reflected in his increasingly
critical analysis of the limits of government action. Such an attitude did not find approval from established academia. When
Mises presented himself for *Staatsexamen* numbers two and
three, he passed with distinction in law, but not in government
science—enough to slow his ambitions in his main field of academic interest. By February 20, 1906, he had passed his juridical, political science, and general law exams. This gained him the
title of *doctor juris utriusque* (doctor of canon and secular law).

---

[50]Ibid., p. 234.
[51]Ibid., pp. 258ff.
[52]Ibid., p. 270.

His mother was proud and his friends probably poked fun at "Dr. Mises"—the pseudonym under which Gustav Theodor Fechner had published satirical pieces attacking early nineteenth-century German materialism.[53]

Years with a Master

The decisive boost to Mises's intellectual development came when Eugen Ritter von Böhm-Bawerk opened his seminar at the University of Vienna in the summer semester of 1905—"a great day in the history of the University and the development of economics."[54] Böhm-Bawerk was Carl Menger's most important follower and had gained international fame as an economic theorist with his *Kapital und Kapitalzins* (Capital and Interest), a two-volume treatise on economics and the history of economic ideas. After a brilliant career as a professor of political economy in Innsbruck and as a four-time Minister of Finance, fifty-four year old Böhm-Bawerk returned to his *alma mater*, where a special position was created for him in the department of government science. For the next nine years, the University of Vienna would host the three best economic theoreticians in the German-speaking world: Böhm-Bawerk, Wieser, and Philippovich. It remains the high point in the teaching of Austrian economics.

Böhm-Bawerk was a towering presence as a teacher and a master of clear thinking and clear speech. His fame attracted outstanding students from all parts of Austria and abroad. But what made these students stay (often for years after graduation) was the razor-sharp mind that could cut through the knottiest problems of economics. Many of his students were critical of the Austrian School, and of his writings in particular, but fearless

---

[53]See for example Dr. Mises, *Beweis, dass der Mond aus Jodine bestehe*, 2nd ed. (Leipzig: Voss, 1832); idem, *Vergleichende Anatomie der Engel—Eine Skizze* (Leipzig: Industrie-Comptoir, 1825).

[54]Mises, *Erinnerungen*, p. 23; *Notes and Recollections*, p. 39.

and thorough, Böhm-Bawerk accepted, examined, and discussed all arguments brought before him, and demonstrated
again and again the usefulness of the Austrian approach.

The very first summer set the tone.
Böhm-Bawerk spent the entire semester discussing the shortcomings of Karl
Marx's labor theory of value, engaging
in extended debate with the brilliant
Austro-Marxist, Otto Bauer. Young
Bauer was the secretary of the parliamentary delegation of the socialist
party and was well-versed in both Austrian and Marxist theory. His main
duty as secretary was to explain and
justify the socialist party's current line.
He was an experienced and impressive
debater who had defended Marx's

Eugen von Böhm-Bawerk

views in countless discussions in and out of academia. He was
also the editor of the socialist journal, *Der Kampf*, and was on
his way to winning great acclaim with a scholarly work on one
of the pressing issues of Austrian politics: the coexistence of
national communities within the Danubian state.[55] Bauer was a
worthy sparring partner for Böhm-Bawerk, but he was no more
than that. He found it impossible to raise a point the old master had not thought of. The spectacle of their encounter left the
other seminar members with the distinct feeling that they had
had the privilege of studying under a true master.

Ludwig von Mises was one of those who continued attending
the seminar after graduation. Critical though he was in all things,
he could not help but feel awe in Böhm-Bawerk's presence. More

---

[55]Otto Bauer, *Die Nationalitätenfrage und die Sozialdemokratie* (Vienna,
1907). On Bauer see Norbert Leser, "Otto Bauer—Friedrich Adler—Max
Adler," *Tausend Jahre Österreich*, Walter Pollack, ed. (Vienna: Verlag Jugend
und Volk, 1974), vol. 3, pp. 258ff.

than half a century later, the celebrated author of *Human Action* had this to say on the occasion of a new English translation of Böhm-Bawerk's *Capital and Interest*:

> There is no doubt that Böhm-Bawerk's book is the most eminent contribution to modern economic theory. For every economist it is a must to study it most carefully and to scrutinize its content with the utmost care. . . . Although Böhm-Bawerk's great opus is "mere theory" and abstains from any practical applications, it is the most powerful intellectual weapon in the great struggle of the Western way of life against the destructionism of Soviet barbarism.[56]

Böhm-Bawerk's seminar decisively reinforced the impact of Menger's *Principles*. Under Böhm-Bawerk's guidance, Mises began to delve more systematically into the literature of economic theory. He began the research that led to his first great book, a treatise on money and banking.[57]

These were years of apprenticeship. Mises continued to liberate himself step by step from his statist prejudices and to become acquainted with the great tradition of monetary analysis in nineteenth-century British and French thought. He started publishing papers on questions related to money and banking, articles that reveal his changing views on the role of

---

[56]Mises, "Eugen von Böhm-Bawerk and the Discriminating Reader," *The Freeman* (August 1959).

[57]His *Habilitation* director was Philippovich. See Franz Baltzarek, "Ludwig von Mises und die österreichische Wirtschaftspolitik der Zwischenkriegszeit," *Wirtschaftspolitische Blätter* 28, no. 4 (1981): 127. Philippovich's *Habilitation* thesis (which he wrote under Menger) dealt with the achievements of the Bank of England. See Eugen von Philippovich, *Die Bank von England im Dienste der Finanzverwaltung des Staates* (Vienna: Deuticke, 1885); translated as *History of the Bank of England and Its Financial Services to the State* (Washington, D.C.: Government Printing Office, 1911). Still Wieser's inaugural lecture might have had a more direct impact on Mises's interest in problems of money and banking.

government in this field. Some of these early opinions are likely to surprise the reader who knows Mises only as the author of *Human Action* or of the *Theory of Money and Credit*. For example, in a 1907 paper on the motivations of Austrian exchange-rate regulations, Mises hailed the policy of suspending cash redemptions so that the central bank could "separate the so-called legitimate demand for gold from the illegitimate one" because it "thereby became possible to keep Vienna inter-bank interest rates lower than in Berlin and London."[58]

He still had a long way to go to become the famously intransigent opponent of all government interventionism. As his earlier writing shows, he did not adopt his later views capriciously or out of ignorance of other perspectives. Ludwig von Mises became the most radical free-market economist of his time only by overcoming the part of himself that was still hostage to the dominant worldview. The *Zeitgeist* had a firm grip on his feelings and instincts, but it could not subdue his will to follow reason wherever it led him.

ᵇ   ᵇ   ᵇ

In his last months as a student, Mises witnessed a great political earthquake, which forebode even more fateful events to come.

Far from Vienna, at the easternmost end of the Eurasian landmass, Russia unexpectedly lost a war against Japan. In one stroke the war smashed Moscow's Far Eastern ambitions, and it was suddenly clear to all of Europe that Russia's energies would be redirected to its western borders. Even more unexpectedly, however, the loss revealed the precarious condition of the Russian monarchy. Insurrection was in the streets of Saint Petersburg and Moscow, and on October 31, 1905 the Tsar capitulated. In

---

[58]Mises, "Die wirtschaftspolitischen Motive der österreichischen Valutaregulierung," *Zeitschrift für Volkswirtschaft, Sozialpolitik und Verwaltung* 16 (1907): 571.

a spectacular October Manifesto, Nicolas II promised Russia a constitution and the election of a parliament.

Vienna and the rest of Europe were shocked to see how far socialist agitation had undermined the Russian power structure, which had been considered the greatest bulwark of reactionary politics in the world. On November 1, Nicolas's October Manifesto was read in the Austrian parliament and the social democrats began singing the *Marseillaise*. Viennese workers took to the streets. On November 2, Mises watched thousands march down the Vienna Ringstrasse. There were bloody encounters with the police. One day later, Emperor Franz Joseph introduced universal male suffrage in both Austria and Hungary.

The turmoil did not subside and was not limited to the capitals of Europe. In the coming years, new revolutions shook old regimes in Turkey, Persia, and China. A contemporary citizen of Vienna later recalled the revolutionary atmosphere:

> The next generation can hardly imagine the depth to which the general consciousness of European society was, at that time, altered and transformed by these events. Until then, the monarchical, statist, and bourgeois order had not been subject to any doubt. They were indestructible. But with one stroke, everything had become problematic.[59]

One positive effect of the new situation was that it finally compelled the emperor to confront the Hungarian problem head-on. For years, the ruling clique of Hungarian landowners had pressed for a revision of the *Ausgleich* agreement of 1867. They demanded in particular that the Hungarian army be allowed to give up German as the language of command, that Hungary should obtain its own central bank, and that it should be severed economically from the rest of the empire through an internal tariff line. When Franz Joseph allowed equal voting

---

[59]Sieghart, *Die letzten Jahrzehnte einer Grossmacht*, p. 74.

rights in all parts of the empire, the Hungarian establishment was doomed. On January 30, 1907 the Austrian estates-based parliament (*Kurienparlament*), which guaranteed a majority of seats to the establishment, was abolished forty-six years after its creation. The first general elections under the new law on May 11, 1907 brought 86 socialist deputies (out of 516) into the *Abgeordnetenhaus*, the lower chamber of parliament. ✍

The Mises family, left to right, *Ludwig, his father Arthur, Richard, his mother Adele, and Karl*

Part II
The Austrian School

Eugen von Böhm-Bawerk

Carl Menger

Ludwig von Mises

4

Fin de siècle Economic Science

THE PROBLEMS AND IDEAS that moved Mises in his early years were addressed by the work of four great economic theorists: Carl Menger, Eugen von Böhm-Bawerk, Friedrich von Wieser, and Joseph Schumpeter.

Menger, Böhm-Bawerk, and Wieser were the incarnation of the Austrian School. Their books and papers (and their physical presence) provided the intellectual background of Mises's scholarly works in *fin de siècle* Austria—the period that lasted until 1914. Mises's major contributions were intended to solve problems raised by their writings. His influence on the succeeding generations of students of Austrian economics—or his lack of influence on them—can only be understood against the background provided by the pre-1914 foundational writings of the Austrian School and by the towering presences of Wieser and Schumpeter on the German and Austrian scene until the late 1920s.

Carl Menger—Pioneer of "Empirical Theory"

Mises knew all four personally, but Menger had retired from teaching a year before Mises discovered Menger's *Principles*. They met for the first time around 1910, when Mises was attending Böhm-Bawerk's seminar and preparing his first treatise, *The Theory of Money and Credit*. It was then customary that young men wishing to pursue an academic career in economics paid Menger a visit. He received them in his house amidst his impressive library and had them talk about their work and projects.[1]

Carl Menger

Menger was born in 1840 in the Galician town of Neu-Sandez (today located in Poland). His father was a lawyer from a family of army officers and civil servants; his mother came from a rich Bohemian merchant family that had moved to Galicia. His full name was Carl Menger Edler von Wolfesgrün, but he and his brothers—the influential politician Max and the socialist legal scholar Anton—did not use their title of nobility.[2]

Menger was a fascinating and energetic personality. Intellectually vigorous into his old age, he was a true polymath in his youth.[3] He had studied law and government science first in Prague and then in Vienna. One of his teachers at the University of Vienna was Peter Mischler, a champion of marginal-value theory, but apparently Menger was not then interested in economics or an academic career. He preferred non-academic writing and in 1863 worked as a journalist for the *Lemberger*

---

[1]Mises, *Erinnerungen* (Stuttgart: Gustav Fischer Verlag, 1978), p. 19; F.A. Hayek, "Einleitung," Carl Menger, *Gesammelte Werke*, F.A. Hayek, ed. (Tübingen: Mohr, 1968), vol. 1, pp. xxxii.

[2]After Menger successfully discharged his commission to tutor Crown Prince Rudolf in economics, he obtained the right to accede to Knighthood. Menger did not apply because he preferred his bourgeois status. See Brigitte Hamann, *Rudolf: Kronprinz und Rebell* (Munich: Piper, 1978), pp. 77, 86.

[3]On Menger see in particular Friedrich von Wieser, "Karl Menger," Anton Bettelheim, ed., *Neue österreichische Biographie: 1815–1918* (Vienna, 1923), vol. 1, pp. 84–92, reprinted in idem, *Gesammelte Abhandlungen* (Tübingen: Mohr, 1929); Hayek, "Einleitung," pp. vii–xxxvi; Yukihiro Ikeda, *Die Entstehungsgeschichte der "Grundsätze" Carl Mengers* (St. Katharinen: Scripta Mercaturae Verlag, 1997).

Zeitung. Around 1864, he began preparing for a doctorate in law and government science and passed the first exam in March 1865. Even at this point his new academic commitment was overshadowed by his literary pursuits.[4] When he passed the last of his four doctoral exams, in March 1867, he was in the process of writing several comedies.[5]

His literary interest was more than academic. Menger founded the journal *Wiener Tagblatt*, which first appeared on November 26, 1865. In an early issue, he began publishing an anonymous novel with the scandalous title *Der ewige Jude in Wien* (The Eternal Jew in Vienna).[6] In March 1866, he joined the economics staff of another Vienna journal, the *Wiener Zeitung.* This paper was

> a pure government organ, controlled by the Council of Ministers and in particular by the President's Office of the Ministry of the Interior. The editorial staff was selected by the government, official articles were written in the ministries, and edited and submitted by the Council of Ministers.[7]

---

[4]Some ten years later, in a diary entry, he said his present health problems were due to the excessive professional activities of the past, as well as to bad nutrition during some periods of his adolescence, too much time spent in cafés, and too many love affairs. He then decided to spend more time in the countryside and to go out for walks regularly. See Karl Menger's biographical sketch of his father Carl's professional career, "X. Beginn der akademischen Laufbahn," Carl Menger Papers, Duke University, Box 21.

[5]Ikeda, *Die Entstehungsgeschichte der "Grundsätze" Carl Mengers*, pp. 65, 170.

[6]This was a fashionable subject of feuilleton novels, a new literary genre at the time. In France, the "king of the feuilleton novel," Eugène Sue had become rich and famous with *Le Juif errant* (1844–45). The protagonist of his novel symbolized the oppression of the Jewish people throughout the centuries.

[7]Kurt Paupié, *Handbuch der österreichischen Pressegeschichte 1848–1959* (Vienna: Braumüller, 1960), vol. 1, pp. 119f. Paupié also claims that Menger's own paper, the *Wiener Tagblatt*, had an official or semi-official character, in particular due to Menger's close ties with Belcredi (p. 119).

Thus Menger became a government employee in a fast-track position that offered prospects to reach the highest strata within the Austrian civil service.[8]

A government position carried great prestige and was highly coveted by the young elites. Competition was fierce even for lesser positions. To succeed one needed *Protektion*—the friendly ear of someone sufficiently high in the government's pecking order to influence the nomination. In Menger's case, the initial *Protektion* might have come through his brother Max, but Carl quickly learned to stand on his own.

One of his tasks as an officer of the *Wiener Zeitung* was to write market surveys. As he later told his disciple, Friedrich von Wieser, this was his practical introduction to price theory.[9] He was struck by the discrepancy between the actual pricing process as explained by traders and the standard textbook explanations he had learned at the university. Upon closer inspection, he came to believe that prices ultimately depended on the value judgments of consumers. It was with this thesis that he eventually earned his *Habilitation* (the traditional central-European university professor's credential) in government science.[10] In 1871 he published his work under the title *Grundsätze der Volkswirtschaftslehre* (Principles of Economics).

In his book Menger presented a theoretical study of fundamental economic phenomena such as economic goods, value,

---

[8]Wieser emphasized: "He entered government service," in "Karl Menger," p. 84. See also F.A. Hayek, "Einleitung," p. xii; Ki'ichiro Yagi, "Carl Menger as Editor: Significance of Journalistic Experience for his Economics and for his Later Life," *Revue européenne des sciences sociales* 30, no. 92 (1992); Hamann, *Rudolf*, p. 78.

[9]Wieser, "Karl Menger."

[10]Apparently Menger did not abandon his literary interests. In January 1869 he published another novel, *Die Bettlerin von St. Marx* (The Beggaress of St. Marx) in another Vienna paper, the *Allgemeine Volkszeitung*. See Ikeda, *Die Entstehungsgeschichte der "Grundsätze" Carl Mengers*, p. 65, n. 168.

exchange, prices, commodities, and money. He explained the properties of these phenomena and the laws to which they are subject at all times and places. This is of course what good economics textbooks always did and still do. What made Menger's book special is the method he used in his explanations. He tried to trace the causes of the properties and laws under scrutiny back to the simplest facts. His purpose was to demonstrate that the properties and laws of economic phenomena result from these empirically ascertainable "elements of the human economy" such as individual human needs, individual human knowledge, ownership and acquisition of individual quantities of goods, time, and individual error.[11] Menger's great achievement in *Principles* consisted in identifying these elements for analysis and explaining how they cause more-complex market phenomena such as prices. He called this the "empirical method," emphasizing that it was the same method that worked so well in the natural sciences.[12]

To the present reader, this label might be confusing, since it is not at all the experimental method of the modern empirical sciences. Menger did not use abstract models to posit falsifiable hypotheses that are then tested by experience. Instead, Menger's was an analytical method that began with the smallest empirical phenomena and proceeded logically from there. This put

---

[11]In the parlance of twentieth century analytical philosophy, Menger's "elements" would have been called "primitives" of economic theory.

[12]Carl Menger, *Grundsätze der Volkswirtschaftslehre* (Vienna: Braumüller, 1871), p. vii. Barry Smith has convincingly argued that Menger applied Aristotelean realism in economic analysis. See Barry Smith, "Austrian Economics and Austrian Philosophy," in Wolfgang Grassl and Barry Smith, eds., *Austrian Economics: Historical and Philosophical Background* (London: Croom Helm, 1986), pp. 1–36; idem, "Aristotle, Menger, Mises: An Essay in the Metaphysics of Economics," Bruce J. Caldwell, ed., *Carl Menger and His Legacy in Economics* (Durham, N.C.: Duke University Press, 1990), pp. 263–88. See also Raimondo Cubbedu, *The Philosophy of the Austrian School* (London: Routledge, 1993), chap. 1, § 1.

Menger in a position to consider market exchanges and prices as macro-phenomena and to explain how they are caused by atomistic, but empirically ascertainable "elements of the human economy" situated in an economic microcosm of individual needs and the marginal quantities owned and acquired. In Menger's words, prices were "by no means the most fundamental feature of the economic phenomenon of exchange," but "only incidental manifestations of these activities, symptoms of an economic equilibrium between the economies of individuals."[13]

As later works and correspondence revealed, Menger was fully aware that his most important innovation was the consistent application of the new "empirical method," which he also called the "exact method," the "analytical-synthetic" or the "analytical-compositive" method. In a February 1884 letter to Léon Walras, criticizing Walras's claim that there was a mathematical method of economic research, Menger wrote:

> It is rather necessary that we go back to the most simple elements of the mostly very complex phenomena that are here in question—that we thus determine in an *analytical* manner the ultimate factors that constitute the phenomena, the prices, and that we then accord to these elements the importance that corresponds to their nature, and that, in keeping with this importance, we try to establish the *laws* according to which the complex phenomena of human interaction result from simple phenomena.[14,15]

---

[13]Menger, *Grundsätze*; translated as *Principles of Economics*, p. 191.

[14]Menger's February 1884 letter to Léon Walras, as translated and published in Étienne Antonelli, "Léon Walras et Carl Menger à travers leur correspondence," *Économie appliquée* 6, nos. 2–3 (1953): 269–87. The passage is quoted from pp. 280f.; the translation is mine.

[15]William Jaffé emphasizes that:

> Carl Menger avoided the use of mathematics in his economics not because he did not know any better, but out of principle. When he wrote to Léon Walras on June 28, 1883 that

Only in this manner was it possible accurately to describe the essence of economic phenomena, and not just the contingent quantitative relationships in which they might stand with other phenomena at certain times and places. Referring to the disagreements between his theory of prices and the price theory of his French correspondent, Menger argued that real-life experience was the only legitimate way to decide the points under contention. The merit of a theory

> always depends on the extent to which it succeeds in determining the true factors (those that correspond to real life) constituting the economic phenomena and the laws according to which the complex phenomena of political economy result from the simple elements.

Menger continues:

> A researcher who arrives by the way of analysis at such elements that do not correspond to reality or who, without any true analysis, takes his departure from arbitrary axioms—which is only too often the case with the so-called rational method—falls necessarily into error, even if he makes superior use of mathematics.[16]

---

he had been for some time thoroughly acquainted with Walras's writings, he did not disclaim, as did other correspondents, sufficient knowledge of mathematics to follow these writings, which we may be sure he would have done if that had been the case. Instead, Carl Menger declared his objection in principle to the use of mathematics as a method of advancing economic knowledge. (William Jaffé, "Menger, Jevons and Walras De-Homogenized," *Economic Inquiry* 14 [December 1976]: 521)

Robert Hébert reports that Menger owned the journals where the mid-nineteenth century French "econo-engineers" published their pioneering studies in mathematical economics. Menger also owned the books of the major representatives of this school of thought. See Robert F. Hébert, "Jevons and Menger Re-Homogenized: Who is the Real 'Odd Man Out'?" *American Journal of Economics and Sociology* 57, no. 3 (1998): 329.

[16]Menger's February 1884 letter to Léon Walras, p. 282.

The empirical foundation of Menger's approach contrasted sharply with the Anglo-Saxon approach of that time, which was inspired by David Ricardo's *Principles* and relied on fictitious postulates and on such arbitrarily constructed aggregates as price level, capitalists, landowners, and laborers. But Menger's approach also contrasted with the dominant fashions on the Continent and in particular in Germany, where economists—in the manner of historians—treated observed complex phenomena such as market prices as the starting point for their analysis rather than trying to explain them as resulting from more fundamental factors.

In one stroke, *Principles of Economics* departed from both paradigms. Menger had found the delicate balance needed to develop economic theory that remained in touch with the real world. The comprehensive architecture of his book also showed that the principle of marginal value, which had played only an obscure role in earlier theories, is of fundamental and all-pervasive importance in economic science.

The core of Menger's book is the chapter on value, which consumes a quarter of its pages. While financial analysts of Menger's experience stressed subjective factors in price formation—the personal judgment of consumers, entrepreneurs, traders on the stock exchange, etc.—academic economists relegated these subjective factors to a secondary position beneath supposedly objective factors independent of human perceptions. The British classical economists (Adam Smith and David Ricardo, most notably) had created a thoroughly objectivist price theory that sought to explain the natural or long-run prices of all goods by reference only to the costs of production, particularly the cost of labor. According to this labor theory of value, subjective factors can cause actual market prices to deviate from "correct" prices, but only temporarily and never by enough to outweigh the impact of the objective costs of labor. The value of a product was therefore ultimately one of its inherent qualities, just like weight or volume. It was "in" the good rather than an accidental feature that stemmed "from outside."

The writings of Smith and Ricardo were overwhelmingly successful in the Anglo-Saxon countries, and had made great inroads on the European continent. The French Revolution had shifted the center of economic research and learning from the Continent to Britain. The Napoleonic era was particularly effective in suppressing the classical-liberal movement on the Continent. Public attention naturally shifted to Adam Smith, the patron saint of the still-vigorous British branch of the movement. Smith became the main authority on economic theory, displacing Quesnay, reducing Turgot to a footnote, and condemning Condillac to oblivion.

Adam Smith, above, and *David Ricardo* below

But his popularity as the intellectual leader of political liberalism did not help Smith in Germany. German economists were far less receptive to the Smithian message than were their peers in the West. German economists tended to be government employees and abhorred unbecoming political affiliations. Wilhelm Roscher, a great historian of economic thought and one of the leading German economists of the nineteenth century, famously observed that it was:

> a national peculiarity of the Germans . . . to deviate from the rule of free trade, which has been imported from England and France, through numerous exceptions made for government interventionism.[17]

---

[17]Wilhelm Roscher, *Geschichte der National-Oekonomik in Deutschland*, 1st ed. (Munich: Oldenbourg, 1874), pp. 1014f.

The German professors read Adam Smith, even read him attentively, but only to dismiss his views as lacking solid foundations. And while they did recognize Smith as an authority in the field, wrongheaded or not, they dismissed Ricardo almost out of hand. Smith's errors were debatable, but in Ricardo they found no scientific merit whatsoever. This preference for Smith over Ricardo grew stronger over the next century and culminated in the works of the very influential Younger Historical School, which rejected economic "theory" altogether.[18]

In his *Principles*, Ricardo had invented what today would be called macroeconomics, stressing the relationships between various aggregates such as price levels, average wages, average profits, but also between social aggregates such as laborers, capitalists, and landowners. On the basis of his insights about the relationships between such aggregate variables, he made the case for a far-reaching *laissez-faire* program. This approach did not meet with enthusiasm among German social scientists. Ever since the French revolutionary army had invaded Germany under the bloody banner of abstract human rights, Germans tended to be suspicious of sweeping political programs derived from theory without basis in observed reality. Under the trauma of the French Revolution, nineteenth-century German historians, jurists, and government scientists tended to stress the particular conditions of concrete human communities, rather than focus on features of an unobservable humanity *en masse*.

Smith did have an extremely able advocate in Jean-Baptiste Say, who was indefatigable in his efforts to promote British classical economics. Say's *Traité d'économie politique* is a masterpiece in its own right, in many ways more sophisticated than the

---

[18]See for example Gustav Schmoller, "Volkswirtschaft, Volkswirtschaftslehre und methode," *Handwörterbuch der Staatswissenschaften*, 3rd ed. (Jena: Gustav Fischer, 1911), vol. 8, p. 426, where Schmoller speaks of a battle of his school against Ricardo's one-sidedness.

books of Smith and Ricardo. Say gave an axiomatic exposition of Smithian (and possibly even Ricardian) economic science, enhancing enormously the prestige of the Scotsman's unsystematic *Wealth of Nations*.[19] He refined the British economists' focus on whole classes or aggregates of goods, subdividing economic science into a macroeconomic trilogy: production, distribution, and consumption of consumers' goods in general. Most important, he gave classical economics an appealing epistemological justification, showing it to be rooted in common experience. This empirically oriented methodology made much more sense to Continental scholars and convinced them that there was a scientific case to be made for Ricardian economics and the political program it seemed to entail.

Jean-Baptiste Say

Say was the central figure in the promotion of British economics on the European continent, but he clearly owed a far greater intellectual debt to the scientific tradition of his own country.[20] By the mid-nineteenth century, thanks to the efforts of Say, British economics had become the academic orthodoxy of Europe and America. It was against the background of this orthodoxy that Menger worked on a restatement of the explanation of the pricing process.

In developing his theory of value and prices, Menger relied on the remnants of an ancient price theory from the late-Scholastic School of Salamanca, which in the sixteenth and early seventeenth centuries had stressed precisely those subjective features of the pricing process that were conspicuously

---

[19]Yet by the same token Say also paved the way to displacing the continental tradition of economic thought that could be traced back to the Spanish late-Scholastics—a tradition that was still alive and vigorous in the Catholic countries of Europe. See below.

[20]Murray N. Rothbard, *Classical Economics: An Austrian Perspective on the History of Economic Thought* (Cheltenham, U.K.: Edward Elgar, 1995), chap. 1.

absent from the British classical school. But the Spanish late-scholastics never produced a treatise on economics, and their discoveries about the nature of value and prices were scattered across thousands of pages.[21]

The subjectivist theory of value survived only in this diffused form with one important exception: Etienne de Condillac's great treatise, *Commerce and Government*. Published in the same year as Smith's *Wealth of Nations* (1776), Condillac's treatment gave the first full axiomatic presentation of political economy on the basis of the subjectivist theory of value. But the impact of his work was minimal because French economists rejected it. Condillac was already a famous philosopher when he published the book, and did not deem it necessary to follow the conventions of the disciples of Quesnay; rather, he presented his thoughts in an independent and original manner—an offense, it turns out, serious enough to prevent the translation of his work into English for more than two hundred years.[22]

Still, *Commerce and Government* was one of the main sources of inspiration for Menger (who of course read French, among other

---

[21]On scholastic economics and the economics of the late-scholastic School of Salamanca in particular, see Joseph A. Schumpeter, *A History of Economic Analysis* (Oxford: Oxford University Press, 1954); Marjorie Grice-Hutchinson, *The School of Salamanca: Readings in Spanish Monetary Theory, 1544–1605* (Oxford: Clarendon Press, 1952); Raymond de Roover, *Business, Banking, and Economic Thought in Late Medieval and Early Modern Europe* (Chicago: University of Chicago Press, 1974); Emil Kauder, *A History of Marginal Utility Theory* (Princeton, N.J.: Princeton University Press, 1965); Murray N. Rothbard, *Economic Thought before Adam Smith* (Cheltenham, U.K.: Edward Elgar, 1995); Jesús Huerta de Soto, "New Light on the Prehistory of the Theory of Banking and the School of Salamanca," *Review of Austrian Economics* 9, no. 2 (1996): 59–81.

[22]Shelagh Eltis and Walter Eltis, "The Life and Contribution to Economics of the Abbé de Condillac," in Etienne de Condillac, *Commerce and Government: Considered in Their Mutual Relationship* (Cheltenham, U.K.: Edward Elgar, 1997).

Étienne Bonnot,
Abbé de Condillac

languages) when he elaborated his economic value theory.[23] Menger pointed out that value can only come into existence once human beings realize that economic goods exist and that each of them has a personal— or, as Menger would say "subjective"— importance.

Most importantly, value always concerns the concrete units of a good, that is, the "marginal" units under consideration, like one cup of water, four loaves of bread, three diamonds, two glasses of milk, etc. It never concerns the total available stock of these goods, except when decisions are actually made about the total stock. This insight is the key to solving an apparent paradox of the subjectivist theory of value, which had prevented a wider acceptance of the theory. If the price of a good really depends on the subjective importance of the good, then how is it that water, which is essential to human survival, commands a far lower price than diamonds, which are much less important than water? This apparent paradox played in favor of the labor theory of value, virtually the only alternative to the subjectivist approach. Whatever the problems of the labor theory of value, it did not contradict reality as strikingly as its subjectivist competitor.

Menger showed that the paradox is only apparent: it vanishes as soon as we stop asking about the value of entire classes of goods, which are economically irrelevant because they are not subject to human decision-making. If we ask instead about the laws that rule the evaluation of individual units of a good, the answer becomes clear. Water is so abundant that it not only serves to satisfy the most important—and thus most highly valued—human need for water, but also far less important needs for water, such as decorative fountains; it is the value of the least

---

[23]Menger quoted Condillac more than any foreign authority other than Adam Smith, and in contrast to Smith, he quoted him only favorably.

important but still satisfied need that determines the economic value of every unit of water, which therefore commands a low market price. By contrast, diamonds are so rare that the available supply can only satisfy the most important needs for them, and as a consequence they are very expensive.

Menger also showed that the value of factors of production is always derived from the value of consumer goods and not the other way around. Contrary to the assertion of cost-of-production theorists, a bottle of wine is not valuable because it has been produced with valuable land and valuable labor; the land and the labor invested in winemaking are valuable in the first place because consumers value the bottle of wine.

Finally, Menger argued that the micro-phenomenon of value exists independent of any social system of the division of labor. Thus he starts analyzing the macro-phenomena of exchange, prices, and money only after his chapter on value.

In the light of Menger's analysis, the market economy appeared as one great organism geared toward the satisfaction of consumer needs. Not only the market prices, but also the institutions of the market such as money are part and parcel of a rational order that can exist and operate without needing the assistance of political authorities.

In a way, Menger delivered a complement to Condillac's thesis that human needs are the great regulator of all human institutions. Condillac had made his case from an economic and, most famously, from an epistemological point of view, arguing that perceptions are determined by needs.[24] He lacked the important element of marginalism, however, and it was on this that Menger built a complete and thorough revision of economic science.

---

[24]See in particular Etienne de Condillac, *Essai sur l'origine des connaissances humaines* (1746); *Traité des sensations* (1754); *Le commerce et le gouvernement* (1776). These works are collected in his *Œuvres complètes* (Paris: Tourneux, Lecointe et Durey, 1822), vols. 1, 3, and 4.

Menger's Work in the German Context

The ancient subjectivist theory of value had survived in fragmentary form in nineteenth-century German economic writings.[25] In this context, the young economist from Vienna was seen as a reformer rather than a revolutionary, thus avoiding the fate of Condillac.

Before Menger, various German economists had criticized the labor theory of value specifically and rejected the doctrine of inherent value in general. Menger's view that value was subjective (personal, individual) in nature was not exceptional among German authors of the first half of the nineteenth century. Indeed, some of them even knew the principle of marginal subjective value.[26] But their insights were merely disconnected observations. None of Menger's German predecessors recognized the central importance of marginal value and none had produced a unified subjectivist theory.

In the 1860s, two unconnected layers of analysis subsisted in the German textbooks. Their price theories typically featured cost-of-production explanations as a dominant component and allowed for an incoherent coexistence with the traditional subjective-value explanations.[27] Karl Marx heaped scorn and ridicule on this blatant display of eclecticism. He was right to do so.

---

[25]In 1807, Gottlieb Hufeland called the subjectivist theory the "traditional view" and recommended never to deviate from it. See Gottlieb Hufeland, *Neue Grundlegung der Staatswirthschaftskunst* (Giessen and Wetzlar: Tasche & Müller, 1807), p. 18.

[26]See in particular Erich Streissler, "The Influence of German Economics on the Work of Menger and Marshall," Caldwell, ed., *Carl Menger and His Legacy in Economics*; idem, "Carl Menger, der deutsche Nationalökonom," B.P. Priddat, ed., *Wert, Meinung, Bedeutung* (Marburg: Metropolis, 1997), pp. 33–88; Ikeda, *Die Entstehungsgeschichte der "Grundsätze" Carl Mengers.*

[27]Erich Streissler points out that Alfred Marshall's *Principles of Economics* (London: Macmillan, 1891) had the exact structure of a typical German textbook. See Streissler, "The Influence of German Economists on the Work of Menger and Marshall," Caldwell, ed., *Carl Menger and his Legacy in Economics*, p. 51.

Menger took what was no more than hinted at in the writings of his predecessors and presented it in a systematic treatise that revolutionized the profession's view on the relations between human needs, value, and prices. Through the systematic attempt to look for the causes of these relations in the simplest facts open to empirical inquiry (the "elements of the human economy"), Menger put the discussion of needs, goods, economic systems, production, prices, income, consumption, etc., on completely new ground.

The contrast to his eclectic German predecessors could not have been greater. Their eclecticism was reinforced by tendencies Menger avoided. In particular, German economists tended to engage in excessive and often pointless record keeping and classification of economic phenomena, an inclination that reflected the political climate of the time. The restoration of monarchy and the concomitant fight against liberalism between 1815 and 1848 made it imprudent to delve too deeply into theoretical considerations, which might lead to a critical appraisal of the limits of government. As William Johnston said: "At a time when it was forbidden to debate matters of fundamental principle, scholars retreated into collecting data."[28] The record-keeping approach to economic analysis reached its climax by the end of the century with the ascension of the Younger Historical School. As did many other academic employees of the new German central state, they saw themselves as "the intellectual bodyguards of the House of Hohenzollern."[29]

---

[28]William M. Johnston, *Vienna, Vienna—The Golden Age, 1815–1914* (Milan: Arnoldo Mondadori, 1981), p. 15.

[29]This point of view was not limited to intellectuals working in "ideological" fields such as history, political economy, or philosophy. In a public lecture given on August 3, 1870, Emil du Bois-Reymond, the rector of the Frederick-William University of Berlin and a pioneer of electro-physiology, proclaimed that his university was the "intellectual bodyguard of the House of Hohenzollern." See Emil du Bois-Reymond, *Über den deutschen Krieg* (Berlin: Hirschwald, 1870).

A related German shortcoming that Menger scrupulously avoided was historicism—the tendency to regard regularities in economic phenomena as "historical laws"—that is, as conditioned by the particular circumstances of time and place. Though the German economists of those days would have agreed with Menger that all economic phenomena were somehow related to one another and that one of the purposes of economic science was to find out what that relationship was, Menger's analysis revealed that these relationships were laws that held true at all times and places; moreover, he showed that they could be studied without reference to the concrete historical context. His book featured many concrete illustrations of the general laws under discussion, but in essence Menger's *Principles* was an exercise in pure theory.

Methodenstreit

Meanwhile, in the universities of the German Reich, a vigorous movement had emerged that pursued an agenda diametrically opposed to Menger's view and advocated a radical break with the traditional approach in economic science.[30] While Menger sought to turn economic theory into an analytical science, the young radicals in Berlin pursued a complete overthrow of theoretical research, replacing it instead with historical studies.

The leader of this group was Gustav Schmoller, a young professor from the University of Halle.[31] Schmoller's great goal,

---

[30]Streissler, "The Influence of German Economics on the Work of Carl Menger and Marshall." Through this work, Streissler has convincingly corrected the heretofore prevailing notion that the Younger Historical School was somehow more deeply rooted in the German tradition of economic science than Carl Menger. As Streissler stated, the real revolutionary was Gustav Schmoller, not Menger.

[31]Schmoller was a professor in Halle from 1864 to 1872. Being one of the first beneficiaries of the Prussian-German victory over France in the Franco-Prussian War, he moved to the University of Strasbourg (1872–1882), before finally receiving a chair at the University of Berlin (1882–1913).

overriding all his theoretical and methodological concerns, was to combat the growing intellectual and practical influence of

laissez-faire liberalism in Germany. His strategy was to promote the discussion of the "social question"—by which he meant the question of how government could promote the welfare of the working classes. That the government could and should promote working class welfare was taken for granted.

Gustav Schmoller

Schmoller put his strategy into practice through an association of like-minded intellectuals and political leaders, most of whom were university professors and civil servants. In October 1872, he convened a first national meeting of

> men of all parties of whom it can be assumed that they have interest in, and moral pathos for, the [social] question and that they do not believe the absolute *laissez faire et laissez passer* to be the right thing as far as the social question is concerned.[32]

Schmoller and two others who would become long-time leaders of the group—the Breslau professor Lujo Brentano and the Berlin statistician Ernst Engel—addressed the meeting with lectures on strikes and labor unions, on German factory laws, and on the housing question.

The distinct anti-market and pro-government orientation of these university professors quickly earned them the sobriquet of *Kathedersozialisten,* or "Socialists of the Chair."[33] Significantly,

---

[32]Gustav Schmoller, "Einladung zur Eisenacher Versammlung von 1872," printed in Franz Boese, *Geschichte des Vereins für Sozialpolitik, 1872–1932* (Berlin: Duncker & Humblot, 1939), p. 241.

[33]The smear term *"Kathedersozialisten"* was coined by Heinrich Bernard Oppenheim in his book *Der Katheder-Sozialismus* (Berlin: Oppenheim, 1872). See Ralph Raico, *Die Partei der Freiheit* (Stuttgart: Lucius & Lucius, 1999), p.

their first meeting took place in the city of Eisenach, which in the same year had hosted the founding convention of the *Sozialistische Partei Deutschlands* (Socialist Party of German). Because the SPD was the very first socialist party in the world, Eisenach had become the symbol of the organized socialist movement. The group now founded the *Verein für Socialpolitik* (Association for Social Policy) with the explicit purpose of promoting welfare policies of the new German central state. The first president was Erwin Nasse, a professor from Bonn. Schmoller, who in 1872 had been a young man, became Nasse's successor in 1890 and remained president until his death in 1917.[34]

The *Verein* organized plenary meetings, which took place every other year, and meetings of an elected committee (*Ausschuss*). These meetings had a deep, and often immediate, impact on German policies because they provided a neutral territory for the representatives of the most powerful organized groups. University professors, labor union officials, high-ranking civil servants, and entrepreneurs met in the *Verein*, got to know one another, and forged political compromises on the issues of the day. The strong practical orientation was also visible in the *Verein*'s publication series. Each volume addressed a different pressing social problem, analyzed its symptoms, and invariably ended with a call for government action. Ralph Raico states:

---

200. The only Austrian participant in the initial 1872 meeting was one Dr. Friedmann (probably Otto Bernhard Friedmann), a journalist from Vienna.

[34]On the history of the *Verein* see Boese, *Geschichte des Vereins für Sozialpolitik, 1872–1932*; Dieter Lindenlaub, *Richtungskämpfe im Verein für Sozialpolitik: Wissenschaft und Sozialpolitik im Kaiserreich vornehmlich vom Begin des "Neuen Kurses" bis zum Ausbruch des ersten Weltkrieges, 1890–1914* (Wiesbaden: Steiner, 1967); Irmela Gorges, *Sozialforschung in Deutschland, 1872–1914*, 2nd ed. (Frankfurt a.M.: Anton Hain, 1986).

Many of the 134 intensively researched volumes that were published until 1914 virtually served as indictments of various flaws and grievances of the existing system, and each of them called for government action. . . . The main goal of the Socialists of the Chair, namely, to change public opinion within the educated bourgeoisie and especially within the bureaucracy, was attained to a large extent.[35]

Through these activities, the *Verein* became one of the most important vehicles for the consolidation and expansion of the new German government's civil service. The professors and the other civil servants saw themselves as neutral mediators among the various contesting social groups. Every solution to any perceived social problem invariably involved either their active participation, or their intermediation.[36] As they saw it, they promoted political compromise between the Left and Right, democracy and monarchy, utilitarianism and justice, laborers and entrepreneurs.[37] They considered themselves neutral

---

[35]Raico, *Partei der Freiheit*, p. 188.

[36]Many years later, Mises characterized their attitude in the following words:

It is the mentality of officialdom—which, according to Brentano, was "the only sounding board of the Association for Social Policy"—that considers as constructive and positive only that ideology which calls for the greatest number of offices and officials. And he who seeks to reduce the number of state agents is decried as a "negative thinker" or an "enemy of the state." (Mises, *A Critique of Interventionism* [New York: Arlington House, 1977], pp. 82–83)

See also Mises, *The Historical Setting of the Austrian School of Economics* (New Rochelle, N.Y.: Arlington House, 1969), p. 31. On the history of the Bismarckian welfare state, and of its predecessor under Frederick II, see Gerd Habermann, *Der Wohlfahrtsstaat: Die Geschichte eines Irrwegs*, 2nd ed. (Frankfurt: Ullstein, 1997).

[37]Gustav Schmoller, "Eröffnungsrede zum 25 jährigen Bestehen des Vereins auf der Kölner Tagung von 1897," printed in Boese, *Geschichte des Vereins für Sozialpolitik, 1872–1932*, pp. 253ff., in part pp. 262f.

arbiters because they considered these conflicts from the "higher" point of view of the new central government, which represented the entire nation.

The era of the *Verein für Socialpolitik* coincided with the heyday of German political centralization. Starting in the early 1890s, however, the government began to turn its back on the *Verein*. Its constant agitation for left-wing political reform had been too successful, and it risked losing its reputation for political neutrality.[38] For a while, Schmoller managed to steer against this trend, but the *Verein*'s very success eventually spelled its doom. At the end of the nineteenth century, it had already attracted a great number of intellectuals and social leaders such as Max Weber, Ludwig Pohle, and Andreas Voigt who were in principle opposed to the *Verein*'s blind pro-government prejudices and had joined only because of its practical importance.[39] Under the leadership of Max Weber, these men repeatedly clashed with the *Verein* establishment over the question of scientific "proof" in political matters; after World War I, Weber's followers would forever change the character of the *Verein*, turning it into a purely academic institution.

But in its glory days of the late 1870s and 1880s, the *Verein* and in particular the person of Gustav Schmoller completely transformed the landscape of German-language economic science. Schmoller also had a lasting influence on German economics through his personal friendship with Friedrich Althoff, a high-ranking civil servant in Prussia's Ministry of Education, who from 1882–1907 controlled the nominations to the chairs of political economy in Prussian universities. It soon became obvious that to obtain a full professorship one had to subscribe

---

[38]Ibid., pp. 260f.

[39]In the early years, the most vociferous opposition to the *Verein*'s agenda came from non-members such as Heinrich Oppenheim and Julius Wolf. See Raico, *Partei der Freiheit*, pp. 200ff. Pohle and Voigt published their influential and devastating critiques of the *Verein* only after they left it in 1905.

without qualifications to the program defined in Schmoller's writings.

Although Schmoller's agenda was targeted primarily against the heroes of the free-trade movement—classical economists such as Adam Smith, Jean-Baptiste Say, and David Ricardo—it effectively killed the teaching of any type of economic theory in German universities. The so-called Younger Historical School under Schmoller went far beyond the healthy skepticism of theoretical abstractions that had characterized the works of the previous generation of German economists. The Schmollerites denied outright that there were any universal social laws at all: there were only certain regularities that changed with the changing institutions of society. The job of government science was only incidentally to study these context-dependent regularities. Its essential task was to study the concrete meaning of the "idea of justice" at a given time and place, because this was the true basis of the "principle of social reform"—adjusting the existing social institutions to the prevailing feelings of what was right and just.[40] Schmoller thus advocated radical relativism and radical legal positivism, the most suitable doctrines for justifying his belief in and adoration of omnipotent government.

Carl Menger had followed the growth of the Schmoller movement for some years. He realized that under the supervening influence of the Younger Historical School, Germany and Austria (which was fully in Germany's intellectual orbit) were in the process of destroying the work of a century of economic scholarship. Menger's first treatise fell on deaf ears. It had found followers in Austria, but this was due in part to his personal influence on academic nominations. The German universities were impenetrable.

---

[40]See for example Gustav Schmoller, "Die Gerechtigkeit in der Volkswirtschaft," *Schmollers Jahrbuch* 5 (1881), pp. 19–54; idem, *Zur Social- und Gewerbepolitik der Gegenwart* (Leipzig: Duncker & Humblot, 1890); idem, *Grundriss der allgemeinen Volkswirtschaftslehre* (Leipzig: Duncker & Humblot, 1900).

Menger decided to lay the foundation for future works in positive economic analysis through a systematic methodological defense of his new approach.[41] The result of these efforts was another great book, *Untersuchungen über die Methode der Sozial-wissenschaften und der politischen Ökonomie insbesondere* (Investigations into the Method of the Social Sciences with Special Reference to Economics).[42] Menger insisted that the economic laws he had discussed were "exact" laws of reality, and that the methods of historical research were entirely unable to discover such economic laws.

These views could not fail to offend the historicist sensibilities of the academic establishment, which were especially strong among economists of Menger's own generation. In fact, while historicism was already noticeable in the works of the Older Historical School (Roscher, Knies, Hildebrand, and others), in the writings of the Younger Historical School (Schmoller, Lexis, and others) it had become a dogma. Schmoller published a highly critical review of Menger's *Investigations*, claiming that Menger had neglected to substantiate his analysis with fitting historical studies; in today's jargon, Menger had indulged in an exercise in pure theory, which lacked "empirical evidence" in its support. This attack could have led to sober scholarly debate if Schmoller had not tried to stigmatize his opponent by labeling his approach the "Mancunian-individualistic method," associating Menger with the supposedly discredited Manchester School.[43]

---

[41]See his important February 1884 letter to Léon Walras, as translated and published in Antonelli, "Léon Walras et Carl Menger à travers leur correspondence," pp. 269–87. The passage referred to is on p. 283.

[42]Carl Menger, *Untersuchungen zur Methode der Sozialwissenschaften und der politischen Oekonomie im besonderen* (Leipzig: Duncker & Humblot, 1883); translated as *Investigations into the Method of the Social Sciences and of Political Economy in Particular* (New York: New York University Press, 1985).

[43]Gustav Schmoller, "Zur Methodologie der Staats- und Sozial-Wissenschaften," *Schmoller's Jahrbuch* n.s. 7, no. 3 (1883): 239ff. See also the review by Norbert Leser in *Conrad's Jahrbücher* n.s. 7, p. 273ff.

The debate between Menger and Schmoller soon drew their disciples into a heated exchange, during which even the grand old man of German economics, Wilhelm Roscher, heaped scorn on Menger.[44] This collective exchange involved several more articles and books.[45] Its unusually polemical and emotional character resulted from the fact that for Schmoller, any kind of economic theory strengthened the case for capitalism.[46] The debate culminated in 1895, when Menger's last great student, Richard Schüller, published his *Habilitation* thesis in which he refuted point by point the criticism of the classical economists that Bruno Hildebrand had expressed in his inaugural lecture at the University of Vienna.[47]

In spite of the heated atmosphere in which it took place, the debate on method between Menger and Schmoller was useful for the clarification of the differences between theoretical and applied economic research. While it did not produce any lasting

---

[44]See the 1886 edition of Roscher's *Grundlagen*, quoted from Karl Milford, "Hufeland als Vorläufer von Menger und Hayek," in Birger Priddat, ed., *Wert, Meinung, Bedeutung: Die Tradition der subjektiven Wertlehre in der deutschen Nationalökonomie vor Menger* (Marburg: Metropolis, 1997), pp. 99f. In 1871, Menger had dedicated his *Grundsätze* to Roscher.

[45]As far as Menger's contributions to the debate are concerned, see Carl Menger, *Die Irrthümer des Historismus in der deutschen Nationalökonomie* (Vienna: Alfred Hölder, 1884); idem "Zur Kritik der politischen Ökonomie," *Zeitschrift für das Privat- und öffentliche Recht der Gegenwart* 14 (1887); idem, "Grundzüge einer Klassifikation der Wirtschaftswissenschaften," *Jahrbücher für Nationalökonomie und Statistik* n.s. 19 (1889). These papers have been reprinted in Carl Menger, *Gesammelte Werke*, F.A. Hayek, ed., 2nd ed. (Tübingen: Mohr, 1970), vol. 3.

[46]The model of opposition between libertarian-minded theorists and statist historians is not a complete reflection of the state of affairs. There were in fact market-friendly historicists such as Lujo Brentano, as well as theorists with strong statist inclinations such as Adolf Wagner, or even Wieser.

[47]Richard Schüller, *Die klassische Nationalökonomie und ihre Gegner* (Berlin: Heymanns, 1895). Hildebrand had succeeded Lorenz von Stein, but stayed only one year in Vienna.

or definitive results, it did renew interest in the topic and high-lighted the importance of certain fundamental distinctions that later economists, philosophers, and historians such as Max Weber, Heinrich Rickert, Ludwig von Mises, and Alfred Schütz would develop. Of particular concern would be the distinction between the fundamentally different natures of natural science, history, and economics.

What is less often seen is that the opposition that rallied all "theorists" behind Menger and all "historians" behind Schmoller caused some important differences within each group to be neglected. This was bound to promote confusion especially within the ranks of the theorists, who tended to be seen (and to see themselves) as adhering to "the" economic the-ory, where they in fact held significantly different notions of the subject matter and contents of their science. Menger's unique contribution tended to be perceived as only one part of a broad consensus on the main outline of "the" new economic theory. Menger did not share this perception.

The Austrian School and the Gossen School

With just two books, Menger had put economic and social thought on completely new foundations. *Principles* pioneered the application of the empirical method in economic theory, and *Investigations* had justified the method and clarified the relationship between the resulting theory and other social sci-ences. Economic science was no longer just the study of visi-ble economic phenomena such as prices, money, production; it had become instead the study of how these phenomena were caused by the interaction between human ideas and an envi-ronment offering limited resources for the satisfaction of human needs.

It took some time for both his opponents and his followers to grasp the full impact of the Mengerian revolution. For his contemporaries, the Mengerian project was attractive for rea-sons other than the grand new vision it implied. In particular, it was Menger's unique analytical method of developing economic theory as a descriptive science of the real world that attracted young disciples.

Menger's "empirical method" fit the ideal of its day. Schools and universities had thoroughly prepared the young scientific elite to appreciate the virtues of empirical research. More than the universities of other countries at that time, Germany's institutions of higher learning insisted on the necessity of empirical investigations in virtually all fields. Surprisingly, this orientation was the product of the "idealist" philosophy of Immanuel Kant, which stressed that knowledge about the objects of the exterior world could only be gained through sensory experience, and in particular through observation. German scientists were more willing than others to leave their armchairs and offices for field research to engage in systematic observation of nature. The famous Alexander von Humboldt was a pioneer of this movement, but others soon began to follow. German science excelled in biology, physics, chemistry, medicine, history, and virtually all other fields of knowledge.[48]

In the field of political economy, however, which was usually taught under the name of government science, the call for an empirical foundation had led to the idealization of historical research. The historicists claimed that there was no other social science but history, and that economic theory, insofar as it had scientific merit at all, had to be a generalization of historical findings. In this context, Menger's approach appeared as an attractive alternative because it showed that economic theory was an independent discipline that could be studied in its own right without abandoning the empirical agenda. The power of

---

[48]For an introduction to nineteenth-century German thought on the nature of science, see the collection of original papers by Humboldt, Gauss, Chamisso, Virchow, Helmholtz, Ranke, Burckhardt, and many others in Wolfgang Schirmacher, ed., *German Essays on Science in the 19th Century* (New York: Continuum, 1996).

this message even attracted scholars of historicist background who had no personal contact with Carl Menger.

A case in point was young Ludwig von Mises. Steeped as he was in the prejudices of interventionism and in the quest for a truly scientific foundation for economic policy, Mises would not have found Ricardo convincing. But Menger convinced him that there was such a thing as a scientific economic theory—a body of propositions about empirical reality, distinctly different from the propositions derived from historical research. Mises yielded to the evidence and became a Mengerian, and he would remain one the rest of his life.

In later works, Mises would modify, generalize, and qualify Menger's views. In particular, he became famous for his interpretation of the epistemological status of the propositions of economic science, that is, for his claim that these propositions are true on *a priori* grounds and therefore cannot be verified or refuted by the evidence of the senses. But these claims were attempts to clarify the position that Mises had inherited from Menger. The difference between Menger's Aristotelian rhetoric and the Kantian phrasing used by Mises is glaring, but the difference is mainly rhetorical. The principal thread of continuity between Menger and Mises is an adherence to the same scientific program of developing economic theory as a descriptive discipline, distinct from other descriptive disciplines such as biology or history. Both Menger and Mises believed that their theories described certain general features of human action that exist and operate at all times and places. This is what set them fundamentally apart from Wieser and Schumpeter, and this is what still sets Mengerian economists apart from all other economists.

Menger's method is also what most sharply distinguished him from Léon Walras and William Stanley Jevons, two authors with whom Menger is often conflated as co-founders of the marginal-utility approach in price theory. It is true that these three men published at about the same time systematic

Léon Walras, top, *and William Stanley Jevons,* bottom

expositions of price theory based on the subjective and marginal nature of value. But apart from a broad agreement on these basic ideas, Menger's theory does not have much in common with the other two.[49]

Walras and Jevons had to overcome great obstacles in expounding their principles. Neither had the German subjectivist tradition to draw on, and both met with fierce resistance from the academic establishment. As far as originality and scientific merit are concerned, however, they cannot compare with Menger.[50] Unlike Menger, Jevons and Walras had a specific predecessor, albeit an obscure one, whom they acknowledged and praised: the independent German scholar Hermann Heinrich Gossen had anticipated their central tenets and their approach to price theory.

---

[49]Accounts of the differences between these authors can be found in J.R. Hicks, "Léon Walras," *Econometrica* (October 1934): 338; Schumpeter, *A History of Economic Analysis*, p. 918; Jaffé, "Menger, Jevons and Walras De-Homogenized," pp. 511ff.; Sandra J. Peart, "Jevons and Menger Re-Homogenized?" *American Journal of Economics and Sociology* 57, no. 3 (1998): 307ff. According to a widespread view, Walras eclipsed Menger and Jevons because he had pioneered general-equilibrium theory and *thereby demonstrated* the interdependency of all economic phenomena. This view is peculiar because this general interdependency is in fact a presupposition of any sort of economic analysis. It is in fact merely another way of saying that there is scarcity. Mark Blaug corrected this erroneous view, stressing that Menger too analyzed economic phenomena in their mutual interdependence. See Mark Blaug, "Comment" [on O'Brien's "Lionel Robbins and the Austrian Connection"], Caldwell, ed., *Carl Menger and His Legacy in Economics*, p. 186.

[50]Jaffé, "Menger, Jevons and Walras De-Homogenized," pp. 513ff., 518. A French predecessor was Jules Dupuit, who published two articles on marginal value in the late 1840s. See Robert Ekelund and Robert Hébert, *Secret Origins of Modern Microeconomics: Dupuit and the Engineers* (Chicago: Chicago University Press, 1999); and Jean-Pascal Simonin et François Vatin, *L'oeuvre*

By following Gossen, Jevons and Walras developed a marginal-utility theory of prices that was markedly less successful at describing observed reality than was Menger's marginal-value approach. The differences between Menger on the one hand, and Gossen, Jevons, and Walras on the other, might seem arcane, but they came to play a major role in the development of Austrian economics, and it is against this background that one must appreciate the significance of Mises's contributions.

Gossen had worked for twenty years on a manuscript that he published in 1854 under the title *Entwickelung der Gesetze des menschlichen Verkehrs* (Deduction of the Laws of Human Interrelationships).[51] In this work he combined two central ideas into a general treatise on human behavior.

First, Gossen thought that economic science concerned laws that rule human psychology as it relates to human action. The most fundamental psychological laws, he claimed, were two laws of want-satisfaction that later came to be known as Gossen's First and Second Law. According to the First Law, the satisfaction derived from the consumption of any good will at some point reach a maximum. Neither higher nor lower consumption will produce greater satisfaction. According to the Second Law of Gossen, all goods should be consumed in such quantities that the contribution to overall satisfaction through the marginal consumption of each good is exactly equal.

Second, Gossen sought to describe human action with algebra and graphs, and relied on several implicit and false postulates in order to attain this goal. For example, he postulated that value is measurable and that the values of different persons can be meaningfully combined.

---

multiple de Jules Dupuit (1804–1866): Calcul d'ingénieur, analyse économique et pensée sociale (Angers: Presses de l'Université d'Angers, 2002).

[51]Hermann Heinrich Gossen, *Entwickelung der Gesetze des menschlichen Verkehrs und der daraus fliessenden Regeln für menschliches Handeln* (Braunschweig: Vieweg & Sohn, 1854).

It was this procedure that made his approach especially contestable in the eyes of the academic establishment of German
economists who abhorred speculations disconnected from the
observed world. Gossen's book also suffered from grave formal
shortcomings, being written in one continuous text, without
chapter headings or a table of contents. This format and his
excessive use of algebra and graphs made his work a tedious and
distasteful reading experience. It fell into oblivion where it
probably would have remained were it not for William Stanley
Jevons.

When Jevons published the first edition of his *Principles of
Political Economy* (1871), he considered his theory unprecedented. In 1878, Professor Adamson, Jevons's successor at
Owens College in Manchester, came across a reference to
Gossen's book in a history of economic thought and informed
his friend Jevons, who celebrated Gossen in the preface to the
second edition of his *Principles* (1879).[52]

Walras was even more enthusiastic than Jevons. He compared Gossen to Copernicus and Newton, and translated
Gossen's book into French.[53] When Menger told him in a letter
that he believed there were significant differences between his
own approach and that of Gossen, Walras waxed indignant and
replied that he found it "odious" to think that Menger would
refuse to recognize such an important predecessor.[54]

---

[52]See the preface of the 1879 second edition of his *Principles of Economics*,
p. il.

[53]Léon Walras, "Un économiste inconnu: Hermann-Henri Gossen,"
Journal des Économistes (April and May 1885). This is the same Walras who in
his correspondence with Menger apologized that his German was not good
enough to digest *Grundsätze*.

[54]See Walras's February 2, 1887 letter to Menger, as translated and published in Antonelli, "Léon Walras et Carl Menger à travers leur correspondence," pp. 269–87. The letter is quoted on pp. 285f. See also the exchange
of letters between Jevons and Walras published in the *Journal des Économistes*

Gossen had indeed anticipated Jevons's and Walras's theories.[55] The three men had developed general theories that were analogous to Menger's general theory of value and prices, but differed from it in their psychological orientation and in the exact type of explanation they offered.

In Menger's theory, the term "value" does not refer to a psychological feeling, but rather to the relative importance for an individual of the marginal unit of good X—that is, to the importance of X *in comparison to* the marginal units of other goods Y and Z. The market price of a good results from the interplay of sellers and buyers, for whom the goods bought and sold have different relative importance. In contrast, in the theories of the other three authors, the price of a good results from the interplay of sellers and buyers whose *feelings or well-being* are differently affected by control of the good. While Menger explained the pricing process as resulting from the importance of a good relative to the importance of other goods, Gossen, Jevons, and Walras explained the pricing process as the impact of a marginal quantity of a good on the psychology of the

---

(June 1874). In a January 27, 1887 letter to Léon Walras, Menger had emphasized that there was only a limited analogy between his approach and Gossen's, but that there was no conformity in the "decisive questions." See Antonelli, "Léon Walras et Carl Menger à travers leur correspondence," pp. 269–87. The letter is quoted on pp. 284f.

[55]Jaffé ("Menger, Jevons and Walras De-Homogenized," pp. 515f.) stresses that Walras initially did not associate diminishing marginal utility with quantities *consumed*, but with quantities *possessed*. It is true that Walras was more cautious than Gossen and Jevons in speculating on the psychological underpinnings of his price theory, even though in his *Eléments d'économie politique* he eventually did bring in Gossen-style psychological analysis. But, as we shall see, the decisive consideration for our purposes is that value is for Walras (just as for Gossen and Jevons) a *two*-sided relationship, involving an acting person and one other object; whereas Menger's analysis of value features at least *three* elements: acting person and two things that are ranked from the point of view of the agent.

actor—an impact they called want-satisfaction (Gossen), utility (Jevons), and satisfied needs (Walras). Jevons's marginal utility thus played structurally the same role that marginal value played in Menger's theory—it delivered an explanation of market prices—but where marginal utility explains the price of a good by the good's direct impact on *human feelings*, Menger's marginal value explains the price of a good by how the good *ranks in importance* compared to other goods, according to the needs of the individuals involved in the pricing process.

In the psychological approach of Gossen, Jevons, and Walras, the human psyche was the great common denominator for the economic significance of all goods; in the theory of Menger, there was no such common denominator. In his approach, "value" cannot be independent of the specific circumstances of time and space; it is inseparable from these circumstances and means different things in different economic settings. According to Gossen, Jevons, and Walras, the *amount* of "utility" derived from a good could be different in different situations, but according to Menger, the entire basis of value is different as soon as the economic context changes—because the good would then be compared to *different* other goods.

Whatever else one might think of the merits of the psychological approach, it had at least one great attraction, namely, that it allowed the possibility of a mathematical price theory based on marginal utility. With the human psyche as the common denominator of all economic values, it became conceivable to represent the want-satisfaction or utility derived from the consumption of a good as a mathematical function of the quantities consumed; it became conceivable to scale satisfaction and utility into units with which one could perform economic calculation completely disconnected from market prices. It also became conceivable to combine individual utility functions into something like an aggregate utility function: one person's satisfaction and another person's satisfaction can be added into a single quantity representing "their" total satisfaction; and one person's gain added to a different person's loss can be mathematically combined to determine whether there is net gain or loss.[56]

These considerations probably played a role in prompting Gossen, Jevons, and Walras to choose the psychological approach. They did not begin with observation and then adopt algebraic and geometric techniques as the most adequate tools for representing what they observed. Rather, they began with an agenda—the need to apply mathematics in economics to make it more "scientific"—and were looking for a plausible hypothesis to justify their preferred approach.[57] This also explains other

---

[56]Gossen, *Entwickelung der Gesetze des menschlichen Verkehrs und der daraus fliessenden Regeln für menschliches Handeln*, pp. 80ff.

[57]This fact is crucial to understanding the history of twentieth-century economic thought. Gossen was already an enthusiastic mathematician and only studied law under the severe pressure of his father; see F.A. Hayek, "Einleitung," introduction to Hermann Heinrich Gossen, *Entwickelung der Gesetze des menschlichen Verkehrs und der daraus fliessenden Regeln für menschliches Handeln*, 3rd ed. (Berlin: Prager, 1927), pp. xf. All of his followers featured the same mindset. As Mark Blaug points out, Jevons first studied chemistry and biology and then turned his attention to economics. His "inspiration was Bentham's 'felicific calculus' of pleasure and pain, supplemented by the works of Dionysius Lardner . . . and Fleming Jenkins . . . , two British engineer-economists of the 1860s" (*Great Economists before Keynes: An Introduction to the Lives and Works of One Hundred Great Economists of the Past* [Cambridge: Cambridge University Press, 1986], p. 100). Walras pursued formal studies in letters, science, and engineering. From his father, the economist Auguste Walras, he adopted the conviction that some concept of utility maximization is the fundamental element of economic science. Walras's great follower Vilfredo Pareto was an engineer and turned to economics only at the age of 42. Similarly, Knut Wicksell's and Irving Fisher's first university degrees were in mathematics. Gustav Cassel, who according to Blaug (ibid, pp. 41ff.) had written the most widely read textbook of the interwar period, was a Ph.D. in mathematics, then became a schoolmaster and then turned to economics, becoming the greatest popularizer of general-equilibrium economics *à la* Walras. In contrast, the predominant formative influence on Austrian economists did not come in the form of mathematical training, but through legal studies. Until the interwar period, all Austrian economists had to obtain a

fictional stipulations to which they resorted, again, in distinct contrast to Menger's method. In their price theories they avoided one of the great pitfalls of economic theory *à la* Ricardo, namely, reliance on aggregates. But because they were eager to make political economy a mathematical discipline they fell prey to the other great pitfall, reliance on fictitious *ad-hoc* postulates. In order to allow for graphical and algebraic representations of utility, demand, and prices, Gossen, Jevons, and Walras assumed that all goods were infinitely divisible. And in order to justify their assumption that the market is in equilibrium, they neglected the existence of error.

Just as the classical economists had done before them, the Gossen School analyzed prices as they would be if certain special conditions were fulfilled: they analyzed hypothetical equilibrium prices rather than actual market prices. It is here, then, that we find the great divide between the Austrian and the Gossen Schools. Menger paved the way for dealing with real-world prices. His work made economics more scientific in the true sense of the word—increasing knowledge about real things—while the writings of Gossen, Jevons, and Walras dealt not with matters of fact, but only conjectures. William Jaffé was entirely right when he wrote:

> Carl Menger clearly stands apart from the other two reputed founders of the modern marginal utility theory. . . . No one familiar with the primary literature can doubt for a moment that Menger's treatment of the structure of wants in relation to *evaluation* was

---

first degree in law before they could turn their research to economic problems. As a consequence, the Vienna economists distinguished themselves by a great capacity to think conceptually and, most importantly, by their eagerness to relate all of their concepts to the observed real world. Their training in law effectively counterbalanced the inclination some of them felt for the natural sciences (for example, Böhm-Bawerk had in his youth a great interest in theoretical physics; see Joseph A. Schumpeter, "Eugen von Böhm-Bawerk," *Neue Österreichische Biographie* [Vienna, 1925], vol. 2, p. 65).

more profound and more penetrating not only than that of Walras who evinced no particular interest in such questions, but also than that of Jevons.[58]

Jaffé went on to identify the root of the greater profundity in Menger's quest for realism, which prevented him from developing "theory" in the sense of a mental construct that is out of touch with concrete experience:

Menger kept too close to the real world for either the verbal or symbolic formulation of the theory; and in the real world he saw no sharply defined points of equilibrium, but rather bounded indeterminacies not only in isolated bilateral barter but also in competitive market trading. . . . With his attention unswervingly fixed on reality, Menger could not, and did not, abstract from the difficulties traders face in any attempt to obtain all the information required for anything like a pinpoint equilibrium determination of market prices to emerge, nor did his approach permit him to abstract from the uncertainties that veil the future, even the near future in the conscious anticipation of which most present transactions take place. Neither did he exclude the existence of non-competing groups, or the omni-presence of monopolistic or monopoloid traders in the market.[59]

At the end of his career, Menger enlarged his approach to deal with social problems. In this respect too he was a pioneer. The very term "sociology" had recently been invented (by the French positivist Auguste Comte), and there were not yet any recognized professional sociologists around. Carl Menger became one of the first economists-turned-sociologist. Many other Austrian economists such as Schumpeter and Mises would follow in his footsteps. Mises later explained that this extension

---

[58]Jaffé, "Menger, Jevons and Walras De-Homogenized," p. 519.
[59]Ibid., p. 520.

of interest is merely a natural consequence of the new viewpoint that Menger had developed in his *Principles*, for the gist of the new approach was an analysis that focused on individual human action and explained all social phenomena as resulting from the interaction of individuals.[60]

The Breakthrough of the Austrian School

At the University of Vienna, Menger faced the determined opposition of Lorenz von Stein, the great champion of French socialism in Germany and Austria.[61] Stein rejected Menger's first petition for the *Habilitation* degree, accepting his application only after Menger had his *Principles* printed by the Vienna publisher Wilhelm Braumüller at his own expense and sent a proof of the first two chapters to Stein. Having accepted his application, Stein still failed Menger for the degree. After several favorable reviews of his book appeared in German professional journals, Menger applied again and this time he passed.

He immediately received offers to teach outside Vienna, but declined because of the heavy financial losses he would sustain if he abandoned his position at the *Wiener Zeitung*. Instead he stayed as a private lecturer at the University of Vienna. A year later the University of Basel made him a very attractive offer. To keep the gifted young professor, the University of Vienna offered Menger a position as *professor extraordinarius*[62] of political economy and allowed him to keep his position with the *Wiener Zeitung*. He accepted and stayed in Vienna for the rest of his career, teaching courses on banking, credit, general economics,

---

[60]Mises, *Money, Method, and Market Process: Essays by Ludwig von Mises*, Richard Ebeling, ed. (Auburn, Ala.: Ludwig von Mises Institute, 1990).

[61]See Karl Menger's biographical sketch of his father Carl's professional career, "X. Beginn der akademischen Laufbahn."

[62]Roughly speaking, this rank corresponded to a present-day associate professor in the United States.

and public finance.[63] In the fall of 1874, he abandoned his position with the *Wiener Zeitung* to have more time to devote to the research that would lead to the publication of *Investigations*.

In all his academic endeavors, Menger met with the continued resistance of the department, which was run by a group under Stein's leadership. Menger decided to form a new coalition and to wrestle down the old oligarchs. And in 1876 he succeeded, because a decisive change had occurred in his career.

The previous fall, he had been approached to become the private tutor of Rudolf von Habsburg, the twenty-two-year-old heir to the throne of Austria-Hungary.

This commission was to be the apex of Menger's pedagogic activities, but it also brought to light his political views, which he had always been careful not to reveal in any of his published writings. After a careful analysis of Prince Rudolf's notebooks, Erich Streissler concludes that these books "show Menger to have been a classical economic liberal of the purest water . . .

Crown Prince Rudolf

with a much smaller agenda for the state in mind than even Adam Smith."[64] Streissler goes on:

> Menger's Rudolf Lectures are, in fact, probably one of the most extreme statements of the principles of *laissez-faire* ever put to paper in the academic literature of economics. There is just cause for economic action only in "abnormal" circumstances. Only when "disaster is impending," only where "government support becomes

---

[63]There must have been some *Protektion* involved. Here it should be remembered that Menger's journalistic activities had early on brought him in touch with established political forces. These connections probably played in his favor when he applied for the chair at the University of Vienna.

[64]Erich Streissler, "Menger's treatment of economics in the Rudolf lectures," Erich W. Streissler, and Monika Streissler, eds., *Carl Menger's Lectures to Crown Prince Rudolf of Austria* (Aldershot, U.K.: Edward Elgar, 1994), pp. 4, 14.

indispensable" should the state step in. Otherwise "government interference" is "always . . . harmful."[65]

Menger was smart enough not to present these views on government as his personal opinion. Rather he worked from carefully selected readings to drive his message home. He even chose as his main textbook Adam Smith's *Wealth of Nations*. Still, Menger's political views seem to have been familiar enough within the Austrian establishment to cause conflict over the question of his nomination as Rudolf's tutor. In fact it came to a confrontation between the conservative councilors of Rudolf's father Franz Joseph, and the more liberal-minded councilors of his mother Elisabeth. The empress eventually had the last word.

Menger took an extended leave of absence from the University for his work with Rudolf, which started in January 1876 and lasted for two years. He became "one of the most trusted teachers of the Crown Prince, trusted by Rudolf himself and by his elders."[66] Menger had made his career. His new monarchical *Protektion* quickly lifted him to the rank of full professor at the University of Vienna, the most prestigious position for an economist in the entire empire. He was now in a position of virtually unrivalled influence on the academic social sciences in Austria-Hungary. Other honors followed almost as a matter of course: he became a lifetime member of the *Herrenhaus*, the upper chamber of the Austrian parliament, member of the academies of sciences

---

[65]Ibid., p. 17. On Menger's liberalism see also Israel Kirzner, "Menger, Classical Liberalism, and the Austrian School of Economics," Caldwell, ed., *Carl Menger and His Legacy in Economics*, pp. 93–106; Ki'ichiro Yagi, "Carl Menger as Editor: Significance of Journalistic Experience for his Economics and for his Later Life," *Revue européenne des sciences sociales* 30, no. 92 (1992); idem, "Carl Menger and Historical Aspects of Liberalism in Austria," essay presented at a symposium on Carl Menger and the Historical Aspects of Liberalism (Center for Historical Social Science Literature, Hitotsubashi University, December 18–19, 2004).

[66]Ibid.

in Vienna and Rome, of the *Institut de France*, and of the Royal Society in Edinburgh.[67]

He used this power to settle conflicts within his department at the University of Vienna. And he also seems to have used it to fill Austria's other chairs of political economy with his followers, including Böhm-Bawerk and Wieser.[68]

Menger saw himself as the founder and leader of a new school of social research, and he strove to raise disciples and to spread them over the land. In a confidential March 1902 letter to the Austrian Ministry of Culture in which he petitioned for early retirement, he claimed that his teaching activities "have

Carl Menger

generated results that surpass the common results of teaching. This concerns in particular the foundation of the Austrian School of economics." He also points out that many excellent young scholars received their university professor's diploma (the *Habilitation*) under his auspices and that these scholars had obtained the majority of the chairs of political economy at the Austrian universities. Besides his main followers, Böhm-Bawerk and Wieser, he referred to Emil Sax, Johann von Komorczynski, Robert Meyer, Gustav Gross, Eugen von Philippovich, Victor Mataja, Robert Zuckerkandl, Hermann von Schullern-Schrattenhofen, Richard Reisch, and Richard Schüller. The list

---

[67]Kurt Rothschild, "Carl Menger," Walter Pollack, ed., *Tausend Jahre Österreich* (Vienna: Verlag Jugend und Volk, 1974), vol. 3, pp. 67ff.

[68]Klaus H. Hennings, *The Austrian Theory of Value and Capital: Studies in the Life and Work of Eugen von Böhm-Bawerk* (Cheltenham, U.K.: Edward Elgar, 1997), pp. 10f., 24, n. 13. Mises's characterization of Menger's and Böhm-Bawerk's attitude gives a somewhat misleading picture of the times. In *Erinnerungen* (p. 22), Mises stresses that these men were not interested in promoting their cause through their personal power (see also Mises, *Historical Setting of the Austrian School of Economics*, p. 39). But that does not mean that they did not have considerable power, nor that they never made any use of it.

of those of his students who had not chosen an academic career is no less impressive. Among them were Moritz Dub, Viktor Grätz, Wilhelm Rosenberg, Rudolf Sieghart, and Ernst Seidler.[69] These men would play an important role in Ludwig von Mises's life and career.

Menger was successful not only in developing the continental tradition of economic science, but also in establishing a network of like-minded young thinkers within the confines of Austria-Hungary.[70] He only failed to get Böhm-Bawerk a chair at the University of Vienna. His favorite disciple applied twice, in 1887 and 1889, but each time the Ministry of Education chose a different candidate. They argued that Böhm-Bawerk represented the same abstract and purely theoretical school as the other chairholder (Menger) and that it was necessary to also have a representative of the new historical school from Germany.[71] Even this did not prove to be a decisive obstacle. In the fall of 1889, Böhm-Bawerk went to Vienna to join the Ministry of Finance and became an adjunct professor at the University of Vienna; in 1905 he obtained a full chair. Hence, in distinct contrast to all other modern (marginalist) schools of economic thought, the Austrian School quickly reached a position of power, protected by intellectual tradition and political patronage. Under the leadership of the next generation, it would obtain a position of unparalleled influence.

---

[69]Hayek, "Einleitung," pp. xxxiiif.

[70]It appears that the main reason why Menger retired at the comparatively young age of sixty-two was that he had caused a scandal through an affair with his housemaid. The affair became public because of the birth of Karl, whom Carl Menger acknowledged as his son. Karl cost Menger his career, and he thereby also changed the history of the Austrian School of economics, which under Carl's guidance certainly would have taken a different course than it did under his successor, Friedrich von Wieser. But Karl's birth also led to a rapprochement between the Austrian School and the mainstream through a more direct route: Karl Menger himself would eventually become a famous mathematical economist.

[71]Shigeki Tomo, *Eugen von Böhm-Bawerk* (Marburg: Metropolis, 1994), pp. 157–62.

Eugen von Böhm-Bawerk

At the time of Menger's petition for early retirement, Eugen von Böhm-Bawerk was his most prominent disciple, serving a fourth term as the head of the Austrian (k.k.) Ministry of Finance.

Böhm-Bawerk had risen to the highest positions in the Austrian state bureaucracy. He would not have done so under normal circumstances. He was a brilliant scholar and an excellent and efficient technocrat, but he was no politician. He abhorred demagogic trickery and despised socialism. He only became a government minister because ethnic conflicts within Austria (especially between Germans and Czechs) made political leadership of the whole country increasingly impossible. During such crises, Austria was ruled by technocratic caretaker governments, and in all of them Böhm-Bawerk served as finance minister. His impeccable scientific credentials commanded respect from all parties and made him the ideal candidate for these emergency situations.[72]

Born in Moravia on February 12, 1851 into a family of high state bureaucrats, Eugen Böhm Ritter von Bawerk was raised in Vienna where he received a thorough education at the *Schottengymnasium*. His father had been entrusted with various delicate negotiations in the revolutionary period leading up to 1848, a term he discharged to the great satisfaction of the emperor. He was knighted in 1854, but died an early death

---

[72]On Böhm-Bawerk see in particular F.X. Weiss, "Eugen von Böhm-Bawerk," F.X. Weiss, ed., *Gesammelte Schriften* (Vienna: Hölder-Pichler-Tempsky, 1926; reprint Frankfurt a.M.: Sauer & Auvermann, 1968), vol. 1, pp. iii–xv; Schumpeter, "Eugen von Böhm-Bawerk;" H. Schullern-Schrattenhofen, "Eugen Ritter von Böhm-Bawerk," Adolf Günther, ed., *Die Universität Innsbruck* (Innsbruck: Tyrolia, 1928), pp. 17–21; Hennings, *The Austrian Theory of Value and Capital*; Tomo, *Eugen von Böhm-Bawerk*; idem, "Eugen von Böhm-Bawerk's Innsbruck Lectures on Economics," Eugen von Böhm-Bawerk, *Innsbrucker Vorlesungen über Nationalökonomie* (Marburg: Metropolis, 1998).

shortly after. His wife then moved to Vienna to assure an adequate upbringing of Eugen, the youngest of her three sons.

In the *Schottengymnasium*, Böhm-Bawerk met his alter ego in Friedrich von Wieser. The two of them would study law and government science at the University of Vienna, discover a common interest in economics, and become followers of Carl Menger. Both of them entered the financial administration of Lower Austria in 1872, passed their doctoral exams—with Menger as one of the examiners—in 1875, and then chose a scholarly career, benefiting from a prestigious government scholarship program that enabled them to study for two years with the greatest German political economists of the time. In 1875 they spent a year in Heidelberg to study in the seminar of Carl Knies, and then spent another year together in the seminars of Wilhelm Roscher in Leipzig and of Bruno Hildebrand in Jena. Later they would both become professors of political economy and accede to international fame as representatives of the new Austrian School of economics. Both would also become cabinet members in emergency situations: Böhm-Bawerk for the Ministry of Finance in 1889–1890, 1895, 1896–1897, and 1900–1904; Wieser in 1917–1918 as trade minister of the last imperial government. Böhm-Bawerk became Wieser's brother-in-law when he married Friedrich's sister Paula.

During their year together in Heidelberg, they presented papers that foreshadowed their later achievements. Both used Menger's *Principles* as their starting point and took his project in new directions—Wieser's paper pioneering the analysis of opportunity costs, and Böhm-Bawerk presenting the first version of his theory of interest.[73]

---

[73]A copy of Böhm-Bawerk's paper with the title "Referat über Kapitalzins im Knies'schen Seminar" is available in the Grove City Archive: Pamphlet Box # 4. Wieser's paper was published after his death in Wieser, *Gesammelte Abhandlungen*, Hayek, ed. (Tübingen: Mohr, 1929).

Thanks to Menger's unwavering support, Böhm-Bawerk obtained his *Habilitation* degree before he was thirty. Menger was aware of an opening for a professor of political economy at the University of Innsbruck—one of the few chairs of its kind in all of Austria-Hungary—and seized the opportunity to place his most gifted follower.

The 1880s were the most productive phase of Böhm-Bawerk's life: he published two massive volumes on the history and positive theory of capital, a work that earned him an international reputation and made him the best-known Austrian economist. He was in fact the first economist of the Austrian School to enjoy immediate English translations of his work.

From 1889 to 1904, however, his government activities as finance minister and in other high functions of the

Eugen von Böhm-Bawerk, Austrian Finance Minister

civil service absorbed virtually all of his energies, and his scholarly output shrank considerably.[74] An exception was his activity

---

[74]Böhm-Bawerk's major accomplishment as a minister of finance was the reform of the Austrian system of direct taxation. He started working on this project in 1889 and his proposals made it, in essentially unaltered form, into a law voted in 1896. Among other things, Böhm-Bawerk's law introduced a personal income tax (top marginal rate: 5 percent), as well as the principle of progressive tax rates into the Austrian code. See Schumpeter, "Eugen von Böhm-Bawerk," pp. 75, 77; Alois Gratz, "Die österreichische Finanzpolitik von 1848 bis 1948," Hans Mayer, ed., *Hundert Jahre österreichischer Wirtschaftsentwicklung, 1848–1948* (Vienna: Springer, 1949), p. 278. The most complete presentation of his activities in the Ministry of Finance is in Tomo, *Eugen von Böhm-Bawerk*, pp. 53–65, 141–78. On Böhm-Bawerk's economic theories, see also Hennings, *The Austrian Theory of Value and Capital.*

as an honorary professor at the University of Vienna and his involvement in the *Zeitschrift für Volkswirtschaft, Socialpolitik und Verwaltung*, which he co-founded and managed starting in the early 1890s and which would become a major outlet for theoretical research in Germany and Austria. After Böhm-Bawerk completed his last term as a Finance Minister, he had more time for scholarly pursuits and was granted a new chair of political economy at the University of Vienna.[75] Wieser had by then succeeded Menger, and thus the University of Vienna enjoyed for a decade an all-star team of Austrian economists.

From 1905 until his death in 1914, Böhm-Bawerk led the life of an elder statesman. His scholarly endeavors were constantly interrupted by his obligations as a lifetime member of the *Herrenhaus* (the upper chamber of the Austrian parliament, which he joined in 1899) and after 1911 as president of the Austrian Academy of the Sciences, which was "the highest scientific honor that Austria had to offer."[76] His main academic activity was a course on advanced economic theory, which he gave in

---

[75]Schumpeter reports that as a minister Böhm-Bawerk followed the maxim, "A finance minister must always be ready to give his demission and always act as if he never intended to quit his job." Böhm-Bawerk quit when another increase in the army budget was no longer covered by corresponding savings or increased taxation. See Schumpeter, "Eugen von Böhm-Bawerk," pp. 79f. Böhm-Bawerk was not opposed to additional government expenditure as a matter of principle. It was in fact the great strategy of the Koerber cabinet (1900–1904) to renew and increase the attachment of the various nations of Austria-Hungary to the central government in Vienna through an ambitious spending program. The strategy succeeded. Conflicts related to national culture suddenly shifted into the background as the economic and financial establishment of the various nations sensed that business with the central government was more important than continuing the policy of obstruction. See Rudolf Sieghart, *Die letzten Jahrzehnte einer Grossmacht* (Berlin: Ullstein, 1932), pp. 56ff.

[76]Schullern-Schrattenhofen, "Eugen Ritter von Böhm-Bawerk," p. 21. The author observes that this election was all the more remarkable because economics had not been considered a prestigious science.

Left, *Eugen von Böhm-Bawerk as Austrian finance minister,* right,
the last Austrian 100 schilling note

the winter semesters, and the direction of a weekly graduate seminar in the summer semesters.[77] This seminar took most of his energy, leaving him completely exhausted at the end of the sessions.

But this was not just any seminar. The group that flocked around Böhm-Bawerk might well have been among the most brilliant crowd of young intellectuals ever gathered in a regular university function. Their names could be taken from any twentieth-century *Who's Who* of social scientists: Ludwig von Mises, Joseph Schumpeter, Richard von Strigl, Franz Weiss, Felix Somary, Emil Lederer, Rudolf Hilferding, Nicolai Bukharin, Otto Neurath, and Otto Bauer. The members of the seminar would come to be known as either great economists or great Marxists. For better or worse, they would leave their mark on the decades to come. The young disciples of the Austrian School considered Böhm-Bawerk to be their undisputed master and under his auspices set out to develop and revolutionize economic science. The young Austro-Marxists, as they were later called, had joined the seminar to confront the man in person who had authored the most devastating attack against Marx's *Das Kapital.* But they came to admire their teacher for

---

[77]Schumpeter, "Eugen von Böhm-Bawerk," p. 80. Both Schumpeter and Mises (*Erinnerungen*, p. 23) state that Böhm-Bawerk declined an offer to become executive director of a major Vienna bank.

his comprehensive knowledge, for his fairness and relentless quest for objectivity, and especially for his willingness and ability to debate them—which he did with great success. Mises attended the seminar until 1913. Böhm-Bawerk left a deep impression on him as a scholar and teacher, setting life-long standards of scholarship. He only admonished that Böhm-Bawerk was too soft on Otto Neurath. Mises considered Neurath a fanatic and found him insufferable because he criticized economics without knowing what he was talking about.[78]

On occasion, the seminar focused intensely on the scientific contributions of individual members. For example, Böhm-Bawerk spent two entire semesters discussing Mises's 1912 book on the theory of money. Many of the seminar members already had a scholarly reputation when they entered the seminar—or soon earned one. The main themes of the sessions, however, developed from Böhm-Bawerk's own work: price theory, the *raison d'être* of economic theory *vis-à-vis* the claims of materialistic Marxism and of the German Historical School, the Austrian versus the Marxist theories of value, and the meaning and importance of economic laws.

Böhm-Bawerk had made important contributions in all these fields. In his *Habilitation* manuscript, he had developed a Mengerian economic theory of rights and of legal and commercial relationships. The manuscript was published as a book the following year (1881) in a substantially abridged form.[79] During the decade or so that he spent in Innsbruck, he concentrated on the development of Austrian price theory. Carl Menger had explained the price of consumers' goods, but had not gone in

---

[78]Mises, *Erinnerungen*, p. 24.

[79]The reference is Böhm-Bawerk, *Rechte und Verhältnisse vom güterwirthschaftlichen Standpunkte* (literally: Rights and legal relationships considered from the point of view of the theory of economic goods]. The original manuscript of his *Habilitation* thesis had 728 pages and the title "Kritische Beiträge zur volkswirtschaftlichen Lehre von der Güternutzung." See Tomo, *Eugen von Böhm-Bawerk*, p. 71.

depth into the pricing of producers' goods. He claimed the latter would not differ fundamentally from the former, except that the price of a producers' good was derivative: it was "imputed from" the value of the consumers' good it produced. Menger's critics had seized on this as a weakness in his system and argued that imputation was impossible because any consumers' good results from the joint cooperation of several producers' goods. How would imputation distribute the value of the final product among the many factors of production? Moreover, was it not obvious that costs of production did have a major impact on the prices of products?

Böhm-Bawerk tackled these problems in a book-length article on the theory of value (1886).[80] He developed in particular what he called the "Law of Costs." Böhm-Bawerk explained that, in the case of consumer goods that could be reproduced *ad libitum* in any quantity, costs of production were in fact the *immediate* cause of the price of the final product. But he showed that even in this special case the costs of production were themselves *ultimately* determined by the value of the *other* consumer goods for the production of which they could also be used. His demonstration was so successful that it brought many economists in Austria and Germany into the Austrian School. Three years later, Böhm-Bawerk incorporated the essence of this article into his *magnum opus*: a two-volume treatise on economic theory and the history of economic thought, with special emphasis on the theory of capital and interest. The first volume had been published in 1884 and gave a systematic exposition and critique of past theories of interest. The second volume of his treatise, entitled *Positive Theorie des Kapitals*, presented his own views on the subject and made him the best-known

---

[80]Böhm-Bawerk, "Grundzüge der Theorie des wirtschaftlichen Güterwerths," *Conrad's Jahrbücher für Nationalökonomie und Statistik* n.s. 13 (1886); reprinted as *Grundzüge der Theorie des wirtschaftlichen Güterwerths* (London: London School of Economics and Political Science, 1932).

Austrian economist outside the German-speaking countries. Here he gave a presentation of the theory of value, prices, and interest that Schumpeter later praised in these terms:

> The *Positive Theory of Capital* gives . . . a theory of the entire socio-economic process, even though the title indicates a more narrow content. . . . It is certain that here the highest goal is aimed at that can be desired within theoretical economics and that this goal is achieved to an extent that few can equal.
>
> Hence, wages, rents, capital, length of the period of production, and the [physical] productivity of the methods of production are variables that mutually determine one another, and thus the entire economic process suddenly appears in an unheard-of simplicity, clarity, and completeness.[81]

In particular, Böhm-Bawerk presented his time preference theory of interest that revolutionized economic thinking in this field. Where his predecessors usually considered interest to be the remuneration of a specific factor of production, Böhm-Bawerk defended the thesis that interest has nothing to do with production per se, but springs from an entirely different source: the unequal valuation of present goods and future goods of the same kind.[82] Production and capital are only indirectly related to interest—related only insofar as capital goods are essentially "future goods" that through the time-consuming production process mature into consumers' goods.

These seemingly subtle distinctions had a momentous political significance at the time Böhm-Bawerk was writing, a time that was characterized by the rise of various socialist movements, most notably the movement led by Karl Marx and

---

[81]Schumpeter, "Eugen von Böhm-Bawerk," pp. 70, 72.

[82]This thesis was no more than hinted at in Menger, *Principles*, pp. 153f.; and William Stanley Jevons, *Theory of Political Economy* (London: Macmillan, 1888), p. 72.

Friedrich Engels. The socialists contested mainstream economic theory, the theory of Jean-Baptiste Say, according to which interest was the specific income of capital. They asserted that labor alone creates value and income and therefore labor alone creates interest. The fact that interest payments went to the capitalists could only mean that capitalists exploited laborers. The working classes did not receive the full value they had produced. But according to Böhm-Bawerk's theory, interest was not produced by anybody; it was a value-spread, existing independent of production per se, that manifested itself only incidentally in the relationship between factors of production and products. As a consequence (and here we come to the far-reaching political implications) interest is not peculiar to capitalism—it would exist under any conceivable system of social organization. No redistribution scheme or any other social policy could abolish interest—not even a fully communist society.

Böhm-Bawerk addressed highly politicized questions on two other famous occasions. After the posthumous publication of the third volume of Marx's *Das Kapital*, which had been edited by Engels, Böhm-Bawerk wrote a 120-page review titled "Zum Abschluss des Marxschen Systems"[83] that was published in an 1895 *festschrift* for Karl Knies. Here Böhm-Bawerk presented a devastating critique of Marx's economics, arguing that while Marx's thought was internally consistent, it was based on assumptions without foundation in observed facts and led to conclusions that were at odds with the real world.

Nineteen years later, shortly before his death, Böhm-Bawerk once again addressed the theoretical foundation of social policies when he published a sixty-five-page essay dealing with the question of whether labor union pressure can improve living conditions for all members of the working classes. More fundamentally, "Macht oder ökonomisches Gesetz?" (Power or

---

[83]Translated and published in 1898 as *Karl Marx and the Close of His System* (London: T.F. Unwin, 1989).

Economic Law?) concerned the question of whether there is such a thing as economic law independent of human will. If such laws exist, then they cannot be "broken" or circumvented by labor union leadership or determined policy makers. In a painstaking case-by-case analysis, Böhm-Bawerk showed that the illusions of labor union leaders and politicians were just that—illusions.[84]

A distinctive feature of Böhm-Bawerk's legacy is his readiness to focus pioneering theoretical research on highly contested questions. This was, in a way, the legacy of the entire "second generation" of Austrian economists. Whereas Carl Menger had concentrated virtually all of his energies on questions of pure theory and could afford the luxury of ignoring Marx and his disciples, Menger's colleagues and followers—men like Sax, Zuckerkandl, Wieser, and Böhm-Bawerk—sought to apply the new theory to the new social movements surrounding them. In this endeavor, Böhm-Bawerk stood out in originality and intellectual vigor, and this was his greatest impact on Mises. Böhm-Bawerk was the very model of a political economist: a man who combined comprehensive historical and theoretical knowledge to take a clear stance on important policy issues. And in at least this one respect, Mises would prove to be a worthy disciple of the master.

Friedrich von Wieser

Mises never studied under Wieser, though it is likely that Wieser, having come to occupy Carl Menger's chair at the

---

[84]This essay was a critical response to Rudolf Stolzmann. Possibly Böhm-Bawerk also wished to preempt a fallacious opinion accepted by some of his most gifted students. A case in point was Ludwig von Mises, who shortly before had argued that labor unions could raise wage rates for all workers, at least in the short run. See Mises, "Die allgemeine Teuerung im Lichte der theoretischen nationalökonomie," *Archiv für Sozialwissenschaften und Sozialpolitik* 37 (1912): 570f.

University of Vienna in 1903, was one of Mises's examiners in government science. Wieser was born in 1851 in Vienna, the son of a high civil servant. He was a tall and handsome man, aristocratic in manners, with clear blue eyes and, in later years, with an impressive long beard. His thorough acquaintance with art and literature was legendary, and he was himself an accomplished piano player. A gentleman of the old world, his personal presence made him the undisputed leader of the Austrian School after Böhm-Bawerk's death in 1914.[85]

His admirers forgave him certain character traits that are unusual in a great scholar and teacher. He never debated or discussed views other than his own and was an extremely slow reader and slow thinker. He rarely quoted anyone, preferring instead to acknowledge his intellectual debt to Menger and Jevons only broadly in the prefaces of his early works. While the combined presence of these traits would exclude any lesser man from the ranks of great intellectuals, in Wieser's case they further aroused the admiration of his followers.

Schumpeter praised Wieser's deficiencies in the following words:

> With sovereign quietness, which we others soon learned to understand as his right, he puts aside the professional literature. He is not even able to read quickly or much. And almost never has he thoroughly dealt with the details of the systems of thought of other people. He has never engaged in polemics, never on a professional level and certainly not on a personal one.[86]

---

[85]For an enthusiastic characterization by his main follower, see Hans Mayer, "Friedrich Freiherr von Wieser," *Neue Österreichische Biographie* (Vienna, 1929), vol. 6, pp. 180–98. A more critical short presentation is in Klaus H. Hennings, "Friedrich Wieser," Walter Pollack, ed., *Tausend Jahre Österreich*, vol. 3, pp. 71ff.

[86]Schumpeter in *Neues Wiener Tagblatt* (July 10, 1921); quoted from F.A. Hayek, "Friedrich Freiherr von Wieser," *Jahrbücher für Nationalökonomie und Statistik* 125 (1926): 523.

Hayek added:

> In his work he never dealt with the present state of
> the science. He has never tried to reconcile existing
> theorems with one another or to deduce new theo-
> rems from them through mere logical operations.
> Rarely has a theoretician been more different from
> the usual image of a theoretician than Wieser. . . .
> [His theoretical contemplations] entirely monopo-
> lized him and did not leave him any time to delve
> into, or systematically analyze, the systems of thought
> of others. He felt the necessity to do this hampered
> his own work on the conceptualization of reality, and
> thus he avoided even oral discussions if they risked
> ending up in something other than the more perfect
> exposition of his own ideas.[87]

Clearly, Wieser differed markedly from Böhm-Bawerk both
in his persona and his scholarship. While his brother-in-law was
widely read in economics, and displayed exhaustive and detailed
knowledge of the literature concerning the theory of capital and
interest, Wieser was exclusively concerned with refining his
own purely contemplative activities. In contrast to Böhm-Bawerk, whose style was often tedious, Wieser knew how to turn a
phrase; for example, he invented the term "marginal utility"
which is still used in mainstream economics. And where Böhm-
Bawerk would always delve into the technical details of an issue,
Wieser cherished the more general features of the theory of
value and prices, and preferred to keep his arguments on that
level of abstraction. For Wieser's admirers, there were definitive
advantages to this approach:

> As a coherent body of thought, Böhm-Bawerk's sys-
> tem might seem to be the greater one in the eyes of
> those who appreciate a system's logical coherence

---

[87]Hayek, "Friedrich Freiherr von Wieser," *Jahrbücher für Nationalökonomie und Statistik*, pp. 523f.

above everything else. Wieser's work, however, presents far more starting points for further development,
often precisely in those passages that have often been
criticized as inconsistent.[88]

While Böhm-Bawerk enjoyed the immediate support of
Menger, Wieser ranked lower on Menger's list of gifted followers
and had to wait longer to be placed in one of the empire's few
full professorships. Menger had known Wieser's unpublished
manuscripts on the theory of value for some years, but had great
reservations about them and did not recommend them for publication. Eventually, however, a chair at the University of Prague
became vacant, and he urged Wieser to submit his work to the
University of Vienna to obtain his *Habilitation*, which he
received in 1883, after Menger had written a highly favorable
review of his work. Menger recommended him for the position
in Prague, where Wieser became a *professor extraordinarius* in
1884. He became a full professor in 1889 and in 1903 he succeeded Menger at the University of Vienna.[89]

Unlike Böhm-Bawerk and the bulk of contemporary German-language theorists, Wieser was inspired by the Gossen
School of marginalist price theory, particularly Jevons's *Theory of
Political Economy*.[90] He was the first German academic economist
to place his stamp of approval on Gossen's work. In fact, in his
Der natürliche Werth (Natural Value, 1889), Wieser presents the
very core of the new marginalist price theory—what he calls the
"elementary theory of value"—as based on Gossen's law of

---

[88]Ibid., p. 524.

[89]Hans Mayer, "Friedrich Freiherr von Wieser," vol. 6, pp. 184, 187.
Hayek, "Friedrich Freiherr von Wieser," p. 518.

[90]He acknowledges his intellectual debt to Jevons in the preface of his
Habilitation thesis, where he mentions the Englishman as one of his two main
sources of inspiration (the other one was Menger); see Friedrich von Wieser,
Über den Ursprung und die Hauptgesetze der wirthschaflichen Werthes (Vienna:
Hölder-Pichler-Tempsky, 1884), p. viii.

want-satiation.[91] These explicit references bear special weight because Wieser's habit was never to cite anyone. Through his eloquent prose, Wieser rescued Gossen's indigestible book from the oblivion into which it had fallen.[92]

---

[91]Friedrich von Wieser, *Der natürliche Werth* (Vienna: Hölder-Pichler-Tempsky, 1889), § 3, p. 7; idem, *Theorie der gesellschaftlichen Wirtschaft*, 2nd ed. (Tübingen: Mohr, 1924), p. 24. Hayek noticed that Wieser had "supplemented" the elementary theory of prices "in regard to its psychological foundations" through Gossen's law of want-satiation (see Hayek, "Friedrich Freiherr von Wieser," p. 520). As we have pointed out above, there was in Menger's value theory no such emphasis on diminishing satisfactions of the same type.

[92]Hayek, "Einleitung," p. xiv. In his introduction to Menger's collected works, Hayek points out that Gossen's work had been favorably mentioned in an 1870 book by F.A. Lange (see Hayek, "Einleitung," p. x, n. 2), but this had no impact. Wieser was not the only Viennese theorist who developed marginal-utility analysis along Jevonsian lines. There were in particular two non-academic economists, Rudolf Auspitz and Richard Lieben, who a few years after Wieser published two books that focused entirely on the graphical (and to a lesser extent, algebraic) exposition of price theory. See Rudolf Auspitz and Richard Lieben, *Zur Theorie des Preises* (Leipzig: Duncker & Humblot, 1887); idem, *Untersuchungen über die Theorie des Preises* (Leipzig: Duncker & Humblot, 1889). Despite the non-academic background of the authors, these works were very well researched and based on a thorough knowledge of the existing literature in the field, in particular the works of Bernoulli, Laplace, Thünen, Dupuit, Gossen, Mangoldt, Menger, Jevons, Walras, Wieser, Böhm-Bawerk, and Launhardt. Just as their contemporary fellow-Jevonsian in Vienna, Auspitz and Lieben emphasized the fictional nature of their style of economic analysis. Thus, noticing that an economic theorist cannot use experiments to isolate causes and their effects, they assert that the economist "is forced to take refuge with his ideas into an abstract world that can be grasped more easily; but then he must try to approximate the real world through gradual changes of his assumptions" (*Untersuchungen über die Theorie des Preises*, p. vii; see also Wieser, *Der natürliche Werth*, part 2). In other words, unrealistic assumptions were absolutely essential for economic analysis. Realism of economic science was at best a matter of approximating the real world, but not a matter of describing it. Auspitz and Lieben were however quite perceptive in regard to the internal logic of mathematical equilibrium economics. They pointed out, for example, that equilibrium obtains only if each individual seeks to maximize his personal satisfaction and if each individual knows

Yet this distinct orientation went largely unnoticed or (to the extent that it was noticed) was considered unimportant. In the homogenizing wake of the *Methodenstreit*, mainstream economists in Germany and Austria thought in much broader categories; to them Wieser was an extreme case of Mengerian "theorist" where he was in fact as far removed from Mengerian theory as he was from German historicism. For example, Wieser's theory featured a strong focus on quantitative relationships where Menger focused on the qualitative relationships between quantities. Wieser's work also had a strong psychological orientation inspired by both the then-fashionable works of the Vienna philosopher Franz Brentano and John Stuart Mill's equally popular attempt to interpret epistemology and logic as psychological disciplines. Wieser also distinguished himself from Menger by his reliance on fictional postulates such as the assumption that value is psychological and measurable.

Friedrich von Wieser

These views were obvious from his first book, *Über den Ursprung und die Hauptgesetze des wirthschaftlichen Werthes*, which was his *Habilitation* manuscript, published at the beginning of the *Methodenstreit* in 1884.[93] Although he used few mathematical expressions, he made frequent reference to "units of value" and to calculations in terms of these units, which

---

how to choose the combination of factors of production most suitable to this end (see for example *Untersuchungen über die Theorie des Preises*, p. 537). Jevonsian German-language writers outside of Vienna were Knut Wicksell, *Über Wert, Kapital und Rente* (Jena: Gustav Fischer, 1893); and Georg Sulzer, *Die wirtschaftlichen Grundgesetze in der Gegenwartsphase ihrer Entwicklung* (Zurich: Müller, 1895).

[93] The literal translation of the title is "On the cause and the principal laws of economic value." No English translation of the work exists.

could be aggregated and otherwise modified through arithmetic operations.[94] In an entry on "marginal utility" that he wrote for the standard German-language economic dictionary of the time, Wieser purported to "develop the rules according to which one scales and computes [*rechnen*] economic utility" or, in other words, to "develop the economic calculation of utility."[95] In Wieser's view, value was a cardinal measure of utility. If an economic good X is not reproducible, then the value of X measures the marginal utility of X itself. But if X is a reproducible good, then the value of X measures the foregone utility of another good, Y, that cannot be enjoyed if the factors of production are used to make X rather than Y. In other words, the value of a reproducible good is a measure of the opportunity costs of producing it.

These fictions about value and the speculations that he based on them in *Ursprung und Hauptgesetze* gained Wieser a reputation as a "pure theorist" in precisely the sense that German mainstream economists disdained: someone who constructs theories without foundation in human experience. The historicist hotspurs must have loved Wieser, for he was living proof that they were not guilty of battling straw men. It had been very difficult to make a case against Menger, who rigorously tied theory to experience, but there could be no doubt that the work of this follower lacked empirical foundation and thus scientific integrity. Young Werner Sombart, to whom Schmoller had

---

[94]In a 1911 essay, he defended the fictions contained in these—as he would call them—idealizing assumptions. See Friedrich von Wieser, "Das Wesen und der Hauptinhalt der theoretischen Nationalökonomie—kritische Glossen," *Jahrbuch für Gesetzgebung, Verwaltung und Volkswirtschaft im deutschen Reich* 35, no. 2 (1911); reprinted in Wieser, *Gesammelte Abhandlungen*, Hayek, ed., pp. 10–34. We will present Wieser's argument below when dealing with Schumpeter.

[95]Friedrich von Wieser, "Grenznutzen," *Handwörterbuch der Staatswissenschaften* (2nd and 3rd editions, Jena: Gustav Fischer, 1900 and later); reprinted in Wieser, *Gesammelte Abhandlungen*, Hayek, ed., pp. 88, 93.

entrusted the job of reviewing Wieser's *Natural Value,* concluded that this work was "entirely unsound."[96]

Ironically, the heated atmosphere of the *Methodenstreit* considerably enhanced the significance of Wieser's work. His elegant prose and his highly developed sense for coining catchphrases like "marginal utility"[97] and "imputation" gained him a widespread reputation as one of the leading representatives of "the Austrian School"—which meant, in the mind of contemporary German mainstream economists, an advocate of theoretical studies dissociated from historical research. Because of this publicity, Wieser was largely successful in promoting among German economists the notion that "the" new economic theory (advocated by Menger and his disciples) was a form of applied psychology.[98]

---

[96]The is review in *Schmollers' Jahrbuch* 13 (1889): 1488–90.

[97]Wieser coined the term *Grenznutzen* in order to convey the meaning of Jevons's "final utility." Through Philip Wicksteed, one of Jevons's students, the new term then made it into English; see Philip H. Wicksteed, *The Alphabet of Economic Science* (reprint, New York: Augustus M. Kelley, [1888] 1970).

[98]For example, Wieser alleged that Menger held that the law of decreasing marginal value was a Gossen-style "law of satiation" (Wieser, "Karl Menger," p. 89). Böhm-Bawerk also shares some of the responsibility for this confusion. His first exposition of the theory of value and prices in 1886 was strongly influenced by Wieser's *Ursprung und Hauptgesetze* (1884), and thus indirectly by Gossen and Jevons. He at least implicitly endorsed the view that value was a psychological phenomenon, pertaining to the sphere of human feelings, and he also believed in the measurability of value and in inter-individual comparisons of value. While these assumptions played a relatively insignificant role in his work (compared to Wieser), the fact that he held them at all promoted the gradual departure from Menger's realist economics toward the emerging neo-classical paradigm. It was symptomatic that Walras complained to Menger (who had shown reluctance to recognize a predecessor in Gossen) that, after all, Böhm-Bawerk shared exactly the same view. Walras believed it was "impossible to deny that he [Gossen] has been the first to conceive clearly and mathematically that what I call *utilité* and *rareté*, and which is nothing but the *subjectiver Wert* or the *Grenzwert* of Mr. von Böhm-Bawerk." Quote from Walras's February 2, 1887 letter to Menger, as translated and

Wieser's views also proved to be fateful in another important respect. As mentioned earlier, he was one of Menger's several followers who addressed the claims of Marxists and other socialist scholars. But while Böhm-Bawerk tried to refine Menger's theory of prices, thus clarifying and confirming Menger's insights about the operation of a capitalist economy, Wieser argued that Menger's theory had no specific political implications whatsoever. It was not a grand apology for the bourgeois class, as critics claimed, but neither could it serve as the basis for objections to socialism.

Wieser's view was rooted in his theory of the relationship between value and prices. Recall that Wieser believed that economic value is subject to arithmetic operations, just as money prices are used in the calculations of businessmen. Thus, there is in this respect no fundamental difference between value and price. Prices are merely "objective exchange value"—they are "subjective exchange value" made visible. Businessmen could theoretically do without money prices and perform their calculations directly in terms of value and so could a socialist planning board. This is still a widely held view among economic laymen. Wieser's achievement was to give a sophisticated presentation of this view and to develop it through the doctrine of his second book, with the telling title *Der natürliche Werth* (*Natural Value*).[99]

According to this doctrine, there can be situations in which entrepreneurs produce certain goods in unnecessary quantities

---

published in Antonelli, "Léon Walras et Carl Menger à travers leur correspondence," pp. 269–87. The passage is quoted from pp. 285f., translation is mine.

[99]A student of Carl Menger's in the late nineteenth century, Robert Zuckerkandl, argued along the same popular lines. In his eyes too, price was but an "expression" of value, and he rejected Böhm-Bawerk's statement that price and value shared virtually no features that would permit them to be lumped together in the same analytical framework. See Robert Zuckerkandl, *Zur Theorie des Preises*, 2nd ed. (Leipzig: Stein & Co, [1889] 1936); reprint (Amsterdam: Liberac, 1968), pp. 24f. and passim.

merely because they command the highest market prices. In these cases, when market prices do not indicate the rationally established or "natural" value, there is a "conflict between objective exchange value [market price] and social utility."[100]

The question then is how social utility is to be understood. Here Wieser refers to the concept of natural value. He asserts that the natural value of economic goods is the value that these goods have only in light of their available quantities and their utility.[101] As soon as any other factors come into play, market prices can deviate from their natural values. Thus the "conflict" between market prices and social utility can be made intelligible by comparing the real world to a fictional state of affairs of ownerless quantities and of homogeneous psychological utilities dissociated from the specific biological and economic characteristics of the individual human being. According to Wieser, this fictional state of affairs obtained in a "communist state"—which he understood to be "a totally unified and utterly rational commonwealth." It follows that real-world market prices give only an imperfect representation of natural value. Not only are they subject to the impact of abuses—individual egotism, error, and other frictions—but they are also subject to the distribution of resources. Thus only in a pure Wieserian "communist state" does the actual value of goods coincide with their natural value.

Wieser offered no proof for these assertions, apparently taking their plausibility for granted; neither did he encounter any objections on these grounds. It hardly needs to be stressed that his views were quite removed from Menger's views both on the conception of value and prices and on the nature of economic science. Menger believed the task of economic theory was to describe certain exact laws of the human economy. It did not deal with all aspects of human action, but it did treat the economy as

---

[100]Wieser, *Der natürliche Werth*, p. 54.

[101]Ibid, p. 60.

it actually exists and is therefore subject to empirical analysis. From Wieser's point of view, economic science addressed only the laws of natural value, which cannot possibly exist in the real world.

Mises did not find Wieser's views appealing.[102] Mises's historicist training had predisposed him to the notion that the essence of science was the discovery of relevant facts, not speculations without empirical foundation.

Because of Wieser's central position in the teaching of economic theory and the general confusion in post-*Methodenstreit* Germany about the various competing approaches to economic theory, he was able to redefine Austrian economics—in a departure from the original Mengerian project—as part of an emerging neoclassical synthesis built on the works of Gossen, Walras, and Jevons.

It is in this light that one has to see Wieser's personal impact on the education of the rising generations of Austrian economists. He held Menger's former position from 1903 to 1920 and continued to teach as an *emeritus* until his death in 1926. During this entire period, it was Wieser who taught the introductory courses in economic science at the University of Vienna. Until 1914, Böhm-Bawerk's presence provided some counterbalance, but after his death, Wieser's position was that of an unquestioned authority in all matters of general economic theory, a position reinforced by the publication that same year of his general treatise, *Theorie der gesellschaftlichen Wirtschaft.*[103]

---

[102]*Erinnerungen*, p. 21. Mises says that despite all his great personal qualities, Wieser was not original in his research and was more harmful than useful for the development of the Austrian School. When Mises explains the meaning of his own contributions, he makes it clear that his work was based on Menger and Böhm-Bawerk, not on Wieser.

[103]Friedrich von Wieser, *Theorie der gesellschaftlichen Wirtschaft*, 1st ed. (Tübingen: Mohr, 1914). An English edition with the title *Social Economics* appeared in 1927 (New York: Adelphi) with a preface by W.C. Mitchell. In

The entire fourth generation of Austrian economists—brilliant young men like Hayek, Machlup, Haberler, Morgenstern, and Rosenstein-Rodan—were thus shaped by the Wieserian mold before they set off on their own intellectual paths. Largely ignorant of Menger's *Principles* (out of print since the 1880s), they were trained in the spirit of the neoclassical synthesis.

As a result of these circumstances, there was strictly speaking no fourth generation of "Austrian" economists in the Mengerian sense. All the young men who are commonly held to be fourth-generation members were in fact lost to the neoclassical school—with the possible exception of Hayek, who decades later rediscovered some Mengerian themes in his work on the *Counterrevolution of Science* (1954).[104]

Third-generation Ludwig von Mises's personal and intellectual influence on these men was limited. He had virtually no impact on their basic training—admitting them to his private seminar only after they had obtained their doctoral degrees. And they probably did not see in him anything more than a reputed expert on monetary theory and a highly controversial political economist. Mises was known for his treatises on the theory of money and on socialism, but none of his students and few of his colleagues grasped the far-reaching implications of these works. He became a recognized authority on general economic theory only many years later, when he spelled out these implications in his general treatise on economic science, *Nationalökonomie* (1940); and it was only in its English-language translation and expansion, *Human Action* (1949), that he eventually

---

foreign countries too, Wieser was therefore perceived as the main interwar authority on Austrian economics. This goes a long way toward explaining the rise of Keynesianism in the mid-1930s.

[104]Yet, significantly, while Hayek's book dealt with virtually all the fundamental errors in the social sciences—in particular, with the errors inherent in scientism (positivism), historicism, and holism—he did not talk about "psychologism" in economic theory.

had a lasting impact on the theoretical outlook of subsequent generations of students.[105]

Joseph A. Schumpeter

With his notable 1902 study on the pre-1848 relationship between Galician lords and peasants, Mises had started off as a star student in the camp of mainstream historicist economics. When he turned to economic theory *à la* Carl Menger, he lost the support of this very influential network. After the death of Böhm-Bawerk, academia had little use for the Mengerian tradition that Mises maintained and developed. He would remain outside both the waning tradition of historicism and the emerging influence of neoclassical economists. His work was respected and he enjoyed an excellent reputation, but he was and would remain for the rest of his life an intellectual outsider—his work did not fit into the general development of the science.

The rising star among the young Vienna economists was another member of Böhm-Bawerk's seminar. Two years younger than Mises, Joseph Alois Schumpeter immediately rose to international fame when, barely twenty-five years old, he published a 600-page treatise on economic methodology with the title *Wesen und Hauptinhalt der theoretischen Nationalökonomie* (The Nature and Essence of Theoretical Economics).[106] In October 1908, he

---

[105]Jeffrey M. Herbener, Hans-Hermann Hoppe, Joseph T. Salerno, "Introduction to the Scholar's Edition," Ludwig von Mises, *Human Action: A Treatise on Economics*, Scholar's edition (Auburn, Ala.: Ludwig von Mises Institute, 1998), pp. vff.; Joseph T. Salerno, "The Place of *Human Action* in the Development of Modern Economic Thought," *Quarterly Journal of Austrian Economics* 2, no. 1 (1999): 35ff.

[106]Joseph A. Schumpeter, *Wesen und Hauptinhalt der theoretischen Nationalökonomie* (Munich: Duncker & Humblot, 1908). On Schumpeter see Eduard März, *Joseph Alois Schumpeter—Forscher, Lehrer und Politiker* (Vienna: Verlag für Geschichte und Politik, 1983); Wolfgang Stolper, *Joseph Alois*

submitted this work to the University of Vienna to obtain a *Habilitation* degree, which he received under Böhm-Bawerk and Wieser's enthusiastic endorsement in March 1909. Six months later, the twenty-six-year old Schumpeter became Austria's youngest professor of political economy, in the provincial capital of Czernowitz. Two years later, after publishing his second, even more influential book *Theorie der wirtschaftlichen Entwicklung* (Theory of Economic Development)—he received a full professorship at the prestigious University of Graz. From there Schumpeter began a long and productive academic career that would lead him via Bonn to Harvard.[107] He held several prestigious positions in more practical fields, but each time his involvement was short-lived and ended in debacle. As Austrian Minister of Finance of the second Renner government he was unable to stop the hyperinflation in 1919, and as president of the Biedermann Bank he went bankrupt in 1924.

Joseph A. Schumpeter

Schumpeter's careers in politics and banking were the products of his personal connections. Due to the influence of his stepfather, General Sigismund von Kéler, he was admitted to the prestigious Theresianum gymnasium—the Eton of pre-1914 Austria. There he befriended Rudolf Hilferding, who later became one of the most brilliant Austro-Marxists and a Minister of Finance of the German Reich. Family money also allowed Schumpeter to stay for a year at the newly founded London

---

Schumpeter: The Public Life of a Private Man (Princeton, N.J.: Princeton University Press, 1994); Richard Swedberg, *Joseph A. Schumpeter—eine Biographie* (Stuttgart: Klett-Cotta, 1994). Also see Stephan Böhm, "Schumpeter and Mises," Klaus Hennings and Warren J. Samuels, eds., *Neoclassical Economic Theory, 1870 to 1930* (Boston: Kluwer, 1990).

[107]He was also a visiting professor at Columbia University in 1913–1914, and at Harvard University in 1927–1928 and 1930.

School of Economics (1906–1907) and to meet Cannan, Marshall, and other British economists. In late 1913 he was a visiting professor at Columbia University and built up a network of contacts in the United States. In the chaotic first months after World War I, Hilferding called Schumpeter, who by then had an excellent international reputation as an economic expert, to join the Commission for the Socialization of German Industry. Schumpeter used the opportunity to prove his political reliability, signing a recommendation to nationalize the German coal mining industry. Shortly thereafter, he became Austrian Finance Minister. Even though he remained in power for only a short time and could realize none of his projects, he at least profited from this engagement on a personal level. He had used his ministerial powers to grant a charter to the Biedermann Bank, which eventually appointed him its president on very comfortable terms. Schumpeter never got involved in managing the bank's daily affairs, but when it went bankrupt in 1924, he felt a deep responsibility toward the stockholders and worked the next eleven years to pay back his debts. He started publishing many paid articles and, when this income proved to be insufficient, accepted a position at Harvard University on very good financial terms.[108]

The most important factor in Schumpeter's career, however, was his intellectual excellence. He had a brilliant mind and was a highly gifted writer.[109] He was sensitive to fine distinctions and the subtle problems of economic analysis, which he presented in appealing prose. Although Mises was skeptical of Schumpeter's work on the fundamental issues of economic theory (as were

---

[108]März, *Joseph Alois Schumpeter—Forscher, Lehrer und Politiker*, pp. 169ff.; Swedberg, *Joseph A. Schumpeter—eine Biographie*, pp. 100f.

[109]His ambitions as a young man were virtually boundless. He sought to become the greatest economist in the world, the greatest horse rider in Austria, and the greatest lover in Vienna. See Swedberg, *Joseph A. Schumpeter—eine Biographie*, p. 71.

Böhm-Bawerk and many other Austrian economists) he did not hesitate to acknowledge Schumpeter's more penetrating insights and to advance them through his own writings.[110] Most notably, Mises was among the many admirers of Schumpeter's colorful portrayal of the role of innovative entrepreneurs in driving social and economic evolution.

Although Mises and Schumpeter were in fundamental disagreement on questions of epistemology and the nature of economic science, they were in essential accord on one subtle but important question: the relationship between economics and psychology. In the mid-nineteenth century, the influential British economist-philosopher John Stuart Mill had popularized an empiricist epistemology according to which all sciences were based on some form of experience. In the case of mathematics and economics, this empirical basis was psychological experience. Mill's epistemology was at first very successful in Austria, where it shaped for example the epistemological views of Friedrich von Wieser. But soon a reaction set in that successfully expelled the Millian approach from central Europe. Around the turn of the century two philosophers, Gottlob Frege and Edmund Husserl, published devastating attacks of psychologism in logic as advocated by J.S. Mill.[111] Their writings had a considerable impact on the rising generation of Viennese

---

[110]Examples of minor importance are Mises's endorsement of the doctrine that later came to be called "demonstrated preference." See Murray N. Rothbard, "Toward a Reconstruction of Welfare and Utility Economics," Mary Sennholz, ed., *On Freedom and Free Enterprise: Essays in Honor of Ludwig von Mises* (New Haven, Conn.: Van Nostrand, 1956. Similarly, Mises agreed with Schumpeter (and the sociologist Georg Simmel) that choice or—as Simmel and Schumpeter put it—"exchange" was the fundamental phenomenon of economic science.

[111]Gottlob Frege, *Function und Begriff* (Concept and Object) (Jena: Pohle, 1892); *Die Grundlagen der Arithmetik* (The Foundations of Arithmetic) (Jena, Pohle, 1884); *Die Grundgesetze der Arithmetik* (Fundamental Laws of Arithmetic) (Jena: Pohle, 1893); Edmund Husserl, *Logical Investigations* (Halle a.S.: Max Niemeyer, 1900).

intellectuals in all fields, and Schumpeter spearheaded the movement to drive psychology out of economic theory. He argued that it was futile to inquire after the psychological or biological causes of human valuations; economic analysis could be based entirely on a formal characteristic of valuation, namely, that the utility of any given unit of a homogeneous good decreased as its quantity increased. This purely formal "law of want satiation" had nothing to do with psychology. It was not even a part of economic science proper, but only a convenient hypothesis that explained market prices better than any other. Economists had to take this formal characteristic of valuation as an "ultimate given" of their deductions, and then compare the results of their deductions to the observed real world.[112] Mises later argued along very similar lines that the laws of economics had nothing to do with the acting person's psychological disposition, but he disagreed with Schumpeter about the nature of economic laws. For Schumpeter, the only basis for scientific propositions was observation of the exterior world. And the only suitable method of economic enquiry was to follow the approach that had proven successful in the natural sciences. In short, he was a positivist who believed that the only method that could yield "facts" was observation of the exterior world. Mises on the other hand followed the program of Menger's very different "empirical theory" and gathered relevant facts wherever he could find them. Unfortunately, however, Mises had written nothing on epistemology until the late 1920s, and Schumpeter's views had a strong impact on the rising generation.

Around 1900, Schumpeter's epistemological views were much more fashionable than those of Menger and Wieser, and they reinforced the general intellectual and esthetic appeal of his work. His positivism allowed Schumpeter to adopt a lofty attitude of "standing above" the issues of the fierce *Methodenstreit*.

---

[112]Schumpeter, *Wesen und Hauptinhalt der theoretischen Nationalökonomie*, pp. 64ff.

Schumpeter took a completely agnostic stance on the issue of price theory, arguing that from a scientific point of view, it was irrelevant whether prices "really" arose from subjective value or from the costs of production. The subjective-value theory was as he saw it only a hypothesis, and it was to be preferred over cost-of-production theories not because the latter were "false" and the former "true" but because the subjective-value hypothesis served to explain a larger realm of price phenomena than did the cost-of-production hypothesis.

Schumpeter was the first real positivist among economic theoreticians, probably inspired by the works of the Vienna physicist-philosopher Ernst Mach, who was an extremely influential thinker at the time and in the decades to come. Mach paved the way for the Vienna Circle of the Logical Positivists in the 1930s. In *The Nature and Essence of Theoretical Economics*, Schumpeter fundamentally argued that modern economic science *à la* Wieser and Walras was a science in the precise sense of Mach's philosophy.[113] He advocated the same views that Milton Friedman presented more than forty years later in his famous essay on economic methodology.[114] But while Friedman's presentation was sketchy and detached from the presentation of the actual doctrine, Schumpeter's *Nature and Essence* made a 600-page case for positivism in economics.

Wieser honored Schumpeter's book with the only review he ever wrote, praising Schumpeter for his achievement in presenting the main contents of economic science.[115] Wieser's only

---

[113]He had anticipated this thesis in a 1906 article on what he called the mathematical method of theoretical economics; see Joseph A. Schumpeter, "Über die mathematische Methode der theoretischen Ökonomie," *Zeitschrift für Volkswirtschaft, Sozialpolitik und Verwaltung* 15 (1906): 30–49.

[114]Milton Friedman, *Essays in Positive Economics* (Chicago: University of Chicago Press, 1953), chap. 1.

[115]Friedrich von Wieser, "Das Wesen und der Hauptinhalt der theoretischen Nationalökonomie—kritische Glossen," *Jahrbuch für Gesetzgebung,*

admonition was a point that he himself usually considered to be of comparatively minor importance: methodology. He severely criticized Schumpeter's positivist methodology and his rejection of psychological introspection as the foundation of economic knowledge. Wieser claimed that as a consequence of his methodological stance, Schumpeter failed to adequately present the *Wesen* (the nature) of economic science. Contradicting Schumpeter's claim that he had adopted his method because it best fitted the subject matter of economic research, Wieser stated:

> The truth is that—without knowing it—he brings in his ready-made methodology from outside. . . . Blinded by the success of the exact natural science he adopts its way of thinking even where it does not at all fit our subject matter, and thus construes an artificial method with which he would never have been able to arrive at the results that he wants to take over from his predecessors.[116]

Wieser then brilliantly addresses Schumpeter's claim that the fundamental economic theorems have the character of hypotheses. He states that the hypotheses of the natural sciences are assumptions about unknowns, whereas the assumptions of economic science always have known real-world correlates, even though they may not always reflect them faithfully. He distinguishes two types of assumptions made by economists: isolating assumptions and idealizing assumptions. The former are needed to engage in *Gedankenexperimenten* or thought experiments;[117] they serve to describe the state of affairs that is the subject of theoretical analysis:

Verwaltung und Volkswirtschaft im deutschen Reich 35, no. 2 (1911); reprinted in Wieser, *Gesammelte Abhandlungen*, pp. 10–34.

[116]Ibid., p. 12.

[117]Wieser did not use this expression in his essay, but it had already been introduced by the physicist-philosopher Ernst Mach. See E. Mach's 1897

> Just like the natural scientist in an experiment, we must make isolations in our mental observations. Complex experiences cannot be interpreted as a whole. We must decompose them into their elements to understand their meaning. Only then are we in a position to deduce the total effect through a composition of the separate particularities.[118]

These isolations must however be strictly realistic because their usefulness depends entirely on their truthfulness. In contrast, the idealizing assumptions do not truthfully reflect a real correlate but deliberately transform it into an "ideal" form—such as *homo oeconomicus*.[119] Thus even in this contestable (and, as Wieser admits, highly contested) form, the fundamental assumptions of economics always have a known real-world correlate in human consciousness. Refusing to make use of them, as Schumpeter suggests, would result in incomplete and ultimately unconvincing economic arguments.[120]

Despite these objections to Schumpeter's misdirected methodology, Wieser praised *Nature and Essence*:

> While [Schumpeter] quickly passes over all those subjects that he thinks others have sufficiently presented,

---

paper "Über Gedankenexperimente," reprinted in his *Erkenntnis und Irrtum*, 5th ed. (Vienna, 1926; reprint Darmstadt: Wissenschaftliche Buchgesellschaft, 1991), pp. 183–200.

[118]Wieser, "Das Wesen und der Hauptinhalt der theoretischen Nationalökonomie—kritische Glossen," p. 22.

[119]Ibid., p. 23.

[120]Wieser warned that Schumpeter-style presentations could hamper the understanding of the meaning of economic relations:

> Schumpeter himself still knows the meaning because he has been introduced to it by his predecessors. But the pupils that he introduces will not know it any longer, because he deprives them of the presentation of those most subtle connections, which only reveal themselves to the inner observation. (ibid. pp. 31f.)

he lingers on the more difficult problems. Having
begun his studies of economics only a few years ago,
he may say with just pride that his book is not written
for beginners, but presupposes quite an exact knowledge of the state of our science.[121]

Schumpeter's appearance, and his promotion through both
Wieser and Böhm-Bawerk, was an important development in
the emergence and consolidation of an international network of
economic theorists following in Gossen's footsteps. Schumpeter
built on the foundations laid by Wieser, making the German-
speaking economic scene safe for what today is known as neoclassical economics. Whereas Wieser had further developed the
theory of Jevons, Schumpeter brought Walras to Vienna. Having thought through the implications of the doctrine of natural
value, he discovered important and far-reaching affinities
between Wieser's system and the general-equilibrium framework developed by Léon Walras in Lausanne. Both Jevons and
Walras had developed a theory of price determination under
fictional "ideal" conditions, disregarding various essential features of the human economy that Menger and to a lesser degree
Böhm-Bawerk had carefully sought to integrate in the new
price theory. For instance, both Walras and Wieser considered
human error to be a mere "friction" preventing the real world
from following the course it should take; and they both implicitly denied that all quantities of economic goods were essentially
related (as private property) to human beings, and that the utility or value of a good was essentially related to the specific situation of the person evaluating the good. Both Walras and
Wieser conceived of price determination as the mechanistic
interplay of freely floating quantities and of equally freely floating (and measurable) utilities. This explanation of economic
phenomena is general-equilibrium theory—implicit in Wieser
and explicit in Walras.

---

[121]Ibid., p. 33.

In *Nature and Essence*, Schumpeter gave a refined and largely verbal restatement of general-equilibrium theory. He remedied certain shortcomings of Walras and Wieser, for example, by accounting for the fact that all quantities of goods are owned quantities, and he came very close to presenting economic science as the science of human choices when he argued that the nature of economic action is exchange. Ludwig von Mises, Richard von Strigl, and Lionel Robbins would develop this insight and argue that the fundamental economic phenomenon was the act of preferring one thing over another thing, and that virtually all economic laws in one way or another relate to this phenomenon.[122]

Schumpeter spent most of his book discussing methodological and epistemological questions, in the course of which he gave the first succinct descriptions of methodological individualism and the method of variations (comparative statics)—terms that he coined. He dealt with economic laws only incidentally, using them as illustrations for his methodological and epistemological claims. His most fateful contribution was to recast the entire general-equilibrium theory in terms of a distinction he borrowed from classical mechanics between statics and dynamics. According to Schumpeter, the "static" economy and the "dynamic" economy are entirely different states of affairs; they present different problems and require different methods of analysis.[123] Schumpeter was not the first economist to stress the usefulness of analyzing static and dynamic economic conditions

---

[122]Schumpeter, *Wesen und Hauptinhalt der theoretischen Nationalökonomie*, pp. 50, 80, 200; Mises, *Theorie des Geldes und der Umlaufsmittel* (Leipzig and Munich: Duncker & Humblot, 1912); idem, *Die Gemeinwirtschaft* (Jena: Gustav Fischer, 1922); idem, *Grundprobleme der Nationalökonomie* (Jena: Gustav Fischer, 1933); Richard von Strigl, *Die ökonomischen Kategorien und die Organisation der Wirtschaft* (Jena: Gustav Fischer, 1923); Lionel Robbins, *The Nature and Significance of Economic Science* (London: Macmillan, 1932).

[123]Schumpeter, *Wesen und Hauptinhalt der theoretischen Nationalökonomie*, pp. 182f.

separately. The American economist John Bates Clark had pioneered this approach a few years earlier in his book *The Distribution of Wealth*, which proved to be very influential among Vienna economists. But Schumpeter produced a mechanistic interpretation of the static-dynamic scheme, holding that in a truly static economy all events of a given day are only repetitions of whatever happened the previous day. He claimed moreover that past economists had dealt exclusively with static conditions, which are the proper subject matter of general equilibrium theory. Dynamic conditions remained virtually unexplored, and economists had yet to even recognize the related problems.

Schumpeter attempted to fill the gap with his *Theory of Economic Development*, which he published in 1911, a year before Mises published his first major work. The book was the dynamic complement so to speak to *Nature and Essence*, which had focused exclusively on static conditions. The second book contained three major theses.

First, Schumpeter argued that economic development was exclusively the result of pioneering "entrepreneurs"—a special breed as different from the rest of mankind as greyhounds are from poodles. Innovative entrepreneurs are the true driving force of social evolution. They impose unheard-of products and methods of production on a reluctant society of mere adjusters. It was this thesis in particular that roused the admiration of Schumpeter's friends and colleagues. Twenty years later, Mises listed the book as one of the top four German-language contributions to economics.[124] It has continued to fascinate some of the best Austrian economists to the present day.[125]

----

[124]Mises to Miss Haider (Brookings Institution), letter dated July 3, 1931; Mises Archive 66a: 87f. He emphasized that he took no account of his own writings.

[125]See for example Kirzner's discussions of Schumpeter in Israel Kirzner, *Competition and Entrepreneurship* (Chicago: University of Chicago Press, 1973), pp. 79–81 and 125–31.

Second, Schumpeter portrayed entrepreneurs as essentially resourceless market participants. They needed new fiduciary bank credit ("credit out of thin air") to finance their projects because all other investment capital was already tied up in other projects. For Schumpeter, capital was essentially "purchasing power" rather than a quantity of real goods that could sustain workers in the production process. Bankers could therefore create "capital" out of nothing by simply printing additional banknotes.

Third, and most importantly, he asserted that under static conditions the phenomenon of interest would not exist. Interest paid on capital invested could only come into being under dynamic conditions, that is, as a result of change. Its primary form was entrepreneurial profit. By contrast, the interest paid on bonds or on bank credits was just a share of profits that entrepreneurs were forced to pay to bankers to secure their cooperation. Schumpeter contested in particular Böhm-Bawerk's theory, according to which time preference creates interest even under static conditions. Arguing along the lines of John Bates Clark, Schumpeter insisted that the passage of time is irrelevant to production under static conditions because consumption and investment are always "synchronized."

Schumpeter's first thesis—that entrepreneurship drives progress—has proven to be the least controversial, but with the other two contentions he opened a Pandora's box of old errors that six preceding generations of brilliant economists, among them his own teachers, had spent their lifetimes fighting.

Böhm-Bawerk immediately recognized the dangerous impact that these skillfully presented views were to have in the future. He wrote a long review of *Theory of Economic Development* in an attempt to offset the damage being done by one of his most gifted students. Böhm-Bawerk made it clear that Schumpeter's "dynamic" theory of interest was completely wrong. Moreover, Schumpeter's economic analysis suffered from a sloppiness that belied the author's great intellectual gifts. One of the review's opening paragraphs came close to charging Schumpeter with a lack of professional integrity:

> Schumpeter has taken pleasure in contemplating an
> ingenious idea, but unfortunately he has not had
> the self-discipline [Selbstüberwindung] to subject
> himself and his idea to a sober and encompassing
> cross-examination, an examination that very soon
> would have shown problems on all sides.[126]

After dissecting some of the most important shortcomings of
the *Theory of Economic Development* in detail, Böhm-Bawerk
went on to identify the spirit of Schumpeter's work:

> I do not intend to give a running critique of all of
> Schumpeter's ideas. I am content with briefly express-
> ing my conviction that Schumpeter commits a fateful
> mistake, which despite all the qualifications that he
> makes is a true mercantilistic mistake of superficial rea-
> soning: When it comes to determining the possible
> scope of productive credit, he accords the essential
> role to money and means of payment, rather than to
> the economy's supplies of real goods. Schumpeter is
> much closer than he thinks—and, maybe, than he
> wishes—to the Laws and McLeods and regrettably he
> is quite removed from Hume, despite all the praise
> that he has for the latter.[127]

Böhm-Bawerk went to great lengths in refuting the doctrines of his former disciple. He knew that ideas have consequences, and that fallacious ideas can ruin a country or an entire
civilization if they are presented with the grace and vigor of
Schumpeter's works. Unfortunately, Böhm-Bawerk died a year
later and the mantle passed to Wieser and Schumpeter. Both
would make sure that the next generation of Viennese economists would be part of the emerging neoclassical synthesis. ◄

---

[126]Eugen von Böhm-Bawerk, "Eine 'dynamische' Theorie des Kapitalzinses," *Zeitschrift für Volkswirtschaft, Sozialpolitik und Verwaltung* 22 (1913);
reprinted *Gesammelte Schriften*, Weiss, ed.; reprint (Frankfurt a.M.: Sauer &
Auvermann, 1968), vol. 2, pp. 520–85; quote is from p. 521.

[127]Böhm-Bawerk, "Eine 'dynamische' Theorie des Kapitalzinses," p. 552.

5
Early Professions

FROM CHILDHOOD, MISES HAD been driven by a progressive outlook and a strong personal urge to contribute to the improvement of the world. Scion of an elevated Jewish family successfully established in post-1867 Vienna, product of a liberal education, he believed that artists and men of science formed the avant-garde of social progress.[1] Enlightenment through scientific discoveries was paramount for the further development of humanity. Mises maintained an unconditional affirmation of truth and intellectual integrity as supreme values, even though this uncompromising stance hurt his career and other material interests. As a consequence, he faced the problems of his time in a series of isolated one-man struggles. Erik von Kuehnelt-Leddihn writes:

> He never fully belonged to a specific camp. He was always a square peg in a round hole. . . . To make matters worse, Mises was consciously a nobleman, a true gentleman, who rejected all compromise and never

---

[1]Carl E. Schorkse, *Fin-de-siècle Vienna* (New York: Knopf, 1980), is famous for his claims that this interest in science and art was a substitute for the political career that the existing monarchical regimes made impossible. Schorke's claim relies on the implicit hypothesis that politics is inherently more satisfying than science or art—an hypothesis that tells us more about Schorske's own value-judgments than about those prevalent among young Germans and Austrians at the time.

concealed his thoughts or his convictions. If some-
body or something was plainly stupid, he said so, nor
could he tolerate cowardice or ignorance . . . this aristocratic Jewish intellectual was an "odd man out," and
fit into no established pattern.[2]

These qualities made a career difficult in Vienna. The inhabitants of the Austrian capital were famous for their sophisticated
taste, humor, and fondness of the pleasures their city could
offer, but they were not known for candor or courage, and they
openly despised those who displayed the qualities they lacked—
especially upstarts from the provinces. A keen connoisseur of
the Austrian mind recalls the mentality in the city on the
Danube:

> People who had their own views and—horribile
> dictu—even championed these views were not well
> received. One had to be "popular" to be welcome,
> and appreciation was given, not to effort, but only to
> success, not to a man himself, but only to his posi-
> tion.[3]

Clearly, Vienna did not provide a favorable climate for
Mises's talents, but he made good use of them anyway, thanks to
immense willpower and his unconditional devotion to truth,
which earned the admiration even of those who resented his
brazenness.

It was this fundamental attitude—to stick to his convictions
at all costs—that had made him receptive to the message of
Menger and Böhm-Bawerk. These thinkers had developed economic theory on fact rather than fancy, and as Mises's own work
in the historicist tradition had shown him, the methodology of

---

[2]Erik von Kuehnelt-Leddihn, *The Cultural Background of Ludwig von Mises*
(Auburn, Ala.: Ludwig von Mises Institute, 1999), pp. 6f.

[3]Rudolf Sieghart, *Die letzten Jahrzehnte einer Grossmacht* (Berlin: Ullstein,
1932), p. 263.

the German mainstream economists was sterile. Ludwig Pohle, the famous critic of the historicists, quoted a satirical magazine that described economic research as the activity of "measuring worker's apartments and stating that they were too small."[4]

When Mises completed his graduate studies in February 1906, he had likely made plans to continue scientific research in some form. At that point he was thoroughly conversant with the Austrian School and with some of the more serious problems left unsolved in the existing literature. He had realized, in particular, that no follower of Carl Menger's had offered a satisfactory integration of the theory of money into the general framework of Menger's theory. This had exposed the Austrian theory to some vigorous criticism, most notably from the German economist Karl Helfferich, who claimed that the theory of money could not be reconciled with Menger's theory of value.[5] Mises dedicated the next five years of his life to filling the gap with a systematic treatise on money that he planned to submit to the University of Vienna as his *Habilitation* thesis.

The *Habilitation* degree was granted on the basis of a comprehensive, scholarly work that not only covered a large field of knowledge and demonstrated the author's ability to shed light on the phenomena under consideration, but also made significant contributions to present knowledge. The idea was that the authorities of the science recognize the candidate as one of their peers. This recognition was far from perfunctory: the *Habilitation* laureates were entitled to apply for full-professorships within the university system, on a par with more senior candidates.

But first the book had to be written and the necessary research to be done. In those days, such an enterprise required unusual private financial means or unusual energy. There were

---

[4]Ludwig Pohle, *Die gegenwärtige Krisis in der deutschen Volkswirtschaftslehre* (Leipzig: Deichert, 1911), p. 52.

[5]See Karl Helfferich, *Das Geld* (Leipzig: Hirschfeld, 1903).

no university positions for these young scholars to earn a living while they pursued a long-term research project. They were private scholars with only loose university affiliations; they could hope for academic employment only after the successful completion of a *Habilitation* thesis. Meanwhile they had to survive a prolonged period of professional and material insecurity. If they could not rely on their family, or did not wish to do so, they had to earn their living in some other occupation while pursuing scholarship at night. This was science the hard way, and it was Mises's way from March 1906 until December 1911, when he finally sent his completed manuscript to the publisher.

He took the hard times lightly. He was a young man full of energy and enthusiasm for his science. Would he have despaired if he had known that this was how his life would be for almost 30 years? He later admitted that it was hopeless for him to obtain one of the few positions at a German or Austrian university. At one point he observed, sarcastically: "I was ill-suited to teach the Royal-Prussian Police-Science."[6] But even in his youth, he had to realize that he would have to make his way without public support. Austria had produced many geniuses only to confine them to lives of independent scholarship. Pioneers like Mendel and Gumplowicz never held university positions. The Austrian government "dismissed from teaching Bolzano and Brentano; it isolated Mach, and did not at all care for Husserl, Breuer and Freud. It appreciated Böhm-Bawerk as a capable official; not as an economist."[7]

However, these failed careers did not deter Mises—or thousands of like-minded young men—from following their examples. Posterity would honor them, they were sure, just as the present society honored the heroes of the past. Books, monuments, and street names were dedicated to scientists and artists

------

[6]Mises, *Erinnerungen* (Stuttgart: Gustav Fischer Verlag, 1978), p. 69f.; *Notes and Recollections* (Spring Mills, Penn.: Libertarian Press, 1978), p. 105.

[7]Mises, *Erinnerungen*, pp. 23; *Notes and Recollections*, p. 39.

who were ignored in their day. The result of their sacrifices was an explosion of creative energies in virtually all fields of human endeavor that made Vienna's glory in the decades before the national socialists rose to power.

The intellectual explosion in Vienna was already visible when young Mises prepared for the life of a private scholar, ready to earn his living in some liberal profession. Scholarly pursuits would be his real life—the one that would give significance to all other activities. His "professional life" would be secondary, a day job to pay the bills. And thus he began, on March 15, 1906, a paid internship with the fiscal administration of Lower Austria in its Vienna district headquarters.[8]

Difficult Start in Professional Life

This was the traditional choice of the sons of civil-servant families. It had been the first station in Böhm-Bawerk's career and thus it was a promising start for Mises, too.[9] A career within the civil service was a highly coveted outlet for law graduates, opening prestigious opportunities within the executive branch of government.[10] The office was then under the direction of Alexander Freiherr von Spitzmüller, who later moved to a top executive position at the Credit-Anstalt and eventually became

---

[8]The most important source of data on Mises's early professional development is a letter of application and *curriculum vitae* that he wrote to the Chamber of Commerce in 1909. This letter is today kept in the files containing the Machlup-Mises correspondence, at the Hoover Institution. See also the undated and non-addressed manuscript of a letter (written in the fall of 1937); Grove City Archive: Kammer für Handel, Gewerbe und Industrie files.

[9]See Joseph A. Schumpeter, "Eugen von Böhm-Bawerk," *Neue Österreichische Biographie* (Vienna, 1925), vol. 2, p. 65; Shigeki Tomo, *Eugen von Böhm-Bawerk* (Marburg: Metropolis, 1994), p. 53.

[10]"The civil service was considered to be the *nobilium officium par excellence*, while top executive positions with private firms were valued far less highly." Sieghart, *Die letzten Jahrzehnte einer Grossmacht*, p. 158.

the last president of the Austro-Hungarian bank, the empire's central bank.[11] Patient and loyal service combined with a dose of clever networking would have put Mises in a position to follow in this great man's footsteps and, given his interest in the theory of money and banking, gain a high position within the central bank.

But Mises soon discovered that this was a mistake. The paralyzing formal procedures, the mental pettiness, and the personal dependence on one's superiors came to him as a shock. He might have been thinking back on this experience when he later wrote on the nature and significance of bureaucracy:

> Government jobs offer no opportunity for the display of personal talents and gifts. Regimentation spells the doom for initiative. The young man has no illusions about his future. He knows what is in store for him. He will get a job with one of the innumerable bureaus, he will be a cog in a huge machine the working of which is more or less mechanical. The routine of a bureaucratic technique will cripple his mind and tie his hands. He will enjoy security. But this security will be rather of the kind that the convict enjoys within the prison walls. He will never be free to make decisions and to shape his own fate. He will forever be a man taken care of by other people. He will never be a real man relying on his own strength. He shudders at the sight of the huge office buildings in which he will bury himself.[12]

---

[11]His 1909 *curriculum vitae* describes his position as that of a *Konzept-spraktikant* at the k.k. Finanzbezirksdirektion in Vienna. Mises's congratulatory letter on Spitzmüller's seventieth birthday in 1932 speaks of a Finanz-Landes-Direktion (head financial office of the regional government). See the June 12, 1932 letter in Mises Archive 71: 151. It is ironic that Mises would become the most outspoken and influential critic of the policies of the Austro-Hungarian Bank under Spitzmüller's governorship.

[12]Mises, *Bureaucracy* (New Haven, Conn.: Yale University Press, 1944), p. 94.

Mises was not going to shudder and bury himself. By the fall of the same year he asked to be honorably released and his request was granted.

This decision must have caused great consternation among his family and friends. How could he give up one of the most coveted positions for young men of his background? "How can someone enjoying the privilege of serving His Majesty quit this service voluntarily?"[13] Mises's choice was indeed remarkable and a vivid testimony to the personality of the young man. Ludwig was not the nice guy who went along with prevailing notions of a good career. He had his own mind and found the civil service utterly dreadful. He was full of ambition and independent judgment. He had far more confidence in his own abilities than in the *Protektion* and prestige accorded to His Majesty's faithful servants.

After his resignation he decided to prepare for a career as a private lawyer. Admission to the bar required that the candidate familiarize himself with the Austrian court system through a two-year internship at the main courts. From October 1906 to September 1908, Mises interned at the court for civil affairs, the trade court, the penal court, the executive court, and the district court of the city of Vienna. The atmosphere in these institutions was not much different from what he had experienced in fiscal administration. But at least there was the prospect of leaving the system one day to become his own man.

In those years, Ludwig must have been the black sheep of the family. Was he unfit for the real world? Did he not know how to compromise? His brother Richard was the white sheep. He had graduated in the same year as Ludwig, then moved as an assistant professor to the University of Brünn (today Brno), and in 1909, at the age of 26, he would land a professorship at the

---

[13]Quoted from Heinrich Treichl, *Fast ein Jahrhundert* (Vienna: Zsolnay, 2003). The question was addressed to Treichl's father Alfred, a friend of Mises's, who had made exactly the same decision a few years earlier.

Richard von Mises

University of Strasbourg. This was a career path Ludwig would have welcomed, but the real world imposed different choices on him.

In the fall of 1908, with the end of his two-year internship approaching, Mises looked for suitable employment in Vienna. He was hired by the prestigious law firm of Robert Pelzer and started working in its office in the Krugerstrasse, right in the center of Vienna, in October 1908.[14] The new position was a vast improvement on the suffocating mental narrowness of courtroom routine. Still, the firm was not a real escape from the bureaucratic atmosphere of the courts. Mises kept looking for other options.

The Parallel Life

During these years, Mises's scholarly enterprises compensated for the dismal courtroom routine. The first result of his research on monetary theory and policy was a published paper on the motives underlying Austrian foreign-exchange controls. The article appeared in Böhm-Bawerk's *Zeitschrift für Volkswirtschaft, Socialpolitik und Verwaltung* and dealt with the ways in which interest groups promoted price and production controls.[15] He followed up in 1908 with a survey of recent literature on money and banking.[16]

It was a welcome addition to his intellectual life when, in October 1907, he was offered a position teaching economics to the senior class of the Trade Academy for Girls. While the

---

[14]Second floor, Krugerstr. 13.

[15]Mises, "Die wirtschaftspolitischen Motive der österreichischen Valutaregulierung," *Zeitschrift für Volkswirtschaft, Socialpolitik und Verwaltung* 16 (1907): 561–82.

[16]Mises, "Neuere Schriften über Geld- und Bankwesen," *Zeitschrift für Volkswirtschaft, Socialpolitik und Verwaltung* 17 (1908): 660–74.

traditionally male Gymnasien offered a broad classical education to prepare a young elite for university studies and the
assumption of high responsibilities within the civil service, girls'
schools had a stronger orientation to concrete professional concerns. Only recently had girls been admitted to the *Matura*
exams and the ensuing university studies. These exams were
organized exclusively by the Gymnasien, however, so the girls
prepared for them in special senior classes (*Abiturientenklassen*)
at their own schools, and on the day of the exam went to the
nearest Gymnasium to take the tests.

Mises taught economics and public finance, and Austrian
government. New to teaching, he must have applied the classic
pedagogy he had inherited from Menger and Böhm-Bawerk.
He would begin with a brief preview of the tenets to be
explained, then turn to an elaboration of his subject, and eventually conclude by repeating some of the more important
tenets.[17] As early as 1907, he would have taught educated young
ladies under the vibrant inspiration of Böhm-Bawerk's example,
whose seminar he continued to attend. Böhm-Bawerk inspired
Mises throughout his life of teaching. All of Mises's students
would praise him for his earnest and engaged style, for the
respect he displayed toward his students, and for the unfailing
encouragement he provided at the slightest signs of interest and
productivity on their part. The first students to profit from
these extraordinary qualities were girls from Vienna's better
families, students of whose names no record has been recovered.

In 1908, Mises became a member of the *Zentralstelle für Wohnungsreform* (Center for Housing Reform), an association of

---

[17]Erich Streissler states that Menger applied exactly this technique in his
lectures to Crown Prince Rudolf; see Streissler, "Menger's treatment of economics in the Rudolf lectures," Erich W. Streissler and Monika Streissler,
eds., *Carl Menger's Lectures to Crown Prince Rudolf of Austria* (Aldershot, U.K.:
Edward Elgar, 1994), p. 11.

politicians and intellectuals striving for an improvement in Vienna's housing conditions.[18] He greatly enjoyed his activity within the Center where he met excellent economists such as the brothers Karl and Ewald Pribram, Emil Perels, Rudolf Maresch, Paul Schwarz, Emil von Fürth, and Robert Meyer. When Meyer became Minister of Finance, Mises was asked to write a policy paper on housing taxes, which was high on the agenda of the Austrian parliament. In his memorandum, Mises argued that the taxes levied on existing buildings were less of a problem than the heavy taxation of joint stock companies, which deterred big capital from investment in real estate. To his great satisfaction, the Center for Housing Reform fully endorsed his report.

At about the same time, Mises was involved in setting up a group for the discussion of problems of economic theory and the fundamental questions of other social sciences.[19] The other leaders of this group—the brothers Karl and Ewal Pribram, Emil Perels, and Else Cronbach—were also members of Böhm-Bawerk's seminar. The weekly sessions with their great teacher were far too brief to allow thorough debate of the problems that came up, so they decided to create an additional forum. The first formal meeting took place on March 12, 1908 and from then on the group met at regular intervals and soon attracted more members. Philippovich, who headed the Center for Housing Reform, allowed the group to use the Center's beautiful premises for its meetings. After World War I, this group would become the *Nationalökonomische Gesellschaft*, the most important German-language forum for the discussion of economic theory. It is likely that the group was already hosting foreign scholars, such as the young Dr. William Rappard who stayed in Vienna for the 1908–1909 academic year and who

---

[18]See Mises, *Erinnerungen*, pp. 14f.
[19]Ibid., pp. 64f.

some twenty-five years later would hire Mises to teach international economic relations in Geneva.[20]

Meanwhile, Mises continued to make progress in his study of money and banking. He was working on two papers that he probably presented in Böhm-Bawerk's seminar and which he submitted to foreign journals. The first one, which was published in the British *Economic Journal*, gave a sympathetic presentation of the foreign exchange policy of the Austro-Hungarian Bank (the central bank).[21] The other paper elaborated on the same subject, dealing more critically with legal aspects of the Bank's policy to redeem its notes in gold. Legally, Austria-Hungary was on a paper-money standard, but Mises argued that a de facto gold standard had been established through the Bank's redemption policy, which by that time it had followed for some years. He concluded that a legal obligation of the Bank to redeem its notes would not represent a new burden or danger, but would be a mere formality.[22] Before he even published the paper, he received an unexpected invitation from a high-ranking officer of the central bank. Mr. Waldmayer offered material that could be useful for the study, but asked that, in exchange, Mises submit the paper to the Bank for approval before publication.

---

[20]See Martine Brunschwig Graf, Jean-Claude Frachebourg, Norman Scott, and Peter Tschopp, *HEI 1927–2002* (Geneva: Graduate Institute of International Studies, 2002), p. 45. This part of the book was written by Norman Scott.

[21]See Mises, "The Foreign Exchange Policy of the Austro-Hungarian Bank," *Economic Journal* 19 (June 1909): 201–11. Edgeworth, the editor of the journal, had asked Philippovich to write this paper, but Philippovich had no time and proposed Mises.

[22]See Mises, "Das Problem gesetzlicher Aufnahme der Barzahlungen in Oesterreich-Ungarn," *Jahrbuch fuer Gesetzgebung, Verwaltung und Volkswirtschaft* (Schmollers *Jahrbuch*) 33, no. 3 (1909): 985–1037. He also expressed these thoughts in his *Theory of Money and Credit* (London: Jonathan Cape, 1934); reprinted (Indianapolis: Liberty Classics, 1980) and commented on the problem in Mises, "Austrian Empire, Finance and Banking," *Encyclopaedia Britannica*, 12th ed. (1921), vol. 30, pp. 323f.

Mises declined.[23] After its publication in Schmoller's *Jahrbuch* the paper prompted a polemical exchange between Mises and two critics: Otto Neurath, another member of Böhm-Bawerk's seminar, and Walther Federn, editor of the journal *Der oesterreichische Volkswirt*.[24]

The issue was of minor importance, and Mises could not understand the heat of the debate. How could there be so much fuss about what seemed to be a clear question of fact? He learned the answer only two or three years later when Böhm-Bawerk briefed him on the background of the affair. The legal obligation to redeem its notes would have curtailed a secret fund out of which the Bank paid bribes and other illicit salaries. The beneficiaries were therefore interested in maintaining the notion that legal note redemption was inadvisable for monetary policy.

How was Mises to take this revelation? Should he unmask his opponents and uncover their corrupt scheme? After much thought, he decided to do nothing of the sort. His mission as an economist was to unmask fallacious economic arguments. If he also discussed the corruption of his opponents, the mission would lose focus. He later summarized his new personal maxim as follows:

> An economist must face his opponents with the ficti-
> tious assumption that they are guided by objective
> considerations only. It is irrelevant whether the advo-
> cate of a fallacious opinion acts in good or bad faith;
> it matters only whether the stated opinion is correct

---

[23]On the incident, see Mises, *Erinnerungen*, pp. 28–32.

[24]See Walther Federn in *Jahrbuch fuer Gesetzgebung, Verwaltung und Volkswirtschaft* (Schmollers *Jahrbuch*) 34 (1910): 151ff.; Otto Neurath, "Gesetzliche Barzahlungen und Kriegsfall," in ibid., pp. 417ff.; Mises, "Zum Problem gesetzlicher Aufnahme der Barzahlungen in Öesterreich-Ungarn: Ein Schlusswort gegenüber Walther Federn," in ibid., pp. 1877–84. Also see Federn's piece in *Der oesterreichische Volkswirt* 44 (July 31, 1909).

or fallacious. It is the task of other people to reveal corruption and inform the public about it.[25]

Kammer

Daily work for the Pelzer law firm was somewhat less rewarding than his early scholarship. Mises kept an eye out for more convenient career opportunities, and one came sooner than expected. His friend Victor Graetz, who was employed as an economic counselor at the local chamber of commerce, proposed Mises as his successor.

Gractz had worked a few years for the executive office of the *Niederösterreichische Handels- und Gewerbekammer* (Lower Austrian Chamber of Commerce and Industry, hereafter *Kammer*). Along with some other young economists such as Alfred Treichl, he had been hired when the *Kammer* made the strategic decision to strengthen its executive office to increase its leverage on Austrian economic policy.[26] The new strategy of the *Kammer* was a reaction both to the expansion of government interventionism in the first decade of the twentieth century, and to the simultaneous elimination of the *Kammer* from the Austrian parliament. Until 1907, the sixty Austrian chambers of commerce had been directly represented in the Austrian parliaments,

---

[25]Mises, *Erinnerungen*, p. 31; *Notes and Recollections*, pp. 51f. He added:

> Throughout my life I have held to these principles. I knew a great deal, if not all, about the corruption of interventionists and socialists with which I had to cope. But I never made use of this knowledge, which was not always properly understood by others. . . . It was often held against me that I politely rejected offers to supply me with proof, admissible in courts of law, of embezzlement and frauds by my opponents.

[26]This decision of the Vienna Chamber of Commerce seems to have been paralleled at many other places in Germany and Austria-Hungary since the late 1890s; see Franz Boese, *Geschichte des Vereins für Sozialpolitik, 1872–1932* (Berlin: Duncker & Humblot, 1939), p. 126.

according to the older parliamentary model where "representation" referred to predefined interest groups, such as the nobility, the clergy, the city dwellers, but also "commerce and industry." Then the introduction of universal suffrage supplanted the
old system and the Vienna *Kammer*, which had traditionally
been the hub of the whole network of chambers of commerce
throughout the country, suddenly found itself without any
direct political influence.[27]

Fortunately for the *Kammer*, however, the hyperactive new
parliamentarians were completely ignorant of economic and
legislative matters. Incapable of anticipating the impact of the
new laws on the market process, they also lacked the ability to
formulate laws in such a way as to ensure their proper enforce-
ment through the bureaucracy. The parliament's incompetence
was obvious and embarrassing, but to the *Kammer* executives it
was an opportunity. They started offering technical assistance
to the various committees and bureaus involved in the preparation of new economic legislation. The services of the *Kammer*,
coming from the official representatives of the Austrian business world, were readily accepted and quite influential. The
Kammer's Executive Office was once again a major player on
Austria's economic-policy scene.[28]

This had positive personal consequences for the members of
the executive office. In early 1909, most of them had been
offered attractive positions within the higher strata of the government bureaucracy and in major corporations. Treichl had left
the *Kammer* in March 1909 for one such. Shortly thereafter he

---

[27]See Franz Geissler, "Die Entstehung und der Entwicklungsgang der
Handelskammern in Österreich," Hans Mayer, ed., *Hundert Jahre österreichischer Wirtschaftsentwicklung, 1848–1948* (Vienna: Springer, 1949), pp. 104,
108. See also Bundeskammer and Wiener Kammer der gewerblichen
Wirtschaft, eds., *100 Jahre Handelskammern in Österreich* (Vienna: Amtsblatt
der Bundeskammer der gewerblichen Wirtschaft, 1948), p. 136.

[28]See Mises, *Erinnerungen*, pp. 45f.

moved on to become vice chairman of one of the major banks.[29] Treichl's friend Graetz had accepted a position as chairman of a large printing company and recommended Mises for the now vacant post at the *Kammer*. Mises applied in February 1909, mentioning his scholarly publications and stressing practical skills such as his command of English and French (as well as Polish and some Italian) and of stenography according to the Gabelsberger system. It is unlikely that the *Kammer* received many applications of this caliber; in fact most candidates with Mises's qualifications sought careers in the more prestigious civil service. He was hired on the spot and began work on the first of April.[30] After three years of wandering, Mises had finally found an agreeable occupation that would support his after-hours scholarship. He remained in this position for the next twenty-five years.[31]

> The *Kammer* offered me the only field in which I could work in Austria. . . . I have created a position for myself. Officially I was never more than an officer (Beamter) in the *Kammer*'s executive office . . . ; I

---

[29]See Treichl, *Fast ein Jahrhundert*, p. 17. After the war, he ran the Biedermann Bank with Schumpeter, its brief-tenured president.

[30]One author claims that he was hired on October 15, 1909 as a provisional *Konzipient* (an aspiring lawyer who has only recently passed his exams). See Alexander Hörtlehner, "Ludwig von Mises und die österreichische Handelskammerorganisation," *Wirtschaftspolitische Blätter* 28, no. 4 (1981): 141. This seems to be wrong. In a May 1909 newspaper report Mises is mentioned as a "representative of the Kammer Bureau." See *Neue Freie Presse* (10 May 1909), p. 4.

[31]At this point, Mises was still living in I., Friedrichstrasse 4. Ludwig and his mother moved to another apartment in 1911. The new address was Wollzeile 24, also in the first district. See the Wohnungszeugnis (housing certificate) in Grove City Archive: file #6/9/1/1. Housing regulations prevented Ludwig from keeping the apartment when his mother died in 1937. By October 31 of that year, he found new tenants who sublet him one room, where he stored his library and personal documents. See his letter to the housing administration, dated September 24, 1937; Grove City Archive: file #6/9/1/1.

always had a nominal superior and colleagues. [But:]
My position was incomparably greater than that of
any other *Kammer* official or of any Austrian who did
not preside over one of the big political parties. I was
the economist of the country.[32]

The chambers of commerce fulfilled three main functions:
they provided the political establishment with a certain level of
control over any emerging commercial power; they provided
the commercial establishment with representation in the state
apparatus; they helped protect established commercial interests
from new competition. Accordingly, the Vienna *Kammer* had
gained its greatest direct impact on Austrian politics in the years
1884–1901, when it most visibly acted as the cartelizing agent
of Austrian industry and opposed free trade in industrial products.[33] In the wake of this campaign, the *Kammer* acquired so
much regulatory power that it was increasingly perceived as an
arm of the central-state administration.[34]

It would be a mistake to think that Mises had quit a bureaucratic life to join a business organization. His job did include
some of the benefits of private institutions, but it also maintained some of the characteristics of the civil service—both the
prestige and the constraints. The main benefit of his new job
was something no government agency could offer: latitude for

---

[32]Mises, *Erinnerungen*, p. 46.

[33]Their opponents were agrarian circles that championed free trade, but
only in industrial products. See Bundeskammer and Wiener Kammer der
gewerblichen Wirtschaft, eds., *100 Jahre Handelskammern in Österreich*, p.
126. Still the *Kammer's* demeanor had to be moderate and reasonable. Some
Austrian industrialist hardliners therefore created a number of other institutions of a more combative character, in particular the *Industriellenklub*
(founded 1875). After World War I, it merged with other similar organizations into the *Hauptverband der Industrie Österreichs*. One of Mises's best
friends, Weiss von Wellenstein, led that organization.

[34]See Bundeskammer and Wiener Kammer der gewerblichen Wirtschaft,
eds., *100 Jahre Handelskammern in Österreich*, p. 135f.

the creative employment of individual energies, and a personal impact on public debate. Mises made ample use of these opportunities to reanimate the spirit of capitalism in an institution where it had become a dead letter.

Mises joined the first section of the *Kammer* as an analyst[35] at the very moment the Austrian tax law was undergoing its first major revision since Böhm-Bawerk and his team of economists had reformed direct taxation in 1896. The Böhm-Bawerkian reforms had established a plan for government finance up to 1909. In 1908, the Ministry of Finance had presented a "reform plan" that did not change anything in the structure of taxation, but increased personal and corporate taxes. Mises's main role within the *Kammer* in the prewar years was to lead an extended campaign against the official proposal.[36] Even though he was a newcomer, he soon surpassed all expectations. Early on he was entrusted with leading the negotiations with the representatives of the Ministry of Finance. He eventually obtained a compromise that reconciled the government's endeavor to increase tax revenue with the interests of the commercial and industrial circles organized in the *Kammer*.

His first mission was to study the impact of the proposed taxation of beer and other alcoholic beverages. He took part in a mid-May 1909 *Kammer* conference on the consequences of the increase of the beer tax. The participants criticized the increase with standard economic arguments, pointing out that it would annihilate marginal business.[37] But when another *Kammer* meeting was held two months later on the taxation of alcoholic beverages, the *Kammer*'s attitude had undergone a seismic shift.

---

[35]The official name of his position was "Konzipist." See Mises Archive 107: 79.

[36]See Alois Gratz, "Die österreichische Finanzpolitik von 1848 bis 1948," Hans Mayer, ed., *Hundert Jahre österreichischer Wirtschaftsentwicklung, 1848–1948*, pp. 265, 307, fn. 70, 309, fn. 123.

[37]Mises Archive 107: 55b.

Mises had taken the bull by the horns and, in the first of many reports he would write in the coming years, raised not only the familiar issue of marginal business, but also the politically delicate issue of the agricultural interests underlying the proposed legislation. Mises pointed out in great detail the existence of inequitable sales quotas for commercial and agricultural producers, and of special subsidies for the agricultural production of alcohol. The meeting denounced these practices, basing all its resolutions on Mises's report.[38]

Mises then turned to proposed legislation concerning private inheritance and donations as well as corporate taxation and corporate law. He reported on the former topic to a plenary *Kammer* meeting in early December 1909.[39] Mises pointed out that the higher taxation and the complicated procedures of the planned law would hurt business life, and he emphasized again that the stipulations of the new law would treat the agrarian population better than urban circles in commerce and industry. But he also brought more far-reaching considerations into play, noticing that the legislation would subject Austria's courts to the control of the financial administration.

Other young economists also gave reports at the meeting, but theirs did not have as great an impact on the public or the press.[40] Mises's reports set new standards both for analytical scope and rigor and for their political audacity. The wind of change blew through the *Kammer*. Even though *Kammer* executives did not always share the views expressed in the reports of their new

---

[38]Mises Archive 107: 55c. In a postwar book, he would point out that the conflict between commercial and agricultural producers had an ethnic aspect, the former being predominantly German and the latter non-German. See Mises, *Nation, Staat und Wirtschaft* (Vienna: Manz, 1919), p. 134; translated by Leland B. Yeager as *Nation, State, and Economy* (New York: New York University Press, 1983), pp. 164f.

[39]Mises Archive 107: 55d, 62.

[40]See for example the press reports in Mises Archive 107: 62, 71a.

employee,[41] they benefited politically from the fact that his seemingly extreme positions were always backed up with such thorough research, that the *Kammer* was able to reach more favorable compromises in the political process.

Storm Clouds

Meanwhile Austrian foreign policy had taken a fateful turn in 1908. A revolution in Turkey had smashed a theocratic establishment that had been unable to enact real reforms for decades, and swept into power a group of ambitious young men who came to be known as the Young Turks.[42] These Young Turks pursued a radical reform program designed to make Turkey more like the secular democracies of the West. European leaders were amazed to see the Young Turks putting their ideas into practice so quickly. Many of them believed that Turkey would soon regain formidable strength, with drastic consequences for the political map of southeastern Europe.

The hawks in Vienna immediately began agitating for the annexation of Bosnia and Herzegovina. The Austro-Hungarian army had occupied these territories since 1878, but they had not been formally incorporated into the empire. The advocates of war insisted that Austria-Hungary could not afford to wait until the Turks were strong enough to reclaim their former colonies. When it became obvious that the hawks would have their way in Vienna, war nearly broke out with Russian-backed Serbia. In the so-called annexation crisis, a great number of troops, Ludwig von Mises among them, were mobilized and dispatched to the southern and northern borders of the empire. The war was averted, however, when the Russians withdrew their support for the Serbs. After a year of negotiations, Bosnia was constituted

---

[41]See for example Mises Archive 107: 71.

[42]All over the world, there were various "Young" movements: among the Czechs, the Chinese, in literature, painting, politics, etc.

as a part of Austria-Hungary. But the event had a lasting negative impact on foreign relations. Austria-Hungary's hawkish Minister of Foreign Affairs, Aehrenthal, successfully lobbied the governments of Russia, France, Italy, and Great Britain to approve the annexation, but the old trust that Austrian statesmen had enjoyed abroad had been destroyed. Rudolf Sieghart, a high government official at the time, said in retrospect that the annexation was "the overture to the World War."[43] An increasing number of crises entangled the major European powers over the next several years. Austria-Hungary mobilized its troops again in 1912 against another Russian-Serb coalition. Once again, the Russians withdrew at the last minute, but two years later they would stand fast.

The annexation campaign had a profound impact on domestic policy as well. The liberal Prime Minister Beck had resigned in November 1908 to protest the annexation. The last phase of bourgeois-liberal rule in Austria ended with his administration. Beginning with Koerber's administration in 1900 (which included Böhm-Bawerk as finance minister) Austria had been ruled for eight years by governments that found their main support in the liberal press and in business and finance. Every prime minister since 1900 had risen to his position through a career in the Austrian bureaucracy, and each ruled on the basis of emergency laws that allowed the emperor to appoint governments without parliamentary approval. But Koerber had pioneered the method of "governing through the press," and his successors Gautsch and Beck skillfully continued this approach. They were not mere administrators for the emperor, but could initiate political change through direct communication with the citizenry, thus bypassing political party organizations.[44]

The succeeding governments could no longer rely on the support of the liberal establishment, especially the press, and for

---

[43] Sieghart, *Die letzten Jahrzehnte einer Grossmacht*, p. 138.
[44] Ibid., p. 143.

this reason alone were unable to address any pressing political problem before the outbreak of war. National conflicts and suppressed democratic longings continued to alienate the citizenry from the empire. Under relentless centrifugal forces, the country was ready to break apart.

Vienna Meeting of the Verein für Socialpolitik

These developments would surface over the next several years and would include two Balkan wars and the Morocco Crisis that preceded World War I, but in 1909, the world had not yet fallen apart. Mises enjoyed his new job at the *Kammer* and continued to pursue his other intellectual interests, including Böhm-Bawerk's seminar and the discussion group he had founded with his friend Perels and others.

In September 1909, the plenary meeting of the *Verein für Socialpolitik* took place in Vienna. It turned out to be one of the most significant intellectual events before World War I. The conference took place at the end of September and featured sessions on the problems of municipally owned companies and on the concept of productivity. Mises probably joined the *Verein* at this point. He certainly attended the sessions that were organized and directed by his teacher Philippovich.[45]

Philippovich, one of the vice-presidents of the *Verein*, had successfully promoted the subject of "the productivity of national economies and the empirical measurement thereof."[46] It was the first time ever that the *Verein* dealt with a problem of pure economic theory. Moreover, it was a problem of fundamental importance for the cause of the social-policy movement

---

[45]See Boese, *Geschichte des Vereins für Sozialpolitik, 1872–1932*, pp. 131, 133; see also Mises's letter to Franz Böse dated September 30, 1919 in Mises Archive 53: 47f.

[46]Other topics dealt with were problems of enterprise owned by local government and a memorial lecture on the German economist Hansen, which was delivered by Georg F. Knapp.

so dear to Philippovich. The productivity debate at the Vienna meeting would become a high point in the history of the *Verein* and of German economics, featuring the confrontation between the historicist majority and a vociferous group of brilliant younger scholars such as Werner Sombart, Bernd Harms, the Weber brothers, and pastor Friedrich Naumann.[47]

Over the years, Max Weber had become the leader of those who contested both premises of the *Verein*: the utility of government interventionism and the historicist methodology. Leadership accrued to him not only because of his imposing personality, but also and especially because he had started his career *within* the *Verein* as both an interventionist and historicist. Other dissenting voices—Dietzel, Wolf, Ehrenberg, Pohle, Passow, and Adolf Weber[48]—had never been Schmollerites in the first place, but Max Weber was elected into the Committee in 1893 as a young star in the *kathedersocialist* tradition. According to Mises:

> He was appointed professor of economics without having dealt with this science before, which was a customary procedure at that time. It reflected the [Historical] School's opinion on the nature of "social sciences" and on the scientific expertise of legal historians. . . . When he accepted the position . . . [the] jurist and historian in him rebelled against the manner in which the School treated legal and historical problems. This is why he began his pioneering methodological and epistemological investigations. It

---

[47]See Mises, "Max Weber und der Kathedersozialismus," *Kritik des Interventionismus* (reprint, Darmstadt: Wissenschaftliche Buchgesellschaft, [1929] 1976, pp. 85ff.); Dieter Lindenlaub, "Richtungskämpfe im Verein für Sozialpolitik," *Vierteljahrschrift für Sozial- und Wirtschaftsgeschichte*, Beiheft no. 52 (1967), pp. 272ff.; Dieter Krüger, "Max Weber und die 'Jüngeren' im Verein für Socialpolitik," Wolfgang Mommsen and Wolfgang Schwentker, eds., *Max Weber und seine Zeitgenossen* (Göttingen: Veröffentlichungen des Deutschen Historischen Instituts London, 1988), pp. 98–136.

[48]Adolf Weber had no family ties with the brothers Alfred Weber and Max Weber.

led him to the problems of materialistic philosophy of history, from which he then approached the religious-sociological tasks. He proceeded finally to a grandiose attempt at a system of social sciences. But all these studies, step by step, led Max Weber away from the political and social ideals of his youth. He moved, for the first time, toward liberalism, rationalism, utilitarianism.[49]

In contrast to the still-dominant Schmollerites, Max Weber and his brother Alfred thought that normative propositions of the type "the government should do this or that" had no scientific basis and reflected only the personal value judgments of their author.[50] These views had been reinforced just the year before the Vienna meeting through Schumpeter's *Nature and Essence*, which championed the claim that economic research could mimic the natural sciences. The Webers also thought that the mainstream systematically overlooked the problems that arose from government intervention.

In 1905, the plenary meeting in Mannheim featured the first open clash between the young radicals and the establishment over the question of cartels and anti-trust policies. In the 1870s and 1880s, the majority of the *Verein* had welcomed the formation of

---

[49]Mises, *Kritik des Interventionismus*, pp. 86f.; the translation is from Mises, *A Critique of Interventionism*, Hans Sennholz, trans. (New York: Arlington House, 1977), p. 103.

[50]Heino Heinrich Nau points out that Max Weber merely elaborated Carl Menger's methodological position. His main contribution was to synthesize Menger's methodology with Heinrich Rickert's theory of value relations. The debate on value freedom itself was therefore a continuation of *Methodenstreit* between Menger and Schmoller. After World War II, there was another round of essentially the same debate in the so-called *Positivismusstreit*, which at the beginning of the 1960s opposed the Marxist Frankfurt School and Karl Popper and his followers. See Nau, "'Zwei Ökonomien.' Die Vorgeschichte des Werturteilsstreit in der deutschsprachigen Ökonomik," Nau, ed., *Der Werturteilsstreit. Die Äusserungen zur Werturteilsdiskussion im Ausschuss des Vereins für Sozialpolitik (1913)* (Marburg: Metropolis, 1996), pp. 9–64.

cartels as an anti-emigration device.[51] In the 1890s, the dominant view was reversed mainly because the civil servants were
jealous of fast-growing corporate power. The Mannheim meeting was meant to be an important milestone of this new orientation. The invited lectures by Brentano, Leidig, Schmoller,
and Kierdorf made the case for various policies designed to
reinforce the position of labor unions within large firms, to curb
corporate power, and to make large firms socially responsible.
Schmoller proposed, for example, that 25 percent of the seats of
the corporate boards be reserved for government representatives.[52]

In the ensuing debate, Friedrich Naumann, Werner Sombart, and Max Weber heavily criticized these analyses and conclusions. Weber accused Schmoller of cultivating old illusory
notions about the nature of the state. But the greatest blow
against the establishment position came through a speech by
pastor Naumann, who seems to have been in his Marxist
phase.[53] He argued that the formation of cartels had resulted
from great secular forces that could not possibly be prevailed
against by some minor state and its middle-class policies in support of the handicrafts. Moreover, anticipating an argument
that Mises would carefully develop many years later, Naumann
pointed out that the proposed government interventions could
not attain the end they were meant to achieve. These interventions were "from a technical and economic point of view, nonsense." Naumann's speech roused the audience to unusually
enthusiastic applause—applause that lasted much too long for

---

[51]The cartels reduced foreign competition and thus they diminished—for
a while at least—the downward pressure on wage rates in the least competitive industries. Workers employed in these industries had less incentive to
emigrate than they otherwise would have had.

[52]"Verhandlungen der Generalversammlung in Mannheim," *Schriften des
Vereins für Socialpolitik* 116 (Berlin: Duncker & Humblot, 1906).

[53]On Naumann see Ralph Raico, *Die Partei der Freiheit* (Stuttgart: Lucius
& Lucius, 1999), chap. 6.

the embarrassed Schmoller, who later scoffed that the response had been "frenetic."[54]

By tradition, Schmoller wrapped up the meeting. He called Naumann a demagogue and said that if he were not allowed to distance himself from Naumann, he would have to step down as president of the *Verein*. Many thought Schmoller's reaction was excessive, and long-time critics such as Ludwig Pohle and Andreas Voigt cancelled their membership. The controversy eventually died down, especially because the next meeting in Magdeburg (1907) dealt with less controversial subjects, such as the training of young economists and problems of city administration. But the stage was set for the Vienna meeting, where core issues of the social-policy movement were on the agenda.

The first two sessions dealt with problems of municipal firms. As usual, the lectures and the discussion concerned technical problems relating in particular to the administration of those firms, their means of finance, and the remuneration of their employees. This cozy exchange of municipal socialists was shaken up, however, when the Weber brothers brought some rather fundamental considerations into play. An eminent historian of the *Verein* who, siding with the mainstream, attended the Vienna meeting, recalled the "sensation" that the Weber brothers stirred with their remarks:

> Whereas, as many speakers stressed, the entire debate had relied on the opinion, shared by all, that municipalization—the transfer of certain suitable industries from private hands into the hands of the municipality—always means social progress, Alfred Weber contested this opinion. He pointed out that municipalization turned ever-greater parts of the population into bureaucrats and presented this without any ambiguity as a great defect.[55]

---

[54]Boese, *Geschichte des Vereins für Sozialpolitik, 1872–1932*, p. 113.
[55]Ibid., p. 133.

Alfred Weber had dared to suggest that there might be something wrong with becoming a civil servant, and something even worse about turning large segments of the population into employees of the state. In doing so, he denounced the very mission of the *Verein*, which was to provide "scientific" underpinnings for ever more government intervention and a larger, more powerful bureaucracy. After his speech, there was too little time for discussion, but the confrontation between the Webers and the Schmollerites would be continued the next day, which dealt with the central concept of national productivity.

The prevailing justification for government intervention stressed the distinction between profitability and productivity. The typical Schmollerite professor would argue that the profit of an investment was, primarily, an indicator of the investment's importance from an individual point of view. Only under very specific and rare conditions was it also indicative of the social value of an investment. From a larger, "social" point of view, it was therefore crucial to judge any decision about the use of society's scarce resources in terms of its "productivity." But is there anything at all like an objective criterion to distinguish more from less productive uses of resources? On this decisive point the *kathedersocialist* professors were silent. Philippovich felt that scientific integrity required a clarification of this theoretical issue and he set up an "Austrian" session on productivity theory, featuring plenary lectures by himself and by his distinguished colleague, Friedrich von Wieser.

Philippovich delivered the first of the two lectures. He gave a brilliant overview of the history of the concept of national productivity, but then evaded the true subject of his lecture, which was supposed to deal with the nature of national-economic productivity and the possibility of measuring it. Philippovich focused entirely on the narrower question of the impact of technological progress on productivity. This evasion derived in part from the difficulty of the subject, but was also due to the fierce opposition that was to be expected from the Weber brothers and their allies.

The second lecture also avoided the crucial question of the concrete meaning of national productivity. Wieser's subject was the measurement of the value of money and of the changes of its value, with special consideration to the problem of productivity. The general idea was that money prices could be used as a yardstick to measure the economy's productivity, or at least changes in productivity. This in turn presupposes that it is possible to analyze and quantify alterations in the yardstick itself—changes in the value of money. Now, Wieser had his own views on what precisely was to be understood by the value of money, and he stated his position in a long essay that appeared in advance of the conference in the *Verein*'s publication series.[56] Based on this essay, he delivered his lecture focusing more narrowly on the technical problems of money-value measurement.[57]

Wieser's discussion highlighted once again that he believed that the natural value of an economic good was not tied to individuals. The natural value of a good was rather its general economic significance within a social context. The difference in value between two goods indicated that the more highly valued good was generally more important than the less valued good— not just for the individual but for all subjects of the commonwealth. In short, the differences between the various values reflected a hierarchy of values. What was better or worse "from an economic point of view" could therefore be determined by reference to differences in value. And despite all problems relating to technical procedure, the value of all things could be ascertained by the inquiring mind. In principle at least it was possible

---

[56]See Friedrich von Wieser, "Der Geldwert und seine Veränderungen," *Schriften des Vereins für Socialpolitik* 132 (Munich, 1909); reprinted in idem, *Gesammelte Abhandlungen*, F.A. Hayek, ed. (Tübingen: Mohr, 1929), pp. 193–242.

[57]The lecture manuscript was also published in the *Verein*'s series. See Friedrich von Wieser, "Über die Messung der Veränderungen des Geldwertes," *Schriften des Vereins für Socialpolitik* 132 (Munich, 1909); reprinted in idem, *Gesammelte Abhandlungen*, Hayek, ed., pp. 243–52.

to measure economic productivity and economic progress, just as it was possible to measure the changing value of money.

These views enabled Wieser to bridge some of the differences that he, the highly prominent "theorist" otherwise had with the predominantly historicist members of the *Verein*. In fact the traditional purpose of the *Verein* was to provide theoretical guidelines for public policy, and on the most fundamental level this required that one be able to distinguish between better and worse economic states of affairs. Wieserian economics promised such a distinction based on the theory of value, even though Wieser himself was reluctant to commit to any policy position.

After Wieser had finished his lecture, the first comments came from Herkner and Knapp, champions of the traditional view, which considered the notion of national productivity to be generally coherent, though it was difficult to give it operational meaning. But then came, as Mises later recalled, "that memorable exchange of arguments in which, for the first time within the *Verein*, the amalgamation of the economic-theoretical and ethical-political viewpoints was fervently attacked."[58] Werner Sombart led the attack, denying that the concept of national productivity was useful for scientific research. Then Gottl-Ottlilienfeld argued, in the same vein, that the notion of national productivity had no correlate in the real world.

It was finally Max Weber's turn to address the question. He had long awaited this opportunity to corner his opponents on the question of the nature of scientific research. He was already known for his ideal of "value-free" scientific research—that is, research with the strict orientation toward the ascertainment of matters of fact.[59] He was himself a passionate man, and he did

---

[58]Mises, "Eugen von Philippovich," *Neue Österreichische Biographie* (Vienna, 1926), 1st section, vol. 3, p. 56.

[59]See Max Weber, *Gesammelte Aufsätze zur Wissenschaftslehre* (Tübingen: Mohr).

not believe that value-freedom required emotional detachment from the object of one's study. But it did imply that the scientist (and especially the social scientist) strictly distinguish between what is and what should be; it implied that he must not conflate his personal preferences with the factual results of his research. In a frontal attack against Philippovich, Weber argued that there was no objective way to speak about the productivity of an aggregate of human beings. The very notion of "national productivity" had a normative rather than descriptive function. It therefore had no place in economic science and should be cast into the economist's dustbin "where it belonged."[60]

Significantly, the main target of Weber's attacks was Philippovich and Schmoller. Weber was implicitly acknowledging Philippovich as the true intellectual leader of the interventionist movement. In his replies to Weber, the latter demonstrated the qualities that had won him this position. As Mises recalled many years later:

> The cause that Philippovich advocated has been defeated; today it is generally recognized that it is not the task of science to establish value judgments. But in that encounter, in which Philippovich was on the wrong side, he was greater than his opponents, who turned out to be right. And these opponents were led by Max Weber! Never has Philippovich's intellectual persona revealed itself in a brighter light, never have his oratorical skills made a deeper impact on the audience than in the final comment of that now-famous debate.[61]

The *kathedersocialist* establishment had spent all its energies justifying the introduction of ethical considerations into economic analysis and insisting that this was "science" too. In Vienna

---

[60]Max Weber, "Verhandlungen des *Vereins für Socialpolitik* in Wien, 1909," *Schriften des Vereins für Socialpolitik* 132 (Munich and Leipzig: Duncker & Humblot, 1910): 583.

[61]Mises, "Eugen von Philippovich," p. 60.

they had won the day, to the great frustration of Max Weber, who no longer believed the *Verein* could be a suitable forum for genuinely scientific questions.[62] After the Vienna meeting, he founded the German Sociological Association, which met for the first time a year later in Frankfurt am Main.[63] This retreat turned out to be unnecessary. After the Vienna meeting, the cause of Schmoller and Philippovich was doomed. They had failed to capture the hearts of the rising generation. After Schmoller's death in 1917, new men would begin to take over the *Verein für Socialpolitik* and set German social research on an entirely different path.

Among these men was Mises, who fully endorsed Max Weber's view of science as a purely fact-oriented discipline, a view that was emphasized in the by-laws of the new sociological association. For the rest of his life—most notably after the death of Böhm-Bawerk—Mises would fight for truly empirical research. During the 1920s, he even upheld Max Weber's use of the expression "sociology"—shorthand for empirical social science, as opposed to the value-laden rumblings of the German

------

[62]The Vienna debate had a follow-up in a meeting of the *Verein's* Committee, which took place on January 5, 1914 in Berlin and was dedicated exclusively to the discussion of the role of value judgments in economic science. In order to avoid unsuitable publicity, the fifteen papers on which the meeting was based were not published, and there are no records of the debate. The meeting was the culmination of the value-judgment debate, which in modified form was continued in the 1960s in the so-called *Positivismusstreit*. Meanwhile those fifteen papers have fortunately been published. See Nau, ed., *Der Werturteilsstreit*.

[63]By early January 1909, Weber had taken part in a meeting in Berlin to prepare the establishment of the sociological association. Among the thirty-nine other participants were Ferdinand Tönnies, Georg Simmel, Werner Sombart, Friedrich Herkner, Paul Barth, Ludwig Goldscheid, Hermann Kantorowicz, Franz Oppenheimer, Ernst Troeltsch, and his brother Alfred. Max Weber was also among the signers of the open letter of invitation to the first meeting of the Association in Frankfurt in 1910, where Tönnies was elected president and Weber himself treasurer.

"government scientists"—to describe his own works. He abandoned this practice when he realized that most other writers used the same word to establish a parallel social science based on foundations completely different from economics. But this is a topic for a later chapter.

Breakthrough at the Kammer

At the end of January 1910, Mises finished a long report that had consumed his energies in the preceding months. He presented the report to a plenary *Kammer* meeting. In it he took issue with proposed legislation to increase corporate income-tax rates, to subject corporate managers to additional taxes, and to give the financial administration access to corporate bookkeeping. Mises criticized the bias of this new legislation, which sought to increase government revenue at the expense of Austrian industry—the *Kammer* clientele—while favoring agricultural producers. Mises suggested that a more reasonable policy would be to apply existing tax laws equitably.[64]

His position with the *Kammer* left him even less time than usual for his academic endeavors, but he seems to have continued his studies with iron discipline. In 1910, he came out with two new publications: an article (in a new French journal) on the reform of government finance in Austria, and a survey of new literature on money and banking for Böhm-Bawerk's *Zeitschrift*.[65]

But he was far better known for his *Kammer* reports, which were followed attentively by friends and foes, and praised in the Vienna daily press as "very thorough," "exhaustive," "very well researched," and "richly documented with statistical material."

---

[64]See Mises Archive 107: 70, 95.

[65]See Mises, "La Réforme financière en Autriche," *Revue Économique Internationale* 7, no. 4 (October 1910): 39–59; idem, "Neue Literatur über Geld- und Bankwesen," *Zeitschrift für Volkswirtschaft, Sozialpolitik und Verwaltung* 19 (1910): 385–95.

The thoroughness of his work and the intellectual leadership that he exercised in *Kammer* circles gained Mises a level of public recognition that allowed him to comment on government policy in the central organ of Austria's ruling elites. Thus, in a *Neue Freie Presse* piece from October 1911, he criticized finance minister Bilinski for his proposed increase of income taxes.[66] And about a year later, he criticized the tax proposals of MP Steinwender, observing that they would reintroduce the bad old (pre-Böhm-Bawerk) habits of making tax laws based only on immediate concerns such as the present balance of power in the Austrian parliament.[67]

The government's constant drive to increase old taxes and to create new ones was a permanent issue on the public agenda. At the end of October 1911, the *Kammer* hosted a meeting of various automobile associations to discuss the government's plan to tax cars. Mises was unhappy with the assembly's toothless resolution to appeal to the government not to exceed German automobile taxes and to tax foreigners only after a stay of more than three months in Austria.[68] He was similarly disappointed in a November 1911 meeting in which the *Kammer* took up the problem of rising meat prices. Mises's report stressed the commonsense point that the easiest solution would be to open the borders for foreign meat imports. But this solution was not "politically viable." The reduction of meat taxes—another simple and effective solution—was equally "unfeasible" because of the government's chronic financial difficulties.

Despite such setbacks, Mises tenaciously pursued his strategy of changing the structure of Austrian taxation, and in March

---

[66]See Ludwig von Mises, "Die neue Regierungsvorlage zur Abänderung des Personalsteuergesetzes," *Neue Freie Presse* (#16931, October 10, 1911); copy is in Mises Archive 106: 7.

[67]See Mises, "Der 'kleine Finanzplan' des Abgeordneten Steinwender," *Neue Freie Presse* (December 5, 1912); copy in Mises Archive 106: 10.

[68]See Mises Archive 107: 81.

1912 he was promoted to the rank of *Konsulent* (councilor). The bottom line of his many reports was that the prevailing tax code enshrined the privileges of various vested interests, particularly Austrian agriculture, and hampered industrial progress.[69] He sought a compromise that would guarantee the government higher revenue while preventing the burden from falling entirely on his clientele. His tenacity eventually paid off. In early 1914, parliament voted a new tax law that granted most *Kammer* demands. The new law stipulated a tax-exempt income of 1,600 schillings (up from 1,200) and also regulated government access to corporate bookkeeping. On the negative side were new taxes on liquor and champagne, as well as an increase of the income tax, which now reached up to 6.7 percent.[70]

Yes: a progressive tax topping out at less than 7 percent. The good old days!

Theory of Money

Despite his workday immersion in the details and intricacies of the Austrian tax policies, Mises had somehow managed to write a treatise on money and banking. He had written no articles for a year, focusing instead on the completion of his book. In mid-December 1911, he put the finishing touches to a manuscript with the title *Theorie des Geldes und der Umlaufsmittel* (Theory of Money and Fiduciary Media—misleadingly published in English as *Theory of Money and Credit*).

---

[69]This line of argument seems to have been especially pronounced at the end of his campaign. A case in point is a report that he probably submitted in May 1913 on the proposed taxation of insurance contracts. Mises here criticized the differential treatment of agrarian and urban segments of the population, and the excessive orientation of the proposal toward the interests of the financial administration. See Mises Archive 107: 92.

[70]See Gratz, "Die österreichische Finanzpolitik von 1848 bis 1948," p. 264.

Excited to see the work of more than five years come to completion, he had already approached several prestigious publishers and now decided to accept the offer of Duncker & Humblot in Leipzig.[71] They had produced the beautiful edition of Schumpeter's spectacular first book and were one of the most prestigious names in economic publishing. Mises worked feverishly revising the proof pages, making last-minute changes, and constantly inquiring about the production process. Under his pressure to speed up production, Duncker & Humblot even hired additional staff.[72] On June 14, 1912, the book was delivered to the book dealers who sold it for the cover price of 10 marks.

The long-term impact of Mises's first treatise can only be called spectacular, and we therefore take a deeper look at its main ideas in the next chapter. After ninety years, it is still in print and remains a source of inspiration for monetary theorists. Despite initial rejection by the majority of German economists, the value of Mises's work was recognized immediately by the profession's greatest minds. Max Weber called it the "most acceptable theory dealing with the substantive monetary problems."[73] Schumpeter praised its "power and originality," noticing that "as usual" the critics had overlooked these qualities in their discussion of unsubstantial side issues.[74] After the war, Albert Hahn would stress the

---

[71]Mises received fifty complimentary copies and had to pay 1372.50 marks (or 26.6 oz of gold) as his share of the total production costs (2264.18 marks). The first edition comprised 1,000 copies plus 100 complimentary copies for reviews and gifts (see Mises Archive 50a: 36f.).

[72]See correspondence in Mises Archive 50a.

[73]Max Weber, *Wirtschaft und Gesellschaft*, 3rd ed. (Tübingen: Mohr, 1947), vol. 1, § 6, p. 40. In the English edition, this passage is not quite correctly translated as "The formulation of monetary theory, which has been most acceptable to the author, is that of von Mises." *Economy and Society: An Outline of Interpretive Sociology*, Guenther Roth and Claus Wittich, eds. (Berkeley: University of California Press, 1978), p. 78.

[74]See Joseph Schumpeter, "Das Sozialprodukt und die Rechenpfennige: Glossen und Beiträge zur Geldtheorie von heute," *Archiv für Sozialwissenschaften und Sozialpolitik* 44 (1917–1918).

Mengerian qualities of Mises's work, saying that its "author, a master of economic theory, never falls for the temptation to pursue fictitious abstractions, but stands on the firm ground of the facts."[75] On the other side of the Atlantic, a young pioneer of economic theory praised the book for essentially the same reasons: "In von Mises there seems to me to be very noteworthy clarity and power. His *Theorie des Geldes und der Umlaufsmittel* is an exceptionally excellent book. Von Mises has a very wide knowledge of the literature of the theory of money. He has a keen insight into the difficulties involved."[76]

The greatest sign of recognition, however, was the fact that Böhm-Bawerk devoted two entire semesters of his seminar to the discussion of Mises's book—an honor shared by no one else, not even Schumpeter. Böhm-Bawerk acknowledged Schumpeter's brilliance but wrote that he wished to see Schumpeter turn to serious work. Apparently, Mises's book was serious theoretical work of the sort Böhm-Bawerk had in mind, and its enduring success proved the old master to be right once again.

Mises submitted the book to the University of Vienna to obtain the *Habilitation* degree and to be admitted as a *Privatdozent*, a private lecturer who could offer the students optional courses. His request was granted in the spring of 1913 and he began lecturing in the summer semester. What glorious days when one could study under Böhm-Bawerk, Wieser, Philippovich, and Mises! But these days were numbered. The all-star Austrian faculty lasted only three semesters. In August 1914, Böhm-Bawerk died and Mises was sent to the front. His best students perished in the war.[77] ◄

---

[75]"The principal advantages of the work are found in that the author, in all mastery of the theory, never allows himself to fall into unrealistic abstractions, but remains fully grounded in fact." Albert Hahn, review in *Archiv für Sozialwissenschaften und Sozialpolitik*, quoted from Mises Archive 87a: 11f.

[76]Benjamin M. Anderson, *The Value of Money* (New York: Macmillan, 1917), p. 100.

[77]See Mises, *Erinnerungen*, p. 18. See also Otto Ehrlich to Mises, letter dated April 29, 1942; Grove City Archive: Ehrlich file.

Mises in the 1920s

D. Ludwig Edler von Mises

6
Treatise on Money

MISES'S GREATEST LIFETIME ACHIEVEMENT was to build an all-encompassing systematic theory of human action, which he first presented in *Nationalökonomie* (1940) and *Human Action* (1949). His system was the result of two large research projects, overlapping in time, the first one concerning economic science as such, while the second dealt with the epistemological and methodological foundations of this science. He published his reflections on epistemology and methodology in the period from 1929 to 1962.[1] His great economic research project extended from 1912 to 1940. It started with a treatise on money, in which Mises unfolds an original theme that he later expands, systematizes, and eventually brings full circle in *Nationalökonomie*.

The great original theme of his economic writings concerned the integration of the theory of money and banking into

---

[1]Landmarks are his essay on "Sociology and History" (1929) and several book publications: *Epistemological Problems of Economics* (first German edition, 1933; translated into English by George Reisman [Princeton, N.J.: Van Nostrand, 1960; 3rd ed., Auburn, Ala.: Ludwig von Mises Institute, 2003]); *Nationalökonomie* (Geneva: Editions Union, 1940); *Human Action* (New Haven, Conn.: Yale University Press, 1949; 3rd ed. [Auburn, Ala.: Ludwig von Mises Institute, 1998]; *Theory and History* (New Haven, Conn.: Yale University Press, 1957; reprinted Auburn, Ala.: Ludwig von Mises Institute, 1985); and *The Ultimate Foundation of Economic Science* (New Rochelle, N.Y.: Arlington House, 1962).

the framework of the Mengerian theory of value and prices. Mises dealt with it in his first treatise, *Theory of Money and Credit*, which had earned him the coveted license to teach at Austrian universities. Carl Menger too had obtained a *Habilitation* for an original theory of money, which he had published as chapter 8 of *Principles*. Mises thus continued a Mengerian tradition by grounding his academic reputation on monetary analysis. He did not submit only one chapter, though, but a complete treatise.

In his theory of money, Carl Menger had been mainly concerned with explaining the origin of money as a social institution. He stressed that money did not come into being like Athena from the brow of Zeus, but developed step by step out of a non-monetary commodity.[2] However, Menger had not applied his marginal-value theory to money itself. The reader of *Principles* could get the distinct impression that value theory only applied to consumers' goods and factors of production, and that money was not subject to the same rules.

What then is the relationship between marginal value and money? This was the question at the heart of *The Theory of Money and Credit*. Mises answered it in the second—the central—part of the book and thereby brought the Austrian theory of value and prices full circle. Money was no longer a special case, but could be fully accounted for by the new marginal-value theory.

In his treatise, Mises went as far as he could to integrate the theory of money and banking into the general theory of value and prices. From the outset he was aware that his exposition would be inadequate. He later explained:

> The greatest difficulty I faced in the preparation of the book was the fact that I meant to give special attention to merely a limited part of the total scope of

---

[2]See Carl Menger, *Grundsätze der Volkswirthschaftslehre* (Vienna: Braumüller, 1871); idem, *Untersuchungen über die Methode der Socialwissenschaften und der Politischen oekonomie insbesondere* (Leipzig: Duncker & Humblot, 1883).

economic problems. But economics necessarily must be a complete and united whole. In economics there can be no specialization. To deal with a part one must do so on the foundation of a theory that comprises all the problems. But I could not use any of the existing theories. The systems of Menger and Böhm-Bawerk were no longer wholly satisfactory to me. I was ready to proceed further on the road these old masters had discovered. But I could not use their treatment of those problems with which monetary theory must begin.

According to prevailing opinion at that time, the theory of money could be clearly separated from the total structure of economic problems—it did not, in fact, even belong with economics; in a certain respect it was an independent discipline. In accordance with this opinion, the universities in Anglo-Saxon countries had created special professorships for currency and banking. It was my intention to reveal this position as erroneous and restore the theory of money to its appropriate position as an integral part of the science of economics.

If I could have worked quietly and taken my time, I would have begun with a theory of direct exchange in the first volume; and then I could proceed to the theory of indirect exchange. But I actually began with indirect exchange, because I believed that I did not have much time; I knew that we were on the eve of a great war and I wanted to complete my book before the war's outbreak. I thus decided that in a few points only I would go beyond the narrow field of strictly monetary theory, and would postpone my preparation of a more complete work.[3]

Unfortunately, his forecast proved to be right, and for many years, the war and its aftermath prevented him from systematically elaborating his more general ideas in print. But these ideas,

---

[3]Mises, *Notes and Recollections* (Spring Mills, Penn.: Libertarian Press, 1978), pp. 55f.

nurtured through the war experience, came to light more pow-
erfully in an essay on the problems of economic calculation in
socialist regimes, which Mises published in 1920 in Max Weber's
Archiv für Sozialwissenschaft und Sozialpolitik, arguably the most
avant-garde German social-science journal of the day. Here he
expanded on the difference between valuation and money-based
economic calculations—a difference he had stressed, but not
elaborated upon, in *Theory of Money and Credit*. Mises observed
that economic calculation consists of the computation of market
prices, prices that can only emerge in the interaction of private-
property owners. Since an extended division of labor is possible
only because decisions can be based on economic calculus, it follows that socialist societies—which by definition have no private
property in the means of production and thus no market prices
for them—could not possibly enjoy an extended division of
labor. Socialism, insofar as it was considered to be a system of
rational division of labor, did not and could not ever exist.

In the manner of Böhm-Bawerk, Mises had derived crucial
political insights from seemingly arcane theoretical distinctions.
He followed his calculation piece with a comprehensive treatise on
socialism (1922); again thoughts he had kept to himself and developed over many years burst forth in the span of a few months.

In *Nationalökonomie* (1940) and *Human Action* (1949) he
finally gave a presentation of the whole body of economic science in light of the difference between valuation and calculation.

> My *Nationalökonomie* finally afforded me the opportu-
> nity to present the problems of economic calculation
> in their full significance. . . . Thus I accomplished the
> project that had presented itself to me thirty-five
> years earlier.[4]

---

[4]Mises, *Erinnerungen* (Stuttgart: Gustav Fischer Verlag, 1978), p. 74;
Notes and Recollections, p. 112. See also Murray N. Rothbard, *Ludwig von Mises:
Scholar, Creator, Hero* (Auburn, Ala.: Ludwig von Mises Institute, 1988), and
James Rolph Edwards, *The Economist of the Century: Ludwig von Mises in the
History of Monetary Thought* (New York: Carlton Press, 1985).

The Nature of Money

As a true disciple of Carl Menger, Ludwig von Mises began the presentation of his theory of money with an analysis of the nature of money itself. He then went on to deal with the determination of money's purchasing power and with the impact of what he called *Umlaufsmittel* (fiduciary media) on the monetary system.

In dealing with the nature of money, Mises relied heavily on the work of Carl Menger. The founder of the Austrian School had shown that money is not to be defined by the physical characteristics of whatever good is used as money; rather, money is characterized by the fact that the good under consideration is (1) a commodity that is (2) used in indirect exchanges, and (3) bought and sold primarily for the purpose of such indirect exchanges.

Menger also stressed that money emerges spontaneously on the market as a response to the lack of the double coincidence of wants. Indirect exchanges are resorted to, for example, by the chair maker seeking to buy a dozen eggs from the farmer who already has enough chairs, or by the painter trying to purchase a glass of beer from the brewer who does not care for art. They first exchange their products into highly marketable commodities, such as salt, wheat, or silver coins, in order to exchange these "media of exchange" against eggs and beer in a subsequent deal. The significance of this fact was that a monetary system could come into being without a prior social contract and without government fiat.[5]

---

[5]Although Menger delivered a painstaking analysis of the process of the emergence of money (a process that was in his view the best illustration of the emergence of social institutions) he was not the first economist to point out that money does not come into being by social contract. Among Menger's predecessors were John Law (1705), Ferdinando Galliani (1751), Étienne de Condillac (1776), Adam Smith (1776), Antonio Genovesi (1788), Jean-Baptiste Say (1802), and Richard Whately (1832). On the emergence of this approach in the eighteenth century see Arthur E. Monroe, *Monetary Theory before Adam Smith* (New York: Augustus M. Kelley, [1923] 1966).

Mises added to and refined this analysis of the nature of money in four ways.

First, he took issue with the idea that the functions of money—being a means of exchange, a store of value, a means of payment, a means of deferred payments, a *numéraire* (measure of value)—were of equal importance. Mises argued that a commodity could play the role of *numéraire* only because it was used as a means of exchange; and, similarly, a commodity was held as a store of value precisely because it was marketable. Thus there was a hierarchical order of the functions of money: the means of exchange was primordial, being a necessary condition for the others.

Second, Mises developed a comprehensive typology of monetary objects—that is, in Mengerian language, of all the things generally accepted as media of exchange. On the most fundamental level, he distinguished several types of "money in the narrower sense" from several types of "money surrogates" or

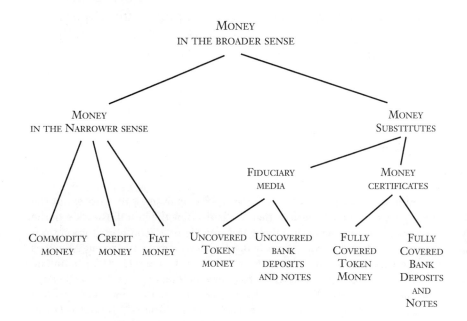

substitutes. Money in the narrower sense is a good in its own right. In contrast, money substitutes were legal titles to money in the narrower sense. They were typically issued by banks and were redeemable in real money at the counters of the issuing bank (see diagram on the previous page).

In establishing this fundamental distinction between money and money titles, he applied crucial insights of Böhm-Bawerk's pioneering work on the economics of legal entities. He stressed: "Claims are not goods; they are means of obtaining disposal over goods. This determines their whole nature and economic significance."[6] As his exposition in later parts of the book would show, these distinctions have great importance, both for the integration of monetary theory within the framework of Menger's theory of value and prices, and for the analysis of the role of banking within the monetary system. At the heart of his theory of banking is a comparative analysis of the economic significance of two very different types of money substitutes. Mises observed that money substitutes could be either covered by a corresponding amount of money, in which case they were "money certificates," or they could lack such coverage, in which case they were fiduciary media—*Umlaufsmittel*. Mises devotes the entire last third of his book to an analysis of the economic consequences of the use of *Umlaufsmittel*.[7]

---

[6]Mises, *Theory of Money and Credit*, p. 65; also Mises quoted Böhm-Bawerk's *Rechte und Verhältnisse vom güterwirthschaftlichen Standpunkte*, pp. 120ff.

[7]Regrettably, this comparative focus of his analysis was lost in the English translation of the title of the book: *Theory of Money and Credit*. The term *Umlaufsmittel*, which literally translates into "means of circulation," was rendered in the English text as "fiduciary media." Consequently the title of the book should have been Theory of Money and Fiduciary Media, but the publisher decided that the unusual terminology would irritate readers and thus opted for the smoother but toothless *Theory of Money and Credit*, failing to honor the fact that even in the original German version the expression was unusual. Mises was hostile to innovations in language that were not justified by the analysis of hitherto neglected phenomena. But the difference between money certificates on the one hand, and *Umlaufsmittel* on the other was such

Third, Mises refuted the idea that money prices are a measure of value. Here he relied on the work of the Czech economist Franz Cuhel who some years earlier, in his *Zur Lehre von den Bedürfnissen* (On the Theory of Needs), had clarified several fundamental issues of the new Mengerian price theory.[8] Cuhel was a champion of the psychological theory of marginal utility (Gossen-Jevons-Wieser), but several of his contributions to the theory of value and utility proved useful despite that fact.

Cuhel refuted Böhm-Bawerk and Wieser's quantitative claims about marginal utility, which referred to homogeneous units of a supply of goods, where each individual unit provides the same utility. According to Böhm-Bawerk, the utilities derived from the use of several units could be added, to the point that the utility, say, of consuming fifteen plums equals exactly fifteen times the utility of consuming one plum. But Cuhel objected that this contradicted the basic idea of the law of diminishing marginal utility, namely, that the satisfaction derived from the consumption of each additional unit of the good is lower than the utility derived from the consumption of the previous unit.[9]

---

a neglected phenomenon, to the point that established scientific terminology even lacked the means for expressing this difference. Mises thus introduced the expression *Umlaufsmittel* for this purpose and even used it in the title of his book to highlight its importance.

[8]See Franz Cuhel, *Zur Lehre von den Bedürfnissen. Theoretische Untersuchungen über das Grenzgebiet von Ökonomik und Psychologie* (Innsbruck: Wagner, 1907).

[9]See ibid., pp. 190f. Böhm-Bawerk had made this claim in a long essay on the theory of value, his first statement on value theory. See Böhm-Bawerk, "Grundzüge der Theorie des wirtschaftlichen Güterwertes," *Jahrbücher für Nationalökonomie und Statistik* n.s. 13 (1886): 48. It was this passage that met with criticism in Cuhel and Mises. Mises said many years later that, in distinct contrast to corresponding passages in Böhm-Bawerk's *Positive Theory of Capital* (New York: G.E. Stechert, 1930), the statement in *Grundzüge* "was incompatible with the whole tenor of Böhm's theory" (Mises to A.E. Foerster, letter dated March 2, 1965; Grove City Archive: Böhm-Bawerk file).

Cuhel also made a devastating case against interpersonal comparisons of satisfactions. The benefits derived from the consumption of two different goods could be compared only indirectly, and only in one narrow case, namely, in the case of individual decision-making at one point of time. From the fact that an individual chooses to enjoy satisfaction A rather than B, one can infer that A yields more satisfaction to this person than B does, because at the time of the choice both A and B were present and competed directly with one another.[10] Hence, the observed choices of individuals provide evidence about the relative size of enjoyment. But this is the only type of evidence available because it is fundamentally impossible to perceive the comparative satisfactions of other people.[11] One can only have direct knowledge of the utilities that the satisfaction of various needs has for oneself. Other people's utilities have to be inferred, indirectly, from their actual decision-making.

It follows that there is no such thing as value calculation or even value measurement. Even money does not have a constant value, and is therefore unable to provide the basis for a value calculus. Moreover, since money prices are the result of individual valuation processes, they are individual historical events, always determined by the particular circumstances in which they emerge. Contrary to what Walras's system of equations

---

This letter raises a certain problem because Mises here said that Böhm-Bawerk eventually realized his error and expressed the correct formulation in a later edition of *Capital and Interest* (South Holland, Ill.: Libertarian Press, 1959, vol. 2, bk. 3, part A, chap. 3, p. 148). But in the second edition of *Theorie des Geldes und der Umlaufsmittel*, 2nd ed. (Munich and Leipzig: Duncker & Humblot, 1924, p. 13), Mises said Böhm-Bawerk had not said anything new on this matter.

[10]See Cuhel, *Zur Lehre von den Bedürfnissen*, pp. 178f.

[11]See ibid., p. 210. Cuhel called subjective utilities by the unusual name of "Egenzen." In an analogous case, Vilfredo Pareto called subjective utility "ophélimité."

suggests, there are no constant relationships between money prices of different times and places.

It was therefore out of the question to follow Irving Fisher in his attempt to establish a quantitative law—such as in physics— of the relationship between the quantity of money and money prices (the price level). Mises placed great emphasis on this cru- cial implication of value theory for the methodology of eco- nomics:

> Because there are no constant relations in the field of human action, the equations of mathematical catal- lactics cannot be made to serve practical problems in the same way the equations of mechanics solve prob- lems through the use of data and constants that have been ascertained empirically.
>
> In my book on money I did not say one contro- versial word against the mathematical school. I pre- sented the correct doctrine and refrained from attacking the method of mathematicians. In fact, I even resisted the temptation to dissect the empty term "velocity." I refuted mathematical economics by proving that the quantity of money and the purchas- ing power of the monetary unit are not inversely pro- portional. This proof demonstrated that the only constant relationship which was believed to exist between "economic quantities" is a variable deter- mined by the data of each individual case. It thus exploded the equations of exchange of Irving Fisher and Gustav Cassel.[12]

Mises's criticism of the mechanical version of the quantity theory had an impact well beyond the theory of money. For this version of the quantity theory represented a larger agenda: a quantitative view of social science in general. Mises showed that there are no quantitative constants linking human actions to

---

[12]Mises, *Notes and Recollections*, p. 58.

repercussions in the social realm. An increased demand for apples would in all cases lead to higher apple prices than would otherwise have existed, but there is no law that tells us that a 10 percent increase of the apple demand will cause, say, an 8 percent or a 14 percent increase of apple prices. Actual quantities will always depend on the particular circumstances of each individual case.

Fourth, and finally, Mises dealt more explicitly than Menger with the claims of the monetary statists or "chartalists." Whereas Menger had argued that money could emerge spontaneously on the market, the statist scholars asserted that money was a creation of the state. Debate on this topic can be traced back to the times of Plato and Aristotle. It ran all through the Middle Ages and was only settled, for a short while, by the classical economists, who had argued along Mengerian lines. But at the end of the nineteenth century the statists struck back. Cernuschi in France, Neupauer in Austria, and Lexis in Germany reasserted the view that money is what the state declares to be such.[13] But the most famous champion of this view was Georg Knapp—the same Knapp who had pioneered the studies on Germanic rule as a liberating force for East-European peasants. In his *Staatliche Theorie des Geldes* (State Theory of Money), Knapp argued that money was a creation of the legal order and that the theory of money therefore had to be studied as a branch of legal history.[14] According to Knapp, money came into being

---

[13]See Henri Cernuschi, *Nomisma; or, "Legal Tender"* (New York: Appleton & Co., 1877); Josef von Neupauer, *Die Schäden und Gefahren der Valutaregulierung für die Volkswirtschaft und die Kriegsbereitschaft* (Vienna: Lesk & Schwidernoch, 1892); Wilhelm Lexis, "Papiergeld," *Handwörterbuch der Staatswissenschaften* (Jena: Gustav Fischer, 1893; 2nd ed., 1901, 3rd ed., 1910). Mises mentions Neupauer's book in Mises, "Die wirtschaftspolitischen Motive der österreichischen Valutaregulierung," *Zeitschrift für Volkswirtschaft, Sozialpolitik und Verwaltung* 16 (1907): 578.

[14]See Georg F. Knapp, *Staatliche Theorie des Geldes*, 2nd ed. (Munich & Leipzig: Duncker & Humblot, 1918), p. 1.

through government proclamation. The state says that this or that is money, and it suddenly becomes a token for some corresponding amount of real goods. The essence of money was therefore to be a government-proclaimed token (*charta* in Latin) that could be used as a legally valid means of payment.[15]

Knapp's views were not well received at first,[16] but did find early support from prominent bankers[17] and eventually won many converts to the state theory of money. His chartalist theory did, after all, perfectly complement the statist convictions already prevalent among German economic professors. As Mises later observed:

> The statist school of German economics has probably reached its high point in Georg Friedrich Knapp's *State Theory of Money*. It is not per se remarkable that this theory has been formulated; after all, its tenets have been championed for centuries in the writings of canonists, jurists, romantics, and certain socialists. What was remarkable was rather the success of the book.[18]

---

[15]See ibid., p. 31. Knapp thought he had to create an entirely new vocabulary to adequately deal with the theory of money and among many other innovations came up with the expression "chartal."

[16]In particular Andreas Voigt, one of the leaders of the small but growing cadre of anti-Schmoller economists, gave Knapp an unfavorable review. See Andres Voigt, "Die staatliche Theorie des Geldes," *Zeitschrift für die gesamte Staatswissenschaft* 62 (1906): 317–40.

[17]See L. Calligaris, "Staatliche Theorie des Geldes," *Münchener Allgemeine Zeitung* (February 1, 1906); idem, "Staatliche Theorie des Geldes," *Österreichische Rundschau* 7, no. 80 (May 10, 1906); F. Bendixen, *Das Wesen des Geldes* (Leipzig: Duncker & Humblot, 1908), p. 3; idem, "Fünf Jahre Geldtheorie," *Bank-Archiv* 10, no. 10 (1911): 145ff.; W. Lexis, "Eine neue Geldtheorie," *Archiv für Sozialwissenschaften und Sozialpolitik* 5 (1906): 557–74; idem, "Die Knappsche Geldtheorie," *Jahrbücher für Nationalökonomie und Statistik*, 3rd series, 32 (1906): 534–45.

[18]Ludwig von Mises, *Staat, Nation und Wirtschaft* (Vienna: Manz, 1919), p. 5, n. 3. Mises referred to Anderson's verdict that Knapp's book "has had wide

Knapp's fundamental error was in failing to see that government orders can only be relevant in the context of presently existing contracts involving deferred payments. *Ex post*, governments can determine what should be counted as "money" and, hence, what should be counted as payment. But it does not have the power to impose on market participants the future use of any means of exchange:

> Business usage alone can transform a commodity into a common medium of exchange. It is not the state, but the common practice of all those who have dealings in the market, that creates money.[19]

Integration of Value Theory and the Theory of Money

Although the new marginalist approach to the theory of value and prices had thoroughly transformed economic science, the theory of money had been left virtually untouched. Here Menger, Jevons, and Walras championed the same view as the classical economists, stressing that money is merely instrumental in acquiring "real" goods—goods which have some beneficial impact on human life—without itself being such a good. From an individual perspective, they argued, the ultimate purpose of market exchanges is never to exchange "real goods" against money, but to exchange real goods against other real goods. And taking the perspective of the national economy, they emphasized that the quantity of money did not affect the overall available quantity of goods.

---

influence on German thinking on money. It is typical of the tendency in German thought to make the State the center of everything." Benjamin M. Anderson, *The Value of Money* (New York: Macmillan, 1917), p. 433. He also quoted Carl Menger's exasperated comment on the success of the *State Theory of Money*: "It is the logical development of Prussian police science. What are we to think of a nation whose elite, after two hundred years of economics, admire such nonsense, which is not even new, as highest revelation?" Mises, *Erinnerungen*, p. 20; *Notes and Recollections*, p. 35.

[19]Mises, *Theory of Money and Credit*, p. 93.

From these insights they concluded that money was irrelevant to the wealth of the nation, and that political economy (which dealt with the economic interests of the whole nation) could afford to ignore money when analyzing the nation's welfare.[20] The most famous metaphor for this view was the "veil of money"—the notion that money is merely an intermediate layer between the human person and the real economy. John Stuart Mill had given clear expression to this perspective:

> Things which by barter would exchange for one another, will, if sold for money, sell for an equal amount of it, and so will exchange for one another still, though the process of exchanging them will consist of two operations instead of only one. The relations of commodities to one another remain unaltered by money: the only new relation introduced is their relation to money itself; how much or how little money they will exchange for; in other words, how the Exchange Value of money itself is determined.[21]

Money, according to Mill, did not influence the wealth of nations whatsoever—it just "reflected" or "corresponded to" the underlying non-monetary reality. Menger, Jevons, and Walras also endorsed this view and, consequently, they accorded all their attention to the supposedly "real" factors of the economy, to the neglect of monetary theory.

Neither champions nor opponents of the new economic theory failed to notice this neglect. The Swedish economist Knut Wicksell observed that the new discoveries in value theory had

---

[20]This particular standpoint for evaluating social problems is also reflected in the standard German names for the discipline of economics: "Nationalökonomie" (national economics) and "Volkswirtschaftslehre" (theory of the economy of the nation).

[21]John Stuart Mill, *Principles of Political Economy* (Fairfield, Conn.: Augustus M. Kelley, [1848] 1976), bk. 3, chap. 7, § 3, p. 488.

not been applied to money,[22] and the brilliant German economist Karl Helfferich even thought the new marginalist approach *could not* be applied to money. In his book *Das Geld*, the future director of Deutsche Bank and German Minister of Finance argued that in the marginal-utility approach (which in his understanding explained the market prices of goods as a consequence of the psychological utility of the various services of these goods) the price-determining utility of a good depended exclusively on the available quantity of the good. But in the case of money, this exclusive dependency could never be given. While the services derived from any other good were independent of its market price, the services derived from the use of money depended directly on its market prices (that is, its purchasing power). In other words, the marginal utility of money depends not only on its quantity, but also on its market prices. Therefore any attempt to explain the value of money on the basis of the marginalist approach involved an inescapable circle: the market price for money could not be inferred from its marginal utility, because its utility itself depended on its market price.[23]

Wieser's Theory of Money

The first reaction from the Austrian camp came from Friedrich von Wieser, when he chose the value of money as the topic for his inaugural lecture at the University of Vienna on October 26, 1903. The lecture was published under the title "*Der Geldwert und seine geschichtlichen Veränderungen*" (The Value of Money and its Historical Changes).[24] It was the first statement of

---

[22]See Knut Wicksell, *Geldzins und Güterpreise* (Jena: Gustav Fischer Verlag, 1898).

[23]See Karl Helfferich, *Das Geld*, 5th ed. (Leipzig: Hirschfeld, [1903] 1921), pp. 544ff. It is noteworthy that in his exposition Helfferich conflates physical and value terms.

[24]See Friedrich von Wieser, "Der Geldwert und seine geschichtlichen Veränderungen," *Zeitschrift für Volkswirtschaft, Socialpolitik und Verwaltung* 13

Wieser's ideas on how the theory of money related to the Austrian theory of value. Monetary theory remained at the center of Wieser's economic research until his death in 1926. He wrote two more lengthy papers for the 1909 Vienna meeting of the *Verein für Socialpolitik*, and also the lengthy entry on money for the postwar edition of the standard German social-science dictionary, the *Handwörterbuch der Staatswissenschaften*. He worked on this last piece until he was virtually on his deathbed.

These publications, which presented the first attempt to integrate marginal-value theory and monetary theory, reserved for Wieser a place of great authority among German-language monetary economists. His impact on German monetary thought was reinforced of course by his authority as one of the founding fathers of the Austrian School. But the main reason he rose to preeminence in monetary economics was that his ideas on money fit well with the established notions of the great majority of his colleagues—far better than the theory of money that Mises was about to present in 1912. Wieser was a representative of the Banking School, whose ideas reigned supreme in turn-of-the-century Germany; Mises developed the theory of the Currency School.[25,26]

(1904); reprinted in Wieser, *Gesammelte Abhandlungen* (Tübingen: Mohr, 1929), pp. 164–92.

[25]Mises later explained that the tenets of the Currency School were unacceptable to the *kathedersocialist* mindset because it seemed to leave no scope for government intervention. The German professors

> favored the Banking School. The victory of the Historical School practically brought excommunication of the Currency School. Karl Marx, Adolf Wagner, Helfferich, Hilferding, Havenstein, and Bendixen held to the doctrines of the Banking School. (Ludwig von Mises, *A Critique of Interventionism* [New York: Arlington House, 1977], p. 94)

Even after World War I, the mainstream opinion among German monetary economists was that the Banking School had won the debate with the Currency School on virtually all substantive issues. The fact that John Stuart Mill, arch-advocate of the veil-of-money theory, endorsed the banking theory with only slight modifications played a crucial role in its sweeping success. See

All essential elements of Wieser's monetary thought were present in his initial 1903 lecture. According to his fundamental assumption, there was no such thing as a demand for money *per se*. To the extent that a good was used in indirect exchanges, it was not demanded as such, but only as an intermediary to obtain a "real good." Money did not have value *per se*, but only represented the value of those other goods that could be exchanged for it. Wieser did not deny that historical media of exchange such as gold and silver were commodity monies, but in his view they were commodities only insofar as they were demanded for non-monetary purposes. Modern media of exchange such as paper money and "money surrogates" (legal claims on money that can be used in place of corresponding amounts of real money), which were used exclusively as exchange intermediaries, were not commodities at all. There was no demand for the paper notes themselves—only for the commodities for which they were exchanged. The value of the former was entirely derived from the demand for the latter.

But if modern money is not a commodity, what is it? And how can it be used in market exchanges if it cannot itself be the object of an exchange? Wieser insisted that while money does enable the "transfer" of commodities from one owner to another, it more importantly *measures* the value of the commodities it helps to transfer.[27] In short, money is essentially a

---

W. Mildschuh, "Geschichtliche Entwicklung der Geldtheorie," *Handwörterbuch der Staatswissenschaften* 4 (1927): 720; J.S. Mill, *Principles of Political Economy*, book 3, chap. 24. Mill's view was probably strongly influenced by the crisis that erupted in 1846 despite the Bank Charter Act (1844), which sought to put the principles of the Currency School into legislation.

[26]In *Geldzins und Güterpreise* (pp. 34ff. and passim), Knut Wicksell had already delivered a scathing critique of the main tenets of the Banking School. His book was pointedly ignored at the time, as was Mises's *Theory of Money and Credit*. Only after World War I did both books enjoy a renaissance.

[27]See Wieser, "Der Geldwert und seine geschichtlichen Veränderungen," pp. 180f. This was also Knut Wicksell's view; see in particular *Geldzins und*

standard of value, a measuring rod or *numéraire*, and it is used in market exchanges to measure the value of the commodities against which it is exchanged. For Wieser, this measuring process is essentially a ranking of the exchanged commodity against the total array of the other commodities from which money derives its value.[28]

It is modern money's "elasticity," according to Wieser, that makes it such an ideal standard of value. Praising Thomas Tooke, the great champion of the Banking School, Wieser argued that increases in the quantity of commodities induce a corresponding rise in the quantity of money surrogates and of the so-called velocity of money. These increases do not exercise an independent influence on money prices. Rather, their elasticity ensures that monetary equilibrium is automatically preserved at the existing purchasing power of money.[29]

What about Helfferich's critique? Is it not circular to assert that money measures the value of commodities, if its own value is entirely derived from commodities? Wieser, who did not bother to mention Helfferich's book, probably thought that he had disposed of the circularity problem by stressing that money is not a commodity. There is no circularity because money is a mere placeholder for those other goods that can be bought with

---

Güterpreise, chap. 3, where he elaborates on the distinction between relative prices and money prices. Wicksell's book had virtually no impact on the German scene at the time it first appeared. But his monetary views seem to have influenced his countryman Gustav Cassel, and through Cassel they eventually reached a broad academic audience after World War I, when Cassel's textbook became the main work of reference on theoretical economics at German Universities. See Gustav Cassel, *Theoretische Sozialökonomik*, 4th ed. (Leipzig: Deichert, 1927), in particular book three.

[28]For similar reasons, Wicksell believed that a cashless payment system or pure credit economy was possible. See his *Geldzins und Güterpreise*, pp. 58, 64ff.

[29]See Wieser, "Der Geldwert und seine geschichtlichen Veränderungen," pp. 169, 175, 179.

its help. The goods measure themselves, so to speak, through money. Of course market prices are not necessarily proportional to values, but as he had already argued in *Natural Value* (1889), this problem vanishes to the extent that the national economy approaches the ideal of a perfect communist society.

Wieser also analyzed the determination of the value of money from a completely different angle by introducing the *diachronic* perspective: how the value of money is based in changes over time. Again, he did not explicitly mention the Helfferich critique, but his diachronic determination of the value of money, implicitly, refutes the charge of circular reasoning. The Helfferich critique applies only to attempts at a *synchronic* determination of the purchasing power of money: one cannot derive market prices for today's money from today's value of money, but this criticism does not apply if the value of today's money depends on yesterday's prices. Wieser showed that this was in fact the case. The apparent circularity vanishes and a pure causal chain appears: money prices from two days ago determine the value of money yesterday, which determines money prices today, etc.

Wieser argued that the value of money had a "historical source" in the needs that are satisfied by those commodities that were first used as money. This original use-value of the original money-commodity was the base from which further changes to the purchasing power of money occurred. At each point, the past value of money served as a basis to evaluate the commodities that were now being exchanged. Insofar as these exchanges modified already existing prices, or added new prices to the total array of commodity prices, the value of money was itself modified, thus changing the basis for future measurements.[30] Wieser stressed that his theory implied that (1) money could come into existence *only* as commodity money, but (2) once it had come into existence and a historical basis for future modifications of its value

---

[30]See ibid., pp. 175, 184.

had been created, it no longer had to remain commodity money. A pure paper money was therefore possible at some later stage.[31]

Wieser placed great emphasis on this point because it alone seemed to explain recent events in the development of the Austro-Hungarian monetary system. Before 1892, Austria-Hungary had officially been on a silver standard. But in order to finance its wars of 1848–1849, 1859–1860, and 1866, the monarchy had issued great quantities of paper notes. These notes were irredeemable at the time of issue, but there were hopes of future redeemability, and thus they were used as money. Their circulation was further bolstered through legal-tender laws. Because redemption was uncertain, the bills circulated at a discount. But in early 1879, something completely unusual occurred: silver sold at a discount and the government bills began circulating at a premium. What had happened? During the previous years, silver production had increased considerably, and in many countries silver had been replaced by gold as a currency. With diminished demand and increased supply, it was only natural that the price of silver fell drastically.[32]

Or was it? Wieser believed that the event was actually a refutation of what he called the "metallistic" theory of money. According to this theory, the value of money did not come from demand, but from the inherent value of the metal that was used as money. The champions of metallism could therefore easily explain why paper circulated at a discount—after all, it was not real money. But they were at a loss to explain how the paper money could ever become more valuable than the supposedly real money. For thirteen years, the Austro-Hungarian monetary system seemed to be real-world proof of the possibility of a pure fiat

---

[31]See ibid., pp. 176f.

[32]See Reinhard Kamitz, "Die österreichische Geld- und Währungspolitik von 1848 bis 1948," Hans Mayer, ed., *Hundert Jahre österreichischer Wirtschaftsentwicklung, 1848–1948* (Vienna: Springer, 1949), pp. 145f.

money. And Wieser's diachronic theory of the value of money delivered the only available explanation of this phenomenon.

But this did not exhaust the explanatory power of Wieser's approach to monetary analysis. Making use of his measuring-rod theory of money, Wieser also gave an original account of the secular rise of money prices.[33] He argued that this phenomenon resulted from a great transformation observable in all developed nations, namely, the abandonment of barter and the adoption of monetary exchanges. In short, the purchasing power of money decreased because the monetary economy became ever more widespread.[34] Wieser argued as follows: because more and more commodities were exchanged against money, the marginal value of these additional commodities constantly decreased; this lower marginal value led in turn to a corresponding decrease of the marginal value of money, that is, to a lower purchasing power of money.

Six years later, he presented important clarifications of his theory in "Der Geldwert und seine Veränderungen" (The Value of Money and its Changes), a lengthy paper he wrote for the 1909 Vienna meeting of the *Verein*.[35] In this paper he made his case for the full integration of monetary theory and general value theory, spelling out how his theory of the value of money related to the subjectivist theory of value.

---

[33]See Wieser, "Der Geldwert und seine geschichtlichen Veränderungen," pp. 184ff.

[34]He admitted that the increased production of commodity money was another factor explaining the secular decline of the purchasing power of money (see ibid., p. 192). Another factor was government expenditures, which were "shifted forward" in the form of taxation and thus "added" to prices, implying a lower purchasing power of money (see ibid., p. 186).

[35]Friedrich von Wieser, "Der Geldwert und seine Veränderungen," *Schriften des Vereins für Socialpolitik* 132 (Munich and Leipzig: Duncker & Humblot, 1909); reprinted in Wieser, *Gesammelte Abhandlungen*, Hayek, ed., pp. 193–242.

The central argument of what later came to be called the "income theory of the value of money" runs as follows: as an individual's income increases, the value of the marginal money unit decreases. Consider an individual agent who, in a given period, spends his entire disposable monetary income *at given prices* on consumers' goods. Wieser argued that the subjective marginal value of money was derived from (equal to) the utility of the least important consumers' good that he could buy with this income. Equipped with the knowledge of his subjective marginal value of money, which henceforth serves him as a personal measuring rod, the agent then sets out to buy and sell goods on the market, always measuring them in comparison to the utility of the least important consumers' good he can afford to buy.[36]

In his 1903 lecture, Wieser had emphasized that because the value of money is merely derivative, it is not really money that is exchanged on the market: real goods are exchanged against one another.[37] Money subdivides "the original exchange" into "two separate parts." First commodity A is exchanged for a sum of money; then this sum is exchanged against some other commodity, B. In 1909, Wieser further clarified this view, stating that demand and supply on the market were manifest only in A and B, whereas money was "merely interposed." According to Wieser this was the *only* difference between direct and indirect exchange. The benefit of this interposition is that money makes a "great social bookkeeping" possible. Wieser uses language borrowed from the warehouse business to describe economic processes within the national economy. In his metaphor, each

---

[36]See ibid., pp. 204f., 208, 211. Wieser stressed that the value of money was determined in monetary *exchanges* of *consumers'* goods only. This precluded taking into consideration, for example, idle cash holdings not used in market exchanges, or monetary exchanges on the markets for producers' goods. The values of producers' goods were in fact merely derived from the values of consumers' goods (see ibid., pp. 214, 219).

[37]See ibid., pp. 165, 173. Wieser here argued that money was an object of exchange only in case it was bought and sold as monetary capital.

quantity of money functions as a deposit receipt that can be easily transferred from one member of the community to another, thereby giving them both access to a common pool where each deposits the fruit of his labor:

> Between all those, who throw commodities into the national-economic process in order to take out commodities in turn, there is some great national book-keeping the meaning of which is that everyone has to throw in a real value that is as large as the value that he wants to take out.[38]

Mises later called this characterization of the nature of money "assignment theory" (*Anweisungstheorie*) because its essence is to conceive of money as a token.[39] The theory goes back to the eighteenth century, to John Law, the greatest champion of inflation before Keynes. Blurring the difference between money and credit, Law wrote:

> Domestick Trade depends on the Money. A greater Quantity employes more People than a lesser Quantity. . . . They may be brought to Work on Credit, and that is not practicable, unless the Credit have a Circulation, so as to supply the Workman with necessaries; If that's suppos'd, then that Credit is Money,

---

[38]Wieser, "Der Geldwert und seine Veränderungen," p. 220. Joseph Schumpeter adopted the same point of view. See his *Theorie der wirtschaftlichen Entwicklung* (Leipzig: Duncker & Humblot, 1911), p. 196.

[39]In the English edition of Mises's book, *Anweisungstheorie* is translated as "claim theory" (see Mises, *Theory of Money and Credit*, appendix). The translation is however somewhat inappropriate. The term "claim" involves an underlying legalistic interpretation of what the assignment theorists hold the nature of money to be. But compared to a legal interpretation of money as a claim, the flaws of the assignment theory look minor. It is obvious that market exchanges are categorically different from the redemption of claims. But assignment theorists never subscribe to such clearly stated (and clearly wrong) interpretations of money. Their doctrine survives precisely because it is ambiguous.

and will have the same effects, on Home, and For-
reign Trade.[40]

In the mid-nineteenth century, the assignment theory came
to be fully developed in the writings of the champions of the
Banking School.[41] From there it made its way into the Germanies. Early German proponents of the *Anweisungstheorie* were
Otto Michaelis and Adolf Wagner. The latter wrote:

> The idea of money is the one of a transferable IOU
> for the services that the money owner has provided to
> civil society. It empowers this money owner to with-
> draw the value equivalent of his services, in terms of
> goods he desires, from any owner of the latter.[42]

In the age of the Historical School, which despised economic
theorizing, Wagner's writings on money became the primary

---

[40]John Law, *Money and Trade Considered with a Proposal for Supplying the
Nation with Money* (Edinburgh: Anderson, 1705), chap. 2. While Mises
rejected this view, he accepted as fundamental the distinction that Law had
made between the monetary and non-monetary demand for money:

> It is reasonable to think Silver was Barter'd as it was valued
> for its Uses as a Mettal, and was given as Money according
> to its Value in Barter. The additional Use of Money Silver
> was apply'd to would add to its Value, because as Money it
> remedied the Disadvantages and Inconveniences of Barter,
> and consequently the demand for Silver encreasing, it
> received an additional Value equal to the greater demand its
> Use as Money occasioned. (ibid., chap. 1)

[41]See in particular Henry D. Macleod, *Theory and Practice of Banking*, 2
vols. (London: Longman, Brown, Green, and Longmans, 1855), vol. 1. In the
first chapter, the author characterizes money as an "evidence of debt being
made transferable." Again, although Mises rejected this opinion, he learned
an important lesson from MacLeod, namely, that bank deposits are substitutes for money in essentially the same way as banknotes. However, while
MacLeod inferred that there was no point in limiting the issuance of new
notes, Mises concluded that deposit creation had to be limited, just as note
issues had been limited through Peel's Bank Charter Act.

[42]Adolf Wagner, *Die russische Papierwährung* (Riga: Kymmel, 1868), p. 44.

source of information on these topics. He converted the next few generations of German-language economists to the principles of the Banking School.[43] In Austria, his ideas were developed by Wieser, Schumpeter, and Hilferding. The very first German-language economist who contested this new orthodoxy was Mises. He sought to vindicate the principles of the Currency School, which he blended with Menger's analysis of money. At the heart of his theory is the insight that money is an economic good in its own right, not just a representation of other goods.

Nothing precise is known about how Mises came to hold these views, but Menger's influence was certainly compounded by Böhm-Bawerk's analogous perspectives on the subject. He had emphasized the crucial points in his university lectures:

> Money is by its nature a good like any other good; it is merely in greater demand and can circulate more widely than all other commodities. Money is no symbol or pledge; it is not the sign of a good, but bears its value in itself. It is itself really a good.[44]

It is not surprising that Böhm-Bawerk and Mises came to radically different policy conclusions from Wieser and Schumpeter. Whereas Mises held that the stock of money was ultimately irrelevant, Wieser stressed that money's function as a measuring rod must not be interfered with. Its value should be as stable as possible, and all destabilizing influences should be eliminated. Wieser suggested that one could optimize the national currency by abolishing commodity money and putting a pure paper money in its place. In fact, paper would be more

---

[43]Mises discusses Wagner's impact in *Money, Method, and the Market Process: Essays by Ludwig von Mises*, Richard Ebeling, ed. (Boston: Kluwer, 1990), chap. 7.

[44]Eugen von Böhm-Bawerk, *Innsbrucker Vorlesungen über Nationalökonomie*, Shigeki Tomo, ed. (Marburg: Metropolis, 1998), p. 211. This is from his Innsbruck lectures in the early 1880s. One must assume that Böhm-Bawerk stressed the same point in his lectures in Vienna.

stable because its value is not subject to the influence of the non-monetary demand for the monetary commodity.[45]

Wieser also clarified his theory that the secular increase of money prices was a consequence of the substitution of monetary exchanges for barter. He argued that the development of the monetary economy brings ever more factors of production within the network of monetary exchanges. The money prices that have to be paid for these factors (which before were paid *in natura*) represent an increase of the monetary costs of production; and these increased costs have to be "added to" the selling prices. It is obvious that in this process aggregate monetary income increases while aggregate real income does not change, thus the value of money decreases. *Quod erat demonstrandum.*[46]

Mises's Theory of the Value of Money

Wieser had not gotten everything wrong. Explaining the present value of money by reference to its past value was a crucial breakthrough in monetary theory. Wieser's work inspired two young Vienna economists—Franz X. Weiss and Ludwig von Mises—to refine the raw idea and hammer out a new doctrine of the value of money.[47]

The "regression theorem," as Mises later called it, would become one of the pillars of his monetary thought, but first, let us consider two related problems of Wieser's version.

First, Wieser could not integrate the regression with the *pricing* process of the market. He had developed a pure *value* theory of the purchasing power of money: his general assumption was that the exchange ratios established between the various goods on the market were only a different expression of their value

---

[45]See Wieser, "Der Geldwert und seine Veränderungen," p. 240.

[46]See ibid., pp. 229f.

[47]See F.X. Weiss, "Die moderne Tendenz in der Lehre vom Geldwert," *Zeitschrift für Volkswirtschaft, Socialpolitik und Verwaltung* 19 (1909): 532ff.

ratios.[48] But Mises thought this assumption entirely untenable. There was no such correspondence between value and price, even in a perfect Wieserian communism. Menger and Böhm-Bawerk had convincingly argued that while market prices did result from individual valuations, they were quantitatively unrelated to the value from which they emerged.

The second fundamental flaw in Wieser's argument was that he did not think of money as a good in its own right. Money was but a token of underlying real goods—a "veil" or "assignment" (*Anweisung*)—and thus had no independent impact on the pricing process. This assumption contradicted one of the main tenets of marginal-value theory. While all other market exchanges result from inverse valuations—with each trading partner preferring the commodity that he bought to the price that he paid—market exchanges in money were, in Wieser's theory, acts that acknowledged *equality* of value.[49] By paying a certain amount of money to take some commodity out of the "social warehouse," one acknowledged it to be of equal value to the good one had sold before ("deposited in the social warehouse") to obtain that sum of money.

Mises's great achievement in his *Theory of Money and Credit* was in liberating us from the veil-of-money myth. Money is a commodity by its very nature, not just by historical accident. By realizing this, Mises was in a position to integrate the theory of money into the general framework of marginal-value theory.

His integration would combine the commodity nature of money with Menger's theory of value and prices as refined by Böhm-Bawerk, and also Wieser's insight that the present value of money required a diachronic explanation. Mises could even rely on Menger's theory of cash holdings, which already contained *in*

---

[48]Wicksell relied on the same assumption. See Wicksell, *Geldzins und Güterpreise*, pp. 17ff.

[49]Again, Wicksell's monetary thought suffered from the same flaw. See ibid. pp. 20f., 64f.

nuce the insight that money is itself an economic good and not just representative of other goods. But to combine these elements into one coherent theory required a radical break with time-honored pillars of monetary economics, in particular, with the classical tradition of presenting money as a mere veil. Mises was fully conscious that this was the key to his theory, which is why, in an introductory chapter of his book, he engaged in the somewhat tedious exercise of distinguishing various types of money proper (money in the narrower sense) from money substitutes. It was these substitutes in fact that were the sort of tokens or place holders that Wieser and the other champions of the assignment theory tacitly had in mind when they spoke of money. Mises's painstaking analysis demonstrated that mainstream theory had unduly generalized the features of money substitutes to money itself. While it is true that the value of a money substitute corresponds exactly to the value of the underlying real good (for example, 1 ounce of gold), the value of the gold money itself does not correspond to anything; rather it is determined by the same general law of diminishing marginal value that determines the values of all goods.

❧   ❧   ❧

Mises *almost* succeeded in dumping the veil-of-money myth. At one place he still reverted to this fallacious doctrine. He claimed that the value of a marginal unit of money is equal to the value of the commodity that the unit is destined to buy. Here is the relevant passage:

> The subjective value of money always depends on the subjective value of the other economic goods that can be obtained in exchange for it. Its subjective value is in fact a derived concept. If we wish to estimate the significance that a given sum of money has, in view of the known dependence upon it of a certain satisfaction, we can do this only on the assumption that the money possesses a given objective exchange value.

> "The exchange value of money is the anticipated use-value of the things that can be obtained with it."[50]
>
> Whenever money is valued by anybody it is because he supposes it to have a certain purchasing power.[51]

His error is precisely the *anticipated-use-value* sentence he quotes from Wieser. It is irreconcilable with his later statements in *Nationalökonomie* and *Human Action*, where he explains that the subjective value of a sum of money is the value of holding this quantity in one's cash balance.[52] The same error seems to be behind his claim that the increase of money substitutes in the previous twenty years or so (up to 1911) had allowed for higher economic growth than would have been possible with the quantity of gold, which grew at a slower pace.[53,54]

By the time he published his treatise *Nationalökonomie* (1940), he had removed these errors from his thinking.[55] But his

---

[50]Mises here quotes Friedrich von Wieser, *Der natürliche Wert* (Vienna: Hölder-Pichler-Tempsky, 1889) p. 46.

[51]See Mises, *Theory of Money and Credit*, p. 119.

[52]See Mises, *Nationalökonomie* (Geneva: Editions Union, 1940), pp. 361f.; *Human Action*, Scholar's edition (Auburn, Ala.: Ludwig von Mises Institute, 1998) p. 408.

[53]Similarly, in his first publication on monetary problems, he had asserted at the beginning of his exposition that the media of circulation need to be "adjusted" to the demand for money. And in the same vein, he talks about conditions for a possible lack of fiduciary media. Such a condition holds when the quantity of the means of payment lags behind the economic development. This would "certainly lead to credit restrictions and, as a consequence, symptoms of economic crises." See Mises, "Die wirtschaftspolitischen Motive der österreichischen Valutaregulierung," pp. 562, 572.

[54]Discussing a somewhat different issue, Mises later admitted that at the time he wrote *The Theory of Money and Credit* he "was still too much under the influence of Mill" (*Notes and Recollections*, p. 60). This prevented him from decisively arguing against Böhm-Bawerk's ideas about money-induced "frictions;" but Mill's influence seems to have reached further than that.

[55]See Nikolay Gertchev, "Dehomogenizing Mises's Monetary Theory," *Journal of Libertarian Studies* 18, no. 3 (2004): 57–90.

earlier monograph on the theory of money was still being taken as his final word on the subject. Don Patinkin, the most influential monetary theorist of the post-1945 era, criticized Mises by referring precisely to the passage quoted above, in which the old veil-of-money notion shows through. Patinkin said that these views implied a circular explanation of the value of money.[56] He was correct in this criticism, but his overall point— that his predecessors had not come up with a coherent explanation of the value of money—ignored Mises's later work: *Nationalökonomie* and *Human Action*.

Money is Not Neutral: Cantillon Effects

The insight that money is a good in its own right and not just a placeholder for other goods led Mises to place special emphasis on the impact of money on the real economy. It was customary to highlight the impact of inflation and deflation on deferred payments. Inflation would entail higher money prices—that is, a lower purchasing power of money—in the future, which in turn benefited debtors at the expense of creditors. Inversely, deflation would benefit creditors at the expense of debtors. So far, so good. Following classical economists such as David Ricardo, Mises stressed that inflation and deflation of the money supply could not possibly enhance the productive potential of the nation as a whole. But such changes did have *other* social consequences, in particular, for the composition of society and the allocation of resources.

Although inflation and deflation could not make society as a whole better off, they modified the distribution of resources among the individual members of society, and this necessarily affected the marginal value of the various uses of these

---

[56]See Don Patinkin, *Money, Interest, and Prices: An Integration of Monetary and Value Theory* (Evanston, Ill.: Row, Peterson, and Co., 1956).

resources. For example, inflation put more money in the hands of individual A (a debtor) and less money in the hands of individual B (a creditor); since these two individuals have different subjective values and different entrepreneurial visions and talents, they will use the money differently, investing it at different times and places, paying different wages to different persons at different rates, etc.

These simple considerations illustrate the pervasive impact of changes in the money supply on the real world—a fact that did not sit well with many of Mises's contemporaries, imbued as they were with the veil-of-money doctrine. Böhm-Bawerk for instance was reluctant to admit the real impact of money, because he was used to thinking of money in aggregate terms—not on the basis of the intra-social distribution and allocation. He tried to minimize the significance of Mises's findings. He thought that the income effect creates some occasional "frictions" but did not alter the long-term state of the economy and the society.[57]

Mises's analysis of the social consequences of inflation and deflation was not limited to the consideration of deferred payments. He also analyzed the redistributive impact of inflation and deflation on spot exchanges. In the case of inflation, for example, he observed that if it affected all members of society at the same time and to the same proportional extent, no redistributive effects would result. But in the real world this condition never holds true. Inflation first affects only some members of society, and through their interaction with others, it eventually affects the rest of society.

---

[57]See Mises, *Erinnerungen*, p. 37. In his lectures, Böhm-Bawerk had stressed the Cantillon effects, but believed that they would "mainly" entail a higher price level. Besides they would merely affect the relationship between debtors and creditors. Böhm-Bawerk, *Innsbrucker Vorlesungen über Nationalökonomie*, pp. 220f.

Let us, for instance, suppose that a new gold mine is opened in an isolated state. The supplementary quantity of gold that streams from it into commerce goes at first to the owners of the mine and then by turns to those who have dealings with them. If we schematically divide the whole community into four groups, the mine owners, the producers of luxury goods, the remaining producers, and the agriculturalists, the first two groups will be able to enjoy the benefits resulting from the reduction in the value of money, the former of them to a greater extent than the latter. But even as soon as we reach the third group, the situation is altered. The profit obtained by this group as a result of the increased demands of the first two will already be offset to some extent by the rise in the prices of luxury goods which will have experienced the full effect of the depreciation by the time it begins to affect other goods. Finally for the fourth group, the whole process will result in nothing but loss. The farmers will have to pay dearer for all industrial products before they are compensated by the increased prices of agricultural products. It is true that when at last the prices of agricultural products do rise, the period of economic hardship for the farmers is over; but it will no longer be possible for them to secure profits that will compensate them for the losses they have suffered. That is to say, they will not be able to use their increased receipts to purchase commodities at prices corresponding to the old level of the value of money; for the increase of prices will already have gone through the whole community. Thus the losses suffered by the farmers at the time when they still sold their products at the old low prices but had to pay for the products of others at the new and higher prices remain uncompensated. It is these losses of the groups that are the last to be reached by the variation in the value of money which ultimately constitute the source of the profits made by the mine owners and the groups most closely connected with them.[58]

---

[58]Mises, *Theory of Money and Credit*, pp. 239–40.

Thus inflation and—by implication—deflation are essentially redistributive phenomena. They cannot enrich society as a whole, but do affect distribution, allocation, and incomes within society.

Mises's analysis of effects of money on the real economy was based on his study of the great inflations of the past[59] and on his study of classical economics.[60] Today these effects are sometimes called the "Cantillon effects"[61]—named for the early eighteenth-century Irish-French banker and economist, Richard Cantillon, who in his *Essay on the Nature of Commerce in General* had first described the redistribution and reallocation effects of inflation.[62] The *Theory of Money and Credit* was one of

---

[59]His teacher Grünberg had analyzed the redistributive impact of inflation during the Napoleonic wars in Grünberg, *Studien zur österreichischen Agrargeschichte* (Leipzig: Duncker & Humblot, 1901), pp. 121ff. Mises had dealt with these cases on pp. 222ff. of the first edition of *Theorie des Geldes und der Umlaufsmittel* (1912). He eliminated these passages from further editions because he believed historical illustrations of the harmful effects of inflation were no longer necessary in light of recent firsthand experiences in Germany and Austria.

[60]He quotes David Hume and David Ricardo. Among his contemporaries, he merely refers to Rudolf Auspitz and Richard Lieben, *Untersuchungen über die Theorie des Preises* (Leipzig: Duncker & Humblot, 1889), p. 65. Mises quotes them on pp. 240f. of his *Theory of Money and Credit*. Other forerunners, whom Mises did not mention, were Mill, *Principles of Political Economy*, bk. 3, chap. 8, § 2, p. 491; Hermann Heinrich Gossen, *Entwickelung der Gesetze des menschlichen Verkehrs und der daraus fliessenden Regeln für menschliches Handeln* (Braunschweig: Vieweg & Sohn, 1854), pp. 205f.; and John E. Cairnes, "Essay Towards A Solution of the Gold Question: The Course of the Depreciation," *Essays in Political Economy: Theoretical and Applied* (London: Macmillan, [1858] 1873), pp. 53ff.

[61]The expression is Mark Blaug's. See Mark Blaug, *Economic Theory in Retrospect*, 4th ed. (Cambridge: Cambridge University Press, 1985), pp. 21ff.

[62]See Richard Cantillon, *Essay on the Nature of Commerce in General* (reprint, New Brunswick, N.J.: Transaction, 2001). Similarly, Mises also revived the analysis of local price differences, which had been neglected since Richard Cantillon. See Eduard Heimann, *History of Economic Doctrines: An Introduction to Economic Theory* (New York: New York University Press, 1945), p. 43.

the last treatises of the subject to highlight their importance. At the time of Mises's writing, Irving Fisher, Gustav Cassel and other economists began to neglect them and concentrate only on the *aggregate* consequences of changes in the money supply.[63] Their approach won the day and thus one of inflation's most pernicious effects came to fall beneath the purview of the new "macroeconomic" radar.[64]

Exchange Rate Determination: Purchasing Power Theory

Mises also took a position at odds with the mainstream view on another important issue: the factors determining the exchange rate between two monies. To do so, he revived an older doctrine that had been displaced by the prevailing veil-of-money myth.

Because mainstream economists conceived of the value of money as a mere reflection of the value of underlying real commodities, it was only natural for them to stipulate that exchange rates too were merely a reflection of some real state of affairs. Thus the balance-of-payments theory enjoyed a virtual monopoly in higher economic education and guided the policies of the German and Austro-Hungarian central banks.[65] According to

---

[63]See in particular Irving Fisher, *The Purchasing Power of Money: Its Determination and Relation to Credit, Interest, and Crises*, 2nd ed. (New York: Augustus M. Kelley, [1913] 1985).

[64]In contrast, Mises's analysis might have influenced John Maynard Keynes, who recognized the great importance of Cantillon effects and advocated monetary stabilization as a strategy for social conservation. See in particular John Maynard Keynes, *A Tract on Monetary Reform* (London: Macmillan, 1923); see also idem, *Indian Currency and Finance* (London: Macmillan, 1913); *The Economic Consequences of the Peace* (London: Macmillan, 1920). Keynes had dismissively reviewed Mises's book in the *Economic Journal* (September 1914): 417–19 in fairly vague and evasive terms. Later he confessed that "in German I can only clearly understand what I know already!" *Treatise on Money* (New York: Harcourt Brace, 1930), vol. 1, p. 199, footnote.

[65]See Otto Heyn, *Irrtümer auf dem Gebiete des Geldwesens* (Berlin, 1900), pp. 30f.; idem, *Die indische Währungsreform* (Berlin, 1903), p. 82; W. Lexis,

this theory, international monetary movements (and thus the exchange rate between different national currencies) tended to equal whatever rate equilibrated the relative weight of imports and exports of commodities and services, and of foreign credit and foreign debts. These real factors were the independent variables, whereas international monetary payments and the exchange rate were dependent variables. The political implication was that, when faced with an undesired depreciation in the exchange rate, governments had to act on those real factors to prevent their expression in monetary flows: they had to curtail imports through tariffs, import quotas, and other measures.

Mises had already rebelled against this orthodoxy in his first publication on monetary policy, his 1907 article on the motives behind the Austro-Hungarian Bank's regulation of exchange rates. There he asserted that the theory of the value of money was not yet sufficiently developed, and the relationship between the quantity of money and the exchange rate was unknown.[66] Five years later, the theory of the value of money was sufficiently well developed in his mind. He demonstrated that the balance-of-payments theorists had turned the real chain of causation on its head. The volume of imports and exports, and of foreign liabilities and credits was not independent of the exchange rate, but entirely dependent on it.

> The balance-of-payments theory forgets that the volume of foreign trade is completely dependent upon prices; that neither exportation nor importation can occur if there are no differences in prices to make trade profitable.[67]

"Papiergeld," *Handwörterbuch der Staatswissenschaften*, 3rd ed. (Jena: Gustav Fischer, 1909–1911), vol. 6, p. 989; Georg D. Knapp, *Staatliche Theorie des Geldes* (Leipzig, 1905), p. 208.

[66]See Ludwig von Mises, "Die wirtschaftspolitischen Motive der österreichischen Valutaregulierung," *Zeitschrift für Volkswirtschaft, Sozialpolitik und Verwaltung* 16 (1907), p. 565.

[67]Mises, *Theory of Money and Credit*, p. 284.

He went on to explain the root of the error:

> It cannot be doubted that if we simply look at the daily or hourly fluctuations on the exchanges we shall only be able to discover that the state of the balance of payments at any moment *does* determine the supply and the demand in the foreign-exchange market. But this is a mere beginning of a proper investigation into the determinants of the rate of exchange. The next question is, What determines the state of the balance of payments at any moment? And there is no other possible answer to this than that it is the price level and the purchases and sales induced by the price margins that determine the balance of payments. Foreign commodities can be imported, at a time when the rate of exchange is rising, only if they are able to find purchasers despite their high prices.[68]

Mises points out that it was Ricardo who had first developed the correct view of exchange rate determination. The exchange rate between two monies depended exclusively on the relative purchasing power of each. In a free market, exchange rates would tend to make it irrelevant which money is used to buy a non-monetary commodity:

> The different kinds of money are exchanged in a ratio corresponding to the exchange ratios existing between each of them and the other economic goods. If 1 kg of gold is exchanged for m kg of a particular sort of commodity, and 1 kg of silver for $m/15\frac{1}{2}$ kg of the same sort of commodity, then the exchange ratio between gold and silver will be established at $15\frac{1}{2}$. If some disturbance tends to alter this ratio between the two sorts of money, which we shall call the static or natural ratio, then automatic forces will be set in motion that will tend to re-establish it.[69]

---

[68]Ibid.
[69]Ibid., p. 207.

The political implications of this analysis are diametrically opposed to the ones suggested by the balance-of-payments doctrine. There is in fact no need to prevent a depreciation of the exchange rate through government intervention, because sooner or later the falling exchange rate would equilibrate the purchasing powers of the two monies, preventing a further fall.

As Mises later acknowledged, this idea was essentially contained already in the classical quantity theory of money, as well as Gresham's Law and the doctrine of the British Currency School. His analysis, which was based on the modern theory of subjective value, had refined these older views and restated them in a more nuanced manner, but the practical conclusion had remained the same. Mises said in retrospect:

> Governmental interventions that seek to regulate international monetary flows to provide the "necessary" quantities of money for the economy are superfluous. In all cases, the undesired outflow of money can only be the result of a governmental intervention that endows differently valued monies with the same legal purchasing power. All that the government must do not to destroy the monetary order, and all that it can do, is to avoid any such interventions. That is the nub of the monetary theory of Classical Economics and of its immediate successors, the theoreticians of the Currency School.[70] It was possible to refine and develop this doctrine with the modern subjective theory, but it was impossible to overhaul it and put something else at its place.[71]

---

[70]Here Mises referred to his treatment of these predecessors in the first edition of *Theorie des Geldes und der Umlaufsmittel*, 1st ed. (Leipzig and Munich: Duncker & Humblot, 1912), pp. 203 ff.

[71]Ludwig von Mises, "Die geldtheoretische Seite des Stabilisierungsproblems," *Schriften des Vereins für Sozialpolitik* 164, no. 2 (Munich: Duncker & Humblot, 1923): 21 f.

His exposition would eventually have an impact on central-bank policy, but at first it was dismissed, and its application prevented. One of the most vituperative dismissals came from a certain Kurt Singer, a follower of Knapp, who had attacked Mises for lack of logic.[72] Years later, Mises commented on Singer in a letter to Emil Lederer:

> I myself regret it very much today that history has proved me right rather than the champions of inflation. My income would be substantially higher if Knapp and his disciples had turned out to be right.[73]

Mises felt it was necessary to return to the subject of exchange-rate determination after World War I because the continued prevalence of the balance-of-payment doctrine had Austria well on its way to hyperinflation. In the feverish days of 1919, he wrote a paper on "Zahlungsbilanz und Wechselkurse" (Balance of Payments and Exchange Rates), which proved to be influential in turning Austrian monetary policy away from the path of hyperinflation before it was too late.

Some years after Mises's book had come out, the Swedish economist Gustav Cassel, who would play an important role in interwar economic science in Germany, developed a variant of the same theory without referring to his contemporary Austrian predecessor.[74] Cassel's exposition had a great deal more success, which was probably due to the fact that he had coined the popular new phrase "purchasing power parity" to describe the equilibrium exchange rate and also because he was less vitriolic than Mises, who had denounced the champions of the

---

[72]See Kurt Singer's book review in *Deutsche Wirtschaftszeitung* (June 1, 1913).

[73]Mises to Lederer, letter dated January 29, 1920; Mises Archive 73: 41f.

[74]See Gustav Cassel, "The Present Situation of the Foreign Exchanges," *Economic Journal* 26 (1916): 62–65; idem, "Abnormal Deviations in International Exchanges," *Economic Journal* 28 (1918): 413–15; idem, *Theoretische Sozialökonomie*, 4th ed. (Leipzig: Deichert, 1927), §§ 60 and 89.

balance-of-payments doctrine as dilettantes and called their analysis superficial—which in fact it was. During the 1920s, then, Ricardo's theory "was called Cassel's theory if one agreed; and Mises's theory if one disagreed."[75]

Fractional-Reserve Banking and Business Cycles

Mises's careful distinction between money proper and money substitutes naturally led to the question of the role of money substitutes. In the second part of his book, Mises showed that bank-issued money substitutes could not affect the value and purchasing power of money, as well as the distribution and allocation of resources as long as they were true representatives of a corresponding amount of money deposited with the bank— that is, in Mises's terminology, as long as they were money certificates. Only if they were issued without being backed 100 percent by a money deposit could they have an influence on prices, distribution, and allocation. These issuances of uncovered or partially covered money substitutes—fiduciary media— added to the quantity of money in the larger sense, increasing money prices and redistributing resources in favor of their first recipients and at the expense of their last recipients. It was therefore necessary to single them out for separate analysis, inquiring after the particular consequences of an expansion of fiduciary media rather than of money proper. The last third of *Theory of Money and Credit* deals with this issue.

First Mises showed why fiduciary media had an impact on money prices. Although they are only legal documents, they are dealt with—bought and sold—as if they were real money, whether or not they are backed by real money. As a consequence, an increase in the quantity of fiduciary media leads to an increase of the price level in the same way and for the same reasons that an increase of real money has this effect.

---

[75]Mises, *Notes and Recollections*, p. 60.

Moreover, there is a tendency in a fractional-reserve banking system steadily to increase the issuance of fiduciary media. No bank can afford drastically to exaggerate its note issues, because it would have faced too many redemption claims at once. But if its increases of fiduciary media are small enough—allowing other banks to follow suit—it can steadily increase the issuances.

This analysis led Mises to one of the central contributions of his book: an entirely new business cycle theory. Here Mises created a synthesis of Böhm-Bawerk's capital theory and the business cycle theory of the Currency School.[76]

Mises argued that the issuance of uncovered money substitutes could depress the interest rate below its equilibrium level, thus inciting entrepreneurs to launch investment projects that consume too many resources. Production takes time and thus requires the support of the human beings engaged in production during the entire production period. For a new project to be successful, one needs a sufficient provision of all the goods that the consumers consider to be more important than the goods that will result from this project. Consequently, the realization of *additional* production projects requires that *additional* consumers' goods be put at the disposal of the entrepreneurs. These additional consumers' goods can only come from net savings. Without sufficient savings, therefore, no extension of the structure of production is possible. It follows that if new projects are started not because of net savings but only because fractional-reserve banks have depressed the interest rate below its equilibrium level, then the resulting structure of production is unsustainable. It is now physically impossible for all production processes to be carried to completion—there are simply not enough savings to sustain the more extensive structure of production.

---

[76]At about the same time, two other members of Böhm-Bawerk's seminar presented original business cycle theories in elaboration of the principles of the Banking School. See Rudolf Hilferding, *Das Finanzkapital* (Berlin: Dietz, 1947 [1910]), part 4, chaps. 17 to 19; Joseph A. Schumpeter, *Theorie der wirtschaftlichen Entwicklung* (Munich: Duncker & Humblot, 1911).

The existence of such an unsustainable situation is not immediately evident because the additional investments are made in "higher" production stages, which are removed in time from their final products, the consumers' goods. But as time goes on, it becomes increasingly evident that something has gone deeply wrong in the entire economy. The day of reckoning is reached in what is commonly called an "economic crisis." Entrepreneurs then discover that not all projects can be carried out as planned for lack of originary capital. Some projects can only be continued in a reduced form, and others have to be stopped altogether. Hence, the material resources and human energies invested in these projects are now seen to have been wasted. Society is impoverished, individuals are out of work, firms go bankrupt, etc.

How can fiduciary media bring about a situation of malinvestment in the first place? Mises argued that this happens when they are brought into circulation through the credit market. In this case, the additional supply of credit reduces the rate of interest, thus pushing it below its equilibrium or "natural" level. Entrepreneurs are able to obtain more credit on better terms and invest these additional funds in new projects in the stages of production most removed from final consumers' goods. Deluded by the increased activities and apparent blossoming of new opportunities, everyone believes at first that the economy is growing faster than before; this is the so-called "boom." But sooner or later the market participants will become conscious of the fact that this boom is unsustainable, at which point the economy goes "bust"—an economic crisis.

In developing his theory, Mises could rely on two important discoveries of previous thinkers. The first was the business-cycle theory of the British Currency School. According to this school of thought, fractional-reserve banking led to a constant increase of fiduciary media, until the banks (in particular the central bank) proved to be unable to satisfy redemption demands. Then the monetary circulation collapsed because the fiduciary media immediately lost all their value, and this in turn ushered in a crisis.[77] The second was Knut Wicksell's discovery that monetary expansion could result from discrepancies between the money rate of interest and the equilibrium rate of interest. Yet none of these predecessors had developed the main theme of Mises's business-cycle theory, namely, the causation and propagation of economy-wide error, as well as the notion that the error-ridden process necessarily has to come to an end because it involves an inter-temporal misallocation of resources.[78]

In Wicksell's famous book *Geldzins und Güterpreise* (Money-Interest and Commodity Prices) he elaborated on David Ricardo's observation that an inflationary monetary policy could reduce the rate of interest only temporarily because sooner or later commodity prices catch up. It followed that any attempt to reduce the interest rate on a permanent basis required constant increases of the money supply. Now, the question was whether any such policy of permanent inflation

---

[77]A group of French economists had developed similar ideas in the mid-1800s. Victor Bonnet argued that excessive investments in fixed capital—excessive meaning disproportionate in comparison to the investments in circulating capital—were responsible for economic crises; and Charles Coquelin had anticipated Knut Wicksell in elaborating the hypothesis that business cycles were caused by credit expansions. See Charles Coquelin, *Du credit et des banques* (Paris: Guillaumin, 1848); Victor Bonnet, *Etudes sur la monnaie* (Paris: Guillaumin, 1870). A good survey of nineteenth-century business cycle theories is in Eugen von Bergmann, *Geschichte der nationalökonomischen Krisentheorien* (Stuttgart: Kohlhammer, 1895).

[78]In 1903, Werner Sombart had presented a "disproportionality theory" of the business cycle at a meeting of the *Verein für Socialpolitik* in Hamburg (*Schriften des Vereins für Socialpolitik* 113; Leipzig: Duncker & Humblot, 1903). Sombart argued that increased gold production had provoked a reallocation of resources that was unsustainable after the gold production ceased. The ensuing crisis, which hit Germany in 1900–1902, was therefore a structural crisis that reflected the unsuitable use that had been made of the capital goods. Sombart's theory does not take into account the problem of inter-temporal misallocation.

could be sustainable. Wicksell answered this question by first pointing out that the notion of "reduced interest rate" did not concern any absolute level of the interest rate, but rather a relative comparison of the market rate of money-interest to what he called the natural rate of interest.[79] He then claimed that indefinite deviations of the money-rate from the natural rate were not possible because the con-

Knut Wicksell

stant influx of new money would sooner or later entail an over-proportional increase of commodity prices, which would induce the banks to adjust the money-rate to the natural rate.[80] But, as Mises pointed out, Wicksell did not substantiate this claim by showing which mechanism forced the banks to perform such an adjustment.[81] Strictly speaking, Wicksell had no explanation of the business cycle at all, and despite his fundamental distinction between the natural and money rates of interest, he did not see that deviations between these two rates entail an intertemporal misallocation of resources.[82]

---

[79]In Wieserian fashion, Wicksell defined the natural rate of interest as the rate that would come into existence under the sole influence of real (non-monetary) factors; see Wicksell, *Geldzins und Güterpreise*, pp. iii, 93ff. He also defined it as the rate at which the price level would remain constant (see ibid., p. 92). Both distinctions led to great confusion among later theorists, but Mises's business cycle theory seemed to show that it was useful to make some such distinction. In *Human Action* he would eventually show that the relevant distinction is between the equilibrium rate of interest and the market rate. Both rates are monetary rates and can therefore coincide.

[80]See ibid., pp. v–vi. Wicksell noticed that Frédéric Bastiat had made a similar point in his polemic against Proudhon. Only Bastiat had not insisted that the concomitant price increase would be over-proportional. See Frédéric Bastiat, *Œuvres completes*, 6th letter to Proudhon.

[81]See Mises, *Theorie des Geldes und der Umlaufsmittel*, 2nd ed., pp. 364ff.

[82]Wicksell comes closest to Mises's discovery when he points out that a low money rate (relative to the natural rate) will incite businessmen to launch additional investment projects and even observes that the low money rate disrupts general equilibrium (see *Geldzins und Güterpreise*, pp. 87f., 97). But he

Mises would later develop and refine the business-cycle theory he had presented in his *Habilitation* work.[83] In 1912 he thought he had found merely one out of a number of conceivably complementary explanations of the business cycle. Thus he qualified his findings right in the opening sentence of the concluding § 5: "It is not the task of this work to develop a theory of economic crises. We take account of crisis phenomena only in so far as they can spring from the mechanism of money and fiduciary media."[84] He goes on in a somewhat lengthy manner to assert that there might be other sources for business cycles, and in particular that they might also exist in a barter economy. It could well be that these qualifications of the significance of his discoveries were meant to shield him against criticisms from his elders—after all the book was the basis on which he sought to be granted his *Habilitation*. Be this as it may, Mises eventually made up his mind and came to adopt more definite views on behalf of business-cycle research. Starting from the second edition of *Theory of Money and Credit*, the qualifications in § 5 are left out, and the first sentence now reads: "Our theory of banking . . . leads ultimately to a theory of business cycles." ∽

---

does not see the implication: that the structure of production is set on a path that is physically impossible to complete.

[83]As far as the exposition of Mises's business-cycle theory is concerned (part 3, chap. 5, in part § 4), there are no differences between the first edition and later editions. But for a few exceptions the text is exactly the same (see 1st ed., pp. 425–36; 2nd ed., pp. 366–75); the same is true for the entire chapter 5, except for § 5 (see below). Thus from the first edition, Mises's business-cycle theory contains the same discussion of forced savings, the reverse movement of prices, the natural rate of interest and deviations from it induced through fiduciary media, the importance of the subsistence fund, etc. as did all later editions. The difference between the first and the second edition relates to the concluding § 5 of chapter 5, where Mises discusses the significance of his own contribution to business-cycle theory.

[84]See Mises, *Theorie des Geldes und der Umlaufsmittel,* 1st ed., p. 433; my translation.

Part III
Officer, Gentleman, Scholar

7
The Great War

LIKE MANY OTHERS, MISES anticipated the outbreak of World War I years in advance. Unlike many others, he dreaded it. He was a Lieutenant of the Austro-Hungarian Army and dearly loved his country, but he was no chauvinist and despised the militarism and statism that were about to drag an entire continent into catastrophe. A number of eminent men and women in all countries—most notably, Bertha von Suttner in Austria and Bertrand Russell in England—felt the same way and dedicated themselves to making the case for peaceful cooperation among nations and to fighting the frenzy of nationalism. These private initiatives proved insufficient to tame the war party. The ruling philosophy of government glorification under the guise of patriotism had made its cause irresistible.

After the war, Mises would write on these subjects in detail. He explained how the war had resulted from state worship, in this case, from worship of the nation-state.[1] But for now he thought that he—the agnostic Jew, cultural German, political individualist, scientific cosmopolitan, and Austrian patriot—

---

[1]See in particular Ludwig von Mises, *Nation, Staat und Wirtschaft* (Vienna: Manz, 1919); translated by Leland B. Yeager as *Nation, State, and Economy* (New York: New York University Press, 1983); and, *Omnipotent Government: The Rise of the Total State and Total War* (New Haven, Conn.: Yale University Press, 1944).

had to fight the nationalists' war. The Austro-Hungarian state was the sole bulwark against the Russian hordes standing ready to invade the land and destroy its Western liberties. Maybe this attitude toward politics was contradictory and anachronistic, but Mises believed he had no choice in the matter, and he continued to believe that all his life. As a contemporary friend and admirer would observe: "A champion of individualism, you cherish strikingly collectivistic orientations. In fact, even under severe duress for your body and total lack of individual comfort, you never lose sight of the whole picture."[2]

First Year in Battle

Early on a Saturday morning, Mises stood ready for departure at Vienna's crowded Nordbahnhof station. He took the eight o'clock express to the city of Przemysl in his native Galicia, where he would join his unit, the field cannon regiment no. 30. The train had special compartments for officers, which made the long journey more comfortable, and thus he spent the day in the company of Ewald Pribram and Count O'Donell, who were both cavalry officers, and the physician Erwin Stransky, a fellow private lecturer at the University of Vienna. None of the young men would ever forget this journey. Stransky later recalled that Mises spoke about his native Galicia, its history, the peculiarities of its church architecture, etc. The time passed somehow and in the evening, around seven o'clock, Mises left the train in Przemysl, wishing his fellow travelers farewell.[3] It was August 1, 1914.

The fighting did not start immediately. Austria-Hungary did not declare war until August 5, after the war between Russia and Germany had broken out. Even then there was no significant fighting for another two weeks. Both camps needed time to mobilize their forces. This should have been easier for

---

[2]Louise Sommer to Mises, letter of September 1917; Mises Archive 4: 143ff.

[3]See Mises Archive 62: 143ff. and 100: 3.

Austro-Hungarian and German troops because of the shorter distances, but the Russians had apparently begun preparations much earlier—shortly after the assassination of Austrian Archduke Ferdinand on June 28.

The fundamental military problem for the Austro-Hungarian and German alliance was a three-front war with numerically superior enemies on all sides—in particular the sheer overwhelming numbers of the Russian army. In 1914, Russia counted a population of roughly 173 million, as opposed to 68 million Germans and 50 million inhabitants of the Austro-Hungarian Empire. Because of the immensity of the Russian Empire, its 250 potential divisions could not be mobilized quickly. Still the Russian generals managed to throw eighty divisions into battle in the first few months. These troops confronted only ten German divisions and thirty-eight Austrian divisions, ninety out of 100 German divisions being bound up on the Western Front and eleven out of forty-nine Austro-Hungarian divisions stuck on the Southern Front in Serbia.[4]

The mission of the Austro-Hungarian troops on the Northern Front was to block the Russians in order to avoid a Russian invasion of the German plains, which lay almost defenseless. They could not retreat into the Carpathian Mountains, which were easier to defend, because the Russians could trap them there with only a small number of their troops and throw their main force into Germany. Hence, in spite of their numerical inferiority, the k.u.k. armies had not merely to resist, but to attack the Russians in an attempt to keep them in the Galician plains. The k.u.k. strategy was to wear the Russians down in a long series of battles. This strategy counted on the Austro-Hungarian Empire's comparative advantages of morale, training, education, and fighting spirit. After the war, Mises said of these

---

[4]See k.u.k. Armee, "Kriegsereignisse im Norden. Von der Mobilisierung bis einschliesslich der Schlacht bei Lemberg," *Österreichisch-ungarische Kriegsberichte aus Streffleurs Militärblatt* (Vienna: Seidel & Sohn, 1915), bk. 1, pp. 7ff.

relentless Austrian offensives that "the flower of the Austrian army was uselessly sacrificed."[5] He considered them "goalless and purposeless" and yet they did have a goal: to keep the Russians in Galicia as long as possible. In this, they succeeded. The human cost included many of Mises's relatives, friends, colleagues, and students.

The battles that followed brought death and destruction on an unheard-of scale. Modern science and technology had profoundly changed all aspects of war, from coordination, to equipment, to tactics and strategy, giving a central place to the use of high-powered and highly mobile artillery. Although the k.u.k. Army was better equipped than its enemy, it was numerically inferior and in almost constant retreat.[6] By the end of September, more than 10,000 civilian refugees from Galicia had poured into Vienna[7] and the k.u.k. Army had been thrown far back behind Przemysl and now stood with its back to the Carpathian Mountains. In the first few weeks and months of the war, almost no day went by that did not see entire k.u.k. batteries (about 100 men each) and even regiments (about 500) being wiped out.

Artillery was not only the main agent of destruction, but also one of the prime targets. Mises's battery constantly had to change position, often under fire. Heavy rainfall set in, hampered their movements, and proved that k.u.k. uniforms were not waterproof. There was no hope of relief any time soon from the military bureaucracy, so Mises resorted to private initiative: he had his mother send clothes for his men.[8]

---

[5]Mises, *Nation, Staat und Wirtschaft*, p. 112n; *Nation, State, and Economy*, p. 138n.

[6]Information on equipment and organization of k.k. artillery batteries is contained in Mises Archive 3: 23ff.

[7]See Mises Archive 100: 28.

[8]See correspondence in Mises Archive 100: 13, 23, 15, 29, 31. Mises later denounced the bad treatment of the common soldiers as a serious impediment to the war effort:

He was himself the special object of motherly care through the army postal system. Adele von Mises sent her son: furred leather gloves, several electric lamps, matches, shoelaces, woolen clothes, camelhair pants and camelhair undergloves, aspirin, cigarettes, glasses and journals, Ludwig's favorite brand of suspenders, eau de toilette, soap, cognac, and tuna cans. Like an accountant, she kept lists of the things she sent and thus controlled both the punctual delivery and the consumption of her son, with a keen eye on his cigarette consumption.[9] She also kept him informed about various events in Vienna, although she could not be too frank or go into too much detail because of the censor. Mises himself probably had access only to official or semi-official journals and newspapers. At the end of August 1914, he read that his beloved teacher, Eugen von Böhm-Bawerk had died in Tyrol on a journey to Switzerland.[10]

Mail could take weeks to reach the soldiers, especially when troop movements were quick and frequent. In September 1914, correspondence was interrupted for three entire weeks and, most unusually, the press no longer ran any reports on Mises's regiment. When, to the great relief of his family and friends his name was eventually mentioned in the *Neue Freie Presse*,[11] Martin Nirenstein wrote him immediately: "this time too victory will be on the side of liberty."[12]

> From the political point of view it was a grave mistake to follow completely different principles in the compensation of the officer and the enlisted man and to pay the soldier at the front worse than the worker behind the lines. That contributed much to demoralising the army! (*Nation, Staat und Wirtschaft*, p. 135, n. 18; *Nation, State, and Economy*, p. 166)

[9]See correspondence in Mises Archive 100: 20, 26, 35; 102: 6, 7, 8, 18, 33.

[10]See Mises Archive 2: 97.

[11]See correspondence in Mises Archive 100: 19, 22.

[12]Correspondence in Mises Archive 2: 98.

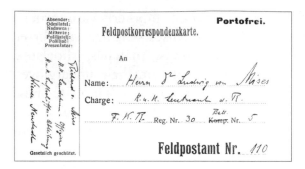

*Postcard to k.u.k.
Lieutenant Mises
from his brother,
Richard, a pilot in the
Austrian army, 1914*

Meanwhile, his brother Richard was stationed in Baden near Vienna. He was experimenting with aircraft motors, commanding a research unit comprised of several soldiers and a lieutenant.[13] A professor of applied mathematics at the Prussian University of Strasbourg since 1909, his interests had centered on aviation. He had become a pilot himself and taught a university course on powered flight in 1913. With his army research unit, he constructed a 600-horsepower plane, which was put to use in 1915. The military research led to the publication of *Fluglehre*, which established Richard as one of the world's foremost aviation pioneers.[14] But the young professor was impatient to get to the front, where the battles continued to be fierce and numerous.

In the first half of October, the united German and Austro-Hungarian armies had driven the Russians back, gaining about 60 miles, only to be driven back again after two weeks of Russian counterattacks. But time was running out for the Russians. The Austrian economy had retained a comparatively large degree of liberty that now increasingly weighed in on the side of the Austro-Hungarian army. The huge profits deriving from

---

[13]See correspondence in Mises Archive 100: 49.

[14]The book was first published 1918 in Berlin, and then remained for decades a standard monograph of aviation theory, being reprinted in a posthumous 6th edition in 1957 (Berlin). Before the war, Richard von Mises had already gained an expert reputation based on his *Elemente der technischen Hydromechanik* (Leipzig: B.G. Teubner, 1914).

the production of war materials were not initially subject to excessive taxation and thus could quickly be reinvested to convert the structure of production to war needs.[15] Many businessmen and industrialists had already started adjusting their plans and their investments to the new situation, and as usual these private ventures reacted quickly and efficiently to subsequent developments on the front. For example, in October 1914, some Austrian businessmen set up a factory to produce ammunition for captured cannons.[16] But long-standing prewar government control of war-related industries did cause problems. Mises later explained:

> Austrian industry not only had to deliver what the war required beyond peacetime provisions; it also had to catch up on what had been neglected in peacetime. The guns with which the Austro-Hungarian field artillery went to war were far inferior; the heavy and light field howitzers and the mountain cannons were already out of date at the time of their introduction and scarcely satisfied the most modest demands. These guns came from state factories; and now private industry, which in peacetime had been excluded from supplying field and mountain guns and could supply such material only to China and Turkey, not only had to produce the material for expanding the artillery; in addition, it also still had to replace the unusable models of the old batteries with better ones. Things were not much different with the clothing and shoeing of the Austro-Hungarian troops.[17]

----

[15]Mises emphasizes that wartime public opinion strongly favored a confiscatory taxation of the great profits made in the armament industries. Initially, the Austrian leadership did not give in to these demands because it was aware of the military importance of having an efficient private production of war materials. See Mises, *Nation, Staat und Wirtschaft*, pp. 142f.

[16]See correspondence in Mises Archive 100: 44.

[17]Mises, *Nation, Staat und Wirtschaft*, p. 114; *Nation, State, and Economy*, pp. 140f. See also Rudolf Sieghart, *Die letzten Jahrzehnte einer Grossmacht* (Berlin: Ullstein, 1932), p. 282.

The higher productivity of private enterprise increasingly came into play and helped bring about an important Austrian victory that ended a month-long battle near the Polish city of Lodz on December 6, 1914. A few days later, the Austro-Hungarian army won another significant victory at Limanova-Lapanow, about fifteen miles from Carl Menger's birthplace in Neu-Sandec. On December 12, the Russians were driven back more than thirty miles, in the course of which 30,000 Russian prisoners were taken.[18] These events marked a decisive turning point on the Eastern war theater. After almost four months of intense fighting, the German and k.u.k. troops had balanced the initial numerical superiority of the Russians and in the coming months would drive them further back east. Richard wrote to Ludwig, in characteristic Mises-family understatement, that he was happy that "it goes better with the Russians."[19]

Apparently, Ludwig even found time now to study the Ruthenian language, possibly to prepare for the establishment of a new local administration.[20] He also wrote frequently to Richard inquiring about the health of their mother, who had been suffering for some months from a foot injury. Richard reported that all cures had failed so far, and that he had also tried in vain to engage the world-famous physician, Professor Adler, with whom the Mises family had personal contact.[21] The

---

[18]See k.u.k. Armee, "Kriegsereignisse im Norden. Von der Mobilisierung bis einschliesslich der Schlacht bei Lemberg," *Österreichisch-ungarische Kriegsberichte aus Streffleurs Militärblatt* (Vienna: Seidel & Sohn, 1915), bk. 2, p. 35.

[19]In the German: "*es mit den Russen besser geht.*" See postcard from Richard von Mises to Ludwig von Mises, dated December 18, 1914; in Mises Archive 2: 102.

[20]At least, this was the guess of Mises's uncle Alfred Landau. In a letter to Mises, dated December 3, 1914, he surmises that Mises's studies of the Ruthenian language will be helpful for the administration of the new "*Gouvernement Tarnopol.*" See Mises Archive 2: 118. Ruthenian was the language of the Ukrainians living under Austrian rule in the eastern part of Galicia.

[21]See correspondence in Mises Archive 2: 102. This must have been Alfred Adler (1870–1937). Up to the 1930s, Adler was the most famous

better news came from the front: Three days before Christmas, Richard and his old friends, Martin and Hugo Nirenstein, read in the Vienna press that Ludwig had been promoted to the rank of a k.u.k. *Oberleutnant* (First Lieutenant).[22] Only two months later, Ludwig was again mentioned as the beneficiary of an *"allerhöchste Belobigung"*—the emperor had praised his achievements in battle.[23]

There followed a brief period of stasis on the battlefield, and public attention turned to the decay the war was causing in the social fabric of the empire. In Vienna, the food supply shrank noticeably and the lines in front of the shops grew longer every day. Ludwig received desperate letters from his mother describing her struggles with Therese, the family cook, who had difficulties with the concept of wartime economizing.[24] And on the front, treason showed its ugly face when, on April 3 and 4, 1915, the infantry regiment no. 28 from Prague was captured without resistance.[25]

Starting early May 1915, however, the German and Austro-Hungarian troops finally began their long march east. Not even Italy's May 23 entry into the war on the side of the Triple Entente (Britain, France, and Russia) could slow down the Central Powers' irresistible drive on the Northern Front. Within a

---

Vienna psychologist. He had first worked with Sigmund Freud, but early on went his own way in placing great emphasis on the particular conditions of each individual patient (*Individualpsychologie*).

[22]See correspondence in Mises Archive 2: 103.

[23]See correspondence in Mises Archive 2: 116. A full description of his military decorations is in Marcel Klang, *Die geistige Elite Österreichs* (Vienna: Barth, 1936), pp. 617f.

[24]See correspondence in Mises Archive 102: 14.

[25]See Mises Archive 2: 21f., 24. He later observed that only the Austrian Germans and the Hungarians fought for the monarchy with full conviction, whereas the service of the Slavs and Romanians was half-hearted at best; many of them actually fought on the other side; see Mises, *Nation, Staat und Wirtschaft*, pp. 112f.

month, they regained Przemysl and continued on, fighting the enemy forces far back into Russia.[26] The causes of this complete reversal of the balance of power in the east were mainly economic in nature. Mises later explained:

> The great technical superiority that the armies of the Central Powers had achieved in the spring and summer of 1915 in the eastern theater of the war and that formed the chief basis of the victorious campaign from Tarnów and Gorlice to deep into Volhynia was . . . the work of free industry, as were the astonishing achievements of German and also of Austrian labor in the delivery of war material of all kinds. . . . The army administrations of Germany and Austro-Hungary knew very well why they did not give in to the pressure for state ownership of the war-supplying enterprises. They put aside their outspoken preference for state enterprises, which would have better suited their world view, oriented toward power policy and state omnipotence, because they knew quite well that the great industrial tasks to be accomplished in this area could be accomplished only by entrepreneurs operating on their own responsibility and with their own resources. War socialism knew very well why it had not been entrusted with the armaments enterprises right in the first years of the war.[27]

In early August, Lemberg was retaken, much to Mises's relief, and he was finally granted a two-week leave. On August 16, he went from the front to Krakow and took the next train to Vienna. He had spent more than a year on the front, survived against the odds, but looked as fresh and vigorous as ever,

---

[26]Mises kept some news clippings about these successes, which were reported on daily. See Mises Archive 102: 29, 31. He later remarked that the success was due to the by-then inferior armament of the Russian troops; see *Mises, Nation, Staat und Wirtschaft*, p. 112, n.

[27]Mises, *Nation, Staat und Wirtschaft*, pp. 114f.; *Nation, State, and Economy*, pp. 141.

though a hip injury had plagued him for months. He helped himself with considerable quantities of Salicyl, the fever and pain reliever his mother sent him.[28] When he started asking for higher doses, she refused to send more, demanding that he return home and stay in bed.[29] The family had already lost his cousin, the physician Max Landau, who died of infection from examining so many typhus cadavers.[30]

Mises did not yet know that he had finished the hardest and most dangerous phase of his military service. After the leave, he would return to the front for about six weeks, and then again from December 1916 to December 1917. But none of these expeditions brought him even close to the chaos he had known in the first months on the Northern Front.

Some time late in 1915, Mises was relieved from active duty and sent to the city of Sopron, in Hungary, where he stayed for about two months, trying unsuccessfully to recover from his hip injury, but happy to be alive. He had survived the worst and finally enjoyed the gratitude and admiration of the civilian population, who celebrated the returning troops as heroes.[31] When he received another medal for outstanding performance before the enemy—the *signum laudis* in silver—the imperial praise for the unpretentious "Reserve Lieutenant whom everybody knows and loves" was enthusiastically reported in the press.[32] The reason for

---

[28]The main substance was willow bark (salix=willow).

[29]See correspondence in Mises Archive 102: 4, 6.

[30]See correspondence in Mises Archive 102: 27.

[31]See Mises Archive 3: 34.

[32]Newsflash *Ödenburger Zeitung* (Sopron), November 28, 1915:

> Our Heroes. The well known and beloved Reserve Lieutenant Dr. Ludwig Edler von Mises, in civilian life an unsalaried lecturer at the University of Vienna, and currently stationed with our Thirtieth, was honored anew with the Signum Laudis in silver for his outstanding efforts before the enemy.

Descriptions of Mises's War Medals

(from left to right)

1. *Militär-Verdienstkreuz (Cross for Military Merit).* Awarded to officers in peace time for distinguished service through zeal and perserverance and in war time for valour and fine leadership. Obverse: German cross with the word "Verdienst" at the center. Swords signify involvement in battle.

2. *Signum Laudis in silver (Medal for Military Merit in Silver).* Awarded for repeated actions worthy of the Royal praise. Obverse: Portrait of Franz Josef and the words "emperor of Austria, king of Bohemia etc. and Apostolic king of Hungary" (in latin, with abbreviations). Swords signify involvement in battle. Reverse: The words "signum laudis" (latin for "sign of praise") within laurel wreaths.

3. *Signum Laudis in gold (Medal for Military Merit in Gold).* Awarded for exceptional merit in war or peace. Obverse: Portrait of Franz Josef and the words "emperor of Austria, king of Bohemia, and Apostolic king of Hungary" (in latin, with abbreviations). Swords signify involvement in battle. Reverse: the words "signum laudis" (latin for "sign of praise") within laurel wreaths.

4. *Karl-Truppenkreuz (Karl-Troops Cross).* Awarded to all troops who served in the field against an enemy for a minimum of 12 months and participated in at least one battle. Obverse: "grati—princeps et patria—Carolus imp et rex" (thankful, prince and fatherland—Charles, emperor and king) Reverse: Two crowns and C (probably for Charles) and "vitam et sanguinem—MLCCCCXVI" (life and blood—1916).

5. *Signum Laudis in gold (Medal for Military Merit in Gold).* General Campain Medal. Obverse: Portrait of Franz Josef and the words "emperor of Austria, king of Bohemia, and Apostolic king of Hungary" (in German, with abbreviations). Reverse: The words "signum laudis" (latin for "sign of praise") within laurel wreaths.

6. *Kriegserinnerungsmedaille (War Commemorative Medal).* Instituted 1932–1933. Awarded to all who served in the First World War. Medal in gold accorded by the Republic of Austria. Obverse: An eagle sitting on a shield with the republican colours of Austria and the words "für Österreich" (for Austria). Swords signify involvement in battle. Reverse: The letters "1914–1918" surrounded by laurel wreaths.

7. *Diamond Jubilee Cross.* Celebrating Franz Josef's 60th anniversary 1848–1908. Golden cross. Obverse: Portrait of Franz Josef, at the center of the cross.

8. *Hungarian Commemorative Medal of the First World War.* Instituted May 1929 by the Regent, Admiral Horthy. Awarded to those who served in the first World War. Obverse: A crest under the crown of Charlemagne. Reverse: Steel helmet and the inscription "pro deo et patria—1914–1918" (for God and fatherland—1914–1918).

his popularity was his reputation as an officer who cared for and took care of his comrades-in-arms.[33]

The Home Front

If Mises could have gotten away earlier, in any honorable manner, he would have welcomed the opportunity. He tried, in the fall of 1914, to use his *Kammer* affiliation to be transferred to some other duty. The *Kammer* had had to give up forty-five men for military service but some others were allowed to remain in their prewar functions or were transferred to the War Ministry, which cooperated very closely with the *Kammer*.[34] Mises was not among the lucky few who never had to expose themselves to harm. He had many talents, but he never mastered the art of maneuvering the hallways and offices of the various war administrations, making oneself indispensable to the bureaucrats and thus unavailable for dangerous missions. The great transformation of all forms of modern leadership toward bureaucratic management, which Max Weber so brilliantly described, was epitomized in many of Mises's former colleagues and fellow students, most notably in the cases of Schumpeter, Lederer, and Karl Pribram.

After the Northern Front had calmed down, Mises was finally considered suitable for bureaucratic employment, and the *Kammer* connections now proved to be effective. During his Christmas holidays in Vienna, on December 22, 1915 he received orders from the War Ministry to join its department no. 13 in Vienna.[35]

---

[33]He would stay in touch with them for the rest of his life. See for example, the correspondence with Col. Ottokar Schulz and with Max Sokal, dating from the 1960s; Grove City Archive: "S" files.

[34]See correspondence in Mises Archive 2: 36.

[35]See Mises Archive 3: 34f.

The most immediate benefit of being stationed in Vienna was the availability of superior medical attention, but curing his hip pain proved slower and more wearying than anticipated. At the end of December, Mises was examined in the k.u.k. army hospital of the town of Baden, a base near Vienna. Dr. Hackmüller found that Mises had typhus and ordered a sulfur-based treatment. This did not bring the hoped-for results. In the following months, Mises was sent to two Vienna experts for special hip treatments, which involved massages, hot-air applications, and walking exercises under supervision.[36]

During this period, he officially resided at a Villa Keller in Baden, but probably spent most nights at the family apartment in downtown Vienna. Thus he came to experience the profound transformations of daily life that his friends in the state bureaucracies had orchestrated to meet the challenges of the war economy. Following the intellectual fashion of the day, in early 1916 these experts had set out to introduce central planning of production and consumption on an increasing scale. Because the existing government apparatus was unable to handle such a task, they turned to the already existing cartel organizations, made them compulsory, and subordinated them to the different k.u.k. ministries. These *Kriegszentralen* or War Centrals controlled the distribution of industrial products and the allocation of raw materials to the firms.[37] Their large-scale activities were financed through the k.u.k. banking establishment in Vienna and Budapest.[38] Götz Briefs later described the step-by-step process, which led wartime Austria-Hungary on the road to the Big Brother state:

---

[36]See Mises Archive 3: 30ff.

[37]Mises later pointed out that wartime central planning started with *Devisenzentralen* or Foreign Exchange Centrals. See Mises, "Austrian Empire. Finance and Banking," *Encyclopedia Britannica*, 12th ed. (1921), vol. 30, pp. 323f.

[38]See Jurij Krizek, "Die Kriegswirtschaft und das Ende der Monarchie," R.G. Plaschka and K. Mack, eds., *Die Auflösung des Habsburgerreiches* (Munich: Oldenbourg, 1970), pp. 43–52; Götz Briefs, "Kriegswirtschaftslehre und

> Commercial advice to the civil administration, import business first in competition with private importers and then on a monopolistic basis, economization and distribution of the stocks—this was the increasing extension of their tasks, which made them assume ever more control functions within their organizations.[39]

These efforts at top-down management of all society did not reach the proportions or intensity attained in the German Reich (Austrians were famous for *Schlamperei*, a jovial carelessness—even sloppiness—that effectively prevented a full-blown, German-style command-economy) but they were effective enough, at least in Mises's eyes, to demonstrate what applied socialism is all about—mass misery—and to confirm every single prejudice he might by then have acquired about the idiocy of government meddling with the free market.[40] "They 'organized' and did not notice that what they were doing was organizing defeat."[41]

Kriegswirtschaftspolitik," *Handwörterbuch der Staatswissenschaften*, 4th ed. (Jena: Gustav Fischer, 1923), vol. 5, pp. 984–1022; H. Wittek, "Die kriegswirtschaftlichen Organisationen und Zentralen in Österreich," *Zeitschrift für Volkswirtschaft und Sozialpolitik* (1922); Otto Göbel, *Deutsche Rohstoffwirtschaft im Krieg* (Stuttgart: Carnegie Stiftung, 1930).

[39]Briefs, "Kriegswirtschaftslehre und Kriegswirtschaftspolitik," p. 1017.

[40]Mises, *Nation, State, and Economy*, p. 146; *Nation, Staat und Wirtschaft*, pp. 118f.:

> It will be the task of economic history to describe in detail the stupidities of the economic policy of the Central Powers during the war. At one time, for example, the word was given to reduce the livestock by increased slaughtering because of a shortage of fodder; then prohibitions of slaughtering were issued and measures taken to promote the raising of livestock. Similar planlessness reigned in all sectors. Measures and countermeasures crossed each other until the whole structure of economic activity was in ruins.

[41]Mises, *Nation, Staat und Wirtschaft*, p. 114; *Nation, State, and Economy*, p. 140.

With retail markets all but eradicated, huge crowds of people lined up in front of a few select food shops that had benefited from official allocations. *Butterstehen, Eierstehen, Milchstehen*—standing in line for butter, eggs, milk, and virtually everything else, often for hours—this was one of the new sad realities of daily life.[42] How to cope with all this without losing one's mind? Mises commended the example of his Uncle Marcus, who somehow managed savings under these conditions—truly a model for living at the existential minimum.[43] But he also offered more substantial support, buying additional food on the black market to supply his mother and other needy ladies. His basic salary in 1916 was 183 kronen[44]—enough to buy some additional potatoes or flour. When he had to leave again for the Eastern Front in December 1916, he asked Emil Perels, a *Kammer* colleague and friend from Böhm-Bawerk's seminar, to take care of these women.[45]

The Mises and Perels circle included one Valerie Adler, who worked as advisor in the *Ernährungsamt* (Bureau of Nutrition), the brothers Karl and Ewald Pribram, one Olly Schwarz, and one Emil Schr.[46] They would often attend opera or theater performances, or just meet at cafés to discuss politics, economics, and literature. Occasionally, these meetings would also take place in a more extended and official setting. For example, on November 16, 1916, Mises took part in a function of the *Österreichische*

---

[42]Around August 20, Mises arrived in Vienna. Zerline, a relative, welcomed him after a week of "Butterstehen, Eierstehen, Milchstehen." See Mises Archive 2: 123.

[43]See Mises Archive 4: 106.

[44]See Mises Archive 2: 43ff., 5: 23. One hundred and eighty-three kronen would be about 200 gold francs or 1.867 ounces of gold.

[45]See Mises Archive 4: 38.

[46]See Mises Archive 4: 35f., 77, 110ff. Ewald Pribram worked for the *Zentralstelle für Wohnungsreform* and as of August 1917 was the fiancé of Marianne Fürth (see Mises Archive 4: 173).

Politische Gesellschaft (Austrian Society for Politics) on current monetary problems. Schumpeter, who had come from Graz to chair the discussion, had urged Mises to debate his old opponent Walter Federn.[47] Schumpeter opened the session, stating the currency problem was manifest as a high price level and low krone exchange rates. He argued that the high prices were the cause of the low krone, and that prices were high because of a shortage of commodities and because of bank note inflation. Normalcy could only be restored through a reduction of the quantity of money; this was the crucial point: the krone had to be restored to its former purchasing power. Mises had few things to add, and limited himself to discussing the inefficiency of foreign-exchange control through the *Devisenzentrale*, whereas Federn gave a balance-of-payments explanation of the present situation, blaming import surpluses for the weak krone. Significantly, most speakers—not only Herr von Landesberger, the head of the *Devisenzentrale*—followed in the same vein.[48]

Mises also resumed his activities as a private lecturer at the University of Vienna, where he discussed in detail the differences between his own theory of money and the various competing views that dominated the scene in German-language universities, in particular the theories of Knapp, Schumpeter, Wieser, and Philippovich.[49] His experience on the frontlines had changed his conduct and appearance, adding a war veteran's personal weight to his exposition. Young Heinrich Treichl, who met him in those

---

[47]See correspondence in Mises Archive 56: 22.

[48]Mises Archive 107: 94.

[49]He published these considerations shortly thereafter in an article for Weber's *Archiv* and later incorporated the piece as a chapter of the second edition of his *Theorie des Geldes und der Umlaufsmittel* (Munich and Leipzig: Duncker & Humblot, 1924). See Mises, "Zur Klassifikation der Geldtheorie" (On the classification of monetary theory), *Archiv für Sozialwissenschaft und Sozialpolitik* 44 (1917–1918): 198–213; idem, *Theory of Money and Credit* (London: Jonathan Cape, 1934), appendix A.

years at the dinner table of his parents, was especially impressed by his dark red mustache.[50] So must have been his army comrades: Mises occasionally had the nickname *Rotwild*.[51]

One of the greatest admirers of the straight and sharp young lecturer was a certain Louise Sommer, who read all of his writings and would soon want to know all his views on everything. Apparently they even met for extended evening discussions, in the course of which *Fräulein* Sommer became a friend—perhaps more. The otherwise unapproachable Mises shared his thoughts and feelings with her, including depressive moods. When he had returned to the front, he mailed her the first flowers of spring.[52] After the war, Louise Sommer became an ardent proponent of Mises's views on liberalism and politics.

On May 5, 1916, Mises received orders to join the Scientific Committee for War Economics, a new committee of the War Ministry.[53] Like many such wartime institutions, the Committee provided privileged employment for the upper class of the intelligentsia. It brought together established senior scholars and bright young students, including Mises, Broda, Karl Pribram, Brockhausen, Adler, Perels, and Bartsch, and possibly also Schumpeter and Alfred Amonn.[54] The whole idea was to establish a forum for in-depth analysis of the economic problems of the war and its strategic "economic goals."

---

[50]See Heinrich Treichl, *Fast ein Jahrhundert* (Vienna: Zsolnay, 2003), p. 15.

[51]The rotwild is a German Red Deer. The word *rotwild* literally translates to "red game animal."

[52]See Mises Archive 4: 69f. See also their correspondence following the publication of his *Nation, Staat und Wirtschaft* (in Mises Archive 53: 56ff.).

[53]See Mises Archive 2: 87. It seems as if shortly before, in April 1916, he had briefly visited his old regiment in Vasarhely in Hungary (see Mises Archive 2: 77).

[54]See, for Kelsen and Amonn, Mises Archive 4: 61f.; for Broda, Mises Archive 4: 97ff.; for Schwarz, Pribram, Brockhausen, Adler, Perels, and Bartsch see Mises Archive 4: 41f.

It was clear from the outset—at least for anyone even faintly acquainted with Mises's views—that he would disagree with some very influential people within the k.u.k. political and military leadership, and also with many Committee members, on the prospective economic benefits of military victory. He definitely did not believe that conquests in the East would convey any economic advantages for the future Austro-Hungarian economy. And in distinct contrast to other committee members, who also knew the rationale for this classical-liberal position, Mises was ready to speak up even to those who were higher in the wartime pecking order and could make his life very unpleasant.

Montesquieu once said that although one had to die for one's country, one was not obliged to lie for it.[55] This seems to have been Mises's maxim too. He had already demonstrated his readiness to give his life for his country. Now he showed his will to honor the truth even if it brought him in conflict with powerful opponents. Committee meetings and presentations featured Mises arguing for the economic irrelevance of political borders. He also worked on an article restating the scientific case for this view. His article was published in December 1916 under the innocent title *"Vom Ziel der Handelspolitik"* (On the Goal of Trade Policy) in Max Weber's *Archiv*.[56]

---

[55]"Être vrai partout, même pour sa patrie [sic]. Tout citoyen est obligé de mourir pour sa patrie; personne n'est obligé de mentir pour elle." Montesquieu, *Oeuvres completes* (Paris: Gallimard / Pléiade, 1996), vol. 1, "Préceptes," p. 1415.

[56]See Ludwig von Mises, "Vom Ziel der Handelspolitik," *Archiv für Sozialwissenschaft und Sozialpolitik* 42, no. 2 (1916): 561–85. After Mises's sudden departure from Vienna, Lederer would eventually read the proof pages (see Mises Archive 4: 37, 217). Mohr Publishers sent a statement of honorarium of 93.75 marks at the end of December, but Mises probably answered this letter only in May 1917. In June, Mohr wired the money to Mises's Postsparkassen account: 142 kronen and 4 Heller (see Mises Archive 2: 94ff.).

Mises argued that, "from a purely economic standpoint," the case for free trade and against protectionism was unassailable. It was true that classical free-trade theory, the theory refined and perfected by Ricardo, had been developed under the assumption that capital and labor were mobile only within national borders, but Mises proceeded to show that the case for free trade stood firm even if these conditions were no longer applicable. In a Ricardian world of free trade, there would be rich and poor countries, and tariffs and import quotas could not change this. In a Misesian world of free international migration, there would be more densely populated countries and less densely populated countries, in all of which the wage rates and interest rates would tend to be equal; and, again, protectionism could not do anything to improve this state of affairs.[57,58]

Mises pointed out that no "economic" case could be made against cross-border movements of people and capital, and then spent most of his paper discussing the paramount "non-economic" rationale, which was nationalism. He stated that international migrations conflict with the "principle of nationality," that is, with the policy goal of promoting the numerical number and the welfare of co-nationals. Emigration leads to the assimilation

---

[57]See Mises, "Vom Ziel der Handelspolitik," pp. 564f. Mises also pioneered a comparative criterion for (relative) over-population and under-population: "We consider a country to be over-populated if it is more densely inhabited than it would be if a system of freedom of migration covered the entire surface of the earth" (ibid., p. 576).

[58]His interest in the theoretical and political implications of modern migration might have been stirred as early as the Philippovich seminar. Since the 1890s, Philippovich had promoted migration research among German economists, even though he never succeeded in getting the subject discussed at any of the meetings of the *Verein für Socialpolitik*. See Eugen von Philippovich, ed., "Auswanderung und Auswanderungspolitik," *Schriften des Vereins für Socialpolitik* 52 (1892); see also the follow-up study on Austrian migration by one of his students: Leopold Caro, "Auswanderung und Auswanderungspolitik in Österreich," *Schriften des Vereins für Socialpolitik* 131 (1909).

of the emigrants to the foreign nation. They are then "lost" to their original nation, and this loss presents a *prima facie* "non-economic" case against free trade. But Mises showed that this anti-free trade conclusion is unwarranted. It is true that emigration to foreign countries weakens the nation, but protectionism cannot correct the problem—at least, Mises contended, it "cannot reach this goal in a manner beneficial to the nation."[59] He observed that even the champions of protectionism had to notice that their proposed policies could not accomplish "those goals that they had set themselves."[60]

By contrast, the anti-German immigration laws of other countries were rational responses to the threat of national alienation resulting from mass immigration.[61] In short, Germany could not change its calamities through protectionism, and was helpless in the face of other countries' policies that further aggravated its problems. Mises soberly summarized this state of affairs, despairing from the point of view of German nationalism:

> The foundations of a global empire [*Weltreich*] are a population that multiplies approximately at the same rate as the population of the other global empires, and a settlement area that offers this population space for its development. Trade policy cannot contribute anything to establish a global empire for a nation if these conditions are not given.[62]

---

[59]Mises, "Vom Ziel der Handelspolitik," p. 567.

[60]Ibid., p. 570.

[61]He pointed out that industrial workers in the (typically Anglo-Saxon) immigration countries could successfully call for anti-immigration laws because the mass immigration from Europe threatened national unity: "There can be no doubt that all countries will effectively close themselves off against immigration that threatens their national composition, just as the countries settled by white men have long since closed themselves off against yellow immigration" (ibid., p. 574).

[62]Ibid., 577.

The isolation of Germany in international politics, Mises surmised, was a result of the fact that it lacked sufficient territories to host its rapidly increasing population. The other nations, which controlled territories suitable to satisfy German expansionism, were united through common interests in defending their possessions and rightly "sensed that Germany must be their natural enemy."[63]

Mises then criticized the plans of the social-democratic leader, Karl Renner, to establish an all-encompassing system of protective tariffs as the foundation of the future relations between the Austro-Germans and the other nations of Austria-Hungary. Renner argued that political unity between the various nations was based on common economic interests, and he thought to create this common basis artificially through protectionism. But Mises objected that, in the present age of nationalism, protectionism actually reinforces the antagonisms between the various nations because it privileges the already industrialized nations. He illustrated this point with the prewar antagonism between Austria's ethnic Germans and the Hungarians, which had made Austria-Hungary's political order so tenuous.

The power of the argument and the place of publication made it impossible for the war party to ignore Mises. Trouble lay ahead.

Back to the Front

At the end of August 1916, Romania entered the war on the side of the Entente powers. With new vigor, the united Russian and Romanian forces pushed forward into Transylvania and started making their way into the Hungarian plains. But their success was short-lived. Within two months, the German armies of Falkenhayn and Mackensen halted the enemy, regained the lost territory, drove the Entente forces back into

---

[63]Ibid., p. 578.

the Transylvanian Alps, and from there into the Romanian heartland around Bucharest. When the Entente abandoned its positions in the mountains, it was clear that they would not be able to hold the Romanian plains either. Within another month, all of Romania had been conquered and the Russian and Romanian troops were driven back into Ukraine.

The entire campaign took place in the midst of a deep crisis in Austrian politics. On October 21, 1916, Friedrich Adler, the radical son of social-democratic leader Viktor Adler, gunned down Prime Minister Count Karl Stürgkh in a Vienna restaurant, ostensibly in protest against the government's longstanding refusal to convene the parliament. Exactly one month later, eighty-six year old Emperor Franz Joseph died. The only man who had successfully held the reluctant nations of the empire together had gone the way of all flesh. His grandnephew, twenty-nine year old Karl, ascended the throne and appointed a new government under Count Clam-Martinic.

In the wake of this regime change, Mises was ordered to leave Department 13. The order came on very short notice. He might have expected a transfer from one part of the War Ministry to another, but it became clear that he had been picked out for another mission on the frontlines.

As details came forward, the picture darkened. Initially he thought he would lead a battery of a regular field cannon regiment, as he had done before, but the last-minute order made it clear that he would be sent on a mountain mission, which implied even greater physical duress.[64] To top it all, his new mountain artillery battery was in terrible shape. It had been created during the February 1916 Italian campaign and had been involved in the bloodiest encounters ever since. They had suffered many losses of men, horses, and material. Just before Mises took over, Romanian forces had destroyed their supply

---

[64]See Mises Archive 4: 74.

line for ammunition.[65] It looked as if someone in Vienna was bent on getting rid of Mises forever, and as things stood, the chances looked good that this someone would succeed.

On December 5, he joined his new unit, the Cannon Battery no. 1 of the Mountain Artillery Regiment no. 22 in the Romanian town of Rammcul Valcery (today Râmnicu Vâlcea). There he obtained a motor vehicle from the German army and moved on to Bucharest. He arrived in the Romanian capital on December 11, received his orders at the headquarters of the Prussian Army, and continued with his regiment to a summit position in the Carpathian Mountains, between Transylvania and the Bukovina.[66]

It took three weeks to receive the first mail from Vienna.[67] His mother's parcels did not reach him at all, and she eventually had Franz Weiss, who held a position with the war administration, send them for her.[68] Meanwhile Mises discovered that the human body can endure amazingly low temperatures without fainting, and he renewed the painful acquaintance with his hip.[69]

The news from Vienna did not help his morale. In mid-February, his Uncle Marcus had had a complete mental and physical breakdown, proving that Ludwig had grossly underestimated minimum living standards.[70] He also received a letter from Karl Pribram who had taken Mises's place at the Scientific Committee. Worried what Mises would think, Pribram wrote

---

[65]See Mises Archive 4: 124ff.

[66]See Mises Archive 2: 852ff. They did not reach their position before December 19, probably because of bad roads and enemy action hampering their moves.

[67]He wrote back to his friends in Vienna for the first time on January 11, 1917, sending New Year's greetings. See Mises Archive 4: 38.

[68]See Mises Archive 4: 229ff.

[69]See Mises Archive 4: 110ff., 115.

[70]See Mises Archive 4: 106.

to give assurances that he had not pushed for his own nomination.[71]

Mises did not suffer from envy and was ready for continued sacrifice even in the face of such injustice. He was a good sport throughout his life. Yet one wonders what he must have felt in March 1917 when, freezing behind a cannon in the Carpathian Mountains, he received news from Perels that Karl Pribram had received the *Ritterkreuz* (Knight's Cross) and had moved on to a position as ministerial secretary in the Trade Ministry's department for social policies.

✎   ✎   ✎

While the climatic conditions in the Carpathian Mountains were severe, the new mission was actually less dangerous and certainly less exciting than the first months of war on the Northern Front. The enemy troops were tired and hardly posed a threat, while there was increasing political resistance within Russia against the Tsar, and against continuing the war in particular. The Eastern Front was relatively quiet, and Mises had time to spend with his fellow officers discussing literature and economics.[72]

On March 14, 1917, the Russian monarchy was overthrown, soon followed by a provisional government under Alexander Kerensky. Three weeks later, Woodrow Wilson, who had been reluctant to ally the United States to the ostensibly autocratic Russian Tsar, led his country into war on the side of the Entente. The old balances on the fronts were disrupted and the troops were repositioned.

In early April, Mises's battery moved to a new strategic position further north. It was also higher in altitude: they set up

---

[71]See Mises Archive 4: 61f. Pribram later on proved that he had great talents for self-promotion.

[72]See Mises Archive 53: 7.

cannons at 6,000 feet.[73] The front remained quiet, however, and the men on both sides were increasingly difficult to motivate. Peace resolutions of the powerful social-democratic parties in Russia, Germany, and Austria had reinforced the general mood of increasing skepticism about the continuation of hostilities.

There were also other distractions, such as handling their new German neighbors. The problem was that the German Army was at least as arrogant as it was efficient. Even its regular soldiers had the tendency to treat foreign allies as incompetent junior partners. On at least one occasion, Mises himself had to confront pretentious German officers claiming jurisdiction over k.u.k. troops;[74] and after the war, when in a high-profile paper he analyzed the problems of the proposed Austro-German monetary unification, he mentioned "the tendency of the North Germans to consider anything South German and in particular anything Austrian to be inferior and alien."[75]

At the end of May and in early June 1917, Mises was in Vienna, probably on a two-week leave.[76] Here he could see first-hand the changes introduced under the new emperor. Karl was about to place his cronies in positions of military and political leadership. Displacing the old elite would have a political cost, but he tried to compensate by attempting to win greater popularity among the general public. Under Franz Joseph, nobody could get in touch with the emperor to discuss political matters except through His Majesty's ministers, but Karl opened his antechamber to anyone who wished to offer advice. It turned out that many of his subjects felt such a calling. Just among Mises's

---

[73]See Mises Archive 4: 54f., 95f., 101.

[74]See Mises's May 3 report on his encounter with a German military police officer in Mises Archive 3: 80.

[75]Mises, "Der Wiedereintritt Deutsch-Österreichs in das Deutsche Reich und die Währungsfrage." Michael Hainisch, ed., "Wirtschaftliche Verhältnisse Deutsch-Österreichs," *Schriften des Vereins für Sozialpolitik* 158 (Leipzig: Duncker & Humblot, 1919), p. 169.

[76]See Mises Archive 4: 18f., 101.

friends, Hans Kelsen and Joseph Schumpeter each wrote several memoranda in which they made detailed policy recommendations. Another witness of the events, Rudolf Sieghart, recalls: "There was a plethora of memoranda and audiences. Everybody gave counsel: Arch-Duchesses and priests, lower skirts and soutanes, profiteers and chats."[77] The new government also convened the upper and lower chamber of the Austrian parliament for the first time in more than three years, on May 30. This too was part of the emperor's strategy to strengthen his bonds with the population—a necessity given the dramatic deterioration of living conditions in the past few months.

Mises was shocked to see how the food supply had collapsed during his six-month absence. He predicted that very soon no more food would be found at the markets, even after hours of standing in line. At one point his grandfather's cook stood three hours in line for meat. His mother had to dismiss her cook, Therese, because she could barely afford to feed her.[78] Sadder news was the loss of his old teacher, Eugen von Philippovich, who died on June 4 from a long illness.

With these impressions he left Vienna on June 9 to return to his battery.[79] He was back in time to prepare the last great action on the Eastern Front. Starting July 1, 1917 the united German and k.u.k. troops completed the re-conquest of the Bukovina in the wake of the so-called Kerensky offensive. At the end of July, Mises and his regiment reached their new permanent field of operations about 60 miles east of their initial position, in the area of Brusztury and Czardaki.[80] One month

---

[77]Sieghart, *Die letzten Jahrzehnte einer Grossmacht*, p. 246.

[78]See Mises Archive 4: 192, 200f.

[79]See Mises Archive 4: 205f.

[80]See Mises Archive 3: 41ff., 54, 71f., 95. The documents also refer to the following places: Kozmacz and Prokaraw (3: 52), Prewarskic Rotc (3: 64), Gutin Tomnatek (3: 101), and others (for example, 3: 46, 104, 110). Mises's code name is *Rotwild* (3: 64). One of their last engagements in battle seems to have taken place on August 8, confronting Romanian troops (3: 67).

later, the war on the Eastern Front was virtually over and his regiment would receive recognition for its performance at the attack on Czardaki.[81]

Meanwhile, his colleagues from the Scientific Committee experienced the war under safer conditions. Mises knew it was the fate of political opponents to become marginalized within the state apparatus—and the ruling war party had an especially successful means of marginalization: it could send its opponents to the front. Still, it was exasperating to see how much the threat of combat intimidated the would-be intellectual leaders of the country. With the opposition to its expansionary plans silenced, and a technocratic elite composed of corrupt cowards, the Austrian war party had carte blanche within the government.

Mises did not capitulate. In the midst of the July battles, with biting pain in his hip,[82] he somehow found the time to write for the *Neue Freie Presse* on public policy.[83] His friends back in Vienna were grateful and amazed. Louise Sommer wrote him:

> How I envy your proficiency in using the method of isolation to suppress disturbing personal problems. . . . I almost envy you your life of narrowly circumscribed activities. Surely you have time to work—you find time even in a shower of bullets.[84]

---

[81]The recognition was pronounced on September 3. See Mises Archive 4: 51.

[82]Apparently, the hip problem deteriorated considerably during the battle. See the remarks in later letters from Helene Meyerson (Mises Archive 4: 79) and Bettelheim (Mises Archive 4: 6).

[83]The pieces were published around August 20 and before. See Mises Archive 4: 102.

[84]August 3 letter to Mises in Mises Archive 4: 87ff. The envious feelings might have originated from the fact that she had taken care of a foster child (4: 143ff.), but was not up to the task. She seems to have been convinced, however, that Mises himself was inexhaustible. She urged him to publish, at last, the typology of monetary theories that he had presented in his course on monetary economics of the year before. See Mises Archive 4: 143ff., 225.

Fortunately, Mises was not showered by bullets in the next two months—the regiment's July and early August battles were the last in the Bukovina. But this did not mean that Mises's frontline mission was over. His battery had orders to join the 1st Corps of the Austrian army on the Southern Front.[85]

With additional troops newly available from the now-quiet Eastern Front, the k.u.k. Army prepared a new offensive against the Italians. The 12th Isonzo Battle in October and November 1917 would be Mises's last engagement in this war, and the last battle he would ever fight with guns. He spent six exhausting weeks on the Southern Front, under fire, enduring cold weather in the Alps, and still suffering a biting pain in his hip. On one of those days, his regiment was stationed on Hoch Rombon, a major peak in the area. Mises reported:[86] "thick fog and snow storm, 50 cm new snow, all ways are stuck, many electric cables are damaged and can be repaired only under life danger." He also mentioned that his men had no more wood to burn and suffered from colds and rheumatism. Fortunately for him and his troops, this was just three days before the decisive breakthrough of the united German and Austro-Hungarian forces in a frontal attack against the better-equipped Italians, pushing them far back into the planes of Frioul and the Veneto.[87] One historian speculates that the "attackers would have moved even faster had they not paused to gorge their rumbling stomachs with the undreamt-of quantities of good Italian food and wine."[88] What a way to escape, once more, the jaws of death.

---

[85]See Mises Archive 51: 107; 4: 103; 7: 12.

[86]The report is dated October 21, 1917. See Mises Archive 4: 15.

[87]In Mises's judgment, the success was due to the inferiority of the Italian soldiers. See Mises, *Nation, Staat und Wirtschaft*, p. 112 n. In the same work, Mises points out (p. 82) that the Austrian army had never been defeated in battle by Italian forces.

[88]Gordon Brook-Shepherd, *The Austrians: A Thousand-Year Odyssey* (New York: Carroll & Graf, 1997), p. 198.

New Life

By mid-November, Mises had left both the front and the Scientific Committee.[89] The details of his departure from the latter are unknown, but it appears to have been part of a general improvement in his situation. From this point on, in fact, his life would continue to improve for quite a while. A few days after quitting the Committee he was promoted to the rank of Captain, and on December 3, 1917 (he had just started an eighteen-day leave in Vienna) he was ordered to join Department 10 of the War Ministry, the department for war economy.[90] The head of the department was one Colonel Linoch with whom Mises enjoyed very good relations. Linoch left him at liberty to engage in academic pursuits.[91] Mises devoted as much time as possible to a new book with the working title of *Imperialismus*,[92] which would summarize his reflections on the war. He also resumed his teaching activities.

The winter semester had already started, so it was too late to set up a seminar, but Mises probably held Sunday lectures at the *Volks-Bildungs-Verein*.[93] If so, the experience dealt a heavy blow to his views about educating the masses. He said in his *Notes and Recollections* (1940), he now realized that the classical liberals had over-estimated the ability of the common people to form independent judgments.

---

[89]See Mises Archive 2: 12.

[90]See Mises Archive 2: 11, 19. Usual abbreviation: 10 K.W. Abt. des k.u.k. KriegsMin. The department was located in the Hotel National in the second Viennese district (the so-called Leopoldstadt) at Taborstrasse 18 (see, e.g., Mises Archive 51: 80).

[91]He also seems to have been involved in *Kammer* activities. See the letters from Schmerling (Mises Archive 51: 23) and Tayenthal (51: 31).

[92]See Mises Archive 54: 2. The book written as *Imperialismus* would later be published as *Nation, Staat und Wirtschaft* (Nation, State, and Economy).

[93]See Mises Archive 51: 47.

In the spring and summer of 1918, he directed a university course on banking theory and advised several students on what to read and which subjects to study.[94] Women would not be admitted to the department of law and government science for another year, but most participants of Mises's course were young ladies. Because of the war, there were few male students left in Vienna. His female students were probably from the department of philosophy, which had admitted women since 1897.

Among the few male students was Dr. Richard von Strigl, who had been a fellow student in Böhm-Bawerk's seminar. Strigl would become one of the most important and influential Austrian economists in the interwar period. The presence of Strigl and of Helene Dub, wife of the economics editor of the *Neue Freie Presse*, highlighted a particular feature of university seminars in those days. The seminars were not mere schooling functions, but also provided a forum for discussions among senior members who were often on a par with the lecturer. Each session began with a presentation on the subject of the day, usually delivered by one of the students. Then Mises commented on both the presentation and the subject itself, and answered questions from other participants.

On May 18, Mises was promoted from an unpaid private lecturer's position to the rank of *professor extraordinarius*.[95] This position does not have an equivalent in the American university

---

[94]His *Banktheoretische Übungen* (exercises in the theory of banking) are mentioned in letters from Käthchen Pick (May 17, 1918; see Mises Archive 51: 32) and one Bermann (June 27, 1918; see ibid. 51: 32). The list with the subjects dealt with is in Mises Archive 17: 15. The list of participants is in Mises Archive 17: 22. Mises had research-related correspondence with Schöndorf (51: 1), anonymous (51: 5), Louise Sommer (51: 21f., 61f., 86), Gama (51: 40f.), and Hilde Oppenheimer (51: 46).

[95]*Ausserordentlicher Universitätsprofessor*. The promotion followed an imperial decision of May 7.

system. An *extraordinarius* position is not a titled full professorship and is unpaid, but it does include tenure and enjoys greater
social prestige than does an associate professorship.

Another welcome event for Mises was his new personal
acquaintance with Max Weber.[96] The German scholar was
already a living legend, but he had not lectured for more than
ten years, pursuing his studies in private at the University of
Heidelberg. Weber now celebrated an unexpected and spectacular comeback in Vienna, and attracted huge crowds of students
and professors. His encounters with Mises produced mutual
admiration. Much of what Mises wrote in the late 1920s on the
logical and epistemological problems of economic science was
in reaction to Weber's position. And in his university courses
and private seminar, Mises relentlessly encouraged the study of
Weber's work. Weber in turn praised Mises's theory of money
as the "most acceptable" in print. And he seemed to have
learned a few things from his young colleague in Vienna. During Weber's 1918 stay in Vienna, Mises convinced him that
there was in the social sciences a discipline separate and distinct
from history. Economic theory was a truly scientific discipline.
Its subject matter was the analysis of the relationships between
means and ends, an analysis that could be performed without
making value judgments.[97] Moreover, Mises persuaded Weber
that economic rationality—that is, economic calculation—
would be absent in a socialist commonwealth.[98]

As the wartime welfare state continued to grow, Mises continued to prefer private alternatives, not just in theory, but in
the actions he took in his own life, from the improvement of his

---

[96]In November 1919, Weber lived at Jaffé's place since his own apartment
had to be repaired (73: 57). Some years after Weber's death, Mises contributed to Rickert's sculpture of Weber (December 1928, 73: 35f.), which
can still be admired in Heidelberg University.

[97]See Mises, *Erinnerungen* (Suttgart: Gustav Fischer, 1978), p. 5.

[98]We will deal with this influence in more detail in a subsequent chapter.

family's food supply (even the black market was deteriorating)
to the professional placement of friends and colleagues eager to
get away from the front.[99] Mises was known to be responsive to
calls for getting people out of the death zone and into an administrative position in Vienna or elsewhere.[100] He was often helped
in these missions of mercy by his friends Victor Graetz and
Ludwig Bettelheim-Gabillon.[101]

Mises's success in placing others was at least in part due to his
increased notoriety. His courageous public opposition to the
war party and its claims for the economic benefits of military
expansion had not changed policy, but it had attracted interest
to him and his work. He had become a public figure when he
was invited to lecture on Austrian public finance to the plenary
meeting of the *Advokatenwählerverein,* an electoral association
of lawyers.[102] It is likely that Mises addressed the same themes
he had two months earlier in an article for the *Neues Wiener*

---

[99]An August 29, 1918 letter by a certain Irene Schmerling is revealing. She
wrote: "Frau Singer recently told me that you had asked for me (I suppose you
were interested in food?—I have only got ersatz honey!)" ("Fr. Singer erzählte
mir kürzlich, dass Sie nach mir gefragt hätten (wohl um Lebensmittel?—es ist
nur Kunsthonig da!"). Mises's annual salary in November/December 1918 was
1,120.51 kronen (see Mises Archive 51: 52). This corresponded to US$71.05,
according to data given in Mises, "Austrian Empire. Finance and Banking,"
Encyclopedia Britannica, 12th ed. (1921), vol. 30, pp. 323f.

[100]Mises helped among others the following persons: the brother of his
fellow I/22-officer Greifs (Mises Archive 51: 45, 72), one Petschek (51: 65f.),
one Steiner (51: 74f.), one Skiem (51: 80ff.), one Sattler (51: 87), one Suss-
mann (52: 2), and possibly also Richard von Strigl (51: 59f.). Other friends of
Mises had a very different reputation. Greifs, who had also approached
Kelsen to help place his brother Karl, wrote to Mises: "If you see Kelsen,
please tell him that I am not astonished about his silence, but embarrassed I
am" (Mises Archive 51: 91). But even complete strangers approached him.
Leo Fishman many years later recalled his visit with Mises. See Fishman to
Mises, letter dated November 11, 1950; Grove City Archive: "F" file.

[101]See Mises Archive 51: 78; 52: 2.

[102]"Wandlungen der österreichischen Finanzpolitik." The invitation came
from Wilhelm Wieselthier and Julius Löw. See Mises Archive 51: 4; 56: 16.

Tagblatt.[103] In this piece, he characterized Austrian tax law as the patchwork product of 100 years of tax reforms, errors, and competing special interests. And he vigorously criticized the government's plan to introduce a one-time emergency tax (*Sonderabgabe*), warning that the new tax would become permanent, and arguing that sound financial policies must consider both government revenue and government expenditures. His lecture was a great success. On Monday, March 11, 1918, Mises started a 15-year public career as *the* economist of Austria.

In May 1918, the Office for the Defense Against Enemy Propaganda invited him to lecture on the "Significance of the War Bond." The lecture took place in the context of an "information course" for officers who were to offer patriotic instructions to the troops.[104] The main purpose of the Office was to promote k.u.k. war bonds. But Mises was unwilling to be an instrument of propaganda and made instead a compelling case for free-market war finance. He especially emphasized the perils of financing the war through inflation. The speech was published from stenographic lecture notes without giving Mises the opportunity to review the transcript.[105]

---

[103]See "Finanzreform und Vermögensabgabe," *Neues Wiener Tagblatt* (January 23, 1918); a copy is in Mises Archive 106: 16.

[104]See Mises Archive 2: 4.

[105]See "Über Kriegskostendeckung und Kriegsanleihen," copy in Mises Archive 10. Mises commented:

> In the summer of 1918 the Army supreme Command organized a course for officers who were to offer patriotic instruction for the troops. . . . My lecture was published from stenographic notes without giving me the opportunity to read the proofs. (*Notes and Recollections* [Spring Mills, Penn.: Libertarian Press, 1978], pp. 66f.)

A Last Mission

After their overthrow of the Kerensky government in November 1917, the Bolsheviks called for an immediate end of the war on the Eastern Front on a status quo ante basis and without reparations for either side. Moreover, they began to make public highly secret prewar Entente plans for punishing Germany in case of victory. These revelations increased the political pressure on the Allies to seek an early peace as their reasons for going to war now appeared in a decidedly less saintly light. The stark contrast between the evil Germanic autocrats and the humane democracies of the West faded away and was slowly replaced by a more realistic picture of the situation. But most of all, the Bolshevik push for peace changed the military situation since it brought the prospect of relieving Austria and Germany from their awkward two-front struggle.

These prospects materialized very slowly, though, because the German side insisted on war reparations that the Bolsheviks would not accept. The peace negotiations started in Brest-Litovsk shortly before Christmas 1917 and were brought to an end only after an Austro-German ultimatum forced the Russian side to sign a treaty by which it ceded military control of the entire Ukraine to its enemies. Thus, what initially promised to be a great military and political success for the Austro-German side had turned into a disaster. Precious time had been lost to move troops to the Western Front. And the imposed "agreement" failed to pacify the Russians, so precious *Mittelmächte* forces were diverted to defend against a possible Russian backlash. In short, all political advantages had vanished. Lloyd George, Wilson, and the Western press immediately presented the treaty of Brest-Litovsk as evidence of the imperial expansionism of their enemies.

The official rationale for a military occupation of the Ukraine was the exploitation of its rich natural resources. Few people in Germany and Austria knew that this idea was flawed. Mises knew it. In his *Archiv* article "On the Goal of Trade Policy" he had pointed out that economic control over resources can be enjoyed even in the absence of political control. Access to Ukrainian resources would have been possible through regular trade channels and did not require military occupation of the entire country. Mises relentlessly insisted on this point with an intransigence that had almost cost him his life.

The real "economic" rationale for the occupation of the Ukraine was the usual one: it brought unearned riches to a select few. In the present case, the economic exploitation of the occupied zone was to be confided to an *"Ostsyndikat"*—a cartel of big industrialists and big bankers with good government connections. Each of them would have monopoly rights to certain Ukrainian products. A May 1918 meeting in Berlin brought all interested men together and determined the broad division of the loot, in particular, each party's "trade contingent"—its exclusive trade domain.[106]

One of the unsettled questions after the Berlin meeting was the future monetary constitution of the Ukraine. The Austrian side had a special interest in the question because Austrian war inflation had swept large quantities of kronen into the occupied zone. Decisions about Ukrainian money and currency would most certainly affect the demand for krone notes and thus could possibly break up the krone's fiat exchange rate.

The fundamental problem was that Austria-Hungary, like all other warring states, had vastly inflated its currency, which consistently lowered its exchange rate with other, less-inflated currencies. The only thorough way to stop both the inflation and its symptoms (higher prices and depreciating exchange rates) was, of course, to stop producing additional krone notes, but

---

[106]See Mises Archive 8: 2ff., 31ff., 36ff.; 9: 14, 162ff. The economic exploitation of occupied territories to finance the war effort has a long tradition. However, World War I added the instrument of all-around planning. See Georg Holzbauer, *Barzahlung und Zahlungsmittelversorgung in militärisch besetzten Gebieten* (Jena: Gustav Fischer, 1939), pp. 1–18.

many statists and money cranks sought schemes to get around this appalling measure. One of these tricks was to make payments in money titles issued on behalf of banks other than the Austro-Hungarian Central Bank in Vienna. The Austrians applied this measure in their occupied territories in Italy. They made payments to their Italian suppliers in *Darlehenskassenscheinen* (Loan Bureau Notes) denoted in lire to bolster the krone exchange rate against the lira.

Similar measures were taken on the Eastern Front. In August 1918, when the Germans had for some time already made ruble payments in the territories they controlled, the *Bankstelle* (bank office) of the East Army Command submitted a memorandum[107] proposing similar measures for the territories occupied by Austrian forces. According to the economists of the *Bankstelle*, the krone surplus on the market resulted from large military payments that were not sufficiently compensated by kronen flowing out as payments for imports from Germany. The German authorities, selfishly concerned with the strength of the mark, were unwilling to cooperate to achieve stable exchange rates. Therefore, the Austrian army should also change its policies by (a) suppressing contraband imports from Austria and exports to Russia and (b) making payments in rubles. These policies would give the *Bankstelle* time to absorb krone surpluses in the Ukraine by offering interest-paying (2 percent) demand deposits with the local exchequer of the East Army, which would assume the function of a branch office of the Austro-Hungarian Central Bank. This would supposedly bring the millions of kronen now being hoarded in private wallets and strongboxes back into circulation where they could be used in the interest of the national economy and of the currency itself. The *Bankstelle* clearly had no idea that these measures were entirely unfit to attain the end that it sought. Few in Austria-Hungary could even comprehend, let alone solve such problems.

---

[107]Dated August 25, 1918; see Mises Archive 51: 69ff.

In June 1918, Otto Katz, director of the Union Bank in Vienna, approached Mises on behalf of a financial policy mission to solve the currency problems in the Ukraine. Mises would be charged with monetary policy in this important occupied territory. The head of the group would be *Exzellenz* Kraus, under whose leadership Mises had already fought the last battles of the Bukovina and the 12th Isonzo battle.[108] The mission represented a great opportunity for Mises. A thirty-six-year-old captain, he still had one of the lower officer ranks, and his position in civilian life was not especially elevated either. His main capital was the solid reputation he had gained as an expert on money and banking. Katz's offer was therefore a unique career opportunity. At the very least it promised exceptional exposure to high-profile policy-making. There was nothing to do but to thank God, fate, and Katz for the offer, and to accept it immediately and wholeheartedly.

Characteristically, however, Mises spelled out his conditions. He would offer his services for this venture only if he had full decision-making power, being the officer with exclusive responsibility for the financial and monetary policy of the Ukraine. This required in turn that he be transferred into the civil service and obtain a position corresponding to that of Bosnian secretary of state.[109] Most importantly, he demanded that his bureaucratic

---

[108]Interestingly, it was the bank director Katz who approached Mises on behalf of a political mission. Apparently, Katz was known to have close ties to top political circles in Vienna, for Mises took his proposals seriously and answered in a letter dated June 20, 1918 (see Mises Archive 51: 104). Presumably Katz had been asked to look out for a suitable currency expert because as a bank director he was supposed to be knowledgeable in monetary matters.

[109]See Mises Archive 51: 104ff.:

> But such a position cannot be accepted by a Captain of the artillery, a charge I hold, neither outwardly, nor within the context of the inner workings of the administration. In my view, the position in question ought to be comparable to that of the Bosnian secretary of state.

authority be completely clarified to avoid later frictions that could turn out to be harmful to the cause. He combined this demand with a hard-hitting attack on the bad habits of Austrian bureaucracy. Unlike their German cousins, he argued, the Austrians lacked the ability for detached commitment to a cause:

> The usual words of appeasement offered in response to claims made about us—"they will get ahead based on character alone" or "things will sort themselves out in time"—are completely false. I am convinced that I could assert myself and secure a "comfortable" position. But what matters is objectivity; for such personal advantages are gained through a yielding of resolve when it comes to things in which one should have remained firm, and through needless caballing, which leaves no time for solid work. One must be capable of pure objectivity. That the Germans are objective is the basis of their success.[110]

Mises had no illusions about the acceptability of his proposals. Setting clear terms of cooperation in the interest of the cause was simply not the style of the Austrian administration, and he therefore thought the negotiations at an end. But some days later, Lieutenant Colonel Maximilian Edler von Becher, a high officer from the Imperial General Staff in Vienna, asked him to name the concrete conditions under which he would be willing to join 2nd Army Command as a financial and monetary consultant. He answered in a letter dated June 26, 1918.

Mises suggested dividing the civil service of the 2nd Army Command into three departments: one for political affairs, one for financial and monetary affairs, and one for public finance. He would become director of the department for financial and monetary affairs. He had to be made a civil servant to have authority in dealing with the other representatives of the state,

---

[110]Mises Archive 51: 108ff.

and he had to be an Imperial (k.u.k.) employee to reduce con-flicts with Austrian, Hungarian, and local state agents. For the same reason, it would not be advisable for him to remain an officer of the *Kammer*. For in his capacity as monetary officer he would have to revise agreements between the Ukraine and the Austrian Trade Bureau, an appendix organization of the *Kam-mer*, which had a monopoly privilege in Ukrainian imports and exports. His negotiations with the Bureau would lack credibil-ity because of the Bureau's executives within the *Kammer*; and they risked inciting nationalist resentments since they could be depicted as an inner-Austrian deal to the detriment of the other nations.

Becher seemed to endorse Mises's arguments and restated them almost word-for-word in an official recommendation to his superiors. In this public paper, of which Mises received a copy, Becher suggested that Mises be invited to go to Odessa for an oral presentation and also to study conditions in Kiev and other large Ukrainian towns.

Behind the curtains of the General Staff, however, plans were made to induce the cooperation of the recalcitrant captain without giving in to his demands. In mid-July, the head of Department 10, Colonel Linoch, received an order to further reduce his staff. The order came from very high up, and it was specific about the staff members to be dismissed. Mises was among them. When he received the news from Linoch, he knew the only choice left to him was between the front and a Ukrainian mission without conditions.[111] Linoch managed to extend Mises's leave in Bad Gastein.[112] Then the commander of the East Army, General Alfred Kraus, sent Mises on a two-week

---

[111]See Oberst Linoch to Mises (in Bad Gastein), letter dated July 20, 1918; Mises Archive 51: 50ff.

[112]His leave was extended through August 25. Mises stayed in the Hotel Badeschloss (see Mises Archive 2: 17f.).

mission to Odessa and Kiev and ordered him to report about Ukrainian currency and finance.[113]

Mises arrived in Odessa on September 7 and quickly learned that the Germans were pushing to establish a Ukrainian fractional-reserve central bank, whereas the Austrians—in particular Herr Pollak from the k.u.k. Ministry of Finance and the Vienna Association of Bankers—resisted this plan.[114] As things stood, it was politically inevitable that any monetary constitution for the Ukraine would have to involve a central bank with a monopoly on the issuance of banknotes. The question was whether the new establishment could be limited to providing currency, or if it would also be drawn into attempts to solve the pressing financial problems of the country.

Such attempts would jeopardize the stability of the new currency, but how else could the financial burdens be shouldered? At a meeting with the local Austrian commander, Mises convinced the Austrian bankers to promote sales of Vienna stocks and bonds to the Ukrainian public.[115]

To avoid the monetary inflation the Germans advocated, the Misesian strategy was to seek a private-business solution through an increase of foreign holdings of Austrian stock and debt. In a later report to General Kraus he made comments and suggestions to improve this proposed institution as much as possible. In particular, he recommended that the future central bank be built on the model of the Bank of the Russian Empire.[116] The Ukrainian central bank should be a pure government institution

---

[113]See Mises Archive 8: 2ff., 9, 26; 18.

[114]See Mises Archive 8: 9.

[115]See Mises Archive 8: 20f.

[116]See "Bemerkungen betreffend die Einrichtung einer ukrainischen Notenbank" (Remarks Concerning the Establishment of a Ukrainian Central Bank) in Mises Archive 51: 114ff. The report was printed without indication of authorship. However, style and content reveal it to be a pure product of Mises's pen. See also the various study materials in Mises Archive 51: 95ff.

(as distinct, for example, from the formal set-up of the Bank of England or the German Reichsbank), and half of its endowment should be held as cash reserves. In its investment policies, the new bank should follow private banking principles: no risky investments and no long-term engagements. Mises also stressed that reserve ratios were "of crucial importance" to create trust and credit for the banknotes. The reserves had to be *in cash*. Anything else would

> not offer any tangible security for the note owner [or] in any way prevent an unlimited note-issue that eventually results in the note's complete devaluation. The history of the French *assignats*, which had been "covered" through liabilities on all of the State's territories, serves here as a warning example.[117]

Mises thus proposed a form of fractional-reserve central banking system better known as the gold exchange standard. He recommended keeping reserves for one third of all circulating banknotes, and these reserves should be either in cash (gold and silver), in foreign currency, or in bills of exchange on foreign currency. Moreover, the management of the bank should "of course" be subordinate to the government, preferably to the trade minister, since the finance minister would be tempted to abuse it for fiscal purposes.

Mises's proposals were never put into practice. A week after his return to Vienna, the Bulgarian front crumbled and after another month, both Austria-Hungary and Germany were in a state of political and military dissolution. The war ended in sudden chaos, and the empire—a centuries-old order—vanished almost overnight. ◈

---

[117]Ibid.

8
Nation, State, and Economy

LIKE MANY INTELLECTUALS OF the time, Ludwig von Mises felt the need to come to grips with the causes and consequences of the war that had destroyed the Old World. For quite some time he had anticipated a dreadful end to the war, and as soon as he had returned from his last mission on the frontlines, he began to put his thoughts on paper. Despite his time-consuming involvement in the new republican government, his *Kammer* activities, and his duties as a professor, he continued working on a new manuscript, which would contain an in-depth analysis of the causes of the war, his personal experience of it, and the political challenges facing postwar Austria.

As usual, he worked on the book in the evening and late-night hours after long workdays spent with other tasks. He finished the manuscript in early July 1919, just before leaving Vienna for a few weeks of vacation in his beloved Bad Gastein. He had written the book as *Imperialismus*, but he published it under the title *Nation, Staat und Wirtschaft* (Nation, State, and Economy).[1] Although it is now one of his less-known works, it made a great impression on many readers at the time, and

---

[1]Mises, *Nation, Staat und Wirtschaft. Beiträge zur Politik und Geschichte der Zeit* (Vienna & Leipzig: Manzsche Verlags- und Universitäts-Buchhandlung, 1919); translated by Leland B. Yeager as *Nation, State, and Economy* (New York: New York University Press, 1983).

established him as the most important intellectual champion of classical liberalism in postwar Austria, and eventually in all of Europe.[2]

The book contains three essays on the theory of imperialism, with applications to the history of Germany and Austria-Hungary. In the first chapter, which comprises almost two-thirds of the book, Mises pioneers what could be called the analysis of the "political economy of nations" to explain German imperialism, which in his view was the main cause of the war. The second chapter contains a thorough critique of the alleged blessings of German war-socialism, and the third dissects the history and politics of the German social democrats.

The book contains most of the political arguments that Mises would develop in more detail during the 1920s. Despite the rather specific nature of the events he was dealing with, none of his observations have lost relevance. As he himself points out in the book, it would be a mistake to think of pre-1914 German imperialism as a specific problem of the Teutonic race. It was rather the necessary result of certain historical conditions, which are likely to produce the same result wherever they come about, and which by 1919 had already resulted in imperialist policies in several other nations.[3]

---

[2]The first impressed reader was the young *Kammer* secretary who typed the manuscript: Therese Thieberger. She would remain his assistant until 1934, when he left for Geneva, and they would remain good friends for the rest of their lives. See Thieberger to Mises, December 5, 1971; Grove City Archive: Thieberger file.

[3]Rudolf Sieghart made this point with great emphasis:

> The peace diktats of the year 1919 have wiped the Austro-Hungarian monarchy off the map, and for the future world history this Empire is likely to be a dead letter. Of all its struggles and sufferings, nothing but some names will remain in history, or so it appears, as in the case of Carthage. But the problems which this Empire has made such painful efforts to solve are not solved in most of its successor states. They reappear everywhere in the world and will for a long time

Migrations, Mixed Populations, and Modern Imperialism

In 1914, the predominant political mentality in Germany was authoritarian: most Germans believed that sheer physical might was the necessary and sufficient condition for successful politics. Because nothing was impossible to a powerful government, the essence of politics was to make the state irresistible. Mises believed this view to be shortsighted. But why did the Germans, of all nations, succumb to imperialism? Why did they not share with so much of the West the classical-liberal enthusiasm for individual liberty, private property, and national self-determination? Mises gave two answers, one relating to Germany's interior conditions, the other concerning its foreign relations. In both cases, he showed that German imperialism resulted from a clash between the principle of national self-determination and the principle of democratic government.

After a brief honeymoon with liberal ideas prior to 1848, the Germans embraced the tenets of statism because of certain particular conditions prevailing in the eastern provinces of Germany and Austria-Hungary. In these areas, the Germans were a small minority among other nations. The introduction of democratic government would have transferred political power from the hands of the German central states to local majorities of Poles, Ukrainians, Romanians, Hungarians, and Slovaks. This in turn would have prevented any political participation of the hitherto-dominating Germans, because, in a democratic system, the command of the language of the majority is an absolute necessity.[4] As long as the liberal parties were in the

---

occupy the minds wherever national minorities struggle for the continued existence of their proper culture. (Rudolf Sieghart, *Die letzten Jahrzehnte einer Grossmacht* [Berlin: Ullstein, 1932], p. 361)

[4]Mises admits that great political *ideas* like liberalism, socialism, etc., are not language-dependent. But he points out (*Nation, State, and Economy*, pp.

opposition, the conflict between German self-determination and majority rule did not become apparent. In the wake of the revolution of 1848, however, popular democracy in the eastern territories threatened the new liberal establishment, and German liberals had been anti-democratic ever since.[5]

The second great problem of the Germans was their relative overpopulation. Classical liberalism had abolished more and more impediments, not only to trade, but also to the free movement of persons. As a result, people migrated to places offering better work conditions, which made their labor more productive. Many Germans had moved to colonies that were predominantly populated by English settlers. Surrounded by an English majority, the German émigrés quickly assimilated and thus were lost to the German nation. In a desperate attempt to counter this development, the German government established a system of protective tariffs, to reduce the incentives of German workers to emigrate under the pressure of more-productive foreign competition. When the failure of this policy became apparent, the government changed its strategy and decided instead to conquer British colonies. It began to build a mighty fleet to combat the Royal Navy, guardian of the British overseas empire. This in turn prompted the British entry into World War I.

Mises identifies population mixes with a German minority as the prime cause of German hostility to government by popular majority. The Germans preferred to rule as a minority over a majority of other nationalities, rather than be ruled by them.

38, 41, 87) that the concrete *application* of such general ideas is conditioned by language and language-dependent culture.

[5] Significantly, the very first and hotly debated problem of the constitutive assembly (*konstituierender Reichstag*) was to select the language for its deliberations starting on July 22, 1848. See Isabel Röskau-Rydel, "Galizien, Bukowina, Moldau," in idem, *Deutsche Geschichte im Osten Europas: Galizien, Bukowina, Moldau* (Berlin: Siedler, 1999), p. 96.

Mises was not moralizing. His purpose was to explain what had happened; he would leave it to others to address what should have happened.[6] The German case was unprecedented: for the first time in the history of liberalism, the principle of national self-determination was incompatible with majority rule.

But imperialism was only partly a product of specific German conditions. It was also nourished through migrations that produced "unfavorable" population mixes elsewhere, and in this respect the German case had a universal significance. In fact, in all countries where great migrations had significantly modified the national balance, imperialism had made an unexpected and powerful return. Mises argued that the Czechs, Russians, Poles, and Hungarians had already followed in the footsteps of the Germans. The United States and Australia, too, treaded on imperialist paths with their immigration policies; mixed-population-induced imperialism had become a world problem.[7]

This modern imperialism was more powerful and destructive than its predecessors, because it could rely on the economic achievements of the brief but very productive era of liberty:

> Modern tyrants have things much easier than their predecessors. He who rules the means of exchange of ideas and of goods in the economy based on the division of labor has his rule more firmly grounded than ever an imperator before. The rotary press is easy to put into fetters, and whoever controls it need not fear the competition of the merely spoken or written word. Things were much more difficult for the Inquisition.[8]

The limits of tyranny in the industrial age were by no means narrow. If it contented itself with mind control and thought

---

[6]See Mises, *Nation, Staat und Wirtschaft*, p. 1.
[7]See ibid., pp. 45, 63f., 74, 90, 107n.
[8]Mises, *Nation, State, and Economy*, p. 216.

control—the crucial elements of political domination—tyranny could last a long time indeed. But the destruction of private property would doom the central authority, because it would destroy the economic foundations of its power. Liberty would eventually be restored, but at least for a while it would be liberty in misery:

> Only one external limit is posed to this rage for destruction. . . . The apparatus of the economy based on division of labor cannot be reproduced, let alone extended, if freedom and property have disappeared. It will die out, and the economy will sink back into primitive forms. Only then will mankind be able to breathe more freely.[9]

A truly ironic and sad aspect of the war was that the German imperialist spirit had won over those who had set out to defeat it.

> Imperialism pressed weapons into the hands of all who do not want to be subjugated. To fight imperialism, the peaceful must employ all its means. If they then triumph in the struggle, they may indeed have crushed their opponent, yet themselves have been conquered by his methods and his way of thinking. They then do not lay down their weapons again, they themselves remain imperialists.[10]

The League of Nations, brainchild of Woodrow Wilson, was designed in a spirit of preserving the postwar power positions of the Anglo-Saxon and French nations, just as a hundred years

---

[9]Mises, *Nation, Staat und Wirtschaft*, p. 178; *Nation, State, and Economy*, p. 217.

[10]Mises, *Nation, Staat und Wirtschaft*, p. 180; *Nation, State, and Economy*, p. 219. Mises here expresses essentially the same idea as William Graham Sumner in his famous essay on "The Conquest of the United States by Spain" (*Yale Law Journal*, January 1899) in which he argued that, although the democratic United States had won the 1898 war with imperialist Spain, the Spanish spirit had conquered the United States.

earlier the Holy Alliance had been designed to conserve the new balance of power after the defeat of Napoleon. In the League, the imperialist "ideas of 1914 are in triumph over those of 1789." While this ironic outcome of the struggle between liberalism and imperialism was tragic for the Germans, it is "less decisive from the standpoint of world history."

> The chief point remains that nations are being "punished" and that the forfeiture theory comes to life again. If one admits exceptions to the right of self-determination of nations to the disadvantage of "evil" nations, one has overturned the first principle of the free community of nations.[11]

Moreover, the League pursued a blind one-size-fits-all agenda of making the world safe for democracy, overlooking the inconvenient fact that democratic government in areas with mixed populations does not mean national liberation but national oppression:

> The League of Nations of Versailles adopts this [nationality] principle . . . only for the nations of Europe. Yet in doing so it overlooks the fact that applying this principle wherever the members of different peoples live mingled together only ignites conflict among peoples all the more. It is still more serious that the League of Nations does not recognize the freedom of movement of the person, that the United States and Australia are still allowed to block themselves off from unwanted immigrants. Such a League of Nations endures so long as it has the power to hold down its adversaries; its authority and the effectiveness of its principles are built on force, to which the disadvantaged must yield but which they will never recognize as right. Never can Germans, Italians, Czechs, Japanese, Chinese, and others regard it as

---

[11]Mises, *Nation, Staat und Wirtschaft*, p. 181; *Nation, State, and Economy*, p. 220.

just that the immeasurable landed wealth of North
America, Australia, and East India should remain the
exclusive property of the Anglo-Saxon nation and
that the French be allowed to hedge in millions of
square kilometers of the best land like a private
park.[12]

Injustice had been perpetrated on the German nation, but
Mises prophetically warned that it would be "the most terrible
misfortune for Germany and for all humanity if the idea of
revenge should dominate the German policy of the future." He
recommended that the Germans turn their backs on imperialism once and for all, and seek instead national self-determination and peaceful relations with all other nations. This was not
an ethical imperative, but a policy in the best interest of the
Germans:

> To retaliate for wrong suffered, to take revenge and
> to punish, does satisfy lower instincts, but in politics
> the avenger harms himself no less than the enemy.
> The world community of labor is based on the recip-
> rocal advantage of all participants. Whoever wants to
> maintain and extend it must renounce all resentment
> in advance. What would he gain from quenching his
> thirst for revenge at the cost of his own welfare?[13]

The Utilitarian Method of Social Analysis

In a highly developed civilization operating under an international division of labor, it was in no one's interest to wage war or
pursue empire. Neither was it in Germany's interest to cultivate
resentments against its present oppressors, nor later to seek

---

[12]Mises, *Nation, Staat und Wirtschaft*, p. 74; *Nation, State, and Economy*, p.
91.

[13]Mises, *Nation, Staat und Wirtschaft*, p. 181; *Nation, State, and Economy*,
p. 220.

revenge. And it was against the considered self-interests of the victorious western allies that they themselves pursued imperialism. Mises believed that such purely utilitarian considerations make a much stronger case for pacifism than any ethical appeal to the powerful to refrain from exercising power.

Mises's rationalist utilitarianism must not be confused with the utilitarianism of Jeremy Bentham, a British philosopher of the late eighteenth- and early-nineteenth century. Bentham had given political utilitarianism its most famous expression, claiming that the purpose of politics should be to promote the greatest happiness of the greatest number of citizens (a normative claim). Although Mises was inspired by Bentham's work, he was not primarily interested in justifying the application of utilitarianism in politics.[14]

Max Weber's work had alerted him to the necessity of discarding normative questions from scientific analysis. Science had to deal with the world as it is, not as it *should* be. Mises was therefore not interested in whether utilitarianism should guide politics, but in its application: is the policy under consideration suitable to attain the proposed end? This, he saw, was the kind of question that could be answered objectively. Any other approach risked entanglement in normative questions. Therefore the value of utilitarianism for the social sciences did not consist in any ready-made political programs advertised under its banner, but in the practical perspective it offered on social problems. Utilitarianism, as Mises understood it, was not a doctrine, but a point of view.[15] It was the perspective of rational suitability analysis; its categories were means and ends.

---

[14]He would later comment on the crucial flaw of Bentham's political thought, which celebrated the democratic majority principle as the foundation for liberty. See Mises, *Theory and History* (New Haven, Conn.: Yale University Press, 1957), pp. 67f.

[15]See Mises, *Nation, Staat und Wirtschaft*, p. 174; *Nation, State, and Economy*, p. 211.

These questions had a venerable tradition in economic thought. John Locke, in his analysis of the debasement of coinage (monetary inflation) had stressed that the crucial question was whether this policy "would at all serve to those Ends for which it is propos'd"[16] and went on to show that this was not the case. Similarly, Adam Smith stressed that colonial trade monopolies reduced national income in all nations, even in those that were meant to benefit from them.[17] At the end of a thorough review of the interventionist trade policies of his time he concluded:

> It is thus that every system which endeavours, either, by extraordinary encouragements, to draw toward a particular species of industry a greater share of the capital of the society than would naturally go to it; or, by extraordinary restraints, to force from a particular species of industry some share of the capital which would otherwise be employed in it; is in reality subversive of the great purpose which it means to promote. It retards, instead of accelerating, the progress of the society toward real wealth and greatness; and diminishes, instead of increasing, the real value of the annual produce of its land and labour.[18]

The same approach characterized the policy analysis of subsequent generations of economists up to Carl Menger, who had

---

[16]John Locke, "Some Considerations of the Consequences of the Lowering of Interest and Raising the Value of Money," Patrick Hyde Kelly, ed., *Locke on Money* (Oxford: Clarendon Press, 1991), vol. 1, p. 304.

[17]See Adam Smith, *Wealth of Nations* (New York: Modern Library, 1994), bk. 4, chap. 7, pt. 3, p. 660 and passim.

[18]Ibid., bk. 4, chap. 9, p. 745. Other contemporary economists also argued along these lines. For example, Etienne de Condillac pointed out that virtually all forms of economic interventionism were in fact "blows against commerce." See Condillac, *Commerce and Government* (Cheltenham, U.K.: Edward Elgar, 1997), second part.

also been a utilitarian in the Misesian sense. In his *Investigations* and several other writings, Menger had argued that economic science deals with exact economic laws, and that these laws in turn concern the optimal use of available means to attain a given end.[19] Menger noticed with great satisfaction that his colleague Heinrich Dietzel championed the same view in two papers he published at the same time that *Investigations* appeared.[20] Dietzel argued that economists need not postulate that human behavior is prompted by primordial "economic" motivations. Economic science is not about motives; it is about finding the optimal means to attain a given end. In short, Dietzel saw economic science as a sort of social technology, and he eventually proposed to rename the science "socio-economics."[21]

Menger's and Dietzel's writings had influenced those younger German-language economists who were outside the ambit of the Historical School, most notably Ludwig Pohle, who criticized the Socialists of the Chair for assuming that good intentions would make for sound policy. Pohle stressed that it

---

[19]See Carl Menger, *Untersuchungen über die Methode der Socialwissenschaften und der Politischen Oekonomie insbesondere* (Leipzig: Duncker & Humblot, 1883), in particular appendix 6, pp. 262ff.; repinted in Carl Menger, *Gesammelte Werke*, F.A. Hayek, ed., 2nd ed. (Tübingen: Mohr, 1969), vol. 2; idem "Zur Kritik der politischen Ökonomie," *Zeitschrift für das Privat- und öffentliche Recht der Gegenwart* 14 (1887); idem, "Grundzüge einer Klassifikation der Wirtschaftswissenschaften," *Jahrbücher für Nationalökonomie und Statistik*, n.s. 19 (1889). The latter two papers have been reprinted in Menger, *Gesammelte Werke*, vol. 3.

[20]See Heinrich Dietzel, "Der Ausgangspunkt der Socialwirthschaftslehre und ihr Grundbegriff," *Zeitschrift für die gesamte Staatswissenschaft* 39 (1883): 1–80; idem, "Beiträge zur Methodik der Wirtschaftswissenschaften," *Jahrbücher für Nationalökonomie und Statistik* 43 (1884): 17–44, 193–259.

[21]See Heinrich Dietzel, *Theoretische Socialökonomik* (Leipzig: Duncker & Humblot, 1895); idem, "Selbstinteresse und Methodenstreit in der Wirtschaftstheorie," *Handwörterbuch der Staatswissenschaften*, 3rd ed. (Jena: Gustav Fischer, 1911), vol. 7, pp. 685–97.

was necessary to analyze whether a proposed policy really had the beneficial consequences that its advocates intended.[22]

Hence, in his utilitarian stance, Mises continued a tradition that reached back well beyond Menger. In *Nation, State, and Economy*, as well as many subsequent works, he showed that suitability analysis was extremely useful for the rational assessment of all the major political questions. In fact, the utilitarian method provided the only possible common ground for a rational comparison of liberalism, socialism, and government interventionism. Mises repeatedly argued that these political systems are merely different strategies for the realization of a common goal: the greatest happiness of the greatest number.[23] Therefore only the utilitarian method of social analysis makes possible a rational choice between these different means:

> It may be that socialism represents a better form of organization of human labor. Let whoever asserts this try to prove it rationally. If the proof should succeed, then the world, democratically united by liberalism, will not hesitate to implement the communist community. In a democratic state, who could oppose a reform that would be bound to bring the greatest gain to by far the overwhelming majority? Political rationalism does not reject socialism on principle.[24]

The Fallacies of German Socialism in War and Peace

Nation, State, and Economy is a rationalist-utilitarian analysis of the three manifestations of German imperialism: (1) past German imperialism for the sake of national greatness, (2) economic central planning in World War I (war socialism), which

---

[22]See Ludwig Pohle, *Die gegenwärtige Krisis in der deutschen Volkswirtschaftslehre* (Leipzig: Deichert, 1911), pp. 13f., 30ff.

[23]See Mises, *Nation, Staat und Wirtschaft*, pp. 141 n., 148f., 150, 182.

[24]Mises, *Nation, Staat und Wirtschaft*, p. 182; *Nation, State, and Economy*, p. 221.

accelerated the introduction of full-blown socialism, and (3) the blossoming imperialism of the social democrats under the banner of syndicalism and the dictatorship of the proletariat.

Although Mises does not define imperialism explicitly, he understands it to be the exact opposite of "self-determination, self-administration, self-rule."[25] Liberal democracy was historically embodied in "the ideas of 1789," which demanded "the most exact and complete application" of the principles of "full freedom of movement of persons and goods, the most comprehensive protection of the property and freedom of each individual," and "removal of all state compulsion in the school system."[26]

He explained that war socialism, far from supporting the German war effort, was one of five disastrous errors that had led the Central Powers to such a crushing defeat.[27] To its advocates, the emergency situation that confronted the German economy at the outset of the war, or the great tasks that it now confronted, were sufficient justification for compulsory central planning on all levels. But such a justification is based in logical fallacy. It was true, Mises granted, that there was an emergency and that the structure of production had to be adjusted as quickly as possible from peacetime to wartime conditions. But it does not follow that the government should then run the economy. The correct question was whether central planning would be better than the free market at achieving the necessary

---

[25]Mises, *Nation, Staat und Wirtschaft*, p. 37; *Nation, State, and Economy*, p. 46.

[26]Mises, *Nation, Staat und Wirtschaft*, p. 79; *Nation, State, and Economy*, p. 96. In contrast, the majority principle was in his eyes merely a means, rather than a constituent part of democracy; see *Nation, Staat und Wirtschaft*, p. 36.

[27]The other errors were military and political. The military errors were, (1) to expect the war to be short, and (2) to expect miracles from unceasing offensives. The political errors were (3) not to anticipate a war on all fronts, and (4) to make the interests of the East-Elbian Junkers supreme in German politics. See Mises, *Nation, Staat und Wirtschaft*, pp. 111ff.

adjustments. Mises proceeded to demonstrate that this was not the case.[28]

He also showed that the apparent blessings of wartime socialism were a dangerous illusion, created by the accompanying inflation. The increase of all prices had falsified the economic calculations of the entrepreneurs. The higher entries in their books falsified their profit-and-loss accounting, to the point that they believed they were making profits when in fact they were consuming their capital. Similarly, he debunked the widespread myth that war finance through government debts was a way of making future generations pay for the war effort. This view, he said, was "completely wrong":

> War can be waged only with present goods. One can fight only with weapons that are already on hand; one can take everything needed for war only from wealth already on hand. From the economic point of view, the present generation wages war, and it must also bear all material costs of war.[29]

General misunderstanding of the economic nature and consequences of wartime central planning was instrumental in reducing resistance to the accelerated introduction of full socialism. The socialists themselves denounced the wartime economic regime, partly because they did not welcome an association in

---

[28]His views on war finance had an impact on young free-market oriented economists of the interwar period such as Stefan Possony (*Die Wehrwirtschaft des totalen Krieges* [Vienna: Gerold, 1938]) and Georg Holzbauer (*Barzahlung und Zahlungsmittelversorgung in militärisch besetzten Gebieten* [Jena: Gustav Fischer, 1939]), but also on interventionists like Adolf Lampe (*Allgemeine Wehrwirtschaft* [Jena: Gustav Fischer, 1938]). Lampe had a preference for "playing markets" though. He suggested that entrepreneurial activities be centrally guided.

[29]Mises, *Nation, Staat und Wirtschaft*, p. 137; *Nation, State, and Economy*, p. 168. He went on to explain that war finance through debts (rather than through taxation or inflation) merely modifies the future distribution of resources.

the minds of the general public between socialism and war, but also in part from their own intellectual confusion. Mises objected:

> [S]ocialism means the transfer of the means of production out of the private ownership of individuals into the ownership of society. That alone and nothing else is socialism. All the rest is unimportant. It is a matter of complete indifference for deciding our question, for example, who holds power in a socialized community, whether a hereditary emperor, a Caesar, or the democratically organized whole of the people.[30]

In the third chapter of *Nation, State, and Economy*, Mises explained that the confusion about the nature of socialism resulted from the fact that the program of the socialist parties in Germany and Austria integrated three distinct elements: Marxist centralist socialism, syndicalism (radical labor-unionism), and democratic government.

The socialists had championed democracy because Karl Marx's theory predicted that socialism would be the rule of the proletarian majority.[31] This part of their program, in which they continued the old classical-liberal agenda that German liberals themselves had abandoned, had created widespread sympathy for the socialist cause even in bourgeois circles. But majority

---

[30]Mises, *Nation, Staat und Wirtschaft*, p. 140; *Nation, State, and Economy*, p. 172.

[31]Mises observes that the German socialists had stuck to the tenet of democracy only because until 1914 they had always been in the opposition and therefore bore no responsibility for their co-nationals in the eastern territories. With the onset of World War I, when they came to power in Germany and Austria, they slowly changed their minds and would have followed in the footsteps of the German liberals, but with the loss of the eastern provinces the problem of mixed nations disappeared as well. See Mises, *Nation, Staat und Wirtschaft*, pp. 105f.

rule was not a central tenet of socialism. The only essential element was central control of all means of production through a
dictatorship of the proletariat. And it was this precept of the
socialist creed that would have to stand up to rational scrutiny,
or else socialism would have to be discarded: is the compulsory
central control of production more efficient than private ownership of the means of production?[32] All other considerations
were secondary. For example, Mises observed that there was no
necessity, in 1919, to wait for the proletarians to become a
majority in Germany and Austria, because the majority of the
general population was already socialist. But if the socialist case
for central planning was invalid, then no power on earth could
maintain a socialist order.

> The dictatorship of the proletariat wants to use terror
> to nip any stirring up of opposition in the bud. Social-
> ism is believed established for all eternity once its
> property has been taken away from the bourgeoisie
> and all possibility of public criticism has been abol-
> ished. It cannot be denied, of course, that much can be
> done in this way, that, above all, all European civiliza-
> tion can thus be destroyed; but one does not thereby
> build a socialist order of society. If the communist
> social order is less suited than one resting on private
> ownership of the means of production to bring about
> "the greatest happiness of the greatest number," then
> the ideas of liberalism cannot be killed even by ter-
> rorist measures.[33]

Mises pointed out that the socialist case crucially relied on
the conviction that once the socialized society is realized, its
members would be guided by entirely different motivations

---

[32]See Mises, *Nation, Staat und Wirtschaft*, p. 152f.; *Nation, State, and Economy*, p. 185f.

[33]Mises, *Nation, Staat und Wirtschaft*, p. 169; *Nation, State, and Economy*,
p. 206.

than from those of their former lives. Rather than pursuing their own interests, they would now think only of serving their community. But if one is skeptical of the feasibility of such a New Socialist Man—if one seeks instead a system that will reconcile the private interests of real-world human beings with those of the larger community, then liberalism had already found such a system: private property.[34]

In their daily politics, the socialists had long since turned away from Marxist orthodoxy to become the political branch of the labor unions, which Marx had despised as "petty bourgeois." They espoused the down-to-earth agenda of their constituency and trumpeted their Marxist heritage only in election speeches. But from both a theoretical and practical point of view, the labor-unionist program was even worse than Marxist socialism. It destroyed the division of labor and the spirit of cooperation:

> Syndicalism deliberately places the producer interest of the workers in the foreground. In making worker groups owners of the means of production (not in so many words but in substance), it does not abolish private property. It also does not assure equality. It does remove the existing inequality of distribution but introduces a new one, for the value of the capital invested in individual enterprises or sectors of production does not correspond at all to the number of workers employed in them. The income of each single worker will be all the greater, the smaller the number of fellow workers employed in his enterprise or sector of production and the greater the value of the material means of production employed in it. The syndicalistically organized state would be no socialist state but a state of worker capitalism, since the individual worker groups would be owners of the capital.

---

[34]See Mises, *Nation, Staat und Wirtschaft*, pp. 157ff. In his later work, based on the socialist-calculation argument, he would show that the problem is the impossibility of identifying what the interests of the commonwealth are.

> Syndicalism would make all repatterning of produc-
> tion impossible; it leaves no room free for economic
> progress. In its entire intellectual character it suits the
> age of peasants and craftsmen, in which economic
> relations are rather stationary.[35]

Labor-unionism is therefore purely destructive. It is locally organized robbery elevated to a general principle. Mises's criticism did not focus on its moral reprehensibility, however, but on its inability to sustain the large-scale division of labor characteristic of modern civilization. Labor-unionism was an utterly unsuitable means to pursue the greatest happiness of the greatest number.

Political Economy of Language Communities

In his criticism of imperialist policies in the service of socialism, labor-unionism, and the socialist war economy Mises could restate many conventional arguments. He faced an unprecedented task in confronting the claim that imperialism can enhance the welfare of a nation. His pioneering analysis brilliantly confirmed Carl Menger's insight that methodological individualism is able to analyze even large collective phenomena.

The main thesis in the first chapter of *Nation, State, and Economy* is that governments are incapable of improving the condition of the nations they rule. The reason is that the origin, emergence, growth, flower, and decline of nations are subject to natural laws. The operation of these laws can be modified by government power but not abrogated, and any alteration will play out to the detriment of the nation. Mises proved his case by first analyzing nations in a free society and then turning to examine the impact of government power on their evolution.

---

[35]Mises, *Nation, Staat und Wirtschaft*, pp. 163f.; *Nation, State, and Economy*, p. 199.

His practical conclusions called for the denationalization of the nation, or more precisely, for keeping government intervention as far as possible out of the life of language communities.

Following Scherer, Grimm, and Otto Bauer, Mises defined nations as language communities. He stressed that as far as democratic regimes are concerned, this definition is more than a mere convention. In democracies, communication—and thus language—is the primary political means. Language communities are therefore of critical political importance.[36,37] What were the natural laws determining the rise and fall of language communities? Mises considered various objective factors determining their evolution.[38] But his decisive considerations start from the fact that the membership in a language community is not something unalterable. Each human person can decide to leave his former nation and join another. In a free society, Mises stressed, nations would be purely voluntary associations:

> No people and no part of a people shall be held against its will in a political association that it does

---

[36]See Mises, *Nation, Staat und Wirtschaft*, pp. 9f. He stated that a nation's specific language generated specific "political constructions" and in particular specific foundational ideas determining the operation of their governments (*Staatsgedanken*); see ibid., pp. 12, 38, 41, 87.

[37]Mises did not argue that language communities are the only factor, or the most important one, in modern politics. He speculated that racial communities were far more important. The problem was that the sociology of race and of race relations was not sufficiently developed to warrant scientific statements. He acknowledged, however, that it had become a "principle of modern political world law" that it is "no longer acceptable to use force on peoples of the white race." That is, the use of force against dark-skinned people in the European colonies was considered legitimate, but not the use of force against fellow-whites. German imperialism made enemies in all quarters by violating this distinction. See Mises, *Nation, Staat und Wirtschaft*, pp. 62, 64f.; *Nation, State, and Economy*, pp. 76, 79f.

[38]For example, he examined the role of written language and stated that it had played a crucial role in the competition between dialects. The first written dialect became the standard language. See Mises, *Nation, Staat und Wirtschaft*, pp. 17ff.

not want. The totality of freedom-minded persons
who are intent on forming a state appears as the political nation; *patrie, Vaterland* becomes the designation
of the country they inhabit; *patriot* becomes a syn-
onym of *free-minded.*[39]

Liberalism knows no conquests, no annexations;
just as it is indifferent towards the state itself, so the
problem of the size of the state is unimportant to it.
It forces no one against his will into the structure of
the state. Whoever wants to emigrate is not held
back. When a part of the people of the state wants to
drop out of the union, liberalism does not hinder it
from doing so. Colonies that want to become independent need only do so. The nation as an organic
entity can be neither increased nor reduced by
changes in states; the world as a whole can neither
win nor lose from them.[40]

What, then, determines individual membership in a language community? Neglecting objective factors such as the
familial, historical, cultural, and political environments of the
individual, Mises focused on the voluntary factor of assimilation. He asserted that, for practical reasons, language minorities
tend to assimilate to the language majorities with whom they
are affiliated through trade and other forms of social intercourse. Therefore, local minority nations *ceteris paribus* tend to
disappear in the course of time. Mises stressed that this assimilation process was dependent on individual membership in certain social classes because social contacts were class-dependent.
Minorities could preserve a separate existence for as long as spatial and social mobility were heavily controlled through custom
and laws. Things changed radically when classical liberalism

---

[39]Mises, *Nation, Staat und Wirtschaft*, p. 27; *Nation, State, and Economy*, p.
34.

[40]Mises, *Nation, Staat und Wirtschaft*, pp. 31f.; *Nation, State, and Economy*,
pp. 39f.

abolished such laws. The result was a dramatic migration—both physical and social—that disrupted the established balances between nations. Mises gave special attention to the impact of the increased spatial mobility, which by the late nineteenth century had already reached a massive scale. These migrations constantly produced areas of mixed cultures, threatening the established groups with their disappearance through assimilation, thus prompting political rivalry and conflict.[41]

Mises did not believe these movements could be stopped because they reflected the self-interest of the migrants.[42] What could be done, then, to alleviate the national conflicts that were the necessary consequence of those migrations? The only viable solution, Mises argued, was to reduce the role of the state within society, because the political conflicts between nationalities primarily concerned control of the state apparatus:

> Of course, the struggle of nationalities over the state and government cannot disappear completely from polyglot territories. But it will lose sharpness to the extent that the functions of the state are restricted and the freedom of the individual is extended. Whoever wishes peace among peoples must fight statism.[43]
>
> The way to eternal peace does not lead through strengthening state and central power, as socialism strives for. The greater the scope the state claims in the life of the individual and the more important politics becomes for him, the more areas of friction are

---

[41]See Mises, *Nation, Staat und Wirtschaft*, p. 48.

[42]*En passant* he mentioned his contribution to the economics of migration by highlighting the importance of relative overpopulation, in distinction to already-known absolute overpopulation. See Mises, *Nation, Staat und Wirtschaft*, pp. 45ff. He had developed the concept of relative over-population in his "Vom Ziel der Handelspolitik," *Archiv für Sozialwissenschaft und Sozialpolitik* 42, no. 2 (1916): 576.

[43]Mises, *Nation, Staat und Wirtschaft*, p. 62; *Nation, State, and Economy*, p. 77.

> thereby created in territories with mixed population.
> Limiting state power to a minimum, as liberalism
> sought, would considerably soften the antagonisms
> between different nations that live side by side in the
> same territory. The only true national autonomy is
> the freedom of the individual against the state and
> society. The "statification" of life and of the economy
> leads with necessity to the struggle of nations.[44]

Mises offered here a radical alternative to the prevalent models for solving national conflicts. Austria had the longest experience with national struggles within a common state, and its intellectual, political, and institutional history was therefore richer than that of any other country in analyzing and solving this problem.[45] For example, the constitution of the Austrian great-dukedom of Siebenbürgen, which existed until 1848, provided for separate parliaments and administrations for Saxons (Germans), Hungarians, and Szeklers. Affairs of general interest were dealt with in a common parliament, which debated in Latin. The ugly side of this otherwise charming arrangement was that the Romanians, who were in the numerical majority in Siebenbürgen, had no representation.[46] During the revolution of 1848, a promising approach was developed to overcome this and similar problems. On March 4, 1849 the deputies of the constitutive assembly (which had by then moved to the city of Kremsier) voted on the proposed Kremsier Constitution, the point of which was to abolish the old territorial units composing the empire (the "kingdoms and lands") and to replace them

---

[44]Mises, *Nation, Staat und Wirtschaft*, pp. 78f.; *Nation, State, and Economy*, p. 96.

[45]For surveys on Austrian language legislation, see Alfred Fischel, ed., *Materialien zur Sprachenfrage* (Brünn: Irrgang, 1902); idem, ed., *Das österreichische Sprachenrecht*, 2nd ed. (Brünn: Irrgang, 1910); Sieghart, *Die letzten Jahrzehnte einer Grossmacht*, pp. 421ff.

[46]See Eduard Bernatzik, *Die Ausgestaltung des Nationalgefühls im 19. Jahrhundert* (Hannover: Helwing, 1912), p. 30.

with administrative counties, the boundaries of which would be drawn according to the national affiliation of the inhabitants. The German nationalists reacted on the very same day with a counter-proposal presented by Prince Schwarzenberg. From then on, the principle of equal legal treatment of the different languages was on the defensive and finally defeated.[47]

The failure of the revolution prevented the practical application of the Kremsier Constitution, but the idea lived on, especially in the various programs of the social-democratic party. At their 1899 convention in Brünn, the social democrats decided to tackle the problem of national conflicts by creating parallel state organizations along national lines. This approach, they believed, would ensure "national autonomy" to each nation and thus prevent struggles between the nations once and for all. To serve as a model for the rest of Austria, they transformed their own party, creating parallel national organizations.[48] In the following years, its intellectual leaders, Karl Renner and young Otto Bauer, revived and refined and popularized the idea of replacing the old territorial units with new national counties.[49] It turned out,

---

[47]See Sieghart, *Die letzten Jahrzehnte einer Grossmacht*, p. 323; Röskau-Rydel, "Galizien, Bukowina, Moldau," p. 97.

[48]The social-democratic faction in the central parliament thereafter called itself "union of social-democratic deputies." See Sieghart, *Die letzten Jahrzehnte einer Grossmacht*, pp. 351ff.

[49]See Otto Bauer, *Die Nationalitätenfrage und die Sozialdemokratie* (Vienna: Verlag der Wiener Volksbuchhandlung, 1907); translated as *The Question of Nationalities and Social Democracy* (Minneapolis: University of Minnesota Press, 2000). Before World War I, Karl Renner published his ideas on the nationality question under the pseudonyms "Synoptikus" and "Rudolf Springer." See Synoptikus, *Staat und Nation* (Vienna: Dietl, 1899); Rudolf Springer, *Die Krise des Dualismus und das Ende der Déakistischen Episode in der Geschichte der Habsburgschen Monarchie: eine politische Skizze* (Vienna: published by the author, 1904); idem, *Grundlagen und Entwicklungsziele der Öster-reichisch-Ungarischen Monarchie* (Leipzig: Deuticke, 1906). At the end of World War I, he published under his true name: *Das Selbstbestimmungrecht der Nationen: in besonderer Anwendung auf Oesterreich* (Leipzig: Deuticke, 1918).

however, that nationalistic passions were too strong to be tamed even by the spirit of socialist solidarity. After the introduction of universal suffrage in 1907, the party quickly dissolved into national organizations and lost all impact on Austrian politics.

With hindsight, and with the help of Mises's theory, we can identify the root cause of these failures. All of his predecessors had tried to use government to solve the problem of national struggles. None of them recognized (or admitted) that coercive association—the *sine qua non* of the state—was the very source of national conflicts. A different government scheme cannot possibly be a solution for a conflict caused by the nature of government itself.

But how far could one go in keeping the state out of society? How far should one go? Mises argued that the only limits are of a technical-administrative nature:

> The size of a state's territory . . . does not matter. It is another question whether a state is viable when its population is small. Now, it is to be noted that the costs of many state activities are greater in small states than in large ones. The dwarf states, of which we still have a number in Europe, like Liechtenstein, Andorra, and Monaco, can organize their court systems by levels of jurisdiction, for example, only if they link up with a neighboring state. It is clear that it would be financially quite impossible for such a state to set up as comprehensive a court system as that which a larger state makes available to its citizens, for example, by establishing courts of appeal.[50]

Hence, Mises advocated a complete liberalization of society. There should be no political limits to this process. And it would in practice be limited only by banal technical considerations. In other words, Mises welcomed the unhampered competition

---

[50]Mises, *Nation, Staat und Wirtschaft*, pp. 66f.; *Nation, State, and Economy*, p. 82.

among national territories, which in a free "inter-national" society would be a peaceful competition between language-based cultures, in which each individual, through his assimilation choices, would determine the fate of the various language communities. Mises sensed that the only dignified attitude toward the reality of cultural competition was national self-confidence:

> A nation that believes in itself and its future, a nation that means to stress the sure feeling that its members are bound to one another not merely by accident of birth but also by the common possession of a culture that is valuable above all to each of them, would necessarily be able to remain unperturbed when it saw individual persons shift to other nations. A people conscious of its own worth would refrain from forcibly detaining those who wanted to move away and from forcibly incorporating into the national community those who were not joining it of their free will. To let the attractive force of its own culture prove itself in free competition with other peoples— that alone is worthy of a proud nation, that alone would be true national and cultural policy. The means of power and of political rule were in no way necessary for that.[51]

Mises argued not only that political rule is unnecessary to improve the condition of a nation, but also that it is incapable of doing so. In a free society people constantly migrate to those locations offering the most favorable conditions for production. Every individual has an incentive to migrate from a relatively poor area to a relatively rich area. These migrations would continue until wage rates and interest rates are equal in all locations.[52]

---

[51]Mises, *Nation, Staat und Wirtschaft*, p. 61; *Nation, State, and Economy*, p. 76.

[52]With this consideration Mises complemented the Ricardian analysis of free trade, which was based on the assumption that capital and labor were mobile only within the borders of the state. See Mises, *Nation, Staat und Wirtschaft*, pp. 51ff.

In a liberalized world, therefore, there would be a tendency away from differences in income. There would eventually be no rich or poor countries in the world. There would only be countries that are more densely populated, and other countries that are less so.

Mises pointed out that government intervention does not change anything about people's motives to migrate from relatively poor areas into relatively rich ones. On the contrary, if government tries to keep its people in the land through a system of protective tariffs, it only exacerbates the problem. Protective tariffs might prevent the emigration of those who would be most affected by foreign competition, but they reduce the per capita income of all the other members of society, further multiplying the incentives for emigration. Again, a dispassionate suitability analysis comes out against government intervention. Mises concluded that the only rational approach in matters of political nationalism was to follow classical-liberal precepts: shrink the state, open borders, and face the cultural competition of international migrations. ⫷

Ludwig von Mises, at age 45, in 1926

9

1919

THE WAR HAD SEEMED like it would never end. Then suddenly, it was over. The Balkan front crumbled in the wake of the armistice in Bulgaria at the end of September 1918. This time it was clear that it would not be possible to liberate enough additional forces from elsewhere to stem the tides in the South East. The Central Powers had lost.

Faced with defeat, the prewar nationalistic tensions within the empire began to reappear even more forcefully. Now Czechs, Croats, Slovenians, Hungarians, and Serbs all sought political independence.[1] The young emperor attempted to save what he could of the centuries-old order by making a peace offer to President Wilson on October 4. Twelve days later, in a last desperate effort to reconcile his recalcitrant nations, Karl abandoned the traditional policy of his family and now tried to spearhead the opposition. He issued a manifesto announcing the reconstruction of Austria-Hungary as a federal state with autonomy for the lands of Czechoslovakia and Yugoslavia.[2] The

---

[1]Jurij Krizek argues that these tensions were amplified during the war because of the compulsory centralization of the k.u.k. economy, which unilaterally benefited the industrial and financial establishment in Vienna and Budapest. See Jurij Krizek, "Die Kriegswirtschaft und das Ende der Monarchie," R.G. Plaschka and K. Mack, eds., *Die Auflösung des Habsburgerreiches* (Munich: Oldenbourg, 1970), pp. 43–52.

[2]For a previous Austrian attempt to enter into peace negotiations with the United States on the basis of a proposed new federal structure for

attempt failed miserably. In fact his manifesto only compounded the crisis—it had been widely interpreted as proclaiming the dissolution of the empire and legalizing the secession of its nations. Rudolf Sieghart later stated: "World history knows no similar case in which the dissolution of an empire has been organized in all forms from above." And in his last speech to the upper chamber of the Austrian parliament, the same writer summed up the ironic essence of the manifesto: "Even before the Austrian nations give up their state, the state gives them up."[3]

Two days after Karl's proclamation, the Entente replied that mere autonomy for Habsburg lands was not enough. The emperor had to give carte blanche to the secessionists and to the enemies of the monarchy. On October 21, the Revolution broke out in the streets of Vienna and in the following weeks spread to Hungary, Bavaria, and Berlin. The South front collapsed when the Hungarian leader Michael Karolyi called back the Hungarian troops, thus preparing a last-minute Italian victory on the battlefield.[4] When Ludendorff's army surrendered on November 11, 1918, Germany was no longer a monarchy and in a process of rapid political dissolution. Even worse was the fate of its southern ally: Austria-Hungary had been entirely wiped off the political map.

The former Habsburg dominions, so rich in territories, individuals, and nations, had shrunk back to—well, to what? It was even difficult to pick a name for the territory that remained after national secessions had amputated most of the old empire. The leftover land hosted a population of 6.3 million,

---

Austria-Hungary, see Erik von Kuehnelt-Leddihn, *Von Sarajevo nach Sarajevo* (Vienna: Karolinger, 1996), p. 21.

[3]Rudolf Sieghart, *Die letzten Jahrzehnte einer Grossmacht* (Berlin: Ullstein, 1932), p. 248.

[4]See Christian Eckert, "Friedensverträge. II. Vom staatswissenschaftlichen Standpunkte," *Handwörterbuch der Staatswissenschaften*, 4th ed. (Jena: Gustav Fischer, 1927), vol. 4, pp. 444ff., 515.

of predominantly German ethnicity. Obviously it could no longer be called Austria-Hungary: Hungary was gone. Neither did it make sense to call it only Austria because historically this name did not refer to national borders, but circumscribed the limits of the Habsburg possessions: *Österreich*—the Eastern Empire. The remaining citizens spontaneously baptized their land *Deutschösterreich* or "German-Austria." The name speaks to their uneasiness and lack of identity.

The emperor's manifesto had proposed that all nations of the empire establish "national councils." The German members of the *Reichsrat* had immediately accepted the idea and formally met on October 21 in Vienna, calling their gathering "provisional national convention of German-Austria." In their second meeting on October 30, then, the provisional parliamentarians had claimed for themselves the supreme control of the German-Austrian state. Even though they did not try to determine the form of the new state (Emperor Karl had not yet formally abdicated), they appointed a government composed of Social Democrats, Christian Socialists, and German Nationalists. Leadership fell to the socialist Karl Renner, who became state chancellor in Austria's darkest hour.

Twelve days after the appointment of the provisional government, the emperor abdicated and left the country. The socialist parliamentarians pushed for both the immediate proclamation of a new republic and its unification with the German Reich, where the socialists were the leading political power. The leaders of the new state had no more urgent business than to dissolve that state. One day after the German armistice, the new German-Austrian republic, in the very act of her brith, declared an *Anschluss* ("annexation") joining the new German Republic. It was November 12, 1918.

New Battlefields

In the years preceding the war, the social democratic party had sunk into political insignificance. By 1911, it had splintered into various national organizations and suffered a terrible setback at the *Reichstag* elections.[5] But the war and eventual defeat had discredited the political establishment to such an extent that the social democrats by virtue of their "outsider" status now seemed to be the most important political force in the country, though elections could not yet be held to confirm the fact. Their hour of glory came at the very moment when they lost their eminent leader. Victor Adler died on November 11 and Otto Bauer—the Austro-Marxist who had debated Böhm-Bawerk as a student in his seminar—became the number one party official. But while Bauer had the strongest backing within the party, he lacked support in the general population, because of his youth and his radicalism. Leadership of the government therefore remained in the hands of the moderate Karl Renner until June 1920.

The radicals under Bauer tried to push Renner to turn the political revolution into a social and economic revolution as well. They sought fully to nationalize the Austrian economy and to incorporate Austria into the German Reich, which was already

Otto Bauer

under firm social-democratic rule. When these attempts failed (largely because of Ludwig von Mises's personal impact on Bauer, as we shall see) the political climate in German-Austria slowly reversed. Elections in February 1919 gave rise to a constitutional convention, and showed the social democrats to be far less powerful than so many had believed. Renner was forced to admit the Christian Social Party's charismatic leader, Monsignor Ignaz Seipel, into his government, and Seipel's party would come to rule German-Austria for most of the 1920s.

In the dramatic winter before the elections, nobody saw those changes coming. People had more immediate concerns. The economic situation in the new Austrian Republic was even worse than in Germany. The average citizen lacked access to

---

[5]See Sieghart, *Die letzten Jahrzehnte einer Grossmacht*, p. 354.

basic goods, especially potatoes, sugar, and coal. Traditionally, the Austrians bought these supplies from other parts of the former empire—from their Czech neighbors in the north, from the Hungarian and Galician plains in the east. But now these regions had gained political independence and their new leadership brought international trade to a standstill. The war was lost, stomachs were empty, people were freezing to death, and there was no relief in sight. From a purely financial point of view, the German-Austrians were the great losers of the war among all nations.[6]

In the winter of 1918–1919, most Austrians were optimistic that the new government, composed as it was of an enlightened elite, would eventually overcome the political and economic chaos that was the aftermath of the war. Yet the new men in charge set out to continue and complete the policies of the previous Imperial governments, which had already put in place a system of war socialism. A contemporary observer and personal acquaintance of many of the country's new leaders, Mises explained:

> From the beginning the intention prevailed in all socialist groups of dropping none of the measures adopted during the war after the war but rather of advancing on the way toward the completion of socialism. If one heard differently in public . . . this had only the purpose of dissipating possible doubts about the rapid tempo of socialization and about individual measures and of stifling opposition to them. The slogan had already been found, however, under which further socializing measures should sail; it was called *transitional economy*.[7]

---

[6]See Mises, *Nation, Staat und Wirtschaft* (Vienna: Manz, 1919), p. 134; translated by Leland B. Yeager as *Nation, State, and Economy* (New York: New York University Press, 1983), pp. 164f.

[7]Mises, *Nation, Staat und Wirtschaft*, p. 144; *Nation, State, and Economy*, p. 176.

During the first year of its existence, the national parliament dedicated its sessions to deliberation on "social legislation" and voted the latest socialist wisdom into law. Within a few months, the new government imposed eight-hour workdays, compulsory vacation for workers, compulsory co-management of firms through worker representatives, coercively financed unemployment insurance, and many other such schemes. The educated public looked on Austria as Americans of 1950 would have looked on a U.S. government run by Milton Friedman, Alvin Hansen, and Paul Samuelson. Power and intellect finally united—*felix Austria*! But the socialists failed, despite their undeniable personal brilliance and economic training.

❧   ❧   ❧

The cornerstone of the new economic system was the printing press of the Austro-Hungarian Bank. Tax revenue was far too low to pay for the various government handouts and increasing the tax rate was both politically impossible and likely to be inadequate to increase the revenue sufficiently in any case. New debts could not be incurred because there was not enough money left over to lend, and the government's credit was terrible: no one expected it to pay back the pile of debts it had amassed during the war. There was therefore only one way for the new government to establish a large-scale welfare state: print more money.

Nineteen-nineteen was a year of crisis. Serious economic and political problems were compounded through a catastrophic policy of inflation-financed socialism. It was a crisis that brought the young republic to the verge of collapse. Civilization prevailed and the specter of anarchy faded only because a few men stood ready to confront all difficulties to make their country safe for liberty and entrepreneurship.

Postwar Socialism and the Specter of Anarchy

Official positions in the new government did not always reflect actual power. For instance, because of the support of the most militant groups within Austrian social democracy, Otto Bauer (who headed the Ministry of Foreign Affairs) was even more influential than Karl Renner, the chancellor. The situation changed only in 1927, when a social-democratic insurrection was defeated with unexpected ease.

The Ministry of Foreign Affairs had a Trade Policy Department that was responsible for the preparation of the trade-related aspects of the forthcoming peace negotiations. The department hired several external consultants strongly affiliated with the Austrian School of economics: Schüller, Mises, Somary, and Steiner.[8] Mises's longstanding personal acquaintance with Bauer, Lederer, and Schumpeter—former fellow-students and colleagues from the War Economics department of the War Ministry—was certainly one of the motives behind the decision to involve him in the new government. Another was that Bauer knew Mises was loyal to the Austrian state. Yet a third motive was the time-honored strategy of containing the most knowledgeable opponent of socialist schemes. But Mises's involvement was a double-edged sword. Had the war not taken place, or the empire not disintegrated, the government and the wider Austrian public would certainly have noticed his views on monetary affairs; after all, he had acquired a solid reputation as an expert on money and banking, and was also the spokesman for the *Kammer* on these questions. But now his views bore the stamp of political authority. While he could not say everything that he knew and believed, what he did say gained immediate

---

[8]Virtually all the higher officials in Bauer's ministry—including Bauer himself—were Jews or of Jewish origin. On November 22, 1918 (Mises Archive 107: 55a) and again on January 11, 1919, the Vienna paper *Reichspost* insinuated that the ministry's takeover by Bauer, "the Jew Dr. Richard von Schüller, a close relative of the recently deceased industrialist Taussig," and Schüller's subordinate "Jews Dr. v. Mieses, [sic] Dr. Broda, and Dr. Steiner" was somehow unacceptable. Yet the fact was, as the *Wiener Morgenzeitung*— a "Jewish National" newspaper—pointed out, that Mises and Somary were Austria's most important currency theoreticians (see Mises Archive 107: 44).

and widespread attention: Still his impact on actual government policy remained moderate. Mises's main mission was to lead tedious negotiations on prewar and wartime financial obligations with foreign businessmen, bankers, and government representatives. Within the government, his colleagues sought his advice, but usually did not heed it.[9]

In the case of Bauer, Mises's influence proved to be short-lived. It was limited to one decision, but it was a critical decision of over-arching importance:

> It was solely due to my efforts that Bolshevism did not then prevail in Vienna. Only a few people had supported me in my efforts and their help was rather ineffective. I, alone, managed to turn Bauer away from seeking union with Moscow. The radical young men who rejected Bauer's authority and were eager to proceed alone and against the will of the Party leadership were so inexperienced, incapable, and torn by mutual rivalry that they could not even form a half-way viable Communist party organization. The events lay in the hands of the leaders of the old Social-Democratic Party, where Bauer had the final word.[10]

Until that fateful winter of 1918–1919, when Mises persuaded Bauer to stop Bolshevism in Vienna, the relationship between the two men was based on mutual esteem. Mises knew personally almost all Marxian theorists of Western and Central Europe, but in his eyes only Bauer "surpassed modest mediocrity." He recognized that Bauer had great knowledge of philosophy, classical economics, history, and the natural sciences, and that he was an excellent speaker who could quickly master the

---

[9]Mises often met with Bauer, Lederer (director of the *Staatskommission für Sozialisierung*), and Schumpeter (who became finance minister in the Spring of 1919). See Mises Archive 53: 13.

[10]Mises, *Notes and Recollections* (Spring Mills, Penn.: Libertarian Press, 1978), p. 77.

most difficult problems—"he could have been a statesman, if he had not been a Marxist." The problem, then, which eventually corrupted Bauer's intellectual, moral, and personal integrity, was that all his learning and all his activities were based on an *a priori* commitment to Marxism.

> Otto Bauer arrived at the University of Vienna as a devout Marxist. . . . [He] had made up his mind never to betray his Marxian conviction, never to yield to reformism or Socialist revisionism, never to become a Millerand[11] or Miquel.[12] No one was to surpass him in Marxian zeal. His wife, Helene Gumplowicz, later strengthened him in this resolve to which he remained faithful until the winter of 1918–1919. At that time I succeeded in convincing the couple that a Bolshevist experiment in Austria would have to collapse in short order, perhaps in a few days. Austria depended on the importation of food from abroad, which was made possible only through relief assistance from former enemies. At no time during the first nine months after the Armistice did Vienna have a supply of food for more than eight or nine days. Without lifting a finger, the allies could have forced the surrender of a Bolshevist regime in Vienna. Few people clearly recognized this state of affairs. Everyone was so convinced of the inevitability of the coming of Bolshevism that they were intent merely on securing for themselves a favorable position in the new order. The Catholic Church and its followers, that is, the Christian-Social Party, were ready to welcome Bolshevism

---

[11]Alexandre Millerand, born 1859, French socialist, was originally radical; when in power, he limited his activities to moderate programs.

[12]John von Miquel, 1821–1901, German statesman, originally was an extreme revolutionary; later he was described as one who had entirely surrendered his radicalism, and aimed only at "practical measures for improving the condition of the people irrespective of the party programs."

with the same ardor archbishops and bishops twenty years later welcomed Nazism. Bank directors and big industrialists hoped to earn a good living as "managers" under Bolshevism. . . .

I knew what was at stake. In a few days Bolshevism in Vienna would have created starvation and terror. Plundering hordes would soon have roamed the streets of Vienna and, in a second blood bath, would have destroyed the remnants of Viennese culture and civilization. Throughout many nights I discussed these problems with the Bauers until I finally succeeded in convincing them. The resulting restraint of Bauer determined the course of events in Vienna.

He went on:

[Bauer] could never forgive me for having made him take the position of a Millerand. The attacks of his fellow Bolsheviks especially hurt him. However, he directed his passionate hatred not against his opponents, but against me. He endeavored to destroy me by inciting chauvinist professors and students against me. But his scheme failed. From that time on I never again spoke with the Bauers.[13]

Bauer and his consorts were subsequently confined to indirect means for achieving their beloved communist state. Rather than copying the Russian model of political revolution they now

---

[13] Mises, *Notes and Recollections*, pp. 16–19. This passage is the only direct source from which we know about Mises's role in preventing Otto Bauer and his wife Helene Gumplowicz from putting their Bolshevist plans into practice. Some collateral evidence is provided in a February 1919 letter to Mises from a certain Dr. Johanna Wallner. She sent him her telephone number and asked him to give Dr. Bauer her greetings. "Under present circumstances," she writes, she does not want to bother (*behelligen*) Bauer with her affairs (see her letter dated February 16, 1919, Mises Archive 53: 30ff.). Thus she knew that Bauer was very busy in his government activities and that Mises was likely to see Bauer precisely in these busy times.

sought to bring about communism in a piecemeal fashion.[14] This involved three major strategies: (1) partial expropriations, (2) supplanting the free market with a system of artificial "prices" for labor and consumers' goods, and (3) eradication of any remnants of old authority.

On this last front, the Viennese socialists achieved at least one lasting victory. On April 3, 1919, a law was enacted prohibiting the use of all titles of nobility and honors. The imposing "von"—concise designation of nobility—was *verboten* in any printed document. And the same order was given in respect to the honorific

Karl Renner

"Edler," the noble predicates "Erlaucht," "Durchlaucht," and "Hoheit," and the noble class designations "Ritter," "Freiherr," "Graf," "Fürst," and "Herzog." As far as business cards, books, and other printed documents were concerned, the prohibition has remained effective to the present day. In interwar Austria, however, the old ways were maintained in personal encounters and oral communications. Mises's name was rendered as "Ludwig Mises" on his book publications and correspondence, but in daily business he would still be addressed as "Professor von Mises."

The major benefit of this unparalleled legislation was to spur Austrian wit. One gentleman of venerable descent circulated his business card with the imprint *geadelt von Karl dem Grossen, entadelt von Karl Renner*—ennobled by Karl the Great, denobled by Karl Renner.

As for the expropriation of private property, the government's policies had a far less lasting impact, but they did do consider-

---

[14]Before he changed his views on the question of socialization, Bauer had been the leader of the left wing of the Austrian socialists. Thereafter he increasingly shifted to the middle ground and reinforced his position within the party apparatus. See Norbert Leser, "Otto Bauer—Friedrich Adler—Max Adler," Walter Pollack, ed., *Tausend Jahre Österreich* (Vienna: Verlag Jugend und Volk, 1974), vol. 3, p. 270.

able damage for the few months they were in effect. A major
agent of this destruction was a new government office headed by
Emil Lederer, called the *Staatskommission für Sozialisierung*
(State Commission for Socialization), which
worked closely with its sister organization in
Germany. The German agency had convened a
group of experts to examine the question of
whether the socialization of coal mining was possible.[15] On February 15, 1919 these experts—
with the cooperation of Joseph Schumpeter—
published a report in which they argued that
socialization was not only possible, but necessary

Emil Lederer

to avoid a mere "governmentization" (*Verstaatlichung*). They
made no attempt to explain the distinction.[16]

The *Staatskommission* epitomized the embarrassment of a
government that was supposed to instigate a socialist revolution,
but had no idea how to do so. The members of the commission
knew they had to come up with a justification for its existence.
Lederer presented it at the first postwar plenary meeting of the
Verein für Socialpolitik, which took place in September 1919 in
Regensburg. He criticized the present state of socialization in

---

[15]The Socialization Commission in Germany first met on December 5,
1918 and also included the Austrian professors Lederer, Hilferding, and
Schumpeter, as well as Theodor Vogelstein (a former chief executive in the
war-socialist economy of Germany), the influential publisher Heinrich
Cunow, labor-union leader Otto Hué, and the German professors Carl Bal-
lod, Robert Wilbrandt, and Eduard Heimann, who acted as secretary general
of the Commission. By March 1919, similar committees had been established
not only in Vienna, but also in Dresden, Munich, and Stuttgart. See the very
informative piece by neo-Spartakist Manfred Behrend, "'Der Wandschirm,
hinter dem nichts geschieht.' Bildung, Tätigkeit und Ende der ersten
deutschen Sozialisierungskommission," *Glasnost* (1998); and the literature
quoted therein.

[16]See Sozialisierungskommission, *Vorläufiger Bericht über die Frage der
Sozialisierung des Kohlenbergbaues* (Berlin, February 15, 1919); quoted from
Behrend, "Der Wandschirm, hinter dem nichts geschieht."

Russia, ridiculing it as a mere "consumers' socialism." The great goal of the German-Austrian government must be the complete socialist transformation of the economy, for which Lederer discussed two strategies. One was to put control of each individual firm in the hands of its workers; this, Lederer claimed, was liable to establish "economic democracy" and was therefore a first step toward democratic socialism in the whole society. The second strategy was to levy a huge one-time capital tax to pay back the war debts.[17] This by itself would immediately put the state in control of industrial capital. The only remaining problem would be to make sure that this "governmentization" would be followed by a true "socialization." But again, this distinction was not explained.[18]

The only concrete proposal on the table seemed to be the one-time capital levy, a measure that had the backing of ostensibly reasonable people such as Schumpeter. Mises tried to lead the *Kammer* into steadfast opposition to this measure.[19] He argued that the imposition of the capital levy would force Austrian entrepreneurs into debt, making them dependent on financial capitalists. Mises also revealed what he perceived to be the long-term

---

[17]Such plans had already been discussed during the war at a meeting of the *Verein für Socialpolitik* on October 14, 1916 in Berlin. Heinrich Herkner had championed the idea of solving the problem posed by the huge war debts through a one-time confiscatory tax. Alfred Weber, who at the time worked for the German Treasury, fiercely opposed any discussion of the issue because it would jeopardize the government's attempt to sell war bonds. See Franz Boese, *Geschichte des Vereins für Sozialpolitik, 1872–1932* (Berlin: Duncker & Humblot, 1939), p. 153.

[18]See ibid., pp. 160f. See also Lederer's paper in "Verhandlungen des *Vereins für Sozialpolitik* in Regensburg 1919," *Schriften des Vereins für Sozialpolitik* 159 (1920); and Alfred Amonn, *Hauptprobleme der Sozialisierung* (Leipzig: Quelle & Meyer, 1919). Amonn belonged to the German-Austrian Staatskommission für Sozialisierung.

[19]Some evidence for his involvement is in correspondence with Frau Fischer, his secretary at the *Kammer*. See the July 1919 correspondence Mises Archive 53: 40. Mrs. Fischer wrote to Mises after his departure to Bad Gastein, where he would spend his summer vacation.

political goals behind the innocuous "one-time" measure. He pointed out that the socialists talked only of sharing the profits, but that this left out the actual structure of enterprise:

> If, however, the state owns shares in all enterprises, it will also share in losses; moreover, it will even be forced to concern itself with the administration of individual businesses, just that, however, is what the socialists want.[20]

The socialist government's impact was most devastating, however, in its perpetuation and extension of the wartime system of price controls. The previous imperial governments had started supplanting the free market by a system of administered "prices" for labor and consumers' goods. Right or wrong, the purpose of this approach was to concentrate all economic energies on the war efforts. When the socialists came to power, they made this system even more encompassing; in their hands, they believed, it would become a means of transforming bourgeois and capitalist Austria into a paradise of the proletariat. Thus government agencies administered higher-than-world-market prices for labor services, and lower-than-world-market prices for agricultural products.

The socialist beggar-thy-neighbor model had set an example for the entire country in ways that had not been anticipated by the rulers in Vienna. The provinces were not willing to comply with Vienna-style socialism. They had their own, homegrown schemes in mind. Each province now sought to loot their local rich, rather than share the booty with Vienna. These conflicts of interest, a natural consequence of the government's socialist

---

[20]Mises, *Nation, Staat und Wirtschaft*, p. 140; *Nation, State, and Economy*, pp. 171. The Austrian experience prepared him well for the American discussion of capital levies of the early 1940s. See his comments in "Report of After-Dinner Discussion, July 30, 1941 on The Prospects for and Extent of A Capital Levy," Grove City Archive: Trusts and Estates file.

agenda, had already made themselves felt under wartime socialism.[21] Now they had broken out full-scale and precipitated town
and country into economic warefare. This left Vienna without
any resources but the monetary printing press. Rapid political
and economic disintegration was accompanied by a deterioration of the krone. Mises wrote to Lederer:

> Here the condition of the currency is hopeless—a
> hopelessness that results from the pitiable state of
> public finance. Only the farmers can still pay taxes,
> and they openly declare that they will not pay any-
> thing. On the other hand, the government deems it
> necessary to spend millions per month to feed an
> urban population that does not work.[22]

Unlike the Russian Bolsheviks, Vienna socialists were unwilling to coerce the provinces into obedience. They perceived the
crisis as constitutional, and hoped to remedy it by legal means.
They failed to see that the real issue was a profound conflict
between Vienna and the provinces that was sparked by their
own economic policies.

Mises analyzed the situation in a December 2, 1919 lecture
to the Association of Austrian Economists on "the political relations between Vienna and the provinces from the overall economic standpoint."[23] He argued that Vienna could only thrive

---

[21]See Mises, *Nation, Staat und Wirtschaft*, p. 119; *Nation, State, and Economy*, pp. 146f. fn.

[22]Mises to Emil Lederer, letter dated October 21, 1919; Mises Archive
73: 58.

[23]Gesellschaft der österreichischen Volkswirte; "Die politischen
Beziehungen Wiens zu den Ländern im Lichte der Volkswirtschaft." See
Mises Archive 107: 20a, 55. The speech was subsequently published in *Neues
Wiener Tagblatt* and *Wirtschaftspolitisches Archiv* and struck a nerve with the
general public. Herr Roth-Seefrid, a businessman and lawyer who knew Austria as well as he knew the back of his own hand, wrote to Mises: "I would
hope that the essay was circulated widely in Germany, where, I must unfortunately admit, a frighteningly unclear impression of the *Anschluss* and the

by a continued participation in the international division of labor. Austria's harvest could never suffice to feed Vienna's workers; only foreign food supplies could, and these had to be bought in exchange for industrial exports. Even the proposed annexation to Germany could not change this state of affairs. The present policy of funding government by printing new money was a typical short-run device that survived only by depleting the capital accumulated in pre-socialist decades. It was bound to wreak havoc on the currency and the economy.

These public comments understated his real perceptions. He was after all a public figure and therefore obliged by law not to harm the nation. Only after World War II, when he no longer held appointed public office, did he become blunt in commenting on public policy. However, one can infer his real views on the state of Austria in late 1919 from a confidential memorandum that he wrote for Vienna's leading bankers and industrialists.[24]

> We are approaching the collapse of our currency. Our monetary policy presently knows only *one* means: printing banknotes, printing ever more new banknotes. There is hardly a prospect of change. One cannot legitimately ask the social-democratic party suddenly to acknowledge that the socialist idea has imploded and that all that it has proclaimed for decades has turned out to be wrong. One cannot expect that the Christian-Social party, whose ideal is a stationary economy of autarchic farmers and small craftsman longing for "subsistence," which for decades has championed professional licenses and

---

like reigns" (Mises Archive 74: 2; translation mine). Roth-Seefrid lived in Berchtesgaden. Mises might have met him there on vacation, for example in August 1927 (Mises Archive 62: 6).

[24]See "Über die im Hinblick auf das Fortschreiten der Geldentwertung zu ergreifenden Massnahmen" (On the measures to be taken on behalf of the decreasing value of money) in Mises Archive 109.

high tariffs, which along with the prince of Liechten-
stein has advocated the program of an "Austria without factories" and has fought with Lueger and
Schlesinger for the "Guilder of the Fathers" and for
"people's money," one cannot expect this party suddenly to become free-trade and liberal. Neither can
one hope that experience will teach any economic
and financial insights to the German Nationalists,
who have always sought to top the social-reform radicalism of the other parties, who today have especially
become the advocates of those broad layers of public
employees whose syndicalism has knocked out our
public finance, and who have learned nothing about
foreign policy and have not forgotten anything
despite the terrible defeat in the world war. It is the
misfortune of this country, which can only exist on the
basis of industrial exports, that the spirit of modern
economic policy has remained alien to its population.
Our policy moves entirely within the intellectual
orbit of imperialism, of mercantilism, of socialism,
and of fantasies about a "national" economy.[25]

Mises pointed out that influential circles within the government believed inflation to be of secondary importance and of no
direct pertinence to the political problems of the day. These
men thought they could suppress the domestic consequences of
inflation (price increases) through price controls, and that the
international consequences (plummeting exchange rates) could
be neglected because they did not directly affect the nation. As
Mises explained, however, this benign neglect for the krone's
plummeting exchange rate was extremely shortsighted. Most of
the working classes' food supply came from abroad through
contraband channels—in fact, these black markets were all that
was keeping the Viennese population alive. If no end was

---

[25]"Über die im Hinblick auf das Fortschreiten der Geldentwertung zu
ergreifenden Massnahmen," p. 1 in Mises Archive 109: 2.

expected for the decline of the krone exchange rate, the contraband merchants would eventually refuse to be paid in krone
banknotes. The consequence would be immediate and impose
dire hardship on the urban masses. Mises went on:

> Given the mentality of our population, this will infal-
> libly lead to excesses. People will first plunder retail
> businesses and then public buildings, bank palaces,
> and private apartments. The last feeble remnants of
> government authority will dwindle; armed bands will
> attempt to rob the country—an attempt that will
> everywhere but in the immediate surroundings of
> industrial centers end in their bloody defeat, because
> today the rural population is armed and is supported
> by well-armed and disciplined local police forces.
>
> This anarchy within the country is the more dan-
> gerous because there are also great dangers threaten-
> ing from abroad. Excesses perpetrated by the popular
> masses can easily lead to hurting foreign citizens, from
> which many a pretext may be derived for an invasion
> by foreign troops. It is true that the Entente does not
> care much for the state of our country and also that
> her present military weakness prevents her from
> intervening. But things are different in the cases of
> Hungary and Czechoslovakia. Both states control
> powerful and well-trained armies. In both countries,
> chauvinistic prestige considerations make for an
> eagerness to occupy parts of German-Austria and
> Vienna in particular. The Czechs are embarrassed by
> the fact that they did not gain their independence
> through glorious military achievements; not without
> reason, the Czech militarists consider the Czech
> Army's cowardly running away from Hungary's Bol-
> shevist troops a dishonor that they want to make good
> for. The Magyar troops too are eager for "national"
> glory; . . . Both Czechs and Magyars will seize any
> opportunity to retaliate for the alleged injustice that
> "Vienna" has perpetrated on them. In truth the
> Czechs seek revenge for the heavy disappointments

occasioned by their young Czech state, and the Magyars seek revenge for the plunder that the Romanians have carried out in Hungary.[26]

Mises knew what he was talking about when he mentioned Hungarian appetites for invading Vienna. In the early summer of 1919, he led negotiations with representatives of the new—and as it turned out, short-lived—Communist government of Hungary, concerning the property rights of Austrian citizens in Hungary. The official leader of the Hungarian delegation was the ambassador to Austria, but this man rarely took part in the meetings and thus the real leaders on the Hungarian side were one Dr. Görög and one Dr. Polanyi. Görög was a colorless bureaucrat without any strong political feelings, but Polanyi had a brilliant mind and was a convinced Communist who clashed at many meetings with Mises, often in long discussions of fundamental questions of social philosophy.[27] One can guess that these clashes concerned not only socialism and capitalism, but also the injustices that Vienna had perpetrated on Hungary. Mises therefore knew that the slightest military weakness in truncated-Austria was likely to culminate in a Hungarian invasion. The present Austrian army was too weak to prevent it. The German army could be relied on, but the Entente probably would not allow its intervention; at any rate, precious time would be lost with diplomatic negotiations—enough for a plundering expedition to Vienna to escape unpunished.

Vienna was in fact invaded before the Treaty of Saint-Germain-en-Laye was signed in September 1919, but the invaders

---

[26]"Über die im Hinblick auf das Fortschreiten der Geldentwertung zu ergreifenden Massnahmen," p. 6 in Mises Archive 109: 7.

[27]See Mises Archive 74: 11ff. Much later, in February 1924, Karl Polanyi sent Mises his paper "Sozialistische Rechnungslegung" which had been published in the *Archiv* 49 (1922) and asked Mises for an offprint of his critique of this article. Polanyi by then lived in the 7th district in Vienna. His letter did not sound very clear (see Mises Archive 80: 87).

were not Czechs or Hungarians—they were Italian troops who forced their way to Vienna to plunder its art collections and libraries.[28] The Hungarian Communists certainly would have followed suit, but they were ousted by a counterrevolution. The Treaty then put some constraints on Czechoslovakia and Hungary. A foreign occupation had thus been ruled out, but the internal dangers could not be stopped. Continued funding of the government's socialist experiments by rampant inflation was likely to lead to complete social breakdown within the country, and possibly to a Communist-Bolshevist insurrection.

Pro-Government Emergencies

Mises was one of the few men who understood that the inflation itself and the inflationary mentality it had produced were the greatest political burdens the war economy had bequeathed to the new republic. But in the socialists' eyes, he was merely a competent technician who knew the money machine well. And during the first months of his involvement with the new administration, Mises did in fact play this role faithfully, preventing on several occasions Austria's fall into lawlessness.

Mises knew that funding the government by printing money contradicted all established principles of public finance. As he had explained in *Theory of Money and Credit*, it was a risky and temporary expedient. If kept up, it had to lead to hyperinflation. Still, as things stood, he believed it was the only way to maintain law and order in Vienna.

> [G]overnment expenditure is today considerably higher than government revenue, and all effort to limit expenditure and to increase revenue until the budget is equilibrated encounter almost irresistible political difficulties. Under such conditions, there is

---

[28]See Christian Eckert, "Friedensverträge. II. Vom staatswissenschaftlichen Standpunkte," p. 511.

> hardly any other solution but to put the printing
> press directly or indirectly to the financial service of
> the state and to provide, by the issue of banknotes,
> those means that cannot otherwise be provided.[29]

It was not the only time Mises would justify and implement emergency monetary policies that are difficult to reconcile with classical-liberal principles. In accord with F.A. Hayek, one could call such positions *desperado policy*: it is "essentially the policy of the desperado who has nothing to lose and everything to gain from a short breathing space."[30] But keep in mind that Mises approached policy matters from a utilitarian point of view. Strictly speaking, there is no such thing as scientific "classical-liberal principle" from his perspective. There are only effective and ineffective policies. Using the monetary printing press in the winter of 1918–1919 was the only suitable way to keep the government going, he thought.

There was also a different sort of emergency that seemed to require a greater use of the printing press. A few months after the political disintegration of the Habsburg empire, the monetary and financial disintegration followed suit. The war bonds had in fact been underwritten mainly by ethnic Germans, who tended to represent the wealthier, urban population of the country. At the end of the war, cash holdings were largely concentrated in predominantly non-German rural areas. The black market had moved food into the cities and cash out into the agricultural countryside. It is not surprising that one of the first measures of the new national governments was to deny responsibility for the war debts incurred by the empire. It was a simple

---

[29]Mises, "Der Wiedereintritt Deutsch-Österreichs in das Deutsche Reich und die Währungsfrage," Michael Hainisch, ed. *Wirtschaftliche Verhältnisse Deutsch-Österreichs* (Schriften des Vereins für Sozialpolitik, vol. 158; Leipzig: Duncker & Humblot, 1919), pp. 155.

[30]F.A. Hayek, *Profit, Interest, and Investment and Other Essays on the Theory of Industrial Fluctuations* (London: Routledge & Kegan Paul, 1939), pp. 63f., n. 1.

political decision that seemed to entail only advantages for their main constituencies, which were the anti-German movements of the seceded territories. The burden of the repayment would fall exclusively on the Germans. As things stood, this was easy enough to justify to both the new nations and the Western powers.[31]

The bondholders soon realized that the small Republic of Austria could not bear the burden of all the war debt on its own. They turned to redeeming their bonds at a discount for cash at the Austro-Hungarian Bank, and the bank granted these requests without fail, printing any quantity of additional banknotes to accommodate the wishes of the bondholders. Thus the urban bondholders had saved at least some fraction of their investment, whereas the rural cash owners saw the purchasing power of their money holdings shrinking under the relentless influx of new money.

Whether or not the Yugoslav, Czechoslovak, and Hungarian leaders had considered the possibility that the central bank could use its control of the production of krone banknotes to counteract their scheme, there was now only one way out for them. They had to abandon the Austro-Hungarian Bank's currency and establish their own. Technically, this involved

---

[31]Mises believed and continued to believe for some time that these popular anti-German laws would prove to be short-lived. On May 9, 1919 he took part in a conference sponsored by the *Währungsschutz* association dealing with the Austrian position in the forthcoming peace negotiations (see Mises Archive 107: 22, 44b). In his comment, which was widely publicized, he stated that the Allies had rejected Russia's refusal to pay the government debts of the old Czarist regime. On the same grounds, therefore, they would have to reject the demands of the new Czechoslovakian, Polish, and Yugoslavian governments, which sought to repudiate debts incurred under the Habsburg monarchy. This would be in accordance with a time-honored principle of international law. Any other stance on this issue would jeopardize international trade, thus harming the Allies' own interests. However, this impeccable argument did not prevent the Allies from siding with the Slavic successor states. Hatred is often stronger than self-interest.

"stamping" the krone notes circulating in their territories, thus making them identifiably separate currencies. Yugoslavia was the first country to put this into practice in early January 1919 and Mises at once commented on the event in an anonymous piece for *Neue Freie Presse*.[32] He anticipated what the next move would be: Yugoslavia, for example, would use a part of its cash surplus to buy financial and other assets in the countries that still used Austrian kronen. This would (1) increase Yugoslavian wealth—trading bad paper for real goods—and (2) provoke a price increase in Austria from which the Yugoslav economy would be protected because of its separate currency.

Such a postwar inflationary reflux of krone notes had been a constant fear during the wartime expansion of the krone currency area. Now it was a reality. Mises started campaigning for immediate countermeasures. The only effective strategy for Austria was to do the same thing—stamping the krone notes circulating in its territory and thus creating a separate Austrian currency. In a truly grotesque episode from mid-January 1919, the champion of sound money provided hands-on support for banknote production.[33] Mises unofficially approached his friend Victor Graetz,

---

[32]"Die Abstempelung der Kronennoten im jugoslawischen Staate," *Neue Freie Presse* (#19536; January 14, 1919); copy is in Mises Archive 106. Such anonymous pieces were often signed by "a leading monetary politician." Mises's authorship is evident from the writing style and vocabulary, as well as from the fact that these pieces are kept in common files (the custodians of the archive in Moscow worked diligently in preserving the "natural" order of the files that they had received from their owner).

[33]He wrote that:

> the money problem, at the moment of the dissolution of the Austro-Hungarian Monarchy, was merely a technical problem of printing, and the question how to obtain printing-plates, banknote-paper and printing-ink appeared for the moment the most important points of currency policy. (Ludwig von Mises, "Republic of Austria. Banking and Finance," *Encyclopedia Britannica*, 12th ed. [1921], vol. 30, pp. 348f.)

who ran a large printing company. His inquiry concerned additional printing facilities for the Austro-Hungarian Bank, whose printing press was unable to handle a rapid replacement of the krone circulation. Graetz responded:

> Coming back to the discussion we had on Tuesday, I venture to inform you that I have made inquires about the question of banknote production, and that very probably it is possible to assure the production in private printing houses within the necessarily short delay. The Steyrermühl [Graetz's company] would be in the position to provide 10 flat-pressing machines which, considering the urgency of the case, could be operated 24 hours in three work shifts, so that the performance would be equal to that of 30 fast-pressing machines.[34]

Because quick action was an imperative, the first step was to stamp the Austrian krone notes. In early February, Mises made the case for this measure in an anonymous piece for *Neue Freie Presse*, urging quick action.[35] The next day, the government issued a decree ordering the stamping of the krone notes circulating in Austria, a process that was completed by June.

When the Czechoslovak government started stamping its notes in late February, it was clear that the Austrians had not acted precipitously.[36] Mises explained the matter in detail in an article he prepared for the *Verein für Socialpolitik* on the question of currency union between Germany and Austria.[37] In the

---

[34]Graetz's letter to Mises, dated January 16, 1919; Mises Archive 53:1.

[35]The article was signed "von einem hervorragenden Währungspolitiker" (from the pen of a leading monetary politician) in *Neue Freie Presse* (February 11, 1919); see copy in Mises Archive 107: 39.

[36]Mises probably commented on this event too in a piece for *Neue Freie Presse*. See Dub's February 25 letter in Mises Archive 53: 16.

[37]This is the paper already quoted as "Der Wiedereintritt Deutsch-Österreichs in das Deutsche Reich und die Währungsfrage," pp. 145–71. Austria's "re-entering" into the German Empire refers to the years before 1867 when its *Kronländer* were part of the *Deutscher Bund* (German Federation). The *Bund*

final version of this piece, which he completed in early July, we read:

> Now German-Austria had to act too. She could not wait until all other states had shifted from the Austro-Hungarian krone to a national krone. She had to separate herself from the Austro-Hungarian krone to prevent those banknotes, which for whatever reasons would not be stamped in the other state territories, from flying back to German-Austria and increasing inflation here. She had to prevent the Czechoslovakian Ministry of Finance, which after the stamping had held back half of the banknotes of its citizens, from using this half to buy stocks and bonds in German-Austria. She had to prevent those krone banknotes circulating in the billions in the Ukraine and in neutral foreign countries from being considered money of German-Austria alone.[38]

He did not mention of course that he himself had already taken the steps he advocated. The government only ratified the *status quo* Mises had already brought into being. On March 15, 1919, Schumpeter was appointed Minister of Finance in Karl Renner's second government, a coalition between Renner's social democrats and the Christian Social Party. Schumpeter immediately put the reform of the currency on his agenda. The matter was apparently settled in a single day of intense discussions with representatives of the Austro-Hungarian Bank and

---

had been established under the leadership of the house of Habsburg as a post-Napoleonic-wars successor organization of the Holy Roman Empire of German Nations, which had disappeared in 1806. The *Bund* ended in 1867 when Prussia defeated it in a short war (battle of Königgrätz).

Mises finished this work in early July 1919, but he circulated a previous version in the wake of his activities in early 1919; see Staatssekretär Urban's letter dated March 5, 1919, which refers to this article, in Mises Archive 53: 29.

[38]Mises, "Der Wiedereintritt Deutsch-Österreichs in das Deutsche Reich und die Währungsfrage," pp. 153f. See also his presentation in Mises, "Republic of Austria. Banking and Finance," pp. 348f.

external experts such as Landesberger, Hammerschlag, Wilhelm König, Walther Federn, and Mises.[39] An executive order of March 25, 1919 conferred the status of legal tender on the stamped krone notes and denied this status to unstamped ones.

This seems to have been one of Schumpeter's few successes as finance minister. He had no power base within either party of the new government. The social democrats trusted him because he had used his academic authority to support the socialization of big industry. The Christian Socialists liked him because of his long-standing opposition to union with Germany. But his only real political asset was the international reputation he enjoyed. He was a recognized authority in economics, and his chancellor correctly anticipated that this could be helpful in negotiations with international creditors. This reputation was no help, however, in his efforts to put government finance back on track. Not a single major point of his program was put into practice: he could not impose a one-time capital levy to pay off the war debt, he could not stabilize the currency, and he failed to create an independent central bank. After the other cabinet members denied support for his financial program, the luckless Schumpeter threw in the towel and quit the government on October 17, 1919.

Toward Sound Money

The stamping of the krone banknotes had prevented a catastrophe, but the great remaining question was of course how Austrian monetary policy and public finance could be restored to sanity. This had to happen quickly, but the average intellectual saw no way of of this mess. Stopping the printing press seemed to imply the destruction of firms and laborers:

> From a theoretical point of view it is correct to put
> the principle of economic freedom into practice, but

---

[39]See Mises Archive 107: 23.

> this principle cannot be realized (because of the destruction of great masses of entrepreneurs and laborers that would result from it) without revolutionary changes; thus the political consequences of putting this principle into practice would prevent it from having its effect.[40]

In reality, this "destruction" would not have been harmful for the workers. Stopping the inflation would have left intact the physical production facilities—and thus the source of the laborers' income; the production sites, factories, and other producers' goods would merely have changed owners. What the inflation did was to prevent such a sweeping redistribution of capital goods from the economic establishment to private entrepreneurs. In a profound sense, the socialist status quo was not pro-working class, but pro-establishment. From this point of view, the argument that Mises's anti-inflationist endeavors were "politically unfeasible" was clearly about what was and was not palatable to the powers that be.

He began an anti-inflation campaign in the winter and spring of 1919. His greatest asset was the readership of the liberal Vienna press—a well-positioned audience. His status as a recognized authority on financial matters put the stamp of officialdom on his pronouncements and he was therefore a carefully read commentator on current events—so carefully read that he preferred to publish some of his pieces anonymously. Mises gladly accepted an offer from his friend Victor Graetz who ran a major printing company and published the daily newspaper *Neues Wiener Tagblatt*. Graetz had no competent journalists to cover economic policy, and monetary policy in particular, and thus wanted Mises to write for his paper. The prolific Mises already wrote on monetary policy for the *Neue*

---

[40]This is Emil Lederer commenting in correspondence on Mises's paper "Zahlungsbilanz und Wechselkurse" (Balance of payments and exchange rates). See Mises Archive 73: 57.

Freie Presse,[41] but Graetz offered attractive terms: Mises would dictate his articles to a stenographer who would come every morning between 8 and 9 o'clock to his apartment. Moreover, Mises would not have to sign the articles and there would be no indication that they were written by a non-staff author.[42]

He also gave public lectures on these problems, almost exclusively to educated audiences (lawyers and businessmen—not politicians) who were taken with his personality and lecture style.[43] One of the obstacles he had to overcome was that the inflation's effects were not yet visible. In Germany and Austria, price controls suppressed domestic price increases thus limiting the most noticeable and painful consequence of inflation to the decreasing number of unregulated markets—and to black markets. The public is thus deceived and fallacious doctrines take hold. These fallacies in turn lead to bad policies, in particular to foreign exchange controls.

The only "official" evidence that something was wrong with the krone was the constant decline of exchange rates, in particular

----

[41]In those days of heated activity, Mises was often asked to deliver on the same day, and seems to have complied (see Mises Archive 53: 16, for an article on the implications of Czech monetary policies in late February 1919).

[42]See Graetz's letter dated March 8, 1919; Mises Archive 53: 44. In the same vein, Mises was also invited to contribute monetary analyses to *Dorn's Volkswirtschaftliche Wochenschrift*, a weekly economics journal edited by a former colleague from the *Wissenschaftlichen Comité für Kriegswirtschaft*. See the editor's letter dated January 27, 1919 in Mises Archive 53: 54. The editor also invited him to lecture before the *Frauenklub* on "Socialization and Economic Planning." Two weeks before, Otto Neurath had given a talk on this subject, and Mises would provide the antidote.

[43]For example, in the lecture he gave on May 2, 1919 on "Means and Ends of Currency Policy" (see Mises Archive 53: 12), he addressed the members of a commerical association. The talk was apparently very successful and dealt a heavy blow to the inflationist party (see newspaper reports in Mises Archive 107: 21, 44a). Mises gave many more talks of this nature during the year, for example, at a common meeting of Austria's chambers of commerce in October 1919 (see Mises Archive 107: 44c).

with the currencies of neutral countries. Yet the champions of inflation successfully prevented this fact from alarming the public. They argued that the declining exchange rates resulted from the mechanics of the balance of payments and that there was no necessary relationship between increases of the money supply and the exchange rate.

In two papers, Mises gave a concise refutation of this balance-of-payments theory and made the case for the quantity theory of money. He pointed out that all shortcomings of the quantity theory could not affect its main tenet: that there is a positive relationship between variations of the quantity of money and variations of the price level.

These articles—"The Quantity Theory of Money" and "Balance of Payments and Exchange Rates"[44]—appeared in a low-circulation professional journal, and Mises had had to be very cautious in wording his critique to protect these papers from the government censor. Nevertheless, his frontal attack on the monetary status quo encountered fierce resistance from several "practitioners" of economic policy, including Siegfried Rosenbaum, the director of the Anglo-Austrian Bank and main sponsor of Walther Federn's journal. But the spell was broken. Mises's papers were widely read and discussed in the following years. Their circulation could have been even larger if Mises had not prevented new printings of "Balance of Trade and Exchange Rates," which he intended to integrate into the second edition of *The Theory of Money and Credit*.

In a parallel effort to his sound money campaign, Mises worked out two plans for monetary reform—an official one proposing action for "normal" times, and a secret contingency plan in case of a sudden emergency. The monetary problem that virtually monopolized the attention of the Austrian government

---

[44]"Die Quantitätstheorie" and "Zahlungsbilanz und Wechselkurse." Copies of both papers are in Mises Archive 39.

and public in the first few months of the republic was a proposed currency union with Germany. Prevailing wisdom—and
the angst Austrians felt from a lack of political or national identity after the collapse of the empire—had it that Austria was
incapable of solving problems without assistance from her big
brother to the north. Mises was charged with defining the Austrian position for the upcoming negotiations with the Germans,
and was invited to contribute an expert report on the question
to a special *Verein für Sozialpolitik* volume that analyzed the Austrian economy. The volume was meant to give a summary of the
situation in Austria and thus serve to inform a larger German
public about the specific conditions of their neighbors to the
south.

The technical details of Mises's report are still relevant to the
modern world of paper money. He pointed out that all problems of Austria's proposed monetary unions with the German
Reich arose from the fact that both countries presently used
paper monies.

> A currency community of two states on the basis of a
> paper currency is hardly feasible if there is not from the
> very outset the intention to abstain from any further
> inflation, and if this intention is not strictly put into
> practice. As soon as inflationary measures are resorted
> to, to add to the state treasury, there must arise differ-
> ences of opinion about the distribution of the new
> quantities of money that are to enter circulation.[45]

The only example of such a currency community based on
paper money was the Austro-Hungarian dual monarchy, which
had been established in 1867 and featured two states using the
same currency, namely the currency of their common predecessor, the *Kaisertum Österreich*. Yet this currency community could
be successful because it was based on the principle that the total

---

[45]Mises, "Der Wiedereintritt Deutsch-Österreichs in das Deutsche Reich
und die Währungsfrage," p. 156.

quantity of banknotes in circulation could not be increased. Thus distributive conflicts were avoided from the outset. But if the proposed currency union involved any inflationary measures, the only way to avoid such distributive conflicts was to establish a common financial administration, he thought.

> It is therefore clear from the outset that German-Austria's adoption of the German Reich's currency can begin only once the political unification has been [if not achieved, then] at least unchangeably decided.[46]

It was Mises's position that Austria should be granted a special subsidy during the first years of the unification because Austrians had made greater contributions to the war effort, and had suffered more from defeat. Also, the financial agreement between the two states had to allow Austrian entrepreneurs to redeem discounted war bonds at the central bank. This was absolutely essential because they had invested much more of their capital in war bonds than had the German entrepreneurs. Mises insisted on these two points, mentioning each of them twice in his 25-page report.

As for the ratio for the conversion of kronen into marks, Mises argued that it should be based on the prevailing market exchange rate between the two currencies. The ratio would also have to account for the future redemption rate of marks into gold. He recommended that this rate be based on the prevailing mark-price of gold. Attempts to reestablish the prewar rate would hurt exports, which would be devastating under the present circumstances, especially for the Austrians.

The transition from the present state of two independent paper monies to the desired currency union could most suitably be achieved through the intermediate creation of a mark-exchange standard. In this scheme, the Austrian central bank would start redeeming its notes for marks, thus making kronen *de*

---

[46]Ibid., pp. 156f.

facto money substitutes for marks. "By this very fact, German-Austria's adoption of the German currency is put into practice. The krone is nothing but a name for a part of the mark."[47] The final step would be the replacement of krone notes by mark notes.

This was a simple and elegant solution, but it was already moot by the time Mises finished the revision of his paper. In early May 1919, the Entente powers issued a decree containing the peace conditions for Germany, and one of them was that Germany could not unite with Austria. The western allies would not budge from this position, and on June 28 the German delegation signed the diktat of Versailles.

Political union had become impossible, and so had Austria's monetary and financial annexation to the German Reich. But Mises pointed out in his report that his plan for currency unification could still work, even under the conditions of the Versailles treaty. In fact, the proposed mark-exchange standard had great legal advantages:

> German-Austria's adoption of the mark-exchange standard does not require any action of the German Reich's government. It therefore does not affect the obligation that the German Reich incurred in the peace treaty on behalf of Austria's independence.[48]

His government colleagues preferred other options. They did not see sound money as a priority. They still sought ways to get around the repayment of wartime debts and to expropriate private savings. Misesian reform—stopping inflation, abolishing price controls, and moving toward *laissez faire*—was out of the question. Apart from all other considerations, these policies would have exposed the enormous redistributive effects of the wartime policies. Renner and Bauer looked for an alternative.

---

[47]Ibid., p. 164.
[48]Ibid., p. 165.

One way to deal with the effects of "surplus money" was to seize cash holdings. Expropriation from German-Austria's former creditors was planned and propagated under the insidious term of *Vermögensabgabe*, which can be translated as "sharing the wealth." This rhetorically philanthropic measure was an all-out attack on the country's capitalists who had heavily invested in war bonds and then redeemed them at a loss from the Austro-Hungarian Bank after the dissolution of the old krone currency area. The proposal encountered the fierce opposition of the *Kammer*, of course, and the socialists were forced to consider other alternatives.

After the peace agreement had been signed on September 10, Austria received loans from the West, giving the government new financial flexibility. Characteristically, the foreign credits were used to buy food for Vienna's now inactive proletarian masses, and many Austrians were already counting on more western help in the future. Mises spoke out against the childish notion that foreign capitalists and governments could have any long-term interest in financing a ruinous socialist experiment in Vienna.

A conference on Austria's currency problems organized by the Vienna Association of Commerce and Industry gives a good sense of his alternative program.[49] Mises and his friend Wilhelm Rosenberg were the main speakers.[50] Rosenberg explained that foreign-exchange controls and banking regulations had stopped the inflow of badly needed foreign credit, and encouraged costly barter and black-market exchanges. The present relief was only temporary. He proposed attracting foreign credit by granting special privileges to foreign companies in such fields as mining, road construction, and tourism. Then Mises observed that strikes and work stoppages were pandemic in Austria. The

---

[49]The conference took place on November 11, 1919. See the newspaper report in Mises Archive 107: 44d.

[50]Wilhelm Rosenberg was already known as a writer on currency problems. See his *Valutafragen*, 2nd ed. (Vienna: Manz, 1918).

only exception was the printing press of Austria's central bank, which worked day and night. If this state of affairs continued, the krone notes would soon become worthless, their circulation would break down, and chaos would ensue. Mises then explained the origins of the present mess: the government itself had created the inflation; it then took the ensuing price rises as a pretext for imposing price controls and many more interventions. As in ancient Rome, the Austrian government was now at the point of providing the means of sustenance for a majority of the metropolitan population. Hoping for more Allied financial support was futile. The only way out was for the government to spend no more than it took in.

But Mises was completely disillusioned concerning the government's capacity to solve the problems that threatened to bring chaos and violence throughout the country. It had taken him time to learn this lesson, and he learned it the hard way. He had had his own ideas about how an enlightened government could enact a thorough monetary reform but he now knew that it would never happen. He developed instead a revolutionary private-enterprise strategy for the establishment of sound money and was resolved to pursue it without delay.

The fundamental paradigm shift at the heart of the Mises Plan was simply to ignore the government, and to make the reform of the monetary system an affair of the country's principal bankers, merchants, and industrialists. In the fall of 1919, Mises distributed a confidential memorandum. He argued that there was an imminent danger that the inflation and the plummeting krone exchange rate would incite people to give up on using krone banknotes altogether, and that it was necessary to prepare for this day.

> One can hardly expect the government to make such preparations. It cannot be assumed that the financial administration that for five years has not only followed, but also repeatedly sought to defend the disastrous inflation policy, and which in complete ignorance of the sole source of the decreasing value of

money has accelerated the decline of the krone, would suddenly change its mind. Leaders responsible for its policies who correctly saw the economic connections have up to now been unable to overcome prevailing in-house traditions. Citizens must seek to achieve through their own powers that which the government fails to bring about. All one can hope for on the part of the government is that it not hamper the initiative of the private sector. It is the duty of the banks—and with the banks, that of big corporations in industry and trade—to make ready the measures that appear necessary to overcome the catastrophic consequences of the collapse of currency. This is in their own interest and also a service to society as a whole.[51]

Mises then gave the details of his plan. He proposed to take measures to replace the krone with a foreign currency. If the inflationary process was sufficiently slow, he argued, no further measures would be necessary. The krone would then be replaced in a continuous process without threatening a disruption of business operations. The danger lay exclusively in the scenario of a sudden collapse that would leave the citizens without money. In this case, disruption could ensue and lead to misery and violence. It was in anticipation of this possibility that he urged the Austrian entrepreneurs to seek a credit of 30 million Swiss francs that could be used for the payment of one month's worth of wages and for retail payments. Moreover, it was of utmost importance that this sum be available in very small denominations lest it be useless for the man on the street.

Austrian law did not allow this, but in the emergency scenario underlying the Mises Plan such legal considerations would be secondary. And he urged his readers not to despair about the possibility of such an emergency, but to see it instead as an opportunity for political improvement:

---

[51]Mises, "Über die im Hinblick auf das Fortschreiten der Geldentwertung zu ergreifenden Massnahmen," p. 7; Mises Archive 109: 8.

Political ideas that have dominated the public mind for decades cannot be refuted through rational arguments. They must run their course in life and cannot collapse otherwise than in great catastrophes. . . .

One has to accept the catastrophic devaluation of our currency as foregone. Imperialist and militarist policy necessarily goes in hand with inflationism. A consequent policy of socializations necessarily leads to a complete collapse of the monetary order. The proof is delivered not only through the history of the French revolution, but also through the present events in Bolshevist Russia and a couple of other states that more or less imitate the Russian example, even though they do not display the atrocious brutality of the Jacobins and Bolshevists, but prefer less bloody methods instead. As unbecoming as the collapse of the currency is in its consequences, it has the liberating effect of destroying the system that brings it about. The collapse of the assignats was the kiss of death for the Jacobin policy and marked the beginning of a new policy. In our country too a decisive change of economic policy will take its impetus from the collapse of the currency.[52]

Vienna Circles

Mises's main occupation was still that of a *Kammer* secretary, in which capacity he profited from the government's attempt to democratize Austria.

---

[52]Ibid., pp. 2f. (Mises Archive 109: 3f.). Without knowing it, Mises had spelled out here an idea that, many years before him, Carl Menger had stated in a private note, saying that ideas must run their course. F.A. Hayek discovered this note at the beginning of the 1930s, when he worked on a new edition of Menger's works. Mises later referred to this note in his *The Historical Setting of the Austrian School of Economics* (Auburn, Ala.: Ludwig von Mises Institute, [1969] 1984), pp. 36f.

The egalitarian wave reached the *Kammer* during the year 1919 and was eventually voted into law on February 25, 1920. The *Kammer* was now renamed the Lower Austrian Chamber of Trade, Commerce, and Industry, and all members now had equal voting rights, irrespective of their tax bill. The internal organization of the *Kammer*'s Executive Office was also changed. The new law stipulated a stronger emphasis on giving the different branches of the economy a more equal representation within the Executive Office—even a level of autonomy within its confines. A new Department of Transport was set up and also a new Department of Banking and Credit. Mises became the executive responsible for questions of money and credit. In his new function, he exercised leadership far beyond the borders of Vienna and Lower Austria due to the privileged status of the Vienna *Kammer*.[53]

He also remained a professor of economics both at the University of Vienna and—briefly—at the *Exportakademie*.[54] He resumed the regular discussions of economic theory that he had organized before the war. These meetings attracted the small number of economists in Austria and Germany sharing a genuine interest in theoretical problems of the social sciences. Mises's group, the nucleus of what would soon after become the more formal *Nationalökonomische Gesellschaft*, enjoyed a virtual monopoly on Vienna's top theorists—especially because Wieser, who was still the most renowned theorist in Vienna, was not interested in this kind of exchange of ideas, and so attracted no

---

[53]On the 1920 reform of the law see Bundeskammer and Wiener Kammer der gewerblichen Wirtschaft, eds., *100 Jahre Handelskammern in Österreich* (Vienna: Amtsblatt der Bundeskammer der gewerblichen Wirtschaft, 1948), pp. 143ff.; Franz Geissler, "Die Entstehung und der Entwicklungsgang der Handelskammern in Österreich," Hans Mayer, ed., *Hundert Jahre österreichische Wirtschaftsentwicklung, 1848–1948* (Vienna: Springer, 1949), pp. 110ff.

[54]For his involvement with the export academy see Mises Archive 53: 3. The export academy would later become the *Hochschule für Welthandel* and then the *Wirtschaftsuniversität*, under which name it is still known today.

such group about himself or his precepts. The Mises circle thus became a crystallization point for the dispersed and isolated theorists in the German-speaking world. Their attitude toward the Vienna group is beautifully summed up by Schumpeter who, having to cancel an appearance at one of the group's meetings, said he had dearly wished "to speak to our circle and graze in congenial company on a theoretical meadow."[55]

The most time-consuming of Mises's intellectual endeavors were the seminars he taught at the University of Vienna, but the activity also gave him relief from the tiresome workdays at the *Kammer* and from hopeless political affairs. He loved being a professor. He loved intelligence and intelligent debate. No amount of political turmoil could deter him from offering his second university seminar as professor of economics, in the winter of 1918–1919. When the first session started, the seminar members were the subjects of a monarchy. When the discussion resumed after a fortnight, they were citizens of a republic. The students must have been impressed by the presence of Dr. Ernst Seidler, who had been one of imperial Austria's last prime ministers. Seidler probably knew Mises from common prewar chamber of commerce activities.[56]

Mises's plan for the seminar was to highlight the importance of the theory of value for the analysis of market phenomena and to stimulate discussions of the major competing theories of value: the subjective theory of value, Marx's theory of value, value in mathematical economics, and Franz Oppenheimer's objective theory of value. He sought to entrust the presentation

---

[55]Schumpeter to Mises, letter dated December 9, 1918, Mises Archive 51: 130f.

[56]Most of the same members assembled for a summer seminar on the issue of free trade versus protectionism. Among the participants was apparently Siegfried Rosenbaum, the president of the Anglo-Oesterreichische Bank and sponsor of Walter Federn's *Österreichischer Volkswirt*. See Rosenbaum's September 1919 letter (Mises Archive 53: 33f) in which he expressed his wish to attend soon another seminar with Mises and Fräulein Dr. Sommer.

of each of these doctrines to one of its adherents. The seminar also featured discussion sessions on the measurement of value and on the differences between classical and modern economics.[57] Rather than taking into account only the most recent articles published in the most prestigious journals, Mises used the seminar to introduce the students to important classical authors. He also encouraged them to do outside research and write articles on particular topics, and offered his assistance with these tasks. He urged them to read broadly without any specific goal or particular agenda—a principle he advocated all his life. He tried to be helpful in various ways, from lending books out of his personal library to finding suitable employment for his students after graduation.

Despite the war and its aftermath, Vienna had remained a great center of learning. Besides the Austrian School of economics, which continued to thrive under Wieser, Mises, and Mayer, there were Austrian or Vienna schools of theoretical physics and philosophy (Moritz Schlick), of law (Kelsen), psychoanalysis (Freud, Adler), history (Dopsch and young Otto Brunner), and art history (Max Dvorak and Josef Strzygowski). But while Mises's classes at the university were a great opportunity for students to become acquainted with theoretical economics, the lectures and exercises were necessarily limited to an elementary level.[58] Mises therefore sought to establish a private seminar for the discussion of more advanced problems. Many such private circles existed in Vienna, and their characters differed widely depending on those involved. Some pioneers of

---

[57]See Mises Archive 17: 25.

[58]Starting in 1919, the University of Vienna offered a new degree in government sciences with a strong emphasis on economics. Students had to attend six semesters of courses in economics, public finance, economic history, statistics, general theory of the state, public administration, and international law. To obtain the Ph.D. in government sciences, they then had to write a dissertation and undergo "two thorough exams." See *Amtsblatt der Universität Wien* 6, no. 9 (June 1919).

various disciplines had instituted private seminars to train their followers in small-group sessions; this was the case, for example, with Sigmund Freud, who had already started a group before World War I, and also for the postwar circle of Hans Kelsen. Other private scholarly circles did not feature a central figure— for example, the student circle that Mises had set up with the Pribram brothers and Emil Perels in 1908 and which would eventually become the *Nationalökonomische Gesellschaft*, or the *Geistkreis*, a student group that Herbert von Fürth and F.A. von Hayek founded in the early 1920s. Some scholars had membership in several circles at once. For example, Felix Kaufmann, a student of Hans Kelsen's and later an assistant professor under him, was a member of the law-oriented Kelsen seminar, the social-science-centered Mises seminar, and the philosophical Vienna Circle. Mises too took part in several groups: in spring and summer of 1919, he was a member both of the *Nationalökonomische Gesellschaft* and of a seminar discussing the writings of Marx.[59] It was probably here that Mises confirmed his less than favorable impression of the socialist intelligentsia. Here he learned that the Party Marxists consisted of two groups: (1) those who had never studied Marx, and who knew only a few popular passages from his books; and (2) those who with all the literature in the world had read as self-taught men nothing except the works of Marx. Max Adler, for instance, belonged to the former group; his Marxian knowledge was limited to the few pages in which Marx developed the "superstructure theory." To the latter group belonged especially the East

---

[59]This last group met on Monday evenings on the premises of the *Staatskommission für Sozialisierung*. Most of its members were Marxists or people with communist leanings such as Lederer and Käthe Pick; see Pick's letter to Mises in Mises Archive 53: 50. Pick had been a member of Mises's seminar already during the 1918 theoretical exercises in the economics of banking. See her correspondence with Mises in Mises Archive 51: 85, 53: 50. She also took part in his subsequent university seminars.

Some of Mises's students from Vienna became famous in the post-World War II era:
Friedrich Hayek, Gottfried Haberler, Alfred Schütz, and Fritz Machlup

Europeans, who were the ardent ideological leaders of Marxism.[60]

Mises's own private seminar started on November 26, 1919 with a talk by Elisabeth Ephrussi on Carver's theory of interest. Subsequent speakers included Strigl, Tugendhat, and Sommer.[61] The sessions of the "privatissimum," as Mises called it, probably took place in his offices in the *Kammer*. In any case this is where the seminar met in later years, when admission would be limited to participants with a doctoral degree. The degree could be in any science; the purpose of the requirement was only to assure the person's aptitude for scientific research.

He wholeheartedly supported his female students as a matter of course, placing for example Marianne von Herzfeld and Helene Lieser as economists with the Association of Austrian Banks and Bankers. Helene Lieser was the first woman in Austria to obtain a doctorate in government science. She went on to become Secretary of the International Economic Association in Paris. Another

---

[60]See Mises, *Erinnerungen* (Suttgart: Gustav Fischer, 1978), p. 11; *Notes and Recollections*, p. 16. The only exception he refers to was Otto Bauer, see above.

[61]See Mises Archive 17: 37. Ephrussi was probably the heiress to the Ephrussi Bank. Margit von Mises mentions Ludwig's occasional joking remark that he could have married a rich heiress had he not met Margit. He was probably referring to Elisabeth Ephrussi. See Margit von Mises, *My Years with Ludwig von Mises*, p. 19.

female student, Martha Stephanie Braun, who later taught at Brooklyn College and New York University, recalled,

> Professor von Mises never restrained any participant in the choice of a topic he or she wanted to discuss. . . . I have lived in many cities and belonged to many organizations. I am sure there does not exist a second circle where the intensity, the interest and the intellectual standard of the discussions is as high as it was in the Mises Seminar.[62]

In these discussions, Mises openly espoused not only classical-liberal economic policies, but a complete classical-liberal worldview—this at a time when the majority of intellectuals in Vienna and the rest of Europe were socialists. Thus Mises was known as *der Liberale*—in today's English we would say he was Mr. Libertarian, the living embodiment of classical-liberal ideas.[63] Many years later, his former student Fritz Machlup would highlight the role of Mises's convictions for his impact on others:

Hans Kelsen

> That Mises could be the center of a school is evidence of his qualities as a teacher. Not that he is a great orator or a brilliant classroom actor, but it is the conviction with which he expounds his ideas which arouses the students' interest, partly by convincing them, partly by provoking their criticism.

---

[62]Margit von Mises, *My Years with Ludwig von Mises*, 2nd enlarged ed. (Cedar Falls, Iowa: Center for Futures Education, 1984). On Mises's private seminar, see pp. 201–11. See also *Notes and Recollections*, pp. 97–100; Martha Steffy Browne [or Martha Stefanie Braun], "Erinnerungen an das Mises-Privatseminar," *Wirtschaftspolitische Blätter* 28, no. 4 (1981).

[63]One of Marianne Herzfeld's letters (October 1, 1919, in Mises Archive 53: 9ff.) is most revealing in this regard. Fräulein Herzfeld's parents were acquainted with Mises and had him occasionally at their house for dinner.

And then Machlup went on to point out the flaws of his former teacher:

> He is usually too reserved and all buttoned up, so to speak. Someone who meets him for the first time may be repelled by his apparent coldness or some lack of sympathy. People who know him better know that he is fully sympathetic. He is a man unwilling to make compromises, even if such compromise might be to his material advantage. He will stick stubbornly to his convictions. Although I feel this is really a merit it sometimes antagonizes people.[64]

Mises did occasionally show his anger addressing a view that he opposed, but apparently he did not let intellectual disagreement turn into personal resentment. He realized that progress must necessarily involve disagreement between the newcomers and the establishment, and thus he encouraged talent regardless of orientation. For example, at the end of the 1920s, Mises recommended mathematical economist Ewald Schams for a Rockefeller Fellowship, praising him as "one of the ablest younger economists of our country."[65] He also recommended Paul Lazarsfeld—the director of a small private outfit dedicated to research into economic psychology[66]—who advocated methodological and political views almost the opposite of those cherished by Mises.[67]

---

[64]Machlup to Walter E. Spahr, letter dated October 24, 1940; Hoover Institution: Machlup-Mises correspondence file. Spahr was the head of the economics department of New York University. Machlup's letter was confidential.

[65]April 1929 letter of Mises to the Rockefeller Foundation, in Mises Archive 62: 125. In May 1931, Schams was a *Sektionsrat* in Vienna. Before that, he must have spent some time in Paris, maybe on a Rockefeller Fellowship; see ibid. 73: 13f.

[66]The Österreichische Wirtschafts-Psychologische Forschungsstelle, of which Mises was a board member.

[67]See Mises Archive 67: 7.

The names of some of his Vienna junior research associates have indeed become legendary in the post-World War II period: Hayek, Haberler, Machlup, Schütz, and Morgenstern, to name just a few. Although these men were usually the official students and collaborators of Mayer and Spann, it was in working with Mises that their theoretical work developed and flourished. It is characteristic of their relationship with Mises that they approached him without any submissiveness. Spann, Mayer, and Kelsen seem to have dealt with their students in a very different way.[68]

In those days he also witnessed the ascendancy of his great rival, Othmar Spann, who was appointed as a full professor of economics and gave his inaugural lecture on May 5, 1919.[69] Spann professed a worldview diametrically opposed to methodological individualism. His method—which he called "universalism"—claimed the importance of starting social analysis with the contemplation of larger wholes, and treating the individual elements of human society as secondary.

Such rivalries and disagreements were commonplace, and were not limited to the university. The intellectual organization of early twentieth-century Vienna was a network of dozens of teachers professing their views to disciples and followers in private settings. The system exemplified the intellectual abundance that results from a free market of ideas. It produced Austro-Marxism, psychoanalysis, legal positivism, logical positivism, and praxeology. But for international reputation and lasting impact, three of these circles stood above the rest: the psychoanalysts, the logical positivists, and the Mises Circle. ∽

---

[68]It is in this regard very revealing to compare Murray Rothbard's biography of Mises (*Ludwig von Mises: Scholar, Creator, Hero* [Auburn, Ala.: Ludwig von Mises Institute, 1988]) with Rudolf Métall's biography of Kelsen (*Hans Kelsen* [Vienna: Verlag Franz Deuticke, 1968]).

[69]Othmar Spann's lecture was printed in the same year under the title *Vom Geist der Volkswirtschaftslehre* (Jena: Gustav Fischer, 1919), and later reprinted as an appendix to *Fundament der Volkswirtschaftslehre*, 3rd ed. (Jena: Gustav Fischer, 1923).

10
A Copernican Shift

THEIR ASCENSION TO POWER at the ballot box had taken the socialists by complete surprise. They were suddenly in charge and had to act. But it turned out that they had no idea how to put their ambitious program of "socializing the economy" into practice.[1] The socialist literature of the previous fifty years had never dealt with the question of how "society" (that is, in practice, the socialist government) should manage the economy. Such questions were deemed to be unscientific because the advent of socialism would come by inexorable law of nature. Marx, Engels, Tawney, Laski, and all other socialist intellectuals until the early 1920s were convinced that socialism would eventually just "be there" full-blown and ready to be admired. In the words of a writer highly sympathetic to their cause:

> They have not sufficiently considered the economic conditions that must be satisfied if a socialist state is to equal or to improve upon the standard of life provided by capitalism. Nor have they given adequate attention, from the technical point of view, to the economic advantages and disadvantages of socialism as compared with capitalism. Yet unless they have some understanding of the economics of a socialist state, and unless they are able to present its case on economic grounds . . .

---

[1] Eduard März, "Die Bauer-Mises-Schumpeter-Kontroverse," *Wirtschaftspolitische Blätter* 28, no. 4 (1981): 66f.

they can hardly hope to persuade the mass of men to believe in the state which they advocate.[2]

By 1919 the socialist movement had swept the political scene in Germany and Austria, but none of its leaders had given any thought to this problem. The greatest champion of wartime central planning, Walther Rathenau (1867–1922), was fully convinced that the central direction of the economy should rest with the state, that is in practice, in his own hands. He celebrated war socialism and made the case for omnipotent government in times of peace. His writings in the period of 1917–1919 in particular were the literary equivalent of carpet bombing and shaped the ideals of the coming generation, F.A. Hayek among them.[3] Other statists had championed the same approach.[4] In the aftermath of

---

[2]Benjamin E. Lippincott, "Introduction," *On the Economic Theory of Socialism* B.E. Lippincott, ed. (New York: McGraw-Hill, 1964), p. 4.

[3]See Walther Rathenau, *Zur Kritik der Zeit* (Berlin: Gustav Fischer, 1912); idem, *Deutschlands Rohstoffversorgung* (Berlin: Gustav Fischer, 1916); idem, *Probleme der Friedenswirtschaft* (Berlin: Gustav Fischer, 1917); idem, *Von kommenden Dingen* (Berlin: Gustav Fischer, 1917); idem, *Die neue Wirtschaft* (Berlin: Gustav Fischer, 1918); idem, *Die neue Gesellschaft* (Berlin: Gustav Fischer, 1919); idem, *Der neue Staat* (Berlin: Gustav Fischer, 1919); idem, *Autonome Wirtschaft* (Jena: Diederichs, 1919). This enormous literary output could not fail to provoke various critical reactions. See for example Walter Lambach, *Diktator Rathenau* (Hamburg: Deutschnationale Verlagsanstalt, 1918); Theodor Fritsch, *Anti-Rathenau*, 2nd ed. (Leipzig: Hammer, 1919). On Rathenau's impact on Hayek see Hans Jörg Hennecke, *Friedrich August von Hayek* (Düsseldorf: Wirtschaft und Finanzen, 2000), pp. 40f.

[4]See Friedrich Bendixen, *Sozialismus und Volkswirtschaft in der Kriegsverfassung* (Berlin: Guttentag, 1916); Richard Riedl, *Die Aufgaben der Übergangswirtschaft* (Vienna: Veröffentlichungen des Generalkommissariates für die Kriegs- und Übergangswirtschaft No. 1, 1917); Karl Pribram, *Die Grundgedanken der Wirtschaftspolitik der Zukunft* (Graz: Leuschner & Lubensky, 1918); Rudolf Wissel, *Die Planwirtschaft* (Hamburg: Auer, 1920); idem, *Praktische Wirtschaftspolitik* (Berlin: Verlag Gesellschaft und Erziehung, 1919). Wissel was a minister of the German government. Among the few critical voices were Andreas Voigt, *Kriegssozialismus und Friedenssozialismus* (Leipzig: Scholl, 1916); and Julius Meinl, *Zwang oder Freiheit?* (Vienna: Manz, 1918).

the war, then, there seemed suddenly to be a radical socialist mass movement that expected immediate action. There were short-lived communist governments in Hungary and Bavaria that by and large continued and amplified wartime central planning. Mises's old nemesis Otto Neurath became a leading member of the Bavarian government and published success stories of his experience and plans for a new society.[5] In the few months until the late summer of 1919, the gates were wide open for complete communism, but the socialist leaders—Karl Kautsky, Otto Bauer, and Max Adler— had no plan for *how* to satisfy this popular demand.

One thing was clear. In distinct contrast to Rathenau, the Vienna socialists (the Austro Marxists) were not at ease with the notion that central planning meant omnipotent government. They wanted the central plan, but the planning was somehow supposed to be done by all of society, not just a technocratic elite. In January 1919, Otto Bauer published a series of articles that he reprinted in a booklet with the title *Der Weg zum Sozialismus* (The Road to Socialism).[6] Bauer advocated the piecemeal expropriation of industrial firms along syndicalist lines: the assets of the firms should henceforth be managed by the workers, or by committees composed of workers, consumers, and civil servants. But neither Bauer nor any of the other intellectual leaders of the socialist movement had given any thought to the effectiveness of their scheme. None of them had cared to compare the performance of socialist and capitalist economies.[7] This turned out to be the crucial strategic weakness of their ideal.

---

[5]See Otto Neurath, *Durch die Kriegswirtschaft zur Naturalwirtschaft* (Munich: Callwey, 1919); idem, *Die Sozialisierung Sachsens* (Chemnitz: Verlag des Arbeiter- und Soldatenrates, 1919); Otto Neurath and Wolfgang Schuhmann, *Können wir heute sozialisieren? Eine Darstellung der sozialistischen Lebensordnung und ihres Werdens* (Leipzig: Klinkhardt, 1919).

[6]Otto Bauer, *Der Weg zum Sozialismus* (Vienna: Verlag der Wiener Volksbuchhandlung, 1919).

[7]This point has been underlined by socialist historian Eduard März. See März, "Die Bauer-Mises-Schumpeter-Kontroverse," p. 70.

In the fall of 1919 the situation in Austria was miserable, particularly in Vienna. Food was scarce, rooms were cold, and the lights were dim or out. Mises had suffered from flu for a couple of weeks. His desk was full and he did not want to work. Yet it was during this time that he completed one of the greatest economics articles ever written.

He had promised Lederer that he would write a series of articles for Weber's *Archiv für Sozialwissenschaften und Sozialpolik*, where Lederer was about to succeed Werner Sombart as the executive editor. On November 14, 1919, Mises told him the title of the first of these pieces: "Economic Calculation in the Socialist Commonwealth."[8] This was to be the centerpiece of the general treatise he was working on, which would contain a systematic and comprehensive critique of all varieties of socialist schemes. He must have begun this project soon after finishing *Nation, State, and Economy* and it would take him two more years to complete the manuscript.

The timing was important: Friedrich von Wieser was close to retirement and although Mises was far from convinced he had much chance of following Wieser in Menger's old position, it was not unreasonable to hope that an impressive book publication shortly before the appointment could tip the balance in his favor.

For various reasons, however, he might have thought it useful to publish the central argument beforehand in a separate work. One was the hope of having an immediate impact on Austrian policies. But there was also a pedagogic rationale for the early publication of the chapter on economic calculation. Mises intended to prove that pure socialism was an economic impossibility and this proof relied on a consideration that had so far escaped the notice of economists. In fact, his proof squarely contradicted one of the most cherished doctrines of the dominant Wieserian paradigm—Wieser's theory of imputation. The

---

[8]"Die Wirtschaftsrechnung im sozialistischen Gemeinwesen." See Mises to Lederer, November 14, 1919; in Mises Archive 73: 56f.

advance publication of the calculation chapter would give his readers time to absorb the central thesis of his larger treatise on socialism.

To prepare himself for the likely criticisms he would encounter from the economic establishment and other interested parties, Mises made use of his seminars to discuss the fundamental problems of the theory of distribution, and more particularly of imputation theory. A short lecture by the mathematical economist Dr. Ernst Seidler opened the first three sessions of the university seminar in October 1919. These were entirely dedicated to the problem of imputation. It is likely that Mises confronted his students at this point with his new ideas.

Unfortunately no records of the meetings have survived. The discussions must have touched on the more subtle problems of economic theory, problems beyond the grasp of most of the students. This was probably Mises's motivation for starting a separate smaller group limited to more advanced members.

The Argument

During the first weeks of the winter semester, Mises finetuned his article on economic calculation, addressing various criticisms and remarks from his seminars. He eventually gave the first formal presentation in early January 1920 in a meeting of the *Nationalökonomische Gesellschaft*. In the assembly were some of the world's best economists and Marxist scholars. Joseph Schumpeter, Alfred Amonn, Max Adler, Helene Bauer, and several other participants at this meeting had known Mises for many years as a passionate champion of individualism and a fierce critic of socialism. He was considered more challenging than most critics, who tended to focus on the past failures of applied socialism. Mises knew in detail socialism's abysmal record, but he focused his criticism on theory, not history. Advocates could always dismiss past failures as irrelevant to the viability of a future socialist commonwealth, but Mises challenged the very possibility of their plans ever succeeding.

In his *Nation, State, and Economy*, he had discussed the standard criticism that the socialists overstated the extent to which people would enjoy work for its own sake. The socialist reply was that people currently loathed hard work only because of the market economy, in which they were objectively alienated from their labor and its products. The future would bring forth a New Socialist Man, who no longer indulged in selfishness but found instead his greatest satisfaction in the good of the collective. Mises countered that no country had ever enjoyed the altruism of so many New Socialist Men more than the German Reich under Wilhelm II. If a socialist government could not succeed in Germany, where else could it possibly ever do so?

This was a good point, but it was a trivial argument compared to the one Mises brought up in that January 1920 meeting. He now proceeded to explain why socialism was economically inferior regardless of the psychological condition and motivations of the population. Even if the future were to produce the New Socialist Man, central planning still suffered a fatal shortcoming.

Mises now presented an elaborated discussion of a problem that he had only briefly touched on in *Nation, State, and Economy*, when he mentioned the role of value and monetary calculation in allocating resources within a national economy. He had observed that capital goods constantly had to be replaced, not just to extend the structure of production, but merely to maintain the existing productive apparatus. Which capital goods should be replaced when? As with all economic decisions there were necessary trade-offs and questions of priority. A rational solution to this problem presupposed that one had clear criteria for judging the extent of wear and tear on the current capital goods. "In a static society" in which capital goods "always are to be replaced only with others of the same kind," Mises argued, one had a physical yardstick, namely, the existing structure of production. But in "an economy subject to change, this simple method does not suffice for most means of production, for the used-up and worn-out means of production are replaced not by ones of the same kind but by others." In such a dynamic context, "Calculation in physical units, which suffices for the primitive conditions of a stationary economy, must therefore be replaced by calculation of value in money."[9] Mises went on to describe the social function of the businessman's calculations:

> Individual capital goods disappear in the production process. Capital as such, however, is maintained and expanded. That is not a natural necessity independent of the will of economizing persons, however, but rather the result of deliberate activity that arranges production and consumption so as at least to maintain the sum of value of capital and that allots to consumption only surpluses earned in addition. The precondition for that is the calculation of value, whose auxiliary means is accounting. The [social] economic task of accounting is to test the success of production. It has to determine whether capital was increased, maintained, or diminished. The [individual] economic plan and the distribution of goods between production and consumption is then based on [previous accounting].[10]

Mises began his January 1920 talk along the same lines, stressing the vital importance of the economic calculus for the allocation of factors of production. His audience concurred. Most of them regretted that economic calculation as it was

---

[9]Mises, *Nation, Staat und Wirtschaft* (Vienna & Leipzig: Manz, 1919), p. 130; translated by Leland B. Yeager as *Nation, State, and Economy* (New York: New York University Press, 1983), pp. 159f.

[10]Mises, *Nation, State, and Economy*, p. 160; *Nation, Staat und Wirtschaft*, pp. 130–31. Mises went on to stress the subjective element in this process:

> Accounting is not perfect. The exactness of its numbers, which strongly impresses the uninitiated, is only apparent. The evaluation of goods and claims that it must work with is always based on estimates resting on the interpretation of more or less uncertain elements.

actually practiced was a "profitability calculus" that reflected the mere private interests of capitalist investors, but none of them questioned the fact that calculation of some sort epitomized rationality in economic affairs. Where all other criteria might be challenged, algebra and arithmetic stood fast. Now Mises came to the heart of his argument, which he presented in two bold theses:

(1) Socialist societies could not rely on economic calculus, such as it is known in market economies, because entrepreneurial calculations are based on money prices for factors of production. Such prices cannot exist in socialism because prices can only come into existence through exchange, and exchange presupposes the existence of at least two owners. Now, the very nature of socialism—its usual definition in fact—is that all means of production are under a unified control. They all belong to one economic entity: society, "the people," the commonwealth or the state—whatever collective entity is named. The crucial fact is that, from the economic point of view, there is in any socialist regime only one owner of all factors of production. Therefore, no factor of production can be exchanged, and there can be no money prices for factors of production. And therefore no socialist community can allocate its factors of production on the basis of economic calculation, as it is known in capitalist markets.

(2) There are no other means of economic calculation. Such economic calculation requires money prices for factors of production, which can only come into existence where factors of production are privately owned.

Insofar as the money calculus epitomizes economic rationality, socialism is inherently irrational.

It was immediately clear to the audience that Mises was treading completely new ground. Socialism had been criticized from many angles, but hardly anyone had doubted that the central planners could achieve gains in efficiency. Mises's thesis, if true, would strike at the heart of the socialist agenda. It would elegantly and crushingly refute Marx and his modern heirs, the

English Guild Socialists and the fashionable Austro-Marxist theoreticians, many of whom were in the audience at Mises's presentation. In short, Mises's paper was an all-out attack on the very foundation of the economic case for socialism—a refutation of its central tenet, which by the end of the war had become universally accepted.[11]

The ensuing debate both clarified the critical aspects of Mises's argument and foreshadowed the various tacks that socialist theorists would take in the coming years as they attempted to defend the viability of their system against the revelation of its fundamental economic irrationality. Mises later summarized the discussion in a letter to Lederer:

> My first concern is to show that economic calculation, as it is practiced in the free economy, is inconceivable in a socialist commonwealth because it is built on the premise that money prices are formed for the means of production. This part of my presentation has generally met with full consent in the discussion in the *Nationalökonomischen Gesellschaft*. Even Max Adler and Helene Bauer have made objections on merely one point, namely, that economic rationality will choose other ways and means in the socialist commonwealth than they will in the free economy. But what these means will be, they could not specify.

---

[11]It later turned out that Mises had an important predecessor in Nicolas G. Pierson, the eminent Dutch economist who was also minister of finance and governor of the Dutch central bank. In an exchange with Austro-Marxist Karl Kautsky, Pierson had argued that any economic system would have to solve the problem of value determination, and that the socialists would have to demonstrate how this determination could be achieved without a system of market prices. See Nicolas Pierson, "The Problem of Value in the Socialist Community," F.A. Hayek, ed., *Collectivist Economic Planning: Critical Studies on the Possibilities of Socialism* (London: Routledge and Kegan Paul, 1935), pp. 41–85. Pierson's original 1902 essay was written in Dutch and therefore did not reach a wider public in Germany and Austria. It was translated into German and English only after Mises's essay had started the debate independently.

Amonn too fundamentally agrees with my argument. I have just told him on the telephone that you would like him to put together some remarks on my paper for the *Archiv*. He replied he could not comply because he fundamentally agreed with the negative side of my argument, but was unable to make a positive proposal for the institution of an economic calculation in the socialist commonwealth.

Schumpeter made the following proposal: The socialist commonwealth gives each comrade a certain amount of accounting money as income and then leaves it to free pricing to bring about prices through exchanges. This proposal is however unsuited to circumvent the problem I have pointed out. For the higher-order goods remain *extra commercium*; consequently it is impossible to sort out prices for them even in terms of this accounting money, and thus economic calculation becomes impossible in the sphere of production.

The substance of my argument, which I believe to have evidenced in my proof, is precisely this: that economic calculation in the free economy is not applicable in the commonwealth; and I also do not see any conceivable economic calculation that the socialist commonwealth could adopt. I believe that this presents the most important problem of socialization—a problem far more important for socialist theory than, formerly, the problem of the average rate of profit.[12]

This was the beginning of what turned out to be the protracted socialist-calculation debate, which continues to be "one of the most significant controversies in modern economics."[13]

---

[12]Mises to Emil Lederer, letter dated January 14, 1920, in Mises Archive 73: 52ff. Mises's comparison in the last sentence refers to a debate initiated by Böhm-Bawerk, who had subjected Marx's theory of the average rate of profit to scathing and devastating criticism.

[13]Mark Blaug, *Economic Theory in Retrospect*, 5th ed. (Cambridge: Cambridge University Press, 1997), p. 557.

The meeting of the *Nationalökonomische Gesellschaft* had ended in triumph for Mises. He had turned the obligatory rearguard action that everybody expected him to deliver into a surprise attack against the very heart of socialism. Vienna's Austro-Marxist elite was left speechless. They had believed that the intellectual war had long been won and that all that was left was the resistance of special interests and the unenlightened. His triumph would become ever more complete over the following weeks, months, and years, when it became increasingly obvious that the objections of his opponents were spurious—and that he had already anticipated most of them.

Emil Lederer's comments are a case in point.[14] Just as Adler and Helene Bauer, he waxed eloquent about the blessings of an as-yet-unknown socialist calculation system, which would incorporate alternatives to capitalist money calculation. But he did not state what such a system would consist in.[15] Lederer also observed that capitalist accounting does not give photographs of reality, but only stylized models which heavily depend on the subjective element of the entrepreneurs' judgments. But Mises had already conceded these points, which were irrelevant to his thesis. In fact, he did not claim that economic calculation was more objective in capitalism than in socialism, but that any economic calculation required the existence of money prices for capital goods. It is true that in capitalism the relevant prices—

---

[14]He did not attend the January 1920 meeting of the *Nationalökonomie Gesellschaft*, but sent Mises his typewritten comments in an undated letter. See Mises Archive 73: 60ff., which is a typewritten reproduction of 73: 49ff.

[15]Lederer claimed that a future socialist economic calculation:

> would be essentially different from capitalistic calculation in that many moments would be included in the calculation, some would be lacking, and some would be evaluated differently; this all points to another kind of system, but a system, nevertheless. It is at that point within a system where universal factors are found that operative methods of calculation for the system originate. (Ibid.)

future money prices—had to be guessed, but the point was that only in capitalism were there any prices to be guessed at all.

Similarly, Lederer misinterpreted Mises's claim that socialist economies could not be rationally directed to mean that socialist societies would not produce any rational leaders. But Mises's real point was that socialism would be deprived of any criteria whatsoever for the rational allocation of resources. Without such criteria even the greatest leader would be unable to organize the structure of production in an efficient way. Mises wrote:

> It is not at all my contention that a socialist commonwealth would not develop leader types. I assume though that these leaders will not excel in the rational, but in the sentimental and intuitive sphere.[16]

A good assumption indeed. Mises here sums up the essence of political leadership in the age of the omnipotent state.

The Intellectual Context

The political implications of Mises's argument were obvious. If Mises was right, full socialism was not a viable option. Only capitalism or some mixed economy that accommodated the market remained on the menu of feasible political constitutions.

Yet Mises's socialist-calculation argument had a much wider theoretical significance than was apparent to most economists in the 1920s and 1930s. It was in fact the first and decisive step toward building the theory of production on completely different foundations from those dominant in the economic mainstream—of which the Austrian School was still a part. Thanks in particular to the writings and towering personal influence of Friedrich von Wieser, most Austrian School economists had unwittingly come to accept John Stuart Mill's dogma, that production and distribution are two separate spheres of human life,

---

[16]Mises to Lederer, letter dated January 14, 1920; Mises Archive 73: 54.

which are separable in both economic analysis and political practice. In Mill's view, production was essentially a matter of technology, whereas distribution was a question of distributive justice. And economic science dealt exclusively with one particular distributive system, namely, the market economy. Says Mill:

> It is . . . evident that of the two great departments of Political Economy, the production of wealth and its distribution, the consideration of Value has to do with the latter alone; and with that, only so far as competition, and not usage or custom, is the distributing agency. The conditions and laws of Production would be the same as they are, if the arrangements of society did not depend on Exchange, or did not admit of it.[17]

Accordingly, questions of ownership and of appropriation were deemed to be the proper subject of legal scholarship, not economic analysis.

This account of the relation between production and distribution did not comport well with Carl Menger's theory of the order of goods, according to which higher-order goods derive their value from lower-order goods and thus ultimately from consumers' goods. Factors of production are valuable only because they serve to produce consumers' goods. The value of streets, machines, cars, petroleum, etc., is thus derived from the value of the enjoyment that they help bring about. This commonsense observation turned classical economics on its head: the cost-of-production theories of value held that consumers' goods are valuable only because they are produced with valuable inputs.

It was not a straightforward task to explain precisely *how* factors of production derive their value from the value of consumers' goods. What does it mean to "derive" value or, in other words,

---

[17]John Stuart Mill, *Principles of Political Economy* (London: Routledge, 1891), bk. 3, chap. 1, p. 298.

what does it mean to say that an actor "imputes" the value of a consumers' good to a factor of production? Carl Menger had only very briefly dealt with the problem of imputation (*Zurechnung*).[18] It is safe to say that he and Böhm-Bawerk believed that the value of consumers' goods depended on the legal situation of the acting individuals—hence in their view production was interrelated with distribution. But in their writings, both focused heavily on the conditions existing in a market economy and neglected the question of how the results of the analysis were modified under the impact of different legal frameworks.

The only early Austrian who addressed the problem of the relationship between value and distribution in any systematic way was Friedrich von Wieser. He recognized the importance of the question and proposed an original answer that he based on an elaboration of Menger's theory of value imputation.[19]

Menger had based his analysis of imputation on the premise that value is a quantity, or at any rate some sort of extensive entity. This assumption was necessary for his imputation theory, because if value did not have such an extended nature it would be unintelligible from what it was that was imputed to something else. It was also an assumption shared by the greatest authorities in German economics.[20] And it certainly did not

---

[18]See Carl Menger, *Grundsätze der Volkswirtschaftslehre* (Vienna: Braumüller, 1871), p. 124. Among the predecessors of his imputation (order-of-goods) theory, see Johann F.E. Lotz, *Revision der Grund-Begriffe der National-Wirthschaftslehre* (Koburg and Leipzig: Sinner, 1811), vol. 1, p. 108; Johann A. Oberndorfer, *System der Nationalökonomie* (Landshut: Krüll, 1822), p. 307; F.B.W. Hermann, *Staatswirthschaftliche Untersuchungen*, 1st ed. (Munich: Fleischmann, 1832), p. 65. Notice however that Menger had no predecessor for his solution of the problem of joint production. See Yukihiro Ikeda, *Die Entstehungsgeschichte der "Grundsätze" Carl Mengers* (St. Katharinen: Scripta Mercaturae Verlag, 1997).

[19]See Friedrich von Wieser, *Der natürliche Werth* (Vienna: Hölder-Pichler-Tempsky, 1889), chap. 3, pp. 67ff.

[20]Consider the number one German economics textbook of Menger's day, Karl Heinrich Rau, *Grundsätze der Volkswirtschaftslehre*, 7th ed. (Leipzig

contradict the dominant interpretation of the new marginalist approach, which thanks to the efforts of Wieser was commonly perceived to be a "psychological" approach dealing with feelings of satisfaction and levels of satiation. And these feelings can vary in strength and duration.

Wieser unquestioningly adopted Menger's premise that value is a quantity and added further speculations on the nature of value to the Mengerian fabric. In particular, he came up with two new claims about value that would prove to have great significance for the political implications of his own value theory, and which foreshadowed the way economic analysis would be practiced during the rest of the twentieth century.

First, Wieser advocated the use of the fiction that one could meaningfully speak of value without respect to the wealth or income of the acting person.[21] The value that is independent of income and wealth is "natural value." Of course the natural value of capital goods is derived from the natural value of consumers' goods. *How* the natural value of consumers' goods is imputed to capital goods is the subject matter of imputation theory.

---

and Heidelberg, 1863), p. 166: "Nobody freely and deliberately enters into a losing deal; that is, a deal in which the exchanged value is of a lesser nature than that which was surrendered."

[21]He himself recognized this stipulation as a fiction, and he justified the use of fictions as a necessary device of scientific analysis. In fact, as significant as the political implications of Wieser's natural-value theory are in their own right, it is equally important to stress the impact of Wieser's methodology on the wider profession. Mathematical economists had made no secret of the fact that their reasoning relied on fictions, even though they believed that the error introduced by unrealistic stipulations was negligible in most cases. In contrast, verbal economists like Menger stressed the necessity for science to describe reality. They were reluctant to use mathematical tools precisely because they saw no way to reconcile the use of such tools with their quest for realism. Wieser broke with this tradition by consciously insisting on the legitimacy of "deductions from fiction." See Wieser, *Der natürliche Werth*, part 2.

Second, natural value is objective in the sense that it is the same for all persons. For example, Wieser claimed that an increase in the quantity of money entailed the same decrease of the value of money for every individual, and he therefore also held that the marginal value of any given amount of money is lower for a rich person than for a poor person. Thus, in spite of some statements in which he stressed that value was always related to an acting individual, in his theory of natural value Wieser completely dissociated the value of goods from any context of concrete human action.

This was the starting point for his theory of the shortcomings of capitalism and also for his policy recommendations. It is obvious that real-life monetary economies are not likely to bring about the same results as an economy in which natural value reigns. According to Wieser, only if all members of society are perfectly equal in their wealth and income position do the values of a monetary economy coincide with natural values. And since natural value is the economic ideal of all possible real economies, it follows that economic policy *should* make sure that all factors of production be treated according to their natural values. This might be achieved in a perfect communist state. But it might also be achieved through heavy government intervention in the market economy.[22]

The practical nub of Wieser's theory, and his great innovation, was to turn upside-down the roles of value theory in production and distribution. In Mill's scheme, value theory played no role in production, but exclusively concerned distributive questions in the contingent framework of a market economy. In contrast, Wieser pointed out that, while the value of goods

---

[22]For an enlightening analysis of the shortcomings of Wieser's value theory, see Samuel Bostaph, "Wieser on Economic Calculation under Socialism," *Quarterly Journal of Austrian Economics* 6, no. 2 (2003); idem, "Friedrich von Wieser's Theory of Socialism: A Magnificent Failure," *Politická ekonomie* 53, no. 6 (2005).

could be neglected in decisions about their distribution, the question of value was central to decisions of production, or a waste of resources would ensue. Modern marginal-value theory not only served to explain the value of all goods in all types of social organization, but could also be applied in all conceivable societies to solve the problem of evaluating and allocating factors of production. Contrary to Mill, therefore, value theory was a truly universal theory.[23] Capitalist calculation in terms of money prices was only one particular application—and a rather deficient one—of the general principles of value calculus.

By the end of World War I, Wieser's analytical framework had become orthodoxy.[24] It is true that the technical details of his imputation theory were challenged, and that it competed with Böhm-Bawerk's slightly different approach.[25] But the

---

[23]And, we might add, it was a truly "scientific" theory because it did not commit the academic economist to any particular political program—just as Maxwell's equations did not commit a physicist to any political party. Wieser fervently denounced the intimate relationship between the various schools of economic thought and the political agendas they were backing up, criticizing these schools for not pursuing "pure knowledge," that is, for Wieser, knowledge untainted by political implications. In contrast, his approach covered "a certain most inner domain of economic truths—truths relating to elements that remain common to all social organizations." Clearly, this guaranteed political impartiality and therefore, in his view, scientific objectivity. See Friedrich von Wieser, "Karl Menger," *Neue österreichische Biographie: 1815–1918* (Vienna, 1923), vol. 1, pp. 91f.

[24]The best illustration is the fact that Max Weber invited him to write a general treatise on economics for the prestigious *Grundriss der Sozialökonomik* series, which was supposed to portray the present state of the social sciences. Wieser thus wrote his *Theorie der gesellschaftlichen Wirtschaft* (Tübingen: Mohr, 1914). The work was first published in 1914 and remained the main work of reference in German-language economics until the early 1930s (a second edition appeared in 1924).

[25]Works on the technical problems of imputation theory abounded from the 1890s and proliferated until the 1930s, without leading to any solution. See for example, Leo Schönfeld-Illy, *Wirtschaftsrechnung* (reprint; Munich: Philosophia, 1924); Wilhelm Vleugels, *Die Lösungen des wirtschaftlichen Zurechnungsproblems bei Böhm-Bawerk und Wieser* (Halle: Niemeyer, 1930).

general postulates and distinctions on which value-imputation theory relied had not met with serious resistance from any major champion of theoretical economics. Most notably, Böhm-Bawerk had no substantial objections to offer. He was not enthusiastic about Wieser's emphasis on the use of fictions in economics, but he too adopted Menger's conception of value as an extended entity that can be imputed to other objects. Thus he compounded the confusion that Wieser had created among younger economic theorists.

The only theoretical challenge to the Wieserian orthodoxy came from a young Russian Marxist who for some time had been a member of Böhm-Bawerk's seminar and who later became Soviet Russia's top economist. In his *Economic Theory of the Leisure Class*, which was first published in Russian in 1917, Nikolai Bukharin presented an all-out attack on the new marginalist price theory, selecting as his prime target the Austrian School because "it is generally known that the most powerful opponent of Marxism is the Austrian School."[26]

One of Bukharin's main objectives was to explain why the Austrian pretensions to the universality of their value theory were untenable. He observed: "while Marx is concerned with the historically determined relations between men, Böhm-Bawerk presents universal forms of the relations between men and things."[27] But, he went on, these universal forms are not sufficient to explain market prices because market prices result among other things from certain contingent features of the capitalist system, most notably private property and the production of commodities. Said Bukharin:

> It is obvious that even the most fundamental phenom-
> enon of political economy, that of value, cannot be
> explained on the basis of the circumstance common to

---

[26]Nikolai Bukharin, *Economic Theory of the Leisure Class* (New York: Monthly Review Press, 1972), p. 9.

[27]Ibid., p. 51.

all times and peoples, that commodities satisfy some human need; yet this is the "method" of the Austrian School.

We therefore reach the conclusion that the Austrian School is pursuing an absolutely erroneous methodological course in ignoring the peculiarities of capitalism.[28]

Mises's socialist-calculation argument buried the old Wieserian approach, but it also overturned the doctrines of Mill and Marx as well.

First, Mises joined with Bukharin in his critique of the older Austrians by arguing that there can be no general principles of value calculation because there is no such thing as value calculation in the first place. There is only price calculation, and it comes into existence only at those times and places where the means of production are privately owned. The existence of economic calculation is a historically contingent event.

Second, Mises showed that this very historical contingency of the economic calculus played out against Marx and the Marxists. Rationality in economic affairs exists only to the extent that capital goods are privately owned. And the reverse holds true as well: the more socialist any given historical order was, the less rational it was. A rational economic order is not a fact of nature, but depends entirely on fragile institutions that need to be cultivated through a sustained cultural and political effort.

Third, Mises smashed Mill's dogma of the separate realms of production and distribution. Production in capitalism is guided by the individual businessmen's calculations. But these calculations are contingent on the existence of private property in the means of production. They cannot be performed in systems lacking such property rights. It follows that production does depend on distribution, and distribution on production. They cannot be separated.

---

[28]Ibid., p. 53.

৵৶   ৵৶   ৵৶

Mises's case for the impossibility of socialist calculation relied on two insights of previous authors, which he had integrated into his brief exposition on value theory in chapter 2 of *Theory of Money and Credit*.

The first of these insights originated from the works of Georg Simmel and Joseph Schumpeter, who had characterized the essence of economic action as exchange; every human action "exchanges" a supposedly superior state of affairs against an inferior one (today one would of course say "choose" rather than "exchange," but the point is the same).[29] As Mises later argued, this essential feature of human action is also the foundation of the phenomenon of value. In the few passages that he devotes to value theory in *Theory of Money and Credit*, Mises decisively elaborates on Menger's definition of value as "the importance that individual goods or quantities of goods attain for us because we are conscious of being dependent on command of them for the satisfaction of our needs."[30]

In Menger's definition of value—which contrasted somewhat with his actual analysis of value[31]—value was a characteristic feature of a single economic good. In contrast, Mises defined the value of one good in explicit context with the value of another good with which it was compared, and he stressed that this "comparison" was based on choice as it involved "acts of

---

[29]See Georg Simmel, *Philosophie des Geldes* (Frankfurt a.M.: Suhrkamp, [1901] 1991), p. 35; Joseph A. Schumpeter, *Wesen und Hauptinhalt der theoretischen Nationalökonomie* (Munich and Leipzig: Duncker & Humblot, 1908), p. 50.

[30]Carl Menger, *Principles of Economics* (New York: New York University Press, 1981), p. 115. Menger also defined value as "a judgment economizing men make about the importance of the goods at their disposal for the maintenance of their lives and well being. Hence value does not exist outside the consciousness of men" (ibid., p. 121).

[31]See chapter 4—"Fin de siècle Economic Science."

valuation." In short, Mises agreed with Schumpeter that value had nothing to do with want satisfaction or any other feelings, and that therefore economists did not have to engage in psychological analysis. Value is ordinal; it is relative; it is a relation. It is not a quantity. Mises emphasized these heterodox observations, then went on to define value as being inextricably bound to human choices:

> Every economic transaction presupposes a comparison of values. But the necessity for such a comparison, as well as the possibility of it, is due only to the circumstance that the person concerned has to choose between several commodities.[32]

With these lines, Mises set the Austrian theory of value—the cornerstone of economic analysis—on a completely new trajectory. Carl Menger had resolutely rejected the notion that the phenomenon of value could somehow depend on human choices. He believed that any reference to free will in this context "would deny economics altogether the status of an exact science."[33] Menger therefore stressed the will-independent factors determining the pricing process. Market prices resulted

---

[32]Mises, *Theory of Money and Credit* (Indianapolis: Liberty Fund, 1980), pp. 51f.

[33]Menger, *Grundsätze der Volkswirtschaftslehre*, p. viii; *Principles of Economics* (New York: New York University Press, 1976), p. 48. He went on:

> Whether and under what conditions a thing is useful to me, whether and under what conditions it is a good, whether and under what conditions it is an economic good, whether and under what conditions it possesses value for me and how large the measure of this value is for me, whether and under what conditions an economic exchange of goods will take place between two economizing individuals, and the limits within which a price can be established if an exchange does occur—these and many other matters are fully as independent of my will as any law of chemistry is of the will of the practicing chemist.

ultimately from individual needs that had to be satisfied with scarce means. He realized that human beings had to have "knowledge of this causal connection" between means and ends, but the Mengerian analysis of the pricing process paid scant attention to this subjective factor.[34] In Menger's account, the theory of value and prices was a subdivision of a Platonic theory of goods. With Mises, it became part of a reality-based theory of human action.

Second, Mises combined this choice-based theory of value with Franz Cuhel's insight that the values underlying individual decision-making cannot be measured. After reviewing the works in the field he was convinced that Franz Cuhel was correct in his emphasis of value as a purely ordinal relationship between economic goods, always tied to the context given by a concrete person at a concrete time and a concrete place.

> Acts of valuation are not susceptible of any kind of measurement. It is true that everybody is able to say whether a certain piece of bread seems more valuable to him than a certain piece of iron or less valuable than a certain piece of meat. And it is therefore true that everybody is in a position to draw up an immense list of comparative values; a list which will hold good only for a given point of time, since it must assume a given combination of wants and commodities. . . . And economic activity has no other basis than the value scales thus constructed by individuals. An exchange will take place when two commodity units are placed in a different order on the value scales of two different persons. In a market, exchanges will continue until it is no longer possible for reciprocal surrender of commodities by any two individuals to

---

[34]The posthumous second edition of his *Principles* (1923) reinforced the stress on the objective factors of the pricing process. Among other things, Menger here distinguishes between "imaginary" and "real" human wants. See our discussion in chapter 14.

> result in their each acquiring commodities that stand higher on their value scales than those surrendered. If an individual wishes to make an exchange on an economic basis, he has merely to consider the comparative significance in his own judgment of the quantities of commodities in question. Such an estimate of relative values in no way involves the idea of measurement.[35]

In these passages Mises almost anticipates his socialist-calculation argument. His 1920 essay on the calculation problem under socialism merely spelled out an important implication of his original revision of Carl Menger's value theory: one cannot calculate with values—only with market prices. But the dependence is mutual. The full scope of the socialist-calculation argument cannot be understood without first understanding that revised value theory.

In the early 1920s, almost nobody understood value the way Mises defined it. It was certainly not difficult to overlook a revision of value theory that was buried in a book on money. Moreover, most of his readers were only superficially acquainted with theoretical problems in the first place. Those with interests in monetary theory typically had only a thin background in general value theory, and economists interested in general value theory were unlikely to search for and ponder the value-theoretical disquisitions of a young monetary economist. As time went on, Mises's position became even more marginalized, with the result that the calculation argument was increasingly difficult to understand for the rising generation of professional economists.

---

[35]Mises, *Theory of Money and Credit*, pp. 52f.

Triumph

By the beginning of 1922, Mises had finished the manuscript of his treatise on socialism and was looking for a good academic publisher.[36] Duncker & Humblot in Munich declined because of the difficult inflationary situation that had begun to wreck the German economy, making the publication of a 500-page scientific treatise a major risk. Mohr in Tübingen was interested but asked Mises to cut 20 percent of the manuscript. Mises kept looking. In February, he signed a contract with Gustav Fischer in Jena.

Their contract had made only vague stipulations about the adjustment of Mises's royalties to the ongoing inflation.[37] When prices rose dramatically between the conclusion of the negotiations in February and the completion of the production process in July, Mises was very happy that Fischer raised the honorarium on a courtesy basis by 50 percent.[38] Thus Fischer turned out to be a good choice and remained Mises's book publisher throughout the 1920s.

The book turned out to be a great success. One decisive factor in its sweeping victory was the growing sense among German economists that the reigning Historicism and the *Kathedersozialisten* had done far more harm than good. Already before

---

[36]See Mises Archive 55: 2ff. He had published parts of it beforehand: the chapter on economic calculation. He also tried to publish chapter 3 ("The Social Order and the Political Constitution") in a *festschrift* for Max Weber. But this project did not materialize because *Socialism* appeared before the other book. See the April 1922 letter from Karl Geibel of Duncker & Humblot to Mises in Mises Archive 55: 6.

[37]This fact is revealing as to Mises's priorities and his sense for business.

[38]Mises received 19,200 marks for the book in July 1922. See Mises Archive 75: 27ff. This was the equivalent of $38.92. A few months later, by October 1922, the mark still in precipitous decline, the dollar equivalent of Mises's honorarium shrank to $6.04. We may suppose, however, that Mises was quick to exchange his marks against kronen, which had a stable dollar exchange rate.

the war, there were signs of decline in German socialist ortho-doxy.[39] The defeat in World War I accelerated the fall, and a wider academic audience became receptive to alternative para-digms. In this situation, Mises's main thesis was confirmed and endorsed by two great authorities in German social science: Max Weber and Heinrich Herkner.

In his *Wirtschaft und Gesellschaft* (Economy and Society), published posthumously in 1922, Weber argued along the same lines as Mises in his 1920 article, that a socialist planning board could not base its allocation of resources on economic calcula-tion.[40] Contrasting capitalist money-price calculation with "cal-culations in kind" that authors like Otto Neurath[41] had pro-posed, Weber observed that

> the comparison of different kinds of processes of production, with the use of different kinds of raw materials and different ways of treating them, is car-ried out today by making a calculation of comparative profitability on terms of money costs. For accounting in kind, on the other hand, there are formidable

---

[39]See Ludwig Pohle, *Die gegenwärtige Krisis in der deutschen Volk-swirtschaftslehre* (Leipzig: Deichert, 1911), p. 6.

[40]See *Max Weber, Economy and Society: An Outline of Interpretive Sociology*, Guenther Roth and Claus Wittich, eds. (Berkeley: University of California Press, 1978), vol. I, pp. 100–03. The following quotes are taken from this pas-sage, in particular, from pages 102f. In the German original see Max Weber, *Wirtschaft und Gesellschaft*, 3rd ed. (Tübingen: Mohr, 1947), vol. 1, chap. 2, § 12, pp. 53–58.

[41]See Otto Neurath, *Bayrische Sozialisierungserfahrungen* (Vienna: Neue Erde, 1920); idem, "Vollsozialisierung: Von der nächsten und übernächsten Zukunft," *Deutsche Gemeinwirtschaft* 15 (1920). In the spring of 1919, Neu-rath was a member of a short-lived revolutionary Bavarian government in Munich, acting as director of the *Zentralwirtschaftsamt* (Office of the Cen-trally Planned Economy). After the suppression of the revolution, Max Weber defended him in court. See Allan Mitchell, *Revolution in Bavaria, 1918–1919: The Eisner Regime and the Soviet Republic* (Princeton, N.J.: Prince-ton University Press, 1965), pp. 293ff.

problems involved here which are incapable of objective solution.

Weber's ensuing discussion showed that he had fully grasped
the nature of the problem, its concrete manifestation, and its
capitalist solution:

> an enterprise is always faced with the question as to
> whether any of its parts is operating irrationally: that
> is, unprofitably, and if so, why. It is a question of
> determining which components of its real physical
> expenditures (that is, of the "costs" in terms of capital
> accounting) could be saved and, above all, could more
> rationally be used elsewhere. This can be determined
> with relative ease in an ex-post calculation of the rela-
> tion between accounting "costs" and "receipts" in
> money terms, the former including in particular the
> interest charge allocated to that account. But it is
> exceedingly difficult to do this entirely in terms of an
> in-kind calculation, and indeed it can be accomplished
> at all only in very simple cases. This, one may believe,
> is not a matter of circumstances which could over-
> come by technical improvements in the methods of
> calculation, but of fundamental limitations, which
> make really exact accounting in terms of calculations
> in kind impossible in principle.

Even the introduction of non-monetary systems of remuneration could not overcome the problem of eradicating irrationalities, because these measures would be unsuitable to identify
irrationalities in the first place.

> The essential question is that of how it is possible to
> discover *at what point* in the organization it would be
> profitable to employ such measures because there
> existed at that point certain elements of irrationality.
> It is in finding out these points that accounting in
> kind encounters difficulties which an ex-post calcula-
> tion in money terms does not have to contend with.

Weber then went on to point out the crucial fact preventing the application of schemes for calculation in kind, namely, that only money imputation works; utility-imputation is a chimera:

> The fundamental limitations of accounting in kind as the basis of calculation in enterprise—of a type which would include the heterocephalous and heteronomous units of production in a planned economy—are to be found in the problem of imputation, which in such a system cannot take the simple form of an ex-post calculation of profit or loss on the books, but rather that very controversial form which it has in the theory of marginal utility. In order to make possible a rational utilization of the means of production, a system of in-kind accounting would have to determine "value"-indicators of some kind for the individual capital goods which could take over the role of the "prices" used in book valuation in modern business accounting. But it is not at all clear how such indicators could be established, and in particular, verified; whether, for instance, they should vary from one production unit to the next (on the basis of economic location), or whether they should be uniform for the entire economy, on the basis of "social utility," that is, of (present and *future*) consumption requirements?

Weber warned against the misconception that this problem was of a merely technical nature—one that could eventually be overcome once enough human resources were invested in finding a solution:

> Nothing is gained by assuming that, if only the problem of a non-monetary economy were seriously enough attacked, a suitable accounting method would be discovered or invented. The problem is fundamental to any kind of complete socialization. We cannot speak of a rational "planned economy" so long as in this decisive respect we have no instrument for elaborating a rational "plan."

Apparently Weber and Mises had developed substantially the same ideas in complete independence from one another.[42] It is likely, however, that Mises provided the initial inspiration for Weber, in their many hours of conversation during Weber's visit to the University of Vienna in the summer semester of 1918. Both men were among the faculty of a course for army officers that dealt with various fundamental political problems. In one of the sessions, Weber delivered a lecture on the general problems of socialism. It was subsequently published with his

approval from stenographical notes.[43] It is significant that Weber does not even hint at the issue of economic calculation in this lecture.

Be that as it may, the important fact is that when Weber died at the age of 56 on June 14, 1920, he and Mises agreed on the socialist-calculation question, and when Weber's *magnum opus* was eventually published in 1922, it weighed in with the full authority of its author

Max Weber

on the side of Mises, causing great consternation among mainstream economists in Germany, who were still steeped in the *kathedersocialist* tradition. As if to reinforce Weber and Mises, Vladimir Lenin—leader of the world's model of socialism—announced a partial retreat on the economic front: Soviet Russia would begin a New Economic Policy, bringing greater freedom for trade and commerce. Attempts to abolish money and markets had produced precisely the chaos that Mises argued was inevitable under full socialism.

---

[42]Weber died on June 14, 1920 and thus might have read Mises's *Archiv* paper, which had come out in February or March of that year. The editors of *Economy and Society* referred to Mises's work at the end of the chapter on "calculation in kind," stating: "During the printing of this work an essay by Ludwig von Mises dealing with these problems came out" (ibid., p. 107).

[43]See Max Weber, *Der Sozialismus* (Vienna: Phöbus, 1918).

But the real knockout for academic socialism in Germany came at the hands of its own vicar. Heinrich Herkner had succeeded Schmoller in his position at the University of Berlin and as the president of the *Verein für Socialpolitik*. For practical purposes, this meant he had become Schmoller's heir as head of the Historical School and of the German social-policy movement. In September 1922, at the *Verein's* fiftieth jubilee meeting in Eisenach, it became obvious that Herkner had to be counted among those who abhorred the excesses of historicism and academic socialism. He called for more moderation, which meant in practical terms a reconsideration of the tenets of classical economics. Herkner stated that even the great Schmoller had confided to him shortly before his death that he was concerned about the inability of the younger generation "to think in terms of free trade." This inability, Herkner argued, had led to exaggerated views about the power of the state relative to the operation of economic law, and the nefarious consequences could be seen.[44]

These views had already become acceptable. Herkner's speech was received with great applause. In the following year, in a widely read paper on "the changed implications of economic science for social policy," Herkner argued that the labor unions had severely hampered economic reconstruction after the war. This concerned in particular their resistance to longer working hours and to any limitations on their power to strike. They were the prime movers behind the political forces that subjected the German economy to an ever more complex web of regulations. Historically astute economists had apprehensions about the ultimate result of this movement: either some perverse guild oligarchy, or a mercantilist police state. As a natural reaction to such excesses there would be excesses in the opposite direction. The influence of the dreaded Manchester School

---

[44]Heinrich Herkner, "Die Zukunft der Sozialpolitik," *Jubiläumstagung des Vereins für Sozialpolitik in Eisenach 1922* (Munich and Leipzig: Duncker & Humblot, 1923), p. 95.

would rebound. Then Herkner singled out Mises's *Socialism* as the single most important work of this liberal resurgence, endorsing virtually all criticisms that Mises had leveled against socialism. Herkner urged his colleagues to thoroughly examine the ideas of these new theoretical economists, stating:

> We encounter by far the most important perform-
> ance of this line of research in the brilliantly written
> and inspired work by the Vienna economist Ludwig
> Mises, *Die Gemeinwirtschaft*. With full command of
> the most recent scientific achievements, and partly on
> the basis of new points of view, the author quite dev-
> astatingly criticizes all variants of socialism and every-
> thing that he considers to be socialism.[45]

This took Mises's *Socialism* from the limited exposure of the ivory tower and made it infamous throughout the socialist movement. The unheard-of concessions and even praise for one of the hated "theorists" caused outrage in the labor unions and angry reassessments of Herkner's position in official socialist circles.[46] Yet Herkner's authority also forced the German main-stream economists to reevaluate their cherished scientific and political tenets. The influential Heinrich Pesch recognized Mises as the head of the new Manchesterism. He explained:

> Because of his clever and original critique of social-
> ism, Mises has met with regard and approval even
> among those authors who, in distinct contrast to him,
> advocate the legal protection of children and women,
> and [compulsory] workers' insurance.[47]

---

[45]Heinrich Herkner, "Sozialpolitische Wandlungen in der wis-senschaftlichen Nationalökonomie," *Der Arbeitgeber* 13, no. 3 (1923): 35.

[46]See Franz Boese, *Geschichte des Vereins für Sozialpolitikx* (Berlin: Duncker & Humblot, 1939), p. 181.

[47]Heinrich Pesch, *Lehrbuch der Nationalökonomie* 5 (Freiburg i.Br.: Herder, 1923), p. ix. Pesch was the leading champion of "solidarism"—a ver-sion of socialism that Mises had criticised in his book.

Many of these authors now began to see that the unsuccessful application of socialist schemes in the postwar period had nothing to do with a lack of psychological or ideological preparedness on the part of the population; it sprang from the inner deficiencies of those schemes themselves—flaws highlighted in the works of Mises and Weber. More and more scholars came to renounce their former socialist ideals. This process came to be known as the "crisis of social policy."[48] How much Mises and his works stood at the center of this "crisis" can be inferred from the fact that by October 1924, more than 20 monographs and papers had been published on the sole subject of economic calculation.[49]

Some thirty-five years later, Mises evaluated the impact of his socialist-calculation argument and found it had shifted the terms of subsequent debate. He observed that

> all arguments advanced in favor of the great reform collapsed. From that time on socialists no longer based their hopes upon the power of their arguments but upon the resentment, envy, and hatred of the masses. Today even the adepts of "scientific" socialism rely exclusively upon these emotional factors. The basis of contemporary socialism and interventionism is judgments of value. Socialism is praised as the only fair variety of society's economic organization.[50]

The Incomplete Revolution

The kernel of Mises's theory of calculation is this: while calculation in terms of money prices is the essential intellectual

---

[48]See Mises, *A Critique of Interventionism* (New Rochelle, N.Y.: Arlington House, 1977), p. 101.

[49]See Mises Archive 75: 50.

[50]Mises, *Theory and History* (New Haven, Conn.: Yale University Press, 1957), p. 65.

tool of entrepreneurs acting in a market economy, calculation in terms of "value" is impossible. A calculus can only be performed with multiples of an extended unit; for example, one can add one apple to another apple or one grain of silver to another grain of silver. In contrast, one cannot add a telephone to a piano concerto and still less can one add wittiness to silence. These things are incommensurable and therefore cannot be linked through mathematical operations. So it is with value. One cannot quantify the value of a thing because value is not extensive and therefore not measurable.

However, value can be qualitatively "imputed" from consumer goods to factors of production, in the sense of a value-dependency: those factors of production are valuable only because they serve to produce valuable consumer goods. But there is no such thing as quantitative value and thus no value calculation; there is only price calculation. In the 1940s, Mises expressed this idea with great clarity in his economic treatise, which summarized a lifetime of reflection on this problem:

> One can add up prices expressed in terms of money, but not scales of preference [that is, value scales]. One cannot divide values or single out quotas of them. A value judgment never consists in anything other than preferring *a* to *b*.
>
> The process of value imputation does not result in derivation of the value of the single productive agents from the value of their joint product. It does not bring about results which could serve as elements of economic calculation. It is only the market that, in establishing prices for each factor of production, creates the conditions required for economic calculation. *Economic calculation always deals with prices, never with values.*[51]

---

[51]Mises, *Human Action*, Scholar's edition (Auburn, Ala.: Ludwig von Mises Institute, 1998), p. 332; emphasis added. A few years later, he wrote:

These insights opened up new perspectives on the social sciences and on the evolution of human societies. If compelled to single out the idea that best characterized Mises's overall contribution to human knowledge, one would have to name his general theory of economic calculation. The 1920 article on socialist calculation was the first step toward the elaboration of this theory.

Against virtually the entire profession of academic economists who, since the days of Adam Smith, had reasoned on the tacit premise that all human action can be based on some sort of economic calculus, Mises held that this possibility exists only in a market economy. Outside the market, there are only personal value judgments. Economic rationality is politically and historically contingent. The extensive and intensive division of labor, capital-intensive production, the rational allocation of factors of production—all the economic premises of human civilization—have existed only in those societies that protected private property rights in the means of production.

Yet when Mises published his original essay on economic calculation under socialism, he did not express himself as unambiguously as he would later. In 1920, it was clear to his readers that he thought that it was impossible to "measure" value; yet he seemed to conceive of value as a feeling.[52] Many readers must

---

> Value is not intrinsic. It is not in things and conditions but in the valuing subject. It is impossible to ascribe value to one thing or state of affairs only. Valuation invariably compares one thing or condition with another thing or condition. It grades various states of the external world. It contrasts one thing or state, whether real or imagined, with another thing or state, whether real or imagined, and arranges both in a scale of what the author of the judgment likes better and what less. (Mises, *Theory and History*, p. 23)

[52]In the first edition of his treatise on money, he had written: "As a feeling, value cannot be measured; it is [however] possible to compare it with

have wondered why it should be impossible, in principle, to measure different degrees of the intensity of a feeling. And if emotional intensity might be measurable, why should it not be possible to calculate in terms of these values so-defined? Mises's own wording actually encouraged speculations of this sort. In the early 1920s, he did not stress that economic calculation "always deals with prices, never with values." Quite to the contrary, in the very article in which he pointed out the problems of economic calculation in socialist regimes, he repeatedly characterized economic calculation as a "value calculation" or "calculation of value."

To some extent, this confusion came out of the terminology. Mises used the word "value" in two distinct ways. The term *wert* has the same ambivalent meaning in German as its English translation "value"—it means value in the qualitative sense but can also mean an exchange ratio on the market. But beyond the issues of terminology, there was genuine, substantial confusion on Mises's part. For example, in his 1922 treatise on socialism (which was after all based on the 1920 essay) he wrote: "Under capitalism, capital and labor move until marginal utilities are everywhere equal."[53] This statement cannot be reconciled with the impossibility of value calculation.

His younger readers, who were most familiar with Friedrich von Wieser's exposition of Austrian value theory, must have assumed that Mises and Wieser were in substantial agreement on value theory. After all, Mises did not contest the notion that

---

other, similar feelings" (*Theorie des Geldes und der Umlaufsmittel,* 1st ed. [Munich and Leipzig: Duncker & Humblot, 1912], p. 16). Significantly, in the second edition of 1924, Mises adopted a non-psychological theory of value, conceiving of value as an act rather than a feeling. He deleted the above sentence from his book and replaced it with the following: "Acts of valuation are not susceptible of any kind of measurement" (*Theory of Money and Credit,* p. 52).

[53]Mises, *Socialism: An Economic and Sociological Analysis* (Indianapolis: Liberty Fund, 1981), p. 203.

economic calculation was essentially a value calculus. He merely pointed out that only in the market economy was there an arithmetic unit—price—that allowed for the calculated use of factors of production, whereas socialist regimes lacked such a unit.

Ironically, the only reviewer who recognized the critical difference between the Cuhel-Mises theory of value and the dominant Wieserian theory was Carl Landauer, a fanatical socialist, who loaded his two reviews of *Socialism* with personal invectives against the author. Landauer wrote:

> With his basic thesis Mises enters into complete opposition to the main idea of the marginal utility school . . . : That economic calculation in terms of marginal utility is not a feature of any particular economic order, but can and must be applied in the communist order just as in the capitalist one.[54]

The statements Mises made around 1920 in his writings and correspondence lead to the conclusion that he himself did not yet fully grasp the connection between his value theory and his theory of economic calculation. In none of these early writings could he bring himself to the categorical judgment that economic calculation "always deals with prices, never with values." It is hardly surprising then that his readers and students missed the point as well. They mistook the 1920 essay for a clever technical challenge to the socialist leadership. They did not see (and possibly could not see) the depth of the issue. Mises had made the first step toward a revolutionary revision of economic science and political philosophy, but he was unable to communicate the full message. As a consequence, he lacked the necessary impact to turn the rising generation of Austrian economists away from Wieserian economics. Brilliant young men such as

---

[54]Carl Landauer, "Übersicht über die neuesten Publikationen Deutschlands und des Auslands," *Jahrbücher für Nationalökonomie und Statistik* 121, no. 2 (1923). Copy in Mises Archive 42: 4.

Hayek, Haberler, Machlup, Morgenstern, and other fourth generation Austrian economists were schooled in the notion that value calculation was an uncontested tenet of economic science.

When Mises recognized his pedagogical shortcomings and spelled out the epistemological implications of his value theory in a series of papers that were published in the late 1920s and early 1930s, it was already too late. Friedrich von Hayek had already begun to rethink and reformulate the socialist-calculation argument from a Wieserian point of view, which made the argument much weaker than it had been in Mises's hands. Characteristically, Hayek himself believed that he was merely clarifying the Misesian position. This confusion plagued the Austrian School for several decades, until the important differences between the Misesian and the Hayekian approaches were highlighted in the early 1990s.[55] ∽

Mises circa 1925

---

[55]Joseph T. Salerno, "Mises and Hayek Dehomogenized," *Review of Austrian Economics* 6, no. 2 (1993); Hans-Hermann Hoppe, "Socialism: A Property or Knowledge Problem?" *Review of Austrian Economics* 9, no. 1 (1996); Jörg Guido Hülsmann, "Knowledge, Judgment, and the Use of Property," *Review of Austrian Economics* 10, no. 1 (1997).

11
A Treatise on Socialism

THE PUBLICATION OF THE essay on economic calculation in socialist commonwealths was the first installment of an entire treatise on socialism that Mises had begun in 1919. This new work would contain a detailed discussion of the profound implications of the calculation problem, but it was far more than that. With penetrating observations on virtually all aspects of socialist practice and doctrine, Mises painted an encompassing and breathtakingly original picture of socialism.

The production of the new opus occurred under the usual circumstances. On top of fulltime workdays and evening seminars, two years of writing after hours produced a 500-page manuscript. But it is safe to assume that his intellectual work during these two years was in creating a synthesis of the previous twenty years of reflection. All the discussions with his friends and opponents, all silent meditations on books he had read and lectures he had listened to ever since he became interested in the problems of social theory, found their way into *Gemeinwirtschaft*. In this way, at least, it was his greatest book to date. Like his other works, it was full of original insights. The present subject provided him with a greater variety of topics than, say, the nature of money and fiduciary media. Yet the subject was not *too* big to prevent him from writing a true treatise—dealing with virtually all aspects of the problem.

Moreover, in contrast with his later treatise on economics (*Human Action*, 1949), he did not burden himself or his readers with lengthy discussions of fundamental epistemological and conceptual problems.[1] The result can only be called astounding. It established Mises's reputation as "the greatest living mind in Austria."[2] And it was the book that turned an entire generation of young intellectuals away from Marxism and toward classical liberalism. Lionel Robbins, Friedrich August von Hayek, Wilhelm Röpke, Eric Voegelin, and many others later testified that *Gemeinwirtschaft* had had a decisive impact on them in their formative years. Hayek compared Mises to Voltaire, Montesquieu, Tocqueville, and John Stuart Mill.[3]

As one correspondent observed, the success could have been even greater if Mises had managed to find a more striking title than the cumbersome *Die Gemeinwirtschaft* (literally: The Commonwealth, or, The Common Economy).[4] Anglo-Saxon readers would have a less difficult time finding out what the book was all about when, thirteen years later, the English edition appeared under the title *Socialism*.

---

[1]The book was also notable in that Mises here used the only diagram he would ever display in one of his publications, depicting typical shapes of the curve of the utility of labor, as a function of labor-time. See Mises, *Gemeinwirtschaft*, 1st ed. (Jena: Gustav Fischer, 1922), p. 154. Significantly, Mises adopted this figure from William Stanley Jevons's *Theory of Political Economy* (London: Macmillan, 1888).

[2]These were the words Felix Kaufmann used to describe Mises to his future wife, Margit Serény, after they first met in 1925. See Margit von Mises, *My Years with Ludwig von Mises*, 2nd enlarged ed. (Cedar Falls, Iowa: Center for Futures Education, 1984), p. 14.

[3]See F.A. Hayek, "Einleitung," introduction to Ludwig von Mises, *Erinnerungen* (Stuttgart: Gustav Fischer Verlag, 1978), pp. xif. See also Erich Voegelin, *Autobiographical Reflections*, vol. 34 of the *Collected Works of Eric Voegelin* (Baton Rouge: Louisiana State University Press, 1989), p. 10.

[4]Fritz G. Steiner to Mises, letter dated December 8, 1930; Mises Archive 66: 23: "It was always my opinion that its current title was the reason this brilliant book did not find the broad circulation it could have earned."

In the opening of part one, Mises analyzed socialism not on its own merits, but from a comparative point of view, contrasting it to the workings of a society organized according to classical-liberal principles. Following in the tradition of Frédéric Bastiat and other libertarian philosophers, Mises here emphasized the central role private property plays in the constitution of free societies. He also stressed the importance of contract and democracy for the peaceful resolution of conflicts, and made a brilliant application of these considerations to the case of the family or, as some would say today, gender relations.

In the next four parts of the book (parts two through five), Mises elaborated four general theses: (1) the promises of socialism were empty because its program for a central direction of production was a theoretical and practical impossibility; (2) there was no process of social evolution that necessarily led to socialist regimes; (3) none of the major ethical justifications of socialism stood up to rational scrutiny; and (4) the true character of socialism was not to improve the human condition, but to worsen it, because socialist policies destroy the capital base of society.

Benefits Derived from the Means of Production under Capitalism

One of the most common charges against the classical-liberal program of elevating the respect of private property into the first principle of human cooperation is that private property benefits the haves at the expense of the great mass of have-nots. As the word "private" insinuates, the have-nots are deprived of the benefits of the goods that are under exclusive control of the haves, who are happy and few. Mises addresses this charge head-on in the opening pages of *Socialism*, by demonstrating the "social" function of private property.

To "have" a good in the economic sense, Mises argues, means to enjoy the benefits derived from this good. There are benefits that can only be enjoyed by one person at a time. This is most notably the case with certain personal services such as haircuts, as well as with a great number of consumer goods, such as foodstuffs, of which a given unit can only be consumed—that is, enjoyed—by one person. Things are somewhat different in the case of durable consumer goods such as TV sets or sofas, which can be enjoyed by several people, though not always at the same time.

But things are fundamentally different once we turn to production goods such as factories, plantations, machine tools and so on. The benefits derived from these goods do not exclusively accrue to their owner, that is, to the person who controls them in the narrow legal sense. Rather, they accrue to the consumers of the final consumer goods that are produced with the help of those production goods. By the very nature of things, therefore, the benefits derived from factors of production cannot be limited to their legal owners. It is therefore not these legal owners who "have" them in the economic sense. The economic "haves" of production goods are all the people who enjoy the consumer goods produced with their help.

Now the crucial point is that this is truly independent of the prevalent social organization. Consumers "have" the factors of production not only in a socialist system, in which they are the (collective) legal owners of those factors, but also in capitalism. Mises explained:

> To have production goods in the economic sense, i.e. to make them serve one's own economic purposes, it is not necessary to have them physically in the way that one must have consumption goods if one is to use them up or to use them lastingly. To drink coffee I do not need to own a coffee plantation in Brazil, an ocean steamer, and a coffee roasting plant, though all these means of production must be used to bring a cup of coffee to my table. Sufficient that others own these means of production and employ them for me. In the society which divides labor no one is exclusive owner of the means of production, either of the material

things or of the personal element, capacity to work. All means of production render services to everyone who buys or sells on the market. Hence if we are disinclined here to speak of ownership as shared between consumers and owners of the means of production, we should have to regard consumers as the true owners in the natural sense and describe those who are considered as the owners in the legal sense as administrators of other people's property.[5]

Ever wary of terminological innovations, Mises stressed that he would not henceforth refer to consumers as the "true" owners of the means of production, but use the accepted terminology according to which the owners of the means of production are those who have immediate legal control over them.

But of course this terminological decision could not alter his findings. Mises had delivered the explanation of the fact—recognized by all serious opponents of classical liberalism, from Marx to Philippovich—that capitalism was not just a rip-off to benefit the happy few at the expense of the great majority. It was no accident that capitalism had incomparably improved the living conditions of the broad masses. It was in the very nature of capital accumulation that its ultimate benefits accrued to the community of consumers, that is, to all members of society.[6] The only question was whether socialistic schemes could enhance the living conditions of the working classes beyond what capitalism had in store for them. And Mises had already

---

[5]Mises, *Socialism: An Economic and Sociological Analysis* (Indianapolis: Liberty Fund, 1981), p. 31.

[6]Some 160 years earlier, Adam Smith had analyzed the economic impact of unequal *land* ownership in very similar terms. He argued that this inequality had a negligible impact on how the land was actually used. Land owners, he said "are led by an invisible hand to make nearly the same distribution of the necessaries of life which would have been made had the earth been divided into equal portions among its inhabitants." Adam Smith, *The Theory of Moral Sentiments* (Indianapolis: Liberty Fund, [1759] 1976), p. 304.

answered this question. In the light of his 1920 article on social-ist calculation, the promise of greater productivity under social-ism looked rather vacuous.

The Utilitarian Case for Democracy

Closer analysis revealed that private property in the factors of production was not just a privilege of the happy few capital-ists, but had a genuine social function. Mises brought the same perspective to bear on government and thus discovered an orig-inal rationale for democracy. This institution was not an end in itself. It fulfilled a social function that no other system of gov-ernment could fulfill.

Traditionally, the champions of democracy had defended this political form with the help of arguments rooted in ethics or natural law. All men are born equal, they claimed, and therefore all men should be equally involved in political decision-making. But this could only be realized in a democracy. Mises did not find this line of reasoning convincing. He believed it was rather obvious that all men were born unequal, and he had little patience with arguments based on claims about natural law, which he considered to be a fiction of the intellect. No agree-ment could ever be reached on a fiction. Rather, it was to be expected that everybody made up his own version of "natural" law, to buttress his political agenda. Thus natural-law consider-ations were simply unfit to be applied in politics, because the very point of politics was, from Mises's perspective at any rate, to resolve conflicts.

In *Socialism*, it became obvious that Mises believed in repub-lican democracy nevertheless. But his rationale for endorsing it differed substantially from the traditional justification of democracy. For Mises, social institutions could be justified only to the extent that they improved the living conditions of the members of society. Accordingly, the starting point for his reflections was that these living conditions could be improved only through productive efforts, and that the division of labor was more productive than isolated individual activities. To improve living conditions as far as possible was therefore tantamount to encouraging the division of labor and to making it as productive as possible. This had been the guiding light in his analysis of the problems of economic calculation, which had led him to the conclusion that in capitalism the division of labor is more productive than in socialism because only in the former could it be based on economic calculation.

In *Socialism*, Mises stressed another implication of the same basic idea. Labor can only be divided among people who live in peace with one another. Violent conflicts necessarily disrupt social cooperation. They split society into parties that work against one another, rather than for one another. They destroy scarce resources rather than producing more resources. The improvement of living conditions therefore requires choosing those political institutions that tend to minimize violent conflicts. This is precisely the function of the democratic form of constitution.

> Its function is to make peace, to avoid violent revolutions. In non-democratic states, too, only a government which can count on the backing of public opinion is able to maintain itself in the long run. The strength of all governments lies not in weapons but in the spirit which puts the weapons at their disposal. Those in power, always necessarily a small minority against an enormous majority, can attain and maintain power only by making the spirit of the majority pliant to their rule. If there is a change, if those on whose support the government depends lose the conviction that they must support this particular government, then the ground is undermined beneath it and it must sooner or later give way. Persons and systems in the government of non-democratic states can be changed by violence alone. The system and the individuals that have lost the support of the people are swept away in the upheaval and a new system and other individuals take their place.

But any violent revolution costs blood and money. Lives are sacrificed, and destruction impedes economic activity. Democracy tries to prevent such material loss and the accompanying psychical shock by guaranteeing accord between the will of the state—as expressed through the organs of the state— and the will of the majority. This it achieves by making the organs of the state legally dependent on the will of the majority of the moment. In internal policy it realizes what pacifism seeks to realize in external policy.[7,8]

Mises did not blindly advocate just any notion of democracy: he warned against the dogmatic excesses derived from certain erroneous natural-law schemes. He noticed in particular that there is no special distinction in *direct democracy*. Politics is a matter of the division of labor, like all other spheres of life.[9] And he also stressed that democracy must not be conceived as the *unlimited* rule of the general will:

---

[7]Ibid., pp. 61f. He notes that Marsilius of Padua seemed to have argued along similar lines in *Defensor Pacis*. Today this line of argument is often attributed to Karl Popper, *The Open Society and Its Enemies* (London: Routledge, 1945), vol. 1, chap. 7. But the young Popper is likely to have learned it, as did many other intellectuals of his time, from *Socialism*.

[8]Notice that the premise of Mises's argument—that governments cannot rule against the will of the majority—had a long tradition in Western thought. See in particular Thomas Aquinas, "Über die Herrschaft der Fürsten," *Staatslehre des Thomas von Aquino*, F. Schreyvogel, ed. (Vienna, [1274] 1923), part 2, chap. 2, pp. 65f. (more recent scholarship argues that this chapter must actually be counted as chap. 10 of part 1); Etienne de la Boétie, *The Politics of Obedience: The Discourse of Voluntary Servitude* (New York: Free Life Editions, [1562] 1975), p. 50; and David Hume, "Of the First Principle of Government," *Essays, Moral and Political* (Minneapolis: Liberty Fund).

[9]Quoting Max Weber, Mises said:

Democracy is not less democracy because leaders come forth from the masses to devote themselves entirely to politics. Like any other profession in the society dividing labour, politics demand the entire man; dilettante politicians are of no use. (*Socialism*, pp. 63–64)

> There is really no essential difference between the unlimited power of the democratic state and the unlimited power of the autocrat. The idea that carries away our demagogues and their supporters, the idea that the state can do whatever it wishes, and that nothing should resist the will of the sovereign people, has done more evil perhaps than the caesar-mania of degenerate princelings.

Mises concluded that "only within the framework of Liberalism does democracy fulfill a social function. Democracy without Liberalism is a hollow form."[10] The great danger inherent in democracy is to turn the libertarian postulate of equality before the law into the postulate of economic equality.

> Here is a fertile field for the demagogue. Whoever stirs up the resentment of the poor against the rich can count on securing a big audience. Democracy creates the most favourable preliminary conditions for the development of this spirit, which is always and everywhere present, though concealed. So far all democratic states have foundered on this point. The democracy of our own time is hastening towards the same end.[11]

Political Economy of the Family

One of the most successful rhetorical ploys in defense of socialism is to present socialism as "going beyond" liberalism in liberating the human being. Socialists such as Karl Marx and Friedrich Engels had praised capitalism for unfettering production. But capitalism had not gone far enough in abolishing the institutions that hampered the flowering of the human race. There was still private ownership in the means of production.

---

[10]Ibid., p. 64.

[11]Ibid., p. 66.

Socialism would do away with this last bulwark of the exploitation of man by man. Only then would the reign of full liberty begin.

The socialist feminists of the eighteenth and nineteenth century had used an analogous argument to make their case. They conceded that the condition of women had vastly improved in the course of the previous centuries. But it had not improved enough. Further progress was prevented through the institution of marriage, which enshrined male domination over the inherently weaker women and curtailed their productive powers. The solution was to outlaw marriage and to replace it with spontaneous and loose bonds between mates.

The exact analogy in the two arguments could not fail to attract Mises's attention. Just as he had shown that the socialist case against the institution of private property was fallacious, so he now proceeded in *Socialism* to denounce the fallacies of the feminist case against the institution of marriage. He showed that the historical progress in the condition of women had resulted from advances of the contractual principle, which was based on the recognition of private property rights, and from the elimination of violence against the property rights of women. Men could dominate women only so long as they owned their wives' person and property.[12] When women came to be recognized as legitimate property owners, the economic basis for that domination was destroyed. It followed that feminism was but a branch of liberalism to the extent that it advo-

---

[12]At the time of his writing, this was still the case in various western countries. For example, in an early case of social engineering, the French Code Napoléon had enshrined male dominance into the law by making the husband the sole legal owner of all family assets; see Xavier Martin, *L'homme des droits de l'homme et sa compagne* (Bouère: Dominique Martin Morin, 2001). The female right to vote had been introduced in Austria only in 1918. The dates for other countries: Germany (1919), Canada (1920), Great Britain (1928), France (1946), Italy (1946), Japan (1947), Switzerland (1971); see article "Wahlen," *Staatslexikon*, 7th ed. (Freiburg i.Br.: Herder, 1989), col. 830.

cated liberty within the confines of private property and full legal equality between men and women. These claims were indeed the rational basis for the development of individual personality.

> Woman's struggle to preserve her personality in marriage is part of that struggle for personal integrity which characterizes the rationalist society of the economic order based on private ownership of the means of production. It is not exclusively to the interest of woman that she should succeed in this struggle; to contrast the interests of men and women, as extreme feminists try to do, is very foolish. All mankind would suffer if woman should fail to develop her ego and be unable to unite with man as equal, freeborn companions and comrades.[13]

But socialist feminists got it wrong. They called for outlawing marriage. They sought to prevent women from associating with men in a way that they, the feminists, thought was harmful for these women. Where did the reasoning go wrong? The case against private property was untenable because private property fulfilled a social function that no other institution could.

But what was the social function of marriage? There had to be such a function; after all, there was no legal obligation for women to get married. They *chose* to marry. Therefore they could easily avoid the fate that, according to the feminists, marriage would

---

[13]Mises, *Socialism*, pp. 90–91. On another page we find:

> So far as Feminism seeks to adjust the legal position of woman to that of man, so far as it seeks to offer her legal and economic freedom to develop and act in accordance with her inclinations, desires, and economic circumstances—so far it is nothing more than a branch of the great liberal movement, which advocates peaceful and free evolution. When, going beyond this, it attacks the institutions of social life under the impression that it will thus be able to remove the natural barriers, it is a spiritual child of Socialism. (p. 87)

entail for them. But why did women choose to marry? He argued that marriage served specific female needs, and that it served them better than any alternative social arrangement. These specific needs were rooted in the fact that the "sexual function," the urge to "surrender to a man" and "her love for husband and children consumes her best energies."[14]

Clearly, Mises would not do well in the court of current left-wing feminist opinion. However, the opinions he professed in *Socialism* were not the idiosyncrasies of a resentful chauvinist. Rather, they were a cautiously worded version of the most widely accepted theory of gender differences of his time, the general theory of men and women that Otto Weininger had construed at the turn of the century, based on a comprehensive review of the scientific data available at the time. Weininger distinguished between a male principle (M) and a female principle (F) that were present in different proportions in each individual. Women were of course dominated by the F principle. Said Weininger:

> The state of sexual arousal is for the woman merely the highest increase of her total being. The latter is always and quite sexual. F is completely immersed in her sex-life, in the sphere of intercourse and repro- duction, that is, in the relation to man and child. Her existence is completely filled up with these things, while M is not merely sexual. . . .
>
> Thus, whereas F is totally fulfilled and taken by sexuality, M knows a dozen of other things: fight and play, sociability and [Gelage], discussion and science, business and politics, religion and art. . . .
>
> F is nothing but sexuality, M is sexual and also something above.[15]

---

[14]Ibid., p. 90.

[15]Otto Weininger, *Geschlecht und Charakter*, 19th ed. (Vienna: Braumüller, 1920), chap 2, pp. 106–08. In chapter 12, Weininger goes on to argue that the only vital positive interest of women is in sexual intercourse. Only because

This is why women had a tendency to choose marriage. And by that same decision, they renounced the achievements they could have realized outside of marriage. In Mises's view, apparently, this went a long way to explaining why female achievements have not matched the achievements of males.

> It may be that a woman is able to choose between renouncing either the most profound womanly joy, the joy of motherhood, or the more masculine development of her personality in action and endeavour. It may be that she has no such choice. It may be that in suppressing her urge towards motherhood she does herself an injury that reacts through all other functions of her being. But whatever the truth about this, the fact remains that when she becomes a mother, with or without marriage, she is prevented from leading her life as freely and independently as man. Extraordinarily gifted women may achieve fine things in spite of motherhood; but because the functions of sex have the first claim upon woman, genius and the greatest achievements have been denied her.[16]

Mises was one of the few men in a leadership position who actively promoted young female intellectuals. Lene Lieser, Marianne Herzfeld, and others wrote their doctoral dissertations under his supervision. Lieser, Herzfeld, Ilse Mintz, Martha Stephanie Braun, Elisabeth Ephrussi, and others were regular members of his private seminar. It is true that he could get none of them a professorship—he could not do this even for his male students, or even for himself. But he could help some

---

women are also essentially passive and receptive, they tend to adopt male values such as chastity and interest in art and science. Thus is comes to an inner conflict between their true sexual nature and the values that they officially endorse. The natural reaction is hysteria, about which Weininger has not much to say except that Breuer and Freud study it with a promising new method.

[16]Mises, *Socialism*, p. 86.

of them to obtain one of those coveted jobs that earn a living while allowing the pursuit of intellectual interests. Again this was the case with Herzfeld and Lieser, both of whom were employed at the Association of Austrian Banks and Bankers.

When Mises rejected the claims of radical feminism, it was not because he lacked sympathy with his female associates or because he was driven by some vicious desire to keep women "in their place." Rather, it was intellectual integrity that led him to insist on his views about gender relations, views that even in his circle were likely to be resented by ambitious women such as M.S. Braun. As Mises saw it, these were the facts, and it was pointless to argue around them:

> the difference between sexual character and sexual destiny can no more be decreed away than other inequalities of mankind. It is not marriage which keeps woman inwardly unfree, but the fact that her sexual character demands surrender to a man and that her love for husband and children consumes her best energies. There is no human law to prevent the woman who looks for happiness in a career from renouncing love and marriage. But those who do not renounce them are not left with sufficient strength to master life as a man may master it. It is the fact that sex possesses her whole personality, and not the facts of marriage and family, which enchains woman. By "abolishing" marriage one would not make woman any freer and happier; one would merely take from her the essential content of her life, and one could offer nothing to replace it.[17]

Implications of the Calculation Problem

The discussion of gender relations closed the first part of the book. In part two, Mises turned to examining socialism on its

---

[17]Ibid., p. 90.

own terms. After the exposition of the socialist-calculation argument (he reprinted the 1920 article), he set out to discuss its further implications.

> Payment for work would be quite arbitrary. For the methods of calculating value used in a free economic society based on private ownership of the means of production would be inaccessible to it since, as we have seen, such imputation is impossible in a socialistic society. Economic facts would clearly limit the power of society to reward the labourer arbitrarily; in the long run the wage total can in no circumstances exceed the income of society. Within this limit, however, the community is free to act. It can decide to pay all work equally, regardless of quality; it can just as easily make a distinction between the various hours of work, according to the quality of the work rendered. But in both cases it must reserve the right to decide the particular distribution of the products.[18]

In practice this meant that the individual members were defenseless against arbitrary decisions taken by the community or rather, as it was in practice, by those in charge of the central decisions. The directors of the socialist commonwealth would decide about the "allocation" of all factors of production. This implied not only that they decide how each stretch of land should be used, but also how to allocate "human resources." The directors would be in a position to give orders to individuals and families, telling them where to move and live, and when to move on. They would do this not out of bad faith or personal abuse of power, but because it was in the very nature of socialism (common ownership of all the means of production, which includes labor) that the individual had to submit to the will of central planners. It was obvious that socialism was anything but a reign of liberty:

---

[18]Ibid., p. 139.

> The Socialist Community is a great authoritarian association in which orders are issued and obeyed. This is what is implied by the words "planned economy" and the "abolition of the anarchy of production." The inner structure of a socialist community is best understood if we compare it with the inner structure of an army.[19]

Socialism could not alter the fact that the individual mind was free, but the mind cannot express itself if all physical means of expression are under the control of the authorities. "No censor, no emperor, no pope, has ever possessed the power to suppress intellectual freedom which would be possessed by a socialist community."[20] This may seem obvious to us now, but in 1922, this assertion seemed to be contradicted by recent events in Russia, where a new artistic avant-garde had risen under the Soviet regime. Mises remained unshaken:

> The nationalization of intellectual life, which must be attempted under Socialism, must make all intellectual progress impossible. It is possible to deceive oneself about this because, in Russia, new kinds of art have become the fashion. But the authors of these innovations were already working, when the Soviet came into power. They sided with it because, not having been recognized hitherto, they entertained hopes of recognition from the new regime. The great question, however, is whether later innovators will be able to oust them from the position they have now gained.[21]

Subsequent events proved his point. Long before the Soviet empire collapsed in 1989, the artistic and intellectual institutions in the countries of Eastern Europe had enshrined the

---

[19]Ibid., p. 163.
[20]Ibid., p. 169.
[21]Ibid., pp. 167–68.

avant-garde of the 1920s and 1930s into eternal standards of truth and beauty, just as the writings of Marx and Engels were treated as holy writ. The Bolshoi Ballet in Moscow dutifully continued the revolutionary tradition, and the Berliner Ensemble faithfully replicated the plays of Bertold Brecht in the same way they had always been played.

Mises also restated the more conventional arguments concerning work and motivation. Starting from the distinction between immediate satisfaction derived from labor (the satisfaction derived from the work itself) and indirect satisfaction (remuneration), Mises contested the assumption that the establishment of a socialist regime would by itself turn whatever work had to be performed into a pure joy. Absurd as it was, this assumption was pervasive among socialists. Mises observed that in a socialist regime, the individual worker would reap but a fraction of the return of his labors. There was therefore a strong incentive for each member of a socialist society to avoid hard work:

> So far as can be judged there is no convincing reason for supposing that labour under Socialism would be more productive than under Capitalism. On the contrary it can be asserted that under a system which provides no incentive to the worker to overcome the irksomeness of labour and to strive his utmost, the productivity of labour must inevitably decline.[22]

Mises argued that this problem went beyond the supply of labor. It also affected the supply of capital. The decision to save one's income increases the capital available for productive ventures. As in the case of all capital goods, the benefits derived from saving do not accrue primarily to the capitalist himself, but to the consumers. In modern parlance, saving is a "public good." But where is the incentive to save in a socialist regime?

> To maintain and accumulate capital involves costs. It involves sacrificing present satisfactions in order that

---

[22]Ibid., p. 161.

greater satisfactions may be obtained in the future. Under Capitalism the sacrifice . . . has to be made by the possessors of the means of production, and those who, by limiting consumption, are on the way to being possessors of the means of production. The advantage which they thereby procure for the future does indeed not entirely accrue to them. They are obliged to share it with those whose incomes are derived from work, since other things being equal, the accumulation of capital increases the marginal productivity of labour and therewith wages. But the fact that, in the main, the gain of not living beyond their means (i.e. not consuming capital) and saving (i.e. increasing capital) does pay them is a sufficient stimulus to incite them to maintain and extend it. And this stimulus is the stronger the more completely their immediate needs are satisfied. For the less urgent are those present needs, which are not satisfied when provision is made for the future, the easier it is to make the sacrifice. Under Capitalism the maintenance and accumulation of capital is one of the functions of the unequal distribution of property and income.[23]

Moral Hazard—The Other Nemesis of Socialism

Having dealt with the consequences that in one way or another resulted from the inability of a socialist management to calculate the contributions of the various factors of production, Mises pointed out that there was another, equally "insurmountable obstacle" for the realization of the socialist scheme:

It is impossible to find a form of organization which makes the economic action of the individual independent of the co-operation of other citizens without leaving it open to all the risks of mere gambling.[24]

---

[23]Ibid., p. 178.
[24]Ibid., p. 186.

In other words, socialism makes subordinate decision makers irresponsible. By socializing the costs of individual action, socialism induces moral hazard at every level of society. All members of a socialist society know that most of the negative consequences of their behavior fall on others. Everyone has an incentive to behave more recklessly than in a strict private-property system, where costs are borne by individual actors.

It is impossible to solve the problem with payment schemes to provide incentives for "suitable" behavior.

> [T]he problem is not nearly so much the question of the manager's share in the profit, as of his share in the losses which arise through his conduct of business. Except in a purely moral sense the property-less manager of a public undertaking can be made answerable only for a comparatively small part of the losses. To make a man materially interested in profits and hardly concerned in losses simply encourages a lack of seriousness. This is the experience, not only of public undertakings but also of all private enterprises, which have granted to comparatively poor employees in managerial posts rights to a percentage of the profits.[25]

In capitalism, the individual responsibility of each property owner for his property is a strong force that harmonizes his actions with those of all other members of society. In contrast, a characteristic feature of socialism is to sever the link between an action and its consequences. Under such conditions, individual actions are necessarily out of step with what is required for the system to perform well.[26]

---

[25]Ibid., p. 191.

[26]This not only concerned questions of business management, but also "private" decisions about the number and timing of offspring. In socialist systems, individuals had no incentive to "harmonize the number of births with the limitations of the means of subsistence." Mises concluded: "Without

There is only one remedy: the imposition of strict rules for subordinate behavior. To safeguard the economic system against the recklessness of irresponsible underlings, the central authorities would have to deprive them of all autonomous power of decision-making, to give detailed prescriptions for the actions of subordinates, and reserve for itself the right of decision-making in all cases not covered by the rules. In short, socialism requires an all-encompassing bureaucratic system.

The Feeble and Compromising John Stuart Mill

Mises devoted particular attention to the discussion of time wages. According to a widespread opinion, the economic theory of time wages had refuted the standard charge against the socialists, namely, that their schemes would suffer from incentives problems that were absent under capitalism. On this issue the socialists had found an unexpected ally in John Stuart Mill,

John Stuart Mill

long regarded as the patron saint of classical liberalism. In his elegant prose, Mill had stressed that capitalism too suffered from an incentive problem as soon as wages were paid for labor time (time wages), rather than for the work performed (piecework).

Mises noticed that Mill's arguments "have provided for decades one of the main props of the socialist idea, and have contributed more to its popularity than the hate-inspired and frequently contradictory arguments of socialist agitators."[27] Nevertheless, Mises found that it was not difficult to unearth the error in Mill, at least for a reader acquainted

---

coercive regulation of the growth of population, a socialist community is inconceivable" (p. 175). This too turned out to be a prophetic statement. The People's Republic of China found it necessary to limit births with the help of the death penalty.

[27]Ibid., pp. 154f.

with marginal-value theory. The English economist had not taken account of the fact that time wages are different for different kinds of work. Therefore, workers under capitalism still do have an incentive to overcome the irksomeness of labor.

> Doubtless the individual working for a time wage has no interest in doing more than will keep his job. But if he can do more, if his knowledge, capability and strength permit, he seeks for a post where more is wanted and where he can thus increase his income. It may be that he fails to do this out of laziness, but this is not the fault of the system. The system does all that it can to incite everyone to the utmost diligence, since it ensures to everyone the fruits of his labour. That Socialism cannot do this is the great difference between Socialism and Capitalism.[28]

This discussion of Mill's mistake on a question of labor economics was Mises's first blow against the hallowed reputation of Mill. He had come to the conclusion that Mill's reputation had done much damage to the intellectual appeal of the case for political liberalism. Five years after the publication of *Socialism*, Mises set the record straight:

> John Stuart Mill is an epigone of classical liberalism and, especially in his later years, under the influence of his wife, full of feeble compromises. He slips slowly into socialism and is the originator of the thoughtless confounding of liberal and socialist ideas that led to the decline of English liberalism and to the undermining of the living standards of the English people. Nevertheless—or perhaps because of this— one must become acquainted with Mill's principal writings.[29]

---

[28]Ibid., pp. 155–56. See also p. 152.

[29]Mises, *Liberalism: In the Classical Tradition* (Irvington-on-Hudson, N.Y.: Foundation for Economic Education, [1927] 1985), p. 195.

The Law of Association

After his analysis of the workings of socialist societies, Mises turned to the doctrine of the inevitability of socialism. Karl Marx and his followers had claimed that social evolution led with the necessity of natural law toward the establishment of socialism. The driving forces in this process were (a) the dialectics of class struggle and (b) the tendency inherent in capitalism for the emergence of monopolies, which centralize economic decision-making and thus prepare the advent of the centrally planned economy of socialism. One might think that addressing this Marxist claim was a waste of Mises's time since he had already shown that socialism was inferior to capitalism. But Mises did not think so. Even though socialism was demonstrably inferior to capitalism, there might still be a tendency for society to evolve toward socialism. The question therefore required a separate treatment.

One of the centerpieces of Marxist sociology was the theory of class struggle, according to which social evolution results from the necessarily conflicting interests of different social classes. History was one long drama featuring the interactions of antagonistic groups. The groups themselves varied over time—kings against nobility, nobility against bourgeoisie, bourgeoisie against proletarians—but the constant theme was the principle of class struggle itself.

In *Socialism*, Mises delivered an in-depth critique of the concept of class struggle, which had been adopted in a modified form by many thinkers outside the Marxist camp, including the champions of Aryan supremacy. Mises did not contest the fact that violent conflict had played a large role in the process of social evolution. Rather, he took issue with the notion that violence had played a *constructive* role. Mises argued that, by its very nature, violence could not have played the role that the advocates of the concept of class struggle ascribe to it. Class struggle could not explain the emergence and growth of human society. At best, it could explain how the members of a given association behaved *vis-à-vis* other given associations. The dynamics of social evolution would remain a mystery without a sound theory of cooperative association.

So why do people cooperate at all? Generalizing a discovery that David Ricardo had famously made in the special case of foreign trade, Mises gave a simple answer: human beings associate with one another because the division of labor is more physically productive than the atomistic production of isolated individuals.

> The theory of the international division of labour is one of the most important contributions of Classical Political Economy. It shows that as long as—for any reasons—movements of capital and labour between countries are prevented, it is the comparative, not the absolute, costs of production which govern the geographical division of labour. When the same principle is applied to the personal division of labour it is found that the individual enjoys an advantage in co-operating not only with people superior to himself in this or that capacity but also with those who are inferior to himself in every relevant way.[30]

---

[30]Mises, *Socialism*, pp. 260f. He goes on to illustrate the principle:

> If, through his superiority to B, A needs three hours' labour for the production of one unit of commodity p compared with B's five, and for the production of commodity q two hours against B's four, then A will gain if he confines his labour to producing q and leaves B to produce p. If each gives sixty hours to producing both p and q, the result of A's labour is $20p + 30q$, of B's $12p + 15q$, and for both together $32p + 45q$. If however, A confines himself to producing q alone he produces sixty units in 120 hours, whilst B, if he confines himself to producing p, produces in the same time twenty-four units. The result of the activity is then $24p + 60q$, which, as p has for A a substitution value of $3 : 2q$ and for B one of $5 : 4q$, signifies a larger production than $32p + 45q$.

Ricardo had barely mentioned what was later called "the theory of comparative cost advantages," relegating the crucial passage to a mere footnote in chapter 7 of his *Principles*. Later economists realized that this principle applied not only to the particular case of foreign trade, but also to the general case of exchange between individuals. Thus is covered all form of division of labor. It explained why human association was worthwhile not only for the inferior worker who found a superior associate, but also for that superior worker. The advantages are mutual, even if not necessarily symmetrical. This explained why children, handicapped, and very old persons could be welcome in the division of labor, even though they might be inferior in all practical respects to their associates. It explained why the members of industrial nations such as the United States or Japan could benefit from the cooperation of the residents of other countries, in which capital was much more scarce and unit-costs therefore higher. In short, the principle that the division of labor between two persons A and B is beneficial even in the "hard case" that A is superior to B in all respects, is a true "law of association."[31]

Mises had independently discovered a general law of human action. More than any other economist, he highlighted its far-reaching implications. The law applies under virtually all circumstances, because it presupposes only that the susceptible associates be *different* in talents or location, which is almost always the case.[32] This led to a surprising conclusion. The very

----

[31]Mises used this expression only in his later treatises on economics. See Mises, *Nationalökonomie* (Geneva: Editions Union, 1940), pp. 126ff.; idem, *Human Action* (New Haven, Conn.: Yale University Press, 1949), pp. 158ff. Here he spoke of "Das Ricardo'sche Vergesellschaftungsgesetz" and of "The Ricardian law of Association." But the generalization of Ricardo's discovery had occurred already in *Socialism*.

[32]Mises, *Socialism*:

> Historically division of labour originates in two facts of
> nature: the inequality of human abilities and the variety of

differences in which the theory of class struggle could see only the causes of violent conflict now appeared in a far more benign light. For these differences between individuals and groups *also* harbored great potentials for mutually advantageous cooperation. The law of association therefore had the power to turn difference from a principle of strife into one of friendship. In the words of Mises:

> The greater productivity of work under the division of labour is a unifying influence. It leads men to regard each other as comrades in a joint struggle for welfare, rather than as competitors in a struggle for existence. It makes friends out of enemies, peace out of war, society out of individuals.[33]

The fact that social differences harbor great potentials for mutual gains through cooperation had of course momentous policy implications. In the light of this fact, it was clear that government should regulate the economy as little as possible, in order not to prevent mutually beneficial associations. This runs directly counter to the notion that government should "level the playing field" on the market, both domestically and in international trade. The Law of Association sustained the case for unilateralism. Many years later, Mises stated in private correspondence:

> Each country, whether small or big, rich or poor, can have a free economy, irrespective of what the others might be doing. It is a widespread error to believe that the Ricardian Law of Comparative Costs presupposes that the other countries too engage in free trade. Also: If one country has the gold standard, it

---

the external conditions of human life on the earth. These two facts are really one: the diversity of Nature, which does not repeat itself but creates the universe in infinite, inexhaustible variety. (p. 259)

[33]Ibid., p. 261.

will enjoy all the benefits of stable money, even if others print notes like crazy. Of course, in the age of international division of labor, socialism in one country or several countries is detrimental to all other people because it diminishes productivity. For example, socialism in Russia and Yugoslavia entails a reduced production of wheat and thus price increases on the world market. But no country can sidestep such repercussions by socializing at home and thus by reducing its own productivity.[34]

After presenting the Law of Association, Mises returned to answering his initial question about social dynamics. Does social evolution necessarily lead to an ever-greater expansion of the division of labor? He examined whether the Darwinian principle of natural selection would answer this question, and found that societies based on a more extensive and intensive division of labor "have more prospect of preserving their members from misery and poverty. They are also better equipped to defend themselves from the enemy."[35] This fact by itself does not provide a satisfying answer. It merely pushes back the question. Why do some societies cultivate a higher division of labor? Quoting the French sociologist Izoulet, Mises answers that the reason is a purely intellectual one:

> It is the social spirit, the spirit of social co-operation, which forms, develops, and upholds societies. Once it is lost, the society falls apart again. The death of a nation is social retrogression, the decline from the division of labour to self-sufficiency. The social organism disintegrates into the cells from which it began. Man remains, but society dies.[36]

---

[34]Mises to Ballvé, letter dated December 26, 1950; Grove City Archive: Ballvé files.

[35]Mises, *Socialism*, p. 272.

[36]Ibid., p. 275. He emphasized:

Mises argued that the social spirit received a decisive boost from classical liberalism, which developed a sophisticated theory of the division of labor and highlighted the social function of private property. In later works, most notably in *Theory and History* (1957), Mises elaborates on the role of ideas in social evolution, presenting them as the ultimate cause of social dynamics. But he had laid the foundation for these subsequent discussions in *Socialism*.

Monopoly Theory

Having dealt with the theory of class struggle, Mises turned to exhibit B in the Marxist case for the historical inevitability of socialism: monopoly theory. To do so, he examined not only the Marxist doctrine that capitalism produces ever more economic concentration, but also the emerging neo-classical theory of monopoly prices, which had been widely used as an indictment of the market economy and as a *prima facie* justification for government intervention in the form of anti-trust policies.

Beginning with the Marxist tenets, Mises observed that the available statistical material contradicted the Marxist contention that there was a higher concentration of capital in private hands.[37] On the other hand, it was clear that industrial production *was* increasingly organized in large plants. The Marxist case seemed to rely on a conflation of very different types of

---

> There is no evidence that social evolution must move steadily upwards in a straight line. Social standstill and social retrogression are historical facts which we cannot ignore. World history is the graveyard of dead civilizations, and in India and Eastern Asia we see large-scale examples of civilization at a standstill.

[37]Schumpeter just recently had endorsed this theory. See Joseph A. Schumpeter, "Sozialistische Möglichkeiten von heute," *Archiv für Sozialwissenschaften und Sozialpolitik* 48, no. 2 (1921): 314. See also idem, *Capitalism, Socialism, and Democracy* (New York: Harper & Row, 1942).

concentration. Mises therefore set out to distinguish and analyze three types of concentration: production plants (establishments), enterprises, and individual fortunes. He showed that
there is indeed a marked tendency toward the concentration of
plants, but stressed that this was merely an offshoot of the division of labor: larger plants can serve larger markets. For similar
reasons, there might also be concentrations of enterprises. But,
Mises emphasized, there was no concentration of individual fortunes, especially of fortunes derived from profitable industrial
enterprise. The main reason was that, contrary to widespread
assumption, capital investment does not guarantee profits. It is
an essentially risky venture that thrives on successful speculation, but is ever exposed to complete ruin. Few families had
more than two or three generations of successful entrepreneurs.
The accumulated riches were then either invested in landed
property, or lost in further speculations.

This analysis reconciled the observations on which the persuasiveness of the Marxist case relied (concentration of plants
and enterprises) with the statistical evidence against any marked
concentration of individual fortunes. Ever-larger plants were
owned by ever-larger *groups*—of stockowners and bondholders.
The beneficial concentration in industry, which allowed for
production at ever-lower unit costs, did not necessarily go in
hand with a concentration of wealth.

This result was directly in line with the position that Max
Weber and Friedrich Naumann had defended before World
War I, when in the meetings of the *Verein für Socialpolitik* they
confronted the champions of anti-trust policies. Economic concentration could be a very beneficial phenomenon. It might
even be necessary to provide for the needs of a growing population. By 1922, Weber and Naumann had died. Now Mises's
discussion of economic concentration in *Socialism* made him the
most prominent advocate of their cause.[38]

---

[38]Mises would defend his position against anti-trust policies for the rest of
his life, often isolated in his stance, most notably when, as an octogenarian, he

During the 1920s, he confronted the anti-trust movement in Austria in his double capacity as a writer and as a secretary of the Vienna *Kammer*, in which Austria's big industrialists and bankers had a forum. He opposed the promotion of the handicrafts by subsidies, not because he disliked small firms or because he ignored their virtues, but because the case for these subsidies was untenable from any larger social point of view. The handicrafts had difficulties because they could not compete against big industry. But it was wrong to jump from this fact to the conclusion that the competition from the big firms was unfair.[39]

Could economic concentration on a free market ever be harmful? Mises answered this question in the affirmative, distinguishing two types of harmful "monopoly" as distinct from beneficial concentration. The first type of monopoly was given when one market participant provided a service that was indispensable, unique, and without substitute. But this case seemed to be a mere theoretical possibility. To which concrete goods would it apply? To air and water? These were certainly indispensable goods, but in most cases they were not *economic* goods at all. Mises argued that this form of monopoly was indeed exceedingly rare:

---

made the case for concentration in the debates of the Mont Pèlerin Society in the 1960s. See for example Mises, "Ein Wort zum Monopolpreisproblem," Peter Muthesius, ed., *Vom Sinn der Konzentration* (Frankfurt: Knapp, 1965).

[39]Quite apart from the corruption that plagued the implementation of anti-trust policies (*Mittelstandspolitik*), these policies often proved to be disastrous in practice because they benefited the more inefficient shops at the expense of the better ones, without improving their overall situation *vis-à-vis* the big industry. There was no critical study accounting for these practical failures. Mises obtained information from Hofrat Pösendeiner, a civil servant charged with the implementation of "industrial policy." He tried to persuade him to put these experiences into print. See Mises to Brodnitz, letter dated April 5, 1927; Mises Archive 62: 21.

> Perhaps the nearest approach to such a monopoly was
> the power to administer grace to believers, exercised
> by the medieval Church. Excommunication and
> interdict were no less terrible than death from thirst
> or suffocation. In a socialist community the State as
> organized society would form such a monopoly. All
> economic goods would be united in its hands and it
> would therefore be in a position to force the citizen
> to fulfill its commands, would in fact confront the
> individual with a choice between obedience and star-
> vation.[40]

Mises turned to the second type of monopoly, which was an
offspring of the theory of prices. A case of "price monopoly"
was given when a seller could restrict his production to increase
his price *and* obtain higher total selling proceeds because the
demand for his product was sufficiently inelastic. Of course this
could work only in the absence of competitors, because any
competitors in the field would expand their production and bid
down the price as soon as our would-be monopolist set out to
restrict his production. But Mises emphasized that, besides the
absence of competition, a second condition had to be given,
namely, a relative inelasticity of demand.

These circumstances brought about an anomaly on the market. Whereas under competitive conditions, each producer had
an incentive to produce as much as possible, thus providing for
the best possible satisfaction of consumer needs, under conditions of "price monopoly" the monopolist had the incentive to
restrict his production.

> The one and only peculiarity of monopoly is that,
> assuming a certain shape for the demand curve, the
> maximum net profit lies at a higher price than would
> have been the case in competition between sellers . . .
> monopoly under such conditions has three results:

---

[40]Mises, *Socialism*, p. 344.

the market price is higher, the profit is greater, both the quantity sold and the consumption are smaller than they would have been under free competition.[41]

However, this argument was vulnerable to the objection that the restriction of production in one firm or industry must not be equated with a reduced overall production in society. When the "price monopolist" restricted his production, he automatically freed up factors of production that henceforth could be used to produce *other* goods and services. The reduced supply of the monopoly good thus entails a larger supply of some other good. And if this is so, then what is wrong with "price monopoly"? Where is the harm? Price monopoly is certainly detrimental to the interests of the consumers of the monopoly good, but it benefits the producers and consumers of other goods. Can purely factual analysis strike a balance between these conflicting individual interests? Mises thought it could. He very clearly saw that "against the smaller production of the monopolized goods one must set the increased production of other goods." Yet he introduced another consideration:

> But these [other goods], of course, are less important goods, which would not have been produced and consumed if the more pressing demands for a larger quantity of the monopolized commodity could have been satisfied. The difference between the value of these goods and the higher value of the quantity of the monopolized commodity not produced represents the loss of welfare which the monopoly has inflicted on the national economy. Here private profit and social productivity are at variance. A social[ist] society under such circumstances would act differently from a capitalist society.[42]

---

[41]Ibid., p. 346.

[42]Ibid., p. 348. Mises, *Gemeinwirtschaft*, 2nd ed. (Jena: Gustav Fischer, 1932), p. 359.

No other writer had even come far enough to see the problem.[43] Many years later he said about the significance of his contribution:

> All those who have dealt with the monopoly problem have emphasized that the limitation of the total consumption of the monopoly good reduces the welfare of the persons concerned. Now in that passage of *Gemeinwirtschaft* . . . I deal with the extension of production that eventually must result from the liberation of non-specific factors of production formerly bound up in the production of the monopoly good. I explain that this extension of production can only concern less important goods (of course, from the point of view of the consumers). They are less important *because* they "would not have been produced and consumed if the more pressing demands for a larger quantity of the monopolized commodity could have been satisfied." . . . There is no proof for the welfare-reducing effect of monopoly prices other than the one I propose.[44]

Mises's devotion to the facts, as he perceived them, was greater than his political inclinations. Certainly he would have been happy to find that the market process always caters to consumers in the best possible way. But he did not find this to be the case, and he insisted on what he did find. Mises would uphold his argument even when his American disciple Murray

---

[43]Before 1922, the most elaborate exposition of the theory of monopoly price could be found in the work of John Bates Clark, who was much admired among Viennese theoreticians. Clark had claimed that monopoly weakens free competition, and that private monopoly was worse than public monopoly. See John Bates Clark, *Essentials of Economic Theory* (New York and London: Macmillan, 1914), pp. 374ff., 397.

[44]Mises to Hans Hellwig, letter dated November 29, 1956; Grove City Archive: Hellwig file. Mises here also refers to a passage in *Nationalökonomie* (p. 336), where he stated the issue even more clearly.

Rothbard, many years later, reformulated monopoly theory in a way that completely exculpated the free market.[45]

While Mises conceded the theoretical possibility of monopoly prices, he stressed that in practice, virtually all cases of monopoly were artificial creations of government intervention.[46] On a free market, monopoly is unlikely to occur in any field other than primary production. "Mining, in the widest sense of the word, is their true domain."[47] But even in this case, monopoly prices are not as harmful as they appear under monopoly theory, because the restricted exploitation of mines means that irreplaceable natural resources are used with greater thrift.

Christian Ethics versus the Market?

Having completed the analysis of the factual questions on socialism, Mises turned to a critique of the ethical doctrines that had served to justify socialist schemes. Here he devoted particular attention to Christianity and examined the question of how much it supported a free society, and how much it would tend to justify violations of private property.

Mises began by noting that of all the great monotheistic religions, Christianity alone was a living faith. Its doctrine covered all dimensions of human existence. It not only addressed the

---

[45]See Murray N. Rothbard, *Man, Economy, and State with Power and Market*, Scholar's edition (Auburn, Ala.: Ludwig von Mises Institute, 2003), chap. 10.

[46]Rudolf Hilferding, *Das Finanzkapital* (Berlin: Dietz, [1910] 1947), chaps. 21 and 22 had made very similar observations in his influential book. However, the Austro-Marxist theoretician argued that state monopolies were an outgrowth of capitalism. Mises was therefore unable to endorse Hilferding's analysis and preferred to recommend a study by the Freiburg professor Robert Liefmann, which detailed how the German government had created monopolies in the recent past. See Robert Liefmann, *Kartelle und Trusts* (Stuttgart: Moritz, 1924).

[47]Mises, *Socialism*, p. 350.

narrowly spiritual questions of man. It also dealt with his ethical concerns, that is, his social and political relationships with
other human beings. This could not be otherwise, Mises
argued, lest religion force its adherents "to look for an answer
elsewhere. This would mean losing its hold on its adherents and
its power over the spirit. Without social ethics religion would
be dead."[48] Thus Mises joined hands with the champions of the
notion that Christianity was a living faith, not in spite of its
meddling with politics, but rather because of its political dimension.[49]

But in 1922, the acknowledgment of Christianity's social
and political dimension was more than a point of doctrine. The
advice of Jesuits, Catholic bishops, and Protestant pastors had
a noticeable impact on daily life. The concrete embodiment of
political Christianity with which Mises had long been
acquainted was the Christian Socialist movement, which had
emerged in the 1860s in the Austrian Alps and other rural areas
predominantly inhabited by Catholic Germans. The movement arose as a reaction to the liberal reforms of the 1850s and
1860s, which had enabled efficient factory production, in con-
junction with bank credit and railways, to displace the old
handicraft-based modes of production. With amazing speed,
this transformation had undermined the social positions of the
old elites—landed nobility and clergy, who were increasingly
challenged and displaced by industrial upstarts who were often

---

[48]Ibid., p. 370.

[49]The same point had been made, though from a completely different
point of view, in Carl Schmitt, *Politische Theologie* (Berlin: Duncker & Humblot, 1922). A great critic of classical-liberal legal doctrines, Schmitt attacked
the notion that modern juridical scholarship had done away with the theological foundation of politics. Othmar Spann too was a Catholic intellectual
of the old school, who believed with Pius IX that all things had to be remade
in Christ. In Mises's own circle of friends, Erich Voegelin was most interested
in these questions. See Voegelin's early work *Die politischen Religionen* (Stockholm: Bermann-Fischer, 1939).

Jewish. Christian Socialism was a product of old-elite intellectuals seeking to discredit these changes by contesting the legitimacy of liberalism and capitalism. Count Egbert Belcredi,
Freiherr von Vogelsang, and Rudolf Meyer called for the
reestablishment of medieval guilds, for credit organizations
under state control, for factory laws, for the protection of
national labor through tariffs and through social insurance
schemes.[50]

This was how Mises experienced political Christianity first-
hand. In chapter 29 of *Socialism*, he gave a theoretical interpretation of this experience. Was Christian Socialism actually
grounded in the teachings of Jesus Christ? Mises answered this
question affirmatively. Christ, he said, had left his disciples no
rules whatever that could be of any use for building a society on
earth, because he believed the Kingdom of God was imminent:

> The expectation of God's own reorganization when
> the time came and the exclusive transfer of all action
> and thought to the future Kingdom of God, made
> Jesus's teaching utterly negative. He rejects every-
> thing that exists without offering anything to replace
> it. He arrives at dissolving all existing social ties. The
> disciple shall not merely be indifferent to supporting
> himself, shall not merely refrain from work and dis-
> possess himself of all goods, but he shall hate "father,
> and mother, and wife, and children, and brethren,
> and sisters, yea, and his own life." Jesus is able to tol-
> erate the worldly laws of the Roman Empire and the
> prescriptions of the Jewish Law because he is indif-
> ferent to them, despising them as things important
> only within the narrow limits of time and not because
> he acknowledges their value. His zeal in destroying
> social ties knows no limits. The motive force behind
> the purity and power of this complete negation is

---

[50]See Rudolf Sieghart, *Die letzten Jahrzehnte einer Grossmacht* (Berlin:
Ullstein, 1932), pp. 299f.

ecstatic inspiration and enthusiastic hope of a new world. Hence his passionate attack upon everything that exists. Everything may be destroyed because God in His omnipotence will rebuild the future order. No need to scrutinize whether anything can be carried over from the old to the new order, because this new order will arise without human aid. It demands therefore from its adherents no system of ethics, no particular conduct in any positive direction. Faith and faith alone, hope, expectation—that is all he needs. He need contribute nothing to the reconstruction of the future, this God Himself has provided for. The clearest modern parallel to the attitude of complete negation of primitive Christianity is Bolshevism.[51]

The very fact that Christ's teachings were utterly unconcerned with the material conditions on earth, Mises argued, explains the great flexibility with which Christianity has adapted to a great variety of political systems throughout the ages.[52] But is the otherworldliness of the teachings of Christ really a sufficient proof for the contention that these teachings are at odds with political liberty? Mises thought so, moving on to exhibit B in the case against Christianity. Not only was it impossible to "find a single passage in the New Testament that could be read as upholding private property," but Jesus Christ also topped this sin of omission with a sin of commission:

> One thing of course is clear, and no skilful interpretation can obscure it. Jesus' words are full of resentment

---

[51]Mises, *Socialism*, pp. 375f.

[52]See ibid., p. 376. Again, this thesis parallels a contemporary work by the anti-liberal Carl Schmitt, *Römischer Katholizismus und politische Form* (Berlin: Duncker & Humblot, 1923). Schmitt however did not believe that Christ's teachings were utterly otherworldly. He held that the Catholic Church survived because she always enjoyed the margin of liberty necessary to accomplish her mission.

against the rich, and the Apostles are no meeker in this respect. The Rich Man is condemned because he is rich, the Beggar praised because he is poor. The only reason why Jesus does not declare war against the rich and preach revenge on them is that God has said: "Revenge is mine." . . . Up to the time of modern Socialism no movement against private poverty which has arisen in the Christian world has failed to seek authority in Jesus, the Apostles, and the Christian Fathers, not to mention those who, like Tolstoy, made the Gospel resentment against the rich the very heart and soul of their teaching. This is a case in which the Redeemer's words bore evil seed. More harm has been done, and more blood shed, on account of them than by the persecution of heretics and the burning of witches.[53]

One can only imagine how these passages must have endeared Mises to his Christian readers. But not only the Christian faithful will wonder if he had a proper understanding of political Christianity. It is clear that the Gospel of Christ had been abused many times in history. There is no doctrine that has been spared this fate, not even the doctrines of Adam Smith and David Ricardo. But Mises's claims seemed to be more than extravagant; they also raised a puzzle. How is it that Western civilization arose under the dominion of Christian doctrine, which seemed to be so steadfastly opposed to anything that makes society possible? Up to 1922, according to Mises's own admission, Christianity was a vibrant faith, and it had been so during the very centuries that witnessed the development of the West. How was this possible?

Mises answered that these cultural achievements were "the work of the Church, not of Christianity" and that the "social ethics of Jesus have no part in this cultural development."[54]

---

[53]Mises, *Socialism*, p. 379.

[54]Ibid., p. 380.

> This evidence leads to the negation of the question
> asked above: whether it might not be possible to rec-
> oncile Christianity with a free social order based on
> private ownership in the means of production. A liv-
> ing Christianity cannot exist side by side with, and
> within, Capitalism.[55]

Liberalism and Christianity were foes by their very nature,
engaged in a struggle of life or death. Either Christianity would
maintain the upper hand, or liberalism would crowd it out. No
compromise was possible.

Ten years later, Mises had changed his mind. In the second
edition of *Socialism*, he added two paragraphs that gave a much
milder and reconciling tone to the conclusion. Mises now
claimed that Christianity and liberalism might not be quite as
antagonistic as he had at first assumed. They could flourish
together, provided there was a new synthesis:

> But there may be an alternative. No one can foresee
> with certainty how Church and Christianity may
> change in the future. Papacy and Catholicism now
> face problems incomparably more difficult than all
> those they have had to solve for over a thousand years.
> The world-wide Universal Church is threatened in its
> very being by Chauvinist nationalism. By refinement
> of political art it has succeeded in maintaining the
> principle of Catholicism through all the turmoil of
> national wars, but it must realize more clearly every

---

[55]Mises, *Gemeinwirtschaft*, 1st ed., p. 421; my translation. For unknown
reasons, the published English translation sounds less categorical than the
original:

> In face of all this evidence, it would seem that only a negative
> answer can be made to the question asked above: whether it
> might not be possible to reconcile Christianity with a free
> social order based on private ownership in the means of pro-
> duction. A living Christianity cannot, it seems, exist side by
> side with Capitalism. (Mises, *Socialism*, p. 386)

day that its continuance is incompatible with nationalist ideas. Unless it is prepared to succumb, and make way for national churches, it must drive out nationalism by an ideology which makes it possible for nations to live and work together in peace. But in so doing the Church would find itself inevitably committed to Liberalism. No other doctrine would serve.

If the Roman Church is to find any way out of the crisis into which nationalism has brought it, then it must be thoroughly transformed. It may be that this transformation and reformation will lead to its unconditional acceptance of the indispensability of private ownership in the means of production. At present it is still far from this, as witness the recent encyclical Quadragesimo anno.[56]

It is not known what changed his mind. It is possible Mises had second thoughts on Christianity and liberalism as a consequence of his activity as a counselor to Monsignor Ignaz Seipel, who according to many Catholic witnesses had a saintly character. He also came to realize that other scholars worked to bridge the gap that he saw between capitalism and Catholicism. Thus he would eventually characterize the influential Jesuit O. von Nell-Breuning as "one of the few German economists who in the Interwar period advocated economic freedom."[57]

Socialism = Destructionism

Mises's analysis of socialism left nothing intact of the grandiose edifice that Marx and many other generations of

---

[56]Mises, *Socialism*, pp. 386f.

[57]Mises to Parker, letter dated May 14, 1953; Grove City Archive: Tax Foundation file. Mises had Nell-Breuning sent a copy of the Tax Foundation's handbook *Fiscal Facts for '53*.

socialist writers had worked to build.[58] But then what was the true significance of socialism? The answer seemed by now to be apparent:

> In fact Socialism is not in the least what it pretends to be. It is not the pioneer of a better and finer world, but the spoiler of what thousands of years of civilization have created. It does not build; it destroys. For destruction is the essence of it. It produces nothing, it only consumes what the social order based on private ownership in the means of production has created. Since a socialist order of society cannot exist, unless it be as a fragment of Socialism within an economic order resting otherwise on private property, each step leading towards Socialism must exhaust itself in the destruction of what already exists.[59]

The work of destruction had been under way for a long time. Intellectuals and artists had been at the forefront of this movement:

> One can say without exaggeration that nothing has been prepared so thoroughly and from all sides for decades than the general collapse of European social order and morals, which we have experienced and still experience daily. All sciences and arts have contributed their part to it.[60]

Here Mises sounds not unlike Carl Ludwig Haller, one of the great nineteenth century European "reactionary" thinkers,

---

[58]The Bolshevist reaction was predictable: he was presented as a "theoretician of fascism." See the article by F. Kapeljush in *The Bolshevik* 15 (August 15th, 1924); Mises Archive 1: 9ff. The file contains a German translation of this piece, which Mises received in the fall of 1925 from the Austrian Mission in Moscow.

[59]Ibid., p. 414.

[60]Mises to an unknown correspondent, letter dated February 9, 1926; Mises Archive 80: 24. The correspondent was presumably the author of the (lost) novel *Polythea*.

who claimed that the egalitarian "spirit of destruction" characterized the Jacobin liberal movement and the French Revolution. Haller argued that egalitarian programs are always smashed on the hard rock of natural social inequalities. Rather than abandoning their impossible goal, the egalitarians set out to transform the world according to their scheme. They led a war against all forms of authority and all social institutions that sprang from them: scholarship, Church, priesthood, nobility, government, family, parents. But because this war merely destroyed the specific social bonds that resulted from inequalities, and not the factual existence of these inequalities, the Jacobins destroyed society. Anticipating Mises, he observed:

> If not everything has collapsed, if we could salvage some fragments of society, this is only thanks to the material impossibility of executing [the Jacobin program], to the sometimes blatant nonsense and the happy inconsistency of human beings, even in evil things.[61]

Mises and Haller certainly agreed on the fact of egalitarian destructionism, but Mises did not join Haller in condemning all institutional innovation after the French Revolution. Neither did he join English professor F.J.C. Hearnshaw in representing socialism as systematized robbery. Bringing the notion of robbery into play was much too moralistic for Mises's taste. The point was a technical one: socialism was just impossible. Commenting on Hearnshaw, Mises wrote to a correspondent at the London School of Economics:

> I entirely agree with you that it is quite wrong to consider socialism as robbery. The socialist system would

---

[61]Carl Ludwig Haller, "Über einige Parteienbenennungen zum besseren Verständnis der Zeitungen und anderer moderner Schriften," *Satan und die Revolution—und andere Schriften* (Vienna: Karolinger, 1991), p. 78.

be just as honest and fair as the capitalist one if a
social order based on common ownership of the
means of production was feasible.[62] ⌁

Mises in his study in the late 1940s

---

[62]Mises to Meyendorff; letter dated July 10, 1928; Mises Archive 88:6.
See also Meyendorff's letter to Mises in 88: 8.

Part IV
Mises in His Prime

12
Fresh Start

AUSTRIA'S SITUATION CONSIDERABLY WORSENED under the impact of the Treaty of Saint-Germain-en-Laye, signed on September 10, 1919. The treaty was a diktat rather than a true agreement, designed to ensure the political weakness of Germans rather than durable peace among the nations.[1] It placed all burdens attributable to the "Austrian" part of the Austro-Hungarian monarchy on German-Austria, and in all questions pertaining to the relations between the successor states of the monarchy, it ruled against German-Austria and in favor of the

---

[1] During the 1920s and 1930s, many testimonies and analyses appeared in France, Britain, and the United States that condemned the treaty as a prolongation of the hostilities by other means, and thus as a heavy burden on future peace in Europe. See for example the account by the French diplomat Alcide Ebray, *La Paix malpropre (Versailles)—pour la reconciliation par la vérité* (Milano: Unitas, 1924); see also the testimony of the British diplomatic journalist Sisley Huddleston, *In My Time* (New York: Dutton & Co., 1938). Useful general discussions of the consequences of Versailles and Saint-Germain by contemporary witnesses are in John Maynard Keynes, *The Economic Consequences of the Peace* (New York: Harcourt, Brace and Howe, 1920); Sisley Huddleston, *War Unless* (London: Victor Gollancz, 1933); idem, *Popular Diplomacy and War* (Rindge, N.H.: Richard Smith, 1954); Christian Eckert, "Friedensverträge. II. Vom staatswissenschaftlichen Standpunkte," *Handwörterbuch der Staatswissenschaften*, 4th ed. (Jena: Gustav Fischer, 1927), vol. 4, in particular pp. 509–12; Felix Ermacora, *Der unbewältigte Friede—St. Germain und die Folgen* (Vienna and Munich: Amaltha, 1989); and Jacques Bainville, *Les conséquences politiques de la paix* (Paris: Fayard, 1920).

other states. This procedure was based on the view that the Habsburg family had pursued a longstanding policy of German hegemony *vis-à-vis* the Czech, Slovenian, Italian, Croatian, and Polish peoples and that therefore the German Austrians now had to bear all costs related to the military defeat and to the dissolution of the empire.

In accordance with this view, the treaty stipulated that the republic of Deutsch-Österreich (German-Austria) change its name into "Republik Österreich"—an unusual provision, to say the least. But the new Republic of Austria had also to endure humiliating demands of a less cosmetic nature. While the principle of national self-determination had been used to justify the separation of Czech, Polish, and Yugoslav lands from the Austro-Hungarian Empire, the goal of "making the Germans pay" trumped principle. In the Czech case, "historical law" was invoked to justify the incorporation of the Sudetenland, which had first been settled by Germans and still had a vast German majority; and in the case of Italy, the establishment of a "natural border" at the Brenner Pass brought South Tyrol under Italian dominion. In German-Austria's own case, "independence" was considered more important than the desire of its inhabitants to join the German Reich. Three months after the Treaty of Saint-Germain had been signed, all the Austrian provincial parliaments voted resolutions in favor of the establishment of economic union with the German Reich. The Entente reacted immediately, on December 17, 1919, insisting that Austria's political and economic independence not be relinquished.

German-Austria lost almost 40,000 square miles—more than a third of its soil—territories that for centuries had been inhabited and cultivated by Germans. Most of the other stipulations of the treaty further humiliated German-Austria and poisoned relations with its neighbors.

The most pressing problems were of a financial nature. The Allies were holding German-Austria alone responsible for the debts of the former Austro-Hungarian Empire. Because war bonds and other war-related debts were denominated in kronen, they could be handled through the printing of more banknotes, but two other financial liabilities proved permanent and pernicious: the salaries of the civil servants and the massive deficits being run up by government-owned industry.

Civil servants in Austria-Hungary had been predominantly German, and a great number of them lived in Vienna. After the dissolution of the empire, German-Austrians found themselves in the awkward position of having five million citizens supporting a civil service developed for fifty million. Various means were tried to reduce the number of civil servants, but in 1922, one out of ten men still received a salary from the public treasury.

While the excessive number of civil servants was an inheritance from the old empire, public firms running huge losses were the achievement of the social democrats, who had "socialized" the coalmines and other industries.

Under these circumstances, it was out of the question for German-Austria to pay damages to anyone. Its citizens were hardly able to feed themselves—especially in Vienna. The traditional trade channels with the eastern provinces no longer existed. Trade with its Czech, Yugoslav, Hungarian, and Polish neighbors—who were even more nationalist and protectionist than the Austrians themselves—had fallen to a minimum. Far from being able to pay reparations, German-Austria depended for survival on the financial support of its former enemies. And from the end of 1919 onwards, it did receive such help.

Hayek and the Bureau for Claims Settlements

According to Article 248 of the Treaty, the new Austria had to pay damages to foreign governments and their citizens. These foreign beneficiaries were not limited to the Entente powers, but included the non-German territories of the old Austria, which according to the stipulations of the Treaty were counted as states "associated" with the Entente. Article 248 had largely been copied from an analogous provision in the Treaty of Versailles, which concerned the much less complicated case of Germany. It was completely unclear how it should be put into practice in the Austrian case. Once again, it was the public-administration experts from the Vienna *Kammer* who had to find a way out.

During the war, Mises's friend Emil Perels had founded an Office for the Protection of Austrian Assets Abroad,[2] the pur-pose of which was to protect the private claims of the citizens of Austria-Hungary, and to establish records of existing claims of these citizens on those of enemy countries. After the ratification of the Treaty of Saint-Germain in the fall of 1920, the Austrian government transformed this organization into the *Abrech-nungsamt*, a governmental bureau for claim settlements. Perels remained the chief executive and several other men were also appointed to its board, Mises among them. The two *Kammer* secretaries shared a predilection for efficient organization and kept the new Bureau for Claims Settlements as small as possi-ble. While its German equivalent in Berlin had more than 1,000 employees by 1922, the Vienna organization, which had to deal with far more complicated cases, had a headcount of 150.[3]

In June of 1922, Perels left the Bureau for a more prestigious appointment and Mises succeeded him. Two and a half years later, Mises quit the position too, ostensibly because his new position as a vice-director of the *Kammer* and his research agenda did not leave him enough time to shoulder the respon-sibilities of the office. His former employees praised him for using his contacts in industrial and banking circles for the suc-cessful floating of a Bureau Bond (*Abrechnungsschuldverschrei-bung*) to finance the payments resulting from the settlement process.[4] But the newspapers reported on conflicts between

---

[2]Schutzstelle für österreichisches Vermögen im Auslande.

[3]See the reports in *Friedensrecht* 1, no. 11 (June 20, 1922). This journal was the official publication of the Bureau.

[4]*Friedensrecht* 4, no. 2 (February 1925).

Mises and the Finance Ministry concerning payments of prewar debts, which the Ministry had delayed.[5] In short, the problem was that Mises had persuaded certain people to finance his government, and now the government refused to pay them back. Mises wanted no part of such an organization.

For Mises himself, the time he spent at the Bureau for Claims Settlements was especially memorable because it brought him in touch with the young student who would eventually become his most important intellectual ally and a friend for many years. By December 1921, Friedrich August von Hayek (1899–1992) had received his first doctorate (in law) when he applied for a position at the Bureau. Mises himself conducted the interview. Hayek presented a letter of recommendation from Friedrich von Wieser, who praised him as a promising young economist.[6] Mises smiled and said he had never seen Hayek in his lectures. But given Wieser's letter it would be rude to reject the young man, so he hired him on the

Friedrich August von Hayek

spot. Mises assigned him to research money and banking theory. Hayek quickly showed himself a useful assistant, alerting Mises to the case for free banking.

More than any of his fellow students, Hayek was an adventurer. His peers Haberler and Voegelin were anxious not to leave the well-trodden career route. They eventually left Vienna to study in the United States when prestigious Rockefeller stipends became available for Austrian students in 1924.[7] But

---

[5]*Neue Freie Presse* (November 18, 1924), p. 12.

[6]F.A. Hayek, "Einleitung," introduction to Ludwig von Mises, *Erinnerungen* (Stuttgart: Gustav Fischer, 1978,) p. xii.

[7]The Laura Spelman Rockefeller Fund had followed a 1922 suggestion by Beardsley Ruml to move into the field of the social sciences. In 1923 the

Hayek was curious enough to travel to New York on his own, with no money and only his capacity and readiness for intellectual hard work. Mises encouraged and supported the project.

Upon receiving his second doctorate (in economics), Hayek left for New York City in March 1923 and stayed until May 1924.[8] He found employment as a translator for economics professor Jeremiah W. Jenks, whom he had met in Vienna in the spring of 1922. Later he also worked for Professor Wesley Mitchell at the National Bureau for Economic Research, collecting data for his book on business cycles.[9] Mitchell was a great admirer of Wieser's, and Hayek provided him with background information that Mitchell used in his preface for the American edition of Wieser's textbook. Hayek also talked to him about Mises. To Mitchell's mild astonishment, Hayek put Mises in the same class as Voltaire, Montesquieu, Tocqueville, and John Stuart Mill.[10]

When Hayek returned to Vienna, he was thoroughly acquainted with American methods of business cycle research, knowledge that would prove to be highly useful two years later, when Mises established an Austrian Institute for Business Cycle Research—mainly to provide Hayek with a suitable position.

Fund started investing in social research with an explicit long-term "scientistic" orientation. In the same year, the Social Science Research Council was established, also on the initiative of Ruml. See Raymond Blaine Fosdick, *The Story of the Rockefeller Foundation* (New York: Harper, 1952), p. 193ff.

[8]On the boat to New York he started translating Pierson's article on the value problem in socialist societies. The translation was probably ready in August and Hayek submitted it to Weiss, who at the time was the editor of the *Zeitschrift*. See Hayek to Mises, letter of August 1923; Mises Archive 79: 15f.

[9]"I also usually have work on the side. At present I am at the National Bureau for Economic Research collecting material for Professor Mitchell's study of the Business Cycle." Hayek to Mises, letter dated January 12, 1924; Mises Archive 81: 23.

[10] Hayek, "Einleitung," p. xi.

Hayek's teacher Wieser had been the main contact of the Rockefeller Foundation among the academic economists in Vienna. He made sure that Hayek was granted the first Rockefeller fellowship, while he was still in Manhattan. But the notification reached the young man only after he had already returned to Vienna.[11] By then he was unwilling to accept the fellowship. Mises then tried to hire Hayek for the *Kammer* library, but it was Haberler who eventually obtained the position.[12] These early problems foreshadowed Hayek's lifetime lack of talent as a careerist.

Fighting Inflation

There was a reason Mises encouraged Hayek and all students he mentored to study the problems of currency and banking. Austrian public finance was in terrible shape and the government paid for substantial parts of its expenditures by printing more money. Wartime controls on foreign exchange were still in place to encourage the belief among the citizens that the government was fighting, rather than creating, inflation.

Mises successfully mobilized the *Kammer* apparatus to oppose foreign exchange controls. In the *Kammer* general assembly, he quoted from letters in which affiliated entrepreneurs described how the current monetary regime made it virtually impossible for them to serve geographically close customers who used a different currency.[13] Mises also had a more direct impact on monetary policy. Owing to his position in the Bureau for Claims Settlements and in the first Renner government, he was one of a handful of senior advisors to the Austro-Hungarian Bank, the

---

[11]F.A. Hayek, *Hayek on Hayek: An Autobiographical Dialogue* (Chicago: Chicago University Press, 1994), p. 67.

[12]Mises to Hayek, letter dated February 8, 1924; Mises Archive 81: 24. Mises here thanks Hayek for sending a report on his time in New York and talks about the position in the *Kammer* library.

[13]See records in the files of the Vienna Chamber of Commerce.

central bank of the old monarchy, which survived several years into the Republic.

The governor of the Bank, Alexander Spitzmüller, was determined not only to stop the fall of the krone, but to increase its exchange rate in a manner similar to what Churchill was about to do in Britain.[14] Mises certainly opposed Spitzmüller's plan and disagreed with his view that a stabilization of the krone at its present low value would amount to a bankruptcy of the state. Mises's position can be inferred from his writings, including the following passage in a 1923 essay:

> It is quite wrong to consider "devaluation" to be a case of state bankruptcy. Stabilization of the present—low—value of money, even if considered only with respect to its effect on existing debts, is something very different; it is both more and less than state bankruptcy. It is more than state bankruptcy to the extent that it affects not only public debts, but also all private debts. It is less than state bankruptcy, on the one hand, to the extent that it also affects the government's assets denominated in paper money; on the other hand, to the extent that it does not affect its obligations denominated in hard money or foreign currency. . . .
>
> The general economic effects, and in particular the trade-political effects of any money-induced change of the purchasing power of money—hence also the effects of a rising purchasing power of money—weigh in against any attempt to raise the value of money before stabilizing it. The present level of the value of money should be stabilized.[15]

---

[14]See for example the documents concerning a May 24, 1921 meeting on the premises of the Bank to discuss exchange rate policies. Among the participants were Spitzmüller, Wieser, Schumpeter, Schwiedland, Schiff, and Mises. See Mises Archive 74: 3ff.

[15]Ludwig von Mises, "Die geldtheoretische Seite des Stabilisierungsproblems," *Schriften des Vereins für Sozialpolitik* 164, no. 2 (1923): 19f.; my

His argument ultimately won the day and provided the basis for the currency reforms of the fall of 1922, but only after fierce resistance from Spitzmüller, who remained unconvinced and clashed with Mises repeatedly. Or, in more diplomatic terms: Spitzmüller had

> taken measures that in my eyes were inadequate. I have publicly spoken against these measures, for example, against foreign exchange controls, and I have frequently explained my standpoint in discussions with Excellency Spitzmüller . . .; I have not succeeded in convincing him of the pertinence of my views.[16]

Spitzmüller later honored Mises as the most important Austrian monetary politician.[17] However, Mises always stressed that his influence was entirely through writing and public lectures. The monetary stabilization of 1922 was the only time official policy met with his approval.

---

translation. Mises pointed out that it was not possible to "compensate the owners of claims denominated in marks for losses they have suffered from 1914 to 1923" because the "present owners of the claims are not always identical with those who have suffered the loss. The bulk of the fungible claims and a considerable part of all other claims have changed hands over the years."

[16]From Mises's second comment at the 1924 meeting of the *Verein für Sozialpolitik*; see Mises Archive 22: 80ff. Spitzmüller remained faithful to his line even many years after the event. In March 1929, he gave two lectures on the policy of the Austrian central bank. He attacked the stance taken by the bank and by the industry, and in his second lecture also dealt several times with Mises whom he criticized for an alleged lack of consistency. See Mises Archive 80: 81.

[17]Mises reacted to a statement to this effect of Spitzmüller's in a comment made at the 1924 meeting of the *Verein für Sozialpolitik*; see Mises Archive 22: 80ff. See also the identical statement by E. Weidenhoffer, secretary of the Hauptverband der Industrie Österreichs in Styria, which he made in a March 1924 letter to Mises; Mises Archive 80: 81.

On October 21, 1921, Mises lectured before the *Österreichis-che Politische Gesellschaft* (Austrian Political Society) on "The Present State of Austria's Public Finance."[18] He argued that the government budget could only be balanced by eliminating food subsidies and selling public enterprises. Every other proposal fundamentally failed to come to grips with the question of how to balance the budget.

The Schober government still preferred the printing press. The ever-increasing production of krone notes was soon followed by a decrease in real purchasing power—the more banknotes the Austro-Hungarian Bank issued the weaker they became. This development became a serious threat to the Austrian economy in the late fall of 1921, increasingly thwarting the financial plans of Austrian firms and choking the division of labor.

In Germany, where the same phenomenon could be observed, the most eminent monetary experts—Reichsbank president Rudolf Havenstein and Finance Minister Karl Helf-ferich—believed there was no causal connection between these events. The decline of the purchasing power of the mark resulted, among other things, from the deficit of Germany's balance of payments, and the Reichsbank's increase of the (nominal) mark supply was necessary to prevent a further decline of the mark supply in real terms.

These views impressed the Austrian public and influential circles within government, but Mises was unconvinced. The purchasing power of money declined faster than the new banknotes were printed, but that was because of the present expectations of money holders concerning the future purchasing power of their money:

> If the future prospects for a money are considered poor, its value in speculation, which anticipates its future purchasing power, will be lower than the

---

[18]See the newspaper report in Mises Archive 107: 24.

actual demand and supply situation at the moment
would indicate. Prices will be asked and paid which
more nearly correspond to anticipated future conditions than to the present demand for, and quantity
of, money in circulation. . . . The monetary units
available at the moment are not sufficient to pay the
prices which correspond to the anticipated future
demand for, and quantity of, monetary units. So trade
suffers from a shortage of notes. There are not
enough monetary units on hand to complete the
business transactions agreed upon. . . . This phenomenon could be clearly seen in Austria in the late fall of
1921.[19]

Thus there was in fact a causal relationship between the
increased production of money and the over-proportional
decline of the purchasing power of money. The decline of Austria's money could not be stopped or even reversed through the
printing press—on the contrary, more inflation would aggravate
the situation even further.

The problem was that Spitzmüller's Austro-Hungarian Bank
was still a stronghold of the party of inflation.[20] The Bank followed the Helfferich-Havenstein line, in a desperate attempt to
catch up with the shrinking krone by printing yet more of them.
Mises tried to steer counter as much as possible, placing two
articles in the *Neue Freie Presse* in March 1922: "Inflation and
the Shortage of Money: Against the Continued Use of the
Printing Press" and "The Austrian Monetary Problem Thirty

---

[19]Mises, "Die geldtheoretische Seite des Stabilisicrungsproblems," pp.
6f.; translated as "Stabilization of the Monetary Unit—From the Viewpoint
of Theory," *On the Manipulation of Money and Credit*, Percy L. Greaves, trans.
(New York: Free Market Books, 1978), pp. 8f.

[20]This concerned in particular the Austrian directors, who were predominantly statist and inflationist. The Hungarian directors were generally advocates of the gold standard. Mises made this point in a 1924 *Verein für
Sozialpolitik* debate with Spitzmüller. See Mises Archive 22: 80ff.

Years Ago and Today: A Commentary."[21] He especially sought
to raise the public's awareness of the destruction that the inflation wrought on the economy. Austria had become a poor country, and already had to pay for at least a part of its imports by
decreasing its capital base, but inflation would destroy it altogether. As he explained to Moriz Dub:

> I think that in evaluating our situation one has to
> strictly distinguish between two things. There is on
> the one hand the inflation, which leads to increasing
> prices for all commodities and for foreign currency;
> on the other hand, there is the fact that our popula-
> tion lives today from capital consumption and pays
> for imported commodities through the export of cap-
> ital assets such as fungible claims and other owner-
> ship titles. Between these two facts there is however
> something of a close connection to the extent that the
> falsification that the inflation has induced in the cal-
> culation of business profits represents the psycholog-
> ical basis for the unrestrained consumption of the
> accumulated capital of the national economy. The
> devaluation of money leads to illusory profits that the
> people have long held to be true profits.[22]

---

[21]Mises Archive 74: 31. The editor of the *Neue Freie Presse*, Moritz Dub,
thanked Mises especially for the latter piece in which he had quoted from a
speech by Carl Menger, who was himself a former editor of the *NFP*.

[22]Mises's letter to Moriz Dub, June 24, 1922, Mises Archive 74: 37. Moriz
(or Moritz) Dub was the economics editor of the *Neue Freie Presse* and author
of several popular books on economic problems. In the postwar period, he
published two works on the "catastrophic boom" induced by inflation of the
money supply. See Moriz Dub, *Katastrophenhausse und Geldentwertung*
(Stuttgart: Enke, 1920); idem, *Die weitere Entwicklung der Katastrophenhausse
in Oesterreich mit Streiflichtern auf Deutschland* (Stuttgart: Enke, 1922).

Seminars

If Mises was waging a campaign against the dangers of economic ignorance, the classroom remained campaign headquarters. The winter semester of 1920–1921 concentrated on business-cycle theory, featuring sessions on the problem of economic crises, on what are "normal" or "good" or "bad" economic conditions, on the historical crises of 1900–1902, 1907, 1873, and on the permanent effects of the business cycle.[23]

In the winter semester of 1921–1922, his university seminar focused on some larger issues of monetary theory. It was a memorable semester because for the first time the participants included several who would become his star students: Hayek, Haberler, Machlup, and Schütz.[24]

While the pedagogical effort made in the "seminars on theoretical economics" was related to the pressing issues of Austria's monetary policy, the subjects discussed in Mises's private seminar were less directly connected to current political events.[25]

In the next few years, the private seminar continued the discussion of basic conceptual problems of economics, but increasingly turned to the discussion of fundamentally different approaches in the social sciences.[26,27]

Hayek sometimes found these debates grueling and felt relieved when he left Vienna to spend a year in New York:

> On the whole I felt somewhat tired of the subjects which had chiefly occupied me in Vienna during the preceding year or so, such as the theory of subjective

---

[23]Mises Archive 17: 53, 53b, 55.

[24]Mises Archive 17: 55, 55b.

[25]Mises Archive 17: 3f.

[26]Mises Archive 17: 5. The record seems to be incomplete.

[27]Mises Archive 20: 7ff. The record seems to be incomplete. There are no records for 1922–1923.

value or the problem of economic calculation under
socialism.[28]

And comparing the way things were discussed in the United
States with what he knew from home, he praised the greater
focus of the American way:

> Insofar as theoretical discussions take place here at
> all, they have one great advantage: there is a certain
> stock of generally recognized doctrine, which corre-
> sponds essentially to that of the Marshallian School
> and which is unquestionably accepted, to the point
> that, when a problem is discussed, the discussion con-
> cerns only this problem and not the entire "founda-
> tions" of economics.[29]

By the time Hayek returned to Vienna in May, 1924, the
seminar had an eminently interdisciplinary character. Fewer
than a third of the members—Strigl, Haberler, Hayek,
Machlup, Morgenstern, Lieser, and Braun—were trained economists, thus the discussions must have been much more "philosophical" than typical present-day debates. The meetings took
place on Friday nights on a fortnightly basis. The twenty-some
participants assembled in Mises's office at the *Kammer* around 7
p.m. One member gave a short introductory talk, which was followed by long discussions until 10:30, at which point the "official" part of the evening ended and the assembly moved to a
restaurant—usually an Italian restaurant called Ancora Verde—
where the "unofficial" debate continued. The most ardent
debaters, Mises usually among them, finally went on to the Café
Künstler and stayed until 2 or 3 a.m. Mises later insisted that in
this circle he was not a teacher and director, but only the first
among equals.

---

[28]Hayek, *Hayek on Hayek*, p. 66.
[29]Hayek to Mises, letter dated August 17, 1923; in Mises Archive 79: 15.

Privatseminar

Ständige Mitglieder: ~~des Privatseminars.~~

Dr.rer.pol. et Dr.jur. Hans Bayer, Assistent am Staatswissenschaft-
Institut der Universität Wien,XIX.,Silberg.15

Dr.jur.Ludwig Bettelheim, Ministerialrat im Bundesministerium für
Finanzen, XIX.,Weimarerstr.71

Dr.rer.pol.Martha Stefanie Braun-Herrmann,III., Arenbergring 19

Dr.jur.Friedrich v. Engel-Janosi, Inhaber der Firma M.Engel,Dampfsäge,
Fußbodenfabrik ,XIX.,Hofzeile 12

Dr.jur.Walter Fröhlich, Rechtsanwaltsanwärter,XIX.,Vegag.10

Privatdozent Dr.rer.pol.et Dr.jur.Gottfried v. Haberler,Bibliothekar
der Kammer für Handel,Gewerbe und Industrie Wien
XIX.,Döblinger Hauptstr.55

Dr.rer.pol.et Dr.jur.Friedrich A.v.Hayek,Leiter des Österreichischen
Institutes für Konjunkturforschung,III.,Leonhardg.3

Dr.phil.Marianne v.Herzfeld,Sekretär des Verbandes österreichischer
Banken und Bankiers,I.,Hohenstaufeng.7

Privatdozent Dr.jur.Felix Kaufmann, Direktor der Österreichischen
Naphta-Import-Ges.m.b.H., I.,Opernring 17

Dr.rer.pol.Helene Lieser,Sekretär des Verbandes österr.Banken und
Bankiers,I.,Hohenstaufeng.7

Dr.rer.Fritz Machlup-Wolf, pol. Gesellschafter der Firma Ybbstaler
Pappenfabriken Adolf Leitner & Bruder,VI.,
Capistrang.4

Dr.rer.pol.Ilse Mintz-Schüller,Assistent am Österreichischen Institut
für Konjunkturforschung,IX.,Hörlg.6

Privatdozent Dr.jur.OskarMorgenstern, VII.,Zollerg.7

Dr.rer.pol.Johanna Paschka, VII.,Zollerg.7

Dr.jur.Paul N.Rosenstein, Assistent am Staatswissenschaftlichen Institut der Universität Wien, I.,Minoritenplatz 3

Dr.jur.Karl Schlesinger, em.Direktor der Anglo-Austrian Bank Ltd.,
IX.,Alserbachstr.16

Dr.jur.Leo Schönfeld,
XVIII.,Türkenschanzplatz 1

Dr.jur.Alfred Schütz,Sekretär des Bankhauses Reitler & Co.,VI.,
Eßterhazyg.20

Dr.rer.pol.Elly Spiro, IX.,Wasag.12

a.o.Universitätsprof.Dr.jur.v.Strigl, Sekretär der Industriellen
Bezirks-Kommission, I.,Singerstr.26

Privatdozent Dr.rer.pol.Erich Voegelin,III.,Untere Viaduktg.35

Student roster for the Privatseminar in 1927

All who belonged to the circle came voluntarily, only imbued by the drive to gain more knowledge. They came as disciples, but in the course of the years they turned into friends. Later, some people of my own age joined the circle too. Scholars from abroad, who paid a visit to Vienna, were welcome guests and took part in the meetings.

The private seminar . . . was and always remained the circle of my—much younger—friends. Outsiders knew nothing of our meetings; they only saw the works published by individual members.

We formed no school, no community, and no sect. We supported one another more through dissent than through assent. We were agreed and united only in one thing: in striving to build up the sciences of human action. Each one went the way that his own law pointed out to him. We have never organized or undertaken anything else that would have resembled the abject "doing research" of the "scientists" of imperial and post-imperial Germany. We have never pondered the thought of publishing a journal or a collective volume. Each one has worked by himself, as it befits the thinker. But each single one of us has contributed to the circle and looked for no other compensation than the recognition—not the applause—of his friends.

There was greatness in this unpretentious exchange of ideas; we all found happiness and satisfaction in it.[30]

Wieser's Long Shadow

The seminars Mises held in Vienna in the 1920s, especially the private seminar that he held in his *Kammer* office, have become legendary due to the prominent role that some of its

---

[30]Mises, *Erinnerungen*, p. 64; my translation.

members played in the social sciences after World War II. The sessions were formative for these young men, even though Mises's personal impact was not as considerable as one might expect, especially in the case of Hayek, Haberler, Strigl, and Machlup, who worked with him, albeit with interruptions, for more than ten years.

For these men, Mises was more role model than teacher. In the discussions of the private seminar, he displayed his ability to dissect all kinds of problems in social analysis, just as he had learned from Böhm-Bawerk. Yet he did not raise a "school" of disciples advocating his doctrines. It is of course the hope of every scholar that others will find his approach interesting and important enough to continue the work where he has left off. But Mises made no efforts to stimulate discipleship, and in fact had no disciples during his Vienna years.

To no small extent this was due to the ideal of individualism. Steeped in the idealism of Schiller, Herder, W.v. Humboldt, and other classical German authors, Mises considered the free development of the individual to be the supreme goal of human achievement. It was more important than any particular creed in religion, politics, or aesthetics. He certainly did not lack firm convictions in politics and science, but in his interactions with students and other people these convictions took only second place to the reverence he paid to the ideal of individualism. After 1926, when he succeeded Wieser as the main contact of the Rockefeller Foundation in Vienna, Mises had the opportunity to provide or withhold material benefits, but he did not use this power to raise epigones. Noble as this attitude was, it gave a competitive edge to some of his rivals who did not have the same scruples.

But the most important factor responsible for the virtual absence of a school of Misesians in the 1920s was that Mises's professional standing was not paramount. When Hayek, Haberler, Machlup, and Schütz first took part in one of his seminars, Mises was a respected expert on monetary economics and the author of a controversial book on contemporary political problems (*Socialism*). Although he was one of the best-known theorists in the German-speaking world, to his students he lacked the fame and brilliance of three other professors of the department of law and government science: Hans Kelsen, Carl Grünberg, and Othmar Spann.[31] Kelsen was the celebrated creator of the Austrian republican constitution and pioneer of the pure theory of law, Grünberg a chief Vienna intellectual of the social-democratic movement, and Spann the author of the most successful social-science textbook ever published in the German language.

In 1919, Spann had obtained Philippovich's position, which had been vacant for two years. Among the professors of economics, he attracted by far the greatest number of students. His theory of "universalism" was a sophisticated development of the older "organic" theories of society, which were widespread and deep-rooted in Catholic countries such as Austria. In the crisis-torn years after the war, universalism was not only more accessible for most people, it also accommodated a deep longing for security and authority. Whereas Wieser and Mises dealt with relatively narrow economic subjects and the technicalities of the Austrian School's marginal-value analysis, Spann confronted the students with a broad picture of social life. His lectures and seminars attracted students whose emotional life was steeped in Catholicism, romanticism, idealism, and nationalism. Spann's best-known student was the later Austrian Chancellor Engelbert Dollfuss, but he also impressed young scholars of the Austrian School such as Hayek and Morgenstern.

He had far less success with his colleagues at the University of Vienna. Initially, he was invited to the sessions of the Nationalökonomische Gesellschaft, but it soon became obvious that a productive debate with members of the Austrian School

---

[31]Eric Voegelin, *Autobiographical Reflections*, vol. 34 of the *Collected Works of Eric Voegelin* (Baton Rouge: Louisiana State University Press, 1989), pp. 2f.

(Wieser, Mises, Mayer, Weiss, and Strigl) was impossible. This was not primarily a question of different political orientations.[32] The problem was that Spann's intuitive approach was diametrically opposed to the analytical approach of the other members. He believed the task of social theory was to grasp the meaning of totalities, whereas the others thought that such undertakings were unscientific. Mises later made it clear that this rejection of Spann's approach had nothing to do with a dogmatic insistence on the virtues of methodological individualism. The point was, rather, that it was the very nature of science to deal with parts rather than wholes. The economic theorist had to identify the relevant parts of social reality and study their interrelations.[33]

The students who did not share Spann's aesthetic, epistemological, and political orientations—a minority—found a ready alternative in the courses of Friedrich von Wieser. In the years after World War I and up to his death in 1926, he was the unquestioned authority in general economic theory in Vienna. With the winter semester of 1922, Wieser's devout disciple Hans Mayer succeeded his master, while Wieser himself continued to lecture as honorary professor on the sociology of power.[34] Because of Mayer's presence and a successful second edition of Wieser's textbook, *Theorie der gesellschaftlichen*

---

[32]Spann's anti-Semitism was notorious. His full professorship in 1919 signaled a somewhat broader anti-Semitic movement that began infecting university life in the early years of the Republic, turning the University of Vienna into a battlefield for Mises and other liberal Jews. Kelsen proved to be one of the last Jews to obtain a full professorship, which he attained in 1918. See ibid., p. 6.

[33]See the discussion of this question in Ludwig von Mises, *Epistemological Problems of Economics* (Auburn, Ala.: Ludwig von Mises Institute, [1933] 2003), pp. 42–50.

[34]F.A. Hayek, "Friedrich Freiherr von Wieser," *Jahrbuch für Nationalökonomie und Statistik* 125 (3rd series vol. 70 [1926]): 526.

Wirtschaft (Social Economics) in 1924,[35] the Wieserian paradigm remained dominant in Vienna long after Wieser's death.

The fact that Hans Mayer—a second-rate scholar by any standard—obtained Wieser's chair speaks volumes about the influence of his predecessor. Mises must have hoped to obtain the position himself. After all, he had already published three books, two of which were brilliant treatises, whereas Mayer had not a single book to his credit and very few papers. But Mayer had been cunning, positioning himself as the primary Wieserian disciple.[36]

It was disheartening that a man like Mayer obtained Wieser's chair. It was not quite as disgraceful as it might seem in retrospect that Mises did not. A more likely candidate was Joseph Schumpeter, who enjoyed great prestige, especially among younger students. He had become a celebrity in the German

---

[35]The book appeared again in the prestigious series *Grundriss der Sozialökonomik* (Outline of Social Economics). The series was published in twelve volumes from 1914 to 1930. Especially the first volumes, some of which have appeared in two editions (prewar and postwar) and which deal with the history of economic science and with general economic theory, still have lasting value. Especially noteworthy is the first volume, *Wirtschaft und Wirtschaftswissenschaft* (1914, 1924) which contains the following essays: Karl Bücher, "Volkswirtschaftliche Entwicklungsstufen;" Joseph Schumpeter, "Epochen der Dogmen und Methodengeschichte;" Eugen von Philippovich, "Entwicklungsgang der wirtschafts- und sozialpolitischen Systeme und Ideale. I. Die Entwicklung bis zum Kriege;" Eduard Heimann, "Entwicklungsgang der wirtschafts- und sozialpolitischen Systeme und Ideale. I. Die jüngste Entwicklung." Equally remarkable is volume three, which contains Friedrich von Wieser's *Theorie der gesellschaftlichen Wirtschaft* (1914, 1924) and volume four, which features Max Weber's famous *Wirtschaft und Gesellschaft* (1922).

[36]Werner Neudeck points out that Mayer was simply higher up in a pecking order that gave much weight to seniority. Mayer had already been a paid professor (*Ordinarius*) in Prague and Graz, whereas Mises had only an unpaid position (*Extraordinarius*) in Vienna. See Werner Neudeck, "Der Einfluss von Ludwig von Mises auf die Österreichische akademische Tradition gestern und heute," *Wirtschaftspolitische Blätter* 28, no. 4 (1981): 26.

orbit through his *Wesen und Hauptinhalt der theoretischen Nation-alökonomie* (1908) and had found international fame with his *Theory of Economic Development* (1911). Both works were published before Mises's first book appeared. Two years younger than Mises, Schumpeter had become Austria's youngest economics professor in 1909 with the active support of Böhm-Bawerk and Wieser. After the war, he was considered the main representative of pure theory, second only to Wieser.

Schumpeter now held a position at the University of Bonn. He was the only major theoretician from Austria ever to obtain a chair at a university of the German Reich. His time in Bonn turned out to be very successful. Under his leadership, the department of economics became a major center of economic theory, with great emphasis on mathematical economics, and one of his students, Erich Schneider, became the leading German neoclassical economist after World War II.

But even Schumpeter was not in the eyes of the profession the number one theorist in interwar Germany. That rank belonged to Gustav Cassel (1866–1945) from Sweden, a mathematician-turned-economist. His core mission was to promote Walrasian mathematical economics. His *Theoretische Sozialökonomik* (Social Economics) quickly became the most widely used interwar textbook on economic theory, and its success became international through translations into virtually all languages of the civilized world.[37] Cassel was famous for his rejection of value theory and utility theory as a foundation of price theory.

Wieser, Schumpeter, and Cassel were "verbal Walrasians."[38] Their books championed the ideas of Walrasian economics,

---

[37]"The simplicity of argument and great accessibility of Cassel's book ensured its success. It was translated into many languages and was probably the most widely-read textbook on economics in the interwar period." Mark Blaug, *Great Economists before Keynes: An Introduction to the Lives and Works of One Hundred Great Economists of the Past* (Cambridge: Cambridge University Press, 1986), p. 42.

[38]Schumpeter and Cassel are self-declared Walrasians. On Wieser's Walrasianism, see Mises, *Erinnerungen*, p. 21; George Stigler, *Production*

without going into mathematical detail. Single-handedly, they not only kept the Walrasian paradigm alive at a critical juncture of its history, but also managed—in what amounted to a revolution—to make it the dominant approach in economic theory within the Reich. Within only a decade, they turned a large number of the younger German economists away from the Historical School and converted them to the Lausanne School of mathematical economics; and through translations of their major books, this influence radiated far beyond the German-speaking world.

The Austrian tradition of Menger had been kept alive through the scattered disciples of Böhm-Bawerk (most notably through Mises) but these followers lacked the paid university positions that would have enabled them to dedicate themselves full time to the development of the Austrian paradigm and to produce students and future professors. At the crucial time when the collapse of the German Reich brought widespread disillusionment with the tenets of the Historical School, Wieser's towering status as the only surviving founder of modern German economic theory provided the verbal Walrasians with a position of supreme authority. Their works introduced an entire generation to mathematical economics, and their style of exposition deluded these uninitiated readers into assuming that there were no significant differences between their works and those of the Mengerian theorists. The confusion was compounded by the fact that Wieser was an economist from Austria.

---

and Distribution Theories: The Formative Period (New York: Macmillan, 1949), p. 158; Hans-Hermann Hoppe and Joseph T. Salerno, "Friedrich von Wieser und die moderne Österreichische Schule der Nationalökonomie," Herbert Hax, ed., Friedrich von Wiesers "Über den Ursprung und die Hauptgesetze des wirthschaftlichen Werthes," in Vademecum zu einem Klassiker der österreichischen Schule (Düsseldorf: Handel und Finanzen, 1999); Bruce Caldwell, "Wieser, Hayek, and Equilibrium Theory," Journal des Economistes et des Etudes Humaines 12, no. 1 (2002); Joseph T. Salerno, "Friedrich von Wieser and F.A. Hayek: The General Equilibrium Tradition in Austrian Economics," Journal des Economistes et des Etudes Humaines 12, no. 2&3 (2002).

Even in the narrower fields of the theory of money, banking, and business cycles, and of the theory of socialism, Mises was not the very highest authority. The great authority in monetary theory was, again, Friedrich von Wieser, who had pioneered the Austrian theory of the value of money and would write the entry on money for the standard German-language dictionary, *Handwörterbuch der Staatswissenschaften*.[39] Wieser's endorsement of banking-school principles and of the assignment theory of money was reinforced through the writings of Schumpeter, the other surviving prewar authority on theoretical economics.[40]

Although Mises's views on money and business cycles found ever more advocates in the course of the 1920s, especially among the younger economists, he lacked the power and influence of the top academic economists.[41] Those who sought to make a career as professional economists were well advised to

---

[39]The *Handwörterbuch* also revealed the pecking order in business cycle theory. Here the lengthy entry came from the pen of Arthur Spiethoff, a Schmollerite to the core who opposed all monetary theories of the trade cycle. See Arthur Spiethoff, "Krisen," *Handwörterbuch der Staatswissenschaften*, 4th ed. (Jena: Gustav Fischer, 1925), vol. 6.

[40]Joseph A. Schumpeter, "Das Sozialprodukt und die Rechenpfennige," *Archiv für Sozialwissenschaften und Sozialpolitik* 44 (1917).

[41]In his contribution to the *festschrift* that celebrated Wieser's seventy-fifth birthday in 1926, Mises picked the subject of "the role of money in the realm of economic goods." Here he attacked the dominant Wieserian income theory of money, arguing that money in general and gold in particular was an economic good—not mere tokens for other "real" goods—and that marginal value theory could therefore be applied directly to money, rather than merely indirectly through the value of some underlying real goods. The piece was published only six years later. Friedrich von Wieser had died in 1926 and the editor of the *festschrift*, Hans Mayer, then chose to publish a comprehensive overview of contemporary economic science in four volumes. Mises's contribution appeared as "Die Stellung des Geldes im Kreise der wirtschaftlichen Güter," Hans Mayer, ed., *Die Wirtschaftstheorie der Gegenwart* (Vienna: Springer, 1932), vol. 2, pp. 309–18; translated as "The Role of Money in the Realm of Economic Goods," *Money, Method, and the Market Process: Essays by Ludwig von Mises*, Richard Ebeling, ed. (Boston: Kluwer, 1990).

immerse themselves in the thought of Wieser and Schumpeter. This was exactly what the younger economists did. The fourth generation of the Austrian School was introduced to Austrian economics primarily through the works of Wieser, and this formative experience shaped their own approach to economic analysis long after the master's death.

Today Hayek is often considered Mises's most famous student. In fact, however, his Wieserian intellectual heritage is striking. In 1922–1923, under the direction of Hans Kelsen and Othmar Spann, Hayek had written his doctoral dissertation (in economics) on the theory of imputation. The work was based on the Wieserian approach to problems of value and price theory, which was incompatible with Mises's socialist-calculation argument.[42] When he updated his thesis three years later for an article in *Conrad's Jahrbücher*, he knew the calculation thesis, but had not changed his mind on the question of imputation. This is what Hayek wrote on the topic, without mentioning Mises by name:

> Of course, in so far as one believes that a completely satisfactory solution to the problem [of imputation] has not yet been found, we cannot exclude the possibility from the very outset that the determinants of the prices of the factors of production are to be found in the exchange economy alone, and therefore that an imputation of value is not applicable, a view held by

---

[42]Hayek, *Hayek on Hayek*, p. 66. The Wieserian approach had found its way into Spann's thought, see Shigeki Tomo, "The Year 1922: A Watershed for Mises and Hayek" (Auburn, Ala.: Ludwig von Mises Institute working paper, September 2003). Similarly, the idea of imputation was familiar to legal theorists. Hans Kelsen had pioneered the pure theory of law, which imputed every single norm back to a fundamental norm. See in particular Hans Kelsen, *Hauptprobleme der Staatsrechtslehre* (Tübingen: Mohr, 1911). In the early 1920s, he had reiterated this thesis in works relating to the problem of sovereignty. See Kelsen, *Das Problem der Souveränität und die Theorie des Völkerrechts* (Tübingen: Mohr, 1920); idem, *Der soziologische und der juristische Staatsbegriff* (Tübingen: Mohr, 1922).

several younger authors. Nevertheless, if this view
were regarded as valid, the result would be that we
would have no satisfactory explanation of economic
processes based on the subjective theory of value, and
it would also follow that these authors too would lack
any basis for many of their investigations.[43]

Hayek went on to explain and develop Wieserian imputation
theory, which in his view was "still today the fundamental and
most detailed treatment of the problem."[44] He explicitly
rejected Mises's argument because it contradicted the Wieserian assumption that all social phenomena are explicable on the
basis of value theory alone. This fact is crucial to understanding
the later stages of the debate on economic calculation under
socialism. Although Hayek entered the debate ostensibly on

Hayek and Mises in 1961

Mises's side, there was a profound disagreement between the two
allies. Mises rejected socialism because factors of production
could only be appraised in a market economy. Hayek did not
endorse this argument because it contradicted the fundamental
framework of his economic thought.

---

[43]F.A. Hayek, "Bemerkungen zum Zurechnungsproblem," *Jahrbuch für
Nationalökonomie und Statistik* 124 (3rd series vol. 69 [1926]): 3; translated as
"Some Remarks on the Problem of Imputation," *Money, Capital, and Fluctu-
ations: Early Essays*, Roy McCloughry, ed. (Chicago: University of Chicago
Press, 1984), p. 35.

[44]Hayek, "Bemerkungen zum Zurechnungsproblem," p. 6; trans., p. 39.

His own opposition to socialism was not yet formulated, but the paper on imputation theory already indicated the future course of his argument. Hayek's main criticism of Böhm-Bawerk's imputation theory was that he treated the value of future consumers' goods as ultimate givens, where in fact they depended on present choices about the use of factors of production.[45] Only a general-equilibrium model could account for these multifarious interdependencies and solve the intricacies of the imputation problem. Hayek concluded his essay mentioning that the Walrasian School of mathematical economics had already successfully tackled problems of a similar nature. But he cautioned against practical problems of applying mathematical imputation theories. Although they could possibly "demonstrate by means of a simplified case that the subjective theory of value is in principle applicable," the complexity of the problem "may make it impossible in practice to apply imputation to any large economic system."[46] This is exactly the line of argument that Hayek later stressed in his critique of socialism.

As a Wieserian value theorist, Hayek could not endorse Mises's argument that a rational socialist economy was impossible because there was no such thing as value imputation. What then were the real reasons for the empirically far better performance of market economies? The solution that Hayek eventually presented in the late 1930s and the 1940s was based on an argument prominent with some economists of the eighteenth and nineteenth centuries. These writers had argued that prices contain information about market conditions (shortages, surpluses) and that they steer production in a market economy.[47]

---

[45]This argument would remain a staple of Hayekian thought. See for example Hayek, "Competition as a Discovery Procedure," *Quarterly Journal of Austrian Economics* 5, no. 3 ([1968] 2002).

[46]Hayek, "Bemerkungen zum Zurechnungsproblem," p. 18; trans., p. 53.

[47]Étienne Bonnot, Abbé de Condillac, *Commerce and Government: Considered in Their Mutual Relationship* (Cheltenham, U.K.: Edward Elgar, 1997), pp. 261f.:

Hayek embedded this argument within a general theory of knowledge, explaining the role of information in human action and economic theory, and argued that market prices have crucial importance in transmitting information between the market participants. Hence, the factual superiority of market economies over centrally planned economies resulted from their communicative superiority. Market prices were a better means for the transmission of information.[48]

The seeds of these later theories were sown in the early 1920s. Hayek's liberalism came from Mises, but the analytical framework of his economic thought was nurtured through the books and classes of Wieser. It was no accident that Hayek became the editor of a posthumous collection of Wieser's most important papers and that he published his first book with Hölder-Pichler-Tempsky, which had published all of Wieser's pioneering studies. All of his life, Hayek perceived himself quite consciously as a member of the Wieserian branch of the Austrian School. In 1978, a few years after Mises had died, Hayek regretted that this branch had been almost entirely displaced by what he called the Mises School:

> In today's world, Mises and his disciples are with some justice regarded as representatives of the Austrian School, albeit he represents only one of the branches into which Menger's teachings had split

---

When trade is perfectly free, the quantity and the need are apparent in all the markets. Then goods put themselves at their true price, and plenty spreads equally everywhere. . . . But when one has once taken all freedom from trade, it is no longer possible to judge, either if there is really an imbalance between the quantity and the need, or what it is.

See also Hermann Heinrich Gossen, *Entwickelung der Gesetze des menschlichen Verkehrs und der daraus fliessenden Regeln für menschliches Handeln* (Braunschweig: Vieweg & Sohn, 1854), pp. 90ff., 231; Adolph Thiers, *De la propriété* (Paris: Paulin, Lheureux & Cie, 1848).

[48]See F.A. Hayek, *Individualism and Economic Order* (Chicago: University of Chicago Press, 1948).

already among his disciples: the close personal friends
and relatives Eugen von Böhm-Bawerk and Friedrich
von Wieser. I admit this only with some hesitation,
because I expected much to come from Wieser's tradition, which his successor, Hans Mayer, tried to
develop. But these expectations have so far not been
fulfilled, even though [that tradition] may yet prove

to be more fruitful than it has been hitherto the case. The "Austrian School"
that today is active almost exclusively in
the United States is basically a Mises
School that goes back to Böhm-Bawerk's
approach. By contrast, the man on
whom Wieser put such great hopes and
who had taken over his chair, has never
made good on the promises.[49]

*Hayek receiving the
Nobel Prize in eco-
nomics in 1974 from
the King of Sweden*

But a year after Mises's death, Hayek
received the Nobel Prize, attracting new
interest to his work and giving the Wieserian
paradigm a second lease on life.

ๆ   ๆ   ๆ

The student on whom Mises apparently had the most profound impact in the early 1920s was Fritz Machlup-Wolf
(1902–1983). Of all later star members of the private seminar,

---

[49]Hayek, "Einleitung," pp. xivf. The Mayer line ended with his student
Wilhelm Weber, who became "the first important teacher of Keynesianism
in Austria." Werner Neudeck, "Der Einfluss von Ludwig von Mises auf die
Österreichische akademische Tradition gestern und heute," *Wirtschaftspolitische Blätter* 28, no. 4 (1981): 32. Neudeck asserts that Mises was the last economist who managed to establish an internationally recognized school in Austria (see ibid., p. 31).

he alone had received his doctorate under Mises's direction.[50] Machlup came from a family of entrepreneurs. His father was a cardboard manufacturer and young Fritz helped him in the management of the firm while he studied economics at the University of Vienna. In 1923, he was involved in setting up a factory for the family business in Hungary even while he was working on a doctoral dissertation under Mises. At the end of the year, the factory was running and Machlup had his doctorate. He was admitted to the private seminar and his relationship with Mises became less formal. Like his mentor, Machlup was an enthusiastic skier and fencer, and they probably spent many hours together in the gym and in the mountains.

Their common Jewish heritage was certainly an important factor in their unusually cordial rapport—in the 1930s, Mises wrote to Machlup in the tone of true friendship, while in his correspondence with other intellectual associates (Hayek for example) there always remained a hint of formality. Being Jewish was also the most important factor hampering both academic careers. Starting around 1922, German-Nationalist and Catholic groups led a campaign to reduce the Jewish presence at the universities.[51] Mises had been appointed adjunct professor under the *Ancien Régime*. In the new Republic he made no further advances. Neither did his disciple. Machlup received his doctorate and that was it.

This situation must have created a mutual sympathy between the two men. Bad as it was, it could not prevent the dynamic

---

[50]"Strictly speaking, only Fritz Machlup was originally a disciple of Mises" (Hayek, "Einleitung," p. xii). On Machlup see Jacob Dreyer, *Breadth and Depth in Economics: Fritz Machlup—The Man and His Ideas* (Lexington, Mass.: Lexington Books, 1978).

[51]Gerhard Jagschitz, *Die Jugend des Bundeskanzlers Dr. Engelbert Dollfuss* (University of Vienna: Doctoral dissertation, 1967), pp. 144f. and passim. The main organizational vehicle in the campaign was the Katholisch-Deutscher Akademikerausschuss.

Machlup from a successful career outside the university system. A few years later, he became a member of the Austrian cardboard cartel and was also appointed secretary of the *Verein österreichis- cher Volkswirte* (Association of Austrian Political Economists). Machlup was a man of great ambition and talents. The drive of the successful entrepreneur never left him even in later years, when he moved to the United States and focused entirely on scholarly pursuits. A poem that Kenneth Boulding composed many years later in his honor testified to the fact:

> *O, happy is the man who sits*
> *Beside or at the feet of Fritz,*
> *Whose thoughts, as charming as profound,*
> *Travel beyond the speeds of sound,*
> *All passing as he speeds them up,*
> *Mach 1, Mach 2, Mach 3, Machlup.*
> *With what astonishment one sees*
> *A supersonic Viennese*
> *Whose wit and vigor, it appears,*
> *Are undiminished by the years.*[52]

Machlup wrote his doctoral dissertation on the gold bullion standard. He published the work as a book in 1925, for the appendix of which he also translated Ricardo's *Proposals for an Economical and Secure Currency* (1816) into German. Six years later, he published a study on the role of bank credit and the stock market in the business cycle.[53] Both books demonstrated that their author had very well assimilated the Misesian approach to monetary analysis, and both of them were brilliant

---

[52]Kenneth Boulding quoted in Gottfried von Haberler, "Fritz Machlup: In Memoriam," *Cato Journal* 3, no. 1 (1983): 14.

[53]Fritz Machlup, *Der Golddevisenstandard* (Halberstadt, 1925); idem, *Börsenkredit, Industriekredit und Kapitalbildung* (Vienna: Springer, 1931).

contributions extending the work of his teacher. Mises praised the second book with words he had never used to describe the work of any other disciple: "a masterpiece."[54]

But it was shortly after its publication that the friendship between the two men became strained. Machlup emigrated to the United States and adjusted (perhaps too readily) to his new intellectual environment. The low point was reached in the 1960s when Machlup started agitating against the gold standard. For several years, his old teacher refused to speak to him. The efforts of Mrs. Mises eventually produced a rapprochement, but the old friendship was gone.

The LSE Connection

The problem of war reparations was the number one issue on the international agenda for the first few years after the war, and remained very prominent until the early 1930s. Initially, the same French and British politicians who had led their countries during the war dominated the negotiations. Steeped in wartime rhetoric, their emotional election campaigns had committed them to hard-line policies against the vanquished. Under such circumstances little progress could be made in regard to Austrian finance and the reparations question. As a result, the second Austrian government under Karl Renner lost the election in June 1920 and a new government under Michael Mayr took over, without significantly greater success in foreign policy.

---

[54]"Dr. Machlup-Wolf is an excellent economist. . . . The second book (*Börsenkredit, Industriekredit und Kapitalbildung*) is really a master piece" (Mises to Kittredge, letter dated March 31, 1933; Mises Archive 67: 5. This was a letter of recommendation for the Rockefeller Foundation.) Mises concluded:

> There is no doubt that Machlup is in all respects the worthiest man for a Rockefeller fellowship. This is not merely my opinion who was his teacher for many years, but everybody's. Last year he lectured at the London School of Economics and Political Science and had a great success.

Things improved slowly after December 1920, when the leadership at the negotiations was shifted to economic experts. But these men too were unable to reach a workable compromise because of public pressure in England and especially in France. No lasting results were achieved at conferences in Brussels, Paris, London, Cannes, Genoa, Paris again, and London again.

It is likely that Mises took part in at least some of these conferences. He was after all an executive of the Bureau for Claims Settlements and his position with the *Kammer* made him an unofficial spokesman for Austrian business and banking. He was an eloquent expert on financial and monetary matters, and his sober voice carried weight with the money men abroad.[55] It was probably here that Mises first met some of the eminent economists from western Europe with whom he would cooperate closely in the following years: Charles Rist from Paris and Theodore Gregory, William Beveridge (later Lord Beveridge), and others from the London School of Economics (LSE).[56] The

---

[55]In those years, Mises was asked to co-author two entries for the new 12th edition of the *Encyclopaedia Britannica* (this edition was in fact a two-volume supplement to the 11th edition). See Mises's contributions in "Austrian Empire," *Encyclopaedia Britannica*, 12th ed. (1921), vol. 30, pp. 323–24; "Republic of Austria," ibid., pp. 348–49.

[56]In November 1922, Mises said he had "talked to an English professor" about a translation of his book *Die Gemeinwirtschaft* into English (see Mises to Zimmermann, letter dated November 22, 1922; Mises Archive 75: 20). This was probably Gregory, who was the only Englishman among the recipients of a complimentary copy (see the list in Mises Archive 75: 8). Documented contacts to William Beveridge date back to the summer of 1924, when Mises had him (and Gregory) sent complimentary copies of the second edition of his *Theorie des Geldes und der Umlaufsmittel* (see correspondence between Mises and his publisher Duncker & Humblot, dated June 24, 1924 in Mises Archive 78: 28, 35). In early November 1924, Mises traveled to London and talked with Robbins about the translation of *Gemeinwirtschaft* (75: 11). He then had him sent a complimentary copy of *Gemeinwirtschaft*, probably as a Christmas gift (see 57: 51). By this time, his command of English was fairly good, as evidenced by his comments on the translation that Robbins (and later also Schwartz) made of parts of *Gemeinwirtschaft* (83: 23ff.,

LSE connection developed slowly and steadily during the 1920s, especially through Mises's impact on the young Lionel Robbins (1898–1984).[57]

Like most young intellectuals of his era, Robbins was a socialist. Nurtured by school readings of Shaw, Wells, and Ruskin, he had become a member of the National Guilds League after World War I and collaborated in the "Labour Campaign for the Nationalisation of the Drink Trade." But these experiences with the real-world labor movement disillusioned the young idealist. He began to read the classical liberal economists and from 1920 to 1923 studied economics at LSE, a creation of the leaders of the guild movement, Sidney and Beatrice Webb.

Because Sidney Webb cherished academic freedom—unlike his wife or their friend, George Bernard Shaw[58]—LSE was spared the fate of becoming the academic mouthpiece of the Fabians. During the 1920s, the school counted a number of excellent economists in its ranks, most notably Edwin Cannan, but also Theodore Gregory and later Robbins himself.

Gregory had Robbins and his other students read the great contemporary economists in America and on the Continent, many of whom he knew personally. Robbins was therefore familiar with the works of Gustav Cassel, Irving Fisher, and Frank A. Fetter. Later he turned to the Austrians, and he probably read *Socialism* in the original German soon after its publication in 1922. He later recalled that the book had a decisive impact on

---

4ff.). Still in his meetings with Gregory and Robbins, Mises probably spoke German. Gregory was an excellent speaker of the language, and Robbins could follow a conversation in German even though he was not himself fluent in it.

[57]On Lionel Robbins see in particular his *Autobiography of an Economist* (London: Macmillan, 1971); D.P. O'Brien, *Lionel Robbins* (London: Macmillan, 1988).

[58]Robbins, *Autobiography of an Economist*, pp. 73–74.

him and solidified his departure from his former socialist ideals.[59]

Two other teachers at LSE, Hugh Dalton and Graham Wallas, reinforced in Robbins the resonance of the utilitarian perspective on political questions that emanated from Mises's work. Wallas in particular was a great teacher and authority on the writings of Jeremy Bentham and the Philosophical Radicals. He constantly emphasized rationalism as the correct approach in politics, especially when it came to choosing political *means*.

And like his young peers in Vienna, Robbins deepened his classroom knowledge through daily discussions with a group of highly gifted friends such as Jacques Kahane, Arnold Plant, and Georg Tugendhat.[60] These men would form the core of British Austrianism in the following years.

Mises probably met Robbins for the first time in the fall of 1924. In October of that year, he wrote to Gustav Fischer that he had received a "very serious offer" for an English translation of the second part of *Gemeinwirtschaft* from a "Mr. Robins," a tutor of economics in Oxford. "Robins" turned out to be Robbins, and he came highly recommended.[61] He had just accepted a temporary position at Oxford University (until 1929, he would alternate between positions at Oxford and LSE). During the next few years, he worked on a translation of *Gemeinwirtschaft* (*Socialism*) and later initiated a translation of Mises's *Theorie des Geldes und der Umlaufsmittel* (*Theory of Money and Credit*). These projects slowed significantly after 1926, when Robbins was charged with various administrative duties at LSE,

---

[59]Ibid., p. 106. In those days, LSE students had to prove their ability to translate from two foreign languages after their first year of study.

[60]Tugendhat was probably the same person who took part in Mises's first private seminar in the winter semester of 1919–1920. In this case there was a strong early personal connection between the circles in London and Vienna.

[61]Mises to Fischer, letter dated October 7, 1924; Mises Archive 75: 49.

to the point that he brought in a co-translator. But his interest in Austrian economics, and especially in the work of Mises, grew constantly. At the beginning of the 1930s, the contacts between Vienna and London had matured to such an extent that Mises and his students were frequent guest lecturers at LSE. The blossoming of Austrian economics in Britain culminated when F.A. Hayek eventually became professor of economics at the London School of Economics in the fall of 1931.

Advent of the Gold-Exchange Standard

It did not take quite as long to find a solution to Austria's postwar financial calamities. The first real breakthrough came at a conference that took place in the fall of 1922 in Genoa and led to the signing of a convention in Geneva on October 4, 1922. The so-called Geneva Protocol was the last in a series of negotiations that had begun at the end of 1921, when Austria was promised loans from the British, French, Czechs, and Italians. The condition was that the Austrian government had to grant institutionalized supervision inside of Austria, and to pledge some of its income and assets to the foreign creditors.

These conditions were at first unacceptable to the Austrian Chancellor, Johann Schober, but time was running out. The only alternative to foreign loans was increased taxation and inflation, and these options were even less acceptable. The social democrats virulently opposed any more taxation of the general population. They were still advocating a special tax on wealth—always a popular proposal, but incapable of balancing the budget. And more inflation would certainly bring monetary breakdown and ensuing civil chaos.

A turning point was reached when, at the end of May 1922, Monsignor Ignatz Seipel assumed the chancellorship with the firm resolution to lead Austria out of the financial nightmare. He already had some experience in handling catastrophic situations in Austrian politics, having been a member of the last imperial government under Heinrich Lammasch in 1918. A

Catholic priest, Seipel was not a man to despair over the unpop-
ularity of the decisions that needed to be made. Living in a
Vienna monastery, he was not as exposed as were his other party
comrades to the many temptations of personal friendship and
the spotlight of fame.[62] He knew that reliance on international
loans under the conditions spelled out by western creditors was
a dangerous strategy because it would lead his country into
dependence on foreign powers.[63] But there was no alternative if
the goal was to rid the country of the poison of inflation. Mises
and his friend Wilhelm Rosenberg convinced Seipel of the
necessity of this reform.[64] With candid foresight, they stressed
that the reform was bound to produce a crisis; there would be
massive unemployment and other interests would be hurt as
well. This crisis would merely bring to light the damage already
done by the previous inflation, but public opinion would blame
the reformer. Seipel appreciated the frankness of his advisors;
Mises later recalled: "he adopted fully my ideas about sound
money and I cooperated with him."[65] In the same month, Mises

---

[62]Himself a monarchist, his great achievement was to reconcile Austrian
Catholicism with the republic and thus to spare Austria the fate of other countries, such as France, Italy, and Spain, where after the establishment of the
republic the political Right split into conservative monarchists and republican
democrats. See Heinrich Dimmel, "Ignaz Seipel," *Tausend Jahre Österreich*,
Walter Pollack, ed. (Vienna: Verlag Jugend und Volk, 1974), vol. 3, pp. 299ff.

[63]For an *ex-post* analysis of this dependence, see the statements of
Spitzmüller and others in *Verhandlungen des Vereins für Sozialpolitik in Zürich
1928. Schriften des Vereins für Sozialpolitik* 175 (1929).

[64]For details see Franz Baltzarek, "Ludwig von Mises und die österreichische Wirtschaftspolitik der Zwischenkriegszeit," *Wirtschaftspolitische Blätter* 28, no. 4 (1981): 132; Mises, *Erinnerungen*, pp. 50–54.

[65]Mises to Mellish, letter dated January 25, 1962; Grove City Archive:
"M" files. See also Mises, Erinnerungen, p. 51. Seipel's economic and political views were of course shaped to a large extent by prevailing Catholic moral
views on social organization, in particular by Pope Leo XIII's encyclical *Rerum
novarum* (1891). He was also known as a sharp critic of racial anti-Semitism;

was appointed the president of the Bureau for Claims Settlements.[66]

⋞ ⋞ ⋞

In one of his first actions after his initial orientation, Seipel dealt a heavy blow to Austria's inflation party, which had its stronghold in the Austro-Hungarian Bank. Following the stipulations of Article 206 of the Treaty of Saint-Germain, he abolished the old central bank and established a new one—under the leadership of Richard Reisch, a former student of Carl Menger's and a civil servant under Böhm-Bawerk in the Ministry of Finance. At the time of his appointment to the presidency of the new central bank, he had just been appointed a vice president under Mises at the Bureau for Claims Settlements.

Seipel's reforms hurt those groups whose incomes had been paid out of the inflation, in particular the nationalized industries and socialist municipal governments that had started creating expensive welfare programs immediately after the war—programs that could only be paid for through the printing press of the Austro-Hungarian Bank. Hurting these interests entailed only moderate political costs for the government, and might have even been a welcome side effect of Seipel's reform in that it promised to hurt groups that were part of the socialist opposition. It turned out, however, that the very success of the reform extended the survival of these groups. The stable monetary framework attracted a great volume of foreign credit to Austria, which was then used to finance local welfare schemes.

---

in his eyes the Austrian Jews were a national minority and should enjoy all minority rights. See his article "Minoritätenschutz und Judenfrage nach dem christlichsozialen Programm," *Volkswohl* 10, no. 2 (February 1919).

[66]The former director, Mises's friend Emil Perels, moved on to another position. He was appointed director of the *Kreditinstitut für öffentliche Arbeiten* (Credit Institute for Public Works).

The reform did visibly curtail Austrian sovereignty in financial and economic matters. Seipel's government accepted the establishment of the office of a Commissar General, who henceforth controlled Austria's public finance. This action effectively surrendered control over Seipel's budget to the Entente-controlled League of Nations. Dr. Alfred Zimmermann, a former mayor of Rotterdam, was appointed Commissar General and stayed for three years in Vienna.[67] With Austria colonized, its government a subject to foreign powers—the socialists did not hesitate to accuse Seipel of giving up the country's sovereignty. The German nationalists in Seipel's coalition saw things the same way.

Mises had been one of the driving forces behind the reform. He thought Austria could have done without the 650 million kronen of credit, but not without the commissar. Austrian politicians needed a fall guy to take responsibility for unpopular policies. He did not exactly have a high opinion of Zimmermann himself, but had great respect for chief executive Hans Patzauer, a civil servant from the Ministry of Finance. Mises was widely perceived as enjoying very good ties to Patzauer. This working relation turned him into a power broker. For example, the leadership of the University of Vienna sought his "advice" (lobbying with Patzauer) whenever it planned an increase of its budget.[68]

◌ ◌ ◌

The Genoa conference had not only provided a solution for Austrian financial calamities, but it also paved the way for the so-called gold exchange standard.[69]

---

[67]Eckert, "Friedensverträge. II. Vom staatswissenschaftlichen Standpunkte," pp. 512ff.

[68]Mises, *Erinnerungen*, pp. 54, 62.

[69]R.G. Hawtrey, *Monetary Reconstruction*, 2nd ed. (London: Longmans, Green & Co., 1926), chap. 6.

In the 1870s, an international monetary system had emerged that covered the entire western world and its colonies: the classical gold standard. The money of this system was gold, but in most cases the currency—that is, the means of payment that actually circulated in the countries taking part in this system—were the fractional-reserve notes of the various national central banks. In a many countries, most notably in Russia, Austria-Hungary, and India, the national currency was backed up not only by physical gold in the vaults of the central bank, but also by other gold-denominated currencies. This practice of holding both gold and gold-denominated foreign banknotes became known as the "gold exchange standard" when it became standard procedure in the interwar period.[70]

During the war, most countries had abandoned the classical gold standard to finance war expenditure through inflation. After the war, many statesmen promoted the reestablishment of an international gold standard. But the accumulated war debts were so huge that redemption at prewar parities would have ruined most governments. On the other hand, these same governments did not wish to create the (correct) impression that they had cheated their creditors and could not fulfill their promises. The natural solution in this context was the adoption of the gold-exchange standard. The advantage of this system was that a central bank could minimize its (non-interest-bearing) gold holdings by trusting other central banks, which held the physical gold needed for redemption. The disadvantages were not as apparent before World War I. It made redemption more uncertain than it had been under the "classical" fractional-reserve gold standard. And because it made redemption dependent on a prior redemption in some other country, it gave

---

[70]Some Austrians then claimed the new international system had been invented by their finance minister, Steinbach, in 1897. In fact, however, the system was devised by David Ricardo in "Proposals for an Economical and Secure Currency," *Works and Correspondence*, Piero Sraffa, ed. (Cambridge: Cambridge University Press, 1951–1973), vol. 4.

political leverage to these foreign central banks. The *Banque de France* acquired a reputation for its ruthlessness in using this leverage.

The first steps toward the creation of the international gold-exchange standard were made at the Genoa conference in the fall of 1922. Here the representatives of the major central banks agreed to cooperate more closely. The idea was to help out central banks that were unable to redeem their notes, as well as, more generally, to "coordinate" central-bank policies. A few years later, Mises stated in plain language what coordination meant: the coordinated central banks would increase their note issues in concert, thus avoiding the embarrassment of the falling exchange rates that inevitably result from unilateral inflation.[71]

Coordination of national inflation policies in order to suppress one of the main symptoms of monetary decay has remained the state of the art to this day. For debtors in a very inflationary currency area, cooperation between the central banks is a boon. Without foreign assistance, the exchange rate of their currency would constantly fall and thus it would be next to impossible to obtain foreign credit. Central bank cooperation solves this problem, at the expense of creditors or would-be debtors in the more stable countries. In the 1920s, this mechanism worked to the advantage of the most ruthless debtors: the socialist municipal and provincial governments in Austria and Germany.

Mises took part in expert meetings at the Finance Ministry, discussing the implications of the Geneva Protocol for Austria.[72] The western loans had given Seipel's government some flexibility in the short run, and the inflation was under control (starting in September 1922, the exchange rate stabilized around 70,000 kronen per dollar) but in the longer run, economic stability and

---

[71]Mises, *Geldwertstabilisierung und Konjunkturpolitik* (Jena: Gustav Fischer, 1928).

[72]Mises Archive 74: 25.

Austrian political independence could only be gained if the budget was balanced without inflation. Large increases of government income were not to be expected because the economy was still in a slump, and a quick recovery was out of the question given the prohibitive trade barriers erected by neighboring countries. The only way out was to cut government spending.

The largest expenses were the heavy food-price subsidies and the payments for the huge deficits of the railroads and the post office.[73] But these were sacred cows of the socialists, and Seipel did not dare touch them for fear of a violent reaction from the opposition, especially because unemployment would rise quickly.[74] He therefore put all his hopes into reducing government expenditure by dismissing 50,000 civil servants.

Eventually the tension in the Austrian budget was reduced through this process. The stabilization of the krone and the virtual dependence of Austrian finance on foreign supervision had reinforced the creditworthiness of Austrian debtors, and especially of Austrian local governments. This tendency was reinforced by those agreements of the Genoa conference that paved the way for the gold exchange standard. And it was further reinforced by the onset of the great U.S. inflation of 1920, which

---

[73]The government had a tobacco monopoly and one for salt, but the receipts were meager. See Mises's statement in Mises Archive 57: 16.

[74]From the end of August till the end of December 1922, the number of unemployed receiving government assistance in the city of Vienna alone rose from 24,000 to 58,000. On February 24, 1923, there were 112,000 unemployed in Vienna and the surrounding districts, of whom 98,000 received government assistance. See Mises's undated letter to an unknown recipient in Mises Archive 57: 16. This document summarizes Mises's view on economic conditions in Austria in early 1923. Mises wrote it in reply to an unknown Anglo-Saxon friend, who had visited Vienna some time earlier. Throughout 1923, unemployment was at 110,000. It would further increase over the following years, reaching some 200,000 by 1929. See Redaktionskomitee der Wirtschaftskommission, *Bericht über die Ursachen der wirtschaftlichen Schwierigkeiten Österreichs* (Vienna: Österreichische Staatsdruckerei, 1930), p. 25.

came into full swing by early 1923 (the United States had overcome a minor postwar depression in 1920–1921). Austrian institutions now benefited from a near limitless inflow of new loans.[75]

This gave a further boost to the ambitious spending plans of
the Austrian socialists, particularly in "Red Vienna." American
funds financed one of the great experiments of communal socialism. Within a decade, Vienna was turned into a miniature nanny
state designed to provide for the needs of the working class from
cradle to grave. One mayor of Vienna boasted in Mises's presence: "The Viennese is born into Social Democracy, he lives in
it and dies as he has lived." To the great dismay of the socialist
bystanders, Mises replied with a Vienna proverb: "Some say that
even the owners of four-story houses are mortal."[76]

The new U.S. loans also supported the violent class struggle
of the Vienna trade unions, which relied on the social infrastructure paid for out of the new public funds. A document from
the time describes the situation from the perspective of Austrian
firms:

> As a consequence of the terror of the Free Trade
> Unions (that is, of the social-democratic trade
> unions), the situation in the factories had become
> unsupportable. The Free Trade Unions forced the
> non-social-democratic workers under threats to join
> their organizations and to contribute to their various
> funds. Threatening strikes, they forced the entrepre-
> neurs to recognize their organizations as the only
> representatives of the interests of the worker classes.
> They prevented the employment of workers with

---

[75]Murray N. Rothbard, *America's Great Depression*, 5th ed. (Auburn, Ala.:
Ludwig von Mises Institute, 2000); Benjamin Anderson, *Economics and the
Public Welfare* (Indianapolis: Liberty Press, 1979), esp. chap. 18. See also the
figures in Milton Friedman and Anna J. Schwartz, *Monetary History of the
United States* (Princeton, N.J.: Princeton University Press, 1963), pp. 710ff.

[76]Mises, *Erinnerungen*, p. 58; *Notes and Recollections* (Spring Mills, Penn.:
Libertarian Press, 1978), p. 90.

other political orientations and even demanded that these persons be fired; thus thousands of workers were condemned to unemployment.[77]

The Christian Socialists sought to introduce legislation outlawing the terror of the trade unions, but the social democratic parliamentarians vetoed all such measures.

The credit-fuelled increase of government power also had a profound impact on the traditional Austrian conflict between industrial and agrarian interests. Austria's conservative landed establishment came under pressure from two sides. While the imports of agrarian products from Hungary and other neighboring countries reduced the price of their products, the Austrian industries had an ever-higher demand for workers and attracted former peasants through higher wages. To counter these trends, the landed interests sought to have the government protect them through tariffs and monopolies, and they sought—unsuccessfully of course—to strike a backroom deal with big industrialists, pointing out that a stable agrarian sector was the backbone of the conservative order. The more peasants were drawn into industrial occupations, the more they would come under the spell of Marxist organizations and Marxist culture. It was therefore in the interest of Austria's industrialists, according to the landowners, not to compete for the agrarian workforce.[78]

A very similar, though less dramatic development took place in other European countries. The general scheme was always the same: wartime inflation had been perpetuated after the end of the hostilities to finance the growth of the welfare state and to cover the deficits of nationalized industries. The governments of Germany and Russia had pursued this dangerous policy up to

---

[77]From the winter 1929–1930 report of the *Industrieller Klub*. See Mises Archive 66a: 53ff.

[78]Ibid.

the bitter end of hyperinflation and the collapse of the monetary system. The other governments were less reckless, but still
followed the same strategy, which they only abandoned once
foreign loans, especially from the United States, became available on a large scale in the framework of the emerging gold-
exchange standard. At that point they shifted from inflation to
debt. With the help of the United States, Europe's initial problem—the lack of discipline to curtail government deficits—
grew worse over the years, reproducing itself, as the Marxists
say, on a higher scale.

Mises repeatedly denounced this practice in the midst of the
Roaring Twenties. In a lecture on the "Therapy of European
Public Finance," which he delivered on February 27, 1925 to
the Hungarian Cobden Association in Budapest, he pointed out
that halting the inflation was not enough.[79] It was only the
beginning, not the end, of monetary and financial reform. What
was needed was a radical reduction on the expenditure side of
the government's budget. "It was an error to start the reform of
public finance by firing officers. One should have begun by
reducing the superfluous government agendas, most of all by
reducing government businesses." And he stressed that it was
"in particular the large issues of bonds which enabled the governments and local administrations to realize their plans for
nationalization and communalization" of industry, culture, and
infrastructure.

---

[79]See Mises, "Die Sanierung der europäischen Staatsfinanzen," in Mises
Archive 40b; 57: 53. The Magyar Cobden-Szövetség (Hungarian Cobden
Association) was a group of free-market businessmen, economists, and journalists in Budapest. Before Mises, Sombart, Oppenheimer, Rist, and George
Paish had spoken at its meetings. They were all received in the most luxuri-
ous conditions (Hotel Ritz) and were probably very well paid as well. One of
Mises's main contacts in Budapest was a certain Felix Schwarz, who was no
academic. Schwarz visited regularly with Mises in Vienna and had contacts
with the *Pester Lloyd*, a Budapest journal that frequently ran reviews of Mises's
books (see Mises Archive 78: 34f., 45; 80: 50).

The seemingly unlimited availability of ever more foreign credit created the impression that the government had endless resources. The demands for government support and the confidence in government omnipotence waxed limitless. The Roaring Twenties set the stage for the roaring dictators of the thirties.

Hyperinflation, Currency Competition, and Monetary Reform

Meanwhile, the *Verein für Sozialpolitik* had put the problem of monetary stabilization on the agenda for its 1923 meeting. Mises had been invited to write one of the expert reports to serve as the basis for the discussions—an unexpected sign of attention.[80] He later recalled that his "monetary theories have been studied only when and where inflationist policies faced immediate collapse, such as in the German Reich."[81] The most fashionable book on money in the years before 1923 was written by Albert Hahn, a young economist in Frankfurt. Developing Schumpeter's theory of capital (in which capital was "abstract" purchasing power), Hahn stressed that fiduciary credit expansion had the beneficial effect of creating "forced savings" and thus higher growth rates than could be obtained

---

[80]Many years later he wrote:

> When my money book appeared in the year 1912, all German reviewers rejected it with very unfriendly words. It was only due to the monetary collapse, which destroyed much more than the monetary system that, when the currency catastrophe approached, even the Verein für Sozialpolitik had second thoughts and asked me—rather than Knapp or Bendixen—to write a report on the problems of monetary stabilization, and that the second edition of my book in 1924 had a much better reception. (Mises to Volkmar Muthesius, letter dated May 18, 1959; Grove City Archive: Hahn files)

[81]Mises to Adolf Grote, letter dated June 29, 1959; Grove City Archive: Grote file.

without inflation. In his book he anticipated virtually all the essential propositions of Keynes's *General Theory* (1936).[82] But in 1923, the German economists started having second thoughts about the blessings of inflation. They wished to listen again to the voice of dissent. At the end of February 1923 Mises submitted his manuscript, "Die geldtheoretische Seite des Stabilisierungsproblems" (The Problem of Stabilization Considered from the Point of View of Monetary Theory).[83]

This title is somewhat misleading. In fact the essay combines a sophisticated analysis of what today would be called the dynamics of currency competition with the first concise statement of Mises's ideas on how to prepare for the transition from an inflationary currency to the gold standard. The essay was one of Mises's most influential works in the sense that it had an immediate and noticeable impact on the economic policy of the German Reich.

Mises began by pointing out that continued inflation would necessarily end up in the collapse of the monetary system:

> In recent months, the German Reich has provided a rough picture of what must happen, once the people come to believe that the course of monetary depreciation is not going to be halted. If people are buying

---

[82]Albert Hahn, *Volkswirtschaftliche Theorie des Bankkredits* (Tübingen: Mohr, 1920). Hahn eventually changed his mind under the impact of the German hyperinflation and of criticism, most notably from Hayek and other members of the Austrian School (see the 1930 third edition of his book). Still later, he wrote a piece comparing his 1920 statements with the corresponding passages in John Maynard Keynes's *General Theory of Employment, Interest, and Money* (New York and London: Harcourt, Brace, 1936). See Albert Hahn, "Continental European Pre-Keynesianism," *The Economics of Illusion*, chap. 16; reprinted in Henry Hazlitt, ed., *The Critics of Keynesian Economics*, 2nd ed. (Irvington-on-Hudson, N.Y.: Foundation for Economic Education, 1995), pp. 287–303.

[83]Duncker & Humblot (the *Verein*'s publisher) to Mises, letter dated February 26, 1923; Mises Archive 78: 6.

unnecessary commodities, or at least commodities not needed at the moment, because they do not want to hold on to their paper notes, then the process which forces the notes out of use as a generally acceptable medium of exchange has already begun. This is the beginning of the "demonetization" of the notes. The panicky quality inherent in the operation must speed up the process. It may be possible to calm the excited masses once, twice, perhaps even three or four times. However, matters must finally come to an end. Then there is no going back. Once the depreciation makes such rapid strides that sellers are fearful of suffering heavy losses, even if they buy again with the greatest possible speed, there is no longer any chance of rescuing the currency. . . . That the German mark is still used as money today [January 1923] is due simply to the fact that the belief generally prevails that its progressive depreciation will soon stop, or perhaps even that its value per unit will once more improve. The moment that this opinion is recognized as untenable, the process of ousting paper notes from their position as money will begin. If the process can still be delayed somewhat, it can only denote another sudden shift of opinion as to the state of the mark's future value. The phenomena described as frenzied purchases have given us some advance warning as to how the process will begin. It may be that we shall see it run its full course.[84]

And indeed it did run its full course, at least as far as Germany was concerned. The process accelerated with exponential growth rates during 1923, culminating in the virtual collapse of the currency in October. In the fall of 1923, the Reichsbank operated some 1,700 printing presses twenty-four hours a day,

---

[84]Mises, "Die geldtheoretische Seite des Stabilisierungsproblems," *Schriften des Vereins für Sozialpolitik* 164, no. 2 (Munich: Duncker & Humblot, 1923); 4f., 8f.; translated as "Stabilization of the Monetary Unit—From the Viewpoint of Theory," pp. 6, 11.

and it used the entire production of thirty paper factories. Eventually the paper supply threatened to become a bottleneck.[85]

For some time, Mises had to fear that his essay would not be published in time to influence policy. In May, he wrote to the publisher, expressing his misgivings about the delay.[86] In his essay, Mises discussed two scenarios of the displacement of the inflationary currency. Either this process can occur in a panic such that the bad money is abandoned in a few days or even in a few hours. Or the currency substitution takes place relatively slowly, thus assuring a smoother transition. Mises had first-hand experience of the slower process. The description given in his essay fits observations he made during the high postwar inflation in Vienna:

> [The] practice of making and settling domestic transactions in foreign money or in gold, which has already reached substantial proportions in many branches of business, is being increasingly adopted. As a result, to the extent that individuals shift more and more of their cash holdings from German marks to foreign money, still more foreign exchange enters the country. As a result of the growing demand for foreign money, various kinds of foreign exchange,

---

[85]Anton Burghardt, *Soziologie des Geldes und der Inflation* (Vienna: Böhlaus, 1977), p. 65. On the German inflation see F.D. Graham, *Exchanges, Prices, and Production in Hyperinflation: Germany, 1920–23* (Princeton, N.J.: Princeton University Press, 1930); Costantino Bresciani-Turroni, *The Economics of Inflation: A Study of Currency Depreciation in Post-War Germany* (London: Allen and Unwin, 1937); Rudolph Stucken, *Deutsche Geld- und Kreditpolitik, 1914–1963*, 3rd ed. (Tübingen: Mohr, 1964), chaps. 3 and 4.

[86]Mises to Duncker & Humblot, letter dated May 25, 1923; Mises Archive 78: 14. The delay was caused by the other contributor to the volume, ex-minister Klein, who was unable to return his proof pages in the agreed time; see Duncker & Humblot's letter to Mises, dated May 18, 1923 in Mises Archive 78: 12. Publications of the *Verein für Socialpolitik* were usually meant to have an impact on current policy; see Franz Boese, *Geschichte des Vereins für Sozialpolitik, 1872–1932* (Berlin: Duncker & Humblot, 1939), pp. 164, 183f.

equivalent to a part of the value of the goods shipped abroad, are imported instead of commodities. Gradually, there is accumulated within the country a supply of foreign monies. This substantially softens the effects of the final breakdown of the domestic paper standard. Then, if foreign exchange is demanded even in small transactions, if, as a result, even wages must be paid in foreign exchange, at first in part and then in full, if finally even the government recognizes that it must do the same when levying taxes and paying its officials, the sums of foreign money needed for these purposes are, for the most part, already available within the country. The situation, which emerges from the collapse of the government's currency, does not necessitate barter, the cumbersome direct exchange of commodities against commodities. Foreign money from various sources then performs the service of money, even if somewhat unsatisfactorily.[87]

Mises contrasted this smooth transition with the panic scenario, which, as he said, was more likely in the context of the 1923 German inflation:

Things will necessarily be much worse if the breakdown of the paper money does not take place step-by-step, but comes, as now seems likely, all of a sudden in panic. The supplies within the country of gold and silver money and of foreign notes are insignificant. The practice, pursued so eagerly during the war, of concentrating domestic stocks of gold in the central banks and the restrictions, for many years placed on trade in foreign moneys, have operated so that the total supplies of hoarded good money have long been insufficient to permit a smooth development of monetary circulation during the early days and weeks after

[87]Mises, "Die geldtheoretische Seite des Stabilisierungsproblems," p. 10; translation p. 13.

> the collapse of the paper note standard. Some time
> must elapse before the amount of foreign money
> needed in domestic trade is obtained by the sale of
> stocks and commodities, by raising credit, and by
> withdrawing balances from abroad. In the meantime,
> people will have to make out with various kinds of
> emergency money tokens.[88]

In the early fall of 1923, several institutions sprang up spontaneously that would lead Germany on the path to replacing the mark. In October, the Hamburger Bank started issuing notes covered by foreign exchange and a similar bank was set up in Kiel. Meanwhile preparations were made in the Rhineland to establish a bank on a gold standard. The disintegration of the German economy into several currency areas was imminent.[89] But history took a different course.

In early August, Karl Helfferich had presented the government with a rescue plan. Helfferich's idea was to create new confidence among the population that the decline of the mark had reached its limit. His strategy was based entirely on speculations about the layman's monetary psychology.[90] Helfferich proposed to establish a new bank to be called the Rentenbank endowed with a claim to 3,200 million marks backed up by all commercial assets in Germany. Thus all German firms including farmers and banks were said to have a collective liability to the Rentenbank. The Rentenbank would then issue Rentenmarks.

In the mind of the average German citizen, the Rentenmark—"founded on value-stable soil"—had successfully stopped the further erosion of the mark. But the end of the crisis had a very different source: on the same day the first Rentenmarks came into circulation, the printing of new marks was

---

[88]Ibid., p. 15.
[89]Stucken, *Deutsche Geld- und Kreditpolitik, 1914–1963*, p. 49.
[90]Ibid., p. 52.

halted. As Mises had emphasized in his report to the *Verein für Sozialpolitik*, the "first precondition of any monetary reform is to halt the printing press."[91]

Mises believed it was also necessary to bring about a return to gold, advocating a "100% marginal gold standard."[92] These two measures were intimately connected. Together they were designed to drive the government out of the monetary arena. He explained:

> The reason for using commodity money is precisely to prevent political influence from affecting the value of the monetary unit. Gold is not the standard money [merely] on account of its brilliance or other physical and chemical characteristics, but because the increase or decrease of its quantity is independent of any orders issued by political powers. The crucial function of the gold standard is that it makes changes in the quantity of money subject to the laws determining the profitability of gold production.[93]

Yet which particular type of gold standard did Mises have in mind? Apparently, he believed that a full-blown gold standard, which involved the circulation of gold coins, was not necessary or advisable under present circumstances. He also believed that a gold exchange standard, in which the currency consists exclusively of fractional-reserve banknotes, was acceptable if bank laws strictly limited the issuance of these banknotes.

His prewar studies had already alerted him to the likelihood that fractional-reserve banknotes would be issued on a growing scale and that there was no natural limit to this type of inflation if it proceeded slowly in a step-by-step manner. His 1923 proposal

---

[91]Mises, "Die geldtheoretische Seite des Stabilisierungsproblems," p. 13.

[92]Ibid. The expression "100% marginal gold standard" is, I believe, Prof. Philippe Nataf's.

[93]Mises, "Die geldtheoretische Seite des Stabilisierungsproblems," p. 16; my translation.

therefore advocated 100 percent reserves for all additional note issues. Mises's plan thus took the present existence of fractional-reserve notes as irreversible and focused instead on the prevention of any further issuance of such notes. All additional issues must be completely covered by gold deposited with the issuing bank.

> The foundation and cornerstone of the provisional new monetary system will be the absolute prohibition of the issue of any notes not completely covered by gold. The amount of Reichsbank banknotes, of banknotes of the Darlehenskassen, of emergency currency of any kind, and of token money will be legislated to be—after deduction of the stocks of gold and of foreign exchange held by the Reichsbank and by the private banks of issue—the maximum amount of German notes in circulation. Any extension of this maximum must be avoided under any circumstances, except for the facilitation of end-of-quarter payments that we have already mentioned. Any note issue beyond this limit must be fully covered by a deposit of gold or of foreign exchange with the Reichsbank. This is obviously the adoption of the main provision of Peel's Bank Act with all its deficiencies. But for the moment these deficiencies hardly have any practical significance. Our present goal is merely to abolish inflation by stopping the printing press. This objective, which alone we presently strive for, is best served through a prohibition of note issues without metallic backing.[94]

To determine the most suitable redemption ratio between gold and the currency, Mises recommended that the monetary authority should proceed by (1) stopping the printing press and then (2) letting the exchange rate between its currency and gold stabilize on the market. In short, stop inflating and then let the market determine the gold value of the mark. Mises maintained

---

[94]Ibid., p. 33; my translation. The deficiences he alludes to concern the absence of legal limitations on checking accounts and other money substitutes.

the same views on the technical aspects of monetary reform for the rest of his career. In 1953, he made the case for a 100 percent marginal gold standard in a more detailed and thorough manner, when he added a fourth section to the English edition of *The Theory of Money and Credit*.[95]

Mises rejected the idea, which would later be maintained by the influential Gustav Cassel, that there might not be enough gold available to put all countries of the world on a gold standard. Mises argued that the pricing process would always equilibrate demand and supply. Moreover, he observed that the global gold supply had increased since 1914 and that trade had decreased, so that there was no great danger of lower-than-1914 prices. Finally, it was not necessary to bring about a full-blown gold circulation.

> [A] return to the gold standard would not necessarily mean a return to the actual use of gold money for small- and medium-sized payments within the country. For even the gold exchange standard developed by Ricardo in his work, *Proposals for an Economical and Secure Currency* (1816), is a true and sound gold standard. The monetary history of the recent decades has clearly shown this.[96]

Following Ricardo further, he even suggested legislating that the Reichsbank only be obliged to redeem gold ingots, rather than gold coins. This would act as an effective deterrent against redemption demands that the Bank might not be able to comply with in its first years of operation under the gold standard. At some later point, it might however be useful to counteract the note-using habits of the population, and thus to replace the

---

[95]But the 1953 Mises Plan was substantially the same plan he first presented in 1923. See Mises, *Theory of Money and Credit* (New Haven, Conn.: Yale University Press, 1953), part 4.

[96]Mises, "Die geldtheoretische Seite des Stabilisierungsproblems," p. 17; my translation.

note circulation by an effective gold circulation, in order to prevent future over-issuance of banknotes.[97]

It turned out that Mises's apprehensions about the remaining inflation dangers in a gold exchange standard were justified. Writing many years later in *Human Action*, he regretted the moderate stance he had taken in his earlier writings because it left too much power in the hands of the government, which through its monetary authority still issued the gold exchange currency. He denounced the root error behind the gold exchange standard, which was in seeing "the costs involved in the preservation of a metallic currency as a waste." This had been the mistake of both Adam Smith and David Ricardo and thus enjoyed immense credibility and prestige. Yet Mises had come to consider it as "one of the most serious shortcomings of the classical economists."

> In dealing with the problems of the gold exchange standard all economists—including the author of this book—failed to realize that it places in the hands of governments the power to manipulate their nations' currency easily. Economists blithely assumed that no government of a civilized nation would use the gold exchange standard intentionally as an instrument of inflationary policy.[98]

Mises's case for the restoration of the gold standard was obviously based on the premise that an inflation-free monetary order would be a good thing. But what if someone objected to this view on fiscal grounds? These "conditional inflationists," as Mises called them, admitted that inflation was not necessary to equilibrate the balance of payments. But they held that in some situations it was suitable and expedient for the government to use inflation as a particular form of taxation. Mises observed that

---

[97]Ibid., pp. 34f.

[98]Mises, *Human Action: A Treatise on Economics* (New Haven, Conn.: Yale University Press, 1949), p. 780.

paper-money production was indeed one of three possible resources of government revenue, the other two being taxation and borrowing.[99] In his view, economic science could not determine which of these techniques should be used. But it had a few things to say about the social and economic consequences of paper-money inflation, and also about its political significance. Mises suggested that inflation was by its very nature undemocratic:

> a government always feels compelled to resort to inflationary measures when it is unable to issue bonds and when it does not dare to increase taxes, because it fears to lose support for its system of government if the latter's financial and general economic consequences become obvious too quickly. Thus inflation becomes one of the most important psychological instruments of an economic policy bent on camouflaging its effects. In this sense it may be called a tool of anti-democratic policy, because it makes it possible, through the deception of public opinion, to perpetuate a system of government, which would have no prospect of public approval if all things were openly explained.[100]

Mises here rediscovers a fact that had been first stressed in the writings of Nicolas Oresme, a fourteenth century scholastic and author of the very first monetary treatise. Oresme pointed out that debasement (the inflation technique of his age) served to enrich the princes at the expense of the community. The princes thereby turned from kings into tyrants:

> I am of the opinion that the main and final cause why the prince pretends to the power of altering the coinage is the profit or gain which he can get from it ... the amount of the prince's profit is necessarily that of the community's loss. But whatever loss the prince

---

[99]Mises, "Die geldtheoretische Seite des Stabilisierungsproblems," p. 30.
[100]Ibid., p. 32; my translation.

> inflicts on the community is injustice and the act of a
> tyrant and not of a king, as Aristotle says. . . . And so
> the prince would be at length able to draw to himself
> almost all the money or riches of his subjects and
> reduce them to slavery. And this would be tyrannical,
> indeed true and absolute tyranny, as it is represented
> by philosophers and in ancient history.[101]

Recalling the intimate relationship between the welfare state
and the warfare state, a relationship emphasized by the nineteenth century free-trade movement of Cobden, Bright, and
Bastiat—Mises stressed that the inflationist mindset, which also
underlies proposals in favor of seemingly moderate conditional
inflation, is not an isolated phenomenon, but part and parcel of
the reigning ideology:

> [Inflationism] belongs to imperialism, to militarism,
> to protectionism, to statism, to socialism—in the
> same way as the sound-money policy of the champi-
> ons of the gold standard had belonged to liberalism,
> to free trade, and to pacifism. And just as the global
> catastrophe that has swept over mankind since 1914
> is not an elementary fact of nature, but the necessary
> consequence of the ideas that rule our times, so is the
> destruction of our monetary system nothing but the
> necessary consequence of the dominance of certain
> ideologies of monetary policy.[102]

෴   ෴   ෴

A few months after the stabilization of the mark, the position
of the banks and other private firms that depended on continued inflation in Germany had become untenable and they

---

[101]Nicholas Oresme, "A Treatise on the Origin, Nature, Law, and Alterations of Money," Charles Johnson, ed., *The De Moneta of Nicholas Oresme and
English Mint Documents* (London: Nelson & Sons, 1956).

[102]Mises, "Die geldtheoretische Seite des Stabilisierungsproblems," p. 36;
my translation.

started scrambling for cash.[103] Many went under, the most prominent case being the Biedermann Bank, whose president was Joseph Schumpeter.

In the interwar period, the large Austrian banks had consciously sought to win economists of Schumpeter's standing as front men to reassure their creditors from abroad. They had also asked Mises for support several times, but he always rejected these proposals because he thought the commercial banks were all bankrupt.[104] This was not a pose. He had in fact always kept his personal account with Austria's postal savings bank.

Theory of Money and Credit Reconsidered

Some time before March 1923, Mises had talked to representatives of Duncker & Humblot about a second edition of *Theorie des Geldes und der Umlaufsmittel*. He planned to incorporate several "major necessary additions" but intended to make cuts elsewhere in order to maintain the overall size of the book. He rejected a first offer as insufficient, both financially and because it stipulated that he cut the book by one sixth. He pointed out that the contract concerning the first edition, which eventually sold out entirely, had been unfavorable to him since he did not even recover his expenses. Eventually he signed a contract on May 31, 1923 that stipulated a production of 2,000 plus 50 complimentary copies and 150 for review.[105]

---

[103]Hawtrey, *Monetary Reconstruction*, chap. 4.

[104]See Mises, *Erinnerungen*. He probably could have increased his revenue several times, if it is licit to extrapolate pre-WW I data. Indeed, before the war, the leading executives of the Credit-Anstalt (Spitzmüller) and of the Bodenkreditanstalt (Sieghart) had a basic annual income of 50.000 kronen, whereas civil servants of the rank Mises attained in the 1920s (Ministerialrat) earned 12.000 kronen. See Bernard Michel, *Banques et banquiers en Autriche au début du 20e siècle* (Paris: Presses de la Fondation nationale des sciences politiques, 1976), pp. 324f.

[105]See the correspondence between Mises and Duncker & Humblot in Mises Archive 78: 7, 9, 17, 38. Mises had Duncker & Humblot send 14 of the

Although the message of the first edition was unaltered in its essentials, he felt obliged to take account of various recent developments in economic theory, as well as changes in his own views, most notably his new perspective on the economics of socialism. He also wanted to further develop the theory of interest and business-cycle theory, about which he now believed he had previously underestimated the significance of his own contribution:

> I have come to the conclusion that the theory which I put forward as an elaboration and continuation of the doctrines of the Currency School is in itself a sufficient explanation of crises and not merely a supplement to an explanation in terms of the theory of direct exchange, as I supposed in the first edition.[106]

He also added a section on current problems of banking policy, a chapter dealing with the monetary theory and policy of statism, and an essay on the classification of theories of money.[107] He deleted long sections dealing with historical cases of hyperinflation. These passages had been necessary in 1912, at the end of a long phase of monetary stability, to illustrate the possibility of inflationary dangers lurking around the corner if the policies of the day continued. In 1924, this was no longer necessary: "the experiences of recent years afford sufficient illustrations of the fundamental argument to allow these discussions now to be dispensed with."[108]

Indeed, Germany's hyperinflation was a striking illustration of Mises's argument. Especially impressive were his predictions

---

50 complimentary copies directly to the recipients. He himself distributed the remaining 36 copies (see Mises Archive 78: 28).

[106]Mises, *Theory of Money and Credit* (Indianapolis: Liberty Fund, 1980), p. 34.

[107]Mises, "Zur Klassifikation der Geldtheorie" (On the classification of monetary theories), *Archiv für Sozialwissenschaft und Sozialpolitik* 44 (1917/1918): 198–213.

[108]Mises, *Theory of Money and Credit*, p. 35.

of inflation's "social consequences"—that is, the redistributive effects. All inflations entail redistribution to the benefit of those who receive the new currency first, but the German inflation entailed redistribution on such a massive, visible scale that few could fail to notice it. While the personal savings of most people had become worthless, some ruthless investors with good political connections had amassed great fortunes.

Mises's anger about these events was not directed against those with political connections, but toward those who made such connections relevant to amassing such fortunes. A passage from an unpublished draft of his introduction to the second edition reveals his state of mind at the end of 1923. Reckoning with the "leaders of the campaign of lies" against his book, he states:

> Between the first and second edition of this book, the European governments waged a war against economic science that was as tenacious as it was unsuccessful. It was the pitiable collapse of their politics that showed those in power the limits of their might. The statist theories have collapsed with the politics of statism, and economic science, long disdained, has reclaimed its place of honor. . . . It was inevitable that the first edition of this book—although it only sought to serve the truth—was passionately, bitterly, and perfidiously attacked by the champions of the theories that prepared the way for monetary debacle.[109]

At the end of March 1924, the last part of the manuscript was in the hands of the publisher, and Duncker & Humblot worked feverishly toward completion of the printing in the summer semester. The first paperback copies were finally ready in the

---

[109]See Mises's manuscript in Mises Archive 78: 32. He had planned to give the new introduction the title "The Place of the Theory of Money and Fiduciary Media Within the System of Theoretical Economics" (see Mises Archive 78: 33), but also abandoned this idea.

second week of July, and the bookbindery delivered the hardcover copies on July 18.[110]

From the start, the book sold exceedingly well for a theoretical treatise, especially one that opposed mainstream views on its subject.[111] This success was not entirely surprising, given Mises's new prominence as a member of Austria's first postwar government and author of *Gemeinwirtschaft*.[112]

The German hyperinflation and the enormous inflation in German-Austria had seriously damaged the credibility of the established authorities. Professional economists and other social scientists were looking for other approaches. In this context, Weber's remark in his posthumous *Wirtschaft und Gesellschaft*—that of all monetary theories, Mises's was the most acceptable—had directed the attention of a broader learned readership to the work of this Austrian economist.

German Economists Return to Classical Liberalism

The second edition of *Theorie des Geldes und der Umlaufsmittel* arrived just in time for the annual meeting of the *Verein für Sozialpolitik*, which took place in late September 1924 in Stuttgart. It provided a welcome antidote to the German edition of John Maynard Keynes's *Tract on Monetary Reform*, which

---

[110]See the correspondence in Mises Archive 78: 7, 20, 22, 26, 38.

[111]Here are the sales figures (see Mises Archive 78: 2, 52): 1924: 839/721, 1925: 420/409, 1926: 144/139, 1927: 78/77, 1928: unknown, 1929: unknown, 1930: 70, 1931: 110. Remaining copies on May 21, 1932: 150. In 1932, Dunckler & Humblot already talked about a third edition of the book, and in light of the sales it is certain that this edition would have been forthcoming. The rise of National Socialism in Germany prevented this project.

[112]Herbert Döring, *Die Geldtheorien seit Knapp*, 2nd ed. (Greifswald: Bamberg, 1922); Melchior Palyi, *Der Streit um die Staatliche Theorie des Geldes* (Munich: Duncker & Humblot, 1922); G.M. Verrijn Stuart, *Inleiding tot de Leer der Waardevastheid van het Geld* (The Hague: Mouton, 1919); Walter Eucken, *Kritische Betrachtungen zum deutschen Geldproblem* (Jena: Gustav Fischer, 1923). The latter work is not mentioned in Mises's book, but Mises refers to it in correspondence; see Mises Archive 80: 52.

Duncker & Humblot had published some months before Mises's book.[113]

Meanwhile Germany's situation had improved considerably. In May, the *revanchiste* Poincaré government had lost the general elections in France and the new leadership under Herriot, Painlevé, and Briand immediately set out to bring about an end to the politics of seizure in the *Ruhr*. As a consequence, the German government was finally able to come to a financial agreement with its former enemies and obtained even better conditions than Austria had in the Geneva Protocols two years earlier. Germany obtained western credit for 800 million gold marks to bolster the reserves of the Reichsbank and thus enable it to operate on a gold exchange standard. In contrast to Vienna, the Berlin government did not have to make any of the far-reaching concessions that would have diminished its political sovereignty. The agreement that was signed in London on August 16, 1924 on the basis of a report from U.S. envoy Charles Dawes was, as all sides agreed, the first true inter-governmental agreement since the war.[114]

A level of optimism finally returned to the population. This apparently helped the German economists face up to the "crisis of social policy" that Weber and Mises had caused with their recent writings. The assembly in Stuttgart broke new ground in the history of the *Verein für Sozialpolitik* when, on the last two days of the meeting, the great majority of the speakers endorsed—with some qualifications—the case for free trade. This ended the more than fifty-year old tradition of monolithic advocacy of the welfare state, inflation, and protectionism.[115]

---

[113]Mises Archive 78: 21. In his book, Keynes had adopted the position of Irving Fisher and Gustav Cassel, according to which monetary policy should strive to stabilize the purchasing power of money.

[114]Eckert, "Friedensverträge. II. Vom staatswissenschaftlichen Standpunkte," p. 490.

[115]Two years before, at the fiftieth anniversary convention in Eisenach, Mises's friend Georg Jahn had unsuccessfully agitated for the transformation

The debate had been put on the schedule at the very last minute. Two considerations came into play: first, in January 1925, the German government was going to recover its sovereignty in matters of foreign trade (it had been denied this freedom by the Treaty of Versailles); second, the Dawes Plan had finally created a reliable basis for policy-making. True to its mission, the *Verein* sought to give intellectual guidance to the forthcoming parliamentary debates—though it was impossible to commission any research papers before the Stuttgart meeting. Herkner's choice of the invited speakers was therefore bound to set the tone for the entire debate. He chose four well-established economists who he knew to be open to free trade: Max Sering, Christian Eckert, Bernhard Harms, and Georg Gothein. At the meeting, these men did indeed call on the German government to pioneer the reestablishment of global free trade, but Gothein and Sering argued that some tariffs should be kept in place, not as a protection for certain industries, but as the basis of future international negotiations to enhance further the freedom of trade.[116]

These statements were so well received that 107 participants went on to sign a "proclamation of university professors" calling for free trade.[117] Mises's friend Georg Jahn expressed the significance of the event in a 1927 essay on the free-trade movement in Germany:

---

of the *Verein* into a pure research association (see Boese, *Geschichte des Vereins für Sozialpolitik, 1872–1932*, pp. 176ff.). Two motivations seemed to be at work in this attempt. On the one hand, Max Weber's ideal of a value-free social science had won many followers among the younger generation. On the other hand, the socialist November revolutions of 1918 had produced a political radicalization of its members and of the larger society. This radicalization diminished the status of the middle-of-the-road mainstream, which in the past had been the main agent of political compromise within the *Verein* and of its application in government policy.

[116]Boese, *Geschichte des Vereins für Sozialpolitik, 1872–1932*, pp. 186ff.

[117]See "Verhandlungen des Vereins für Sozialpolitik in Stuttgart 1924," *Schriften des Vereins für Sozialpolitik* 170 (1925): 139ff.

> [The new free-trade initiatives] have found expression in a proclamation that was agreed upon, in Stuttgart (1924), in the wake of a meeting of the *Verein für Sozialpolitik* dealing with the reform of trade policy and which was signed by a great number of academic economists. The proclamation says: "Germany's new economic structure, the implications of the London Agreement, and important changes in the forces cooperating on the world market have confronted Germany with an entirely new trade-political situation. The undersigned representatives of the economic and social sciences, among them many who before the war had advocated the basic principles of [then protectionist] German trade policy, emphasize that under current conditions Germany is forced to make the advantages of world trade its own, most notably in order to rationalize its agriculture and its industry. Hence, they can concur with industrial and agrarian tariffs only to the extent that these are necessary and adequate means to make international trade more liberal.

Jahn went on:

> What these academic economists demand is nothing less than restoration of trade policy to the free-trade ideas of the nineteenth century. . . . Major parts of agriculture and industry might continue to be in need of protection. But the greater interest of the state is in free trade and not in the conservation of a system of protective tariffs, which increases rather than diminishes the problems.[118]

It was probably the most joyful experience that Mises ever had at a *Verein* meeting, even though he did not fully concur

---

[118]Georg Jahn, "Freihandelslehre und Freihandelsbewegung," *Handwörterbuch der Staatswissenschaften*, 4th ed. (1927): 369f., vol. 5.

with all provisions of the proclamation.[119] The events most certainly took him by surprise. Returning from his summer vacation in Bad Gastein, Mises had spent only a couple of days in Vienna and then traveled to Stuttgart. He did not plan to take part in the discussions, but eventually gave in to the demands of the other participants who rightly saw in him one of the main driving forces behind the apparent new orientation.[120]

Thus, in a comment he made after the trade sessions, when the convention had turned to problems of currency and inflation, Mises observed that the meeting had featured "remarkable progress toward a de-mercantilizing of economic thought." Protectionist ideas had

> lost much, if not all, of their old attractiveness for this
> group. And it is not different in the field of monetary
> theory. All advocates of the State Theory of Money
> have disappeared and some who not long ago advo-
> cated abolishing the gold standard now advocate cal-
> culation in gold and the gold standard.

He also took a shot at those who, like Alfred Schmidt-Essen (in those days an influential writer on monetary questions) claimed that the gold standard is a monetary order in the exclusive interest of the United States and England. Turning this argument on its head, Mises said: "It was not a foreign commodity that depreciated our currency, but a foreign doctrine—the fight against and the rejection of the quantity theory—that we accepted with the banking theory." Then he recollected the story of how, on an

---

[119]By the end of October 1924, he had not signed it. See the copy of the proclamation and the list of its supporters in Grove City Archive: "I" file.

[120]Mises spoke from notes consisting of keywords. He later developed these notes into two manuscripts that he sent to the Verein's manager, Franz Boese, who handled the publication of the proceedings (see Mises Archive 80: 56). The manuscripts with Mises's comments are contained in Mises Archive 22: 71ff.

evening three years earlier, he walked with a German visitor through the streets of Vienna. While most factories stood silent or had significantly reduced their operations, only the printing presses of the Austro-Hungarian Bank were busy.

Things had definitely improved. The inflation had been stopped and the party of inflation and its theories—most notably the banking theory of money—had lost much of their authority. At the *Verein* meeting, Mises's views did not encounter any serious resistance. Melchior Palyi merely objected that his criticism of the banking theory had gone too far.[121] The only view that Mises himself opposed was Felix Somary's contention that monetary reform was a matter of constitutional amendment. Anticipating a tenet of the late twentieth century school of constitutional economics, Somary claimed that monetary stability was essentially a legal issue that could be solved through a suitable monetary constitution that limited the powers of the central bank management. Mises objected that this approach does not get to the root of the problem, namely, the inflationist mindset. Ultimately, central bank policies are determined by ideas, not by legal codes.[122]

Silver Linings on the Horizon

The successful second edition of the *Theorie des Geldes* and the reorientation of the *Verein für Sozialpolitik* were symptoms of a changed intellectual and political climate that came into full

---

[121]Mises Archive 80: 55.

[122]Criticizing the effectiveness of monetary policy, Mises also seemed to advance an early version of the rational-expectations argument. He stressed that he did not want to argue that future inflation would be prevented by more enlightened monetary authorities. His point was rather that economic enlightenment of the general public would deny inflationary monetary policy any effect. As soon as the public became aware of falling exchange rates, everybody would turn to smuggling, at which point the government could not finance itself by printing banknotes.

swing after 1923, the year of the "crisis of social policy" and of the stabilization of the mark. Central to both events were Mises's writings. This fact did not reach the attention of the larger public, but was obvious to all leading circles in academia and in monetary policy.

His impact in those years was limited primarily by his deficiencies as a communicator. He was not an orator and lacked the charismatic personality to win over an audience. He had a fine and dry wit, but was often too subtle for those outside Europe's higher society. And when he gave talks in foreign languages, his wit abandoned him. He certainly was not at ease in French or English. His accent was strong when speaking English, and his French, although significantly better, was far from perfect. Who knows what turn the history of the 1920s might have taken had Mises enjoyed the communicative gifts of a Maynard Keynes, an Irving Fisher, a Werner Sombart, or an Othmar Spann?

Still Mises did have a significant impact. After 1924, he became a sought-after speaker, and also, after 1925, the official representative of the Austrian chambers of commerce at the International Chamber of Commerce. These meetings and the connections he was building at the London School of Economics provided Mises with the opportunity to disseminate his views throughout Europe.[123] He was a vocal champion of a return to a gold standard. His efforts were crowned with the introduction of a gold-exchange standard in Austria.

It was only a gold-exchange standard—a fractional-reserve system with a lower reserve ratio than its predecessor, the classical gold standard—but at least notionally, gold was once again

---

[123]Mises to Eric Voegelin, letter dated June 12, 1925; Mises Archive: 79: 11:

> Next week I will travel to Brussels [to the Chamber of Commerce convention] . . . and then to London, where I will again look up my English friends. I have great expectations for the visit, even if I can only stay in London for a short time.

the money of the country. The new gold-based currency, the schilling, replaced the krone on January 1, 1925.[124] Little Austria thus spearheaded a movement that came into full swing when Great Britain returned to gold a few months later, on April 25. In many ways this reform paralleled the 1892 reform that had first introduced the krone, itself a gold-based currency. Both reforms enjoyed the decisive support of Austrian economists. Just as the original krone could be called the brainchild of Carl Menger, so the original schilling was the fruit of Mises's labor.[125]

In the preceding year, Mises had been given a prominent forum to explain and justify the necessity of the reform. He did so in a widely publicized lecture that he delivered to the annual plenary meeting of an association of German industrialists in the new Czechoslovakian Republic. Mises made the case that the return to the gold standard was the most pressing problem of present-day monetary policy.[126] A local newspaper had been given a long abstract of his manuscript based on which it presented, on the same evening, a detailed report on the meeting and Mises's speech. The story was picked up by all major papers of the former empire and widely publicized.[127] Eventually the

---

[124]The conversion rate was 10,000 kronen = 1 schilling. The krone had been introduced in 1892 in substitution for the Gulden banknotes, which however circulated during the next few years. The substitution process was ended by January 1, 1900.

[125]For Menger's writings in the context of the 1892 reform, see Carl Menger, *Gesammelte Werke*, F.A. Hayek, ed. (Tübingen: Mohr, 1968), vol. 4.

[126]The name of the association was *Deutscher Hauptverband der Industrie*. The meeting took place at the association's headquarters in Teplitz on March 15, 1924; see Mises Archive 57: 20ff. Mises might have given a similar talk to the Association of Merchants and Industrialists in Berlin (*Verein Berliner Kaufleute und Industrieller*). See Oscar Heimann to Mises, letter dated December 31, 1923; Mises Archive 57: 1.

[127]Mises Archive 57: 24.

full speech was published as "Present-day Questions of Financial and Monetary Policy."[128]

The circumstances of this appearance are interesting in that they give a taste of the conditions under which Mises had to operate in those days. The secretary of the association, a certain Dr. Janovsky, had approached Mises to give a talk on present-day problems of public finance and monetary policy. When Mises chose the title "Return to the Gold Standard, the Main Problem of Present-Day Monetary Policy," Janovsky feared the speech would seem irrelevant to people interested in practical affairs. He also feared that Mises's remarks would be too controversial. The meetings of the association did attract considerable attention among political circles in Czechoslovakia and neighboring countries, and statements from the keynote speakers were commonly interpreted as reflecting the official position of the association. According to Janovsky, the association had not yet come to a firm opinion on the question of Czechoslovakian monetary policy. Janovsky mentioned however that the last resolution the association passed on monetary questions had endorsed the policies advocated by John Maynard Keynes, who opposed the return to prewar parities for all strongly depreciated currencies.[129] He did not mention that he himself was an advocate of banking-theory style economic policies and had engaged in infights with local admirers of Mises such as Fritz Wolfrum.[130]

---

[128]Mises, "Finanz- und währungspolitische Fragen in der Gegenwart," *Mitteilungen des deutschen Hauptverbandes der Industrie* 5 (12): 201–09, Teplitz-Schönau, March 20, 1924.

[129]Mises Archive 57: 11.

[130]Mises Archive 80: 64. Janovsky later became a Misesian. See his February 3, 1932 letter to Mises, in which he criticizes the currency proposal of a certain Jellinek as not conducive to the aims he has set himself (in Mises Archive 71: 62). In the fall of 1932, Janovsky gave a speech before the *Gesellschaft österreichischer Volkswirte*. Mises was instrumental in arranging this talk (see Mises Archive 71: 126).

Mises criticized the reform proposals of Keynes, Josiah Stamp, and Fisher as overrating the usefulness of price indices to measure the value of money. He stressed that the great advantage of the gold standard was not any sort of value stability, but rather its independence from the political process. The prewar decline in the purchasing power of gold had not resulted from the production of this metal, but from the production of fiduciary media. Whatever its deficiencies, the gold standard was superior to government-managed money.[131]

∾ ∾ ∾

For Mises, 1925 also brought a significant breakthrough on an entirely different level. He finally met the woman who would become his wife.

Margit Serény had been one of six guests at a dinner party held by Fritz Kaufmann, a young lawyer and member of Mises's private seminar. It is almost a miracle that Mises won the heart of the lady sitting next to him, for he spent most of the meal discussing economics. On the other hand, his preoccupation gave her the opportunity to observe him. This is how she perceived him:

> What impressed me were his beautiful, clear blue eyes, always concentrated on the person to whom he talked, never shifting away. His dark hair, already a little grayish at the sides, was parted, not one hair out of place. I liked his hands, his long slim fingers, which clearly showed that he did not use them for manual work. He was dressed with quiet elegance. A dark custom-made suit, a fitting silk necktie. His posture indicated that he must have been a former army officer.[132]

---

[131]Mises, "Die Goldwährung," *Neues Wiener Tagblatt* (April 12, 1925). A copy is in Mises Archive: 106: 18.

[132]Margit von Mises, *My Years With Ludwig von Mises*, 2nd ed. (Cedar Falls, Iowa: Center for Futures Education, 1978), p. 13. The book is, as the

He talked to her after dinner, and they went to a dance club. Apparently Mises was a poor dancer—at least by Margit's standards—and so they spent most of the night talking. Actually she did most of the talking and he listened attentively. Margit was an attractive woman of five-foot-four, with brown hair and grey-blue eyes. Now, as they talked, he discovered she was also a witty and warm person. He must have fallen in love with her that evening. The next day, he sent her red roses and asked her out for dinner. It was the first of many such dinners over the next two years.

Margit Serény was an actress from a bourgeois background in Hamburg. During the war, she had performed on one of the leading stages in Vienna, the *Deutsches Volkstheater*. When Mises met her, she was thirty-five years old and a very attractive widow with two children, Guido and Gitta. Shortly after her arrival in Vienna in early 1917, she had married Ferdinand Serény, a Hungarian aristocrat who died in 1923, bequeathing to her assets that had lost most of their value during the inflation.

Characteristically, Mises was cautious even when his feelings might have threatened to overwhelm him. Could he trust an actress? As Margit later pointed out, most people in polite society considered actresses to be high-class call girls. Ludwig

---

author correctly points out, the only available testimony on Mises the man from a firsthand source. But its statements are not fully reliable, as two examples show. First, the author lied about her age, claiming to be six years younger than she really was. Even on her gravestone, the birth year is incorrectly given as 1896. Her correct birth year is stated, in her marriage certificate as well as in U.S. immigration paperwork, as 1890 (see the 1941 U.S. "Affidavit of Identity and Nationality;" a copy is in Grove City Archive: Mexico 1942 files). Second, Margit states that she "was the only woman he wanted to marry from the first moment he met her." While this statement might be true, the following sentence, in which she claims that Ludwig "never changed his feelings or his mind about this decision," is demonstrably wrong, as we will see in a later chapter. These examples show that Margit von Mises's biographical recollections must be read with caution. The present work uses her statements only where other evidence does not contradict them.

Margit Serény in 1919. She was a member of the Deutsche Volkstheater and the left-hand picture was on a postcard sold in Vienna at the time.

seems to have shared this prejudice. At any rate he took precautions. As he later confessed to his wife, he had checked some of her statements about her professional development by consulting the records in the archives of the *Neue Freie Presse*.[133] He probably also talked to his cousin, Rudolf Strisower, who had been Ferdinand Serény's physician. These investigations confirmed Margit's version of things.

But there were more fundamental obstacles that hampered the development of their romance. On the one hand, Ludwig's mother Adele had great reservations about Margit. Actually none of his girlfriends had ever met with her approval. She must have imagined a different sort of wife for her beloved son, and her opinion had a great weight for Ludwig, especially since he held certain philosophical views that would have deterred him from marriage anyway. These concerned the nature of marriage and the possibility of being both a husband and a

---

[133]Ibid., pp. 3, 9.

scholar. A thoroughly unromantic passage from *Socialism* says it all:

> As a social institution marriage is an adjustment of the individual to the social order by which a certain field of activity, with all its tasks and requirements, is assigned to him. Exceptional natures, whose abilities lift them far above the average, cannot support the coercion which such an adjustment to the way of life of the masses must involve. The man who feels within himself the urge to devise and achieve great things, who is prepared to sacrifice his life rather than be false to his mission, will not stifle his urge for the sake of a wife and children. In the life of a genius, however loving, the woman and whatever goes with her occupy a small place. We do not speak here of those great men in whom sex was completely sublimated and turned into other channels—Kant, for example— or of those whose fiery spirit, insatiable in the pursuit of love, could not acquiesce in the inevitable disappointments of married life and hurried with restless urge from one passion to another. Even the man of genius whose married life seems to take a normal course, whose attitude to sex does not differ from that of other people, cannot in the long run feel himself bound by marriage without violating his own self. Genius does not allow itself to be hindered by any consideration for the comfort of its fellows even of those closest to it. The ties of marriage become intolerable bonds which the genius tries to cast off or at least to loosen so as to be able to move freely. The married couple must walk side by side amid the rank and file of humanity. Whoever wishes to go his own way must break away from it. Rarely indeed is he granted the happiness of finding a woman willing and able to go with him on his solitary path.[134]

---

[134]Mises, *Socialism: An Economic and Sociological Analysis* (Indianapolis: Liberty Fund, 1981), pp. 85f. Mises's treatment of the genius (p. 166) was

This passage survived all editions of the book. Ludwig was slow to allow Margit onto his hitherto solitary path. But on the other hand he was longing for the love of a true companion. Margit later surmised that a deep-seated dissatisfaction with his (entirely public) life was the true cause of his infamous temper. The most terrible outbursts he reserved for the woman he loved:

> His temper was as astonishing as it was frightening. Occasionally he showed terrible outbursts of tantrums. I do not really know what else to call them. . . . Suddenly his temper would flare up, mostly about a small, unimportant happening. He would lose control of himself, start to shout and say things, which coming from him were so unexpected, so unbelievable, that when it happened the first few times I was frightened to death. Whatever I said would enrage him even more. It was impossible to reason with him.[135]

After a few years of married life, however, he became much more reasonable and less easy to anger. ✄

Margit during the 1930s

---

anticipated by George Bernard Shaw in his "Earning a Living and Creative Work." Mises did not know this passage from Shaw at the time. Twenty-five years later, a German correspondent pointed out the parallel. See Johannes Bahner to Mises, letter dated June 12, 1947; Grove City Archive: "B" file.

[135]Margit von Mises, *My Years with Ludwig von Mises*, p. 36.

*Ludwig and
Margit von Mises*

13

A System of Political Philosophy

SINCE ITS EMERGENCE IN eighteenth century France, economic science has focused on the practical problems of policymaking. Government's impact on the economy was central to economic books and pamphlets; all other problems tended to be dealt with only as much as was necessary to achieve a better understanding of the policy issue under consideration.

The marginalist revolution of the 1870s then focused the attention of theorists on the analysis of the market economy—somewhat one-sidedly. Academic energies were now dedicated to the solution of the new theoretical problems. The discipline lost much of its focus on policy questions.

Did the new marginal-value theory change any of the political implications traditionally derived from economic science?

Virtually all of Mises's publications from the 1920s in one way or another dealt with this question. He could rely on some of the work done by his predecessors—in particular, Böhm-Bawerk's essay "Power and Economic Law," which analyzed government intervention in the labor market from a Mengerian perspective. But in Mises's view, the question of the political implications of economic science required a more comprehensive approach. His great contribution was to show how the utilitarian method, which he had outlined in his *Nation, State, and Economy*, could be used to promote such an approach.

During the 1920s, Mises developed an all-encompassing utilitarian theory of social organization. The kind of theory he had in mind would deal with the suitability, not only of all economic systems that had ever existed in the past, but of all conceivable ones. His theory of socialism was an important step toward the realization of such a conception because he had come to the conclusion that the idea of assessing "all conceivable economic systems" was far less ambitious than it sounds.

There are, he maintained, only three categories of which all conceivable systems are particular instances: capitalism, socialism, and interventionism.

Capitalism is a system of division of labor based on private ownership of the means of production. It is characterized by the cooperation of many individuals or groups, none of whom control all capital goods. Their cooperation is based on respect for existing property rights and is regulated through contract, gift, and exchange.

In contrast, socialism is a system with only one individual or group controlling all means of production. There can be no exchange-based cooperation in this system, because exchange presupposes that the items traded have different owners.

Thus, by 1922, the bulk of the work had been done. Mises could now turn to the third system, interventionism, which had been the traditional subject of economics. His great task was to reconstruct the traditional analysis of government interventionism by applying the utilitarian method of the classical economists from a Mengerian point of view. Mises published his research in a series of articles written primarily between 1922 and 1926 and later republished as chapters of the book *A Critique of Interventionism*.[1]

---

[1] Mises, *Kritik des Interventionismus* (Jena: Gustav Fischer, 1929; reprint Darmstadt: Wissenschaftliche Buchgesellschaft, 1976); *A Critique of Interventionism*, Hans F. Sennholz, trans. (New York: Arlington House, 1977). Just how important Mises considered this project can be gathered from the fact

First Outline of a Theory of Interventionism

Economists had traditionally asked whether government interventions into the otherwise unhampered market could benefit the national economy. Their characteristic answer was that this was not possible. For the rest of the eighteenth, and much of the nineteenth century, this verdict continued to be one of the defining features of what it meant to be an economist. Each succeeding generation refined the explanation of why government intervention was unsuitable.

When Mises set out to reformulate and systematize this traditional field of economic inquiry at the beginning of the 1920s, he had already made one significant contribution to the analysis of government intervention through his generalization of the Ricardian theory of international trade.[2] Whereas Ricardo had studied a world in which only commodities could be transferred from one country to another, Mises dropped the assumption of immobility for labor and capital. In his 1916 article on the goal of trade policy, he described the impact of free migrations and capital flows on the global allocation of factors of production and on the composition of nations. Most importantly, he dealt with the question of whether trade policy (tariffs, quotas, subsidies) could be helpful in enhancing or maintaining "national greatness"—the number of persons belonging to the national community, and their welfare. His answer was negative. Trade policy "cannot reach this goal in a manner beneficial to the nation," and he observed that even the champions of protectionism had to

---

that during those years he worked on hardly any other research project and even rejected an offer to write a standard textbook on monetary policy. See Mises's letter to the editor of the prestigious series *Grundriss der Wirtschaftspolitik*, dated December 12, 1924; Mises Archive 80: 57. Mises said he was very busy and had "a number of projects" that he wanted to complete before accepting any new obligations.

[2]It is significant that Mises presented his theory of international trade as a generalization of Ricardo's model, rather than of John Stuart Mill's.

notice that their proposed policies could not even advance, much less reach, "those goals that they had set themselves."[3]

He restated this argument more forcefully three years later, in *Nation, State, and Economy*. Combining detailed theoretical and historical analysis, he showed that the protective tariffs the German government introduced after 1879 did not achieve their purpose, which was to halt the emigration of German workers into foreign lands.[4]

The next occasion for him to elaborate on this traditional field of economics came rather unexpectedly. In 1922, Friedrich von Wieser invited him to contribute to the new fourth edition of the standard social-science dictionary, *Handwörterbuch der Staatswissenschaften* (Concise Guide to the Political Sciences). Wieser's invitation had an air of reluctance and condescension.[5] Rather than soliciting an article on a topic covered by Mises's previous research, he asked him to write on price controls—a subject that could have been given to any average economist. All entries relating to money, banking, business-cycle theory, and socialism were written by other authors, including Wieser himself. Mises tried to decline, but when Wieser insisted, he eventually agreed to write about the *theory* of price controls.[6]

---

[3]Mises, "Vom Ziel der Handelspolitik," *Archiv für Sozialwissenschaft und Sozialpolitik* 42, no. 2 (1916): 567, 570.

[4]Mises, *Nation, Staat und Wirtschaft* (Vienna & Leipzig: Manz, 1919), pp. 57ff.

[5]"But I do not want to forgo your cooperation on the new edition of the *Handwoerterbuch der Staatswissenschaften*. Would you not be able to pen the entry on price controls?" Wieser to Mises, letter dated April 1, 1922; Mises Archive 74: 32.

[6]Mises, "Preistaxen. I. Theorie," *Handwörterbuch der Staatswissenschaften*, 4th ed. (Jena: Gustav Fischer, 1925), vol. 6; reprinted as "Theorie der Preistaxen" in Mises, *Kritik des Interventionismus*, pp. 123–36; *A Critique of Interventionism*, pp. 139–51.

The theory of price controls was a contested field, where two incompatible views dominated. On the one hand, free-market economists denied outright that price controls were possible at all. Laws of nature governed society and economy, and no government decree could violate such natural law. It might therefore be possible to create a socialist society (though this would not be advisable for several reasons) but it is impossible to create a society based on government decree. On the other hand, the *kathedersocialist* professors of Government Science objected that legislation and government decrees regulating prices obviously did exist. No law of nature had prevented them from coming into existence and from modifying prices according to the wishes of the authorities. The facts proved that it was possible to create such a thing as a mixed economy, or "Third Way," which could be made to combine the advantages of capitalism and socialism while avoiding the disadvantages of either extreme.

Now Mises definitely believed that economic laws are as unbreakable as the laws of nature.[7] How, then, could he handle the *kathedersocialist* objection? He applied the utilitarian method of analysis that he had discussed in *Nation, State, and Economy*. The decisive question, Mises argued, was not whether it was possible to enforce price controls (it evidently was), but whether price controls can attain the goals of the policy makers—and he proceeded to show in his article that they actually detract from the very goals they were supposed to attain. They are therefore destructive from the policy makers' own subjective point of view.

It follows that the old liberals (and some of the old socialists, too) had it right: there is no Third Way, in the sense of a meaningful, non-destructive economic system. Mises emphasized that this was the political significance of the theory of price controls. And this insight in turn led straight to the adoption of *laissez-faire* policies. By this reasoning, classical liberalism was not

---

[7]Mises, *Kritik des Interventionismus*, p. 125.

an ideology, in the value-laden sense, but only the straightforward application of economic science.[8]

Only in one sense could it be meaningful to talk about mixed
economies, namely, "in the sense that some means of production may be publicly owned while others are owned privately."[9]
In other words, a meaningful economic system presupposed
clearly defined and respected property rights. When the government blurred property rights through decrees and legislation, making itself a virtual co-owner of the factors of production, then the original owners would use the remaining control
in a way contrary to the stated purposes of the government.
Price controls prevent factor owners from using their property
the way they think best. They "fix prices in deviation from those
prices that would be formed on the unhampered market."[10]
Thus the factor owners turn to various second-best actions that
jeopardize the government's plans.

Mises showed that these unintended reactions of the factor
owners would prompt the government to encroach ever further
on the property rights of the citizens, thus instigating a downward spiral of interventionism. Each additional intervention
would be counteracted by another round of reactions contrary-
to-purpose, and so on. The process can stop only when the government controls all factors of production—that is, once a system of pure socialism comes into existence. The German and
Austrian economies in World War I are perfect examples:

---

[8]Ibid., p. 123. Following Archbishop Whately, Mises called economics
the "science of catallactics." See Richard Whately, *Introductory Lectures on
Political Economy*, 3rd ed. (London: Parker, [1832] 1847), p. 5.

[9]Mises, *Kritik des Interventionismus*, p. 136; *A Critique of Interventionism*, p.
151.

[10]Mises, *Kritik des Interventionismus*, p. 128; my translation. Mises distinguished these "genuine" price controls from controls that merely sanctioned
the state of affairs that the market would have brought about anyway.

> He who traces back the war-economy policies can
> easily find the phases mentioned above: at first price
> controls, then forced sales, then rationing, then reg-
> ulation of production and distribution, and, finally,
> attempts at instituting central planning of the entire
> process of production and distribution.[11,12]

Mises also discussed various other examples to illustrate the
counterproductivity of price controls. His most important
example of the destructiveness of price floors was the minimum
wage rate that labor unions enforced with the passive support of
the government. This case also had a wider theoretical significance because it showed that it was "irrelevant for our analysis
whether the apparatus of coercion imposing the controls is the
'legitimate' state apparatus or a sanctioned apparatus with public power."[13]

---

[11]Ibid., p. 131; my translation.

[12]Mises's account of the dynamics of wartime interventions into the price
system came to be reflected in Götz Brief's entry for the *Handwörterbuch der
Staatswissenschaften*:

> The beginning of war-economy prices meant highest price
> policies in Austria as well. Experiences here were exactly like
> those in Germany: artificially high prices misallocated goods
> so that they were not directed to the most desired channels
> of trade and consumption. After the Italians entered the war
> and the blockade became a reality in Austria, in particular,
> the growing scarcity of raw materials and goods left no alter-
> native but the path down which Germany had already
> turned: official confiscation, centralized rationing and dis-
> bursement of goods. (Götz Briefs, "Kriegswirtschaftslehre
> und Kriegswirtschaftspolitik," *Handwörterbuch der Staatswis-
> senschaften*, 4th ed. [1923], vol. 5, p. 1017)

[13]Mises, *Kritik des Interventionismus*, p. 133; *A Critique of Interventionism*,
p. 31, 56ff.

Critique of the "Anti-Marxists"

Having restated, in his piece on price controls, the classical-liberal case against government meddling with market prices, Mises further developed his system of political philosophy through a systematic critique of the two major variants of pro-interventionist theory that dominated the German scene in the mid-1920s: non-Marxist socialism and social liberalism.

The abject practical failure of the Marxist revolutionaries in the postwar period had done much harm to their image as the vanguard of social progress. The explanation for this failure in the writings of Mises, Max Weber, and Boris Brutzkus had led many economists to revise their views about the suitable scope of government within society. But others remained unrepentant advocates of the total state. They merely rejected the specifically egalitarian agenda of the socialists.

The uncontested leader of this group was Werner Sombart, the greatest star among the interwar economists in Germany. Sombart had started his career popularizing Marxism in academic circles with his 1896 book *Sozialismus und soziale Bewegung im 19. Jahrhundert* (Socialism and Social Action in the Nineteenth Century).[14] Later editions testified to Sombart's increasing estrangement with his initial Marxist ideals. The tenth edition, which appeared under a new title in 1924, featured an outright demolition of Marxist socialism.[15] Sombart had turned back to the mainstream Schmollerite socialism,

---

[14]Before Sombart's appearance, the German universities received Marx's writings very critically. In the United States, too, the rise of Marxism encountered the same reservations in academic circles until, some forty-five years after Sombart, Joseph Schumpeter popularized Marx as an important thinker in his *Capitalism, Socialism, and Democracy* (New York: Harper & Row, 1942).

[15]Werner Sombart, *Der proletarische Sozialismus ("Marxismus")*, 10th ed., 2 vols. (Jena: Gustav Fischer, 1924).

which advocated the total state without an egalitarian agenda.[16]

Sombart's intellectual qualities had gained him a place of pre-eminence. Where most Marxist intellectuals held dogmatically to the tenets of Marx and Engels, Sombart sought to analyze and develop their doctrines with a critical mind in quest of objectivity. This made his work the perfect target for a thorough criticism of the intellectual current of anti-Marxist socialism, and Mises provided such a criticism in an article with the title "Antimarxismus" (Anti-Marxism).[17]

Already in his article on price controls, Mises had pointed out that the shortcomings of interventionism did not result from the egalitarian agenda that some governments pursued, but from the very nature of government intervention itself, namely, the infringement of private property rights. Socialism and interventionism were destructive economic systems whether explicitly egalitarian or not. They would be unsuitable forms of social organization even if they pursued some other ideal of distribution—even meritocracy. There might be certain superficial similarities between a free society and a non-egalitarian one controlled by a total state, but these two would still be essentially different:

> On the surface the social ideal of etatism does not differ from the social order of capitalism. Etatism does not seek to overthrow the traditional legal order and

---

[16]Here is the most favorable thing Mises had to say about Sombart: "He was highly gifted, but at no time did he endeavor to think and work seriously. . . . And yet, it was more stimulating to talk to Sombart than to most other professors. At least he was not stupid and obtuse." Mises, *Erinnerungen* (Stuttgart: Gustav Fischer Verlag, 1978), p. 68; *Notes and Recollections* (Spring Mills, Penn.: Libertarian Press, 1978), p. 103.

[17]Mises, "Antimarxismus," *Weltwirtschaftliches Archiv* 21 (1925) reprinted in Mises, *Kritik des Interventionismus*, pp. 91–122; translated as "Anti-Marxism," in *A Critique of Interventionism*, pp. 107–38.

formally convert all private property in production to
public property. . . . But in substance all enterprises
are to become government operations. Under this
practice, the owners will keep their names and trade-
marks on the property and the right to an "appropriate" income or one "befitting their ranks." Every
business becomes an office and every occupation a
civil service. . . . Prices are set by government, and
government determines what is to be produced, how
it is to be produced, and in what quantities. There is
no speculation, no "extraordinary" profits, no losses.
There is no innovation, except for that ordered by
government. Government guides and supervises
everything.[18]

Mises showed that the error in the idea of the omnipotent
state has nothing to do with the state's particular agenda. The
government is not omnipotent if its goal is to improve "collective life" (as opposed to that of mere aggregates of individuals).
But neither is it omnipotent if it seeks to enhance the welfare of
the totality of individual citizens. In both cases, government
intervention is counterproductive. It follows that the time-honored and seemingly significant distinction between individualism and collectivism is of only secondary importance. The primary distinction is between policies that work and policies that
do not work, which leads in turn to the distinction between a
social order based on private property (which works) and those
social orders that depend on infringements of private property
rights (and do not work). It is therefore beside the point
whether individuals or collectives run the economy—provided
only that the property rights of all individual members of the
collectives are preserved. It also follows that the size of the firm
is of no importance. As long as private property is respected, the

---

[18]Mises, *Kritik des Interventionismus*, pp. 124f.; *A Critique of Interventionism*, pp. 140f.

buying decisions of the consumers reward only those companies that offer the best products. If these companies are larger than others, so be it.[19]

Mises emphasized this fact against the doctrines of Dietzel, Karl Pribram, and Spann, which had a great influence on interwar political thought in Germany and, after World War II, in the wider western world. Dietzel and Pribram sided with individualism, whereas Spann championed collectivism, but they all agreed that these were the ultimate categories and that all political points of view derived from them.[20] Mises disagreed. He argued that there was a point of view that was derived from neither individualism nor collectivism, namely, the utilitarian method of social analysis.[21] He had already proved how successful this method was in analyzing the static and dynamic problems of social "wholes" such as language communities, and

---

[19]Keynes was convinced that, in attacking and criticizing individualism, he had destroyed the case for *laissez-faire*. See John Maynard Keynes, *The End of Laissez-Faire* (London: Hogarth Press, 1926), pp. 39f. The postulate of a dichotomy between individualism and collectivism led Keynes to anticipate the now-famous Coasean view on the problem of optimal social organization. Thus Keynes surmised that the "ideal size for the unit of control and organization lies somewhere between the individual and the modern State" (ibid., p. 41). The Coasean theory is best expressed in Ronald Coase, *The Firm, the Market, and the Law* (Chicago: University of Chicago Press, 1988).

[20]Heinrich Dietzel, "Individualismus," *Handwörterbuch der Staaswissenschaften*, 4th ed. (1923), vol. 5; Alfred Pribram, *Die Entstehung der individualistischen Sozialphilosophie* (Leipzig: Hirschfeld, 1912); Othmar Spann, *Der Wahre Staat* (Leipzig: Quelle & Meyer, 1921).

[21]Mises, *Kritik des Interventionismus*, pp. 95f., 111. He stated:

> In the final analysis, there is no conflict of interest between society and the individual, as everyone can pursue his interests more efficiently in society than in isolation. The sacrifices the individual makes to society are merely temporary, surrendering a small advantage in order to attain a greater one. This is the essence of the often cited doctrine of the harmony of interests. (*A Critique of Interventionism*, pp. 112f.)

he emphasized that the analysis of such wholes is the very point of theoretical social science.[22] It was fallacious to believe that individual action could be understood out of its wider social context, just as it was false that the proper understanding of social wholes required that the social analysis itself be holistic.

The utilitarian method alone was a truly scientific one because it traced all social phenomena back to facts of experience:

> The utilitarian social doctrine does not engage in metaphysics, but takes as its point of departure the established fact that all living beings affirm their will to live and grow. The higher productivity of labor performed in division of labor, when compared with isolated action, is ever more uniting individuals to association. Society is division and association of labor.[23]

Each person seeks to enhance his welfare, and cooperative labor is more productive than isolated labor. Therefore, insofar as the growth of a person's welfare presupposes greater quantities of material goods, the person can best attain his ends by engaging in a division of labor. This is how society comes into being.

All elements in this economic explanation of society are ascertainable facts. In contrast, the doctrines of individualism and collectivism do not lend themselves to any such causal

---

[22]"What society is, how it originates, how it changes—these alone can be the problems which scientific sociology sets itself." Mises, *Socialism: An Economic and Sociological Analysis* (Indianapolis: Liberty Fund, 1981).

To be perfectly clear, Mises believed that the positive analysis of the emergence and transformation of social wholes had to rely on methodological individualism. Based on this analysis, one could apply the utilitarian method, that is, raise the question whether any given policy was suitable to attain its goals. Othmar Spann rejected not only individualism as a political orientation, but also as a methodological device.

[23]Mises, *Kritik des Interventionismus*, p. 96; *A Critique of Interventionism*, p. 112.

explanation of the origin of society because they are based on postulates rather than on analysis of fact. And Mises proceeded to show that the same criticism also applied to the Marxist theory of proletarian class struggle. He did not deny that human history featured many group conflicts and that they often had great importance for the course of events. Rather, he argued that the fashionable struggle theories—of which the Marxist theory of class struggle was but one particular instance—purported to be much more than they really were. Group conflicts were not, and could not possibly be, the basic elements of human life. The real question was how any group could come into existence in the first place. One first had to explain the formation of groups before one could explain the struggle between them. But all struggle theorists, Marx included, failed on this front.

> The reason for this negligence is not difficult to detect. It is impossible to demonstrate a principle of association that exists within a collective group only, and that is inoperative beyond it. If war and strife are the driving forces of all social development, why should this be true for classes, races, and nations only, and not for war among all individuals? If we take this warfare sociology to its logical conclusion we arrive at no social doctrine at all, but at "a theory of unsociability."[24]

Mises pointed out that Marx's theory of class struggle even failed to give an empirical account of its most basic concept. What is a "class" in the Marxist sense? Marx had never defined it. "And it is significant that the posthumous manuscript of the third volume of *Das Kapital* halts abruptly at the very place that was to deal with classes." Mises went on:

---

[24]Mises, *Kritik des Interventionismus*, p. 100; *A Critique of Interventionism*, p. 116. Mises quotes here Paul Barth, *Die Philosophie der Geschichte als Soziologie*, 3rd ed. (Leipzig: Reisland, 1922), p. 260.

> Since his death more than forty years have passed, and
> the class struggle has become the cornerstone of mod-
> ern German sociology. And yet we continue to await
> its scientific definition and delineation. No less vague
> are the concepts of class interests, class condition, and
> class war, and the ideas on the relationship between
> conditions, class interests, and class ideology.[25]

Werner Sombart, along with the great majority of German
sociologists of whom he was the undisputed leader, had adopted
the Marxist view that proletarian class struggle was the ultimate
driving force in modern societies. He was now an opponent of
Marxist ideology, but his analyses still remained Marxian. He
mercly refrained from drawing all the practical conclusions,
which Marx and the Marxists had consistently deduced, from
the theory of class struggle. He did not and could not provide
an alternative to the Marxist scenario of social evolution. His
only objection came in the form of a postulate: things *should not*
happen as they would happen according to the theory of class
struggle, therefore government *should* resist such developments.
Yet with this admission, Sombart and the bulk of the German
sociologists had again left the realm of science and entered that
of religion and ethics. Sombart in fact championed a return to
medieval forms of social organization—the guilds—just as
Keynes in England proposed "a return, it may be said, towards
medieval conceptions of separate autonomies."[26] Similarly, the
few theorists who had thoroughly criticized Marx's concept of
class struggle, like Othmar Spann, marveled at the alleged blessings of national socialism in the middle ages. Mises concluded:

> for every scientific thinker the objectionable point of
> Marxism is its theory, which seems to cause no offence

---

[25]Mises, *Kritik des Interventionismus*, pp. 101f.; *A Critique of Interventionism*, pp. 117f.

[26]Keynes, *The End of Laissez-Faire*, pp. 42f.

to the Anti-Marxist. . . . The Anti-Marxist merely objects to the political symptoms of the Marxian system, not to its scientific content. He regrets the harm done by Marxian policies to the German people, but is blind to the harm done to German intellectual life by the platitudes and deficiencies of Marxian problems and solutions. Above all, he fails to perceive that political and economic troubles are consequences of this intellectual calamity. He does not appreciate the importance of science for everyday living, and, under the influence of Marxism, believes that "real" power instead of ideas is shaping history.[27]

∽ ∽ ∽

"Anti-Marxism" caused outrage among the Marxists. What was Mises's sin? First, he had dared criticize the great master with a penetrating analysis of the incurable shortcomings of Marx's theory of class struggle. Second, he had again contended that from an economic point of view Marxist socialism was not essentially different from the various new brands of national socialism that had begun to spring up in the 1920s, mostly in reaction against Marxist movements. Thus a fraction of Italian socialists, who rejected the teachings of Marx and called themselves "Fascists," rose to power under the leadership of Benito Mussolini. There was also a movement of non-Marxist "National Socialists" in Germany. The father of this movement was Friedrich Naumann who, by a strange coincidence, later came to be regarded as the godfather of twentieth-century German liberalism.[28] The leader of the National Socialists from the 1920s until their bitter end was, of course, Adolf Hitler.

---

[27]Mises, *Kritik des Interventionismus*, p. 121; *A Critique of Interventionism*, p. 137.

[28]See Ralph Raico, *Die Partei der Freiheit* (Stuttgart: Lucius & Lucius, 1999), chap. 6.

Marxist socialists vociferously object to being classified under the same heading that includes Fascist Socialists and National Socialists. But as Mises showed, all distinctions between these groups are on the surface. Economically, they are united.

Critique of the New Liberals

After dealing with Sombart and others who had remained unrepentant champions of powerful central government, Mises turned to a critique of the more moderate branch of the *kathedersocialist* movement.[29] In the wake of the "crisis of social policy" these intellectuals had lost their faith in the blessings of an omnipotent government. They thought of themselves as "social liberals"—meaning that they recognized certain fundamental defects of free markets, and advocated government interventions to fix them. The leaders of this group were Heinrich Herkner, Lujo Brentano, and Leopold von Wiese. Their most important prewar predecessors were Eugen von Philippovich and Friedrich Naumann.[30]

The German social-liberal movement's endeavor to appropriate the term "liberal" paralleled the strategy of Leonard Hobhouse in England and John Dewey in the United States.[31] Both groups championed a much broader scope for government action than the classical liberals, whom they derided for their *laissez-faire* position. So why did they call themselves "liberals"?

---

[29]Mises, "Sozialliberalismus," *Zeitschrift für die gesamte Staatswissenschaft* 81 (1926); reprinted in Mises, *Kritik des Interventionismus*, pp. 55–90; translated as "Social Liberalism," in *A Critique of Interventionism*, pp. 71–106.

[30]As Raico, *Die Partei der Freiheit*, chap. 6 explains, Naumann inspired several postwar movements with often contradictory agendas.

[31]Hobhouse (1864–1929), a professor of sociology at LSE, became famous with his *Liberalism* (London: Williams and Norgate, 1911). Among the writings of John Dewey (1859–1952), see in particular *Liberalism and Social Action* (New York: Putnam, 1935).

Their only claim to the word was that they did not believe in the ideal of all-out central planning. The omnipotent state threatened the core of individual freedom: the "civil liberties" of individual citizens. But in contrast to classical liberals, these new social liberals had no principled objection to far-reaching limitations of citizens' "economic liberties." Such intrusions into private property rights could, they contended, be justified on various grounds, for example, the "principle" that there should be no income without work, or the contention that government intervention was needed to make the economy better resemble the model of perfect competition. They also argued that economic liberty was not truly liberal because it entailed a certain cold-heartedness to one's fellow citizens.

The rest was marketing. Anticipating an important maneuver of twentieth century party politics in western democracies, they presented themselves as liberals because of the positive connotations of the still-popular notion of individual liberty. The strategy worked so well that today the words "liberal" and "liberalism" are often taken to be the exact opposite of their original meaning.

Mises objected to this intellectual and practical confusion. He emphasized that what was at stake was not the use of words, but the substantial differences between an economy unhampered by government intervention, and an economic system characterized by such interventions. To use the word "liberal" in the new sense was to obscure these differences.

The new liberals gave the impression that politics concerned only the ends to be attained. The choice, they implied, was between cold-hearted and parasite-friendly economic liberties on the one hand, and warm-hearted, equitable civil liberties on the other.[32] But Mises explained that this view was entirely

---

[32]An extreme case of this confusion was Keynes, who not only held that politics was about the ends to be pursued, but about emotional attitudes to these ends. Thus he held that the "essential characteristic of Capitalism [was]

unfounded. Politics is not about ends but about means. Classical liberals often cherished the same ideals as their socialist rivals. What set them apart was their practical program to attain those ideals: where classical liberalism championed the inviolability of private property, the defining mark of all other political orientations was that they sought to attain their ends through violations of private property rights.

In an ideal classical-liberal society, every man is sovereign within the boundaries of his property. All relations between human beings are based on mutual consent. Each person cooperates with others to promote common interests; if one side is unwilling, cooperation stops. This withdrawal from cooperation might appear brutal in the eyes of the other party, but the only way to prevent it would be to force the first party to continue against his will, which would no longer promote the common interests of both. What might seem to be the unsocial excesses of the capitalist order are therefore, in truth, desirable consequences of the fact that cooperation is based on mutual consent:

> If, in a capitalistic society, the buyer seeks to buy an economic good wherever it is least expensive, without regard for other considerations, he does not act with "insensitivity toward suffering." If the superior enterprise successfully competes with one working less economically, there is no "brutal use of elbows," or "struggle to overpower and enslave fellow men." The process in this case is no undesirable concomitant effect or "outgrowth" of capitalism, and unwanted by liberalism. On the contrary! The sharper the competition, the better it serves its social function to improve economic production. That the stagecoach driver was replaced by the railroad, the hand weaver

---

the dependence upon an intense appeal to the money-making and money-loving interests of individuals as the main force of the economic machine" (Keynes, *The End of Laissez-Faire*, p. 50).

by mechanical weaving, the shoemaker by the shoe factory, did not happen contrary to the intentions of liberalism. And when small ship-owners with sailing vessels were replaced by a large steamship company, when a few dozen butchers were replaced by a slaughterhouse, a few hundred merchants by a department store, it signifies no "overpowering and enslaving of fellow men."[33]

It is true that an ideal classical-liberal society has never existed: "the picture of what fully developed capitalism can achieve is incomplete at best, even if we reflect upon British society at the zenith of capitalism when liberalism was leading the way."[34] Capitalism was thus an "unknown ideal," as Ayn Rand would later say.[35] It is neither impossible nor undesirable to bring such a society about. Economic science shows both that it is a practical political option, and that all the alternatives to it are inferior. Socialism is necessarily less efficient than capitalism because it cannot rely on economic calculation; and interventionism does not work at all. Mises asserted: "Economic knowledge necessarily leads to liberalism."[36] The best proof was that the social liberals had been unable to develop an alternative economic theory that would substantiate their agenda.

---

[33]Mises, *Kritik des Interventionismus*, pp. 67f.; *A Critique of Interventionism*, p. 84. Similarly, he observed:

> In fact, unearned income flows from control over the means of production. He who opposes unearned income must oppose private property in the means of production. Therefore, a liberal cannot sympathize with such efforts. If he does so nevertheless, he is no longer a liberal. (*Kritik des Interventionismus*, p. 65; *A Critique of Interventionism*, p. 81)

[34]Mises, *Kritik des Interventionismus*, p. 68; *A Critique of Interventionism*, p. 84.

[35]See Ayn Rand, *Capitalism: The Unknown Ideal* (New York: Penguin, 1967).

[36]Mises, *Kritik des Interventionismus*, p. 70; *A Critique of Interventionism*, p. 86.

The outstanding example of the social liberals' intellectual impotence was the theory of wages. As the Webbs had done before him, Brentano attempted to prove that labor unions could raise the wage rates of all workers above the level they would have attained on the free market. Their writings had already received devastating criticism from Böhm-Bawerk, Pohle, and Adolf Weber.[37] In his article on "Social Liberalism" Mises finished the job. He added that even if it were possible for labor unions to raise wage rates to some degree for all workers, there was another fundamental question to be asked:

> If labor unions actually had the power to raise the average wage of all workers above the rate that would prevail without their intervention, the question remains, How high can wages go? Can average wages go so high that they absorb all "unearned" income and must be paid out of capital? Or is there a lower limit at which this rise must stop? This is the problem the "power theory" must answer with regard to every price. But until today no one has ever tried to solve the problem.[38]

In other words, if the labor unions (or whoever else) really can increase wages rates for all by a mere display of power, that is, if prices really depend on power rather than on economic law, then why ask for wage increases of, say, 10 percent? Why not ask increases of 100 percent or 1,000 percent or 1,000,000 percent? To ask this question is to answer it. The wages-are-a-matter-of-bargaining-power theory is an absurdity.

---

[37]Mises himself had, in an early article, explained that labor unions could possibly raise wage rates for all workers in the short run; see Mises, "Die allgemeine Teuerung im Lichte der theoretischen nationalökonomie," *Archiv für Sozialwissenschaften und Sozialpolitik* 37 (1912): 570f. His studies on interventionism in the 1920s convinced him that this short-run rise was invariably bought at the price of capital consumption.

[38]Mises, *Kritik des Interventionismus*, p. 80; *A Critique of Interventionism*, p. 96.

Because the social liberals were aware of these problems, they denied the validity of economic science altogether. But, as Mises showed, this self-serving attitude amounted to an intellectual abdication and served to create a dangerous political vacuum. The social liberals even denied that present problems would ever be solved. For decades they had accustomed the German people to the notion that willpower and strength are the driving forces of all social processes. Now, at a time when they themselves had lost their faith in the omnipotent state, they left the people with old prejudices and no outlet. In his conclusion, Mises spelled out the grave political dangers of a situation in which the masses demand the establishment of socialism and their political leaders are unwilling to comply:

> Politics does not dare introduce what the prevailing ideology is demanding. Taught by bitter experience, it subconsciously has lost confidence in the prevailing ideology. In this situation, no one, however, is giving thought to replacing the obviously useless ideology with a useful one. No help is expected from reason. Some are taking refuge in mysticism, others are setting their hopes on the coming of the "strong man"— the tyrant who will think for them and care for them.[39]

∽ ∽ ∽

Mises submitted the manuscript of "Social Liberalism" at the end of February 1926.[40] At this point he had already made up his mind about his next two books. The first would be a collection of his papers criticizing the different manifestations of the interventionist creed. It would feature his "Anti-Marxism" and

---

[39]Mises, *Kritik des Interventionismus*, p. 90; *A Critique of Interventionism*, p. 106.

[40]See his letter to Brodnitz, editor of the *Zeitschrift für die gesamte Staatswissenschaft*, dated February 26, 1926; Mises Archive 80:20.

"Social Liberalism" as well as one or two new pieces to generalize his thesis from the "Theory of Price Controls." The second book would spell out the political implications of these findings from a classical-liberal point of view. As it turned out, the second book appeared first, in 1927, under the title *Liberalismus* (Liberalism); the other book was published only two years later under the title *Kritik des Interventionismus* (Critique of Interventionism).

The Transformation of Economic Science

By early 1926, Mises had worked out four elements of a general theory of interventionism: two case studies, in the fields of international trade and price controls, a critique of the spurious anti-Marxist socialism prevalent in Germany, and a critique of the social liberals. Now he had to pull these elements together into one unified theory of interventionism. The occasion came when he delivered two lectures in Rotterdam and Utrecht in October 1926. The manuscript of these lectures was subsequently published as an article for the *Archiv für Sozialwissenschaften und Sozialpolitik*.[41] The article generalized the thesis contained in the piece on price controls, and placed great emphasis on the continuity between Mises's work and that of previous generations of economists.

One of the objections that Mises sought to counter was that his theory made it seem that virtually all government activities were necessarily contrary to their professed purpose. Was he some sort of anarchist? Replying to this objection, Mises sought to delineate precisely which government actions constituted

---

[41]Mises, "Interventionismus," *Archiv für Sozialwissenschaften und Sozialpolitik* 56 (1926); reprinted in *Kritik des Interventionismus*; translated as "Interventionism," in *A Critique of Interventionism*, pp. 15–55.

"intervention" and which did not. His answer in a nutshell was that government does not "intervene" if it respects the will of private owners to use their own property as they please. Interventions are only those public actions meant to determine the use of property in deviation with the will of the owner.

> Intervention is a limited order by a social authority forcing the owners of the means of production and entrepreneurs to employ their means in a different way than they otherwise would.[42]

Mises stressed that interventionism is a larger phenomenon than the ill-suited actions of governments. The characteristic feature of interventionism is an "authorized" violation of private property. If committed by anyone other than the "social authorities," invasions of private property would be considered a crime. So what are these social authorities? Their characteristic feature is that their actions are legitimated by an "intellectual power" (*geistige Macht*). Thus their interventions are deemed to be *legitimate* violations of property. Intellectual power can give a monopoly over property rights violations to a particular agent; such is the case with all statist theories, which justify violations of property only by a special body of persons (the "state" or the "government"). But intellectual power can also be such as to enable violations of property without a central agent. This is so, for example, when religious doctrine prohibits payment of "high" prices as usury.[43]

The characteristic feature of intervention is that it brings about *unwanted co-ownership*. The government (or whoever else intervenes) claims a level of control over the property, but otherwise leaves it in the hands of its owner. Even outright expropriations do not count as interventions according to Mises, because they involve a clear-cut change of ownership.

---

[42]Mises, *Kritik des Interventionismus*, p. 6; *A Critique of Interventionism*, p. 20.

[43]See Mises's university lecture of November 16, 1927; Mises Archive 24: 6.

Most important, measures that serve to protect the physical integrity of private property are not interventions. Since this protection is the proper function of government in the classical-liberal vision of society, Mises's theory of interventionism cannot be interpreted as making the case for anarchism.[44] However, Mises stressed that "protection of property" should not be interpreted too loosely. In response to the particular notion, increasingly popular among economists of the 1920s, that a free market essentially resembled a Walrasian model of "perfect competition," Mises warned:

> Regulations for the preservation of competition do not at all belong to those measures preserving the private property order. It is a popular mistake to view competition between several producers of the same product as the substance of the ideal liberal order. In reality, the central notion of classical liberalism is private property, and not a certain misunderstood concept of free competition. It does not matter that there are many recording studios, but it does matter that the means of record production are owned privately rather than by government. This misunderstanding, together with an interpretation of freedom that is influenced by the natural rights philosophy, has led to attempts at preventing the development of large enterprises through laws against cartels and trusts.[45]

---

[44]Mises used the term "anarchism" to refer to the Proudhonian idea of a society without the defense of private property rights, and "anarchy" to designate the chaos he believed to be inevitable for such a society. He did not have in mind the anarchism of his later student Murray Rothbard, who used these same words to advocate a free market society without a modern state—a system in which even the defense of property rights would be provided privately. See Murray N. Rothbard, *For a New Liberty*, 2nd ed. (San Francisco: Fox & Wilkes, 1978); idem, *The Ethics of Liberty*, 2nd ed. (New York: New York University Press, 1998).

[45]Mises, *Kritik des Interventionismus*, p. 4; *A Critique of Interventionism*, p. 18.

Here Mises addressed for the first time a fallacy that he would have to confront on many occasions and for the rest of his life—especially after World War II, when the neoclassical movement swept the academic world, and perfect-competition models were taken to be ideal representations of a market economy.[46] The political implications were disastrous. The new approach opened an endless agenda for government agencies which, through endless novel interventions, sought to shape the real world to their impossible model.

Mises sensed this danger. Economic science had been the intellectual foundation of the nineteenth century's liberty. It was a science that dealt with real human life, not with the fictitious constructions that were at the heart of the rising neoclassical movement. Moreover, it was a science with clear political implications, not a mere intellectual exercise. The very nature of the science made it odious to the powers that be. Its results violated the political correctness of the day, which suddenly found itself exposed to the cold light of rational criticism. Mises knew he was making no friends when, at the height of the debate on the introduction of a national unemployment-relief program in Germany (established 1927), he stated:

> In the capitalist social order unemployment is merely a transition and frictional phenomen. Various conditions that impede the free flow of labor from place to place, from country to country, may render the equalization of wage rates more difficult. They may also lead to differences in compensation of the various

---

[46]See on this change of views of the economics profession Thomas DiLorenzo and Jack High, "Antitrust and Competition, Historically Considered," *Economic Inquiry* (July 1988). The authors show that, during the 1920s, the rising neoclassical movement more and more abandoned the project of modeling reality, in favor of squeezing reality into the Procrustean bed of their models. See also Frank Machovec, *Perfect Competition and the Transformation of Economics* (London: Routledge, 1995).

types of labor. But with freedom for entrepreneurs and capitalists they could never lead to large-scale and permanent unemployment. Workers seeking employment could always find work by adjusting their wage demands to market conditions.

If the market determination of wage rates had not been disrupted, the effects of the World War and the destructive economic policies of the last decades would have led to a decline in wage rates, but not to unemployment. The scope and duration of unemployment, interpreted today as proof of the failure of capitalism, results from the fact that labor unions and unemployment compensation are keeping wage rates higher than the unhampered market would set them.[47]

Mises knew that by insisting on these truths he was making life difficult for the vast majority of his colleagues. He also understood why so few of them dared to articulate even the most elementary lessons of their science: most of them depended on government support. Opposing their employer or benefactor would have been both impolite and impolitic.

He who timidly dares to doubt the justifications of the restrictions on capitalists and entrepreneurs is scorned as a hireling of injurious special interests or is, at best, treated with silent contempt. One can easily fall under the suspicion of serving "capital." Anyone using economic arguments cannot escape this suspicion.[48]

Because of this ostracism of genuine economists, those who held (or hoped to hold) academic positions in political economy became eager to avoid any behavior that could offend the powers that be. The most innocent strategy was to understate one's

---

[47]Mises, *Kritik des Interventionismus*, p. 20; *A Critique of Interventionism*, p. 34.
[48]Mises, *Kritik des Interventionismus*, p. 17; *A Critique of Interventionism*, p. 31.

findings when they risked upsetting certain powerful social groups. Thus Mises observed about Richard Strigl's book *Angewandte Lohntheorie* (1926), which essentially confirmed the old insight that labor unions cannot increase wages rates for all workers: "All Strigl's statements are carefully worded in the same manner that authors of previous centuries worded theirs in order to escape inquisition or censure."[49]

In a similar vein, an increasing number of young economists turned their attention to abstract and technical problems that did not have any political implications unwelcome to their employers. This helps explain the success of mathematical economics, econometrics, Keynesian economics, and game theory after World War II.

Mises observed that this retreat from traditional economic inquiry was in part the result of a perverse interpretation of value-freedom in the social sciences. According to this view, any critique of practical politics, by the very fact that it deals with a political problem, cannot possibly be scientific. Such was the strongly held opinion of Friedrich von Wieser and others.[50] Mises did not concur. Economic analysis is suitability analysis; it examines whether a proposed means is fit to attain a purported end. This is a factual question and thus subject to a scientific answer.[51,52] Economists can invoke the authority of their

---

[49]Mises, *Kritik des Interventionismus*, p. 39; *A Critique of Interventionism*, p. 53.

[50]See Friedrich von Wieser, "Karl Menger," Anton Bettelheim, ed., *Neue österreichische Biographie: 1815–1918* (Vienna, 1923), vol. 1, pp. 84–92, reprinted in idem, *Gesammelte Abhandlungen*, F.A. Hayek, ed. (Tübingen: Mohr, 1929).

[51]The personal values of the economist do not come into play here at all. Mises illustrated this point with the following example:

> When I say that price controls are illogical, I mean to assert that they do not achieve the objective they are usually meant to achieve. Now, a Communist could reply: "I favor price controls just because they prevent the smooth functioning of the market mechanism, because they turn human society into

science when they reject a policy that does not achieve what its proponents say it will. Mises concluded by pointing out that erroneous notions of value-freedom threatened to make the research of the rising generation sterile:

> We destroy economics if all its investigations are rejected as inadmissible. We can observe today how many young minds, who under other circumstances would have turned to economic problems, spend themselves on research that does not suit their talents and, therefore, adds little to science. Enmeshed in the errors described above, they shun significant scientific tasks.[53]

What Mises was describing was the beginning of the process through which economic science was being redefined—altered to suit the needs of the young and the ambitious, who in their mercenary way were willing to elevate certain comfortable errors to the level of principle. Mises was only a bystander in this process and did not see it as clearly then as he would see it in the 1950s and 1960s. In 1926, he did perceive that the

---

a 'senseless chaos' and all the sooner lead to my ideal of communism." Then, the theory of price controls cannot answer him, as physiology cannot answer the man who wants to kill with hydrocyanic acid. (*Kritik des Interventionismus*, p. 27; *A Critique of Interventionism*, p. 41)

[52]Economic analysis shows that all government interventions *are* unsuitable to attain the ends they are professed to attain (statement of matter of fact). In the light of this result, classical liberalism advocated that there *shall* be no intervention (judgment of value):

> government shall be limited to the protection of private property and the elimination of all obstacles to free market access for individuals or groups of individuals. This is nothing but another wording of the principle: laissez faire, laissez passer. (Mises, *Kritik des Interventionismus*, pp. 37f.; *A Critique of Interventionism*, pp. 51f.)

[53]Mises, *Kritik des Interventionismus*, p. 28; *A Critique of Interventionism*, p. 41.

replacement of economic science—which had shaped the modern world because of its practical implications for public policy—would entail grave danger for civilization. The transformation of economics into a self-absorbed technical discipline made it politically toothless. A mere "theory" based on fictitious stipulations and therefore without scientifically valid implications for public policy was no threat to vested interests, and the champions of this theory did not have to fear reprisals. Clearly, this state of affairs suited the majority in the economics profession, both employers and employees. But it was disastrous for science, human liberty, and economic progress.

The transformation of economics amounted to the abandoning of the authority that previous generations of economists had gained for their science. But even those who championed real economic science could still destroy through their self-promotion what remained of its credibility. These men—good writers and speakers, authors of very successful textbooks—claimed that there was no economic science prior to them. Robert Liefmann, Franz Oppenheimer, and Friedrich von Gottl-Ottlilienfeld had inherited the rhetorical strategy of Karl Marx, who thought he could enhance the respectability of his own arguments by belittling the efforts of his predecessors and contemporaries.[54] Owing to the eloquence of these authors, their condemnations of all previous accounts of economic law reached a broad audience.[55] The average lay reader almost inevitably

---

[54]See Robert Liefmann, *Allgemeine Volkswirtschaftslehre* (Leipzig: Teubner, 1924); Franz Oppenheimer, *Theorie der reinen und politischen Ökonomie*, 2nd ed. (Berlin: Reimer, 1911); Friedrich von Gottl-Ottlilienfeld, *Wirtschaft und Technik*, 2nd ed. (Tübingen: Mohr, 1923).

[55]Of course Liefmann did not intend to discredit economic science. Mises's point was that the effect was the unintentional result of Liefmann's rhetoric. Things were completely different in the case of Keynes, who consciously sought to discredit economic science in his crusade to vindicate government interventionism. Keynes claimed that the case for *laissez-faire* had no scientific basis, but was entirely founded on postulates of political philosophy

came away with the impression that at its best economic science relied on the work of a single author.

> The public, unfortunately, is led to believe that in economics everything is uncertain and problematic, and that economic theory merely consists of the personal opinions of various scholars. The excitement created by these authors in German-speaking countries succeeded in obscuring the fact that there is a science of theoretical economics which, despite differences in detail and especially in terminology, is enjoying a good reputation with all friends of science.[56]

The result was that government interventionism was no longer subject to scrutiny. Clearly, if there is no such thing as an economic science in the first place—if all views on the real impact of economic policy are just personal opinions—then it is pointless to change policy because of them.

Mises not only believed that there was such a thing as economic science, but also and in particular, that its core analysis of government economic policies had survived all changes of fashion and schools of thought. In other words, economic science was most constant and most unshakable precisely in that field where it mattered most: in economic-policy analysis. There was

---

(private property as a natural right) and theology (harmony of interests). See Keynes, *The End of Laissez-Faire*, pp. 11, 26. Without quoting Keynes, Mises showed that these claims missed the point. Private property does not require natural law for justification, but can be vindicated on the basis of suitability analysis alone. Further, the theological garment of the harmony-of-interest doctrine was just that. Already in his "Anti-Marxism," Mises had proven that the "attacks on the thought of 'preestablished harmony' do not touch the substance, merely the wording, of the utilitarian social theory." *Kritik des Interventionismus*, p. 98; *A Critique of Interventionism*, p. 114.

[56]Mises, *Kritik des Interventionismus*, pp. 29f.; *A Critique of Interventionism*, pp. 43f.

an unbroken line of continuity in economic thought on this question. It ran from the eighteenth century Physiocrats, via the classical economists and the nineteenth century French Laissez-Faire School, and via the marginal revolution with its different schools, up to Mises's own work in the 1920s.

Mises recognized of course that there were often profound differences between the various schools of thought, but he stressed that these differences had never affected the practical results. When it came to stating the impact of government intervention on the economy, there were no relevant differences of opinion between the schools. By and large, economists agreed on the practical issues. Notable disagreement existed only between economists and those who denied that there was such a thing as economic science at all.

> We need not here deal with the deeper epistemological question of conflicting systems. Nor need we discuss a multiplicity of opposing systems. To investigate the problems of interventionism there are, on the one hand, modern economics together with classical theory and, on the other hand, the deniers of system and theory, no matter how carefully they word their denial of the possibility of theoretical knowledge. Our answer to them is simple: try to create a system of theoretical knowledge that pleases you more than ours. Then we can talk again.

Concluding the essay he drove home this essential message:

> But surely it is as futile today as it was in the past to defend interventionism as meaningful and purposeful from the point of view of economic theory. In fact, it is neither meaningful nor purposeful from any point of view. There is no road from economics to interventionism.[57]

---

[57]Mises, *Kritik des Interventionismus*, p. 41; *A Critique of Interventionism*, p. 55.

⊰   ⊰   ⊰

At the beginning of the twenty-first century, Mises's emphasis on the continuity of economic thought in practical matters and the characterization he made of "economists" no longer seems true. But this is because the transformation whose beginnings he noticed in the mid-1920s has since been completed. Present-day mainstream economics is heavily focused on purely technical problems of modeling reality with mathematics, econometrics, and game theory.[58] As a consequence, the professional economists of today are not really economists in the sense in which Mises used the word—the same sense in which it was used throughout the nineteenth century. The Austrian School of Mises and Hayek (after the latter had repudiated his early neoclassical views) was in fact the only twentieth-century school of economic thought in the classical sense. Significantly, John R. Hicks said many years later about the Austrian School:

> I am writing in their tradition; yet I have realised, as my work has continued, that it is a wider and bigger tradition than it at first appeared. *The "Austrians" were not a peculiar sect, out of the mainstream; they were in the mainstream; it was the others who were out of it.*[59]

But Mises's ecumenical stress on the homogeneity of the different schools of economic thought (in regard to the necessity of economic theory in general, and the analysis of government interventionism in particular) has turned out to be problematic. Present-day historians of economic thought, well acquainted with Mises's work, have claimed that until the early 1930s,

---

[58]The relationship between these models and the real world that they supposedly portray is still as problematic as it has been from the outset.

[59]John R. Hicks, *Capital and Time: A Neo-Austrian Theory* (Oxford: Clarendon Press, 1973), p. 12.

Mises and virtually all other Austrian economists were unaware of the profound differences between the Mengerian approach to economic analysis and that of the other marginal-utility schools. These historians claim that it was the socialist-calculation debate of the 1930s that radicalized Mises and Hayek, spurred them to reflect on the uniqueness of their approach, and to distinguish themselves more sharply from the followers of William Stanley Jevons and Léon Walras.[60]

But Mises's ecumenism was not meant to cover all problems or branches of economic theory. The message he sought to convey was that there was such a thing as *economic science relevant to policymaking*, and he thought the best evidence for this claim was that there were some economic laws on which all schools agreed. The disciples of Carl Menger could not subscribe to Ricardo's theory of value, but they could endorse almost everything he had written on political economy.[61] Mises stressed these common points, not because he believed that the remaining disagreements were unimportant, but because he sought to drive home the fact that the practical implications of economics were not just a matter of personal opinion. Interventionism does not work. All economic theory agreed on this point.

---

[60]See in particular Israel Kirzner, "The Austrian School of Economics," *New Palgrave Dictionary of Economics* (New York: Macmillan, 1986); idem, "The Socialist Calculation Debate: Lessons for Austrians," *Review of Austrian Economics* 2 (1987).

[61]Mises later wrote that political economy, "as developed by several generations of English thinkers, brilliantly expounded by Hume and Adam Smith and perfected by Ricardo, was the most exquisite outcome of the philosophy of the Enlightenment." And regarding the classical theory of free trade and protectionism, he observed that the "critics did not embark upon the (hopeless) task of discovering some false syllogisms in the chain of Ricardo's reasoning." Mises, *The Historical Setting of the Austrian School of Economics* (Auburn, Ala.: Ludwig von Mises Institute, [1969] 1984), pp. 20, 23.

Liberalismus

With the analysis of interventionist dynamics, Mises had gained a complete picture of all possible forms of the economic organization for human society. The time was ripe for publishing his first book-length synthesis of the results. He sought to make the case for a free society, a case that was not based on aesthetic or ethical considerations, but on the rock-solid foundation of economic science. From there he would spell out the further implications of the case for liberty in fields such as monopoly and anti-trust, the state, colonialism, democracy, foreign trade, and foreign policy. The book would be a synthesis of his post-World War I writings, summarizing the politically relevant results from *Nation, State, and Economy* as well as from *Socialism* and his more recent writings on interventionism. Mises packed all these subjects into a book of a mere 175 pages and published it in 1927 under the title *Liberalismus*.[62] It remains one of the most important manifestos of political liberalism. It was not addressed to economists or to the larger community of scholars. It did not contain any new contributions to the social sciences. Rather, it was an exposition and application of the state of the art in economic science—a book for the public, for the citizens of Austria and Germany, and for the citizens of the world.

That "state of the art" was largely shaped by Mises's own efforts. *Socialism* had been published five years earlier, and his essay "Interventionismus" had only just appeared in print. But Mises presented his views as being held by "the" liberals, and it was not improper for him to do this. He *had* defined the state of the art. His views on socialism and interventionism were unrefuted and did bring up-to-date the classical-liberal position on both topics. Still, while Mises expounded the views of "the"

---

[62]Mises, *Liberalismus* (Jena: Gustav Fischer, 1927; reprint Sankt Augustin: Academia Verlag, 1993).

classical liberals on property, liberty, peace, equality, government, democracy, socialism, free trade, and so on, what the book essentially did was to give a concise presentation of the results of his own work, spelling out for the first time their political implications in detail.

Mises began his argument by stressing two fundamental facts: first, the division of labor is physically more productive than the work of isolated individuals;[63] second, all men—save a handful of ascetics—prefer a higher productivity of their labor to a lower one. These two facts represented common ground: neither socialists nor fascists denied them. The question then arises, which way of dividing labor is *most* productive? All members of society can agree that this is the decisive question; where they disagree is on which answer is correct. The liberals want to entrust all aspects of the division of labor to the decisions of individuals who work out competing schemes of cooperation based on mutual consent and recognition of private property. The socialists want to expropriate all private property—or at least abolish all private property in the means of production; for them, the division of labor is to be organized by a central plan, which regulates all instances of cooperation between individuals. The social democrats and other partisans of a "Third Way" champion partial expropriations to curb what they believe are the excesses of capitalism.

In light of Mises's insights concerning socialism and interventionism there can be no doubt as to which is the correct answer. Socialism cannot possibly be as productive as capitalism

---

[63]Emphasis on the centrality of this point had a venerable tradition in western thought ever since Saint Thomas Aquinas wrote on the nature of government in the thirteenth century. See Thomas Aquinas, "Über die Herrschaft der Fürsten," F. Schreyvogel, ed., *Staatslehre des Thomas von Aquino* (Jena: Gustav Fischer, 1923), part 1, chap. 1, pp. 11f. It is more than likely that Mises was acquainted with this edition of Saint Thomas's classic work, because it was published in a series under the direction of Othmar Spann.

because it cannot have recourse to monetary calculation and therefore lacks the wherewithal to compare physically heterogeneous production alternatives. Interventionism is intellectually incoherent. It does not achieve the self-proclaimed aims of its champions, which is why even Marx loathed it.[64] And it cannot be the foundation of a permanent economic order because it has the tendency to move toward socialism. The unbiased observer is therefore forced to admit that capitalism is the only rational, productive economic order since all other alternatives squander resources and destroy wealth. One might like capitalism or hate it; one might deem it ethically justified or offensive; the fact is that there is nothing else that can possibly take its place. Economizing and a large-scale division of labor are possible only in a free market based on private property. The free market, then, is necessarily more productive and happiness-enhancing (insofar as happiness is *at all* enhanced by material things) than any other social system.

Hence, the primary goal of liberalism is to ensure a productive division of labor, and the fundamental postulate of its political program is the protection of private property as the means to achieving that goal. All other postulates are secondary. For example, the postulate of personal freedom for all members of society (rejection of slavery) relies on the fact that free men work better than slaves. It is therefore not only in the interest of all other citizens but also in the interest of the slave masters, that the chains of slaves be broken. Similarly, the postulate of legal equality of all men is not based on some notion of natural law according to which all men are born equal. To Mises it was obvious that men are born *unequal*. Still he held that they should enjoy *legal* equality. Why? Because if they were not treated equally before the law—if some have a privileged legal

---

[64]An analysis of Marx's views on interventionism is in Mises, "Marxism and the Labor Movement," *Omnipotent Government* (New Haven, Conn.: Yale University Press, 1944), chap. 7, sect. 2.

position compared to others—then group conflicts are artificially brought about, disturbing the peace that is the very basis for the division of labor.[65] The same consideration applies in the case of democracy. Mises restated the utilitarian justification of democracy that he first presented in *Socialism*. In a letter to Anton Erkelenz, the editor of the influential left-liberal (Naumannian) journal *Die Hilfe*, Mises elaborated on the significance of his approach in the context of the 1920s:

> You claim with some regret that I am "not a democrat as a matter of principle," but only for economic reasons. It is certain that political principles are to be desired or repudiated only from the point of view of their social consequences. Can one refute those opposed to democracy if one cannot offer any argument in favor of democracy other than one claiming that every individual should have the same rights? Does this not leave one defenseless, then, against the objection that human beings are extraordinarily varied and that it is illicit to grant equal rights to the good and the evil? That young academics have turned against democracy is, above all, because the common way of defending democratic principles is thoroughly flawed.[66]

---

[65]Here again Mises championed essentially the same view as Saint Thomas, who stressed that the maintenance of peace was the supreme goal of government, precisely because the fruits of the division of labor could not be obtained otherwise. See Thomas Aquinas, "Über die Herrschaft der Fürsten," part 1, chap. 2, p. 19.

[66]Mises to Erkelenz, undated letter; Mises Archive 56: 6ff. He made the same point in a 1942 lecture on the "principle of equality and social order," in which he distinguished two currents of thought in eighteenth-century liberalism: the natural-law doctrine stressing the inborn equality of men, and the "more realistic" utilitarian point of view: "Men are different, but the laws should not discriminate." See the two versions of his lecture notes contained in Grove City Archive: Mexico 1942 file 3.

He brought the same considerations to bear on the case of fascism, which he emphasized was a movement that arose in reaction to the ruthlessness of the Bolshevist parties organized in the Third International. To the extent that the fascists used naked force to combat the violence of the Bolshevists, Mises said, it was unobjectionable. There was no other remedy against force but force itself. But the danger of the fascists was their blind faith in the omnipotence of this means. Ultimately, peace and social cooperation can only be founded on victories in the realm of ideas.[67] "Fascism was an emergency makeshift. To view it as something more would be a fatal error."[68] Unfortunately, that fatal error was not avoided, and the lesson was not learned. Fascism was not wrong for condoning the use of force (all social systems do), but for idolizing its use.

For Mises, the important lesson was that fascism's error was not in its collectivist roots, but in its rejection of the social

---

[67]Presciently, he stated:

> The victory of Fascism in a number of countries is only an episode in the long series of struggles over the problem of property. The next episode will be the victory of Communism. The ultimate outcome of the struggle, however, will not be decided by arms, but by ideas. It is ideas that group men into fighting factions, that press the weapons into their hands, and that determine against whom and for whom the weapons shall be used. (Mises, *Liberalism: In the Classical Tradition*, Ralph Raico, trans. [Irvington-on-Hudson, N.Y.: Foundation for Economic Education, 1985], p. 51)

[68]This sentence is preceded by the following statement that is often quoted out of context to "demonstrate" the absurd contention that Mises endorsed fascism:

> It cannot be denied that fascism and similar movements aiming at the establishment of dictatorships are full of the best intentions and that their intervention has, for the moment, saved European civilization. The merit that fascism has thereby won for itself will live on eternally in history. But though its policy has brought salvation for the moment, it is not the kind which could promise continued success. (ibid., p. 51)

function of private property. Many modern libertarians still think that capitalism is an outgrowth and reflection of individualism, whereas socialism, both left and right, results from collectivism. Whatever the merits of this view, Mises did not subscribe to it. He stressed that the question of how best to organize the division of labor has nothing to do with the question of whether society should serve the needs of the individual or if the individual should serve society.[69] Neither is there a collectivist science as opposed to individualist sciences. There are only facts and the one true science to deal with them. And to Mises the facts were clear: there is only one way to make society work at all, namely, the mutual respect for private property rights. It is therefore beside the point whether society in some sense precedes the individual or the other way round; it is also irrelevant to ask who should be served by social cooperation since there is only one type of social interaction that merits the name "cooperation" at all.

His book did not have the desired effect. Many years later, Mises wrote in private correspondence that in "Germany and Austria, it had no success, and neither could a Swedish translation stop the drive to the planned economy."[70] A few years later, after Hitler came to power, the authorities ordered the publisher to destroy all remaining copies.[71] ⤳

---

[69]Ibid., p. 60.

[70]Mises to Faustino Ballvé, letter dated October 29, 1949; Grove City Archive: Ballvé files.

[71]Gustav Fischer to Pierre Hamilius, letters dated December 8, 1950 and November 14, 1951; Grove City Archive: Hamilius files. Hamilius sent these letters to Mises following a meeting they had in New York in early September 1959.

Mises lecturing at his NYU seminar in 1960. Henry Hazlitt was a regular participant.

The Mises Dinner Circle in New York in 1959
top, *Mises, Hayek, and Percy Greaves;* middle, *Mises, Bettina Bien Greaves, and Hazlitt;* bottom, *Mises and Hayek*

Portrait of Mises by Gregory Floyd West

14
Booms

THE YEAR 1923 WITNESSED a political paradigm shift in Austria and Germany. Previously, socialism had been an almost nondebatable ideal and inflation an uncontested means of economic policy. After 1923, most Central European intellectuals were disillusioned with the former and outright opposed to the latter. Policy debates had not only shifted topics: they had changed orientation.[1] More and more economists and other social scientists recognized that the use of government to improve social affairs was problematic. A young generation arose that learned to think more critically than their elders about government interventionism and socialist schemes. This burgeoning anti-statist movement was still a minority when it crumbled under the ascent of Hitler in early 1933, but to the very end, it had been a vigorous and growing movement. And there is no doubt that its protagonist was Ludwig von Mises.[2]

---

[1]This is one of the central findings of Irmela Gorges's comprehensive study of the research subjects and methodological orientations of three representative social science organisations of the time: the Verein für Sozialpolitik, the Deutsche Gesellschaft für Soziologie, and the Cologne Forschungsinstitut für Sozialwissenschaften. See Gorges, *Sozialforschung in der Weimarer Republik 1918–1933* (Frankfurt a.M.: Anton Hain, 1986), pp. 694–98.

[2]One observer who met him first as a young man in 1928 would later recall:

The year 1926 brought another improvement in Mises's good fortune. He started cooperating with the Rockefeller Foundation and established an Austrian Institute for Business Cycle Research, which allowed his young political allies—most notably Friedrich Hayek—to earn a living in economic research. In the following years, Mises also became involved with various European free-trade organizations and used the International Chamber of Commerce as a platform for networking and for promoting classical-liberal policies. But because none of his major writings had been translated into French or English, his primary influence remained limited to Germany and Austria. What could be called the first Mises Revolution took place between 1929 and 1932, during which time he became a board member of the *Verein für Sozialpolitik*, his works were discussed in all major economics textbooks, and more and more young economists were pursuing Misesian themes in their research.

It was also in these years that Mises completed his system of thought—at least in broad strokes—with a series of path-breaking essays on value theory and on the epistemology of economics. Had it not been for the rise of Hitler, this quiet revolution would have had a significant impact on the German world. Instead, these ideas had to wait for another place and time—the

---

What Edwin Cannan has been for England, Frank H. Knight for the USA and Luigi Einaudi for Italy, Ludwig von Mises was for the German speaking world: Austria, Germany and Switzerland, the initiator for a renaissance of liberalism and the market economy. (Albert Hunold, editorial of *The Mont Pèlerin Quarterly* 3, no. 3 [October 1961]: 3)

This leadership in policy debate was based on similar leadership in the field of positive analysis, as can be inferred from a 1925 *festschrift* for Lujo Brentano that set out to portray the state of the art in economics after World War I. Here Mises figures among the thirteen most-cited authors, along with Böhm-Bawerk, Brentano, Cassel, Eulenburg, Keynes, Marx, J.S. Mill, Ricardo, Schumpeter, Sombart, Spann, Walras, and Wieser. See Moritz J. Bonn and Melchior Palyi, *Die Wirtschaftswissenschaft nach dem Kriege* (Leipzig: Duncker & Humblot, 1925).

United States in the 1950s—to become the basis of a second Mises Revolution.

1926 Journeys

The 1926 congress of the International Chamber of Commerce took place in the United States, and Mises made his way across the Atlantic for the first time. He left by way of London, where he met Cannan and Robbins at a critical juncture in the history of LSE's economics department.

Lionel Robbins had returned to LSE from Oxford the previous fall and his continued interest in Austrian economics and in Mises's work in particular would become highly important in the coming years.

Mises in 1926

Edwin Cannan, however, offered less promising news. He was about to retire, and LSE's management planned to hire the Harvard professor Allyn Young as his successor. Young was known as a diehard positivist, and he was expected to make the economics department a center for the transformation of economic science into applied mathematics. This had been a longstanding plan of the socialist founders of the school, and of the New York-based Laura Spelman Memorial, which donated large sums to LSE for research on the "natural bases" of economics.[3,4] Mises must

---

[3]See William H. Beveridge, *The London School of Economics and Its Problems, 1919–1937* (London: Allen & Unwin, 1960), esp. pp. 50, 83, 85, 88ff., 109. The founders of LSE were Sidney and Beatrice Webb. The Laura Spelman Memorial was named after the wife of John D. Rockefeller, and later absorbed into the Rockefeller Foundation. In 1923–1924, LSM donated almost $100,000 to LSE; in 1926, it gave another $500,000 for research on the "natural bases" of economics, and $175,000 for other projects.

[4]The idea that economics could be turned into applied mathematics or applied biology is a good illustration of Keynes's famous dictum that each

have seen dark clouds over London as he sailed for New York. Eventually, however, two events slowed the pace of LSE's transformation: Young's unexpected death in 1929, and Lionel Robbins's conversion to Austrian economics.

Mises remained in the States for about two months.[5] Besides his participation in the ICC meeting, he made various public appearances, which at least in part had the purpose of attracting U.S. investors to Austria. By the time of Mises's visit, Austria was enjoying a good press in the United States thanks to the public-relations efforts by Mises and others. He must have noticed with satisfaction that the U.S. Department of Commerce circulated reports stating that Austria

> during 1925 maintained in general the advance made in 1924 and in several respects made considerable progress—especially in fiscal, currency, and credit matters—according to the annual report of the Board of Directors of the Austrian National Bank.[6]

In New York City, he also met the leadership of the Rockefeller Foundation and seems to have made an excellent impression. The

---

generation labors under the ideas "of some defunct economist." See John Maynard Keynes, *General Theory of Employment, Interest, and Money* (Cambridge: Cambridge University Press, [1936] 1973), p. 383. William Stanley Jevons and his followers such as Edgeworth had been very influential within British academia in pressing the case for mathematics in economic science. The great champion of the case for biology was Alfred Marshall: "The Mecca of the economist lies in economic biology rather than in economic dynamics" (*Principles of Economics: An Introductory Volume*, 8th ed. [London: Macmillan, 1920], p. xiv). Keynes knew what he was talking about.

[5]He had a mailbox with the Laura Spelman Rockefeller Memorial in New York City. See Mises to Brodnitz, letter dated February 26, 1926; Mises Archive 80: 20.

[6]See the Department's report in Mises Archive 57: 79; see also the Baker-Kellog investment letter, dated April 24, 1926; Mises Archive 57: 70. Mises obtained this letter apparently through a certain Mr. W.W. Welsh in Chicago.

timing could not have been better, for shortly after Mises's return to Vienna, Friedrich von Wieser died and Mises became the foundation's main contact among Vienna's economists.[7] He later recalled that the Rockefeller Foundation had "taken a kind interest in my teaching and research work."[8] In Austria, Mises had a decisive influence on the selection of the future Rockefeller Fellows. When he moved to Geneva, the foundation paid his salary at the Graduate Institute for International Studies, and when he eventually moved to the United States, the foundation provided again the lion's share of his income during the first four years.

The acquaintances he made in New York had made his trip a splendid success, but the reactions of academic audiences must have been disappointing. In American universities, there was a marked lack of interest in theoretical work and exaggerated hopes for empirical research, particularly in statistical studies.

Mises had already noticed, in meetings of the International Chamber of Commerce, an ever-greater number of American representatives championing interventionist views. His stay in the United States confirmed his impression that Americans were abandoning liberalism. Back in Vienna, he summarized his impressions in several lectures, in particular in a talk on "Changes in American Economic Policy," which he delivered in November 1926 before a relatively small circle of top Austrian

---

[7]"After the death of Böhm-Bawerk and Wieser . . . Mises was manifestly the leader of the school" (Fritz Machlup, "Ludwig von Mises: The Academic Scholar Who Would Not Compromise," *Wirtschaftspolitische Blätter* 28, no. 4 [1981]: 9). See also Werner Neudeck, "Der Einfluss von Ludwig von Mises auf die Österreichische akademische Tradition gestern und heute," ibid., p. 27.

[8]Mises to U.S. Department of State, letter dated December 20, 1941; Grove City Archive: Mexico 1942 files. The local coordinator for the Rockefeller Foundation in Vienna was British-born Alfred Francis Pribram (not related to Karl and Ewald Pribram).

entrepreneurs in the *Industrieller Klub*. In December he lectured
to a larger audience on the less sensitive topic of "America and
the Reconstruction of the European Economy."[9]

On the ship back to Europe, Mises read the proof pages of
his "*Sozialliberalismus*" and was already planning his longer
work on interventionism, which he eventually delivered at an
October conference in Rotterdam.[10,11] Before leaving for the
Netherlands, however, he attended two conferences: John Maynard Keynes's lecture at the University of Berlin and the 1926
plenary meeting of the *Verein für Sozialpolitik* in Vienna.

Mises traveled to Berlin sometime in early September
1926.[12] Keynes's lecture was based on his book, *The End of Laissez-Faire*, which had been published two months earlier. In the
mid-1920s, Keynes already enjoyed an excellent reputation in
Germany. He had been among the first western intellectuals to
criticize the Treaty of Versailles, which in his view was a manifesto of shortsighted vengefulness. He also thought it was
impossible to implement in practice.[13] Thereafter, his writings
were eagerly translated into German, and several German

---

[9]This lecture was delivered to the German *Hauptverband der Industrie* in
Czechoslovakia. See Mises to *Magazin der Wirtschaft*, letter dated December
20, 1926; Mises Archive 80: 10.

[10]Mises Archive 57: 65ff.; 83a.

[11]He probably also delivered a version of this paper, in the fall of the same
year, in a two-hour lecture on "Government and the National Economy." He
gave the talk at a summer university designed for American students visiting
Vienna (*Internationale Hochschulkurse*). See Mises to Martha Stefanie Braun,
letter dated July 20, 1926; Mises Archive 83: 59.

[12]Mises to Brodnitz, letter dated September 16, 1926; Mises Archive 80: 5.

[13]John Maynard Keynes, *The Economic Consequences of the Peace* (New
York: Harcourt, Brace and Howe, 1920). For a critique of the fundamental
errors in Keynes's assessment of Germany's ability to comply with the
Treaty's economic stipulations (war reparations), see Henry Hazlitt, "The
1919 Prophecies of Maynard Keynes," *New York Times Book Review* (March
11, 1945), p. 5; Etienne Mantoux, *The Carthaginian Peace or The Economic
Consequences of Mr. Keynes* (Oxford: Oxford University Press, 1946).

economists attended his courses in Cambridge. Mises later recalled that Keynes was himself influenced by the *katheder* socialists, who he eventually "outdid . . . in many points."[14] His new book would endear Keynes even more to the German public, especially to his German colleagues, who had cultivated a tradition of criticizing what they believed to be the many shortcomings of liberty.[15]

John Maynard Keynes

The End of Laissez-Faire reads like a parody of anti-liberalism. For example, Keynes listed several features of real-world economies that did not fit the model of "perfect competition," and then went on to claim that these were problems for *laissez-faire* rather than for the perfect-competition concept itself.[16] Anticipating the views he would

---

[14]Mises to Montes de Oca, letter dated February 26, 1949; Grove City Archive: Montes de Oca files.

[15]To what extent Keynes was welcomed with open arms can be gathered from Friedrich von Wieser's endorsement in his very last work, of Keynes's proposals for replacing the gold exchange standard by fiat paper money:

> An economist with the broad vision and scientific acuity of Keynes could raise the question of whether it would be possible to replace the gold standard altogether with another system that would allow for stable exchange rates at lower costs. (Friedrich von Wieser, "Theorie des Geldes," *Handwörterbuch der Staatswissenschaften*, 4th ed. [Jena: Gustav Fischer, 1927], vol. 4, p. 716)

[16]These complications arise, according to Keynes,

> (1) when the efficient units of production are large relative to the units of consumption . . . , (2) when overhead costs or joint costs are present, (3) when internal economies tend to the aggregation of production, (4) when the time required for adjustments is long, (5) when ignorance prevails over knowledge, and (6) when monopolies and combinations interfere with equality in bargaining. (John Maynard Keynes, *The End of Laissez-Faire* [London: Hogarth Press, 1926], pp. 32f.)

expound in more detail ten years later in his *General Theory*, he argued that many of "the greatest evils of our time are the fruits of risk, uncertainty, and ignorance," as if these would be banished by socialism or interventionism. Keynes did not seem to realize how absurd this diagnosis of "contemporary" social problems was.

To cope with the universal problems of human existence, Keynes advocated the following policies: (1) "deliberate control of the currency and of credit by a central institution," (2) "collection and dissemination on a great scale of data relating to the business situation, including full publicity, by law if necessary, of all business facts which it is useful to know," (3) complete control of savings and investment, and (4) control of the population. This last point required, according to Keynes, that the government try to control both the number and the quality of its population—much as a breeder controls livestock.[17]

Mises was thoroughly unimpressed by Keynes's case against *laissez-faire*. As he later wrote in a review of the event, the intellectual significance of Keynes's book was negligible. Its author had merely restated arguments that had been advanced and refuted many times in the past.[18] What made Keynes important were his personality and the prestige he enjoyed from his status at the University of Cambridge. This prestige had been further enhanced by his critique of the Treaty of Versailles, which had gained him an international reputation as an impartial observer.

When Mises returned to Vienna, Richard Schüller caused a scandal at the *Verein für Sozialpolitik* through his account of the

---

[17]Ibid., pp. 47f.

[18]Mises, "Das Ende des Laissez-Faire, Ideen zur Verbindung von Privat- und Gemeinwirtschaft" (The end of laissez-faire: ideas for combining the private and public economy), *Zeitschrift für die gesamte Staatswissenschaft* 82 (1927): 190–91. Apparently, Mises sent a pre-publication copy of this review to Gregory in London; see Mises Archive 83: 58.

cause for growing unemployment in Germany and Austria.[19] He argued that the permanent unemployment resulted from the consolidation of political power for both labor unions and entrepreneurs. Organized labor and organized capital had eclipsed the self-healing processes of markets, which involved falling prices and wages rates.[20] These statements offended many of the assembled economists, but it was no longer taboo to bring them up. The *Verein* moved slowly, but it was moving in the direction of the free-market radicals. This intellectual change was reflected in the improved social standing of former outcasts such as Mises. Even left-wingers such as the young Adolf Löwe in Kiel now maintained friendly relations with the Vienna champion of *laissez-faire*.[21]

Institute for Business Cycle Research

One thing that impressed Mises on his 1926 trip to America was the empirical research on business cycles conducted at Harvard University. More precisely, he was impressed by the commercial success of the monthly reports. The price of an annual subscription was on the order of $100, a small fortune at the time.[22] Many years later, a member of the sales team that

---

[19]Mises was probably in attendance, but it is possible that he was among those "Austrian gentlemen" who reportedly did not attend the sessions they were supposed to attend, to the great dismay of the *Verein*'s secretary, Franz Boese.

[20]Franz Boese, *Geschichte des Vereins für Sozialpolitik, 1872–1932* (Berlin: Duncker & Humblot, 1939), pp. 194f.

[21]Immediately after the 1926 *Verein für Sozialpolitik* meeting in Vienna, Mises recommended Konrad Zweig to Adolf Löwe for a position in Kiel. Zweig was just about to receive his doctorate. Mises knew him from his University seminar. Löwe eventually hired Zweig, emphasizing the "angenehmen Beziehungen" (pleasant relationship) he had established with Mises. See Löwe to Mises, letter dated October 2, 1926; Mises Archive 80: 17f.

[22]One hundred dollars could buy roughly five ounces of gold, thus at present (February 2006) more than $2,500.

marketed these reports, Frederick Nymeyer, would become a devoted Misesian and set up the Libertarian Press, a publishing house to disseminate Mises's writings. Mises did not meet Nymeyer in 1926, but his trip to Harvard provided the inspiration to establish a similar institute in Austria. His idea was to use the money generated through the sale of reports to fund young libertarian intellectuals, who had little chance of obtaining one of the rare positions at public universities.

Vienna enjoyed a living scientific tradition and still attracted great numbers of excellent students. But the Austrian government's financial calamities after World War I made it impossible to exploit this potential; whatever private means had once been available had been eaten up by the inflation of the early 1920s. The result was a shortage of research positions. The selection of candidates and the funding of research projects were increasingly a function of party allegiance. The universities were politicized in general, but particularly so in the social sciences.

In this context, the establishment of private research institutions that financed themselves by the sale of products, rather than by state funds, offered an attractive alternative. Mises had thoroughly prepared the project, studying the operation and organization of comparable foreign institutes and consulted with experts throughout the world. In fact, he was not the first to think along these lines. The League of Nations had for some years encouraged the creation of business cycle institutes in the United States and in Europe.[23] After Harvard (1919), the NBER (established by Mitchell in 1921) and London (1922), the wave had spread to Germany with establishments in Berlin,

---

[23]See Manfred Mautner and Franz Nemschak, *Zum 25 jährigen Bestand des Österreichischen Institutes für Wirtschaftsforschung* (Vienna: Österreichisches Institut für Wirtschaftsforschung, 1952), p. 9. The study of business cycles was at the time one of the most fashionable topics and one that seemed to be relevant for international economic cooperation. The League's initiative could rely on funding by the Rockefeller Foundation.

Hamburg, Kiel, and Essen (all in 1925). In the same year, a group of businessmen and academics had set up a private *Konjunktur-Gesellschaft* as a department of the Frankfurt chamber of commerce, which in turn was affiliated with the Frankfurt stock exchange. The director of the Society was Eugen Altschul, who personally trained young economists in statistics and other methods used in Anglo-Saxon-style business cycle research. Similarly, another group of young men around Paul Lazarsfeld would establish a private institute of consumer research in Vienna a few years later, with Mises on its board.

In the fall of 1926, Mises coordinated the final preparations for the establishment of the *Österreiches Konjunkturforschungsinstitut*—the Austrian Institute for Business Cycle Research (hereafter "*Institut*").[24] The composition of the board (the *Kuratorium*) reflected Mises's connections as well as the need to involve, at least nominally, all major stakeholders. Mises found academic front men in Hans Mayer and Karl Pribram; obtained funds from his friends in the Vienna community of bankers and industrialists such as Viktor Graetz, Helene Lieser, and Gustav Weiss-Wellenstein; received support from *Kammer* colleagues such as Otto Geiringer and Emil Perels, as well as from the *Kammer* itself, which provided office space. Other board seats were occupied by representatives of public administrations such as the Chamber of Labor, the *Nationalbank* and the federal railways. Chairman of the Board was Richard Reisch. Mises himself was one of the two vice chairmen, but he was in fact the main force behind the new organization.

---

[24]From a legal point of view, the *Institut* was set up as a private association and publicly registered on December 2, 1926. See the copy of the bylaws in Mises Archive 57: 85ff. On the early years of the Institut, see Mautner and Nemschak, *Zum 25 jährigen Bestand des Österreichischen Institutes für Wirtschaftsforschung*; see also Carl Theodore Schmitt, "The Austrian Institute for Business Cycle Research," *Journal of Political Economy* 39, no. 1 (February 1931): 101–03.

The *Institut* had an executive committee chaired by a Kammer representative. But its daily operations were in the hands of an executive with the title of Director. Mises made sure that Hayek would be appointed to this position. At first, his most important duty was to insure the publication of the *Institut*'s main product: the monthly reports on Austrian business conditions, which he fashioned after the three-curve barometer of the Harvard Committee of Economic Research. Hayek himself wrote the first, very lengthy report, which contained a detailed description of the definitions and quantitative methodologies used in the Institut's research activities. Over the years, he relied more and more on contributions from others. By April 1931, the monthly reports of the *Institut* had a circulation of 500 copies.[25] In the fall of that year, Hayek left Vienna to become a professor of economics in London and Morgenstern assumed leadership of the *Institut*.

In addition to the monthly reports, the *Institut* had the mission of organizing meetings and lectures, and to act as a focal point for further research in theoretical economics. Thanks to funding from the Rockefeller Foundation, it also published a series of monographs on problems of business cycle theory that became the most visible outlet for the work of the coming generation of Austrian economists.[26]

---

[25]Mohr/Siebeck to Mises, letter dated April 25, 1931; Mises Archive 93: 13.

[26]The Rockefeller Foundation provided funding from 1929 to 1938. See Mautner and Nemschak, *Zum 25jährigen Bestand des Österreichischen Institutes für Wirtschaftsforschung*, p. 12. The first seven volumes in this series have passed the test of time and are today classics of Austrian economics: F.A. Hayek's *Geldtheorie und Konjunkturtheorie* (1929); Fritz Machlup's *Börsenkredit, Industriekredit und Kapitalbildung* (1931), Hayek's *Preise und Produktion* (1933), Erich Schiff's *Kapitalbildung und Kapitalaufzehrung im Konjunkturverlauf* (1933), Oskar Morgenstern's *Grenzen der Wirtschaftspolitik* (1934), Machlup's *Führer durch die Krisenpolitik* (1934), and Richard Strigl's *Kapital und Produktion* (1934). After Mises's departure from Vienna in 1934, Morgenstern, who in 1931 had succeeded Hayek as the director of the Institute, began to publish works with a markedly less Austrian orientation:

It was the only institution that Mises ever established and it turned out to be a great success. Mises set it up as a private association, which secured a maximum of political independence. Many years later, the then director of the *Institut* acknowledged that the private character of his institution was the basis for the constructive role it played in Austrian politics. He also mentioned that in difficult times he found inspiration and encouragement in reading Mises's inaugural speech, in which he had made the case for independence.[27]

Austrian Politics at the Onset of the Gold-Exchange Standard

The establishment of the *Institut* and the beginning of Mises's liaison with the Rockefeller Foundation coincided with a fundamental change of the business environment in Austria. The Geneva Protocols of October 1922 and the simultaneous currency reform had eliminated the government's financial disasters, but came at the price of Austria's sovereignty. Inflation continued but at a much lower pace, while unemployment soared from 49,000 in 1922 to 150,000 in 1925. Red Vienna and other socialist municipalities grew larger with the help of foreign loans. Business expanded too, especially because the financial and industrial community in Vienna had successfully renewed its prewar ties with other regions of the former Austro-Hungarian

---

Ragnar Nurkse's *Internationale Kapitalbewegungen* (1935), Gerhard Tintner's *Die Preise im Konjunkturverlauf* (1935), and Abraham Wald's *Berechnung und Ausschaltung von Saisonschwankungen* (1936). Apart from this series of monographs, the most important outlet for theoretical research was the *Zeitschrift für Nationalökomonie* (established in 1930), which under the editorship of Hans Mayer featured many pioneering articles on the role of time in economics, on equilibrium analysis, on capital theory, and on business cycle theory.

[27]Franz Nemschak to Mises, letter dated January 3, 1964; Grove City Archive: Österreichisches Institut für Wirtschaftsforschung files.

Empire. The wounds the war had left in the social fabric of Central Europe seemed to be healing. The quiet growth began to leave its mark on Austrian psychology. Many now believed that the country was destined to act as intermediary between East and West. Optimism and wishful thinking combined in extrapolating the debt-financed expansion into an indefinite future.

These fantasies were crushed by the establishment of the gold exchange standard in 1925. The new monetary system stimulated the international division of labor and brought greater growth to all participating countries. But it also exposed mercilessly the limits of their interventionist governments.[28] International competition drove down prices, and while the consumers rejoiced, firms found it nearly impossible to cut costs accordingly because of labor-union power and entrenched economic regulations.

> The inflation of the early 1920s reduced the harm done by labor unions and regulations because rising costs were paired with rising prices. But with the return to an international gold standard in 1925 sales prices stabilized and even decreased, while there was still no downward flexibility on the cost of labor. Doing business in Austria became ever more difficult and discouraging. Industrial firms found it harder to raise new funds through equity capital or bonds. Labor unions, local politicians, and newspapers began pressuring the banks to fill the gap. They "had to fulfill an economic duty" of bailing out "the threatened firms during bad times."[29]

---

[28]Mises later summarized the experience of the second half of the 1920s in a report to the Austrian government that he co-authored at the government's behest in 1930. See Redaktionskomitee der Wirtschaftskommission, *Bericht über die Ursachen der wirtschaftlichen Schwierigkeiten Österreichs* (Vienna: Staatsdruckerei, 1930).

[29]Rudolf Sieghart, *Die letzten Jahrzehnte einer Grossmacht* (Berlin: Ullstein, 1932), p. 195. Sieghart went on:

This was the context in which Mises wrote and spoke during the second half of the 1920s on monetary problems and public finance. Shortly after the creation of the *Institut*, he gave a widely publicized public address on the consequences of Austria's interventionist policies.[30] Mises argued that, after a year of doing business under the gold standard, the time had come for a sober analysis of the impact of Austrian economic policies. The effects of inflation on business accounting had been exhausted and the new gold-denominated balance sheets provided a more realistic picture of the state of the economy. The past policies had not merely taxed the income streams of business, but had actually eaten up their capital.[31]

Mises demanded an immediate reduction of taxes and of the companies' contributions to the government's social insurance schemes. He also called for the privatization of public firms such as postal savings offices, railroads, postal and telegram services, forestry, and coal and steel firms, arguing that their deficits amounted to more than 170 million schillings, which was more than the federal government's 1927 budget deficit of 135 million schillings.[32] This calamity, Mises argued, was the

---

Later these same circles reproached the directors of the bank [he means the large and influential Boden-Credit-Anstalt, which he directed in those years] with having too generously complied with the credit wishes of these same industries.

[30]He delivered the address to the plenary meeting of the *Niederösterreichischen Gewerbeverein* (Commercial Association of Lower Austria). A copy of the published version of his talk is in Mises Archive 62: 41.

[31]Prior to 1925, tax laws and other regulations prohibited Austrian firms from calculating capital consumption in terms of gold prices. The legally permissible balance sheets therefore presented an unrealistically optimistic picture of the firms. See Redaktionskomitee der Wirtschaftskommission, *Bericht über die Ursachen der wirtschaftlichen Schwierigkeiten Österreichs*, p. 12.

[32]Also, because of the rent control laws, the local, state, and federal governments, which already in 1914 owned more than half of all urban rental housing, significantly reduced their income.

inevitable result of two entirely incorrect principles of public finance: that (1) public expenditure comes first, and public income follows public expenditure; and (2) taxation of capital and private enterprise does not affect the broad masses of the people.

The proposal to privatize the deficit-prone public firms was a slap in the face of the statists in all parties. The main bastion of statism was Otto Bauer's socialist party, and one of their preferred means of political "persuasion" was the open threat of violent insurrection. A few months after Mises's talk, however, the credibility of those threats received a serious setback in a showdown between the socialists and the Vienna police. The event occurred in the wake of a questionable court decision that had, in the socialists' view, been slanted in favor of a political right-winger. The socialists now called for a general strike and demonstrations on Friday July 15, 1927. To the government, this was a thinly disguised attempt at its overthrow.[33] When the crowd gathered in front of the palace that hosted the department of justice, someone set the building on fire and the police stepped in immediately. In the resulting carnage, ninety demonstrators were killed even before the army arrived. Mises commented in a private letter to a former student in Paris:

> Friday's putsch has cleansed the atmosphere like a thunderstorm. The social-democratic party has used all means of power and yet lost the game. The street

---

[33]In those days, demonstrations were armed demonstrations as a matter of course. The socialist party had its own private army, the *Republikanische rSchutzbund* or "republican alliance for mutual protection." Established in 1924, it counted some 80,000 men in 1928; see Ernst Hoor, *Österreich 1918–1938* (Vienna: Bundesverlag für Unterricht, Wissenschaft und Kunst, 1966), p. 101. Similarly, on the other side of the political spectrum, there was the *Heimwehr* or "home defence" movement, a private military organisation that had emerged shortly after 1918 and which later split into a patriotic "Austrian" and a national socialist wing; in September 1933, the Austrian wing joined the new *Vaterländische Front* or "patriotic front."

fight ended in complete victory of the police. . . . All troops are loyal to the government.

The general strike has collapsed and the leaders of the social democrats then had to cancel it.

The threats by which the social-democratic party has up to now permanently tried to bully the government and the public have proved to be far less dangerous than one had believed.[34]

The failure of the general strike and the accompanying massacre also had an unexpected personal impact on Mises's life, as we will see at the end of the present chapter.

Free Trade, Monetary Stabilization, and Cyclical Policy

Mises was reluctant to become involved in any organized political campaign. In a November 1924 letter, he declined an honorary executive position in an Austrian free-trade association, stating, "As a matter of principle, I do not belong to any political or economic-political organizations."[35] This attitude changed over the next couple of years, as he enjoyed the early successes of the European free-trade movement. But his original apprehensions proved correct and his involvement, while intense and high profile, was also short-lived. Among his international associates in the movement, he saw political maneuvering, nepotism, and other forms of questionable behavior at the expense of the free-trade cause. Mises waited for the right opportunity to take his leave.

---

[34]Mises to Steiner, letter dated July 21, 1927; Mises Archive: 62: 20. Fritz Georg Steiner had been one of the top students in Mises's seminar at the University of Vienna. See Martha Steffy Browne [Braun], "Erinnerungen an das Mises-Privatseminar," *Wirtschaftspolitische Blätter* 28, no. 4 (1981): 111.

[35]Mises to Freihandelsbund gegen Teuerung und Wirtschaftszwang, letter dated November 11, 1924; Mises Archive 80: 60.

The opportunity came when the International Committee of the *Europäischer Zoll-Verein*—the European free trade organization of which Mises had founded the Austrian chapter— campaigned against Austria's annexation to the German Reich (the *Anschluss* question). Neither Mises nor his Austrian colleagues could afford to be associated with either side of the dispute, and when the committee ignored Mises's urging to withdraw from its campaign, Mises left the organization in February 1929.

Disillusioned with the official free-trade movement, Mises returned his focus to the battle of ideas.

ക്ക   ക്ക   ക്ക

At the height of his involvement with the *Europäischer Zoll-Verein*, Mises had written an update of his theory of money in light of more recent developments, to take account in particular of the workings of the gold-exchange standard.

In February 1928, he published a concise presentation of the main events in the modern history of money for a more general public.[36] A few weeks after this publication, he was in the process of completing a monograph on monetary stabilization and economic policy designed to combat business cycles. On March 17, he offered the manuscript to Gustav Fischer. Mises emphasized that the time was right for such a book, both because of the increased general interest in business cycles and because the *Verein für Sozialpolitik* would deal with these problems at their annual meeting in the fall.[37] Fischer was convinced. *Geldwertstabilisierung und Konjunkturpolitik* (Monetary

---

[36]Mises, "Die Lehre vom Gelde," *Forschungen und Fortschritte* (Berlin, February 1928).

[37]Mises to Fischer, letter dated March 17, 1928; Mises Archive 87a: 17.

Stabilization and Cyclical Policy) was sent to bookstores on May 22.[38]

In the book, Mises delivered a systematic critique of Irving Fisher's views on monetary reform, which had gained great support in the world of academic economists. It had prompted men such as John Maynard Keynes and Gustav Cassel to endorse similar schemes. According to Fisher, the deficiency of commodity money—such as gold and silver coins—was that it did not provide a standard of constant purchasing power. As a consequence, long-term investment and contracts for deferred payments involved excessive risk. His proposed solution was to replace the gold standard with a currency of stable purchasing power as defined by a price index.

Mises pointed out that stability of the purchasing power of money was not a requisite of capital-intensive production. Market participants could very well take account of expected changes in the purchasing power of money when they made any long-term investments or contracts. Moreover, because the purchasing power of money could not be defined without arbitrary assumptions, Fisher's index-number standard would not be different in essence from the prevailing commodity standards. In terms of an arbitrary index number it might be stable, but no price index could possibly represent the relevant purchases of all market participants. So any single index number would necessarily fail to stabilize purchasing power for many market participants. Fisher's scheme could not possibly establish money of stable value, but only a transfer of value other than that which would occur on the free market.

---

[38]Mises received a fee of 550 marks. He had Fischer send him a check from a German bank. Fischer sent 15 complimentary copies directly to their recipients, and 15 complimentary and 10 more paid copies to Mises. See the correspondence in Mises Archive 87a: 3, 7.

The crucial issue from Mises's point of view was not value stability but distribution. While it was certainly true that the gold standard did not produce stable purchasing power, its virtue was that its distribution effects were free from political interference. Any artificial currency such as paper money would constantly invite political manipulation and thus lead to a redistribution of resources based on political bargaining power rather than the will of consumers.

Fisher had completely overlooked this problem. Like all those who endorsed price stabilization, he focused exclusively on redistribution resulting from variations of the price level. But as Mises showed, this problem was already addressed in the market and expressed as "price premiums" in the gross interest rate. But there was no such counterbalance for the redistribution that resulted from "Cantillon effects"—new money reaching different market participants at different times. Fisher's diagnosis did not cover this problem and his scheme for monetary reform ignored it.

In the second part of the book, Mises presented a revised version of his business-cycle theory. He introduced the distinction between two types of inflation: inflation of fiduciary media and inflation of money proper. Mises argued that the *recurrence* of the business cycle—its cyclical nature—resulted exclusively from the inflation of fiduciary media. Increases of the money supply were more or less one-time shots. They could entail malinvestment, but this was only one time for all. In contrast, there was a tendency to repeat experiments with fiduciary media, because businessmen and politicians believed that the issuance of additional fiduciary media was a suitable way to reduce interest rates.[39] With this explanation Mises complemented his previous analyses of the business cycle, which had

---

[39]Mises, *Geldwertstabilisierung und Konjunkturpolitik* (Jena: Gustav Fischer, 1928), p. 58.

focused on the process linking boom and bust, but which had not yet included an explanation of the *recurrence* of cycles.

Mises also radicalized his praise for free banking. In the second edition of his treatise on money he had said that future money reformers would be well advised to reconsider the case for free banking. Now he added that, historically, fiduciary media have become a large-scale problem only because the state had gotten involved in banking. Governments privileged certain banks with a monopoly on note issuance; they also intervened to bail out these banks when the fractional-reserve scheme collapsed in bank runs. As a consequence, the crises of fractional-reserve banking had reached far greater proportions than they would have in a free market. And the cooperation between (fractional-reserve) central banks—which had been reinforced in the wake of the 1922 Genoa conference and which had become standard practice under the gold-exchange standard— only further increased the dimensions of the problem.

Free banking would have minimized these crises. But Mises did not believe that it was possible to overcome the political resistance against the establishment of this system. He hoped that monetary policymakers would be wiser in the future and heed the teachings of his business-cycle theory.[40]

The New Theoreticians

Mises's hope for a wiser future monetary policy did not seem quite as naïve at the time as it now seems in retrospect. The year 1928 marked the high point of his influence on German monetary thought. The majority of the contributions to the meeting of the *Verein für Sozialpolitik* in Zurich elaborated on his writings. One of the many participants from Vienna later recalled: "In the year 1928, almost all professors and other members held

---

[40]Ibid., pp. 61, 65f., 73ff., 81ff.

Mises in high esteem and admired him."[41] Another sign of his influence was the international recognition he received on a May 1928 lecture tour in England.

Mises visited England just when his new book on monetary stabilization was about to come out. He had already written his lectures, which dealt with "private property and socialism," and he offered the manuscript to the University of London Press for publication. The Press eventually declined, saying the manuscript was not voluminous enough.[42]

Still, the 1928 lecture tour marked one of the high points of the golden age of the Vienna-London "Austrian axis." Mises later recalled that he had first joined the British Royal Economic Society in the 1920s because it did not yet promote a left-wing agenda. "At the time Lionel Robbins and Sir William (now Lord) Beveridge were dubbed 'Austrians' by their critics because they agreed with me."[43]

A few months after Mises's lecture tour in England, the annual convention of the *Verein für Sozialpolitik* was held in Zurich. The subject of the discussions, "goals and methods of business-cycle research," had been determined at the 1926 Vienna meeting. Already at that point, it was clear that the second edition of *Theory of Money and Credit* had been received far more positively than the 1912 edition. General experience with wartime inflation and postwar hyperinflation had made the

---

[41]Browne [Braun], "Erinnerungen an das Mises-Privatseminar," p. 116. See also Gertrud Pütz-Neuhauser, "Zur Entwicklung der Konjunkturtheorie im deutschen Sprachraum in der Zwischenkriegszeit," B. Schefold, ed., *Studien zur Entwicklung der ökonomischen Theorie VIII* (Berlin: Duncker & Humblot, 1989), pp. 97f. The conference was attended by about 300 participants.

[42]University of London Press to Mises, letter dated May 25, 1928; Mises Archive 62: 69.

[43]Mises to Frederick Nymeyer, letter dated May 14, 1953; Grove City Archive: Nymeyer files. He had also joined the American Economic Association, for the same reasons.

Meeting of the Verein für Socialpolitik, *at the University of Zurich, September 11–13, 1928.* Third and fourth rows include: *Sombart, Hayek, Machlup, Mayer, Strigl, Degenfeld, Mises, Spitzmüller, Bettelheim, Hunold.* Top two rows include: *Morgenstern, Schams, Löwe, Rosenstein-Rodan, Rüstow, Dietze*

Misesian message—that business cycles were the result of fiduciary credit—more palatable to a broad public. In the following years the popularity of the monetary theory of the trade cycle increased to such an extent that, by 1933, Mises himself believed that it had become the dominant theory in Germany and Austria.[44]

The 1928 Zurich meeting was an important milestone in this progress. In preparation for the meeting, the *Verein*'s subcommittee on economic theory published a 370-page volume on

---

[44]Mises to Ugo Papi, letter dated March 17, 1933; Mises Archive 94: 3. In his 1922 *Habilitation* monograph on business cycles, Wilhelm Röpke did not even mention Mises; see Wilhelm Röpke, *Die Konjunktur* (Jena: Gustav Fischer, 1922). Ten years later, he had read the Austrians; see his *Krise und Konjunktur* (Leipzig: Quelle & Meyer, 1932). He had first met Mises in 1922 at the meeting of the *Verein*. In the early 1920s, he worked in the German reparations office. It is likely that he often met Mises at international conferences dealing with war debt.

business cycle theory, containing papers written predominantly by economists of the rising generation—those who had turned away from historicism toward the study of theoretical problems. Among them were Eucken, Hayek, Hahn, Löwe, and Kuczynski. Mises himself took an active part in the sessions and concluded with the statement that the present discussion was a proof of progress, even though no agreement had been reached and many problems still remained. Only sixteen years earlier, he had been the only German to develop the monetary theory of the trade cycle. He was proud that many of his ideas, rejected at the time, were now commonplace for the majority of economists. The progress was even more pronounced when the comparison was to the meeting of 1903 (twenty-five years earlier), which was the only other time the *Verein* had even dealt with the problem of economic crises.[45]

A few months later, Mises was one of six new members elected to the board of the *Verein*.[46] Although he himself did not

---

[45]Mises Archive 22: 8ff. At the heart of the German-language debate on business cycle theory in the late 1920s was the question whether this theory was, or could be, part of Léon Walras's general equilibrium theory; or whether it required a different approach. Christof Rühl discusses the approaches of Hayek, Löwe, Lutz, and Schumpeter, in Rühl, "Der Beitrag deutschsprachiger Ökonomen zur konjunkturtheoretischen Debatte der Zwischenkriegszeit," H. Hagemann, ed., *Zur deutschsprachigen wirtschaftswissenschaftlichen Emigration nach 1933* (Marburg: Metropolis, 1997), pp. 243–92. Mises took no active part in this methodological debate. He later addressed the main issues when he set out to formulate his own equilibrium theory in the late 1930s. We will deal with his contribution in chapters 16 and 17. On the development of monetary business cycle theories from Wicksell to Hayek, see Carl-Ludwig Holtfrerich, "Zur Entwicklung der monetären Konjunkturtheorien: Wicksell, Schumpeter, Mises und Hayek," in Schefold, ed., *Studien zur Entwicklung der ökonomischen Theorie* 8, pp. 103–40.

[46]Mises was elected *in absentia* at the meeting of the reform committee on March 6–7, 1929. He received a report from one of his closest allies in those years, Georg Jahn, a professor from Halle. See Jahn to Mises, letter dated March 9, 1929; Mises Archive: 22: 42.

attach much importance to the event, it symbolized better than anything else his professional standing in those days. Starting as an eccentric in 1912, Mises had become a respected academic leader. The *Verein* establishment may not have appreciated him, but it was realistic enough to recognize him as the representative of a growing movement among the members. More importantly, however, his rise epitomized the new respectability of theoretical research, which the *Verein's* founding generation had despised.

The Theory of Value Reconsidered

For Mises, it was a sign of hope that a new generation of students had risen to fill the ranks of the theoreticians. The spell of the Historical School was definitely broken. But another danger loomed on the horizon—bad theory.

One important area where the danger was very real was value theory. Carl Menger had applied his "exact method" with great success in this field; Mises himself had refined Menger's analysis by stressing the relationship between value and choice. But these works had had virtually no impact on the younger generation. Many new theoreticians believed that economic theory applied only to those human actions that were guided by "economic considerations"—which made sense only if there were also non-economic considerations, which in turn seemed to presuppose that there were two types of values, economic and non-economic.

This error was reinforced when, in 1923, Carl Menger's *Principles of Economics* was published in a revised second edition. The book had been out of print for many years and Menger had never authorized a new printing. The revisions contained in the new edition had been found in manuscripts that Menger had left at the time of his death. Most important, Menger had introduced the distinction between "real wants" and "imaginary wants," a distinction that seemed to confirm the notion that economic science dealt only with a specific type of value, namely, with real values that could be used in economic calculations.

Mises had been convinced at least as early as *Theory of Money and Credit* that the notion of value calculation was a chimera. The only economic calculation was calculation with money prices. But in discussions of his socialist-calculation argument, he must have seen how much he had underestimated the extent to which the notion of value calculation had taken hold of the minds of the rising generation. Because of ambiguities in the exposition of that argument, those who were not perfectly acquainted with Mises's views on value theory were unlikely to notice the foundational claim that there is no such thing as value calculus, only price calculus.[47] These difficulties were barely visible in the early 1920s. When Mises first presented his case for the impossibility of socialist calculation at the Vienna *Nationalökonomische Gesellschaft*, he talked to a generation that had been raised in Böhm-Bawerk's seminar. But in the course of the next few years, the conditions for a genuine understanding of his case diminished rapidly because of two factors:

One, the emphasis on value theory had always been a specialty of the Austrian School. Where Mengerian value theory was a theory of value judgments, Jevons and Walras had based their price theories on the concept of utility, which remained entirely in the realm of felt satisfactions. After Böhm-Bawerk's death, value theory in Austria was completely dominated by Wieser, the least Mengerian of the Austrian economists.

Two, in the German-speaking countries, Gustav Cassel started promoting Vilfredo Pareto's idea that price theory could do without value theory.[48] Ironically, Mises himself had indirectly revitalized the use of the Walrasian general-equilibrium

---

[47]See the discussion in "A Copernican Shift," chapter 10 in this volume.

[48]Vilfredo Pareto, *Manuel d'économie politique*, 4th ed. (Geneva: Droz, 1966 [1909]), vol. 3, § 36; Gustav Cassel, *Grundgedanken der theoretischen Ökonomie* (Leipzig and Erlangen: Hatschek & Scholl, 1926).

approach: his case against socialism had pushed socialist-minded economists into the general-equilibrium camp, which seemed their only escape from the problems of value theory and economic calculation.

By the end of the 1920s, it had become impossible for Mises to ignore the widespread confusion about the difference between value and price. A case in point was his 1929–1930 correspondence with Leopold von Wiese, a sociologist at the University of Cologne. Wiese argued that the Italian mathematical economist Enrico Barone had shown that general equilibrium models of the economy could be used to solve the problem of economic calculation in socialist commonwealths. Mises replied that Barone's entire demonstration was based on the untenable assumption that the subjective values of different individuals could be reduced to a common denominator.[49]

At that point, Mises had already recognized that part of the problem was his own ambiguity in previous writings and he began correcting himself. Thus in the second edition of *Theory of Money and Credit* (1924), he had "de-psychologized" his exposition of value theory, deleting the ominous sentence "As a feeling, value cannot be measured; it is [however] possible to compare it with other, similar feelings" and replacing it with "Acts of valuation are not susceptible of any kind of measurement."[50]

---

[49]Enrico Barone in F.A. Hayek, ed., *Collectivist Economic Planning: Critical Studies on the Possibilities of Socialism* (London: Routledge, 1935). Mises referred to §§ 17, 80, and 168 of this work. See Mises to Wieser letter dated December 12, 1929; Mises Archive 91: 4. The correspondence was a follow-up to personal discussions in Cologne. On Tuesday, December 3, 1929, Mises had lectured in Cologne on "economic interests and political parties." Rudolf Seyffert, who was the head of the department of economics and social sciences, directed the lecture series "contemporary political theories" and invited Mises to give one of the talks. See Seyffert to Mises, letter dated October 18, 1929; Mises to Seyffert, letter dated October 28, 1929; Mises Archive 62: 107, 112.

[50]In the original texts we read: "Als Gefühl ist der Wert jeder Messung unzugänglich; Vergleiche mit anderen, gleichartigen Gefühlen sind

Although this change did not affect his actual analysis of the problems of conceiving of value as a quantifiable entity, it marked a conscious transition from a psychological conception of value to one in which value was an *act* rather than a *feeling*.

His next step was much bolder. For the first and only time, Mises published an article whose only purpose was to criticize his scientific forebears. He took issue with passages in Menger and Böhm-Bawerk that had given rise to "objectivist" interpretations of their value theories. Mises criticized the ethical connotations of Menger's concept of imaginary wants as unnecessary for the explanation of market prices; in the same vein, he criticized Böhm-Bawerk's psychological distinction between economic and non-economic motives as equally unnecessary. Mises stressed that "the essence of the modern theory" that Menger and Böhm-Bawerk had developed was to recognize that human behavior results from choice, and that choice always concerns the relative importance of quantities at stake in the concrete choice in question—the "marginal" quantities. Psychology does not come into play here:

> For catallactics the ultimate relevant cause of the exchange ratios of the market is the fact that the individual, in the act of exchange, prefers a definite quantity of good A to a definite quantity of good B. The reasons he may have for acting exactly thus and not

---

möglich," *Theorie des Geldes und der Umlaufsmittel,* 1st ed. (Munich and Leipzig: Duncker & Humblot, 1912), p. 16. Twelve years later, he changed this to: "Der Wertungsakt ist jeder Messung unzugänglich" (2nd ed., Munich and Leipzig: Duncker & Humblot, 1924, p. 11). In the English edition: "Acts of valuation are not susceptible of any kind of measurement," *Theory of Money and Credit* (Indianapolis: Liberty Fund, 1980), p. 52. Similarly, speaking about his book *Nation, Staat und Wirtschaft* in the fall of 1925, Mises said in a letter to Robbins that he would have to rewrite the book thoroughly for a new edition. See Mises to Lionel Robbins, letter dated October 9, 1925; Mises Archive 83: 61.

> otherwise . . . are of absolutely no importance for the
> determination of a market price.[51]

Other disciplines such as psychology, physiology, and cultural history may try to determine the factors that prompt a given choice. Economic science is exclusively concerned with individual ("subjective") values *per se*; it "is independent of all psychological and ethical considerations."[52] Why then did so many economists bring these considerations into play? Mises explained that this unfortunate habit was the result of an accident of the history of economic thought. The development of subjective-value theory coincided with the development of a psychological "law of the satiation of wants and of the decrease in the marginal utility of the unit in an increasing supply."[53]

This piece ("Remarks on the Fundamental Problem of the Subjective Theory of Value") was published in February 1928, more than eight years after Mises's first exposition of the socialist-calculation argument. It had its impact: the *Verein für Sozialpolitik* decided to discuss the problems of value theory at an annual convention. Mises and Arthur Spiethoff were appointed editors of a special volume on value theory to be published in

---

[51]Mises, "Remarks on the Fundamental Problem of the Subjective Theory of Value," *Epistemological Problems of Economics*, 3rd ed. (Auburn, Ala.: Ludwig von Mises Institute, 2003), chap. 5, p. 178. The original publication was "Bemerkungen zum Grundproblem der subjektivistischen Wertlehre," *Archiv für Socialwissenschaft und Sozialpolitik* (February 1928).

[52]Mises, "Remarks on the Fundamental Problem of the Subjective Theory of Value," p. 180.

[53]Mises went on:

> All attention was turned toward this law, and it was mistakenly regarded the chief and basic law of the new theory. Indeed, the latter was more often called the theory of diminishing marginal utility than the doctrine of the subjectivist school, which would have been more suitable and would have avoided misunderstandings." (Ibid., p. 180)

preparation for these discussions, which were delayed several times, but eventually took place in the fall of 1932 in Dresden.[54]

Mises wrote two entries for this volume, one giving an exposition of the development of the subjectivist theory of value, the other analyzing the psychological motivations of its critics. In the first piece, Mises gave a systematic exposition of the theory of value; in light of this account he explained previous contributions to the theory of value. Again he stressed the act of preferring, or human choice, as the "basic element in human conduct."[55] But he also spelled out for the first time the implications of the difference between value and price. He now saw the wider theoretical significance of his socialist-calculation article of 1920: it had been the first and decisive step toward the development of a general theory of economic calculation, in light of which economics was only a sub-discipline of a more general theory of human action. In the 1920s, Mises called this discipline "sociology" but he eventually came to call it "praxeology"—the logic of action.

Where praxeology deals with the general principles behind all human action, economics deals more narrowly with the laws of human action in a system where the means of production are privately owned. The characteristic feature of such a system is

---

[54]See Ludwig von Mises and Arthur Spiethoff, *Probleme der Wertlehre* (Munich and Leipzig: Duncker & Humblot, 1931). This was volume 183/I in the series of the *Verein* publications. A companion volume 183/II, which contained the proceedings of the Dresden meeting, was published in 1933.

[55]Mises, "On the Development of the Subjective Theory of Value," *Epistemological Problems of Economics*:

> All conscious conduct on the part of men involves preferring an A to a B. It is an act of choice between two alternative possibilities that offer themselves. Only these acts of choice, these inner decisions that operate upon the external world, are our data. We comprehend their meaning by constructing the concept of importance. If an individual prefers A to B, we say that, at the moment of the act of choice, A appeared more important to him (more valuable, more desirable) than B. (p. 149)

that it enables a profitability calculus to guide actions. Business-men can contrast the money prices they expect to receive for a product with the expected money expenditure related to its pro-duction. And they can compare the expected profit from any investment to the profit expected from any available alternative. The selection of the projects that will secure the available resources, and prevent the alternative projects from being financed, can therefore be based on an evaluation of alternatives in common quantitative terms.[56] In short, the money calculus of the businessman makes it possible for him to compare alterna-tives in common terms. Thus he is in a position to pass summary judgments on states of affairs involving physically heterogeneous goods.[57] One can now define "income" as "proceeds minus costs"; one can define "savings" as "income minus consumption";

---

[56]The actual selection process merely *can* be based on the profitability calculus, but does not preclude other decisions. Nothing prevents a busi-nessman from building a social hall for his friends rather than a factory for his customers. Yet the benefit of the money calculus remains even in this case, for it tells the businessman exactly what he is giving up for his per-sonal consumption—the satisfaction of providing unpaid catering for his friends. Without prices, he could not calculate the opportunity cost of his decision.

[57]It is not possible to say whether 1,000,000 gallons of milk are somehow more (or less) than the 1,000 cows that produce this milk, just as it is impos-sible to say whether a palace garden is more (or less) than the 100 gardeners who brought it into shape. The reason is that all these things are heteroge-neous and therefore cannot be compared quantitatively—the problem of adding apples and oranges. For the same reason it is also impossible to tell whether using the cows to produce the milk is *more efficient* than using the gardeners to bring the garden into shape. But once all these things are exchanged against money, we can make such quantitative comparisons, namely, by comparing their money prices. Depending on what these prices are, we can say that the milk exchanges for more (or less) money than the cows, and that the garden exchanges for more (or less) money than the serv-ices of the gardeners. And depending on the ratios of selling and buying prices (the profitability) we can assert that our money is more (or less) effi-ciently used in producing milk than in producing a palace garden.

and one can give exact and meaningful definitions of capital, profit and loss, etc.

Economic calculation thus produces phenomena absent in other systems of social organization. Dealing with them is the task of economic science. Where praxeology deals with human choices (value judgments), the sub-discipline of economics deals with those value judgments that can be based on quantitative economic calculations.

In contrast, other economists believed economic calculation was possible outside the framework of a market economy. They assumed that calculation in terms of market prices was only one form of economic calculation. More to the point, they believed that it was possible in principle for the members of society to perform calculation in terms of utility, which they assumed to be quantifiable. It followed that *all* elements of economic science—the science of calculated action—had the same general applicability as marginal value theory. Categories such as saving, consumption, capital, profit, loss, and efficiency were not just categories of the market, but of human action in general.

Mises's 1931 essay on value theory highlighted the differences between the approach of the Austrians and that of the neoclassicals. The former is a truly general and realistic approach that applies to every single human action. It does not deal merely with "rational" choices reflecting "rational" values, but with *all* choices and values. In contrast, the emerging neoclassical analysis of choice did not apply to all human behavior, but only to those actions that *would be* observed if the acting person strictly followed the results of a utility calculus. From this point of view, therefore, economic science does not deal with human action *per se*, but only with one aspect of human action—"right" action or "logical" action.

This was the position espoused by Friedrich von Wieser, who was also consistent enough to advocate, in one of his rare methodological statements, the use of "idealizing abstractions" such as *homo oeconomicus*.[58] It was also the stance of Vilfredo Pareto, according to whom the theoretical social sciences deal mainly with "logical actions" rather than with human action in general.[59] And although he placed a little less emphasis than Wieser on the central idea of utility calculus, Pareto was quite explicit in stating that market prices are just helpful "auxiliary variables" to solve the fundamental economic equations. These equations are the same in each economic system—they do not depend on the political organization of society—and their ultimate elements are individual tastes and obstacles (costs).[60] Market prices for factors of production could be dispensed with, because the general-equilibrium equations would produce any "prices" needed as accounting devices for the central planning agency:

> even if the socialist state abolished all right of exchange and prohibited all buying and selling, prices would not disappear on that account; they would remain at the very least as an accounting device in connection with the distribution of goods and their transformation.[61]

---

[58]Friedrich von Wieser, "Das Wesen und der Hauptinhalt der theoretischen Nationalökonomie—kritische Glossen," *Gesammelte Abhandlungen*, F.A. Hayek, ed. (Tübingen: Mohr, [1911] 1929).

[59]Pareto, *Manuel d'économie politique*, chap. 2, §§ 1–18. Pareto is a subjectivist only in the sense that he recognizes the subjective character of the goals of human action (see ibid., chap. 3, §§ 29f.), which is why he strictly distinguishs between (objective) utility and (subjective) "ophelimity." Yet Pareto's subjectivism stops short when it comes to dealing with the means of action because here he professes to consider only the case of "logical action."

[60]Ibid., chap. 3, § 152.

[61]Vilfredo Pareto, *Manual of Political Economy* (New York: Augustus M. Kelley, 1971), chap. 3, p. 155. He went on:

> The use of prices is the simplest and easiest means for solving the equations of equilibrium; if one insisted on not using them, he would probably end up by using them under another name, and there would then be only a change of language, and not of things.

Mises recognized that his Austrian value theory could explain every single instance of conscious behavior, whether calculated or not, thus generalizing the theory of *homo oeconomicus* into a theory of *homo agens*. In contrast, other economists and sociologists believed that while it was true that marginal utility theory could explain only calculated (logical, rational) behavior, it was still a "general" theory of human action because utility is a pervasive factor determining all human actions. For the neoclassicals, economics was still the theory of *homo oeconomicus* it had already been in the hands of the classical economists, but its protagonist was no longer confined to the market—*homo oeconomicus* now lived everywhere.

To the present day, this has remained a dividing line between the Misesians and a distinguished group of thinkers in the Wieserian-Paretian lineage, in particular Gary Becker and the movement he has inspired.[62] It also accounts for the fact that Misesians markedly deviate from the present-day mainstream when it comes to explaining phenomena such as growth, monopoly, welfare, the relationship between law and economics, money, conflict, etc.

The problems of value theory and economic calculation are far more important than the single chapter they might get in some textbooks (if they are covered at all). In the late 1920s, Mises showed that these problems were at the very heart of the social sciences. In the 1940s, he would present the theory of economic calculation as one of the main building blocks of his general theory of human action.

---

[62]See in particular Gary Becker, *Economic Theory* (New York: Knopf, 1971); idem, *A Treatise on the Family* (Cambridge, Mass.: Harvard University Press, 1991).

Toward a New Epistemology of the Social Sciences

Mises's reflections on the scientific and political significance of value theory were part of a more general effort on his part to pull together the different strands of his previous works, to discuss their implications, and to fill in the gaps.

One area in which the case for liberty and private property had been less than airtight was epistemology. The famous *Methodenstreit* between Menger and Schmoller had not produced the necessary clarification. The crucial question was whether there was such a thing as a theoretical social *science*—or whether the scientific rhetoric of the economists was just hot air.

In previous works, Mises had argued along the lines of Walter Bagehot that a social theory is necessary to interpret the wealth of data presented by observation. Therefore the social analyst first needed a theory, and only as a second step could he approach the object of his inquiry.[63] He also criticized the "empiricists" who thought they could explain the observable real world without relying on theory.[64] In 1926, these statements were made only for the record. With the benefit of hindsight, however, we know that they heralded the beginning of a research program that Mises pursued for the next thirty-five years. He discovered that the most underdeveloped area of the social sciences was epistemology—the meta-theory explaining how these sciences relate to reality.

His very first contribution to this field was an essay on the relationship between "sociology" and "history."[65] Mises here

---

[63]Mises, *Kritik des Interventionismus* (Jena: Gustav Fischer, 1929; reprint Darmstadt: Wissenschaftliche Buchgesellschaft, 1976), p. 72; see also idem, *Gemeinwirtschaft*, 1st ed. (Jena: Gustav Fischer, 1922), p. 355.

[64]Mises, *Kritik des Interventionismus*, p. 28.

[65]Mises, "Soziologie und Geschichte," *Archiv für Sozialwissenschaft und Sozialpolitik* 61, no. 3 (1929): 465–512; reprinted in Mises, *Grundprobleme der Nationalökonomie* (Jena: Gustav Fischer, 1933), chap. 2; translated as "Sociology

stated that the *Methodenstreit* of the 1880s and 1890s had banished the teaching of economics from the universities of the German Reich, but that it had not clarified the central question of whether there was such a thing as a social theory that could claim the status of a science. Meanwhile, however, great progress had been achieved on a different front. The works of Wilhelm Windelband, Heinrich Rickert, Max Weber, and Henri Bergson had clarified the epistemological nature of historical research.[66] The works of these scholars had yielded two important insights.

First, the application of the methodology of the natural sciences to human action did not exhaust the task of the historian. The genuine purpose of historical research was to explain concrete human behavior in the unique circumstances influencing this behavior.

Second, historical research could not do without theoretical tools. There was no such thing as historical analysis untainted by theoretical interpretation. For example, the mere classification of observed phenomena such as "he was a king" or "she is my neighbor" or "they were Germans" involved more than a description of naked facts. The very words used in the description were in fact theoretical tools. Max Weber had set out to develop an epistemology to characterize the logical character of

---

and History," *Epistemological Problems of Economics*, 3rd ed. (Auburn, Ala.: Ludwig von Mises Institute, 2003), chap. 2.

[66]Mises praised in particular the "Southwest German School of New Criticism" (Windelband, Rickert, and Weber) for developing the concept of "understanding"—the specific tool of the science of history. See Wilhelm Windelband, *Präludien*, 8th ed. (Tübingen: Mohr, 1922), vol. 2, pp. 136ff.; Heinrich Rickert, 2nd ed. (Tübingen: Mohr, 1913); idem, *Kulturwissenschaft und Naturwissenschaft*, 3rd ed. (Tübingen: Mohr, 1915); Max Weber, *Gesammelte Aufsätze zur Wissenschaftslehre*, 7th ed. (Tübingen: UTB, 1988); Henri Bergson, *L'évolution créatrice* (Paris: Presses Universitaires de France, [1907] 1991).

the theoretical tools needed in the science of history, arguing that they were "ideal types."[67]

Building on these insights, Mises set out to explain that "sociology"—the term he used as shorthand for the "theoretical science of social phenomena"[68]—was one of the theoretical tools needed in historiography. Much of his long essay was devoted to a critical discussion of Max Weber's approach. Mises emphasized Weber's merits as a logician of historical research, but also stressed that, even though Weber held a chair of economic science, he could not be considered an economist. In Mises's view, Weber was simply unacquainted with economic theory. He acquired his reputation as a theoretician because he cultivated a new, very general form of historiography, which Mises proposed to call "universal history":

> The investigations collected in Weber's posthumously published major work, *Wirtschaft und Gesellschaft*, belong to the best that German scientific literature of the last decades has produced. Yet in their most important parts they are not sociological theory in our sense. Nor are they history in the customary meaning of the term. History deals with one town or with German towns or with European towns in the Middle Ages. Until Weber's time it knew nothing like the brilliant chapter in his book that deals simply with the "town" in general, a universal theory of town settlement for all times and among all peoples, the ideal type of the town in itself.[69]

---

[67]Max Weber, *Wirtschaft und Gesellschaft*, 3rd ed. (Tübingen: Mohr, 1947), chap. 1, § 1.

[68]The essay "Sociology and History" would be the last time Mises would use the term in this sense. He had used it in the first edition of *Gemeinwirtschaft* (Jena: Gustav Fischer, 1922).

[69]Mises, *Epistemological Problems of Economics*, pp. 114f.

Brilliant though Weber's achievement was, it had nothing to do with universally valid sciences such as economics. The point was that ideal types such as the universal town were fictitious; they did not fit all or even any observed phenomena they were designed to describe. Weber had used the expression "ideal" in the same sense as Friedrich von Wieser—as a fictitious assumption. These fictions vitiated the scientific and political conclusions derived from their use: "propositions involving them must be similarly deficient."[70] Economic laws, in contrast, concerned universally existing causal relationships inherent in human action. In every single instance in which the cause was given, it produced the effect according to the law. Mises explained:

> The laws of sociology are neither ideal types nor averages. Rather, they are the expression of what is to be singled out of the fullness and diversity of phenomena from the point of view of the science that aims at the cognition of what is essential and necessary in every single instance of human action. Sociological concepts are not derived "through one-sided *intensification* of *one* or *several* aspects and through integration into an immanently consistent *conceptual representation* of a multiplicity of scattered and discrete individual phenomena, present here in greater number, there in less, and occasionally not at all, which are in congruity with these one-sidedly intensified aspects." They are rather a generalization of the features to be found in the same way in every single instance to which they refer.[71]

Mises argued that the subject matter of both historical and theoretical social analysis is "human action." The salient point was that not all observable human behaviors count as action.

---

[70]Ibid., p. 118.

[71]Ibid., p. 98. Mises here quotes Weber, *Gesammelte Aufsätze zur Wissenschaftslehre* (Tübingen: Mohr, 1922), p. 191.

Rather, human action is a particular sub-class of behavior. It is behavior determined by conscious decision-making, that is, behavior constrained by scarcity. "Only as far as [scarcity] does exist does action take place; as far as it is lacking, action is also lacking." Mises went on:

> Once one has realized this, one also implicitly realizes that every action involves choice among various possibilities. All action is economizing with the means available for the realization of attainable ends. The fundamental law of action is the economic principle. Every action is under its sway. He who wants to deny the possibility of economic science must begin by calling into question the universal validity of the economic principle, i.e., that the necessity to economize is characteristic of all action by its very nature. But only one who has completely misunderstood the principle can do this.[72]

But what was the epistemological status of the universally valid theory of human action? In his 1929 essay, Mises had touched on this question only when he observed that economic theory was "rationalistic in the sense that it makes use of the methods of reason—*ratio*." And he further characterized these methods of reason as "discursive reasoning" and "scientific reasoning."[73] Only four years later would he make his famous statement that the theoretical social sciences were *aprioristic* disciplines whose validity does not depend on the evidence of the senses.

The 1929 article on "Sociology and History" contained already, *in nuce*, the argument by which Mises would refute the claim of extreme historicism that there is no such thing as a

---

[72]Mises, *Epistemological Problems of Economics*, pp. 85f.
[73]Ibid., pp. 98f.

generally valid social theory because the structure of the human mind was in a state of constant flux. He demonstrated that the empirical evidence offered to substantiate this claim failed to do so. Moreover, he argued that the historicist claim was self-contradictory:

> What the proponents of historicism fail to see is that even propositions like; "The theorems of classical economics possessed relative truth for the age in which they were constructed" can be enunciated only if one has already adopted a supertemporal, universally valid theory.[74]

Mises also addressed the opposite error of assuming social theory could have exactly the same logical character as the theories of the natural sciences. While it is true that human action is strictly determined by external factors, the knowledge *that* they are so determined is not sufficient to construct mathematical models of human behavior. One would also have to know *how* these factors affect human choice, and no such knowledge was available. Mises argued:

> However, we do not know how these external factors are transformed within the human mind to produce thoughts and volitions directed and operating upon the outer world. We are able to ascertain this only *post factum*, but in no way can we deduce it in advance from a known regularity formulated as a law.[75]

It was therefore necessary for the social scientist to take concrete human action as the starting point of his analysis—as an

---

[74]Ibid., p. 114.

[75]Ibid., pp. 122f. A year earlier, in *Geldwertstabilisierung und Konjunkturpolitik* (Jena: Gustav Fischer, 1928), Mises still maintained more empiricist notions about the epistemology of economics. Although he emphasized that some sort of theory was necessary to interpret observed fact (pp. 39–42), he at one point went so far as to assert that the Harvard business barometer delivered a statistical verification of the circulation-credit theory (p. 69).

ultimate given. He could not hope to determine human behavior with any degree of quantitative exactitude. The propositions of the economist were *qualitatively* exact.

In this argument, Mises drew on his previous work in the field of monetary theory:

> Mathematics has a significance in the natural sciences altogether different from what it has in sociology and economics. This is because physics is able to discover empirically constant relationships, which it describes in its equations. The scientific technology based on physics is thereby rendered capable of solving given problems with quantitative definiteness. The engineer is able to calculate how a bridge must be constructed in order to bear a given load. These constant relationships cannot be demonstrated in economics. The quantity theory of money, for example, shows that, *ceteris paribus*, an increase in the quantity of money leads to a decrease in the purchasing power of the monetary unit, but the doubling of the quantity of money does not bring about a fifty percent decline in its purchasing power. The relationship between the quantity of money and its purchasing power is not constant. It is a mistake to think that, from statistical investigations concerning the relationship of the supply of and the demand for definite commodities, quantitative conclusions can be drawn that would be applicable to the future configuration of this relationship. Whatever can be established in this way has only historical significance, whereas the ascertainment of the specific gravity of different substances, for example, has universal validity.[76]

---

[76]Mises, *Epistemological Problems of Economics*, pp. 128f.

A Private Boom-Bust

Mises had been surprised and delighted by the failure of the general strike on July 15, 1927. What did not surprise him was the massacre that took place when the masses rallied in the streets of Vienna. One of his first thoughts was to alert Margit Serény of the danger. Under no circumstances should she let the children out. Margit was away during the day, however, and Mises left detailed instructions with the housekeeper.[77]

When Margit returned in the late afternoon, she was deeply touched to learn how much Mises cared about her and her children. She had held him in great esteem, but in no way reciprocated the attentiveness he had bestowed on her during the two years since they had first met in Kaufmann's apartment. Red roses and expensive perfume could not conquer her heart. She just could not understand this man:

> In the first years of our relationship, Lu was almost an enigma to me. I never had seen such modesty in a man before. He knew his value, but he never boasted. . . . I think it was the extreme honesty in Lu's feelings that attracted me so strongly to him. These feelings were so overpowering that he, who wrote thousands of pages about economics and money, could not find the words to talk about himself, and explain his feeling.[78]

Fortunately, actions sometimes speak for themselves. On that day of July 1927, for the first time, Margit felt something like love for him and grew more open to his advances. It was the beginning of a short-lived boom in their friendship, which less than two months later ended in a resounding crash.

---

[77]On this and the following see Margit von Mises's typewritten record of the events—Mises Archive 105—which was probably written in November 1927.

[78]Margit von Mises, *My Years with Ludwig von Mises*, 2nd enlarged ed. (Cedar Falls, Iowa: Center for Futures Education, 1984), pp. 18f.

That night, Mises visited Margit to see if everything was in order. Telephone lines were down and he had been unable to call her. He took her for a walk on the Ringstrasse, where the turmoil of the day could still be felt: only men were out; she did not see another woman. At the end of their excursion he proposed to go dancing. When she said yes, he knew it indicated progress. Some days later, he held her hand for the first time, in a dance club, and on the following weekend, he kissed her for the first time in a dark corner of the Prater, Vienna's central park—like a couple of high school kids, as she would later recall. When she had to leave for Hamburg a few days later, he told her that he would ask her to marry him, but that he first had to make up his mind to be a stepfather to her children. They parted with plans to meet in Berchtesgaden, a resort town in the Bavarian Alps, at the end of August.

On August 25, she took the train from Munich to Berchtesgaden and was happily surprised when Mises suddenly entered the train at one of the intermediate stations. They took adjacent hotel rooms in Berchtesgaden. Concerned about appearances, Mises presented Margit as his sister. They enjoyed a wonderful training period for marriage, as he would say. They talked about the problems facing their potential union: she could not fulfill his wish to have a child together; she would have to become Jewish again to appease his mother; his mother would have to be kept out of all marriage preparations because she might jeopardize everything, as she had done on an earlier occasion.[79]

On Sunday, September 4, they returned to Vienna, where events took a fateful turn. Mises had fallen ill without noticing

---

[79]We are still paraphrasing Margit von Mises's rather vague record of the events (document in Mises Archive 105). From the phrase "she would have to become Jewish again" one must infer that she had been Jewish before getting married to Ferdinand Serény, a protestant. The phrase "training period for marriage" is liable to several plausible interpretations and has probably been selected for precisely this reason.

at first. He met her for supper on the following Tuesday, and on Wednesday he saw her again, shaken by fever and a severe headache. Given these circumstances, he would not talk about marriage. He had to have a clear head to make the most important declaration of his life. Yet Margit felt she had already been waiting for quite a while and was growing impatient. She told him she would not wait a single day more and pressed him for a decision. He later wrote her of the event:

> "Today or never! I will not allow you to postpone the decision by even a couple of hours." No loving woman talks that way. A single warm word from you would have made me happy, would have bound me to you forever. But you said no such word. You did not meet me as a loving woman, but as a cold adversary.
>
> It was the greatest disappointment of my life. I had hoped to find love and goodness in you, and I found hardness, uncompromising hardness. I had already overcome all prior apprehensions, which I have not hidden from you, because I thought true love was stronger than the difficulties that stood in the way of our union.[80]

It seemed to be the end. They departed under the mutual declaration that the problems in their relationship were irreconcilable. She even returned the love letters he had written to her in Hamburg.

The next morning, Margit felt remorse and wrote to him, but he remained silent. She continued to write every day, without response, and a few days later finally got him on the phone.

---

[80]Mises to Margit Serény, letter dated November 3, 1927; Mises Archive 62: 35f. Mises wrote this letter at the behest of Professor Adler, Margit's doctor, who had conveyed Margit's wish that he explain in full why he refused to see her again. The physician in question must have been Ludwig Adler; see Margit von Mises, *My Years with Ludwig von Mises*, p. 8.

Mises reiterated what he had said on the preceding Wednesday. It was over, forever.

Not much later, he must have discovered the true cause of his fever—a rare condition known as acute surgical abdomen—and checked into the hospital for surgery.[81] Margit had stopped writing him, but she sought news on the state of his health from his second cousin, Strisower, the doctor of her late husband. She even prayed to God for his recovery, admitting later that she had always thought of herself as an atheist, but this emergency had revealed otherwise.

Eventually she started writing him again. When he did not reply, she begged Professor Adler, her physician, to ask Mises to write and explain in full the reasons for his obstinacy. With this request coming from a colleague as a quasi-official request, Mises felt he had to comply. He wrote a strongly worded and unflattering letter, and emphasized that he would have preferred to spare her the embarrassment of reading his account. Margit sent the letter back, saying it was unworthy of him.

At some point in late 1927 or 1928, he started calling her again. He would not speak. He just let her answer the phone and listened to her voice, sometimes twice a day. And then one day he showed up again at her apartment, without any explanation, and they continued the relationship where they had left off in September 1927. She still waited for him to propose, but he was still unable to make this step. Later she wrote:

> Before we married, this love must have been a very distressing factor in his life—so upsetting that he knew he could fight a battle in the Carpathian Alps but could never win the battle against himself.[82]

---

[81]On September 16, he was still in the hospital. See the letter that Mises's secretary sent to the *Königsberger Hartungsche Zeitung*, dated September 16, 1927; Mises Archive 62: 10.

[82]Margit von Mises, *My Years with Ludwig von Mises*, p. 19.

Eventually, she could not bear it any more. She left Vienna and went to London for work as a translator. She would return to Vienna only after she had met him again on the Thames. ⊰

Mises in profile

15
Crises

THE MELTDOWN OF THE New York Stock Exchange in October 1929 sent shockwaves through the world economy. Central Europe was particularly affected. Corporate profits in Austria had been squeezed under the combined impact of increased taxation and labor-union power. As a consequence, private entrepreneurs were increasingly unable to attract the capital needed to cope with the changes. Moreover, the economy of Germany and Austria had come to rely increasingly on public expenditure, which in turn was financed through a steady stream of U.S. and French credit. The main players in this process were not the federal governments, but second-level authorities and municipalities. Loyal to the prevailing socialist ideology of the time, city mayors had used postwar foreign loans as a means to communalize firms, especially in the fields of transport and public utilities. The performance of these companies plummeted under the new public management, but this was compensated for by ever more credit from abroad. Until 1928, the inflationary policies of the capitalist West could be relied on for promoting the growth and perseverance of the Central European welfare states. Then the June 1928 stabilization of the franc stopped capital exports from France and the volume of new foreign loans floated in the United States dropped by some 50 percent when the Federal Reserve started increasing its interest rates. The party was over.

One of Mises's professional duties was to help attract capital to Austria. In the international meetings for the semi-public *Kammer*, he represented his country and sought to protect its interests by promoting Austria's reputation as a good credit risk.[1] For example, in late March and early April 1930, Mises went on a mission to London to promote an English-language brochure that Hayek's Institute for Business Cycle Research had prepared for the *Kammer*'s propaganda department (what we would now call a public relations office) in London.[2]

He also was on a private mission: he had to see Margit again. She had never written after leaving Vienna the year before. He somehow learned her address and they met on his very first evening. She recalled: "From the first look—from the first moment—everything was as it had been before. We both knew it never would change."[3] A few months later, she returned to Vienna—private mission accomplished.

Mises's official mission was one of his less successful undertakings. After the Wall Street crash in October 1929, U.S. loans quickly became unavailable for Austria and Germany. Even Mises's persuasiveness could not prevent the crisis from spilling over to Austria. It soon turned out that the Austrian

---

[1]Mises, *Erinnerungen* (Stuttgart: Gustav Fischer Verlag, 1978), p. 53.

[2]Mises to Simon, letter dated April 9, 1930; Mises Archive 66a: 28; see also Mises to unknown correspondent, letter dated April 28, 1930; Mises Archive 66a: 45. Mises used the occasion to meet his friends at LSE, although he had not announced the trip to them much in advance, if at all. Thus he missed Robbins, who had been out of town for some time and then tried to meet him for lunch, but met Meyendorff in King's College on Monday, April 1. Meyendroff probably introduced him to Alistor Phillips from Trinity College Dublin. They had also planned to meet Hearnshaw, but the latter was not in London. See Mises to Robbins, letter dated April 12, 1930; Mises Archive 83: 21; Meyendorff to Mises, letter dated March 30, 1930; Mises Archive 88: 2.

[3]Margit von Mises, *My Years with Ludwig von Mises*, 2nd enlarged ed. (Cedar Falls, Iowa: Center for Futures Education, 1984), p. 21.

entrepreneurs, crippled by a decade of communal socialism, labor unions, and soaring taxes, were unable to provide relief. Stock markets plummeted all over Europe and within a year reached an all-time low.

As usually happens in a financial crisis, all sorts of real and self-appointed experts advertised their plans to solve the problem. These plans invariably involved increased government intervention. The great panacea was meddling with the gold standard. Several well-intentioned amateurs sent their reform proposals to Mises. Not one of them had actually studied any of his writings. They just sought a renowned monetary expert to give leverage to their ideas. One of them actually proposed a currency based on electricity! Mises usually replied, and in one case even said he would welcome a publication of the gentleman's proposal; a public discussion of these views would be instructive and help to bring about a solution to the present monetary problems.[4] This was no idle talk; he sometimes arranged such discussions himself. A case in point was Charlotte von Reichmann, a young economist from the University of Frankfurt. Unlike the cranks, she had actually read Mises's monetary theory. In fact, she had devoured all of his books and admired them very much. Still, in her doctoral dissertation she had advocated a substantially different (inflationary) point of view on the nature of credit, claiming that even paper-money credit was true capital. When she sent her dissertation to Mises in December 1931 and solicited his comments, she was quite surprised to receive a very appreciative response, plus an invitation to give a talk to the *Nationalökonomische Gesellschaft*.[5]

---

[4]Mises to Fritz Arnstein, letter dated December 17, 1931; Mises Archive 95: 6.

[5]She could not believe her eyes when she saw she was invited to give a talk, and her teachers laughed at her, saying it could not possibly be a serious invitation: Mises was only being polite to a student of his friends from the Frankfurt circle. But Mises was serious. When he thanked her for accepting

In 1930, the Austrian government asked Mises to join an *ad hoc* Economic Commission to study the causes of the difficulties that plagued the country: permanent high unemployment (in 1929, some 200,000 or 14 percent of the workers in industry and commerce were without jobs), numerous bankruptcies, idle production facilities, and the lack of profitability for a large number of Austrian businesses. Mises was one of the three members of the anonymous Editorial Committee that eventually issued the final report of December 1930.[6] The other two members were Edmund Palla, a labor-union leader and Secretary of the Chamber of Labor, and Engelbert Dollfuss, a rising leader of the Christian-Socialist Party who would later become Austrian chancellor.

The report detailed the factors that weakened the competitiveness of the Austrian economy. It pointed out that the inflation years (1914–1925) had produced an inflationist mentality in the Austrian population. Continual increases of prices and incomes were now considered to be the normal state of affairs.[7] This mentality conflicted with stable or declining selling prices on world markets, to which Austria was exposed after the introduction of the gold-exchange standard in 1925. Once on the standard, wholesale prices could be increased only for local products and only to a limited extent, while production costs continued their increase. Taxation had risen by more than 30 percent, payments for the public social-security systems by

---

the invitation to Vienna she exclaimed, "But it is I who have to thank you for letting me rise, as if through the touch of a magic wand, from the mass of nameless scientists!" See the correspondence in Mises Archive 71: 22–35.

[6]Richard von Schüller was the official president of the committee, but he did not take part in the writing. See Franz Baltzarek, "Ludwig von Mises und die österreichische Wirtschaftspolitik der Zwischenkriegszeit," *Wirtschaftspolitische Blätter* 28, no. 4 (1981): 136; Mises, *Erinnerungen*, p. 49.

[7]Redaktionskomitee der Wirtschaftskommission, *Bericht über die Ursachen der wirtschaftlichen Schwierigkeiten Österreichs* (Vienna: Staatsdruckerei, 1930), p. 19.

more than 50 percent, and the wage rates of the 1.3 million industrial workers by some 24 percent. The increase of production costs had squeezed corporate profits, which in turn made it impossible to attract the foreign capital direly needed for a quicker adjustment of Austrian industry. The committee therefore recommended a reduction of public expenditure and of public revenues, as well as a renegotiation of wage contracts in order to reduce total labor costs.

Mises was not happy with the report.[8] He thought it failed to identify the main culprits—the welfare state and the labor unions. He used his next opportunity to set the record straight, writing under his own name. He also put the discussion of crisis-related topics on the agenda of his private seminar, which in the academic year 1930–1931 dealt for the first time in many years exclusively with economic problems.[9] Similarly, in the winter semester, the university seminar dealt with the formation, maintenance, and consumption of capital.[10] The summer semester was to deal with methodological problems, but it was unexpectedly cancelled because Mises had to travel to the United States for a meeting of the International Chamber of Commerce.

These sessions were far more satisfying for Mises than were the public debates into which he had been drawn by his reputation as Austria's greatest monetary theorist. During the crisis, he confronted some of the more influential money cranks in public debate. He argued that the Great Depression was more

---

[8]Neither were the other members of the committee. The report was widely perceived as a manifesto of Manchester capitalism. Mises's hand in it was obvious. See Baltzarek, "Ludwig von Mises und die österreichische Wirtschaftspolitik der Zwischenkriegszeit," p. 136. The author states that Mises's views had a major impact on Austrian policy debates in the early years of the crisis.

[9]See the syllabus in Mises Archive 40: 14.

[10]See syllabus in Mises Archive 17: 219; see also the letter by Bloch referring to Köppel's lecture in Mises Archive 17: 202a, 203.

lengthy and severe than any former bust because it resulted from the combined effect of inflation and the regimentation of businesses.

In one of his public appearances, in late October 1930, Mises debated Robert Eisler, an Austrian economic historian affiliated with the Paris office of the League of Nations.[11] Eisler had written a book on the history of money and taught courses on his monetary policy schemes at the Sorbonne in Paris and the prestigious private *Institut Universitaire des Hautes Études Internationales* in Geneva. He advocated the entire program of anti-crisis policies that later became known as Keynesianism. Eisler claimed that the post-1929 crisis had resulted from previous deflationary policies and in particular from the deflationary gold standard. In his view, the crisis could be overcome by a simple change in the technique of international currency management: the abolition of any form of gold standard and the creation of an international fiat money system. This would solve various problems in the labor market, agriculture, housing and other fields. It would finance huge public works, give sufficient wages and old-age pensions to workers, and guarantee extraordinary bull markets for entrepreneurs and bankers. It would even appease social antagonisms within society.

No written account of the Mises-Eisler debate remains, but Mises's argument can be inferred from a public lecture that he delivered a few months later to the plenary meeting of the *Deutsche Hauptverband der Industrie*, the association of German industrialists in Czechoslovakia. The title of the lecture was "The Causes of the World Economic Crisis."[12] He delivered it

---

[11]Österreichischer Klub in Wien to Mises, letter dated October 14, 1930; Mises Archive 66: 2f. Mises apparently also gave another public talk, in Vienna, on Monday December 1, 1930; see Steiner to Mises, letter dated December 8, 1930; Mises Archive 66: 23. On Eisler see Irving Fisher, *Stabilised Money: A History of the Movement* (London: George Allen & Unwin, 1935), pp. 100–02.

[12]Mises to Siebeck, letter dated February 19, 1931; Mises Archive 92: 36.

on February 28, 1931, and it was soon published under a slightly different title in a major economics series that also featured many socialist and interventionist analyses of the crisis.[13]

The Causes of the Great Depression

In a mere 34 pages, Mises presented a concise and penetrating analysis of the crisis. He pointed out that the market economy was regulated by the requirement that entrepreneurs satisfy consumer preferences. Inflation disrupts this self-regulation of the market. It induces businessmen to overestimate the possibilities for profitable investment, so that they make bad investment decisions and squander resources. These errors become apparent in a crisis—the U.S. stock market crash of 1929, in this case. The market participants now revise their plans and adopt more sober views on economic conditions. Employment opportunities and capital goods are shifted from the unsustainable production projects to those firms and industries that are now most important to consumers and therefore most profitable. The unemployed find new jobs at lower wages, production resumes, and the economy grows again.

Mises stressed that this scenario, while typical for previous business cycles, did not exactly fit the conditions of the present

---

[13]Mises, *Die Ursachen der Wirtschaftskrise* (Tübingen: Mohr, 1931). On February 19, 1931, Mises had approached Mohr's CEO Paul Siebeck for the publication of his lecture in Czechoslovakia in the series "Recht und Staat." Siebeck was glad to accept this proposal and by March 2, they had agreed on the terms: Mises would obtain 30 complimentary copies, 80 marks per 16 pages, and the total number of copies in any edition would not exceed 2000 (see Mises Archive 92: 32ff.). Mises then also changed the title of the work from "The Causes of the World Economic Crisis" to "The Causes of the Economic Crisis" (see Mises Archive 92: 11). In mid-April, shortly before leaving for the United States, he was through with the revisions. On top of his thirty complimentary copies he ordered another twenty-five copies, and had twenty out of these fifty-five copies sent directly to their recipients. The money (170 marks, see Mises Archive 93: 14) was wired to his Postscheck account (see Mises Archive 92: 13).

one. Before, there was virtually no unemployment in the boom phase, and even during the bust unemployment and stagnation were temporary. They lasted only as long as it took market participants to find the most profitable new division of labor. But this time, Mises observed, things were markedly different—so much so that he had to adjust his business cycle theory. This time, despite enormous inflation, there was no corresponding general boom economy in Europe.

> In light of past experience and of our theory one should have assumed that the crisis would therefore be milder. But it is far more severe and, it seems, business conditions will not improve anytime soon.[14]

It would have been plausible to assume that the present bust would not be as painful as it would have been in the case of a more sweeping boom. The relatively weak boom should have induced a relatively moderate bust. But this was not the case. Why? Mises answered that the present stagnation was the combined result of two causes layered one over the other. The current business cycle had merely aggravated the problems of unemployment and the lack of profitability. But these problems had existed, and continued to exist independent of the cycle.

> Both the lack of profitability and unemployment are being intensified right now through the general depression. However, in the postwar period they have become lasting phenomena that have not disappeared entirely even in the upswing. We are confronted here with a new problem, one that cannot be answered by the theory of cyclical changes alone.[15]

What were the causes of the permanent postwar crisis? Mises argued that there were several. Each one, however, was an instance of government intervention. Mises thus explained the

---

[14]Mises, *Die Ursachen der Wirtschaftskrise*, p. 14.
[15]Ibid, pp. 14f.

Great Depression by combining his theory of business cycles with his theory of interventionism. The least controversial of his candidate causes was the nefarious influence of price controls and public finance. Most economists agreed that price ceilings created shortages of consumers' goods and that price floors resulted in unmarketable surpluses without benefiting anyone. They also accepted that the growth of the state increased the costs of production and that taxation of capital induced capitalists to consume rather than reinvest their wealth. More controversial, however, was Mises's stance on the labor market, where he was one of the few economists with the courage to stand fast on the law of supply and demand, even as it applies to employment and wages. The main cause of unemployment was clear: government-supported labor unions.[16]

On the unhampered market, he argued, unemployment could only be a temporary phenomenon. There are "probably always a certain number of job-seekers . . . just as on the unhampered housing market there are always unoccupied apartments and apartment-seekers."[17] Today we would say that search costs cause a certain amount of natural unemployment.[18]

---

[16]His opinion was already on record. See his remarks in the 1926 essay "Sozialliberalismus," reprinted in *Kritik des Interventionismus* (Jena: Gustav Fischer, 1929). In January 1926, the *Neues Wiener Tagblatt* approached Mises to get his opinion on how unemployment was to be reduced (see Mises Archive 80: 26). And on March 6, 1930 the Vienna journal *Welt am Morgen* published Mises's advocacy of the abolition of unemployment relief (see Mises Archive 66a: 40). Among the other economists who argued along these lines, see in particular, A.C. Pigou, *Industrial Fluctuations* (London: Macmillan, 1927); Jacques Rueff, "L'assurance chômage cause du chômage permanent," *Revue politique et parlementaire* (December 10, 1925); Lionel Robbins, *The Great Depression* (London: Macmillan 1934).

[17]Mises, *Die Ursachen der Wirtschaftskrise*, p. 15.

[18]Five years before, in his piece on "Interventionism," Mises had characterized this free-market unemployment as a "frictional phenomenon" that would not exist in a static state—that is, in equilibrium. See Mises, *Kritik des Interventionismus*, pp. 13, 20.

Except for this natural residue, however, the market cleared at a wage rate resulting from a competitive demand by entrepreneurs and a competitive supply of workers. "Now this self-regulation of the market is strongly obstructed through the intervention of the labor unions acting under the protection and support of government power." The labor unions seek to establish the wage rates of their members at higher than market rates. "This goal the unions pursue by the use of violence." Mises went on to explain:

> Only those workers who belong to the union, who demand the wage rates prescribed by the union, and who do their work in the manner prescribed by the union are permitted to work in the firms. Should the entrepreneur refuse to accept the conditions of the union, a strike ensues. Those workers who wish to work despite the union's imposed ban will be forced by acts of violence to refrain from their plan. These union tactics naturally presuppose that the government tolerates this behavior, at the least. Were it to proceed in its usual way and interfere with the criminals who abuse jobseekers and vandalize the machines and other of the entrepreneurs' facilities, then circumstances would be different. But that it has capitulated to the unions is the precise feature that characterizes the modern state.[19]

Owing to this position of power, which enables them to abuse the property rights of the capitalists as well as the human rights of workers and would-be workers, the unions can push wages above the market rate. But at this higher level it is impossible to hire all those who would have found employment otherwise. The result is unemployment and the concomitant misery of a great many people. For some time, the masses might tolerate their immiseration, but sooner or later they would demand jobs.

---

[19]Mises, *Die Ursachen der Wirtschaftskrise*, pp. 16f.

Even the unions could not resist such a large-scale popular movement and therefore the institution of tax-financed unemployment relief was created. He concludes:

> Unemployment as a permanent and mass phenomenon results from the labor-union policy of pushing up wage rates. Without unemployment relief, this policy would long since have collapsed. Unemployment relief is therefore not, as misguided public opinion assumes, a measure to alleviate emergencies caused by unemployment. To the contrary, it is an element in the chain of causes that create unemployment as a permanent and mass phenomenon in the first place.[20]

In short, the crisis had turned into a great depression through government interventionism. And this economic calamity in turn accentuated political antagonism within states and between states, spurring yet another round of destructive policies.[21]

How to break out of the vicious circle? Mises argued that ultimately there was no choice but to abolish all government intervention and to confront union power head on. The confrontation had better be sooner rather than later. The longer it is delayed—for example, through inflation—the more capital will be consumed, which in turn causes ever-decreasing wages and living standards.[22] And yet this idea continued to enjoy great popularity. As Mises wrote some months after publication of his lecture to a friend in Paris:

> Today, with the exception of a dozen or two reasonable individuals, the whole world is in complete agreement on two points: debts should remain unpaid, and the economy should be stimulated through strong inflation.[23]

---

[20]Ibid., p. 18.

[21]Ibid., pp. 26, 32.

[22]Ibid., pp. 31f.

[23]Mises to Fritz Georg Steiner, letter dated January 29, 1932, Mises Archive 71: 11.

Not all criticisms of his views were based on this opinion, however. Some critics charged Mises with one-sidedness. Some of his colleagues in the *Kammer* thought it was illegitimate to focus only on the problems of government interventionism. There was also something like entrepreneurial interventionism, which brought about very similar problems.[24] The nub of Mises's response to this argument is contained in a letter he wrote to *Kammer* colleague Rudolf von Bermann, who agreed with Mises on questions of government interference, but insisted that the government was not the only agency to engage in interventionism.[25] In his answer, Mises stressed the particular features of the selection process of the market:

> It is certain that entrepreneurs too commit errors; this has never been denied. But the characteristic feature of the capitalist economy is that the entrepreneur diminishes his own position as entrepreneur and property owner to the very extent to which he commits errors. . . . A capitalist social order unhampered by interventions, therefore, provides for a permanent selection among the capitalists and entrepreneurs. . . . Why can incompetent people in the German Reich and in Austria remain CEOs for many years? Because in an interventionist state these executives are selected primarily in regard to whether they enjoy a good reputation with the higher authorities (which

---

[24]Otto Conrad, "Der Interventionismus als Ursache der Wirtschaft-skrise—eine Auseinandersetzung mit Ludwig Mises" (Interventionism as cause of the economic crisis—a dispute with Ludwig Mises"), typewritten manuscript, Mises Archive 23: 42ff. Mises's response had the title "Interventionismus der Unternehmer? Entgegnung auf die vorstehenden Ausführungen Otto Conrads" (Interventionism of the entrepreneurs? Reply to Otto Conrad's aforesaid remarks), typewritten manuscript, Mises Archive 23: 31ff.

[25]Bermann to Mises, letter dated August 24, 1931; Mises Archive 95: 23ff. Bermann had been a student of Mises's in 1918. Later Mises brought the gifted Bermann into the *Kammer* and also maintained close private contact. See their correspondence in Mises Archive 51: 31f.; 95: 32.

possibly are the "lower" ones) and because firms that are long since bankrupt are artificially carried along for years, under the pressure of all sorts of interventions.[26]

The most popular alternative explanation of unemployment in those days, at least in intellectual circles, was the one that Emil Lederer had published in the same series in which Mises's brochure appeared. Lederer ridiculed "the primitive notion that, faced with unemployment, one could always restore equilibrium by reducing wage-rates." He argued that the crisis was a consequence of fast technological progress—so fast indeed that an adjustment of the market participants was somehow intrinsically impossible. As long as innovations applied only to consumer products, according to Lederer, unemployment would not result: the new industries would absorb any remaining idle labor. But when innovations occurred in the form of fast technological progress, which replaced labor by cheaper machinery at such a speed that entrepreneurs could not keep pace, unemployment ensued.[27]

The problem with this argument was not only its implicit premise that entrepreneurial speculation could not possibly keep up with fast technological progress, but the even deeper assumption that technological progress could somehow take place independent of entrepreneurs. In a chapter that Mises contributed to a *festschrift* for the Dutch professor C.A. Verreijn Stuart, he discussed why the very idea of technological progress

---

[26]Mises to Bermann, letter dated September 10, 1931; Mises Archive 95: 22.

[27]Emil Lederer, *Technischer Fortschritt und Arbeitslosigkeit* (Tübingen: Mohr, 1931). He had advocated these views for many years, along with the opinion that inflation can somehow create additional goods. See for example his editorial "Der technische Fortschritt" in the Vienna journal *Arbeiter-Zeitung* (September 4, 1927): 12.

outpacing adjustments was completely baseless.[28] Mises pointed out that capital was inherently conservative in the sense that the value of the existing capital structure forced the entrepreneurs constantly to weigh its maintenance against its displacement. It is not the case that any new technology, merely by virtue of being technologically superior to those presently in use, would displace the older ones. Such a complete replacement would occur only if it were warranted by market prices.

While Lederer, Conrad, and others had tried to counter Mises's analysis of the causes of the crisis by proposing alternative explanations, other economists confronted his main thesis head-on. They criticized Mises's argument that in an unhampered economy nothing prevents the clearing of the market through price adjustments. Erich Carell claimed that each change of supply and demand would induce cumulative (Wicksellian) effects that amplified the initial disequilibrium.[29] And Wilhelm Röpke argued:

> In the present phase of the crisis it seems to me it is wrong to expect that a reduction of the level of wages would re-establish equilibrium. This is wrong because, given the total paralysis of investment, each reduction of prices and incomes would lead to a continued sterilization of means of payment—in the form of an increase of the liquidity of the banking system—and thus to an extended disequilibrium. Mises and his fellow-travelers apparently do not sufficiently take account of the fact that today we have monstrous productive reserves that are unused; in other words, we have a gigantic "capital surplus" that requires credit expansion to become visible. For this

---

[28]Mises, "Das festangelegte Kapital," *Economische Opstellen: Aangeboden aan Prof. C.A. Verrijn Stuart* (Haarlem: De Erven F. Bohn N.V., 1931), pp. 214–28.

[29]Erich Carell, review of Mises's *Ursachen der Wirtschaftskrise* in *Jahrbücher für Nationalökonomie* 135 (1931): 924f.

reason it is not correct that government investment would deprive the private economy of its means. The paradoxical fact, which cannot be grasped on the basis of purely static ideas, is that the means of the private economy would thereby be multiplied.[30]

Mises had anticipated this line of argument in "The Causes of the Economic Crisis." He noticed that some economists had come up with a new theory of how inflation could be beneficial. These economists knew full well that unemployment resulted from excessive wage rates. But rather than confronting the unions with the demand to stop their harmful practices, they "suggest to cheat the unions." Mises summarized the argument and identified its crucial flaw:

> In the next inflation, nominal wage rates shall not be changed, which would be equivalent to a reduction of real wage rates. This blithely assumes that in the next boom the unions will not demand further wage increases, but quietly contemplate a reduction of real wages.[31]

It was not reasonable to expect such union behavior. Mises's refutation of the new pro-inflation argument was grounded in common sense. And by analogy it also applied to the owners of all other "monstrous productive reserves that are unused," as Röpke had claimed. It was unreasonable to assume that these owners would quietly contemplate a reduction of the real prices they obtained for selling or renting out their resources. But in the heated atmosphere of the early 1930s, with growing economic problems and a ruling statist ideology presenting government action as a panacea, reasonable argument was rare and dissenters were highly unpopular. As one reviewer of "The Causes of the Economic Crisis" explained:

---

[30]Wilhelm Röpke, review of Mises's *Ursachen der Wirtschaftskrise* in *Zeitschrift für Nationalökonomie* 4, no. 2 (1932): 273–75.

[31]Mises, *Die Ursachen der Wirtschaftskrise*, p. 31.

> The labor unions have become so powerful and such
> an important political factor in state and public opin-
> ion that nobody ventures to tell the truth—neither
> the journals, which seek to avoid being accused of
> antisocial sympathies, nor the government, which is
> afraid of becoming unpopular and of exposing itself
> to the unfettered demagoguery of all those parties
> that, not surprisingly, attract the masses with their
> bellicose cries against any reduction of wages.[32]

The plague of political correctness existed well before the
end of the twentieth century. Some of Mises's critics could not
help admiring his courageous stance faced with overwhelming
opposition. Eugen Altschul, while calling Mises "one of the
most extreme representatives of liberalism," admitted that he
was unafraid to argue consistently.[33] Another reviewer said, "the
Vienna professor Mises, who has been called the 'last knight of
liberalism,' fights indefatigably against government intervention in the market process."[34]

Even an otherwise fearless ally like Fritz Wolfrum criticized
him for stressing labor-union intervention as the primary factor
responsible for the crisis. Wolfrum would have preferred Mises
to stress other factors such as price controls "because everybody
is better at recognizing a fault in others and, after all, our purpose must be to enlighten the broad masses."[35]

⋙   ⋙   ⋙

Enlightenment of the broad masses! Often, Mises felt that it
was precisely the elites who were in need of more light. A case

[32]Walter Tschuppik in *Süddeutsche Sonntagspost* (November 8, 1931);
Mises Archive 45: 66.

[33]Dr. Eugen Altschul in *Magazin der Wirtschaft* (June 19, 1931).

[34]Albert Lauterbach in *Der Holzarbeiter* 40, no. 4 (February 18, 1932).

[35]Wolfrum to Mises, letter dated May 4, 1931; Mises Archive 77: 22.

in point was his 1931 trip to the United States and Canada, where he took part in a congress of the International Chamber of Commerce (ICC) and met many other colleagues and economists.[36]

The trade policy of the United States was one of the top problems discussed at the ICC meeting. In June 1930, the U.S. Congress had passed, and President Hoover had signed into law, the Smoot-Hawley Tariff Act, which authorized the highest tariffs on imports of agricultural products and manufactured items in the history of the United States. Within a year, it was already obvious that the act was devastating for international trade. It protected the farmers and manufacturers who produced for domestic markets, but hurt the consumers and farmers and manufacturers who produced for foreign markets. It undermined the international gold-exchange standard. The American political leadership would not admit this. The president, Congress, and the American representatives at the ICC meeting were firmly committed to the cause of what some of them called the "new economics"—rescuing the capitalist economy through more government intervention (fighting the disease by torturing the patient). A few months later, Hoover signed the 1932 Revenue Act, which brought about the largest peacetime increase of tax rates in the history of the United States, but this did not raise the absolute amount of taxes collected and did not keep Hoover from losing reelection at the end of that year. Starting in 1933, the new president, Franklin Delano Roosevelt, would intensify the New Deal policies that had begun with Smoot-Hawley.[37]

---

[36]See correspondence in Mises Archive 66: 28; 66a: 85, 98, 109, 129; 68: 51; 83: 14.

[37]See Murray N. Rothbard, *America's Great Depression*, 5th ed. (Auburn, Ala.: Ludwig von Mises Institute, 1999), esp. chap. 11: "The Hoover New Deal of 1932."

At the 1931 Washington meeting of the ICC, the interventionist spirit that produced these policies was evident. Mises wrote in correspondence:

> at the Congress I saw again how difficult it is today to battle against increasing protectionism. The US government and political parties energetically oppose all attempts to impose a moderation of US tariffs.[38]
>
> What I saw in America was not very pleasant. The official circles of the United States hold fast to a policy of high tariffs. . . . To be certain, the United States pursues the most pernicious interventionist ideas in its domestic and foreign economic policies.[39]

But the situation in Austria was certainly no better and declined quickly. In March, at the general meeting of the stockholders of *Oesterreichische Nationalbank*, Mises had publicly pointed out that the bank had succeeded in stabilizing the exchange rate of the schilling.[40] That was probably the best thing that could be said about Austrian finance. But he knew that grave problems lay ahead. Several times he had rejected executive positions with some of the major banks, because he believed they were bankrupt and it was only a matter of time before this state of bankruptcy would become apparent.

In early May 1931, the day of reckoning came. The default of Austria's largest bank, the Rothschild-dominated Credit-Anstalt, put the Austrian payments system into immediate jeopardy.[41] Upon his return to Vienna, Mises had to decline several

---

[38]Mises to Wilhelm Klein, letter dated June 10, 1931; Mises Archive 66a: 100.

[39]Mises to Fritz Wolfrum, letter dated June 10, 1931; Mises Archive 77: 23.

[40]The meeting took place on March 20, 1931. See the report by Gustav Linert in Mises Archive 66a: 175.

[41]Anselm von Rothschild had founded the Credit-Anstalt in 1855 as a public-private venture to stimulate economic development. Its difficulties in 1931 were essentially due to the fact that, two years before, the Rothschild

invitations to comment on the event and its implications for the Austrian government's efforts to balance its budget, saying such public statements could not be reconciled with his position as secretary of the *Kammer*. A penal lawsuit was brought against the executives of the bank, and Austrian law prohibited any initiative to influence public opinion before the verdict of the judges.[42] Too big to fail, the Credit-Anstalt was bailed out by Reisch's central bank. In exchange, it and other leading banks were coopted into reintroducing foreign exchange controls through the backdoor.[43] They were asked to hamper any gold exports of their customers. Mises must have felt this resurgence of mercantilist ideas was the beginning of the end. To the editor of *Deutsche Wirtschafts-Zeitung*, one of the journals that had solicited a comment, he confided:

> Our financial situation is far worse than the official view admits. And yet parliament opposes any hard-hitting measures out of concern for the voters—in particular, the many civil servants.[44]

The reluctance of "the official view" to admit the true extent of Austria's socialist plight stemmed also from the corruption of the media. This concerned in particular reports on the city of

---

family had given in to demands from the Austrian government to save the semi-public Boden-Credit-Anstalt after it had been subject to a bank run of several weeks. Merging with this bankrupt institution proved to be too much even for the financial acumen of Louis von Rothschild, who owned some 30 percent of the Credit-Anstalt.

[42]Only three years later did he feel free to analyze these events in an article published in a prominent review: "Der Weg der österreichischen Finanzpolitik" [The path of Austrian financial policy], *Wirtschaftliche Nachrichten* 18, no. 1 (January 10, 1935): 38–39.

[43]See Aurel Schubert, *The Credit-Anstalt Crisis of 1931* (Cambridge: Cambridge University Press, 1991); Howard S. Ellis, *Exchange Control in Central Europe* (Cambridge, Mass.: Harvard University Press, 1941).

[44]See Mises's letter, dated June 10, 1931 in Mises Archive 66a: 107.

Vienna, which had become an international showcase for communal socialism. As Mises pointed out in correspondence with a fellow Rotary Club member from the Netherlands, none of the Vienna newspapers dared oppose rent control or criticize the budget and other financial reports of the city of Vienna because the newspapers depended in so many ways on the city administration.[45] Few economists were critical enough to see through the public propaganda, and even fewer dared to speak out against it. Again it was the group around Mises that filled this gap, most notably when Hayek published his study on rent control.[46]

Mises was so convinced that all the major Austrian banks were bankrupt[47] that he kept personal bank accounts elsewhere. These prophecies materialized at an amazing speed. Bankruptcy of the Credit-Anstalt could be prevented only with help from the Rothschild banks in Paris and London. Few other establishments had saviors from abroad. Within two months, financial collapse spread throughout Austria, and on Black Monday, July 13, 1931, it reached Germany. One of the best-reputed German banks, the *Darmstädter und Nationalbank* closed its counters, triggering a chain reaction that quickly involved all payments

---

[45]Mises to Josephus Jitta, letter dated June 10, 1931; Mises Archive 66a: 102. Jitta was the president of the Rotary Club in Den Haag. Mises never met him on his prewar trips to Holland (1926–1936). The two men met for the first time at the second (1949) Mont Pèlerin Conference. See the correspondence in Grove City Archive: Jitta file.

[46]F.A. Hayek, *Das Mieterschutzproblem. Nationalökonomische Betrachtungen* (Vienna: Steyrermühl-Verlag, 1930). Mises was fond of this publication and recommended it in private correspondence; see for example Mises to Wolfrum, letter dated June 10, 1931; Mises Archive 77: 23. Another good study was published by Josef Schell, *Gerechtigkeitsidee und Mietengesetzgebung* (Vienna: Manz, 1927). Schell was married to a young woman who had attended Mises's classes at the Handelsakademie. See Schell to Mises, letter dated January 29, 1955; Grove City Archive: Schell file.

[47]He held this opinion after 1921. See Mises, *Erinnerungen*, p. 46.

within Germany. When the government decreed a compulsory holiday for the banks and the capital markets, international payments came to a halt.

A Lieutenant in London

In the spring of 1931, the political prospects for Europe were bleak. The Roaring Twenties had turned out to be a short interlude of relative liberty and international economic cooperation. Now the pendulum had swung back to interventionism and state idolatry. The only signs of hope were those few individuals and groups that had liberated themselves from the political prejudices of the time. The most promising group was the one led by Lionel Robbins at the London School of Economics.

Lionel Robbins

Robbins's career had been on a fast track. After a two-year stay at Oxford, he had become the chair of LSE's economics department in 1929 following the unexpected death of Allyn Young. Robbins gathered around himself a group of brilliant students who would become stars of twentieth century economic science: Ronald Coase, William Hutt, John Hicks, Nicholas Kaldor, Abba Lerner, Tibor de Scitovsky, George Shackle, Ludwig Lachmann, Paul Sweezy, and Ursula Webb (who married Hicks).[48] They were exposed to Mises's ideas like no other group outside Vienna.

Mises's influence on Robbins was mainly based on his writings, but it had been nurtured through personal contacts since

---

[48]Coase started his recollections of his early years at LSE with the following words: "I will be discussing what happened in economics in England, but these were times when, to a very considerable extent, this was what happened in economics." Ronald Coase, *Essays on Economics and Economists* (Chicago: University of Chicago Press, 1994), p. 19.

the early 1920s. By 1931, Mises was thoroughly familiar with the school's staff and faculty, and could give detailed instructions to foreign visitors about how to meet people at LSE. In a January 1931 letter to Walter Sulzbach, for example, he recommended that Sulzbach get in touch with Gregory and Robbins, "the best economists and freest minds in contemporary England." They had to be looked up in their offices and, if not there, called on at home. Meyendorff and Schwartz would certainly be willing to receive him if he gave their secretaries his calling card, mentioning that he was a friend of Mises's. He recommended the same procedure to solicit the assistance of Mr. Headicar, the librarian.[49]

In those days, Robbins's admiration for Mises was boundless. He eagerly proselytized among his countrymen and had already converted his friend Arnold Plant to the cause of Austrian economics. He also sought to increase the Misesian profile of the economics department through regular guest lectures by Mises and his closest students. His long-term plan was to build up an effective counterweight against the pernicious influence of John Maynard Keynes, whose advocacy of inflation and government intervention had swept the universities of Cambridge and Oxford, as well as the Bank of England.

Robbins also sought to stem the tides within his own school. This concerned not only political orientation, but also fundamental questions pertaining to the nature and method of economics. For years, LSE's management had sought to make the school a center of economic research in the image of mathematics and biology. The few remaining old-style economists did not believe the young Robbins was strong enough to fend off the positivist crusaders.

But then an unexpected opportunity arose when Hayek visited the department in late January and early February 1931 to

---

[49]Mises to Sulzbach, letter dated January 12, 1931; Mises Archive 66a: 70.

present his theory of business cycles, which was based on an elaboration of Böhm-Bawerk's theory of capital. It was Hayek's first personal encounter with Robbins, who had known him only through his writings.[50] Robbins had liked in particular Hayek's critique of the doctrines of the American economists William Trufant Foster and Waddill Catchings, two highly influential champions of the notion that excessive savings might prevent economic growth.[51] Similar views were prominent also in the United Kingdom and in particular in Cambridge, where—as we now know—Keynes went so far as to make plans for the euthanasia of the coupon-clipping classes.[52] Thus Robbins invited the talented young Austrian to join the cause in Britain.

Hayek delivered four lectures to an audience composed of professors and students. They met with mixed success. The senior faculty, most of whom did not know much about Austrian economics, found Hayek's tall figure far more impressive than his arguments. But the younger audience members were stunned. Robbins had prepared his students to receive a revelation from the epicenter of theoretical research. And under the impact of such passionate guidance, they indeed felt that Hayek's lectures were a great success. One of them, later to become a Nobel laureate, wrote about them in retrospect:

---

[50]Martha Braun later said that Robbins had tried for years to get Hayek to LSE. Martha Steffy Browne [Braun], "Erinnerungen an das Mises-Privatseminar," *Wirtschaftspolitische Blätter* 28, no. 4 (1981): 115.

[51]This work earned Hayek a *Habilitation* degree at the University of Vienna. It was published in 1929 as "Gibt es einen Widersinn des Sparens?" *Zeitschrift für Nationalökonomie* 1, no. 3 (1930).

[52]Keynes suggested that a deliberate policy of lowering interest rates "would mean the euthanasia of the rentier, and, consequently, the euthanasia of the cumulative oppressive power of the capitalists to exploit the scarcity-value of capital." John Maynard Keynes, *General Theory of Employment, Interest, and Money* (New York and London: Harcourt, Brace, 1936), p. 376.

They were undoubtably the most successful set of public lectures given at LSE during my time there. . . . The
audience, notwithstanding the difficulties of understanding Hayek, was enthralled. What was said
seemed to us of great importance and made us see
things of which we had previously been unaware.
After hearing these lectures, we knew why there was
a depression. Most students of economics at LSE and
many members of the staff became Hayekians or, at
any rate, incorporated elements of Hayek's approach
in their own thinking.[53]

Robbins himself later characterized the Hayek lectures as "a
sensation" that was "at once difficult and exciting."[54] He immediately prepared their publication and began lobbying to get
Hayek a position at LSE. Hayek, probably at the behest of Robbins, wrote a review of Keynes's *Treatise on Money* and sent the
manuscript to Robbins, who was the editor of LSE's journal
Economica. The Cambridge economist's book had just appeared,
in December 1930, and Hayek's review of it was brilliant and
devastating. Robbins now persuaded LSE director William
Beveridge to make him an offer. Hayek became the Tooke Professor of Political Economy. His lectures were published under
the title *Prices and Production* and his review of Keynes's book
appeared in *Economica*.

The last knight of liberalism had found a worthy lieutenant
in London.

---

[53]Coase, *Essays on Economics and Economists*, p. 19.

[54]Lionel Robbins, *Autobiography of an Economist* (London: Macmillan,
1971), p. 127. Robbins went on (p. 128):

I do not think nowadays that the analytical constructions
which excited us so much in the lectures on Prices and Production had all the width or appropriateness of assumption
which some of us—including conspicuously the present
writer—were disposed to claim for them.

In the fall of the same year, Hayek and Robbins co-taught Hayek's first LSE seminar. The entire economics teaching staff was in attendance when he explained and defended the Austrian theory of capital. In a letter to Mises, Hayek reported on the atmosphere of the discussions:

> Some of the junior (rank-wise, not age-wise!) colleagues—in particular Hicks, Benham, or Toysonby—are excellent, too. There is much opportunity for me to learn, and I am hindered in doing so only because Robbins presented me as an eminent authority, so that people always want to hear my opinion on all matters. I am aware, for the first time, that I owe to you virtually everything that gives me an advantage as compared to my colleagues here and to most economists even outside my narrow field of research (here my indebtedness to you goes without saying). In Vienna one is less aware of [this intellectual debt to you] because it is the unquestioned common basis of our circle. If I do not deceive too many expectations of the people here at LSE, it is not to my credit but to yours. However, [my] advantage [over the others] will disappear with your books being translated and becoming generally known.[55]

Mises was certainly happy with this development. Commenting on the work of Hutt, one of Robbins's students, who had just published a revisionist account of the impact of capitalism on the condition of the nineteenth-century English working classes (an account that was devastating for the established view that the free market had worsened the plight of the working poor) he wrote in December 1931:

---

[55]Hayek to Mises, letter dated November 21, 1931; Mises Archive 81: 19ff. Hayek went on: "I must tell you this because I here feel more indebted to you than anytime before. Moreover, given that Robbins and Plant provide excellent support to championing your ideas, I hope to have some success."

> In England one can observe a decided turning away
> from the atheoretical direction. The movement that
> today is centered in the London School of Economics
> and in the person of Robbins will have the greatest
> scientific and political impact.[56]

Robbins and Hayek in turn encouraged their Viennese Meister
to visit London more frequently. Mises had a standing invitation to stay at Robbins's home. Hayek argued: "Here you have
at least as many honest admirers as anywhere else, and it would
be good if you could reinforce the influence that you exercise
anyway through frequent personal visits."[57] The absolute high
point of Mises's impact was reached with the publication of
Robbins's *Nature and Significance of Economic Science*. Sending a
copy to Mises, the author called it a "modest attempt to popu-
larize for English readers the methodological implications of
modern Economic Science," and he apologized "for my crudi-
ties of exposition."[58]

But the love affair between LSE and Misesian economics did
not last. The new Austrian doctrines had initially benefited
from their exoticness and novelty, but their policy implications
prevented certain long-term conversions. A case in point was
William Beveridge, who during the late 1920s had been
infected by Robbins's enthusiasm for the logical rigor of Mises's
writings, which had made him more tolerant toward classical-
liberal policy prescriptions.[59] But by the time Hayek delivered
his inaugural lecture in early 1933, Sir William had become

---

[56]Mises to Hayek, letter dated December 7, 1931; Mises Archive 81: 18.

[57]Hayek to Mises, letter dated January 11, 1932; Mises Archive 81: 2.

[58]Robbins to Mises, letter dated May 25, 1932; Mises Archive 83: 1.
Lionel Robbins, *Nature and Significance of Economic Science* (London: Macmillan, 1932).

[59]He was a notorious champion of intervention most notably in the free
labor market. See William Beveridge, *Unemployment: A Problem of Industry*,
2nd ed. (London: Longmans, Green & Co., 1930).

"again a socialist of the purest sort." Hayek surmised that this was "an emotional reaction to *Gemeinwirtschaft*, which he had just read and not understood."[60]

Hayek himself was instrumental in turning the LSE group away from Mises and toward the emerging verbal-Walrasian movement that had begun in Germany a decade earlier under the leadership of Wieser, Cassel, and Schumpeter. Given Hayek's background, this was hardly surprising. His economic thought had been nurtured in the classes of Friedrich von Wieser, and he had never made a secret of this intellectual heritage. Mises knew this perfectly well.[61]

Hayek not only stressed the common features of the Austrian and the Lausanne Schools, but also believed the latter to be far more technically advanced and therefore better suited to deal with the more demanding problems of economic analysis, in particular with the problem of value imputation. He would have presented these views from his very first LSE seminar on capital theory, where he must have found the ready support of the young John Hicks, who at that time had already embarked on his project of bringing Walras and Pareto to LSE.[62] Their combined influence came to be felt most notably in the second edition of Robbins's *Nature and Significance of Economic Science*,

---

[60]Hayek to Mises, letter dated March 10, 1933; Mises Archive 81: 5. Mises replied: "I am sorry that the impact of *Gemeinwirtschaft* on Sir William was not the intended one. By the way, has he already read the English version?" Mises to Hayek, letter dated March 17, 1933; Mises Archive 81: 6. Thus the manuscript must have been available by March 1933. Beveridge's opposition could explain why the book came out only in 1936.

[61]Significantly, he hailed Hayek's article on "Capital Consumption" as the best and clearest of all his writings—after Hayek had published his two early books on money and the trade cycle. See Mises to Hayek, letter dated December 18, 1931; Mises Archive 81: 17.

[62]Hicks had taught advanced classes in economics from 1929 onwards, that is, from the moment Robbins assumed leadership of the department. See Robbins, *Autobiography of an Economist*, p. 129.

which appeared in 1935. While the first edition almost completely neglected the Lausanne School, the new edition was replete with references to mathematical economists.

Hayek acquainted Robbins's group with the views of the fourth-generation Austrian economists. He championed the notion that general equilibrium theory was the state of the art and that all verbal economists, including Mises, worked within the very same framework. They were convinced that all further elaborations had to depart from here. Morgenstern and Hayek most vividly felt the need for reform, but neither of them grasped that the alternative was already at hand. It had escaped their notice that the logical structure of Mises's arguments against socialism and interventionism was squarely outside the Walrasian paradigm.

Hayek's two books on money appeared in English before any of Mises's works.[63] And he was the first Austrian economist ever to have a direct personal impact on the Anglo-Saxon world—the last best hope for Austrian economists after Germany and Austria turned socialist in the 1930s. It was Hayek therefore who was responsible for the impression of most English and American economists about modern Austrian economics during those critical years before the publication of Keynes's *General Theory*. It seems he made his case less successfully than his great rival from Cambridge.

Hayek later regretted that he had not refuted Keynes's *General Theory* in 1936 as he had done earlier with his *Treatise on Money*, and he seems to have believed that his failure to do so was crucial to the success of the Keynesian Revolution. But this was certainly an exaggeration of the influence he had with his British colleagues at the time. Hayek failed to do in 1930s

---

[63]F.A. Hayek, *Prices and Production* (London: Routledge, 1931); idem, *Monetary Theory and Trade Cycle Theory* (London: Routledge, 1933); Mises, *Theory of Money and Credit* (London: Jonathan Cape, 1934); idem, *Socialism* (London: Jonathan Cape, 1936).

Britain what Mises had done in 1920s Germany: reverse the orientation of the profession by the sheer power of his arguments. Hayek had his chance, but in the perception of the British mainstream his writings were at best controversial. Sraffa's review of *Prices and Production* had at least the same negative impact on Hayek's influence as Hayek's review of the *Treatise on Money* had had on Keynes's.

To a certain extent this resulted from the inconsistencies and contradictions Hayek had inherited from his real mentor. Hayek was and would remain throughout his life a disciple of Wieser's. This was so despite the fact that of the entire fourth generation of Austrian economists, he was the one closest to Mises in both methodological and political views.[64] The main reason, however, was that Hayek, still in his early thirties, was simply overburdened by the amount of work involved in trying to live up to Robbins's expectations. He never managed to publish more than essays or excerpts of much larger (but unfinished) manuscripts, a fact he constantly lamented. He never had the time to think through the fundamental problems of economic theory in its relationship to all other elements of Austrian economics. His presentations of monetary theory, capital theory, and business-cycle theory were mainly syntheses of already existing doctrines. Where he could not rely on the work of others as a supporting framework he lost himself in the analysis of details and never produced a coherent picture of his subject.[65]

When Keynes's *General Theory* appeared, in the same year as the English translation of Mises's *Socialism*, the initial curiosity

---

[64]In the few years following the creation of the *Institut für Konjunkturforschung*, his political views became indistinguishable from those of Mises. See the description of his activities in Hans Jörg Hennecke, *Friedrich August von Hayek* (Düsseldorf: Wirtschaft und Finanzen, 2000), pp. 87–91.

[65]The best illustration of this is F.A. Hayek, *Pure Theory of Capital* (London: Macmillan, 1941). The product of ten years at LSE, it was a book with neither head nor tail.

about Austrian economics had faded. The stage was set for the return of the local champion. Hayek had made no progress in promoting Austrian economists among the group of brilliant students who after World War II would shape economic teaching and research throughout the world. After ten years at LSE, he had used up the authority he inherited from Mises and lost former allies to the burgeoning Keynesian revolution.

This might seem in retrospect like a lost opportunity. Hayek was in a pivotal position to prepare for the rise of Austrian economics in England and the United States. And he certainly could have done more to promote Austrian economics in London had the circumstances been different. But the circumstances were what they were: Hayek had come to LSE at a time when the chair of the economics department was politically weak, and when the efforts of the school's management to turn economics into applied mathematics had attracted a number of highly gifted students eager to explore this new direction. Moreover, Austrian economics was not yet what it was about to become. The school was still in the phase before Mises's quantum leap. The encompassing system of economic thought that would first be expressed in *Nationalökonomie* (1940) and then in *Human Action* (1949) was then only visible in its broadest outlines.

Finally, there is the simple fact that Hayek was not a Misesian. In the early 1930s, Hayek was a pillar of the very same general-equilibrium movement that he decried a few years later. It would be meaningless to regret, in hindsight, that Hayek did not do what he had never set out to do, what he could not have succeeded in doing had he tried. He could not explain and defend a doctrine in the 1930s that was not fully developed until the 1940s.

Return to Foreign-Exchange Controls

After his return from the ICC meeting in Washington, Mises spent two busy months trying to limit the political damage of the Credit-Anstalt crisis. When he left Vienna at the end of July, he had helped beat back attempts to officially establish a system of foreign-exchange controls that would have thrown Austria back to 1922. He returned to Vienna in mid-September—just in time to learn that the Bank of England had abandoned the gold standard, refusing to redeem its notes in gold.[66] Mises was shocked and feared the worst. He surprised the members of his seminar, but especially his English student Ursula Webb with the announcement that "In one week, England will be in a hyper-inflation!"[67] He still did not fully anticipate the political landslide that soon set in. A week later he left Vienna again, this time for lectures in London and Frankfurt.[68] When he returned to Vienna on October 6, the government had officially reintroduced foreign exchange controls, instituting a return to the bad old days he had thought were gone forever. As he wrote to one of his friends:

> Events in Austria are taking a turn that causes me to fear the worst. We have found ourselves in a controlled economy once again. Foreign currency stocks are being "managed," a kind of Central Economic Agency, albeit under a different name, is being set up for each of the various branches of industry . . . usury laws and seizures lie just ahead. People have learned nothing and have forgotten

[66]See the correspondence in Mises Archive 66a: 142; 69: 8. The Bank of England suspended payments on September 19, 1931.

[67]The incident is reported in John R. Hicks, *A Market Theory of Money* (Oxford: Clarendon, 1989), p. 101. Ursula Webb was at the time studying in Vienna. A few years later she married John Hicks.

[68]In London, Mises stayed at Robbins's house. See Mises to Robbins, letter dated November 23, 1931; Mises Archive 83: 9. See also Mises to Lederer, letter dated October 6, 1931; Mises Archive 73: 10. He had probably arranged this trip at the end of September in order to avoid celebrations of his fiftieth birthday in Vienna. He asked his secretary to stifle all such attempts. He would be more agreeable if the organizers of birthday parties returned in twenty years. See Thieberger to Mises, letter dated August 12, 1941; Grove City Archive: Thieberger files.

everything. You can imagine my disposition under such circumstances.[69]

The collapse of the brief period of free trade that had blossomed in the second half of the 1920s was now at hand. More bad news poured in. Some of Mises's former allies were now advocating inflation using theories that had been refuted countless times.[70]

One incident epitomized the entire situation: In July 1930, Mises had been invited by the League of Nations to write a memorandum for the League's Gold Delegation. The mission of the delegation was "to examine into and report upon the causes of fluctuations in the purchasing power of gold and their effect on the economic life of the nations." Among its members were Keynes, Cassel, Sprague, and Janssen—certainly a bad sign. Still Mises complied and in early October 1930 sent his paper to Alexander Loveday, the head of the League's (Rockefeller-sponsored) economic intelligence unit.[71] Publication was delayed, however, and a year later Mises was notified that none of the memoranda that had been solicited for the Gold Delegation would be published, ostensibly for budgetary reasons.[72]

---

[69]Mises to Wolfrum, letter dated October 24, 1931; Mises Archive 77: 21.

[70]For example, Reisch published a paper arguing that, although all fiduciary media are by their very nature inflationary, this inflation was not harmful if the fiduciary media were issued only as short-term commercial credits. See Richard Reisch, "Das Kreditproblem der Volkswirtschaft," *Zeitschrift für Nationalökonomie* 3, no. 1 (1932). Reisch, it will be recalled, was the president of the *Oesterreichische Nationalbank*. Mises commented on the paper in private correspondence: "horrendous." Mises to Steiner, letter dated January 29, 1932; Mises Archive 71: 11.

[71]Loveday (League of Nations) to Mises, letter dated July 1, 1930; Mises Archive 91a: 3ff.

[72]League of Nation to Mises, letter dated October 13, 1931; Mises Archive 66a: 141. Keynes and others had meanwhile published the Macmillan Report (London: HMSO, 1931), which made a highly successful case for inflationary finance to stop the fall of the price level.

Mises was invited to sit on the new Foreign Exchange Board, whose job was to do everything of which he disapproved. He probably accepted the position in order not to hurt Austrian credit abroad: his absence from the Board would have disquieted foreign investors.

In a letter to Robbins he described the new system and his function within it:

> Just when I returned to Vienna, the crazy foreign-exchange control was introduced. At the top of this unfortunate system is a Foreign Exchange Board, which decides everything pertaining to our foreign commerce and thus is some sort of a general director of the national economy. I am the only non-interventionist member of this body, into which I fit as well as into the executive council of the 3rd International in Moscow. . . .
>
> There is a general enthusiasm for new interventionist measures and for "state capitalism" and "hyper-interventionism." Any resistance against this policy is peremptorily opposed . . . by pointing out that England too is now going to adopt a policy of high protective tariffs.[73]

The power of the Board was soon cut back quite drastically, possibly as a consequence of Mises's agitation from within. Only two weeks after Mises had presented it as a central planning bureau in a letter to Robbins, he wrote to Hayek that the Board was "a totally superfluous institution since it has no power" and that he regretted having agreed to spend his time there.[74]

Still, a Board position seems to have been powerful enough to influence the allocation of foreign currency to individual

---

[73]Mises to Robbins, letter dated November 23, 1931; Mises Archive 83: 9. The original German term for the Board was "Devisenbeirat" or, more explicitly, "Beirat für die Devisenzuteilung in der Nationalbank."

[74]Mises to Hayek, letter dated December 7, 1931; Mises Archive 81: 18.

firms, giving Mises the unwanted power to grant favors to special interests. In January 1932, for example, he received a letter from Abraham Frowein, an important German industrialist and vice-president of the International Chamber of Commerce. Frowein owned a silk factory in Vienna. The firm's activities depended crucially on access to foreign currency to pay for imported raw materials. Mises ignored the offer to "return any services as a matter of course" and instead referred Frowein's representative to a colleague on the Board who was responsible for the silk industry.[75]

Since no Austrian could buy foreign currency or take schillings out of the country, traveling was almost impossible for ordinary citizens—a considerable problem for Mises, who often went abroad for lectures.[76] But he had just concluded a new contract with Gustav Fischer for a new edition of *Socialism*, and Fischer agreed to become Mises's unofficial banker. He did not pay royalties to Mises's account in Vienna, but kept the money and sent it piecemeal to the hotels where Mises stayed on his trips in Germany.[77] This is how Mises was able to participate, for example, in board and committee meetings of the *Verein für Sozialpolitik* in Berlin in early January 1932, and in the *Verein's* annual convention in September of the same year.

---

[75]Frowein to Mises, letter dated January 16, 1932; Mises Archive 71: 16; Mises to Frowein, letter dated January 21, 1932; Mises Archive 71: 17. After the war, Frowein became the honorary president of the ICC and remained on good terms with Mises. See their correspondence in Grove City Archive: "F" files.

[76]And for other private reasons: he had a small account at the *Österreichisches Creditinstitut für öffentliche Unternehmungen und Arbeiten*, through which all foreign payments were channeled. Mises used it to pay for his books, for example, for the *Encyclopaedia of the Social Sciences*, to which he had subscribed before the foreign exchange controls were instituted. Yet this "private clearing" involved a markup of 22 percent. See the correspondence in Mises Archive 71: 107ff.

[77]See for example Fischer to Mises, letter dated September 26, 1932; Mises Archive 68: 7.

Back home in the fall of 1931, Mises organized a meeting of the *Nationalökonomische Gesellschaft* and in a passionate speech attacked the notion that the current crisis resulted from shortcomings of capitalism and required the remedy of more government intervention. The only rational response to the present calamity was finally to stand against the labor unions, which were the root cause of the inflationary policies behind the crisis. The lecture drew international attention.[78]

Some reacted with hysteria, especially after Mises published his position as "Die Krise und der Kapitalismus" (Crisis and Capitalism).[79] His former student Hedwig Lemberger claimed that economic science was bankrupt if it had no other solution for unemployment than to allow the unhampered market to reduce wage rates. She argued that Mises's Manchester-liberal analysis applied only to the conditions of the nineteenth century, while in the present crisis unemployment resulted from unmanageably fast technological progress, as Emil Lederer had explained.[80] Mises replied:

> I cannot understand why it is a declaration of bankruptcy for economic science to see one of the causes of disruptions of economic life in the labor-union policy of keeping wage rates above the level that would be established on the unhampered market, and in the fact that government supports this policy through unemployment relief and the refusal to protect job-seekers. . . . Streamlining has nothing to do with unemployment. There was streamlining also in the nineteenth century, maybe even to a relatively greater extent than today. But because at the time

---

[78]Hayek in London had heard reports about it. See Hayek to Mises, letter dated November 21, 1931; Mises Archive 81: 21.

[79]Mises, "Die Krise und der Kapitalismus," *Neue Freie Presse* (October 17, 1931).

[80]Hedwig Lemberger to Mises, dated November 15, 1931; Mises Archive 66a: 158.

there were no interventions in the formation of wage rates, the fired workers found employment in new and extended industries. They would even have been absorbed far quicker but for a number of government regulations that hampered their freedom of migration and change of profession. My assumptions do not merely rely, as you believe, on the experience of times long past, but especially on irrefutable theoretical considerations.[81]

Eventually the crisis was settled the same way as the post-war crisis ten years earlier: more foreign debt. In July 1932, Austria secured a foreign credit of 300 million schillings from the League of Nations. The road was free for a new beginning.

✥   ✥   ✥

The crisis prompted a renewed interest in business-cycle research, and in seeking the means for government to steer the economy away from the increasingly dramatic swings between boom and bust. The Vienna Institute for Business Cycle Research published two monographs that were to become classics in the literature of economic science: Hayek's *Preise und Produktion*, and Fritz Machlup's *Börsenkredit, Industriekredit und Kapitalbildung*. Mises was very proud of these works, especially of Machlup's book, which he called a masterpiece. Austrian analyses of the fundamental practical issues of the day were much needed to counter prevailing anti-capitalist views. Mises's educational mission over the past ten years now paid off. Many years later, a member of the Mises orbit recalled in correspondence the "die-hard [*kämpferische*] group of Mises, Hayek, Strigl, Morgenstern, and Meinl"[82] that used all available media

---

[81]Mises to Lemberger, dated November 21, 1931; Mises Archive 66a: 157.

[82]Jorge Radványi to Mises, letter dated May 21, 1959; Grove City Archive: Buenos Aires file.

and institutions to plead the case for economic liberty and against government interventionism.[83]

These activities had their impact on public policy. In distinct contrast to the massive proto-Keynesian deficit-spending policies that in the early 1930s came to be applied in other western countries, the Austrian government pursued a program of comparative austerity—with some very positive results. From 1932 to 1937, national production dramatically increased in industry and agriculture, the government's budget was balanced, foreign public debt was cut in half, central-bank reserves doubled, and unemployment shrank from 310,000 to 220,000.[84]

One ally of this group, Fritz Wolfrum proposed a radical remedy to the situation: total liberalization of the monetary sector. Wolfrum not only recommended rescinding foreign-exchange controls. He also called for the abolition of all impediments to private minting and the private issue of banknotes. This reform, he argued, would not only be a way out of the present calamity and prevent similar crises in the future, it would also lead to monetary liberalization in other countries. This in turn would raise the price of precious metals, further rewarding the early adopters:

> It is certain that the country that first liberates the monetary economy will benefit most from its fructifying benefits; and it is obvious that, once the process is set in motion, each country must follow the others.[85]

---

[83]A collection of press articles that Machlup, Morgenstern, Haberler, Hayek, and others wrote from 1931 to 1934 for Graetz's *Neues Wiener Tagblatt* has recently been published in Hansjörg Klausinger, *Machlup, Morgenstern, Haberler, Hayek und andere* (Marburg: Metropolis, 2005).

[84]See Ernst Hoor, *Österreich 1918–1938* (Vienna: Bundesverlag für Unterricht, Wissenschaft und Kunst, 1966), pp. 142f.

[85]Fritz Wolfrum, "Das Geldproblem," typewritten manuscript dated November 12, 1931, pp. 8f.; Mises Archive 77: 17f.

As Wolfrum's case demonstrates, the crisis divided the wheat from the chaff within the classical-liberal movement. Some abandoned liberalism and returned to interventionism, while others became more radical in their defense of liberty. Lionel Robbins wrote to Mises:

> Every day reveals fresh incursions of the system of free exchange and private property and it becomes clear that the number of persons capable of putting up an intelligent defense of capitalist institutions is very small. Behind the scenes we do what we can but there are not many of us to carry on the battle. . . . The sad thing about this crisis is that it seems to be driving so many who at one time were good liberals over to the other side. With me it has been just the opposite: all sorts of doubts and mental reservations have been cleared up and I am conscious of being much more "*streng*" than in the past. . . . Certainly to judge from the quality of the argument on the other side, it ought not to be difficult to defeat it on that plane.[86]

Mises agreed. At the end of December, he wrote a two-part article for the *Neue Freie Presse* on the gold standard and its enemies. He argued it was impossible to replace gold in international exchanges. And even in domestic exchanges, the position of this metal would only grow stronger the more the national governments followed their inflationary policies.[87]

Mises accepted a proposal of the journalist Robert Scheu who, in February 1932, had invited him to take part in what was then an entirely new format: the talk show.[88] Scheu's idea

---

[86]Robbins to Mises, letter dated December 19, 1931; Mises Archive 83: 5ff. "Streng" means severe.

[87]Mises, "Die Goldwährung und ihre Gegner," *Neue Freie Presse* (December 25 and 30, 1931).

[88]See their correspondence and related documents in Mises Archive 71: 52, 58f., 158ff.

was to conduct live interviews with prominent experts on the pressing economic issues of the day. The interviews would be held in a public auditorium and broadcast to a radio audience. The first interviewee, in early March 1932, was Othmar Spann. The evening was apparently a great success despite the fact that Spann had rarely given public lectures. Still Mises hesitated. From previous correspondence Mises knew Scheu to be a money crank, so he sought to establish a list of questions to which he would reply. Mises eventually appeared on the talk show, on Thursday, March 17, to discuss the gold standard compared to other monetary systems, the regulation of the monetary circulation of a national economy, the role of central banks in monetary policy, the creation of national currencies, and the theories of Silvio Gesell—Germany's most popular money crank who advocated new laws to encourage the spending of money by a special tax on "hoarding," that is, on savings.[89]

In early April 1932, then, Mises eventually got the *Kammer* to adopt a resolution against the artificial exchange rate of the schilling. Albert Hahn wrote from Frankfurt, asking Mises to what extent he was responsible for the contents of the *Kammer* report, to which Mises replied:

> The resolution has resulted from a first draft that I wrote, but after difficult and lengthy negotiations it has been revised to obtain unanimity through compromise. Hence, I myself cannot of course take public responsibility. I would have stated things less ambiguously.[90]

The Austrian government did not change its course, and by June a return to the old gold parity was no longer possible without

---

[89]Gesell's views found a spokesman in the eloquent and authoritative Keynes. See Keynes, *General Theory of Employment, Interest, and Money*, chap. 23, sec. 6.

[90]Mises to Hahn, letter dated April 9, 1932; Mises Archive 71: 45.

upsetting the price system, which had adjusted to the circumstances. The economic situation had considerably deteriorated and Mises was furious, fulminating in a letter to his Dutch colleague and friend G.M. Verrijn Stuart:

> In Austria we stand on the debris of the interventionist and state-socialist system. All of the public firms have passive balances . . . and considerable sums of tax money must be used to compensate for these deficits. Unemployment grows and unemployment relief devastates public finance. . . . But the peak of the madness is the foreign-exchange controls.
>
> He who seeks to study the consequences of thoroughgoing state socialism, city socialism, and interventionism should pursue these studies in Austria, where we enjoy government interventionism "without gaps." We have reached the point where those who "merely" argue in favor of protective tariffs and against the prohibition of imports are decried as free traders.[91]

It was probably in these days that Mises became a "metallist"—having supported the gold exchange standard, he now advocated a metallic currency as a way to keep government out of monetary policy altogether.[92] More than twenty years earlier, in the first edition of his *Theory of Money and Credit*, he had come close to poking fun at the simpletons who believed coins of precious metal were money in some stronger sense than banknotes were.[93] As a

---

[91]Mises to G.M. Verrijn Stuart, letter dated June 30, 1932; Mises Archive 71: 136.

[92]Mises to James Gardner, letter dated March 30, 1964; Grove City Archive: "G" file. Mises here states that he advocated "the classical old gold standard (and not . . . the gold exchange standard)" and that "I changed my mind concerning the functioning of the gold exchange standard as it happened more than 30 years ago."

[93]See Mises, *Theorie des Geldes under Umlausfmittel*, 1st ed. (Leipzig: Duncker & Humblot, 1912), pp. 44, 48, 56f.

young man, he had come across gold and silver coins only as collector's items (his father had a famous collection). He had always understood the merit of a metallic *standard* to keep the quantity of money independent of political manipulation, but he had never advocated the actual *circulation* of gold or silver coins. But now the evidence was undeniable: governments could not be trusted even with the production of money.

He remained a monetary metallist for the rest of his life. In a roundtable discussion on the gold standard that took place in January 1948 Mises spoke only once, and only to underline a point made by another speaker:

> Under present conditions no return to the gold standard is possible without a return to an effectual circulation of gold coins. . . . If gold coins are employed in daily transactions, if everybody is used to receiving and giving away gold pieces, if people are accustomed to carrying gold coins for retail purposes, the public becomes aware of the fact that gold is the nation's standard money and that the country is under a gold standard. This cognizance has not merely pedagogic value. It enables the average citizen to realize in time whether his government is clinging to sound monetary policies or whether it is tampering with the currency system. The weakness of a gold standard without effectual circulation of gold coins consists precisely in the fact that it makes it extremely difficult for the average citizen to discern inflation in its early stages. . . . An effectual gold coin circulation makes the voter the guardian of the gold standard. This is its main function.[94]

---

[94]He was underlining something said by Spahr. See the typewritten manuscript of Mises's comment in Grove City Archive: Courtney files. Mises later incorporated these views in *Human Action: A Treatise on Economics* (New Haven, Conn.: Yale University Press, 1949, p. 780) and in the new 1953 edition of his *Theory of Money and Credit* (London: Jonathan Cape, 1934), pp. 450ff.

Second Edition of Socialism

The battles on the political front had their impact on Mises's academic pursuits, especially on his teaching. The 1931–1932 private seminar met more irregularly, or at any rate was less well planned than usual. At least some of the sessions apparently dealt with the theory of capital and the business cycle, featuring lectures by Machlup, Morgenstern, and Bloch.[95]

His university seminar now focused on methodological problems of the social sciences.[96] Subjects dealt with in the winter semester were the relationship between theory and praxis, and between facts and theories; the implications of the is-ought distinction; the universal validity of economic knowledge; quantitative and qualitative knowledge; the relations between statistical, historical, and theoretical research; the meaning of *verstehen*; behaviorism; the mathematical method; forecasting in economics; and economics and sociology.

Mises had to begin the 1932 summer semester late because he had to attend two conferences of the International Chamber of Commerce, and also take part in a world economic conference in Berlin, which reunited politicians and experts from all over the world to discuss the implications of the present crisis for international commerce and finance.[97,98] The seminar sessions continued the discussions of the winter semester, dealing in particular with behaviorism and its relationship with the

---

[95]See their thesis papers in Mises Archive 40: 21f.

[96]See the schedule in Mises Archive 17: 233.

[97]The ICC conference in Innsbruck took place in the third week of April, the Welthandels-Woche in the first week of May, and the ICC conference in Munich started on May 18. See correspondence in Mises Archive 68: 10, 13; 71: 38; 81: 14; 85: 5.

[98]The *Weltwirtschaftskonferenz Berlin 1932* was part of a *Welthandels-Woche*, a weeklong conference organized by the newspaper *Berliner Tageblatt*. Mises was back in Vienna by Friday morning, May 6, for urgent *Kammer* business. See documents and correspondence in Mises Archive 71: 10; 77: 6.

approach of German historicism; the meaning of "meaning" in the social sciences and its connections with utilitarianism; the concept of *homo oeconomicus*; economics and sociology; sociology and history; and again, forecasting in economics.[99]

Mises's biggest academic project in 1931–1932 was the preparation of the second edition of *Socialism*. Upon his return from the United States, he found on his desk a letter from Gustav Fischer, announcing that Fischer was running out of copies of *Socialism* and inquiring whether Mises would be interested in doing a second edition.[100] Of course he would. The first edition comprised 2,000 copies plus 100 complimentary and review copies, more than a thousand of which had been sold within two years of publication, to the point that in 1924 already Fischer anticipated a second edition for some time after 1925.[101] Eventually, however, the sales did not confirm these hopes.

Mises's friend F.G. Steiner, a Paris-based banker, believed the main reason the book was not more popular was the inadequacy of its German title. The prospect of learning something about *Gemeinwirtschaft*—the "communal economy"—did not appeal to less-educated readers. He hoped a new edition would soon be forthcoming:

> Even more so than when your book was first published, there is today a kind of defeatism spreading among members of the capitalist class. Arguments of the type so brilliantly presented in your book could provide the necessary encouragement.[102]

Mises began revising the manuscript, probably in the summer of 1931. In order not to increase the length of the book, he

---

[99]See the schedule in Mises Archive 17: 258, 261.

[100]Fischer to Mises, letter dated April 24, 1931, Mises Archive 68: 52.

[101]See their correspondence in Mises Archive 57: 34; 75: 15, 37.

[102]Steiner to Mises, letter dated December 8, 1930; Mises Archive 66: 23.

had to cut some parts to compensate for additions.[103] Following suggestions by Robbins, for example, he added a comment on the impossibility of syndicalism, and also added a discussion of Heimann's *Mehrwert und Gemeinwirtschaft* (1922) as an appendix to the new edition.[104] The passages on Heimann stress the dynamic nature of the problem of pricing. Prices for factors of production cannot simply be imputed backwards from the prices for consumers' goods since the entrepreneur produces for future consumption, and future prices for consumers' goods cannot be directly inferred from present prices.

Mises sent the first 405 pages of the revised manuscript to Fischer at the end of October 1931. Then the process slowed due to Mises's greater involvement in the campaign against foreign-exchange controls. In order not to lose too much time, Mises had asked four friends to help him review the proof pages.[105] The division of labor worked well, and on February 26, 1932 Mises sent the last pages to Fischer by courier. Fischer received it the next day and immediately forwarded it to Lippert & Co. in Naumburg. A month later, Fischer held the first copies in his hands and on April 1, Mises received his complimentary copies in Vienna.[106,107]

---

[103]Mises to Fischer, letter dated October 26, 1931; Mises Archive 68: 47.

[104]See the correspondence between Robbins and Mises, dated November 12 and 23, 1931; Mises Archive 83: 9f. Mises in fact reproduced in his book the entire survey on recent contributions to the analysis of socialist calculation that he had published some years before in the Archive. See Mises, "Neue Beiträge zum Problem der sozialistischen Wirtschaftsrechnung," *Archiv für Sozialwissenschaft und Sozialpolitik* 51 (December 1923): 488–500.

[105]See correspondence between Mises and Fischer, dated October 26 and 27, 1931; Mises Archive 68: 46f.

[106]See their correspondence in Mises Archive 68: 31ff., 46.

[107]He received thirty complimentary copies of the book, ten of which were hardcover. Twenty of these (six with hard covers) were sent to Vienna. Mises had Fischer send the remaining ten, plus nine more copies for which he himself paid, to the following people: hardcover copies went to Robbins,

The book was a financial success for Mises. He received a pre-paid 15 percent of the selling price, of a total volume of 1,500 copies and with royalties totaling 4,050 marks. But the most gratifying result lay in the reactions from both friends and foes who honored the new edition as "the leading anti-socialist and affirmatively liberal work within scientific economic literature."[108] Critics charged that Mises had not taken account of the most recent attempts to solve the problem of socialist calculation. But they made no attempt to name or describe these alleged new solutions. Another typical criticism was to qualify Mises's ideas as "utopian." Some critics apparently felt pity for Mises, whose radicalism had left him few allies. One such critic wrote about Mises's "tragic fate":

> [He] advocates the liberalism of the so-called "classical" economists so unshakably and bluntly that he has become an embarrassment to those who would normally agree with him. Mises disdains any concessions in matters of social policy and ideology and hence, he provides a cheap opportunity to many liberal theoreticians who are just not as courageous as he is to differentiate themselves from him in a self-serving and "compassionate" way.[109]

Anderson, Sulzbach, and Beveridge; paperbacks went to Gregory, Hayek, both Verrijn Stuarts, Adolf Weber, Passow, Wiese, Oswalt, Vleugels, Halm, Hahn, Röpke, Wolfrum, Brutzkus, and Lederer.

[108]Anonymous, "Die Gemeinwirtschaft," *Der Deutsche Volkswirt. Literatur-Beilage* no. 1 (December 23, 1932). One reviewer said:

> The battle between individualism and socialism, which by now has been waged almost one hundred years, has now entered its final phase. In a few years or decades, at most, victory will be on one side or the other. At the high point of this battle, Mises's book is a crucial action. It is impossible to estimate its intellectual, economic, and, in the long run, even its political implications. (Anonymous, "Sozialismus—eine Utopie," *1. Handelsbeilage der "Berliner Börsen-Zeitung"* [November 3, 1932])

[109]E.W.E., "Die Planwirtschaft und ihre Gegner," *Die Tat* 24 (10).

Inadvertently, this critic had pointed out a great service that Mises provided for all those who were, like the critic himself, opposed to government omnipotence, but did not want to reduce the scope of the state as radically as did the Vienna economist. Mises put these half-baked liberals in a comfortable middle-of-the-road position. They could make use of his arguments without a full commitment to their practical implications. Mises made them appear less radical.

It is true that Mises's radicalism alienated some of those who might otherwise have been closer allies. But it also altered the thinking of many open-minded readers, those who were willing to weigh his arguments against their prejudices. These readers often acknowledged the pertinence of his analysis of socialism and interventionism. Mises's work made them understand that capitalism must not be confused with the observed reality of the "traditional economic order."

One reviewer said:

> Possibly the greatest merit of the work is that it shows that the present-day shortcomings of capitalism, the so-called economic system of individualism, result to a large extent from the fact that, for some time now, we have not had such a system, but ever more distort it in the interest of domestic and foreign policy.[110]

Another:

> In some circles Mises is called the last consistent representative of a liberal economic order. He is certainly not the last, but after many years the first who has dared to think through all the consequences of such an order, and to erect and demonstrate a doctrine with unshakable logic.[111]

---

[110]Review of "Die Gemeinwirtschaft," *Kartellrundschau* 7/8 (1932).

[111]W.W. [Weiss-Wellenstein], "'Die Gemeinwirtschaft.' Die zweite Auflage des Werkes von Ludwig Mises," *Mitteleuropäische Wirtschaft. Wochenbeilage der "Neuen Freien Presse"* (December 10, 1932).

The most enthusiastic responses came from younger economists, but these followers did not expect Mises's argument to convert the mainstream anytime soon. One of them, Georg Halm from the University of Würzburg, said Mises himself was too optimistic:

> I could name no work that is as revolutionary within its field as your *Gemeinwirtschaft*. Later generations will probably recognize this much more clearly than the bulk of your contemporaries. I believe you overestimate the latter considerably in your statement that your views are rarely contested today. Isn't the discussion of your *Gemeinwirtschaft* in Lederer's brochure, "Planned Economy," mind-boggling?[112]

Dresden Meeting of the Verein für Sozialpolitik

On January 4 and 5, 1932, in meetings of the board and of the committee of the *Verein für Sozialpolitik* in Berlin, Mises met some of these colleagues whom he so overestimated. He had unsuccessfully encouraged Hayek to attend the sessions, saying, "doubtlessly it will be interesting; maybe it is the last

---

[112]Halm to Mises, letter dated April 16, 1932; Mises Archive 71: 89. The response:

> I find that Lederer in his amply unclear brochure "Centrally Planned Economy" makes it obvious that socialist theory is completely bankrupt. In fact, the use of money is in his eyes the only basis for economic calculation, but he fails to see that, in a society in which the means of production are not privately owned, there is no pricing process for means of production. Moreover, and characteristically, he falls prey to the other error of Kautsky in that he wants to use past prices as a starting point. The few pages dedicated to this problem deliver nothing new and are even more confused than the previous justification attempts by socialist writers. (Mises to Halm, letter dated April 26, 1932; Mises Archive 71: 37)

meeting before the abolition of usury [*Brechung der Zin-sknechtschaft*]."[113]

Mises hoped to convince the committee to have value theory and the economics of cartels discussed at the forthcoming plenary meeting in Dresden. Both projects were thwarted when the committee, after a heated debate, decided to set the issue of national autarky—economic "self sufficiency" through trade isolation—on the agenda. Mises thought this decision was completely unacceptable and that it had the potential to destroy the *Verein*. There was no common ground for the discussion of autarky. Making it the subject of discussion was bound to intensify rather than alleviate the clashes among members.[114]

Disillusioned with the *Verein's* willingness to promote productive scientific cooperation, he did not even plan to attend the Dresden meeting, but changed his mind when he learned from Spiethoff that there would finally be a subcommittee meeting on value theory.[115] In preparation for this meeting, Spiethoff and Mises edited a volume on the problems of value theory: *Probleme der Wertlehre*. The chapters of this book were solicited from proponents and opponents of the Austrian theory of value and prices.[116] The selection of the authors ensured that all major points of view could be expressed. Superficially, the

---

[113]Mises to Hayek, letter dated December 18, 1931; Mises Archive 81: 17. The phrase "abolition of usury" alludes to point 11 of the National Socialist Worker Party program of February 24, 1920.

[114]Mises to Lederer, letter dated April 9, 1932; Mises Archive 73: 4; Mises to Amonn, letter dated April 27, 1932; Mises Archive 71: 143.

[115]"I have not yet entirely abandoned all hope that it will be possible to do fruitful work within the *Verein für Sozialpolitik*. All depends on the course of the Dresden meeting and on the new president." Mises to Georg Jahn, letter dated July 15, 1932; Mises Archive 71: 133.

[116]See Mises and Arthur Spiethoff, eds., *Probleme der Wertlehre* (Schriften des Vereins für Sozialpolitik 183/I, Munich and Leipzig: Duncker & Humblot, 1931), vol. 1.

great divide was between the moderns (that is, advocates of marginal-value theory as the basis of price theory) and their Casselian (Kromphardt), historicist (Gottl), Marxist (Oppenheimer), and universalist (Spann) opponents. This divide was also reflected in the co-editorship of Mises and Spiethoff, who were known to be in different camps. But more to the point the book was part of Mises's strategy to spread the message that economic science was not a matter of mere personal opinion. There are certain fundamental facts on which all past and present economists agreed, despite all the differences separating the various schools.

The subcommittee meeting took place immediately after the plenary meeting, which was held on September 28 and 29, 1932. Mises gave the opening talk, emphasizing that marginal-value theory alone was able to explain all economic phenomena and that the different forms in which the marginal principle was advocated were not nearly as incompatible as the opponents of economic science claim.[117] As one newspaper report put it, the meeting was attended by a large delegation from Vienna and by "advocates of the marginal-utility school working in foreign countries." These participants showed "how productively the theories of the Vienna and the Lausanne schools could be further developed."[118]

---

[117]His speech was subsequently printed, without title, in Mises and Arthur Spiethoff, eds., *Probleme der Wertlehre* (Schriften des Vereins für Sozialpolitik 183, no. 2, Munich and Leipzig: Duncker & Humblot, 1933), vol. 2, pp. 1–12; reprinted with the title "Der Streit um die Werttheorie" in Mises's book *Grundprobleme der Nationalökonomie* (Jena: Gustav Fischer, 1933), chap. 7; translated by George Reisman as "The Controversy Over the Theory of Value," *Epistemological Problems of Economics*, 3rd ed. (Auburn, Ala.: Ludwig von Mises Institute, 2003), chap. 7.

[118]Martha St. Braun, "Die diesjährigen Verhandlungen des Vereines für Sozialpolitik," *Neue Freie Presse* (October 8, 1932).

The discussion was less controversial than might have been expected because the main opponents of value theory—Liefmann, Cassel, Spann, and Oppenheimer—had not even come to take part in the meeting. Neither had any of their disciples appeared. This was a remarkable fact in its own right and was duly noticed in the preface of the proceedings. The debate was then to a large extent a Viennese affair.

But the Dresden meeting was also a breakthrough from the point of view of contemporary history. It was a high point of the renaissance of political economy in Germany. During the preceding decade, economic theory had again become palatable in the places of higher learning where the Historical School had for a long time reigned supreme. Three publications in 1931 epitomized this change and the central role Mises played in it.

The most important of these publications was the third edition of Adolf Weber's textbook, which in Mises's judgment was the most significant German-language textbook of economics in its day.[119] Similarly, the Frankfurt professor Budge published his textbook on monetary economics, *Lehre vom Geld*, in which he acknowledged Mises's achievements and critically discussed Mises's views.[120] Last but not least, Georg Halm published a revised edition of the late Ludwig Pohle's standard textbook on capitalism and socialism, based on Pohle's notes. The great bulk of the extensive additions brought a more radical rejection of socialist schemes, bolstered by quotations from *Socialism* and other of Mises's works.

---

[119]Weber had sent Mises a copy of his book in November 1931. Mises replied: "I greet the success of your book as a sign that public opinion is beginning a gradual shift in the direction of sound ideas." Mises to Adolf Weber, letter dated November 15, 1931; Mises Archive 66a: 156.

[120]Mises was very grateful. See his letter to Budge, dated June 13, 1931; Mises Archive 66a: 98. Some two years later, shortly after Hitler had seized power in Germany, Mises stated that his monetary theory had become in Germany, after World War I, the dominant theory of the business cycle. See Mises to Ugo Papi, letter dated March 17, 1933; Mises Archive 94: 3.

In the same year, a Ph.D. student of Halm's in Würzburg, Karl Wagner, defended a doctoral thesis that ripped National Socialist ideology apart and received praise from Mises.[121] Wagner was one of several promising young economists who were eventually swept aside by German National Socialism. The seeds Mises had planted in German soil were in for a long winter. Most of them died during the Nazi episode. Those few that survived experienced a short blossoming in the late 1940s and 1950s, and helped re-establish a market economy in the land of Bismarck and Hitler.

The 1932 Dresden meeting of the *Verein* gave a taste of what might have been possible if Mises's campaign to demonstrate the libertarian political implications of economic science had been allowed to run its course. The first day of the meeting featured a session on "industrialization and unemployment." Werner Sombart was now a vice president of the *Verein* and in charge of selecting the invited lecturers. He had difficulty finding lecturers he considered suitable. Eventually he opted for his disciple Manuel Saitzew of Zurich and for Gerhard Colm of Kiel. But neither one endorsed the Sombartian line, which presented the massive unemployment in Germany and Austria as a consequence of economization and streamlining in industry. They argued that such technological changes could not cause unemployment on a massive and permanent scale. Saitzew contended that the real reasons included high tariffs, and Colm pointed to the inflexibility of wage rates and other prices, which resulted from powerful labor unions and cartels. Colm also stated that the selection process of the market was hampered by modern bankruptcy laws, which were too lenient on debtors, and by subsidies paid to unprofitable firms.

---

[121]Mises said: "Your work needs to be welcomed not only as a scientific achievement, but also as a political deed." Mises to Karl Wagner, letter dated June 8, 1931; Mises Archive 66a: 117.

Clearly, these views were not to the liking of Sombart or the *Verein* establishment.[122]

The next day of the meeting, Thursday September 29, 1932, demonstrated even more forcefully how much economic common sense had displaced the old allegiance to the interventionist creed. The sessions were supposed to deal with the question of autarky, but the meeting once again took an entirely different course from what the *Verein* leadership had anticipated. Here too, Sombart had had difficulties finding suitable candidates who could make a substantial case in favor of autarky. He eventually settled on Constantin von Dietze and Emil Lederer, who were only moderate autarkists at best.[123] Dietze half-heartedly defended autarky by arguing that "food freedom" was necessary in war and that agrarian workers were physically better suited as soldiers. But he concluded his talk insisting that autarky offered no solution to unemployment, and that his real confidence lay with the forces of the free market. The high point of the meeting approached when Emil Lederer, with the full authority of his position at the University of Berlin, "in a brilliant speech that was based on the traditional arguments of the free-trade doctrine and on the most recent statistical data,"[124] argued that no country was less suited to engage in protectionism than Germany. In the ensuing debate on autarky, almost all the speakers emphasized that it was wrong to oppose free trade as contrary to the national interest and that it would be wrong to make free-trade policies conditional on the trade policies of other countries.

Commenting on the meeting for a major Vienna business newspaper, Louise Sommer noticed the historical irony of the

---

[122]Franz Boese, *Geschichte des Vereins für Sozialpolitik, 1872–1932* (Berlin: Duncker & Humblot, 1939), pp. 229ff.

[123]Ibid., pp. 232ff.

[124]Martha St. Braun, "Die diesjährigen Verhandlungen des Vereines für Sozialpolitik," *Neue Freie Presse* (October 8, 1932).

Verein majority's now advocating free trade and free markets. Sommer traced the emergence of this new majority to the early 1920s when Heinrich Herkner's endorsement of Mises's *Socialism* caused a "crisis of social policy." Mises's ideas, wrote Sommer, were the primary agent of the transformation of Germany's intellectual landscape in the 1920s:

> The ideas that Mises developed [in this book] have affected the entire ideology of the *Verein für Sozialpolitik* and turned it toward an endorsement of the free-market economy. It is from this point on that the *Verein* has unmistakably changed its goals. It has now become a battlefield for the debate of questions of economic principle and economic order. It is a milestone of the history of this association . . . that free-market ideas have had a renaissance at this year's meeting, that the fight against autarky, against the whole system of restraints and regulations that fetters economic life, has been taken up at the meeting with much energy.[125]

Just as Mises was finally beginning to stir the spirit of liberty among the young generation of German economists, the old *Kathedersozialisten* had a final and devastating triumph. On January 30, 1933, their intellectual scion, Adolf Hitler, was appointed chancellor of the German Reich.

When the Nazis rose to power, they immediately began with their program of *Gleichschaltung* (enforced conformity, literally "synchronization"), whose goal was to subordinate all organizations to the central Nazi organizations that controlled the federal government. Faced with the choice of becoming part of the Nazi apparatus or self-dissolution, the *Verein*, honorably, chose

---

[125]Louise Sommer, "Für die freie Verkehrswirtschaft! (Die Dresdner Tagung des Vereines für Sozialpolitik)," *Wiener Wirtschafts-Woche* (October 12, 1932), pp. 7f. Sommer was by then a private lecturer in economics at the University of Geneva.

to disband in December 1936. Even more honorably, Mises quit the *Verein* three years earlier, in immediate protest against the *Gleichschaltung* laws.[126]

❦   ❦   ❦

Mises was also one of the initiators of an international effort to provide new career opportunities to the academics whom the Nazis expelled from Germany. At the end of March 1933, Beveridge and Robbins were in Vienna and met Mises for dinner. Their Austrian friend stormed into the lobby of the Hotel Bristol, breaking the news that the Nazis had fired a number of Jewish academics such as Bonn, Mannheim, and Kantorowicz. On the spot, the three men discussed what could be done to help these German socialists. Would it be possible to set up relief funds in France and Britain to employ them? Beveridge announced that he himself would oversee a relief action at LSE. Back in London, Robbins organized a meeting of LSE's Professorial Council, which voted for a scheme of "voluntary" deductions from staff salaries to finance the relief fund. He also convinced Beveridge to support an even larger scheme, and eventually a relief fund was created on a national scale. In a letter to Mises, in which he reported on progress, Robbins praised his correspondent for having seen the practical implications of the new situation and for initiating an effective response.[127]

Economic Theory Completed

In the Dresden discussions of value theory, Mises had emphasized that a productive debate could take place only

---

[126]See the letters and other materials printed in ibid., pp. 273ff. The *Verein* was re-established after World War II, in 1948. Mises did not wish to have anything to do with this postwar organization. See Mises to Sommer, letter dated June 11, 1957; Grove City Archive: Sommer file.

[127]Robbins to Mises, letter dated May 19, 1933; Grove City Archive: Robbins files. See also Robbins, *Autobiography of an Economist*, pp. 143f.

among those who did not rule out the possibility of a universally valid social theory. Those who excluded this possibility on a priori grounds were forced to endorse what Mises would eventually call *polylogism*—the extreme historicist hypothesis that there is no such thing as a generally valid social theory because the structure of the human mind was in a state of constant flux. According to this hypothesis, there is not just one universally valid theory of human action; there are in fact several different "logics of action."

The most explicit champion of polylogism had been the socialist Josef Dietzgen (1828–1888), who had developed a materialistic philosophy independent of Marx and Engels.[128] In 1929, the case for polylogism came into the spotlight of scientific debate with the publication of Karl Mannheim's *Ideologie und Utopie*.[129] It quickly found support in all political camps. Polylogism was an expedient tool to avoid the scrutiny of arguments—especially those made by economists—and to replace the sober process of reasoning with the emotional appeal of name-calling. Advocates of polylogism "could simply declare all theories they disliked as bourgeois theories, without entering into a detailed discussion of their contents and arguments."[130] Not surprisingly, the German racists were eager to adopt the same comfortable strategy to avoid critical debate of the ideology of the Aryan master race. Mises recalled:

> Professor Biberbach of the University of Breslau distinguishes between Anglo-Saxon-Franco-Jewish mathematics and German mathematics. Professor Lenard, the winner of the Nobel Prize, believes that

---

[128]See Eugen Dietzgen, ed., *Gesammelte Werke*, 3rd ed. (Stuttgart: Dietz, 1922), in particular vol. 3, which contains Josef Dietzgen's "Letters on Logic" and his "Excursions of a Socialist into the Field of Epistemology."

[129]Karl Mannheim, *Ideologie und Utopie* (Bonn: Cohen, 1929).

[130]Mises, "Economics and Politics," Grove City Archive: Mexico 1942 file 6.

only German physics are true, whereas the physics of all the other nations are simply nonsense.[131]

A few years later, Mises explained the historical setting of this intellectual current:

> Until the middle of the nineteenth century everybody took it for granted that the logical structure of the human mind is the same with every human being. All . . . human relations are based on this assumption. Wherever men met men, they never had any doubt in this respect. All philosophers and all laymen agreed— were unanimous in this belief.
>
> But in the middle of the nineteenth century Karl Marx expounded a different view. According to Marx the logical structure of mind is different with the members of different classes. The human mind does not find truth but ideologies. Ideologies seem true in the eyes of the members of the same class, but are meaningless in the eyes of members of other classes. Every class produces its own ideologies, which later are debunked by ideologies of other classes. In this way Karl Marx stigmatized the philosophy of John Locke as a "bourgeois philosophy." Later Marxians called Schopenhauer the philosopher of the *rentier* class and Nietzsche the philosopher of big business. Lenin, the founder of the Third International, and Frederick Adler, the secretary general of the Second International, investigated whether the physical theories of Mach are bourgeois or not. The Einstein theory of relativity is branded by some Bolsheviks as "bourgeois and reactionary."[132]

---

[131]Ibid. See also Lothar Gottlieb Tirala, *Rasse, Geist und Seele* (Munich: Lehmann, 1935). The author was a medical doctor.

[132]Mises, "Economics and Politics," lecture given at the National University of Mexico, January or February 1942; quoted from Margit von Mises's handwritten lecture notes contained in Grove City Archive: Mexico 1942 file 6. In this lecture Mises presented material that he eventually published in

In the 1932 debate in Dresden, Mises pointed out that any defense of the polylogistic hypothesis involves a self-contradiction, since the exchange of arguments only makes sense if the logical structure of the human mind is independent of social or racial class:

> A Marxist—and I understand by this term not only the members of a political party that swears by Marx, but all who appeal to Marx in their thinking concerning the sciences of human action—who condescends to discuss a scientific problem with people who are not comrades of his own class has given up the first and most important principle of his theory. If thought is conditioned by the thinker's social existence, how can he understand me and how can I understand him? If there is a "bourgeois" logic and a "proletarian" logic, how am I, the "bourgeois," to come to an understanding with him, the "proletarian"? Whoever takes the Marxist point of view seriously must advocate a complete division between "bourgeois" and "proletarian" science; and the same is also true, *mutatis mutandis*, of the view of those who regard thought as determined by the race or the nationality of the thinker. The Marxist cannot be satisfied with separating classes in athletic contests, with a "bourgeois" and a "proletarian" Olympics. He must demand this separation above all in scientific discussion.
>
> The fruitlessness of many of the debates that were conducted here in the *Verein für Sozialpolitik* as well as in the *Gesellschaft für Soziologie* are to be attributed more than anything else to the neglect of this principle. In my opinion, the position of dogmatic Marxism is wrong, but that of the Marxist who engages in discussions with representatives of what he calls "bourgeois science" is confused. The consistent Marxist

---

Omnipotent Government (New Haven, Conn.: Yale University Press, 1944), chap. 6, sect. 6.

> does not seek to refute opponents whom he calls "bourgeois." He seeks to destroy them physically and morally.[133]

In a paper he had written in preparation for the Dresden meeting, Mises had highlighted the wider significance of polylogism, characterizing it as a "romantic revolt against logic and science" and pointing out that it "does not limit itself to the sphere of social phenomena and the sciences of human action. It is a revolt against our entire culture and civilization."[134]

In Dresden, Emil Lederer argued that this argument was considerably overblown. Mises was wrong in assuming that the being-generates-consciousness theory implied that every single instance of thought is ideology, in the Marxist sense of an intellectualization of economic interests. According to Lederer, nobody claimed that there were no universally valid theories. Logic and mathematics certainly counted. But neither could it be denied that there were other disciplines, the basic categories of which were largely dependent on "the historical situation, that is, on the social structure of the time and on the social position of the thinker." Lederer went on:

> Now the question is whether economics belongs to the first category of sciences, which totally rely on pure intuition [*reine Anschauung*] and logic, or to the socially determined fields of knowledge in the sense of modern sociology or, if you wish, in the sense of Marxism. Herr von Mises apparently shares the view

---

[133]Mises, "The Controversy over the Theory of Value," chap. 7 of *Epistemological Problems of Economics*, pp. 218f. He had only touched on this point, which he now regarded as fundamental, in a paper he wrote for *Probleme der Wertlehre*, the volume that served as a basis for the discussion in Dresden. See Mises, "The Psychological Basis of the Opposition to Economic Theory," chap. 6 of *Epistemological Problems of Economics*, p. 201.

[134]Mises, "The Psychological Basis of the Opposition to Economic Theory," p. 214.

of the Physiocrats: the latter believed that the physio-
cratic theory was as obliging for each rational thinker
as the theorem of Pythagoras. . . . Herr von Mises
apparently claims the same rank, the same validity for
economic theory in its entire scope, and this is what I
deny. It is true that economic theory has a kernel that
is independent of historical economic developments.
But this general or exact or pure theory, for which I
feel affinities, is not the theory of economic action
per se, in all its historical phases. The substance of
this theory is a narrow one; it essentially covers the
static process or stationary circulation [*Kreislauf*]. It
ultimately deduces all consequences from the principle of economizing, as applied to man in his dependency on nature.[135]

In his rejoinder, Mises pointed out that static economic theory did not merely apply to static processes, but especially to
change. The word "static" did not mean that the subject of
inquiry was a stationary economy; rather it referred to a specific
method of analysis, which studied the implications of a change
of one datum, *ceteris paribus*, i.e., under the assumption that all
other data remained unchanged.[136] But Mises still had not clarified his views about the epistemological character of economic
science. This was the task to which he proceeded upon his
return to Vienna, where he finished an essay on "the task and
scope of the science of human action."

Mises planned to publish this piece as the introductory chapter of a new book on fundamental problems of economic analysis. The book would contain various essays he had published in
the past five years in the fields of epistemology and value theory. The idea was to clarify the very foundations of economic

---

[135]Lederer in Mises and Spiethoff, eds., *Probleme der Wertlehre*, vol. 2, pp.
114f.

[136]Mises in ibid., p. 117.

science, not only by a general discussion of its philosophical character, but also by restating the core concepts of value and capital theory. The book would therefore contain both an introduction to economics from the point of view of the philosophy of science, and actual economic analyses of value and of inconvertible capital. The first three chapters, on epistemology, consumed some 60 percent of the volume. The next four chapters dealt with value theory, and the concluding essay was his contribution to the Verreijn Stuart *festschrift*.

Mises finished revising the manuscript over Christmas 1932 and on January 3, 1933 wrote to Gustav Fischer to propose the book for publication. Fischer did not believe the book would sell well, but agreed to publish it. By mid-April, Mises received the first copies of *Grundprobleme der Nationalökonomie* (Fundamental Problems of Economics).[137]

His new essay on "the task and scope of the science of human action" was chapter one. It would be the keystone of the system of economics Mises had been working on for years. Taking up Lederer's challenge, Mises argued that economic laws were true a priori, on a par with the laws of logic and mathematics.[138] To the present day, this has remained one of his most controversial tenets, but the debate resulted in most cases from a misunderstanding of his position. Twentieth-century social scientists typically argued that science was always based on "experience" and that any proposition that was based instead on some arbitrary "a

[137]Mises, *Grundprobleme der Nationalökonomie: Untersuchungen über Verfahren, Aufgaben und Inhalt der Wirtschafts- und Gesellschaftslehre* (Jena: Gustav Fischer, 1933). Almost three decades later, Mises's American student George Reisman produced a translation. The American edition eventually appeared under the somewhat different title of *Epistemological Problems of Economics* (Princeton, N.J.: Van Nostrand, 1960).

[138]Mises, "Aufgabe und Umfang der allgemeinen Wissenschaft vom Handeln," *Grundprobleme der Nationalökonomie*, chap. 1; translated as "The Task and Scope of the Science of Human Action," *Epistemological Problems of Economics*, chap. 1, pp. 1–69.

priori" principle was therefore not scientific. Mises agreed. He had been a proponent of rigid fact-orientation since his early years as a student. He had enthusiastically supported Max Weber in the controversy on value judgments, arguing that the proper sphere of science was the world as it is—not as it should be. Mises himself rigorously held to the notion that true science was always concerned with verifiable facts.

So why were his epistemological views controversial? Most other social theorists believed that the facts relevant for the social sciences could be known through observation-based methods of inquiry. Here Mises disagreed. In the tradition of Carl Menger's quest for "empirical theory," he believed that economic theory describes facts of the real world such as the one that human beings make choices.[139] But facts of this sort *cannot be observed*—it is impossible for example to look at choices, to smell them or touch them. Economics is not an empirical science in this sense, but it is a science nevertheless, because the facts it deals with are true even though they are unavailable to the human sensory apparatus. The proper method to analyze them is through "discursive reasoning."

Mises stressed again his conviction that economics is part of a more general social theory. And now he gave more precision to what this general theory was all about. It was a theory of human action:

---

[139]Thus he insisted: "For the purposes of science, we must start from the action of the individual because this is the only thing of which we can have direct cognition" (ibid., p. 44). And he also stated:

> Science cannot proceed otherwise than discursively. Its starting points must have as much certainty as human knowledge is capable of, and it must go on from there, making logical deductions step by step. It can begin as an aprioristic science with propositions necessary to thought that find their support and warrant in apodictic evidence; or as an empirical science it can start with experience. (ibid., p. 49)

> The science of human action that strives for univer-
> sally valid knowledge is the theoretical system whose
> hitherto best elaborated branch is economics. In all of
> its branches this science is a priori, not empirical.
> Like logic and mathematics, it is not derived from
> experience; it is prior to experience. It is, as it were,
> the logic of action and deed.[140]

How did Mises address Lederer's argument that only a part
of economic theory was universally valid, namely, the aspect
that dealt with the equilibrium relationship between human
action and nature? Mises argued that "universal validity" does
not imply that all laws of human action apply in every single
instance of human behavior. Rather, it means that a law applies
whenever the conditions specified by it are given. Whether or
not they are is an empirical question; but once this is stipulated,
the law holds true on a priori grounds.

> For example, we are unable to grasp the concept of
> economic action and of economy without implying in
> our thought the concept of economic quantity rela-
> tions and the concept of an economic good. Only
> experience can teach us whether or not these con-
> cepts are applicable to anything in the conditions
> under which our life must actually be lived. Only
> experience tells us that not all things in the external
> world are free goods. However, it is not experience,
> but reason, which is prior to experience, that tells us
> what is a free and what is an economic good.[141]

---

[140]Ibid., pp. 13f. He went on to argue that the theory of human action
ultimately coincides with the science of logic:

> Human thought serves human life and action. It is not
> absolute thought, but the forethought directed toward pro-
> jected acts and the afterthought that reflects upon acts done.
> Hence, in the last analysis, logic and the universally valid sci-
> ence of human action are one and the same.

[141]Ibid., p. 15.

Some of the empirical conditions under which human action can take place are universally given. For example, all human actions occur during the passage of time and all acting persons age in the course of time. Other empirical conditions such as the use of money are of a more contingent nature. But however universal or contingent these conditions are, it remains true that *once* they are given, they cause certain objective effects, which are the subject matter of the a priori theory of human action.

Because the theory of human action does not rely on data gathered through the senses, but rather on a priori facts that we come to know through discursive reasoning, it cannot possibly be verified or refuted by experience gained exclusively through observations. Mises highlighted the practical implications of this fundamental epistemological fact:

> Human action always confronts experience as a complex phenomenon that first must be analyzed and interpreted by a theory before it can even be set in the context of an hypothesis that could be proved or disproved; hence the vexatious impasse created when supporters of conflicting doctrines point to the same historical data as evidence of their correctness. The statement that statistics can prove anything is a popular recognition of this truth. No political or economic program, no matter how absurd, can, in the eyes of its supporters, be contradicted by experience. Whoever is convinced a priori of the correctness of his doctrine can always point out that some condition essential for success according to his theory has not been met. Each of the German political parties seeks in the experience of the second Reich confirmation of the soundness of its program. Supporters and opponents of socialism draw opposite conclusions from the experience of Russian bolshevism. Disagreements concerning the probative power of concrete historical experience can be resolved only by reverting to the doctrines of the universally valid theory, which are independent of all experience. Every theoretical

argument that is supposedly drawn from history necessarily becomes a logical argument about pure theory apart from all history.[142]

Twilight in Vienna

The discussion of the epistemology of economics was continued in Mises's private seminar in Vienna, where his views
found far more opposition (and more competently offered) than
in Dresden. Several members of the seminar, including Felix
Kaufmann and Robert Wälder, were also members of a discussion group of the positivistic philosophers, the Vienna Circle.
These men brought a completely different perspective to the
problems, and the clash of their views with the opinion of the
seminar director was a highlight in the history of those gatherings. Much of the fame that later accrued to the seminar
through the recollections of its prominent participants was due
to the methodological debates in the last years of its existence.
Mises characterized them as "vivid, even outright passionate."[143]

The brilliance of the discussions in the academic year
1933–1934 happily combined with the presence of a significant
number of distinguished guests. Mises was at this point more
than just a well-known author. He was a recognized leader
among German-speaking economists. After his election to the
Board of the *Verein für Sozialpolitik* in early 1929, the private
seminar attracted an increasing number of guests, especially
from foreign countries. Alvin Hansen came in 1929, Frank
Knight for a stint in May 1930, Carver, Batson, and others in
1931. But the absolute high point was in 1933–1934, when four
scholars from Japan (Itschitani, Midutani, Otaka, Takemura),
plus Hugh Gaitskell, Ragnar Nurkse, Karl Pribram, François

---

[142]Ibid., p. 30.

[143]Mises to Machlup, letter dated July 12, 1934; Hoover Institution:
Machlup-Mises correspondence file.

Perroux, Gerhard Tintner, and Emmanuel Winternitz, to name just the more prominent guests, attended the sessions.[144]

On March 9, Mises gave the opening talk to a debate that would fill the next three months and which more narrowly concerned the question of whether economics was an aprioristic science of human action. Mises presented his case and also addressed the position of Kaufmann, who held that economic science was based on (potentially fictional) stipulations arrived at through conventions.[145] Mises's paper highlights the reason why his position was not very convincing to the other participants. More than in his previous written essays, he stressed that economic theory was an a priori discipline because it could not be verified or refuted in laboratory experiments. This line of argument was rather unsatisfactory because it seemed to draw epistemological conclusions from a mere technical difficulty. At any rate, it was unpersuasive to the next four presenters.[146]

❧   ❧   ❧

---

[144]During his sojourn in Vienna, Hugh Gaitskell set out to make a new translation of Böhm-Bawerk's *Capital and Interest*, which was still available only in a translation from the first edition. Mises later recalled that other English economists too were ready to shoulder the task, and even publication was not a problem in these days when the public interest in Austrian economics was at its peak in Great Britain: "They abstained from this undertaking because they expected that Gaitskell would execute his plan." But the young man in Mises's Vienna seminar never finished the job. Gaitskell opted instead for an acceleration of his career in politics, becoming Minister of Fuel and Power in the postwar British Labour government. See Mises to Nymeyer, letters dated November 22, 1947 and November 8, 1950; Grove City Archive: Nymeyer files.

[145]Mises, "Leitsätze zur Erörterung der methodologischen Probleme der Sozialwissenschaften und zur Kritik des Kaufmann'schen Standpunktes" (Basic principles for the discussion of the methodological problems of the social sciences and for a critique of the Kaufmannian position); typewritten manuscript, dated March 9, 1934, 6 pp.; Mises Archive 32: 2–4.

[146]Felix Kaufmann, Robert Wälder, Erich Schiff, Oskar Morgenstern.

In the wake of the economic crisis in 1931, the Christian Socialists had proposed a coalition government to the socialists under Bauer. When Bauer refused, voters shifted increasingly to the Austrian National Socialists. Christian Socialists now believed that the best way to hold back the tide of national socialism was to use authoritarian methods to suppress opposition to the government. These tactics were decisively intensified after the National Socialists rose to power in Germany on January 30, 1933. Many observers expected that Austria too would now fall into their hands, especially since they supported their Austrian branch organization through media campaigns and terror bombings against the Austrian government and its allies.[147]

Desperate in its quest to stop the Nazi tide and keep Austria independent, the government under Engelbert Dollfuss concluded an alliance with Fascist Italy, but also resorted to authoritarian methods in its domestic policies.[148] Dollfuss abolished the parliamentary republic, using a suitable opportunity on March 4, 1933 when all three presidents of the parliament stepped down in protest against a questionable procedure. The last of the three officially convened the parliament for March 15, but now Dollfuss stepped in, convinced the Christian Socialist parliamentary faction to support his *coup d'état*, and sent in the police to prevent a consolidation of the (pro-German) social democrats and German nationalists on March 15. In the course of the next few months, Dollfuss also abolished the Communist party and the Austrian branch of the German Nazi party. Henceforth he ruled dictatorially, on the basis of an emergency law passed in 1917. On May 20, he established the *Vaterländische Front* (Patriotic Front) to rally all forces loyal to the Austrian state. Dollfuss proclaimed

---

[147]See Erik von Kuehnelt-Leddihn, *Von Sarajevo nach Sarajevo* (Vienna: Karolinger, 1966), p. 47; Hoor, *Österreich 1918–1938*, pp. 74, 106, 114.

[148]The alliance with Italy was cemented in the "Protocols of Rome," signed on March 17, 1934.

at a rally on September 11, 1933 that his fatherland would now become the "socialist, Christian, and German State Austria, based on its estates and with a strong authoritarian leadership."[149]

Ideologically, the Dollfuss regime relied on state-of-the-art Catholic political and social theory, as embodied in the writings of Othmar Spann and Pope Pius XI, both of whom glorified social order based on the respect of the professional *Stände* or estates.[150] While Spann's views had a deep impact on the German-speaking world, his influence could not match Pius XI's encyclical *Quadragesimo Anno* (1931), which was a shot in the arm for the corporatist movement. As one of Mises's correspondents from Switzerland reported, young Catholic politicians were entirely imbued with its ideas, even more than those of Othmar Spann.[151]

In February 1934, the socialists rose one last time against the Dollfuss dictatorship, when the police tried to seize a social democratic arms depot in the provincial town of Linz. Dollfuss

---

[149]Mises became a member on March 1, 1934 at the Patriotic Front's *Kammer* branch office. Membership was probably mandatory for all employees of public and semi-public organizations. Mises's membership card (number 282632) can now be found in the Grove City Archive: file #6/9/1/1. He was also a member of the "Werk Neues Leben," a subdivision of the Patriotic Front. See his membership card (number 406183) in Grove City Archive: Kammer der gewerblichen Wirtschaft für Wien file.

[150]Arguably, his true significance lay elsewhere. Historian Ernst Hoor presents Dollfuss as the first and only stateman of the first Austrian republic who consciously and explicity reclaimed an Austrian nation—as distinct from the German nation—and who framed his policies accordingly. See Hoor, *Österreich 1918–1938*, p. 75.

[151]Lauchenauer to Mises, letter dated December 30, 1932; Mises Archive 97: 3. Arguably, these young politicians gave the papal encyclical a stronger statist reading than was really warranted by its contents. Mises would later acknowledge that the man who wrote the first draft of the encyclical, Jesuit Pater O. von Nell-Breuning, was "one of the few German economists who in the Interwar period advocated economic freedom." See Mises to Parker, letter dated May 14, 1953; Grove City Archive: Tax Foundation file.

had their revolt bloodily repressed and lost no time using the opportunity to oust the social democrats from parliament. The leftover deputies then voted for a "new constitihn" that in its essential lines returned to the pre-1907 constitutional model. Members of parliament were no longer elected by universal suffrage, but appointed from among members of the major "estates" such as landowners, clerics, labor unions, industrialists, etc. The new constitution was proclaimed on May 1, 1934. On July 25, 1934, Engelbert Dollfuss was murdered in the wake of an attempted national socialist *coup d'état*. German troops then marched onto the northern border of Austria and were called back only because Mussolini had concentrated his army on the southern border, pledging to guarantee the country's independence. From that day on, Austria's fate lay in the hands of the Italian government.[152]

In the course of these events, life in Vienna became increasingly unpleasant for Mises. As in World War I, there was once again an official government censor. For some years, Fritz Machlup had written weekly editorials for the *Neue Freie Presse*. He stopped in May 1934 when it became pointless to write on the few topics still free from censorship. At that point, Machlup received a Rockefeller stipend to go to the United States, following in the footsteps of Voegelin and Haberler. Now Mises himself would leave, to the great regret of his circle of friends and colleagues, who bid him farewell at the high point of their many years in his private seminar.

Felix Kaufmann rhymed one last time:

---

[152]See Mises, *Erinnerungen*, pp. 89–91; Kuehnelt-Leddihn, *Von Sarajevo nach Sarajevo*, p. 52; Hoor, *Österreich 1918–1938*, p. 115. Italy changed its alliances in the autumn of 1936, when France and Great Britain sanctioned the Italian invasion and annexation of Abyssinia. The new alliance between Hitler and Mussolini spelled the doom for Austrian independence.

Farewell to Professor Mises

What is going to become of the Mises Kreis
In the year that's coming?
Geneva can't for all suffice,
My fingers won't stop drumming.
The question will not leave me be,
The seminar means everything to me. . .[153]

ABSCHIED VON PROFESSOR MISES

by Felix Kaufmann

Melody: O alte Burschen-
herrlichkeit

1. Was   soll denn mit dem   Miseskreis   im nächsten Jahr ge-
2. Bald   wird die hohe   Fakultät   mit Schaudern es er-
3. Die   Schüler, die so   eifervoll   für Mises' Lehre
4. Nun   zieht der Meister   selber fort   und lehrt auf andrem

schehen?   Wir können doch nicht   dutzendweis von
fassen,   dass mit dem einen,   der da geht, gar
stritten,   die gegen jeden   Einfuhrzoll, so
Stuhle   und schafft ein neues   Zentrum dort, der

hier nach Genf mitgehen.   Ich raufe mir das
viele Wien verlassen.   Für England und für
kühn Attacken ritten.   Sie weilen längst im
alten Wiener Schule.   Wir hoffen, dass sein

letzte Haar. Was   mach ich ohne   Seminar!   O
USA, wird   Wien jetzt fern doch Genf ganz nah.   O
fernem Land, weil   man sie hier so   schlecht verstand.   O
starker Geist, dem   Völkerbund die   Wege weist.   Und

jerum, jerum,   jerum,   o   quae mutatio   rerum.
jerum, jerum,   jerum,   o   quae mutatio   rerum.
jerum, jerum,   jerum.   o   quae mutatio   rerum.
denken sein in   Treuen   und   denken sein in   Treuen.

---

[153]Translations by Arlene Oost-Zinner.

Das Mises-Kreis-Lied

Liebe Kinder, weil heute Freitag ist,
Gibt es Mises-Privatseminar.
Und dort geh ich hin, auch wenn ein Maitag ist,
Süß und duftend wie keiner noch war.
Denn der Blütenduft muß vergehen,
Doch die Wahrheit die bleibt bestehen.
Und die Wahrheit findest Du im Mises-Kreis
Jeden Abend zentner- und scheffelweis.
Fängt man richtig zu streiten erst an,
Denn Debatten die habn dort an Schan!

I geh heut abend zum Mises hin,
Weil ich so gern dort bin,
Man spricht ja nirgends so schon in Wien
Über Wirtschaft, Gesellschaft und Sinn.
Und willst Du recht das Verstehen verstehen,
Mußt à tout prix Du zu Mises auch gehn,
Weil man das nirgends sonst deutlich weiß
Als nur im Mises-Kreis.

Is auch ein Problem noch so konsistent,
Traut sich gar nicht zur Tiire herein,
Denn es weiß sehr wohl, daß Gefahr es rennt,
Aufgelost binnen kurzem zu sein.
Sind auch noch so hart manche Niisse,
Knackt man doch sie durch kluge Schliisse,
Bis die Kerne uns auf der Zung zergehn,
Wie sonst nur noch die siiBen Pralineen,
Die ein glitiger Geist offeriert,
Daß das Schweigen nicht gar zu schwer wird.
(Refrain)

1st der Geist urn zehn Uhr mit Weisheit voll,
Flihit der Magen sich traurig und leer,
Doch erhalt er bald seinen Einfuhrzoll,
Denn wir gehn in den grünen Anker.
Dort ist die Frohlichkeit unser Motto
Bei Spaghetti und bei Risotto.
Wie die Zeit vergeht, keiner hatts gedacht,
Denn auf einmal schlagt es schon Mitternacht,
Doch jetzt kommt die genialste Idee:
Man geht noch in das Kunstlerkaffee.
(Refrain)

Manchmal denkt man sich, hat denn einen Sinn
Diese ganze Problemspalterei?
Draußen fließt derweil froh das Leben hin
Und selbst ist man so wenig dabei.
Wars nicht kliiger, im Strom zu schwimmen,
Als die Wasserkraft zu bestimmen?
Ließ man nicht besser alles Denken sein,
Lebte einfach froh in den Tag hinein
Und genosse des Augenblicks Rausch?
Doch man weiß ja, hier gibts keinen Tausch.
(Refrain)

The Song of the Mises Circle

Come and gather all around, it's Friday
Time for Mises's *Privat Seminar.*
I'll be there for sure, even if it's May
And the day is the sweetest thus far.
Oh, the fragrance fades, it is certain
But truth, you'll find, knows no curtain.
In the Mises Kreis, it's always center stage
Buckets full of truth, remain the latest rage.
And when you begin to debate,
You know that the hour will grow late!

You'll find me with Mises tonight, tonight
No longer do I need to roam.
Society, Economy and Truth, that's right
Are debated, defended, I'm home!
And if you desire Verstehen's made clear
At all costs, you must come, get yourself here!
For clarity, wisdom and truth entice,
Here at the Mises Kreis.

Do you know a problem full of nasty quirks,
Come escort it to Mises's door.
It will know full well this time that danger lurks
As it's whittled right down to its core.
Many shells, of course, know the same fate
Nuts so hard to crack, but at this rate
They will melt on tongues that know deductive
    prose,
Like the chocolate creams, our friend so kindly
    chose,
Making silence a happy refrain,
But now let us all sing again:
(Refrain)

Ten O'clock comes 'round, and wisdom's filled
    our minds,
But our bodies demand ever more.
That Green Anchor calls, and here our stomachs
    find,
Import tariffs to even the score.
Here's where ERE is our motto,
Have spaghetti, and eat risotto.
No one ever dreams how fast the time can race
Midnight rings, we take our favorite place
In that nice little Kunstler Café;
An ingenious end to the day.
(Refrain)

Oh the time, it comes, when we must question
    why,
Is such questioning really that smart?
Life goes on and on, it just keeps flowing by,
And we all play a very small part.
We could swim along, take no notice
Of the tide's direction, the world's focus.
Should we not, keep these thoughts at bay,
Push our cares aside, and relish what's today.
And yet there's no tradeoff at hand,
Somehow we must take a stand.

Part V
Mises in Geneva

16
The Geneva Years

THE ECONOMIC CRISIS HEIGHTENED political antagonisms throughout Europe. Fewer and fewer citizens believed democracy could meet the current challenges. Only two alternatives seemed available, both based on violence: either the dictatorship of the proletariat (or more precisely the dictatorship of labor union bosses and socialist party leaders), or an authoritarian dictatorship bent on restoring the old order.

In the wake of a financial scandal, on February 6, 1934, two right-wing mass organizations demonstrated in the streets of Paris. The angry mobs tried to storm the Palais Bourbon, whereupon the police opened fire, killing fifteen and wounding many hundreds. The French government under Daladier stepped down, and the violence spread to other countries, including Austria.

Mises later said that it was the growing power of the Nazi party in Austria that prompted him to leave the country.[1] With this remark, he did not refer to the government of Engelbert Dollfuss, which had reintroduced authoritarian corporatism into Austrian politics to resist the socialism of both the Marxist and the Nazi variety. Mises meant the Austrian branch of the

---

[1] See the report on an interview with him in "Von Mises to Speak Tonight," *Santa Ana Register* (October 17, 1944); a copy is in Grove City Archive: Hoiles files.

National Socialist German Workers Party, which enjoyed strong backing from Berlin and fought a daily battle to conquer the streets of Vienna. Dollfuss's authoritarian policies were in his view only a quick fix to safeguard Austria's independence— unsuitable in the long run, especially if the general political mentality did not change.

In March 1934, Mises was delighted to receive an offer from the Geneva-based Graduate Institute of International Studies to become a visiting professor of international economic relations. He accepted immediately.[2] However, he did not flee Austria, as he would when the Nazis seized control of the country four years later. He moved to Geneva in disgust, but he considered the move temporary.

Mises had been an employee of the *Kammer* long enough to qualify for early retirement, but he did not wish to burn his bridges and eventually arrived at an agreement according to which he would do some work for it during his school vacations and be paid half his former salary.[3] In early December 1934, he returned to Vienna for the first time and worked some weeks in his old position. Thereafter he continued to work as a consultant and liaison officer for the Vienna *Kammer*.

He often came to the Austrian capital in the middle of the week, for one or two days. Whenever he was in Vienna, he visited with Margit. She was still waiting for him; he could not make his mind up about proposing. For another three years, their love could not get out from under the shadow of his mother.

---

[2]Rappard to Mises, letter dated March 19, 1934; Mises to Rappard, letter dated March 23, 1934; Grove City Archive: Graduate Institute Archive.

[3]Kammeramtsdirektor to Mises, letter dated October 31, 1934; Grove City Archive: Kammer für Handel, Gewerbe und Industrie files. The file also concerns salary statements for the years 1936 and 1937. In both years, Mises had a gross annual income of 14,620 schillings.

Institut des Hautes Études Internationales

Geneva had been a quiet town before World War I, even though it already hosted the International Red Cross Committee. After the war, it became the home of the International Labor Office (1919) and of the League of Nations (1920). The latter was the result of an initiative of U.S. President Woodrow Wilson. The idea was to create an international political organization that would resolve conflicts between nation states without resorting to war. Ironically, Wilson did not receive the necessary ratification from the U.S. Senate for the United States to join the new organization. The League began its operations in 1921 without the participation of the man who had created it. Geneva was chosen for its location because of the longstanding neutral status of Switzerland—a status that in those days had more than mere nominal significance—and because Geneva was culturally a French city.

One of the most pressing problems for the new international bureaucracies was the lack of qualified employees. To cope with this problem, a Swiss director of the League named William E. Rappard (1883–1958) proposed the creation of a special bilingual school for the advanced scientific study of problems of international politics and administration. The school was to offer courses in French and English and make "full use of the resources of the League and the ILO in the form of specialized knowledge, documents and direct observation of how international affairs were conducted in the new context of multilateralism."[4]

Rappard was a diplomat and constitutional historian who combined in himself all the qualifications necessary to breathe

---

[4]Martine Brunschwig Graf, Jean-Claude Frachebourg, Norman Scott, and Peter Tschopp, *HEI 1927–2002* (Geneva: Graduate Institute of International Studies, 2002), p. 40. See also p. 50.

life into this project.[5] He was not only a brilliant diplomat with connections to politicians, scholars, and statesmen, private firms and foundations, as well as government institutions in France, Britain, Switzerland, and the United States, but was also a highly respected scholar with appointments at Harvard University and the University of Geneva, where he served as an influential member of the academic senate and even briefly headed the university itself.

William Rappard, Bertrand de Jouvenel, Karl Popper, and Mises at the first Mont Pèlerin meeting in April 1947

Last but not least, he had the good fortune to enjoy the personal friendship of Woodrow Wilson, his colleague at Harvard from 1911 to 1913.[6] This certainly proved to be helpful in more than one respect.

Elected as rector in 1926, Rappard launched the new school of international political relations as a joint venture of the University of Geneva, which provided academic affiliation and oversight, and the Rockefeller Foundation in New York, which pledged to finance the school in cooperation with the city of Geneva and the Swiss federal government.

Rappard had been in touch with the Rockefeller Foundation since 1924 (or more precisely, with the Laura Spelman

---

[5]His mother was a scion of the Hoffmann-Laroche family from Basel. In July 1919, William Emmanuel Rappard became secretary general of the new League of Red Cross Societies, a position he quit in 1921. Before 1919, he was already a member of the International Committee of the Red Cross. His *magnum opus* was *Die Bundesverfassung der Schweizer Eidgenossenschaft, 1848–1948—Vorgeschichte, Ausarbeitung, Weiterentwicklung* (Zurich: Polygraphischer Verlag, 1948).

[6]See the testimonies by Léopold Boissier and Carl J. Burckhardt in the memorial volume edited by Rappard's family: *William-E. Rappard* (Geneva: Kundig, 1961), pp. 45, 57.

Rockefeller Memorial Fund). In 1926, Rockefeller representative Dr. Abraham Flexner[7] pledged five annual payments of 20,000 U.S. dollars to the Geneva Department of Education, giving the green light to the creation of the school. Rappard hired the Frenchman Paul Mantoux as its first director. The school opened its gates in September 1927 under the name *Institut des Hautes Études Internationales* (Graduate Institute of International Studies).[8] The Rockefeller Foundation's pledge of financial support was extended and increased in subsequent years and the Foundation would "continue to be the main financial sponsor for nearly twenty years." By 1938, the school was receiving annual payments of 80,000 U.S. dollars and by March 1948, it had received a total of $1.4 million.[9]

Rappard and Mantoux had first met at the Versailles Peace Conference in 1919. Rappard had been granted special diplomatic observer status due to his personal acquaintance with Woodrow Wilson, and Mantoux was the principal interpreter in the allied camp and wrote the official records of the Council of Four.[10] Rappard had known Mantoux already through his writings on economic history, which had won Mantoux an excellent international reputation. As a young man, he had published a

---

[7]This was the same Flexner who had written the famous Flexner Report: *Medical Education in the United States and Canada: A Report to the Carnegie Foundation for the Advancement of Teaching* (1910) which led the the closure of four out of six medical schools in the United States.

[8]Brunschwig et al., *HEI 1927–2002*. Of particular interest is the section dealing with the years 1927 to 1978, authored by Norman Scott.

[9]Ibid., pp. 37, 72, 81.

[10]During the war, he had served as a personal interpreter between his college friend Albert Thomas and Lloyd George, both of whom were commissioned to coordinate the reorganization of the British and French munitions industries. At the end of the war, George was Prime Minister and Thomas would soon become the first president of the International Labour Organization in Geneva. "The die was cast. Mantoux's new career was made" (ibid., p. 51).

monograph on the industrial revolution in the eighteenth century, which brought him quick fame and catapulted him into the higher strata of French academics and politics. A few months after the Versailles conference, he became Rappard's colleague in the directorate of the League of Nations. Given his academic and political background, he was an obvious—and excellent— choice for the new school.

Rappard later joined Mantoux in the management of the Institute, and together they led it for about twenty years. The harmonious cooperation between the two men proved to be the foundation of the Institute's success and its cordial atmosphere, which made it attractive as a destination for scholars from around the world. The position that Mises would hold for six years was a one-year (renewed) visiting position for economists of international reputation. His predecessors had been Samuel Patterson (Philadelphia), Frank Graham (Princeton), and Jacob Viner (Chicago). Other recent visiting economists of international pedigree were Gustav Cassel (Stockholm), and Theodore Gregory (London). It might well have been Gregory who brought Mises to Geneva—they had known each other for many years, and in 1933–1934 cooperated closely in the International Chamber of Commerce.[11] Or the initiative could have come from someone else—Professor Alfred Zimmern, for example, who ran the Geneva School of International Studies and had asked Mises in December 1929 to recommend suitable students for scholarships.[12] In any case, it is fairly certain that

---

[11] See the untitled typewritten statement dated July 9, 1934; Grove City Archive: Kammer für Handel, Gewerbe und Industrie file. Michael Heilperin later stated that Rappard and the economists had particular affinities with Charles Rist, Jacques Rueff, Jacob Viner, and Lionel Robbins. See his statement in *William-E. Rappard*, p. 78.

[12] Alfred Zimmern to Mises, letter dated December 12, 1929; Grove City Archive: Institut des Hautes Etudes Internationales files. Zimmern was a professor at the University of Geneva and head of international affairs at the Institute for Intellectual Cooperation. Before the establishment of the *Institut*, he

Mises's long-standing and close association with the Rockefeller Foundation proved to be beneficial once again. He himself had been very active in helping colleagues from Germany find new jobs abroad after Hitler rose to power in January 1933, and at least some of these new positions were likely financed by the Rockefeller Foundation. It was natural therefore that he himself receive support once the political situation in Austria became untenable for him. This was certainly the case after the violence of February 1934 and its aftermath. While it would be an exaggeration to say that Mises was on the payroll of the Rockefeller Foundation (this was effectively precluded both by Rappard's insistence that funds be received with no strings attached and by the co-financing of the Institute from Swiss sources) the fact remains that during the Geneva years Mises's salary was paid to a large extent out of Rockefeller money, and so things would remain for the next decade.[13]

Academic Life

Rappard quipped that the Institute owed the excellence of its teaching staff to Hitler and Mussolini. A case in point was

---

had run "summer vacation schools on international affairs"—the *Zimmern School*—for some years. He then moved to Oxford University. See Scott in Brunschwig et al., *HEI 1927–2002*, p. 29.

[13]This strong financial connection (dependence) was downplayed by all sides. In 1942, Tracy Kittredge wrote in a letter to the U.S. State Department that the

> Foundation has been familiar with the work of Professor von Mises for more than ten years and has contributed toward research projects under his direction in Vienna and in Geneva, and to his present stipend at the National Bureau of Economic Research.

Kittredge to Acheson, letter dated January 5, 1942; Grove City Archive: Mexico 1942 files. In fact, the Rockefeller Foundation paid the NBER stipend in full.

Guglielmo Ferrero, who had been under house arrest in Italy before coming to Geneva as a professor of history; and it was also true for men like Mises, Kelsen, and Röpke, who found in the Institute a political safe haven. In Kelsen's case, language also played a role to the extent that he was fluent in French, but had difficulties with the English language.[14] Mises's command of English was also much weaker than his French.

Once they located on the shores of Lake Geneva, these refugee scholars discovered that their new school also offered a congenial social and intellectual atmosphere. Mises arrived in the fall of 1934 and took an apartment on 16 *chemin Krieg*—literally the "war path"—but after the first extension of his visit, he moved to nicer accommodations on 3 chemin Dumas. At that point, the permanent faculty featured, in addition to Rappard and Mantoux: Eugène Borel, Mack Eastman (economics), Hans Wehberg (international law), Maurice Bourquin (diplomatic history), Pitman Potter (political science), Paul Guggenheim (international public law), Guglielmo Ferrero (modern history), Carl Burckhardt (modern history), and Hans Kelsen (law). The personal relationships among these men appear to have been extraordinarily cordial—by the standards of academic life at any rate. What is amazing is that there was something like a social life there at all—these famous scholars did what other professional groups did as well: exchange visits, entertain one another at home, and become acquainted with the family members of their colleagues. And they liked it. Mises was apparently most at ease with Rappard, Mantoux, Bourquin, and Ferrero.[15]

---

[14]When Kelsen was ousted from his chair at the University of Cologne in 1933, he received offers from the Institute, from LSE, and from the New School for Social Research. The language issue prompted him to opt for Geneva, where professors could teach in French. See Rudolf Aladár Métall, *Hans Kelsen* (Vienna: Verlag Franz Deuticke, 1968), p. 64.

[15]Mises to Wilhelm Hertz (Geneva), letter dated November 9, 1961; Grove City Archive: "H" files. In this letter Mises recalled the quiet years of

He also associated with scholars from the League of Nations's Economic Intelligence Unit (Loveday, Haberler, Tinbergen, Meade, Koopmans, Polak, Fleming, Nurkse, Condliffe, and Hilgerdt), the International Labor Office (Karl Pribram), and the Geneva Research Center (John B. Whitton). The most immediate common bond among these groups was that they all depended on funding from the Rockefeller Foundation, which in those very years launched a massive international program of business-cycle research with a special focus on economic stabilization. The Foundation not only funded the economists working at the League of Nations and at Rappard's Graduate School, but also business cycle institutes in Louvain, New York, Paris, Sofia, Vienna, and Warsaw. Its officers were careful not to impose any research agenda, but their wishes could not be ignored. Thus a group of financially endowed laymen had a decisive impact on the path that business-cycle research would follow over the course of the coming decades. The League's authority and Rockefeller's money gave leadership to people such as Alexander Loveday and Alvin Hansen; business-cycle research would henceforth be conducted with an increasingly quantitative orientation.[16] By the time Mises moved to Geneva, he was already an anachronism—a vestige of the early Rockefeller involvement in the social sciences.

These developments were noticeable but not yet dominant in 1934. Mises and others could conduct their research as they saw fit, and in Geneva they could do it under the most pleasant circumstances. Much of the Institute's conviviality was related to size: throughout the 1930s, the school remained small and

---

study and exchange with like-minded friends and mentioned in particular these four.

[16]Neil de Marchi, "League of Nations Economists and the Ideal of Peaceful Change in the Decade of the 'Thirties," C.D. Goodwin, ed., *Economics and National Security* (Durham, N.C.: Duke University Press, 1991), pp. 143–78.

virtually free from the plague of bureaucracy—its administration counted a mere six heads and one part-time accountant. Student numbers almost never exceeded 100 and just under half of them were enrolled in the doctoral program. The permanent faculty had twelve members at its peak in 1938—including Rappard and Mantoux.[17] These residential scholars were complemented by one or two visiting professors who stayed for a semester or a year, and there were also guest lecturers who gave high-profile short courses, which typically ran for a week. The combination of these circumstances made for something approaching academic paradise. Rappard explained the recipe:

> I know of no better . . . means of being useful to advanced students . . . than placing at their disposal as completely and as informally as possible the most eminent specialists available. If these specialists are well chosen, not only for their intelligence and erudition, but also for their character, and if they are made to realize that their sole professional duty is to contribute to the progress of science through their own work, and to advise and assist the advanced students . . . I believe our job is practically done.[18]

Each professor was free to choose the subject of his courses and seminars. The only constraint was to give from time to time some introductory class for non-specialists. In practice this meant that Mises, on top of the three hours he was required to teach anyway, occasionally had to give an introductory course

---

[17]Scott in Brunschwig et al., *HEI 1927–2002*, pp. 53f. Mantoux was not present all the time—already in 1928, he had moved his home to Paris because the city on the Seine offered better educational possibilities for his children and also because he continued to work on the official records of the Versailles Conference. This had prompted Rappard to join him as a co-director of the *Institut* in the same year.

[18]Rappard quoted from Scott in Brunschwig et al., *HEI 1927–2002*, p. 56.

on economics for non-economists, which he did in rotation with the other economists.

The school occupied the basement and first floor of the splendid Plantamour mansion, located on the border of the old city center at 5 Promenade du Pin. Mises started lecturing on October 25, 1934. He gave a two-hour seminar on International Finance, and a one-hour course on "The International Aspects of Monetary Policy," which he held Thursdays from 5:15 to 6:00 p.m. In one of the first sessions, on November 15, 1934, he gave his inaugural lecture on the gold standard and the problems of controlled currency.

Apart from the three hours of required teaching, Mises was free to pursue his research as he saw fit—and all of this at the very comfortable annual salary of 25,000 Swiss francs or 233.375 oz of gold, which corresponded to some US$8,177 in the 1930s and fifteen times as much in our day.[19]

For years he had told his students that high salaries combined with few obligations were the prime factor for the low productivity of university professors. (And a few years after he had gone to Geneva, Hayek told him about a discovery he had just made: Adam Smith too had held this opinion of the consequences of high salaries for academics![20]) Now was the opportunity for

---

[19]Rappard to Mises, letter dated March 19, 1934; Graduate Institute Archive. The dollar amount can be calculated on the basis of the following data: 20 SWF = 0.1867 ounces of gold; 35 USD = 1 ounce of gold. The essential terms of his contract (3 hours of teaching, 25,000 SWF compensation) applied throughout the entire period of his employment at the Institute; see the certificate from André Mussard (the Institute's secretary-general), dated June 6, 1940; Graduate Institute Archive.

[20]Adam Smith quoted in Hayek to Mises, letter dated October 15, 1937; Grove City Archive: Hayek files:

> I have thought a great deal upon this subject, and have inquired very carefully into the constitution and history of several of the principal universities of Europe; I have satisfied myself that the present state of degradation and contempt into which the greater part of these societies had fallen in almost

Mises to prove himself wrong by finally writing his general treatise on economic science—a project he had postponed twenty
years earlier in anticipation of the coming war.

His appointment and the lectures on money coincided with
the publication of the English edition of his monetary treatise.
After many years, Batson had finally completed the translation
with Robbins's help and published the work under the title *The
Theory of Money and Credit.* It was the first foreign edition of a
Mises book—perfect timing to support the new professorship in
international economic relations. Mises had pursued a hands-off
policy with his translator, a policy he maintained for the rest of
his life. But while *laissez-faire* is an unshakable maxim as far as
the limitation of governments is concerned, it does not always
apply in private affairs. Many years later, Mises complained in
correspondence with a young colleague from Austria that good
translators were hard to find. "I am outright horrified about the
sense-distorting errors that I have found in French and German
translations of my English publications, and in English and
French translations of my German books."[21] In the present case,
for example, the title of the English edition: "theory of money
and credit" certainly made for smoother reading than the more
literal "theory of money and fiduciary media," but it blunted the
title's edge. The point of the original title was precisely to highlight the particular character of fiduciary media, which the book
showed distorted the operation of a monetary economy.

For future scholarship, Mises had to develop his English. In
a letter to Machlup he observed that one of the practical consequences of Hitlerism was to reduce the importance of the

---

       every part of Europe arises principally, first, from the large
       salaries which in some Universities are given to professors, and
       which render them altogether independent of their diligence.

[21]Mises to Rudolf Berthold, letter dated November 4, 1959; Grove City
Archive: Berthold file.

German language.[22] The future belonged to English, and to practice, Mises decided to give his Institute lectures in English instead of French. In light of subsequent events his decision turned out to be extremely fortunate. It was the general policy of the Institute that professors and students were required to understand both French and English, but it was customary to speak the language in which one felt most at ease. It was therefore entirely normal that a question be asked in English and the answer given in French. Similarly, in written examinations students could use either language, regardless of which language had been used for the question. Even greater liberties existed for written homework and doctoral dissertations, which could also be written in German or Italian.[23]

But Mises did not master the English language. Tape recordings made in the late 1950s and early 1960s reveal a very strong accent even after some thirty years of lecturing in English. One might therefore assume that his early lectures in Geneva were quite a challenge to the patience of his audiences. Mises did his best to compensate for his linguistic deficiencies by writing his lectures out in advance, but his delivery remained poor. He was a solid lecturer, but never a brilliant one, and could not compete in the classroom with charismatic speakers such as Bourquin and Rappard, who impressed and overwhelmed their audience through personality and oratorical skills. Harvard graduate Parker T. Hart, who attended the Institute in 1935–1936, wrote a revealing student evaluation. At the end of his first semester, Hart did not even mention Mises, but at the end of the second semester, he praised him in the following words:

> I have gradually come to the conclusion that Professor Mises ranks as one of the best here, as an analyzer

---

[22]Mises to Machlup, letter dated October 23, 1934; Hoover Institution: Machlup-Mises correspondence file.

[23]This information is taken from the school's catalogue pertaining to the 1939–1940 academic year.

of current economic problems. The title of his course is likely to have little relation to the topics treated, but his lectures are always stimulating and lucid— and, as a unique feature—always carefully written out in advance. His English leaves a good bit to be desired, from a grammatical point of view; and a first impression is likely to be unfavorable. However, his vocabulary is rich and his meaning always clear. In short, he "wears well" indeed; and for those interested in the economic riddle left by the break-up of the old Austro-Hungarian Empire he has an especially valuable contribution to make. Best of all, he is able to enliven his discussions and lectures by concrete experience and first hand observations drawn from wide travel and research "on the spot."[24]

The report suggests one of the reasons why he did not produce any outstanding students during his years in Geneva. An even more important reason was the typical mindset of the students at the Institute, who were eager to obtain employment in an international organization—that is, in a government bureau. It is safe to assume that such students were not especially receptive to Mises's message. His two best-known students from these years became experts in the economics of war: Stefan Possony and Edmund Silberner.[25]

Still, overall relations between Mises and his students were quite good, reflecting the general atmosphere in the Plantamour mansion. A student who was at the Institute during

---

[24]Typewritten copy of an extract of Parker T. Hart's report to the Institute of International Education of New York. Rappard had obtained a copy of the report from the president of the Federal Technical University of Zurich, Mr. Rohn, who organized student exchanges between the United States and Switzerland. See Rappard to Mises, letter dated March 25, 1937; Graduate Institute Archive.

[25]Haberler later singled out J. Marcus Fleming and Alexandre Kafka. See Gottfried von Haberler, "Mises's Private Seminar" in "Erinnerungen an das Mises-Privatseminar," *Wirtschaftspolitische Blätter* 28, no. 4 (1981): 123.

Mises's first two years later recalled a scene from one of the soirées that brought students and faculty together playing charades:

> Monsieur Mantoux found himself paired with Roland Sharp in the role of the classical lovers, Leander and Hero. Sharp, despite his little black moustache, managed to achieve a certain feminine charm by tying a bright red ribbon around his hair, mounted a chair behind a high screen, and held aloft a candle to light the way for Leander. Monsieur Mantoux bravely cast aside his coat, crossed the Hellespont with a vigorous swimming motion on the floor, and won both first prize of the evening and an abiding place in our hearts as one who was not only a distinguished scholar but also a very good sport.[26]

Mises also had great fun pursuing a new hobby: driving. While in Vienna all of his activities took place within the confines of the city center, his new life in Geneva required greater mobility. To make excursions into the mountains and into France, he needed an automobile. At some point in 1935 or 1936, he must have started taking lessons. In late 1936, he had obtained his driver's license and a car. During his training he had become so enthusiastic that he bought his first vehicle—a black eight-cylinder Ford called "Grand Tourisme Luxe"—some six weeks before he got his license.[27] The initial rides he took only with a chauffeur; then step-by-step, he set out for excursions on his own. His first guest for a day tour was Heilperin. And in the spring of 1937, he set out with Margit for

---

[26]Hal Lary quoted from Scott in Brunschwig et al., *HEI 1927–2002*, p. 67.

[27]See the sales contract (dated September 30, 1936) and his driver's license (dated November 13, 1936) in Grove City Archive: file # 6/10/1/1. The price of the car was 5,900 Swiss francs, about a quarter of his annual salary.

a two-week vacation to the Côte d'Azur.[28] He was and would always remain a poor driver, but he greatly enjoyed it nevertheless. And he truly wanted to share his new passion with the woman he loved. He made arrangements for Margit to take driving lessons in Vienna.[29] Together they spent many happy hours on the road.

Alienation from Former Associates

The 1930s witnessed the first phase in a process that distanced Mises from some of his closest associates. The most dramatic cases were those of Fritz Machlup and Lionel Robbins, both of whom would in the course of the years change their views on a number of important issues, particularly on money and the gold standard. In Machlup's case, Mises eventually broke off all contact for a few years. The issue for him was integrity. It was one thing to disagree on the importance of the gold standard, but he believed Machlup's change of heart to be unprincipled.[30]

In the 1930s, the seeds of this alienation were newly sown, and only hindsight allows us to see where the process began. In 1934, Machlup left Vienna for the United States on a Rockefeller stipend. From February to June 1935, he lectured at Harvard, and then moved on to a full professorship at a new Rockefeller

---

[28]See the route protocols in Grove City Archive: file #6/10/1/2. His first independent ride was on December 20, 1936 (85 km). The day tour with Heilperin took place on January 17, 1937 (235 km).

[29]Margit von Mises, *My Years with Ludwig von Mises*, 2nd enlarged ed. (Cedar Falls, Iowa: Center for Futures Education, 1984), p. 27.

[30]At a 1965 conference, Machlup had attributed the attempt to restore a gold standard to special interest politics. Mises was in the audience and thereafter refused to talk to Machlup. According to his wife he said: "He was in my seminar in Vienna . . . he understands everything. He knows more than most of them and he knows exactly what he is doing." Margit von Mises, *My Years with Ludwig von Mises*, p. 146. Machlup's view of the event is reprinted in ibid., pp. 192f.

creation: the University of Buffalo. Rather than a stalwart of the Austrian School, however, Machlup became part of the new economics movement. Mises must have sensed the shift in his former student. In January 1936 he appealed to him:

> I hope that you will not become American over there,
> but, to the contrary, that you convert the Americans
> to liberalism and Austrianism. They need it indeed.[31]

Seventeen months later, he asked rhetorically what the Austrian economists could learn from the new theory of monopolistic competition. Machlup wrote on Mises's letter: "That's not the issue—but if we raised the question anyway, the answer would be: quite a lot."[32]

The break with Lionel Robbins was less severe. At the end of Mises's first academic year in Geneva, Robbins had come to the Institute to give one of the prestigious week-long short courses that attracted not only the entire faculty of the Institute, but also "representatives of the local authorities, the diplomatic missions and the international organisations."[33] Robbins delivered a series of lectures in the summer of 1935 on problems of international economic organization.[34] He had brought his family and took them mountain climbing with Mises. The Robbins children would later recall how after a day of climbing Mises had filled their rucksacks with Swiss chocolate. But correspondence between the two men stopped after December 1935, and was resumed—somewhat reluctantly on Robbins's part—only in

---

[31]Mises to Machlup, letter dated January 11, 1936; Hoover Institution: Machlup-Mises correspondence file.

[32]Mises to Machlup, letter dated June 29, 1937; Hoover Institution: Machlup-Mises correspondence.

[33]Scott in Brunschwig et al., *HEI 1927–2002*, p. 63.

[34]The product of these lectures was a book with the title *International Economic Planning* (London: Macmillan, 1937).

1943, when Mises made a last attempt to win Robbins back to the side of liberty.[35]

Robbins later distanced himself very clearly from the ideas he had cherished in the early 1930s. He said in his autobiography that he wished he had never written his book *The Great Depression* (1934). *Economic Planning and International Order* (1937), the book in which he published his Geneva lectures, was to be his last "Austrian" work. In *The Economic Basis of Class Conflict* (1939), Robbins started having second thoughts about "idle resources" the presence of which, he felt, undermined the applicability of the Austrian business cycle theory. From then on, the Austrian influence on Robbins's thought receded more and more into the background. Although he remained on friendly personal terms with Mises, they were no longer intellectual comrades in arms.[36]

In contrast to Machlup and Robbins, Mises's friendship with Hayek grew stronger during these years, especially during the war. It was Hayek who managed Mises's bank accounts in London. He paid Mises's subscriptions for *Economica* and the *Review of Economic Studies*, and bought books for him—a sign of the great trust Mises put in his former Vienna associate. Apart from his bankers and Gustav Fischer (a quasi-banker for Mises in the

---

[35]Mises to Robbins, letter dated December 10, 1935; Grove City Archive: Robbins file. Mises commented on the second edition of Lionel Robbins, *The Nature and Significance of Economic Science* (London: Macmillan, 1932) in particular on Robbins's use of the word "experience." Speaking about the significance and role of tautologies, Mises said that he had learned from Meyerson. See Émile Meyerson, *De l'explication dans les sciences* (Paris: Fayot, 1927).

[36]For a concise presentation of the Austrian impact on Robbins's intellectual development see Denis P. O'Brien, "Lionel Robbins and the Austrian Connection," Bruce J. Caldwell, ed., *Carl Menger and His Legacy in Economics* (Durham, N.C.: Duke University Press, 1990), pp. 155–84. O'Brien stresses Robbins pervasive eclecticism. He points out that Mises's impact on Robbins was at all times matched, if not surpassed, by Wieser's and Mayer's.

early years of German credit controls), the hyper-cautious Mises never let anybody peek into his financial records.[37]

The crucial factors in their friendship were Hayek's integrity and appreciation for free markets, not any one point-by-point correspondence in outlook on politics or economics—although Hayek felt it necessary to assure his former mentor that he "need have no fear about my becoming converted to Keynesianism."[38] Their friendship grew despite rather significant disagreements. While they did not affect the personal and professional relations between the two men, these disagreements would come to play a role in the rebirth of the Austrian School after 1974.

What were these disagreements? Wieser's impact on Hayek's economic thought made itself felt in Hayek's theories of monetary equilibrium and of "neutral" money—both theories that Mises would explicitly reject. Other points of contention appeared when Hayek turned to capital theory. In the spring of 1934, Fritz Machlup queried the inner circle of Austrian economists—Mises, Hayek, Strigl, Haberler, Machlup—about capital theory in general and the concept of the period of production in particular. Mises had answered Machlup's five questions in May, stating that three of them seemed to be based on an untenable interpretation of the period-of-production concept. Machlup replied with some astonishment:

> I should be very grateful for you to write to me whether you totally maintain your fundamental

---

[37]The deposit account would be quite substantial after the publication of *Theory of Money and Credit* and *Socialism*. In February 1936, Mises had more than 237 pounds in the account; by May 1939 it was almost 780 pounds. See Hayek to Mises, letter dated February 15, 1936, as well as the typewritten statement of the development of the accounts until May 1939 in Grove City Archive: Hayek files.

[38]Hayek to Mises, letter dated January 12, 1941; Grove City Archive: Hayek files.

> objections against my (and Hayek's) conceptions.
> Hayek's new book on capital would from A to Z be
> subject to your objections, if strictly interpreted.[39]

Another difference emerged when Hayek turned his attention to the theory of socialism. In 1935, Hayek edited a volume
of essays making the case for the impossibility of socialist economic calculation. The volume contained an introductory essay
by Hayek, the two classic pieces by Pierson and Mises, and two
concluding essays discussing the current state of the debate in
the continental literature (Halm) and in English-language publications (Hayek).[40]

In his introduction, Hayek pointed out that Mises had been
the first writer to emphasize that the "pricing process" must
cover intermediate products and factors of production lest economic calculation be impossible. Yet by "pricing process"
Hayek seemed to mean the mere *expression* of prices in terms of
money—in other words, his argument seems to be based on the
Wieserian assumption that money prices were just one convenient way of expressing values and performing value calculations.[41] In his discussion of the proposal to use mathematical

---

[39]Machlup to Mises, letter dated September 25, 1934; Grove City
Archive: Machlup files. Copies of Machlup's original questionnaire, and the
answers formulated by Mises, Hayek, Haberler, Marschak, and Machlup
himself are in the same file. One year later, Oskar Morgenstern demolished
the idea that the average period production was an adequate measure of cap-
ital-intensity. See Morgenstern, "Zur Theorie der Produktionsperiode,"
Zeitschrift für Nationalökonomie 6 (1935): 196–208. Historian Harald Hagemann suggests that this critique was instrumental for Hayek to abandon the
period-of-production concept in later works. See Hagemann, "Einführung,"
Harald Hagemann, ed., *Zur deutschsprachigen wirtschaftswissenschaftlichen Emigration nach 1933* (Marburg: Metropolis, 1997), pp. 13f.

[40]F.A. Hayek, ed., *Collectivist Economic Planning: Critical Studies on the Possibilities of Socialism* (London: Routledge, 1935). An appendix of the volume
featured Barone's 1908 article arguing that a socialist directorate could use a
system of general equilibrium equations as a planning device.

[41]Hayek, "The Nature and History of the Problem," in ibid., p. 33.

equation systems as economic planning tools, Hayek then admits that this proposal is "not an impossibility in the sense that it is logically contradictory." Rather, the true problem of central planning was, according to Hayek, a result of the type and quantity of *information* required.[42]

Central planners would first need precise information about the location and the physical characteristics of every single economic good. Second, they would need to centralize all available technical knowledge as well as knowledge about how to gain new technical knowledge ("techniques of thought"). And third, they would need "data relative to importance of the different kinds and quantities of consumers' goods." Given these requirements, socialist economic calculation was clearly impracticable, even though it was not—as Mises had contended—impossible. Hayek emphasized:

> all the difficulties which have been raised are "only" due to the imperfections of the human mind. But while this makes it illegitimate to say that these proposals are impossible in any absolute sense, it remains

---

[42]Hayek, "The Present State of the Debate," in ibid., pp. 208ff. This distinctive perspective on the problem of economic calculation under socialism was a consequence of Hayek's acceptance of mathematical general equilibrium analysis as the most advanced expression of modern economic science. This was correctly noticed on all sides. For example,

> Professors Hayek and Robbins of the London School of economics, who next to Mises are the leading opponents of socialism among economists, have apparently been influenced by Barone. They have taken up a second line of attack, the line that is usually taken after a principle has been admitted. They admit that a rational allocation of resources is theoretically possible in a socialist state, but deny that it can be worked out in practice. (Benjamin E. Lippincott, "Introduction," *On the Economic Theory of Socialism*, ed., B.E. Lippincott [New York: McGraw-Hill, 1964], p. 13)

See also Eduard März, "Die Bauer—Mises-Schumpeter-Kontroverse," *Wirtschaftspolitische Blätter* 28, no. 4 (1981): 73.

> not the less true that these very serious obstacles to
> the achievement of the desired end exist and that
> there seems to be no way in which they can be over-
> come.[43]

Hayek's conclusion was that socialist calculation posed insuperable practical difficulties. For him the formidable cognitive
problem of economic calculation without money prices was the
beginning and end of his economic argument against central
planning. Mises too recognized the existence and importance of
knowledge problems.[44] But he had *also* perceived a deeper problem of an altogether different nature. For Mises, the "pricing
process" was not just the solution to an intellectual puzzle—it
did not merely "express" the knowable reality of value in terms
of some other knowable reality of money prices. Rather, the
pricing process *created* a reality that could not possibly be
known otherwise. Hayek would contend—following Wieser—
that *if* the fundamental knowledge problems could be solved,
one could calculate the correct prices for factors of production.
Mises denied this as even a theoretical possibility. Socialist calculation was for him a conceptual impossibility.

In 1938, Mises published an article on using the equations of
mathematical economics as the tools of a socialist planning board.[45]

---

[43]Hayek, "The Present State of the Debate," p. 238.

[44]He pointed out these problems in his original 1920 article and throughout his later works. See for example *The Ultimate Foundation of Economic Science* (Irvington-on-Hudson, N.Y.: Foundation for Economic Education,
2002), p. 110.

[45]Mises, "The Equations of Mathematical Economics and the Problem of
Economic Calculation in a Socialist State," *Quarterly Journal of Austrian Economics* 3, no. 1 (2000). The original version of this article was written in German, but never published. A French translation by Gaston Leduc appeared in
1938 in Charles Rist's *Revue d'économie politique* 97, no. 6 (1938): 899–906.
The quoted English translation by Vera Smith was originally prepared for
Economica, but not published there because the editorial board of the journal
rejected all submissions that had already appeared elsewhere.

Here he argued that Hayek had underrated the significance of the assumption that the socialist planning board knows future consumer preferences. Hayek had pointed out that the quest for such knowledge encounters great practical problems. Mises concurred. But there was also a logical riddle, one that subsists even with foreknowledge of the future. One cannot simply plug such known future consumer preferences into a system of equations and obtain a solution of the resource allocation problem. The equations of Walras, Pareto, and Barone merely describe how the economy would look in a state of general equilibrium. They describe an economy in equilibrium, not an economy tending toward equilibrium. The real-world economy is always in a state of flux; it is continually in *dis*equilibrium. The fundamental economic problem is to choose the best actions to approach the equilibrium state, and to do this in the most efficient way. For a person confronted with real-world decisions in the present—whether an entrepreneur or a socialist dictator— it is therefore no help whatsoever to know the hypothetical future consumer preferences according to some theoretical construct. His crucial problem is to decide the next step to get closer to equilibrium. The general equilibrium equations themselves offer no information for solving this problem.

Mises argued that the decisive advantage the market economy has over socialism is in the use of *present experience*. For a socialist dictator, the knowledge of present conditions can be no more than a starting point for speculations about the ultimate equilibrium state of the economy; but these speculations are overthrown every day by unforeseen changes. In contrast, the entrepreneurs of a market economy can apply present-day experiences in present-day decision-making. They can use their knowledge of current *conditions* (supply side) and current entrepreneurial *opinions* about conditions in the future (demand side) to bring about piecemeal improvements of the existing structure of the economy.

Apparently Mises had presented several versions of the paper to Hayek without gaining his approval. Even the version that was eventually published in the *Revue d'économie politique* did not convince Hayek. He wrote to Mises in private correspondence:

> There would be much to say about the paper, but the problem it raises is so broad that it is very difficult to deal with it adequately in a letter. As I mentioned in Paris I am not yet entirely satisfied even with the new version of the last section. Suppose all knowledge of the individual entrepreneurs about the future had come together in the head of the economic dictator, and suppose it were conceivable that he solve the countless equations into which these data were to fit. Would then really only one other problem remain, a difference between the position of the entrepreneur and of the dictator? I do not quite see it.[46]

At that point, Hayek had already published his now-famous paper on "Economics and Knowledge," in which he had argued that general equilibrium economics *à la* Walras, Pareto, and Wieser was a system of tautological propositions—a "pure logic of choice" as it were—and as such unassailable. It did not give an adequate explanation of how real economies work because it assumed from the outset that a fundamental problem has already been solved, namely, the problem of knowledge acquisition. Hayek argued that the market could solve this problem because market prices act as a mechanism of communication, and that the great deficiency of socialism was precisely that it lacked such a mechanism.

Thus Hayek had found his way out of the general-equilibrium box. The views he adopted on the theoretical and practical importance of information and the acquisition of knowledge were part and parcel of his attempt to reconcile his Walrasian outlook with the facts of life. The problem was, however, that

---

[46]Hayek to Mises, letter dated October 20, 1938; Grove City Archive: Hayek files.

he projected these problems onto all other theorists and in particular onto Mises. His 1937 essay on "Economics and Knowledge" was directed against what he believed to be the apriorism of Mises.[47] In fact it was at best a criticism of the unwarranted a priori suppositions of Walrasian general equilibrium theory, which Hayek himself was instrumental in spreading.

Hayek's speculations about the importance of knowledge and information did not change Mises's views about the a priori nature of economic science. Hayek attributed this fact to the intellectual inflexibility of his 66-year-old mentor. Yet it was the young Hayek who lacked openness to new ideas. When Mises published his first pioneering essays on the nature of value and the relationship between economic theory and the real world, Hayek and his fellow students had already made up their minds on these questions.[48]

Despite all this, Hayek did continue to be Mises's favorite student and closest ally. He visited Geneva in the spring of 1937 to conduct a brilliant and successful *cours temporaire*. The lectures were published a year later in one of his best books ever: *Monetary Nationalism and International Stability*. Unfortunately, Mises could not attend the entire course. Soon after Hayek's arrival, he received terribly bad news about his mother and

---

[47]Hans Jörg Hennecke, *Friedrich August von Hayek* (Düsseldorf: Wirtschaft und Finanzen, 2000), pp. 131–34. The author quotes from a 1981 letter that Hayek wrote to Terence Hutchinson:

> But the main intention of my 1936 lecture was to explain gently to Mises why I could not accept his a priorism. Curiously enough, Mises who did not readily accept criticism from his juniors, accepted my argument but insisted that it was not incompatible with his view.

[48]See section "Wieser's long shadow" in chapter "Winds of Change," above.

immediately left for Vienna.[49] Adele von Mises suffered only for a few days. She died on April 18, 1937 and was buried four days later in the presence of her sons.

Ludwig had been very close to her—so close that she was an obstacle to marriage with Margit. Now the gates were open for this union.

Mises and the Neo-Liberals

The disagreement on the question of socialist calculation was but a symptom of a larger dissent between Mises and his erstwhile comrades-in-arms.

Not only did Mises unabashedly defend the central tenets of the Manchester School, which had by then fallen into general disrepute, he went beyond them. He showed that any third-way system was inherently unstable because it could not solve the problems it purported to solve, and thus motivated ever more government intervention until the interventionist system had been transformed into outright socialism. But socialism was not viable. There remained only one meaningful option: 100 percent capitalism. Again and again, Mises insisted that there was no choice in this matter. It was ludicrous to speculate about some particular third-way policy that would fit the sensibilities of a given group. Society was viable only to the extent that private property rights were respected, and that was that.

This message resonated well with the old liberals, who marveled at such a splendid restatement of the ideals of their youth. But Mises's views were received less wholeheartedly by the rising generation, which had been raised in an intellectual environment soaked in statism. Their school teachers and university professors had come to endorse all the main ideas behind the case for socialism: the doctrine of class conflict and class

---

[49]Hayek to Mises, letter dated May 10, 1937; Grove City Archive: Hayek files.

struggle, the notion of the immiseration of the working classes under capitalism, and the belief that an unfettered capitalist system tended toward monopoly.

On the positive side, Mises had definitely dethroned full-blown socialism as a policy ideal. The energies of Hayek, Machlup, Haberler, Robbins, Perroux, and Röpke—men who would play a significant role in shaping post-World War II policies in the western world—no longer served the idol of omnipotent government. This proved to be of decisive importance for the course of history. But Mises's influence proved too weak to inspire in them the courage necessary for a wholehearted return to the kind of vibrant liberalism that had characterized the Manchester School and the worldwide *laissez-faire* movement of the nineteenth century.

Mises had not yet published the systematic treatise on economic science that would have clarified the scientific case for unfettered capitalism. He had presented some important elements of his general economic theory of social systems, but before 1940 it was not yet clear how these elements interrelated and on which general analytical framework they relied. In 1940, Mises finally published such a general treatise under the title of *Nationalökonomie—Theorie des Handelns und Wirtschaftens*. But by 1940, Hayek was fifty-one years old and an established scholar; the book came too late for him, and it also came too late for the rest of his generation—for the Röpkes and Machlups and Robbinses and all the others Mises had steered away from socialism in the 1920s. In the minds of these men, Mises's early work on the impossibility of socialism and the ineffectiveness of interventionism had created a paradox. Mises had convinced them that full-blown socialism was neither feasible nor desirable; they were also persuaded that third-way systems were overrated. But many of them did not yet question the claim that nineteenth-century liberalism had failed because its economic program, *laissez-faire* capitalism, had not delivered the goods. They believed it to be a simple matter of fact that the unfettered free market tends toward monopoly, and that the nineteenth-century working classes had lived in misery because of *laissez-faire* capitalism.[50]

For these men, theory had disproved the viability of socialism, and history had proven the defects of capitalism. What was needed was a third way—a third way that could somehow get around Mises's demonstration that interventionism was necessarily counter-productive. The solution that emerged in the 1930s was based on an intellectual construct that split the social economy into two elements: (1) an institutional framework, and (2) the processes that played themselves out within that framework—most notably the pricing process. According to this new creed, government should not meddle with the processes but it did have to establish and maintain the institutional framework. This set of assumptions is characteristic of what has come to be called neo-liberalism.

We find a clear expression of the neo-liberal worldview in a paper Hayek wrote in 1935. Commenting on Mises's theory of interventionism, Hayek observes that it did not follow from Mises's argument that "the only form of capitalism which can be rationally advocated is that of complete *laissez faire* in the old sense." He continued:

> The recognition of the principle of private property does not by any means necessarily imply that the particular delimitation of the contents of this right as determined by the existing laws are the most appropriate. The question as to which is the most appropriate permanent framework which will secure the smoothest and most efficient working of competition is of the greatest importance and one which

---

[50]A revision of the historical performance of nineteenth-century capitalism set things straight after World War II. The feeble beginnings are in F.A. Hayek, ed., *Capitalism and the Historians* (Chicago: University of Chicago Press, 1954).

must be admitted has been sadly neglected by economists.[51]

The roots of the neo-liberal ideology went back at least to
the 1880s and 1890s, when German economists of the Historical School and their American disciples became convinced that
industrial concentration has harmful effects and required moderation through government intervention. One of the visible
consequences of this mindset was the Sherman Act, which to
the present day has replaced the power of consumers with that
of bureaucrats. In Germany, the philosophy of the third way
became pervasive in the *Sozialpolitik* instigated under Kaiser
Wilhelm. France followed, invoking the necessity of a *tierce
solution*, as did the United States under the New Deal.

Still the first programmatic statements of neo-liberalism
were published only in the 1930s—again, unsurprisingly, in
Germany and the United States. The most influential statement
came from Chicago economist Henry Simons, who in 1934 circulated a working paper with the title "A Positive Program for
Laissez Faire"—in which the word "positive" indicated that this
program justified ample government intervention, whereas classical *laissez faire* was a "negative" program in that it did not provide such a justification. Simons called on government to regulate money and banking, prevent the formation of monopolies,
and provide minimum income for the destitute—a departure
indeed from *laissez-faire* liberalism.[52]

These ideas perfectly expressed the feelings of a generation
of economists who had been raised in a thoroughly statist intellectual environment, but who still knew the teachings of the

---

[51]Hayek, "The Nature and History of the Problem," in *Individualism and
Economic Order* (Chicago: University of Chicago Press, 1948), p. 135.

[52]H.C. Simons, *A Positive Program for Laissez-Faire. Some Proposals for a
Liberal Economic Policy* (Public policy pamphlet no. 15; Chicago: University of
Chicago Press, 1934).

classical liberals. F.A. Hayek, Wilhelm Röpke, Fritz Machlup, Milton Friedman, Michael Polanyi, Walter Eucken, and many others received their university training and their decisive intellectual impulses during the 1920s and early 1930s. During the later 1930s they began to acquire more senior positions and would, after the World War II, assume intellectual leadership on the Right.[53] Their neo-liberalism animated the work of the postwar institutions that would stem the tide of growing statism, in particular, the Mont Pèlerin Society and the Institute for Economic Affairs in London. In more recent years, the neo-liberal agenda is carried forward by a new wave of educational institutions, such as the Institute for Humane Studies, the Cato Institute, and the Atlas Research Foundation.

Popular Fronts

Meanwhile the enemies of civilization made further inroads. By the mid-1930s, Stalin had launched a new offensive both in national politics and in the international theater. Through a series of show trials he effected the wholesale execution of his most important rivals as well as their constituencies within the Communist Party. In Geneva, his foreign minister, Litvinov, forged an "anti-fascist" alliance that for the first time brought the democratic western states into coalition with the internationalist socialists in Moscow.[54] The common ground of the alliance was, of course, opposition to the nationalist socialists in Rome and Berlin. As things turned out, Litvinov's move proved

---

[53]Some of them, most notably Hayek, later turned toward a more *laissez-faire* stance. But this turn came at a time when the neo-liberal steamroller was already well underway.

[54]For an eyewitness account of these events, see Sisley Huddleston, *In My Time* (New York: Dutton & Co., 1938). Mises was also an eyewitness. He commented on the change of Soviet tactics in *Theory and History: An Interpretation of Social and Economic Evolution* (New Haven, Conn.: Yale University Press, 1957), p. 350.

to be successful. In retrospect it seems to have been by far the most effective strategy in the twentieth century for undermining western resistance to statism of the Russian variety.[55]

At first western diplomats in Geneva resisted the Russian advances. But this reluctance crumbled under the impact of the Spanish Civil War (1936–1939). In Western Europe, all attention was thenceforth focused on nationalist socialism. The presence of fascist governments in Berlin, Rome, and Madrid posed an immediate threat to the security of France and the United Kingdom, while the menace of internationalist socialism seemed remote. None of the diplomats in Geneva could yet imagine the Red Army standing on the Elbe and in Vienna. This lack of imagination was reinforced by the Communist infiltration of the Roosevelt administration in the United States. Mrs. Roosevelt in particular entertained an entire coterie of Communist intellectuals.[56]

Roosevelt had swept the States with a panoply of new laws and bureaus that made the country increasingly resemble Old Europe.[57] The New Deal was new for America, but old for

---

[55] Western journalists and intellectuals played a shameful role covering up the reality of the Soviet regime. See for example Sally J. Taylor, *Stalin's Apologist: Walter Duranty, the New York Times's Man in Moscow* (Oxford: Oxford University Press, 1990), and Paul Hollander, *Political Pilgrims*, 4th ed. (New Brunswick, N.J.: Transaction, 1998).

[56] John T. Flynn, *The Roosevelt Myth* (New York: Devin-Adair, 1948); reprinted with an introduction by Ralph Raico (San Francisco: Fox & Wilkes, 1998).

[57] To mention just a few of these new laws and bureaus: the Tennessee Valley Authority (1933), the Agricultural Adjustment Act (1933) establishing a system of price controls, the National Recovery Administration as part of the National Industrial Recovery Act, the Wagner Act (1935) attempting to establish compulsory unionization, the Undistributed Profits Tax (1936) confiscating up to 74 percent of profits, the Wages and Hours Act (1938) establishing compulsory higher minimum wages and a compulsory 40–hour work week.

Europeans. Mises recognized in the American events the very follies he and others had denounced ever since the war socialism of World War I. He wrote:

> President Roosevelt's New Deal has been greeted with enthusiasm, not only in its country of origin, but also throughout the world. The reason for this general affinity is that the essential idea of the New Deal conformed exactly to public opinion. Everyone believed that it was necessary to replace capitalism and private enterprise with more government intervention. Although certain isolated measures were criticized, the new policy as a whole was received favorably.[58]

Most economists believed that American capitalism was now effectively doomed. Schumpeter, who in the year of Roosevelt's election had moved from Bonn to Harvard, was widely quoted as complaining that he could just as well have stayed in Germany.[59]

One of the remaining differences between the new American policies and the new policies in Germany concerned Communism. It quickly became obvious that the new American administration was pursuing a policy of rapprochement in its relations with Soviet Russia. One of Roosevelt's very first actions was to establish a bank to channel funds to the Bolsheviks. Though not a member of the League of Nations, the United States had nevertheless joined the anti-fascist alliance.

In the spring of 1936, Communist-initiated "popular fronts" won elections in France and Spain. Although the Communists

---

[58]This is the first paragraph of Mises's preface to A.S.J. Baster, *Le crépuscule du capitalisme américain—étude économique du New Deal* (Paris: Librairie de Médicis, 1937).

[59]These premonitions turned out to be justified. See Thomas DiLorenzo, "Franklin Delano Roosevelt's New Deal: From Economic Fascism to Pork-Barrel Politics," John V. Denson, ed., *Reassessing the Presidency* (Auburn, Ala.: Ludwig von Mises Institute, 2001), pp. 425–51.

stayed in the background, ostensibly to fend off any concerns about secret ambitions for Bolshevik-style *coups d'état*, the fact remains that for the first time ever, these countries had socialist governments. The French socialists now did what their Austrian and German comrades had done eighteen years earlier. Léon Blum and his government nationalized the arms industries, outlawed right-wing political organizations, increased compulsory education, outlawed resistance against labor-union violence, imposed a mandatory increase of wage rates, coercively increased minimum wage rates even further by reducing the labor time to forty hours per week without reducing weekly salaries, imposed a minimum annual vacation of two weeks for every employee (along with subsidized train tickets courtesy of the taxpayer), and forced each firm with more than ten employees to pay for worker "delegates" to supervise the application of the new policies.

Not surprisingly, a great number of small and medium-sized firms had to cease operations under this wave of regulations, and many of the workers who lost their jobs in this process could not find employment elsewhere because the surviving firms could not afford to hire them at the new minimum wage rates. Capitalists fled the country, and Léon Blum soon had to rely on public debt and inflation to keep his government functioning at all. In June 1937, he resigned after little more than a year in power. In April 1938, the new Daladier government took over, reversing virtually all the new socialist laws and crushing labor-union power in short but violent confrontations.

In Spain, the correction was far less swift and far more violent. Mises traveled to Madrid in May 1936 to attend a conference for the promotion of international studies. In a press interview he said that the conference was a step forward in improving international relations.[60] But Spain's relations with other

---

[60]See the front page of *El Sol* (May 31, 1936). A copy is in Grove City Archive: Madariaga file.

nations made no further progress before the country imploded. Mises reported to Machlup: "The anarcho-syndicalists are preparing the takeover, and the people on the 'right' sharpen their long knives."[61]

In July 1936, the new Popular Front government had hardly taken office when civil war erupted. After more than two years of extremely bloody fighting, in the course of which more than one million Spaniards lost their lives, the authoritarian insurrectionists under General Franco marched victoriously into Madrid.

The Spanish translation of *The Theory of Money and Credit* had appeared just a couple of weeks before the outbreak of the war.[62] Now it was condemned to oblivion until, decades later, a group of determined economists resuscitated this work. Outside Spain, the case for *laissez-faire* fell on deaf ears too while the opponents of the free society found a growing audience—especially if the rhetoric for more government control was flexible enough to accommodate a wide variety of political regimes. Thus John Maynard Keynes made a splash in Germany, where the translation of his *General Theory* appeared the very same year as the original. In the preface to the German edition, Keynes boasted that his theory was particularly well suited for totalitarian regimes and lamented that it was less fit for the conditions prevailing in freer societies.[63]

---

[61]Mises to Machlup, letter of June 1936; Hoover Institution: Machlup-Mises correspondence.

[62]Mises to Baus, letter dated November 6, 1938; Grove City Archive: Baus file.

[63]John Maynard Keynes, *Collected Writings* (London: Macmillan, 1973), vol. 7, p. xxvi:

> Nevertheless the theory of output as a whole, which is what the following book purports to provide, is much more easily adapted to the conditions of a totalitarian state, than is the theory of production and distribution of a given output produced under conditions of free competition and a large measure of laissez-faire.

Mises did not comment on Keynes's *General Theory* when it appeared in 1936. He reacted only when the Keynesian movement came into full swing and elevated the British economist to the status of a guru of the profession. In Mises's eyes, the Keynesian revolution was insignificant from the point of view of the history of ideas. Keynes had not brought forth a single new doctrine.[64] Even his major fallacies were old and had been refuted hundreds of times. The proper way to deal with Keynesianism, therefore, was to consider it from a sociological point of view. In 1948, Mises wrote:

> For a correct appraisal of the success which Keynes' *General Theory* found in academic circles, one must consider the conditions prevailing in university economics during the period between the two world wars.

Similarly, in 1933, Keynes allowed a German translation of his paper on "national self-sufficiency" to be purged of passages that might have been offending to the new Hitler government. See Knut Borchardt, "Keynes' 'Nationale Selbstgenügsamkeit' von 1933. Ein Fall von kooperativer Selbstzensur," *Zeitschrift für Wirtschafts- und Sozialwissenschaften*, vol. 108, pp. 271–84.

[64]At the onset of the Keynesian Revolution, a few eminent historians of thought had pointed out that Keynes's views about the relationship between variations of the money supply, employment, and output had been anticipated and stressed in mercantilist thought. See Eli Heckscher, *Mercantilism*, 2nd ed. (New York: Macmillan, [1930] 1955); Jacob Viner, *Studies in the Theory of International Trade* (New York: Harper and Bros, 1937), chaps. 1 and 2. The implication is that Keynes was not so much a revolutionary, but a reactionary champion of the *ancien régime*. The single most detailed study of his *magnum opus* confirmed this implication in rather devastating terms:

> Now though I have analyzed Keynes's *General Theory* in the following pages theorem by theorem, chapter by chapter, and sometimes even sentence by sentence, to what some readers may appear a tedious length, I have been unable to find in it a single important doctrine that is both true and original. (Henry Hazlitt, *The Failure of the "New Economics,"* 2nd ed. [Irvington-on-Hudson, N.Y.: Foundation for Economic Education, (1959) 1994], p. 6)

Among the men who occupied the chairs of economics in the last few decades, there have been only a few genuine economists, i.e., men fully conversant with the theories developed by modern subjective economics. The ideas of the old classical economists, as well as those of the modern economists, were caricatured in the textbooks and in the classrooms; they were called such names as old-fashioned, orthodox, reactionary, bourgeois, or Wall Street economics. The teachers prided themselves on having refuted for all times the abstract doctrines of Manchesterism and *laissez-faire*.[65]

Two years later, he added:

The great [classical] economists were harbingers of new ideas. The economic policies they recommend were at variance with the policies practiced by contemporary governments and political parties. As a rule many years, even decades, passed before public opinion accepted the new ideas as propagated by the economists, and before the required corresponding changes in policies were effected.

It was different with the "new economics" of Lord Keynes. The policies he advocated were precisely those which almost all governments, including the British, had already adopted many years before his "General Theory" was published. Keynes was not an innovator and champion of new methods of managing economic affairs. His contribution consisted rather in providing an apparent justification for the policies which were popular with those in power in spite of the fact that all economists viewed them as

---

[65]Mises, "Stones into Bread, The Keynesian Miracle," Henry Hazlitt, ed., *The Critics of Keynesian Economics*, 2nd ed. (Irvington-on-Hudson, N.Y.: Foundation for Economic Education, 1995), p. 313. This paper was first published in the March 1948 issue of *Plain Talk*.

disastrous. His achievement was a rationalization of the policies already practiced.[66]

Profound Transformations

From August 1 to August 6, 1937, Mises took part in the meetings of the ninth international congress of philosophy, where he presented a paper on "The Logical Character of the Science of Human Conduct." Here he met the Polish philosopher Tadeusz Kotarbinski, who delivered a fascinating paper on the "idea of the methodology of general praxiology."[67] Though the paper itself did not have a lasting impact on Mises's thought, he was intrigued by the fact that Kotarbinski had used the word "praxiology" to designate a general theory of human action. Mises had already come across it in a 1926 paper from another Polish scholar, the mathematical economist Eugen Slutzky.[68] He had occasionally used this term in the discussions of his

---

[66]Mises, "Lord Keynes and Say's Law," in Hazlitt, ed., *The Critics of Keynesian Economics*, p. 319. This paper was first published in the October 1950 issue of *The Freeman*.

[67]See the volumes of the *Travaux du IXe Congrès International de Philosophie* (Paris: Hermann & Co., 1937). These conference proceedings appeared in the series *Actualités scientifiques et industrielles*. Mises's paper is printed in volume 5, pp. 49–55, Kotarbinski's in volume 4, pp. 190–94.

[68]Eugen Slutsky, "Ein Beitrag zur formal-praxeologischen Grundlegung der Ökonomik," *Annales de la classe des sciences sociales-économiques* (Kiev: Académie Oukraïenne des Sciences, 1926), vol. 4. Mises quotes this paper in *Epistemological Problems of Economics*, 3rd ed. (Auburn, Ala.: Ludwig von Mises Institute, 2003), chap. 1, p. 6. This very passage contains the phrase "a universal praxeology" and thus suggests that Mises had adopted the word already in 1933. But in the original text, Mises used a slightly different expression, namely, "eine allgemeine Praktik," meaning a general science of human practice or human action. See *Grundprobleme der Nationalökonomie* (Jena: Gustav Fischer, 1933), p. 14. The translation is however justified in the light of Mises's later adoption of the term.

Vienna private seminar.[69] But because he abhorred terminological innovations he had been reluctant to use it in print, even
though he needed a good label for the cumbersome "general
theory of human action." Throughout the 1920s, he had used
the word "sociology," but by the early 1930s he had to acknowledge that most other social scientists had come to understand
something completely different by this term. Under the influence of fanatic anti-economists such as Othmar Spann and
Werner Sombart, "sociology" had become shorthand for an
alternative social science—one that did not integrate the tenets
of economics, but instead denied them and sought to replace
economics with other explanations of the market economy,
socialism, and the hampered market economy.

But now there was a new term: *praxeology*. It was gaining
ground in the academic literature and, what is more, its champions seemed to use it in a way congruent with Mises's understanding of what a general science of human action was all
about. Kotarbinski probably talked to Mises about his "general
theory of fighting" in which he applied the general praxeological method to the phenomenon of war.[70] And it was probably
also Kotarbinski who referred Mises to some of the pioneers of
praxeology such as the French philosopher Alfred Espinas.[71]

---

[69]Robert Wälder, "Diskussionsbemerkungen zu den Leitsätzen von Professor v. Mises zur Erörterung der methodologieschen Probleme der Sozialwissenschaften," typewritten paper, dated April 19, 1934, 10 pp.; Mises
Archive: 32: 7–11. On page 6 of this paper, Wälder states that Mises had
talked about "Praxeologie," and on page 5 he uses the expression "System des
praxeologischen A priori."

[70]This work was published one year later as a French-language appendix
to one of Kotarbinski's works. See Tadeusz Kotarbinski, "Considérations sur
la théorie générale de la lutte," *Z Zagadnien Ogólnej Teorii Walki* (Warsaw,
1938), pp. 65–92.

[71]Alfred Espinas, "Les origines de la technologie" *Revue philosophique* 15
(July to December 1890); idem, *Les origines de la technologie* (Paris: Felix Alcan,
1897). Mises apparently did not have direct access to Espinas's work. Hayek

Mises found that the meaning of "praxeology" in Espinas's work was quite different from what he had in mind. Slutsky's use of the term was somewhat closer to his own views, but still did not quite hit the nail on the head.[72] In any case, "praxeology" had not yet come to be as closely associated with anti-economics as had the term "sociology" (and Hayek reported from London that the term was unknown in English) and thus Mises eventually adopted it as a label for his general theory of human action.

Work on his great treatise also progressed in other fields. One of the important areas that he had neglected for the past two decades was methodology. He had written on the epistemology of economic science, but he had not yet dealt with the more narrowly technical aspects of economic analysis. Mises now proceeded to this task by elaborating on the scattered methodological observations he had made in previous writings.[73]

---

looked up the reference for him in London, and it was also Hayek who discovered that the relevant passage from Espinas's book was taken verbatim from an article that Espinas had published some years earlier. See Hayek to Mises, handwritten note dated November 12, 1939; Grove City Archive: Hayek files.

[72]Mises to Rudolf Berthold, letter dated November 4, 1959; Grove City Archive: Berthold file. Mises thus initiated a *second* praxeological tradition. Present-day followers of the early French school call themselves "praxiologists" and their discipline "praxiology." These scholars, most of whom are academics from France and Poland, publish the series *Praxiology: The International Annual of Practical Philosophy and Methodology* (New Brunswick, N.J.: Transaction, 1992); see in particular vol. 7: *The Roots of Praxiology—French Action Theory from Bourdeau and Espinas to Present Days*, V. Alexandre and W.W. Gasparski, eds. (2000). Mises himself kept up with the praxiologists at a distance. In 1956, he noticed with interest the existence of a *Journal of Praxiology* that was edited by a scholar at the University of Melbourne in Florida (Grove City Archive: Hugh P. King file). He distinguished the two approaches in a letter to Stephen B. Miles, dated April 19, 1961; Grove City Archive: "M" files.

[73]Occasionally he made interesting observations on the methodology and the logical character of economics in his correspondence. Of particular interest is a letter to Lionel Robbins commenting on the second edition of *The

He presented his very first paper dealing with purely methodological questions in early March 1938 in Venice, at a conference
held in memory of the French pioneer of mathematical economics, Augustin Cournot.[74] Fittingly, Mises dealt with one of
the core elements of mathematical economics, namely, the concept of economic equilibrium. He argued that this concept did
have an important role in economic analysis, but not nearly as
important as the champions of mathematical economics made it
out to be. The equilibrium construct was necessary as the logical opposite of entrepreneurial profit and loss. In equilibrium,
there would be no such thing as profit or loss. Only in disequilibrium did these phenomena come into being. But where these
statements only refined the basic conceptual framework that
had already been elaborated by Frank Knight, Mises also
emphasized that the equilibrium construct was necessary *only*
for the correct conception of profit and loss—and for no other
economic phenomena.[75]

Nature and Significance of Economic Science (New York: Macmillan). See Mises
to Robbins, letter dated December 10, 1935; Grove City Archive: Robbins
files. The letter also demonstrates that Mises was in touch with the positivistic Vienna Circle; he refers to correspondence with the mathematical economist Karl Menger (the son of the founder of the Austrian School).

[74]Mises to Machlup, letter dated March 5, 1938; Hoover Institution:
Machlup-Mises correspondence file. The paper was eventually published in
the proceedings of the conference, as "Les Hypothèses de Travail dans la Science Économique" (Working hypotheses in economic science), *Cournot nella
economia e nella filosofia* (Padua: Cedam, 1939), pp. 97–122. In previous writings, he had no more than touched on methodological questions. See for
example his observations on "the static method" and the possibility of
"dynamic laws" in Mises, "Sociology and History," in *Epistemological Problems
of Economics*, pp. 117f.

[75]For some time, he had also advocated the use of equilibrium as a
methodological device for the analysis of dynamic changes. See Mises, *Gemeinwirtschaft*, 1st ed. (Jena: Gustav Fischer, 1922), p. 151. Compare with Mises,
Human Action (Auburn, Ala.: Ludwig von Mises Institute, 1998), p. 248.
Notice that Mises was perfectly familiar with the pioneering works on

≈ ≈ ≈

At about the same time the Austrian Chamber of Commerce was completely reorganized. Mises asked to be retired by January 1, 1938, emphasizing that he would continue to work for the new chambers of commerce if they sought his services.[76] They did. In early February 1938, Wilhelm Becker, right hand man to the new president of the *Bundeskammer*, asked Mises to become the chief of the department for monetary and financial affairs. The only caveat was that Mises had to give up his position in Geneva. Mises probably went to Vienna around February 20 to discuss the project.[77] One reason for his renewed interest in returning to Vienna might have been the precarious financial situation of the Institute: in the course of 1936 it had become clear that certain elements within the Rockefeller Foundation were increasingly reluctant to lend further support.

Thus in the fall of 1937, Mises seriously considered a return to Vienna. He then gave much thought to the central political problem of his fatherland: preserving the liberty of its citizens against the encroachments of the mighty neighbors north and south. Mises was convinced that this problem could only be solved within a federation of the east-European language communities (nations) under a strong Danubian central state. In early 1938, he laid out a confidential master plan for the necessary reforms in a ten-page paper with the title "Principles for

---

mathematical equilibrium theory that Wald, Rosenstein-Rodan, Morgenstern and others had just published in the *Zeitschrift für Nationalökonomie*.

[76]See undated and non-addressed manuscript of a letter (written in the fall of 1937); Grove City Archive: Kammer für Handel, Gewerbe und Industrie files.

[77]Becker to Mises, letters dated February 8, 1938 and February 14, 1938; Grove City Archive: Kammer für Handel, Gewerbe und Industrie files. Eventually the reforms turned the *Kammer* into a pure bureaucracy. For an eyewitness account of the changes, see Mader to Mises, letter dated October 31, 1949; Grove City Archive: "M" file.

the Creation of a New Order in the Danube Area."[78] Here he
argued that such a new order would require the east-European
countries to overcome their protectionism, which Mises saw as
the root cause of conflict among them, which was in turn the
cause of their weakness confronted with their three mighty
neighbors: Russia, Germany, and Italy. But to abandon protectionism requires far more than the legal abolition of customs and
import quotas. It also implies abolishing the special privileges
that come through monetary policy, taxation, health and safety
regulations and construction codes, public works, railway rates,
and many other fields of public administration. From this Mises
draws a far-reaching conclusion. It is not sufficient to limit the
sovereignty of the different governments through a customs
union. Indeed, their whole administration would have to be run
by a federal government. Without a central government over-
arching all national governments, the latter would engage in
nationalistic policies against the minorities within their territory, thus creating tensions and conflicts that would ultimately
explode the confederation.

In short, Mises proposed to counteract the military threat of
the moment through a political federation with other smaller
states of the Danube area, but such a federation could work only
if national protectionism could be eliminated. It followed that
the political institutions of the federation had to be radically
centralized.[79]

---

[78]Mises, "Leitsätze für die Neuordnung der Verhältnisse im Donauraum,"
undated manuscript, 10 pp. He left a copy at the Graduate Institute in Geneva,
but also took copies with him when he left for the United States in 1940.

[79]He went into more detail: The local governments and courts must take
account of minorities by using all languages spoken by more than 15 percent
of the local population. Because economic legislation, in particular free trade
and the regulation of banking and money, must be uniform in all countries,
one needs a central parliament and a central jurisdiction. The proceedings of
these institutions would be in an official language, and Mises believed French

It needs to be stressed that the primary purpose of Mises's proposal was not to create closer economic cooperation in the Danube area. This could have been achieved, without any political unification whatsoever, through the simple unilateral adoption of free trade by each government. The point of his scheme was to secure a maximum of political liberty under present conditions. In his eyes, Austria and the other countries of the area had the choice between abandoning a part of their autonomy—to become strong enough to resist foreign pressure—or losing their autonomy altogether. Either they would become subservient provinces ruled by Germany, Russia, and Italy, or they would rule themselves in a common central state.

A majority of Austrian leaders abhorred the prospect of political centralization. They sought national self-determination first and foremost. The point of Mises's paper was to show that they were in error. National independence was not a suitable means, under present circumstances, to attain the end of national self-determination. Those who rejected a supra-national central government for the Danube basin implicitly believed that England and France were going to defend them permanently. But these two countries would become tired of fighting wars on behalf of the Eastern states and would eventually demand that they create a political system that could survive on its own.

With these plans in mind, Mises went to Vienna in February 1938.[80] He had other reasons to return to the city on the Danube:

---

or English should be chosen. The central organizations would have to be located in Vienna, which would have a special status corresponding to the status of Washington, D.C. within the United States. In order to avoid jealousy among the national populations, some of the federal officers would have to be of French or British nationality.

[80]He later developed his plan for the establishment of an Eastern Democratic Union in much more detail in two major papers that have only recently been published: "Entwurf von Richtlinien für den Wiederaufbau Österreichs" (May 1940, 51 pages) and "An Eastern Democratic Union: A Proposal

getting the paperwork done for marriage. For some ten years, Margit had waited patiently for him to propose. Eight months after the death of his mother, at Christmas 1937, Ludwig was finally ready. True to himself, he left out all ornamental talk and went on to propose with his habitual concision: "I cannot go on further. I cannot live without you, darling. Let's get married."[81] Margit was incredulous and the happiest she had ever been. They lost no time making plans. One of the formalities was the public announcement of their wedding plans six weeks before the ceremony.

But world events conspired against personal happiness. During those weeks before their announced wedding date, Adolf Hitler threatened Austrian Chancellor Schuschnigg: Germany would provoke civil war in Austria, and invade the country. On extremely short notice, Schuschnigg announced a general referendum on Austria's unification with Germany. The vote was to take place the next Sunday, March 13. Mises was in town on one of his short visits, probably coming in from the Cournot conference he had attended in Venice. In the course of the week, it became clear that the Germans were preparing to invade Austria to prevent the referendum from ever taking place. The cautious Mises knew that he was high on the Nazi enemy list, and he left Vienna on Thursday the 10th or early on Friday the 11th of March—not a moment too soon, as it turned out.

On Friday, March 11, 1938, S.S. Chief Heinrich Himmler arrived in Vienna with an advance contingent to arrest the most important adversaries of Hitler and seize their property.[82] Two days later, on March 13, after the German army had reached

---

for the Establishment of a Durable Peace in Eastern Europe" (October 1941, 43 pages); both papers have been translated and published in Richard Ebeling, ed., *Selected Writings of Ludwig von Mises: Political Economy of International Reform and Reconstruction* (Indianapolis: Liberty Fund, 2000).

[81]Quoted from Margit von Mises, *My Years with Ludwig von Mises*, p. 27.

[82]Joachim Fest, *Hitler* (Berlin: Deutsche Buch-Gemeinschaft, 1973), p. 753.

Vienna at the end of a triumphant march through the country, a group of men broke into Mises's apartment and searched it. At the end of March, the Gestapo came and took twenty-one boxes full of Mises's possessions and sealed the apartment when they left. In the fall, the Gestapo returned and took the rest. They looted everything they could find—the books Mises had lovingly collected over decades, his personal correspondence, paintings, silver, personal and administrative documents—everything, even the laundry. Mises would never see these belongings again and never learn what happened to them.[83] At the end of World War II, the Red Army found his personal files, together with the documents of other prominent enemies of the Nazi regime, in a train in Bohemia. They were then sent to a secret archive in Moscow. In 1991, eighteen years after Mises's death, they were rediscovered and are today a most precious tool for biographers of the great economist.[84]

---

[83]See Mises, "Information" (March 4, 1939)—a rough list of the items that were in the room he had sublet in the apartment; Hoover Institution: Hayek-Mises correspondence.

[84]Mises's personal library went in different directions. The Nazis sent his book collection to a new *Judenbibliothek* in Berlin. This library was under the control of R. Heydrich's Sicherheitsdienst (SD) and located at Eisenacher Strasse 12. However, it is not known where Mises's books are today. During World War II, the collections of the *Judenbibliothek* were sent back and forth to the provinces to protect them against Allied bombings. They were also subject to various transfers, book exchanges with other libraries, and plunder. See Werner Schroeder, "Bestandsaufbau durch Plünderung—Jüdische Bibliotheken im RSHA 1936–1945," paper presented at an international congress on *Raub und Restitution in Bibliotheken* (Vienna City Hall, April 23–24, 2003). By 1956, Mises knew that some of his books had "turned up in German second hand bookshops" and opined that some of his letters—two letters he had received from Sigmund Freud, for example—would "be found one day in the possession of an autograph dealer." Mises to Eissler, letter dated October 11, 1956; Grove City Archive: Sigmund Freud Archives file.

The looting of his apartment was only the beginning. The new authorities soon discontinued his salary and pension payments and attached his bank account for an "escape tax" (*Reichsfluchtsteuer*) and a Jewish tax (*Judenabgabe*).[85] They also confiscated the most marketable part of Ludwig and Richard's inheritance: a widely known collection of some 150 rare gold coins and more than 3,000 other coins and medals that their father, Arthur von Mises, had bequeathed to his sons in 1903.[86] Mises family property had become free booty.

The Nazis had prepared the takeover of Austria with diligent care. They had studied all writings that even remotely questioned the Nazi cause or any of its ideals. After the takeover, they sought the authors of these works. Perfectly harmless men such as Carl Brockhausen, a philanthropist and pacifist of some international reputation, were interviewed by the German secret police.[87] But the Gestapo also took on the greatest champion of national socialism in Vienna, Othmar Spann. The author of *Der wahre Staat* was all in favor of strong government, but it would have to be a government in the service of the right

---

[85]Nine years later, speaking of the reluctance of the *Kammer* to make restitution for those payments, his former secretary wrote: "But how right you were when you prophesied that we would be cheated of everything." Thieberger to Mises, letter dated December 16, 1947; Grove City Archive: Thieberger files.

[86]See Mises to Köhler, letter dated November 17, 1955; handwritten manuscript of a letter written after May 25, 1959; letter dated April 1, 1960; Grove City Archive: Köhler files. See also the summary list of stolen coins that Mises composed in 1960 but apparently did not submit to the authorities. Köhler was a lawyer in Vienna. Mises got in touch with him after learning about the ratification of a U.S.-Austrian treaty in 1955. But the deadline for claims had already expired in 1953. Most of the gold coins were Polish and pre-1892 Austrian coins. In 1962, Mises eventually obtained restitution—not from Austrian, but from German authorities—in the value of the estimated weight of the collection: some 25 troy ounces.

[87]See Brockhausen's typewritten report on the incident in Grove City Archive: Brockhausen file.

ideas—his ideas. Attempts to co-opt him as a Hitler propagandist quickly failed, and he and his son Raphael ended up in the Dachau concentration camp, where he was tortured and partially lost his eyesight.[88]

This was not a time of people with backbone. It was the time of the Hans Mayers of the world. A few weeks after the *Anschluss*, Mayer wrote the members of the *Nationalökonomische Gesellschaft*, announcing that the membership of non-Aryans had been cancelled. Mayer kept his chair at the university, just as he would retain it when the social democrats returned to power after World War II.

Decades afterward, Lionel Robbins recalled exactly the time when his love affair with Vienna came to an abrupt end, namely,

> when to his eternal shame, Hans Mayer, the senior Professor of Economics in the University of Menger, Wieser and Böhm-Bawerk, whom I myself had more than once heard denouncing Hitler and all his works, instead of closing down, as he could honourably have done, expelled the Jewish members from the *Nationalökonomische Gesellschaft* of which he was the president. I have never been able to screw myself up to go back since.[89]

---

[88]Mises later testified:

> not all those persecuted were anti-Nazis. For instance, Professor Othmar Spann, one of the outstanding champions of the Nazi doctrine, spent some time in a concentration camp because he was connected with Gregor Strasser, the personal rival of Hitler. ("Nazis and Democrats in Austria," typewritten manuscript dated March 18, 1946; Grove City Archive: U.S. Government Agencies file)

Ironically, the prison term that he served under Hitler eventually whitewashed him after the war. Spann's doctrines continued to be taught in Vienna until the late 1960s. See Karl Milford and Peter Rosner, "Die Abkopplung der Ökonomie an der Universität Wien nach 1920," Harald Hagemann, ed., *Zur deutschsprachigen wirtschaftswissenschaftlichen Emigration nach 1933*, p. 481.

[89]Lionel Robbins, *Autobiography of an Economist* (London: Macmillan, 1971), p. 91.

This is also how Mises felt about the incident. It took him many years after the end of the war before he could bring himself to return to his once-beloved city.

Many scholars had to leave Austria to make way for the Hans Mayers of the new era, and a great number of them passed through Switzerland. In the coming months and years, Mises increased his efforts to find employment for Austrian expatriates abroad.[90] This came at a time when his own position in Geneva became financially precarious. Together with his brother Richard he also took care of relatives and personal friends who had not managed to flee in time. These efforts were instrumental in bringing about a rapprochement of the Mises brothers, even though it could still not be called a warm relationship. When Ludwig married Margit in July, he did not deem it necessary to mention the fact in their correspondence. Richard found out about it a month later through their aunt Fanny and asked Ludwig for a confirmation, yet even then it was not Ludwig who replied, but Margit. Through her warmth and charm she eventually eased the relationship between the recalcitrant brothers when they were later in some proximity on the western shores of the Atlantic.

Margit and her daughter Gitta had remained in Vienna for several weeks after the *Anschluss* because they did not have the necessary paperwork to leave the country. At this time, their lives would have been in great danger if their relationship with

---

[90]Engel-Janosi could not find a job in Turkey, where only Turks were allowed to teach modern history. See Richard von Mises to Mises, letter dated June 30, 1938; Grove City Archive: Richard von Mises files. To Machlup, Mises wrote: "I am completely clueless what to do with the masses of Viennese that turn to me for help. Nobody is allowed to stay in Switzerland." Mises to Machlup, letter dated June 17, 1938; Hoover Institution: Machlup-Mises correspondence file. Margit later recalled: "We helped whenever we could. Our living room looked like a miniature Red Cross office. I was always writing, packing, shipping" (*My Years with Ludwig von Mises*, p. 39).

Mises had been known. Eventually they were able to leave, and Ludwig greeted them at the train station in Zurich, flowers in hand. She later recalled:

> In the thirteen years we shared before our marriage,
> I had never seen Lu cry. Nor did I ever see him cry in
> all the thirty-five years of our married life. He wept—
> unrestrained and unabashed. Tears were streaming
> down his face, and he was not ashamed of them.[91]

On July 6, 1938 they were married in Geneva.[92] It was a simple administrative ceremony before a civil judge and two witnesses: Hans Kelsen and Gottfried von Haberler. Ludwig and Margit spent their honeymoon in the French Alps. It was a grand opening to a happy period of their lives. Ludwig now worked quickly and productively on the completion of his *magnum opus*. And he had the time and money to live a joyful life in the company of Margit (her children were at boarding schools and stayed with them only during vacations).

His years with Margit brought about a profound positive transformation of Mises's personality. He was still obstinate in his opinions and formal in his demeanor, but in interacting with other people he became much less buttoned-down. Most importantly, his temper improved. The outbursts and tantrums that Margit had so dreaded disappeared completely after a few years.[93] He greatly needed her love, and he got it. Even though she herself had a great ego, she adapted her life to make him happy. Arriving in Geneva, she had to start at square one. Mises's good friend, Weiss-Wellenstein, had warned her that

---

[91] Margit von Mises, *My Years with Ludwig von Mises*, p. 31.

[92] The original marriage certificate is in the files of the Graduate Institute of International Studies. Margit's records: Hungarian nationality, born on July 3, 1890, father's name was Albert Herzfeld, mother's name was Selica Fontheim.

[93] Margit von Mises, *My Years with Ludwig von Mises*, p. 36.

her life with Ludwig would not be easy. And indeed, it was quite difficult at first. Mises introduced her to his closest associates only *after* the marriage, and not without warning: "Here in Geneva, when men talk, women have to be silent. They only listen."[94] Even Kelsen and Haberler, who were after all their witnesses, she met only shortly before the wedding. And only afterward did Margit move into Ludwig's apartment. There she found—to no surprise—a bachelor's residence:

> The furniture was first class and beautifully kept. But the whole apartment looked to me like a display in a department store. It was cold and impersonal.[95]

But right from the first day, the transformation of his personality set in. Mises had changed his attitude. Margit was no longer just a friend and lover. She was now Mrs. von Mises, the comrade he had longed for and the object of his true and deep love. So complete and radical was this change that he would henceforth refuse to even talk about the thirteen years before the wedding. "It was as if he had put the past in a trunk, stored it in the attic, and thrown away the key."[96] For Margit, this total break with the past would always be a burden, but the benefits were obvious:

> From the day of our marriage, Lu was a changed person. Not that he spoiled me with gifts or presents— he would not have known how to do that—but he was relaxed, affectionate, and his eyes were sparkling with happiness. Every little thing I did was of interest to

---

[94]Quoted from ibid., p. 33.

[95]She went on:

> For the first time I saw a refrigerator—we did not have them yet in Vienna—and it was a real marvel to me. I loved Lu's sparkling kitchen, but otherwise I had my doubts. The apartment was small . . . I would not have known where to put my belongings. (Ibid., p. 31)

[96]Ibid., p. 36.

him. The world had changed for him. . . . Lu was
overpowering in his love and affection for me. Never
was he cross or dissatisfied with anything I did; he
could not nag. There was not one day, to the very end
of his life, that he did not tell me: "I love you, darling,
oh . . . how I love you." It seemed to me, after our
marriage, that for the first time in his life he felt really
fulfilled and happy.[97]

The events in Austria had brought a number of their former
Vienna friends to Geneva, and it was almost like the old days:
lunches and dinners with Helene Lieser, Louise Sommer, Lise
Berger, Hans Kelsen, and the Nirensteins.[98] They went out
almost every weekend for a drive across the French border, and
with the help of the Michelin Guide they explored the delights
of French cuisine and the beauties of the Alpine landscape on
both sides of the border. Margit bravely assisted her new husband on the road. He definitely had an adventurous side and
enjoyed the thrills of high speed and the centrifugal pull of
mountain curves. On one of these curves, he lost control of the
car, which suddenly lurched over the roadside barrier into the
valley's abyss. Margit and Ludwig held their breath, but the car
did not move. Then he pulled back slowly and they continued
the rest of the way in a more civilized composure.[99]

They had other scary moments for completely different reasons. One day a dark car stopped them on one of their excursions, and a man in a long dark coat told Mises he had to talk to
him. He asked Mises to follow him into the other car, which of

---

[97]Ibid., pp. 35–36.

[98]Mises also visited frequently with the local Guggenheims and Gins-
bergs. See Ginsberg to Mises, letter dated June 19, 1941; Grove City Archive:
"L" file.

[99]This would never change. They were both thoroughly fond of driving,
but they were terrible drivers. They had at least two other serious car acci-
dents: in 1948 and 1966.

course Mises refused to do. There were veiled threats, but the situation was resolved when a friend, who was a high official of the League of Nations, presented himself to the strangers, who hurried back to their car and left. Mises and family had the distinct impression that they had just avoided an attempted kidnapping.

Such events made them think about leaving Europe entirely and emigrating to the United States. They considered this option seriously in the fall of 1938.[100] Personal danger in Switzerland was not the only factor involved. Mises knew that his school was in financial difficulties, and that it was possible his contract would not be extended.

The Walter Lippmann Colloquium

Seven weeks after his wedding, Ludwig attended a historic meeting of the champions of both "old" Manchester-style liberalism and of neo-liberalism. His new bride probably forgave him and may even have joined him on the trip: the conference took place in Paris.

Neo-liberalism was at first a purely informal phenomenon. Virtually all of its proponents were economists who cooperated in a spontaneous network within a few institutions such as the International Chamber of Commerce in Paris. By the mid 1930s, the network had reached the critical mass needed for a more formal organization under the banner of the new third way. One important step toward the organized appearance of the emerging neo-liberal network was made when, in 1937, the American journalist Walter Lippmann published a neo-liberal

---

[100]Richard von Mises refers to such statements from Margit in a letter to Ludwig, dated December 29, 1938; Grove City Archive: Richard von Mises files. At this point, Mises's treatise *Nationalökonomie* was "already very close to completion." Mises to Machlup, letter dated December 18, 1938; Hoover Institution: Machlup-Mises correspondence file.

manifesto with the title *Inquiry into the Principles of the Good Society*.[101]

The book appealed to European neo-liberals because Lippmann gave eloquent expression to their own deeply held views about the roots of the present political and economic crisis. Those who still called themselves liberals rejected socialism but did not want to be too strongly associated with the Manchester doctrine of *laissez-faire*. Lippmann placed himself in opposition both to the old liberals and to the contemporaneous socialist agitators. Lippmann's middle-of-the-road position suited the pragmatic mentality of his countrymen. Americans tended to take a businesslike approach to political conflicts, seeking to solve them through negotiation and compromise. Lippmann shrewdly presented both the socialists and the Manchestermen as stubborn doctrinaires. He contrasted these "extremists" with his own practical-minded scheme. This resonated with the neo-liberal continental European economists of the interwar period, who differed from Lippmann only in the details they envisioned for the Good Society.

One of these was Louis Rougier (1889–1982), a philosopher at the University of Paris and director of a "Centre Danubien." Rougier considered Lippmann's book a brilliant exposition of a consensus that had emerged among liberal scholars in the recent past, most notably in books by Mises, Robbins, Lavergne, Marlio, and Rueff.[102] He quickly arranged for a French edition of the *Good Society*[103] and seized the occasion to convene a five-day colloquium in Paris "with the idea of reviewing the process of capitalism and of trying to define the doctrine, the conditions

---

[101]Walter Lippmann, *Inquiry into the Principles of the Good Society* (Boston: Little, Brown & Co., 1937).

[102]Louis Rougier, "Préface," *Le Colloque Walter Lippmann* (Paris: Librairie de Médicis, 1938).

[103]Walter Lippmann, *La Cité Libre* (Paris: Librairie de Médicis, 1938).

necessary for its implementation, and the new responsibilities of a true liberalism."[104]

The event took place on August 26–30, 1938 at the International Institute of Intellectual Cooperation and it assembled representatives of very different liberalisms. These men fell into at least four groups with distinctly different views on the history, theory, and political agenda of modern liberalism.

The first group, which represented the mainstream of neo-liberalism, promoted not only practical, but also theoretical compromise with coercive socialism. They were willing to compromise on any particular item to make their general agenda more palatable to the voter. Their position can be thought of as "pro-market" social democracy.

Second, there was a small group of men such as Hayek who were dissatisfied with various aspects of classical liberalism and endorsed a somewhat larger scope for government intervention. In contrast to the first group, however, their fundamental concern was with individual freedom and in time they therefore took an increasingly radical stance, moving ever closer to the classical-liberal position.

Third, there was an equally small group of men such as Alexander Rüstow who were reluctant to endorse classical liberalism root and branch, but their main objection was to the egalitarianism, such as it was, of its advocates. They argued that hierarchy was absolutely necessary for the maintenance of a free society, because only the authority implied in it would effectively transmit the cultural tradition of liberty. The great error of the French Revolution was that it had not only abolished the coercive hierarchy of the *Ancien Régime*, but also jettisoned the principle of hierarchy *per se*. In its egalitarian fervor, it had

---

[104]Louis Rougier, "Préface." He later emphasised that the purpose was to define neo-liberalism. See Louis Rougier, "Le Néo-libéralisme," *Synthèses* (December 1958).

tossed out the natural-hierarchy baby with the coercive-hierarchy bathwater.

Fourth, and finally, Ludwig von Mises upheld nineteenth-century *laissez-faire* policies on refined theoretical grounds that he himself had developed over the past eighteen years. By the 1930s, he was acknowledged both within and outside libertarian circles as the most important contemporary representative of the Manchester School.[105]

The Lippmann Colloquium showed that three of Mises's insights had had a profound impact on the neo-liberals. First, his demonstration that socialist calculation was impossible had liberated them from all notions that a full-blown socialist commonwealth was feasible or even desirable on economic grounds. Second, the socialist-calculation argument had convinced them that competitive pricing is of utmost importance and a defining characteristic of the free market. Third, they endorsed Mises's original case for liberalism, which stressed that a private-property order was the only feasible system for the division of labor.

---

[105]See the leftwing Eduard Heimann, *History of Economic Doctrines: An Introduction to Economic Theory* (New York: New York University Press, 1945), p. 19. The anonymous reviewer of the French edition of *Gemeinwirtschaft* presented the author as "the uncontested head of the School of Austrian Economists" (Review of *Le Socialisme in Les Industries Mécaniques* [Paris, June 1938]). When Louis Baudin invited Mises to join the scientific committee of a new French journal of comparative economics in 1939, he told him that all political orientations would be represented in this committee, reason enough to have liberalism defended by masters such as Mises (see Baudin to Mises, letter dated May 18, 1939; Grove City Archive: Baudin file). The uniqueness of Mises's role was still recognized some twenty years later by one of the last surviving students of the French laissez faire school. Writing to Mises in September 1957, the professor A. Bastet said that Mises was the successor "to our master Yves Guyot"—who himself was the successor to Gustave de Molinari (1819–1912). And Molinari was successor to the great "proto-Austrian" Frédéric Bastiat (1801–1850). See Bastet to Mises, letter dated September 5, 1957; Grove City Archive: "B" file.

The latter two insights, however, came to be twisted so as to fit the neo-liberal interventionist agenda. Whereas Mises had simply stated that a calculation-based division of labor could take place only where private property exists, the neo-liberals set out to manipulate the legal and judicial systems in order to "improve" on the spontaneous division of labor that would have resulted from political *laissez-faire*. For these men, the market was critically important, but they believed that government intervention could enhance the "efficiency" and "fairness" of the market process. Unlike socialists, neo-liberals believed that the market took society in the right direction, but unlike classical liberals, they believed that the unhampered market fell short of its true potential.

In a preface to the first German edition of the *Good Society* (1945), Wilhelm Röpke emphasized the orientation of neo-liberal policies toward the optimization of the social machine:

> Thus the question is not: For or against *laissez-faire*? Rather it is: Which judicial order [*Rechtsordnung*] fits an economic constitution that is just, free, of the highest productivity, and based on a sophisticated division of labor?[106]

As a consequence of this particular interpretation of Mises's theory of social systems, the neo-liberals also reinterpreted the significance of Mises's insights about the importance of competitive pricing. Mises had argued that a rational division of labor could be based only on market prices for factors of production, which in turn required private ownership of these factors. In contrast, the neo-liberals focused exclusively on the prices themselves, neglecting the conditions under which free

---

[106]Wilhelm Röpke, "Einführung," in Walter Lippmann, *Die Gesellschaft freier Menschen* (Bern: Francke, 1937), p. 32. As this preface shows, Röpke was deeply impressed by Lippmann's work, which he believed had had a tremendous impact on the neo-liberal movement.

pricing occurs. For them, the practical conclusion of the social-ist-calculation argument was not that government should not interfere with property in general, but rather that it should be kept from meddling *with prices* specifically. At the Colloquium, Lippmann was praised for his distinction between "market compatible interventions" and interventions incompatible with the operation of a market economy.[107] Only direct interference with the working of the price mechanism was illegitimate. If the government limited itself to controlling only the legal frame-work within which the market participants would be left free to pursue their projects as they wished, then this intervention would be unobjectionable from a neo-liberal point of view.

The unifying principle of postwar neo-liberal theories was an attempt to justify liberty in some cases *and* state-sponsored vio-lence in others, through one and the same theory. The most important products of these endeavors were the theory of public goods and the Chicago (Coasean) theory of law and economics.

Mises relentlessly criticized the neo-liberal interpretation of the significance of the socialist-calculation argument. From his point of view, the arbitrary distinction between the "play of the price mechanism" and the "framework of the market" was non-sensical. The nature of government intervention is to violate private property rights, thereby affecting the price mechanism *in all cases*. While it is true that certain phenomena result only from direct interference with the pricing process—shortages and surpluses, most notably—the larger issue of economic cal-culation remains. It is ultimately irrelevant whether govern-ment intervention meddles directly with prices or indirectly through the "framework" of price formation; in *either* case, market prices are perverted.

---

[107]Rüstow prided himself on having coined the phrase "liberaler Inter-ventionismus" (classical-liberal interventionism) as early as 1932. See the copy of his letter to Volkmar Muthesius, dated May 23, 1955; Grove City Archive: Muthesius file. He probably referred to his talk at the 1932 Dresden meeting of the Verein.

Plans for after the War

Parallel to the work on his treatise of economics—or praxe-ology, as he now called it—Mises spent much time writing and teaching about concrete contemporary political problems.[108] He applied the general theory of praxeology to explain the rise of Nazism, and he probably also presented his plans for the time after Hitler. He also wrote down these thoughts in a book man-uscript and in several lengthy memoranda.

By 1938 he had already composed a book manuscript that described "The Way of the German People toward National Socialism"—the working title in June 1940, when he left a copy of the manuscript with his colleague Potter. The work would eventually be published in an English translation in 1944 under the title *Omnipotent Government*. Here Mises elaborates on the thesis developed in his 1919 book *Nation, State, and Economy*, in which he had explained the rise of German imperialism. He now stressed that the age of nationalist protectionism had cre-ated an incentive for war. Protectionism promoted the interests of some citizens at the expense of all other citizens subject to the government that applied protectionist measures. But it also came at the expense of foreigners, who therefore stood to gain from a violent overthrow of that government. Mises would later make this point in a paper delivered to an American audience:

> The reasoning of the old liberals can be condensed in one sentence: war is useless in a liberal world. This theorem is absolutely correct, but we must not forget the condition "in a liberal world". . . . Our world is very different and in this world you cannot say that war is useless. It is not true that the individual citizen

---

[108]"In my course at Geneva dealing with the economic and sociological doctrines in modern political thought I used to devote many hours to [a full refutation of the Nazi doctrines]" (Mises, "Post-war Reconstruction," type-written manuscript dated May 28, 1941, 22 pages, quote is from p. 9). Trans-lated and publishd in Ebeling, ed., *Selected Writings of Ludwig von Mises*.

> cannot derive any advantage of a victorious war. . . .
> In the world of state interventionism the territorial
> expansion of his own state is of the utmost impor-
> tance to each individual citizen. Every benefit which
> he derives from his own government is the more
> valuable the larger its territory is. Every new con-
> quest further restricts the area in which discrimina-
> tion is applied against him.[109]

When World War II broke out in September 1939, Mises
was already thinking about the time after the war—a war that
Mises was absolutely convinced Hitler would lose. When the
war eventually reached the western theater in May 1940, Mises
had reached the conclusion that the major economic problem of
the postwar period would be shortage of capital. To attract foreign capital and to stimulate capital accumulation, governments
would be forced to accept far-reaching curtailments of their
sovereignty:

> These states will have to renounce any powers in the
> field of money, credit, trade, and taxation on behalf of
> foreign capital. They will have to submit themselves
> unconditionally to the jurisdiction of international
> courts, and accept that the decisions of these courts
> be imposed by an international police force.

This might sound somewhat strange, Mises concedes, but a
state is free to choose whether it accepts these conditions for
receiving foreign capital, and there is a strong political rationale for the abandonment of national sovereignty.

> Small states must have an effective protection against
> aggression by bigger states. States engaging in secret
> rearmament must be prevented from the execution of
> their plans by an international police. Governments

---

[109]Mises, "Post-war Reconstruction," pp. 3, 4, 12.

that violate peace must be treated as robbers and
murderers are treated within each state.[110]

By May 1940, Mises had elaborated a fairly detailed plan for
Austria's postwar reconstruction. This plan is of some interest
because (1) it is representative of the applied work he did, for
example, in the context of his *Kammer* activities and (2) shows
the relatively large scope Mises allowed for government activity
within the framework of a market economy.[111]

The starting point for his considerations was that Austria
could feed its population of 6.5 million people only as an industrialized nation, which requires entrepreneurs who know how
to produce for the world market. In old Austria there had been
about a thousand such men. Today, these entrepreneurs were
gone because the government, the trade unions, and the whole
country had fought a war against them. At least two-thirds of
them were Jews. Their firms were "Aryanized" according to the
Marxist idea that the workers and the means of production are
all that matter in a firm: the entrepreneurs are mere exploiters.
"However, without the spirit and the energy of the entrepreneur a firm is just a heap of junk and scrap." And even those
entrepreneurs who were not murdered or tortured could not
continue their business because of foreign exchange controls
and central planning.

As a consequence, Austria would face a far more difficult situation than it faced after World War I, when the creative and
industrious entrepreneurs saved the country despite the obstruc-
tions thrown up by the government. This time Austria would
not be able to count on postwar imports of foreign capital.

---

[110]Mises, "Gedanken über die Wirtschaftspolitik nach dem Kriege"
(Thoughts on postwar economic policy), undated manuscript (probably
1940), 19 pages; see pp. 17f.

[111]Mises, "Entwurf von Richtlinien für den Wiederaufbau Österreichs,"
report dated May 1940, 51 pages. In the Grove City Archive there is also a
first version of this report, which contains 48 pages.

Mises's positive program for the postwar period contained several standard classical-liberal positions: that the currency must be based on gold, that the central bank must be obliged to redeem its notes and demand deposits against gold at the legal rate; no foreign exchange control would be permissible, and Austria would have to follow a strict free-trade policy.[112]

But Mises also recommended several measures of government intervention. He said that Austria should never impose import duties on luxury goods (which implies that such duties could be taken on other goods) because a major part of its own export is composed of such goods. Interdictions of imports for public-health and veterinary reasons were legitimate, and weapons imports must be reserved for the government. Interdictions of exports should be allowed only from military considerations in times of political tension. Similarly, restrictions of business activity are permissible in the production and trade of weapons, drugs, and poisons.

Mises championed a program of thorough political centralization. On behalf of taxation he claimed: "All taxes and duties accrue directly to the State. The communal authorities have no power of taxation. They get their means from the State."[113] In

---

[112]Then, however, Mises proceeded to an astounding contention:

> Free trade does not mean that all import duties are abolished. It only means that one does not try to increase domestic prices through import duties in order to enable domestic producers to sell their products at higher prices than their foreign competitors. Thus two kinds of import duties are in accordance with free trade: (a) financial duties [which have to correspond to domestic sales taxes], and (b) retortion duties on the import of all, or certain, commodities from countries pursuing a policy which is hostile to the interests of Austrian trade. ("Entwurf von Richtlinien für den Wiederaufbau Österreichs," p. 24)

[113]Ibid., p. 26. He spelled out a definite list of taxes: (a) sales taxes for alcohol and tobacco; (b) a sales tax that is only levied on commodities bought

order to avoid "expensive double administrations," the state alone should direct the whole administration of the county. The only other level, under the central institutions of the state, was that of the county administrations and courts. The communal authorities would have to execute the tasks set for them by the general legislation. Their only revenue would come from the state and from public firms and property. The purpose of this ultra-centralized structure was to avoid corruption and waste of public money. The postal, telegram, and telephone services would be organized by a single post office in Vienna. Employment in the public administration was to be regulated according to the French competitive system, to prevent protectionism, nepotism, and corruption.

Mises goes on to discuss how to deal with the Austrian government officials who served under the Nazis. Whether they may stay in the public services is to be decided case by case in the "Interest of the State."

The system of education "has to be radically re-structured."[114] The *Volksschule* (elementary school) needed to be nationalized, and all institutions of higher education had to fall under the direct responsibility of the Department of Education. Mises even made proposals on the specific content of education: in the *Gymnasien* pupils should be obliged to learn English and French, and the requirements to pass exams should be considerably increased because "only extraordinarily talented and

---

by consumers; (c) an income tax on wages to finance the social security system; (d) a progressive tax on housing expenditures; (e) a tax on luxury cars; (f) a tax on lottery gains; (g) a tax on playing cards; (h) fees for certain administrative acts [registering of patent rights, brands, etc.]; (i) a "moderate taxation" of yields of more than 6 percent on capital, which are paid out to the stock owners of corporations with limited liability. Mises emphasized that, apart from point c, there should be no income taxes. Penalizing income kills the goose that lays the golden eggs. Moreover, all public enterprises would have to be sold or closed if their proceeds did not cover costs.

[114]Ibid., p. 31.

industrious pupils merit that the State incurs special expenses for their education."[115]

Mises's pronouncements on the Austrian universities were severe. While their expenses constantly increased, the scientific level decreased ever further. The University of Vienna would therefore have to be established anew with the help of Western European scholars and of Austrian professors teaching abroad. The universities of Graz and Innsbruck would have to be closed altogether, since they had long since lost the right to call themselves universities.[116]

In order to reduce the postwar scarcity of capital, Mises suggested publicizing the new Austria's free-trade policies to foreign capitalists and entrepreneurs and attracting old Austrian entrepreneurs back to their home country.[117] He also recommended a study of "the methods of the French cultural propaganda" to improve Austria's image in the world by reference to the great "cultural achievements of its sons."[118] The selection of Austria's representatives would therefore have to be more careful. To the western capitals Austria should only send men "who because of their scientific importance or because of other outstanding qualities command a great personal reputation and thereby can purvey Austria's representation with a prestige that it would lack otherwise. Here too France may serve as an example."[119]

Mises never put these proposals into print under his name. He always kept a strict separation between his scientific work, for which he would stand unreservedly, and his work as an economic and political consultant. His plan for Austria's postwar reconstruction fell into the latter category.[120] It applied his

---

[115]Ibid., pp. 31–32.

[116]Ibid., p. 32.

[117]Ibid., p. 36.

[118]Ibid., p. 37.

[119]Ibid., p. 38.

[120]One historian of his *Kammer* activities pointed out:

scientific insights about suitable and unsuitable policies to Austria's concrete historical situation on the eve of World War II. It took into account the political forces at work, as well as the political orientation of the men for whom he wrote his report.

Escape from Europe

The summer of 1939 was exceptionally beautiful. Ludwig and Margit spent a vacation in Aix-les-Bains, which had a magnificently Alpine setting, almost as Bad Gastein, their regular vacation spot in Austria.[121] Richard von Mises paid them a visit on his way to the United States. In June he had come to the conclusion that Turkey was no longer safe and decided to accept a visiting position at Harvard University.[122] He would soon learn how good his timing was.

The war broke out on September 1, 1939, when Mises must have been in the process of reviewing the proof pages of his *Nationalökonomie*. Strangely enough, during the first eight

---

At the university and in his books, he showed himself as an uncompromising champion of the free market. As a practitioner and *Kammer* politician he was rather flexible and ready for compromise if nothing essential had to be given up. But even in compromise he then remained hard and would not deviate from the course of action that had been recognized and agreed upon. (Alexander Hörtlehner, "Ludwig von Mises und die österreichische Handelskammerorganisation," *Wirtschaftspolitische Blätter* 28, no. 4 [1981]: 142)

[121]On August 7, 1939, Mises wrote from Aix-les-Bains to a Giovanni Demaria; Grove City Archive: Demaria file. He granted permission for an Italian translation of his *Theorie des Geldes und der Umlaufsmittel*, stating that he alone had all rights for translations into foreign languages. This translation probably never came into existence, but the incident showed that Italian Fascism was far more tolerant than German Nazism. Mises compared Russian freedom and Fascist freedom in *Anti-Capitalistic Mentality* (Princeton, N.J.: Van Nostrand, 1956), chap. 4, section 4 and chap. 5.

[122]See Richard to Ludwig, letters dated June 13, and July 23, 1939; Grove City Archive: Richard von Mises files. They probably met on August 8.

months of the war, everything was quiet on the western front. The governments of France and Britain had declared war on Germany in fulfillment of the guarantees they had extended to Poland. But they did nothing to prevent the *Wehrmacht* from completing its invasion of Poland within two weeks; and they did not even declare war on the Soviet Union, which also invaded Poland, in visible execution of a secret agreement between Hitler and Stalin to divide Poland between them— thus continuing the tradition of Frederick II and Catherine II.

The simple fact was that France and Britain were utterly unprepared for a new war—militarily, economically, and mentally. There was widespread sentiment, especially in France, that the cause was not worth another round of mass slaughter. They believed that World War I had been fought in vain, and the Treaty of Versailles had humiliated the Germans without creating justice. It had given protection to former ethnic minorities through the creation of the Czechoslovak and Polish states, but the Germans who remained there were now exposed to an oppression that was virtually indistinguishable from the one that the Czechs, Slovaks, and Poles had experienced in pre-1914 Germany and Austria. Under Hitler, the Germans set out finally to protect their co-nationals in the East, and a great number of western Europeans found this foreign policy unobjectionable. This attitude did not express passivity or apathy. It resulted naturally from the political dogma that ruled the West in those days, namely, that ethnic self-determination was the highest political principle.

But while most citizens of the West did not feel the *Wehrmacht* threatened their existence, their governments were ready to draw a line in the sand. In September 1939, the resolution to stop Hitler was not much more than a moral resolve—a resolve, moreover, that was half-baked and corrupted by several years of "anti-fascist" lobbying by the Bolshevists in Geneva. But it marked the beginning of the efforts that would eventually lead to the German defeat in World War II.

Mises was silent on the subject, but Margit became nervous. In anticipation of a German invasion, she asked him to consider emigration to America or elsewhere. Reluctantly, Mises began to explore the possibility in correspondence with his brother Richard and Fritz Machlup, both of whom had already crossed the Atlantic.[123] Machlup had discussed the idea of a "California vacation" for Mises with Benjamin Anderson and other friends from the University of California. Anderson had just moved to the Los Angeles campus of the University of California and was the most influential man in the hitherto unprestigious department of economics. UCLA showed interest, and the chairman of the department wrote two letters to Machlup, who then mediated between the two parties. In this process things got mixed up. At first Mises declined when Machlup told him UCLA could offer only a comparatively low salary.[124] Mises asked his friend to tell Dudley Pegrum, the chair of the department, that his Austrian passport had expired and that he could therefore not accept the offer at the moment, and would be grateful if the invitation could be postponed a year. While Mises's letter was on its way, Machlup wrote again, this time pointing out that an invitation from UCLA would "procure you a permanent non-quota immigration visa for the United States, which might be considered an asset these days."[125] This convinced Mises. Meanwhile he had received a cable from his friend Unger, a former Geneva student of his, who was already in New York City and who told him in telegraphic language

---

[123]See the correspondence in Grove City Archive: Machlup files.

[124]Machlup's guess was that UCLA could pay at most $4,000 per annum. Mises said that his means were very limited and that his family-related expenditures were so big that he knew not how to arrange things with the prospective salary from UCLA. See Mises to Machlup, letter dated February 28, 1940; Grove City Archive: Machlup files.

[125]Machlup to Mises, letter dated February 15, 1940; Grove City Archive: Machlup files.

that he, Mises, was making a mistake. As soon as he received Machlup's letter on February 28, Mises wrote back that his concerns about passport and visa questions had been dispelled and that he would be ready to go to California. If he had cabled this message to Machlup, Mises might have begun a career in California in August 1940, and history would have been different. But Mises sent the letter by surface mail, and it reached Machlup only after he had already declined the offer on Mises's behalf. When Machlup wrote to Anderson "trying as diplomatically as I could to reopen the negotiations" he received a response from Anderson's secretary that her boss was on a short vacation.[126] One month later, Pegrum gave him a definitive no.

⤳ ⤳ ⤳

Meanwhile, Mises himself had been in touch with Anderson, though on less vital matters. In March 1940, *Nationalökonomie* was at the printer, and there was no sign that the war would soon reach Western Europe.[127] To most citizens of the West it was not clear that it ever would. Writing Mises from his new position in Los Angeles, Benjamin Anderson announced his intention to come to Europe in the summer. He hesitated to do so, though not from fear of danger:

> I have a feeling that coming to Europe at this time, even to the neutral States, is almost like going to a friend's house when a member of the family is undergoing an operation, and that I might simply be an additional burden on busy and wary men who have

---

[126]Machlup to Mises, letter dated April 17, 1940; Grove City Archive: Machlup files.

[127]The printing of *Nationalökonomie* had started by January 1940. Mises half-jokingly surmised that it might be the last economics book published in the German language. See Mises to Machlup, letter dated January 30, 1940; Hoover Institution: Machlup-Mises correspondence file.

more important things to do than to carry on discussions with a foreign economist.[128]

In his response, Mises assured his American friend that these fears were groundless: "Your doubts about a visit in Europe are unfounded. It is just the right time for you to come and to see what is going on."[129]

Mises had been convinced that the new war would start just as the last war had ended—in the trenches. He was convinced that France and its allies would withstand any German attack. Modern conditions had made defense the most effective military strategy:

> But the time of battles of the old style, which permitted getting around the opponent's flank, was past on the great European theaters of war, since the massiveness of the armies and the tactics that had been reshaped by modern weapons and means of communication offered the possibility of arranging the armies in such a way that a flank attack was no longer possible. Flanks that rest on the sea or on neutral territory cannot be gotten around. Only frontal attack still remains, but it fails against an equally well armed opponent.[130]

With these comforting thoughts in his mind, Mises had the pleasure of holding in his hands the freshly bound *Nationalökonomie*, the work of a lifetime. The joy lasted only for a few days before it was overwhelmed by unexpected and devastating news. In May 1940, the *Wehrmacht* ended the "phony war" and

---

[128]Benjamin M. Anderson to Mises, letter dated March 1, 1940; Grove City Archive: Anderson file.

[129]Mises to Anderson, undated letter manuscript; Grove City Archive: Anderson file.

[130]Mises, *Nation, Staat und Wirtschaft* (Vienna: Manz, 1919), p. 112, n.; translated by Leland B. Yeager as *Nation, State, and Economy* (New York: New York University Press, 1983), p. 138 note.

overran Western Europe in a series of blitzkrieg attacks. Mises was completely taken by surprise. He had not realized that conditions had once again changed profoundly. Tank divisions had become sufficiently fast to attack the flanks of even very large armies, especially when the divisions operated under air support. A few military theoreticians had perceived this threat during the interwar period, but it was only in the spring of 1940 that General Heinz Guderian and his men proved the threat a reality.[131] Mises could hardly believe what he read in the newspapers. "Belgium! Holland!" he exclaimed in his notebook on May 10. Less than two weeks later, Guderian reached the Channel and cut off the allied supply lines. The British escaped at Dunkirk and now the Germans took on the eighty-some remaining French divisions one by one.[132] On June 14, Mises exclaimed again: "Paris!" and three days later "Armistice!" It was an ordeal. May 1940 was, as he later recalled, "the most disastrous month of Europe's history."[133] It was the only time he was ever wrong in forecasting an important political or economic event.

---

[131]In their purely tactical use of the air force in direct confrontations with enemy troops, the Germans applied the theory of the chief engineer of the French navy, Rougeron, who at the beginning of the 1930s had synthesized the experiences of World War I. In distinct contrast, the western allies would eventually apply the theories of the Italian general Giulio Douhet, according to which the air force should bomb the cities and supply lines in the hinterland of the enemy, thus destroying his economy and the morale of the population. Douhet's theory had already been anticipated in the strategic planning offices of the British Royal Air Force, directly after its creation in the spring of 1918. The end of the war prevented the application of the plans at this point. See Giulio Douhet, *Luftherrschaft* (Berlin: Drei Masken Verlag, 1935); Colston Shepherd, *The Airforce of Today* (London & Glasgow: Blackie & Son, 1939). I am indebted to Philipp Egert for these references.

[132]On June 3, 1940, Louis Baudin wrote to Mises that Paris was calm. "I was not surprised by our early failures. We needed to get rid of our bad leaders and to correct people's mindsets. The Popular Front has cost us dearly!"

[133]Mises to Royal Wilbur France, letter dated October 31, 1946; Grove City Archive: France file.

After the allied debacle at Dunkirk, Mises knew it was a question of days or weeks before it would be impossible to leave Geneva. His residence in Geneva would soon be unsafe. He had to act. He was high on the German government's list of wanted men. The Germans had already tried to kidnap him and had almost succeeded. They had already been pressuring the Swiss authorities to surrender Mises. The Swiss had refused, but they had also let Mises know they had acted out of charity, and that his visa was still subject to extension on a yearly basis. This situation was already dangerous (and insulting) when the Germans were still on the other side of the Alps. But now the Axis troops were about to encircle Switzerland from all sides, and Mises felt his days in Geneva were numbered.

Hans Kelsen and Wilhelm Röpke were in the same situation. At least for some time, Rappard and Mantoux planned to provide all three of them with jobs in Vichy France. But neither of them believed this was sufficient protection, and during the next days and weeks they actively sought admission to the United States—which they received within two weeks of the capitulation of Paris.[134] Holding their invitation letters for the United States in his hands, Mises and Röpke weighed again the pros and cons of another emigration. Eventually Mises and Kelsen left, while Wilhelm Röpke remained in Switzerland. Röpke too was high on the Nazi list of wanted men and was thus at the mercy of the Swiss authorities. But he was courageous and trusted that the influence of his friends would keep him in the country; he believed that sooner or later the West would win this war against Germany, as it had won the last one.[135] This was apparently the prevailing opinion in their circle. Hayek wrote to Mises:

---

[134]Rappard to Kelsen, Mises, and Röpke, letter dated May 27, 1940; Mantoux to Rappard, letter dated May 24, 1940; Grove City Archive: Mantoux file.

[135]Surrounded by fascist regimes, Switzerland naturally adapted to the new political landscape as part of a strategy of conflict minimization. In

I agree with all you say about the prospects. I have no
doubt that we shall have a dreadful time but that in the
end we shall win. But the old Europe we shall never
see again. . . . It does not seem unlikely that at some
future date we shall all rejoin on the other side of the
ocean. I have no intention of running away while the
war lasts, but after it I may find that if I want to continue my work at all I may have to follow you.[136]

In retrospect one might think that Röpke's decision was the
correct one. Mises could have remained in Geneva, where he
had spent some of the happiest years of his life and enjoyed ideal
conditions for his scholarly work. For him personally, the U.S.
move was a disaster. But what would the world of ideas and the
world at large look like today had Mises remained in Europe?
He might never have written in English. *Human Action* would
not have seen the light of day, and thus would not have reached
the group of brilliant students whom Mises inspired in the New
York of the 1950s and 60s—those students who carry on his
ideas to this day.

❧ ❧ ❧

Mises now accepted an invitation to Berkeley that Machlup
arranged to be sent to him by radiogram on May 16.[137] He

September 1940, for example, Switzerland temporarily introduced Nazi designations for its political offices and institutions, creating "Gauleiter" and an
"Arbeitsfront" organization. However, the émigrés who had stayed on in the
small mountain country could never be sure they would not be surrendered
to the governments they had escaped. See Hermann von Grimeisen to Mises,
letter dated November 25, 1940; Grove City Archive: Grimeisen file. Röpke,
too, seems to have considered emigration to the United States. See Hayek to
Mises, letters dated June 1, 1940 and August 29, 1940; Grove City Archive:
Hayek files.

[136]Hayek to Mises, letter dated June 1, 1940; Grove City Archive: Hayek
files.

[137]A copy is in Grove City Archive: Hayek files. A month later, Professor
Penrose from the University of California wrote another "official" letter of

quickly proceeded to get his paperwork done: visa, transatlantic fare from Lisbon to New York, etc. This took a few weeks, however, which proved to be too long. Kelsen had departed on May 28 with the last plane leaving Switzerland from Locarno to Barcelona. When Ludwig and Margit were ready to go, Italy had entered the war on the German side, attacking France on its southeastern flank. Although the Italian onslaught was unsuccessful, it still made air travel out of Switzerland impossible. The German and Italian armies were about to close the circle around Switzerland. Already they controlled air traffic and would not allow unauthorized planes to leave the country. There was just one escape route left: by bus, but it would take them until July 3 to obtain passage.[138] On the afternoon of that day, a Wednesday, they were told they could leave with the American Express motorcar on the following morning at six o'clock. Although the suitcases had been packed for many days, there was no more time for last visits with Mantoux and Rappard. Mises wrote a good-bye letter and left.[139]

The Germans had not yet occupied the entire French territory between the Swiss and the Spanish border, but their troops were already setting up control posts at strategically important intersections. The bus driver therefore had to drive through the

---

support, which was ostensibly addressed to Professor Pitman B. Potter of the Geneva Research Center, urging him to facilitate Mises's passage to the United States. The letter predicted negative consequences on American public opinion for any country that would hinder Mises's safe passage.

[138]Hayek had urged Mises to get in touch with Rougier for the French transit visa. "He has worked miracles in other cases. To avoid any loss of time I am cabling him at the same time and you may possibly hear from him." Hayek to Mises, letter dated June 1, 1940; Grove City Archive: Hayek files.

[139]He had already written a goodbye letter to Mantoux and Rappard on June 10. See Grove City Archive: Mantoux file. He had also left a gift, possibly on this occasion, for the library: a copy of George F. Knapp, *Staatliche Theorie des Geldes*, 2nd ed. (Munich & Leipzig: Duncker & Humblot, 1918) with Carl Menger's annotations. See Silberner to Mises, letter dated December 11, 1940; Grove City Archive: Silberner file.

German lines, avoiding any direct contact with them. Fortunately, he was experienced and cautious, and he could rely on the help of the local population. Again and again he stopped to talk to people who would alert him to the presence of German troops in his path. Then he would leave the highway and take a detour on some of the more obscure lanes, often driving miles out of the way. From their windows, the passengers saw women standing in line for bread. They learned that butter was unavailable and that meat had become very scarce. The bus of predominantly Jewish refugees moved slowly but steadily through several southeastern provinces of France. Every stop must have made them anxious; each bit of news about German troops ahead fuelled their fear, each of the many detours ate away at their nerves. Margit got upset about the couple sitting in front of them—young Charles Kindleberger and his pregnant wife—because they insisted on keeping the window open. Nerves. The ride must have seemed endless, but eventually, at the end of the day, they reached the Spanish border at Cerbères.

Here they learned at the inspection house of the Spanish authorities that the border had already been closed for a week. A diplomatic solution had been found only for American and English citizens, who were allowed to enter Spain and continue their trip. On the next day, the Swiss citizens were granted entry for similar diplomatic reasons—which meant in practice that the Portuguese and the Jewish passengers of German and Austrian origin were left stuck at the border. They stayed the night in hotels on the French side, where Ludwig and Margit found cheap accommodation. The Spanish officers had advised them to talk to the Spanish Consul in the nearby city of Perpignan. The consul found their papers in good order and wrote a letter of recommendation to the border officers, but to no avail. The officers now insisted they needed a special order from Madrid and also claimed (falsely, it turned out) that the passengers' Portuguese visas were no longer valid.

It was Saturday. Two days wasted. How far were the Nazi troops from Cerbères? Mises had to act and did the only thing he could do on a Saturday afternoon: send cables soliciting the help of William Rappard and Louis Rougier.[140]

Rougier had joined the new French government of Marshal Pétain. The hour of glory for the octogenarian Marshal Pétain had been World War I, which had turned him into one of France's greatest heroes. Now he had agreed to lead his country in its darkest hour, because those who had steered France into the current debacle had abandoned their positions and fled the country in panic. He could rely only on a handful of men, one of whom was Rougier, whom he used as a foreign liaison officer with his British ally and possibly also with Spain. Rougier therefore had the necessary personal connections to plead on behalf of Mises and the other stranded bus passengers. Somehow Mises managed to get in touch with his office and was told to get new visas at the Spanish consulate in Perpignan. Meanwhile, Rappard had taken care of the Portuguese visa problem.

On Monday, July 8, Mises traveled by train to Toulouse, alone, taking the passports of all the remaining bus passengers with him. From Toulouse, where he received the new Portuguese visas, he went to Perpignan to obtain the new Spanish stamps. It was late at night when he returned to the border town where the other passengers had been waiting for him with anxiety. He had visas for everybody except the Portuguese.

The next morning, the bus drove again to the border control station, and this time it was allowed to pass. After six days of paralysis in a "very difficult situation that seemed to be without issue," as Mises later wrote, the passengers received a new lease on their lives.[141]

---

[140]Rappard reacted immediately and cabled on the same day to Professor Amzalak in Lisbon. See the transcript of the cable in Graduate Institute Archive.

[141]The quote is from Mises to Rappard, letter dated July 14, 1940; Graduate Institute Archive. This letter contains Mises's report on their adventure at the French border. See also the slightly different (and probably

❧ ❧ ❧

It took them a few hours to reach Barcelona where they reserved places on the next available plane to Lisbon. Upon their arrival in Portugal, Mises lost no time getting in touch with his travel agent. The ship for which they had made reservations had already departed. The next ship for which bookings were still available left in three weeks. Mises arranged two places on the waiting list. Renting a room in the Park Hotel, they lived out of a single suitcase and would not unpack any of the others, so as to be ready for immediate departure.

As it turned out, they only spent a few days in Lisbon. Margit was amazed to see that her husband seemed to have friends and colleagues everywhere—the city was full of foreigners waiting for passage to America. They visited with a couple of academics and former colleagues from the International Chamber of Commerce. She herself was mainly concerned about the fate of her daughter Gitta. Hayek made inquiries, but could not get in touch with the director of her school in France.

The morning of Thursday, July 25, 1940, Margit received a call from the travel agent. There was a cabin available on a ship leaving in a few hours. They had to move fast.

That same day, Ludwig and Margit von Mises left Europe on a ship called the *Europe*. It would take almost eight years for Mises to again set foot east of the Atlantic. By then he would be an American citizen, on his way to rebuilding the Austrian School of economics in the United States. ❧

---

less accurate) account in Margit von Mises, *My Years With Ludwig von Mises*, pp. 51–56. Official documents and correspondence relating to their escape from Europe are in Grove City Archive: files #6/10/1/2 and #6/10/1/3.

Mises in 1944

17

A Treatise on Economics

NATIONALÖKONOMIE CAME OFF THE press in May 1940, just in time to survive the collapse of its publisher, only to be buried under the avalanche of the war. Many of the copies Mises sent to friends and colleagues never reached their destinations. Mises took it with some humor: "I suppose the Nazis used them as fuel."[1]

The book survived only because its English-language successor, *Human Action*, drew incomparably more attention from readers all over the world. But it was in *Nationalökonomie* that Mises first presented the entire system of thought that he had developed during more than thirty years of intense study.[2] The

---

[1]Mises to François Perroux, letter dated September 28, 1946; Grove City Archive: Perroux file.

[2]*Human Action: A Treatise on Economics* (New Haven, Conn.: Yale University Press, 1949; Scholar's edition [Auburn, Ala.: Ludwig von Mises Institute, 1998]), and *Nationalökonomie* (Geneva: Editions Union, 1940) are virtually identical in general architecture. There are a few substantive differences between the two books, but these differences pale in comparison to the differences that separate both of them from all similar works. In the present chapter, we will therefore quote *Human Action* wherever possible. In *Human Action*, Mises placed a greater emphasis on refuting positivism, whereas in *Nationalökonomie* he had refuted in particular Spann and Marx. Moreover, in *Human Action* he added a chapter on general probability theory, and he expanded the "conclusion" of *Nationalökonomie* into a comprehensive seventh part of *Human Action* that dealt with the social and cultural significance

typical economics textbook was, then as now, just an amalgamation of incompatible bits of theory. Mises's treatise presented
social laws as one coherent whole, and it drew an encompassing
picture of social reality in a step-by-step manner, moving from
the most general phenomena to the most specific. It was social
philosophy in the best sense.

Mises understood the importance of a full treatise. A book of
smaller scope and size could not put the various ideas in context.
Mises had to educate his readers before he could convince
them—an essential task in the age of interventionism, in which
the average citizen was constantly exposed to pro-government
propaganda. Replying to a reader he once said:

> I tried to answer the questions you are asking me in
> my books. A book is, in fact, a letter written to all
> one's friends, to those the author has already acquired
> as well as to those he hopes to acquire in the future.[3]

But Mises did not have exaggerated confidence in the power
of the written word. In a 1957 letter to a friend from Mexico, he
expressed his wish to discuss very soon the theoretical problems
that this friend had raised in his previous letter. A personal
meeting would be necessary because a thorough discussion of
those problems "can, in writing, only be done in the form of a
book. And the written word can never replace the spoken
word."[4]

---

of praxeology. He had planned an American edition early on and had anticipated modifications of his text to accommodate the particular background of
his American readers. See Mises to Machlup, letters dated December 18,
1938, June 15, 1939, and January 30, 1940; Hoover Institution: Machlup-
Mises correspondence file.

[3]Mises to Ernest Anthony, letter dated June 19, 1953; Grove City
Archive: Anthony file.

[4]Mises to Ballvé, letter dated May 13, 1957; Grove City Archive: Ballvé
files.

The System in an Overview

In the introduction (virtually identical in *Human Action*), Mises set the agenda for the book. The treatise would present the system of economic science in the light of two central problems that had been neglected in all previous works in the field: epistemology and value theory.[5]

He then offered his system in 751 pages, organized into six parts. Now all his previous discoveries could appear in their correct context, along with the new elements that he had developed during his Geneva years.

Part 1 deals with the features of human action that exist under all conceivable conditions of action. After a first chapter in which he gives an initial characterization of action, emphasizing in particular the distinction between behavior and action, Mises deals with the epistemological problems of the science of action (chapter 2).[6] He then turns to a more detailed analysis of action (chapter 3) in which he argues that phenomena such as exchange, price, costs, success and failure, and profit and loss are not given only in the context of a market economy, but are features of human action in general; they are categories of action.

In chapter 3 he also deals with the categories of means and ends, and of preference. Mises did not follow the terminology of the older Austrian School in speaking of *value*. Instead he used the term *preference*, which better conveys that the category of action is rooted in human choice. This terminological decision certainly helped to avoid confusion, especially since

---

[5]This emphasis demonstrates in turn the crucial importance of *Grundprobleme* for the development of *Nationalökonomie*.

[6]A fine point to notice: the treatment of epistemology came after the definition of action, because science and epistemology are themselves instances of action. Another fine point: In *Human Action*, Mises adopts the pragmatist definition of truth ("that which works in practice") and maintains this definition throughout all later writings.

Menger, the father of Austrian value theory, had emphasized
that value had nothing to do with human free will.[7] According
to Menger's *Principles*, economic science studies the relation
between man's needs and the economic goods necessary to satisfy those needs. In Walras's *Éléments*, as well as in the mainstream of the 1930s and 1940s and up until the 1980s, economic science was essentially about prices and quantities
traded on the market. But in *Nationalökonomie*, the true object
of the science was understood to be human action, and in particular choice.

In another noteworthy passage of part 1, Mises presents for
the first time the law of diminishing marginal utility as a praxeological law.[8] It has nothing to do with the psychological phenomenon of satiation. Rather, the law concerns the simple fact
that larger supplies of a homogeneous good can serve more
ends than smaller supplies. Yet these additional ends are, by
virtue of the very fact that they are additional ends, less important than those already served with the smaller supply. Here
Mises departs from all other economists, most notably from
Wieser, who had adopted Gossen's psychological interpretation
of the law. Mises draws a sharp line between praxeology and
psychology, and he emphasizes the ramifications of this in other
important passages of the book. We will take a look at some of
these below.

In part 2, our author deals with those features of human
action that come into play whenever an individual interacts with
other individuals. Later in the book, he analyzes the particularities of the three fundamental types of social systems: the market economy (part 4), socialism (part 5), and the hampered market economy (part 6).

---

[7]Carl Menger, *Grundsätze der Volkswirtschaftslehre* (Vienna: Braumüller,
1871), p. vii.

[8]Mises, *Nationalökonomie*, chap. 5, sect. I.

He also restates the theory of society that he had presented in *Socialism*, but this time in its proper context.[9] He stresses the "Ricardian Law of Association" and the crucial role of reason in shaping human society.

In part 3, he completes twenty years of intellectual assimilation of his 1920 essay on the impossibility of economic calculation in socialist commonwealths. In some thirty-five pages, he finally offers a general theory of economic calculation; what is more, he presents it in its proper place, namely, *before* turning to the analysis of any concrete system of human cooperation (parts 4–6). Of course he had anticipated this architectonic necessity in the essays on value theory he wrote in the late 1920s. But it is one thing to stress the difference between valuation (preference) and calculation in a general argument; it is quite another to apply this insight in concrete analysis.

Part 4, on the market economy, is over 400 pages—more than half the book. Here Mises restates a good number of the theories he had developed in previous works: the theory of monopoly prices, the theory of money and credit, his famous business cycle theory, the theory of wages, and the doctrine of the harmony of interests of all market participants. But rather than simply repeating himself, he presents thoroughly revised versions of his previous thoughts. He expands the monopoly theory he first developed in *Socialism*, placing special emphasis on the discussion of Marxist monopoly theory. He presents the theory of the harmony of interests in an entirely new formulation, and rejects the Anglo-Saxon theories of Keynes and of Robinson and Chamberlin (imperfect competition). In the theory of money, he brooks no exception to the rule that political modifications of the money

---

[9]In *Socialism: An Economic and Sociological Analysis* (Indianapolis: Liberty Fund, 1981), the theory was presented not in the first part, which dealt with fundamentals, but in one of the subsequent parts that dealt with particular problems of socialist orders.

supply are unwarranted from an economic point of view, and, finally, he integrates his business cycle theory with interest theory, a subject he had never addressed before in writing.

Besides interest, the central novelty in his analysis of the market economy was his emphasis on the role of the entrepreneur. Mises carefully distinguished between entrepreneurs as those who take successful action in an uncertain world, and entrepreneurship in the sense of a fundamental economic *function*—the bearing of risk under uncertainty. It is this economic function that gives rise to the specific income component of profit and loss. It was one of the great contributions of *Nationalökonomie* to clarify the role of this entrepreneurial function in the workings of the market economy. Yet Mises felt he could not achieve this without a somewhat roundabout exposition. To define entrepreneurship, it is necessary to give a proper definition of profit and loss. But for Mises this was impossible without a clarification of the nature of equilibrium and its role in economic science. He therefore saw himself forced to start part 4 with a somewhat basic chapter dealing with the methods necessary for the discursive analysis of the market economy—with various equilibrium concepts in particular. Only then did he feel that the ground had been laid to explain the nature and significance of entrepreneurship.

In part 5, which deals with socialist societies, Mises does not restate all the main findings of *Socialism*. Rather, he concentrates on the centerpiece of his refutation of the socialist program: the impossibility of economic calculation wherever the means of production are collectively owned. Thus part 5 must be considered an extension of part 3. Mises discusses the schemes of socialist calculation developed in the 1930s, most notably in the Anglo-Saxon world. He refutes the idea of generating prices through an artificial market and also contests the notion that mathematical economics could overcome the calculation problem, even theoretically.

In part 6, he delivers a far more comprehensive and detailed discussion of interventionism than he had in his essays from the mid-1920s. The general line of the argument remained the same: interventionism is counterproductive because it does not attain the professed ends of its authors.

Nationalökonomie featured entirely new and important contributions. Even in those places where Mises restates his older doctrines, he has revised them—often substantially. It was therefore highly unusual for Gottfried von Haberler to claim a few years later, in a confidential evaluation for Yale University Press, which considered commissioning a translation of the book, that it contained hardly anything new.[10]

Anti-Psychologism

Mises's exposition of economic science differed decisively from all modern authors in that it drew a sharp line between praxeology and psychology. This has remained a defining feature of the works of his disciples.

Mises did not contest that the psychological background of a person, his worldview, knowledge, conscious motivations, subconscious urges, and so on have an immediate impact on his behavior. Neither did he ignore the important psychological problems that his friend F.A. Hayek began to stress in those years, in particular, that of knowledge acquisition. Mises's point was that there were *also* laws of human behavior that exist in complete independence of these psychological dispositions.

For example, in chapter 4, Mises discusses ends and means, scales of values, and scales of needs. He does not deal with the question of how or why people select ends and means, or how or why they have certain values and certain needs. He argues that in every human action we *do* use means to attain ends, and

---

[10]Haberler to Davidson, letter dated January 23, 1945; Yale University Press Archive.

that needs and values can be *ranked*.[11] In chapter 15 ("The Market") he points out that consumers are sovereign because their buying decisions steer the market.[12] This is obviously true, irrespective of *what* consumers buy or the reason *why* they make these purchases. Therefore he does not deal with these questions. In chapter 16 ("Prices") Mises states that the number of market participants determines *how narrow* the margins are within which prices are determined. Yet this implies that the number of market participants has no influence on *how prices are formed*. Irrespective of the number of market participants, market prices are *always* determined by the decisions of marginal buyers and sellers.[13] Thus, all prices can be explained as a result of the mere fact *that* market participants prefer one good A to another good B.[14]

Praxeology is the science of these laws. It examines the ramifications of the mere fact *that* a man makes this or that choice. Considering the relationship between a choice and its consequences, praxeology examines the suitability of different means to attain particular ends. In praxeological analysis, the ends are "given," not in the sense that human beings cannot choose them or that the choice of the right end is not problematic, but in the sense that the choice of ends is outside the scope of this particular science.[15]

---

[11]Murray Rothbard later argued that as a consequence of the mere fact that people rank their choice alternatives, it follows that demand curves must slope downward to the right. See Murray N. Rothbard, *Man, Economy, and State*, 3rd ed. (Auburn, Ala.: Ludwig von Mises Institute, 1993), chap. 2. Mises made no such inference. He was skeptical about the use of graphical methods in exact analysis (he did accept them as pedagogical devices).

[12]Mises, *Human Action*, p. 270.

[13]Ibid., p. 324.

[14]Ibid., pp. 328f.

[15]Mises would later discuss the irrelevance of *homo oeconomicus* for modern economics in *Human Action*, pp. 62ff. He concluded that "theorems concerning commodity prices, wage rates, and interest rates refer to all these

With respect to the knowledge of market participants, Mises emphasized the fact that the individual market participants are not equally well informed. Yet even if they all *had* the same information they would appraise this information differently.[16]

As to equilibrium, he stated again and again that the market never reaches such a state, that it is a mere mental construct the only function of which is to analyze profits and losses. That is, the equilibrium construct is needed to explain a particular component of price *spreads*. It is not required to explain prices (wages, interest, commodity prices) as such.[17]

Consequently, in Mises's view, equilibrium is not the right benchmark for the evaluation of the market. To critics of economic science who complain that the market never produces a perfect balance between different goods and services, Mises replies in two steps.[18] First, he points out that this fact of imbalance does not refute economic doctrine because economic science explains *any* state of affairs as it results from the fact that consumers make certain valuations. Second, he observes that the relevant benchmark for the market is government intervention. And because government officials are not supermen, one cannot make the a priori assumption that entrusting them with the maintenance of the market will bring improvement. As the analysis of government interventionism shows, the very opposite is the case.

Capitalism and Liberalism are Rational

In *Socialism* and *Liberalism*, Mises had argued that human society was founded on the basis of the higher physical productivity of human cooperation, as compared to individuals acting

---

phenomena without any regard to the motives causing people to buy or to sell or to abstain from buying or selling" (p. 64).

[16]Ibid., p. 325.

[17]Ibid., pp. 245ff.

[18]Ibid., p. 647, for example.

on their own. This was the crux of the classical-liberal social philosophy and the cornerstone of the political program of *laissez-faire* Manchesterism. In *Nationalökonomie*, Mises set out to contrast this social philosophy with competing worldviews. He stressed that economic analysis had given a purely fact-based account of the origin of human society:

> The scientific theory as developed by the social philosophy of eighteenth-century rationalism and liberalism and by modern economics does not resort to any miraculous interference of superhuman powers. Every step by which an individual substitutes concerted action for isolated action results in an immediate and recognizable improvement in his conditions. The advantages derived from peaceful cooperation and division of labor are universal. They immediately benefit every generation, and not only later descendants. For what the individual must sacrifice for the sake of society he is amply compensated by greater advantages. His sacrifice is only apparent and temporary; he foregoes a smaller gain in order to reap a greater one later. No reasonable being can fail to see this obvious fact. When social cooperation is intensified by enlarging the field in which there is division of labor or when legal protection and the safeguarding of peace are strengthened, the incentive is the desire of all those concerned to improve their own conditions. In striving after his own—rightly understood—interests the individual works toward an intensification of social cooperation and peaceful intercourse. Society is a product of human action, i.e., the human urge to remove uneasiness as far as possible.[19]

He then went on to point out the larger cultural and philosophical significance of this discovery:

---

[19]Ibid., p.146.

> The historical role of the theory of the division of labor as elaborated by British political economy from Hume to Ricardo consisted in the complete demolition of all metaphysical doctrines concerning the origin and the operation of social cooperation. It consummated the spiritual, moral and intellectual emancipation of mankind inaugurated by the philosophy of Epicureanism. It substituted an autonomous rational morality for the heteronomous and intuitionist ethics of older days. Law and legality, the moral code and social institutions are no longer revered as unfathomable decrees of Heaven. They are of human origin, and the only yardstick that must be applied to them is that of expediency with regard to human welfare.[20]

Thus the economists had explained society as a human creation, designed and implemented by cooperating individuals to satisfy individual needs. In contrast, alternative approaches such as universalism and collectivism stipulated that society could be defined independently of individual action. To the collectivists,

> society is an entity living its own life, independent of and separate from the lives of the various individuals, acting on its own behalf and aiming at its own ends which are different from the ends sought by the individuals.

Mises went on to point out that this conception of society has a natural conclusion:

---

[20]Ibid., p. 147. A few years later, Joseph Schumpeter pointed out that the social analysis of the classical economists had its roots in medieval scholasticism. Saint Thomas Aquinas and his followers had pioneered methodological individualism and utilitarian justifications of social institutions. By contrast, divine law and omnipotent government were protestant inventions. See Joseph A. Schumpeter, *History of Economic Analysis* (New York: Oxford University Press, 1954), part 2, chap. 2, pp. 91–93.

> Then, of course, an antagonism between the aims of society and those of its members can emerge. In order to safeguard the flowering and further development of society it becomes necessary to master the selfishness of the individuals and to compel them to sacrifice their egoistic designs to the benefit of society.[21]

What is needed, therefore, is a definition of the proper interests of "society" thus conceived. Mises observed that science was at a loss to provide such a definition. As a consequence,

> all these holistic doctrines are bound to abandon the secular methods of human science and logical reasoning and to shift to theological or metaphysical professions of faith.[22]

Mises emphasized the epistemological dimension of this problem:

> The essential problem of all varieties of universalistic, collectivistic, and holistic social philosophy is: By what mark do I recognize the true law, the authentic apostle of God's word, and the legitimate authority. For many claim that Providence has sent them, and each of these prophets preaches another gospel.[23]

Equilibrium, Profit and Loss, and Entrepreneurship

It was through the writings of Carl Menger and Eugen von Böhm-Bawerk that Mises had come to understand the market economy as a rational social order in which all factors of production are geared toward the satisfaction of consumer wants. Not only the allocation of the production factors, but also the incomes of the owners of these factors ultimately depended

---

[21]Ibid., p. 145.
[22]Ibid., p. 145.
[23]Ibid., p. 147.

exclusively on their relative contribution to the satisfaction of human wants. All values, all prices, as Frank Fetter had put it, depend on a daily referendum in the market democracy.[24]

But in none of his predecessors did Mises find a satisfactory account of the process through which the structure of production was brought in line with consumer preferences. His fellow Böhm-Bawerk seminar member, Joseph Schumpeter, had brilliantly shown how entrepreneurs drive the market. According to Schumpeter's *Theory of Economic Development*,[25] entrepreneurs are innovators who constantly interrupt the smooth operation of an inert economy.

Schumpeter had a point. Innovation does play a central role in the market economy. But how does this fit with the Mengerian picture of the market economy as a rational social order? Was there a contradiction between the Schumpeterian notion that entrepreneurs reap profits for innovation and the Mengerian insight that all incomes depend on consumer wishes? In *Nationalökonomie*, Mises reconciles Schumpeter with Menger. From Schumpeter, he adopted the idea that entrepreneurs are the motor of the market process. But they cannot earn a profit for innovation *per se*—only for innovations that improve the satisfaction of consumer wants.

Entrepreneurs constantly adjust the structure of production to what they expect will be the future preferences of consumers. The different entrepreneurs act in effect as advocates for different consumer needs. Based on their estimates of what they expect to obtain for an imagined product in the future, they go to the

---

[24]"The market is a democracy where every penny gives a right of vote." Frank A. Fetter, *The Principles of Economics* (New York: The Century Co., 1905), p. 395. A few pages later he states: "So each is measuring the services of all others, and all are valuing each. It is the democracy of valuation" (p. 410).

[25]Joseph A. Schumpeter, *Theorie der wirtschaftlichen Entwicklung* (Munich: Duncker & Humblot, 1911).

factor markets where they compete with other entrepreneurs, bidding up prices for the available factors of production—workers and material supplies. This pricing process determines the incomes of all factors of production, and it ensures that only the most important investment projects ("important" in terms of future consumer spending) will be realized.

The driving force of entrepreneurship is the profit motive. Profit is the specific remuneration a person receives for bearing uncertainty. In the market economy, entrepreneurs act with due caution and responsibility because they are personally liable for any wrong decisions. Loss is the punishment for unsuccessful entrepreneurship. Profit and loss are together the measure of entrepreneurship.

Are all businessmen entrepreneurs? Are all entrepreneurs businessmen? If not, how could entrepreneurs be distinguished from "regular" businessmen and other market participants? Mises answered these difficult questions by defining entrepreneurship as a social *function*, namely, as the function of assuming responsibility for the uncertainty of the future. The entrepreneur in Mises's theory is not a person but a role played by people—and it is not at all limited to businessmen. Ultimately *anyone* can be an entrepreneur to the extent that he assumes the repercussions of uncertainty. Profits and losses do not only determine the income of businessmen, but also of wage-earners and capitalists. They always come mixed with specific factor incomes such as wages and interest.

One of the great problems Mises had to solve in this theory was to give a precise definition of profit and loss. In particular, he had to distinguish profit and loss from interest. His solution was that profit and loss were the results of human error. In other words, profits and losses can only exist in situations of disequilibrium. In contrast, money interest ultimately springs from time preference and has nothing to do with whether the market participants make good or bad decisions. Money interest exists both in general equilibrium and in disequilibrium, whereas profit and loss exist only in the latter case.

But then this line of argument makes it necessary to clarify the precise meaning of general equilibrium, as well as its role in economic analysis. Mises argued that general equilibrium—which he called the stationary economy (*stationäre Wirtschaft*)[26] —is a purely *methodological* device. It is an imaginary construct (*Gedankenbild*) that has no counterpart in the real world. Its only purpose is for the definition of profit and loss.

Consumer Sovereignty and Interest

In *Nationalökonomie*, Mises finally delved into interest theory, the primary research area of his revered teacher, Böhm-Bawerk. In his classes at the University of Vienna in the 1920s, Mises had frequently dealt with contemporary interest theories. In those years, he had also planned to write a paper on the subject, but there had always been other projects that seemed more important.[27] In Geneva, he was finally at leisure to fill this gap.[28]

Böhm-Bawerk had initiated the Austrian tradition of defining the phenomenon that was at issue in interest theory. He argued that the "interest rates" paid in the context of credit operations are in fact a secondary aspect of a larger phenomenon. The primary aspect of this phenomenon was given in certain price differences that could be observed on the market. The starting point for Böhm-Bawerk's theory was the common observation that successful business was characterized by a positive spread between the sum total of the prices paid for its factors of production and the sum total of prices received as proceeds for its

---

[26]In *Human Action*, he called it the "evenly rotating economy," p. 246–47.

[27]Mises to an unknown correspondent, letter dated November 24, 1930; Mises Archive 66: 14.

[28]He started lecturing on capital and related problems in the winter semester of 1936–1937. See Mises to Machlup, letter dated February 15, 1937; Hoover Institution: Machlup-Mises correspondence file. By then, Mises must have made his mind up about these questions.

products. Entrepreneurs earned more money by selling their products than they spent on the factors of production that brought these products into being.

This phenomenon raised the fundamental question of whether the entire spread between selling proceeds and cost expenditure can be "arbitraged away" through entrepreneurial competition, or whether at least part of this spread could never be eliminated. In other words, is there a part of it that contains a pure interest component? And if so, what is its cause?

Böhm-Bawerk's great achievement was to formulate the problem of interest theory as a value problem—a question of demonstrated preference between goods. Interest results from human choice and exchange, rather than being caused by some factor outside of human action. As the result of preference in action, interest reflects a fundamental value *inequality*—the choice of a more valuable alternative over a less valuable one. Observable interest rates manifest an inequality between the value of products and the total value of the corresponding means of production, including "waiting" or the "use" of capital. This way of putting the problem departed sharply from previous approaches, such as the interest theory of Carl Menger, which were based on the premise that there was a fundamental equality between these two values.[29] In Menger's view, interest was the value of a component part of the factors of production, whereas Böhm-Bawerk saw it as a value *differential*.

But where did such a value differential come from? According to Böhm-Bawerk, "*Present goods have in general greater subjective value than future goods of equal quantity and quality.*"[30] The American economist Frank Fetter later coined the term "time

---

[29]Menger, *Grundsätze*, pp. 133ff.

[30]Eugen von Böhm-Bawerk, *Capital and Interest* (South Holland, Ill.: Libertarian Press, 1959), p. 265: emphasis in the original. See also Böhm-Bawerk, *Positive Theorie des Kapitals* (Innsbruck, 1889), p. 327, and Böhm-Bawerk, *Capital and Interest*, p. 259.

preference" to designate this phenomenon.[31] It is because of a time preference for present goods over future goods that factors of production (which will yield products in the future) are less valuable than the corresponding quantity of otherwise equal products existing here and now.

Böhm-Bawerk emphasized that time preference is only the *proximate* cause of interest. The *ultimate* cause is something even more fundamental. He famously argued that time preference is itself caused by two psychological dispositions: (1) that current needs are usually less well satisfied than future needs, and (2) that human beings tend to underestimate future needs. He also argued that time preference is caused by the higher physical productivity of more roundabout methods of production—his famous "third cause" of time preference.[32]

Mises rejected Böhm-Bawerk's psychological explanation of time preference. Psychology, Mises argued, could never establish that time preference was an element of the very nature of human action. In some actions, the psychological forces that Böhm-Bawerk described were at work and led to a preference of present over future goods of the same kind. But in other instances, the very opposite was the case. Böhm-Bawerk himself had admitted this point, which is why he held that time preference existed only "in general" but not in all cases of human action.[33]

The Böhm-Bawerkian view of the nature of time preference had two related shortcomings. First, it was difficult to reconcile

---

[31]See Frank A. Fetter, *Economic Principles*, 2 vols. (New York: The Century Co., 1915); idem, *Capital, Interest, and Rent*, Murray N. Rothbard, ed. (Kansas City: Sheed Andrews and McMeel, 1977).

[32]Böhm-Bawerk, *Positive Theorie des Kapitals* (Jena: Gustav Fischer, 1921), pp. 328ff.

[33]Mises, *Nationalökonomie*, pp. 439ff.; *Human Action*, pp. 485ff. Mises also criticized Böhm-Bawerk for having failed to develop a truly praxeological theory of the period of production.

with the fact that values and prices are manifested in human choice. If choice is free, how is it that future values by their very nature—or at least "as a rule"—stand in a determinate relationship to present values? Second and more importantly, the Böhm-Bawerkian approach was in conflict with the theory of subjective value. His view of time preference concerns the value differential between *homogeneous* present and future goods, but the very fact that two goods exist at different points in time automatically makes them *heterogeneous* goods. Böhm-Bawerk himself admitted this implicitly when he emphasized that the values of present and future goods is liable to be different because they "are intended for a service of a different set of wants."[34] This second point is devastating for the old time-preference theory, for one cannot even make claims with respect to present and future goods "of the same quality" without contradicting oneself.

Moreover, as can be seen from Böhm-Bawerk's equivocal description of the time preference phenomenon, which stresses that only "in general" are present goods preferred over identical future goods, he did not assert that time preference was universally positive.[35] In the hands of Mises's predecessors, then, time preference theory was a mere assertion that a determinate relationship between the values of future and present goods of the same kind existed. None of its champions proposed a tenable explanation for this supposed relationship other than the intuitive reference to the visible facts of the market: that the selling proceeds from products were higher than the expenditure on the corresponding factors of production. But these are

---

[34]Böhm-Bawerk, *Positive Theorie des Kapitals*, p. 327.

[35]Neither did Irving Fisher and Frank Fetter think this was the case; they even argued that time preference could be negative. See Irving Fisher, *The Rate of Interest* (New York: Macmillan), p. 184; and Frank A. Fetter, "Interest, Theories: Old and New," *American Economic Review* (1914): 238f.; idem *Economic Principles*, 2 vols. (New York: The Century Co., 1915), p. 237.

the very facts to be explained by interest theory—they cannot themselves be their own explanation.

How did Mises solve these problems? He asserted on *a priori* grounds that time preference is at all times and places positive. Human action by its very nature involves a preference for sooner rather than later fulfillment of one's ends. Thus Mises asserted—contra Böhm-Bawerk, Fetter, and Fisher—that time preference is not the result of the psychological dispositions of man, but of the temporal nature of action. Years later, Mises nicely summarized this point in private correspondence:

> Time preference is not a "psychological assumption," but the effect of the physical and chemical structure of the universe in which man lives and acts. It refers to the fact that in order to be alive in March a man must first survive the month of February.
>
> If the phenomenon we call time preference were not to exist, people would only consume what is subject to speedy decay. Other things they would always only save and invest as the outcome of such a behavior would in their eyes mean a greater yield than the result of investing them for a shorter period.[36]

Mises had not so much clarified the phenomenon that his predecessors had in mind when they used the term *time preference*, but had instead given a complete restatement of the theory. When Böhm-Bawerk, Fetter, and Fisher used the term *time preference*, they referred to an observable value differential between two physically similar goods existing at two different times. But when Mises used the term, he referred to a *counterfactual* value differential between two alternative uses of one and the same good. Time preference concerns the value differential between a present use of a good and an alternative future use of this good that could only have been realized had a different

---

[36]Mises to Robert Fleming, letter dated May 13, 1969; Grove City Archive: "F" file.

choice been made. When I use a good now rather than later, I demonstrate that I prefer to use the good now rather than later. And this in turn necessarily means that the value of its present use is higher for me than the value of the use I might have made of it in the future.

Like Böhm-Bawerk, Mises believed that time preference was only the *proximate* cause of interest. But rather than seeing the ultimate cause in certain psychological dispositions of the human being, he followed Frank Fetter and Franz Cuhel in arguing that the ultimate cause was the necessity of consumption.[37] The fact is that human beings cannot survive if they do not consume. Hence there must be *some* time preference in human action or the human race would perish. This does not mean that time preference is the only factor determining human actions. It means that in order to survive, human beings must *at some point* prefer shorter production processes to longer ones, even though the longer ones would be more physically productive.

Mises argued that one would always choose the longest production process if one could disregard the need for survival through time.[38] It is the need to survive that prompts the acting person *also* to consider the passage of time and to prefer, at some point, sooner results to later ones.

Consider three alternative fishing processes: the first one leads to catching one fish at the end of one hour, the second to catching ten fish but only at the end of one day, and the third to catching 100 fish all of them at the end of a week. Assume we observe a person pursuing the production process leading to a

---

[37]Mises, *Nationalökonomie*, pp. 443f. Here he quoted Fetter, *Principles of Economics*, p. 144, and Franz Cuhel, *Zur Lehre von den Bedürfnissen* (Innsbruck: Wagner, 1907), p. 304. For an earlier statement of this argument, see Mises, *Grundprobleme* (Jena: Gustav Fischer, 1933), pp. 23f.

[38]Mises, *Nationalökonomie*, p. 446; *Human Action*, p. 483.

catch of ten fish at the end of a day. Mises explains: the person did not pick the 100-fish alternative because his time preference was stronger than the additional gain he would have gotten from the longer process. He does not want to wait a week. The only reason he picked the ten-fish alternative at all, rather than the one-fish alternative, is that *in this case* the attraction of the additional gain was strong enough to overcome his time preference.

Let us highlight the significance of this explanation within the overall theoretical framework of Misesian economics. Consumption here appears as the root of all economic phenomena. Carl Menger and his disciples had argued that consumer choices directly determine the prices of consumers' goods, and that indirectly they also determine the prices of producers' goods. Now time preference, too, and with it the phenomena of capital and interest appear to be rooted in consumption. The great attraction of this explanation (at least from Mises's point of view) was that it did not stress any psychological dispositions of man, but relied on the fundamental fact that there can be no human action without consumption. The consumption-theory of time preference thus seamlessly integrates the theory of capital and interest into the general theory of prices. In the field of interest—as in the broader market process—the consumer is sovereign.

Business Cycle Theory Restated

In light of his theory of interest, Mises now clarified the relationship between interest and changes in the quantity of money. The Austrian (Misesian) theory of the business cycle asserts that intertemporal misallocations result from inflation-induced reductions of the interest rate. But what was the precise meaning of "reduction"? Mises did not mean to assert that simple changes of the interest rate would induce a business cycle. The fact that today's interest is lower than yesterday's does not by itself mean that a misallocation has occurred.

In his *Theory of Money and Credit*, Mises had based his analysis on the Wicksellian distinction between the natural rate of interest and the money rate. But this distinction was untenable in light of Mises's work on economic calculation and on the non-neutrality of money. There is no such thing as a natural rate of interest, defined as the rate of interest that would prevail in a barter economy. And even if there were such a "natural" rate of interest, it would still be irrelevant for the analysis of a monetary economy. Money is not just a veil over a barter economy. It affects all economic relations. Prices, incomes, allocation, and social positions in an economy using money are completely different from what they would be in a society with no common medium of exchange. And so the interest rate in a monetary economy is necessarily different from what it would have been in the same economy if the market participants had decided to forgo the benefits of money. Even if one could hypothetically compare "natural" and money interest rates—which is not the case—it would not follow that intertemporal misallocations would ensue whenever the "natural" rate was higher than the money rate.

In *Nationalökonomie*, Mises gave a new exposition of his business cycle theory. He came up with a new benchmark to identify pernicious reductions of the monetary interest rate. The relevant benchmark was no longer the Wicksellian natural rate that would exist if the economy were a barter economy. It was rather the monetary interest rate that would exist in the absence of credit expansion.[39]

Any increase in the supply of credit on the market will reduce the interest rate, but if the increase comes from printing paper money or banknotes (rather than from savings) then the artificially lower interest rate falsifies the entrepreneurial profit calculus. In light of the decreased interest rate, a greater number of

---

[39]Mises, *Nationalökonomie*, p. 502.

business projects appear to be profitable and are launched. But the material factors of production necessary for the physical completion of the greater number of projects do not exist. Credit expansion does not mean expansion of the real factor endowment of the economy; it merely means expansion of the money supply through the credit market. It follows that it is physically impossible to sustain the new structure of production that resulted from the credit expansion. The boom must eventually end in a bust.[40]

Update of the Socialist-Calculation Debate

Mises did not believe that the argument in favor of socialist calculation had made any progress. But the new pro-socialist arguments provided an opportunity for further elaboration from his side. He distinguished four types of proposed solutions to the problem he had pointed out in 1920.

The first candidate solution seeks to perform economic calculation in terms of labor time *à la* Neurath. But this approach cannot work because of the material factors of production and the heterogeneity of different types of labor.

The second candidate parallels the first in that it seeks to unearth a substitute for money prices as a medium of calculation. Only here the proposed substitute is not labor time, but utility, as in Wieser's theory. In his rebuttal, Mises points out that human beings cannot measure utility but only rank it. The utilities of units in differently sized supplies are necessarily unequal. Because of this lack of homogeneity, they cannot serve as units in a calculus of value.

According to the third proposal, socialist communities could create an artificial market by ordering the plant managers to

---

[40]Ibid., pp. 502–10. Mises stresses that the boom is not a phase of "overinvestment," but of misallocation. There is too much consumption and too much investment at the same time.

behave as if they were employed in capitalist firms. The idea was to combine the benefits of a price system *and* "social" control through government-appointed managers, but without creating bureaucracy and monopoly. Such schemes had become fashionable during the 1930s, and by the time *Nationalökonomie* was published they were achieving the status of a new orthodoxy that would survive half a century.[41]

One of the new theoreticians, the Polish socialist Oskar Lange thought some compensation for Mises might be in order, given that it was his "powerful challenge that forced the socialists to recognize the importance of an adequate system of economic accounting to guide the allocation of resources in a socialist economy." Lange therefore proposed that "a statue of Professor Mises ought to occupy an honorable place in the great hall of the . . . Central Planning Board of the socialist state."[42]

No socialist state was generous enough to follow up on this suggestion, but the University of Wroclav created a statue of Oskar Lange and preserved it into our day, surely as a monument to the perennity of his message. Generations of students were taught that socialism was, in theory at least, a viable economic system; some authors even went so far as to argue—statistics in hand—that the Soviet economies of Eastern Europe were superior or about to become superior to the capitalist

---

[41]See in particular Fred Taylor, "The Guidance of Production in a Socialist State," *American Economic Review* 19 (1929); Carl Landauer, *Planwirtschaft und Verkehrswirtschaft* (Leipzig: Duncker & Humblot, 1931); H.D. Dickinson, "Price Formation in a Socialist Community," *Economic Journal* 43 (1933); A.P. Lerner, "Economic Theory and Socialist Economy," *Review of Economic Studies* 2 (1934); Oskar Lange, "On the Economic Theory of Socialism," *Review of Economic Studies* 4, no. 1 (October 1936); idem, "The Computer and the Market," *Review of Economic Studies* 4, no. 1 (October 1936); idem, *Price Flexibility and Employment* (Bloomington, Ind.: Principia Press, 1944).

[42]Oskar Lange in *On the Economic Theory of Socialism*, B.E. Lippincott, ed. (New York: McGraw-Hill, 1964), p. 57.

economies of the West.[43] This notion evaporated in 1989.[44] The fall of the Berlin Wall opened everyone's eyes to the stark reality that seventy years of socialism had created nothing but misery, pollution, and slavery. The world learned the hard way what it could have learned in 1922 from a readily available book. In *Socialism*, Mises had analyzed the idea of market socialism even before any socialist had thought of it. And he had already identified its Achilles heel: moral hazard.

Artificial markets would make managers irresponsible. Some of the benefits of successful management would still be private (the increased reputation and career advancement of successful managers), but all of the costs of mismanagement would have to be borne by the citizenry at large. As a consequence, the managers of the state would take on excessive risks; they would

---

[43]See in particular the various editions of the most important Western textbook of the postwar years, Paul Samuelson's *Economics* (New York: McGraw-Hill, 1948). Up to the very last edition that appeared before the collapse of the Soviet empire, Samuelson stated: "The Soviet economy is proof that, contrary to what many sceptics had earlier believed, the socialist command economy can function and even thrive" (*Economics*, 13th ed., 1989, p. 837). A good study of this issue is in Mark Skousen, "The Perseverance of Paul Samuelson's *Economics*," *Journal of Economic Perspectives* 11, no. 2 (Spring 1997): 137–52.

[44]In actual practice, market socialism had never played a big role in the Eastern Bloc. Some intellectuals were allowed to discuss the calculation problem and the market-socialist solution; see in particular Wlodzimierz Brus, *Funktionsprobleme der sozialistischen Wirtschaft* (Frankfurt a.M.: Suhrkamp, [1961] 1971). But in practice there was central planning, not any form of competitive pricing. Significantly, in the early 1960s, the Soviet professor Yevsey G. Liberman received worldwide attention with his proposals to steer production with the help of price incentives. For a concise presentation see Alec Nove, "The Liberman Proposals," *Journal of Soviet and East European Studies* 47 (April 1963): 112–18. Needless to say, Liberman did not address, much less solve, the problems Mises had pointed out in 1922. Mises himself commented on this newest fad of economic planning in his "Observations on the Russian Reform Movement," *The Freeman* 16, no. 5 (May 1966): 23–29.

squander society's capital. Eighteen years later, in *Nation-alökonomie*, Mises did not miss the opportunity to note the irony that, according to this proposal, the market economy was such a bad thing that it had to be reintroduced through the back door as soon as the new socialist regime is established. He went on to chastise the champions of artificial markets for narrow-mindedness. The problem of the allocation of resources is not primarily a managerial problem within each plant. It is a problem of choosing where to place available capital. Which of the existing plants should be expanded, which ones should be cut back, which new production sites should be established? These decisions lay in the hands of "capitalists, entrepreneurs, and speculators." And it was out of the question to extend the scheme of the artificial market to *them*. Restating the analysis of moral hazard along the lines given in *Socialism*, Mises argued that "playing capitalists" would be completely irresponsible. No risk would be too high for the make-believe capitalists because they themselves would hardly bear any negative consequences. Such a system would be neither socialism nor capitalism. It would be no system at all. "It would be chaotic."[45]

He then turned to the fourth scheme, according to which socialist societies should use the equations of mathematical economics to solve the problem of economic calculation. Here Mises restates the argument he had presented in his 1938 French-language article of the same title: those mathematical equations describe a state of affairs that is already in equilibrium, but not the concrete steps through which any equilibrium could ever be reached.

> It was an error to suppose that one could calculate the equilibrium state with data taken from an economy that is not in equilibrium. It was another error to believe that acting man, for his present-day calculations, needs

---

[45]Mises, *Nationalökonomie*, pp. 639f.

to know the evaluations and appraisals that would obtain in the equilibrium state.[46]

He went on to conclude that this fundamental conceptual problem made it superfluous to deal with the practical problems of central planning that Pareto and Hayek had raised.

A Pure Cash Balance Approach

Nationalökonomie and *Human Action* completed the project Mises had started in 1912 with his treatise on money. In certain crucial respects, he decisively improved upon his earlier exposition of monetary theory. The author of *Nationalökonomie* is a better monetary theorist than the author of the *Theory of Money and Credit*. In his biographical recollections Mises is somewhat diffident on this point. He merely says that his work from the 1940s had "completed" the great initial project of integrating marginal value theory with the theory of money.[47] Some years later, he used the harsher term "misstatements" to characterize the shortcomings of his early work. To a German correspondent he wrote:

> You cannot avoid going astray [*Entgleisungen*] if you take money out of the total context of market phenomena and deal with it separately. I have experienced this in my own case. The market process is an indivisible whole. One cannot subdivide it into pieces. My theory of money has reached maturity only in *Human Action*.[48]

The keystone of the mature theory concerned the central importance of the cash balance approach, which alone would

---

[46]Ibid., p. 645.

[47]Mises, *Erinnerungen* (Stuttgart: Gustav Fischer Verlag, 1978), p. 74; *Notes and Recollections* (Spring Mills, Penn.: Libertarian Press, 1978), p. 112.

[48]Mises to Hans Hellwig, letter dated April 10, 1958; Grove City Archive: Hellwig file.

explain money prices in terms of human action, rather than in terms of mechanistic metaphors such as the "velocity" of money.[49] Mises now stressed that the demand for money was truly a demand for cash balances. The value of the cash balances was not simply borrowed from the value of the goods against which they could be exchanged.[50] There was an independent source of value in the services that these cash balances rendered in providing liquid purchasing power.[51]

Mises also radicalized his stance on the usefulness of expansions of the money supply. In *Theory of Money and Credit* he held that monetary expansion might be needed to accommodate greater growth, at least under plausible circumstances. From 1940 onward, he categorically rejected this notion. All benefits that might result from monetary expansion were now presented as being strictly ephemeral. They had no systematic positive impact—quite to the contrary. ⋖

---

[49]Mises, *Nationalökonomie*, pp. 361–65; *Human Action*, pp. 395–402.

[50]This was the view he championed, at least in one crucial passage, in *Theory of Money and Credit* (London: Jonathan Cape, 1934; Indianapolis: Liberty Fund, 1980). See our discussion in chapter 6.

[51]His later theory was already present in the first edition of his *Theory of Money and Credit*, but it was presented side by side with other statements taking the opposite point of view. Mises developed the cash-balance approach to the demand for money starting from Menger's article "Geld," *Handwörterbuch der Staatswissenschaften*, 1st to 3rd eds. (Jena: Gustav Fischer, 1891–1909), chap. 14. One possible source of Mises's second thoughts on this question was a short book that Edwin Cannan had published at the end of World War I. See Edwin Cannan, *Money: Its Connexion with Rising and Falling Prices* (London: King & Son, 1918). In his 1942 lectures in Mexico City, Mises stressed that the individual demand for money was in fact identical with the individual's cash holdings and referred the audience to p. 83 of Cannan's book. See the lecture notes in Grove City Archive: Mexico 1942 files.

Part VI
Mises in America

18
Émigré in New York

MISES KNEW THAT IT would be hard for him to find a suitable position in the United States—fortunately he had no idea just how hard. He was thoroughly out of step with positivism or, as he called it, pan-physicalism, which had begun to shape the development of American economics during the past two decades, and which at the very moment he arrived on American shores, was being promoted with large grants from the Rockefeller Foundation, among others. And his political views were of course also highly unfashionable. In the land of the free—the very cradle of radical *laissez-faire* policies—the philosophy of the founding fathers of the American republic was all but dead in 1940. A few years later, one correspondent summed up the situation:

> Dickens, Carlyle, Coleridge, Charles Kingsley, Charlotte Brontë, Byron, Hood (*The Song of the Shirt*), Elizabeth Barrett Browning and a host of others are still remembered and read today by millions, while the works of Adam Smith, Malthus, Ricardo, McCulloch, and Mill lie undusted except by scholars.[1]

---

[1]Royal Wilbur France to Mises, letter dated November 7, 1946; Grove City Archive: France file.

The contemporary American intellectual world was deeply anti-capitalistic. How could a man like Mises integrate himself into such an environment?

Arrival in New York

On August 3, 1940 the ship docked in New York City. Mises had not been there since 1931 when he had attended a conference of the International Chamber of Commerce in the midst of the Great Depression. In that year, he had come as a distinguished representative. Now he arrived almost empty-handed. Fifty-eight years old, he had to start his life anew. The worst year of his life lay ahead.

Friedrich Unger had booked them a room, and Alfred Schütz was waiting for Ludwig and Margit at the dock. Their happiness upon seeing him was short-lived. Schütz had the unpleasant task of delivering a letter from Robert Calkins, the dean of UC Berkeley, who told Mises that the school had no budget to hire him. They could raise some money in the form of a stipend, but this would be modest, and Calkins would therefore understand if Mises chose to accept a more attractive position elsewhere.[2] A few days later, Howard Ellis wrote from Berkeley thanking Mises for sending a copy of *Nationalökonomie* and wishing him good luck. And that was it for Berkeley.

Machlup wrote from California, where he had met Dean Calkins, and recommended that Mises get in touch with the Rockefeller Foundation regarding a position at UCLA. In many other cases, the Foundation had facilitated the transition of émigré scholars by cosponsoring chairs for them. This, Machlup believed, should be no problem in the present case. Mises thus spoke to his friends at the Foundation, and they gave him the green light by August 15. All hope was now on

---

[2]Calkins to Mises, letter dated August 1, 1940; Grove City Archive: Machlup files.

Machlup to work something out. But to Mises's great disappointment, the attempt failed.

What should they do now? Ludwig and Margit decided to stay in New York for the time being, where many of their European friends and acquaintances had also found refuge under similar conditions. They had already found suitable accommodation in a hotel. The next step was incomparably more difficult: finding new sources of income. Without the job at Berkeley and with much of his assets frozen in Europe, Mises could count the days until his money would run out. He hoped to find academic employment in New York or elsewhere, but there was not much of a job market for economists. A few years later, the G.I. Bill would create a panoply of new positions for professors in colleges and universities, but in 1940 there were only a few full-time positions available. It is true that the federal government had started hiring economists for New Deal agencies such as the National Resources Planning Board, and after the United States entered World War II in December 1941, federal employment became a boon for economists.[3] But Mises had already been found unsuitable for government employment in World War I in his native Austria, at a time when he was far less infamous as an opponent of interventionism. Imagine Mises in the U.S. Office of Price Administration, working under the young John Kenneth Galbraith, or with Milton Friedman in

---

[3]Roosevelt signed the G.I. Bill in 1944. The Bill provided funds to send returning soldiers to colleges and universities, thus keeping them off the labor market. It cost the American taxpayers some $14 billion between 1944 and 1956. See Theda Skocpol, "Delivering for Young Families: The Resonance of the GI Bill," *American Prospect* 28 (September 1996), pp. 66–72. In 2003, the federal government employed more than 3,000 economists or about 15 percent of all members of the American Economic Association. Peter Klein has argued that, due to these circumstances, World War II radically changed the outlook of American economics profession, which turned statist. See Klein, "Why Academic Intellectuals Support Socialism," unpublished manuscript, presented at the New Zealand Business Roundtable, April 2003.

Columbia University's Statistical Research Group, working out the technical details of the withholding tax that Friedman had just invented.[4] Many European expatriates—among them many former Mises students and associates such as Fritz Machlup, Oskar Morgenstern, and Abraham Wald—were accepted into wartime government service. But Mises had to go private or he would go nowhere.[5]

To get into the private market for economists would take time, however, and time he did not have. It is true he enjoyed an excellent international reputation as a theoretician, but he lacked demonstrated experience in the American economy and he was about to turn fifty-nine.[6]

Nevertheless he had to find a job. He used his old contacts to arrange talks at various organizations in New York. On

---

[4]Friedman restored his honor through late repentance, sighing: "Truly, the road to Leviathan is paved with good intentions." Milton and Rose D. Friedman, *Two Lucky People: Memoirs* (Chicago: University of Chicago Press, 1998), p. 123.

[5]During the 1930s, U.S. universities had absorbed many Communist and social democrat economists from Germany. For example, Emil Lederer, Adolf Loewe, and Eduard Heimann found employment at the Graduate Faculty of Political and Social Science (New School for Social Research) in New York, and Carl Landauer became a professor at Berkeley. On the New School for Social Research see Gary Mongiovi, "Emigré Economists at the New School, 1933–1945," Harald Hagemann, ed., *Zur deutschsprachigen wirtschaftswissenschaftlichen Emigration nach 1933* (Marburg: Metropolis, 1997), pp. 383–403.

[6]"I have already passed the age limit." Mises to Machlup, letter dated August 7, 1940; Hoover Institution: Machlup-Mises correspondence file. This alone cannot have been a decisive obstacle. Richard Schüller, some ten years older than Mises, found a position at the New School for Social Research. Margit called on Machlup for help, stating that her husband was deeply depressed. "He is able to serve and fight for an idea, but not for his personal destiny." Margit von Mises to Machlup, letters dated August 6, 1940 and October 8, 1940; Hoover Institution: Machlup-Mises correspondence file.

November 7, for example, he addressed the Banking Seminar of Columbia University's School of Business on the problem of "Post-War Reconstruction of Europe."[7] Two weeks later, he gave a presentation on his contributions to economic theory before the New York University department of economics. He lectured at Princeton University on December 19 and at the turn of the year attended a meeting of the American Economic Association in New Orleans.[8] And on February 11, 1941, he gave a talk to the exclusive Accountants Club of America in the Perroquet Suite of Manhattan's Waldorf-Astoria hotel. The invitation came from John T. Madden, the dean of NYU's school of commerce, who also told him that for the first time ever, the Club had consented to pay an honorarium ($50). The subject of the talk was postwar economic conditions in Europe. The Club did not seem to be under the spell of academic economists, for it advertised for the talk by pointing out that Mises, "although [!] one of the leading economists of the world, is noted for his practical viewpoint and his ability to express himself in terms intelligible to the layman."[9] Mises produced the usual result in his audience. One participant recalled that it was "the clearest, soberest and most thought provoking analysis that

---

[7]Published in *Trusts and Estates* (January 1941), reprinted in Richard Ebeling, ed., *Selected Writings of Ludwig von Mises: Political Economy of International Reform and Reconstruction* (Indianapolis: Liberty Fund, 2000), vol. 3. The publishers of *Trusts and Estates* "distributed some 3,000 copies over and above our usual circulation to leading educators and economists, as well as institutional investors." Luhnow to Mises, letter dated March 17, 1941; Grove City Archive: Trusts and Estates file.

[8]The NYU address was eventually published as "My Contributions to Economic Theory," *Planning for Freedom and Sixteen Other Essays and Addresses*, 4th ed. (South Holland, Ill.: Libertarian Press, [1952] 1980). The Princeton invitation came from Morgenstern. In New Orleans, Mises met Irving Fisher and his German assistant, Hans Cohrssen. See Fisher to Mises, letter dated February 3, 1941; Grove City Archive: Fisher file.

[9]See Grove City Archive: Accountants Club of America file.

I have heard" and arranged a follow-up meeting with Mises to continue the discussion.[10]

His other presentations produced similar results.[11] The vigorous intellectual from Vienna impressed his audiences, but none of these appearances led to anything resembling a contract. The situation was desperate. However, one good side effect of these activities was to make him better known among like-minded intellectuals and businessmen.

Of course Mises also sought direct contact with ideological allies and potential allies. The most important case in point was Henry Hazlitt (1894–1993), who a few years before had written a very favorable book review of *Socialism*, stating that Mises had "written an economic classic in our time."[12] Hazlitt later recalled how they met in New York:

> Sometime in 1940 I got a telephone call. The voice on the other end said "This is Mises speaking." As I've told many of my friends since, it was as if someone had called and said, "This is John Stuart Mill speaking." I had referred to Mises as "a classic," and you don't expect a classic to call you on the telephone! Anyway, that led to our acquaintance.[13]

It was August 1940. Hazlitt had a weekly column in the *Times* and a few months later he brought Mises onboard.

---

[10]Seidman to Mises, letter dated February 19, 1941; Grove City Archive: Accountants Club of America file.

[11]Mises to Machlup, letters dated November 14, 1940 and November 27, 1940; Hoover Institution: Machlup-Mises correspondence file.

[12]*New York Times Book Review* (January 9, 1938). On Hazlitt see Jeffrey Tucker, "Henry Hazlitt: The People's Austrian," Randall G. Holcombe, ed., *15 Great Austrian Economists* (Auburn, Ala.: Ludwig von Mises Institute, 1999), chap. 11.

[13]Henry Hazlitt, "An Interview with Henry Hazlitt," *Austrian Economics Newsletter* (Spring 1984). See also Margit von Mises, *My Years with Ludwig von Mises*, 2nd enlarged ed. (Cedar Falls, Iowa: Center for Futures Education, 1984), p. 58.

Hazlitt might well have been Mises's first close American friend. Benjamin Anderson had moved to Berkeley, and Seligman had died in 1939. During the first years in the new world, Mises in his social life could rely largely on friends and acquaintances from the old world. Manhattan had become the nexus of European opposition elites trying to survive the war years on the American side of the Atlantic.

Henry Hazlitt

Politicians, academics, artists, entrepreneurs, and bankers whose lives were not secure under the Nazi regime had chosen New York as their safe harbor.[14] Naturally, most of these people had a bourgeois or upper-class background, and many were Jews. Ludwig and Margit were certainly amazed when they discovered how many friends, colleagues, students, and even relatives had found their way to Manhattan: the Ungers, the Geiringers, the Schüllers, the Kleins, the Kallirs, the Fürths, the Schuetzes, the Hulas, Eric Voegelin, Felix Kaufmann, Emmanuel Winter, Emmanuel Winternitz, Robert Michels, Engel-Janosi, and many others. In fact, Mises could have resumed his old private seminar: all of its members were in New York City! Even his Vienna family doctor was there.[15]

Many other people, among them his closest friends from Vienna, had not made it. During the coming months and years, news of their terrible fates made it to New York. Emil Perels and his wife died in a German concentration camp.[16] Ludwig

---

[14]Marianne Herzfeld, who spent the war years in London, asked Mises to extend her greetings to all her friends in New York and said, "there are, I think, about a hundred people there whom I would like to see." Herzfeld to Mises, letter dated August 23, 1941; Grove City Archive: Herzfeld file.

[15]Thieberger to Mises, letter dated October 31, 1940; Grove City Archive: Thieberger files.

[16]Susi Schoelson (Chris Butler) to Mises, letter dated September 12, 1948; Grove City Archive: Butler file. Schoelson was a niece of Perels's wife,

Bettelheim-Gabillon was first separated from his family and forced to reside in a mass residence in Vienna; he was later deported and never seen again.[17] Viktor Graetz had died after the *Anschluss*, and only his wife Emmy had managed to emigrate to the States.[18] Ewald Pribram and his wife had committed suicide when they could not leave Belgium.[19]

There was still no news from Margit's daughter, Gitta, and the Miseses went through months of apprehension about her fate. By April 1941, however, they knew that she was secure in the company of Louis Rougier's stepson and on her way to America. By that time, Margit's mother too resided in New York.[20]

Lilli Roth. Their last sign of life was a letter Perels wrote in 1943 to his sister, Frieda Becher von Rüdendorf. Schoelson, the Perels, and Mises had often skied together in the Austrian Alps. In July 1946, Mises wrote to Otto Friedländer that the "terrible fate" of Perels had "deeply shaken" him (letter dated July 13, 1946; Grove City Archive: Friedländer file). As late as February 1944, he did not yet know of Perels's fate; see Grove City Archive: Hoover Library file.

[17]Mises to Hans Cohrssen, letter dated February 12, 1946; Grove City Archive: Cohrssen file. Newspaperman Richard Charmatz met Bettelheim on the eve of his deportation. See Charmatz to Mises, letter dated February 26, 1947; Grove City Archive: Charmatz file. Charmatz survived the war in Vienna because he was married to an Aryan wife, but they lost all their material belongings.

[18]Elsa Brockhausen to Mises, letter dated May 4, 1947; Grove City Archive: Brockhausen file.

[19]Marianne Herzfeld to Mises, letter dated August 23, 1941; Grove City Archive: Herzfeld file. Ewald's brother Karl had made it to Washington, where he continued his career in international organizations. On Nazi crime victims among Mises's friends and acquaintances, see also Mises to Passow, letter dated January 29, 1947; Grove City Archive: Passow file.

[20]Mises to Potter, handwritten manuscript of a letter dated April 17 (1941); Grove City Archive: Geneva Research Center file. See also Karl Hagedorn to Margit Mises, letter dated May 2, 1947; Grove City Archive: Hagedorn file. Mises to Hayek, handwritten manuscript of a letter dated April 18 (1941); Grove City Archive: Hayek files.

Mises established contact with Austrian political expatriates. After about a year in exile, he became more formally involved in the work of various Austrian exile organizations, which mushroomed after the United States entered the war in December 1941. From the beginning, Mises was often asked for help—by friends, acquaintances, and often people who only knew him indirectly. In many cases, these were former students or employees who had no records from Europe. He patiently wrote letters of recommendation and certificates of class attendance, and in some cases, this was instrumental in providing them with a job.[21] He also tirelessly wrote letters of support and made other efforts to help those who had not yet made it to the safe haven of America.[22]

The letters that Machlup and a few others wrote for Mises did not bring the desired result. He must have started to envy Hayek, who wrote from London of business as usual, or almost:

> Although the German planes have become a nuisance during the last week or so and there is of course a small chance that one may be hit by a stray bomb, one gets very soon used to this and it does not really affect normal life. We are comfortable and I am carrying on with my work as always and if things do not change very much indeed there is no reason why this should not go on.[23]

---

[21]For example, Henry Bund, Otto Ehrlich, Bert Hoselitz, Karl Kapp, Leon Koeppel, Rudolf Loebl, Edmund Silberner, Louise Sommer, Walter Sulzbach.

[22]For example, in the cases of legal historian Hermann von Grimeisen and of Paul Mantoux and his family.

[23]Hayek to Mises, letter dated August 29, 1940; Grove City Archive: Hayek files. In the same letter, Hayek confidentially announced his plan to leave the country at some later point on a foundation grant for work in the United States. Jacob Viner was involved and had promised help. During the remainder of the war, though, Hayek stayed in London and Cambridge, and did not allow himself to be disrupted by the events of the war. At one time he lamented the risk of destruction of his books through firebombs. These risks

Mises too would have had the nerves to live under occasional bombings, but he could not live indefinitely without income, and his funds were running out. He had some money in the United Kingdom, revenue from the sale of his books, which could keep him going for some more weeks or months. Hayek managed his bank account in England, but wartime foreign exchange controls made it impossible to transfer these sums out of Britain, and it was only a matter of time until it would become impossible to withdraw anything from the account. It was however possible to export commodities, and thus Hayek entered the book merchant business. He withdrew the money from Mises's account and started buying precious books—among them a first edition of the *Wealth of Nations* and two sets of the complete works of Jeremy Bentham—which he then forwarded to Mises through Haberler in Harvard. This would certainly not have been efficient in normal times, but under the circumstances it was the only way to get any money out of the country.[24]

National Bureau of Economic Research

The New School for Social Research had absorbed many social scientists from Central Europe, and even some of Mises's associates such as Richard Schüller. Mises never received an offer. Hayek received one in August 1940, but declined out of loyalty to his colleagues at LSE.[25]

---

were "not inconsiderable in an empty house with nobody on the spot to put out a firebomb—which, if one gets there promptly, is the easiest thing in the world." Hayek to Mises, letter dated January 12, 1941; Grove City Archive: Hayek files.

[24]Hayek to Mises, letter dated June 1, 1940, and subsequent correspondence; Grove City Archive: Hayek files. They used this device at least until 1948, because the United Kingdom maintained a regime of foreign exchange controls even in the postwar period.

[25]Hayek to Mises, letter dated August 29, 1940; Grove City Archive: Hayek files. Rougier and Hula's affiliation is mentioned on an undated handwritten list of Mises's contained in Grove City Archive: Montes de Oca files.

Eventually it would once again be the Rockefeller Foundation that would fund Mises. Joseph H. Willits, who at the time headed the Foundation's social sciences division, signed a $2,500 grant to the National Bureau of Economic Research to put Mises on its payroll for one year starting December 15, 1940.[26] The stipend was less then a third of his salary in Geneva, but given the circumstances Mises would have been satisfied to find anything at all.[27]

Mises's contacts with other NBER economists seem to have been ephemeral. He ran a seminar at NBER's Hillside offices but found it uninspiring. To Hayek he wrote:

> My seminar is going on. Last week M. and L. took part. I think that their impression was that it is still far below the Stubenring standard. But everything takes time.[28]

It turned out, however, that he did not have the time to build up a group of permanent participants as in Vienna. All of the attending students were quickly absorbed in government jobs—the war years were a strong growth period for the federal

---

[26]William J. Carson to Mises, letter dated December 24, 1940; Grove City Archive: NBER files.

[27]Barzun observed in those years that "professorial salaries in American universities [reached] the not very dizzy height of nine or ten thousand dollars a year" and then added the following remark: "The lower depths of the profession's earning power are painful to think of and undercut any irony; e.g. in 1940 there were 433 junior colleges, whose salary scale ranged, on average, from $1,572 to $2,130 a year; and 177 teachers' colleges, for which the figures are $2,433 and $3,600." Jacques Barzun, *Teacher in America* (Indianapolis: Liberty Press, [1945] 1981). Fritz Machlup's starting salary at the University of Buffalo in 1935 had been $6,500. See Machlup to Mises, letter dated May 6, 1935; Hoover Institution: Machlup-Mises correspondence file.

[28]Mises to Hayek, handwritten manuscript of a letter dated April 18 [1941]; Grove City Archive: Hayek files. "M." probably stood for Machlup and "L." for Lieser.

government, which hired thousands of young graduates all over the country.[29]

During the first year at NBER, Mises continued to write in German, which few or none of his colleagues could read. He must have thought he would one day return to an academic position in Europe. But was there any real chance that this could happen? When he arrived in New York, this might have been his plan and his hope, but the prospect grew ever dimmer over the course of 1941.

His manuscripts were translated into English. The NBER officer responsible for handling publication matters, a certain Martha Anderson, also tried to find a translator for one of his book manuscripts—probably the original German manuscript of what was later published as *Omnipotent Government*. In November 1941, Anderson proposed Max Eastman for the job. Eastman was a New York journalist who had already translated *Das Kapital*. Mises replied that he would like to meet Eastman, and might have done so in Eastman's home in March 1942, but no professional relationship would come of it.

Dark Hours and New Plans

The money from the Rockefeller Foundation was not enough to live on, and in 1941 it was almost all the income they had. He had never known such destitution. His family had not been wealthy but they had always been comfortable, had always had help in the household. But now they could barely pay for a restaurant or for tickets to the theater or opera. Margit started training as a secretary.

Even more depressing was the ideological state of affairs in the very countries that were at present the bulwark against international Communism and National Socialism. Things had deteriorated considerably since his last trip to the States in 1931,

---

[29]Mises to Rappard, letter in Graduate Institute Archive.

when "progressive" interventionism was already at a previous high point. In the years of Roosevelt's New Deal, the political gospel preached from the press and the pulpits had shifted yet further to the left. The Soviet Union was now held in high regard and Communistic schemes were discussed seriously, while the free market was derided as an atavism of an unenlightened past. It was only a matter of time before the United Kingdom and the United States would become fascist or Communist or some variant thereof. Was this a future worth dying for? Without hope for the future, was it worth living in the present? Where were the voices of dissent, except for a scattered few like Henry Hazlitt and Lawrence Fertig? Where were the economists with enough backbone to resist the Keynesian temptation—the very embodiment of statist longings? How long could his disciples hold out, insecure as they were in their status as émigrés?

It was at this point that Hayek, to whom he must have confided his desperation, reassured him that he "need have no fear about my becoming converted to Keynesianism"—though for Hayek too the future looked bleak:

> I agree entirely with what you say about the horrible state of economic thinking here and in the U.S.A. That at the present time when one can at least have some hope for the immediate future the long run outlook should be so dark is really dreadful.[30]

---

[30]Hayek to Mises, letter dated January 12, 1941; Grove City Archive: Hayek files. He went on:

> I am trying hard to show to people how this present trend leads inevitably to economic decay and fascism and I shall follow up my pamphlet with a more popular booklet (probably in one of the sixpenny series) on which I am now working, apart from the larger book, which is slowly progressing.

Three months later, Hayek reported the publication of his first article on the influence of scientism on social thought.

Mises did not believe he could contribute to turning the tide. His career was in a deep slump. He was completely at odds with the prevailing scientific fashions in the United States and he saw no way to have any impact on public opinion. Ironically, one factor that barred him from reaching an audience through his writings was that U.S. publishers strictly aimed at the mainstream. The greatest champion of capitalism could not make himself heard because in a world dominated by the statist ideology his books did not seem profitable enough to enjoy the support of commercial publishers. He wrote to Hayek:

> I have been very busy these last months in writing my posthumous works. I do not believe that it will be possible for me to publish anything other than small articles in periodicals.[31]

Mises reached an absolute low point in April 1941. Margit had been ill since early March—a flu and sinus troubles—to the point that she could not even bring herself to keep up her diary. Mises, usually extremely discreet about his emotions, lamented in a letter to Hayek: "Margit is not yet totally recovered. The thing seems interminable."[32] It was also quite impossible to cheer her up because she was still anxious about the fate of her daughter. Thus he was left alone with his sorrows and apprehensions. He had left Switzerland because he refused to depend entirely on the goodwill of one party, the Swiss government. But in the United States he fared no better. All his money came from the Rockefeller Foundation, which made it clear to Mises

---

[31]Mises to Hayek, handwritten manuscript of a letter in response to Hayek's letter dated May 6, 1941; Grove City Archive: Hayek files. To Machlup he wrote: "I do not know why I am working, but I have been very productive." Mises to Machlup, letter dated May 20, 1941; Hoover Institution: Machlup-Mises correspondence file.

[32]Mises to Hayek, letter dated April 18, 1941; Grove City Archive: Geneva Research Center file.

what his status was now. While left-wing lunatics and the cranks of the imaginary science of quantitative economics received lucrative contracts with the New School of Social Research, Mises had to live on the equivalent of a post-doctoral stipend. And he was made to understand that even this amount was not meant as compensation for his service to economic science, but as something between a pension and charity for an old man who could not get along otherwise.

Mises was not a man to attach too much importance to material things. He once told Margit that, if she was after riches, she had married the wrong man. But neither was he the type of intellectual that Ayn Rand depicted in her novel *Atlas Shrugged*: the libertarian philosopher who in dire straits would descend stoically from his chair at the university to work behind the counter of a small-town burger joint. Had Mises ended up flipping hamburgers, his heart would have broken. And what would have happened to economics, the Austrian School, and human liberty if Mises had had to give up intellectual work? He had not yet published a single piece written in English. He had not yet encountered even one of his later-famous American students. He had left the world a revolutionary treatise on economics that nobody could read during the war, and which nobody would care about when the war was over. Mises would have remained an important figure in the history of economic thought, but the *laissez-faire* Austrian School would never have come into being.

∾ ∾ ∾

These darkest days were not without some good news, even though it may have seemed insubstantial at first. Henry Hazlitt had brought Mises in touch with the *New York Times*, and in March 1941 Mises wrote his first editorial.[33]

---

[33]See the correspondence between Hazlitt and Mises in Grove City Archive: Hazlitt files. Apparently, this was his only editorial in 1941. In the

In May 1941, he took part in the meetings of a group closely associated with the Austrian-American League. The group included Dietrich von Hildebrand, Richard von Schüller, Raoul Auernheimer, Erich Hula, and Otto Kallir (Nirenstein). The front man in the League was von Hildebrand, but the organizational driving force was the secretary, Otto Kallir, who had probably brought his cousin Mises on board. In June 1941, Mises and other members of this group formed the Austrian Committee to promote the independence of Austria after the end of the war. Leadership lay apparently in the hands of Richard von Schüller. Most members of the Committee were at least sympathetic to the prospect of reestablishing a monarchy in Austria. This alone would have been a decisive stumbling block for the cooperation of the Committee with Austrian expatriates of republican convictions, especially with the social democrats.[34] They still could not agree on the fundamental principle of Austrian independence. They still pursued the old *Anschluss* agenda—this time without Hitler.[35]

Planning for after the war still occupied a prominent place in Mises's work. On May 20, 1941, he reported to Young that he had made good progress on his research project: a study of the social and economic problems of Central and Eastern Europe, which Mises hoped could serve as a basis for postwar

---

spring of 1942, he published three further editorials, all of which dealt with the crucial logistical problems of Germany's war effort. In 1943, then, he published the last four editorials, which dealt primarily with problems of postwar reconstruction, especially monetary problems. For each of these articles he received $10. The pay slips are in Grove City Archive: NYT files.

[34]Otto Kallir (Nirenstein) to Mises, letter dated July 19, 1941; Grove City Archive: Austrian National Committee files.

[35]Ernst Hoor pointed out that, until 1945, the expatriate leadership of the social democrats avoided making any statement that could have been interpreted as a commitment to Austrian independence, or to the existence of an Austrian nation. See Hoor, *Österreich 1918–1938* (Vienna: Bundesverlag für Unterricht, Wissenschaft und Kunst, 1966), p. 46.

reconstruction in this region. He said he would start writing it soon, and he must have finished it by mid-July, when he sent out copies to friends and colleagues. In this 43-page memorandum, Mises restated the political and economic case for the establishment of an East-European Union with a strong central government: growth through free trade and *laissez-faire*, response to the problems of linguistic minorities, and protection against the three mighty neighbors.[36]

In another paper that he had finished writing by the end of May, he pointed out that his plan for an Eastern Union would complement similar ideas for the establishment of a Western Union. This approach—the formation of political blocs, as they in fact eventually came to be established after World War II (NATO in the West and Warsaw Pact in the East)—was more promising than the approach of the League of Nations in the interwar period, which consisted in providing "for the lack of a peace ideology by the establishment of a bureau and a bureaucracy."[37]

---

[36]The new plan differed from the proposals he had made in early 1938 in that the proposed Eastern Democratic Union (EDU) was to include not only the countries in the Danube basin, but virtually all of Eastern Europe, including the territories that in 1933 formed the sovereign states of Albania, Austria, Bulgaria, Czechoslovakia, Danzig, Estonia, Greece, Hungary, Latvia, Lithuania, Poland, Rumania and Yugoslavia, as well as large parts of Prussia. The proposed new political entity would thus cover 700,000 square miles with about 120,000,000 residents using 17 different languages. See Mises, "An Eastern Democratic Union: A Proposal for the Establishment of a Durable Peace in Eastern Europe," dated October 1941, 43 pp. A typewritten first draft of this paper is dated July 1, 1941 and contains 15 pp. Through the British Embassy in Washington, D.C., Mises sent copies of the July version to Hayek and Robbins (see Noel Hall to Mises, letter dated July 18, 1941; Grove City Archive: "H" files). In May 1941, Mises possibly gave a lecture at Yale discussing his plan for an Eastern European Union. See Irving Fisher to Mises, letter dated June 11, 1941; Grove City Archive: Fisher file.

[37]Mises, "Post-war Reconstruction," dated May 28, 1941, 22 pages, quote from, p. 16. He went on:

> It is the general belief today that the sovereignty of the small nation has proved its impracticability and that they have to

≼ ≼ ≼

The late spring of 1941 greeted Mises with a most welcome opportunity. He happened to meet again with Señor Montes de Oca, a high official of the Mexican Treasury and executive president of the Banco Internacional, whom he had known from his days with the International Chamber of Commerce. Luis Montes de Oca was a hard-nosed businessman and a great admirer of Mises's work. As early as 1937 or 1938 he had invited him to visit Mexico City for a series of lectures, but Mises had not accepted the invitation. It must have been a most pleasant surprise for both of them to meet again in good health in Manhattan, and Montes de Oca instantly renewed his invitation: Mises should come for two months to Mexico.[38] It was the first true sign of recognition in eighteen months. Mises was happy, and Margit was happy that her husband was happy.

Mises and Montes de Oca also discussed the project of translating Mises's *Socialism* into Spanish. Montes de Oca proposed to do the translation himself from the French edition when Mises praised this edition for its accuracy and style. (Montes de Oca did not read German.) He also proposed a concrete price for the rights to the Spanish edition: $200—a

---

disappear as independent states. This is true under present conditions . . . even the United States must be reckoned among these "small" nations . . . I believe that the only thing which the Western democracies can do is to form a Union for . . . defense. . . . I do not see any other reasonable solution for the postwar problem than a closer political and military union between the menaced democracies. (pp. 17f.)

The great weakness of his own plan was that it, too, was mute on the question of the "peace ideology" that could provide for the political and economic integration of Eastern Europe. Some ten years later Mises implicitly confessed this in private correspondence with Salvador de Madariaga (see Grove City Archive: Madariaga file).

[38]Mises to Velasco, letter dated December 16, 1958; Grove City Archive: Velasco files.

month's salary for Mises at that point. All this was very good news, and as soon as his Mexican friend departed, Mises set out a syllabus for his projected visit to the National University of Mexico. He proposed eight lectures in English on the economics of capitalism, socialism, and interventionism; moreover, one lecture in French on the gold standard and managed currency; and also two seminars, one dealing with money and banking, the other with the "part played by economic and social doctrines in political controversies of today." He sent these proposals to Montes de Oca on June 12.[39]

৶   ৶   ৶

A few weeks later, Ludwig and Margit left Manhattan for a long vacation in New Hampshire's White Mountains. They traveled by train on July 16 and arrived on the same day at their destination: Glen House in Gorham, New Hampshire, at the base of Mount Washington, the highest peak in northeastern America. Almost every day they hiked in the mountains.[40] Although Mount Washington was a much-visited site, Ludwig and Margit were by themselves as soon as they were far enough away from the roads.[41] The scenery of the White Mountains reminded them of the Alps—just the setting he needed to renew

---

[39]This letter is mentioned in Montes de Oca to Mises, letter dated August 29, 1941; Grove City Archive: Mexico 1942 files. The content of the course, lecture, and seminars is mentioned in Mario de la Cueva to Mises, letter dated October 10, 1941; Grove City Archive: Mexico 1942 files.

[40]On the first weekend, he briefly returned to New York City. On July 21 and 23 he lectured at NYU's School of Commerce on the "Economics of Government Regulation of Business." See correspondence in Grove City Archive: Dorau file.

[41]"Many hundred cars pass our place every day, as all people are eager to glance 5 minutes at the peak, to take a snapshot and to rush away" (Mises to Hayek, handwritten manuscript of a letter of August 14, 1941; Grove City Archive: Hayek files).

his strength, as in Europe he
had needed to spend one month
each year in those mountains.
In the serenity of defiant rocks,
cool air, and wide views, where
sky and earth held court in
splendid majesty, he too could
elevate his mind again above
the material circumstances into
which great events had catapulted him. Here he considered
again the big picture, and his

*Mises on vacation in the White
Mountains*

place within it. It was probably here that Mises resolved himself
to begin a new life in the United States, to become a citizen of
the country, and to continue the fight for liberty from American
soil.

Margit must have been extremely pleased to see her husband
regaining energy to such an extent that he climbed most of
Mount Washington's 6,288 feet.[42] Near the end of their stay at
Glen House, more good news came with the publication of the
Atlantic Charter on August 14. The U.S. government seemed
determined after all to support the United Kingdom in the war
and to create a postwar order based on liberty.[43]

The holiday had come just in time. After the United States
entered the war, vacationing was seen as unpatriotic and the
Miseses abstained from it. Back in New York, he threw himself
into work with new verve. From now on, things would improve
in his life, slowly but steadily. In early October, he and Margit
moved into the apartment where they would remain for the rest

---

[42]Mises to Anne Robbins, undated letter (probably January 1943); Grove
City Archive: Robbins files.

[43]Mises also felt greatly relieved by the Russian entry into the war against
Germany. Margit von Mises to Machlup, letter dated September 3, 1941;
Hoover Institution: Machlup-Mises correspondence file.

*Mises's New York City
West End apartment*

of their lives. (It was subject to rent control laws.) Margit had found the three-bedroom apartment at 777 West End Avenue in Manhattan.[44]

Mises continued to work for a few weeks on the proposal for the establishment of an Eastern Democratic Union. By October, he had completed the memorandum, one of the first pieces that he himself had written in English and which contained his political testament for Eastern Europe. Mises's thoughts now turned to America. To Hayek he wrote:

> As I do not want to increase further the collection of my posthumous works I am writing now in English. I hope that I will succeed to finish within a year a volume dealing critically with the whole complex of "anti-orthodox" doctrines and their consequences.

He went on:

> Your essays on the Counter-revolution of Science are the most valuable contribution to the history of the decay of western civilization. I hope that you will pretty soon publish the whole book.
>
> I am, however, rather skeptical in regard of the practical results of our endeavors. It seems that the age of reason and common sense is gone forever. Reasoning and thinking have been replaced by empty slogans.
>
> A few days ago, Alvin Hansen delivered a lecture on post-war economic reconstruction. The old stories about full employment, scarcity of foreign exchange, the need for foreign exchange control and

---

[44]Mises to Machlup, letter dated September 19, 1941; Hoover Institution: Machlup-Mises correspondence file.

planning, more self-sufficiency etc. He did not even mention the problem of capital shortage. He seems to believe that taxing the rich would make it possible to maintain the pre-war standard of living of the masses. Two centuries of economic theory were in vain, as they could not kill the mercantilist prejudices. The audience—many ex-members of the *Verein für Sozialpolitik*—expressed full agreement with the lecturer.[45]

While they made preparations for the trip to Mexico, another piece of news made Mises's day and gave him hope for the future. On December 8, 1941, the United States declared war on Japan after the Japanese raid on Pearl Harbor. The Americans were finally in business. Nothing could save Hitler now. A few months later, Mises wrote to a friend, a German protestant minister in Massachusetts:

> Of course, the war is a very unfortunate thing. But, you are quite right, it was inevitable and it has to be fought to the end. It is necessary to establish a new order where people who break the peace have to be treated like those who resort to violence within each country.[46]

Mises seems to have fallen back into what in more sober moments he called the dictatorship complex. He blithely assumed that the institutions entrusted with the "new order" would use their enormous power only for those purposes of which he, Mises, approved.[47]

---

[45]Mises to Hayek, handwritten manuscript of a letter in response to Hayek's letter of October 24, 1941; Grove City Archive: Hayek files.

[46]Mises to Otto Loverude, handwritten manuscript of a letter dated March 7, 1942; Grove City Archive: Churches files.

[47]See Mises, "The Dictatorship Complex," *Omnipotent Government* (New Haven, Conn.: Yale University Press, 1944), chap. 11, sect. 2. In his monetary thought he had overcome this error, most notably in the context of his eventual rejection of the gold exchange standard.

The American entry into the war prompted various Austrian personalities to join forces and create more formal organizations to prepare the reconstruction of Austria after the war, which, they were sure, would end with an allied victory. Already in anticipation of the event, and prompted by Roosevelt and Churchill's Atlantic Charter, Richard von Coudenhove-Kalergi, a close ally of Otto von Habsburg, had submitted a petition to the U.S. government for a separate treatment of Austria after the war. Mises signed the petition, along with many other leading Austrian expatriates.[48]

After Pearl Harbor, the Austrian Committee assembled in several meetings during the month of December to discuss how to proceed. After a meeting on December 13, Mises prepared a one-page manifesto that outlined a political postwar order in Austria that would be based on the principle of individual liberty. The paper probably resulted from the discussions of this meeting; Mises wrote it but did not sign his name. In any case, the document enthusiastically welcomed the Atlantic Charter as the "constitution of a new community of all free people," and it expressed the wish for an independent Austria after the war. According to the most important stipulations of the document, the new Austria would be a state of freedom and democracy, even though the question of the concrete form of state (parliamentary democracy, monarchy, etc.) was explicitly left open. Moreover, the new Austria would not insist on the title of a "sovereign" country, because sovereignty was no longer consonant with the spirit of the time, but would instead seek integration into an Eastern European Union and a new league of nations.

But the Austrian Committee was but one of many similar groups that started popping up, and Mises was also a member of Austrian Action, a group led by Ferdinand Count von Czernin.[49]

---

[48]Coudenhove-Kalergi to Mises, letter dated November 20, 1941; Grove City Archive: Austrian National Committee files.

[49]Austrian Action to Mises, letter dated February 4, 1942; Grove City Archive: Austrian National Committee files.

It was clear that an effective representation of Austrian interests in America was impossible under these conditions, and the leaders of the various groups decided to join forces. In early February 1942, Mises, then in Mexico City, received a telegram with the invitation to join the newly formed Austrian National Committee. The telegram was signed by Walter Schuschnigg (possibly a relative of the last Chancellor of free Austria) and Hans Rott.[50] Mises accepted membership, though he could not personally appear at the founding meeting in Manhattan, where his colleague Erich Hula represented him.[51]

Six Weeks in Mexico

The trip to Mexico (late January to March 1942) by far surpassed their expectations. They were treated with the highest respect—hotel reservations had been made at the local Ritz— and Mises found an audience prepared for and receptive to his message. He started lecturing on January 14 and finished his program by February 20. Besides his course at the School of Economics, which he taught in English, he also gave two lectures in French at the Independent School of Law.[52] The course

---

[50]Rott and Schuschnigg to Mises, telegram dated February 10, 1942; Grove City Archive: Austrian National Committee files. In 1941–1942, Schuschnigg was the driving force behind attempts to bring a group of mostly Jewish refugees from Austria, who had been stranded in Lisbon, to the United States; see Grove City Archive: Schuschnigg file. Mises was in touch with Schuschnigg throughout the war. See the 1944–1945 correspondence with Pitman Potter in Grove City Archive: Potter file. Potter had moved to Oberlin College in Ohio and edited the *American Journal of International Law*.

[51]Hula to Mises, letter dated February 20, 1942; Grove City Archive: Austrian National Committee files.

[52]The course at the School of Economics paid US$800, and for the lectures at the law school he received US$50. See Montes de Oca to Mises, letter dated October 4, 1941; Grove City Archive: Mexico 1942 files. The same files contain his very detailed lecture notes—at that point, he probably did not yet feel quite comfortable speaking in English—which allow for a detailed reconstruction of the matters he dealt with.

only attracted some 8–14 students—still Mises thought it was "a great success. The audience was of course small, as the students mostly do not understand foreign languages."[53] Montes de Oca attended each session, but Mises had particularly animated discussions with Señor Eduardo Hornedo.

Margit stayed in and around the hotel, and in the evenings Ludwig joined her and often took her out. They also spent many evenings at the home of Montes de Oca. At these meetings Mises again and again expressed his pessimism about the future, and again and again his Mexican host protested that it was not too late to start a fight for liberty and sound economic policies. Montes de Oca was indeed firmly convinced that the best place to start this fight was Mexico. He had made Mises a job offer by correspondence even before his Austrian guest had left New York. The Bankers' Association and the Chamber of the Mining Industry—two of the three most important Mexican business associations—were interested in hiring Mises for "an extended stay" as an economic advisor.[54] Mises wrote back that the offer was "very flattering and tempting" and that he was "anxious to get more detailed information about the functions which it is expected I would fulfill."[55] Six weeks later, Montes de Oca replied with a firm offer. According to his proposition, Mises would become the head of the economics departments of the two business associations, with sufficient personnel to assist him and at a comfortable monthly salary of 1,000 Mexican pesos (a lunch for one person at the Ritz cost three or four

---

[53]Mises to Hayek, handwritten undated manuscript to a letter dated March 18, 1942; Grove City Archive: Mexico 1942 files. The date of the letter can be inferred from Hayek's response dated May 19, 1942; Grove City Archive: Hayek files.

[54]Montes de Oca to Mises, letter dated October 4, 1941; Grove City Archive: Mexico 1942 files.

[55]Mises to Montes de Oca, handwritten manuscript of a letter dated October 7, 1941; Grove City Archive: Mexico 1942 files.

pesos). He would also be teaching courses and seminars at any department he wished at the National University of Mexico and at the Colegio de Mexico, and he would be free to take up other (paid) teaching assignments. The offer was for three years and could become effective any time—Mises would not even have to return to the United States after his upcoming visit.[56]

This was a great temptation. Had the offer come a year earlier, Mises would probably have accepted it on the spot. But he had since made new plans. Was his future not in the United States? Montes de Oca tried to bring Mises to an early commitment by correspondence, but his Austrian friend remained steadfast: He would first pay a visit to each of the two business associations before making a decision.

Upon his arrival in Mexico City, Mises conducted very wide-ranging talks with his Mexican hosts. He even started to write a couple of words in Spanish, and at the request of his hosts began working on a memorandum analyzing Mexico's economic problems. In the course of the next few weeks, he perused the statistical yearbooks of the country and became acquainted with other literature on Mexican conditions. He read the press to the best of his ability and led many discussions with his host and other people. Slowly a more concrete picture of Mexico became clear to him, which he later described in a letter to Hayek:[57]

> Mexico is a country without industry and very short of capital. The soil is in the greater part of the country very poor. The result . . . is that they have to import wheat and mais [Mises meant what Americans call "corn"], but the rulers—generals, trade

---

[56]Montes de Oca to Mises, letter dated November 29, 1941; Grove City Archive: Mexico 1942 files.

[57]Mises to Hayek, handwritten undated manuscript to a letter dated March 18, 1942; Grove City Archive: Mexico 1942 files. The date of the letter can be inferred from Hayek's response dated May 19, 1942; Grove City Archive: Hayek files.

union leaders and pink intellectuals—intend to start industrialization by ruthless confiscation of capital. Neither this attitude nor its effects differ from conditions in other countries. But really amazing is the fact that there are some people—of course a small elite only—who have a very keen insight into the problems involved and try to educate the intellectuals.

Then Mises went on to compare this Mexican elite very favorably with the "small group of economists" who, according to Hayek, resisted the trend toward government omnipotence in Great Britain.[58] Speaking of his Mexican hosts, Mises said:

You cannot find such men in other countries. Contrary to your statement in the "Nature" article everybody in this country advocates allround planning. Sir William's ideas (published in the London *Times* a few days ago) all economists, businessmen and pressure groups sympathize with. They are convinced that current events have demonstrated in an irrefutable way the superiority of the "post office" system. People do not learn anything; they despise theory and they interpret facts from the point of view of their errors and prejudices.[59]

Still the fact remained that Mexico was a very poor country and that the forces of reason were weak. Luis Montes de Oca must have sensed that Mises was not exactly enthusiastic about another Chamber of Commerce career, and brought up the prospect of a research organization under Mises's leadership—a private "Institute of the Social Sciences." This was much more to the liking of his Austrian guest, and when Mises departed he

---

[58]F.A. Hayek, "Planning, Science, and Freedom," *Nature* (November 15, 1941): 580.

[59]Mises to Hayek, handwritten undated manuscript to a letter dated March 18, 1942; Grove City Archive: Mexico 1942 files. "Sir William" is Lord Beveridge.

promised that he would write a paper for *Cuadernos Americanos*—a journal managed by one of Montes de Oca's associates—as well as a short memorandum on the establishment of an Institute of the Social Sciences, as a basis for further deliberation. He complied with this request after his return, and wrote two memoranda—one concerning the general aspects of the venture, the other concerning more concrete institutional aspects of the proposed Institute—in June 1942.[60]

The Austrian National Committee

Ludwig and Margit returned to New York in March. A letter from Machlup had arrived, informing them of another unsuccessful attempt to secure a suitable job for Mises, this time at Rochester. The chairman of the department had told Machlup that he "should be ashamed to approach so distinguished an economist as Professor Mises with the small salaries at our disposal."[61]

Fortunately, the Rockefeller grant to NBER had been extended, though apparently not without resistance. Mises applied for the extension in December 1941, based on a six-page report on his research activities in the previous year. The extension was not confirmed until mid-February, but it is possible that the delay was the result of his trip to Mexico. For the next few months, Mises took an active role in the meetings of the newly constituted Austrian National Committee. As he said

---

[60]Both memoranda are in Grove City Archive: Montes de Oca files. The paper was translated and published as "Ideas sobre la Política Económica de la Postguerra," *Cuadernos Americanos* 4, no. 4 (July-August 1942): 87–99. The original manuscript had the title "Economic Nationalism and Peaceful Economic Cooperation," and was published many years later in *Money, Method, and the Market Process*, Richard M. Ebeling, ed. (Boston: Kluwer, 1990).

[61]Machlup to Mises, letter dated March 16, 1942; Grove City Archive: Machlup files.

on many occasions in private discussions and correspondence, he was extremely pessimistic with regard to Europe's future:

> You can't have a reasonable state of affairs with unreasonable people. I do not believe that a member of the Hitler youth or of the equivalent groups in Italy, Hungary or so on can ever turn toward honest work and non-predatory jobs. Beasts cannot be domesticated within one or two generations.[62]

But true to his motto, this was no reason for him to step back in resignation. On the contrary, he threw himself into work preparing postwar policies and he encouraged his correspondents to do the same.[63]

Mises and Otto von Habsburg in 1960

The Austrian National Committee was a creation of Otto von Habsburg, who had the ear of the American administration and turned out to be the common denominator for the feuding groups of Austrian patriots. Otto delivered an excellent diplomatic performance during the war years that eventually prompted the allies to reestablish an independent Austrian state after the war (a decision to this effect was made at a conference of the foreign ministers of the United States, Britain, and Russia in October and November 1943 in Moscow). Otto's success also boosted the monarchical principle.[64] He must have at least toyed with

---

[62]Mises to Alexander Hirsch, undated manuscript of a letter in response to Hirsch's letter dated May 12, 1943; Grove City Archive: "H" files.

[63]Mises contributed several memoranda dealing with the principles of postwar reconstruction (see Habsburg file). "Entwurf von Richtlinien für den Wiederaufbau."

[64]For years, the leaders of the legitimist movement had been the most ardent champions of Austrian nationhood. The movement had been suppressed before

the idea of reestablishing his dynasty after the war, and many devoted followers (as well as the usual careerists, who sensed an opportunity for political windfall profits) encouraged him to pursue this strategy. These circles of Austrian expatriates generally referred to Otto von Habsburg as "His Majesty, Kaiser Otto" and called him "Imperial Highness." Mises himself would continue to use this title in correspondence with Habsburg long after the prospect of a restoration of the Austrian monarchy had faded.[65]

In the heated days of World War II, many Austrian expatriates were betting on a political return of the Habsburg dynasty after the war. Mises's former colleague at the University of Vienna, Heinrich Graf von Degenfeld, was one of the staunch supporters of a monarchical restoration on legitimist grounds. In mid-April 1942, Habsburg asked Mises and a few other men for their detailed opinion on some forty to fifty questions concerning strategic and tactical problems that Habsburg confronted in his double capacity as the leader of the Austrian National Committee and of the House of Habsburg. Mises put this job on the front burner and answered the questionnaire within a week. Only one part of Mises's confidential report survived: the one in which he comments on the conditions under which a restoration could be achieved. Mises wrote that there was no contradiction between national self-determination and a monarchical regime, provided that the monarchy was established by a free referendum.

1933 because Austria's neighbors and its former war enemies had threatened with diplomatic and military sanctions in case of attempted restoration. When the suppression stopped, the legitimists very quickly gained political ground. By 1938, Otto von Habsburg had been nominated honorary citizen in 1,540 out of 4,400 Austrian cities and towns. See Hoor, *Österreich 1918–193*, pp. 64–66.

[65]See his letter to Habsburg dated May 20, 1960; Grove City Archive: Habsburg files.

This point of view reflected the Polish heritage of its author.[66] Poland had in fact had an elective kingdom from 1573 to 1795; the aristocratic parliament (the *Sejm*) elected the king by unanimous vote. But Mises did not base his argument on historical precedent. Rather, he argued that only an elected monarch enjoyed a secure basis for his reign. Enthronement on the basis of legitimist claims against the will of the people could not last. It was likely to be resisted and eventually overthrown. As an alternative approach, Mises sent along the memorandum containing his proposal for the establishment of an Eastern Democratic Union.[67]

The Austrian National Committee united all Austrian right-wingers and provided them with political representation in Washington, D.C. (in the person of Egon Ranshofen-Wertheimer). One success of this group was the proclamation of "Austrian Day" on July 25, 1942, by twelve state governors. And U.S. Secretary of State Cordell Hull declared that the United States government had never recognized Hitler's annexation of Austria. This dissociation of German villains and Austrian victims would remain the one common position of the various Austrian right-wing expatriate groups throughout the war, and here they achieved a clear success. (The expatriate social democrats never wavered from the agenda of a greater Germany.)

Mises took part in a plenary meeting of the Austrian National Committee on April 22, 1942, and a month later he was elected to a subcommittee on postwar reconstruction. In June 1942, he also took part in a subcommittee on foreign policy, where it appears that he had a major impact. The first sessions discussed and drafted a "Declaration of the United Free Austrians" based on the December 1941 manifesto of the Austrian Committee. In

---

[66]See chapter "Roots."

[67]Degenfeld to Mises, letter dated April 11, 1942; Mises to Degenfeld, letter dated April 20, 1942; the three-page questionnaire; and Mises's manuscript "Monarchismus, nicht Legitimismus;" Grove City Archive: Habsburg files.

contrast with that document, however, the Declaration asserted that Austria had been coercively taken over by the Nazis and that it was therefore under *de facto* occupation by a foreign army. The Declaration also deemphasized integration into international political federations and emphasized the concept of sovereignty. Most important, the Declaration avoided the question of which form of government Austria should adopt after the war. According to the earlier manifesto, the form of government should be determined through the deliberation of a national assembly. But the Declaration was mute on this point, because a monarchist faction under the leadership of Mises's former colleague Count Degenfeld wished to maintain the option of a legitimist foundation for a future Austrian constitutional monarchy.[68]

For the time being, the compromise was good enough for Mises and other republicans. The important thing was that some agreement be reached as a basis for the rest of the agenda. Mises outlined this agenda in an *"Aktions-Kalender"*—a project schedule he seems to have circulated within the Committee. According to this schedule, the next step would be to enter in negotiations with two left-wing groups of Austrian expatriates to support a common declaration. Then the result should be published and further negotiations started, this time with the Czechs and the Poles, and then with other nations that Mises recommended for an East-European Union. Finally, there would have to be negotiations with bankers and businessmen to address the issue of financing the first few months and years of the new state.

But it did not come to pass, and apparently Mises gave up active participation in the committees and did not even attend

---

[68]Compare the version of the Declaration dated June 20, 1942, the revisions of June 25, Degenfeld's annotations dated July 1, 1942, and the final version of July 12, 1942; Grove City Archive: Austrian National Committee files.

the dinner in honor of Otto von Habsburg's thirtieth birthday on November 20, 1942. Work in the Committee must have convinced him that he had no future in Europe. The old continent was ravaged by war because it had been in the firm grip of statist illusions. The expatriates who were making plans for postwar Austria were entirely under the same spell. It is true that they despised National Socialism, but they did not despise socialism per se. Each of them had his own little scheme, and invariably all of these involved the state running the country. Many years later he wrote in correspondence: "As the Bourbons of the Restoration, many Austrians have learned nothing and forgotten nothing."[69] These must have been his feelings in 1942 as well.

New Friends

The honorarium for the Mexican lectures supplemented their income and things looked far rosier in 1942 than they had in their first year in the new country. But the financial situation was still bleak, with no permanent source of income and Ludwig's retirement fund frozen in Austria. On December 18, 1942 he reported on the activities of the year and applied for another extension of his research grant. He also tried to convince NBER to finance a large-scale research project to elucidate the origins of modern totalitarianism. He planned a comprehensive seminar with people like Rougier, Röpke, Hayek, and others. The project did not materialize, but his research grant was extended in January 1943. Mises even received a two-year extension under the same conditions as before. It was the normal policy of

---

[69]Mises to Rudolf Berthold, letter dated December 8, 1959; Grove City Archive: Berthold file. Among the few groups who showed any interest in his analysis of the necessity for and the problems of a postwar Eastern European Union was the (socialist) Central and Eastern European Planning Board, an organization that envisaged a postwar federation among Czechoslovakia, Greece, Poland, and Yugoslavia. See Olgierd Langer to Mises, letter dated February 18, 1943; Grove City Archive: "C" file.

the Rockefeller Foundation to subsidize the integration of European émigré scholars into American universities for about two years. Thus Mises could be happy to obtain twice as much support. However, it was to be the very end of their cooperation. The second year's bonus was a not-so-subtle good-bye. The Rockefeller Foundation's Willits made it clear, and NBER's Carson made it even more stark, that this extension would be the last one.[70]

Fortunately for Mises, he had found a more amenable source of support independent of the Rockefeller Foundation: the National Association of Manufacturers. NAM leadership opposed the New Deal and other statist projects. These men were determined to prepare a counterattack, starting a large-scale campaign to educate the American public about the benefits of what they called the free enterprise system. NAM needed intellectual leadership from people who were conversant both in the world of business and in the world of ideas. By February 1943, they had discovered what they were looking for in the person of Ludwig von Mises. Many years in the Vienna chamber of commerce had accustomed him to dealing with businessmen and to communicating effectively his economic and political insights to this audience. Just when the Rockefeller Foundation made it clear that they were no longer interested in supporting the Austrian economist, NAM immediately stepped in and offered to hire Mises as a consultant—"starting today."[71] Mises became a member of the Economic Policy Advisory Group. He later became a member of NAM's Economic Principles Commission and of its Advisory Group on International Economic Relations. The contract provided for an annual honorarium of $3,000,

---

[70]Meanwhile, Willits was on very good personal terms with Wesley C. Mitchell. See his letter to Mitchell dated January 2, 1944; Grove City Archive: AER files.

[71]Noel Sargent to Mises, letter dated February 10, 1943; Grove City Archive: NAM files.

which was 20 percent more than what Mises earned at NBER. The contract was extended on an annual basis. In the 1944–1945 period, Mises's honorarium increased to $3,600.[72]

Mises worked closely with NAM secretary Noel Sargent, who in 1943 commissioned a study from him on "international monetary reconstruction" after World War II. By the fall of the year, Mises had written a 68-page memorandum on the subject, in which he advocated a return to the gold standard and criticized reconstruction plans that Harry Dexter White and Keynes had made in preparation for the 1944 Bretton Woods conference. A few months later, he took part in a NAM-sponsored expert meeting to discuss the Keynes and White Proposals. The group included Rufus Tucker from General Motors, Princeton professor Edwin Kemmerer, and Mises's old acquaintance, Albert Hahn, who became a good friend during their years in Manhattan.

By June 1944, Mises had prepared another memorandum, this time on monopoly.[73] A few months later, he addressed two Advisory Committee luncheons on the West Coast. At that point, he had already acquired a solid reputation through the publication of *Bureaucracy* and *Omnipotent Government* in the same year by Yale University Press. Accordingly, he was presented as "the most eminent and uncompromising defender of English liberty and the system of free enterprise which has reached its highest development here in the United States."[74] He addressed the local NAM chapters in San Francisco (October

---

[72]His taxable income increased to almost $6,100 in 1943 and almost $7,100 in 1944. See tax returns in Grove City Archive: NBER files.

[73]Probably this is the manuscript that was published posthumously as "Monopoly Prices," *Quarterly Journal of Austrian Economics* 1, no. 2 (1998).

[74]Introduction to Mises's address to the Southern California NAM Advisory Committee meeting on October 18, 1944; Grove City Archive: NAM files.

18) and Los Angeles (October 25) and met "such excellent men as Leonard Read, [Orval] Watts and R.C. Hoiles."[75]

The encounter with Leonard Read was a fateful one. They may have met a few years earlier, shortly after his arrival in the United States. Read later recalled such a first meeting in 1940, at which he had been much impressed by the purity of Mises's opposition to any government power beyond the minimum necessary for the preservation of domestic peace and the market. Mises had reportedly attended a party in Read's home.[76] One of the other guests asked Professor Mises:

> All of us will agree with you that we are headed for troubled times but, Dr. Mises, let's assume that you were the dictator of these United States and could impose any changes you think appropriate. What would you do?

Read clearly recalled the answer:

Quick as a flash, Mises replied, "I would abdicate!"[77]

Mises had remained in touch with Read through correspondence. He may also have been on Read's mailing list and received one of the 1.5 million copies of Read's four-page pamphlet, "Why Not 1,900?"—a reaction against FDR's proposed

---

[75]Mises to Fuller, handwritten manuscript of a letter dated November 14, 1944; Grove City Archive: Fuller files. Read had invited Mises for a lecture on behalf of the Los Angeles Chamber of Commerce. He had learned about Mises's NAM-related trip to the West Coast through their mutual friend, Walter Sulzbach. See Read to Mises, letter dated August 7, 1944; Grove City Archive: Read files.

[76]Earliest extant correspondence started in June 1943, when Read asked Mises whether he would be ready to give lectures in the framework of a business education campaign. Read invited Mises for dinner to his house on October 19 or 20, 1944. See correspondence in Grove City Archive: Read files.

[77]Quoted from Mary Sennholz, *Leonard E. Read: Philosopher of Freedom* (Irvington-on-Hudson, N.Y.: Foundation for Economic Education, 1993) p. 145.

Leonard Read

legislation to seize all annual salaries in excess of $25,000. Read had argued that there was no objective reason not to seize all salary in excess of the national average salary, which happened to be $1,900.

Read was a self-made businessman who had spent the greater part of his career as an executive for various West-Coast chambers of commerce. He had the good luck to manage the chamber of Palo Alto in 1928, when that city's most prominent resident was elected president of the United States. Read organized a sort of a pilgrimage for 700 Californians to Washington, D.C., and caught the eye of Herbert Hoover's entourage. His career was made. He moved on to ever-higher positions within the larger network of California chambers of commerce and eventually became general manager of the world's largest chamber of commerce, in Los Angeles. By that time, he had become a champion of *laissez-faire* capitalism, had published his first book—a critique of New Deal economic policies—and had for many years managed the Western School for Commercial Organization Secretaries.

Once in his new position in Los Angeles, he hired V. Orval Watts, a professor of economics who had been a popular instructor at the Western School.[78] Watts thus became the first economist ever hired by a U.S. chamber of commerce on a full-time basis. Together they fought the New Deal rather effectively, organizing many courses and other educational conferences throughout California. Mises's lectures were part of this effort. On the evening of Tuesday, October 17, one day before his NAM luncheon talk, Mises gave a lecture to the Rotary

---

[78]Watts was a disciple of Harvard professor Thomas N. Carver, who had lectured for Read's Western School for Commercial Organization Secretaries in the 1930s. Watts took over from Carver when Carver's honorarium became unaffordable for Read.

Club on "credit expansion and depression" and that same evening addressed an audience at the Santa Ana High School on the "causes of the war." Mises stayed as a guest at the home of R.C. Hoiles, who published the predecessor of the present-day Orange County *Register*.[79] Several weeks before the talks, the Los Angeles Chamber of Commerce and the Register started promoting the event through articles and columns, and it turned out to be a success. Read in particular was much impressed by what he had seen and heard. A year later he would move to New York and eventually establish the mother of all libertarian think tanks in collaboration with Mises. The association would last for the rest of Mises's lifetime.

The alliance with NAM, in contrast, did not last long. Mises continued to "advise" NAM, co-authoring a two-volume study on the *American Individual Enterprise System*, which was published on April 1, 1946. The book was part of a large-scale NAM campaign aiming at the abolition of the wartime Office of Price Administration. The campaign succeeded and the Office expired, but so did Mises's contract. He continued to serve on NAM's Advisory Group on International Economic Relations, but resigned at the end of 1948, when NAM became increasingly agnostic on the question of inflation and its consequences. The final straw for Mises was when NAM started championing the view that increased productivity was the proper antidote to inflation.[80]

---

[79]See the 1944 correspondence in Grove City Archive: Hoiles files. Hoiles published several newspapers and had learned about Mises through Walter Sulzbach.

[80]Nymeyer to Brown, letter dated October 2, 1952; Grove City Archive: Nymeyer files. Many years later, he got another contract on the NAM staff, starting January 1954, for $6,000 per annum plus $2,400 expenses. Mises speaks about his first cooperation with NAM in a letter to Albert Hunold, dated December 27, 1947; Grove City Archive: Hunold files.

❧ ❧ ❧

At about the same time he began his work for NAM, Montes de Oca wrote from Mexico City that he had made good progress in the preparation of the International Institute of the Social Sciences. He now asked Mises to submit a list of prospective permanent professors, and some indication of the salaries they would require. Mises replied that Walter Sulzbach, Alfred Schütz, Louis Rougier, Jacques Rueff and he himself—all European expatriates living in New York without American citizenship—would be available for permanent employment in Mexico City for an annual compensation of some $6,000 per head. This was a fairly generous salary, and proved to be a major stumbling block for the establishment of the Institute. But in early 1943 everything seemed possible: a group of first-rate intellectuals with classical-liberal pedigree was at least potentially available and another group of men was interested in financing the venture. Moreover, there was a plan: Louis Rougier would be invited to the University of Mexico City for a series of lectures; Mises was to prepare a study on Mexican politico-economic conditions (which Montes de Oca had commissioned for his Banco Internacional); and Montes de Oca continued to work on a translation of *Socialism*.[81]

In planning for the future teaching staff of an institute in Mexico City, Mises had also brought up the names of Plant, Machlup, Rappard, Röpke, and Robbins.[82] He also made one

---

[81]See their correspondence of January and February 1943; Grove City Archive: Montes de Oca files.

[82]Mises to Montes de Oca, letter dated July 22, 1945; Grove City Archive: Montes de Oca files. It is not clear whether these were the only names he suggested, or if they were the only ones Montes de Oca mentioned in his reply. Mises had drafted a longer list of prospective staff (permanent and temporary), and also a short list of the subjects to be taught. The staff included: Machlup, Haberler, Nurkse, Sulzbach, Voegelin, Poetter, Schutz, Rougier,

last attempt to win Lionel Robbins over. In early 1943, he invited Robbins to come to New York. Robbins combined his scientific authority and personal network with great organizational skills and an unusual ability at clear and convincing expression in spoken and written language. The fate of Britain, and thus of Europe, depended on where he weighed in. Mises sought to get him out of his Cambridge and London milieu, to breathe the fresh air of liberty. But Robbins never came to New York: instead he became a champion of the British interventionist government.[83]

Mises eventually delivered the study on Mexican economic conditions to his Mexican friend when the latter came to New York in December 1944. Montes de Oca was now eager to have an epilogue for the forthcoming Spanish edition of *Socialism*.[84] He had still not given up on the Institute of the Social Sciences, although another problem besides the salary question had so far prevented any progress. Most of the prospective permanent and temporary teaching staff—Robbins, Plant, Machlup, Sulzbach, and others—were by then employed in war offices of the French, British, and U.S. governments, and were either unable

---

Kelsen, Hula, Rueff, Baudin, Hayek, Robbins, Plant, Hutt, Wiese, Einaudi, Rappard, Strigl, Heckscher, and Bourquin. The main subjects to be taught were (1) economics, (2) history and critical analysis of socio-economic doctrines in the last two hundred years, (3) constitutional history since 1776, (4) economic and social history since 1750, and (5) modern public finance. See Grove City Archive: Montes de Oca files.

[83]See correspondence from January 1943; Grove City Archive: Robbins files. There is no surviving correspondence between December 1935 and early January 1943; and then it was Robbins's wife Iris who wrote, thanking for a Christmas parcel with sweets (chocolate, lemon juice, and more) that the Miseses had sent. Two days later, her daughter Anne wrote too, and on January 25, Lionel himself also renewed their correspondence.

[84]Montes de Oca to Mises, letter dated January 2, 1945; Grove City Archive: Montes de Oca files.

or unwilling to leave until the war was over.[85] Montes de Oca invited Mises to return to Mexico City as a visiting professor during the year, but Mises declined because he planned to apply for U.S. citizenship in August—five years after his arrival—and sought to avoid any complications that might result from a trip abroad.

≼ ≼ ≼

Mises's social integration into the cosmopolitan milieu of New York accompanied a more general integration into American society. One sign of adjustment was the change of Mises's

Mises and Philip Cortney in the 1950s

manners, which became less formal in his dealings with friends. During 1942, when he wrote a series of editorials for the New York *Times* and other journals, Henry Hazlitt felt comfortable enough addressing his Austrian friend to leave behind the deferential "Professor Mises" in favor of "Dear Ludwig" (July 1942) and later "Dear Lou" (December 1942).

In April 1945, he made another important and lasting acquaintance, when he started correspondence with Philip Cortney, at the time the vice-chairman and treasurer of Coty, the perfume company. Mises wrote to congratulate Cortney on a paper in which he had criticized Keynesianism. Cortney, who already knew Mises's work, wrote back saying there was "no person in the world whose opinion I value more than yours"

---

[85] Mises to Montes de Oca, letter dated July 22, 1945; Grove City Archive: Montes de Oca files.

and that he hoped to meet him soon at dinner with their mutual friend, André Maurois.[86]

On the professional level, however, Mises's integration proceeded more slowly. The essential reason was his unwillingness to trade away his convictions for social acceptance. By 1944, he was a member of the New York Overseas Rotary Fellowship, which meant nothing to him—he found the meetings extremely boring and after a short while stopped attending them.[87] He also had some access to the national press through Hazlitt at the *Times*, but quickly ran into confrontations.

A case in point is a letter to the editor of the *New York Times* published on January 3, 1943. Here Mises explained that mere organizational devices would not make for world peace after the war. In particular, he rejected the idea that some new version of the League of Nations would make international relations better than they had been in the interwar period. Only a "radical change in political mentalities and social and economic ideologies" toward the classical-liberal position could make the world safe for peace and prosperity.[88] The letter provoked the editor of *Barron's* to solicit similar pieces from Mises.[89] But this cooperation was not fated to last very long. Mises contributed only one article on "Big Business and the Common Man," which was

---

[86]Cortney to Mises, letters dated April 9, 1945 and March 7, 1955; Grove City Archive: Cortney files. Mises had met Maurois at Louis Rougier's apartment in New York City. The dinner at Maurois's apartment probably took place on May 21 or 22, 1945. See Maurois to Mises, letter dated May 13, 1945; Grove City Archive: "M" files.

[87]Mises to R.C. Hoiles, letter dated June 21, 1944; Grove City Archive: Hoiles files.

[88]Mises, "Super-National Organization Held No Way to Peace: Radical Change in Political Mentalities and Social and Economic Ideologies Viewed as Necessary in Order to Eradicate Economic Nationalism," Letter to the Editor, *The New York Times* (January 3, 1943), p. E–8.

[89]George Shea to Mises, letter dated February 3, 1943; Grove City Archive: Barron's file.

published in February 1944 and only after sharp protestations from some "associate" of *Barron's*.[90] The essential point under contention was whether or not Mises had exaggerated in claiming that the inventive spirit was absent in Russia. Mises wrote:

> As far as I know the best that the Russians have achieved was imitating foreign models. The major attraction of their exhibitions at the World's Fairs in Paris and in New York were imitations of American agricultural implements and of Ford cars and tractors. Their planes and tanks were not original. Today they are fighting almost entirely with lend-lease material.
>
> Incidentally I want to remark that Germany also contributed very little to the improvement of weapons. The iron ship, the armored ship, the torpedo, the submarine, the plane, the machine-gun, the tank came from England, France and America. The German General Staff mistrusted the airplane and the tank and Tirpitz, before the first War, belittled the U-boat. The Zeppelin is a genuine German invention. But it is both commercially and militarily impracticable.[91]

The cooperation with *Barron's* ended soon after.

Similarly, Mises's integration into professional organizations of American economists suffered a setback. Just when Fritz Machlup joined the *AER* editorial board in October 1943, Mises felt he had to stop further cooperation with the journal. What had happened? He reviewed books for various journals, focusing on works dealing with postwar reconstruction in Europe. Two of

---

[90]Mises, "Big Business and the Common Man: High Living Standards in U.S. Came from Big Mass Production Enterprise," *Barron's* 24, no. 9 (February 28, 1944), p. 3.

[91]Mises to Shea, letter dated January 19, 1944; Grove City Archive: Barron's file. See also Mises to Stringham, letter dated June 13, 1946; Grove City Archive: "S" files.

these were invited reviews for the *American Economic Review*[92] and the *AER* had published a rejoinder by a certain Alfred Braunthal to the first of the two reviews, without giving Mises the opportunity to respond. To Mises this was a clear sign of discrimination. Writing to Machlup, Mises said that he was

> no longer prepared to contribute to a periodical whose editors fail to comply with the principles of literary decency for partisan considerations. They should rather send their books directly to Mr. Braunthal or other comrades.[93]

American Citizen

Mises had applied for citizenship at the earliest possible date—August 1945—and on January 14, 1946, he became an American citizen.[94]

One of the first things he did was to get in touch with his old employer to reclaim the retirement funds that he rightfully owned, but which had been denied to him in an August 1938

---

[92]Mises reviewed Adolf Sturmthal's *The Tragedy of European Labor, 1918–1939* (New York: Columbia University Press, 1943), *The American Economic Review* 33, no. 3 (September 1943): 702–05; as well as S. Leon Levy's *Nassau W. Senior: The Prophet of Modern Capitalism* (Boston: Bruce Humphries, 1943), *The American Economic Review* 34, no. 2 (June 1944): 359–61.

[93]Mises to Machlup, letter dated November 26, 1944; Grove City Archive: AER files. Five years later, he wrote in similar fashion to the dean of the School of Business Administration of the University of Buffalo: "Referring to your letter of May 11 I am sorry to inform you that I have no suggestions to offer for the program of the Econometric Society. Yours very truly etc." Mises to Somers, May 17, 1949; Grove City Archive: "S" files.

[94]Mises to Köhler, letter dated November 21, 1959; Grove City Archive: Köhler files. He renounced his title of hereditary Austrian nobility, but kept the name Ludwig *von* Mises as a *nom de plume*. See his curriculum vitae dated May 13, 1958; Grove City Archive: U.S. Army War College files.

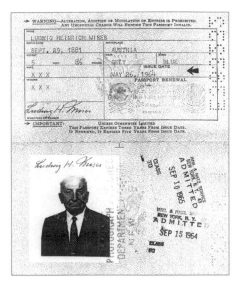

Mises's American passport issued on May 26, 1964

letter from a Nazi offi-cial.[95] He was told he was entitled to a monthly pay-ment of 953.95 schillings, starting May 1, 1945. The money was transferred to his old bank account in Vienna. Foreign exchange controls were still in place, however, and Mises could not transfer the money to an American account unless he provided an authorization from the Nationalbank.

Did he ever think about returning to Vienna? He did not. Mises was still in touch with some prewar acquain-tances, for example, with Carl Brockhausen and historian and writer Richard Charmatz. He had Idaho publisher J.H. Gipson send them CARE packages.[96] He also took care of the surviving

---

[95]Mises to Kammer, letter dated February 10, 1946; Grove City Archive: Kammer für Handel, Gewerbe und Industrie files.

[96]Gipson owned Caxton Printers Ltd. in Caldwell, Idaho. His brother was the noted American colonial historian Lawrence Henry Gipson. He made his money as a commercial printer and with an office supply company. The profits he invested in his hobby: publishing literature he personally liked, such as libertarian conservative books (for example, Albert J. Nock's *Our Enemy, The State* [1935], Garet Garrett's *The Revolution Was* [1938], and Erik von Kuehnelt-Leddihn's *Liberty or Equality* [1952]). Mises first met him in January 1947. Gipson spontaneously offered help for those Mises thought deserved support in the hard postwar years. Mises named three Austrians (Brockhausen, Charmatz, and Friedrich Köhler, his long-time attorney in Vienna), and three Germans (Passow, Eugen Fink, a professor of philosophy in Freiburg and former assistant to Edmund Husserl, and Karl Hagedorn,

mother of Ludwig Bettelheim-Gabillon, who had died at the hands of the Nazis.[97] Still Mises did not use the opportunity to visit Germany or Austria. Both countries were still occupation zones and access required special permits.[98] From correspondence with Charmatz he knew that Vienna was in even worse shape than after World War I, and this time lacked the leadership to prevent the rampant socialization of the entire country. As Charmatz wrote, many Austrians had been looking forward to allied victory, from which they expected liberation—quite literally. Instead they got even more government regimentation than before. Even the so-called "liberal" professions were now coerced into state-controlled organizations; and as in the worst years of the war, the population lived on food rations, the only difference being that the rations were smaller and that the food coupons could not always be redeemed.[99]

But Mises's disinclination to visit Vienna also had another source. As he wrote to his friend Carl Brockhausen, a former professor of constitutional and administrative law at the University of Vienna: "I do not yearn for an encounter with the mob who applauded the massacre of excellent men."[100] It is not

---

an attorney in Hamburg and friend of Margit's family). The next year, Gipson repeated his offer (and did so once more in the spring of 1953). Mises then brought Gipson in touch with Erik von Kuehnelt-Leddihn, who became another author of Caxton Printers. In a letter dated October 25, 1952, he enthusiastically endorsed Kuehnelt-Leddihn's *Liberty or Equality*, as well as three of Garrett's books (Grove City Archive: Gipson files).

[97]Mises to Hans Cohrssen, letter dated February 12, 1946; Grove City Archive: Cohrssen file. Mises here asks Cohrssen to transmit a food parcel to Helene Bettelheim-Gabillon.

[98]Elsa Brockhausen to Mises, letter dated May 4, 1947; Grove City Archive: Brockhausen file.

[99]Charmatz to Mises, letters dated February 26, 1947 and May 4, 1947; Grove City Archive: Charmatz file.

[100]"Ich sehne mich nicht danach, dem Pöbel zu begegnen, der bei dem Niedermetzeln ausgezeichneter Männer Beifall geklatscht hat." See Carl

quite clear whom Mises had in mind. The good-hearted Brock-hausen tried to convince Mises that this severe judgment was not borne out by the facts—there had been no lynch mobs in Vienna.[101] But by "mob" Mises probably meant men such as Hans Mayer, Othmar Spann, Srbik, and Nadler, who had actively supported the Nazi takeover of Austria and yet were once again in positions of influence. Mises did eventually make his way back to Vienna, but only to visit. ᦊ

Mises with Margit's grandson,
Chris Honeyman, in 1958

Brockhausen to Mises, letter dated July 22, 1947; Grove City Archive: Brockhausen file. Brockhausen brought this issue up in later letters too, asking Mises where he had received his information. In a letter dated July 4, 1949, Brockhausen, more than ninety years old, said he was about to look into the accounts of Nazi war crimes.

[101]In early March 1940, Mises had declared his readiness to contribute to the reconstruction of "our devastated [*verwüstetes*] Austria." See Mises to Plöchl, letter dated April 2, 1940; Grove City College Archive: Plöchl file. Clearly the early use of such vocabulary made it difficult to keep pace with the subsequent devastations.

Mises in 1956

19
Birth of a Movement

IF MISES EVER HAD any illusions about the state of the American mind before he came to the United States in 1940, he had certainly lost them by the end of the war. American public opinion was under the sway of statism and the old American liberties were at an all-time low. As Mises wrote to a German correspondent: "Unfortunately one can become acquainted with the fruits of the planned economy here in the U.S.A. too."[1] Similarly, to a promising young economist in Austria he wrote that the American literature on economics was, if anything, worse than the European:

> There is a great enthusiasm for unbalanced budgets, deficit spending, low interest rates and all sorts of regimentation. Those who dare to disagree are simply brushed aside as "orthodox and reactionary."[2]

---

[1]Mises to Johannes Bahner, letter dated June 12, 1947; Grove City Archive: "B" file. Johannes Bahner was the owner and CEO of the Elbeo textile corporation.

[2]Mises to Reinhard Kamitz, letter dated October 18, 1946; Grove City Archive: Kamitz file. Kamitz eventually became Minister of Finance and then president of the Österreichischen Nationalbank. Mises respected him very much and paid him the following tribute about his time as a Minister of Finance: "under the most adverse circumstances you have proved yourself to be a worthy successor to the two Pleners and to Böhm-Bawerk." Mises to Kamitz, letter dated November 14, 1961; Grove City Archive: Kamitz file.

And on the same theme:

> The intellectual ravages caused by Keynesianism are
> very bad. For example, everyone here is delighted
> that national income has "increased" from 77.6 bil-
> lion dollars in 1940 to 161.0 in 1945.[3]

But the forces of resistance were slowly emerging. There was
a seedbed of libertarian opposition, a network of leaders—
thinkers and organizers, some alone, others in small groups—
who were preparing the counterattack. One historian has called
these years "the nadir of individualistic, Jeffersonian thought in
the United States."[4] Yet the nadir was only in political *practice*.
The *thinking* was no longer in disarray, but in the initial phase of
a long-term resurgence. It is true that these thinkers and organizers were still scattered. They had only to find one another.

There were journalists like Henry Hazlitt, Lawrence Fertig,
Frank Chodorov, Suzanne LaFollette, Garet Garrett, John T.
Flynn, and John Chamberlain. There were writers like Albert J.
Nock, Isabel Paterson, Rose Wilder Lane, Ayn Rand, and Felix
Morley. There were organizers such as Leonard Read, Freder-
ick Nymeyer, and Loren Miller. There were businessmen ready
to sponsor educational ventures to promote *laissez-faire* policies,
such as Jasper Crane, Harry Earhart, Alfred Kohlberg, Howard
Pew, Claude Robinson, Pierre Goodrich, and William Volker.
And there were academics such as Benjamin Anderson, H.J.
Davenport, Fred Fairchild, Leo Wolman, Frank Knight, Henry
Simons, and Ludwig von Mises. These men and women
reversed the course of events in a mere fifteen years. They were
not strong enough to rid America of its creeping statism, but
they succeeded in slamming on the brakes and reorienting public debate.

---

[3]Mises to Hans Ilau, letter dated May 17, 1947; Grove City Archive:
NAM files.

[4]Robert M. Crunden, *The Mind and Art of Albert Jay Nock* (Chicago:
Henry Regnery, 1964), p. 179.

By the beginning of the 1960s, classical liberalism had risen from the ashes, and it had done so under the decisive impact and intellectual leadership of Mises.[5] These fifteen years of his life saw a last great blossoming of his creative powers, which paved the way for a new liberty in the western world. During this period, Mises's impact was amplified and deepened through several new organizations that rallied a hitherto disparate and unaware public around the banner of liberty. And for the first time in his life, Mises worked on a permanent basis with a group of students who had learned economic science through his writings. These first Misesians soon became even more coherent and radical advocates of *laissez-faire* than the master himself—something unprecedented for Mises: in his Vienna seminars, he had been in the awkward position of being more radical than his students.

Libertarian Seedbeds

Many Americans had grown weary of the New Deal during the second term of President Roosevelt's administration. More and more people realized that their president had brought about a revolution in the American system of government. But the majority gave FDR a third term. The president promised to keep America out of the new European war that would eventually turn into World War II. When Roosevelt went back on his word, the majority started to wane. The population still stood behind the commander in chief in a time of war, but the disenchantment with New Deal policies became ever more manifest. People started listening to critical voices, and these voices could now be heard everywhere.

Isabel Paterson in *The God of the Machine* (1943) and Rose Wilder Lane in *The Discovery of Freedom* (1942) had delivered passionate and widely noticed indictments of the omnipotent

---

[5]Julian Joseph DelGaudio, *Refugee Economist in America: Ludwig von Mises and American Social and Economic Thought, 1940–1986* (Ann Arbor, Mich.: University Microfilms International, 1988).

Top: *Isabel Paterson, Albert Jay Nock, John T. Flynn, Rose Wilder Lane*
bottom: *Henry Hazlitt, Benjamin Anderson, Frank Chodorov, and John Chamberlain*

state undermining individual liberty. John T. Flynn had exposed the socialist agenda and impact of the federal government's interventions in *The Roosevelt Myth* (1948) and *As We Go Marching* (1945). In early 1944, Felix Morley, John Chamberlain, and Frank Hanighen founded the weekly journal *Human Events*. Their mission was to educate the American public about the uncomfortable fact that their federal government had been taken hostage by socialist and Communist ideologues. The public also listened for the first time to the voice of two Austrian émigrés. Mises came out with two books in 1944: *Omnipotent Government* and *Bureaucracy*, both of which were calculated to diminish the faith in the necessity and expediency of solving social problems with the brutal force of state power. And in the same year Friedrich August Hayek published *The Road to Serfdom*, the book that made him famous.

Intellectuals held no monopoly on critical inquiry into the nature and scope of the Roosevelt government. Ordinary citizens without any scientific pretensions now rediscovered the old

American virtue of distrusting their government. Wherever they looked, they found their worst fears confirmed. And now they not only noticed, but also recorded and spread their discoveries. One example illustrates the situation: An entrepreneur from Houston running a small printing company had started wondering just how many federal agencies had actually been created under the New Deal. There was no ready reference for the information, so he decided to create one himself. He produced an alphabetical listing of all the agencies, the length of which must have been breathtaking—at least in those days. At first he had just printed a small number of flyers for his friends, acquaintances, and people on his local mailing list. The response was overwhelming. After a few months, he had sold almost 200,000 copies—and in each case it was the buyer who approached him.[6]

The most visible turning point for the fortunes of classical liberalism came on September 18, 1944. On this day, F.A. Hayek's book *The Road to Serfdom* appeared in the United States and met with huge and immediate success. *Reader's Digest* condensed the book and had more than one million copies distributed by the Book-of-the-Month Club.[7] Overnight, Hayek became an international celebrity.

Nobody was more surprised by these events than Hayek and his publisher. There were four major factors to his unexpected success. First, Hayek did not come up with any new argument, but just gave a particularly eloquent and sophisticated presentation of a position that, before the war, had already found wide acclaim among the American public. The central argument of *The Road to Serfdom* was in fact that increased powers for government were tantamount to reduced sovereignty for the individual

---

[6]E.M. Biggers to Congressman H.P. Fullmer, letter dated June 5, 1943; Grove City Archive: "B" files.

[7]George H. Nash, *The Conservative Intellectual Movement in America Since 1945* (New York: Basic Books, 1976), pp. 6f.

citizens, and that total government control turned the citizens into slaves—regardless of whether the totalitarian state was fascist or Communist. Second, the war years had dramatically accelerated this increase of powers of the U.S. federal government and thus raised awareness of and misgivings about this fact among a greater number of people. Third, again echoing other neo-liberals, Hayek defended what seemed to be a pragmatic middle-of-the-road solution that appealed to the American mind. He emphasized that he did not advocate *laissez-faire* but a new brand of liberalism.[8] Fourth, and finally, Hayek weighed in with the full authority of an academic economist who was well-known and respected in the United Kingdom, a fact that to the present day can arouse Americans' intellectual inferiority complex.

For staunch defenders of liberty, Hayek's neo-liberalism was of course far too soft on government. The positive program of *The Road to Serfdom* left the government in control of economic life. The economy was still to be a planned one, with the government in charge of all the planning. Hayek merely suggested that this planning be for competition rather than the detailed control of all market participants. This was a naïve approach from any realistic political point of view, and some thought it was indefensible from an intellectual point of view as well. Commenting on Hayek's program, Frank Chodorov exclaimed: "How silly!" and made it clear that he thought the program verged on intellectual cowardice.[9]

Mises was very happy about the success of the book. However, he too thought that Hayek had made his case in misleading terms. Hayek had singled out economic planning as the root cause of the various policies that threatened political and economic freedom. But there is no danger in planning *per se*. The

---

[8]F.A. Hayek, *The Road to Serfdom* (Chicago: University of Chicago Press, 1944), pp. 17, 36.

[9]Frank Chodorov, "What This Country Needs Is Guts," *analysis* 2 (February 1946): 3.

real question is: *who* should do the planning, and how should the plans be applied? Should there be only one plan imposed by the power of the state on all citizens? Or should there be many different plans, made by each individual or head of household? Mises emphasized this crucial distinction in a speech delivered on March 30, 1945 to the American Academy of Political Science. He left implicit the fact that his speech was a critical review of Hayek's book.[10]

A few days later, on April 3, Hayek arrived in New York to start a *Road to Serfdom* lecture tour. It was the first time he saw his old mentor in America.[11] The book and the lecture tour trumpeted the dawn of a new era. The sale of thousands of copies signaled to everyone that the American population still harbored strong affections for liberal ideas, and that these feelings had huge political potential.

The most momentous initiative to exploit this potential was, we can see in retrospect, the decision of Leonard Read to quit his lucrative position at the Los Angeles chamber of commerce

---

[10]Mises's speech was first published as "Planning for Freedom," together with a speech by Rufus S. Tucker, delivered before the same audience, in a 24-page pamphlet: *Economic Planning* (New York: Dynamic America, 1945), pp. 3–12. Later the essay was reprinted in Mises's book *Planning for Freedom* (South Holland, Ill.: Libertarian Press, 1952). In correspondence with A. Dauphin Meunier, a professor in Paris, Mises mentioned that he disliked the title and subtitles of the printed version of his talk. The French translation was published in 1947 in the *Revue de l'Économie Contemporaine* under the title "L'interventionnisme et le salaire." See Grove City Archive: Dauphin Meunier file. In a letter to Selma Fuller, Mises praises the virtues of *Road to Serfdom*, but concedes the appropriateness of Fuller's critical stance on the book.

> The positive program developed by Hayek matters little when compared with these virtues of his book. However, it is a very comforting fact that your friends were shrewd enough to see the contradictions in this program. (Mises to Fuller, handwritten manuscript of a letter dated November 14, 1944; Grove City Archive: Fuller files)

[11]Mises to Montes de Oca, handwritten manuscript of a letter dated April 3, 1945; Grove City Archive: Montes de Oca files.

at the end of April 1945, and to move to New York as an Executive Vice President of the National Industrial Conference Board. Read sensed the potential for a huge interest in *laissez-faire* liberalism and its underpinnings in economic science *à la* Mises. And he understood that liberty had to be defended as an integrated whole, not in a piecemeal fashion with many concessions. But looking around in 1945, he was amazed to discover that there was not one institution to satisfy this demand for information, and certainly none ready to support or promote classical-liberal scholars and students. Many years later, he summarized his discoveries in four points:

> Number one, [the freedom philosophy] wasn't issuing from any place on the face of the earth. Number two, there wasn't a magazine in the country that would take one of our articles. Three, there wasn't a book publisher that would take one of our books. Number four, just twenty-six years ago [in 1945] there did not exist a consistent literature of this philosophy written in modern American idiom. That's how far down the drain this philosophy was.[12]

The National Industrial Conference Board was an educational institution the purpose of which was to provide information about economic science and the functioning of the American economy to classroom teachers all over the country. Read had been hired along with Garet Garrett and others to establish a new nationwide educational program. The express purpose of the new program was to inform teachers, journalists, and intellectuals (the "secondhand dealers in ideas" as Hayek called them[13]) about the importance of individual liberty for economic

---

[12]Read in an interview with George H. Nash, quoted in Nash, *The Conservative Intellectual Movement in America*, pp. 22f.

[13]F.A. Hayek, "The Intellectuals and Socialism," *University of Chicago Law Review* 16 (1949): 417–33, reprinted in Bruce Caldwell, ed., *The Collected Works of F.A. Hayek*, vol. 10: *Socialism and War: Essays, Documents, Reviews* (Chicago: University of Chicago Press, 1997), p. 222.

prosperity and society at large. Read's mission was to raise the necessary funds.

Mises was aware of Read's effort. When, in May 1945, he received a request from Mr. Allman, the vice president of the Fruehauf Trailer Company, inquiring what could be done in terms of organizational work to give the "individual, private enterprise way of living and doing business" political leverage, Mises replied that friends of his were elaborating a plan for imminent action.[14] He had probably talked again with Read about his pet project: the establishment of a libertarian journal of opinion. *Human Events* had been launched the year before, but Mises was not happy with its one-sided focus on anti-Communism. The problem was not just the increase of government interventionism in the name of Communist ideals; the problem was that the government intervened at all. A libertarian journal of opinion would have to educate the public about basic economic laws.

The Long Visit at New York University

One great limitation to Mises's effectiveness in spreading the gospel of liberty was that he lacked an academic base. Like most other champions of the free market, he frequently lectured to businessmen and other civic leaders. But he had no direct impact on future intellectuals who studied at the universities. It was quite often a frustrating experience for him. In a letter to Machlup he wrote:

> Again and again various organizations invite me to refute Marxism and the union doctrine (which are held to be identical), and as an aside also Keynes and Hansen, in a short paper that can be read in not more than thirty minutes and which every high-school

---

[14]Allman to Mises, letter dated May 10, 1945; Mises to Allman, letter dated May 18, 1945; Grove City Archive: "A" files.

graduate can easily understand. "Refute Marx, but don't use high-brow terms such as value, dialectical materialism, average rate of profit, etc. Refute Keynes, but do not speak of the multiplier, of liquidity preference, etc."[15]

Unlike many of his former students and associates, Mises had been unable to obtain a suitable position at one of the major universities.[16] He had offers from smaller schools such as the University of Rochester, but would not settle for second-rate institutions. At some point in 1944, some of his friends and admirers in New York took the initiative to provide him a visiting professorship at New York University. Led by Lawrence Fertig, an NYU trustee, these men eventually came to an agreement with NYU's Graduate School of Business Administration: the School would invite Mises to give an economics seminar, and Mises's salary would be from private funds.[17] This arrangement continued on a regular basis. Mises started his

---

[15]Mises to Machlup, letter dated December 15, 1946; Grove City Archive: Machlup files.

[16]Herbert von Beckerath, Goetz Briefs, Gottfried von Haberler, Georg Halm, and Joseph Schumpeter had obtained positions at Harvard; Machlup was at the new (Rockefeller-funded) University of Buffalo, and Morgenstern at Princeton. Apparently they were all unwilling or unable to get Mises into their departments.

[17]Nash, *The Conservative Intellectual Movement in America*, pp. 13, 351, n. 47. Nash mentions that Hazlitt and Read were among those involved. Nash also mentions (ibid., p. 20) that Hayek's position at the University of Chicago was similarly subsidized out of private funds. It is not clear who, apart from Fertig, contributed to paying Mises's salary. It is however most likely that a major part of the money came from the Volker Fund. Other potential donors were among the men who would later back *The Freeman*, in particular Alfred Kohlberg (importer), Jasper Crane, Howard Pew (Sun Oil), Herbert Hoover (former U.S. president), W. Prentis (Armstrong Cork), W.F. Peter (Chicago, Rock Island, and Pacific Railroad). See Charles H. Hamilton, "*The Freeman*: The Early Years," R. Lora and W.H. Longton, eds., *The Conservative Press in Twentieth-Century America* (London: Greenwood, 1999).

Mises's NYU seminar met in the Gallatin House on the campus of NYU

classes in February 1945.[18] He was a "visiting" professor at NYU for more than twenty years.[19]

Despite the humiliating circumstances, the seminar proved to be an enormous success. From the outset, it was not only attended by NYU business students, but also attracted a colorful group of personalities from outside: journalists, businessmen, writers, and students from other universities. In a manner reminiscent of Mises's seminars in Vienna, it became a rallying point for New York-based intellectuals interested in the scientific case for *laissez-faire*, as well as a point of attraction for visitors from abroad. In Vienna, the Mises Circle would move from Mises's *Kammer* offices to Ancora Verde for dinner, then to the Café Künstler to continue the conversation late into the night. In New York, the participants in Mises's NYU seminar could follow the classroom session by joining their professor in Child's Restaurant, followed by the Café Lafayette.

Seminar students such as Hans Sennholz, William Peterson, George Reisman, Israel Kirzner, and Ralph Raico eventually formed—together with Murray Rothbard—the solid core of Misesians to hold out through the long libertarian winter of

---

[18]Mises to Machlup, letter dated December 26, 1944; Hoover Institution: Machlup-Mises correspondence file.

[19]When he was looking for a job right after his arrival in the United States, Machlup had brought him in touch with New York University's department of economics. In November 1940, the department head (Spahr) invited Mises to give a talk on his contributions to economic theory. Spahr was slow (or unwilling) to follow up with a job offer and Mises then accepted the position at NBER.

the 1960s and 1970s, thus enabling the breakthrough of Misesian ideas of the 1980s and 1990s. Mises inspired them to contribute to the great project of hammering out a systematic and encompassing libertarian philosophy—a project that had attracted courageous and innovative thinkers from the time of the sixteenth-century Spanish late scholastics to the time of the Manchester School. In retrospect, the results can only be called amazing. It is one thing indeed for students to follow the example of a passionate and encouraging teacher. It is quite another thing to actually produce anything of value. A surprising number of Mises's NYU students later became important scholars and even pioneers in economics, history, and philosophy.

One example of the international significance of the seminar was the case of the Japanese students drawn to attend. Mises's prewar work had been favorably received in Japan and several professors from this far-eastern country had taken part in his Vienna seminar. After the war, a correspondent from the Yasuda Bank wrote Mises that his *Theory of Money and Credit* had "made a very strong impression in Japanese financial circles and is regarded most highly."[20] The impact would increase when a Japanese edition appeared in May 1949—just in time to provide intellectual ammunition against the wave of Keynesianism that swept the country with the American occupation forces.[21] One

---

[20]Yoneo Azuma to Mises, letter dated July 13, 1948; Grove City Archive: Azuma file. Azuma was a student of Mitsutaro Araki, to whom Mises had already in 1925 granted permission to translate and publish *Theory of Money and Credit*. Araki never completed the translation, but his student finished it in the early years of the war. When he wrote to Mises in 1948, the manuscript of the translation had survived the war years in a vault of the publisher. Azuma also kept Mises informed about intellectual developments in Japanese economics.

[21]Machlup reported a few years later from a meeting with Japanese colleagues in Tokyo: "there was a discussion of whether certain parts of your *Theory of Money* were already in the first edition or only added in the second edition. There were several present who were able to discuss this question."

classical-liberal from Japan later recalled the chain of events in his country:

> The names of von Mises and Hayek are well known in Japan. The latter's *Road to Serfdom* was published, during the War about the time when Japan started experimenting in state socialism; my own experience confirms completely the exactness of the professor's prognostications. When the War was over, we had to throw everything overboard and I expected a return to free enterprise. Then a curious thing happened; the Americans arriving in Japan in the wake of the landing forces started putting into effect policies which were hardly distinguishable from state socialism![22]

Leonard Read and FEE

About a year after the inception of Mises's NYU lectures, another institution would be established that would prove to be a pillar of the classical-liberal renaissance and give further leverage to Mises's ideas. Leonard Read had come to the conclusion that his engagement with the National Industrial Conference Board was a waste of time and money. One of the main reasons for this ineffectiveness was that the Board was committed to a policy of "hearing both sides." In practice this meant, for example, that at the bimonthly public conferences that the Board sponsored at the Waldorf-Astoria, both the champions of the free market and the advocates of government intervention were granted equal time to present their cases. Leonard Read believed this policy was based on a severe misunderstanding of

---

See Machlup to Mises, letter dated March 28, 1955; Hoover Institution: Machlup-Mises correspondence file.

[22]Jujiro Iwai to Nymeyer, letter dated January 23, 1952; Grove City Archive: Nymeyer files.

what hearing both sides truly meant in the present context. In the words of his biographer:

> The "other side" was everywhere—in government, education, and communication. Even businessmen had come to rely on government for restrictions of competition, for government contracts and orders, easy money and credit, and other favors. . . . How do you present "both sides" when "one side" is all around you, pre-empting the public discussion, and the "other side" is barely audible in the deafening noise of the former?[23]

Read thought any funds spent on yet another presentation of the statist view was money down the drain, and he felt he could not in good conscience justify this expenditure. At the end of 1945, he resigned his position and started visiting the donors to apologize.[24] One of them, New York City businessman Pierre Goodrich, encouraged Read to think about setting up his own organization. Two months later, Read established the Foundation for Economic Education (FEE), which in July 1946 would move to the pastoral premises in Irvington-on-Hudson, several miles north of Manhattan, where it is still located.

Read mobilized substantial corporate backing for this venture. He had a full address book and was personally acquainted

---

[23]Mary Sennholz, *Leonard E. Read: Philosopher of Freedom* (Irvington-on-Hudson, N.Y.: Foundation for Economic Education, 1993), p. 69.

[24]Mises continued to be invited to other NICB conferences. For example, on May 16, 1946, he discussed the subject of postwar interest rates with Woodlief Thomas (a Federal Reserve economist), Friedrich Lutz, and Paul Samuelson. And on January 22, 1948, he took part in a symposium that dealt with the question: "Should we return to a gold standard?" Here he met Philip Cortney; among the other contributors were Albert Hahn and Michael Heilperin. See Grove City Archive: NICB files. He was probably also instrumental in providing his friend Walter Sulzbach with a job at NICB in 1946 or 1947; see Grove City Archive: Sulzbach file.

with many executives and owners of the large corporations, some of whom also joined FEE as trustees.

The main activity of FEE was to send out pamphlets and letters explaining the "freedom thesis" to some 30,000 households.[25] Read himself gave a great number of public lectures and together with his other staff, he would soon start offering weekend seminars and other educational programs. The pamphlets and conferences brought students throughout the country in touch with the writings of

Foundation for Economic Education, Irvington-on-Hudson, New York

Mises and other champions of classical liberalism. Mises himself was one of the first economists hired for lectures and seminars on FEE's premises, and would eventually become its intellectual center for more than two decades.[26]

It would be hard to overstate the significance of the appearance of FEE. Though its activities were not noticed by a larger national audience, the very existence of this organization gave the scattered classical-liberal forces focus and orientation. It gave them what they had not had since the heyday of nineteenth-century liberalism: a home. FEE provided the material and infrastructure for an enthusiastic return to the ideals of the nineteenth-century *laissez-faire* liberals. To the key question about the proper functions of government, FEE's Manchesterian

---

[25]The number of 30,000 was attained by early 1949. See Read's memorandum dated March 23, 1949; Grove City Archive: FEE files.

[26]He was "paid a uniform amount at regular intervals" and therefore became, for technical reasons (tax laws), an employee of FEE in October 1946. See Curtiss to Mises, letter dated October 8, 1946; Grove City Archive: FEE files.

Larry Fertig, Mises, Leonard Read, and Henry Hazlitt

answer was that government should be strictly limited to the prevention of "aggressive force" or physical violence.[27]

Most importantly, it attracted young people interested in the intellectual case for liberty and ultimately brought Mises in touch with a self-selected group of students, who were much more receptive to the political implications of his ideas than were many of the attendees of his NYU seminar. Several students he first met at FEE conferences later joined the weekly seminar at NYU, where Mises could go into much more detail.

Last but not least, FEE provided some intellectual counterweight to the neo-liberal orthodoxy that was about to emerge from the University of Chicago's economics department. In 1947 and 1948 respectively, Frank Knight and Henry Simons (posthumously) had published collections of articles making their case for a libertarianism that was so watered-down as to be indistinguishable from social democracy.[28] Other members of the Chicago School were Aaron Director and Milton Friedman. FEE's impact was of course comparatively minor, but without it,

---

[27]See Nash, *The Conservative Intellectual Movement in America*, p. 24.

[28]Frank Knight, *Freedom and Reform* (New York: Harper, 1947); Henry C. Simons, *Economic Policy for a Free Society* (Chicago: University of Chicago Press, 1948).

the Chicago School would have totally dominated the American free-market scene.

Frederick Nymeyer

At about the same time Read was setting up FEE in Irvington, New York, Mises made another acquaintance who would eventually turn into a long-term ally. In May 1946, Chicago businessman Frederick Nymeyer had finished reading Mises's *Theory of Money and Credit*, which prompted him to write to the author and inquire about any further writings of his on the subject.[29] During the following months, Nymeyer read *Omnipotent Government* and other available English-language writings of the Austrian professor. He was the ideal reader for Mises. He had received his economics education in the early 1920s, then worked for a while as a field representative of the Harvard Business Cycle Index. He was well acquainted with the monetary thought that prevailed in the United States. The *Theory of Money and Credit*, he found, "was a radically different approach than the mechanical Quantity theory" and he therefore "had some difficulty to adjust all my thinking to your exposition." Part of the difficulty seemed to be the different use of terms, and Nymeyer then went on to raise questions about one of the crucial concepts of the theory: the demand for money.[30] Mises agreed that the way he had put it—the demand for money being the demand for purchasing power—was ambiguous, and that a better way of putting it was to say that the market participants had a demand for cash holdings. He promised to revise his writings accordingly and to consider this point in his forthcoming treatise on economics.

---

[29]Nymeyer to Mises, letter dated May 20, 1946; Grove City Archive: Nymeyer files.

[30]Nymeyer to Mises, letter dated June 12, 1947; Grove City Archive: Nymeyer files.

This exchange was the beginning of a long-lasting alliance (though never really more than a personal friendship). Nymeyer soon commenced to read other Austrian works available in English, in particular Böhm-Bawerk's *Capital and Interest*. Slowly, he became a dedicated admirer of the Austrian School. He was also a dedicated Calvinist and claimed, "Böhm-Bawerk has gone as far beyond Adam Smith as Calvin did beyond Luther."[31]

Mises's agnosticism did not diminish Nymeyer's admiration for the Austrian economist. And it did not prevent Mises himself from cooperating openly and productively with Christian libertarians in America. In Austria, such cooperation was almost out of the question, because the Christian Socialists had pushed the Catholic Church into an intellectual dead end. Only outstanding personalities such as Monsignor Seipel could overcome the socialist resentments against the liberal Mises. But in the States, things were different. A great number of the Protestant clergymen in America loved individual liberty and the free market and considered this love to result quite naturally from their Christian religion. Many of these men felt that Mises's theories were complementary to their faith.

In correspondence with a high clergyman of the Church of England in Canada, who had read *Human Action*, Mises wrote:

> I fully agree with your statement that the Gospels do not advocate anticapitalistic policies. I dealt with this problem years ago in my book *Socialism*. . . . I furthermore fully agree with your proposition that one does not find in *Human Action* "one word which is in opposition to the Christian faith."[32]

---

[31]Nymeyer to Mortimer Adler, letter dated February 14, 1948; Grove City Archive: Nymeyer files.

[32]Mises to P.C. Armstrong, letter dated January 16, 1950; Grove City Archive: Armstrong file.

Mises enthusiastically welcomed the publication of the monthly periodical *Faith and Freedom* by Spiritual Mobilization, a Los Angeles based organization in December 1949. Of course he knew very well that the majority of Protestant leaders championed some form of socialism or interventionism, and that while the Catholic Church "valiantly fights communism," it did not oppose socialism. But these problems were outside of his field: "I think that only theologians are called to deal with the issue."

This was also the opinion of Frederick Nymeyer. One of the mainsprings of his motivation for spreading Mises's writings was precisely the complementary relation he perceived between *laissez-faire* capitalism and Christianity.

Mises and Nymeyer probably met for the first time in late January 1948. Nymeyer then started thinking about why the Austrian School of economics was not prevalent in the United States and he came to the conclusion that Austrian works were not sufficiently well known. In the fall of that year, he was ready to take action, relying in particular on his voluminous address book ("I know several of the outstanding entrepreneurs in the country. I sit on some important Boards of Directors."[33]). And at the end of January 1949, after several more encounters with Mises, Nymeyer came up with a plan: The idea was to set up a "Liberal Institute" under Mises's leadership at the University of Chicago—Nymeyer was a friend of the dean of the business school—or at some other suitable university in the Chicago area.[34] Nymeyer had already won over his associate Robert W. Baird and his friend John T. Brown, vice-president of the J.I. Case Company. By May 1949 they had talked to several other businessmen in the area.

---

[33]Nymeyer to Mises, letter dated October 12, 1948; Grove City Archive: Nymeyer files.

[34]Nymeyer to Mises, letter dated January 25, 1949; Grove City Archive: Nymeyer files.

At the end of April, the university had told Nymeyer that they would favor "unrestricted gifts" to be used with "academic freedom"—which meant that the university would select the staff of the proposed Liberal Institute. Mises commented:

> Based on this slogan ["academic freedom"] the universities are boycotting all those economists who dare to raise objections against interventionism from another point of view than that of socialism. The question of academic freedom is today not: should communist teachers be tolerated? It is rather: should only communists, socialists or interventionists be appointed?[35]

But the resistance did not come only from within the universities. A few years later (and that much the wiser), Mises acknowledged the existence of another factor:

> One of the worst features of the present state of affairs is the misplaced loyalty of the alumni. As soon as somebody dares to criticize something concerning a university, all alumni come to the rescue of their alma mater. Then we have the spectacle of big business defending the boycott launched by the faculties against all those who do not sympathize with interventionism, planning and socialism.[36]

In any case, the plan for a Chicago-based "Liberal Institute" under Mises's leadership did not materialize. But Nymeyer and his friends probably had some influence in bringing Hayek to Chicago, and in the early 1950s he played a significant role in raising funds for Mont Pèlerin Society meetings.[37]

---

[35]Mises to Nymeyer, handwritten manuscript of a letter in response to Nymeyer's letter dated April 26, 1949; Grove City Archive: Nymeyer files.

[36]Mises to Nymeyer, letter dated May 17, 1952; Grove City Archive: Nymeyer files.

[37]Nymeyer to Hayek and others, correspondence of spring and summer 1952; Grove City Archive: Nymeyer files.

Mises Debates American Libertarians

With the NYU seminar, FEE, and individual organizers and publishers such as Nymeyer, Mises enjoyed for the very first time in his entire life a truly congenial network of students and supporters. He had always been a respected scholar, but few of his readers and associates really appreciated the radical anti-statist gist of his theories. This held true in particular in the case of the neo-liberals, who prided themselves on their pragmatic position and on their good sense in wanting to place the government to be in charge of creating competition. These men accused Mises of exaggerated logical argument in the intellectual battle for liberty. If this is a valid charge, then Mises was surely guilty. As one historian put it, he fought "with a supreme logical rigor that even his friends sometimes considered excessive."[38] An example of such a friend was Chicago professor of economics Henry C. Simons, who praised Mises as "the greatest living teacher of economics" and "the toughest old liberal or Manchesterite of his time." But alas, he added, "he is also perhaps the worst enemy of his own libertarian cause."[39]

Things were completely different in the circle of his new friends. Many of the new people who came to Mises through his NYU seminar and FEE were even more libertarian than he was. Suddenly it was Mises who on several occasions turned out to represent the more statist position in his seminar. American libertarians such as Leonard Read and R.C. Hoiles placed great emphasis on the definition of political liberty in terms of non-initiation of force. After the publication of *Human Action*, for example, Hoiles criticized Mises in private correspondence for having admitted that public education "can work very well" in monolingual countries if it is limited

---

[38]Nash, *The Conservative Intellectual Movement in America*, p. 10.

[39]Henry C. Simons, *Annals of the American Academy of Political and Social Science* 236 (November 1944): 192.

to reading, writing, and arithmetic. Hoiles saw this as an unnecessary concession. Public education, even if limited to the case under discussion, was unjustifiable:

> the fact that some people were compelled to pay who did not want to have their children taught or who had no children, was teaching by example that the majority had a right to coerce the minority to pay for anything the majority wanted. If that is not the worst kind of government intervention, I do not know what intervention means.
>
> When you make this one concession you are denying that our government is limited in what it has a right to do. It seems to me that intervention by the government is just the same thing as initiating force. Understand, I am not opposed to the use of force to stop someone from initiating force, but the government has no right to initiate force. The only purpose of a government is to stop people from intervening in an unhampered market and to stop people from initiating force to make someone pay for anything he doesn't want to pay for.[40]

This perspective was entirely outside Mises's utilitarian approach to political problems. He believed that the question of who initiated force was politically irrelevant because one could hardly ever reach agreement on it. The only relevant question was whether the initiation of force was suitable to attain the end of the acting person, even if his action was somehow wrong from an ethical point of view. A two-sentence letter he sent some ten years later to an American correspondent, a publisher in Wisconsin, speaks volumes: "I read your stimulating letter with great interest. As I see it, the main argument in favor of the

---

[40]Hoiles to Mises, letter dated September 7, 1949; Grove City College Archive: Hoiles file.

capitalist system is that it has raised the standard of living of the common man in an unprecedented way."[41]

Another, even more substantial point of disagreement between Mises and many American libertarians was the question of democracy. A few months after FEE set up shop, F.A. "Baldy" Harper saw the need to write a four-page confidential memorandum defending Mises's views on democracy against the criticisms of Orval Watts, who had pitted democracy against American-style liberalism.[42] Mises would also come to taste the particular American flavor of hostility to democracy in a 1947 exchange of letters with Rose Wilder Lane. Apparently they had met for lunch with Hoiles and others, and Lane had the impression that Mises believed they shared the same outlook on fundamentals. At the meeting she did not feel it was the right moment to start a discussion on the subject, but later wrote him to set the record straight:

> as an American I am of course fundamentally opposed to democracy and to anyone advocating or defending democracy, which in theory and practice is the basis of socialism.
>
> It is precisely democracy which is destroying the American political structure, American law, and the American economy, as Madison said it would, and as Macauley [sic] prophesied that it would do in fact in the 20th century.[43]

Mises did not even bother to address the issue, but observed that he never addressed people who called his writings "stuff"

----

[41]Mises to M.H. Johnson, letter dated October 25, 1956; Grove City Archive: "J" files.

[42]See the memorandum dated January 13, 1947 in Grove City Archive: FEE files.

[43]Lane to Mises, letter dated July 5, 1947; Grove City Archive: Lane files.

and "nonsense"—as Lane had done in a book review.[44] And that
was that for more than two years, after which the debate
resumed on more civilized terms, probably because of Lane's
friendship with Howard Pew. Mises's basic objection to Lane
was that she had misunderstood him. He had never advocated
any concrete regime of parliamentary democracy. He merely
stressed the fact that all political systems ultimately hinge on
mass opinion.[45]

Mises's American friends disagreed and the discussions and
correspondence between them remained without conclusion.
But the confrontation between the Austrian scholar and his
American readers and disciples would be a driving force in the
development of libertarian theory. Mises's student Murray Rothbard would eventually work out the radical implications of Misesian economics with great care, combining the non-initiation-
of-force criterion with the typical Misesian focus on private
property rights. Rothbard thus created the blend of libertarian
economics and natural-law ethics that continues to attract many
intellectuals to this day.

The new radical environment contrasted sharply with the
mentality of Mises's old associates, who had been libertarians by
central European standards, but were moderate interventionists
in an American context. A case in point was Fritz Machlup. In a
1946 letter to Mises he asked his old master to bless his evasive
way of addressing pro-labor-union audiences. He wrote:

---

[44]According to Lane, Mises had fallen prey to the confusion of egalitarianism. She quotes Mises: "It is obvious that every constitutional system can
be made to work satisfactorily when the rulers are equal to their task." There-
upon she comments: "Stuff and nonsense! . . . The basic fallacy [of Germany]
was in the lack of a rational political thought, and this book admirably displays that lack." Rose Wilder Lane in *Economic Council Review of Books* 2, no.
10 (November 1945), p. 3.

[45]See the fall 1949 and fall 1950 correspondence in Grove City Archive:
Lane files.

I would like your advice: I must soon give a lecture
for the U.S. Chamber of Commerce on "Monopolistic Wage Determination as Part of the General Problem of Monopoly." The lecture is to be published,
and will probably receive more attention than suits
my liking. If the lecture were to be presented in a scientific forum, I could go into the history of ideas, and
in particular Mill and so forth. But for the Chamber
I must be practical and political. I will have no choice
but to say that monopoly wages are the only purpose
of labor unions, and that strong labor unions mean
unemployment and inflation and lead to an authoritarian state. Can an honest man avoid such statements? Are there any alternatives? . . .

If it is politically unthinkable to outlaw labor
unions—and I assume this is the case today—can one
consider government limitations on private wage
increases? I am not thinking, of course, of a fixing of
wages through the state, but of a general interdiction
to increase wages . . . by more than 10% in three
years, or something of this sort. Of course this is
entirely fantastic. Would it be smarter not to mention
such makeshift solutions at all? They have no
prospect of being accepted.[46]

Mises replied that he would tell the Chamber: "First of all,
liberate yourself from false ideas. *Study economics.* Then go on to
convince others." And he emphasized: "I reject any outlawing
or limitation of the liberty of association. No liberties shall be
abolished, only coercion."[47]

Correspondence between the two men had already become
quite infrequent and would cool even further. Their estrangement

---

[46]Machlup to Mises, letter dated December 13, 1946; Grove City College
Archive: Machlup files.

[47]Mises to Machlup, letter dated December 15, 1946; Grove City College
Archive: Machlup files.

thawed before Mises's eightieth birthday, but would sink to an all-time low by the mid-1960s.

Planned Chaos

Montes de Oca had already talked to Mises in 1943 about writing an epilogue to the Spanish edition of *Socialism*, but Mises probably did not turn to the task before 1945. Until then, the rate of progress on the translation was unclear, and Mises may well have been wary of engaging in another task for Montes de Oca, who so far had not completed any of the projects they had discussed in 1942. Mises had not even received agreed-upon payment for a study of Mexico. The prospective Mexican publishers of *Socialism* asked for an epilogue dealing with the Soviet experiment, both because dealing with the question was interesting in its own right and since it would bring the book up to date. Mises replied evasively, suggesting that the best solution would be to write a special introduction for the Spanish edition.[48]

In early January 1946, Mises finally received payment for the study on Mexico he had written in 1943. He also worked rapidly on the completion of the epilogue his Mexican partners had asked for. The typewritten manuscript was probably finished at the end of the month.[49]

In July and August 1946, Mises lectured again in Mexico City. In the last days of July, Hayek joined him.[50] They also toured the

---

[48]See their correspondence of June and July 1945; Grove City Archive: Montes de Oca files.

[49]Mises to Montes de Oca, letter dated January 12, 1946; Grove City Archive: Montes de Oca files. Mises received $590 for the study. He finished the epilogue at the end of December 1945. See Mises to Schmidt, letter dated December 31, 1945; Grove City Archive: Schmidt file.

[50]Mises to Karl Brandt, letter dated September 7, 1946; Grove City Archive: Brandt file.

Central Plateau and spent some days on Lake Chapala.[51] On the tour he also gave a talk in Guadalajara (August 27). Montes de Oca acted as a translator to attract a larger audience.

One purpose of Mises's visit was to discuss the long-standing project of an Institute for the Social Sciences. This prospect must have been put to rest on that occasion—the subject did not come up again in any subsequent correspondence. But another project now took on ever-more concrete shape. Hayek was trying to rally classical-liberal scholars on both sides of the Atlantic to establish an international scholarly society devoted to the promotion of individual liberty. He planned to set up a meeting during the next year and sought to secure Mises's participation.

At the end of the year, Montes de Oca was appointed as the Director General of the Mexican central bank, the Banco de Mexico. His group later invited Hazlitt (early January 1947), as well as Hansen and Haberler for lectures (January 1947). Mises himself was invited again for August 1947, to give a series of lectures critically analyzing Marxism.[52]

Upon his return to New York, Mises learned that Henry Hazlitt had had to leave the *New York Times*. This was not the first time Hazlitt's politics forced him out of a job. In 1933, he had quit his position as literary editor of *The Nation*, which did not welcome his hostility to the New Deal. Leaving the *New York Times* was a serious setback, but Hazlitt immediately found a new position at *Newsweek*, where he enjoyed the same liberty of opinion he once had enjoyed at the *Times*. He would write his *Newsweek* column for exactly twenty years, until he had to leave, once again, for ideological reasons.

Mises himself fared much better and continued his "visit" at NYU, where he taught a course on currency reform in the

---

[51]Mises to Hayek, letter dated December 31, 1946; Grove City Archive: MPS files.

[52]Mises to Hayek, letter dated December 31, 1946; Grove City Archive: MPS files.

spring term of 1947. In the fall of 1946, Mises also met a substantial number of European economists such as Jacques Rueff,
François Perroux, Trygve Hoff, and others, who had traveled to
the United States and were lecturing at FEE and other institutions.[53] One likely subject of discussion was Hayek's plan for an
international society of classical-liberal scholars.

A Conference at Mont Pèlerin

Exactly one year after the establishment of the Foundation
for Economic Education in New York, another organization
was brought into existence to provide a forum for the
exchange and development of ideas from a classical-liberal
perspective. Unlike FEE, this organization did not have any
permanent headquarters; it was conceived as a society of academic scholars, and it mainly consisted of annual meetings,
which have subsequently taken place at different cities
throughout the world. Most importantly, however, this society
was founded in the spirit of neo-liberalism, and ever since,
neo-liberal scholars, politicians, and journalists have represented the bulk of its members.[54]

The society was a follow-up to the 1938 Lippmann Colloquium that Louis Rougier had organized in Paris. This time,
the initiative fell quite naturally into the hands of Hayek, who
was well known on both sides of the Atlantic—due to the success of *The Road to Serfdom* and also because he was among the
first western intellectuals to renew contacts with his continental counterparts after the war.[55] In these meetings the idea of a

---

[53]Mises to Hayek, letter dated December 31, 1946; Grove City Archive:
MPS files.

[54]For an overview see R.M. Hartwell, *History of the Mont Pèlerin Society*
(Indianapolis: Liberty Fund, 1995).

[55]For example, by January 1949, Hayek had already paid several visits to
Austria. See Charmatz to Mises, letter dated January 27, 1949; Grove City
Archive: Charmatz file.

libertarian association slowly emerged. Hayek certainly discussed the issue when he met Mises at the end of July 1946 in Mexico, but at that point there was not yet any concrete plan. From Mexico City he flew to Oslo, where Trygve Hoff organized a preparatory meeting to discuss rather vague plans for the establishment of a neo-liberal association of European intellectuals. There the plan for an "Acton-Tocqueville Society" must have taken shape.[56] By the end of the year, he had found the necessary funds to sponsor the event from Swiss (through Hunold) and American (Volker Fund) sources, and he wrote a letter of invitation to some fifty persons for a ten-day conference in the Swiss Alps, at the foot of Mount Pèlerin on Lake Geneva.

Hayek was probably anticipating trouble with Mises: on the invitation letter to him, Hayek added a hand-written apology that he had not had the time to discuss his plan with him in any detail. His apprehension turned out to be correct. Mises went through the roof, writing to Hayek that he could not leave NYU in April and that he "abhorred the idea of going to Europe. I have seen enough decline already."[57] At Hazlitt's request, he had written a four-page memorandum containing

---

[56]Hayek to Mises, letter dated December 28, 1946; Grove City Archive: MPS files. Mises to Karl Brandt, letter dated September 7, 1946; Grove City Archive: Brandt file. Mises had been in touch with Hoff prior to June 28, 1946. Hoff had written a libertarian manifesto during the war. He sent the manuscript to Sweden, from where an American diplomat was supposed to send it to Alfred A. Knopf in New York. But the diplomat never did so. Hoff learned after the war that this was because the diplomat found the manuscript "undemocratic"—which probably meant that it was too critical of the fundamental dogmas of America's war ally. Hoff had also come to an independent discovery of the impossibility of economic calculation in socialism. Mises had the highest opinion of the Norwegian economist. Hoff was "one of the few contemporaries whose judgment on the problems dealt with in *Human Action* is of consequence." Mises to Hoff, letter dated January 11, 1950; Grove City Archive: Hoff files.

[57]Mises to Hayek, letter dated December 31, 1946; Grove City Archive: MPS files.

his "Observations on Professor Hayek's Plan." Here he stated that many similar plans to stem the tide of totalitarianism had been pursued in the past several decades—he himself had been involved in some of these projects—and each time the plan failed because these friends of liberty had themselves already been infected by the statist virus: "They did not realize that freedom is inextricably linked with the market economy. They endorsed by and large the critical part of the socialist programs. They were committed to a middle-of-the-road solution, to interventionism." At the end of the memorandum, he stated his main objection:

> The weak point in Professor Hayek's plan is that it relies upon the cooperation of many men who are known for their endorsement of interventionism. It is necessary to clarify this point before the meeting starts. As I understand the plan, it is not the task of this meeting to discuss anew whether or not a government decree or a union dictate has the power to raise the standard of living of the masses. If somebody wants to discuss these problems, there is no need for him to make a pilgrimage to the Mount Pèlerin. He can find in his neighborhood ample opportunity to do so.[58]

In his letter to Hayek, he was more specific:

> I am primarily concerned about the participation of Röpke, who is an outspoken interventionist. I think the same holds true for Brandt, Gideonse, and Eastman. All three of them are contributors to the purely socialist—even though decidedly anti-Soviet—*New Leader*.[59]

---

[58]Mises, "Observations on Professor Hayek's Plan," typewritten memorandum dated December 31, 1946; Grove City Archive: MPS files.

[59]Mises to Hayek, letter dated December 31, 1946; Grove City Archive: MPS files. Mises suggested that Hayek invite Montes de Oca and Velasco from Mexico, Maestri from Cuba, and Hytten from Australia.

Still Mises did not rule out his participation, but he did suggest a postponement of the conference until September. This turned out to be impracticable, though, and Hayek undertook another attempt to convince his old mentor in early February. He downplayed the significance of Brandt, Gideonse, and Eastman's connections to the *New Leader*, mentioning that he himself had written for this magazine. But more importantly, he argued that the program of the conference was still quite open and that the main purpose of the meeting on Lake Geneva—and of subsequent meetings—would be to win over especially those historians and political scientists, who still harbored wrong ideas on a number of issues, but who were willing to learn.[60] This seems to have been enough to convince Mises to attend. At Hayek's suggestion, he got in touch with the main sponsor of the conference, the Kansas City-based William Volker Fund, and within a week, travel arrangements were made through FEE.

∽ ∽ ∽

It was probably the first time Mises personally got in touch with Harold W. Luhnow and the well-endowed Volker Fund. The contact would prove to be highly beneficial in the course of the next fifteen years, until the Fund was liquidated in the early 1960s.

German-born William Volker (1859–1947) had made a fortune with a home furnishing business he had established in 1882 in Kansas City.[61] In 1911, after finally marrying at the age of 52, he became a philanthropist. He eventually established in 1932 a private fund to protect his capital against the encroachments of the tax code—especially the new income tax of 1916. It may

---

[60]Hayek to Mises, letter dated February 3, 1947; Grove City Archive: MPS files.

[61]On Luhnow, see the special collections of the Kansas City Public Library, which also contain photography.

have been Volker himself who approved
the support of the Mont Pèlerin Society
meeting, which took place some seven
months before he died. But it is more
likely that this was already the decision of
his nephew, Harold Luhnow, who became
the director of the Fund in 1944 and
turned it into the principal sponsor of libertarian scholarship.[62] Apparently Luhnow's main source of libertarian inspira-

William Volker 1911

tion had been Loren Miller, who from 1942 to 1944 had been
an executive of the Kansas City Civic Research Institute (a
Volker Fund outfit), before he departed for the Detroit Bureau
of Governmental Research—another source of funding of postwar libertarianism.

The influence of the Volker Fund radiated far beyond the
United States. By the end of 1953, it paid the membership
fees for virtually all non-U.S. members of the Mont Pèlerin
Society.[63] The Fund's cooperation with Mises was very close,
especially after Luhnow hired former FEE employees Herbert
and Richard Cornuelle.[64]

Most other libertarian think tanks and funds have been perverted over time, turning away from their initial principles. The
Volker Fund escaped this fate. It was liquidated in the early
1960s, when its directorship fell into the hands of those who
could not identify with the libertarian orientation of its founder.

---

[62]Shortly after Volker's death, the Fund moved from Kansas City to
Burlingame, California. This must have been between April 1949 and June
1951. See correspondence in Grove City Archive: Herbert Cornuelle file.

[63]Hazlitt to Mises, letter dated December 21, 1953; Grove City College
Archive: Mont Pèlerin Society files.

[64]Liaison Officers were Richard Cornuelle and Kenneth Templeton. Herbert Cornuelle left the Fund in November 1953 for a business job in Hon-
olulu.

❧ ❧ ❧

The Mont Pèlerin Conference started on April 1, 1947 and lasted for ten days. Mises left New York on March 25, curious to see Europe again after almost seven years. The meeting had only a minimal agenda and left a great deal of leeway for the participants to determine the subjects they wished to discuss in the course of the next days.

Mises and Read, Harper, and Watts from FEE, as well as Hazlitt, and Davenport (*Fortune* Magazine) represented the Manchesterite fringe of the meeting. Hayek, Friedman, and Machlup were neo-liberals; people like Walter Eucken, Harry Gideonse, Bertrand de Jouvenel, Frank Knight, Michael Polanyi, Karl Popper, Wilhelm Röpke, and George Stigler were

Mises and Walter Eucken at 1947 Mont Pèlerin

liberal social democrats. Maurice Allais and Lionel Robbins represented the far left of the Conference. Allais could not even bring himself to endorse the vague "statement of aims" that all other participants approved on April 8.

In his opening address Hayek set the agenda for the postwar ideological reconstruction of the classical-liberal movement. It involved, Hayek explained, on the one hand "purging traditional liberal theory of certain accidental accretions which have become attached to it in the course of time" and, on the other hand, "facing up to some real problems which an over-simplified liberalism has shirked or which have become apparent only since it has turned into a somewhat stationary and rigid creed."[65] As later developments would show, the concrete

---

[65]F.A. Hayek, "Opening Address to a Conference at Mont Pèlerin," *Studies in Philosophy, Politics, and Economics* (Chicago: University of Chicago Press,

First meeting of the Mont Pèlerin Society in 1947; Robbins far left, Machlup, in front of left window, Hayek, center, group on right, Rappard, Mises, Eucken, Stigler

meaning of this program was (1) to exculpate classical liberalism from certain widely held criticism, for example, that the policies it had inspired had led to mass misery; (2) to distinguish the "modern" liberalism from its *laissez-faire* predecessor.

Some of the other scheduled talks, however, were more "neo" and less "liberal." For example, the German economist Walter Eucken explained that anti-monopoly legislation was not sufficient to combat monopolies. Further legislative inference was needed in the field of corporate law, patent law, and trademark law. He championed two maxims of economic policy. First, although there was to be freedom of contract, this freedom was not to be allowed to limit in any way the freedom of contract of others. Second, monopolistic market participants should be forced to behave as if they were in "competition"— produce the same quantities and sell them at the same prices that would prevail under "competition."

In short, Eucken dished up the same interventionist agenda that had already dominated the Lippmann Colloquium in 1938. At that time, Mises had been on his honeymoon in Paris, which might

---

1967), p. 148. See also the very moderately worded "Statement of Aims." A copy is in Grove City Archive: Intercollegiate Society of Individualists file (filed around 1964).

explain why his contributions to the discussions had been unusually tame. Nine years later, the honeymoon was over. He reacted with great determination and defended his *laissez-faire* position so vigorously that many years later his friend Lawrence Fertig still recalled the debate. Milton Friedman eventually concurred:

> our sessions were marked by vigorous controversy over such issues as the role of religion and moral values in making possible and preserving a free society; the role of trade unions and the appropriateness of government action to affect the distribution of income. I particularly recall a discussion of this issue, in the middle of which Ludwig von Mises stood up, announced to the assembly "You're all a bunch of socialists," and stomped out of the room, an assembly that contained not a single person who, by even the lowest standards, could be called a socialist.[66]

Friedman did not specify what he meant by "the lowest standards." In any case, while Mises was able to hold socialists in high esteem, the incident showed that he had little patience with socialists parading as liberals. The exchange between Mises and his neo-liberal opponents set the tone in the Mont Pèlerin Society for years to come. Wilhelm Röpke would later pay a friendly tribute to Mises, even though the latter made "sarcastic comments upon the unenlightened spirit of so many of its members" including Röpke himself.[67] Although the libertarians around Mises were a small minority, it was they who had the financial backing of the main American sponsors such as the Volker Fund, without which the Society would quickly have died out in those early years. As long as Mises took an active

---

[66]Milton Friedman and Rose D. Friedman, *Two Lucky People: Memoirs* (Chicago: University of Chicago Press, 1998), p. 161.

[67]Wilhelm Röpke, "Homage to a Master and a Friend," *The Mont Pèlerin Quarterly* (October 1961): p. 5.

part in the meetings, therefore, it was
impossible to move on to discussing the
technical details of an approved government
interventionism. *Laissez-faire* had made a
comeback. It was not the majority opinion,
but it was a debatable and debated political
option—too much for some initial members
such as Maurice Allais, who soon left the
Society for precisely this reason.[68]

Mont Pèlerin in 1947

Despite fundamental disagreements, the meeting was a success. On April 9, some forty participants established the Mont
Pèlerin Society and elected Hayek as their president.[69]

Preparing the Counter-Revolution

By March 1945, Yale University Press had decided to publish
an American edition of *Nationalökonomie*. The idea of a simple
translation was never really an option. All sides agreed to publish
a revised edition.[70] For the next three and a half years, Mises
worked busily on this project. The revisions were not to be substantive. Their primary purpose was to adapt the work to the

---

[68]Possibly Allais's visit to FEE in October 1947 reinforced his concerns
that the American libertarians were far too radical for his taste. The visit is
mentioned in Herbert Cornuelle to Mises, letter dated October 14, 1947;
Grove City College Archive: FEE files.

[69]Eventually Hunold from Zurich and Aaron Director became secretaries;
Eucken, Jewkes, Knight, Rappard, and Rueff were elected vice-presidents; and
Hardy became the Treasurer. Mises, Antoni, Gideonse, Iversen, Robbins, and
Röpke became members of the Council. See "President's Circular No. 1,"
dated November 17, 1947; Grove City Archive: MPS files. On December 10,
Albert Hunold announced that Mises would soon receive a photo album with
some seventy pictures of the conference as a Christmas present.

[70]In June 1945, Mises still said the book was "to be published in an American edition next year." Handwritten manuscript of letter to Tietz; Grove
City Archive: Tietz file.

intellectual background of his American readers. In this task, Mises benefited enormously from the experience of Henry Hazlitt and Yale editor Eugene Davidson, both of whom suggested many areas of improvement. For example, Mises now dealt with doctrines and policy proposals that had specific importance in the United States, such as the Georgist theory of land taxation.[71] But he especially modified his discussion of the fundamental philosophical problems of the science of human action. For example, in his German book, Mises felt he had to refute Othmar Spann's "universalist economics" in great detail; he now dropped this discussion almost entirely and focused instead on the refutation of positivism and the use of quantitative methods in economic theory.

He added an entirely new chapter—the only chapter with no counterpart in *Nationalökonomie*—to discuss the basic problems of probability theory, which was at the heart of the quantitative approach that dominated economic analysis in the Anglo-Saxon countries. In this chapter, Mises seized the opportunity to build on and elaborate the works of his brother Richard, who had pioneered the so-called relative-frequency theory of probability. Mises considerably simplified the axiomatic exposition of the theory and argued, without mentioning his brother by name, that the standard account was redundant.

Beyond the scholarly aspect of this contribution, the correction of his brother was a sequence in a typical "Austrian" literary squabble. Twelve years earlier, Richard had ventured into the field of his elder sibling, and claimed in one of his books that

---

[71]He addressed the issue on pp. 632–33 of *Human Action: A Treatise on Economics* (New Haven, Conn.: Yale University Press, 1949), and in a later letter to his French friend Lhoste Lachaume. See Ballvé to Mises, letter dated March 18, 1955; Grove City Archive: Ballvé files. See also Mises to Lidia Alkalay, letter dated February 19, 1952; Grove City Archive: "A" files.

laissez-faire policies had no scientific merit.[72] Now Ludwig struck back by demonstrating what an elegant exposition of the relative-frequency theory looked like.

Human Action almost became Mises's first posthumous publication. In October 1948, he and Margit had a very serious car accident.[73] But the couple survived and Ludwig put the finishing touches on the book by the spring of 1949. He sent copies of the manuscript to receptive publishers and friends, among them Jasper Crane, who ran the Van Nostrand Publishing Company and whom he knew well through FEE.[74]

A Neo-Liberal Coup in Germany

The 1947 Mont Pèlerin Society meeting was enough to satisfy Mises's curiosity about Europe and European scholars for quite some time. Europe lay in shambles; even Paris was in rags. He did not even wish to think about traveling to Austria. All that was good and memorable about Europe was in the past. No need for him to return to the old continent just to witness the misery induced by those very statist follies he had spent a lifetime fighting. When he was invited to the next Mont Pèlerin Society meeting, scheduled for July 1949 in the Swiss town of Seelisberg, he declined.[75]

---

[72]Richard von Mises, *Kleines Lehrbuch des Positivismus: Einführung in die empiristische Wissenschaftsauffassung* (The Hague: Van Stockum & Zoon, 1939).

[73]Hayek to Mises, letter dated November 15, 1948; Grove City Archive: Hayek files. Mises to François Perroux, letter dated November 13, 1948; Grove City Archive: Perroux file. Perroux had learned about the accident from Helene Berger Lieser.

[74]Crane to Mises, letter dated June 28, 1949; Grove City Archive: Crane file.

[75]Apparently he also declined an invitation to lecture at the University of Vienna in a U.S.-sponsored program in 1948. Fritz Machlup took part. See Thieberger to Mises, April 18, 1948; Grove City Archive: Thieberger files.

But his American friends at the Volker Fund thought it was crucial to have him on board, lest the interventionists have a free hand. The Mont Pèlerin Society provided American libertarians not only with some cosmopolitan flair, but it also put them in touch with a mass of intellectuals close to their cause that could not be found at home.

Moreover, in one of the great ironies of history, liberal principles had just been applied with overwhelming success in Germany, and a thorough acquaintance with Ludwig Erhard and the intellectual leaders of the German reforms promised to be helpful for American libertarians in their struggles at home. Nobody in the States knew the reformers, and curiosity was great.[76] Prompted by the news from Germany, Leonard Read asked Mises about Erhard. The reply:

> The only fact I know about Professor Erhard is that he is the chairman of the Economic Advisory Board. This council is moderately interventionist and opposes the radical New Dealism of the German political parties and of the outright socialist British Military Government. It is possible that the Board's firmness in this matter is an achievement of Erhard's uncompromising attitude and the persuasiveness of his exposition of the principles of true liberalism.[77]

The only way to find out, however, was to go to Europe and meet the man and his supporters. But from Luhnow's point of view, this would only be worthwhile if men like Mises could be brought along to give the meetings the right orientation. Through the intermediation of Herbert Cornuelle and Loren

---

[76]There was no similar curiosity for Italy, where Luigi Einaudi, after leading three years the country's central bank, had just been elected Italian president.

[77]Mises to Read, letter dated December 4, 1948; Grove City Archive: FEE files.

Miller, Luhnow urged Mises to attend the Seelisberg meeting. Mises acceded. It would be his second return to Europe after emigration.[78]

He left New York at some point in June, and then went to Seelisberg from July 3 to 10. The meeting was supposed to deal in particular with questions relating to the labor market.[79] But as was to be expected, it was entirely overshadowed by the discussion of recent events in West Germany.

In March 1948, Ludwig Erhard had been appointed the director of the economic administration of the British-American occupation zone. A disciple of the social-liberal sociologist Franz Oppenheimer, Erhard was unknown in the world of libertarianism—which was probably why he got the job in the first place.[80] But the virtually unknown Erhard lost no time in setting out a liberal coup. Three months after his appointment, he

---

[78]In March 1950 he said that he had been to Europe twice, but not to Austria. See Mises to Ernest Neurath, letter dated March 13, 1950, Grove City Archive: Neurath file.

[79]Miller to Mises, letter dated March 26, 1949; Grove City College Archive: MPS files. See the front-page report in *Neue Zürcher Zeitung* (July 25, 1949). In June 1949, Mises was in Europe. See Margit von Mises to R. Ziegler; Grove City Archive: Cluett, Peabody & Co. file.

[80]On Franz Oppenheimer's influence on his student Ludwig Erhard, see for example the interview with Erhard in *Deutsche Zeitung* (December 30/31, 1961), p. 20. During the Nazi era, Erhard had worked for two economic research institutes. After the war, he became the Bavarian minister of the economy and also attended the private seminar of Mises's friend, Adolf Weber, who in those days was probably the most "Austrian" professor of economics (see *Der Spiegel*, October 16, 1963, mentioned by Gibson to Mises, letter dated March 3, 1964; Grove City Archive: "G" file). Weber championed a theory of the market process and of consumer sovereignty that was virtually indistinguishable from Mises's views; see for example, Adolf Weber, *Weltwirtschaft* (Munich: Richard Pflaum Verlag, 1947), pp. 86, 102, 106, 108. It was probably under the impact of the discussions in the Weber circle that Erhard received the vision and inspiration for his reforms of June 1948.

made two bold decisions. Against the regulations of the British military government, he (1) abolished virtually all price controls and (2) introduced a new currency: the German mark.

The very next day the stores and shops were filled with merchandise. Businessmen had cut back production during the postwar years, and retailers held back commodities, reserving them for sales on the black market, where higher prices could be obtained. This lamentable state of affairs had resulted from the Nazi system of price controls, which had made profitable production impossible and turned the open market into a black market. The allied occupation forces had maintained it at the behest of a small group of influential left-wing economic advisers, for whom central planning and government controls was state of the art.[81] Erhard overthrew this system, thus creating the economic foundations of the (western) Federal Republic of Germany, which came to be established in the fall of 1949. More than that, he had put into practice a classical-liberal alternative to the Marshall Plan for postwar reconstruction.[82]

A year before the Erhard reforms, on June 5, 1947, U.S. Secretary of State George Marshall had presented his proposal for the economic reconstruction of Europe through the large-scale

---

[81]In those days, Walter Eucken, one of the intellectual leaders behind the Erhard reforms, wrote to Mises about the need for further deregulation: "The German authorities, with whom I am in constant touch, try everything to this effect. But American economic policies in Germany are still essentially based on central planning." Eucken to Mises, letter dated June 25, 1948; Grove City Archive: Read files.

[82]A few years later, the banking theorist Heinrich von Rittershausen speculated in private correspondence with Mises that *Gemeinwirtschaft* had laid the foundation for Erhard's success, "because all of the significant young people read it carefully during the 12 bookless years." Rittershausen to Mises, letter dated August 22, 1957; Grove City Archive: Rittershausen file. Of all postwar monetary theorists in Germany, Rittershausen was probably most sympathetic to Mises's views.

spending of U.S. tax money.[83] In subsequent years and decades, the story of the Marshall Plan has been told and retold from the point of view of its sponsors, thus becoming part of modern welfare-state mythology. High school students in all western countries learn that Marshall Plan-funded government spending initiated a new phase of economic growth after World War II.

In the cold light of economic reasoning, however, we can see that the Marshall Plan was in essence a scheme for postponing the bankruptcy of socialism and the welfare state. In private correspondence, Mises pointed out that the European countries had already "nationalized railroads, telegraph, electric power, telephone, mines, and many factories," and he went on to add:

> They have already expropriated by taxation all higher incomes and cannot expect any additional revenue from pushing further the policy of soaking the rich. Thus they want the American taxpayer to foot the bill for the deficits incurred by their glorified socialization policy. They call this scheme the Marshall plan.[84]

In December 1948, when Leonard Read asked him for his opinion of Erhard, Mises did not know the man. In the following years, however, he familiarized himself with the writings of Erhard and found that they closely reflected the opinions of his advisers: Cologne professor of economics Alfred Müller-Armack, as well as Wilhelm Röpke and Walter Eucken. During the 1950s, Mises realized that the very success of Erhard's free-market reforms was liable to be used against the market economy, because the reforms were "sold" in terms of interventionist

---

[83]Adolf Wittkowski, *Schrifttum zum Marshallplan und zur volkswirtschaftlichen Integration Europas* (Bad Godesberg: Bundesministerium für den Marshallplan, 1953).

[84]Mises to Mark Jones, letter dated March 31, 1948; Grove City Archive: Jones file.

rhetoric. He therefore honored the German reformers with a lengthy comment in his most prominent book:

> [The] supporters of the most recent variety of inter-ventionism, the German "soziale Marktwirtschaft," stress that they consider the market economy to be the best possible and most desirable system of society's economic organization, and that they are opposed to the government omnipotence of socialism. But, of course, all these advocates of a middle-of-the-road policy emphasize with the same vigor that they reject Manchesterism and laissez-faire liberalism. It is neces-sary, they say, that the state interfere with the market phenomena whenever and wherever the "free play of the economic forces" results in conditions that appear as "socially" undesirable. In making this assertion they take it for granted that it is the government that is called upon to determine in every single case whether or not a definite economic fact is to be considered as reprehensible from the "social" point of view and, consequently whether or not the state of the market requires a special act of government interference.
>
> All these champions of interventionism fail to realize that their program thus implies the establish-ment of full government supremacy in all economic matters and ultimately brings about a state of affairs that does not differ from what is called the German or the Hindenburg pattern of socialism. If it is in the jurisdiction of the government to decide whether or not definite conditions of the economy justify its intervention, no sphere of operation is left to the market. Then it is no longer the consumers who ulti-mately determine what should be produced, in what quantity, of what quality, by whom, where, and how—but it is the government. For as soon as the outcome brought about by the operation of the unhampered market differs from what the authorities consider "socially" desirable, the government inter-feres. That means the market is free as long as it does

precisely what the government wants it to do. It is
"free" to do what the authorities consider to be the
"right" things, but not to do what they consider the
"wrong" things; the decision concerning what is right
and what is wrong rests with the government. Thus
the doctrine and the practice of interventionism ultimately tend to abandon what originally distinguished
them from outright socialism and to adopt entirely
the principles of totalitarian all-round planning.[85]

Mises's reservations did not grow weaker through personal
contact with representatives of the German "Ordo" school of
neo-liberalism. Quite the contrary: in private correspondence
from the mid-1950s, he stated, "I have more and more doubts
whether it is possible to cooperate with Ordo-interventionism
in the Mont Pèlerin Society."[86]

ᵍ   ᵍ   ᵍ

The site of the 1949 Mont Pèlerin Society meeting was one
of the legendary places of European libertarianism: the town of
Seelisberg, located at the foot of a mountain of the same name.
It was on the *Rütliwiese*, one of the adjacent meadows that, in
early August 1291, Swiss patriots deliberated in secret meetings
to prepare the overthrow of the regime of Emperor Rudolf,
who had imposed a wide variety of new laws and taxes. The
Mont Pèlerin Society convened more comfortably in hotel
facilities, and not all of its participants were eager to overthrow

---

[85]Mises, *Human Action: A Treatise on Economics*, 3rd ed. (Chicago: Regnery, 1966), pp. 723–24. Until the mid-1950s, Mises was apparently reluctant
to even meet with Erhard. Röpke thought this was because Mises was under
the influence of his closest German intellectual ally, Volkmar Muthesius, a
sharp and relentless critic of Erhard's economic policies. See Muthesius to
Mises, letter dated January 2, 1954; Grove City Archive: Muthesius file.

[86]Mises to Muthesius, letter dated June 1, 1955; Grove City Archive:
Muthesius file.

the burgeoning new welfare state. Wilhelm Röpke for example was more concerned about defining a role for government in fighting against "proletarianization." Karl Popper tried to do the same thing for the field of education and research.[87]

A New Yorker

After a brief return to Manhattan, Mises went to Mexico City for the month of August to lecture at the Asociacion Mexicana de Cultura. He and Margit arrived on the night of July 29, and he soon started his twelve-session course on economic theory, seasoned with a survey of the past 200 years of European history and excursions into the history of thought. Among other things, he explained "how Keynes was influenced by the German socialists of the chair and how he outdid them in many points."[88] The seminar participants enjoyed the privilege of receiving advance copies of *Human Action*.[89]

During this trip, Montes de Oca delicately raised the question again of whether Mises would stay permanently in Mexico. Mises apparently replied that he now desired "to stay in New York City because it has become the intellectual center of the present day." Montes de Oca would have left it at that, but a few months later he felt the need to raise the question yet again in writing:

> There has been what might be termed a movement among Mexican business men to invite you to become advisor for various business organizations,

---

[87]There is a summary of the programs of the first four Mont Pèlerin Society meetings in Grove City College Archive: MPS files. Folder #9. Summary of all meetings until 1970 in folder #33.

[88]Mises to Montes de Oca, letter dated February 26, 1949; Grove City Archive: Montes de Oca files. A handwritten note with keywords for a (later) talk on Keynes is in Grove City Archive: May file.

[89]Mises to Montes de Oca, letter dated July 22, 1949; Grove City Archive: Montes de Oca files. They stayed at the Ritz, and he received $1,500 for the seminar (stated in earlier correspondence).

> more or less in the capacity you performed this func-
> tion in the Vienna Chamber of Commerce.[90]

After serious reflection Mises again declined, referring this
time to his advanced age, which would prevent him from acquiring a sufficient command of the Spanish language. But he emphasized that if he "were twenty years younger, I would not refuse
your kind proposition" and he also said that the invitation was very
tempting from another point of view: "My three visits to your
country have shown me that the climate of opinion is today in
Mexico more favorable to the acceptance of sound economic ideas
than in any other country."[91] But this did not alter his decision.

Not only had Mises become an American—he was now a
New Yorker. ✦

Mises, top, *vacationing in the White
Mountains; hiking in Austria; and, behind the
wheel of their car in 1950;* left, *Mises in 1955*

---

[90]Montes de Oca to Mises, letter dated February 24, 1950; Grove City
Archive: Montes de Oca files.

[91]Mises to Montes de Oca, letter dated March 13, 1950; Grove City
Archive: Montes de Oca files.

20
Human Action and Its
Consequences

BY THE LATE 1940S, Mises was well integrated in the emerging
network of American libertarians. His NYU seminar, his lectures
at Mont Pèlerin Society meetings and other conferences, and his
writings had established his impact on the rising generation. And
even beyond the circles of organized libertarianism he had gained
a nationwide reputation as an economist and social analyst of the
first order, though for most academics his methods and political
orientation smacked too much of times past.

The publication of *Human Action* in September 1949 produced a quantum leap in his prominence and impact. Overnight,
Mises turned into the central intellectual figure of the entire
American Right, an event that was paralleled during the next
decade only in the case of *Atlas Shrugged*, the novel that catapulted Ayn Rand to even greater fame, at least among the general
public. Mises now appeared to the public not merely as a scholar
of the old school, but as one of the great minds of western civilization, a creative genius who had not only mastered all aspects
of his science, but had completely transformed this science to
offer a new way of looking at social processes and relationships.

Human Action was a success without precedent. His 1922
treatise on socialism had been a sensation too, but only because
of the general recognition that theoretical socialism offered no
help with the problems of postwar reconstruction. The socialist
avant-garde had seized power in Germany and Austria, but then

had no idea what to do. And this crisis quickly turned from a theoretical one to a political one when socialist governments drastically aggravated conditions rather than improving them. Mises's comprehensive analysis in *Gemeinwirtschaft* delivered a breathtakingly lucid explanation of this mess. But while the book provoked outrage and fury in the socialist camp and initiated a paradigm shift in the thinking of an entire generation, it had not become the rallying banner of a movement. Its author had been a relatively junior economist and no institutions were in place to concentrate and organize the readers the book had convinced.

American ground was more fertile. It had been prepared by a long tradition of individual liberty and a recent reorientation toward that tradition. There were, in effect, the makings of a movement just waiting for *Human Action* to form its intellectual nucleus. And just as important, there were institutions and individual promoters eager to accelerate it. Moreover, Mises himself was already one of the intellectual leaders of this grassroots movement. He knew writers and journalists who would promote his book, and there were men who stood ready to sponsor his subsequent work. Supporters now came in droves, asking Mises to give lectures and seminars. Wealthy businessmen sought his advice and often did what he recommended. And *The Freeman*, the first libertarian journal of a distinctly Misesian flavor, might never have seen the light of day without the glory that *Human Action* brought to its author.

Mises now became the true *spiritus rector* at FEE, which had previously featured him as one among several consultants. To get a taste of the pre-1949 character of FEE, consider the case of Murray Rothbard. The man who would become Mises's most important disciple had learned about FEE through a small brochure with the title "Roofs or Ceilings?"[1] attacking rent

---

[1] Milton Friedman and George Stigler, "Roofs or Ceilings?" (Irvington-on-Hudson, N.Y.: Foundation for Economic Education, 1946).

control laws. Leonard Read had printed 500,000 copies. The authors of the brochure were two young Chicago economists by the names of Milton Friedman and George Stigler. This was in September 1946. Rothbard continued to read FEE publications and attended their conferences; yet in the spring of 1948, the future pillar of the Misesian renaissance had never even heard of Austrian economics. It appears that neither Leonard Read's FEE nor, for that matter, any of the other emerging libertarian organizations, had placed any special emphasis on Mises or the tradition he represented. Then *Human Action* came in one mighty blow and rendered FEE devotedly Misesian.

First Reactions

Neither Mises nor his friends expected the success the book would have. After his return from Mexico, Mises left for a two-week vacation in the Berkshire Mountains.[2] The book was released to the bookshops while he was away, on September 14, 1949. In his weekly *Newsweek* column, Henry Hazlitt announced and praised it, anticipating the role it would play in subsequent events:

> *Human Action* is, in short, at once the most uncompromising and the most rigorously reasoned statement of the case for capitalism that has yet appeared. If any single book can turn the ideological tide that has been running in recent years so heavily toward statism, socialism, and totalitarianism, *Human Action* is that book.[3]

This was almost a self-fulfilling prophecy. Not three months later, by December 6, more than 4,000 copies had been sold and

---

[2]Mises to Jitta, letter dated October 22, 1949; Grove City Archive: Jitta file.

[3]Henry Hazlitt, "The Case for Capitalism," *Newsweek* 34 (September 19, 1949), p. 70.

the book was in its third printing.[4] With the reports of ever more sales, Mises's euphoria lasted for months.[5] His NYU seminar addressed "fundamental problems and theorems of economics and their relationship to philosophical, historical, and political ideas."[6] It started on his birthday, September 29.

When Ludwig and Margit spent New Year's Day 1950 with Hazlitt, Schütz, and Hayek at their Manhattan apartment on West End Avenue, it was already clear that *Human Action* was a phenomenal success, especially for a 900-page scientific treatise. Even his ideological opponents had to admit that the sixty-eight-year-old economist had written a "Capitalist Manifesto"[7] and "a truly unvarnished and unconditional defense of laissez-faire."[8]

Many other reviews followed over the course of the next several months. Most of these were insubstantial and their criticisms boiled down to carping at the book's pontifical style.[9] One

---

[4]Mises to Armin Spitaler, letter dated December 6, 1949; Grove City College Archive: Spitaler file; Mises to Ziegler, letter dated July 16, 1949; Grove City Archive: Cluett, Peabody & Co. file.

[5]The only dark cloud was that Margit had been ill in November.

[6]See the flyer dated August 9, 1949 in Grove City Archive: Fertig files. The flyer mentioned that the seminar was sponsored by the Volker Fund.

[7]Seymour E. Harris, "Capitalist Manifesto," *Saturday Review* 32 (September 24, 1949): 31.

[8]John Kenneth Galbraith, "In Defense of Laissez-Faire," *New York Times Book Review* (October 30, 1949), p. 45. The New Year's party is mentioned in Mises to Hayek, letter dated December 13, 1949; Grove City Archive: Hayek files.

[9]In private correspondence, Oskar Morgenstern declared that he could not agree with Mises's statements on game theory. He did not explain why he disagreed, but said:

> that the matter is far deeper and that it actually does produce results that cannot be had without it. I can see this from certain applications which are now being made in various fields, but these are all matters of difference that are, fortunately, on a level of common understanding.

reviewer had the audacity to complain that as a reader of the work one "continually has the sense of being argued out of existence."[10] But other reviews were receptive to its monumental contributions. Young Murray Rothbard praised *Human Action* as a masterpiece of original synthesis. The book contained "a complete structure of economic science," which was "firmly grounded in *praxeology*, the general principles of individual action."[11] Similarly, Richard C. Cornuelle highlighted that Mises had integrated value and price theory, and was therefore in a position to defend capitalism without basing his reasoning on such fictions as *homo oeconomicus*.[12]

The book also found an exceptionally friendly reception in Germany, were Cologne University professor Armin Spitaler published a long review in the *Weltwirtschaftliches Archiv*. In South Africa, a young professor adopted Mises's epistemological point of view without reservations in his fall 1950 inaugural lecture at the University of Witwatersrand in Johannesburg. The man who lectured on "Economics as a Social Science," Ludwig Lachmann, was a graduate of the London School of Economics, where he had studied in the 1930s under Hayek and Robbins. Before that, he had been a student of Werner Sombart's in Berlin. Lachmann was already acquainted with Mises's aprioristic epistemology, which the Vienna economist had first outlined in his 1933 *Grundprobleme der Nationalökonomie* (Epistemological Problems of

---

This was certainly helpful. Mises must have been somewhat bemused, however, that Morgenstern did not quite remember the title of the book that he professed to have read "to a great extent." (In his letter he thanked Mises for having sent him a copy of "Economic Action.") See Morgenstern to Mises, letter dated January 12, 1950; Grove City Archive: Morgenstern file.

[10]Alfred Sherrard, "The Free Man's Straightjacket," *New Republic* 122 (January 9, 1950): 18–19.

[11]Murray N. Rothbard, "Review of *Human Action*," *Faith and Freedom* (September 1950): 14; idem, "Praxeology," *analysis* (May 1950): 4.

[12]Richard Cornuelle, "A New Philosophy of Laissez Faire," *American Affairs* (January 1950): 47–51.

Economics), and which now for the first time hit the Anglo-Saxon intellectual scene.[13]

A member of Mises's NYU seminar, George Koether, arranged for chapter 35—"The Economics of War"—to be reprinted by the New York based Christian Freedom Foundation (CFF) in September 1950, as a reaction to the Korean War which should soon entail a new round of price controls and economic regimentation. Koether worked at the time both for CFF

Mises and George Koether

and for FEE. The Foundation reprinted the chapter in its fortnightly newspaper, *Christian Economics*.[14] This publication reached some 100,000 clergymen spread out over the entire country. This might have been Mises's first contact with CFF and its staff, and it became a productive and beneficial collaboration that would last a lifetime. George Koether continued to attend Mises's NYU seminar for many years and became a personal friend of Ludwig and Margit's. After Ludwig's death, he helped Margit write her autobiographical recollections, *My Years with Ludwig von Mises*.[15] In the 1950s, he worked in the New York area, first for CFF and FEE, then as an automotive and transportation editor of *Look Magazine*, and eventually as an economist of the U.S. Steel Corporation.[16]

---

[13]Lachmann must have sent Mises a copy of this lecture. See Mises to Ballvé, letter dated December 26, 1950; Grove City Archive: Ballvé files.

[14]See correspondence in Grove City Archive: Christian Freedom Foundation file. CFF was at the time located on 26 West 58th Street in Manhattan. Around 1957, its offices moved to 250 West 57th Street.

[15]Margit von Mises, *My Years with Ludwig von Mises* (Cedar Falls, Iowa: Center for Futures Education, 1978).

[16]The latter position is mentioned in a March 1959 letter from Mises to Hayek. Koether also initiated the creation in 1956 of a Mises bust by his

Mises had another disciple and admirer on the CFF staff. Brooklyn-born Percy Laurie Greaves (1906–1984) was the American self-made man *par excellence*. Before he began to work at the Christian Freedom Foundation in 1950, he had been a bookkeeper, seaman, advertising manager, instructor in economics, financial editor, ghostwriter, and research assistant to the U.S. Congress, where he had collaborated in the investigation of the Pearl Harbor Attack and in the drafting of the Taft-Hartley Act.[17] Greaves faithfully attended all sessions of Mises's NYU seminar and, together with his future wife Bettina Bien, wrote minutes for each one of them.[18] Eventually he

Percy Greaves and Mises in 1959

made a career out of promoting Misesian economics in public lectures and seminars. But most importantly, the Greaveses cared for their professor in the late 1960s and early 1970s, when

---

sculptor friend, Mrs. Erickson. Thereafter his relationship with the Mises couple quickly turned into fond friendship (Grove City Archive: Koether files).

[17]*Who's Who in America*, monthly supplement of September 1952. Greaves had left *Christian Economics* no later than March 1959. See Greaves to Frederick Nymeyer, letter dated March 21, 1959; Grove City Archive: Greaves files. In his job search, he then presented himself as "a leading disciple of Professor Ludwig von Mises, the world famous analyst of socialist fallacies and leading exponent of the free market society." Greaves to Edward Duning, letter dated May 26, 1959; Grove City Archive: Greaves files. By then he had met Bettina Bien (Greaves had previously been married in 1930 and had three children).

[18]These lecture notes are now in the process of being edited and published as "Mises Seminar Lectures." The first volume has just appeared. See Mises, *The Free Market and Its Enemies* (Irvington-on-Hudson, N.Y.: Foundation for Economic Education, 2004).

*Mises, Margit, Bettina
and Percy Greaves at the
airport in 1959*

Mises and his octoge-
narian spouse became
frail. After Mises died
in 1973, they contin-
ued to assist Margit
von Mises. When Percy died, Bettina continued to take care of
her revered teacher's widow, until Margit too died in 1993, at
the age of 103. Bettina then became the curator of Ludwig von
Mises's literary estate, as she still is today.

The president of CFF and editor of *Christian Economics* was
Howard Kershner, but the man behind the organization and its
journal was the wealthy Philadelphia industrialist, J. Howard
Pew, who had inherited the Sun Oil Company from his father
and was an extremely successful entrepreneur in his own right.
Pew assumed various social responsibilities besides sponsoring
CFF. He was the chairman of the board of Grove City College in
western Pennsylvania, and he owned the Chilton Press, which
published the *Pathfinder* and the *Farm Journal*.[19] Mises had
known him at least since March 1945, when the National Association of Manufacturers sent him the manuscript of a talk in which
Pew had explained how cartels threaten economic progress.[20]

---

[19]See the "Statement to the Directors of *Freeman* Magazine, Inc. by its
active editors," attachment to a letter to the *Freeman*'s Board of Directors
dated October 2, 1952, p. 4; Grove City Archive: *Freeman* files. The Pew
family had a solid track record of opposition to interventionism. It sold virtually all of its (highly profitable) European business when confronted with
the alternative of joining government-sponsored cartels. See Pew to Mises,
letter dated November 5, 1954; Grove City Archive: Pew files.

[20]Vada Horsch to Mises, memorandum dated March 23, 1945; Grove
City Archive: NAM files.

The two men had entered into direct correspondence in November 1948, when Pew asked Mises to write a letter to the editor of the *New York Times*, in response to what they both believed was a shameful column by a certain Edward Collins. Mises declined the request, responding that any such attempt was futile:

> First of all, they have the habit of "editing" and shortening such letters so that they lose a good deal of their persuasive power or even become completely garbled. Secondly the editor or the columnist has the privilege of the last word. The effect on the uncritical reader is always that "his" paper is right.
>
> What is needed to fight such allegedly "non-dogmatic" dogmas as those advanced by Mr. Collins (and a host of other writers) is an independent journal of opinion.[21,22]

---

[21]Mises to Pew, letter dated November 27, 1948; Grove City Archive: Pew files.

[22]Mises later explained in private correspondence with a reader of *Human Action* who wondered why the libertarian message did not make it into the press:

> The newspapers and magazines published in this country are either operated on a commercial basis or are newspapers and magazines of opinion. . . . The publishers and editors of the first group are anxious not to antagonize the feelings of the majority or a considerable part of their readers. If they cannot refuse printing an article or a letter to the editor which attacks the popular errors concerning the "Fair-Deal" and similar policies, they "edit" it. They cut down the arguments of the author in such a way that they become clumsy nonsense. The effect upon the reader is just the contrary of what the author intended. They get the impression that the market economy is advocated exclusively by bunglers and half-wits. . . . The second group consists almost exclusively of outright communists, half-communists and other "pink" publications. . . . There are a few exceptions. One is the *Wall Street Journal*, another one is *Plain Talk*. But the *Wall Street Journal* is solely read by bankers and businessmen, *Plain Talk* does not get sufficient backing and may be forced to go out of

Pew was quick to react. In early December 1948, he met with the team running *Plain Talk* magazine—Alfred Kohlberg, Isaac Don Levine, and Eugene Lyons—to discuss the advisability of "making it into just such a journal of opinion."[23] Pew's idea was to provide a forum for Mises, Hazlitt, and other select economists. These talks did not lead to the desired result, but two years later, one year after the publication of *Human Action*, Pew stood again first in line to finance a libertarian journal of opinion, *The Freeman*, which for a few glorious years would spread Austrian economics among a larger public.

Pew had the habit of giving away shares of his corporation, Sun Oil, to all of his employees. Starting in 1951, he also gave such shares to Mises as Christmas gifts. He did this every year until 1968. He wrote:

> While you have been devoting your life to saving the world from those processes which inevitably lead to Communism, the rest of us have been devoting our time to operating industry to the exclusion of everything else, so that we have been blinded to the future. And so I hope you will accept from me, at this Christmas Season, a small token of my appreciation in the form of a few shares of stock in the Company to which I have devoted my life.[24]

---

business." (Mises to Walter Harrison, letter dated November 5, 1949; Grove City Archive: "H" files)

Mises had had personal experiences with this type of journalism. In 1944, for example, the *New York Times* had published a smear-job review of *Omnipotent Government* by a notorious Stalinist, who had obviously never read the book.

[23]Pew to Mises, letter dated December 7, 1948; Grove City Archive: Pew files.

[24]Pew to Mises, letter dated December 3, 1951. Apparently, the two men had started socializing around October of 1949, when Pew was a lunch guest in the Mises's apartment.

Misesians

Mises and his circle of friends were not the only libertarians who had not believed *Human Action* could become a bestseller. Herbert C. Cornuelle and the people at the Volker Fund had sensed that the Misesian edifice was too intellectual to be digested by the general American public. What was needed was a more boiled-down version of the book, which would facilitate

Murray Rothbard

the penetration of the message into the larger public. But who could write such a work?

Cornuelle thought he had found the right person in Murray Rothbard, who had been in touch with FEE from at least 1946.[25] Apparently he met Mises for the first time at a FEE lecture in the summer of 1948.[26] By that time, Rothbard held degrees in mathematics and economics, but knew almost nothing about Austrian economics. By the spring of 1948, when he passed his oral exams, he had never heard of Austrian economics, except, as he later recalled, "as something that had been integrated into the main body of economics by Alfred Marshall sixty years before."[27] Rothbard had a distinct recollection of his pre-*Human Action* economic worldview:

> I had a definite, instinctive feeling or insight or what-
> ever that there was something wrong with all the

---

[25]See William M. Curtiss (Executive Secretary of FEE) to Rothbard, letter dated November 25, 1946; Rothbard Papers.

[26]Leonard Read to Rothbard, letter dated June 24, 1948; Rothbard Papers (also in Grove City Archive: Read files). This was an invitation to attend a meeting on July 8, when Ludwig von Mises would be speaking.

[27]Rothbard to William F. Campbell, letter dated April 1951; Rothbard Papers.

schools of economics. I was very unhappy with all the economic theory. I thought that the institutionalists, when the institutionalists were criticizing the orthodox, Anglo-American economics that they were right and, when the orthodox people were criticizing the institutionalists, they were right. The criticisms were right, and I believed that the simple supply and demand stuff was correct, but I didn't really have a good theoretical base. I wasn't happy with any theories offered. And then when I read *Human Action*, the whole thing just slipped into place, because everything made sense.[28]

Shortly before he left FEE to work for the Volker Fund, Herbert Cornuelle asked Mises to keep an eye on the Columbia University graduate. He called him "one of the most outstanding liberal economic students I know" and mentioned that Rothbard would be interested in attending the NYU seminar.[29] Some weeks before the publication of *Human Action*, then, Mises and Rothbard seem to have discussed Rothbard's project of writing a Misesian textbook on economics—a "guide for the intelligent layman." After Mises's approval of an outline of the proposed book, Rothbard wrote to Cornuelle in November 1949, declaring that he was interested in the subject and that Mises had asked him to draft a representative chapter on "Money and Banking on the Unhampered Market."[30]

During those months, Rothbard took part in Mises's NYU seminar, which dealt that winter with Marxism and in the

---

[28]Walter Block and Walter Grinder, "Rothbard Tells All: Interview with Murray Rothbard," December 1972, p. 6, in Rothbard Papers.

[29]Herbert Cornuelle to Mises, letter dated June 17, 1949; Grove City Archive: FEE files.

[30]See Rothbard's letter to Herbert C. Cornuelle, November 28, 1949, Rothbard Papers. This sample chapter is later referred to as "the money chapter."

spring moved on to the discussion of other schools of thought. It reinforced the main message Rothbard had derived from reading *Human Action*: "From you I have learned for the first time that economics is a coherent structure, and I am sure that this has been impressed on the other members of the seminar as well."[31]

By early January 1951, less than sixteen months after the publication of *Human Action*, Cornuelle and Mises had received the representative chapter. Cornuelle was enthusiastic about the work and Mises also thought that Rothbard would be the right person to write a textbook on Austrian economics—*after* getting his Ph.D.

He wrote to Cornuelle:

> I think that Rothbard's Chapter on Money and Banking is very satisfactory. It certainly proves his ability to write a textbook much better than those I have had an opportunity to see. I hope he will continue his work as soon as he will have finished his thesis.[32]

But Cornuelle did not wait. He offered Rothbard financial support from the Volker Fund so that the project could go forward. Rothbard began working for the Fund on January 1, 1952, and continued his intensive work for them for the next six years.[33]

∽ ∽ ∽

Murray Rothbard was the first in a long line of whiz kids who found a new intellectual home in *Human Action* and in Mises's

---

[31]Rothbard to Mises, letter dated May 18, 1950; Grove City Archive: Rothbard files.

[32]Mises to Cornuelle, letter dated February 10, 1951; Rothbard Papers.

[33]Memo to Volker Fund: Progress Report, January 1 to October 1, 1952, 13 pp., Rothbard Papers.

seminars. Over the next fifteen years it happened with great regularity that highly gifted young men such as George Resch and Paul Cantor suddenly sought admission to the NYU seminar. Some of them even sought admission to Mises's residence. One day Mises was ready to go out for dinner when the doorbell rang. Two youngsters were standing at the door and offered a subscription to *The Freeman* magazine. Mises declined the offer, saying he was already on their mailing list. He did not know that this was his first contact with two of his most ardent followers: Ralph Raico and George Reisman.

Raico and Reisman were both fifteen years old. They had been reading *The Freeman* for a year or two and had also read some of Mises's books. Inspired, they had established "the Cobden Club, an organization of right-wing students" to fight the good fight. One day they decided to pay their hero a visit and came up with the ruse of presenting themselves as salesmen. Fortunately, they then decided to do things the proper way and paid a visit to the FEE offices in Irvington, where they met with Ivan Bierly, who was so impressed by their knowledge that he asked Mises whether he would be willing to receive them. Within ten days the meeting was arranged, and the old man— who fortunately did not remember their faces—advised the boys "about the proper way to study economics and spend [their] time in college."[34] He persuaded them that they had to invest more time learning about economics and liberty, rather than propagandizing theories that they did not really understand. As a token of his trust in their talents, he invited them to attend his NYU seminar—on the condition that they did not make noise.

---

[34]Raico and Reisman to Mises, letter dated February 24, 1953; Grove City Archive: Raico file. That first meeting took place on February 23. Bierly's letter of February 13 is in the same file.

They would attend his seminar for many years and became important advocates of Misesian economics. They both learned German on Mises's advice. Raico translated *Liberalismus* into English and Reisman did the same for *Grundprobleme*.[35]

Speeches and Papers

Encouraged by the success of *Human Action*, Mises turned again to fighting the prevailing ideology of interventionism. On April 18, 1950 he attended a reception of New York's University Club held in honor of the author of *Human Action*, and addressed the audience in an after-dinner speech on "The Economics of the Middle-of-the-Road Policy."[36] Two weeks later, the lecture was printed in the *Financial and Commercial Chronicle*, and at the end of the year, Frederick Nymeyer printed one thousand copies of it as a pamphlet for his campaign to counter the growing socialism among his fellow Calvinists.

Mises went on to write a series of articles on various aspects of interventionism, which he published mainly in three journals: *Commercial and Financial Chronicle*, *Plain Talk*, and *The Freeman*. These pieces both drew on the success of *Human Action* and spurred further interest in the book within the grassroots libertarian movement. Yet Mises certainly harbored no illusions about their short-run impact. The libertarian tradition was old in America, and it was still strong, but he was well aware that current trends were eroding it relentlessly: "If interventionism

---

[35]*Epistemological Problems of Economics*, trans. George Reisman (Princeton, N.J.: Van Nostrand, 1960); *The Free and Prosperous Commonwealth*, trans. Ralph Raico (Princeton, N.J.: Van Nostrand, 1962). The title of the latter book was changed in subsequent editions to *Liberalism: A Socio-Economic Exposition* (Kansas City, Kansas: Sheed Andrews and McMeel, 1978). The Volker Fund sponsored Raico's translation, which he began in the summer of 1956.

[36]The talk was a huge success. See the correspondence between Mises and Shelby Cullom Davis in Grove City Archive: "D" files.

continues to be the policy of the U.S., this country will before long go outright totalitarian."[37] This concern was soon confirmed by the policies adopted in the wake of the Korean War. When war broke out in the fall of 1950, the U.S. government immediately reinstituted the wartime regime of price controls and regulations.

In the spring of 1950, Mises attended a conference dedicated to analyzing the impact of the current Korean War mobilization on the American economy. The conference took place on April 5–8 in White Sulphur Springs, West Virginia and was sponsored by the William Volker Fund.[38] He then wrote a lengthy paper for the 1951 Mont Pèlerin Society meeting in Beauvallon. Its subject was the nature of entrepreneurial profit and loss, which, Mises explained, resulted exclusively from the relative quality of entrepreneurial decision-making and therefore could not possibly be abolished through legislation or any other form of government intervention. He also demonstrated the social utility of profit and loss: profits direct resources into those hands that use them in the way most desired by consumers; losses help eliminate incompetent entrepreneurs, thus preventing a waste of resources. The work was ready by early June and Mises sent it to Nymeyer.[39] His Calvinist friend immediately recognized its suitability for widespread dissemination. Even before the Mont Pèlerin Society meeting began, Nymeyer had

---

[37]Mises to P.C. Armstrong, letter dated March 1, 1950; Grove City Archive: Armstrong file.

[38]See the proceedings in Aaron Director, ed., *Defense, Controls, and Inflation* (Chicago: University of Chicago Press, 1952).

[39]At the same time he must have finished at least the first draft of another important work. By June 1951, he had written a manuscript on Dialectical Materialism, a later version of which was probably incorporated as a chapter in *Theory and History* (New Haven, Conn.: Yale University Press, 1957). See Cornuelle to Mises, letter dated June 6, 1951; Grove City Archive: Herbert Cornuelle file.

agreed to publish the paper and set out to print 5,000 copies, of which the Volker Fund immediately ordered 1,500 copies.[40]

In his renewed effort to combat interventionism, Mises began by writing on such topics as middle-of-the-road policies, inflation, and profit and loss rather than free trade or direct foreign investments. He believed that it was important to target domestic interventionism. To one correspondent in Sweden, who sought to launch a campaign for free trade, Mises explained why this campaign could only be based on a preceding campaign focused on domestic policies:

> One could take into consideration the abolishment of protectionism in the time of Cobden and Chevalier, as freedom of commerce existed within each state, or it was at least on its way toward being established.
>
> Things are very different in the age of interventionism. Each country has a system of varying privileges for individual interest groups (pressure groups). None of these measures would work if foreign countries were to freely supply the domestic market of this country. Keeping away foreign competition is for this reason an indispensable complement to domestic economic policy.
>
> U.S. representatives occasionally indulge in talk of free trade. This is pure illusion. American agricultural policies—parity prices, subsidies, limitation of crop surfaces, destruction of supplies (potatoes!), among other things—would collapse overnight if foreign imports were freely allowed into the country. Can you imagine a present-day England or present-day France with a regime of free trade?
>
> The more a country proceeds toward comprehensive control of all business activities, the more it must close itself to foreign countries. The battle for

---

[40]Nymeyer to Mises, letter dated May 28, 1951; Mises to Nymeyer, letter dated June 21, 1951; Grove City Archive: Nymeyer files.

> free trade must therefore first attack domestic pro-
> tectionist measures.[41]

Of course this does not mean that he would now downplay the
importance of free trade. He discussed it in his lectures and
occasionally also in correspondence. A master of concision,
Mises sometimes addressed the point better in correspondence
than in his books. For example, in response to the perennial
question of whether free trade would cost American jobs, he
replied:

> Wages are cheaper in almost all foreign countries
> than they are in this country. But total costs of pro-
> duction are for most commodities—practically for all
> manufactured goods—lower in this country than they
> are abroad. What counts in competing on the market
> is not the height of one item of the total bill of costs,
> but total costs of production.
>
>   There are, of course, some minor and less impor-
> tant branches of manufacturing which under free
> trade would lose a part of their customers to foreign
> competition. But such an increase of imports can,
> other things being equal, only occur if there is to
> some extent an increase in American exports. If the
> Swiss are "flooding" America with watches, America
> must "flood" Switzerland with some other goods as
> payment for the increased amount of Swiss watches

---

[41]Mises to Friedrich Hoenig, letter dated December 6, 1951; Grove City
Archive: "H" files. Similarly, he wrote a few years later to Rougier:

> An interventionist government can virtually annul all the
> expected advantages of the disappearance of customs barriers
> by domestic intervention. Under the conditions of interven-
> tionism a really common market can be achieved only by a
> common government that has the power to delimit strictly
> the jurisdiction of the various national governments. (March
> 18, 1959; Grove City Archive: Rougier files)

received. For the Swiss do not give the watches away as gifts. They are *selling* them.[42]

The Freeman

The success of *Human Action* prompted the creation of another important libertarian institution. Mises had long been arguing the need for a free-market journal of opinion. Now organizers, journalists, and, especially, financial backers rallied to establish such a journal. Its explicit purpose would be to promote the ideas Mises stood for. The Austrian economist became the intellectual standard-bearer of *The Freeman*, which reinforced the infant network of Mises's NYU seminar, FEE, and the Mont Pèlerin Society. Despite its eventual departure from its founding auspices, *The Freeman* would play a significant role in the revival of American libertarianism under new Austrian auspices. Two historians have aptly summarized this role:

> It is difficult to convey a sense of the crucial role of *The Freeman* at the height of its prestige, between 1950 and 1954. The American Left, in these years, had many well-known and reputable journals from which to choose; the American Right had almost none.[43]
>
> By the end of 1955, when new owners changed the nature of the magazine, a self-conscious and relatively coherent movement had evolved. If "creeping conservatism" was "the grand trend of the 1950s" . . . then *The Freeman* had been its professional and articulate journal of opinion.[44]

---

[42]Mises to Ernest Anthony, letter dated June 19, 1953; Grove City Archive: Anthony file.

[43]George H. Nash, *The Conservative Intellectual Movement in America* (New York: Basic Books, 1976), pp. 28f.

[44]Charles H. Hamilton, *"The Freeman*: The Early Years," R. Lora and W.H. Longton, eds., *The Conservative Press in Twentieth-Century America* (London: Greenwood, 1999).

The Freeman began as a successor to the journal *Plain Talk*, which for some time had been in financial trouble and could

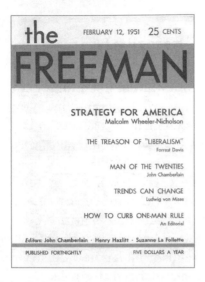

only survive on subsidies from New York businessman Alfred Kohlberg. Initial financing of *The Freeman* came through the fundraising efforts of Jasper Crane, which had resulted in a substantial donation from Herbert Hoover and sizeable loans from Howard J. Pew and Crane himself.[45]

The explicit motivation of Pew and Crane was to provide a forum for the author of *Human Action* and like-minded intellectuals, but to ensure editorial independence all initial funds came in the form of donations and loans, rather than by stock.[46] Leadership of *The Freeman*

---

[45]See "Battle for the *Freeman*," *Time*, January 26, 1953. In a note dated October 3, 1952, John Chamberlain called Hoover the "principal founder of the *Freeman*." Later Leo Wolman successfully set up an advertisement program, which was then followed through by Kurt Lassen. See Hazlitt to Chamberlain, letter dated October 24, 1952; Grove City Archive: *Freeman* files.

[46]See the "Statement to the Directors of *Freeman* Magazine, Inc. by its active editors," attachment to a letter to the *Freeman*'s Board of Directors dated October 2, 1952, p. 5; Grove City Archive: *Freeman* files. Shortly after the establishment of *The Freeman*, Frederick Nymeyer had written to business friends that

> Dr. von Mises has been the prime mover on the program to put out a truly liberal (meaning by that laissez-faire capitalism) periodical to counter-influence the flood of Leftist publications. The man who finally organized the financial matters for such a publication is Mr. Jasper Crane. (Nymeyer to Choate and others, letter dated February 13, 1951)

was in the hands of its three editors: Henry Hazlitt, John Chamberlain, and Suzanne LaFollette. Chamberlain became the president and Hazlitt the vice-president of the journal. They published *The Freeman* as a fortnightly review, with Mises on an eleven-man board of directors. The first issue appeared on October 2, 1950.[47]

Many observers greeted the new publication as the necessary exception in a media landscape dominated by the Left. Raymond Moley explained to his readers in *Newsweek*:

> It is difficult to realize how firmly entrenched in this country are the forces which would pervert the free institutions of this country into the reality of a socialist state. The drift toward more state power, particularly Federal power, began many years ago under such names as "progressivism" or "liberalism." This movement as organized politics ultimately captured the Democratic Party under FDR. It pervades most of the economic and political thinking in our colleges and universities. It has seized ascendancy in our literary criticism and book reviewing. And finally, through the political arms of the CIO and AFL it has measurably brought together into a hard core the immense financial and voting strength of the unions.
>
> No little credit for this is due to two journals of opinion, *The Nation* and *New Republic*. These journals,

---

See also Nymeyer to Dalton, letter dated April 6, 1953; Grove City Archive: Nymeyer files. Crane was at the time a director of DuPont and member of its executive committee.

[47] *The Freeman* had two predecessors by the same name. The first *Freeman* was published for a couple of years in the 1920s; the editor was Albert Jay Nock. In the 1930s, then, a former assistant to Nock, Suzanne LaFollette, published a successor for about fourteen months. LaFollette also joined the editorial team of Chamberlain's and Hazlitt's *Freeman* in 1950. See Nash, *The Conservative Intellectual Movement in America*, p. 27; Hamilton, "*The Freeman*: The Early Years."

once the voice of minority protest, have become the
gospel of what has almost become an established
order of thinking. A whole generation of teachers and
other leaders of thought have to a measurable degree
taken their political bearings from these journals.

The Freeman's great role is that of a protest
against the new orthodoxy which holds that all good
comes from the state. This new protest has the virtue,
however, of conformity to the oldest and best traditions of American freedom—traditions that if neglected too long will wither and die.[48]

The journal had an excellent start. Subscriptions increased
from 5,203 in the first issue to 12,200 in May 1951. By March
1952, *Time* and *Newsweek* reported that the new kid on the
block distributed close to 20,000 copies. At the end of March
1952, Alfred Kohlberg dropped out as treasurer and returned to
his import business. In came Alex Hillman, publisher of *Pageant*
and *People Today* and other magazines. This was the first great
blossoming of Austro-libertarianism in America. Mises now felt
that things had substantially improved, and he wrote in correspondence that the case for liberty had made great progress
since the dark days of 1945.[49]

The Freeman not only provided Mises with a forum for his
ideas, but also with an organizational basis through which he
could reach out directly to students. At the initiative of Henry
Hazlitt, *The Freeman* sponsored a two-week Mises seminar in
the afternoons of June 25 through July 6, 1951 in the alumni
room of the NYU Faculty Club on Washington Square.[50] In

---

[48]Raymond Moley's column in *Newsweek* (November 13, 1950).

[49]Mises to V. Casimir-Lambert, letter dated May 15, 1951; Grove City
Archive: Casimir Lambert files. Casimir Lambert, who left the United States
in 1946, had just returned. Mises wrote to him that meanwhile "many things
have changed" for the better.

[50]Mises was not in New York during the first three weeks of June, and left
New York City again on July 10 (probably for the Mont Pèlerin Society

the first week, Mises dealt with fundamental problems of economic analysis, and in the second turned to monetary economics. Young Leland Yeager, at the time a graduate student in monetary economics, was one of the thirty-nine participants. The second week would leave a lasting impression him.[51] He wrote:

> Reading your books is very instructive, but seeing and hearing you in person is a genuine inspiration. You revealed yourself not only as a great economist but as a great humanitarian too. The interventionists who cite you as an example of a "die-hard reactionary" are only showing their own complete ignorance. What a pity that the world has so few intellectually courageous men like you![52]

Yeager was one of the few student participants. Most members of the seminar were teachers, journalists, businessmen, and professors. The two weeks were a great success and led to a second Mises seminar in June and July 1952, in San Francisco's Public Library, before an audience of forty-six participants.[53] Again the first week was dedicated to fundamentals. Mises here delivered his analysis of dialectical materialism, which a few years later

---

meeting in Beauvallon). See Mises to Richard von Mises, letter dated May 7, 1951; Grove City Archive: Richard von Mises files.

[51]Herbert Cornuelle to Mises, letter dated October 30, 1950 and subsequent correspondence; Grove City Archive: *Freeman* files. Yeager to Mises, letter dated June 26, 1955; Grove City Archive: Buck Hill Falls file.

[52]Yeager to Mises, letter dated July 7, 1951; Grove City Archive: *Freeman* files. Bettina Bien took lecture notes of this seminar. In the 1980s, Yeager held the Ludwig von Mises Chair in political economy at Auburn University in Alabama. He is the author of a famous textbook on international monetary relations.

[53]There was also another 1951 meeting in White Sulphur Springs, which Mises did not like at all because of the presence of too many statists. See Nymeyer to Brown, letter dated October 2, 1952; Grove City Archive: Nymeyer files.

appeared as a chapter of his book *Theory and History*. In the second week, he dealt with capital theory (saving, investment and the accumulation of capital, the demand for capital, and the economic and political significance of foreign investment).

Again the seminar was very successful, but it did not go to his head. When invited to appear on television in California, he declined saying, "my foreign accent prevents me from appearing on television or radio. These media of communication intensify the shortcomings of the speaker's pronunciation."[54]

ও ও ও

In the tradition of *Plain Talk*, one of the concrete goals of *The Freeman* was to expose Communism as a totalitarian scheme. Anti-Communism also provided a unifying theme for dealing with foreign policy and domestic policies, which could be denounced as Communist-inspired. Yet there was no fundamental agreement on the strategic role of anti-Communism. Chamberlain and LaFollette saw in it the very essence of their mission. For Mises and Hazlitt, Communism was just a particularly gruesome species of the more general disease of statism, which manifested itself most notably in domestic government interventionism.

Many of *The Freeman* articles in the decisive early years dealt with American foreign policy, especially with the role of the

---

[54]Mises to James Fifield, handwritten manuscript of a letter, undated response to Fifield's letter dated July 8, 1952; Grove City Archive: Churches files. Mises left Manhattan for San Francisco some days after June 18. After the seminar, he spent a vacation in California and returned to Manhattan after Labor Day. The fall term started on September 22. See Mises to Cobrin, letter dated June 18, 1952; Grove City Archive: "C" files. The vacation is mentioned in Mises to Hamilius, letter dated June 3, 1952; Grove City Archive: Hamilius files. The place (San Francisco) and length of the seminar is mentioned in Mises to Julier, letter dated September 22, 1953; Grove City Archive: "J" files.

United States in confronting the Soviet-led East Bloc. The focus on anti-Communism in foreign policy was certainly convenient in that it allowed the editors to expand their readership without offending those who were both anti-Communist and pro-interventionist.

Even on the issue of foreign policy, however, there was no unity in the libertarian camp. One faction advocated political isolationism combined with cultural and commercial openness to foreign countries. On the other side, there were the interventionists who championed American government opposition to Communism on a worldwide scale. The latter tended to be less interested in combating Communism by intellectual and educational means, focusing instead on the denunciation of Communist infiltrators, the prosecution of domestic traitors, and military action against Communist troops abroad. The confrontation crystallized in a semi-public correspondence between Leonard Read and Lawrence Fertig. Read had championed a resolute anti-war stance, because he recognized that war was the great mainspring of government power. Fertig commented:

> Your philosophy seems to trend toward non-resistance and even slightly toward anarchism. I believe that the raising of an army is a perfectly legitimate function of government. Your implication that we must wait on these shores before striking back at an aggressor, makes no sense to me. Your statement that a man in the army shooting Communists in Korea is just as guilty as a man blowing the head off a baby in Centerport, is a statement that I reject completely.[55]

And he went on to say that the fundamental problem cannot be coercion *per se* because taxes are after all coercively levied on the citizenry. Read replied:

---

[55]Fertig to Read, letter dated March 15, 1951; Grove City Archive: Fertig file.

> Personally, I am unable to concede that there is any
> right that comes into being by reason of you and me
> acting collectively. From a moral standpoint can the
> collective be right in doing what is wrong for the per-
> son? I concede that you have a moral right to protect
> your life and property against violence otherwise ini-
> tiated. Collectively we have the same right, but no
> more. This reasoning is not anarchical nor is it paci-
> fistic. It is nothing more than the limitation of force
> to what I think is its proper scope.[56]

Mises's views on the issue are revealed in a letter that he
wrote some years later to Anthony Fisher, the founder of the
neo-liberal Institute of Economic Affairs in England. Mises
deplored the pro-socialist leanings of public opinion on the
western side of the Iron Curtain, which "paralyzes all political
actions of the West and makes it possible for the Russians to do
what they want in Hungary, Poland and the Near-East." He
continued:

> The average American intellectual condemns Eng-
> land and France as aggressors. But he does not con-
> sider as aggression what the Russians are doing in
> Hungary. He admits that the Russians are rather harsh
> in Hungary. But he excuses this harshness. It is, he
> thinks, rather unrealistic to apply to eastern affairs the
> yardstick of Western civilization. What in America
> would have to be qualified as brutality is in the East
> merely behaving as everybody does.[57]

Otherwise Mises did not get involved in these debates. In
Liberalism, he had argued that the Russians should be allowed to
do in their own country whatever they wished; that they should

---

[56]Read to Fertig, letter dated March 19, 1951; Grove City Archive: Fertig file.

[57]Mises, to Fisher, letter dated December 10, 1956; Grove City Archive:
Fisher file.

be free to spread their ideology in the West, even with the help of clandestine hirelings; and that businessmen and other citizens of the Western countries should be free to make loans to Bolsheviks in Russia and elsewhere. What he opposed was Western *governments* actively supporting the destructive policies of Communism, whether through premiums paid on exports to the Soviet Union, or through propaganda on their behalf.[58] He had espoused this position a quarter-century earlier and he had not retracted a single world. He was convinced that Communism first and foremost posed an intellectual challenge and had to be fought with the weapon of the mind.[59] Mises wanted *The Freeman* to run more articles and book reviews dealing with economic principles but he was aware that the journal lacked the manpower to do so.

This dispute over American foreign policy foreshadowed dividing lines within the American libertarian movement that have continued to the present day, but in the early 1950s, it was only a side show in the unfolding drama that led to the early demise of *The Freeman*.

The main factor in this drama was a disagreement between Hazlitt and Chamberlain on strategic issues of editorial policy. Then, too, there was the fact that Hazlitt, who had the backing of the main sponsors, was unwilling to give up his position at *Newsweek* to run *The Freeman* full time. Conflicts between the Hazlitt-Mises camp and the Chamberlain-LaFollette camp were inevitable, given their different outlooks on what *The Freeman* was and should be. For Mises and Hazlitt, the essential mission of the journal was to educate the larger public, not to take part in the daily strife of political factions:

---

[58]Mises, *Liberalism*, pp. 153f.

[59]He expressed this opinion in a letter to Louis Rougier, dated May 9, 1950; Grove City Archive: Rougier files.

> As I see it, the function of *The Freeman* is to make it
> possible for dissenters to challenge the ideas of the
> Left. . . . The issue is not so much to fight commu-
> nism as this task is to some extent accomplished by
> other media of communication. What matters is to
> expound sound economics and to expose current eco-
> nomic fallacies.[60]

In contrast, Chamberlain favored a more aggressive tone
both attacking and endorsing specific persons, parties, and
political candidates. With an eye on Mises, Röpke and other
academic contributors, he later argued against "sterile" journalism:

> We believe that it was the intention of the founders
> that *The Freeman* should be a comprehensive fort-
> nightly review of the contemporary scene and not
> merely a journal of classical economics, allowing a
> selected group of economists to talk to each other via
> their papers.[61]

In short, Chamberlain held that the magazine must have "cru-
sading zeal . . . wit, satire and editorial bite."
  Hazlitt replied:

> Exactly. But one man's crusading zeal is merely
> another man's vehemence; one man's wit and satire
> merely another man's trivial wisecracks; one man's
> "editorial bite" merely another's vituperation.

After two years of experience, Hazlitt found his concerns
confirmed. He quoted Chicago economist Frank Knight, who
had told him in correspondence that *The Freeman*

---

[60]Mises to Jasper Crane, letter dated April 27, 1954; Grove City Archive:
Crane file.

[61]See the "Statement to the Directors of *Freeman* Magazine, Inc. by its
active editors," attachment to a letter to *The Freeman*'s Board of Directors
dated October 2, 1952, pp. 4–5; Grove City Archive: *Freeman* files.

seems to "scream" in a way that may tickle the ears of those already converted or "overconverted," but it would hardly convert anybody, at least nobody open to reason, and they are the only ones I'm personally interested in.[62]

Hazlitt himself was later reported to object to putting out the "kind of magazine in which McCarthy is a sacred character." And Fertig was quoted in the same source, saying that *The Freeman* "should have convinced by logic and reason, with less shrillness, less direct hysteria."[63] Hazlitt stated his own opinion in October 1952:

A libertarian journal of opinion is only worth publishing, as I see it, if it can have a real effect in turning the tide of national thought in this crucial era. To have such an effect, it must command the respect of the intellectuals—even (in fact, particularly,) of those we are trying to convert. And it cannot command this respect unless it has dignity and a note of authority. Of course the magazine must also be lively to reach as wide an audience as possible without sacrificing these qualities.[64]

Even though Hazlitt was only a part-time editor, his work with *The Freeman* proved to be a severe drain on his energies.

---

[62]Hazlitt to Chamberlain, letter dated October 24, 1952; Grove City Archive: *Freeman* files. This seems to have been a widely shared perception. One company executive explained why he would advertise in *The Freeman* in 1953, but not in 1952 (when the old editorial team was still in place):

We did consider *The Freeman* last year, but at that time it was too inflammatory and not objective enough. But now, since they have been reorganized, this magazine is very liberal in the conservative sense of the word. (Dalton to Nymeyer, letter dated April 8, 1953; Grove City Archive: Nymeyer files)

[63]Quoted from "Battle for the *Freeman*."

[64]Hazlitt to Chamberlain, letter dated October 24, 1952; Grove City Archive: *Freeman* files.

By May 1952, he brought a new man onto the editorial team: Forrest Davis, a former Washington editor for the *Saturday Evening Post*. But just a few days after his arrival, it was clear that Davis was not to be Hazlitt's man. Isolated in his editorial stance, Hazlitt resigned in June. Officially, he took a "leave of absence of four months" at the request of Mises, Fertig, and other friends on the board of directors, who did not want to abandon control of *The Freeman* to the remaining editors.[65]

So far so good for Chamberlain, LaFollette, and Davis. Their major problem in the long run was to find funding independent of the financial fathers of the magazine, Pew and Crane, who backed the Hazlitt line. This problem seemed to find a convenient solution in the form of a fundraising dinner at the occasion of *The Freeman*'s second anniversary. One month before the event, however, the Hazlitt camp started torpedoing the dinner preparations.

It is not entirely clear what prompted them to this action. The following scenario seems most likely: During Hazlitt's leave of absence, Howard Pew had made it clear both to the Chamberlain camp and to the members of the Board of Directors that he stood ready to finance *The Freeman* single-handedly if it focused on the communication of broad principles of the free-market philosophy, rather than engaging in partisan attacks on persons and programs—that is, if it followed the Hazlitt editorial line.[66] When Chamberlain and his associates did not yield, Mises and the others started a last desperate attempt to direct *The Freeman* toward Hazlitt's position by scuttling the fundraiser that would have made the editors financially independent of Pew and Crane.

---

[65] Hazlitt to Chamberlain, letter dated October 24, 1952; Grove City Archive: *Freeman* files.

[66] See the "Statement to the Directors of *Freeman* Magazine, Inc. by its active editors," attachment to a letter to *The Freeman*'s Board of Directors dated October 2, 1952; Grove City Archive: *Freeman* files.

The struggle got uglier and more personal. Chamberlain now wrote nasty letters accusing Hazlitt of being Pew's lapdog, and in a heated board meeting in October 1953, Mises said Chamberlain and LaFollette were second-rate journalists compared to Hazlitt.[67]

Hazlitt himself resigned both from the board of editors and as vice-president on October 8, 1952, as he had intended since May. Meanwhile Crane and Fertig lined up a majority behind their position, and at a board meeting on January 21, 1953, Hazlitt was elected editor-in-chief, whereupon Chamberlain, LaFollette, and Davis resigned immediately.[68]

But this was only a symbolic victory. More than six months of quarrels had brought *The Freeman* to the verge of bankruptcy. Jasper Crane desperately tried to raise new money with fundraising letters, and Frederick Nymeyer tried to acquire new advertisers, but to no avail.[69] After a few months, Hazlitt, who still continued to write for *Newsweek* and to fulfill other contractual obligations, became discouraged by the desperate financial situation.

In 1955, the magazine was taken over by the Irvington Press, a subsidiary of FEE, with Frank Chodorov as editor. Mises contributed an article on "Inequality of Wealth and Income" to the first issue, May 1955. By January of the next year, *The Freeman*

---

[67]Chamberlain to Mises, letter dated October 27, 1952; Grove City Archive: *Freeman* files. On October 31, 1952 a vote of confidence in favor of the present editors brought to light the composition of the two factions. A "yes" vote came from the three editors themselves and from Hillman, Peters, and Kohlberg. A vote of no confidence came from Read, Fertig, Mises, and the Robinsons. See the handwritten note in Grove City Archive: *Freeman* files.

[68]Chamberlain eventually became an editor of *National Review* as well as of the *Princeton Panel* and a regular contributor to the *Wall Street Journal*.

[69]Henry Regnery's response to Crane was symptomatic: "I think this is a lost cause." Regnery to Nymeyer, letter dated April 6, 1953; Grove City Archive: Nymeyer files.

was officially the journal of FEE. Paul Poirot would be its editor for the next few decades, and it would continue to publish the work of Mises and promote the economics of the Austrian School. But it never reached a mass audience.

The Nymeyer Connection

Frederick Nymeyer had printed one thousand copies of "The Economics of the Middle-of-the-Road Policy," which he distributed for free among his fellow Calvinists. The campaign had a resounding echo. A few months later, the Edison Company ordered 3,100 copies, the Norfolk and Western Railway Company ordered 800 copies, and other orders followed.[70] At least one copy had found its way over the Atlantic and fell on fertile ground. The young English businessman Anthony Fisher asked that forty-eight copies be sent to him as a gift—because of the foreign exchange controls—which he duly received.[71] And at least one other copy made it over the Pacific. A Japanese correspondent of Nymeyer's wrote him:

---

[70]Nymeyer to Delafield, letter dated April 4, 1951; Smith to Nymeyer, letter dated June 11, 1951; Grove City Archive: Nymeyer files. Following instructions from Mises, Nymeyer published the piece under the title "Middle-of-the-Road Policy Leads to Socialism." See Mises to Nymeyer, letter dated October 28, 1950; Grove City Archive: Nymeyer files. Mises received a 10 percent royalty on the sales. See for example Nymeyer to Mises, letter dated June 6, 1951; Grove City Archive: Nymeyer files. The total number of copies Nymeyer printed was 10,000. Shortly after the end of 1961, when a stock of 1,380 copies was left, there was a reprint, and another reprint of 30,000 (!) copies in 1965. See Nymeyer to Lipsett, letter dated October 9, 1961; Nymeyer to Mises, letter dated July 15, 1965; Grove City Archive: Nymeyer files.

[71]Nymeyer wrote: "Mr. Fisher's request may be a 'racket,' but my assumption is that he is an advocate of free and competitive markets and that the use he makes of this pamphlet will promote a good cause." Nymeyer to Mises, letter dated April 23, 1951; Grove City Archive: Nymeyer files. In Latin America, the Federation of the Mexican Chambers of Commerce planned to translate the piece (Mises to Nymeyer, letter dated June 21, 1951).

> What I find revealing is the fact that such of his pam-
> phlets as I received from you had to be published at
> all in a country which is supposed to be the only
> remaining fortress of free enterprise . . . if the Amer-
> icans themselves are to be told about the benefits of
> free enterprise by Austrians of all peoples, it seems to
> me that the world's malady is pretty far gone.[72]

In the fall of 1950, spurred by the success of his campaign,
Nymeyer set up the publishing company "Consumers-Produc-
ers Economic Service" in South Holland, Illinois. This would
later become the "Libertarian Press," which still exists today.
Throughout the 1950s, Nymeyer came to New York for two or
three days at the beginning of each month and had regular dinner and lunch meetings with Mises. They never became close
friends but there were more than mere professional ties
between the Jewish agnostic and the Dutch-American Calvinist.
Nymeyer eventually convinced himself that Mises was "the
greatest living champion of the innermost rampart of Christianity." In various letters to Howard Pew, Nymeyer summarized many years of reflection on the significance of Mises's
work for Christianity:

> If there is to be a re-Reformation, it will have to be,
> in my opinion, on the basis of what the praxeological
> and the natural sciences have contributed to human
> knowledge since the days of the reformation. In
> regard to questions of ethics, I have come to the con-
> clusion that the economics of Dr. von Mises consti-
> tutes by far the most satisfactory means to modernize
> the ethics of the Hebrew-Christian religion. When
> that kind of a synthesis is made, one turns out to be
> an extraordinarily conservative adherent of the

---

[72]Jujiro Iwai to Nymeyer, letter dated January 23, 1952; Grove City
Archive: Nymeyer files.

Christian religion. But also some of the absurdities
are removed.[73]

৯ৎ   ৯ৎ   ৯ৎ

Nymeyer's publishing venture began as all start-ups do: small
scale with big ideas. At first he published copies of Mises's "Middle-of-the-Road Policy Leads to Socialism," but he already had
larger-scale projects in mind; in particular, he planned an
American edition of *The Theory of Money and Credit* and a translation of the final edition of Böhm-Bawerk's three-volume
magnum opus.[74] Mises warned him that the major problem was
not to print good books, but to spread the message in a hostile
environment:

> As conditions are today in this country, such books
> would be boycotted by the universities, the libraries
> and the influential newspapers and periodicals. It
> seems to me that the main problem is to raise the
> money for counter-acting such a boycott.[75]

Nymeyer knew Mises was right and he knew what to do about
it. Many years of networking in American industrial circles had
filled his address book, and he was astonishingly capable of
bypassing the distribution channels of established publishers to

---

[73]Nymeyer to Pew, letter dated April 22, 1959; Grove City Archive:
Nymeyer files. The statement that Mises is the "the greatest living champion
of the innermost rampart of Christianity" is in Nymeyer to Pew, letter dated
February 10, 1959; Grove City Archive: Nymeyer files. See also Nymeyer to
Pew, letter dated September 17, 1956; Grove City Archive: Pew files.

[74]Nymeyer was also in touch with Hayek, who recommended Böhm-
Bawerk's "Macht oder ökonomisches Gesetz" [Control or Economic Law]
for translation. Nymeyer then made inquiries about the copyrights for a 1931
translation by John Richard Metz. See Nymeyer to Sennholz and Huncke,
letter dated June 5, 1951; Grove City Archive: Nymeyer files.

[75]Mises to Nymeyer, letter dated January 16, 1951; Grove City Archive:
Nymeyer files.

reach the public directly. Mises was impressed. He started giving serious thought to Nymeyer's plan to hire a qualified German-English translator for Böhm-Bawerk's work.

Mises now remembered a young man from Germany who had been attending his NYU seminar for some time. He had come to the United States a year earlier, as one of the first immigrants after the German quota had been opened in the summer of 1949. Hans Sennholz had already studied economics in Marburg and Cologne, and he had received a Ph.D. in economics from the University of Cologne in the spring of 1949. In Marburg, a fellow-student had advised him to read the treatise on money by that "sharp Jew" from Vienna, so when Sennholz decided to continue his studies, he recognized Mises's name in the faculty list of New York University. He attended his seminar with great enthusiasm and after some months asked Mises to supervise a Ph.D. dissertation. Sennholz later recalled:

> In his twenty-four years at New York University Professor Mises sponsored only four candidates who wrote their dissertations under his tutelage (Sennholz, Spadaro, Kirzner, Reisman). When I first broached my plan to study with him and earn the degree he bluntly rejected me: "Many would like me to sponsor them but only very few are qualified." I was stunned and hurt but understood his reaction when I learned that the school conferred very few terminal degrees in a year. Professor Mises was not about to sponsor a potential failure. In fact, the four he actually accepted may have been his full share of successful candidates. When I repeated my request six weeks later he reacted quite differently; he readily and courteously accepted me as his candidate and even suggested a number of topics for my dissertation.[76]

---

[76]He went on: "He probably changed his opinion about me when he learned that I was a German doctor with a degree from Cologne University, which I had earned at the age of 27 after nearly seven years in the armed

During the following years, Sennholz would not only write his doctoral dissertation but also translate Böhm-Bawerk. At Mises's suggestion, Nymeyer also hired native English speaker George D. Huncke as a co-translator.[77] Many years later, the Nymeyer-Sennholz connection proved to be important in maintaining the mission of Libertarian Press, when Sennholz took over the company.

Nymeyer had another publishing idea that proved to be highly successful. He had given much thought to the question of how Mises's ideas could be presented to the greater public in a more accessible form than a 900-page treatise. He found the answer when, in 1952, his Libertarian Press published a collection of articles that Mises had written during the previous seven years.[78] The book was titled *Planning for Freedom*. This was also the title of the first essay, which Mises had written in 1945 in reaction to Hayek's phrase of government planning for competition. The other chapters criticized various aspects of interventionist theory, history, and practice; they also contrasted the interventionist record with the operation of the free market. Each chapter could be read independently of the others, and thus the total made for an excellent "light" introduction to Misesian economics. Sales proved very satisfactory. One order came from the Soviet Union. Mises commented: "I hope

---

services (November 15, 1939—September 14, 1946)." Hans F. Sennholz, "Finding My Way," a speech delivered at the Schlarbaum award ceremony (San Mateo, California, October 16, 2004). Edward Facey also received his Ph.D. under Mises.

[77]Mises's proposal is in his letter to Nymeyer dated January 27, 1951; Grove City Archive: Nymeyer files. By December 1952, conflicts had arisen between the two translators. See Nymeyer to Mises, letter dated December 11, 1952; Grove City Archive: Nymeyer files.

[78]About a year later, Nymeyer had another idea, suggesting that *Human Action* be made more accessible by the creation of a glossary. Nymeyer to Mises, letter dated November 25, 1953; Grove City Archive: Nymeyer files. Later on, Percy Greaves put this idea into practice.

that the purchase of *Planning for Freedom* will complete the Moscow collection of my publications."[79]

American Edition of
Theory of Money and Credit

The success of *Human Action* paved the way for a new edition of *The Theory of Money and Credit* in 1953. By the late 1940s, the book had been out of print for some years.[80] Nymeyer was willing to publish a new edition, but Mises chose the more prestigious Yale University Press, which was interested in publishing more of its bestselling author. In true Christian spirit, Nymeyer promoted the book through a flyer campaign. Five thousand flyers were sent to bankers and another 10,000 to other potential buyers.[81]

Mises used the opportunity to add a new fourth part to the book on "monetary reconstruction" which argued for reintroducing the gold standard. Here he restated ideas he had expressed in previous works, but greater intellectual maturity had made the exposition simpler. He combined these older, more technical ideas with the case against the only possible alternative to the gold standard, namely, inflation. Mises thought that the United States was on the verge of the steep decline of inflationism and interventionism he had seen in Europe. In only one respect did the American situation differ from Germany in 1914 and 1923: the presence of a vocal opposition against this decline.[82]

---

[79]Mises to Nymeyer, letter dated March 24, 1955; Grove City Archive: Nymeyer files.

[80]Nymeyer files, around 1950.

[81]He may have sent Mises's paper "About Things to Come" along with the flyer. See Nymeyer to Mises, letter dated October 22, 1953; Grove City Archive: Nymeyer files.

[82]Mises to Hagemann, letter dated January 6, 1955; Grove City Archive: Hagemann file.

But he also added two crucial insights he had gained since the last edition of his book.

The first of these insights was that there was not even an "emergency case" for inflation. The champions of emergency inflation agreed that there is no economic case for this policy under normal circumstances, but they argued that inflation was justified as a last resort when a national emergency (such as war) required the continued operation of the government and taxation and debt failed to do the job.[83]

Mises noticed that, *if* a majority of citizens truly stood behind the government and its project, no inflation would be necessary. In this case, the political determination of the majority would come to be expressed in higher taxation. There was only one conceivable scenario in which the emergency argument applied: if the majority disagreed with the government. Either they believed that the government already had the resources it required, or that there was no emergency in the first place. Either way, resorting to inflation is tantamount to establishing an antidemocratic minority rule. He had raised this point already in 1923 at the height of the German hyperinflation. But his wording then was cautious and he did not insist on the point.[84] In 1954, he stated unambiguously that inflation was the financial aspect of tyrannies. It is not an instrument of legitimate revenue, but an instrument of oppression:

---

[83]He observes:

> This political argument is only rarely resorted to in books, articles, and political speeches. It does not lend itself to such public treatment. But the underlying idea plays an important role in the thinking of statesmen and historians. (Mises, *Theory of Money and Credit* [Indianapolis: Liberty Fund, 1980], p. 500)

[84]Mises, "Die geldtheoretische Seite des Stabilisierungsproblems," *Schriften des Vereins für Sozialpolitik* 164, no. 2 (Munich: Duncker & Humblot, 1923): 32. See also our discussion in chap. 12.

There is no need to raise the question whether the government's or the majority's opinion is right. Perhaps the government is right. However, we deal not with the substance of the conflict but with the methods chosen by the rulers for its solution. They reject the democratic way of persuading the majority. They arrogate to themselves the power and the moral right to circumvent the will of the people. They are eager to win its cooperation by deceiving the public about the costs involved in the measures suggested. While seemingly complying with the constitutional procedures of representative government, their conduct is in effect not that of elected officeholders but that of guardians of the people. The elected executive no longer deems himself the people's mandatory; he turns into a führer.

He went on:

It is not just an accident that in our age inflation has become the accepted method of monetary management. Inflation is the fiscal complement of statism and arbitrary government. It is a cog in the complex of policies and institutions which gradually lead toward totalitarianism.[85]

The second insight Mises added to the 1954 edition also represents a departure from his thinking in 1934, and even more so from his views of 1912, when he first published the book. The insight concerns the necessity of an actual circulation of gold coins. In 1912, he almost disparaged such "metallistic" views, but forty years of experience had made him wiser. He now emphasized:

Gold must be in the cash holdings of everybody. Everybody must see gold coins changing hands, must

---

[85]Mises, *Theory of Money and Credit*, p. 468.

> be used to having gold coins in his pockets, to receiving gold coins when he cashes his paycheck, and to spending gold coins when he buys in a store.[86]

Of course Mises had not become a gold bug. He had no fetish about the yellow metal or any other metal. The point was that only a commodity currency made the citizens sovereign in monetary matters. As long as they had real money in hand, they were truly in charge of it and they would immediately notice any departure from sound policies. Any bank or government refusal to redeem checks would immediately be recognized as fraud.

> What is needed is to alarm the masses in time. The workingman in cashing his paycheck should learn that some foul trick has been played upon him. The President, Congress, and the Supreme Court have clearly proved their inability or unwillingness to protect the common man, the voter, from being victimized by inflationary machinations. The function of securing a sound currency must pass into new hands, into those of the whole nation.[87]

At the end, Mises noticed, there were no arguments against the gold standard; there was only the cynical claim that reintroducing it was a utopian undertaking. He replied very much along the same lines by which he had concluded his critique of socialism:

> Yet we have only the choice between two utopias: the utopia of a market economy, not paralyzed by government sabotage on the one hand, and the utopia of

---

[86]Ibid., p. 493. Similarly, he wrote in private correspondence: "There is only one effective method of avoiding inflation: All government expenditure must be covered by taxes and by borrowing from the public, not by borrowing from the commercial banks." Mises to Howard Pew, letter dated November 6, 1951; Grove City Archive: Pew files.

[87]Mises, *Theory of Money and Credit*, p. 494.

totalitarian all-round planning on the other hand. The choice of the first alternative implies the decision in favor of the gold standard.[88]

Grey Eminence and Itinerant Scholar

The success of *Human Action* was not the only instance of Mises's influence on the libertarian movement and on the American Right in general. Another factor was, ironically, his relative isolation among academic economists. By the late 1940s, Mises was already the odd man out in both his methods

Mises in their New York apartment in the 1950s

of research and his political orientation. Then *Human Action* put him in the spotlight, and suddenly his authority weighed heavily in the decision-making of the few but substantial funds that had been created to support free-market scholarship.

Thirty years of social science research funding through the Rockefeller Foundation and others who pursued an explicit "scientistic" orientation had left their mark on the state of economics and other disciplines. The money from Rockefeller, Ford, Carnegie, and others was channeled into the universities through the Social Science Research Council, a 1923 Rockefeller creation. To the exterior world, the Council represented seven major social science societies, but in fact it was a self-perpetuating

---

[88]Ibid., p. 500. He had little doubt that these warnings would go unheeded. See his letter to Rougier, dated January 3, 1952; Grove City Archive: Rougier files.

body. In January 1954, Karl E. Ettinger, a private research consultant, commented on the role of the Council in a letter to F.A. Hayek. Quoting extensively from R.B. Fosdick's *History of the Rockefeller Foundation*, he concluded:

> there seems to be strong evidence that the emergence of an orthodoxy of quantitative sociology has been greatly influenced by the magnetism of money and the control of available funds by a foundation bureaucracy that knew what it wanted and favored the imitation of the methods of natural scientists by social scientists.[89]

Only a small number of private individuals and institutions still supported social philosophers of the old type. Mises knew them all, and *Human Action* had given a great boost to his authority. The Volker Fund had been funding him since 1945. But after the publication of his treatise, the Fund began supporting lectures and extended seminars for Mises, and it even started funding his students. Thus from 1955 to 1969, the Volker Fund sponsored a one-year fellowship in political economy at NYU's Graduate School of Business Administration. Mises nominated the recipient.[90] For some time, he also

---

[89]Ettinger to Hayek, letter dated January 5, 1954; Grove City Archive: Ettinger file. Ettinger refers to Raymond B. Fosdick, *The Story of the Rockefeller Foundation* (New York: Harper, 1952). The political explosiveness of these observations stemmed from the tax-exempt status that the big foundations enjoyed. See on this Harry D. Gideonse, "Changing Issues in Academic Freedom in the United States Today," *Proceedings of the American Philosophical Society* 94, no. 2 (1950); Mises's letter dated May 24, 1954; Grove City Archive: U.S. Congress files. Mises had known Ettinger at least since 1946. Ettinger coordinated research on consumers' cooperatives on behalf of the Petroleum Industry Research Foundation. See Grove City Archive: Petroleum Industry Research Foundation file.

[90]The first recipient was Hans Sennholz (1955–56). Israel Kirzner was the laureate in 1956–57 and Toshio Murata in 1959–1960 (upon his return to Japan, he began to spread Mises's theories and also translated *The Ultimate*

controlled an annual budget of $12,500 at NYU.[91] And other institutions started doing the same thing, for example, the Earhart Foundation undertook travel expenditures and student scholarships, the National Association of Manufacturers organized and paid for seminars, and Howard Pew and others subsidized *The Freeman*. For several years, funding Mises and his projects was almost a matter of course. His judgment on persons and projects was often final.[92]

This sudden concentration of resources on Mises reflected more than the respect owed to the man—it was also the sign of an important problem in the free-market movement: by the early 1950s, substantial money was available for scholarship, but there were not many libertarian scholars of Mises's stature. The situation was quite bleak, as Lawrence Fertig stated in a letter:

> Take the faculty of Columbia University. Aside from Dr. George Stigler and Dr. Leo Wolman, I doubt if there is another member on the entire economics faculty who presents the free-market, liberal point of view. At Yale, out of thirty members of the economics faculty, until recently just two—Professor Henry Fairchild and one other—represented the old liberal point of view. The Harvard faculty is dominated by men like Professor Seymour Harris, Alvin Hansen, Sweezy and others like them, who range all the way

---

Foundation of Economic Science and *Human Action* into Japanese). Only two students received the fellowship for three consecutive years. One of these students was Robert Guarnieri, from 1963 to 1966. See the correspondence in Grove City Archive: Guarnieri file. Guarnieri had been a student of Hans Sennholz's in Grove City. He later set out for a business career.

[91]These payments started after December 1958. See Bierly to Taggart, letter dated March 17, 1960; Grove City Archive.

[92]In the fall of 1958, historian of economic thought Emil Kauder advised Raymond de Roover, who was looking for funding of a research project, not to write directly to the Volker Fund, but to get first in touch with Mises or Hayek. See the correspondence in Grove City Archive: Roover files.

from Keynesians to outright Socialists. This faculty
[NYU] is definitely under the major influence of
Keynesians and collectivists, although there are a few
eminent men, like John D. Williams and Sumner
Slichter, who have not gone entirely that way. The
same is true of smaller colleges, such as Williams,
Amherst, etc. The New School for Social Research
doesn't have a single libertarian on its faculty. Sarah
Lawrence College probably couldn't produce a single
one either.[93]

The men on Fertig's short list of libertarians were less original than Mises, less radical, and less outspoken in their support
of *laissez-faire* capitalism—a fact that was obvious to all parties
involved. Mises himself considered many of them to be moderate interventionists, an opinion that his financial backers had
learned to respect. He occasionally recommended textbooks
written by these other men, for example, Fairchild and Shelly's
Understanding Our Free Economy, and Van Sickle and Rogge's
Introduction to Economics. But the most he could say of these
books was that the interventionism advocated within them was
less radical than that promoted in all the other textbooks, which
he believed were "*totally* flawed from a theoretical point of view
(Marx, Keynes, econometrics) and had a radical interventionist,
if not outright socialist orientation."[94]

In short, there was no substitute for Ludwig von Mises, and
this fact would have unfortunate consequences for American
libertarianism in the following decades.

---

[93]Fertig to Paul McGhee, letter dated April 3, 1952; Grove City Archive:
Fertig files.

[94]Mises to Ballvé, letters dated February 13, 1956 and May 13, 1957;
Grove City Archive: Ballvé files.

New York Circles

Mises's activities in New York centered on his NYU seminar. By the early to mid-1950s, four major groups attended the NYU seminar.

First, there was a group of NYU students who took the seminar for credit. The great majority of them were thoroughly uninterested in scientific questions of economic analysis. Yet there were exceptions. One early student who cooperated more closely with Mises was Hugh P. King, who from 1951 to 1953 was his assistant and later became a business counselor.[95] Then there was Morton Cobrin, who in 1952 wrote a 300-page master's thesis that condensed some of the main ideas of *Human Action* in more accessible language. Cobrin then attended Mises's seminar on "Government Control and the Profit System."[96] But there were also more important exceptions. At least three regular NYU students would eventually become important Misesians who, each in his own way, took up where their teacher had left off: Hans Sennholz, Israel Kirzner, and George Reisman.[97]

Hans Sennholz, who had translated Böhm-Bawerk, received his American Ph.D. under Mises in 1954 and published his dissertation in early 1955 under the title *How Can Europe Survive?* With Mises's support, Sennholz had received a $3,000 Earhart research grant for the academic year 1953–1954, when the fellowship program started.[98] Mises praised him as outstanding in

---

[95]King to Mises, letter dated June 4, 1953; Grove City Archive: King file.

[96]Cobrin to Mises, letter dated June 10, 1952; Grove City Archive: "C" files. Cobrin had written his master's thesis under the supervision of a Dr. Dorau.

[97]Notable but less important were Louis Spadaro and Edward Foley.

[98]He was still the only student Mises had recommended until March 1955. By then Mises hoped that "also other members of my Seminar will soon comply with the requirements." Mises to Loren B. Miller, letter dated March 21, 1955; Grove City Archive: Earhart Foundation file.

his "professional ability, pedagogic talent and personal character."[99]

In contrast to Sennholz, young Israel Kirzner had not known anything about Mises before attending his seminar. He was not even a student of economics, but an accounting major who had to take one economics seminar to fulfill his requirements. Since he knew nothing of economics, he decided to attend the classes of the most published economics professor at NYU. Starting in September 1954, Kirzner attended Mises's seminar for many years, acting eventually as a (Volker-sponsored) tutor for the younger students. He switched from accounting to economics and studied under Mises to obtain his Ph.D., which he received

Israel Kirzner

in 1957 with *The Economic Point of View*. Kirzner eventually became a professor of economics at NYU, a famous theoretician of entrepreneurship with numerous book publications, and retired in 2002.[100]

The third important Misesian from the ranks of Mises's regular students was George Reisman, who got a Ph.D. under Mises in 1963 for a theoretical study of interest rates with the title: *The Theory of Aggregate Profit and the Average Rate of Profit*. His lifelong research project was the creation of a great synthesis between classical economics, Austrian economics, and Ayn

---

[99]Mises to Chellevold, letter dated March 1, 1956; Grove City Archive: Sennholz files.

[100]Kirzner was a Volker fellow in 1956–1957 and in early 1957 obtained a research grant from the Earhart Foundation. At that point, he had already defended his dissertation and was about to submit the final version. See Mises to Ware, letter dated January 28, 1957; Grove City Archive: Kirzner files. Mises praised Kirzner as "a young man who promises to become a highly competent teacher and author." Mises to Ware, letter dated February 7, 1957; Grove City Archive: Kirzner files.

Rand's "objectivist" social philosophy. As a result of these endeavours, he eventually published his *magnum opus*, *Capitalism* (1996). He is now an emeritus professor at Pepperdine University in California.

The second group at the seminar was composed of professionals and businessmen. This group included personal friends of Mises's, such as Henry Hazlitt, Lawrence Fertig, and George Koether. But there were also men such as Doctor Richard Fruin, a commander in the U.S. Navy, who had come to know Mises through his publications and who seized the opportunity to attend the seminar sessions from the end of 1954 to the end of 1961.

The third group came from FEE. It included Foundation staff and students who had been introduced to Austrian economics through FEE. The staunchest attendees were Bettina Bien and Percy Greaves, who would form the core of the seminar until its very end.

The fourth group was a spin-off of the FEE crowd. It was composed of radical young free-marketeers around Murray Rothbard, including Ralph Raico, George Reisman, Leonard Liggio, and Robert Hessen. They called themselves the Circle Bastiat.

The Circle Bastiat: left to right, *Ralph Raico, Murray Rothbard, George Reisman, Leonard Liggio, and Robert Hessen*

When Rand's novel *Atlas Shrugged* appeared in 1957, it had a deep impact on the Circle Bastiat, and also impressed Mises and other senior members of his seminar.[101] Rothbard read the novel that fall and discussed it endlessly with Reisman. They also had continuing discussions on the question of whether capital accumulation implied a declining interest rate. For Reisman, these discussions were the point of departure for a lifelong research program.[102]

≼   ≼   ≼

By all standards, the seminar was of very high quality. In its first ten years, it featured Mises at the peak of his teaching career. One participant who had attended the sessions from the very start in 1945 wrote a thank-you note in 1952, stating that he had been especially impressed by two facts:

> First, it has attracted a serious-minded group of individuals whose varied occupational and professional interests serve to stimulate a fruitful discussion; secondly, unlike most seminars, each succeeding year of attendance builds upon the intellectual acquisitions of the past one without leaving any impression that the student is repeating a previous course.[103]

---

[101]In 1954, Rothbard began to socialize with Ayn Rand's group and then backed away, having decided that she was not really a libertarian. After *Atlas Shrugged* came out, however, there was a temporary rapprochement and the Circle Bastiat was introduced to Rand. This eventually led to the breakup of the Circle Bastiat. See Rothbard to Mises, letter dated July 17, 1958; Grove City Archive: Rothbard files. See also Justin Raimondo, *An Enemy of the State: The Life of Murray N. Rothbard* (Amherst, N.Y.: Prometheus Books, 2000), p. 109ff.

[102]Reisman to Ware, letter dated July 14, 1963; Grove City Archive: Reisman files. See also the preface to Reisman's *Capitalism* (Ottawa, Ill.: Jameson books, 1996).

[103]Frank Dierson to Mises, letter dated June 10, 1952; Grove City Archive: "D" files.

What makes the seminar especially important for the later dissemination of Mises's ideas is that it brought together a group of excellent students for whom *Human Action* was the starting point for further intellectual work. No previous group of his students had had this privilege, and it had a noticeable effect on their further intellectual development and on the schools they created. It is revealing to contrast the cases of Sennholz and Rothbard with the case of Fritz Machlup, who had been Mises's star student in the 1920s and early 30s. All three men were high-caliber intellectuals, but only the former two became genuine Misesians. A possible difference lay in the existence of the treatise.

As he had done with his students in Vienna and Geneva, Mises inspired his American students to apply rigorous deductive reasoning to the analysis of politically relevant subjects. But they did more: they followed the logic to its politically radical conclusions. Murray Rothbard in his youthful exuberance once boasted that his forthcoming defense of the market economy "will be far more right-wing than Mises because of its grounding in 'welfare economics,' which theory I have basically set forth in my *Festschrift* article."[104] It is unthinkable that one of Mises's Vienna students would have boasted that he was more libertarian than his professor—the Vienna students thought Mises tended to exaggerate the case for the market economy.

But Rothbard was merely an extreme case of the entire species of Misesian students in the post-*Human Action* period. Their favorite sport was to find statist arguments and premises in Mises's works. They relished in "unveiling" his socialism and

---

[104]Rothbard, Report to R. Cornuelle, July 19, 1955, 6 pp., Rothbard Papers (at least one page is missing). Rothbard had written a precursor to this paper in 1954 and submitted it (unsuccessfully) to *Economica*. See Rothbard to Mises, letter dated September 22, 1954; Grove City Archive: Rothbard files.

had a good laugh when Rothbard called the old master "a member of the non-Communist left."[105]

This new radicalism radiated beyond Mises's NYU seminar. Inspired by *Human Action*, several authors set out to defend liberty, property, and capitalism as absolute principles of social order. The best known case is Ayn Rand, who shocked the political correctness of her day with a proud, assertive defense of individualism and capitalism that announced itself right in the titles of her books. Works such as *Capitalism—The Unknown Ideal* and *The Virtue of Selfishness* were inspired by *Human Action*, an intellectual debt that she graciously acknowledged. Yet Rand's case was no exception. In September 1955, Mises received a massive manuscript with the title "The Capitalist Manifesto." The author, a certain Joe Abrahamson, asked him for comments.[106] It was the work of an enthusiastic amateur but it showed where ever more of his readers were headed.

The high point of these glorious years was the publication of a *Festschrift* for Mises on the occasion of the fiftieth anniversary of the doctorate that Mises had earned at the University of Vienna in 1906. Mises received the book at a celebration on March 7, 1956 in Manhattan. Hans and Mary Sennholz organized the event.[107] Roughly a year before the celebration, they had invited contributions from seminar members such as Hazlitt,

---

[105]As quoted from Ralph Raico's recollections of Rothbard in Llewellyn H. Rockwell, Jr., ed. *Murray N. Rothbard: In Memoriam* (Auburn, Ala.: Ludwig von Mises Institute, 1995), p. 3.

[106]Abrahamson to Mises, letter dated September 7, 1955; Grove City Archive: Abrahamson file. Mises replied he hoped soon to find the leisure to study it carefully.

[107]Hayek and Machlup had thought about undertaking a festschrift for Mises's seventieth birthday in 1951. However, none of them was willing to make the effort and thus they turned to Hazlitt "to do all the technical work connected with the editing of such a volume." See Machlup to Hazlitt, letter dated November 28, 1950; Hoover Institution: Machlup-Mises correspondence file. Hazlitt was too busy to become a part-time assistant to Hayek and

On the occasion of the 50th anniversary of Mises's doctorate. Top with Mary Sennholz and Hayek; left, with Margit and Hayek, bottom left, autographing the Festschrift volume with Machlup and Hayek, bottom right, with Machlup and with Margit

Rothbard, and Sennholz, and from various other intellectuals who had in some way been close to Mises.[108]

The Sennholzes took pains to avoid any closer involvement of Mises's former students and colleagues from Vienna, whose political orientation was considerably less liberal than that of the NYU seminar. Among the twenty contributors, only three—Röpke, Machlup, and Hayek—had been friends with Mises in Vienna. Thus the *Festschrift* became a faithful reflection of the change of Mises's intellectual environment. It was to be a celebration of the intellectual case for human liberty and the free market, and of the man who had done so much to develop this case. The title made it clear: *On Freedom and Free Enterprise*.[109]

A Misesian Treatise

It was in these high years of the new American Misesians—the *Human Action* years—that Murray Rothbard completed his "textbook" rendering of Austrian economics. At first he stuck to the original project of a mere popularization of *Human Action*, trying "to do for Mises what McCulloch did for Ricardo."[110] But

---

Machlup, but the decisive obstacle was financial: no publisher could be found. See Machlup to Mary Sennholz, letter dated November 1, 1954; Hoover Institution: Machlup-Mises correspondence file.

[108]Faustino Ballvé had received the request to make a contribution by March 1955. See Ballvé to Mises, letter dated March 18, 1955; Grove City Archive: Ballvé files. Louis Rougier withdrew his contribution because he thought it was poorly translated into English, and Alfred Müller-Armack declined, saying he had no time; see Grove City Archive: Mary Sennholz files.

[109]This does not mean that critical voices were banished. William Rappard contributed an important critique of Mises's theory of interventionism. Rappard here published thoughts he had long since expressed in private correspondence. See for example on the occasion of the publication of *Nationalökonomie*. Rappard to Mises, letter dated May 31, 1940; Grove City Archive: Rand file.

[110]Rothbard to H. Cornuelle, letter dated March 14, 1951; Rothbard Papers. "What McCulloch did for Ricardo" refers to John Ramsay McCulloch, *Principles of Political Economy* (New York: Augustus M. Kelley, [1864] 1965).

*Murray Rothbard at the
Festschrift dinner honoring
Mises in 1956*

by October 1952, he had already decided to pursue a more independent exposition of economic science. Rothbard ended up writing an entire treatise of economic science, covering in some 900 pages the theory of the market economy and of government interventionism. The work was a masterpiece and had a deep impact on subsequent generations of Misesian economists.

During the winter semester of 1952, Rothbard presented several chapters of his work in Mises's seminar.[111] It was here that he might have defended for the first time some of the doctrines that set him apart from Mises. The professor handled the situation in his usual manner, namely, with scholastic *laissez-faire*. He encouraged Rothbard to follow the path he had chosen.[112]

This might have had to do with the specific American flavor of the exceptions Rothbard took to Mises's approach. For example, Rothbard had come to believe that there was a "science of rational ethics based on human nature and what is good for human nature." Thus he had abandoned Max Weber's position, which Mises cherished, that there can be no *science* of ethics, but only subjective value judgments. Rothbard had probably come to adopt this new viewpoint under the influence of discussions with Ayn Rand's group. In the first version of his manuscript of chapter one, where he explained the first principles of human action, Rothbard had adopted the Weberian position, which was the "standard" position at Columbia. Probably, therefore,

---

[111]See Rothbard's memorandum to the Volker Fund: "Progress Report, January 1 to October 1, 1952;" Rothbard Papers.

[112]Rothbard to Richard Cornuelle, letter dated January 3, 1953; Rothbard Papers.

Rothbard attended meetings of Rand's group during 1952 and in the course of these encounters changed his mind on the question of scientific ethics.[113]

Rothbard also took exception to the philosophical pessimism that seemed to form the foundation of Mises's theory of human action. Mises had asserted that man acts to relieve dissatisfaction, which implied that man did not act when he was happy. Rothbard thought that such a view was "contrary to the natural state of man, which is at its happiest precisely when it is engaged in productive activity."[114]

But Rothbard would soon disagree with Mises on a more fundamental issue. During the winter semester 1953, he was in the process of reviewing conventional price theory, which stressed cost curves and other remnants of classical "objective" price theories. His rejection of these approaches had led him to some original conclusions. Rothbard became convinced that the entire neo-classical theory of monopoly prices relied on a completely unwarranted fiction, namely that it was possible to distinguish these monopoly prices from competitive prices. He believed that Mises too had fallen prey to this fiction. Mises held indeed that the sovereignty of consumers was impaired in the presence of monopoly prices. Rothbard disagreed:

> I have come to the conclusion that this theory is outright nonsense. I do not differ with Mises rashly on matters of economic theory, but in this particular case I think he has not freed himself from the shackles of the old neo-classical approach. The key question here is this: How do we know what the "competitive price"

---

[113]There were indirect contacts between Rothbard and Rand ever since November 1947. By May 7, 1953 Rothbard was asked to introduce Reisman and Raico to Ayn Rand, which suggests that at that point he was a regular member of her group.

[114]Rothbard, Progress Report (Rothbard Papers: Memo to Volker Fund, April 1, 1953).

is? If we go to the illustration of this approach in, for example, Fetter's *Economic Principles*, we find a competitive price, and the monopolist assessing his demand curve at this price. But, in reality, we never know the competitive price. The competitive price is a *result* of action, and not a given. Even if we can observe a man restricting his investment and production in a product, and raising price, we can never know if this is a movement from "competitive price" to "monopoly price" or from "sub-competitive price" to "competitive price." As Mises has told us again & again, a concept divorced from real action and employed as an actual reality and even an ideal, is invalid. Therefore, the whole concept of competitive price vs. monopoly price has to go by the board. On the free market there is only the "free market price" which in turn is competitive, since buyers and sellers freely compete with each other. And this is true not only for the individual seller, but also for a *cartel*. For I have come to the perhaps even more revolutionary conclusion that there is nothing in the world wrong with a cartel when it is *voluntary*. When many firms merge or form a cartel, what happens? In effect, the assets of many individuals are pooled and directed by them all, in accordance with their proportionate ownership and their contract. But how does this process differ from the *formation of an ordinary corporation*, when different individuals pool their capital and assets according to their voluntary contract? Not in the slightest.[115]

Another year later, at the beginning of the academic year 1954–1955, Mises concentrated in his NYU seminar on price theory and other aspects of the theory of the market economy, possibly because he sensed that Rothbard was in a decisive

---

[115]Rothbard to R. Cornuelle, Memo ("Textbook or Treatise?") dated February 1954; Rothbard Papers.

phase of his work and close to completion. He had Rothbard deliver several presentations, in particular, on Robinson's and Chamberlin's theory of monopolistic competition and on selling costs.[116]

Rothbard was better prepared than ever. He had spent the summer discussing economics for endless hours with young George Reisman. In the course of these discussions they developed an important extension of Mises's theory of economic calculation. Starting from the "question of how extensive the number of firms in the economy must be in order to have calculation," they "came to the conclusion that for every 'vertical integration' within a firm, in order for the firm to allocate costs, etc., *internally*, there would have to be a market for that area *external* to the firm. Thus, the inability of a Socialist government to calculate is a special case of the inability of any firm to calculate for departments internal to itself, if there is no external market to which to refer."[117]

Murray Rothbard, Henry Hazlitt, and Ludwig von Mises

---

[116]Rothbard to R. Cornuelle, letter dated November 5, 1954; Rothbard Papers.

[117]Rothbard to R. Cornuelle, Memo dated August 9, 1954; Rothbard Papers.

Combined with the Mises seminar, this intensive exchange gave a decisive boost to Rothbard's writing, to the point that, by July 1955, the manuscript had almost reached the form it would have when it was eventually published in 1962.[118] Most important, Rothbard had by then completed the chapter explaining the conceptual framework within which he would analyze both the operation of the market economy and government interventions. In distinct contrast to all previous economists—with the notable exception of Gustave de Molinari, the dean of the French nineteenth century *laissez-faire* school—Rothbard did not present the modern state as an integral part of society. Rather, he distinguished between two types of production of security: coercive and free. The former was characteristic of the modern state, whereas the latter would exist only in a hypothetical free society.[119]

These statements, which Rothbard made in his July 1955 report to the Volker Fund, must have set off alarm bells with Luhnow and other Volker Fund people. For the first time, Rothbard had spelled out his thoroughly anti-statist worldview and tried to prove that this view found support in the tenets of economic science. This brazen display of political anarchism was apparently too much even for the Volker Fund. Rothbard was given another extension of his research grant, which he used, during the academic year 1955–1956, to polish his manuscript (by July 1956 it amounted to 1900 typed pages) and finally to finish his Ph.D. in economics at Columbia University. But it must have been made clear to him that he could not count on Volker Fund support in the future, at least not to the extent he had enjoyed it in the past. By April 1956, he applied for a new research grant for work on the Great Depression—this time

---

[118]Rothbard to R. Cornuelle, letter dated July 19, 1955; Rothbard Papers.

[119]For a partial list of Rothbard's main contributions to economics, see Joseph Stromberg's introduction to the fourth edition of *Man, Economy, and State* (Auburn, Ala.: Ludwig von Mises Institute, 2003).

from the Earhart Foundation.[120] Mises supported him unequiv-
ocally, stating that he was "fully convinced that [Rothbard] will
one day be counted among the foremost economists."[121]

Rothbard's treatise was put on hold. He worked part-time for
FEE writing a short book on money (*What Has Government
Done to Our Money?*) and he continued to polish the manuscript
of his treatise for the next few years.[122] The directors of the
Volker Fund needed quite some time to ponder the question of
what to do with this explosive material, which threatened to dis-
integrate the nascent libertarian movement. In May 1959,
Rothbard reported completion of the manuscript in a letter to
Mises. He also expressed his regret that he had only rarely been
attending Mises's seminar.[123]

This version of the manuscript was passed on to the Volker
Fund's Frank S. Meyer, ostensibly in an effort to bring the project to completion. (Or the decision might have been related to
already existing plans to close down the Fund.) Meyer was no
Rothbardian. He was chosen as a third-party or "objective"
opinion on the merits of the book. He delivered a report that
would allow both the author of the book and his sponsor to
agree on how to proceed without losing face. Meyer said the
book was "one of the two or three most important discussions
of economics to be written in this century," and he lavishly
praised it for its radical break with the traditional utilitarian

---

[120]Rothbard to Mises, letter dated April 2, 1956; Rothbard to R. Cornuelle, letter dated May 30, 1956; Rothbard to H.W. Luhnow, letter dated
July 29, 1956; all in Rothbard Papers. The Earhart Foundation grant, which
Rothbard duly received, made up for the ending of the Volker Fund grant,
which had supported his writing of the treatise.

[121]Mises to Kennedy, letter dated April 5, 1956; Grove City Archive:
Rothbard files.

[122]Mises commented on the September 1957 version of the book at the
request of FEE. See correspondence in Grove City Archive: Rothbard files.

[123]Rothbard to Mises, letter dated May 5, 1959; Grove City Archive:
Rothbard files.

underpinnings of economic theory, a break that opened the prospect of integrating the economic rationale against collectivism into certain strands of conservative thought.[124] On the other hand, Meyer admonished that certain chapters were "fundamentally political in their scope and written from the point of view of an uncompromising anarchism." These chapters should be removed and their economic content be collected into a single chapter.

And so it happened. Rothbard's treatise (with anarchism excised) was published in 1962 as *Man, Economy, and State*. His discussion of a stateless market society would eventually appear eight years later in a separate book with the title *Power and Market*.

Sennholz at Grove City College

While Rothbard was still busy writing and polishing the manuscript of his *magnum opus*, Hans Sennholz was already a quality product of Mises's NYU seminar. He had written a very thorough doctoral dissertation and published it in 1955 with Jasper Crane's Van Nostrand Company. And in distinct contrast to Rothbard, who spent nights working or discussing with friends, slept through much of the day, missed deadline after deadline, and tended to be messy and disorderly, Sennholz featured the Teutonic personal virtues of punctuality, orderliness, and reliability. By the mid-1950s, he was visibly Mises's most important student.

Sennholz was not only an intellectual heir to the Austrian tradition, but also had the vision, the drive, and the enthusiasm to lead the Austrian School and the burgeoning libertarian intellectual movement into the second half of the twentieth century. Not only did he realize that the decisive battle in politics was the battle of ideas—and that for the time being this battle was

---

[124]Frank Meyer, Memo: On Murray Rothbard's Manuscript, late 1959 or January 1960; Rothbard Papers.

mainly fought in institutions of higher learning—but he also saw quite clearly that there was no hope whatsoever in "turning around" mainstream academia from within. The success of the libertarian movement depended on its ability to set up parallel academic institutions to compete with the socialist academic establishment from the outside.

The tragedy for Sennholz, and for the libertarian movement at large, was that most of his initiatives to establish parallel libertarian institutions did not find the necessary support. For example, starting in August 1955, he tried for some years without success to establish a libertarian journal.[125] And at the end of the 1950s, he tried to establish an American School of Economics with the mission of producing future university professors, equally without success. These failures might have been due to the timidity of potential donors, or to Sennholz's youth and assertiveness. He was a born leader who could not suffer subservience; he needed to be his own man in all of his endeavors. For some time, he threw himself into working for FEE and took up residence in Irvington-on-Hudson. But the presence of another great ego—Leonard Read's—made it impossible for Sennholz to turn FEE into the instrument of his far-reaching plans. After completion of his Ph.D. in 1955, he began looking for a new position.

Hans Sennholz

It was not easy for Sennholz to find academic employment because of a triple disadvantage: he was an old-fashioned economist, a libertarian, and a German.[126] Eventually however he found a position at Grove City College, a liberal arts college in

---

[125]Grove City Archive: American School of Economics files.

[126]Vada Horsch tried to place him at Yale. See Ryan to Mises, letter dated July 9, 1956; Grove City Archive: NAM files.

western Pennsylvania that had been sponsored by the Pew family for generations. It was once again the longstanding connection between Mises and J. Howard Pew that proved so useful. When Sennholz first saw the facilities, he could hardly believe his eyes:

> The chapel is fashioned after European Gothic cathedrals. Its beauty is superb. The reception room in the library would have flattered European royalty, with thick Persian rugs on the floor and expensive originals on the wall, the furniture of French antique style. The indoor swimming pool is built according to Olympic standards—only Esther Williams is missing. The bowling alley is patterned according to Westchester club standards. The girls dormitory boasts a gold leaf Steinway piano besides other beautiful furniture. I am beginning to understand why most professors go to Grove City and are never heard of again.

On the other hand, Sennholz did not wax enthusiastic about the students, who did not nearly live up to the hopes of Pew and other sponsors who had wanted their contributions to help educate the future champions and supporters of a free society: "In spite of all this splendor offered by a few capitalists, the 1,300 students constitute the usual sample of 75% collectivists and 25% without opinion."[127]

---

[127]He went on to urge the establishment of a new graduate school for the education of future professors, a school squarely built on the tradition of classical liberalism. See Sennholz to Mises, letter dated November 7, 1956; Grove City Archive: American School of Economics files. During the next few years, Sennholz would spend much time and energy on this project; but it did not materialize, mainly due to financial reasons. In another letter, he mentions that the plans for establishing a graduate school of economics had been longstanding with FEE. See Sennholz to Mises, letter dated January 10, 1959; Grove City Archive: American School of Economics files.

Clearly, there was a lot of work to do. Sennholz grabbed the bull by the horns and threw himself into the battle of ideas. During the next five decades, he educated a new generation of Austrian School scholars, among them Walter Grinder, Jeffrey Hummel, Alejandro Chafuen, Philippe Nataf, and Peter Boettke. He would publish hundreds of articles and dozens of books and booklets. He and Rothbard almost single-handedly created a modern Austrian—Misesian—literature. Until the early 1960s, they were not alone in this endeavor. Mises himself made a number of contributions that we will discuss in the next chapter. ✍

Mises lecturing at the NYU seminar

Pictures from the NYU seminar

21

The Epistemological Case
for Capitalism

IN THE EARLY 1950S, Mises's NYU seminar dealt increasingly with epistemological questions. As he said to Ludwig Lachmann, he felt that the analysis of epistemological problems would be the number one task in the social sciences in the coming years.[1] It was the topic of his last two monographs: *Theory and History* (1957) and *The Ultimate Foundation of Economic Science* (1962).

The subject had been prominent in his thoughts and reflections since the publication of "Sociology and History" (1929) and "Conception and Understanding" (1930). It was one of the two areas in which he felt contemporary economics was most deficient (the other one being the theory of economic calculation). In *Nationalökonomie* and *Human Action* he had stressed the historical significance of the problem:

> It is a complete misunderstanding of the meaning of the debates concerning the essence, scope, and logical character of economics to dismiss them as the scholastic quibbling of pedantic professors. It is a widespread misconception that while pedants squandered useless talk about the most appropriate method of procedure, economics itself, indifferent to these

---

[1]He had said this in a July 1956 meeting with Lachmann. See Lachmann to Mises, letter dated September 17, 1956; Grove City Archive: Lachmann file.

idle disputes, went quietly on its way. In the Methodenstreit between the Austrian economists and the
Prussian Historical School, the self-styled "intellectual bodyguard of the House of Hohenzollern," and
in the discussions between the school of John Bates
Clark and American Institutionalism much more was
at stake than the question of what kind of procedure
was the most fruitful one. The real issue was the epistemological foundations of the science of human
action and its logical legitimacy.[2]

He had come to the conclusion that political motivations were
behind these epistemological critiques of economic science:

The main motive for the development of the doctrines of polylogism, historicism, and irrationalism
was to provide a justification for disregarding the
teachings of economics in the determination of economic policies. The socialists, racists, nationalists,
and etatists failed in their endeavors to refute the theories of the economists and to demonstrate the correctness of their own spurious doctrines. It was precisely this frustration that prompted them to negate
the logical and epistemological principles upon which
all human reasoning both in mundane activities and
in scientific research is founded.[3]

Thus the epistemology of economics was not just an idle pas-
time for ivory tower intellectuals. It was of direct practical relevance. How does economic theory relate to reality? Most economists believed—and still believe today—that their propositions concern only hypothetical conditions never actually given
in real life. To Mises, this point of view was paradoxical:

It is strange that some schools seem to approve of this
opinion and nonetheless quietly proceed to draw

---

[2]Mises, *Human Action*, 3rd ed. (Chicago: Regnery, 1966), p. 4.
[3]Ibid., p. 6.

> their curves and to formulate their equations. They
> do not bother about the meaning of their reasoning
> and about its reference to the world of real life and
> action.[4]

He himself felt it was a necessity to explain the epistemology of economic science and devoted chapters two and three of *Human Action* (a total of 62 pages) to these issues.

However, despite its fundamental importance, epistemology did play only an incidental role in *Human Action*. The great organizing theme of *Human Action* was the theory of economic calculation. Mises began with an analysis of the conditions under which no economic calculation could take place, then turned to the discussion of economic calculation in general, then within the market economy, and finally to those social settings that render economic calculation impossible (socialism) or pervert its use (interventionism). From a philosophical point of view, *Human Action* made a sweeping case for utilitarian social philosophy—"utilitarian" with a distinct Misesian flavor. And the scientific core of this case was economics and the theory of economic calculation in particular.

In his new book, Mises made another case for his utilitarian philosophy. This time, the argument turned on the epistemology of social analysis. Mises argued that the only scientific interpretation of social reality was based on economics and history, and that the conclusions of both these disciplines led to the more speculative generalizations of utilitarian philosophy as he understood it. He showed that the major alternative approaches—Marxism, positivism, and historicism—despite their pretensions to science, were untenable on epistemological grounds. They were essentially metaphysical doctrines; that is, their claims were not based on ascertainable fact, but on speculations (many of which, as Mises would show, were incoherent).

---

[4]Ibid.

The new book was eventually published under the title *Theory and History* and subtitled *An Interpretation of Social and Economic Evolution.*[5] It has remained one of his least read and least understood works. The difficulty lay only partly in the abstract nature of its subject. The main hurdle was, as in several of his other writings, a lack of pedagogical effort on his part. Many people know what to expect when they consult a treatise on economics. But few have any idea about the relationship between theoretical and historical approaches to social analysis.

Mises's new book was not about narrating mankind's social and economic evolution. It dealt instead with the epistemological problems of the various competing narratives. In *Human Action*, he had referred to these problems incidentally. He had stressed that economic analysis, starting from the actions of individual persons, gave a purely fact-based account of the origin of human society. The holistic approaches had been unable to do this. They explained society by "theological or metaphysical professions of faith."[6] In *Theory and History*, he amplified this argument into a sweeping epistemological vindication of the case for liberty and capitalism.

The book is divided into four parts. Part one deals with the central phenomenon of the social sciences: value. Mises explains the nature of value and studies the implications for a scientific analysis of human behavior. In part two, he argues that, while all endeavors to discover scientific laws must be built on the *assumption* of strict determinism, all attempts to find laws that determine the origin of ideas and of value judgments have been in vain. Marxist dialectical materialism and other theories that explain ideas in terms of more fundamental material conditions are merely metaphysical speculation. The same holds true for

---

[5]Mises, *Theory and History: An Interpretation of Social and Economic Evolution* (New Haven, Conn.: Yale University Press, 1957).

[6]Mises, *Human Action*, p. 145. See also ibid., pp. 145–47.

those philosophies of history that explain the evolution of society in terms of some final destination. In part three, Mises gives an in-depth discussion of the problems of scientific historical analysis, developing the approach of the Southwest German School of historiography. In part four, finally, he critically dissects various speculations about history. In what follows, we will discuss the major elements of his contribution.

The Argument in a Nutshell

For Mises, the starting point is that "[a]ny epistemological speculation must lead toward determinism." This is so because the human mind is the instrument through which we learn about all things, and our human mind has a determinist bent. It cannot help thinking that all things are strictly determined by certain causes.

> Whatever the true nature of the universe and of reality may be, man can learn about it only what the logical structure of his mind makes comprehensible to him. . . . The logical structure of his mind enjoins upon man determinism and the category of causality. As man sees it, whatever happens in the universe is the necessary evolution of forces, powers, and qualities which were already present in the initial stage of the X out of which all things stem. All things in the universe are interconnected, and all changes are the effects of powers inherent in things. No change occurs that would not be the necessary consequence of the preceding state. All facts are dependent upon and conditioned by their causes. No deviation from the necessary course of affairs is possible. Eternal law regulates everything. In this sense determinism is the epistemological basis of the human search for knowledge. Man cannot even conceive the image of an undetermined universe. In such a world there could not be any awareness of material things and their changes. It would appear a senseless chaos. Nothing could be identified and distinguished from anything

else. Nothing could be expected and predicted. In the
midst of such an environment man would be as helpless as if spoken to in an unknown language. No
action could be designed, still less put into execution.
Man is what he is because he lives in a world of regularity and has the mental power to conceive the relation of cause and effect.[7]

This point of view implies that human action could be
explained, at least in theory, in terms of underlying material
forces. We know that human action is *immediately* determined
by the ideas and value judgments of the acting individuals. But
these ideas and value judgments must in turn be determined by
more fundamental causes. If such causes were physical or chemical processes, then the explanation of human behavior could
become a branch of applied physics or applied chemistry.

However—and this is the crucial consideration that Mises
had stressed already in previous work—at present nobody
knows anything about the more fundamental causes of human
behavior. Up to now all attempts to identify laws that would
explain ideas and value judgments in terms of physical, chemical, or other processes have been in vain. There are various
hypotheses about what such basic determination could look
like. But not a single one of them has ever been validated.[8] All

---

[7]Mises, *Theory and History*, pp. 73–74. He emphasizes that from the point
of view of a perfect being such as God, things might look completely different. This position can best be characterized as a Leibnizian rationalism. On
the importance of Leibnizian rationalism for Austrian intellectual life, see
William M. Johnston, *The Austrian Mind* (Los Angeles: University of California Press, 1972), chap. 19. Johnston is however not convinced that the
Austrian School of economics was influenced by the Leibnizian tradition. See
ibid, pp. 86f.

[8]Thirteen years before, he had written:

We may reasonably assume as hypothesis that man's mental
abilities are the outcome of his bodily features. Of course, we
cannot demonstrate the correctness of this hypothesis, but
neither is it possible to demonstrate the correctness of the

such hypotheses are therefore mere speculation. They are philosophical or metaphysical constructs, not scientific knowledge.[9]

Our deficient knowledge about the more remote causes of human behavior has two straightforward methodological implications. All efforts to explain the causes and consequences of human behavior must, at least for the time being, take individual human behavior as an ultimate point of departure. They must accept the principle of *methodological individualism*. The older economists had applied this principle intuitively and even Schumpeter, who coined the term, defended it merely on grounds of expediency. Mises delivered an epistemological demonstration of its necessity. Methodological individualism is rooted in deficient human knowledge.

The causal analysis of individual human behavior must take account of the fact that any human action has certain *invariant* consequences—that is, consequences that result from like action at any place and any time. For example, an increase of the quantity of money tends to entail an increase of the price level above the level it would otherwise have reached, irrespective of when and where the money supply is increased. The study of such consequences is the task of praxeology and economic science.

---

opposite view as expressed in the theological hypothesis. We are forced to recognize that we do not know how out of physiological processes thoughts result. We have some vague notions of the detrimental effects produced by traumatic or other damage inflicted on certain bodily organs; we know that such damage may restrict or completely destroy the mental abilities and functions of men. But that is all. (*Omnipotent Government* [Spring Mills, Penn.: Libertarian Press, 1985], p. 156)

[9]This point also applied to F.A. Hayek's *The Sensory Order* (Chicago: University of Chicago Press, 1952), a book that Mises did not cite. Hayek had attempted to analyze the mechanism through which physiological impulses come to be translated into mental perception. Apparently, Mises was not convinced that Hayek delivered more than metaphysical speculation.

But human action also has *contingent* causes and consequences. The very same action—increasing the quantity of money—can be inspired by very different ideas and value judgments. And the objective consequences resulting from any action can provoke very different individual reactions at different times and places. In other words, the causal chains through which ideas and value judgments are connected with human action are contingent. The elucidation of these contingent causal chains is the task of historical research.[10]

Mises stressed that this is as far as scientific analysis of human action can go. Starting from observable human behavior we can explain its invariant consequences (with the help of economics); we can also explain its contingent consequences (by historical understanding); and we can to some extent explain how this behavior resulted from the ideas and value judgments of the acting person in the particular case under consideration (again by understanding). Mises did not exclude the possibility that individual value judgments and ideas had invariant causes, but again, neither he himself nor anybody else knew what they were. At present, only some of the contingent causes of human action could be identified by historical understanding on a case by case basis. And even this analysis was not likely to give the full picture. There was an unfathomable remnant that defied any explanation whatever: historical individuality. Mises explained:

---

[10]Individual value judgments and actions

> are ultimately given as they cannot be traced back to something of which they would appear to be the *necessary* consequence. If this were not the case, it would not be permissible to call them an ultimate given. But they are not, like the ultimate given in the natural sciences, a stopping point for human reflection. They are the starting point of a specific mode of reflection, of the specific understanding of the historical sciences of human action. (Mises, *Theory and History*, p. 310; emphasis added)

> The characteristics of individual men, their ideas and
> judgments of value as well as the actions guided by
> those ideas and judgments, cannot be traced back to
> something of which they would be the derivatives.
> There is no answer to the question why Frederick II
> invaded Silesia except: because he was Frederick II.[11]

It follows that the social sciences, at least for the time being,
cannot be bound with the natural sciences into a unified body
of scientific knowledge. "This ignorance splits the realm of
knowledge into two separate fields, the realm of external events,
commonly called nature, and the realm of human thought and
action."[12] For methodological reasons, the social sciences are
separate from the natural sciences. Mises called this the principle of *methodological dualism*.

Social analysis, if it just sticks to the known facts, must
explain all social phenomena as resulting from individual action,
and the causal chain of events must start and end with the ideas
and value judgments of individuals. Scientific endeavors within
the constraints of methodological individualism and methodological dualism entail the development of the disciplines called
"praxeology" and "history." The former is the discipline that
describes the invariant consequences of human action that
result regardless of time and place. The latter is the discipline
that (1) describes value judgments from the point of view of the
acting person and (2) describes how individual actions and other
relevant factors combine with one another in a given objective
context to produce a definite outcome. History describes in retrospect how the acting person perceived the situation in which
he had to act, what he aimed at, what he believed to be the
means at his disposition. And it uses the general laws provided
by economics and the natural sciences to describe the objective

---

[11]Mises, *Theory and History*, p. 183.
[12]Ibid., p. 1.

impact that the acting person had through his behavior. Thus the mission of history is to describe the drama of social and economic evolution from the point of view of its protagonists. Its specific tool is "psychology" or "specific understanding" or— Mises's favorite expression—"thymology."

Of the two disciplines, economics had the most momentous practical implications.[13] In *Human Action*, Mises had shown that economic analysis leads directly to *laissez-faire* conclusions. He demonstrated that government intervention entails consequences that are unwanted even from the point of view of the champions of these interventions.

In *Theory and History*, he completed the case for capitalism from the epistemological point of view. In particular, he took on those theories that were grounded on an explicit or implicit rejection of methodological individualism and methodological dualism. His basic argument against the approaches of Marxism, teleological philosophies of history, and positivism was that they had no scientific underpinning whatever. They were based on certain *beliefs* about social and economic evolution, but they had

---

[13]Mises, *Theory and History*:

> Thymology has no special relation to praxeology and economics. The popular belief that modern subjective economics, the marginal utility school, is founded on or closely connected with "psychology" is mistaken. . . . [P]raxeology is not concerned with the events which within a man's soul or mind or brain produce a definite decision between an A and a B. It takes it for granted that the nature of the universe enjoins upon man choosing between incompatible ends. Its subject is not the content of these acts of choosing but what results from them: action. It does not care about what a man chooses but about the fact *that* he chooses and acts in compliance with a choice made. (p. 271; emphasis added)
>
> The thymological analysis of man is essential in the study of history. It conveys all we can know about ultimate ends and judgments of value. But as has been pointed out above, it is of no avail for praxeology and of little use in dealing with the means applied to attain ends sought. (p. 280)

not delivered the goods. Their most fundamental tenets could neither be refuted nor verified with the tools of science: reason and observation. Moreover, to the extent that they did make propositions about ascertainable facts, they were wrong (or incoherent) at the crucial junctures of the argument. For example, Marxism and the various philosophies of history could not explain how the general direction in which they believed society was moving resulted from individual action. Positivism blithely disregarded the fact that there are no constant relationships in observable human behavior. The champions of historicism contradicted themselves whenever they championed any government policy whatever, while holding to the notion that there was no such thing as economic law. Strictly speaking, these were metaphysical or quasi-religious doctrines, not science.

Science and the Culture of Salutary Dissent

As Mises saw it, the task of metaphysics, philosophy, and religion was to slake the unquenchable human thirst for knowledge and certainty. He remarked:

> Those divines who saw that nothing but revelation could provide man with perfect certainty were right. Human scientific inquiry cannot proceed beyond the limits drawn by the insufficiency of man's senses and the narrowness of his mind.[14]

And even more clearly, a few years later:

> The human mind in its search for knowledge resorts to philosophy or theology precisely because it aims at an explanation of problems that the natural sciences cannot answer.[15]

---

[14]Ibid., p. 9.

[15]Mises, *The Ultimate Foundation of Economic Science* (Irvington-on-Hudson, N.Y.: Foundation for Economic Education, [1962] 2002), p. 117.

There were questions to which science had not yet provided an answer ("What determines the behavior of atoms?"); and there were questions to which science *could not* give any answers ("Was there a beginning of time?" "Does the soul die?"). Science could give answers only to the extent that it could rely on ascertainable facts. There was a scientific interpretation of social and economic evolution only to the extent that there were ascertainable facts that warranted this interpretation. And even then, there were basic assumptions underlying any scientific analysis of facts that could not themselves be demonstrated:

> It is contradictory to expect that logic could be of any service in demonstrating the correctness or validity of the fundamental logical principles. All that can be said about them is that to deny their correctness or validity appears to the human mind nonsensical and that thinking, guided by them, has led to modes of successful acting. . . . There is no deductive demonstration possible of the principle of causality and of the ampliative inference of imperfect induction; there is only recourse to the no less indemonstrable statement that there is a strict regularity in the conjunction of all natural phenomena. If we were not to refer to this uniformity, all the statements of the natural sciences would appear to be hasty generalizations.[16]

Now Mises did believe that metaphysics, philosophy, and religion also relate to reality in some way, but the problem is that their interpretation of reality cannot be verified by reason and observation. Therefore they *cannot be demonstrated* as a scientific proposition can be demonstrated. And the espousal of a metaphysical or religious doctrine therefore cannot be grounded on such a demonstration, but must rely essentially on a value judgment. And Mises insisted that value judgments and ultimate

------

[16]Mises, *Theory and History*, p. 9.

ends are "beyond any rational examination." They could only be examined by applying some standard of evaluation, but as soon as one applies such a standard, the end under consideration would no longer be an ultimate end; rather, it would become a means for the attainment of the proposed standard. It follows that truly ultimate ends could not possibly be demonstrated by reason and observation:

> The characteristic mark of ultimate ends is that they depend entirely on each individual's personal and subjective judgment, which cannot be examined, measured, still less corrected by any other person. Each individual is the only and final arbiter in matters concerning his own satisfaction and happiness.[17]

Even the venerable idea of justice, interpreted as an ultimate end, cannot be demonstrated. One has to rely on intuition and interpretation of one's inner voice—yet how can disagreements between different intuitions and different inner voices be settled? Moreover, and most importantly, justice is not an ultimate end; it is a means for the attainment of social cooperation:

> All these ethical doctrines have failed to comprehend that there is, outside of social bonds and preceding, temporally or logically, the existence of society, nothing to which the epithet "just" can be given. A hypothetical isolated individual must under the pressure of biological competition look upon all other people as deadly foes. His only concern is to preserve his own life and health; he does not need to heed the consequences which his own survival has for other men; he has no use for justice. His only solicitudes are hygiene and defense. But in social cooperation with other

---

[17]Ibid., p. 12. Notice that Mises admitted the existence of errors in regard to one's value judgments (ibid., p. 174). He also took it for granted that one could enjoy art (ibid., p. 63). The point was, again, that each individual is his own judge.

men the individual is forced to abstain from conduct
incompatible with life in society. Only then does the
distinction between what is just and what is unjust
emerge. It invariably refers to interhuman social relations. What is beneficial to the individual without
affecting his fellows, such as the observance of certain
rules in the use of some drugs, remains hygiene.

The ultimate yardstick of justice is conduciveness
to the preservation of social cooperation. Conduct
suited to preserve social cooperation is just, conduct
detrimental to the preservation of society is unjust.[18]

This raises an important practical problem for all systems of
social organization that, because they cannot be built on scientific demonstration, must rely exclusively on value judgments.
The problem appears as soon as one raises the question: How
do the members of such systems deal with dissenters? This
question concerns in particular the members of different collectivist systems of social organization. Their starting point is the
moral postulate that the collective takes precedence over the
individual:

If a man assigns a higher value to the concerns of a
collective than to his other concerns, and acts accordingly, that is his affair. So long as the collectivist
philosophers proceed in this way, no objection can be
raised. But they argue differently. They elevate their
personal judgments of value to the dignity of an
absolute standard of value. They urge other people to
stop valuing according to their own will and to adopt
unconditionally the precepts to which collectivism
has assigned absolute eternal validity.[19]

What happens though when individuals are reluctant to
espouse the collectivist agenda? Mises emphasized that the collectivists depend on violence to solve this problem:

---

[18]Ibid., p. 54.
[19]Ibid., pp. 59f.

> There is, of course, but one way to make one's own
> judgments of value supreme. One must beat into sub-
> mission all those dissenting. This is what all repre-
> sentatives of the various collectivist doctrines are
> striving for. They ultimately recommend the use of
> violence and pitiless annihilation of all those whom
> they condemn as heretics. Collectivism is a doctrine
> of war, intolerance, and persecution. If any of the col-
> lectivist creeds should succeed in its endeavors, all
> people but the great dictator would be deprived of
> their essential human quality. They would become
> mere soulless pawns in the hands of a monster.[20]

Again, the basic problem of all collectivist schemes is that in
their argument they willy-nilly have to rely on value judgments,
and value judgments cannot be proven to be right or wrong. In
contrast, the facts of science are ascertainable by all people.
Anyone can check for himself the veracity of what the scientists
say. He can convince himself that one course of action is feasible while another is not, or that one course of action leads to a
desired outcome while another one fails to do so. Science has
nothing to say about ultimate ends or value judgments, but it
does provide knowledge about the earthly means to attain
earthly ends. It is therefore the foremost tool for men to find a
minimal agreement for cooperation in the world, *despite* their
differences in beliefs and value judgments. Catholics, Protestants, Jews, and Muslims might not agree on theological questions, but all of them can check for themselves that a greater
division of labor is more productive than a smaller one, or that
money prices are needed for economic calculation. It follows
that a free society *can* work even if its members do not share the
same ultimate value judgments.

> The characteristic feature of a free society is that it
> can function in spite of the fact that its members dis-
> agree in many judgments of value. In the market

---

[20]Ibid., pp. 60–61.

> economy business serves not only the majority but
> also various minorities, provided they are not too
> small in respect of the economic goods which satisfy-
> ing their special wishes would require. Philosophical
> treatises are published—though few people read
> them, and the masses prefer other books or none—if
> enough readers are foreseen to recover the costs.[21]

A few years later, Mises went beyond this defense of dissent
to a position of advocacy. Not only is dissent compatible with
the functioning of a free society, it was actually the driving force
behind the cultural and economic development that culminated
in the nineteenth century:

> What transformed the stagnant conditions of the
> good old days into the activism of capitalism was not
> changes in the natural sciences and in technology, but
> the adoption of the free enterprise principle. The
> great ideological movement that started with the
> Renaissance, continued in the Enlightenment, and in
> the nineteenth century culminated in Liberalism pro-
> duced both capitalism—the free market economy—
> and its political corollary or—as the Marxians have to
> say, its political "superstructure"—representative
> government and the individuals' civic rights: freedom
> of conscience, of thought, of speech, and of all other
> methods of communication. It was in the climate cre-
> ated by this capitalistic system of individualism that
> all the modern intellectual achievements thrived.
> Never before had mankind lived under conditions
> like those of the second part of the nineteenth cen-
> tury, when, in the civilized countries, the most
> momentous problems of philosophy, religion, and
> science could be freely discussed without any fear of
> reprisals on the part of the powers that be. It was an
> age of productive and salutary dissent.[22]

---

[21]Ibid., p. 61.

[22]Mises, *The Ultimate Foundation of Economic Science*, p. 123.

This culture of salutary dissent was ultimately the product of freedom of thought and speech, but its more proximate cause was the discovery and dissemination of economic science. The "development and practical application" of this new discipline, concluded Mises, "was the most spectacular event of modern history."[23]

Heroic Elites in a Mass Democracy

Yet by the mid-1950s, capitalism and classical liberalism were everywhere on the retreat. How was it possible that the great majority of westerners had forgotten, or failed to appreciate, the most spectacular event of modern history? In *Theory and History*, Mises outlined his account of the rise and fall of classical liberalism. In the center of his reflection was the relationship between elites and masses, a relationship that he analyzed within the framework of his epistemological reflections.

In other writings he had already stressed the fundamental historical fact that social progress, in particular the rise of capitalism, had resulted from the efforts of a small group of individuals:

> The most amazing thing concerning the unprecedented change in earthly conditions brought about by capitalism is the fact that it was accomplished by a small number of authors and a hardly greater number of statesmen who had assimilated their teachings. Not only the sluggish masses but also most of the businessmen who, by their trading, made the laissez-faire principles effective failed to comprehend the essential features of their operation. Even in the heyday of liberalism only a few people had a full grasp of the functioning of the market economy. Western civilization adopted capitalism upon recommendation on the part of a small élite.[24]

---

[23]Ibid., p. 3.

[24]Mises, *The Anti-Capitalistic Mentality* (Princeton, N.J.: Van Nostrand, 1956), chap. 2, sect. 1.

How was this possible? Because ultimately society is ruled by ideas. Small groups who spread their ideas can therefore have, in due time, a disproportionate impact on social organization.

> A rather superficial and shallow view of the problems of government saw the distinction between freedom and despotism in an outward feature of the system of rule and administration, viz., in the number of people exercising direct control of the social apparatus of coercion and compulsion. . . . The way toward a realistic distinction between freedom and bondage was opened, two hundred years ago, by David Hume's immortal essay, On the First Principles of Government. Government, taught Hume, is always government of the many by the few. Power is therefore always ultimately on the side of the governed, and the governors have nothing to support them but opinion.[25]

Now Mises combined this insight with his epistemology of the social sciences. If Hume was right that ideas rule society and if it was true that no scientific account could be given of how new ideas emerge in general, then it follows that new ideas were the true driving force in human history:

> History is the record of human action. Human action is the conscious effort of man to substitute more satisfactory conditions for less satisfactory ones. Ideas determine what are to be considered more and less satisfactory conditions and what means are to be resorted to alter them. Thus ideas are the main theme of the study of history. . . . The genesis of every new idea is an innovation; it adds something new and unheard of before to the course of world affairs. The reason history does not repeat itself is that every historical state is the consummation of the operation of

---

[25]Mises, *Theory and History*, pp. 65–66.

ideas different from those that operated in other historical states.[26]

It follows that *intellectual* elites were the true elites in comparison to which the mighty and powerful of any age are just the executors of ideas developed in previous ages. The creative genius was the hero, the true driving force of history:

> Every man, whether great or small, lives and acts within the frame of his age's historical circumstances. These circumstances are determined by all the ideas and events of the preceding ages as well as by those of his own age. The Titan may outweigh each of his contemporaries; he is no match for the united forces of the dwarfs. A statesman can succeed only insofar as his plans are adjusted to the climate of opinion of his time, that is to the ideas that have got hold of his fellows' minds. He can become a leader only if he is prepared to guide people along the paths they want to walk and toward the goal they want to attain. A statesman who antagonizes public opinion is doomed to failure. No matter whether he is an autocrat or an officer of a democracy, the politician must give the people what they wish to get, very much as a businessman must supply the customers with the things they wish to acquire.
>
> It is different with the pioneers of new ways of thinking and new modes of art and literature. The path-breaker who disdains the applause he may get from the crowd of his contemporaries does not depend on his own age's ideas. . . . The genius' work too is embedded in the sequence of historical events,

---

[26]Mises, ibid., pp. 224–25. He continued: "The essence of civilization is ideas. If we try to distinguish different civilizations, the *differentia specifica* can be found only in the different meanings of the ideas that determined them" (ibid.) See also ibid., pp. 261f. and Mises, *The Ultimate Foundation of Economic Science*, pp. 92f.

is conditioned by the achievements of preceding generations, and is merely a chapter in the evolution of
ideas. But it adds something new and unheard of to
the treasure of thoughts and may in this sense be
called creative. The genuine history of mankind is the
history of ideas. . . . And in searching for their origin
we inevitably come to a point at which all that can be
asserted is that a man had an idea. Whether the name
of this man is known or not is of secondary importance.[27]

In Mises's worldview, in which all things and all thoughts are
the necessary consequence of antecedent causes, ideas were the
one dynamic element of social evolution. The discoverers and
promoters of new ideas—the creative geniuses—were the social
vanguard, the elite that led humanity onto new paths, both good
and bad.[28] But in order to play this role, they had to be aware of
their responsibility.

---

[27]Mises, *Theory and History*, pp. 186–88.

[28]Mises's stress on the particularities of the genius is a pervasive feature of
his thought, running from *Gemeinwirtschaft* (Jena: Gustav Fischer, 1922) via
Human Action (1949) to *Theory and History* (1957) and *Ultimate Foundation of
Economic Science* (1962). It is not known where his inspiration came from, but
it cannot be excluded that he took it for granted that educated people would
know the theoretician who had insisted on the categorical difference between
"mere" talent (be it ever so great) and true genius. Weininger wrote at the
beginning of the century:

Someone may have a talent, for example, the mathematical
talent, by birth and to an extraordinary degree; he will then
be able to digest the most difficult chapters of this science
with but small effort; but it does not follow that, for this reason, he has any genius, which is the same thing as originality,
individuality, and condition of his own productivity. Con-
versely, there are great geniuses who have not developed any
special talent to a high degree. Just think of Novalis or Jean
Paul. . . . Talent is hereditary, it may be the common good of
a family (the Bachs); genius is not transferable, it is never
general, but always individual (Johann Sebastian). (Otto

Now, the problem was that the majority of the rationalist philosophers who pioneered the capitalist revolution of the eighteenth and nineteenth centuries were not sufficiently self-aware. They did not perceive themselves as a small elite, and did not see social progress as necessarily driven by small elites. Rather they indulged in egalitarian fantasies about society.

> [They] assumed that all men are endowed with the same power of reasoning. They ignored the difference between clever people and dullards, even that between the pioneering genius and the vast crowds of simple routinists who at best can espouse the doctrines developed by the great thinkers but more often are incapable of comprehending them. As the rationalists saw it, every sane adult was intelligent enough to grasp the meaning of the most complicated theory. If he failed to achieve it, the fault lay not in his intellect but in his education. Once all people have enjoyed a perfect education, all will be as wise and judicious as the most eminent sage.[29,30]

Weininger, *Geschlecht und Charakter*, 19th ed. [Vienna: Braumüller, 1920], part 2, chap. 4, p. 126)

[29]Mises, *Theory and History*, p. 270. He added:

The second shortcoming of rationalism was its neglect of the problem of erroneous thinking. Most of the rationalist philosophers failed to see that even honest men, sincerely devoted to the search for truth, could err. This prepossession prevented them from doing justice to the ideologies and the metaphysical doctrines of the past. A doctrine of which they disapproved could in their opinion have been prompted only by purposeful deceit. Many of them dismissed all religions as the product of the intentional fraud of wicked impostors.

[30]Schumpeter had discussed the shortcomings of the classical doctrine of democracy along very similar lines. See Joseph A. Schumpeter, *Capitalism, Socialism, and Democracy* (New York: Harper & Sons, 1942), chap. 21. Both Schumpeter and Mises would highlight the crucial role of leadership in the operation of the market and in politics. In distinct contrast to Schumpeter,

Mises held that as a consequence of this error of the eighteenth-century rationalists (and perpetuated by the nineteenth-century socialists) the dull masses were increasingly reluctant to accept intellectual leadership from anyone but those who flattered them. They were imbued with the mystical notion that the mass of the people can never be wrong—that society could do without the guidance of intellectuals.

Faced with this situation, the classical liberals still endorsed democracy, and so did Mises. It was true that mass democracy had led straight to "the 'dictatorship of the proletariat' and the autocracy of Hitler, Mussolini, Peron, and other modern successors of the Greek tyrants."[31] But the crucial question was whether any alternative political system could have prevented these excesses. Despite the political and humanitarian catastrophes of the twentieth century, Mises did not abandon the case for democracy. Rather he appealed to the elites to accept their responsibilities by engaging in public debate and enlightening their fellow citizens about the right course of action:

> If the small minority of enlightened citizens who are able to conceive sound principles of political management do not succeed in winning the support of their fellow citizens and converting them to the endorsement of policies that bring and preserve prosperity, the cause of mankind and civilization is hopeless. There is no other means to safeguard a propitious development of human affairs than to make the masses of inferior people adopt the ideas of the elite. This has to be achieved by convincing them. It cannot be accomplished by a despotic regime that instead of enlightening the masses beats them into submission. In the long run the ideas of the majority,

---

however, Mises stressed *intellectual* leadership. He also insisted that leadership could be good or bad; it could promote the preservation and flourishing of society, but it could also hurt and destroy it.

[31]Mises, *Theory and History*, p. 66.

however detrimental they may be, will carry on. The
future of mankind depends on the ability of the elite
to influence public opinion in the right direction.[32]

What does this imply more specifically for libertarian intellectuals who wish to steer social evolution toward greater freedom? Do they have to make the case for a particular form of government or for a particular design of constitutions? Mises would have none of this. The form of government was a completely secondary problem because tyranny could exist under any of the possible systems. He argued that the primary challenge for libertarian intellectuals was to preserve a climate of opinion that tolerated dissent. Hume's insight, that governors have nothing to support them but opinion,

> logically followed to its conclusion, completely
> changed the discussion concerning liberty. The
> mechanical and arithmetical point of view was abandoned. If public opinion is ultimately responsible for
> the structure of government, it is also the agency that
> determines whether there is freedom or bondage.
> There is virtually only one factor that has the power
> to make people unfree—tyrannical public opinion.
> The struggle for freedom is ultimately not resistance
> to autocrats or oligarchs but resistance to the despotism of public opinion. It is not the struggle of the
> many against the few but of minorities—sometimes
> of a minority of but one man—against the majority.
> The worst and most dangerous form of absolutist
> rule is that of an intolerant majority. Such is the conclusion arrived at by Tocqueville and John Stuart
> Mill.[33]

Without an elite defending tolerance, there could be no culture of dissent, no competition and progress in the economic

---

[32]Mises, *The Ultimate Foundation of Economic Science*, p. 95.

[33]Mises, *Theory and History*, pp. 66f.

sphere. Mises was not being naïve in ascribing this responsibility to intellectuals. They were the heroes of the drama of human history, yes, but they also had to be truly heroic in their attitude toward life. He knew from bitter personal experience that a pro-capitalist intellectual could not expect lavish material rewards. A case in point was the commercial book market. A true pioneer could not expect a high income on a free market:

> Reverence to the great authors and artists has always been limited to small groups. . . . The book market is flooded by a downpour of trivial fiction for the semi-barbarians. But this does not prevent great authors from creating imperishable works.[34]

The decisive consideration was, again, that no alternative social system held better promise:

> It is, of course, true that in the market economy not those fare best who, from the point of view of an enlightened judgment, ought to be considered as the most eminent individuals of the human species. The uncouth hordes of common men are not fit to recognize duly the merits of those who eclipse their own wretchedness. They judge everybody from the point of view of the satisfaction of their desires. Thus, boxing champions and authors of detective stories enjoy a higher prestige and earn more money than philosophers and poets. Those who bemoan this fact are certainly right. But no social system could be devised that would fairly reward the contributions of the innovator whose genius leads mankind to ideas unknown before and therefore first rejected by all those who lack the same inspiration.[35]

The only consolation for great but unsuccessful intellectuals was that the pioneers in business did not fare any better:

---

[34]Mises, *Anti-Capitalistic Mentality*, chap. 4, sect. 2.

[35]Mises, *The Ultimate Foundation of Economic Science*, p. 113.

The much defamed acquisitiveness of promoters and speculators succeeds daily in providing the masses with commodities and services unknown before. A horn of plenty is poured upon people for whom the methods by means of which all these marvelous gadgets are produced are incomprehensible. These dull beneficiaries of the capitalistic system indulge in the delusion that it is their own performance of routine jobs that creates all these marvels. They cast their votes for rulers who are committed to a policy of sabotage and destruction. They look upon "big business," necessarily committed to catering to mass consumption, as upon the foremost public enemy and approve of every measure that, as they think, improves their own conditions by "punishing" those whom they envy.[36]

The Study of History

Mises devoted all of part three to the discussion of the nature, scope, and methods of historical research. This might be surprising from the pen of an economist. But keep in mind that Mises was interested in economics as a tool to guide action. In his early years as a student at the University of Vienna, this practical concern had made him dissatisfied with the methods taught by the Historical School. A passage from *Theory and History* sums up the problem:

The historicists' fateful error consisted in the belief that this analysis of the past in itself conveys information about the course future action has to take. What the historical account provides is the description of the situation; the reaction depends on the meaning the actor gives it, on the ends he wants to attain, and on the means he chooses for their attainment.[37]

---

[36]Ibid., p. 114.
[37]Mises, *Theory and History*, p. 288.

By the 1950s, a sort of a neo-historicism was in full swing and about to conquer western academia. The new movement was led by statisticians and econometricians who held precisely the views that Mises had rejected more than fifty years earlier. In correspondence with Nymeyer, he lamented:

> They are full of contempt for what they call "meta-physical economics." Only "facts", they say, count. That these "facts" are history and not facts in the sense in which the natural sciences employ this term, remains unknown to them.
>
> The official doctrine of all these research institutions, government economists, university economists and so on is, for instance, that the socialist program is not to be refuted by "metaphysics", but by "facts". They point out, e.g., that profits are "only" x% of the national income or "only" y% of the sales dollar and that "therefore" the socialists are wrong. But the socialists believe that all profits as such are wrong, and are to be confiscated. They use the same figures to corroborate their own contentions.[38]

Mises had turned to economics because this discipline provided knowledge about something on which historical research was mute—even with the advanced techniques of econometrics—namely, the objective suitability of means to attain social ends. Yet the same overarching practical motivation preserved his lifelong interest in the study of history. In *Theory and History* Mises set out to explain why and how historical knowledge had to complement economics as a guide for human action. Thus he closed a great parenthesis opened during his days in the Grünberg seminar.

In his previous works he had outlined the division of labor between praxeology and history. He had presented history as a

[38]Mises to Nymeyer, letter dated June 19, 1953; Grove City Archive: Nymeyer files.

sort of residual discipline that sought to come to grips with problems that could not be addressed by the exact disciplines.[39] He had singled out in particular the problem of assigning relative quantitative weights to different causes that combine into an observable effect. Mises called this the problem of "relevance." The only way to tackle it was to apply the specific tool of the historian, understanding or *Verstehen*:

> The historian can enumerate all the factors which cooperated in bringing about a known effect and all the factors which worked against them and may have resulted in delaying and mitigating the final outcome. But he cannot coordinate, except by understanding, the various causative factors in a quantitative way to the effects produced. He cannot, except by understanding, assign to each of n factors its role in producing the effect p. Understanding is in the realm of history the equivalent, as it were, of quantitative analysis and measurement.

But the understanding of the relative quantitative contribution of any one cause to a combined effect could not be independently verified or refuted. As a consequence, the problem of relevance was the source of insuperable disagreement between men of science. And Mises stressed that it was in fact the only source of lasting disagreement:

> Historical understanding can never produce results which must be accepted by all men. . . . Historians may disagree for various reasons. They may hold different views with regard to the teachings of the

---

[39]Mises, *Human Action*, p. 50:

> The scope of understanding is the mental grasp of phenomena which cannot be totally elucidated by logic, mathematics, praxeology, and the natural sciences to the extent that they cannot be cleared up by all these other sciences. It must never contradict the teachings of these other branches of knowledge.

nonhistorical sciences; they may base their reasoning on a more or less complete familiarity with the
records; they may differ in the understanding of the
motives and aims of the acting men and of the means
applied by them. All these differences are open to a
settlement by "objective" reasoning; it is possible to
reach a universal agreement with regard to them. But
as far as historians disagree with regard to judgments
of relevance it is impossible to find a solution which
all sane men must accept.[40]

In *Theory and History* Mises wanted to flesh out his theory of
understanding. He did not believe that the necessarily subjective judgments of relevance somehow made history otiose.
Despite its deficiencies, only the discipline of history could
solve certain problems that were of utmost practical importance. In particular, history alone could provide an analysis of
the context of action. Mises stressed that human action was
always embedded in concrete circumstances of time and place.
Action was a conscious response to a given situation and it could
succeed only if the acting person understood the present. But:

There is no such thing as a nonhistorical analysis of
the present state of affairs. The examination and
description of the present are necessarily a historical
account of the past ending with the instant just
passed. The description of the present state of politics
or of business is inevitably the narration of the events
that have brought about the present state. If, in business or in government, a new man takes the helm, his
first task is to find out what has been done up to the

---

[40]Ibid., pp. 57–58. In *Theory and History*, speaking of the same problem:

The precariousness of forecasting is mainly due to the intri-
cacy of this . . . problem. It is not only a rather puzzling question in forecasting future events. It is no less puzzling in retrospect for the historian. (p. 314)

See also *The Ultimate Foundation of Economic Science*, pp. 67, 103.

> last minute. The statesman as well as the businessman learns about the present situation from studying the records of the past.[41]

Mises knew what he was talking about. Reporting on current business and political conditions had been his daily bread for many years. Moreover, at two critical junctures he had analyzed the state of affairs in politics: in *Nation, State, and Economy* (1919) and in *Omnipotent Government* (1944) he had analyzed the forces at work in the rise of aggressive nationalism and statism as well as their cataclysmic endings in the two world wars. At the onset of the Cold War he had added a third piece, *Planned Chaos* (1946), which told the tale of the rise of the Soviet Union to its position of power. Thus he was in a good position to challenge those of his readers who might disagree:

> Let those who want to reject the preceding statements undertake to describe any present situation—in philosophy, in politics, on a battlefield, on the stock exchange, in an individual business enterprise—without reference to the past.[42]

But how far back should history be studied? Was it practical or necessary for statesmen and business leaders to seek instruction about more than the past few years before they took office? He observed that there "is no point in history at which we can stop our investigation fully satisfied that we have not overlooked any important factor."[43] There was no a priori rule that could be helpful in deciding where to stop historical research. The usefulness of further knowledge could only be determined *after* completion of additional research. In any case, it was a grave error to believe that increasing remoteness in time meant decreasing practical relevance:

---

[41]Mises, *Theory and History*, pp. 287–88.
[42]Ibid., p. 289.
[43]Ibid., p. 290.

> The mere fact that an event happened in a distant
> country and a remote age does not in itself prove that
> it has no bearing on the present. Jewish affairs of three
> thousand years ago influence the lives of millions of
> present-day Christian Americans more than what
> happened to the American Indians as late as in the
> second part of the nineteenth century. In the present-
> day conflict of the Roman Church and the Soviets
> there are elements that trace back to the great schism
> of the Eastern and Western churches that originated
> more than a thousand years ago.[44]

The specific intellectual tool applied in historical research
was "understanding" or *Verstehen*—the term introduced by the
Southwest German School of historiography. In his previous
writings, Mises had referred to and endorsed the historical
works of this school. In *Theory and History*, he developed his
own account of the theory of *Verstehen*. He presented it as a tool
to unearth facts provided by introspection and by contact with
other human beings:

> It signifies the cognition of human emotions, motiva-
> tions, ideas, judgments of value and volitions, a fac-
> ulty indispensable to everybody in the conduct of
> daily affairs and no less indispensable to the authors
> of poems, novels, and plays as well as to historians.
> Modern epistemology calls this mental process of the
> historians the specific understanding of the historical
> sciences of human action. . . . [However it] is not a
> mental process exclusively resorted to by historians.
> It is applied by everybody in daily intercourse with all
> his fellows. It is a technique employed in all interhu-
> man relations. It is practiced by children in the nurs-
> ery and kindergarten, by businessmen in trade, by
> politicians and statesmen in affairs of state.[45]

---

[44]Ibid., p. 290.
[45]Ibid., pp. 264–65.

Mises was reluctant to use the word "psychology" to describe this approach, because by the early 1950s the new discipline of experimental psychology had become fairly entrenched and was about to become identified with psychology *per se*. In order to avoid confusion, he introduced a new term to designate the traditional humanistic discipline of psychology:

> Thymology is . . . what everybody learns from intercourse with his fellows. It is what a man knows about the way in which people value different conditions, about their wishes and desires and their plans to realize these wishes and desires. It is the knowledge of the social environment in which a man lives and acts or, with historians, of a foreign milieu about which he has learned by studying special sources.[46]

Mises observed that the members of the Southwest German School were unaware of the existence of economic theory, but this did not diminish their achievements in the clarification of the logical nature of history. In *Theory and History*, Mises made an important contribution to the theory of *Verstehen*. He pointed out that the main application of *Verstehen* was not in the analysis of the past, but as a tool for anticipating the future. There were in fact two types of historians: "the historian of the past as well as the historian of the future, i.e., acting man."[47] The Southwest German School and its followers such as Alfred Schütz had in their writings exclusively dealt with the historian of the past. But the most urgent questions related to the historian of the future:

> The main epistemological problem of the specific understanding is: How can a man have any knowledge of the *future* value judgments and actions of other people? The traditional method of dealing with this problem, commonly called the problem of the

---

[46]Ibid., p. 266.
[47]Ibid., p. 320.

alter ego or Fremdverstehen, is unsatisfactory. It
focused attention upon grasping the meaning of
other people's behavior in the "present" or, more correctly, in the past. But the task with which acting
man, that is, everybody, is faced in all relations with
his fellows does not refer to the past; it refers to the
future. To know the future reactions of other people
is the first task of acting man. Knowledge of their past
value judgments and actions, although indispensable,
is only a means to this end.[48]

What then is the logical character of the *Verstehen* of future
action? Mises is unequivocal: the historian of the future is
essentially an intellectual entrepreneur. All his knowledge concerns contingent data of the past that cannot be generalized.
How can such information about particular circumstances of
time and place be used to forecast the future? There is only one
way: the historian of the future must *guess* what the future will
be. Forecasting is inherently speculative and uncertain when it
comes to anticipating future human behavior:

Psychology in the sense of thymology is a branch of
history. It derives its knowledge from historical experience. . . . All that thymology can tell us is that in the
past definite men or groups of men were valuing and
acting in a definite way. Whether they will in the
future value and act in the same way remains uncertain. All that can be asserted about their future conduct is speculative anticipation of the future based on
the specific understanding of the historical branches
of the sciences of human action.[49]

---

[48]Ibid., p. 311.

[49]Ibid., p. 272. On thymology being an empirical rather than an a priori
discipline, see also ibid., p. 311. He later gave a more operational description
of the intellectual process involved:

Out of what we know about a man's past behavior, we construct a scheme about what we call his character. We assume

This insight delivered a clue to the vexed problems of cultural history, a discipline riddled with chauvinistic and nihilistic prejudices. Mises would have nothing of the sort of cultural relativism that the young Lévi-Strauss had championed just a few years before.[50] He believed in the superiority of western culture, the evidence being that all other cultures were eager to copy the institutions they believed had brought affluence to the West. And he did not dance around the fact that this culture had been created by white men. However, this was in no way a scientific vindication of racist policies:

> Historical experience warrants the statement that in the past the efforts of some subdivisions of the Caucasian race to develop a civilization have eclipsed those of the members of other races. It does not warrant any statement about the future. It does not permit us to assume that this superiority of the white stock will persist in the future. . . . In 1760 a historian would have been right in declaring that Western civilization was mainly an achievement of the Latins and the British and that the Germans had contributed little to it. . . . But if somebody had inferred from these facts that the Germans are culturally inferior and would rank in the future far below the French and the British, his conclusion would have been disproved by the course of later history. . . . All that can be said about racial issues on the ground of historical experience boils down to two statements. First, the prevailing differences between the various biological strains of men are reflected in the civilizatory achievements of the group members. Second, in our age the main achievements in

----

> that this character will not change if no special reasons interfere, and, going a step farther, we even try to foretell how definite changes in conditions will affect his reactions. (Mises, *The Ultimate Foundation of Economic Science*, pp. 50f.)

[50]Claude Lévi-Strauss, *Race et Histoire* (Paris: UNESCO, 1952).

civilization of some subdivisions of the white Cau-
casian race are viewed by the immense majority of the
members of all other races as more desirable than
characteristic features of the civilization produced by
the members of their respective own races.[51]

The Anti-Capitalistic Mentality

One year before the publication of *Theory and History*, Mises
had published a short book in applied thymology. Here he dealt
with the psychological causes of anti-capitalism—with what he
called the *Anti-Capitalistic Mentality*. It is significant that he
published this work only *after* an exhaustive discussion of the
merits of the intellectual case against the market economy. Thymology, we need to keep in mind, was for Mises a residual discipline. The purpose of *Verstehen* was to explain those aspects of
human behavior that could not be explained by other disciplines. If economic analysis could disprove the case against the
market, then what could explain the worldwide popularity of
socialism and the omnipotent state? This is the question that he
dealt with in this slim volume and, as usual, he did not mince
words. He singled out two factors: intellectual error, and the
base passions of envy and hatred.

> From the very beginnings of the socialist movement
> and the endeavors to revive the interventionist poli-
> cies of the precapitalistic ages, both socialism and
> interventionism were utterly discredited in the eyes

---

[51]Mises, *Theory and History*, pp. 335–37. He remarked:

> A prediction about the future behavior of those races which
> today are considered culturally backward could only be made
> by biological science. If biology were to discover some
> anatomical characteristics of the members of the non-Cau-
> casian races which necessarily curb their mental faculties,
> one could venture such a prediction. But so far biology has
> not discovered any such characteristics.

of those conversant with economic theory. But the ideas of the immense majority of ignorant people [are] exclusively driven by the most powerful human passions of envy and hatred. . . . They are socialists because they are blinded by envy and ignorance. They stubbornly refuse to study economics and spurn the economists' devastating critique of the socialist plans because, in their eyes, economics, being an abstract theory, is simply nonsense. They pretend to trust only in experience. But they no less stubbornly refuse to take cognizance of the undeniable facts of experience.[52]

The book appealed to a wider audience, and the indefatigable Nymeyer willingly served the market. He had Van Nostrand print 2,000 paperback copies at sixty cents each.[53] The reviews were predictable. Hazlitt, Rothbard, Raico, and a few others praised it, while most of the reviewers were bewildered or scandalized. *The Economist* disparaged it out of hand. Mises took this as a good sign. The book was having its impact. He wrote to a Greek correspondent:

That the London Economist, that harbinger of the policies that are ruining British prosperity and civilization, does not like my *Anti-Capitalistic Mentality* is, in the eyes of discerning people, a recommendation.[54]

---

[52]Mises, *Anti-Capitalistic Mentality*, chap. 2, sect. 2. He had alluded to the fundamental role of envy in *Socialism* (Indianapolis: Liberty Fund, 1981, p. 384) quoting Mandeville, Hume, and Schatz. In October 1952, he had recommended Helmut Schoeck's proposed study on envy to the Volker Fund. Schoeck's application was successful, and he reported to Mises on the progress of his studies; see Grove City Archive: Schoeck file.

[53]Nymeyer to Johnson, letters dated October 31, 1956 and January 10, 1957; Grove City Archive: Nymeyer files.

[54]Mises to M.E. Constantacatos, letter dated May 16, 1957; Grove City Archive: Constantacatos files.

And in another letter he expressed his satisfaction over the severe fire the Swedish edition of the book had drawn:

> The only proof that the time bestowed upon the production of a book was not wasted is the fact that it is rejected by all conformists and champions of the prevailing popular doctrines. I am not ashamed of belonging to a very small minority. Actually this minority, although small, is not negligible for it includes the most eminent men of our age.[55]

Christianity Reconsidered

One of the most striking features of *Theory and History* and *The Ultimate Foundation of Economic Science* is the frequent allusion to theological problems. At the same time, there is an equally noticeable change of nuance in the discussion of religion, and of the Christian faith in particular. Whereas in *Socialism* and *Human Action* Mises had been skeptical that Christianity could ever be reconciled with the principles of a free society, in the late 1950s and early 1960s he had lost much of this skepticism. Consider the following statement from the first edition of *Socialism* (1922):

> [Our] evidence leads to the negation of the question asked above: whether it might not be possible to reconcile Christianity with a free social order based on private ownership in the means of production. A living Christianity cannot exist side by side with, and within, Capitalism.[56]

By 1949, he had reached an intermediate phase in which he thoroughly distinguished between theocracy and religion. The

---

[55]Mises to Trygve Hoff, letter dated June 11, 1957; Grove City Archive: Hoff files. Mises had told Hoff that he never replied to criticism.

[56]Mises, *Gemeinwirtschaft*, p. 421; my translation.

latter was not necessarily in contradiction with classical liberalism, provided that it did not impose its views on mankind. The pious just had to tolerate debate on issues they found sensitive, such as birth control and divorce. Moreover, Mises seemed to prefer the kind of religion that was a purely inward affair for each individual. It was not allowed to have any social impact whatever. He referred at length to the work of William James, for whom religion was

> a purely personal and individual relation between man and a holy, mysterious, and awe-inspiring divine Reality. It enjoins upon man a certain mode of individual conduct. But it does not assert anything with regard to the problems of social organization.[57]

Eight years later, Mises had moved still closer to the Christian position. We read in *Theory and History*:

> There is nothing in any ethical doctrine or in the teachings of any of the creeds based on the Ten Commandments that could justify the condemnation of an economic system which has multiplied the population and provides the masses in the capitalistic countries with the highest standard of living ever attained in history. From the religious point of view, too, the drop in infant mortality, the prolongation of the average length of life, the successful fight against plagues and disease, the disappearance of famines, illiteracy, and superstition tell in favor of capitalism.[58]

In the same work, he stressed that it was "justifiable if ethics and religion tell people that they ought to make better use of the well-being that capitalism brings them." And he even pointed out that the champions of natural-law theory had anticipated at least

---

[57]Mises, *Human Action*, p. 156.

[58]Mises, *Theory and History*, p. 343.

some discoveries of the economists.[59] He merely admonished that it was "irresponsible to condemn one social system and to recommend its replacement by another system without having fully investigated the economic consequences of each."[60] And another five years later he wrote in *The Ultimate Foundation of Economic Science*:

> According to the fundamental doctrine of Christian theology and philosophy, God has created the human mind in endowing man with his faculty of thinking. As both revelation and human reason are manifestations of the Lord's might, there cannot be ultimately any disagreement between them. God does not contradict himself. It is the object of philosophy and theology to demonstrate the concord between revelation and reason. Such was the problem the solution of which patristic and scholastic philosophy tried to achieve.[61]

---

[59]Ibid., p. 45. This was probably under the impact of reading Raymond de Roover and Schumpeter, possibly also Marjorie Grice-Hutchinson, on the sixteenth- and seventeenth-century School of Salamanca.

[60]Ibid., p. 343.

[61]Mises, *The Ultimate Foundation of Economic Science*, pp. 106f. In *Theory and History*, he had not yet been convinced that the antagonism between reason and faith could be overcome within Christian theology.

> We may leave aside the genuine dogmas such as Creation, Incarnation, the Trinity, as they have no direct bearing on the problems of interhuman relations. But many issues remain with regard to which most, if not all, Christian churches and denominations are not prepared to yield to secular reasoning and an evaluation from the point of view of social utility. Thus the recognition of natural law on the part of Christian theology was only conditional. It referred to a definite type of natural law, not opposed to the teachings of Christ as each of these churches and denominations interpreted them. It did not acknowledge the supremacy of reason. It was incompatible with the principles of utilitarian philosophy. (Ibid., pp. 46f.)

One intellectual influence that seems to have contributed to the formation of Mises's mature judgment on the relationship between economic science, liberalism, and the Christian faith was apparently Karl Barth, whose work he probably started reading in the 1950s.[62] In Barth's theology, God is the "wholly other" who could not possibly be grasped in terms of human reason. Barth made a passionate case for revealed theology and against the intellectualist presumptions of natural theology.[63] This line of argument appealed to the extreme rationalist in Mises, who must have been intrigued to find in Barth a brother in spirit when it came to pointing out the contradictions of the notion of an "acting God." He acknowledged:

> The repudiation of naive anthropomorphism that imagined a supreme being either as a dictator or as a watchmaker was an achievement of theology and of metaphysics. With regard to the doctrine that God is wholly other than man and that his essence and nature cannot be grasped by mortal man, the natural sciences and a philosophy derived from them have nothing to say. The transcendent is beyond the realm about which physics and physiology convey information. Logic can neither prove nor disprove the core of theological doctrines. All that science—apart from history—can do in this regard is to expose the fallacies of magic and fetishistic superstitions and practices.[64]

Government interventionism and socialism clearly fell into the latter category. Mises argued:

> A conscientious moralist or churchman would not consider meddling in controversies concerning technological or therapeutical methods without having

---

[62]Barth is mentioned in *Anti-Capitalistic Mentality*, chap. 2, sect. 2.; but not in *Human Action*, p. 671, n. 8.

[63]Karl Barth, *Der Römerbrief* (Munich: Kaiser, 1922).

[64]Mises, *The Ultimate Foundation of Economic Science*, p. 38.

sufficiently familiarized himself with all the physical, chemical and physiological problems involved. Yet many of them think that ignorance of economics is no bar to handling economic issues. . . . The truth is that those fighting capitalism as a system contrary to the principles of morals and religion have uncritically and lightheartedly adopted all the economic teachings of the socialists and communists. Like the Marxians, they ascribe all ills—economic crises, unemployment, poverty, crime, and many other evils—to the operation of capitalism, and everything that is satisfactory—the higher standard of living in the capitalistic countries, the progress of technology, the drop in mortality rates, and so on—to the operation of government and of the labor unions. They have unwittingly espoused all the tenets of Marxism minus its—merely incidental—atheism. This surrender of philosophical ethics and of religion to the anticapitalistic teachings is the greatest triumph of socialist and interventionist propaganda. It is bound to degrade philosophical ethics and religion to mere auxiliaries of the forces seeking the destruction of Western civilization.[65] ⮜

*One of Margit's
favorite pictures
of Lu*

---

[65]Mises, *Theory and History*, pp. 344–45.

22
Fragmentation of the Movement

THE EMERGENCE OF THE Austro-libertarian movement in America reached its high point in the year 1956. Ten years of continuous expansion ushered in a torrent of important publications and other breakthroughs. In 1955, Hans Sennholz published his first book. In early 1956, his wife Mary edited a *Festschrift* for Mises that documented the Austro-libertarian network of intellectuals. Mises himself published *The Anti-Capitalistic Mentality* and gave the opening address at the 1956 Mont Pèlerin Society meeting in Berlin on "The Permanent Inflation." Also in 1956, Murray Rothbard received his Ph.D. in economics from Columbia University and Sennholz obtained his first position at Grove City College.

Nineteen fifty-six was also the year when Mises began to receive outward signs of recognition. Unlike several of his friends and colleagues, such as Hans Kelsen and Joseph Schumpeter, Mises had never been fortunate enough to receive prizes, honorary doctorates, prestigious positions, and influence in politics. He had spent his life swimming against the tide and by now he probably did not even expect the applause of his contemporaries. In 1937, the Vienna *Kammer* sought to have Mises promoted to the rank of a *Hofrat* or Court's Counselor—the highest rank attainable for non-political appointees among the Austrian civil servants—but Hitler's takeover prevented this. Mises then had to wait until he was almost seventy-five to

receive public recognition. In June 1956, he was accorded a $15,000 William Volker Distinguished Service Award.[1] A year later, he received an honorary doctorate from Grove City College, and other honors followed over the next few years. The most lasting sign of the veneration that Mises enjoyed in those days is the bronze bust that George Koether arranged to be made, also in 1956.

Recognition for lifetime achievement is usually accompanied by a winding down. So it was in the case of Mises and of the movement he inspired in the 1950s. In personal public appearances, he began to feel his age. He had never been an orator, but had always been impressive, especially in smaller settings, for

Mises during a NYU seminar

his encompassing knowledge of the subject and for his lucid and systematic exposition. This flame shone for the last time at the Princeton Mont Pèlerin Society meeting in 1958, and in a series of lectures he gave in Buenos Aires in 1959. Thereafter, his frailty weighed ever more heavily.[2] He was increasingly hard of hearing and was soon unable to conduct seminar discussions without the assistance of Percy Greaves.

It was at this point that a strategic weakness of the burgeoning Austro-libertarian movement began to be felt quite painfully: the age gap. Between the almost-octogenarian Mises and his major thirty-something disciples—Sennholz, Rothbard, and Kirzner, in particular—there

---

[1]*New York Times* (June 21, 1956).

[2]Already in 1956–1957, he had not felt well for many months. In May, at the end of the academic year, he looked forward to spending a long vacation in Austria and Switzerland. See Mises to M.E. Constantacatos, letter dated May 16, 1957; Grove City Archive: Constantacatos files.

was no intermediate generation to take leadership from Mises's faltering hands. Henry Hazlitt and Leonard Read were the right age, but were thought of as mere popularizers of the ideas

Mises and Alberto Benegas Lynch in Buenos Aires in 1959

of others. They lacked the authority to lead what was after all an intellectual movement.[3]

The libertarian movement now came under the influence of those who were already intellectual authorities and in the prime age for leadership, but not really Misesians in the Austro-libertarian sense. By the early 1960s, Friedrich Hayek, Milton Friedman, and Ayn Rand had acquired solid reputations as writers and were ready for national recognition as the leaders of an intellectual movement. It was due to their unrivaled impact that in the 1960s Austro-libertarianism came to be largely supplanted by other libertarian and conservative movements. The most visible signs of this paradigm shift were the displacement of *The Freeman* by *National Review* (established in 1955), the takeover of the Mont Pèlerin Society by Chicago School neoliberals in the 1960s, and the emergence of an organized Randian or "Objectivist" movement.

All this occurred while American mass opinion was being converted to the gospel of interventionism and socialism. Mises must have been shocked about the results of a survey among American high-school seniors, as reported in a 1955 letter to the editor of the *Wall Street Journal*. Asked about their attitudes toward free enterprise, 82 percent said they did not believe that

---

[3]Mary Sennholz has argued that Read was underestimated as an intellectual figure. See *Leonard E. Read: Philosopher of Freedom* (Irvington-on-Hudson, N.Y.: Foundation for Economic Education, 1993).

there was business competition in the United States; 60 percent said owners received too much profit; 76 percent believed owners got most of the gains from new machinery; 55 percent championed the postulate "from each according to ability, to each according to needs"; 61 percent rejected the profit motive as the driving force of the economic system; and 60 percent said workers should not produce all they could.[4]

Austro-libertarianism simmered on a low flame for the next two decades. It lingered as an underground movement centered around Hans Sennholz, Murray Rothbard, and, starting in the 1970s, also around Israel Kirzner and Ludwig Lachmann. The movement was further weakened through internal strife. The most important disagreement concerned the "anarchy" question: is a minimal state necessary to preserve a free society? The Rothbardian anarchists rejected the state entirely, claiming that its protection and contract-enforcement functions were (like all other services) better served by free-market competition than government monopoly. This stance cost them the support of the classical-liberal groups around Leonard Read and Hans Sennholz, who advocated minimal-state (or "minarchist") solutions. Yet the coherence and radicalism of Rothbard's views attracted many of the brightest young minds, and when Austro-libertarianism reemerged as a powerful intellectual force in the 1980s and 90s—with the Ludwig von Mises Institute at its epicenter—it did so under the intellectual leadership of Murray Rothbard.

In the late 1950s and early 1960s, Mises witnessed the rise of an American "conservative" mass movement and of the neo-liberal Chicago School within the Mont Pèlerin Society. He saw some of his most promising students abandon their support for free enterprise.

---

[4]Ernest C. Hasselfeldt, letter to the editor, *Wall Street Journal* (February 24, 1955); copy in Grove City Archive: NAM files.

Conservative Movement and Libertarian Remnant

By the mid-1950s, *The Freeman* had accomplished its goal of rallying the disparate libertarian forces—"the Remnant" as Albert Jay Nock would call them. Yet its financial and organizational difficulties had opened the gates for another non-leftist periodical, which would consolidate the forces on the American Right from a far less libertarian point of view than *The Freeman*.

National Review burst onto the American scene in the fall of 1955. Its driving force was the young editor-in-chief William F. Buckley, Jr., a Yale graduate with a strong anti-Communist pedigree: during his studies, he had gathered information on professors and fellow students for the FBI.[5] Buckley absorbed the editorial talent that was unable to find a home at *The Freeman*, in particular, Suzanne LaFollette and William Henry Chamberlin, but also such men as Russell Kirk, Frank Meyer, Max Eastman, and Erik von Kuehnelt-Leddihn.

When Buckley announced *National Review* as "frankly, conservative,"[6] old-world men such as Mises must have thought that, frankly, Buckley did not know what he was talking about. Mises did contribute a few pieces in the course of the first few years of *National Review*'s existence. But on more than one occasion, he emphasized the difference between libertarianism and conservatism. In response to birthday greetings in 1957, he wrote: "Unfortunately this cannot be changed. I am a surviving contemporary of Karl Marx, Wilhelm I, and Horatio Alger, in short: a paleo-liberal [*Paläo-liberaler*]."[7]

---

[5]See Sigmund Diamond, *Compromised Campus: The Collaboration of Universities with the Intelligence Community, 1945–1955* (New York: Oxford University Press, 1992).

[6]See Buckley's mass-mailed letter, dated November 4, 1955; Grove City Archive: Buckley file. The letter contains no definition of "conservatism."

[7]Mises to Muthesius, letter dated October 3, 1957; Grove City Archive: Muthesius files.

In October 1954, Mises declined an invitation from Yale University to participate in a series called "Conservative Lectures" which was promoted with the promise that "each lecturer will work consciously toward restoration of . . . the power of the word conservative." He noted that the word "conservative" had no political roots in America and that in Europe it meant the very opposite of the principles for which America stood:

> To conserve means to preserve what exists. It is an empty program, it is merely negative, rejecting any change. . . . To conserve what exists is in present-day America tantamount to preserving those laws and institutions that the New Deal and the Fair Deal have bequeathcd to the nation.[8]

The sudden emergence of the word "conservative" highlighted a more general unease of the counter-revolutionary forces in the United States. They were quite sure what they were against: Communism, fascism, socialism, the New Deal, the Fair Deal, etc. But what did they stand *for*? The fact is that even in the leadership of the new movement, economic knowledge and staunch libertarian convictions were rare. The recourse to words like conservatism reflected a widespread unease about adopting any clear positive message. It was easier to be evasive than to state clearly that at the center of the new movement's agenda stood the principle of private property. Other terms started floating around too, such as "limited government," "federalism," and "decentralization." When Mises emphasized in a paper the crucial importance of an independent judicial apparatus "that protects the individual and his property against any violator, whether king or common robber,"[9] the secretary of the Earhart

---

[8]Mises to John Belding Wirt, letter dated October 23, 1954; Grove City Archive: Conservatism files. See also similar statements in Mises to Richard Cornuelle, letter dated November 1, 1965; Grove City Archive: Richard Cornuelle file.

[9]Mises, "Economic Freedom in the Present World," *Economic Freedom and Interventionism: An Anthology of Articles and Essays* (Irvington-on-Hudson,

Foundation wondered whether this might not be too radical. After all, judges in the United States were all appointed and paid by the government.

Mises replied that the American judges were independent insofar as they could not be removed or prosecuted even if their decisions were not palatable to the executive. In contrast, the insistence on limited government was at best useful "in the present-day American fight against the attempts to make the Government step by step totalitarian." Mises went on:

> But there is no doubt that outside of this special field this term is meaningless as it does not indicate in what regard the government ought to be limited. Union bosses could, for instance, refer to this slogan to justify non-interference on the part of the government whenever strikers commit acts of violence, sabotage, etc.

It was therefore of vital importance that one advocate clearly the supremacy of private property and its offshoots: capitalism and the market economy. Insistence on federalism and decentralization would not do:

> Decentralization on a federal basis gives in itself no guarantee that freedom will be preserved. Medieval feudalism had both decentralization and federalism; but only the lords were free (and tax-exempt); burghers and peasants had to endure legal disabilities, had no share in the government and had alone to pay taxes.[10]

N.Y.: Foundation for Economic Education, 1990), chap. 47. See also Henry Hazlitt's call for a change of the too "rigid" U.S. Constitution in his long letter to the editor of the *New York Times* (February 8, 1942); Grove City Archive: Hazlitt files. See also Henry Hazlitt, *A New Constitution Now* (New York: McGraw Hill, 1942)

[10]Mises to Richard Ware, letter dated October 24, 1957; Grove City Archive: Earhart Foundation files.

These were very good reasons not to use the label "conservative" for the new American movement that rejected Communism, socialism, the New Deal and the emerging anti-market mentality of the ever-more-statist mainstream. But the die was cast. Four years after the establishment of *National Review*, the label "conservative" held the public arena. By that time, at the latest, Mises must have outlived the optimism he had felt in the early days of *The Freeman*. He reverted to the pessimistic outlook that had become almost second nature. When his student George Reisman said he had the impression that the *laissez-faire* liberals were growing in numbers, Mises replied that this was the natural impression of a person who was still in the process of getting to know the other scattered individuals of the Remnant. Such a person might think there are ever more individuals to share his views, because he comes to know ever more such individuals. But Mises believed that the growth was only in personal acquaintance and not in absolute numbers. On another occasion, he commented that his writings were like the Dead Sea Scrolls that someone would find a thousand years from now.[11]

But pessimism did not prevent Mises from fighting the good fight, and from encouraging others to be strong in the battle of ideas. In a letter to Hayek, who had also vigorously rejected the label of "conservative," Mises wrote:

> I completely agree with your rejection of conservatism. In his book *Up from Liberalism*, Buckley—as a person a fine and educated man—has clearly defined his standpoint: "Conservatism is the tacit acknowledgment that all that is finally important in human experience is behind us; that the crucial explorations have been undertaken and that it is given to man to know what are the great truths that emerged from them. Whatever is to come cannot outweigh the importance to man of what has gone before." (p. 154)

---

[11]Jeffrey A. Tucker, "Mises as Mentor: An Interview with George Reisman," *Austrian Economics Newsletter* 21, no. 3 (Fall, 2001): 4.

Origines, Augustinus, and Thomas Aquinas have said the same thing in other words. It is a sad truth that this program is more attractive than everything that has been said about liberty and about the idealistic and materialistic benefits of the free economy.[12]

What were the reasons for this sad truth? Mises felt there was here an unexplored question. He went on:

I assume that you, just as I, do not write to console yourself with the proverb: *Dixi et salvavi animam meam* [I have spoken and thus saved my soul]. Hence there is the question: How is it possible that the elite of our contemporaries is absolutely clueless *vis-à-vis* all these things? How does it come, for example, that the sugar price policy of the American government is hardly ever contested, even though out of 500 or 1,000 voters there is at most one who can expect advantages from an institutionally increased sugar price?

The problem I have in mind is not the behavior of the mass of "intellectuals" and of those who count themselves among the intellectuals. I mean those authors, both fiction and non-fiction, who for example speak about affluence and simultaneously about an over-population that brings mankind close to starvation. Or the Civil Liberties Union, which, on the one hand, moves heaven and earth when it finds that a tennis club admits Negroes to its courts only as guests, but denies them membership, but which declares on the other hand that it is no civil right to work without a union card.

---

[12]Mises to Hayek, letter dated February 18, 1960; Grove City Archive: Hayek files. See also F.A. Hayek, *The Constitution of Liberty* (Chicago: University of Chicago Press, 1960), postscript.

Demise of the Circle Bastiat

The only work that matched *Human Action* as a literary monument to the libertarian renaissance of the early postwar period was Ayn Rand's novel *Atlas Shrugged*. Mises was a great admirer of this work and said so in a letter to its author:

> "Atlas Shrugged" is not merely a novel. It is also—or may I say: first of all—a cogent analysis of the evils that plague our society, a substantiated rejection of the ideology of our self-styled "intellectuals" and a pitiless unmasking of the insincerity of the policies adopted by governments and political parties. It is a devastating exposure of the "moral cannibals," the "gigolos of science" and of the "academic prattle" of the makers of the "anti-industrial revolution." You have the courage to tell the masses what no politician told them: you are inferior and all the improvements in your conditions which you simply take for granted you owe to the effort of men who are better than you.
>
> If this is arrogance, as some of your critics observed, it still is the truth that had to be said in this age of the Welfare State.[13]

In the original Rand circle in Manhattan, and in many of the later Randian groups throughout the United States, many members cultivated a religious reverence for the writings and opinions of Ayn Rand. Their attitude to Rand's writings did not differ essentially from the attitude that Christians hold toward the Bible, and consequently they were in more than one respect the acolytes of a Randian church. Rothbard, who had personally attended the meetings of Rand's group for several months,

---

[13]Mises to Rand, letter dated January 23, 1958; unknown provenance. Before he read *Atlas Shrugged* (New York: Random House, 1957), Mises had not counted Ayn Rand among the foremost contemporary artists and philosophers. See Mises, *Anti-Capitalistic Mentality* (Princeton, N.J.: Van Nostrand, 1956), chap. 4, p. 2.

stated that "the fanaticism with which they worship Rand and Branden has to be seen to be believed, the whole atmosphere being a kind of combination of a religious cult and a Trotskyite cell."[14] They demanded unconditional allegiance to their creed and harassed and ousted anyone who would not go along with the party line.

One position of the creed particularly dear to these Randians was atheism—the religious belief in the non-existence of God. For Ayn Rand and her disciples it has always been a matter of course to contest any evidence purporting to prove the existence of God, and to emphasize any argument or piece of evidence that was deemed to prove His non-existence. But this argumentative approach was chosen only when they confronted neophytes. With more senior members of the group, they felt they could expect a more "mature" stance on the God-question: the unconditional adoption of atheism. And they did not forgive deviance; in particular, they would not tolerate an avowed Christian in their midst and even went so far as to harass members who, although atheists or agnostics themselves, were married to unrepentant Christians. This was the case with Murray Rothbard, whose wife JoAnn was unapologetically Protestant.[15]

One might argue that the Randian insistence on action in conformity with its atheistic ideal was a healthy attitude to preserve and cultivate purism; and indeed from this point of view, Randianism might be as legitimate as any other religion. It was however not the attitude that Murray Rothbard brought to his encounters with fellow human beings. He had a firm opinion on various questions, but he was mainly interested in argument and debate as the best method to test positions and opinions. When it became obvious that he preferred being married to JoAnn to

---

[14]Rothbard to Mises, letter dated July 17, 1958; Grove City Archive: Rothbard files.

[15]See Murray N. Rothbard, *The Sociology of the Ayn Rand Cult* (Port Townsend, Wash.: Liberty Publishing, 1987).

being numbered among the Randians, things turned ugly. In early summer 1958, Rothbard was asked to abandon his theistic wife. He refused to comply.

This incident had direct repercussions on the Austro-libertarian movement in that it led to the disintegration of the Circle Bastiat—the Misesian study group that met at Murray Rothbard's apartment and had included Hessen, Liggio, Raico, and Reisman. Hessen and Reisman remained in the Randian orbit and had no further contact with their former friends—who had in their view betrayed Reason.

Rothbard in turn pulled no punches about what he came to call the Ayn Rand Cult. He later had telephone shouting matches with Nathaniel Branden, a man who took pride in outdoing everyone else in worshipping his mistress (in both connotations).[16] Branden charged Rothbard with plagiarism and threatened him with a lawsuit, alleging that Rothbard in a recent paper had adopted ideas from Ayn Rand and Branden's wife Barbara without duly acknowledging this intellectual debt. The charge was baseless. It cost Rothbard's friend Leonard Liggio only a couple of hours of work in the public library to document that the "stolen ideas" had been part of the western intellectual heritage for several centuries, and had originated in many cases with Catholic scholastic thinkers.

Mises had taken part in the Symposium on Relativism at which Rothbard had presented the original version of the paper under dispute.[17] He was speechless at the Randians' charge of

---

[16]On Branden and Rand see Barbara Branden, *The Passion of Ayn Rand* (New York: Doubleday, 1987).

[17]The symposium took place in 1959 at Emory University. The Volker Fund sponsored it. Helmut Schoeck, a professor of sociology at Emory, organized the event. Schoeck also wrote the most scathing indictment of the charges made against Rothbard. About Rand and Barbara Branden he said: "They clearly suffer from a serious case of what Sorokin (*Fads and Foibles*) calls the discoverer's complex. They seem to think that they, the female

plagiarism against Rothbard, but he avoided any direct involvement in the controversy, which he was sure would resolve itself in Rothbard's favor. Mises had good reason not to create even more bad blood between his disciples and the Randians. At the beginning of the 1960s, Branden's organization was very successful in selling Mises's writings, in particular, *Planning for Freedom*. At the end of 1961, the book was almost sold out and Nymeyer planned an extended second edition, including an additional essay.[18] Ayn Rand and Nathaniel Branden also tried to establish closer ties with Mises, inviting him to attend their lecture evenings and social gatherings.[19]

Mises reciprocated to a certain extent. He appreciated intellectual affinities with the Randians, but he was not fond of their fanatical zeal. He liked to persuade other people through detached speech and writing, whereas the Randians strove to make converts to the cause of Objectivism by applying the same techniques used by religious cults: group sessions, psychoanalysis, and group pressure. Mises could perfectly well respect and even befriend people with whom he disagreed, even when these disagreements concerned questions of fundamental importance. This was the case for example with Louis Rougier (a positivist), Gottfried von Haberler (an interventionist), Louise Sommer (a protectionist), and Murray Rothbard (an anarchist).[20] Leland Yeager (a monetarist) once wrote to Mises:

---

innovators of unique ideas, were robbed by a bad male." Schoeck's letter to unknown recipient, dated August 13, 1958; Grove City Archive: Rothbard files.

[18]Nymeyer to Lipsett, letter dated October 9, 1961; Nymeyer to Mises, letter dated December 27, 1961; Grove City Archive: Nymeyer files. Another organization that was very successful in selling Mises's books was the Intercollegiate Society of Individualists.

[19]Nathaniel Branden to Mises, letters dated January 16, 1961 and May 26, 1961; Grove City Archive: Branden files.

[20]It goes without saying that he did not avoid socializing with (honest) socialists. Cases in point were the Bauers until their fallout with Mises in

> I hope you agree that among people who are united
> in favor of economic liberalism, there can be healthy
> controversy on such details as the admissibility of the
> price-level concept and whether the gold standard or
> price-level stabilization is the better rule for mone-
> tary policy.[21]

And this hope was entirely justified, despite the fact that Yeager's disagreements with Mises concerned more than mere
details. Mises would not hold anyone in low esteem just because
the person in question held opinions that Mises believed were
entirely wrong. Steeped in the humanism of the Christian Occi-
dent, he held the individual above anything else. He was not
concerned about individual souls, of course, but he did care
supremely about individual liberty. He was happy for each new
convert to the cause of liberty, but he would have been unable
to rejoice over conversions obtained through group pressure
and other forms of harassment.

For Mises, only one sin was unforgivable: lack of integrity.
Speaking and behaving against one's better knowledge could not
be excused. This is why Mises maintained a lifelong friendship
with Gottfried Haberler, whom he believed to be an honest
interventionist, but broke with Fritz Machlup when he started
qualifying the case for the gold standard. At the same time
Mises recommended Leland Yeager for Mont Pèlerin Society
stipends even though Yeager was no less skeptical of gold
money than Machlup.

1919, as well as his critic Carl Landauer, whom he probably met in 1952 in
Berkeley. See Landauer to Mises, letter dated June 16, 1952; Grove City
Archive: Ernest Offen file. And he wrote letters of recommendation for
interventionist professors. See for example the letter he wrote for Alexander Kokkalis, dated January 4, 1954; Grove City Archive: Kokkalis file.

[21]Yeager to Mises, letter dated June 26, 1955; Grove City Archive: Buck
Hill Falls file.

But the Randian mind was not overly concerned with the tri-fling virtue of integrity. There was only Reason (always capital-ized), and whoever did not come to endorse Reason as defined by the Ayn Rand church had to be stupid, evil, or hard of hear-ing. Being friends with such a person was out of the question. The Randian way of dealing with disagreements was to con-front the dissenter with a stark choice: *either* undergo an endless series of discussions with the foregone conclusion that the dis-senter had fallen prey to the heresy of irrationalism, *or* be expelled from the group and shunned by all its members.

In the fall of 1961, Nathaniel Branden showed once again that bullying his opponents was his *forte*. The *New Individualist Review*, a journal edited by Ralph Raico, who was by then a doc-toral student in Chicago under Hayek, had published a critical piece on Ayn Rand. This prompted Branden to ask Hayek, who was on the editorial board of the *Review*, publicly to dissociate himself from the author of the article, and to "insist an apology to Miss Rand be printed in The *New Individualist Review* on your behalf and in your name."[22] He also sent a copy of the let-ter to Mises, who was certainly happy to have kept the Randi-ans at arm's length. Of course Hayek never complied.

Mises abhorred such bullying. He had a different way of dealing with smears. In the fall of 1961, Mises and Rand met at a party in Henry Hazlitt's house.[23] After dinner, a discussion between them turned into an argument on philosophical prin-ciple and drew the attention of the bystanders. It is not clear

---

[22]Nathaniel Branden to Mises, letter December 15, 1961; Grove City Archive: Branden files.

[23]It was not their first personal meeting. They also met in early July 1961 and they discussed "the problems which we both consider as vital." Mises to Rand, letter dated July 10, 1961; Grove City Archive: Rand file. It is possible they stayed in touch in the 1960s. In June 1970, Mises promised his Mexican friend Velasco that he would talk to her about him and his work. See Mises to Velasco, letter dated June 27, 1970; Grove City Archive: Rand file.

what was said, even though there were a number of topics on which they heartily disagreed.[24] In any case, Russell Kirk, a notorious critic of Randianism who had witnessed the discussion, was later reported to have said in his lectures before student audiences that Mises had called Ayn Rand "a silly little Jew girl." When the report was brought to Mises's attention, he immediately wrote to Kirk: "I never called Mrs. Ayn Rand—or for that matter, anyone else—'a silly little Jew girl.' I should be obliged if you would not repeat this false story in the future."[25]

Kirk denied it all:

> Your informant, with the eccentricity and fanaticism characteristic of the Randian cult, seems to have combined details from several accounts of the meeting between yourself and Miss Rand which she had heard, and to have attributed the composite story to me. Any anti-Jewish prejudice, or suggestion thereof, was not contained in my second-hand account, nor in the account which I heard. But I am glad to have from Mr. Hazlitt a more accurate report of the encounter, before receiving your letter.[26]

------

[24]For example, Mises did not believe that scientific value theory could establish an objective ranking of choice alternatives. He also had recently asserted in print that the essence of art and beauty is "that which pleases." See Mises, *Theory and History: An Interpretation of Social and Economic Evolution* (New Haven, Conn.: Yale University Press, 1957), p. 62. On the other hand, he certainly did agree with Rand's writings in most other respects. In correspondence with Muthesius he said that Ayn Rand was the most energetic opponent of anti-trust policy. See Mises to Muthesius, letter dated March 22, 1962; Grove City Archive: Muthesius files.

[25]Mises to Russell Kirk, letter dated July 5, 1962; Grove City Archive: Branden files. See also Hazlitt, to Kirk, undated letter; Grove City Archive: Hazlitt file # 9.

[26]Kirk to Mises, letter dated July 13, 1962; Grove City Archive: Kirk file.

Against the Neo-Liberals

The Mont Pèlerin Society had begun as an "ecumenical" undertaking, bringing together purebred liberals of the classical tradition and neo-liberals, who endorsed interventionist schemes to one degree or another. From the beginning, Mises had been skeptical about the ecumenical concept, but for the first five or six years his apprehensions seemed unwarranted, even though the organization of all Mont Pèlerin activities lay in the hands of a devout neo-liberal: Albert Hunold from Switzerland, whom Mises had first met at the 1928 Zurich meeting of the *Verein für Sozialpolitik.*

An admirer of *Road to Serfdom*, Hunold had been among those who encouraged Hayek to convene the foundational meeting of the Society at Mont Pèlerin, and he had also raised substantial funds for the event. At this meeting, the ambitious Hunold was elected secretary of the Society, but after a few years he was no longer satisfied with his position under Hayek. His long-term goal was to become Mont Pèlerin Society president; his strategy was to make himself irreplaceable. He dealt with the smallest details of organization and by the mid-1950s started to handle correspondence without consulting Hayek, who resented these encroachments from a man he did not exactly love in the first place. After 1956, the conflict between the two men grew more intense and eventually came to a clash that brought the Society to the verge of dissolution.

In the early years, this clash was barely visible. With the support of Hunold and others, the neo-liberals steadily increased their numbers, but they did not dominate the Society. The main reason was probably that, although Hunold had financial backing in the Swiss business community, he could not match the funds that were mobilized on the other side of the Atlantic. Hayek, Mises, and a few other classical liberals had a primordial impact on the selection of topics to be discussed. On the one hand, this was due to their scientific pedigree. On the other, they enjoyed substantial financial backing from the Volker Fund and from individuals such as Nymeyer, Grede, and Crane. At least until the end of 1953, the Volker Fund paid the membership fees, and often also covered travel expenditure, for virtually all non-U.S. members of the Mont Pèlerin Society.[27] And the Fund was eager to accommodate Mises's wishes (and probably Hayek's wishes also) when it came to securing financially the presence of certain members at the meetings. For example, when Mises declared that he would not attend the 1954 meeting in Venice, because of insufficient French and British participation, the Volker Fund asked him to handpick the beneficiaries of financial assistance in order of their relative importance.[28] At the end of that first phase of the history of the Mont Pèlerin Society, therefore, the leadership around Hayek was far more radically libertarian than most of the regular members—especially those from Europe.

The coexistence within the Mont Pèlerin Society of groups with such different orientations was well known by its members.[29] It was also fairly obvious even for newcomers. A case in point was Jean-Pierre Hamilius, a young professor of business and economics in Luxembourg, whom Mises knew through

---

[27]For the list of the beneficiaries of membership subscriptions, see Hazlitt to Mises, letter dated December 21, 1953; Grove City Archive: Mont Pèlerin Society files.

[28]Mises named among the French economists: (1) Louis Baudin, (2) Daniel Villey, (3) François Trevoux, and (4) Bertrand de Jouvenel; among the British: (1) Jewkes, (2) Plant, and (3) Dennison; as well as the Irishman Duncan. See Mises to Richard Cornuelle, letter dated June 4, 1954; Grove City College Archive: Mont Pèlerin Society files. Mises did not attend the Venice meeting because he had to undergo gallbladder surgery. Two years later, he approved the funding of Coase, Nutter, Alchian, Philbrook, and Yeager. See Mises to Luhnow, letter dated December 7, 1956; Grove City College Archive: Mont Pèlerin Society files.

[29]"There are within the Mont Pèlerin Society, on the whole, two antagonistic camps: the laissez-faire liberals . . . and the neoliberals. . . . Everybody knows that." Albert Hunold, "How Mises Changed My Mind," *The Mont Pèlerin Quarterly* III, no. 3 (October 1961): 17.

correspondence.[30] Hamilius had recently discovered the literature of classical liberalism, which he devoured and translated
into French and German. Mises had him invited for the 1953
Mont Pèlerin Society meeting in Seelisberg.[31] Hamilius immediately noticed that the Society was divided along the lines of
ideological orientation and language into "different groups and
clans." He himself felt closest affinities to the American group
of Mises, Hayek, Hazlitt, Morley, Fertig, and Miller. From the
other participants, who did not know that he had gotten his
invitation through Mises, he heard reservations about "the old
guard (Mises, Hayek, . . .)" who were sometimes called the "old
conservatives." The young professor from Luxembourg was
eagerly taking notes and discussing the interventionist schemes
of various members who were not yet part of the old guard.
Thus John van Sickle proposed taxing rich heirs, Wilhelm
Röpke favored subsidies for homeowners, and Otto Veit argued
that heavy taxation would not deter entrepreneurs from working.[32] Ludwig Erhard, fresh from the victory of his party in the
1953 elections in Germany, also gave a talk at the meeting.

Hamilius's report shed light on the change of relative
weights within the Society that resulted from the apparent success of Ludwig Erhard's neo-liberal policies in Germany, the so-
called *Wirtschaftswunder* or economic miracle. To the socialists
and social democrats who dominated the climate of mainstream
economic opinion at the time, it was truly miraculous that the
abolition of price controls and the transition from a centrally

---

[30]Hamilius to Mises, letter dated February 26, 1952; Grove City Archive:
Hamilius files. At that point Hamilius was 29 years old.

[31]He also suggested invitations for Fertig, Cortney, and Nymeyer. These
three men were admitted as new members in a Council meeting of Hayek,
Rappard, Jitta, Mises, and Hunold. See Mises to Hunold, letter dated June
26, 1953, and the protocol of the Council meeting of September 9, 1953;
Grove City Archive: Mont Pèlerin Society files.

[32]Hamilius to Mises, letter dated October 11, 1953; Grove City Archive:
Hamilius files.

planned economy toward a market economy would yield sub-stantial economic benefits. For unrepentant classical liberals such as Mises there was no miracle at all. But Erhard's success was problematic because it gave unwarranted credentials to his middle-of-the-road philosophy. This also applied to his closest advisers, who were often referred to as champions of the "social market economy" or leaders of the "Ordo School" of econom-ics: his undersecretary of state Müller-Armack, and the profes-sors Wilhelm Röpke (Geneva), Alexander Rüstow (Heidelberg), and Walter Eucken (Freiburg). In short, the success of Erhard's initial classical-liberal policies was used to vindicate subsequent interventionist policies, in particular, anti-trust laws and infla-tion.

Even before the war, Mises did not have the highest opin-ion of most German economists. After his emigration, he had avoided any closer involvement with them. He would acknowledge Erhard's achievements by contributing to a *Festschrift* in Erhard's honor, but he declined to write an entry for the new standard social science dictionary, the *Hand-wörterbuch der Sozialwissenschaften*; only after Gottfried Haber-ler pleaded the case of the editors did Mises agree to write a piece on "Economic Liberalism," a complement to Hayek's article on "Political Liberalism."[33] And the prospect of cooper-ating with the fashionable Ordo School, be it in the Mont Pèlerin Society or elsewhere, did not exactly warm his heart either. He believed the Ordo people were hardly better than the socialists he had fought all his life. In fact, he eventually called

---

[33]His contribution was eventually published under the title "market." See Mises, "Markt," *Handwörterbuch der Sozialwissenschaften* (Stuttgart: Gustav Fischer, 1959), part 27, pp. 131–36. He delivered the work before the end of March 1955. The publishers "improved" his article after having received the proof pages from him. See Mises to Hermann Bente, letter dated January 15, 1960; Grove City Archive: "B" file. A translation of this piece by Edmund A. Gibson is in Grove City Archive: "G" file. See also Haberler's letter dated May 19, 1953 in Grove City Archive: Haberler file.

them the "Ordo-interventionists."[34] And his New York associates seem to have harbored essentially the same views—but without Mises's hesitation to express such views in print.

There were classical liberals in Germany who opposed the interventionist excesses of the Erhard ministry and the Ordo School. The leaders of this *laissez-faire* group were Volkmar Muthesius and Hans Hellwig.[35] But they could do no more than fight an honorable rear-guard action. Being denied professorships at the universities, their foremost means of action was Muthesius's journal, to which Mises contributed several articles. Hellwig wrote to Mises:

> Men such as Erhard and maybe even more so Prof. Rüstow have strictly speaking not much to do with classical liberalism. Earlier classical liberals would have made no bones calling them social democrats. They would not have called them even social-liberals or socialists of the chair.[36]

---

[34]Mises to Muthesius, letter dated June 1, 1955; Grove City Archive: Muthesius files. It must be said, however, that he supported them whenever common ground could be found. Thus in June 1950, he recommended the translation of Röpke's textbook *Die Lehre von der Wirtschaft* to the University of Chicago Press. See correspondence in Grove City Archive: Röpke files.

[35]Muthesius, who was based in Frankfurt am Main, ran two successful journals: *Zeitschrift für das gesamte Kreditwesen* and *Monatsblätter für freiheitliche Wirtschaftspolitik*.

[36]Hellwig to Mises, letter dated January 12, 1962; Grove City Archive: Hellwig file. Hellwig had expressed such views in published writings from 1955 onwards. In a piece for Muthesius's journal, he had argued that antitrust policies were counterproductive and that the champions of such policies—most notably Eucken, Miksch, and Böhm—could therefore not properly be called classical liberals. Moreover, he had the indelicacy to point out that Böhm's and Miksch's monographs had been published in the Nazi era, and could only have been published at the time because the Nazis did not perceive neo-liberalism as a fundamental threat. On the contrary, quite a few of them took a liking to the idea of government imprinting its "order" on competition. Hellwig knew what he was talking about: he had been a Berlin-based journalist during those very years. But Walter Eucken's widow, Edith,

Mises replied:

> I have no illusions about the true character of the pol-
> itics and politicians of the "social market economy."
> [Erhard's teacher Franz Oppenheimer] taught more
> or less the New Frontier line of [President
> Kennedy's] Harvard consultants (Schlesinger, Gal-
> braith, etc.)[37]

But because of the near total ignorance of foreign languages,
Mises explained, the American public had a very unrealistic
notion about what the German "social market" model stood for.
The only issue of German politics included in the American
debate was the monetary policy of the German central bank,
which was much less inflationary than the policies of the U.S.
Federal Reserve. Thus the ruling class in Germany was perceived as devoted to classical-liberal principles such as sound
money and international trade.

Erhard's success changed the Mont Pèlerin Society, sweeping
in the very themes Mises had stressed should be excluded—such
as the need for anti-trust and the possible virtues of credit expansion. On both issues Mises sided with Volkmar Muthesius, who
argued that the best way to combat monopolies was to abolish
the policies and government institutions that created them in the
first place. Mises was especially wary of yet another round of discussions of anti-trust laws. In his youth he had witnessed the

---

and Wilhelm Röpke protested with great vehemence and recrimination to
Muthesius for publishing such politically incorrect views. Mises sided with
Muthesius. See the May 1955 correspondence in Grove City Archive:
Muthesius file.

[37]Mises to Hellwig, letter dated January 19, 1962; Grove City Archive:
Hellwig file. Mises also knew well the pro-inflationist views of Erhard's
undersecretary of the economy, Alfred Müller-Armack. In 1932, Müller-
Armack had published a book amplifying the case for inflation presented by
Joseph Schumpeter. He had argued that credit expansion had the character of
a self-fulfilling anticipation of growth. See Alfred Müller-Armack's *Entwicklungsgesetze des Kapitalismus* (Berlin: Juncker & Dünnhaupt, 1932).

anti-cartel agitation that followed their rise in the 1890s. At the time, the debate had been propelled by the *Verein für Socialpolitik*, which was always seeking a new rationale for more interventionism. For decades now he had not come across new arguments on either side, and he expected that any debate in the Mont Pèlerin Society would quickly turn toward an interventionist agenda, rather than addressing the main case of present-day monopoly prices: the U.S. price policies for agricultural products. It was probably due to his influence that the topic did not appear until the 1956 Mont Pèlerin Society meeting in Berlin, by which point many German professorial members had urged Hayek to set the monopoly question on the program. The issue could no longer be avoided.[38]

The meeting fully confirmed Mises's expectations.[39] It turned out to be the overture for some five years of internal struggle for the Mont Pèlerin Society. A few months later, Hayek tried to mobilize his allies to attend the next meeting in Saint Moritz (1957), which he felt would be decisive for the future of the Society, but to no avail.[40] Personal tensions between Hayek and Hunold became obvious in the following year, which for the first time brought a Mont Pèlerin Society meeting to the United States—to Princeton.[41]

---

[38]Hayek to Mises, letter dated October 25, 1955; Grove City Archive: Hayek files.

[39]A few months later he wrote: "I hope that this year's Mont Pèlerin meeting will be more interesting than the Berlin meeting." Mises to Pierre Goodrich, letter dated April 3, 1957; Grove City Archive: Goodrich files. Goodrich's company (Indiana Telephone Corporation) issued annual reports highlighting the consequences of the ongoing inflation for the American economy and for corporate accounting (the problem of "illusory profits"). Mises liked them very much and urged Goodrich to seek wider circulation of his message.

[40]See Hayek's circular letter dated November 27, 1956; Grove City Archive: Hayek files.

[41]In the early 1950s, the American libertarians tried to hold a Mont Pèlerin Society meeting in the United States, but for financial reasons (the

The Princeton meeting was positively memorable, however, in that Mises here delivered one of his last lectures to the Mont Pèlerin Society, on the subject of "Liberty and Property." The topic had been suggested by Hayek, who was desperate to organize something like a debate on fundamental questions among the members of the Society. All his previous attempts had ended in a fiasco, as he himself recognized. But Mises rose to one of his last great public appearances. His talk survives as a tape recording and testifies to the fact that he was still at the height of his powers. The printed version of the lecture has remained one of the best concise expositions of the case for classical liberalism.[42]

During the next three years, the conflict between Hayek and his recalcitrant secretary lurked beneath the surface. Hayek could not get substantial support to oust Hunold. Most American members were on Hayek's side but feared that an open conflict would destroy the Society. It eventually came to a showdown at the Kassel meeting in 1960.[43] Both Hayek and Hunold

---

Europeans had no money) this project materialized only in 1958, when Jasper Crane managed the fundraising. The outbreak of tensions at the Princeton meeting is stated in Hunold to Röpke, letter dated April 4, 1960. About that time, Mises's student from his Geneva years, Stefan Possony, had difficulties being accepted into the society. See his inquiry in a December 1958 postcard to Mises; Grove City Archive: "P" file.

[42]Bettina Bien Greaves, *Austrian Economics: An Anthology* (Irvington-on-Hudson, N.Y.: Foundation for Economic Education, 1996), pp. 77–82. A digital file of the audio is available at http://www.Mises.org/Media/.

[43]See the correspondence in the Cortney, Fertig, Hunold, and Leoni files. Hunold presented his view on the events before the Kassel meeting in a letter to Röpke, dated April 4, 1960, a copy of which he also sent to Mises. Hayek then declared in another open letter, dated July 3, 1960, that Hunold's replacement as secretary of the Society would be the most important task of the forthcoming general meeting. After careful examination of the evidence, Röpke became more and more convinced that several of Hayek's charges against Hunold were baseless and that, on the contrary, Hayek himself had occasionally overstepped the bounds of his authority. Hunold in turn believed that Hayek had come under the bad influence of Machlup and others (Friedman?) who sought to abuse the Society for their personal purposes. After the

stepped down from their positions, but Hunold would become vice president of the Society and wreak havoc for a while longer. The 1961 meeting was to celebrate Mises's eightieth birthday, but Hunold turned it into yet another battle between neo-liberalism and *laissez faire*. The Ordo-liberals would soon be pushed into the background for a while; the power vacuum was not to be filled with Austro-libertarians, but economists from the Chicago School. ∽

Mises and Hazlitt at the NYU seminar in 1960.
Mises had just said "The Communist censor bans
bad books—My books!"

Turin meeting, member Wolfgang Frickhöffer concurred; he had the impression that a group around Friedman had poisoned the atmosphere with intrigue and pettiness. In early January 1962, Bruno Leoni presented his negative experiences with Röpke and Hunold in an open letter to all Mont Pèlerin Society members. See Grove City Archive: MLS files. And he went into more (ugly) detail in a confidential letter to Koether, which of course reached Mises. See Leoni to Koether, letter dated October 14, 1961; Grove City Archive: Leoni file.

*Mises giving his "Liberty and Property" talk at the Mont Pèlerin
meeting in Princeton, 1958*

23
Last Years

MISES REMAINED VIGOROUS UNTIL about 1962. In the early 1960s, he completed four major writing projects and gave several public lectures per year. At his public appearances the frailty of his condition became increasingly obvious. More and more his feeble voice and his virtual deafness weighed against his legendary reputation. He had become a living icon of liberty, yet a fading icon after all.

In 1962, he still had a substantial number of speaking engagements, addressing for example The Remnant (a group associated with Edmund Opitz), a 150 student audience at the Nathaniel Branden Institute, the Young Americans for Freedom (YAF) at Madison Square Garden, the Coast Federal Savings and Loan Association, the NYU Faculty Club, the American Management Association, and the Free Enterprise Institute. In the same year, on the night of May 16, his voice was heard for the first time in a long while at Harvard University. As one might guess, it was not the University who had invited him. He was not even physically present. The United States Steel Corporation had sponsored a series of radio shows featuring a six-minute taped speech on economic subjects. Mises spoke on the conflicts of interest between workers and employers. He was on the air simultaneously at Harvard, Brown, and Cornell universities. The next day the same speech was aired at Dartmouth and Yale.[1]

---

[1]See documents and correspondence in Grove City Archive: Karras file.

After 1962, public appearances became less frequent and Mises focused on his regular teaching activities. Until May 1969, he taught his NYU seminar; he lectured at FEE seminars

Mises and Percy Greaves

until 1972. In these very last years, only his most faithful friends and admirers—most notably Percy Greaves, and Bettina Bien—continued to take part in his regular seminar sessions. They had become used to the short-comings of the presentation and still wrote diligent notes

of each meeting. Greaves always sat right next to Mises to facilitate all communication between the old master and his seminar. When a student asked a question, Greaves would shout this question into Mises's ear, receive the answer from the old man's feeble lips, and then repeat Mises's words with his booming voice to the audience. New people showed up from time to time out of curiosity, but did not stay because it was difficult to follow the lectures and impossible to engage the speaker. Such newcomers often wondered why the seminar had such visible success with the regular participants. Some had the impression of a prayer meeting involving a bunch of fervent disciples around an enigmatic guru—with Percy Greaves as the high priest and Bettina Bien as the devoted abbess of a Mises Cult.

Mises did not ignore his physical condition and true to his nature prepared well in advance for the approaching end. He started skipping Mont Pèlerin Society meetings, which usually took place in Europe. The last one Mises attended was in 1965 in Stresa, Italy. He saw his beloved Vienna for the last time in September 1964.[2] He began selling off his library of scholarly

---

[2]Mises to Harry Hoiles, letter dated February 25, 1969; Grove City Archive: "H" files. At the end of July 1964 he gave a talk at the Walter

journals. In October 1958, he parted with his collection of *Econometrica* (the complete set, vols. 1–26)[3] and in July 1965 cancelled his membership in the Royal Economic Society.[4] Eventually, by the end of 1968, Percy Greaves assisted him in selling the rest of his periodicals.[5]

Mises preserved his health almost until the end of his long life.[6] He slowed down smoothly and was still around after many of his younger American friends and associates had already gone. Nymeyer died in 1967, Cortney in 1971, Harper in April 1973. Just when Mises was starting to feel really old and somehow left over, it was time to congratulate Richard Schüller on

---

Eucken Institute in Freiburg. He followed an invitation by Hayek (Eucken file). He then attended the Mont Pèlerin Society meeting in Semmering and also went to Vienna. There he visited the Institute for Business Cycle Research (now Institute for Economic Research), which recognized him as its founder (see Franz Nemschak to Mises, and Franz Nemschak to Libertarian Press, letters dated September 3, 1964; Grove City Archive: Österreichisches Institut für Wirtschaftsforschung files).

[3]Mises to Swets & Zeitlinger, correspondence of October 1958; Grove City Archive: Swets & Zeitlinger file. In other correspondence Mises emphasized that he was a member of the Econometric Society only to receive its periodical. See Mises to Nymeyer, letter dated May 14, 1953; Grove City Archive: Nymeyer files.

[4]Letter to Robinson; Grove City Archive: "R" files.

[5]International University Booksellers to Greaves, letter dated February 1, 1969; Grove City Archive: Greaves files.

[6]In February 1962, he had to undergo surgery (see Mises to Muthesius, letter dated February 21, 1962; Grove City Archive: Muthesius files; see also March 1962 correspondence with Magnus Gregersen; Grove City Archive: Gregersen file). In the spring of 1966, Mises must have suffered for a long time from a viral infection. See Thieberger to Mises, June 6, 1966; Grove City Archive: Thieberger file. On July 3, 1966, Ludwig and Margit had a car accident. Margit later had to undergo surgery. At the end of October, she was recovering well. See Mises to Nymeyer, letter dated October 25, 1966; Grove City Archive: Nymeyer files. In January 1968, Mises had at least one tooth pulled. See Thieberger to Margit von Mises, January 18, 1968; Grove City Archive: Thieberger file. In June 1969, he and Margit were sick most of the month. See letter to Rougier, June 23, 1969; Grove City Archive: Rougier files.

the occasion of his 100th birthday.[7] The last Habilitant of Carl Menger's was still around!

During a 1971 summer vacation in Manchester, Vermont, Ludwig fell ill with a serious infection.[8] Even though he recovered physically, he had lost the ability to concentrate and was incapable of doing any work from then on. His wife recalled him saying: "The worst is that I still have so much to give to the people, to the world, and I can't put it together anymore. It is tormenting."[9] During the last two years of his life, Mises was no longer himself and needed assistance and supervision. In this critical phase, to Margit's great relief, Bettina Bien and Percy Greaves were ready to provide generous assistance.[10]

In July 1973, Margit took Ludwig for a last trip to Europe, to a spa up in the mountains above the Swiss town of Luzern. Upon their return to New York, Mises's condition deteriorated and the very next day he was brought to Saint Vincent's Hospital. There he died on the morning of Wednesday, October 10, 1973. A memorial service was held at the Universal Funeral Chapel, 52nd Street and Lexington Avenue in New York City on Tuesday, October 16, at noon.

Last Writings

In the last phase of his life, Mises completed four major writing projects: *The Ultimate Foundation of Economic Science* (1962),

---

[7]In June 1970; see Grove City Archive: Schüller file.

[8]Fertig files, "S" files, letter from Schiff. See also American Whig-Cliosophic Society to Mises, letter dated July 25, 1971; Margit from Mises to the same society, letter dated August 1, 1971; Grove City College: "A" files.

[9]Margit von Mises, *My Years with Ludwig von Mises*, 2nd enlarged ed. (Cedar Falls, Iowa: Center for Futures Education, 1984), p. 180.

[10]After the end of the Mises seminar at NYU they had offered help: "We consider ourselves deeply indebted to you. If either of us can be of any assistance at any time—to you or to Margit—we hope you will feel free to call on us. We shall always be at your service." Greaves and Bien to Mises, letter dated June 6, 1969; Grove City Archive: Greaves files.

the second edition of *Human Action* (1963), a booklet on the *Historical Setting of the Austrian School of Economics* (1969)[11], and the third edition of *Human Action* (1966). Apart from this, Mises produced a few articles.

The most important publication of this period, and in fact the only book-length work, was *The Ultimate Foundation of Economic Science*. The culmination of more than thirty years of meditation on the epistemological problems of the social sciences, it deals with the most difficult problems in this field, written, as were all of his works, in accessible language and with a clear presentation. In many ways it is one of Mises's finest books and clarifies important points that he had introduced in his previous work. The central thesis is (1) that there is such a thing as economic law that cannot be identified with the methods of the natural sciences; and (2) that the arguments of those who advocate these methods in economics have no scientific foundation whatever, but are based on metaphysical speculation. In short, Mises's last book was an all-out frontal attack against positivism.[12]

---

[11]This work was first published in a Spanish edition in Argentina in 1962. See Mises, *El Establecimiento Histórico de la Escuela Austriaca de Economía* (Colección Investigaciones No. 43, La Plata: Universidad Nacional de la Plata, 1962), pp. 691–727. It was probably a outgrowth of the lecture he gave on May 2, 1962 to the NYU Faculty Club on "The Austrian School of Economics at the University of Vienna," printed in Bettina Bien Greaves, *Austrian Economics: An Anthology* (Irvington-on-Hudson, N.Y.: Foundation for Economic Education, 1996), pp. 77–82.

[12]This attack concerned not only the "verificationist" positivism of the Vienna Circle (Schlick, Carnap, Frank, and others), but also Karl Popper's "falsificationist" positivism. Popper's theory made ample room for the use of deduction, whereas the Vienna Circle advocated strict induction; he also claimed that only falsifiable statements can be "scientific," while the Vienna Circle posited that all non-verifiable statements are simply nonsensical. Such differences are certainly important in many respects. However, they are irrelevant as far as Mises's critique is concerned, because it aims at the common ground of both versions of positivism. For more detail see Hans-Hermann Hoppe, *Economic Science and the Austrian Method*, 2nd ed. (Auburn, Ala.: Ludwig von Mises Institute, 2006); Jörg Guido Hülsmann, "Facts and Counterfactuals in Economic Law," *Journal of Libertarian Studies* 17, no. 1 (2003).

He stressed in particular that the positivist precept—testing economic theories by confronting them with observed data—is not itself derived from any empirical knowledge. Rather this precept is an a priori postulate that *contradicts* the most elementary empirical facts known about human action, in particular, that human beings make choices and that there are no known laws that determine those choices. It follows that the observed data in the social sciences have a completely different nature from the data used in the natural sciences. The latter are elements in an inexorable chain of cause and effect. Every single one of them can therefore be used to verify or refute the theories of physics, chemistry, and so on.[13] But the observed data in the social sciences do not stand in such a universally present chain of cause and effect. More precisely, the only thing that is known about them is that they are not part of such a chain. They are singular events and must therefore be interpreted on a case-by-case basis. They cannot be used to derive any general laws. They are not a benchmark for verifying or refuting economic theories. Observation-based testing simply makes no sense in economics.

Just as the Marxists claim to have knowledge about the operation of "productive forces" that determine the course of events in ways unknown and unknowable to other people, so the positivists are unshakable in their confidence that there are some hidden constant relationships in human action that will in the future be identified with testable theories, even though all available evidence suggests that such relationships do not exist.

Mises goes to great lengths to bolster his thesis. He shows that the existence of non-Euclidean geometry does not invalidate the case for an a priori economic science. Similarly, he argues that the development of probability theory cannot possibly be a device to

---

[13]Mises accepts Popper's theory in this regard: "The positivistic principle of verifiability as rectified by Popper is unassailable as an epistemological principle of the natural sciences." Mises, *Ultimate Foundation of Economic Science* (Irvington-on-Hudson, N.Y.: Foundation for Economic Education, [1962] 1996), p. 120. See also ibid., pp. 70f.

avoid the case for determinism. And in discussing the implications of the theory of evolution for a priori disciplines such as economics, he comes to conclusions very different from those of his friend Rougier and others. Mises stresses the hard fact that nothing is known about the future evolution of the human mind. Therefore, the logical and praxeological structure of this mind must be considered *as if* it were unchanging. For all practical purposes, it is an a priori for the social sciences.

In clarifying the logical nature of economic science, Mises stressed that pure reasoning can give us empirical knowledge about the real world because reasoning and acting have the very same nature. Analyzing his own thought processes in an armchair, the economist can identify the basic economic categories.

> Following in the wake of Kant's analysis, philosophers raised the question: How can the human mind, by aprioristic thinking, deal with the reality of the external world? As far as praxeology is concerned, the answer is obvious. Both a priori thinking and reasoning on the one hand and human action on the other, are manifestations of the human mind. The logical structure of the human mind creates the reality of action. Reason and action are congeneric and homogeneous, two aspects of the same phenomenon. In this sense we may apply to praxeology the dictum of Empedocles: γνῶσις τοῦ ὁμοίου τῷ ὁμοίῳ.[14]

The point had been overlooked in traditional epistemology because the philosophers

> dealt with thinking as if it were a separate field cut off from other manifestations of human endeavor. They dealt with the problems of logic and mathematics, but

---

[14]Mises, *Ultimate Foundation of Economic Science*, p. 43. The Greek phrase means "knowledge of the same through the same." Mises stressed that the "questions whether the judgments of praxeology are to be called analytic or synthetic and whether or not its procedure is to be qualified as 'merely' tautological are of verbal interest only" (ibid., p. 45).

they failed to see the practical aspects of thinking. They ignored the praxeological a priori.[15]

Mises argued that, because economic theorems were deduced from the praxeological a priori, they provide knowledge of apodictic certainty:

> Every theorem of praxeology is deduced by logical reasoning from the category of action. It partakes of the apodictic certainty provided by logical reasoning that starts from an a priori category.[16]

And he emphasized that even the most radical skepticism cannot affect this conclusion, precisely because acting and thinking

> stem from the same source and are in this sense homogeneous. There is nothing in the structure of action that the human mind cannot fully explain. In this sense praxeology supplies certain knowledge.[17]

Yet right on the next page of his book, he was quick to emphasize that praxeological knowledge is but one ingredient of information necessary to succeed in the world. Future choices cannot be determined in advance and for this reason alone there is therefore an all-pervading uncertainty in human affairs that the apodictic certainty of praxeology cannot alter or diminish:

> Man is at the mercy of forces and powers beyond his control. He acts in order to avoid as much as possible what, as he thinks, will harm himself. But he can at best succeed only within a narrow margin. And he can never know beforehand to what extent his acting will attain the end sought and, if it attains it, whether this action will in retrospect appear—to himself or to the other people looking upon it—as the best choice

---

[15]Ibid., p. 2.

[16]Ibid., p. 45.

[17]Ibid., p. 65.

among those that were open to him at the instant he embarked upon it.[18]

Most importantly, uncertainty also stems from our ignorance about nature in general. Mises did not at all share the conceit displayed by positivists such as Bertrand Russell that the natural sciences will ultimately penetrate all secrets of the world.[19] In his view, human science barely scratches the surface of things. Important though it may be—and Mises was convinced that science was the most important tool for human progress— it is not an intellectual panacea and does not make superfluous the virtues of humility and religion:

> Although the progress of the natural sciences tends to enlarge the sphere of such scientifically directed action, it will never cover more than a narrow margin of possible events. And even within this margin there can never be absolute certainty. The result aimed at can be thwarted by the invasion of forces not yet sufficiently known or beyond human control. Technological engineering does not eliminate the aleatory element of human existence; it merely restricts its field a little. There always remains an orbit that to the limited knowledge of man appears as an orbit of pure chance and marks life as a gamble. Man and his works are always exposed to the impact of unforeseen and uncontrollable events. He cannot help banking upon the good luck not to be hit by them. Even dull people cannot fail to realize that their well-being ultimately depends on the operation of forces beyond man's wisdom, knowledge, prevision, and provision. With regard to these forces all human planning is vain. This is what religion has in mind when it refers to the unfathomable decrees of Heaven and turns to prayer.[20]

---

[18]Ibid., p. 66.

[19]Bertrand Russell, *Religion and Science* (Oxford: Oxford University Press, [1936] 1997).

[20]Mises, *Ultimate Foundation of Economic Science*, pp. 66–67.

≼ ≼ ≼

Mises probably started working on the second edition of *Human Action* in early 1962. Percy Greaves provided assistance and had already made suggestions for changes in the fall of 1961. While the two men worked together smoothly and productively, cooperation with the publisher was far less successful. For reasons that were never entirely clarified, Yale University Press butchered the book. Mises's life achievement now featured many misprints, different shades of print, displaced and omitted paragraphs and pages, and no more running heads. He was more than a little angry and suspected political motives:

> The present management of the Press regrets, for political reasons, the fact that their predecessors published my book. They are especially angry about the great success of *Human Action*. If they had any sense of propriety at all, they would openly tell the author that they do not want any longer to publish his books and that he is free to look for another publisher.[21]

Eventually Yale University Press did show that sense of propriety and Mises went on to publish a third edition with Henry Regnery in Chicago, possibly with the intermediation of his friend Nymeyer.[22] This time things worked out as planned and he enjoyed a beautiful new edition.

With one exception, the new editions did not feature any major changes or elaborations.[23] The exception concerned the

---

[21]Quoted from Margit von Mises, *My Years with Ludwig von Mises*, p. 110.

[22]Mises had probably first heard about Regnery through Nymeyer in 1953. See Nymeyer to Mises, letter dated April 13, 1953; Grove City Archive: Nymeyer files.

[23]For an overview of the major changes and a discussion see Jeffrey M. Herbener, Hans-Hermann Hoppe, and Joseph T. Salerno, "Introduction to the Scholar's Edition," Mises, *Human Action*, Scholar's edition (Auburn, Ala.: Ludwig von Mises Institute, 1998). Mises sent exhaustive lists of the changes to Reig in Madrid, who sought to keep the Spanish translation up-to-date.

definition of freedom. This elaboration was prompted by the fact that, in the 1950s, some of Mises's most brilliant students—most notably Murray Rothbard and his Bastiat Circle—had carried the case for the free market and against government interventionism to what they felt was its logical conclusion: political anarchism.

Last Skirmishes with the Anarchists

In 1949, Mises had defined freedom by stating that a "man is free as far as he can live and get on without being at the mercy of arbitrary decisions on the part of other people."[24] The crucial word here is "arbitrary"—a term that was left undefined and that the young anarchists had interpreted in their way. In 1963, therefore, Mises set out to give more meat to his theory. He wrote:

> The concepts of freedom and bondage make sense only when referring to the way in which government operates. . . . As far as the government—the social apparatus of compulsion and oppression—confines the exercise of its violence and the threat of such violence to the suppression and prevention of antisocial action, there prevails what reasonably and meaningfully can be called liberty. . . . Such coercion does not substantially restrict man's power to choose. . . . If, however, the government does more than protect people against violent or fraudulent aggression on the part of antisocial individuals, it reduces the sphere of the individual's freedom to act beyond the degree to which it is restricted by praxeological law. Thus we may define freedom as that state of affairs in which the individual's discretion to choose is not constrained by governmental violence beyond the margin within which the praxeological law restricts it anyway.[25]

---

[24]Mises, *Human Action*, p. 279.

[25]Mises, *Human Action: A Treatise on Economics*, 2nd ed. (New Haven, Conn.: Yale University Press, 1963), pp. 281–82. See also *Human Action*, 3rd ed. (Chicago: Regnery, 1966), p. 281.

This elaboration of his position did not dissuade the anarchists, and it is not difficult to see why. In the above passage, Mises gives two definitions of freedom.

According to the first, freedom prevails if force is limited to the suppression of "antisocial" behavior. Mises gives only one example—robbery—to illustrate what he means by this term.[26] If this was meant to imply that the use of force is legitimate if it concerns the protection of property rights, then Mises's definition of freedom was essentially compatible with the views of the anarchists, who would merely add that the government must play by the same rules, and therefore cannot obtain its revenue through the violation of property rights. Mises never brought himself to analyze this proposal in detail. His occasional remarks on the question show that he believed the case for anarchism would only hold in a world inhabited by angels.[27] But as Rothbard's writings on the question show, he was not that naïve.[28]

Mises's second definition of freedom was equally unlikely to steer the anarchists away from their orientation, though for a different reason. According to this one, human action is said to be subject to two distinct influences: praxeological law and government intervention. The influence of the latter is presented as

---

[26]*Human Action*, 2nd ed., p. 280.

[27]A typical example from about the same period:

> A shallow-minded school of social philosophers, the anarchists, chose to ignore the matter by suggesting a stateless organization of mankind. They simply passed over the fact that men are not angels. They were too dull to realize that in the short run an individual or a group of individuals can certainly further their own interests at the expense of their own and all other peoples' long-run interests. (*Ultimate Foundation of Economic Science*, p. 100)

[28]Rothbard published *Power and Market* (Princeton, N.J.: D. Van Nostrand, 1970) only in 1970, but the manuscript of the book (which was originally conceived as a part of *Man, Economy, and State* (Princeton, N.J.: D. Van Nostrand, 1962) was certainly available for Mises in the early 1960s.

somehow adding to the influence of the former. But this does not square well with what Mises said in the rest of his book about praxeological laws. At all times and all places, the impact that government intervention has on human beings is *mediated* through the laws of human action. Praxeological laws are not "forces" in the sense that human action (for example, governmental action) is a force; rather, they are the relations that tie up any given force in a chain of causes and consequences.

In private correspondence with Bruno Leoni he regretted that anarchist ideas were "supported by some of the most intelligent men of the American rising generation," but he had a ready psychological explanation at hand: anarchism was a "reaction to the deification of the state."[29]

He had come in touch with the burgeoning anarchist movement already in the years leading up to the publication of *Human Action*, especially through his contacts with west-coast libertarians but also in correspondence with Rose Wilder Lane. His debates with these American radicals had remained fruitless. But after some twenty years, their extreme anti-statism had gained momentum. The best proof was the existence of the Circle Bastiat involving Rothbard, Raico, and Liggio. Raymond Cyrus Hoiles, publisher of the Freedom Newspaper chain, boasted of this growing impact in a letter to Mises, their first correspondence in thirteen years. Answering Mises's contention that no rational man ever proposed that the production of security be entrusted to private associations, Hoiles said:

> I happen to know several people who so believe. Robert LeFevre, the founder of the Freedom School, I believe, believes that the market place is the best way to protect life and property. F.A. Harper, Orval Watts, my son, Harry Hoiles, Rose Wilder Lane, all certainly believe the Declaration of Independence is

---

[29]Mises to Bruno Leoni, letter dated February 15, 1965; Grove City Archive: Mont Pèlerin Society files.

exactly what it says, because nobody can give a man's consent but that individual himself.[30]

Mises replied in a Hobbesian manner, objecting that in the absence of a monopoly of the use of coercive force, "everybody would have continually to defend himself against hosts of aggressors." He concluded:

> I think you err in assuming that your principles are those of the Declaration of Independence. They are rather the principles that led a hundred years ago the Confederate States to refuse to recognize the President elected by the majority. Wherever and whenever resorted to, these principles will lead to bloodshed and anarchy.[31]

Now this point of view seems to be at odds with the principle of self-determination, at least in the form in which Mises had championed it for many years. Had Mises changed his mind? He had discussed this issue in correspondence from the early 1950s with Salvador de Madariaga in Oxford. In one of his letters, Mises held that Ernest Renan had settled the question "unambiguously" in his famous lecture on the nature of nations. Self-determination is the right of peoples to "decide their own fate." However, according to Renan a "nation" could be just *any* voluntary association of persons. What if a subgroup of an existing nation suddenly decided to go its own way? Would this not be an instance of self-determination? Mises was of course perfectly familiar with the problem. He had known it from his native Austria, where the old nation was divided in the late

---

[30]Hoiles to Mises, letter dated May 7, 1962; Grove City Archive: Hoiles file. In a subsequent letter of May 21, Hoiles argued that the production of security in a free market would be organized by insurance companies, thereby anticipating an important argument in later analysis of this problem.

[31]Mises to Hoiles, letter dated May 14, 1962; Grove City Archive: Hoiles file. Notice that in the 1860 election Lincoln received far less than a majority of the votes.

nineteenth century along linguistic lines. Referring to the secession of language communities, he admitted that the case for
secession was unassailable on logical grounds. Only brute force
could be held up against it:

> It is a fact that no ideology has been developed which
> would have approved of the existence of a state com-
> posed of people speaking different languages. In the
> absence of such doctrine there is no argument avail-
> able against the ambitions of the majority of a terri-
> tory's population asking for independent statehood.
> There is only the recourse to the *ultima ratio regum*.[32]

And he concluded: "To construct such an ideology of states
including various linguistic groups is one of the great tasks left to
coming generations."[33] But this conclusion begged the question.
Self-determination is relevant only if there are disagreements
between individuals and groups on ideological questions. How
should secessionist movements be handled at a time when no
great overarching ideology exists? The only solution available
for classical liberals relied on the principle of self-determination. But when Mises applied this principle to the concrete case
of the American Civil War, he felt it had to yield to other considerations of equally fundamental importance:

---

[32]Mises to Salvador de Madariaga, letter dated September 9, 1952; Grove
City Archive: Madariaga file. Mises had criticized Madariaga in *Omnipotent
Government* (Spring Mills, Penn.: Libertarian Press, 1985). Still he had held
the Spaniard in great esteem—until this correspondence led to their falling
out. He said in fact in the same letter: "I think that I have never paid a higher
tribute to the achievements of any living author than I did in speaking of you
on page 15 of my book."

[33]See *Omnipotent Government*. He probably owed the idea that nations
result from the "construction" of ideologies to his friend Louis Rougier, who
had argued that there are no objective or scientific criteria to delimit nations
from one another. The true foundation of a nation is a specific "political
myth." See Louis Rougier, *Les mystiques politiques contemporaines et leurs incidences internationales* (Paris: Recueil Sirey, 1935).

> It is of no avail for the discussion of our problem
> whether or not we qualify Lincoln's attitude as lib-
> eral. In denying to the Southerners the right to
> secede, the very right on which the existence of the
> United States was morally founded, he certainly did
> not behave as a liberal. But there was another prob-
> lem in the case: slavery. One could argue: The real
> issue is not self-determination, but slavery. In fact,
> most of the contemporary European liberals argued
> this way and sympathized with the Unionists.[34]

The quote shows how uneasy Mises was at discussing this
problem. He just could not reach a clear conclusion. Ten years
later he wrote: "When every territory can by majority vote
determine whether it should form an independent state or a
part of a larger state, there will no longer be wars to conquer
more provinces."[35] But still he did not address de Madariaga's
argument that the very problem is to decide who should take
part in the "independence voting"—that is, who should be
counted as belonging to the nation. Mises evaded the issue:

> The liberals have always maintained that it does not
> matter for the people as a whole and for individual cit-
> izens whether their own state's sovereignty stretches
> over a larger or smaller territory. The size of the
> realm, the integration of provinces whose inhabitants
> do not voluntarily want to be or to remain integrated,
> concerns only royalty and aristocracy.[36]

Mises ended their 1952–1953 correspondence rather
abruptly, saying that de Madariaga's point of view was "the most

---

[34]Mises to Salvador de Madariaga, letter dated September 9, 1952; Grove
City Archive: Madariaga file.

[35]Mises, *Ultimate Foundation of Economic Science*, p. 94.

[36]Mises to de Madariaga, letter dated April 1, 1953; Grove City Archive:
Madariaga file.

anti-liberal proposition I have ever heard."[37] He put an equally abrupt end to his 1962 correspondence with Hoiles when the latter expressed his regret to see Mises "advocate any form of socialism, or any form of tyranny."[38] But this did not prevent his continued association with other members of the anarchist camp. In January 1964, he taught a course on money at Robert LeFevre's Freedom School.[39] This was the same LeFevre who had praised Hoiles's succinct statement of the case for anarchism. Mises even served on the Advisory Board of the Freedom School and eventually also on the Council of Advisors for F.A. "Baldy" Harper's Institute for Humane Studies (IHS) in California.[40] (A champion of formal manners, Mises was close enough to Harper to address him as Baldy.[41]) He also continued his affiliation with Frank Chodorov's Intercollegiate Society of Individualists, which he had supported from the very beginning in 1952. Moreover, he praised the *New Individualist Review* that graduate student Ralph Raico had established at the University

---

[37]See de Madariaga to Mises, letter dated March 11, 1953; Mises to de Madariaga, letter dated April 1, 1953; Grove City Archive: Madariaga file.

[38]Two similar cases might be mentioned in which Mises did not pursue correspondence touching on the necessity of coercion: a Mr. Kuhlmann, who favored an increase in inheritance taxes in order to decrease income taxes, reminded him: "And remember you say 'Taxes are necessary'." (Kuhlmann to Mises, letter dated April 7, 1962; Grove City Archive: Kuhlmann file.) And a Mrs. Powell Moffit complained about his endorsement of conscription in the 2nd edition of *Human Action*. See Virginia Powell Moffit to Mises, letter dated February 21, 1964; Grove City Archive: "M" files.

[39]Grove City Archive: Freedom School files.

[40]McLeod to Mises, letter dated March 10, 1965; Grove City Archive: IHS files. Baldy Harper had founded IHS in 1963. After leaving FEE, he had for some time worked for the Volker Fund and then lectured at Wabash College.

[41]See Mises's letter to Harper dated May 8, 1969; Grove City Archive: *Farmand* file. In another letter he wrote that he could only stay for three days because he had to return for his NYU seminar. He also mentioned that his health was not very good. Mises to Harper, letter dated June 5, 1969; Grove City Archive: IHS files.

of Chicago (on behalf of a local chapter of the Intercollegiate
Society of Individualists). He wrote for it a review of Rothbard's
Man, Economy, and State and seemed to rate it higher than *The
Freeman* or any other journal.[42]

Mises also followed Rothbard's subsequent writings and
activities, often to his chagrin. A 1968 letter that Fertig wrote to
Mises probably conveys Mises's own feelings as well:

> Among the things which are really disturbing is the
> case of Murray Rothbard. I enclose the current issue
> of *National Review*. . . . Now he is allied with the New
> Left. Imagine that! Just a short while ago he was on a
> Committee that favored Castro and Cuba. It's sad to
> see a brilliant mind like his go to pot that way.[43]

Last Skirmishes with the Monetarists

Rothbard's apparent decline was not the main worry for the
aging Mises. He followed with great concern how the American
monetary system, and the global monetary system built on it,
unraveled all through the 1960s. In the middle of the decade,
the alarm bells were ringing at the headquarters of the U.S.
monetary authorities. Foreign central banks and individuals
were following the lead of France in redeeming dollars in gold.
The United States government's stock of gold shrank on a daily
basis and at an accelerating rate. The new economists were
quick to repeat their endless lamentation that all of this was the

---

[42]Mises to Meehl, letter dated July 25, 1963; Grove City Archive: "M"
files. He also praised the work in correspondence with one of the thinkers he
most admired, the French philosopher Louis Rougier. See his letter to
Rougier, dated December 6, 1962; Grove City Archive: Rougier files. The
letter ends with: "But, please, first of all read the book of Rothbard. It is very
interesting also from the epistemological point of view."

[43]Fertig to Mises, letter dated July 12, 1968; Grove City Archive: Fertig
files.

consequence of the "unfavorable balance of payments" and they demanded measures against greedy businessmen driving up prices in the States; some were even calling for controls of foreign exchange. Philip Cortney wrote to Mises, inquiring why he had not published anything on the present calamity. Mises replied that in his books he had said everything on the issue. But then he set forth his view anyway:

> Those ascribing inflow and outflow of money in or out of a country to the sales and purchases of the country's inhabitants are committed to a fallacy. They assume that the size of an individual's cash-holding is not planned by the man but is merely the unintentional outcome of his buying and selling. A man (or a business firm or a department of the public administration) may one morning be surprised to discover that there is no money left in his pocket to buy a postage stamp. What a catastrophe if this happens to a considerable part of the nation! The supporters of this doctrine are inconsistent as they think that this calamity can only occur in the mutual transactions of the inhabitants of sovereign nations and not also in the business relations of the administrative subdivisions. . . .
>
> There prevails in the world the opinion that the inflationary policy of the American Government will continue, that sooner or later the gold hoard in Fort Knox will be exhausted and the American Administration will be forced to abandon its policy of selling the ounce to foreign governments and central banks at $35. This explains the drain upon the American Government's gold holdings.
>
> If our civilization will not in the next years or decades completely collapse, the gold standard will be restored.[44]

---

[44]Mises, typewritten manuscript, probably of February 17, 1965; Grove City Archive: Cortney files.

Cortney replied with news about his talks with Jacques Rueff. And he reported that the French press had quoted Fritz Machlup's testimony before a congressional committee in Washington, D.C., in which Machlup had pronounced himself against a return to the gold standard.[45] Mises had already been informed, by Machlup himself. His former student asked him for "hints about books or articles that may contain pertinent material" to bolster his claim that the French monetary authorities in the 1920s had successfully abolished the "self-restriction" that comes with the gold standard.[46]

This must have come as a shock for Mises. In the fall of the same year, he met Machlup at the Mont Pèlerin Society meeting in Stresa, only to witness him reiterating his new views. He got very upset and told Margit not to talk to Machlup any more.[47] Here is Machlup's version of the event:

> Philip Cortney made his customary plea for an immediate return to the gold standard with a substantial increase in the official price of gold. After listening to the reasons he gave for raising the price of gold, I used the chairman's prerogative to make a comment in the subject. I compared the plea of the gold-boosters to the pleas of trade-union leaders who want wage rates to be raised after a period of falling prices . . . and want wage rates to be raised also after a period of rising prices. . . . Similarly, the gold lobby wants the price of gold to be raised after a period of falling commodity prices . . . and want the price of gold to be raised also after a period of increasing commodity prices.[48]

---

[45]Cortney to Mises, letter dated April 24, 1965; Grove City Archive: Cortney files.

[46]Machlup to Mises, letter dated March 22, 1965; Hoover Institution: Machlup-Mises correspondence file. Mises apparently never replied.

[47]Margit von Mises, *My Years with Ludwig von Mises*, p. 146.

[48]He went on: "When the session was over, I tried to talk to Professor Mises, but he abruptly turned around and marched away. The break in

No wonder Mises was upset. His former student, an erstwhile champion of the gold standard, had now publicly reduced the issue to a question of special interest politics.

Another year later Mises sensed a seismic shift in the quality of the developing crisis. He wrote:

> What not so long ago could be called a monetary crisis is more and more—at least for the U.S.—developing into a most serious political crisis. The federal Government as well as the States and the Municipalities have since 1960 wasted fabulous sums of money for more or less unnecessary expenditures and are now facing tremendous deficits. There cannot be any question of a serious monetary reform because the ruling party (for many years probably Leftists) thinks—probably correctly—that its popularity could not survive a return to balanced budgets. This means that inflation is now the main financial basis of the nation's political actions and that no "practical" man, no man who counts in an election campaign, gives any thought to a state of affairs without a continuous increase in the quantity of money in circulation.[49]

Mises planned to take part in an April 1968 conference on international monetary problems organized by the Graduate Institute of International Studies. The invitation came from Jacques Freymond, who then headed the Institute, but had been extended at the behest of Philip Cortney. Mises was looking forward to the event, but then Cortney explained that the agenda and the conclusions were already set, and that academic discussion was to be kept to a strict minimum. "For your guidance: we

---

friendly relations lasted for several years." Machlup, "Ludwig von Mises: The Academic Scholar Who Would Not Compromise," *Wirtschaftspolitische Blätter* 28, no. 4 (1981): 13.

[49]Mises to Cortney, letter dated June 27, 1966; Grove City Archive: Cortney files.

do not recommend putting an end to the I.M.F."[50] Mises immediately declined participation.

Last Honors

On October 20, 1962, Mises received the Austrian Medal of Honor (*Ehrenzeichen*) at the Austrian embassy in Washington. He had the embassy invite Otto Kallir for the luncheon. They also asked some of his other former students, probably those residing in Washington.[51] In June 1963, he obtained an honorary doctorate from NYU; in 1964, an honorary doctorate in political science from University of Freiburg (Hayek was there during those years). In March 1969, prob-ably in anticipation of his retirement, he was elected a Distinguished Fellow of the American Economic Association. His election may have been an attempt to influence the Nobel committee, which in the fall of the same year would grant the first Nobel Prize in economics. The prize went instead to Ragnar Frisch and Jan Tinbergen, economists who are all but forgotten today. Mises would never receive the Nobel Prize, but one year after his death, Hayek won it for his elaboration of the Misesian business cycle theory.

Mises with the Austrian Medal of Honor for Science and Art, October 1962

These official acknowledgements were gratifying, of course, but Mises did not pride himself too much on this type of recognition. Throughout his life, he remained dedicated more to his ideas than to the applause of his contemporaries. Thus he must

---

[50]Cortney to Mises, letter dated March 26, 1968; Grove City Archive: Institut des Hautes Etudes Internationales files.

[51]Wilfried Platzer to Mises, letter dated September 25, 1962; Grove City Archive: Österreichische Botschaft files.

have been even more pleased with the continued success of his books. Nymeyer had reprinted *Planning For Freedom* in 4,000 copies by September 1965.[52] Jonathan Cape republished *Socialism* in 1969 and FEE ordered 1,000 copies. At the same time, Yale University Press ceded its rights to *Bureaucracy*, *Omnipotent Government*, and *Theory and History*, which were now republished by Arlington House.[53]

A young Arlington House senior editor by the name of Llewellyn H. Rockwell, Jr. was in charge of these projects. He had been a subscriber to *The Freeman* as a high-school student and in 1968 had moved to New York City, where he took part in FEE seminars and got in touch with George Roche.[54] Rockwell only met Mises once, but he eagerly absorbed and digested his ideas. In 1982, he would establish the now famous Ludwig von Mises Institute.

A very different kind of recognition that he was happy to experience at the end of his life was the virtual vindication of his theory of economic calculation by the practitioners—the economists of the East Bloc. In the fall of 1967, a group of young economists in Communist-ruled Czechoslovakia had started reviving the socialist-calculation debate of the 1920s and 1930s in light of postwar experiences with centrally planned economies. One of them, Dr. Karel Kouba, entitled his study "Plan and Market in Socialism." This was circulated for "internal" use of the Czechoslovak Academy of the Sciences. He studied Mises's original paper from 1920 and Hayek's later modification of the argument, as well as Oskar Lange's scheme for

---

[52]Nymeyer to Mises, letter dated September 28, 1965; Grove City Archive: Nymeyer files.

[53]Grove City Archive: FEE files.

[54]Rockwell followed Roche in 1971 to Hillsdale College to run its ideological and publications programs, which included a Mises Lecture Series, the newsletter *Imprimis*, and Hillsdale College Press, and a few years later joined the staff of Congressman Ron Paul, a serious student of Mises, and a lifelong opponent of central banking.

market socialism, about which he wrote: "Based on today's experiences one can say that this is a purely theoretical demonstration." A colleague of Kouba's, Oldrich Kyn, went so far as to rehabilitate Mises's point of view in an article for the *Ekonomická Revue*, which had an international circulation and also

reached Mises's desk.[55] Another Czechoslovakian economist confided to Fritz Machlup: "We have now learned that Mises and Hayek were right and that Oskar Lange was an idealist."[56] A few months later, this intellectual rebellion ushered in the short-lived "Prague Spring" of 1968—almost eight months of political and economic liberalization, crushed by Soviet tanks.

A commemorative issue of the Libertarian honoring Mises's 100th birthday

Most of all, Mises must have enjoyed the sort of recognition that comes from the concrete actions of people he had inspired. In April 1967, a man from Hollywood bound for the Vietnam War, made FEE his life insurance beneficiary. "In the event of my death I would want this money [$15,000] to be used *only* to place copies of *Human Action* by Ludwig von Mises in any libraries which will accept them."[57]

On a lighter note, after a "Libertarian Conference" in Orange County, California, with Mises among the participants,

---

[55]Karel Kouba, *Plan a trh za socialismu* (Prague: Economic Section of the Czechoslovak Academy of the Sciences, 1967); Oldrich Kyn, "Vyzva marxisticke ekonomicke teorii," *ekonomicka revue* 7 (1967): 289ff.

[56]Machlup to Mises, letter dated April 18, 1967; Hoover Institution: Machlup-Mises correspondence file.

[57]William S. Cushman to FEE, undated letter; Grove City Archive: "C" files. Mises wrote to Cushman on May 1, 1967.

local lefties carried around pictures of Marcuse, Mao, and others at a May Day demonstration on the UC Irvine campus. Mises's host wrote and asked Mises for photos to use in a counterattack.[58]

And on his ninetieth birthday, the CBS television show *Spectrum* featured a birthday special on Ludwig von Mises. The speaker, Jeffrey Saint John, called Mises "the de Tocqueville of modern economics" and observed that he had explained long ago that Nixon-style price controls are economic dictatorship and have in the past produced Communism, Nazism, and fascism.[59] For the same occasion, Harper's IHS had sponsored a two-volume *Festschrift*, six copies of which were sent to Mises at the end of October. He was touched and commented to Margit: "The only good thing about being a nonagenarian is that you are able to read your obituaries while you are still alive."[60]

However, there were a few magnificent obituaries that Mises would not be able to read.[61]

American Economic Review, "In Memoriam: Ludwig von Mises, 1881–1973," volume 64, no. 3 (June 1974): 518. Drafted (but unsigned) by Fritz Machlup:

> Mises was certainly not a popular economist; by his blunt criticism of popular views and policies, by his unrelenting attacks on inflationism, interventionism, and socialism, and by his uncompromising steadfastness in arguing the case for private enterprise and free markets, he acquired as many intellectual enemies and detractors as any of the renowned economists of the twentieth century. At the same time, Mises was a

---

[58]Schureman to Mises, May 2, 1969; Grove City Archive: "S" files.

[59]Grove City Archive: "D" files.

[60]Quoted from Margit von Mises, *My Years with Ludwig von Mises*, p. 181.

[61]The following obituaries were compiled by Bettina Bien Greaves and Robert W. McGee in *Mises: An Annotated Bibliography* (Irvington-on-Hudson, N.Y.: Foundation for Economic Education, 1993) pp. 315ff.

beloved teacher and friend of a host of students who came to appreciate the integrity and profundity of his teachings in courses and seminars but particularly in his private seminars.

Bidinotto, Robert James. "Von Mises—A Final Salute." *Unbound!* Boston: Individuals for a Rational Society 2, no. 1 (September-October 1973): 1–2:

> Our age may well be labeled by future historians as "the Age of Mediocrity." Nothing is so characteristic of this century as the ever-shrinking stature of men. Yet if these times are to be vindicated, it will be solely by the grace of a few lonely giants who stood tall and strode far, guided down unexplored paths by unflinching courage and unwavering vision. . . .
>
> On October 10, 1973, one of those giants fell. . . .
>
> Dr. Ludwig von Mises is dead at the age of 92. And it is difficult to conceive of any person in our time who has given the world so much, yet been rewarded so little in return.

Chamberlain, John. "Unsung Economist Who Was Prophet." *Chicago Tribune*. Section 1 (October 13, 1973), p. 14:

> Genuine innovators such as von Mises have to wait for death to gain their rightful recognition. It is all very unfair, but the truth does eventually catch up with the showmen, relegating them to the historical footnote positions where they belong. . . . Von Mises' great work, *Human Action*, a study of the conditions needed to release an optimum amount of productive energy in a society . . . will live long as a monument to von Mises.

Daily Telegraph. U.K. "Ludwig von Mises." (October 11, 1973):

> With the death of Prof Ludwig von Mises yesterday, aged 92, the world's liberal economists lose their most prolific pen, and Austria loses the last lingering reminder of the intellectual pre-eminence of Vienna at the turn of the century. . . .

As an authoritative exponent of liberal economics he has enjoyed a popularity, never foreseen, in the Asian liberal economies of Japan, Hong Kong and Formosa, and a respect, never foreseen, in the Communist countries, for his exposition of the impossibility of calculation in a full socialist society. . . .

The gentle, witty but tenaciously logical teaching of von Mises in Europe and America earned him a loyal army of auxiliary writers and pamphleteers.

Hazlitt, Henry. Remarks at Mises's Memorial service, October 16, 1973, pp. 6–8. Multilithed by the Foundation for Economic Education (Irvington, N.Y.), pp. 6–8:

His outstanding moral quality was moral courage, the ability to stand alone, and an almost fanatical intellectual honesty and candor that refused to deviate or compromise an inch. This often cost him personally dear, but it set an ideal to strengthen and inspire his students and all the rest of us who were privileged to know him.

International Herald Tribute. "Economist Ludwig von Mises; Advanced Libertarian Theory" (October 12, 1973), p. 5:

Mr. von Mises was recognized as a brilliant contributor to economic thought not only by his disciples but also by many who disagreed radically with his political and social philosophy.

Kirzner, Israel M. Tribute in *National Review* 25, no. 45 (November 9, 1973): 1246, 1260:

To those who knew him, Ludwig Mises was, in the face of shocking neglect by so many of his contemporaries, a living exemplar of incorruptible intellectual integrity, a model of passionate, relentless scholarship and dedication. It will not be easy to forget these stern lessons which he so courageously personified.

McFalls, John, investment advisor. "The Passing of Ludwig von Mises." Broadcast memorial to Ludwig von Mises, October 14–16, 1973, during Value-Action radio programs:

> Mises was a master of synthesis. He brought wholeness out of the fractured field of economics. He was a scholar of great patience and integrity who believed that the movement toward collectivism and state intervention posed a grave threat to Western civilization.

Monatsblätter für Freiheitliche Wirtschaftspolitik. "Der letzte Liberale" [The last liberal] 11 (November 1973): 645:

> With the passing of "the last liberal," a liberal of the old school who occasionally said, "Liberalism, that is what I am," the last survivor of the epoch-making Viennese School of Economics is gone at 92 years of age. Now honored by a diminishing band of followers, he has almost become a legend, on the one hand in the field of money and business cycle theory, and on the other hand and above all in the world of economic and political theory. (Translated from the German)

Peterson, William H. "Ludwig von Mises: In Memoriam." *The Wall Street Journal* (October 12, 1973):

> Mr. von Mises believed in choice. He believed that choosing among options determines all human decisions and hence the entire sphere of human action. . . .
>
> While man could destroy himself and civilization, he could also ascend—in a free society, i.e., a free economy—to undreamed-of cultural, intellectual and technological heights. In any event, thought would be decisive. Mr. von Mises believed in the free market of not only goods and services but of ideas as well—in the potential of human intellect. . . .
>
> He held that a free society and a free market are inseparable. He gloried in the potential of reason and man. In sum, he stood for principle in the finest tradition of Western Civilization."

La Prensa. Buenos Aires. "Ludwig von Mises: Murió en Nueva York" [Ludwig von Mises: Died in New York] (October 18, 1973):

> Mises' life, his works and his conferences were all dedicated to rounding out the thesis that men are not automatons; they act rationally and the ideas that motivate them are the original cause of the course of history. His concepts make clear that government intervention leads inevitably not only to conflicts within a country, but also to international conflicts. (Translated from the Spanish)

Read, Leonard. Remarks at memorial service, October 16, 1973, pp. 8–9. Multilithed by the Foundation for Economic Education (Irvington, N.Y.), pp. 8–9:

> Ludwig Mises is truly—and I use this term in the present tense—a Teacher. More than two generations have studied under him and countless thousands of others have learned from his books. Books and students are the enduring monuments of a Teacher and these monuments are his. This generation of students will pass away but the ideas set in motion by his writings will be a fountain source for new students for countless generations to come.

Rothbard, Murray N. "Ludwig von Mises: 1881–1973." *Human Events*. Washington, D.C. (October 10, 1973): 847.

> Readers of Mises' majestic, formidable and uncompromising works must have often been surprised to meet him in person. Perhaps they had formed the image of Ludwig Mises as cold, severe, austere, the logical scholar repelled by lesser mortals, bitter at the follies around him and at the long trail of wrongs and insults that he had suffered.
>
> They couldn't have been more wrong; for what they met was a mind of genius blended harmoniously with a personality of great sweetness and benevolence. Not once has any of us heard a harsh or bitter word escape from Mises' lips. Unfailingly gentle and

courteous, Ludwig Mises was always there to encourage even the slightest signs of productivity or intelligence in his friends and students. . . .

And always there as an inspiration and as a constant star. Inserted by Philip M. Crane in *Congressional Record* 119:159 (October 23, 1973) E6696– 6697.

Murray Rothbard later added:

When Mises died, and I was preparing an obituary, Professor Raico kindly sent me a deeply moving passage from *Adonais*, Shelley's great eulogy to Keats, that, as usual for Raico, struck just the right note in a final assessment of Mises:

> *For such as he can lend—they borrow not*
> *Glory from those who made the world their prey:*
> *And he is gathered to the kings of thought*
> *Who waged contention with their time's decay,*
> *And of the past are all that cannot pass away.*[62] ⚜

---

[62]Murray N. Rothbard, *Ludwig von Mises—Scholar, Creator, Hero* (Auburn, Ala.: Ludwig von Mises Institute, 1988) p. 74. The original cites Ralph Raico, "The Legacy of Ludwig von Mises," *The Libertarian Review* (September 1981): 22.

Epilogue

> If ever it could be said that one man stood against the ideological tide of an era, that was von Mises. But whether his efforts have turned that tide is a question to be resolved in the future by those who understand his theories and share his love of liberty.[1]

LUDWIG VON MISES WAS the "last knight of liberalism" but to think of him as a political thinker only is to underestimate his place in the history of ideas. He pioneered the integration of monetary theory into value theory (macro- and microeconomics), the theory of economic calculation, and the inquiry into the a priori foundations of economic science. Even more than that, he excelled as a systematic thinker. He created a comprehensive system of economic theory and also highlighted the place of economics among the sciences and its role within human civilization. More than any other economist before or after him, he has clarified its political, social, and cultural implications. Economics was not merely the foundation of a comprehensive political program centered on private property rights; it was the scientific cornerstone of an entire worldview in which peace, cooperation, and tolerance reigned supreme.

---

[1]Bettina Bien Greaves and Robert W. McGee, *Mises: An Annotated Bibliography* (Irvington-on-Hudson, N.Y.: Foundation for Economic Education, 1993), p. 317. The original cites Howard S. Katz, "Ludwig von Mises Dies at Age 92," *Rip-Off Resistance* 1, no. 4 (December 1973): 3.

As he saw it, opting for a free society did not demand cold-heartedness or mistrusting the intellect. It was the type of society that was demonstrably best at promoting the material, cultural, and spiritual well-being of the overwhelming majority of mankind—of all those who did not aspire to live off spoliation. Human reason, despite its limitations, was the most precious tool in man's pursuit of happiness; and it led straight to the case for classical liberalism and the market economy. Other thinkers, most notably F.A. Hayek, had criticized socialism and statism as the fruit of excessive rationalism. For Mises, the planning state and the interventionist state were not reasonable enough. Their intellectual champions were quite simply wrong on the essential questions. But rather than admitting the case for liberty and capitalism, these advocates spent their time finding ever new justifications for government interventionism—by contesting the very existence of economic laws if necessary. This was not so much an intellectual hubris as it was a moral one. It was not, above all, an empty pretense of knowledge. It was a "revolt against reason."[2]

The chief contribution of *Human Action* is to make this point. Ever since its first publication in 1949, Mises's *magnum opus* has remained for our time what the *Enquiry into the Nature and Causes of the Wealth of Nations* was for the eighteenth and nineteenth centuries: a handbook of the science of human liberty, a treatise of the scientific foundations underpinning political liberalism. Just as Adam Smith's work was based on comprehensive acquaintance with the economic knowledge of his day, *Human Action* portrays the grammar of modern economics. The foundation of "modern" economic thought is the theory of subjective value, developed by Menger and others. Mises complemented this theory by a general theory of economic calculation.

---

[2]This expression is taken from the title of chapter 3 in *Human Action*. See on this question Joseph T. Salerno, "Ludwig von Mises as a Social Rationalist," *Review of Austrian Economics* 4 (1990): 26–54.

Its central idea is that economic rationality is logically and historically contingent. Contradicting on this point all economic literature since Adam Smith—as well as fellow Austrians including Wieser and Hayek—Mises stressed that calculation in terms of money prices is not just one form of economic calculus; it is the only type of economic calculus there is.

It follows that human civilization is the fragile fruit of certain cultural conditions that are necessary for the emergence of money and monetary calculus. Here economics comes again into play. Learning, developing, and spreading the teachings of economic science has brought about an unheard-of increase of living standards after the eighteenth century, along with the cultural achievements of a great number of people who then became affluent enough to dedicate their lives to the arts and the sciences. To preserve these cultural standards it is necessary not to lose sight of their economic foundations. It is necessary to learn economics. Mises stresses: "This is, in our age, the primary civic duty."[3] And he insists that the matter is too important to be entrusted to public education and government experts:

> Economics must not be relegated to classrooms and statistical offices and must not be left to esoteric circles. It is the philosophy of human life and action and concerns everybody and everything. It is the pith of civilization and of man's human existence.[4]

In the concluding chapters of his *magnum opus* he emphasized the importance of private education. It was an important lesson he had learned firsthand in his long life: government sponsorship introduces a pro-government bias into economic education and economic research, thus undermining the social

---

[3]Mises, *Human Action*, Scholar's edition (Auburn, Ala.: Ludwig von Mises Institute, 1998), p. 875.

[4]Ibid., p. 874.

function of economic science. He concluded *Human Action* with this statement:

> The body of economic knowledge is an essential element in the structure of human civilization; it is the foundation upon which modern industrialism and all the moral, intellectual, technological, and therapeutic achievements of the last centuries have been built. It rests with men whether they will make the proper use of the rich treasure with which this knowledge provides them or whether they will leave it unused. But if they fail to take the best advantage of it and disregard its teachings and warnings, they will not annul economics; they will stamp out society and the human race.[5]

When he wrote these lines, Mises could look back on a lifetime invested in the development of economics. Little by little he had come to realize that this discipline was the intellectual foundation of modern civilization and that all people who care about other people and the progress of human civilization had to become acquainted with it. This was not a conviction he had adopted in youthful exuberance when he first came across the writings of Menger and the classical economists. It was an opinion that grew in him, even after he had already reached a fairly advanced age. The passage just quoted is from *Human Action*. Nine years earlier, in *Nationalökonomie*, Mises could not bring himself to assign to economics quite such an elevated place. But then he was only fifty-eight years old.

By "economics" Mises meant the science that came from classical figures such as Hume, Smith, Ricardo, Say, and Bastiat; that had been transformed by Menger and others in the light of the new subjective value theory; which had further been transformed by Mises and others in the twentieth century; and which

---

[5]Ibid., p. 881.

Mises expected to be transformed ever further by future generations. It was the science that analyzed the logical implications of human action dealing with scarce goods. It was the science that demonstrated, again and again, that government interventionism could not work miracles, but was bound by inexorable laws of cause and effect.

This science came to be supplanted in the course of the twentieth century, and in particular after World War II, by a new discipline that, while being taught under the same name as the old economics, set out to apply the methods of the natural sciences to elucidate phenomena such as prices, income, unemployment, inflation, and growth. Mises digested the challenges that the various strands of this new discipline raised for the old economics. When he published *Human Action*, then, it was not merely a summary of his own previous works, but a new synthesis, developed in critical response, not only to historicism and Marxism, but also to positivism, experimental psychology, and game theory—disciplines that still dominate the social sciences in our day. Ironically, the very success of the ideas that Mises combated in a lonely struggle more than thirty years ago now make for the lasting importance of his own system of thought.

Misesian economics is today a strong and fast-growing paradigm, as witnessed by the number of publications that elaborate where he left off, as well as by the increasing attention paid to this paradigm in textbooks on contemporary and historical economic thought. The most surprising aspect of this growth is that it has virtually no institutional backing. Mises himself turned politically incorrect at an early stage of his career and later on he fell even more out of fashion due to his epistemological views. The colleges and universities shunned him. The political parties in power did not listen and were certainly glad that nobody else seemed to do so either. Mises enjoyed some personal backing by private foundations, most notably the Volker Fund and the Earhart Foundation. After his death, his legacy was promoted actively by the Ludwig von Mises Institute in Alabama. But these few and financially insignificant institutions had a hard time competing with organizations that bore the stamp of official (government) approval. It was and still is an uphill battle.

Thus the main explanation of the present-day growth of the Misesian paradigm is the extraordinary vigor of the ideas that inspire it. Mises is a classic, but in our day he is more than that. A classic author has given mankind a timeless formulation of essential questions and, sometimes, time-tested answers. Yet these questions and answers are not necessarily the ones that move us today or are relevant to solve the problems that we confront. Not so in the case of Mises. More than thirty years after his death his writings still strike the reader, academic and layman alike, as relevant and thought provoking. His books and articles are still bought by the thousands each year and—most of all—read. How many economics students today actually read something Adam Smith or David Ricardo have written? Any teacher of economics knows the answer. The same answer holds true for the writings of twentieth-century luminaries such as Gustav Cassel or Frank Knight. It holds true even for the writings of John Maynard Keynes; the greatest champion ever of interventionism is constantly referred to in the classroom and in the media, but few people have ever held one of his books in their hands. In contrast, Mises is still read and studied attentively all over the world, second only to the fashionable textbook authors of our day.

What is it that makes for this continued relevance? Looking back, at the end of this volume on the life and work of Mises, many plausible answers could be given to this question. One could single out a substantial number of path-breaking contributions in various fields of economic analysis. One could refer to his personal virtues entailing admiration and inspiration on the part of many close associates. But we would like to stress another consideration, an aspect of overriding importance that helps explain both the fascination of his work and his place in the history of thought: realist epistemology. Mises's work stands for the idea or hypothesis that some aspects of social reality cannot be adequately analyzed with the methods used in the natural sciences and in historical investigation. Yet this layer of the social world can be described with praxeology and economics. There are time-invariant causes and effects in human action. Praxeology is the descriptive knowledge of these causes and effects. It was this idea that attracted Mises to Menger and that turned him into an economist once he convinced himself that Menger was on to something. It is the same idea that still attracts people to Mises's writings as a radical alternative to the great number of contemporary approaches that, while discarding the realist hypothesis from the outset, seem to fail to deliver the goods.

Whoever wishes to engage in the analysis of the causes and effects that prevail in the social world would do well to start with Mises, unless he wishes to go even further back and find his own way from the classical economists or from the School of Salamanca. As things stand today, Mises's writings provide the only continuous link between modern economic thought and the long tradition of realist social analysis that reaches back to Nicolas Oresme in the fourteenth century.

This is not to say, of course, that the Misesian paradigm defines some sort of perfection in the social sciences. But it has given us the most recent system of social thought from a realist point of view; and thus it seems to be at present the most useful starting point to engage in that great intergenerational venture that we call the social sciences. It has also given us a most fruitful intellectual apparatus for understanding the workings of society in all times and places. ✑

*Mises at the Festschrift dinner honoring
the 50th anniversary of his doctorate*

Bibliography

Akademisches Gymnasium Wien. *Jahres-Bericht über das k.k. Akademische Gymnasium in Wien für das Schuljahr 1899/1900*. Vienna: Verlag des k.k. Akademischen Gymnasiums, 1900.

Alexandre, V, and W.W. Gasparski, eds. *Praxiology: The International Annual of Practical Philosophy and Methodology*. New Brunswick, N.J.: Transaction, 1992. Vol. 7: *The Roots of Praxiology—French Action Theory from Bourdeau and Espinas to Present Days*. New Brunswick, N.J.: Transaction, 2000.

Altschul, Eugen. Book Review in *Magazin der Wirtschaft* (June 19, 1931).

Amaroso, Luigi, ed. *Cournot nella economia e nella filosofia*. Padua: Cedam, 1939.

Amonn, Alfred. *Hauptprobleme der Sozialisierung*. Leipzig: Quelle & Meyer, 1919.

———. *Objekt und Grundbegriffe der theoretischen Nationalökonomie*. Vienna: Deuticke, 1911.

Anderson, Benjamin. *Economics and the Public Welfare*. Indianapolis: Liberty Press, 1979.

———. *The Value of Money*. New York: Macmillan, 1917.

Anonymous. "Die Gemeinwirtschaft." *Der Deutsche Volkswirt. Literatur-Beilage* no. 1 (December 23, 1932).

———. "Sozialismus—eine Utopie." *1. Handelsbeilage der "Berliner Börsen-Zeitung"* (November 3, 1932).

Antonelli, Étienne. "Léon Walras et Carl Menger à travers leur correspondence." *Économie appliquée* 6, nos. 2–3 (1953).

Aquinas, Thomas. "Über die Herrschaft der Fürsten." In *Staatslehre des Thomas von Aquino*, edited by F. Schreyvogel. Jena: Gustav Fischer, 1923.

Archive of the Hoover Institution at Stanford University. Palo Alto, California.

Archive of the Wirtschaftskammer. Vienna, Austria.

Auspitz, Rudolf, and Richard Lieben. *Untersuchungen über die Theorie des Preises*. Leipzig: Duncker & Humblot, 1889.

———. *Zur Theorie des Preises*. Leipzig: Duncker & Humblot, 1887.

Bainville, Jacques. *Les conséquences politiques de la paix*. Paris: Fayard, 1920.

Baltzarek, Franz. "Ludwig von Mises und die österreichische Wirtschaftspolitik der Zwischenkriegszeit." *Wirtschaftspolitische Blätter* 28, no. 4 (1981).

Barth, Karl. *Der Römerbrief*. Munich: Kaiser, 1922.

Barth, Paul. *Die Philosophie der Geschichte als Soziologie*, 3rd ed. Leipzig: Reisland, 1922.

Barzun, Jacques. *Teacher in America*. Indianapolis: Liberty Press, [1945] 1981.

Bauer, Otto. *Der Weg zum Sozialismus*. Vienna: Verlag der Wiener Volksbuchhandlung, 1919.

———. *Die Nationalitätenfrage und die Sozialdemokratie*. Vienna: Verlag der Wiener Volksbuchhandlung, 1907. Translated as *The Question of Nationalities and Social Democracy*. Minneapolis: University of Minnesota Press, 2000.

Becker, Gary. *A Treatise on the Family*. Cambridge, Mass.: Harvard University Press, 1991.

———. *Economic Theory*. New York: Knopf, 1971.

Behrend, Manfred. "'Der Wandschirm, hinter dem nichts geschieht.' Bildung, Tätigkeit und Ende der ersten deutschen Sozialisierungskommission." *Glasnost* (1998).

Bendixen, Friedrich. *Das Wesen des Geldes*. Leipzig: Duncker & Humblot, 1908.

———. "Fünf Jahre Geldtheorie." *Bank-Archiv* 10, no. 10 (1911).

———. *Sozialismus und Volkswirtschaft in der Kriegsverfassung*. Berlin: Guttentag, 1916.

Bergmann, Eugen von. *Geschichte der nationalökonomischen Krisentheorien*. Stuttgart: Kohlhammer, 1895.

Bergson, Henri. *L'évolution créatrice*. Paris: Presses Universitaires de France, [1907] 1991.

Bernatzik, Eduard. *Die Ausgestaltung des Nationalgefühls im 19. Jahrhundert*. Hannover: Helwing, 1912.

Beveridge, William. *The London School of Economics and Its Problems, 1919–1937*. London: Allen & Unwin, 1960.

———. *Unemployment: A Problem of Industry*, 2nd ed. London: Longmans, Green & Co., 1930.

Blaug, Mark. "Comment" [on O'Brien's "Lionel Robbins and the Austrian Connection"]. In *Carl Menger and His Legacy in Economics*, edited by Bruce Caldwell. Durham, N.C.: Duke University Press, 1990.

———. *Economic Theory in Retrospect*, 5th ed. Cambridge: Cambridge University Press, 1997.

———. *Great Economists before Keynes: An Introduction to the Lives and Works of One Hundred Great Economists of the Past*. Cambridge: Cambridge University Press, 1986.

Boese, Franz. *Geschichte des Vereins für Sozialpolitik, 1872–1932*. Berlin: Duncker & Humblot, 1939.

Boétie, Etienne de la. *The Politics of Obedience: The Discourse of Voluntary Servitude*. New York: Free Life Editions, [1562] 1975.

Böhm-Bawerk, Eugen von. *Capital and Interest*. South Holland, Ill.: Libertarian Press, 1959.

———. "Eine 'dynamische' Theorie des Kapitalzinses." *Zeitschrift für Volkswirtschaft, Sozialpolitik und Verwaltung* 22 (1913). Reprinted in *Gesammelte*

Schriften, edited by Weiss. Reprint, Frankfurt a.M.: Sauer & Auvermann, 1968. Vol. 2.

———. "Grundzüge der Theorie des wirtschaftlichen Güterwertes." *Conrad's Jahrbücher für Nationalökonomie und Statistik* n.s. 13 (1886). Reprinted as *Grundzüge der Theorie des wirtschaftlichen Güterwerths.* London: London School of Economics and Political Science, 1932.

———. *Innsbrucker Vorlesungen über Nationalökonomie*, edited by Shigeki Tomo. Marburg: Metropolis, 1998.

———. *Karl Marx and the Close of His System.* London: T.F. Unwin, 1989.

———. *Positive Theorie des Kapitals.* Innsbruck, 1889. Reprinted Jena: Gustav Fischer, 1921.

———. *Positive Theory of Capital.* New York: G.E. Stechert, 1930.

Stephan Boehm. "Schumpeter and Mises." In *Neoclassical Economic Theory, 1870 to 1930*, edited by Klaus Hennings and Warren J. Samuels. Boston: Kluwer, 1990.

Bois-Reymond, Emil du. *Über den deutschen Krieg.* Berlin: Hirschwald, 1870.

Bonnet, Victor. *Etudes sur la monnaie.* Paris: Guillaumin, 1870.

Bostaph, Samuel. "Friedrich von Wieser's Theory of Socialism: A Magnificent Failure." *Politická ekonomie* 53, no. 6 (2005).

———. "Wieser on Economic Calculation under Socialism." *Quarterly Journal of Austrian Economics* 6, no. 2 (2003).

Branden, Barbara. *The Passion of Ayn Rand.* New York: Doubleday, 1987.

Braun [Browne], Martha St. "Die diesjährigen Verhandlungen des Vereines für Sozialpolitik." *Neue Freie Presse* (October 8, 1932).

Briefs, Götz. "Kriegswirtschaftslehre und Kriegswirtschaftspolitik." *Handwörterbuch der Staatswissenschaften*, 4th ed. 1923. Vol. 5.

Brook-Shepherd, Gordon. *The Austrians: A Thousand-Year Odyssey.* New York: Carroll & Graf, 1997.

Browne [Braun], Martha Steffy. "Erinnerungen an das Mises-Privatseminar." *Wirtschaftspolitische Blätter* 28, no. 4 (1981).

Bresciani-Turroni, Costantino. *The Economics of Inflation: A Study of Currency Depreciation in Post-War Germany.* London: Allen and Unwin, 1937.

Bukharin, Nikolai. *Economic Theory of the Leisure Class.* New York: Monthly Review Press, 1972.

Bundeskammer and Wiener Kammer der gewerblichen Wirtschaft, eds., *100 Jahre Handelskammern in Österreich.* Vienna: Amtsblatt der Bundeskammer der gewerblichen Wirtschaft, 1948.

Burghardt, Anton. *Soziologie des Geldes und der Inflation.* Vienna: Böhlaus, 1977.

Cairnes, John E. "Essay Towards A Solution of the Gold Question: The Course of the Depreciation." In *Essays in Political Economy: Theoretical and Applied.* London: Macmillan, [1858] 1873.

Caldwell, Bruce, ed. *Carl Menger and His Legacy in Economics*. Durham, N.C.: Duke University Press, 1990.

———. "Wieser, Hayek, and Equilibrium Theory." *Journal des Economistes et des Etudes Humaines* 12, no. 1 (2002).

Calligaris, L. "Staatliche Theorie des Geldes." *Münchener Allgemeine Zeitung* (February 1, 1906).

———. "Staatliche Theorie des Geldes." *Österreichische Rundschau* 7, no. 80 (May 10, 1906).

Cannan, Edwin. *Money: Its Connexion with Rising and Falling Prices*. London: King & Son, 1918.

Cantillon, Richard. *Essay on the Nature of Commerce in General*. Reprint, New Brunswick, N.J.: Transaction, 2001.

Carell, Erich. Review of Mises's *"Ursachen der Wirtschaftskrise."* *Jahrbücher für Nationalökonomie* 135 (1931).

Caro, Leopold. "Auswanderung und Auswanderungspolitik in Österreich." *Schriften des Vereins für Socialpolitik* 131 (1909).

Cassel, Gustav. "Abnormal Deviations in International Exchanges." *Economic Journal* 28 (1918).

———. *Grundgedanken der theoretischen Ökonomie*. Leipzig and Erlangen: Hatschek & Scholl, 1926.

———. "The Present Situation of the Foreign Exchanges." *Economic Journal* 26 (1916).

———. *Theoretische Sozialökonomie*, 4th ed. Leipzig: Deichert, 1927.

Cernuschi, Henri. *Nomisma; or, "Legal Tender."* New York: Appleton & Co., 1877.

Chamberlain, John. "Battle for the *Freeman*." *Time*. January 26, 1953.

Chodorov, Frank. "What This Country Needs Is Guts." *analysis* 2 (February 1946).

Clark, John Bates. *Essentials of Economic Theory*. New York and London: Macmillan, 1914.

Coase, Ronald. *Essays on Economics and Economists*. Chicago: University of Chicago Press, 1994.

———. *The Firm, the Market, and the Law*. Chicago: University of Chicago Press, 1988.

Condillac, Étienne Bonnot, Abbé de. *Commerce and Government: Considered in Their Mutual Relationship*. Cheltenham, U.K.: Edward Elgar, 1997.

———. *Essai sur l'origine des connaissances humaines* (1746). Included in *Œuvres complètes*. Paris: Tourneux, Lecointe et Durey, 1822. Vol. 1.

———. *Le commerce et le gouvernement* (1776). Included in *Œuvres complètes*. Paris: Tourneux, Lecointe et Durey, 1822. Vol. 4.

———. *Traité des sensations* (1754). Included in *Œuvres complètes*. Paris: Tourneux, Lecointe et Durey, 1822. Vol. 3.

Cornuelle, Richard. "A New Philosophy of Laissez Faire." *American Affairs* (January 1950).

Coquelin, Charles. *Du credit et des banques.* Paris: Guillaumin, 1848.

Crunden, Robert M. *The Mind and Art of Albert Jay Nock.* Chicago: Henry Regnery, 1964.

Cubbedu, Raimondo. *The Philosophy of the Austrian School.* London: Routledge, 1993.

Cuhel, Franz. *Zur Lehre von den Bedürfnissen. Theoretische Untersuchungen über das Grenzgebiet von Ökonomik und Psychologie.* Innsbruck: Wagner, 1907.

DelGaudio, Juilan Joseph. *Refugee Economist in America: Ludwig von Mises and American Social and Economic Thought, 1940–1986.* Ann Arbor, Mich.: University Microfilms International, 1988.

Dewey, John. *Liberalism and Social Action.* New York: Putnam, 1935.

Diamond, Sigmund. *Compromised Campus: The Collaboration of Universities with the Intelligence Community, 1945–1955.* New York: Oxford University Press, 1992.

Dickinson, H.D. "Price Formation in a Socialist Community." *Economic Journal* 43 (1933).

Dietzel, Heinrich. "Beiträge zur Methodik der Wirtschaftswissenschaften." *Jahrbücher für Nationalökonomie und Statistik* 43 (1884).

———. "Der Ausgangspunkt der Socialwirthschaftslehre und ihr Grundbegriff." *Zeitschrift für die gesamte Staatswissenschaft* 39 (1883).

———. "Individualismus." *Handwörterbuch der Staaswissenschaften*, 4th ed., 1923. Vol. 5.

———. "Selbstinteresse und Methodenstreit in der Wirtschaftstheorie." *Handwörterbuch der Staatswissenschaften*, 3rd ed. Jena: Gustav Fischer, 1911. Vol. 7.

———. *Theoretische Socialökonomik.* Leipzig: Duncker & Humblot, 1895.

Dietzgen, Josef. *Gesammelte Werke*, 3rd ed. Stuttgart: Dietz, 1922.

DiLorenzo, Thomas J., and Jack High. "Antitrust and Competition, Historically Considered." *Economic Inquiry* (July 1988).

Dimmel, Heinrich. "Ignaz Seipel." *Tausend Jahre Österreich*, edited by Walter Pollack. Vienna: Verlag Jugend und Volk, 1974. Vol. 3.

Director, Aaron, ed., *Defense, Controls, and Inflation.* Chicago: University of Chicago Press, 1952.

Douhet, Giulio. *Luftherrschaft.* Berlin: Drei Masken Verlag, 1935.

Döring, Herbert. *Die Geldtheorien seit Knapp*, 2nd ed. Greifswald: Bamberg, 1922.

Dreyer, Jacob. *Breadth and Depth in Economics: Fritz Machlup—The Man and His Ideas.* Lexington, Mass.: Lexington Books, 1978.

Dub, Moriz. *Die weitere Entwicklung der Katastrophenhausse in Oesterreich mit Streiflichtern auf Deutschland.* Stuttgart: Enke, 1922.

———. *Katastrophenhausse und Geldentwertung.* Stuttgart: Enke, 1920.

Ebeling, Richard M., ed., *Selected Writings of Ludwig von Mises: Political Economy of International Reform and Reconstruction*. Indianapolis: Liberty Fund, 2000.

Ebray, Alcide. *La Paix malpropre (Versailles)—pour la reconciliation par la vérité*. Milano: Unitas, 1924.

Eckert, Christian. "Friedensverträge. II. Vom staatswissenschaftlichen Standpunkte." *Handwörterbuch der Staatswissenschaften*, 4th ed. Jena: Gustav Fischer, 1927. Vol. 4.

Edwards, James R. *The Economist of the Century: Ludwig von Mises in the History of Monetary Thought*. New York: Carlton Press, 1985.

Ekelund, Robert, and Robert Hébert. *Secret Origins of Modern Microeconomics: Dupuit and the Engineers*. Chicago: Chicago University Press, 1999.

Ellis, Howard S. *Exchange Control in Central Europe*. Cambridge, Mass.: Harvard University Press, 1941.

Elster, Ludwig. "Philippovich von Philippsberg, Eugen." *Handwörterbuch der Staatswissenschaften* 6 (1925).

Eltis, Shelagh, and Walter Eltis. "The Life and Contribution to Economics of the Abbé de Condillac." In Etienne Bonnot, Abbé de Condillac, *Commerce and Government: Considered in Their Mutual Relationship*. Cheltenham, U.K.: Edward Elgar, 1997.

Ermacora, Felix. *Der unbewältigte Friede—St. Germain und die Folgen*. Vienna and Munich: Amaltha, 1989.

Espinas, Alfred. "Les origines de la technologie" *Revue philosophique* 15 (July to December 1890). Reprinted, *Les origines de la technologie*. Paris: Felix Alcan, 1897.

Eucken, Walter. *Kritische Betrachtungen zum deutschen Geldproblem*. Jena: Gustav Fischer, 1923.

Fechner, Gustav Theodor. ("Dr. Mises"). *Beweis, dass der Mond aus Jodine bestehe*, 2nd ed. Leipzig: Voss, 1832.

———. *Vergleichende Anatomie der Engel-Eine Skizze*. Leipzig: Industrie-Comptoir, 1825.

Fest, Joachim Fest. *Hitler.* Berlin: Deutsche Buch-Gemeinschaft, 1973.

Fischel, Alfred, ed. *Das österreichische Sprachenrecht*, 2nd ed. Brünn: Irrgang, 1910.

———. *Materialien zur Sprachenfrage.* Brünn: Irrgang, 1902.

Fisher, Irving. *The Purchasing Power of Money: Its Determination and Relation to Credit, Interest,* and *Crises*, 2nd ed. New York: Augustus M. Kelley, [1913] 1985.

———. *Stabilised Money: A History of the Movement*. London: George Allen & Unwin, 1935.

Flexner Report. *Medical Education in the United States and Canada: A Report to the Carnegie Foundation for the Advancement of Teaching*, 1910.

Flynn, John T. *The Roosevelt Myth*. New York: Devin-Adair, 1948. Reprinted with an introduction by Ralph Raico. San Francisco: Fox & Wilkes, 1998.

Fosdick, Raymond Blaine. *The Story of the Rockefeller Foundation*. New York: Harper, 1952.

Fetter, Frank A. *Capital, Interest, and Rent*, edited by Murray N. Rothbard. Kansas City: Sheed Andrews and McMeel, 1977.

———. *Economic Principles*. 2 Vols. New York: The Century Co., 1905 and 1915.

Franz, Georg. *Liberalismus—Die deutschliberale Bewegung in der habsburgischen Monarchie*. Munich: Callwey, 1955.

Frege, Gottlob. *Function und Begriff*. Jena: Pohle, 1891.

———. *Die Grundlagen der Arithmetik*. Jena: Pohle, 1884.

———. *Die Grundgesetze der Arithmetik*. Jena: Pohle, 1893. Vol. 1; Jena: Pohle, 1903. Vol. 2.

Friedman, Milton. *Essays in Positive Economics*. Chicago: University of Chicago Press, 1953.

Friedman, Milton, and Anna J. Schwartz. *Monetary History of the United States*. Princeton, N.J.: Princeton University Press, 1963.

Friedman, Milton, and Rose D. Friedman. *Two Lucky People: Memoirs*. Chicago: University of Chicago Press, 1998.

Fritsch, Theodor. *Anti-Rathenau*, 2nd ed. Leipzig: Hammer, 1919.

Galbraith, John Kenneth. "In Defense of Laissez-Faire." *New York Times Book Review* (October 30, 1949).

Gall, Franz. *Alma Mater Rudolphina 1365–1965—die Wiener Universität und ihre Studenten*. Vienna: Austria Press, 1965.

Garrett. Garet. *The Revolution Was*. Caldwell, Idaho: Caxton Printers, 1938.

Geissler, Franz. "Die Entstehung und der Entwicklungsgang der Handelskammern in Österreich." *Hundert Jahre österreichische Wirtschaftsentwicklung, 1848–1948*, edited by Hans Mayer. Vienna: Springer, 1949.

Gertchev, Nikolay. "Dehomogenizing Mises's Monetary Theory." *Journal of Libertarian Studies* 18, no. 3 (2004).

Gideonse, Harry D. "Changing Issues in Academic Freedom in the United States Today." *Proceedings of the American Philosophical Society* 94, no. 2 (1950).

Göbel, Otto. *Deutsche Rohstoffwirtschaft im Krieg*. Stuttgart: Carnegie Stiftung, 1930.

Görres-Gesellschaftliche zur Pflege der Wissenschaft, *Staatslexikon*, 7th ed. Freiburg i.Br.: Herder, 1989. Vol. 5

Gorges, Irmela. *Sozialforschung in Deutschland 1872–1914*, 2nd ed. Frankfurt a.M.: Anton Hain, 1986.

———. *Sozialforschung in der Weimarer Republik 1918–1933*. Frankfurt a.M.: Anton Hain, 1986.

Gossen, Hermann Heinrich. *Entwickelung der Gesetze des menschlichen Verkehrs und der daraus fliessenden Regeln für menschliches Handeln.* Braunschweig: Vieweg & Sohn, 1854.

Gottl-Ottlilienfeld, Friedrich von. *Wirtschaft und Technik,* 2nd ed. Tübingen: Mohr, 1923.

Graduate Institute Archive. Mises files in the Graduate Institute of International Studies. Geneva, Switzerland.

Graf, Martine Brunschwig, Jean-Claude Frachebourg, Norman Scott, and Peter Tschopp. *HEI 1927–2002.* Geneva: Graduate Institute of International Studies, 2002.

Graham, F.D. *Exchanges, Prices, and Production in Hyperinflation: Germany, 1920–23.* Princeton, N.J.: Princeton University Press, 1930.

Grassl, Wolfgang, and Barry Smith, eds. *Austrian Economics: Historical and Philosophical Background.* London: Croom Helm, 1986.

Gratz, Alois. "Die österreichische Finanzpolitik von 1848 bis 1948." *Hundert Jahre österreichischer Wirtschaftsentwicklung, 1848–1948,* edited by Hans Mayer. Vienna: Springer, 1949.

Graetz, Heinrich. *History of the Jews.* Vol. 5. Philadelphia: Jewish Publ., 1895.

Greaves, Bettina Bien, ed. *Austrian Economics: An Anthology.* Irvington-on-Hudson, N.Y.: Foundation for Economic Education, 1996.

Greaves, Bettina Bien, and Robert W. McGee, eds. *Mises: An Annotated Bibliography.* Irvington-on-Hudson, N.Y.: Foundation for Economic Education, 1993.

Grice-Hutchinson, Marjorie. *The School of Salamanca: Readings in Spanish Monetary Theory, 1544–1605.* Oxford: Clarendon Press, 1952.

Grove City Archive. Mises files in the Grove City College Library. Grove City, Pennsylvania.

Grünberg, Carl. *Die Bauernbefreiung und die Auflösung des gutsherrlich-bäuerlichen Verhältnisses in Böhmen, Mähren und Schlesien,* 2 vols. Leipzig: Duncker & Humblot, 1893–1894.

———. *Studien zur österreichischen Agrargeschichte.* Leipzig: Duncker & Humblot, 1901.

Gugitz, Gustav. *Das Wiener Kaffeehaus. Ein Stück Kultur- und Lokalgeschichte.* Vienna: Deutscher Verlag für Jugend und Volk, 1940.

Guglia, Eugen. *Das Theresianum in Wien.* Vienna: Schroll, 1912.

Haberler, Gottfried von. "Fritz Machlup: In Memoriam." *Cato Journal* 3, no. 1 (1983).

———. "Mises's Private Seminar." In Ludwig von Mises, *Planning for Freedom,* 4th ed. South Holland, Ill.: Libertarian Press, 1980.

———. "*Erinnerungen* an das Mises-Privatseminar." *Wirtschaftspolitische Blätter* 28, no. 4 (1981).

Habermann, Gerd. *Der Wohlfahrtsstaat: Die Geschichte eines Irrwegs*, 2nd ed. Frankfurt: Ullstein, 1997.

Haller, Carl Ludwig, "Über einige Parteienbenennungen zum besseren Verständnis der Zeitungen und anderer moderner Schriften." *Satan und die Revolution—und andere Schriften.* Vienna: Karolinger, 1991.

Hamilton, Charles H. *"The Freeman*: The Early Years." In R. Lora and W.H. Longton. *The Conservative Press in Twentieth-Century America.* London: Greenwood, 1999.

Hahn, L. Albert. "Continental European Pre-Keynesianism." *The Economics of Illusion.* New York: Squier Publishing, 1949. Chap. 16. Reprinted in *The Critics of Keynesian Economics,* Henry Hazlitt, ed., 2nd ed. Irvington-on-Hudson, N.Y.: Foundation for Economic Education, 1995.

———. *Volkswirtschaftliche Theorie des Bankkredits.* Tübingen: Mohr, 1920.

Hamann, Brigitte. *Rudolf: Kronprinz und Rebell.* Munich: Piper, 1978.

Harris, Seymour E. "Capitalist Manifesto." *Saturday Review* 32 (September 24, 1949).

Hartwell, R.M. *History of the Mont Pèlerin Society.* Indianapolis: Liberty Fund, 1995.

Hawtrey, R.G. *Monetary Reconstruction,* 2nd ed. London: Longmans, Green & Co., 1926.

Hayek, F.A. "Bemerkungen zum Zurechnungsproblem." *Jahrbuch für Nationalökonomie und Statistik* 124, 3rd series, vol. 69 (1926). Translated as "Some Remarks on the Problem of Imputation." In Hayek, *Money, Capital, and Fluctuations: Early Essays,* edited by Roy McCloughry. Chicago: University of Chicago Press, 1984.

———. *Das Mieterschutzproblem. Nationalökonomische Betrachtungen.* Vienna: Steyrermühl-Verlag, 1930.

———, ed. *Capitalism and the Historians.* Chicago: University of Chicago Press, 1954.

———, ed. *Collectivist Economic Planning: Critical Studies on the Possibilities of Socialism.* London: Routledge, 1935.

———. "Competition as a Discovery Procedure." *Quarterly Journal of Austrian Economics* 5, no. 3 (1968/2002).

———. "Einleitung." Introduction to Hermann Heinrich Gossen, *Entwickelung der Gesetze des menschlichen Verkehrs und der daraus fliessenden Regeln für menschliches Handeln,* 3rd ed. Berlin: Prager, 1927.

———. "Einleitung." In Carl Menger, *Gesammelte Werke.* Tübingen: Mohr, 1968.

———. "Einleitung." Introduction to Ludwig von Mises, *Erinnerungen.* Stuttgart: Gustav Fischer, 1978.

———. "Friedrich Freiherr von Wieser." *Jahrbuch für Nationalökonomie und Statistik* 125, 3rd series, vol. 70 (1926).

————. *Geldtheorie und Konjunkturtheorie*. Vienna: Holder-Pichler-Tempsky, 1929.

————. "Gibt es einen Widersinn des Sparens?" *Zeitschrift für Nationalökonomie* 1, no. 3 (1930).

————. *Individualism and Economic Order*. Chicago: University of Chicago Press, 1948.

————. *Hayek on Hayek: An Autobiographical Dialogue*. Chicago: Chicago University Press, 1994.

————. "The Intellectuals and Socialism," *University of Chicago Law Review* 16 (1949). Reprinted in *The Collected Works of F.A. Hayek*, vol. 10: *Socialism and War: Essays, Documents, Reviews*, edited by Bruce Caldwell. Chicago: University of Chicago Press, 1997.

————. *Monetary Theory and Trade Cycle Theory*. London: Routledge, 1933.

————. "The Nature and History of the Problem." In *Individualism and Economic Order*. Chicago: University of Chicago Press, 1948.

————. "Opening Address to a Conference at Mont Pèlerin." *Studies in Philosophy, Politics, and Economics*. Chicago: University of Chicago Press, 1967.

————. "Planning, Science, and Freedom." *Nature* (November 15, 1941).

————. "Postscript." In *The Constitution of Liberty*. Chicago: University of Chicago Press, 1960.

————. *Prices and Production*. London: Routledge, 1931.

————. *Preise und Produktion*. Vienna: Julius Springer, 1933.

————. *Profit, Interest, and Investment and Other Essays on the Theory of Industrial Fluctuations*. London: Routledge & Kegan Paul, 1939.

————. *Pure Theory of Capital*. London: Macmillan, 1941.

————. *The Road to Serfdom*. Chicago: University of Chicago Press, 1944.

————. *The Sensory Order*. Chicago: University of Chicago Press, 1952.

Hazlitt, Henry. *A New Constitution Now*. New York: McGraw Hill, 1942.

————. "An Interview with Henry Hazlitt." *Austrian Economics Newsletter* (Spring 1984).

————. "The Case for Capitalism." *Newsweek* 34 (September 19, 1949).

————. "The 1919 Prophecies of Maynard Keynes." *New York Times Book Review* (March 11, 1945).

Hébert, Robert F. "Jevons and Menger Re-Homogenized: Who is the Real 'Odd Man Out'?" *American Journal of Economics and Sociology* 57, no. 3 (1998).

Heimann, Eduard. *History of Economic Doctrines: An Introduction to Economic Theory*. New York: New York University Press, 1945.

Helfferich, Karl. *Das Geld*, 5th ed. Leipzig: Hirschfeld, [1903] 1921.

Hennecke, Hans Jörg. *Friedrich August von Hayek*. Düsseldorf: Wirtschaft und Finanzen, 2000.

Hennings, Klaus H. *The Austrian Theory of Value and Capital: Studies in the Life and Work of Eugen von Böhm-Bawerk*. Cheltenham, U.K.: Edward Elgar, 1997.

Herbener, Jeffrey M., Hans-Hermann Hoppe, Joseph T. Salerno. "Introduction" to Ludwig von Mises, *Human Action: A Treatise on Economics*, Scholar's Edition. Auburn, Ala.: Ludwig von Mises Institute, 1998.

Herkner, Heinrich. "Die Zukunft der Sozialpolitik." *Jubiläumstagung des Vereins für Sozialpolitik in Eisenach 1922*. Munich and Leipzig: Duncker & Humblot, 1923.

———. "Sozialpolitische Wandlungen in der wissenschaftlichen Nationalökonomie." *Der Arbeitgeber* 13, no. 3 (1923).

Hermann, F.B.W. *Staatswirthschaftliche Untersuchungen*, 1st ed. Munich: Fleischmann, 1832.

Heyn, Otto. *Die indische Währungsreform*. Berlin, 1903.

———. *Irrtümer auf dem Gebiete des Geldwesens*. Berlin, 1900.

Hicks, John R. *A Market Theory of Money*. Oxford: Clarendon, 1989.

———. *Capital and Time: A Neo-Austrian Theory*. Oxford: Clarendon Press, 1973.

———. "Léon Walras." *Econometrica* (October 1934).

Hilferding, Rudolph. *Das Finanzkapital*. Berlin: Dietz, [1910] 1947.

Hobhouse, Leonard T. *Liberalism*. London: Williams and Norgate, 1911.

Holcombe, Randall G., ed. *15 Great Austrian Economists*. Auburn, Ala.: Ludwig von Mises Institute, 1999.

Hollander, Paul. *Political Pilgrims*, 4th ed. New Brunswick, N.J.: Transaction, 1998.

Holzbauer, Georg. *Barzahlung und Zahlungsmittelversorgung in militärisch besetzten Gebieten*. Jena: Gustav Fischer, 1939.

Hufeland, Gottlieb. *Neue Grundlegung der Staatswirthschaftskunst*. Giessen and Wetzlar: Tasche & Müller, 1807.

Hoppe, Hans-Hermann. "Socialism: A Property or "Knowledge Problem?" *Review of Austrian Economics* 9, no. 1 (1996).

Hoppe, Hans-Hermann, and Joseph T. Salerno. "Friedrich von Wieser und die moderne Österreichische Schule der Nationalökonomie." In *Friedrich von Wiesers. Vademecum zu einem Klassiker der Nationalökonomie*. Düsseldorf: Verlag Wirtschaft und Finanzen, 1999.

Hörtlehner, Alexander. "Ludwig von Mises und die österreichische Handelskammerorganisation." *Wirtschaftspolitische Blätter* 28, no. 4 (1981).

Huerta de Soto, Jesús. "New Light on the Prehistory of the Theory of Banking and the School of Salamanca." *Review of Austrian Economics* 9, no. 2 (1996).

Huddleston, Sisley. *In My Time*. New York: Dutton & Co., 1938.

———. *Popular Diplomacy and War*. Rindge, N.H.: Richard Smith, 1954.

———. *War Unless*. London: Victor Gollancz, 1933.

Hülsmann, Jörg Guido. "Knowledge, Judgment, and the Use of Property." *Review of Austrian Economics* 10, no. 1 (1997).

———. "Facts and Counterfactuals in Economic Law." *Journal of Libertarian Studies* 17, no. 1 (2003).

Hume, David. "Of the First Principle of Government." *Essays, Moral and Political*, edited by Eugene F. Miller. Minneapolis: Liberty Fund, 1987.

Hunold, Albert. "How Mises Changed My Mind." *The Mont Pèlerin Quarterly* 3, no. 3 (October 1961).

Husserl, Edmund. *Logical Investigations*. Halle a.S.: Max Niemeyer, 1900.

Ikeda, Yukihiro. *Die Entstehungsgeschichte der "Grundsätze" Carl Mengers*. St. Katharinen: Scripta Mercaturae Verlag, 1997.

Inama-Sternegg, K.T. von. *Deutsche Wirtschaftsgeschichte*, 4 vols. Leipzig: Duncker & Humblot, 1879–1901.

Jaffé, William. "Menger, Jevons and Walras De-Homogenized." *Economic Inquiry* 14 (December 1976).

Jagschitz, Gerhard. *Die Jugend des Bundeskanzlers Dr. Engelbert Dollfuss*. University of Vienna. Doctoral dissertation, 1967.

Jahn, Georg. "Freihandelslehre und Freihandelsbewegung." *Handwörterbuch der Staatswissenschaften*, 4th ed. (1927). Vol. 5.

Jevons, William Stanley. *Theory of Political Economy*. London: Macmillan, 1888.

Johnston, William M. *The Austrian Mind*. Los Angeles: University of California Press, 1972.

———. *Vienna, Vienna—The Golden Age, 1815–1914*. Milan: Arnoldo Mondadori, 1981.

Kamitz, Reinhard. "Die österreichische Geld- und Währungspolitik von 1848 bis 1948." In *Hundert Jahre österreichischer Wirtschaftsentwicklung, 1848–1948*, edited by Hans Mayer. Vienna: Springer, 1949.

Kann, Robert A. *A Study in Austrian Intellectual History: From Later Baroque to Romanticism*. New York: Praeger, 1960.

Katz, Howard S. "Ludwig von Mises Dies at Age 92." *Rip-Off Resistance* 1, no. 4 (December 1973).

Kauder, Emil. *A History of Marginal Utility Theory*. Princeton, N.J.: Princeton University Press, 1965.

Kautsky Karl. *Erinnerungen und Erörterungen*. The Hague: Mouton, 1960.

Kelsen, Hans. *Das Problem der Souveränität und die Theorie des Völkerrechts*. Tübingen: Mohr, 1920.

———. *Der soziologische und der juristische Staatsbegriff*. Tübingen: Mohr, 1922.

———. *Die Staatslehre des Dante Alighieri*. Vienna: Deuticke, 1906. .

———. *Hauptprobleme der Staatsrechtslehre*. Tübingen: Mohr, 1911.

Keynes, John Maynard. *A Tract on Monetary Reform*. London: Macmillan, 1923.

————. *Collected Writings*. London: Macmillan, 1973. Vol. 7.

————. *The Economic Consequences of the Peace*. New York: Harcourt, Brace and Howe, 1920.

————. *The End of Laissez-Faire*. London: Hogarth Press, 1926.

————. *General Theory of Employment, Interest, and Money*. New York and London: Harcourt, Brace, 1936.

————. *Indian Currency and Finance*. London: Macmillan, 1913.

————. "Review of *Theorie des Geldes und der Umlaufsmittel*." *Economic Journal* (September 1914).

————. *Treatise on Money*. New York: Harcourt Brace, 1930.

Kink, Rudolf. *Geschichte der kaiserlichen Universität zu Wien*, 2 vols. Vienna: Gerold, 1854.

Kirzner, Israel. "The Austrian School of Economics." *New Palgrave Dictionary of Economics*. New York: Macmillan, 1986.

————. *Competition and Entrepreneurship*. Chicago: University of Chicago Press, 1973.

————. "Menger, Classical Liberalism, and the Austrian School of Economics." In *Carl Menger and His Legacy in Economics*, edited by Bruce Caldwell. Durham, N.C.: Duke University Press, 1990.

————. "The Socialist Calculation Debate: Lessons for Austrians." *Review of Austrian Economics* 2 (1987).

Klang, Marcel. *Die geistige Elite Österreichs*. Vienna: Barth, 1936.

Klein, Peter G. "Why Academic Intellectuals Support Socialism." Unpublished manuscript, presented at the New Zealand Business Roundtable. April 2003.

Knapp, Georg F. *Die Bauernbefreiung und der Ursprung der Landarbeiter in den älteren Teilen Preussens*, 2 vols. Leipzig: Duncker & Humblot, 1887.

————. *Staatliche Theorie des Geldes*, 1st ed. Leipzig, 1905. 2nd ed. Munich & Leipzig: Duncker & Humblot, 1918.

————. *Die Landarbeiter in Knechtschaft und Freiheit*. Leipzig: Duncker & Humblot, 1891.

Knight, Frank. *Freedom and Reform*. New York: Harper, 1947.

Kotarbinski, Tadeusz. "Considérations sur la théorie générale de la lutte." *Z Zagadnien Ogólnej Teorii Walki*. Warsaw, 1938.

Kouba, Karel. *Plan a trh za socialismu*. Prague: Economic Section of the Czechoslovak Academy of the Sciences, 1967.

Krizek, Jurij. "Die Kriegswirtschaft und das Ende der Monarchie." In *Die Auflösung des Habsburgerreiches*, edited by R.G. Plaschka and K. Mack. Munich: Oldenbourg, 1970.

Krüger, Dieter. "Max Weber und die 'Jüngeren' im Verein für Socialpolitik." In *Max Weber und seine Zeitgenossen*, edited by Wolfgang Mommsen and Wolfgang Schwentker, 98–136. Göttingen: Veröffentlichungen des Deutschen Historischen Instituts London, 1988.

Kuehnelt-Leddihn, Erik von. *Liberty or Equality.* Caldwell, Idaho: Caxton Printers, 1952.

Kuehnelt-Leddihn, Erik von. *The Cultural Background of Ludwig von Mises.* Auburn, Ala.: Ludwig von Mises Institute, 1999.

————. *Von Sarajevo nach Sarajevo.* Vienna: Karolinger, 1996.

k.u.k. Armee. "Kriegsereignisse im Norden. Von der Mobilisierung bis einschliesslich der Schlacht bei Lemberg." *Österreichisch-ungarische Kriegsberichte aus Streffleurs Militärblatt.* Vienna: Seidel & Sohn, 1915.

Kyn, Oldrich. "Vyzva marxisticke ekonomicke teorii." *ekonomicka revue* 7 (1967).

Lambach, Walter. *Diktator Rathenau.* Hamburg: Deutschnationale Verlagsanstalt, 1918.

Lampe, Adolf. *Allgemeine Wehrwirtschaft.* Jena: Gustav Fischer, 1938.

Landauer, Carl. *Planwirtschaft und Verkehrswirtschaft.* Leipzig: Duncker & Humblot, 1931.

————. "Übersicht über die neuesten Publikationen Deutschlands und des Auslands." *Jahrbücher für Nationalökonomie und Statistik* 121, no. 2 (1923).

Lane, Rose Wilder. Book Review in *Economic Council Review of Books* 2, no. 10 (November 1945).

Lange, Oskar. "The Computer and the Market." *Review of Economic Studies* 4, no. 1 (October 1936).

————. "On the Economic Theory of Socialism." *Review of Economic Studies* 4, no. 1 (October 1936).

————. *On the Economic Theory of Socialism,* edited by B.E. Lippincott. New York: McGraw-Hill, 1964.

————. *Price Flexibility and Employment.* Bloomington, Ind.: Principia Press, 1944.

Lauterbach, Albert. Book Review in *Der Holzarbeiter* 40, no. 4 (February 18, 1932).

Law, John. *Money and Trade Considered with a Proposal for Supplying the Nation with Money.* Edinburgh: Anderson, 1705.

Lederer, Emil. "Der technische Fortschritt." *Arbeiter-Zeitung* (September 4, 1927).

————. *Technischer Fortschritt und Arbeitslosigkeit.* Tübingen: Mohr, 1931.

————. "Verhandlungen des *Vereins für Sozialpolitik* in Regensburg 1919." *Schriften des Vereins für Sozialpolitik* 159 (1920).

Lerner, Abba P. Lerner. "Economic Theory and Socialist Economy." *Review of Economic Studies* 2 (1934).

Leser, Norbert. "Otto Bauer—Friedrich Adler—Max Adler." *Tausend Jahre Österreich,* edited by Walter Pollack. Vienna: Verlag Jugend und Volk, 1974. Vol. 3.

Lévi-Strauss, Claude. *Race et Histoire.* Paris: UNESCO, 1952.

Levy, S. Leon. *The American Economic Review* 34, no. 2 (June 1944).

———. *Nassau W. Senior: The Prophet of Modern Capitalism.* Boston: Bruce Humphries, 1943.

Lexis, Wilhelm. "Die Knappsche Geldtheorie." *Jahrbücher für Nationalökonomie und Statistik*, 3rd series, 32 (1906).

———. "Eine neue Geldtheorie." *Archiv für Sozialwissenschaften und Sozialpolitik* 5 (1906).

———. "Papiergeld." *Handwörterbuch der Staatswissenschaften.* Jena: Gustav Fischer, 1893; 2nd ed., 1901, 3rd ed., 1910.

Liefmann, Robert. *Allgemeine Volkswirtschaftslehre.* Leipzig: Teubner, 1924.

———. *Kartelle und Trusts.* Stuttgart: Moritz, 1924.

Lindenlaub, Dieter. "Richtungskämpfe im Verein für Sozialpolitik." *Vierteljahrschrift für Sozial- und Wirtschaftsgeschichte*, Beiheft no. 52 (1967). Reprinted as *Richtungskämpfe im Verein für Sozialpolitik: Wissenschaft und Sozialpolitik im Kaiserreich vornehmlich vom Begin des "Neuen Kurses" bis zum Ausbruch des ersten Weltkrieges, 1890–1914.* Wiesbaden: Steiner, 1967.

Lippincott, Benjamin E. "Introduction." In *On the Economic Theory of Socialism*, edited by B.E. Lippincott. New York: McGraw-Hill, 1964.

Lippmann, Walter. *Inquiry into the Principles of the Good Society.* Boston: Little, Brown & Co., 1937.

———. *La Cité Libre.* Paris: Librairie de Médicis, 1938.

Locke, John. "Some Considerations of the Consequences of the Lowering of Interest and Raising the Value of Money." In *Locke on Money*, edited by Patrick Hyde Kelly. Oxford: Clarendon Press, 1991. Vol. 1.

Lotz, Johann F.E. *Revision der Grund-Begriffe der National-Wirthschaftslehre.* Koburg and Leipzig: Sinner, 1811. Vol. 1.

Mach, Ernst. "Über Gedankenexperimente." Reprinted in Mach, *Erkenntnis und Irrtum*, 1897. Reprint, 5th ed. Vienna, 1926. Reprint, Darmstadt: Wissenschaftliche Buchgesellschaft, 1991.

Machlup, Fritz. *Börsenkredit, Industriekredit und Kapitalbildung.* Vienna: Springer, 1931.

———. *Der Golddevisenstandard.* Halberstadt, 1925.

———. *Führer durch die Krisenpolitik.* Vienna: Springer, 1934.

———. "Ludwig von Mises: The Academic Scholar Who Would Not Compromise." *Wirtschaftspolitische Blätter* 28, no. 4 (1981).

Machovec, Frank. *Perfect Competition and the Transformation of Economics.* London: Routledge, 1995.

Macleod, Henry D. *Theory and Practice of Banking.* London: Longman, Brown, Green, and Longmans, 1855. Vol. 1.

Mannheim, Karl. *Ideologie und Utopie.* Bonn: Cohen, 1929.

Mantoux, Etienne. *The Carthaginian Peace or The Economic Consequences of Mr. Keynes.* Oxford: Oxford University Press, 1946.

Marchi, Neil de. "League of Nations Economists and the Ideal of Peaceful Change in the Decade of the 'Thirties." In *Economics and National Security,* edited by C.D. Goodwin. Durham, N.C.: Duke University Press, 1991.

Martin, Xavier. *L'homme des droits de l'homme et sa compagne.* Bouère: Dominique Martin Morin, 2001.

Marshall, Alfred. "The Mecca of the economist lies in economic biology rather than in economic dynamics." In *Principles of Economics: An Introductory Volume,* 8th ed. London: Macmillan, 1920.

———. *Principles of Economics: An Introductory Volume.* London: Macmillan, 1891.

März, Eduard. *Joseph Alois Schumpeter—Forscher, Lehrer und Politiker.* Vienna: Verlag für Geschichte und Politik, 1983.

———. "Die Bauer—Mises-Schumpeter-Kontroverse." *Wirtschaftspolitische Blätter* 28, no. 4 (1981).

Mautner, Manfred, and Franz Nemschak. *Zum 25 Jährigen Bestand des Österreichischen Institutes für Wirtschaftsforschung.* Vienna: Österreichisches Institut für Wirtschaftsforschung, 1952.

Mayer, Hans. "Friedrich Freiherr von Wieser." *Neue Österreichische Biographie.* Vienna, 1929. Vol. 6.

McCulloch, John Ramsay. *Principles of Political Economy.* New York: Augustus M. Kelley, [1864] 1965.

Meinl, Julius. *Zwang oder Freiheit?* Vienna: Manz, 1918.

Menger, Carl. *Die Irrthümer des Historismus in der deutschen Nationalökonomie.* Vienna: Alfred Hölder, 1884.

———. "Geld." *Handwörterbuch der Staatswissenschaften,* 1st to 3rd eds. Jena: Gustav Fischer, 1891–1909.

———. *Gesammelte Werke,* edited by F.A. Hayek. Tübingen: Mohr, 1968.

———. *Grundsätze der Volkswirtschaftslehre.* Vienna: Braumüller, 1871.

———. "Grundzüge einer Klassifikation der Wirtschaftswissenschaften." *Jahrbücher für Nationalökonomie und Statistik,* n.s. 19 (1889).

———. *Principles of Economics.* New York: New York University Press, [1976] 1981.

———. *Investigations into the Method of the Social Sciences and of Political Economy in Particular.* New York: New York University Press, 1985.

———. *Untersuchungen über die Methode der Socialwissenschaften und der Politischen oekonomie insbesondere.* Leipzig: Duncker & Humblot, 1883. Translated as *Investigations into the Method of the Social Sciences and of Political Economy in Particular.* New York: New York University Press, 1985.

———. "Zur Kritik der politischen Ökonomie." *Zeitschrift für das Privat- und öffentliche Recht der Gegenwart* 14 (1887).

Menger, Karl. "X. Beginn der akademischen Laufbahn." Carl Menger Papers, Duke University, Box 21.

Métall, Rudolf Aladár. *Hans Kelsen*. Vienna: Verlag Franz Deuticke, 1968.

Meyerson, Émile. *De l'explication dans les sciences*. Paris: Fayot, 1927.

Mildschuh, W. "Geschichtliche Entwicklung der Geldtheorie." *Handwörterbuch der Staatswissenschaften* 4 (1927).

Mill, John Stuart. *Principles of Political Economy*. London: Routledge, 1891.

Milford, Karl. "Hufeland als Vorläufer von Menger und Hayek." In *Wert, Meinung, Bedeutung: Die Tradition der subjektiven Wertlehre in der deutschen Nationalökonomie vor Menger*, edited by Birger Priddat. Marburg: Metropolis, 1997.

Mises, Adele von. "A Day in the House of My Parents." *Tante Adele erzählt*. Unpublished manuscript, 1929.

Mises Archive. Mises files in the Special Archive for Historico-Documentary Collections. Moscow.

Mises, Ludwig von. *A Critique of Interventionism*. Translated by Hans Sennholz. New York: Arlington House, 1977.

———. *Anti-Capitalistic Mentality*. Princeton, N.J.: Van Nostrand, 1956.

———. "Antimarxismus." *Weltwirtschaftliches Archiv* 21 (1925). Reprinted in Mises, *Kritik des Interventionismus*. Jena: Gustav Fischer, 1929. Reprint Darmstadt: Wissenschaftliche Buchgesellschaft, 1976. Translated as "Anti-Marxism." In *A Critique of Interventionism*. Translated by Hans Sennholz. New York: Arlington House, 1977.

———. "Austrian Empire. Finance and Banking," *Encyclopedia Britannica*, 12th ed. (1921). Vol. 30.

———. *Bureaucracy*. New Haven, Conn.: Yale University Press, 1944.

———. "Das Ende des Laissez-Faire, Ideen zur Verbindung von Privat- und Gemeinwirtschaft" (The end of laissez-faire: ideas for combining the private and public economy). *Zeitschrift für die gesamte Staatswissenschaft* 82 (1927).

———. "Das festangelegte Kapital." *Economische Opstellen: Aangeboden aan Prof. C.A. Verrijn Stuart*. Haarlem: De Erven F. Bohn N.V., 1931.

———. "Das Problem gesetzlicher Aufnahme der Barzahlungen in Oesterreich-Ungarn." *Jahrbuch fuer Gesetzgebung, Verwaltung und Volkswirtschaft (Schmollers Jahrbuch)* 33, no. 3 (1909).

———. "Der 'kleine Finanzplan' des Abgeordneten Steinwender." *Neue Freie Presse* (December 5, 1912).

———. "Der Weg der österreichischen Finanzpolitik." *Wirtschaftliche Nachrichten* 18, no. 1 (January 10, 1935).

———. "Der Wiedereintritt Deutsch-Österreichs in das Deutsche Reich und die Währungsfrage." In *Wirtschaftliche Verhältnisse Deutsch-Österreichs*, edited by Michael Hainisch. *Schriften des Vereins für Sozialpolitik* 158. Leipzig: Duncker & Humblot, 1919.

———. "Die Abstempelung der Kronennoten im jugoslawischen Staate." *Neue Freie Presse* (January 14, 1919).

————. "Die allgemeine Teuerung im Lichte der theoretischen Nationalökonomie." *Archiv für Sozialwissenschaften und Sozialpolitik* 37 (1912).

————. "Die Entwicklung des gutsherrlich-bäuerlichen Verhältnisses in Galizien (1772–1848)." E. Bernatzik and E. von Philippovich, eds. *Wiener staatswissenschaftliche Studie* 4, no. 2 Vienna & Leipzig: Deuticke, 1902.

————. "Die geldtheoretische Seite des Stabilisierungsproblems." *Schriften des Vereins für Sozialpolitik* 164, no. 2. Munich: Duncker & Humblot, 1923. Translated as "Stabilization of the Monetary Unit—From the Viewpoint of Theory." In *On the Manipulation of Money and Credit*, translated by Percy L. Greaves. New York: Free Market Books, 1978. Reprinted in *The Causes of the Economic Crises*. Auburn, Ala.: Ludwig von Mises Institute, 2006.

————. *Die Gemeinwirtschaft*. Jena: Gustav Fischer, 1922; 2nd ed. 1932.

————. "Die Goldwährung," *Neues Wiener Tagblatt* (April 12, 1925).

————. "Die Goldwährung und ihre Gegner." *Neue Freie Presse* (December 25 and 30, 1931).

————. "Die Lehre vom Gelde." *Forschungen und Fortschritte*. Berlin, February 1928.

————. "Die neue Regierungsvorlage zur Abänderung des Personalsteuergesetzes." *Neue Freie Presse* (October 10, 1911).

————. "Die Stellung des Geldes im Kreise der wirtschaftlichen Güter." In *Die Wirtschaftstheorie der Gegenwart*, edited by Hans Mayer. Vienna: Springer, 1932. Vol. 2. Translated as "The Role of Money in the Realm of Economic Goods." In *Money, Method, and the Market Process: Essays by Ludwig von Mises*, edited by Richard Ebeling. Boston: Kluwer, 1990.

————. "Die wirtschaftspolitischen Motive der österreichischen Valutaregulierung." *Zeitschrift für Volkswirtschaft, Sozialpolitik und Verwaltung* 16 (1907).

————. "Economic Freedom in the Present World." In *Economic Freedom and Interventionism: An Anthology of Articles and Essays*. Irvington-on-Hudson, N.Y.: Foundation for Economic Education, 1990. Chap. 47.

————. "Ein Wort zum Monopolpreisproblem." In *Vom Sinn der Konzentration*, edited by Peter Muthesius. Frankfurt: Knapp, 1965.

————. *El Establecimiento Histórico de la Escuela Austriaca de Economía*. Colección Investigaciones No. 43. La Plata: Universidad Nacional de la Plata, 1962.

————. *Epistemological Problems of Economics*. Translated by George Reisman. Princeton, N.J.: Van Nostrand, 1960. 3rd. ed. Auburn, Ala.: Ludwig von Mises Institute. First German edition, 1933.

————. "The Equations of Mathematical Economics and the Problem of Economic Calculation in a Socialist State." *Quarterly Journal of Austrian Economics* 3, no. 1 (2000). Translation by Vera Smith for *Economica*, but not published. Original German version never published. French translation by Gaston Leduc in *Revue d'économie politique* 97, no. 6 (1938).

————. "Eugen von Böhm-Bawerk and the Discriminating Reader." *The Freeman* (August 1959).

———. "Eugen von Philippovich." *Neue Österreichische Biographie*. Vienna, 1926. Vol. 3.

———. "Finanzreform und Vermögensabgabe." *Neues Wiener Tagblatt* (January 23, 1918).

———. "The Foreign Exchange Policy of the Austro-Hungarian Bank." *Economic Journal* 19 (June 1909).

———. *The Free and Prosperous Commonwealth*, translated by Ralph Raico. Princeton, N.J.: Van Nostrand, 1962. The title of the book was changed in subsequent editions to *Liberalism: A Socio-Economic Exposition*. Kansas City, Kansas: Sheed Andrews and McMeel, 1978.

———. *Geldwertstabilisierung und Konjunkturpolitik*. Jena: Gustav Fischer, 1928.

———. *Grundprobleme der Nationalökonomie: Untersuchungen über Verfahren, Aufgaben und Inhalt der Wirtschafts- und Gesellschaftslehre*. Jena: Gustav Fischer, 1933. Translated by George Reisman as *Epistemological Problems of Economics*. Princeton, N.J.: Van Nostrand, 1960.

———. *The Historical Setting of the Austrian School of Economics*. Auburn, Ala.: Ludwig von Mises Institute, [1969] 1984.

———. *Human Action: A Treatise on Economics*. New Haven, Conn.: Yale University Press, 1949; 2nd ed. New Haven, Conn.: Yale University Press, 1963; 3rd ed. Chicago: Regnery, 1966. Scholar's edition. Auburn, Ala.: Ludwig von Mises Institute, 1998.

———. "Interventionismus." *Archiv für Sozialwissenschaften und Sozialpolitik* 56 (1926). Reprinted in *Kritik des Interventionismus*. Translated as "Interventionism," in *A Critique of Interventionism*. Translated by Hans Sennholz. New York: Arlington House, 1977.

———. *Kritik des Interventionismus*. Jena: Gustav Fischer, 1929. Reprint Darmstadt: Wissenschaftliche Buchgesellschaft, 1976.

———. "La Réforme financière en Autriche." *Revue Économique Internationale* 7, no. 4 (October 1910).

———. *Liberalism: In the Classical Tradition*. Translated by Ralph Raico. Irvington-on-Hudson, N.Y.: Foundation for Economic Education, [1927] 1985.

———. *Liberalismus*. Jena: Gustav Fischer, 1927. Reprint Sankt Augustin: Academia Verlag, 1993.

———. "Lord Keynes and Say's Law." In *The Critics of Keynesian Economics*, edited by Henry Hazlitt. Irvington-on-Hudson, N.Y.: Foundation for Economic Education, 1995. First published in *The Freeman* (October 1950).

———. "Markt." *Handwörterbuch der Sozialwissenschaften*. Stuttgart: Gustav Fischer, 1959.

———. *Money, Method, and the Market Process: Essays by Ludwig von Mises*, edited by Richard Ebeling. Boston: Kluwer, 1990.

———. "Monopoly Prices." *Quarterly Journal of Austrian Economics* 1, no. 2 (1998).

———. *Nationalökonomie*. Geneva: Editions Union, 1940.

———. *Nation, Staat und Wirtschaft.* Vienna: Manz, 1919. Translated by Leland B. Yeager as *Nation, State, and Economy.* New York: New York University Press, 1983.

———. "Neue Beiträge zum Problem der sozialistischen Wirtschaftsrechnung." *Archiv für Sozialwissenschaft und Sozialpolitik* 51 (December 1923).

———. "Neue Literatur über Geld- und Bankwesen." *Zeitschrift für Volkswirtschaft, Sozialpolitik und Verwaltung* 19 (1910).

———. "Neuere Schriften über Geld- und Bankwesen." *Zeitschrift für Volkswirtschaft, Sozialpolitik und Verwaltung* 17 (1908).

———. *Notes and Recollections.* Spring Mills, Penn.: Libertarian Press, 1978.

———. "Observations on the Russian Reform Movement." *The Freeman* 16, no. 5 (May 1966).

———. *Omnipotent Government: The Rise of the Total State and Total War.* New Haven, Conn.: Yale University Press, 1944. Reprint, Spring Mills, Penn.: Libertarian Press, 1985.

———. *Planning for Freedom and Sixteen Other Essays and Addresses,* 4th ed. South Holland, Ill.: Libertarian Press, [1952] 1980.

———. "Preface." In A.S.J. Baster, *Le crépuscule du capitalisme américain—étude économique du New Deal.* Paris: Librairie de Médicis, 1937.

———. "Preistaxen. I. Theorie." *Handwörterbuch der Staatswissenschaften,* 4th ed. Jena: Gustav Fischer, 1925. Vol. 4. Reprinted as "Theorie der Preistaxen," *Kritik des Interventionismus.* Jena: Gustav Fischer, 1929. Reprint Darmstadt: Wissenschaftliche Buchgesellschaft, 1976. Translated by Hans Sennholz as "Theory of Price Controls." In *A Critique of Interventionism.* New York: Arlington House, 1977.

———. "Republic of Austria. Banking and Finance." *Encyclopedia Britannica,* 12th ed. [1921]. Vol. 30.

———. *Socialism: An Economic and Sociological Analysis.* London: Jonathan Cape, 1936. Reprinted Indianapolis: Liberty Fund, 1981.

———. "Soziologie und Geschichte." *Archiv für Sozialwissenschaft und Sozialpolitik* 61, no. 3 (1929). Reprinted in Mises, *Grundprobleme der Nationalökonomie.* Jena: Gustav Fischer, 1933. Chap. 2. Translated as "Sociology and History." In Mises, *Epistemological Problems of Economics,* 3rd ed. Auburn, Ala.: Ludwig von Mises Institute, 2003. Chap. 2.

———. "Stones into Bread, The Keynesian Miracle." *The Critics of Keynesian Economics,* edited by Henry Hazlitt, 2nd ed. Irvington-on-Hudson, N.Y.: Foundation for Economic Education, 1995. First published in *Plain Talk* (March 1948).

———. "Super-National Organization Held No Way to Peace: Radical Change in Political Mentalities and Social and Economic Ideologies Viewed as Necessary in Order to Eradicate Economic Nationalism." Letter to the Editor. *The New York Times* (January 3, 1943).

———. *Theorie des Geldes und der Umlaufsmittel,* 1st ed. Munich and Leipzig: Duncker & Humblot, 1912. 2nd ed. Munich and Leipzig: Duncker & Humblot, 1924.

———. *Theory and History: An Interpretation of Social and Economic Evolution.* New Haven, Conn.: Yale University Press, 1957.

———. *Theory of Money and Credit.* London: Jonathan Cape, 1912 and 1934. Reprinted Indianapolis: Liberty Classics, 1980.

———. *The Ultimate Foundation of Economic Science.* Irvington-on-Hudson, N.Y.: Foundation for Economic Education, [1962] 2002.

———. "Sozialliberalismus." *Zeitschrift für die gesamte Staatswissenschaft* 81 (1926). Reprinted in Mises, *Kritik des Interventionismus.* Jena: Gustav Fischer, 1929. Reprint Darmstadt: Wissenschaftliche Buchgesellschaft, 1976. Translated as "Social Liberalism." In *A Critique of Interventionism.* Translated by Hans Sennholz. New York: Arlington House, 1977.

———. "Vom Ziel der Handelspolitik." *Archiv für Sozialwissenschaft und Sozialpolitik* 42, no. 2 (1916).

———. "Zum Problem gesetzlicher Aufnahme der Barzahlungen in Öesterreich-Ungarn: Ein Schlusswort gegenüber Walther Federn." In *Jahrbuch fuer Gesetzgebung, Verwaltung und Volkswirtschaft (Schmollers Jahrbuch)* 34 (1910).

———. "Zur Geschichte der österreichischen Fabriksgesetzgebung." *Zeitschrift für Volkswirtschaft, Socialpolitik und Verwaltung* 14 (1905).

———. "Zur Klassifikation der Geldtheorie" (On the classification of monetary theories). *Archiv für Sozialwissenschaft und Sozialpolitik* 44 (1917/1918).

Mises, Ludwig von, and Arthur Spiethoff, eds. *Probleme der Wertlehre.* Schriften des Vereins für Sozialpolitik 183/I. Munich and Leipzig: Duncker & Humblot, 1931.

———, eds. *Probleme der Wertlehre.* Schriften des Vereins für Sozialpolitik 183/II. Munich and Leipzig: Duncker & Humblot, 1933.

Mises, Ludwig von, Edmund Palla, and Engelbert Dollfuss. *Bericht über die Ursachen der wirtschaftlichen Schwierigkeiten Österreichs.* Vienna: Staatsdruckerei, 1930.

Mises, Margit von. *My Years with Ludwig von Mises.* Cedar Falls, Iowa: Center for Futures Education, 1978.

Mises, Richard von. *Elemente der technischen Hydromechanik.* Leipzig: B.G. Teubner, 1914.

———. *Kleines Lehrbuch des Positivismus: Einführung in die empiristische Wissenschaftsauffassung.* The Hague: Van Stockum & Zoon, 1939.

Mitchell, Allan. *Revolution in Bavaria, 1918–1919: The Eisner Regime and the Soviet Republic.* Princeton, N.J.: Princeton University Press, 1965.

Monroe, Arthur E. *Monetary Theory before Adam Smith.* New York: Augustus M. Kelley, [1923] 1966.

Montesquieu. *Oeuvres completes.* Paris: Gallimard / Pléiade, 1996. Vol. 1.

Morgenstern, Oscar. *Grenzen der Wirtschaftspolitik*. Vienna: Springer, 1934.

Müller-Armack, Alfred. *Entwicklungsgesetze des Kapitalismus*. Berlin: Juncker & Dünnhaupt, 1932.

Nash, George H. *The Conservative Intellectual Movement in America Since 1945*. New York: Basic Books, 1976.

Nau, Heino Heinrich. "'Zwei Ökonomien.' Die Vorgeschichte des Werturteilsstreit in der deutschsprachigen Ökonomik." In *Der Werturteilsstreit. Die Äusserungen zur Werturteilsdiskussion im Ausschuss des Vereins für Sozialpolitik (1913)*, edited by Nau. Marburg: Metropolis, 1996.

Neudeck, Werner. "Der Einfluss von Ludwig von Mises auf die Österreichische akademische Tradition gestern und heute." *Wirtschaftspolitische Blätter* 28, no. 4 (1981).

Neupauer, Josef von. *Die Schäden und Gefahren der Valutaregulirung für die Volkswirtschaft und die Kriegsbereitschaft*. Vienna: Lesk & Schwidernoch, 1892.

Neurath, Otto. *Bayrische Sozialisierungserfahrungen*. Vienna: Neue Erde, 1920.

———. *Die Sozialisierung Sachsens*. Chemnitz: Verlag des Arbeiter- und Soldatenrates, 1919.

———. *Durch die Kriegswirtschaft zur Naturalwirtschaft*. Munich: Callwey, 1919.

———. "Gesctzliche Barzahlungen und Kriegsfall." In *Jahrbuch fuer Gesetzgebung, Verwaltung und Volkswirtschaft* (Schmollers *Jahrbuch*) 34 (1910).

———. "Vollsozialisierung: Von der nächsten und übernächsten Zukunft." *Deutsche Gemeinwirtschaft* 15 (1920).

Neurath, Otto, and Wolfgang Schuhmann. *Können wir heute sozialisieren? Eine Darstellung der sozialistischen Lebensordnung und ihres Werdens*. Leipzig: Klinkhardt, 1919.

Nock, Albert J. Nock. *Our Enemy, The State*. Caldwell, Idaho: Caxton Printers, 1935.

Nove, Alec. "The Liberman Proposals." *Journal of Soviet and East European Studies* 47 (April 1963).

Nurkse, Ragnar. *Internationale Kapitalbewegungen*. Vienna: Springer, 1935.

Oberndorfer, Johann A. *System der Nationalökonomie*. Landshut: Krüll, 1822.

O'Brien, Denis, P. *Lionel Robbins*. London: Macmillan, 1988.

———. "Lionel Robbins and the Austrian Connection." In *Carl Menger and His Legacy in Economics*, edited by Bruce Caldwell. Durham, N.C.: Duke University Press, 1990.

Oppenheim, Heinrich Bernard. *Der Katheder-Sozialismus*. Berlin: Oppenheim, 1872.

Oppenheimer, Franz. *Theorie der reinen und politischen Ökonomie*, 2nd ed. Berlin: Reimer, 1911.

Oresme, Nicholas. "A Treatise on the Origin, Nature, Law, and Alterations of Money." In *The De Moneta of Nicholas Oresme and English Mint Documents*, edited by Charles Johnson. London: Nelson & Sons, 1956.

Österreichische Akademie der Wissenschaften. *Österreichisches biographisches Lexikon, 1815–1950*. Vienna: Verlag der österreichischen Akademie der Wissenschaften, 1975. Vol. 6.

Palyi, Melchior. *Der Streit um die Staatliche Theorie des Geldes*. Munich: Duncker & Humblot, 1922.

Pareto, Vilfredo. *Cours d'économie politique*. Geneva: Droz, [1986], 1964. Vol. 2

———. *Manuel d'économie politique*, 4th ed. Geneva: Droz, [1909] 1966.

———. *Manual of Political Economy*. New York: Kelley, 1971.

Patinkin, Don. *Money, Interest, and Prices: An Integration of Monetary and Value Theory*. Evanston, Ill.: Row, Peterson, and Co., 1956.

Paupié, Kurt. *Handbuch der österreichischen Pressegeschichte 1848–1959*. Vienna: Braumüller, 1960. Vol. 1.

Peart, Sandra J. "Jevons and Menger Re-Homogenized?" *American Journal of Economics and Sociology* 57, no. 3 (1998).

Pesch, Heinrich. *Lehrbuch der Nationalökonomie* 5. Freiburg i.Br.: Herder, 1923.

Philippovich, Eugen von, ed. "Auswanderung und Auswanderungspolitik." *Schriften des Vereins für Socialpolitik* 52 (1892).

———. *Die Bank von England im Dienste der Finanzverwaltung des Staates*. Vienna: Deuticke, 1885. Translated as *History of the Bank of England and Its Financial Services to the State*. Washington, D.C.: Government Printing Office, 1911.

———. *Die Entwicklung der wirtschaftspolitischen Ideen im 19. Jahrhundert*. Tübingen: Mohr, 1910.

———. *Grundriss der politischen Oekonomie* (Outline of political economy), 3 vols., 9th ed. Tübingen: Mohr, 1911.

Pierson, Nicolas. "The Problem of Value in the Socialist Community." *Collectivist Economic Planning: Critical Studies on the Possibilities of Socialism*, edited by F.A. Hayek. London: Routledge and Kegan Paul, 1935.

Pigou, A.C. *Industrial Fluctuations*. London: Macmillan, 1927.

Pogonowski, Cyprian. *Jews in Poland: A Documentary History*. New York: Hippocrene Books, 1993.

Pohle, Ludwig. *Die gegenwärtige Krisis in der deutschen Volkswirtschaftslehre*. Leipzig: Deichert, 1911.

Popper, Karl. *The Open Society and Its Enemies*. London: Routledge, 1945.

Possony, Stefan. *Die Wehrwirtschaft des totalen Krieges*. Vienna: Gerold, 1938.

Pribram, Alfred. *Die Entstehung der individualistischen Sozialphilosophie*. Leipzig: Hirschfeld, 1912.

Pribram, Karl. *Die Grundgedanken der Wirtschaftspolitik der Zukunft*. Graz: Leuschner & Lubensky, 1918.

———. *Der Lohnschutz des gewerblichen Arbeiters nach österreichischem Recht*. Vienna: Deuticke, 1904.

Raico, Ralph. *Die Partei der Freiheit*. Stuttgart: Lucius & Lucius, 1999.

———. "The Legacy of Ludwig von Mises." *The Libertarian Review* (September 1981).

Raimondo, Justin. *An Enemy of the State: The Life of Murray N. Rothbard*. Amherst, N.Y.: Prometheus Books, 2000.

Rand, Ayn. *Atlas Shrugged*. New York: Random House, 1957.

———. *Capitalism: The Unknown Ideal*. New York: Penguin, 1967.

Rappard, William. *Die Bundesverfassung der Schweizer Eidgenossenschaft, 1848–1948—Vorgeschichte, Ausarbeitung, Weiterentwicklung*. Zurich: Polygraphischer Verlag, 1948.

Rathenau, Walther. *Autonome Wirtschaft*. Jena: Diederichs, 1919.

———. *Der neue Staat*. Berlin: Gustav Fischer, 1919.

———. *Deutschlands Rohstoffversorgung*. Berlin: Gustav Fischer, 1916.

———. *Die neue Gesellschaft*. Berlin: Gustav Fischer, 1919.

———. *Die neue Wirtschaft*. Berlin: Gustav Fischer, 1918.

———. *Probleme der Friedenswirtschaft*. Berlin: Gustav Fischer, 1917.

———. *Von kommenden Dingen*. Berlin: Gustav Fischer, 1917.

———. *Zur Kritik der Zeit*. Berlin: Gustav Fischer, 1912.

Rau, Karl Heinrich. *Grundsätze der Volkswirtschaftslehre*, 7th ed. Leipzig and Heidelberg, 1863.

Reisch, Richard. "Das Kreditproblem der Volkswirtschaft." *Zeitschrift für Nationalökonomie* 3, no. 1 (1932).

Riedl, Richard. *Die Aufgaben der Übergangswirtschaft*. Vienna: Veröffentlichungen des Generalkommissariates für die Kriegs- und Übergangswirtschaft No. 1, 1917.

Renner, Karl. *Staat und Nation*. Vienna: Dietl, 1899.

Ricardo, David. "Proposals for an Economical and Secure Currency." In *Works and Correspondence*, edited by Piero Sraffa. Cambridge: Cambridge University Press, 1951–1973. Vol. 4.

Rigg, Bryan Mark. *Hitler's Jewish Soldiers*. Lawrence: Kansas University Press, 2004.

Robbins, Lionel. *Autobiography of an Economist*. London: Macmillan, 1971.

———. *The Great Depression*. London: Macmillan 1934.

———. *International Economic Planning*. London: Macmillan, 1937.

———. *The Nature and Significance of Economic Science*. London: Macmillan, 1932.

Rockwell, Llewellyn H., Jr., ed. "Heart of a Fighter." *The Free Market* 23, no. 7 (2005).

————, ed. *Murray N. Rothbard: In Memoriam*. Auburn, Ala.: Ludwig von Mises Institute, 1995.

Rodakiewicz, August. *Die galizischen Bauern unter der polnischen Republik: eine agrarpolitische Untersuchung*. Brünn: Rohrer, 1902.

————. Book Review in *Zeitschrift für Volkswirtschaft, Sozialpolitik und Verwaltung* 11 (1902).

Roover, Raymond de. *Business, Banking, and Economic Thought in Late Medieval and Early Modern Europe*. Chicago: University of Chicago Press, 1974.

Röpke, Wilhelm. *Die Konjunktur*. Jena: Gustav Fischer, 1922.

————. "Einführung." In Walter Lippmann, *Die Gesellschaft freier Menschen*. Bern: Francke, 1937.

————. "Homage to a Master and a Friend." *The Mont Pèlerin Quarterly* (October 1961).

————. *Krise und Konjunktur*. Leipzig: Quelle & Meyer, 1932.

————. "Review of Mises's *Ursachen der Wirtschaftskrise*." *Zeitschrift für Nationalökonomie* 4, no. 2 (1932).

Roscher, Wilhelm. *Geschichte der National-Oekonomik in Deutschland*, 1st ed. Munich: Oldenbourg, 1874.

Röskau-Rydel, Isabel. "Galizien, Bukowina, Moldau." In Röskau-Rydel, *Deutsche Geschichte im Osten Europas: Galizien, Bukowina, Moldau*. Berlin: Siedler, 1999.

Rosenberg, Wilhelm. *Valutafragen*, 2nd ed. Vienna: Manz, 1918.

Rothbard, Murray N. *America's Great Depression*, 5th ed. Auburn, Ala.: Ludwig von Mises Institute, 2000.

————. *Classical Economics: An Austrian Perspective on the History of Economic Thought*. Cheltenham, U.K.: Edward Elgar, 1995.

————. *Economic Thought before Adam Smith*. Cheltenham, U.K.: Edward Elgar, 1995.

————. *The Ethics of Liberty*, 2nd ed. New York: New York University Press, 1998.

————. *For a New Liberty*, 2nd ed. San Francisco: Fox & Wilkes, 1978.

————. *Man, Economy, and State*, 3rd ed. Auburn, Ala.: Ludwig von Mises Institute, 1993.

————. *Man, Economy, and State with Power and Market*. Scholar's edition. Auburn, Ala.: Ludwig von Mises Institute, 2003.

————. *Power and Market*. Princeton, N.J.: D. Van Nostrand, 1970.

————. "Praxeology." *analysis* (May 1950).

————. "Review of *Human Action*." *Faith and Freedom* (September 1950).

————. *Ludwig von Mises: Scholar, Creator, Hero*. Auburn, Ala.: Ludwig von Mises Institute, 1988.

————. *The Sociology of the Ayn Rand Cult*. Port Townsend, Wash.: Liberty Publishing, 1987.

————. "Toward a Reconstruction of Welfare and Utility Economics." In *On Freedom and Free Enterprise: Essays in Honor of Ludwig von Mises*, edited by Mary Sennholz. New Haven, Conn.: Van Nostrand, 1956.

Rothschild, Kurt. "Carl Menger." In *Tausend Jahre Österreich*, edited by Walter Pollack. Vienna: Verlag Jugend und Volk, 1974. Vol. 3.

Rougier, Louis. "Le Néo-libéralisme." *Synthèses* (December 1958).

————. *Les mystiques politiques contemporaines et leurs incidences internationales*. Paris: Recueil Sirey, 1935.

————. "Préface." In *Le Colloque Walter Lippmann*. Paris: Librairie de Médicis, 1938.

Rueff, Jacques. "L'assurance chômage cause du chômage permanent." *Revue politique et parlementaire* (December 10, 1925).

Russell, Bertrand. *Religion and Science*. Oxford: Oxford University Press, [1936] 1997.

Salerno, Joseph T. "Friedrich von Wieser and F.A. Hayek: The General Equilibrium Tradition in Austrian Economics." *Journal des Economistes et des Etudes Humaines* 12, no. 2&3 (2002).

————. "Ludwig von Mises as a Social Rationalist." *Review of Austrian Economics* 4 (1990).

————. "Mises and Hayek Dehomogenized." *Review of Austrian Economics* 6, no. 2 (1993).

————. "The Place of *Human Action* in the Development of Modern Economic Thought." *Quarterly Journal of Austrian Economics* 2, no. 1 (1999).

Samuelson, Paul. *Economics*. New York: McGraw-Hill, 1948.

Schell, Josef. *Gerechtigkeitsidee und Mietengesetzgebung*. Vienna: Manz, 1927.

Schiff, Erich. *Kapitalbildung und Kapitalaufzehrung im Konjunkturverlauf*. Vienna: Springer, 1933.

Schirmacher, Wolfgang, ed. *German Essays on Science in the 19th Century*. New York: Continuum, 1996.

Schmitt, Carl. *Politische Theologie*. Berlin: Duncker & Humblot, 1922.

————. *Römischer Katholizismus und politische Form*. Berlin: Duncker & Humblot, 1923.

Schmoller, Gustav. "Die Gerechtigkeit in der Volkswirtschaft." *Schmollers Jahrbuch* 5 (1881).

————. "Einladung zur Eisenacher Versammlung von 1872." In Franz Boese, *Geschichte des Vereins für Sozialpolitik, 1872–1932*. Berlin: Duncker & Humblot, 1939.

————. "Eröffnungsrede zum 25 jährigen Bestehen des Vereins auf der Kölner Tagung von 1897." In Franz Boese, *Geschichte des Vereins für Sozialpolitik, 1872–1932*. Berlin: Duncker & Humblot, 1939.

————. *Grundriss der allgemeinen Volkswirtschaftslehre.* Leipzig: Duncker & Humblot, 1900.

————. "Volkswirtschaft, Volkswirtschaftslehre und -methode." *Handwörterbuch der Staatswissenschaften*, 3rd ed. Jena: Gustav Fischer, 1911. Vol. 8.

————. "Zur Methodologie der Staats und Sozial-Wissenschaften." *Schmollers Jahrbuch* n.s. 7, no. 3, (1883).

————. *Zur Social- und Gewerbepolitik der Gegenwart.* Leipzig: Duncker & Humblot, 1890.

Schönfeld-Illy, Leo. *Wirtschaftsrechnung.* Reprint, Munich: Philosophia, 1924.

Schorske, Carl E. *Fin-de-siècle Vienna.* New York: Knopf, 1980.

Schroeder, Werner. "Bestandsaufbau durch Plünderung—Jüdische Bibliotheken im RSHA 1936–1945." Paper presented at an international congress on *Raub und Restitution in Bibliotheken* (Vienna City Hall, April 23–24, 2003).

Schubert, Aurel. *The Credit-Anstalt Crisis of 1931.* Cambridge: Cambridge University Press, 1991.

Schüller, Richard. *Die klassische Nationalökonomie und ihre Gegner.* Berlin: Heymanns, 1895.

Schullern-Schrattenhofen, H. "Eugen Ritter von Böhm-Bawerk." In *Die Universität Innsbruck*, edited by Adolf Günther. Innsbruck: Tyrolia, 1928.

Schumpeter, Joseph A. *Capitalism, Socialism, and Democracy.* New York: Harper & Row, 1942.

————. *A History of Economic Analysis.* Oxford: Oxford University Press, 1954.

————. "Das Sozialprodukt und die Rechenpfennige: Glossen und Beiträge zur Geldtheorie von heute." *Archiv für Sozialwissenschaften und Sozialpolitik* 44 (1917–1918).

————. "Eugen von Böhm-Bawerk." *Neue Österreichische Biographie.* Vienna, 1925. Vol. 2.

————. "Sozialistische Möglichkeiten von heute." *Archiv für Sozialwissenschaften und Sozialpolitik* 48, no. 2 (1921).

————. *Theorie der wirtschaftlichen Entwicklung.* Munich: Duncker & Humblot, 1911.

————. "Über die mathematische Methode der theoretischen Ökonomie." *Zeitschrift für Volkswirtschaft, Sozialpolitik und Verwaltung* 15 (1906).

————. *Wesen und Hauptinhalt der theoretischen Nationalökonomie.* Munich and Leipzig: Duncker & Humblot, 1908.

Seipel, Ignaz. "Minoritätenschutz und Judenfrage nach dem christlichsozialen Programm." *Volkswohl* 10, no. 2 (February 1919).

Sennholz, Mary. *Leonard E. Read: Philosopher of Freedom.* Irvington-on-Hudson, N.Y.: Foundation for Economic Education, 1993.

Shahak, Israel. *Jewish History, Jewish Religion: Hitler's Jewish Soldiers: The Untold Story of Nazi Racial Laws and Men of Jewish Descent in the German Military.* London: Pluto Press, 1994.

Shepherd, Colston. *The Airforce of Today.* London & Glasgow: Blackie & Son, 1939.

Sherrard, Alfred. "The Free Man's Straightjacket." *New Republic* 122 (January 9, 1950).

Sieghart, Rudolf. *Die letzten Jahrzehnte einer Grossmacht.* Berlin: Ullstein, 1932.

Simmel, Georg. *Philosophie des Geldes.* Frankfurt a.M.: Suhrkamp, [1901] 1991.

Simonin, Jean-Pascal, and François Vatin. *L'oeuvre multiple de Jules Dupuit (1804–1866): Calcul d'ingénieur, analyse économique et pensée sociale.* Angers: Presses de l'Université d'Angers, 2002.

Simons, Henry C. *A Positive Program for Laissez-Faire. Some Proposals for a Liberal Economic Policy.* Public Policy Pamphlet No. 15. Chicago: University of Chicago Press, 1934.

———. *Economic Policy for a Free Society.* Chicago: University of Chicago Press, 1948.

Singer, Kurt. Book review in *Deutsche Wirtschaftszeitung* (June 1, 1913).

Skocpol, Theda. "Delivering for Young Families: The Resonance of the GI Bill." *American Prospect* 28 (September 1996).

Slutsky, Eugen. "Ein Beitrag zur formal-praxeologischen Grundlegung der Ökonomik." *Annales de la classe des sciences sociales-économiques.* Kiev: Académie Oukraïenne des Scienccs, 1926.

Smith, Barry. "Aristotle, Menger, Mises: An Essay in the Metaphysics of Economics. In *Carl Menger and His Legacy in Economics*, edited by Bruce J. Caldwell. Durham, N.C.: Duke University Press, 1990.

———. "Austrian Economics and Austrian Philosophy." In *Austrian Economics: Historical and Philosophical Background*, edited by Wolfgang Grassl and Barry Smith. London: Croom Helm, 1986.

Sombart, Werner. *Der proletarische Sozialismus ("Marxismus"),* 10th ed. 2 Vols. Jena: Gustav Fischer, 1924.

Somary, Felix. *The Raven of Zurich: The Memoirs of Felix Somary.* London: Hurst & Co., 1960.

Sommer, Louise. "Für die freie Verkehrswirtschaft! (Die Dresdner Tagung des Vereines für Sozialpolitik." *Wiener Wirtschafts-Woche* (October 12, 1932).

Sozialisierungskommission. *Vorläufiger Bericht über die Frage der Sozialisierung des Kohlenbergbaues.* Berlin, February 15, 1919.

Spann, Othmar. *Der Wahre Staat.* Leipzig: Quelle & Meyer, 1921.

———. *Vom Geist der Volkswirtschaftslehre.* Jena: Gustav Fischer, 1919. Reprint, appendix to *Fundament der Volkswirtschaftslehre*, 3rd ed. Jena: Gustav Fischer, 1923.

Spiethoff, Arthur. "Krisen." *Handwörterbuch der Staatswissenschaften*, 4th ed. Jena: Gustav Fischer, 1925. Vol. 6.

Springer, Rudolf. *Das Selbstbestimmungrecht der Nationen: in besonderer Anwendung auf Oesterreich.* Leipzig: Deuticke, 1918.

————. *Grundlagen und Entwicklungsziele der Österreichisch-Ungarischen Monarchie.* Leipzig: Deuticke, 1906.

————. *Die Krise des Dualismus und das Ende der Déakistischen Episode in der Geschichte der Habsburgschen Monarchie: eine politische Skizze.* Vienna: published by the author, 1904.

Staatsarchiv. Vienna, Austria.

Stadler, Karl R. "Victor Adler." *Tausend Jahre Österreich*, edited by Walter Pollack. Vienna: Verlag Jugend und Volk, 1974. Vol. 3.

Stigler, George. *Production and Distribution Theories: The Formative Period.* New York: Macmillan, 1949.

Stolper, Wolfgang. *Joseph Alois Schumpeter: The Public Life of a Private Man.* Princeton, N.J.: Princeton University Press, 1994.

Streissler, Erich. "Carl Menger, der deutsche Nationalökonom." *Wert, Meinung, Bedeutung*, edited by B.P. Priddat. Marburg: Metropolis, 1997.

————. "The Influence of German Economics on the Work of Carl Menger and Marshall." In *Carl Menger and His Legacy in Economics*, edited by Bruce Caldwell. Durham, N.C.: Duke University Press, 1990.

Streissler, Erich W., and Monika Streissler, eds. *Carl Menger's Lectures to Crown Prince Rudolf of Austria.* Aldershot, U.K.: Edward Elgar, 1994.

Strigl, Richard von. *Die ökonomischen Kategorien und die Organisation der Wirtschaft.* Jena: Gustav Fischer, 1923.

————. *Kapital und Produktion.* Vienna: Springer, 1934.

Stuart, G.M. Verrijn. *Inleiding tot de Leer der Waardevastheid van het Geld.* The Hague: Mouton, 1919.

Stucken, Rudolph. *Deutsche Geld- und Kreditpolitik, 1914–1963*, 3rd ed. Tübingen: Mohr, 1964.

Sturmthal, Adolf. Book Review in *The American Economic Review* 33, no. 3 (September 1943).

————. *The Tragedy of European Labor, 1918–1939.* New York: Columbia University Press, 1943.

Sulzer, Georg. *Die wirtschaftlichen Grundgesetze in der Gegenwartsphase ihrer Entwicklung.* Zurich: Müller, 1895.

Swedberg, Richard. *Joseph A. Schumpeter—eine Biographie.* Stuttgart: Klett-Cotta, 1994.

Taylor, Fred. "The Guidance of Production in a Socialist State." *American Economic Review* 19 (1929).

Taylor, Sally J. *Stalin's Apologist: Walter Duranty, the New York Times's Man in Moscow.* Oxford: Oxford University Press, 1990.

Thiers, Adolph. *De la propriété.* Paris: Paulin, Lheureux & Cie, 1848.

Tietze, Hans. *Die Juden Wiens.* Vienna & Leipzig: Tal, 1933.

Tintner, Gerhard. *Die Preise im Konjunkturverlauf.* Vienna: Springer, 1935.

Tirala, Lothar Gottlieb. *Rasse, Geist und Seele.* Munich: Lehmann, 1935.

Tomo, Shigeki. "Eugen von Böhm-Bawerk's Lectures on Economics." In Eugen von Böhm-Bawerk, *Innsbrucker Vorlesungen über Nationalökonomie.* Marburg: Metropolis, 1998.

———. "The Year 1922: A Watershed for Mises and Hayek." Auburn, Ala.: Ludwig von Mises Institute Working Paper, September 2003.

Treichl, Heinrich. *Fast ein Jahrhundert.* Vienna: Zsolnay, 2003.

Tschuppik, Walter. Book Review in *Süddeutsche Sonntagspost* (November 8, 1931).

Tucker, Jeffrey A. "Mises as Mentor: An Interview with George Reisman." *Austrian Economics Newsletter* 21, no. 3 (Fall, 2001).

Vleugels, Wilhelm. *Die Lösungen des wirtschaftlichen Zurechnungsproblems bei Böhm-Bawerk und Wieser.* Halle: Niemeyer, 1930.

Voegelin, Erich. *Autobiographical Reflections.* Vol. 34 of the *Collected Works of Eric Voegelin.* Baton Rouge: Louisiana State University Press, 1989.

———. *Die politischen Religionen.* Stockholm: Bermann-Fischer, 1939.

Voigt, Andreas. "Die staatliche Theorie des Geldes." *Zeitschrift für die gesamte Staatswissenschaft* 62 (1906).

———. *Kriegssozialismus und Friedenssozialismus.* Leipzig: Scholl, 1916.

Wagner, Adolf. *Die russische Papierwährung.* Riga: Kymmel, 1868.

"Wahlen." *Staatslexikon,* 7th ed. Freiburg i.Br.: Herder, 1989. Col. 830.

Wald, Abraham. *Berechnung und Ausschaltung von Saisonschwankungen.* Vienna: Springer, 1936.

Walras, Léon. "Un économiste inconnu: Hermann-Henri Gossen." *Journal des Économistes* (April and May 1885).

Weber, Adolf. *Weltwirtschaft.* Munich: Richard Pflaum Verlag, 1947.

Weber, Max. *Economy and Society: An Outline of Interpretive Sociology.* Guenther Roth and Claus Wittich, eds. Berkeley: University of California Press, 1978.

———. *Gesammelte Aufsätze zur Wissenschaftslehre.* Tübingen: Mohr, 1922. 7th ed. Tübingen: UTB, 1988.

———. *Der Sozialismus.* Vienna: Phöbus, 1918.

———. *Wirtschaft und Gesellschaft,* 3rd ed. Tübingen: Mohr, 1947. Vol. 1.

Weininger, Otto. *Geschlecht und Charakter,* 19th ed. Vienna: Braumüller, 1920.

Weiss, F.X. "Die moderne Tendenz in der Lehre vom Geldwert." *Zeitschrift für Volkswirtschaft, Socialpolitik und Verwaltung* 19 (1909).

———. "Eugen von Böhm-Bawerk." In *Gesammelte Schriften,* edited by F.X. Weiss. Vienna: Hölder-Pichler-Tempsky, 1926. Reprint, Frankfurt a.M.: Sauer & Auvermann, 1968. Vol. 1.

W.W. [Weiss-Wellenstein]. "'Die Gemeinwirtschaft.' Die zweite Auflage des Werkes von Ludwig Mises." *Mitteleuropäische Wirtschaft. Wochenbeilage der "Neuen Freien Presse"* (December 10, 1932).

Whately, Richard. *Introductory Lectures on Political Economy*, 3rd ed. London: Parker, [1832] 1847.

Wicksell, Knut. *Geldzins und Güterpreise.* Jena: Gustav Fischer Verlag, 1898.

———. *Über Wert, Kapital und Rente.* Jena: Gustav Fischer, 1893.

Wicksteed, Philip H. *The Alphabet of Economic Science.* Reprint, New York: Augustus M. Kelley, [1888] 1970.

Wieser, Friedrich von. "Das Wesen und der Hauptinhalt der theoretischen Nationalökonomie—kritische Glossen." *Jahrbuch für Gesetzgebung, Verwaltung und Volkswirtschaft im deutschen Reich* 35, no. 2 (1911). Reprinted in *Gesammelte Abhandlungen*, edited by F.A. Hayek. Tübingen: Mohr, [1911] 1929.

———. "Der Geldwert und seine geschichtlichen Veränderungen." *Zeitschrift für Volkswirtschaft, Sozialpolitik und Verwaltung* 13 (1904). Reprinted in Wieser, *Gesammelte Abhandlungen*, F.A. Hayek, ed. Tübingen: Mohr, 1929.

———. "Der Geldwert und seine Veränderungen." *Schriften des Vereins für Socialpolitik* 132 (Munich, 1909). Reprinted in Wieser, *Gesammelte Abhandlungen*, edited by F.A. Hayek. Tübingen: Mohr, 1929.

———. *Der natürliche Werth.* Vienna: Hölder-Pichler-Tempsky, 1889.

———. "Grenznutzen," *Handwörterbuch der Staatswissenschaften*, 2nd and 3rd editions. Jena: Gustav Fischer, 1900. Reprinted in Wieser, *Gesammelte Abhandlungen*, edited by F.A. Hayek. Tübingen: Mohr, [1911] 1929.

———. "Karl Menger." In *Neue österreichische Biographie: 1815–1918*, edited by Anton Bettelheim. Vienna, 1923. Vol. 1. Reprinted in Wieser, *Gesammelte Abhandlungen*, edited by F.A. Hayek, ed. Tübingen: Mohr, 1929.

———. *Theorie der gesellschaftlichen Wirtschaft.* Tübingen: Mohr, 1914. Translated as *Social Economics.* New York: Adelphi, 1927.

———. "Theorie des Geldes." *Handwörterbuch der Staatswissenschaften*, 4th ed. Jena: Gustav Fischer, 1927. Vol. 4.

———. *Über den Ursprung und die Hauptgesetze der wirthschaflichen Werthes.* Vienna: Hölder-Pichler-Tempsky, 1884.

———. "Über die Messung der Veränderungen des Geldwertes." *Schriften des Vereins für Socialpolitik* 132 (Munich, 1909). Reprinted in *Gesammelte Abhandlungen*, edited by F.A. Hayek. Tübingen: Mohr, 1929.

Windelband, Wilhelm. *Kulturwissenschaft und Naturwissenschaft*, 3rd ed. Tübingen: Mohr, 1915.

———. *Präludien*, 8th ed. Tübingen: Mohr, 1922. Vol. 2.

Winter, Balduin. "Die Rückkehr zum Kind. Wirklichkeit ist mehr als Realität. Drohobycz, die Heimat des Dichters und Traumtänzers Bruno Schulz im vergessenen Europa." *Freitag. Die Ost-West-Zeitung* (literature section; March 30, 2001).

Wissel, Rudolf. *Die Planwirtschaft.* Hamburg: Auer, 1920.

———. *Praktische Wirtschaftspolitik.* Berlin: Verlag Gesellschaft und Erziehung, 1919.

Wittek, H. "Die kriegswirtschaftlichen Organisationen und Zentralen in Öster-reich." *Zeitschrift für Volkswirtschaft und Sozialpolitik* (1922).

Wittkowski, Adolf. *Schrifttum zum Marshallplan und zur volkswirtschaftlichen Integration Europas.* Bad Godesberg: Bundesministerium für den Marshallplan, 1953.

Yagi, Ki'ichiro. "Carl Menger as Editor: Significance of Journalistic Experience for his Economics and for his Later Life." *Revue européenne des sciences sociales* 30, no. 92 (1992).

———. "Carl Menger and Historical Aspects of Liberalism in Austria." Essay presented at a symposium on Carl Menger and the Historical Aspects of Liberalism. Center for Historical Social Science Literature, Hitotsubashi University (December 18–19, 2004).

Zuckerkandl, Robert. *Zur Theorie des Preises,* 2nd ed. Leipzig: Stein & Co, [1889] 1936. Reprint, Amsterdam: Liberac, 1968.

Zweig, Stefan. *Die Welt von Gestern—Erinnerungen eines Europäers.* Frankfurt a.M.: Gustav Fischer, 1988.

Index of Names

Index of Subjects

Page numbers followed by an *i*, *n*, or *p* indicate illustrations, notes, or photographs.

Non-English titles are indexed under the initial letter of their article if appropriate (i.e., *Die...* will be found under the Ds).